Seventh Edition

A Global History: From Prehistory to the 21st Century

L. S. Stavrianos

PRENTICE HALL
Upper Saddle River, New Jersey 07458

Library of Congress Cataloging-in-Publication Data

STAVRIANOS, LEFTEN STAVROS.
    A global history: from prehistory to the 21st century / L.S.
STAVRIANOS.—7th ed.
        p.   cm.
    Includes bibliographical references and index.
    ISBN 0-13-923897-2
    1. World history. I. Title.
    D20 .S827   1999
    909—dc21   98-45072

Editorial director: *Charlyce Jones Owen*
Acquisitions editor: *Todd Armstrong*
Production editor: *Edie Riker*
Buyer: *Lynn Pearlman*
Marketing manager: *Sheryl Adams*
Photo editor: *Lorinda Morris-Nantz*
Photo researcher: *Beth Boyd*
Photo permissions: *Tony Arabia*
Cover director: *Jayne Conte*
Cover art: *National Geographic Society*
Editorial assistant: *Holly Jo Brown*

This book was set in 10/12 Stone Serif by East End Publishing Services and was printed and bound by Courier Companies, Inc. The cover was printed by The Lehigh Press, Inc.

 © 1999, 1995, 1991, 1988, 1982, 1975, 1970, by Prentice-Hall, Inc.
Simon & Schuster / A Viacom Company
Upper Saddle River, New Jersey 07458

Printed in the United States of America

10 9 8 7 6 5 4 3 2 1

ISBN   0-13-923897-2

Prentice-Hall International (UK) Limited, *London*
Prentice-Hall of Australia Pty. Limited, *Sydney*
Prentice-Hall Canada Inc., *Toronto*
Prentice-Hall Hispanoamericana, S.A., *Mexico*
Prentice-Hall of India Private Limited, *New Delhi*
Prentice-Hall of Japan, Inc., *Tokyo*
Simon & Schuster Asia Pte. Ltd., *Singapore*
Editora Prentice-Hall do Brasil, Ltda., *Rio de Janeiro*

Dedicated to Agustina Franco Serrano
with appreciation for her contribution
to the preparation of this edition

Brief Contents

Contents

Chapter 6
Indian Civilization   *117*

Chapter 7
Chinese Civilization   *128*

Chapter 8
End of Classical Civilizations   *141*

What It Means for Us Today   *158*

Chapter 20
Expanding Civilization of the West:
Renaissance and Reformation   *305*

Chapter 21
Expanding Civilization of the West:
Economic Growth and State Building   *319*

What It Means for Us Today   *333*

PART VI
WORLD OF THE EMERGING WEST,
1500–1763   *337*

Chapter 22
West European Expansion: Iberian Phase,
1500–1600   *339*

Chapter 23
West European Expansion:
Dutch, French, British Phase, 1600–1763   *357*

Chapter 24
Russian Expansion in Asia   *368*

Chapter 25
Beginning of Global Unity   *380*

Chapter 44
Second Industrial Revolution:
Global Repercussions   *635*

List of Maps

From the Author to the Reader

Ours is a time of problems, of gigantic problems. Everything is being transformed under the magic influence of science and technology. And every day, if we want to live with open eyes, we have a problem to study, to resolve.

Pope Pius VI, May 18, 1969

WHY A TWENTY-FIRST CENTURY GLOBAL HISTORY?

Each age writes its own history. Not because the earlier history is wrong, but because each age faces new problems, asks new questions, and seeks new answers. This precept is self-evident today when the tempo of change is increasing exponentially, creating a correspondingly urgent need for new history posing new questions and offering new answers.

Our own generation, for example, was brought up on West-oriented history, and naturally so, in a West-dominated world. The nineteenth and early twentieth centuries were an era of Western hegemony in politics, in economics, and in culture. But the two World Wars and the ensuing colonial revolutions quickly ended that hegemony, as evidenced by the disappearance of the great European empires from the maps of the world. The names and the colors on those maps changed radically, reflecting the new world that had emerged by the mid-twentieth century.

Slowly and reluctantly we recognized that our traditional West-oriented history was irrelevant and misleading in this world. A new global perspective was needed to make sense of the altered circumstances. The transition from the old to the new was achieved, albeit with much soul searching and acrimony. By the 1960s the reality of the shift was evident in the emergence of the World History Association, in the appearance of the *Journal of World History*, and in the publication of the first edition of this text.

This brings us back to our original question: Why publish a new edition for the twenty-first century, only a few decades after the first edition? The answer is the same as the answer given to justify the first edition: Namely, a new world requires a correspondingly new historical approach. The postcolonial world of the 1960s necessitated a new global history. Today the equally new world of the 1990s, and of the twenty-first century, requires an equally new historical approach. The new world of the 1960s was in large part the product of the colonial revolutions. The new world of the 1990s, as Pope Pius VI noted, is the product of the "magic influence of science and technology." The pervasiveness of this influence is evident in the "gigantic problems" it has created in all aspects of our lives. For example, students of the late twentieth century doubtless remember their daily prostration under their wooden desks, probaby wondering what protection those flimsy structures could offer against nuclear bombs.

That generation of students had to face up to not only new dangers to human life, but also to unprecedented peril to the mother Earth which had given birth to that life. Oceanographer Jacques Cousteau has warned: "Mankind has probably done more damage to the Earth in the twentieth century than in all previous human history."[1] Likewise the environmental organization Worldwatch Institute concluded in 1989: "By the end of the next decade the die will pretty well be cast. As the world enters the twenty-first century, the community of nations either will have rallied and turned back the threatening trends, or environmental deterioration and social disintegration will be feeding on each other."[2]

This dismal prospect of species and planet destruction has prompted the publication of a stream of books with titles such as *End of the American Century*, *End of the World*, *End of the Future*, and *End of History*. These gloomy titles seem to be justified if we view ourselves as but one link in a long species chain. Approximately 40 million different species of plants and animals now exist on planet Earth. Beyond that, somewhere between 5 and 40 billion species have existed at one time or another. Thus only one in a thousand species is still alive, making the survival record of Earth species a 99.9 percent failure. This record seems to provide statistical support for the current popularity of "end of" books.

The statistics are misleading, however, because of a fundamental difference between the human species and all those extinct species. The latter became extinct primarily because they proved incapable of adapting to changes in their environment, as occurred, for example, during the Ice Age. *Homo sapiens*, by contrast, being endowed with superior intelligence, was able to adapt environment to its needs by mastering fire, fashioning clothes, constructing shelters, and so forth. Thus *Homo sapiens* stands out as a unique species capable of adapting environment to its needs and thereby becoming the master rather than the creature of its destiny.

The crucial difference between master and creature is currently being dramatically illustrated by the changing relationship between humans and the smallpox virus, the most universally feared of all diseases. Appearing first in the Far East at least two thousand years ago, it reached Europe in the eighth century C.E. and then spread to the Americas after Columbus. With the European dispersal over other continents, the virus decimated overseas populations lacking immunity. Hence the genocidal disaster suffered by Amerindians, Australian aborigines, and island populations in Polynesia and the Caribbean. The virus also persisted in Europe, reaching plague proportions, and ultimately carrying off one-third of the continent's population.

The taming of the virus began in 1796 when the English physician Edward Jenner discovered that a person inoculated and infected with cowpox was protected against smallpox. Today the smallpox-Homo sapiens relationship is completely reversed with a few stocks of the virus isolated in American and Russian laboratories. The last known case of smallpox was recorded in Somalia in 1977, and in 1980 the virus was declared eradicated in the wild.

Scientists have been recommending that the remaining stocks of the virus be destroyed lest it escape from storage, but a final decision has been deferred because of concern that the virus might be needed for future research. This concern has abated because scientists have been producing harmless clones of DNA fragments of smallpox and believe they now have the full genetic blueprint that will enable them to conduct research tests even if the virus itself were eliminated. In January 1996 the executive board of the United Nations World Health Organization agreed to set June 30, 1999 as the destruction date for all remaining stocks. So the killer virus, which for so long has tormented the human species, is now under lock and key, awaiting execution (and extinction) on a date set by its erstwhile victims. Thus *Homo sapiens* reigns supreme in both the animate and inanimate worlds.

"For the first time in the course of history," concludes physicist Werner Heisenberg, "man on earth faces only himself; he finds no longer any other partner or foe." The great irony of our era is that this primacy is a root cause of our current global malaise and apprehension. Having eliminated all possible rivals, we humans no longer confront any foes. We confront only ourselves.

This new confrontation with our inner self rather than with the outside world is a formidable undertaking. It requires not merely the acquisition of more knowledge and technology, an enterprise in which we have proven unequaled. It requires also the crowning of that knowledge with an ethical compass to provide it with direction and purpose. In the seventeenth century, when the scientific revolution was emerging, the English philosopher Francis Bacon noted its potentiality and warned against its perils. He enthusiastically endorsed the pursuit of "knowledge and skill" through science, but he added that the pursuit should be conducted with "humility and charity," and not "for the pleasure of mind, or for contention, or for superiority to others, or for profit or fame, or power, or any of these inferior things; but for the benefit and use of life."[3]

The degree to which we have ignored Bacon's warning against "inferior things" is painfully registered in what we see daily on our TV screens, and also in Fordham University's annual report, *The Index of Social Health*. This monitors the well-being of American society on the basis of Census Bureau statistics regarding teenage suicide, unemployment, drug abuse, high school drop-out rate, and the availability of affordable housing. The *Index* recorded a drop from 75 in 1970 to 36 in 1991, which the director of the annual report labeled "awful."

The "awful" deterioration in social health is not limited to the United States. Oceanographer Jacques Cousteau recognized this in the course of a one-day walk in Paris from 7 A.M. to 7 P.M. During his walk he had a counter, which he clicked "every time I was solicited by any kind of advertising for something I didn't need. I clicked it 183 times in all by the end of the day."

This experience is scarcely unique. It is the norm, regardless of whether one is walking in Paris or Athens or Los Angeles or Mexico City. But Cousteau, being the thoughtful scientist that he was, set out to probe the social significance of his personal experience. "It is the job of society, not of the individual person," he concluded from his probing, "to control this destructive consumerism. I am not for some kind of ecological statism. No. But when you are driving in the street and see a red light, you stop. You don't think the red light is an attempt to curb your freedom. On the contrary, you know it is there to protect you. Why not have the same thing in economics? . . . Responsibility lies with the institutions of society, not in the virtues of the individual."[4]

This conclusion, set forth in Cousteau's article entitled "Consumer Society Is the Enemy," is significant because throughout the world, consumer societies are becoming the norm. In China, for example, when Mao began his rule in 1949, the popular clamor was for the "big four" (bicycle, radio, watch, and sewing machine). Since then, consumer expectations have escalated to the "big eight," adding items such as color TV, refrigerator, and motorcycle. The list continues to lengthen, an outstanding recent addition being the automobile, which is becoming a status symbol among the billions of "have-nots" in the Third World. Between 1990 and 2000 the number of automobiles will increase in Indonesia from 272,524 to an estimated 675,000; in India from 354,393 to 1,100,000; and in China from 420,670 to 2,210,000.[5]

Environmentalists are concerned about the impact of millions of additional automobiles on the global atmosphere. Norway's former prime minister Gro Harlem Brundtland notes, however, that Western Europeans who initiated the industrial revolution and the ensuing atmospheric pollution, cannot now condemn "have-nots" to the status of "never-will-haves."[6]

These developments raise profound issues for individuals and for societies, today and in the forseeable future. So we now find ourselves at a point where we can no longer avoid facing up to fundamentals. What is the meaning of life? What is the purpose of human existence? Francis Bacon confronted this head-on when he urged that the newly emerging discipline of science be employed for the "benefit and use of life" and not for "inferior things" such as "profit, or fame, or power." Thus Bacon posed the issue squarely: must *Homo sapiens* end up as *Homo economicus*, dedicated to achieving a bloated stomach and a bloated bank account?

The first objective of every society must be to satisfy basic human needs—food, shelter, health, education—so priority must be given to improving economic efficiency until those needs are satisfied. But once they are met, should economic productivity continue to receive priority regardless of individual, social, and ecological costs? This basic question has not received the consideration it warrants, so that by default, a mindless consumerism and materialism have spread over the planet, as Cousteau discovered during his walk in Paris.

Such equivocation cannot be sustained indefinitely. Consequently *Homo sapiens* now is engaged willy-nilly in a search for an alternative to *Homo economicus*, or more precisely, for an ethical compass to direct our rampant technology. This represents a great challenge to the human species—

the greatest in its meteoric career. Hitherto it has used its superior intelligence to master its environment, leading to its current primacy on planet Earth. But with this primacy achieved, and crumbling quickly into the current worldwide social and environmental degradation, humanity is confronted now with the novel challenge of achieving transcendence from the intelligent *Homo sapiens* to the wise *Homo humanus*—in short, from intelligence to wisdom.

In the forthcoming chapters we shall see that humans are facing up to the challenges of today, as they have repeatedly and triumphantly to those of the past. Consequently the world on the eve of the twenty-first century is undergoing unprecedented social experimentation and innovation. Their extent and significance are evidenced by the recent transformations throughout the globe. In China, for example, hardened revolutionaries are groping for "a communism with a Chinese face;" in the former USSR the economist Nikolai Shmelev advises his fellow countrymen not to fear losing their "ideological virginity"[7]: and even in the dominant market economies, capitalism itself is emerging in alternative forms. These include the American variety emphasizing untrammeled free enterprise; the German and Scandinavian varieties stressing the welfare state and worker participation in decision making; and the proliferating Asian melange with varying combinations of national economic planning, huge interlinked conglomerates, lifetime jobs in large companies, and government aid to export-oriented domestic industries.

Such effervescence suggests a twenty-first century of great potentiality as well as great peril. Lacking a crystal ball, historians cannot predict the outcome with any certainty. But they can predict with reasonable assurance a twenty-first century that is neither utopian nor dystopian, but a century of possibilities. Which of these will actually be realized will be determined by the readers of these lines who will be making fateful actions and decisions in forthcoming decades.

Given these circumstances, this is not a time for self-deluding utopian fantasies, nor is it a time for gloomy foreboding. Rather it is a time for hardheaded reappraisal of existing practices and institutions, retaining what works and discarding what does not—which is precisely what is going on now throughout the world. This new edition of the text has been prepared with the hope of facilitating the reappraising process and thereby contributing to Francis Bacon's espousal of that which "benefits" life, and also to his rejection of "inferior things."

NOTES

1. *New Perspectives Quarterly* (Summer 1996), pp. 48, 49.
2. *Worldwatch Institute Reports, State of the World 1987, 1989* (W.W. Norton, 1987–1989), pp. 194, 213.
3. Cited in A. Pacey, *The Culture of Technology* (MIT Press, 1983), pp. 114–15, 178–79.
4. J. Cousteau, "Consumer Society Is the Enemy," *New Perspectives Quarterly* (Summer 1996) pp. 48, 49.
5. *New York Times*, June 6, 1996.
6. *New Perspectives Quarterly* (Spring 1989) pp. 4–8.
7. *New York Times*, June 25, 1987.

Acknowledgments

Grateful acknowledgment is made to the following authors and publishers for permission for quotation of the chapter opening epigraphs. Chapter 1, Clyde Kluckholn, *Mirror for Man* (New York: McGraw-Hill, 1949), p. 11. Chapter 2, R. J. Braidwood, "Near Eastern Prehistory," *Science* vol. 127 (June 20, 1958), 1419–30. Chapter 8, Robert Lopez, *The Birth of Europe*, © 1962 by Max Leclerc et Cie, Prop. of Librairie Armand Colin and © 1966 trans. by J. M. Dent & Sons, Ltd., and published in 1967 by M. Evans and Co., Inc., New York, by arrangement with J. M. Dent & Sons, Ltd. Chapter 9, Lynn White, Jr., "Tibet, India, and Malaya as Sources of Western Medieval Technology," *American Historical Review* XLV (April 1960), 515, 526. Chapter 12, W. C. Bark, *Origins of the Medieval World* (Stanford: Stanford University Press, 1958), p. 66. Chapter 14, Lynn White, Jr., "Technology and Invention in the Middle Ages," *Speculum*, XV (1940), 156. Chapter 17, A. J. Toynbee, *Civilization on Trial*, © 1948 by Oxford University Press, Inc. Chapter 21, Lynn White, Jr., "Technology and Invention in the Middle Ages," *Speculum*, XV (1940), 156.

Chapter 24, B. H. Sumner, *A Short History of Russia* (New York: Harcourt Brace Jovanovich, 1943), p. 1. Chapter 26, Herbert Butterfield, *Origins of Modern Science* (London: G. Bell & Sons, Ltd., 1957), p. 179. Chapter 28, Peter Chaadayev, *Apology of a Madman*, cited in H. Kohn's *The Mind of Modern Russia* (New Brunswick, N.J.: Rutgers University Press, 1955), p. 50. Chapter 29, H. A. R. Gibb, "Social Change in the Near East," in P. W. Ireland, ed., *The Near East* (Chicago: The University of Chicago Press, 1942), p. 43. Chapter 30, Arnold J. Toynbee, *The World and the West* (London: Oxford University Press, 1953). Chapter 31, J. K. Fairbank, "The Influence of Modern Western Science and Technology on Japan and China," from *Explorations in Entrepreneurial History*, VII, No. 4. Chapter 36, K. M. Panikkar, *Asia and Western Dominance* (London: George Allen & Unwin, Ltd., 1969). Chapter 39, Arnold J. Toynbee, *Survey of International Affairs, 1931*, (London: Oxford University Press, 1932) under the auspices of the Royal Institute of International Affairs, p. 1.

Photo Credits

Elisofon / National Museum of African Art/Smithsonian Institution; p. 257 Julius Kirschner / American Museum of Natural History; p. 258 © Werner Forman Archive, Art Resource, National Museum, Lagos, Nigeria; p. 259 The British Museum, London, Courtesy of the Trustees.

Chapter 16: p. 264 Josephus Daniels / Photo Researchers, Inc.; p. 266 The Metropolitan Museum of Art, The Michael C. Rockefeller Memorial Collection, Bequest of Nelson A. Rockefeller, 1979 (1979.206.1063); p. 268 Boltin Picture Library; p. 269 Robert Frerck/Chicago / Odyssey Production; p. 271 Marilyn Bridges.

Chapter 17: p. 277 Foto Marburg / Art Resource, New York.

Chapter 18: p. 288 Ray Roberts / Camera Press, Ltd.; p. 289 The Granger Collection; p. 291 Michel Gotin; p. 293 National Maritime Museum, London.

Chapter 19: p. 300, 301 Corbis-Bettmann.

Chapter 20: p. 307 Gallerie del'Accademia, Venice; p. 309 Henry E. Huntington Library and art Gallery; p. 311 Corbis-Bettmann; p. 312 The Toledo Museum of Art, Toledo, Ohio, purchased with funds from the Libbey Endowment, Gift of Edward Drummond Libbey; p. 314 Musee Cantonal des Beaux Arts, Palais de Rumine, Lausanne.

Chapter 21: p. 320 Giraudon / Art Resource, New York; pp. 322, 327 Library of Congress; p. 323 Scala / Art Resource, New York; p. 325 Erich Lessing / Art Resource, New York.

Chapter 22: p. 342 The British Library; p. 344 Reprinted from *Admiral of the Ocean Sea* by Samuel Eliot Morison. Copyright 1942 © renewed 1970 by Samuel Eliot Morison. By permission of Little, Brown and Company, Boston, Mass.; p. 345 Culver Pictures, Inc.; p. 346 The Granger Collection; p. 347 Peter Greenberg; p. 351, 352 Corbis-Bettmann; p. 354 Comstock.

Chapter 23: pp. 359, 363, 365 Library of Congress; p. 360 Giraudon / Art Resource, New York; p. 361 National Maritime Museum; p. 362 Museum of the City of New York, The J. Clarence Davies Collection; p. 366 Bildarchiv Preussischer Kulturbesitz.

Chapter 24: p. 372 The National Museum, Copenhagen; p. 374 The Granger Collection; p. 375 Library of Congress; p. 376 New York Public Library, Rare Book Division.

Chapter 25: p. 381 Culver Pictures, Inc.; p. 383 Jerry Jacka Photography; p. 385 Michael Campbell / Library of Congress; p. 389 Hulton / Corbis-Bettmann; p. 391 Ackermann and Johnson Ltd., London, UK/Bridgeman Art Library, London/New York; p. 392 Library of Congress; p. 393 Detail from the Bressani Map / National Archives of Canada.

Chapter 26: p. 404 Museo della Scienza, Florence, Italy, Scala / Art Resource, New York; pp. 405, 406, 419 Bildarchiv Preussischer Kulturbesitz; p. 409 Board of Trustees of the National Museums and Galleries on Merseyside, Walker Art Gallery, Liverpool; p. 412 The Granger Collection; pp. 414, 423 Library of Congress; p. 421 Mary Evans Picture Library; p. 422 portrait of the Bellelli family by Degas, Giraudon / Art Resource, New York; p. 425 Hulton / Corbis-Bettmann.

Chapter 27: p. 431, Stock Montage, Inc. / Historical Pictures Collection; pp. 438, 454 Library of Congress; p. 433 by courtesy of the National Portrait Gallery, London; p. 434 Genf, Musee d'Art et d'Histoire, Bildarchiv Preussischer Kulturbesitz; p. 435 courtesy The Henry Francis DuPont Winterthur Museum; p. 439 The Granger Collection; pp. 440, 449 Corbis-Bettmann; pp. 442, 444, 452 Musee de la Ville de Paris, Musee Carnavalet, Paris, France, Giraudon / Art Resource, New York; pp. 447, 451 Bildarchiv Preussischer Kulturbesitz.

Chapter 28: p. 457 Library of Congress; p. 458 The Granger Collection; pp. 459, 463 Corbis-Bettmann; pp. 461, 467 Bildarchiv Preussischer Kulturbesitz; p. 462 L. S. Stavrianos.

Chapter 29: p. 470 The Granger Collection; p. 473 Mary Evans Picture Library; p, 474 Tony Stone Images; p. 475 Corbis-Bettmann.

Chapter 30: p. 477 UN/DPI John Isaac; p. 479 E. T. Archive; pp. 480, 481 Hulton / Corbis-Bettmann; p. 482 Culver Pictures, Inc.

Chapter 31: pp. 488, 494 Corbis-Bettmann; p. 489 Hulton / Corbis-Bettmann; p. 490 Library of Congress; p. 491 Brown Brothers; p. 493 Stock Montage, Inc. /Historical Pictures Collection.

Chapter 32: p. 498 The British Museum; p. 499 Library of Congress; p. 501 Peter Greenberg; p. 505 Kyrkans Internationella AV-tjanst / Upsala Cooperative Creamery Association.

Chapter 33: p. 510 UPI/Lewis W. Hine / Corbis-Bettmann; p. 511 Library of Congress; p. 513 courtesy of American Antiquarian Society; p. 514 The State Museum of Pennsylvania, Pennsylvania Historical and Museum Commission; p. 515 UPI / Corbis-Bettmann.

Chapter 34: p. 517 Mayer / Liaison Agency, Inc.; p. 519 Index Stock Photography, Inc.; p. 520 Bishop Museum; p. 521 Helen Birch Bartlett Memorial Collection, 1926, photograph © 1994, The Art Institute of Chicago, all rights reserved; p. 522 George Holton / Photo Researchers, Inc.

Chapter 35: p. 526 Union Pacific Railroad; p. 528 Corbis-Bettmann; p. 529 Keystone Press Agency.

Chapter 36: p. 536 National Archives; p. 537 Bildarchiv Preussischer Kulturbesitz; p. 540 (top, bottom) Brown Brothers; p. 542 Hulton / Corbis-Bettmann; pp. 545, 547 Library of Congress; p. 546 Roger Violet / Liaison Agency, Inc.; p. 549 American Stock, Archive Photos; p. 550 Corbis-Bettmann.

Chapter 37: p. 556 Corbis-Bettmann; pp. 557, 561 AP/Wide World Photos; p. 558 Library of Congress; p. 559 UPI / Corbis-Bettman.

Chapter 38: pp. 563, 566 Bildarchiv Preussischer Kulturbesitz; p. 567 Corbis-Bettmann; p. 569 UPI / Corbis-Bettmann; p. 570 Bettmann/Hulton / Tony Stone Images.

Chapter 39: p. 574 Library of Congress; pp. 575, 581 Bildarchiv Preussischer Kulturbesitz; p. 577 Brown Brothers; p. 580 Heinrich Hoffman / Bildarchiv Preussischer Kulturbesitz.

Chapter 40: p. 585 AP/Wide World Photos; p. 588 Archive Photos; p. 589 Mary Evans Picture Library; p. 590 Ullstein Bilderdienst.

Chapter 41: p. 594 AP/Wide World Photos; p. 597 Roger Violet / Liaison Agency, Inc.; pp. 599, 600 National Archives; pp. 602, 605 Archive Photos; pp. 604, 607 Library of Congress.

Chapter 42: p. 613 Magnum Photos, Inc.; p. 614 AP/Wide World Photos; p. 615 Black Star; p. 616 Owen Franklin / Stock Boston; p. 617 Brown Brothers; p. 619 David Brauchli / AP/Wide World Photos; p. 620 Reuters/Gary Hershorn / Archive Photos.

Chapter 43: p. 625 Franklin D. Roosevelt Library; p. 626 Yutaka Nagata / United Nations; pp. 628, 632 Archive Photos; p. 629 Brown Brothers; p. 630 National Archives; p. 631 John F. Kennedy Library.

Chapter 44: p. 637 Steve Murez / Black Star; p. 638 Ed Clark/Life Magazine © Time, Inc.; p. 639 P. F. Bentley, Time Magazine © Time, Inc.; p. 642 Shone / Liaison Agency, Inc.; p. 643 Lehtikuva Oy / Woodfin Camp & Associates; p. 644 Robert Wallis / SABA Press Photos, Inc.; p. 646 Utarbekov Nabihan/Press Studio/Lehtikuva / SABA Press Photos, Inc.; p. 647 A. Ramey / Woodfin Camp & Associates; pp. 649, 652 UPI / Corbis-Bettmann; p. 651 reprinted by permission of Ms. Magazine, © 1972; p. 653 Baldeu / Sygma; p. 658 Eric Pasquier / Sygma; p. 660 Tim Carlson / Stock Boston; p. 662 John Coletti / Stock Boston; p. 663 by courtesy of the National Portrait Gallery, London; p. 665 Elizabeth Mangelsdorf/S.F. Examiner / SABA Press Photos, Inc.; p. 668 Bildarchiv Preussischer Kulturbesitz; p. 669 (top) Kevin Carter /Sygma, (bottom) Elliott Erwitt / Magnum Photos, Inc.; p. 670 Ajit Kumar / AP/Wide World Photos; p. 671 John McConnico / AP/Wide World Photos.

PART I

Before Civilization

P art I is concerned with the 4 million years before human civilization. The other parts of this book are devoted to history since humans became civilized, less than 6,000 years ago. Thus, by far the longest phase of human evolution will receive by far the briefest consideration. The reason for the disproportionate emphasis on the story of civilized people is the constantly accelerating tempo of human history. Geologic time is measured in billions of years, and human prehistory in thousands, but since the advent of civilization, the time unit has shrunk progressively to centuries and to decades, until fateful events now daily crowd us, unceasingly and inexorably. Indeed the pace of change has reached such proportions that it is a very real question whether the human species is capable of adjusting quickly enough to avoid obsolescence, or even extinction.

The disparity in the pace of events, and the corresponding disparity in emphasis in this study, should not lead us, however, to minimize the significance of what happened during prehistory. During those millennia, two developments provided the bedrock foundation for all later history. One was the gradual transition from hominid to Homo sapiens, or thinking human being. The other was the transformation of the human newcomer from a food gatherer who was dependent on the bounty of nature to a food producer who became increasingly independent of nature—the master of its own destiny. These two epochal events—the appearance of human beings and their invention of agriculture—are the subjects of the two chapters of Part I.

1

Humans as Food Gatherers

Anthropology holds up a great mirror to man and lets him look at himself in his infinite variety.

Clyde Kluckhohn

One of the outstanding achievements of modern peoples is their study and reconstruction of the past. The ancients had little understanding of what had happened before them. Thucydides, the most objective of Greek historians, began his study of the Peloponnesian War by stating that nothing of great importance had happened before his time. His ignorance of history prevented him from recognizing the unique glory and contribution of Athens. By contrast, our age is more history-minded than any other. We know more about the early history of the Egyptians, the Greeks, or the Chinese than they themselves knew. Furthermore, knowledge of our early human ancestors is being increased every year by the findings of scientists in various fields such as geology, archeology, anthropology, paleontology, and biology. To this list of fields should be added

space technology, which is being used to survey the surface and even the subsurface of the earth from satellites, space shuttles, and airplanes. These are equipped with sensors that can measure subtle variations in temperatures on the ground. Because sand, cultivated soil, vegetation, and different types of rocks have distinctive temperatures and emit heat at different rates, the sensors can identify loose soils that had been prehistoric agricultural fields or were covering ancient caravan routes or architectural ruins. Thus radar imaging systems have been used to map the ancient intercontinental Silk Road traversing Central Asia, as well as Maya causeways in the Guatemalan jungle and footpaths along the shore of Lake Arenal in Costa Rica.

A spectacular recent example of technology enabling us to recover lost chapters of our human past is the discovery of obliterated sections of the Great Wall of China. Segments of the Great Wall have been lost for centuries under layers of shifting desert sand. These segments were brought to light by radar images taken from the space shuttle *Endeavor* in April 1994. The images disclosed a 47-mile stretch of the wall in a remote section of China 430 miles west of the capital, Beijing. In Beijing's environs, the Wall was carefully preserved through the centuries, providing photo opportunities, showing, for example, President Nixon and Chairman Mao striding atop the Wall. By contrast, the Wall was allowed to crumble in remote areas. There the Wall was not constructed with stones. Mud and branches were often substituted. Thus long segments deteriorated and disappeared from view until the recent uncovering by the wizardry of modern technology.[1]

This type of investigation and research has extended our knowledge back before the beginning of civilization, even before there were written records. This is very important, for it was only about 5,000 years ago that humans learned to write, whereas their hominid beginnings have been traced back over 4 million years. We shall consider these long prehistoric millennia when people became human. They existed, as did the other animals, by collecting food wherever it was to be found, rather than by growing it as their agriculturist descendants would learn to do.

I. FROM HOMINIDS TO HUMANS

Our globe revolves around the sun, which is one of 10 billion stars in our galaxy. This in turn is one of millions of galaxies that make up the universe. The enormity of this scale should be kept in mind while we trace through our human experiences and human concerns in the following pages. It is well to remember that in the context of the universe our planet earth is literally like a speck of dust on the Pacific Ocean.

Earth took form about 5 billion years ago, and the first life appeared on it about 4 billion years ago in the form of single-celled creatures. Although such primitive life traditionally has been viewed as qualitatively different from nonlife, scientists no longer accept this assumed dichotomy between organic and inorganic.

Rather they think of living matter as having evolved naturally from nonliving matter. They classify all matter into a hierarchy of states of organization. At a certain level in this hierarchy the transition occurs from inorganic to organic. More specifically, electrons, protons, and neutrons combine to form atoms, and the atoms form molecules. The molecules become more or less well organized aggregates, and one class of these is living matter.

Organic matter in turn went through a comparable hierarchical evolution: from the original microorganisms to primitive plants such as seaweeds, to animals without backbones (invertebrates) such as jellyfish and worms, and ultimately to animals having backbones (vertebrates). These vertebrates, with some of their invertebrate and plant cousins, began their successful adaptation to life on land about 300 million years ago. First came the amphibians, followed by the great army of prehistoric reptiles, then the birds, and finally the mammals. For the past 60 million years, mammals have been the dominant form of life on earth.

Almost all scientists accept the proposition that humans belong to the animal kingdom—more specifically to the order of Primata, which they share with the tree shrews, lemurs, tarsiers, monkeys, and apes. Evidence from several fields of study supports this conclusion. Anatomists have found basic similarities between humans and the other higher animals in the general plan of their skeletal, muscular, and organic structures. Embryologists have noted that the human embryo displays, at different stages of its development, characteristics of some of the lower forms of life, such as gill arches at the end of one month and a rudimentary tail at two months. Anthropologists have shown that human fossil remains show a consistent trend away from the general anthropoid type, or hominids, toward Homo sapiens. Other scientists have discovered many similar indications of our ties to the other animals, including close resemblance between the chemical composition of the blood of apes and of humans, possession of common parasites, and similarities in their ways of learning.

The differentiation of the human stock occurred during the Pleistocene epoch, with its six or seven glacial and five or six interglacial periods. These drastic environmental changes compelled all animals to adapt and readapt themselves continually to new conditions. Success in this crucial matter depended not on brute strength nor on the ability to resist cold but rather on the continuous growth of intelligence and the use of that intelligence to work out satisfactory adaptations. This, of course, is the secret of the unchallenged primacy of human beings on earth. Humans have been, first and foremost, generalists. They never adapted exclusively to one type of environment, as the gibbon did to the forest with its long lithe arms, or the polar bear to the arctic with its heavy white fur. Rather humans relied on their brains, not their bodies, to adapt to any environment.

The human species is the product of natural selection from a succession of humanlike ancestors, or hominids, some of which were capable of using simple stone tools and weapons. The earliest of these hominids was Australopithecus, believed to have appeared first in the savannas of eastern and southern Africa over 4 million years ago. The pelvis and leg of this hominid were strikingly similar to those of modern humans, but the cranial capacity was only about one-third that of a human, or hardly larger than that of living apes. Thus a humanlike system of walking erect on two legs rather than on all fours was combined with an apelike brain.

The African savannas were ideal for primates at that level of development. The climate was warm enough to make the lack of clothing bearable, and the open grasslands, in contrast to dense forests and deserts, afforded both water and animal foods. Thus, despite their simple tools, the Australopithecines subsisted on an adequate diet, including eggs, crabs, tortoises, birds, rodents, and young antelopes. The last were easy prey because they "freeze" in the grass when faced with danger.

Australopithecus roamed the African plains for over 2 million years, during which time several species of this hominid appeared, flourished, and disappeared. Anthropologists are not agreed on details because many new finds are made each year, and theories change with these finds. For example, recent fossil discoveries in Java challenge the traditional "out-of-Africa" theory that earliest humans originated in Africa and fanned out from there to Asia, Europe, the Americas, and Australia. The Java fossils are of such surprising antiquity that they strengthen the position of the multiregionalists who believe that early humans originated and evolved independently in many parts of the world.[2] Doubtless many more discoveries will be made in the years to come, and many more new theories about human origins will be formulated to take into account the new fossil findings.

Regardless of the exact date and exact location, human beings or Homo sapiens (thinking humans) eventually did appear, certainly by 40,000 years ago, though recent excavations indicate a much earlier date. Viewed in the broadest perspective, this development represents the second major turning point in the course of events on this planet. The first occurred when life originated out of inorganic matter. After that momentous step, all living forms evolved by adapting to their environments through mutation and natural selection. That is, the genes adapted to the environment, as was evident during the climatic upheavals of the Pleistocene. But with the appearance of humans, the evolutionary process was reversed. No longer did genes adapt to environment; instead, humans adapted by changing the environment to suit their genes. Today, a third epochal turning point appears imminent as humans' growing knowledge of the structure and function of genes may soon enable them to modify their genes as well as their environment.

Humans, and only humans, have been able to create a made-to-order environment, or culture, as it is called. The reason is that only humans can symbolize, or envision, things and concepts divorced from here-and-now reality. Only humans laugh, and only they know that they will die. Only they have wondered about the universe and its origins, about their place in it and in the hereafter.

With these unique and revolutionizing abilities, humans have been able to cope with their environment without mutations. Human culture became the new, nonbiological way of having fur in the arctic, water storage in the desert, and fins in the water. More concretely, culture consists of tools, clothing, ornaments, institutions, language, art forms, and religious beliefs and practices. All these have served to adapt humans to their physical environment and to their fellow humans. Indeed, the story of humanity as related in the following chapters is simply the story of a succession of cultures that we have created, from our Paleolithic origins to the present day.

When humans used their superior brains to change their environment to suit their genes rather than the opposite, as had been the prevailing pattern in the past, they made a quantum leap ahead of all other species on this planet. This explains why humans today are the dominant species after a modest beginning in Africa's savanna. But this raises a puzzling question. Why are humans today seemingly incapable of controlling their environment, which they themselves have created? Why are they discovering that their own homemade environment is becoming less and less fit for habitation?

The answer seems to lie in the basic difference between genetic and cultural evolution. Genetic evolution functions via gene mutations which, if favored by selection, become dominant in a population in the biologically brief period of a few thousand years. This was the evolutionary path that led through a succession of hominids from Australopithecus to Homo sapiens.

By contrast, cultural evolution, occurring through the introduction of new tools or ideas or institutions, can change and has changed societies almost overnight. Witness how steam power affected the entire globe in the nineteenth century, how the internal combustion engine did likewise in the twentieth, and how nuclear power and computers are transforming our environment today—so much so that Albert Einstein warned us that humanity now faces either new "ways of thinking" or "unparalleled catastrophe."

The key problem appears to be the time lag between technological change and the social change it necessitates. The reason for the lag is that technological change usually is welcomed and quickly adopted because it improves productivity and living standards, whereas social change is commonly resisted because it requires self-appraisal and adaptation, which are threatening and uncomfortable. This explains today's paradox of humans' acquiring more and more knowledge, and being more and more able to

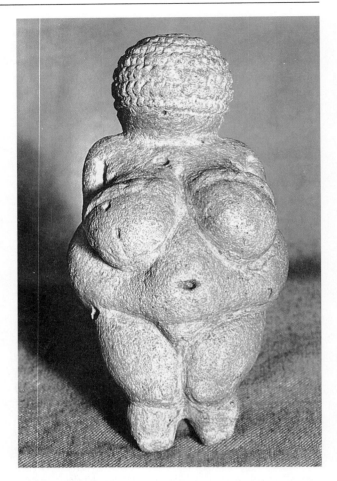

Venus of Willendorf, a stone figure dating between 15,000 and 10,000 B.C.E. Because of the proportions of this figure, it can be considered a manifestation of early fertility cults.

change their environment as they wish, yet their not being able to change their environment to make it more livable. In short, our problem as a species is to balance our ever-expanding knowledge with wisdom in how we use that knowledge. We shall see in the following chapters that learning how to balance knowledge and wisdom is becoming so urgent that, as Einstein has warned us, our future as a species depends on the outcome.

We shall see that this problem of balance has risen repeatedly throughout human history and is rising today more frequently and urgently as our knowledge is growing with ever-increasing speed, and our wisdom failing to keep up.

II. LIFE OF THE FOOD GATHERERS

Homo sapiens with their superior intelligence developed the so-called "blade technique." They used the long, sharp flakes, or "blades," struck off the core of a stone to fashion a variety of new tools as well as "tools to make tools." Some of the new tools were composites of different materials, such as spears with hafted heads of bone, antler, or flint, and flint blades set in bone or wooden handles. Another departure was the construction of projectiles such as the bola, sling, spear thrower, and bow and arrow. The latter must have been relatively inefficient at first, but it was gradually improved until it became the most formidable weapon prior to modern firearms. Other inventions of the upper Paleolithic included bone and ivory bodkins, bone needles with eyes, belt fasteners, and even buttons—all of which indicate that Magdalenian hunters wore sewn skin garments with fitted sleeves and trousers.

Although this late Paleolithic technology was advanced compared to that of the early Paleolithic a million years before, it still was primitive in the sense that productivity was low. Food gatherers had no formal political structure with full-time political leaders. Rather they formed autonomous bands that usually numbered twenty to fifty persons. Larger groups were possible, and some did exist in areas that yielded plentiful food supplies, such as the American Northwest, with its inexhaustible salmon runs, and the Dordogne valley in southern France, with its great reindeer herds in Magdalenian times. Judging from contemporary hunting societies, authority in Paleolithic times was rigidly limited and lacked an established and recognized power to control people. Leaders arose naturally for specific purposes; an old man might be the accepted planner of ceremonies because of his ritual knowledge, whereas a young person with proven skill in the chase might take the lead in hunting parties. But the important point is that all such leaders were persons of influence rather than authority since there were no institutions for imposing one's will upon others.

Social organization necessarily was as simple as political organization, if indeed the two can be distinguished at this stage. The basic unit was the family, consisting of the parents and their immature and unmarried children. Extra wives usually were permitted, but in practice polygamy was rare. Relations between the sexes were more equal during the Paleolithic millennia than at any time since. The chief reason seems to have been that women contributed to the food supply of the band as much as did the men, if not more so. Consequently for most of human history there was none of the dependence and inferior status that is commonly associated today with the "weaker" female sex.

From a study of ninety food-gathering bands surviving to the present, anthropologists have found that the men hunt animals and provide meat, whereas the women gather everything they can find around their camp—roots, berries, nuts, fruits, vegetables, insects, lizards, snakes, rodents, shellfish, and so forth. Although the meat the men bring in is highly prized, the fact is that what the women collect is the main part of the diet. The women usually gather twice as much food as the men are able to hunt and kill and bring back to the camp. Thus the sexes have different tasks, but these tasks are equally important. Food-gathering women not only bear the children and rear them but also provide most of the food.

It is true that the men were responsible for the defense of the band and had control over the weapons, but they did not use the weapons against the women to intimidate and subjugate them. In fact, when Europeans first came into contact with food-hunting peoples in overseas lands, they usually were surprised and shocked by the equality that food-gathering women enjoyed compared to European women. The Jesuit missionary Paul le Jeune spent the winter of 1633–1634 with a band of Montagnais-Naskapi Indians on the Labrador Peninsula of eastern Canada. "The women have great power here," le Jeune reported, and he urged the Indian men to assert themselves. "I told him that he was the master, and that in France women do not rule their husbands." Another Jesuit father reported, "The choice of plans, of undertakings, of journeys, of winterings, lies in nearly every instance in the hands of the housewife." It is significant that anthropologist Eleanor Leacock

A Stone Age Saharan rock painting, the Fresco of Tassili n'Ajjer, Algeria. One scholar believes this strikingly beautiful painting represents women gathering grain (represented by the dots, presumably). If so, it would have likely been wild grain unless cereal crops were cultivated very early here—something for which we have no evidence. Whether gathering grain or engaged in graceful dance, the figures here remind us of the ancient human presence in the once-green Saharan regions.

found the same quality in sex relations among the Montagnais-Naskapi when she studied them in 1950–1951. "It was beautiful to see the sense of group responsibility . . . and the sense of easy autonomy in relationships unburdened by centuries of training in deferential behavior by sex and status."[3]

Not only was there sex equality among the food gatherers but there were also strong kinship ties. Each person had duties toward the other tribal members and in turn enjoyed rights and privileges. All helped each other in the quest for food and in providing shelter from the elements and defense from their enemies. Some fighting between tribal groups arose from personal feuds and from competition for hunting and fishing grounds. But Paleolithic society lacked both the manpower and the resources essential for large-scale warfare, which did not become possible until the rise of agriculture, with its greatly increased productivity and correspondingly increased population. In short, the essence of Paleolithic social organization was cooperation. Families and bands were primarily mutual-aid societies working together in the harsh struggle for existence.

After observing the daily life of food gatherers in various parts of the world, anthropolo-

Detail from American Museum of Natural History representation of a Neolithic village in Denmark, about 2700 B.C.E. Note the variety of occupations: hunter, wood-gatherer, fire tender, grain-grinder, potter, and weaver.

gist R. B. Lee concludes: "A truly communal life is often dismissed as a utopian ideal, to be endorsed in theory but unattainable in practice. But the evidence for foraging peoples tells us otherwise. A sharing way of life is not only possible but has actually existed in many parts of the world and over long periods of time."[4]

Anthropologists recently have focused on the diets as well as the social institutions of our prehistoric ancestors, especially because what they ate seems to hold lessons for us today. What people ate thousands of years ago can be determined in two ways. One is by examining coprolites, or fossilized feces. They reveal many things, such as pollen, plant crystals, feathers, bones, hair, and eggshells, so a coprolite provides a capsule record of what passed through a person's digestive tract millennia ago. The other way to determine the diets of our food-gathering ancestors is to observe what present-day food gatherers eat, whether they be the aborigines of Australia or the !Kung of South Africa's Kalahari

desert. Such observation has revealed that present-day food gatherers have a surprisingly abundant and reliable food supply, even though they are living on undesirable lands that nobody else wanted. One reason for the plentiful food is that the food gatherers have an extraordinary knowledge of their home territory and all its plant and animal life. They cannot read or write, but they can learn and remember. The !Kung, for example, remember so much that they are now using some 500 different types of plants and animals as food and for medical, cosmetic, toxic, and other purposes. Among the insects they eat and enjoy are beetle grubs, caterpillars, bee larvae, termites, ants, and cicadas. Because of our customs, we do not consider most of these as food, yet they are nutritious. Termites, for example, are 45 percent protein, an even higher proportion than in dried fish.

The great number of foods that the food gatherers are willing to eat provides a valuable life insurance for them. Depending on a multitude of different plants and animals for their food supply, they are better off in this regard than agriculturists who grow only a few crops, and who are in danger of starvation if those crops fail because of drought, flood, frost, or pests. The food gatherers run no such danger; if they find some plants or animals in short supply, they are certain to make up the lack with the hundreds of others that they know they can find. For example, anthropologists who were studying the !Kung in the summer of 1964 noted that a serious drought that summer was hurting the neighboring Bantu farmers. Their crops had failed and their families were starving. So the Bantu women joined the !Kung women when they started out on their daily expeditions in search of roots, greens, berries, nuts, birds, eggs, and so forth. There was no shortage of these hundreds of different foodstuffs, so the Bantu as well as the !Kung families survived easily despite the drought.

The food supply of !Kung and other gatherers is not only abundant but also healthy. It is low in salt, saturated fats, and carbohydrates, and high in polyunsaturated oils, roughage, vitamins, and minerals. This diet, together with the active life they lead as nomads, explains why few food gatherers suffer from the diseases common in industrialized societies—medical problems such as high blood pressure, obesity, varicose veins, ulcers, and colitis. On the other hand, many !Kung die from accidental injuries that cannot be treated because of the lack of doctors and hospitals. So scientists find that about one-tenth of the !Kung population is over sixty years of age, which is roughly the same percentage as in industrialized countries where doctors and hospitals are readily available.

The above conclusions about prehistoric diet have been tested by the anthropologist Vaughn M. Bryant, Jr., of Texas A&M University. While doing fieldwork in an archeological dig in southwest Texas, he switched his diet to that of the prehistoric people of that region—a diet that he knew well from his coprolite research. Pleased with the results of the new diet, he continued it after returning to his campus. He also added exercise to his daily routine in order to approximate the rigors of prehistoric life. He rode his bike to school, climbed stairs instead of

taking elevators, and walked across the campus instead of driving. Since changing to his new way of life, he reports:

I've felt much better, both physically and mentally. I just have more energy than I used to. . . . I haven't had a serious illness in the past four years. I haven't missed a day of work. . . . In three months or so, I lost 30 pounds . . . without counting calories and without having to go hungry. . . . Those fruits and vegetables are so low in calories. . . . I think snacking helped, too. It seems when you snack all day you eat less than if you sit down and gorge yourself at three meals. . . . When you think about it, there's nothing weird about this diet. I think we were designed by nature to eat foods similar to what primates—the great apes—generally eat: fruits and other plant foods, a little meat, a lot of complex carbohydrates and fiber, and not very much fat. Until just a few thousand years ago, everyone probably ate the way I do.[5]

Turning our discussion from social institutions and practices to general beliefs, we find that primitive humans were basically ahistorical and nonevolutionary in their attitudes toward themselves and their society. They assumed that the future would be identical to the present, as the present was to the past. Consequently there was no notion of change, and hence no inclination to criticize or to tamper with existing institutions and practices. To their way of thinking, everything, including themselves, their culture, and their habitat, had appeared with the creation and was destined to continue unaltered into the future. The creation myths of hunting peoples are strikingly similar, involving heroes who fashioned the landscape, stocked it with game, brought forth the people, and taught them the arts and their customs.

The following origin myth of the Andaman islanders is fairly typical:

The first man was Jutpu. He was born inside the joint of a big bamboo, just like a bird in an egg. The bamboo split and he came out. He was a little child. When it rained he made a small hut for himself and lived in it. He made little bows and arrows. One day he found a lump of quartz and with it he sacrificed himself. Jutpu was lonely, living all by himself. He took some clay (kot) from a nest of the white ants and moulded it into the shape of a woman. She became alive and became his wife. She was called Kot. They lived together at Teraut-buliu. Afterwards Jutpu made other people out of clay. These were the ancestors. Jutpu taught them how to make canoes and bows and arrows, and how to hunt and fish. His wife taught the women how to make baskets and nets and mats and belts, and how to use clay for making patterns on the body.[6]

Primitive humans were very knowledgeable concerning nature. They had to be, for their very existence depended on it. Their knowledge was passed on orally from generation to generation, and much of it is only now being recognized and utilized. An example is the manifold uses of India's neem tree, a fast-growing evergreen. For millenia it has been prominent in village culture and in ancient texts. Its bark, leaves, flowers, seeds, and fruit were used to treat diseases ranging from diabetes to ulcers and constipation. Neem twigs were used as an antiseptic toothbrush, and its oil is now used in the preparation of toothpaste and soap. Neem extract also is a potent insecticide, effective against two hundred insects, including locusts, mosquito larvae, and boll weevils.

Despite their abundant first-hand contact with and knowledge of nature, early humans had little explanatory knowledge; they could give no naturalistic explanation if floods or droughts came or if the hunting or fishing was poor. Not knowing how to cope with nature by naturalistic means, they had to resort to the supernatural. They turned to magic and spent much time in efforts to persuade or fool nature into yielding a greater abundance. By making each useful animal or plant the totem of a particular group, and by using images, symbols, and imitative dances, primitive people believed that the animal or food could be encouraged to flourish and multiply. As long as the rules of the totems were strictly observed, the reproduction of the group and of its food supply could be assured.

All group members seem to have participated at first in the ritual ceremonies, but toward the end of the Paleolithic, part-time specialists in the form of medicine men or shamans seem to have appeared. These people were thought to have peculiar relations with the forces that were supposed to control those parts of the universe or environment that mattered—primarily food and fertility but also health and personal luck. More and more, as they were relieved from the full-time work of food and tool production, they used their magical arts for the common good. Shamans are still found today in nearly every surviving food-gathering culture, including those of the Bushmen, the Eskimos, and the Australian aborigines. The earliest pictorial representation of these shamans is the "Sorcerer" of the cave of Trois-Frères in France. This "terrible masterpiece," as it has been called, is a Paleolithic painting of a man clad in a deerskin, with the horns of a stag, the face of an owl, the ears of a wolf, the arms of a bear, and the tail of a horse. Other nearby paintings suggest that the cave was a meeting place where a sorcerer invoked animal spirits for success in the hunt and worked up his audience to the emotional pitch necessary to face danger.

Paleolithic technology, however, was not productive enough to support anything approaching a hierarchy of priests, so no cohesive theology could be developed. Conceptions of gods and spirits were hazy, and much emphasis was placed on individual visions. Religion was not used as a method of social control. Benefits did not depend on the morality of the individual. People begged or bargained with the supernatural, as we can see from the following statement made by an Eskimo to the Arctic explorer Knud Rasmussen:

We believe our Angakut, our magicians, and we believe them because we wish to live long, and because we do not want to expose ourselves to the danger of famine and starvation. We believe, in order to make our lives and food secure. If we do not believe the magicians, the animals we hunt would make themselves invisible to us; if we did not follow their advice, we should fall ill and die.[7]

Fear of what couldn't be understood and the desire to bring the supernatural under human control were expressed in art as well as religion. By far the outstanding example of Paleolithic art consists of its extraordinary cave paintings, the best of which are located in southern France and northwestern Spain. The

Two prehistoric cave paintings from France.

subjects of the drawings are usually the larger game: bison, bear, horse, woolly rhinoceros, mammoth, and wild boar. The best of the drawings are in full color, remarkably alive, and charged with energy. Despite their extraordinary artistic quality, the cave drawings apparently were designed for utilitarian reasons. They were drawn in the darkest and most dangerous parts of the caves, although the people lived only in or near the cave entrances. The artists also commonly painted one picture over another, with no apparent desire to preserve their works. Hence it appears that the reason these Paleolithic artists made their way to the depths of the earth and created the most realistic reproductions possible of the animals they hunted was the belief that they thereby gained some sort of magic power over their game.

In conclusion, the recent findings of scientists in various fields have led us to recognize and appreciate the achievements of our prehistoric ancestors as constituting a major and decisive element in our total human heritage. Even in the realm of technology, where we consider ourselves today to be especially successful, the hunter-gatherers acquired a vast amount of data that is basic for us to the very present. They knew their habitats intimately, so they used those species of plants and animals that were beneficial and avoided those that were useless or injurious. They developed a great variety of tools including knives, axes, scrapers, hammers, awls, and needles. They also created an equal variety of weapons such as spears, harpoons, clubs, shields, armor, blowguns, and bows and arrows. Some of their inventions—such as the nonsubmersible kayak, the snowhouse, and the outrigger canoe—and the use of numerous poisons—such as hydrocyanic acid, which South American Indians learned to remove from a species of manioc which became a staple article of their diet, and other poisons such as curare, snake venoms, hemlock, and alkaloids that were used to kill game and human enemies—required considerable knowledge and skill. In preparing and preserving foods, our early ancestors used virtually all the techniques known to us today. They had earth ovens, they practiced stone boiling, they froze food in the arctic, they preserved it by drying, and they sealed foods airtight with tallow. Apart from recent inventions such as plastic containers and the harnessing of gas and electricity, Paleolithic cooks would have felt at home with modern kitchens and cuisines.

In coping with illnesses, prehistoric peoples were by no means wholly dependent on magic. They knew how to set broken bones with splints, to use tourniquets, to employ poultices and bandages, to use steam baths and massage, to practice bloodletting as therapy, and to administer enemas (which South American tribes did with rubber syringes). Preliterate peoples also had knowledge of heavenly bodies, distinguishing and naming constellations of stars. Finally, oceanic navigation was achieved in prehistoric times by the Polynesians, who made regular voyages between Hawaii and Tahiti, a distance of 2,350 miles. After reviewing these achievements in all phases of life, anthropologist Leslie A. White concludes: "The accumulated knowledge, skills, tools, machines, and techniques developed by primitive, preliterate peoples laid the basis for civilization and all the higher cultures. . . . It is indeed remarkable to see how close to the present day, primitive peoples have come at many points on the technological level."[8]

As impressive and significant as Paleolithic technology was the Paleolithic society. The everyday life of our prehistoric ancestors was in many ways very attractive. Its members were equal with one another. Warm bonds of kinship permeated and determined their social relationships. Paleolithic life offered everyone specific and accepted obligations and rewards. There was no problem of alienation or of anxiety in the face of an uncertain or unpredictable future. To the present day, an Australian aborigine can take a piece of broken glass, fashion it skillfully into an arrowhead or spear point, fit it to a spear thrower or to a bow that he has strung himself, set forth and kill his game, prepare his dinner with due attention to ceremony, and after dinner, round out the day with storytelling, sharing his adventures with the stay-at-homes. In this manner the Paleolithic hunter was a "complete man" to a degree that has not been approached since the agricultural revolution.

But the bonds that held Paleolithic society together were restricting as well as comforting. The individual was wholly subordinate to the band or tribe, which was viewed as a timeless procession of the dead, the living, and the unborn, attended by all the unseen powers of the spirit world. To this procession of life the individual was completely subject. Doubtless the overwhelming majority of individuals felt themselves to be participants rather than captives. Yet the fact remains that the result was stagnation along with security. Although the Paleolithic way of life was psychically satisfying, it was also a dead-end street. Sometimes deviance from tradition actually ended in death—for example, among the Arunta of Australia, whose elders arranged with the enemy to kill those individuals who had not been living in accordance with tribal tradition. It was this stultifying and constraining tradition that was the all-important other side of Paleolithic society.

Not only were some Paleolithic nonconformists killed, but so were the infants and the infirm in case of food shortage. The food gatherers had to move perpetually because sooner or later they exhausted the food supplies in the vicinity of their camp. This inescapable mobility forced them to prune ruthlessly their material possessions. It also forced them on certain occasions to prune equally ruthlessly some of their band members—the infants, the aged, and the infirm. A food-gathering mother obviously could carry only one infant at a time. A second born before the first had been weaned had to be killed at birth, as were also all but one infant in cases of multiple birth. Only a few food gatherers could support themselves in a given area.

THE LIFE OF THE FOOD GATHERERS

We may assume that the style of human life during the Paleolithic millennia was basically the same as that of the food gatherers that fifteenth- and sixteenth-century Europeans discovered in the New World. The accounts left by the explorers, and by the settlers and missionaries who followed them, are valuable in giving us a glimpse into our common human past. The following report is by the Jesuit father Jacob Baegert, who lived between 1750 and 1767 among the Indians of California.* His description of the "Californians" gives us a picture of Paleolithic ancestors, and also challenges common assumptions about "human nature."

With all their poor diet and hardships, the Californians are seldom sick. They are in general strong, hardy, and much more healthier than the many thousands who live daily in abundance and on the choicest fare that the skill of Parisian cooks can prepare. . . .

For the small-pox the Californians are, like other Americans, indebted to Europeans, and this disease assumes a most pestilential character among them. A piece of cloth which a Spaniard, just recovered from the smallpox, had given to a Californian communicated, in the year 1763, the disease to a small mission, and in three months more than a hundred individuals died. . . .

From what I have already said of the Californians, it might be inferred that they are the most unhappy and pitiable of the children of Adam. Yet such a supposition would be utterly wrong, and I can assure the reader that . . . they live unquestionably much happier than the civilized inhabitants of Europe. . . . Throughout the whole year nothing happens that causes a Californian trouble or vexation, nothing that renders his life cumbersome and death desirable. . . . Envy, jealousy, and slander embitter not his life, and he is not exposed to the fear of losing what he possesses, nor to the care of increasing it . . . the Californians do not know the meaning of meum [mine] and tuum [thine], those two ideas which, according to St. Gregory, fill the few days of our existence with bitterness and unaccountable evils.

Though the Californians seem to possess nothing, they have, nevertheless, all that they want, for they covet nothing beyond the productions of their poor, ill-favored country, and these are always within their reach. It is no wonder, then, that they always exhibit a joyful temper, and constantly indulge in merriment and laughter, showing thus their contentment, which, after all, is the real source of happiness.

*Smithsonian Institution, *Annual Report for 1863* (Washington, D.C., 1864), pp. 352–369.

Consequently they were easily swept aside when the agricultural revolution made possible the sustenance of relatively large numbers of food producers, or peasants, who spread irresistibly into the sparsely populated hunting grounds. This fact explains why food-gathering bands were inevitably doomed once the agricultural revolution got under way, and why today only a few such bands survive in out-of-the-way places where agriculture is not feasible for one reason or another.

We shall see that the agricultural revolution also set off a chain reaction of urbanization, class differentiation, and social cleavage that undermined the appealing equality of primitive society. But in doing so it also broke the restricting bonds of tribal traditionalism and thereby launched humanity, for good or ill, on the fateful course that was to lead from hunting ground to megalopolis, from human muscle to atomic power. Before turning to the agricultural revolution, however, it is necessary to consider the global spread of Paleolithic peoples and the ensuing repercussions this dispersal created, affecting us to the present day.

III. APPEARANCE OF RACES

It is commonly assumed that population explosion is a phenomenon peculiar to our times, but this is not so. Spectacular population spurts have occurred with each major technological breakthrough in history, and for the obvious reason that an advance in technology leads to increased productivity, which can support a larger number of people. By human standards of the time, the differential between early and late Paleolithic technology did represent a major advance. This in turn led to a population jump from an estimated 125,000 hominids in the early Paleolithic to 5.32 million Homo sapiens at the end of the Paleolithic 10,000 years ago, on the eve of the agricultural revolution. This increase of over forty-two times is thus comparable to the population explosions that, as we shall see, were to accompany each of the later technological revolutions.

Another demographic pattern set at this time and repeated in the future was the disproportionate increase of any population that took the lead in technological innovation, and hence the spread of that population over larger areas. This pattern has prevailed since the first appearance of life on earth, in accordance with the Law of Cultural Dominance propounded as follows by the anthropologists M. D. Sahlins and E. R. Service:

... that cultural system which more effectively exploits the energy resources of a given environment will tend to spread in that environment at the expense of less effective systems. ... Higher forms characteristically exploit more different kinds of resources more effectively than lower; hence in most environments they are more effective than lower; thus their greater range.[9]

At all times, the best-adapted species, or that which is most efficiently exploiting the physical environment, is the species that has prevailed and extended its domain. Thus the Australopithecines, with their primitive pebble tools and lack of clothing, were unable to extend their range beyond the warm savanna lands. Homo sapiens, with more advanced technology and correspondingly more efficient adaptation, were able to push north into the Siberian tundra as well as south into the African and Southeast Asian tropical rain forests.

Part of the superior human technology was the construction of various devices for crossing bodies of water. Depending on local natural resources, these devices were of four basic types: skin boat, bark boat, raft, and dugout. With this variety of boats, early humans were able to cross rivers and lakes and even the wider expanses of water from Africa to Europe, from Southeast Asia to Australia, and from Siberia to North America. This spreading out was greatly helped by the Ice Age, which sucked the ocean waters up into the ice caps, thus lowering the level of the oceans and creating land bridges between continents. Under these circumstances, humans occupied all continents except Antarctica. They became, together with their inseparable dog, the most widespread animal in the world. (See map of Early Human Migrations, p. 16.)

Hand in hand with the dispersal of Homo sapiens went race differentiation. A variety of so-called races appeared, with distinguishing characteristics in skin color, hair texture, and facial

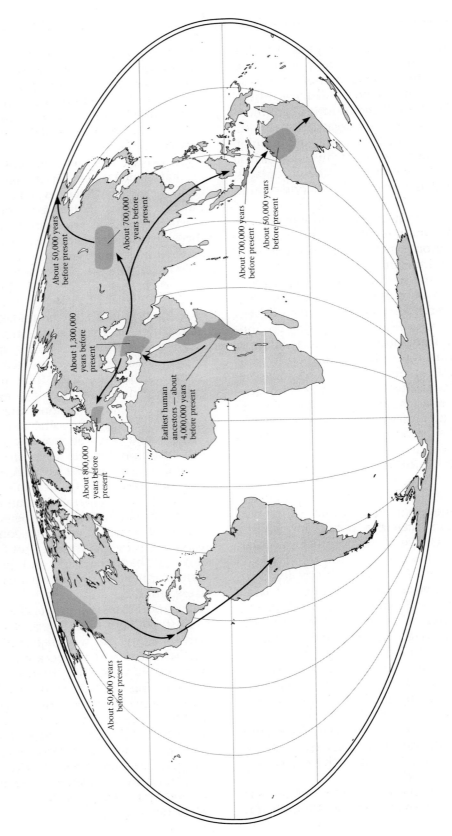

Early Human Migrations

structure. These races are believed to have emerged because of the relative isolation of the various human populations and their adaptation to differing local environments. The significant point concerning this differentiation within the human species is that it occurred so late—well after the emergence of Homo sapiens. All modern races, then, stem from a common stock, and after it had attained its full human development. This explains why the Europeans were able to interbreed with all the races in the lands they discovered. It also explains why, as virtually all anthropologists agree, there are no significant differences in innate mental capacity among all races. Representatives of late Paleolithic or of the contemporary Australian aborigines would stand as much chance of graduating from a university as would representatives of any other living races.

The details about how the races appeared in various regions are not known and probably never will be. Archeologists have long accepted the "out-of-Africa" theory about human origins, which holds that humans appeared first in Africa, whence they migrated to other continents. This theory, along with others, is being questioned because of discoveries being made virtually every year in new excavations throughout the world. For example, stone tools recently found in northern Australia indicate human settlements in that region as early as 176,000 years ago, which undermines past theories that dated earliest immigrations at 50,000 to 60,000 years ago. Equally disparate are past theories about the date of early migrations to Central Asia, compared to much older bones and stone tools recently found there in caves.

So great and numerous are the disparities disclosed by ongoing excavations that archeologists now are reassessing cherished past assumptions. Some are asking whether the original human birthplace was in Africa or in Asia. Others, known as multiregionalists, believe the cradle of the human race will never be found because a single source for all humans does not exist anywhere. Rather they find more plausible the theory of multiple origins for the human species at different places.

Despite the present uncertainty about human origins and evolution, we do know that by the end of the latest Ice Age, about 10,000 years ago, the global distribution of races was beginning to be the same as today. The Caucasoids occupied Europe, North and East Africa, and the Middle East, extending into India and central Asia. The Negroids were in the Sahara (better watered then) and a bit southward, whereas the Pygmies and Bushmen, in contrast to later times, occupied the remainder of Africa. Other Pygmies, the Negritos, lived in the forests of India and Southeast Asia, while in the open country of these regions and in Australia were the Australoids. Finally in East Asia and the Americas were the Mongoloids.

Although that racial pattern is vaguely similar to today's, the map of Global Race Distribution (p. 18) shows that basic changes had occurred by 1000 C.E. and still more by today. These changes, as we shall note later, came as a direct result of later technological revolutions. It was the failure to keep up with these revolutions that explains the virtual disappearance of the Bushmen and Pygmies and Australoids, as well as the swamping of the American Indians in most of the New World. Put in other words, it explains why 10,000 years ago blonds probably were no more numerous than Bushmen, whereas today there are 100,000 blonds for every living Bushman.

The very different experiences of the Bushmen, compared with those of the Caucasoids or other races, had nothing to do with differences in ability. We will return to this important point at the end of Part IV, "Races in History," where we shall consider the reasons for the varied racial experiences.

In conclusion, it is noteworthy that while humans were dividing into various races, they were also growing in height. Whereas our early ancestors reached an average height of four feet, six inches, today our average is five feet, ten inches. This growth is believed to be due to abundant and reliable food supplies, especially animal protein, and to immunization during childhood, which has curbed growth inhibiting diseases. The body growth has continued through modern times, as evident in the size of the body armor of medieval knights, into which most adult males today would be unable to squeeze.

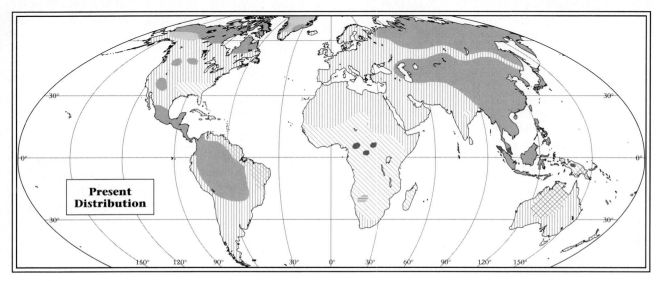

Global Race Distribution

SUGGESTED READINGS

Essential aids for the study of world history are G. Barraclough, *The Times Atlas of World History* (Times Books, 1991); W. L. Langer, *An Encyclopedia of World History* (Houghton Mifflin, 1972), and the superbly illustrated *National Geographic Atlas of World History* (Washington, 1997).

Important recent books on early human history are by J. E. Pfeiffer, *The Emergence of Man* (Harper & Row, 1985); R. Lewin, *In the Age of Mankind* (Smithsonian Book, 1988), presents current theories about prehistory and human prospects today; and M. Wolpoff and R. Caspari, *Race and Human Evolution* (Simon & Schuster, 1997), which deals with the Afro-centric-multicentric controversy. The most recent and colorful survey of human origins, with superb illustrations, is by R. Gore, "The Dawn of Humans," *National Geographic* (May 1977).

For the status of Paleolithic women, see M. Ehrenberg, *Women in Prehistory* (British Museum, 1989); R. R. Reiter, ed., *Toward an Anthropology of Women* (Monthly Review Press, 1975); M. K. Martin and B. Voorhies, *Female of the Species* (Columbia University, 1975); and R. Bridenthal and C. Koonz, eds., *Becoming Visible: Women in European History* (Houghton Mifflin, 1977).

NOTES

1. *New York Times*, April 23, 1996.
2. C. C. Swisher et al., "Latest Homo erectus of Java," *Science* (December 13, 1996): 1870–1874; *New York Times*, December 13, 1996.
3. Cited by E. Leacock, "Women in Egalitarian Societies," in R. Bridenthal and C. Koonz, eds., *Becoming Visible: Women in European History* (Houghton Mifflin, 1977), pp. 21, 22.
4. B. Spencer, *Native Tribes of the Northern Territory of Australia* (London, 1914), p. 36; and R. B. Lee, *The !Kung San* (Cambridge University, 1979), p. 246.
5. V. M. Bryant, Jr., "I Put Myself on a Caveman Diet Permanently," *Prevention*, Vol. 3 (September 1979), pp. 128–137. More details on this subject can be found in Bryant's articles in *Scientific American*, Vol. 232 (January 1975); and in *American Antiquity*, Vol. 39, No. 3 (1974).
6. A. R. Radcliffe-Brown, *The Andaman Islanders* (Free Press, 1948), p. 192.
7. K. Rasmussen, *People of the Polar North* (Lippincott, 1980), p. 124.
8. L. A. White, *The Evolution of Culture: The Development of Civilization to the Fall of Rome* (McGraw-Hill, 1959), pp. 271, 272.
9. M. D. Sahlins and E. R. Service, eds., *Evolution and Culture* (University of Michigan, 1960), pp. 75, 79.

2

Humans as Food Growers

It is probably very difficult for us now to conceptualize fully (or to exaggerate) the consequences of the first appearance of effective food production. The whole range of human existence, from the biological (including diet, demography, disease, and so on) through the cultural (social organization, politics, religion, esthetics, and so forth) bands of the spectrum took on completely new dimensions.

Robert J. Braidwood

During Paleolithic times humans became "human" by learning to speak, to make tools, and to use fire. These advances gave them an enormous advantage over the other animals about them, and yet in one fundamental respect humans remained akin to animals: They were still hunters among other hunters. They were still food gatherers, as were countless other species that were completely dependent on the bounty of nature. And being dependent on nature, humans were dominated by nature. They had to be constantly on the move in order to follow animals and to locate berry patches or fishing grounds. They had to live in small groups or bands because not many could find enough food to support themselves in a given area. It is estimated that even in fertile areas with mild winters only one or two food collectors could support themselves per square mile. And as much as twenty or even thirty square miles were needed for each individual in regions of cold climate, tropical jungle, or desert.

The shift from being food gatherers to being food producers changed every aspect of human life. Why the shift was made and what its results were are the subjects of this chapter.

I. ORIGINS OF AGRICULTURE

When humans became food producers a new world with limitless horizons opened before them. They left behind them the Paleolithic (old stone) age and entered the Neolithic (new stone) age.

Neolithic humans differed from their Paleolithic predecessors in two respects: They made stone tools by grinding and polishing rather than by chipping and fracturing; and, even more important, they obtained food wholly or primarily from agriculture and/or stock raising rather than from hunting animals or gathering plants. The new cutting tools made of ground stone were more durable than earlier tools and facilitated important inventions like the plow and the wheel, which appeared toward the end of the Neolithic period. But still, the trick of grinding a chipped or hewn axe to a smooth, polished edge was a rather trivial matter compared to the transformation of humans from food collectors to food producers.

This transformation was not the result of sudden inspiration. It was not a case of some prehistoric Archimedes shouting "Eureka!" as he suddenly realized how plants grow. People actually understood the mechanics of plant growth before the agricultural revolution, just as they knew before Columbus's voyage that the earth was round—and just as modern hunting societies that are wholly without agriculture are nevertheless thoroughly familiar with the nature and behavior of plants in their habitats. They know that plants sprout from seeds, that they usually need water and sunshine to flourish, and that they grow better in one type of soil than in another. Such knowledge is acquired naturally by modern primitives because their very existence depends on practical understanding of the surrounding flora and fauna. There is no reason for doubting, and plenty of evidence for believing, that prehistoric people acquired the same practical understanding when they were in similar circumstances.

If the basic principles of plant life were known to humans thousands of years before the agricultural revolution, why did they delay so long before putting them into practice? One reason is that there was no incentive to do so. Hunting peoples did not normally live on the brink of starvation. Nor did they increase rapidly in numbers and outstrip the available food supply. Being nomads, they were always on the move and, therefore, could not have large families. Mothers had to breast-feed each of their babies because they did not have farm animals to provide milk. If a new baby was born too soon after the previous birth, the mother had to let it die because she could not breast-feed and carry two infants at one time from camp to camp. Usually mothers were spared the tragedy of infanticide because breast-feeding tends to suppress ovulation, so mothers did not normally become pregnant during the several years they fed each baby. If this natural form of birth control failed, then our ancestors resorted to such practices as infanticide, abortion, and lactation taboos, which kept their numbers low enough to pull through the lean months of each year. Thus hunting societies continued to exist for millennia at a comfortable equilibrium and consequently lacked stimulus for radical change.

Not only did the hunters under normal circumstances have plenty to eat, but also they had a rich variety of food. The Bushmen of South Africa provide a modern example. Although these hunters live in an unfavorable desert environment, they nevertheless collect food from 85 edible plant species and 223 animal species. Thus their diet is much richer in vitamins, minerals, and protein than that of peasants who rely on the few types of grains or tubers they grow. Historically, hunters also had a more dependable supply of food because they could draw on such a large number of plants and animals. By contrast, peasants always faced the danger of starvation if bad weather spoiled their crops.

Not only did hunters have a better and more dependable food supply than food-growing peasants, but in addition they had to work less for their food. Again, adult Bushmen living in a harsh desert spend an average of only fifteen hours per week hunting or collecting food. This is little more than two hours a day. It is not surprising, then, that Bushmen are exceptionally healthy, with 10 percent of their adults being over sixty years of age. Aiding their good health is their nomadic way of life. Since they are always on the move, they avoid diseases that develop from unsanitary conditions, such as from the human excreta and garbage that collect in the villages where peasants spend their lives.

For all these reasons, hunters did not shift to agriculture until 10,000 years ago, even though they knew much earlier how to grow things. Another reason for the late beginning of agriculture was the scarcity of plants and animals suitable for domestication. Throughout history humans have been able to domesticate only a few hundred plants and a few dozen animals, ones that happen to possess certain essential characteristics. Plants must be potentially high-yielding and be adaptable to a variety of environments. If not, domesticating them will have little effect. This explains why, out of approximately 200,000 species of flowering plants, only about 3,000 have been used to any extent for food. Of these, fewer than 30 are of major importance. They include four grasses (wheat, rice, maize, and sugar), starchy staples (potato, yam, manioc, and banana), and legumes, which are the meat of the poor (lentils, peas, vetches, beans, peanuts, and soybeans).

Like plants, animals also must be domesticated. They must be capable of overcoming their instinctive fear of humans, of breeding in captivity, and of accepting the diet provided by humans. The peoples of the Old World were fortunate in having available a variety of such animals to provide them with meat, milk, wool, and beasts of burden. The progress of American Indians, by contrast, was retarded because they had nothing comparable; they had to make do with a group of half-domesticated Andean cameloids: the llama, alpaca, and vicuna.

As we can see from this discussion, no breakthrough to agriculture could be expected unless some change occurred to upset the comfortable equilibrium of the hunting societies, and even then agriculture could occur only in areas where domesticable plants or animals were available. This is precisely what happened.

During the comparatively short period between 10,000 and 2,000 years ago, the great majority of humans on this planet shifted to agriculture. Obviously this was a forced shift, for no hunter would voluntarily leave his easy and secure way of life for the never-ending work of the peasant tied to his fields and his cattle. What forced the change was population pressure. Over tens of thousands of years, the number of humans had increased slowly, causing the migrations in Africa, Asia, Europe, Australia, and the Americas. Finally all the continents, except Antarctica, were populated. As the number of humans continued to grow slowly but steadily, hunters were forced to supplement the food they gathered with food they grew. Undoubtedly they were unhappy about staying in one area to grow crops and raise cattle, but the fact is that many more people per square mile can be supported by agriculture than by food gathering.

Agriculture first became a full-time occupation in those few regions where there were plants and/or animals that could be domesticated. In the process of domestication the wild plants and animals became larger and provided more food. Thus the hunters spent more and more of their time as food producers rather than food gatherers, until they ended up as peasants living in villages. From the first few centers of this agricultural revolution, the new way of life gradually spread over most of the globe.

II. SPREAD OF AGRICULTURE

The process of transition from hunting to agriculture was gradual and took place independently in many parts of the world. Agriculture developed independently in the Middle East—the Nile Valley in Egypt and Sudan, the valley of the Tigris and Euphrates in Syria and Iraq, and the eastern coast of the Mediterranean in the areas of Turkey, Syria, Lebanon, and Israel—as well as in Mexico, northern China, and Peru. New discoveries being made yearly suggest that there were other independent centers in Southeast Asia, West Africa, and elsewhere. We know the most about the Middle East and Mesoamerica (roughly tropical America north of Panama), both of which had an especially large number of domesticable plants and/or animals.

In the Middle East, ancient peoples found the ancestors of modern wheat, oats, rye, and barley, as well as those of the modern goat, sheep, cattle, and pig. In Mesoamerica, the two small republics of Costa Rica and El Salvador, although comprising only 1 percent of the area of the United States, yield as many plant species as do both the United States and Canada. This extraordinary diversity is the result of the variety of climates created by the wide range of altitude, temperature, and rainfall within a small area. Consequently, dozens of plants were successfully domesticated in Mesoamerica. The most important ones were maize, beans, and squashes.

Over a period of many centuries the various plants were adapted by humans to a variety of environmental conditions and spread to other areas, thereby creating a regional complex of multiple-species agriculture. This advanced type of agriculture had two great advantages: a high level of productivity and subsistence security. If one crop failed for climatic reasons, another with different requirements could survive. So agriculture provided the dependable food supply essential for dense populations and for the civilizations they produced.

The transition from the earliest domestication to agricultural revolution, or full dependence on agriculture, was very gradual and prolonged. Known as the phase of incipient agriculture, in the Middle East it lasted from roughly 9500 to 7500 B.C.E. In the New World it lasted even longer. One of the earliest centers of domestication in the New World was the Mexican valley of Tehuacán, where incipient agriculture began in approximately 7000 B.C.E. It is estimated that 2,000 years later only 10 percent of the diet of the local Indians was derived from their domesticated plants, primarily maize. By 3000 B.C.E., still only a third of the food came from domesticated sources. It was not until about 1500 B.C.E. that maize and other plants were hybridized to the point where their yield was sufficiently high to provide most of the food, thus completing the transition from incipient agriculture to the agricultural revolution.

From these two original centers of full-fledged agriculture, from northern China, and from other centers that will be identified in the future, the new mode of living spread to all parts of the globe. The diffusion process was sparked by the inefficiency of early agriculture, which was an intermittent or shifting type of cultivation. The land was cleared and used for crop growing for a few years; then it was abandoned to natural growth for eight to ten or more years to allow the fertility to be restored. As a result, the ratio of abandoned or recuperating land to that under cultivation at any specific time was

between five and ten to one. This very land-wasteful agriculture, together with increasing population, required constant extension of the limits of the tilled land into new regions. There was a continual "budding-off" or "hiving-off" from the agricultural settlements into the less densely populated lands of the food-gathering peoples. In this way agriculture was diffused in all directions from the original centers. (See maps of Expansion of Agriculturists, p. 24, and Dispersal of Agriculture, p. 26.)

This doesn't mean that agriculture eventually spread all over the globe. A great variety of local conditions determined where agriculture was to appear early, where late, and where not at all. In the Afro-Asian desert belt and in the arctic regions, agriculture was impossible for obvious reasons. Agriculture was also absent in parts of Africa and the Americas, as well as in all of Australia, because of a combination of isolation and unfavorable physical environment. In other regions such as central and western Europe, agriculture was hampered because the heavy forests were an almost insurmountable obstacle until the Iron Age, when cheap and effective implements became available. When the iron axe replaced the stone, it was possible to increase the efficiency of forest clearing and thereby to allow larger plots to be cultivated in areas where agriculture was already practiced. Hence efficient cultivation extended from the Mediterranean coastlands to the European interior, from the Indus River valley to the Ganges, from the Yellow River valley to the Yangtze, and from Africa's savannas to the tropical rain forests.

Very little is known concerning the precise details of the spread of agriculture from region to region. From the Middle East it spread eastward to the Indus valley, northward to central Asia and eastern Europe, and westward to central and western Europe. In China, wheat and barley were introduced from the Middle East about 1300 B.C.E., but recent research shows that native plants had been domesticated and cultivated in that region 3,000 years earlier. These plants included rice and tea grown in south China and millets, sorghum, and soybeans grown in north China. Distinctively Chinese was the mulberry tree, whose leaves fed the silkworms, and the lacquer tree, which yielded its famous varnish or lacquer.

Expansion of Agriculturists

Women were the principal farmers in most Native American societies, growing corn, beans, and other crops that made up most of their food supply. This sixteenth-century French engraving shows Indian men preparing the soil for cultivation and Indian women sowing seeds in neat rows.

Agriculture in Africa developed independently about 5000 B.C.E. around the headwaters of the Niger and in the Nile valley about 4000 B.C.E. Whatever its origins, African agriculture for many centuries was confined to the open savanna lands and failed to penetrate southward into areas of tropical rain forest. This was partly because the millet and sorghum commonly grown in the savanna did not do well in the rain forest. But about the beginning of the Christian era this obstacle was overcome by two important developments. One was the appearance of iron working, which may have reached Africa from its place of origin in the Middle East. The other was the arrival, apparently from Southeast Asia, of bananas and Asian yams, which flourished under forest conditions. Thus two new crops along with iron tools brought about the rapid expansion of agriculture down to the southern part of the continent.

In modern times, with the partition of Africa among Western empires, African agriculture suffered a setback. European missionaries, officials, and scientists brought with them their familiar European cereals such as wheat and corn and assumed that the unfamiliar African cereals were inferior. With modern packaging and advertising, European cereals were generally accepted as being truly superior. Today, however, it is gradually being realized that this assumption is unjustified. The U.S. National Academy of Sciences began publishing in 1996 a series of reports entitled *Lost Crops of Africa*. The reports state that Africa has more indigenous varieties of cereal than any other continent, including an African variety of rice (tef), an Ethiopian staple rich in protein and iron, and sorghum, which is used largely for animal feed in the United States but which yields a high quality flour. "Africa is called the hungry continent," concludes the National Academy report, "yet it is a cornucopia of food plants people are not taking advantage of."[1]

In the Americas agriculture arose independently in Mexico and Peru; we will focus our attention on maize in Mexico. The kernels of maize are clustered together on a corn cob, and unlike other grains (such as wheat), they do not fall to the ground and germinate. Thus the cultivation of maize requires human assistance, as evidenced by the presence of maize in archeological sites. Some kind of wild maize provided the base for modern domesticated maize, as seen in fossilized maize pollen discovered in the area

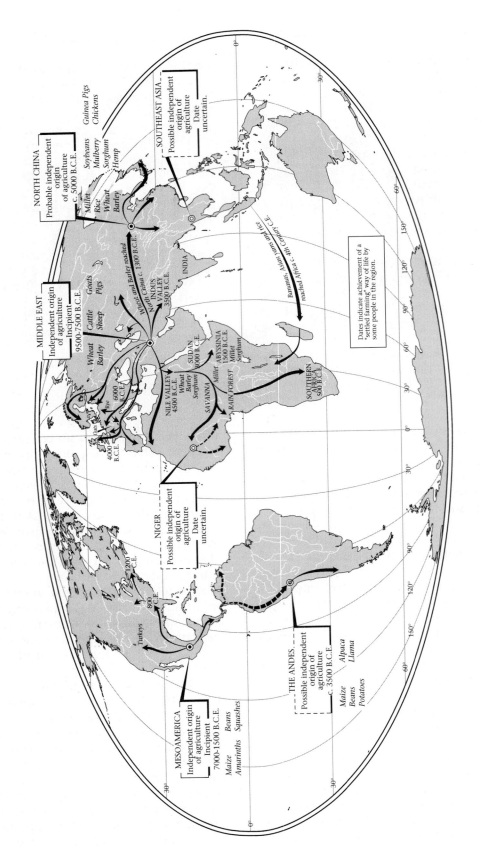

Dispersal of Agriculture

of Mexico City. Modern varieties of maize seem to be the result of a cross between this ancestral strain and wild teosinte grass. The hybrid was domesticated in the area of Mexico about 1500 B.C.E. Other domesticated crops in the Mexican region include squash (about 7000 B.C.E.) and beans (between 3000 and 5000 B.C.E.).

Many of the agricultural products in the area of Mexico were not domesticated at the same time. One must conclude that there was probably a long period of transition when the people of this area continued to forage for food while raising other crops.

Agriculture also seems to have become important in the mountains of Peru about 5600 B.C.E. Domesticated crops in this area include tomatoes, peanuts, lima beans, and potatoes. Also, maize different from the Mexican variety has been found there dating from between 4300 and 2000 B.C.E. From this original Mesoamerican center, agriculture spread both north and south. Maize arrived in the American Southwest about 3000 B.C.E. but did not have much effect until 750 C.E., when improvements over the first maize made its cultivation more productive than simple food collecting. Likewise, in eastern North America the Indians did not shift to dependence on agriculture until about 800 C.E., when they developed field cropping based on several varieties of maize, beans, and squash.

III. VARIETIES OF AGRICULTURE

The worldwide diffusion of agriculture led to the domestication of a variety of plants suitable to a variety of local conditions. In the Middle East wheat and barley had been the most common crops. But as the farmers moved northward they found that these crops did not do as well as rye, which originally had been a weed sown unintentionally with the wheat and barley. Hence there was a shift to rye in central Europe and, for the same reasons, another shift to oats further north.

Likewise, the extension of agriculture to sub-Saharan Africa led to the cultivation of native millets and of one type of rice, while around the shores of the Mediterranean the olive became one of the most important sources of edible oil. Across the Iranian plateau and in

northwest India an essentially Middle Eastern type of agriculture was practiced. But a dividing line running north and south through central India marks the transition to an entirely different climatic zone with correspondingly different plant life. This is the monsoon region, with heavy seasonal rainfall, constant heat, and dense jungles. Seed-bearing plants of the Middle Eastern variety, which require plenty of sun, cannot thrive here, so in their place we find the yam, taro, banana, and above all, rice. Finally, in the Americas the main crop everywhere was maize, supplemented by beans and squash in North America and by manioc and potatoes of both the sweet and "Irish" varieties in South America.

The net result of this agriculture diffusion was, very generally speaking, three great cereal areas: the rice area in East and Southeast Asia; the maize area in the Americas; and the wheat area in Europe, the Middle East, North Africa, and central Asia to the Indus and Yellow River valleys. During the several millennia between the agricultural and industrial revolutions these three cereals were as fundamental for human history as coal, iron, and copper were to become later. Recently wheat has been overtaking rice as the world's most important grain. The reason is that agricultural scientists have developed wheat varieties that are more resistant to heat, cold, drought, and pests. So wheat can be grown now in many more regions than in the past. Hence a global harvest of wheat in 1995 totaling 542 million tons.

Early farmers not only grew different crops in different regions of the world, but also they developed different types of agricultural techniques to raise those crops. One of the earliest is known as the "slash-and-burn" method. This slash-and-burn technique was carried on against forests because the land had to be cleared of trees and bushes so that the farmers could plant their seeds. But the clearing was a very hard job because the farmers had only stone tools in those early times. So they used fire to burn down the forests and thus clear the land for farming. Live trees, however, do not burn easily because they are full of sap. So the early farmers slashed a ring around the trunk of each tree, which stopped the flow of sap and caused the tree to die. The dead and dry trees were easy to burn, and the remaining ashes were a good fertilizer. So the farmers planted their seeds in the cleared and enriched land, watered and weeded the plants that sprouted, built fences to keep out wild animals such as rabbits or deer, and finally harvested the crop when it was ripe. This slash-and-burn technique made possible the extension of farming into large areas formerly covered by forests. It is a technique still practiced in many regions of the world.

Another technique still common on all continents is terrace agriculture. It remains the preferred method in mountainous areas where, in case of heavy rains, farmers face the danger of losing their crops to flash floods pouring down hillsides. To prevent such damage, farmers built stone walls on mountain slopes and then collected soil and piled it up behind the walls. Soil washed down the slopes and accumulated behind the walls as well. When enough soil piled up to fill the terraces, the farmers then had small level fields on which they could plant their crops without fear of losing them to floods. This is how potatoes are grown today in the Andean highlands of Peru, maize in the highlands of North China, and grapes in Mediterranean countries such as Spain, Italy, and Greece.

A third type of agriculture, vegetative root farming, is widely practiced in tropical regions. Live shoots of root plants such as taros, yams, and manioc are partly buried in moist ground where they grow into large tuberous roots that can be pulled up and fried, boiled, or baked into soup, paste, or cake. These are staple food crops that can be grown year round which provide a dietary mainstay when their starch is supplemented with fish (a common practice in East and Southeast Asia).

Finally, we should note raised field agriculture, which was developed about three thousand years ago in Peru's highlands. It was then dropped and has been forgotten for centuries. Scientists are very interested in this old technology because after discovering its secrets and using it to grow local Peruvian crops, they find it produces bigger crops than can be grown with the more expensive modern agricultural techniques with their chemicals and machinery. The raised fields range from 13 to 33 feet wide, are 33 to 330 feet long, and are about 3

feet high. Crops are planted on those earthen platforms, which are separated from each other by canals of similar size. The platforms are constructed from earth that was shoveled out when the canals were dug. Growing crops on these individual raised fields rather than on the surrounding flat countryside gives the farmers several advantages, which are shown in the accompanying illustration.

- Crops are protected by the canal water heat against frost, which is common during the cold nights of the Andean highlands.
- Crops are protected against floods because surplus water flows into the canals.
- Crops are protected against drought by capillary action from the canals and by the ease of hand watering.
- Crops are fertilized with organic muck (green algae, cattle droppings, and dead plant matter), which is raised from the canal bottoms to the raised fields and provides fertilizer superior to the chemical varieties and costs nothing but the labor, which is plentiful in local villages.
- Fish raised in the canals improve substantially the diet of local farmers by increasing the protein in their diet.

Thanks to these advantages, experimental raised fields in Peru were yielding 30 tons of potatoes per acre in 1984, compared to 8 tons from surrounding fields cultivated in the usual manner with imported machinery and fertilizers. Because the raised field technology is a self-sustaining as well as a more productive system, it is being tried out in the United States and in Indonesia, as well as in several Latin American countries. Perhaps a type of agriculture developed originally in the Andean highlands, then forgotten for centuries and recently rediscovered and revived by scientists, may end up reappearing all over the world. The success of this ancient technology shows that lessons can be learned from our prehistoric successors, even in technological matters, despite all the marvels of modern "high technology."

In addition to these varieties of domesticated plants and of agricultural techniques, we should note that in those regions where there was too little rainfall for agriculture, the inhabitants turned to stock raising. They domesticated local animals rather than local plants. The first

Raised-platform fields, used in the Andes in ancient times, yield bumper crops without modern tools or fertilizers; the main expense is for labor to dig canals and build up platforms.

Water in the canals absorbs the sun's heat by day and radiates it back by night, helping protect crops against frost. The more fields cultivated this way, the bigger the effect on the microenvironment.

The platforms are generally 13 to 33 feet wide, 33 to 330 feet long, and about 3 feet high, built with soil dug from canals of similar size and depth.

Sediment in the canals, nitrogen-rich algae and plant and animal remains, provides fertilizer for crops. In an experiment, potato yields outstripped those from chemically fertilized fields.

Reconstructed fields can be managed by relatively small groups of workers, recent experiments showed. The size of the platforms allows for hand-watering in time of drought, and capillary action feeds the roots. The elevation also protects crops from flooding. The method may be of value in many Third World areas.

Raised Field Agriculture

wild animal they domesticated was the dog. At first they killed and ate dogs, as they did other animals. Then they found that dogs were useful to keep in the camp because they frightened off wild animals by their barking and they also helped the hunters to find game. By 10,000 B.C.E., hunting bands on all continents had their packs of domesticated dogs.

Soon afterwards, humans domesticated other animals that were useful to them in one way or another. Thus those people became pastoral nomads, and many continue today to live in this way, roaming the vast steppes and desert lands from the Sahara to Manchuria and the broad savannas of sub-Saharan Africa. Pastoral

nomadism was late in developing because it had to await the domestication of the horse and camel, which provided suitable transport in open country. But once pastoral nomadism got under way, between 1500 and 1000 B.C.E., a variety of forms developed. Some nomads depended on a single animal—camels in Arabia and cattle in East and South Africa—whereas others relied on a mix of livestock—herds of horses, cattle, camels, sheep, and goats in central Asia.

Yet regardless of the variety of animals, the pastoral nomads were poor compared to those who lived in the rich valleys of the Tigris-Euphrates, Nile, Indus, and Yellow rivers. In

This scene on an Attic jar from late in the sixth century B.C.E. shows how olives, one of Athens' most important crops, were harvested.

these valleys, a permanent type of irrigation agriculture was developed that was very productive and that in time supported great and wealthy civilizations. These valley civilizations were irresistible magnets to the comparatively poverty-stricken nomads of the central Eurasian steppes and of the Middle Eastern and North African deserts. Thus Eurasian history to modern times has been in large part the history of the rise and fall of great civilizations, with the pastoral nomads always ready to contribute to the fall of any civilization weakened by internal discord.

IV. LIFE OF THE FOOD GROWERS

The most obvious impact of the agricultural revolution was the new sedentary existence. Humans now had to settle down to care for their newly domesticated plants and animals. Thus the Paleolithic nomadic band gave way to the Neolithic village as the basic economic and cultural unit. Indeed the village remained the basis for a pattern of life that was to prevail until the late eighteenth century and that persists to the present day in the vast underdeveloped regions of the world.

Recent archeological excavations reveal that our early ancestors were not always restricted to a choice of nomadic hunting and gathering or sedentary farming. If local plant and animal food resources were unusually rich, it was possible for the local inhabitants to settle down in year-round villages, even though they depended entirely on hunting and gathering. This was the case in Abu Hureyre in northern Syria, where wild cereals, pulses, and legumes grew so densely that they yielded harvests as rich as though they were in planted gardens. Therefore it was possible for a large village of 300 to 400 gatherer-hunters to flourish in Abu Hureyre for several hundred years. Similar favorable conditions enabled food collectors to exist in permanent settlements in other regions such as the Pacific Northwest (Oregon, Washington, and British Columbia), where bountiful fish resources were available year-round. Likewise in the Southern Pacific, along the Peruvian coast, favorable sea currents nurtured marine life across the whole ecosystem, from phytoplankton to birds and sea mammals. So here also, food gatherers settled down in permanent villages, supported comfortably by the varieties of marine life swarming in the coastal waters. Yet such villages were the exception: Nomadism was the natural corollary of food gathering, just as a settled life was of food producing.

It is easy to romanticize Neolithic village life, but to do so would be grossly misleading. Everyone—men, women, and children—had to work, and work hard, to produce food and a few handicraft articles. Productivity was low since people learned slowly and painfully about soils, seeds, fertilizers, and crop rotation. Despite hard labor, famine was common; it often followed too much or too little rain or a plague of pests. Epidemics swept the villages repeatedly as sedentary life introduced the problem of the disposal of human excreta and other refuse. Although dogs helped with sanitation and personal modesty presumably caused people to deposit stools away from habitation, neither of these was sufficient to prevent the various diseases that follow the route from the bowel to the mouth. Furthermore, malnutrition was the rule because of inadequate food supply or unbalanced diet. Life expectancy under these circumstances was exceedingly low, but the high birthrate increased village populations everywhere until famine, epidemic, or emigration restored the balance between food supply and number of mouths to feed.

Yet Neolithic village life was not all misery and suffering. It was a time when people made technological progress at an infinitely more rapid rate than in the preceding Paleolithic period. Primarily, it was not because they had more leisure time than the hunters; we have seen that this was not so. Rather, the new sedentary life made a richer material existence physically possible. The living standards of the nomadic hunters were limited to what they could carry, whereas the Neolithic villagers could indulge in the building of substantial housing together with furnishings, utensils, implements, and assorted knickknacks. They learned to make pottery out of raw clay, at first imitating the baskets, gourds, and other containers of pre-agrarian times. Gradually they grasped the potential of pottery materials and techniques and began to fashion objects that no longer resembled the earlier containers. By the end of the Neolithic period, people in the Near East were building kilns, or ovens, that could fire pottery at a higher temperature and so allow for glazing. The glazed surface sealed the pottery and prevented seepage or evaporation. The agriculturist then had vessels that could be used not only for storing grain but also for cooking and for keeping liquids such as oil and beer.

Similar progress was made with textiles. Late Paleolithic peoples may have twisted or spun wild mountain sheep, goat, dog, or other animal fibers into coarse threads and woven them to make belts, headbands, or even rough blankets. Indeed they probably also modeled clay into crude containers. But it was during the Neolithic that people developed the textile art. They used fibers of the newly domesticated flax, cotton, and hemp plants and spun and wove the fibers on spindles and looms they had gradually

evolved. Neolithic villagers also learned to build dwellings that were relatively substantial and roomy. The materials varied with the locality. The Iroquois of northern New York were known as the people of the long house because they lived in huge bark and wood structures that accommodated ten or more families. In the Middle East adobe was used for the walls, whereas in Europe the most common material was split saplings plastered with clay and dung. The roofs were usually of thatch. Dwellings were furnished with fixed beds that might be covered with canopies. Also there were modern-looking dressers with at least two tiers of shelves and various wall cupboards. Light and warmth were provided by an open fire, generally placed near the center of the room. There was no chimney to let out the smoke—only a hole in the roof or a gap under the eaves.

Sedentary life also made possible a tribal political structure in place of the individual bands of the hunting peoples. Tribes were made up of the inhabitants of the villages of a given region, and they were identified and distinguished from others by distinctive characteristics of speech and custom. Some tribes, usually those with primitive economies, were so loosely organized that they were almost at the hunting-band level. Others boasted powerful chiefs and primitive nobilities distinct from the commoners, though the lines were blurred and never reached the exclusive class structures characteristic of the later civilizations.

The basic social unit of the Neolithic village customarily was the household consisting of two or more married couples and their children. This extended family was more common than the independent nuclear family because it was better suited for coping with the problems of everyday living. If an individual producer was temporarily or permanently out of commission, the extended family could absorb the loss. It could function more efficiently during intense work periods when many hands were needed for clearing forest, harvesting, or pasturing livestock. It could also exploit a large area effectively by sending members for long periods to care for distant gardens or grazing herds, while others tended nearby plots and did household chores.

The distinctive feature of the Neolithic village was social homogeneity. All families had the necessary skills and tools to produce what they needed, and, equally important, all had access to the basic natural resources essential for livelihood. Every family was automatically a component part of the village community, which owned the farmlands, pastures, and other resources of nature. Hence there was no division between landed proprietors and landless cultivators in tribal society. "Hunger and destitution," reports an American anthropologist, "could not exist at one end of the Indian village . . . while plenty prevailed elsewhere in the same village. . . ."[2]

Precisely because of this equality, tribal societies, whether of Neolithic times or of today, have a built-in brake on productivity. Output is geared to the limited traditional needs of the family, so there is no incentive to produce a surplus. This in turn means that labor is sporadic, diversified, and correspondingly limited. The daily grind—the eight-hour day, five-day week—is conspicuously absent. The typical tribe member worked fewer hours per year than a modern man or woman and, furthermore, worked at his or her pleasure. The basic reason was that a person then labored and produced in a specific social role—as a husband or father or brother, a wife or mother or sister, or a village member. Work was not a necessary evil tolerated for the sake of making a living; rather it was a concomitant of kin and community relations. One helped one's brother in the field because of kinship ties and not because one might be given a basket of yams. This tribal society was a comfortable egalitarian society. But for precisely that reason it was a low-productivity society, as can be seen from the work schedule of the Bemba tribe. (See p. 33.)

The equality in tribal social relations extended also to tribal gender relations. This equality was firmly grounded in the free access to land that tribal women enjoyed along with the men. An anthropologist who observed the Siang rice growers of central Borneo reported that widows continued to cultivate their own plots after losing their husbands. "On the whole, the women can swing an axe as effectively as the men." If the widow was encumbered by small children, "she is usually assisted by the others in the village, through gifts of rice and wild pig or by help in clearing her field, at least

until such time as the children have become old enough to help her."[3]

Women had equal rights not only in agriculture but also in the new village crafts. Excavations at Catal Huyuk, a seventh-millennium-B.C.E. settlement in Asia Minor, reveal that women cultivated indigenous plants, baked bread in communal ovens, wove wool and cotton textiles, made mats and baskets out of the wheat straw, and fired pottery for cooking and storage. In this particular settlement, women appear to have enjoyed not merely equal status but a superior one. Pictorial representations, house furnishings, and burial remains all indicate that the family pecking order was first the mother, next the daughter, followed by the son, with the father in last place.

Turning finally to religion, the new life of the soil tillers gave rise to new beliefs and new gods. The spirits and the magic that had been used by the hunters were no longer appropriate. Now the agriculturists needed, and conceived, spirits who watched over their fields and flocks and hearths. Behind all these spirits stood a creator, usually vaguely defined. But most important, almost everywhere there was a goddess of the earth or of fertility—the earth mother. She was the source of productivity of plants and animals and of the fecundity of women. Life and well-being, the annual cycle of death and birth, ultimately depended on her, hence the creation of many fertility-goddess cults. Such cults were symbolized by the numerous clay figurines with exaggerated female characteristics—pendulous breasts and heavy thighs. They reflect the spread of agriculture from the Middle East and have been found throughout Europe and as far east as India.

V. DEMOGRAPHIC AND RACIAL RESULTS

We have seen that population increase was responsible for the agricultural revolution, but that revolution in turn caused still more population increase. Many more people can be supported per square mile by growing rather than gathering food. It is no surprise, therefore, that between 10,000 and 2,000 years ago the human population jumped from 5.32 million to 133 million, a twenty-five-fold increase within 8,000 years.

LOW PRODUCTIVITY OF TRIBAL SOCIETY

A Western observer kept the following record of the work of the Bemba tribe of Northern Rhodesia (now Zambia) during the month of September 1933. Admittedly this is a slack time of the year, when more beer is drunk than normally. Nevertheless the following selections from the record show that the Bemba tribe members do not have to cope with the "daily grind" of modern industrial society.*

September 1st, 1933. Two gourds of beer ready, one drunk by old men, one by young men. A new baby born. Women gather from other villages to congratulate, and spend two or three days in the village. Women's garden work postponed during this time.

2nd. Old men go out to clear the bush. Young men sit at home finishing the sour dregs of the beer. More visits of neighbouring women to see the new baby. Few women go out to do garden work.

3rd. Young men and women go to a church service conducted in a neighbouring village by a visiting Mission doctor. No garden work.

6th. Old and young men working by 6:30 A.M. and hard at it till 2 P.M. Two gourds of beer divided between old and young in the evening. Women working in their gardens normally.

7th. A buck shot by observer's party. Young men go out to fetch the meat. Women grind extra flour to eat with it. Two gourds of beer also made ready and drinking begins at 2 P.M. By 4 o'clock young men swaggering around the village, ready to quarrel, which they finally do. Dancing at night. Old women hilarious, and rebuked by their daughters for charging into a rough dance on the village square. Not enough beer for the younger women. They remain sober and express disapproval of the rest. No garden work done, except by old men.

8th. Every one off to their gardens in high spirits at 8 A.M. Back at 12 A.M. Young men sit in shelter and drink beer dregs for two hours, singing Scotch Mission hymns in sol-fa. Young girls go out on a miniature fish-poisoning expedition, but catch nothing.

15th. Three men begin digging dry-weather gardens by the river. Little boys go bird-snaring. Young women still away at the capital. Nobody to get relish. No proper meal cooked.

17th. Great heat. Young men sit about in shelter all day, comb each other's hair, shave, and delouse each other. No relish available. Women too tired to cook.

19th. Nine men clear bush. One woman hoeing. Three women piling branches. Young women go fish-poisoning and catch one fish (about 2 lb.).

22nd. Three men clear bush. One man hoes. Four young men go fishing with three of the wives. Three piling branches.

24th. Four gourds of beer divided between whole village. Sufficient for women as well as men. Beer-drinking lasts two days off and on.

25th. Two old men only able to tree-cut. Young men afraid to climb trees because of 'beer before the eyes.' They sit in their shelter and make baskets. One woman only does garden work. Young boys snare birds. Remains of beer drunk.

30th. More beer. Four men clear bush.

*A. I. Richards Land, *Labour and Diet in Northern Rhodesia* (Oxford University, 1939), pp. 162–164.

Not all the scattered peoples of the earth increased to the same degree. Those who switched to agriculture the earliest grew the fastest. We saw earlier that food-gathering women had few children because they breast-fed each baby for several years and they were less likely to become pregnant while they were breast-feeding. But with the agricultural revolution, mothers had cows, sheep, and goats that provided them with plenty of milk in addition to their own. So mothers now began using that milk to feed their babies and, therefore, they did not need to breast-feed each baby for several years. But they were more likely to become pregnant as soon as they stopped breast-feeding. So mothers living in villages with domesticated animals began having an average of six children, as compared to the average of four children they had had during the long centuries when they were nomadic food gatherers. That is why the population of the human race skyrocketed, as we have seen, between 10,000 and 2,000 years ago.

While agriculturists were increasing so rapidly and spreading all over the world, food gatherers were left far behind in numbers and were crowded out of the most fertile lands. Since early agriculture was not very productive, population pressure soon built up in the villages. The surplus population migrated to nearby fresh lands used by the food gatherers. Sometimes the outnumbered gatherers fled to other lands that were not suitable for farming. This happened in Africa to the Bushmen, who ended up in the Kalahari Desert, and to the Pygmies, who now live in dense jungles. (See map of Global Race Distribution, p. 18, and map of Recession of Hunters, p. 35.)

More commonly, the agricultural immigrants and the local food gatherers intermarried and produced a new hybrid people. Then as population pressure built up again, the new hybrid population would "bud-off" in turn to fresh lands, where further interbreeding would take place with native peoples. In this way agricultural techniques and crops were transmitted long distances, and the people who emerged at the end of the line were of an entirely different racial type from the originals. Thus the immigrants who brought wheat, cattle, the wheel, and the plow into north China were thoroughly Mongoloid, even though these materials originated in the Middle East.

The net result of these migrations that spread agriculture over the globe was that by 1500 B.C.E. the hunters, who in 8000 B.C.E. had comprised 100 percent of the human race, had shrunk to little more than 1 percent of the population. This occupational shift led in turn to a racial shift. Ten thousand years ago the race map of the globe showed a rough balance among six races—the Caucasoid, Mongoloid, Negroid, Bushman, Pygmy, and Australoid. (See map of Global Race Distribution, p. 18.) By 1000 C.E. this balance was drastically changed in favor of the agriculturist Mongoloids, Caucasoids, and Negroids, and against the Bushmen-Pygmies, who had remained food gatherers. The only reason the Australoids held their own was that their isolated island home had not yet been discovered by any agriculturists. This had to wait for the European explorers of the eighteenth century, and, when the discovery did take place belatedly, the consequences were all the more catastrophic for the hapless aborigines. Considering the globe as a whole, then, the racial effect of the agricultural revolution was to end the millennia-old racial equilibrium and to establish the Mongoloid-Caucasoid-Negroid predominance that persists to the present.

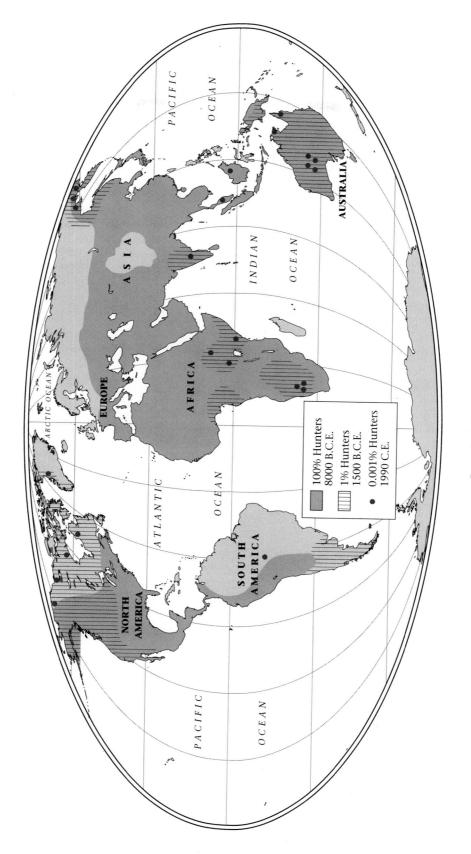

Recession of Hunters

SUGGESTED READINGS

Theories about the origins and nature of the agricultural revolution are constantly changing with new findings. The latest thinking is given in C. Wesley Cowan and Patty Jo Watson, *The Origins of Agriculture* (Smithsonian Institution Press, 1992); R. D. Hurt, *Indian Agriculture in America: Prehistory to the Present* (University Press of Kansas, 1987). See also M. N. Cohen, *The Food Crisis in Prehistory* (Yale University, 1977); S. Struever, ed., *Prehistoric Agriculture* (Natural History Press, 1971); L. R. Binford and S. R. Binford, eds., *New Perspectives in Archeology* (Aldine, 1968); and B. M. Fagan, ed., *Avenues to Antiquity* (W. H. Freeman, 1976). The independent origin of Chinese agriculture is described in Ping-ti Ho, *The Cradle of the East* (University of Chicago, 1975); and D. N. Keightly, ed., *The Origins of Chinese Civilization* (University of California, 1983). The cultural results of the spread of agriculture across Europe are analyzed in C. Renfrew, *Archeology and Language* (Cambridge University Press, 1988). The end result of the agricultural revolution for today's world is evident in J. Bertin, *Atlas of Food Crops* (Paris, 1971). The emergence of sedentism among food gatherers is analyzed in D. Price and J. A. Brown, *Prehistoric Food-Gatherers, the Emergence of Cultural Complexity* (Academic Press, 1985).

NOTES

1. Cited in *New York Times*, April 23, 1996.
2. L. H. Morgan, *Houses and House-Life of the American Aborigines* (New York, 1881), p. 45.
3. J. H. Provine, "Cooperative Ricefield Cultivation Among the Siang Dyaks of Central Borneo," *American Anthropologist*, Vol. 39, No. 1 (1937), pp. 80–91.

What It Means for Us Today

THE NATURE OF HUMAN NATURE

The world was surprised and excited in 1971 by the discovery of the Tasaday, a tribe of twenty-seven food-gathering people who had been living in complete isolation on Mindanao Island in the Philippines, where their tribal ancestors had lived similar lives for at least six centuries. The most striking and significant characteristic of this small band is their complete lack of aggressiveness. They have no words for weapon, hostility, anger, or war. Since contact with outsiders, they have eagerly adopted the long Filipino knife, the bolo, because it is superior to their stone tools for gathering food, chopping wood, and slashing through jungle brush. But they have turned down the spear and the bow and arrow because they cannot use them for food gathering. And all the food they collect (yams, fruit, berries, flowers, fish, crabs, frogs) they divide carefully and equally among all members of the band.

The validity of the Tasaday finding has been both questioned and defended. However, other small groups with similar social characteristics have been found all over the world, so the Tasaday remain significant as a common prehistoric type recognized by anthropologists. And the Tasaday are significant because they are food gatherers, as were all human beings before the agricultural revolution—in other words, for over 80 percent of human history. If, during all those tens of thousands of years, people everywhere were as peaceful as the Tasaday, then we cannot accept the common belief that Homo sapiens are innately aggressive.

Unfortunately, at the same time the world was learning about the Tasaday, another band of thirty people, the Fentou, were discovered in New Guinea. These tribesmen are fierce warriors, continually fighting with bows and arrows. Similar contradictions appeared historically among the American Indians. The Comanches and Apaches raised their children to be fighters, whereas the Hopis and Zunis raised theirs for peaceful living—and still do.

So where does this leave us regarding the nature of human nature? The record of history suggests that human beings are born neither peace-loving nor war-loving—neither cooperative nor aggressive. What determines how human beings act is not their genes but how their society teaches them to act. The psychologist Albert Bandura, who has specialized on this subject, has concluded that human nature is "a vast potentiality that can be fashioned by social influences into a variety of forms. . . . Aggression is not an inevitable or unchangeable aspect of man but a product of aggression-promoting conditions within a society."[1]

This question about human nature is of life-and-death significance for us all. With the development of technology, wars have become more deadly. They have also become more frequent. There were not many wars during the Paleolithic period, which covers most of human history, because the small food-gathering bands could use only so much territory. They had nothing to gain by trying to take over territory of a neighboring band. In fact, they had everything to lose because bloody wars might very well have destroyed the human race at a time when so few were scattered about the globe. Human young, after all, are wholly dependent not for one year like monkeys or three to four years like apes, but for six to eight years. The survival of the human young during their long years of dependence was best assured by a system of cooperative base camps that afforded the necessary food and protection. In short, cooperative kinship societies prevailed during the Paleolithic millennia precisely because they were so well suited to the survival of the species.

All this changed with the agricultural revolution. As agriculture became more productive, populations increased, villages grew into cities, and cities grew into empires with great palaces and temples and accumulated wealth. With so much now to fight over, wars became more and more frequent. They also became more and more destructive. Although relatively few people were killed by Roman soldiers with their short swords or by medieval knights in their heavy armor, by modern times the carnage had become general. During World War I, 8.4 million military and 1.3 million civilians were killed. During World War II, the score was 16.9 million military and 34.3 million civilians. A third world war would involve a far greater jump in casualties. The International Council of Scientific Unions, comprising scientists from thirty nations, reported in September 1985 that direct blast and radiation effects of nuclear attacks would take several hundred million lives, but from 1 billion to 4 billion of the world's 5 billion people would die of famine. This would result from a "nuclear winter," when huge clouds of sooty black smoke from nuclear blasts would envelop the earth and rob global crops of warmth and light from the sun.

The important lesson that history teaches us is that such wars are not inevitable. They have occurred not because of human nature but because of human societies. And human societies have been made by human beings and can be remade by human beings. This is the gist of the following conclusion by anthropologist Ashley Montagu concerning human nature: "Certainly we are born with genetically based capacities for many kinds of behavior, but the manner in which these capacities become abilities depends upon the training they receive, upon learning. . . . Our true inheritance lies in our ability to make and shape ourselves, not the creatures but the creators of destiny."[2]

SUGGESTED READINGS

The following authors argue that humans are by instinct aggressive creatures: R. Audrey, *African Genesis* (Atheneum, 1961), and his *Territorial Imperative* (Atheneum, 1966); also D. Norris, *The Naked Ape* (McGraw-Hill, 1967). The opposite view, that human conduct is molded by social environment, not heredity, is presented in the popular work by M. F. A. Montagu, *The Nature of Human Aggression* (Oxford University, 1976); in A. Bandura, *Aggression* (Prentice Hall, 1973); and in R. C. Lewontin, S. Rose, and L. J. Kamin, *Not in Our Genes* (Pantheon, 1984). The latest work on this subject is the provocative *War before Civilization* by L. H. Keeley (Oxford University, 1996).

NOTES

1. A. Bandura, *Agression* (Prentice Hall, 1973), pp. 113, 322.
2. *New York Times*, February 3, 1983 (Letters to the Editor).

PART II

Classical Civilizations of Eurasia, to 500 C.E.

We have seen in Part I that after hominids became humans, their first major achievement was the agricultural revolution. This revolution made it possible for the ancient river valley civilizations to develop in the Tigris-Euphrates, Nile, Indus, and Yellow river valleys. Beginning about 3500 B.C.E., the ancient civilizations lasted to the second millennium B.C.E., when they were uprooted by nomadic invaders from the steppes of central Asia and the deserts of the Middle East. Thus the ancient civilizations gave way to the new classical civilizations, which were different in several respects.

Whereas the ancient civilizations had been confined to river valleys, the classical civilizations expanded outward until they all had contact with one another. Civilization during the Classical Age, then, stretched without interruption across Eurasia, from the Atlantic Ocean to the Pacific. The classical civilizations were distinctive in content as well as in range. Like the ancient civilizations, each of the classical civilizations developed its own special style—its own social, religious, and philosophical systems—which persist to modern times. This creativity, it should be noted, was not limited to the Middle East, as it was at the time of the ancient civilizations. During the centuries of the Classical Age, all regions of Eurasia interacted as equals. All made their distinctive contributions, which still affect human beings throughout the globe to the present day.

3

First Eurasian Civilizations, 3500–1000 B.C.E.

The city came into being for the sake of life; it is for the sake of good life.

Aristotle

Every city is two cities, a city of the many poor and a city of the few rich; and these two cities are always at war.

Plato

The first light of civilization dawned on a desert plain scorched by the sun and nourished by two great rivers, the Tigris and the Euphrates. Although at one time it was believed that the Nile valley gave birth to civilization, it is now agreed that the earliest centers were in Sumer, the Old Testament's "land of Shinar." This area comprised the barren, wind-swept plains at the head of the Persian Gulf, in the southern part of what used to be known as Mesopotamia and is now the state of Iraq. About 3500 B.C.E. certain communities of agriculturists who had developed techniques for cultivating this arid wasteland successfully completed the transition from Neolithic tribalism to civilization.

The date given is an approximation, pinpointed merely for the sake of convenience. In fact, no one year, or decade or even century, can be specified. We have seen that the shift from food gathering to food growing did not suddenly occur when someone discovered the idea of agriculture. Likewise the transition to civilization did not happen at the moment that someone had the idea of developing urban centers and urban civilization. What happened, in short, was not an event but a process. The purpose of this chapter is to examine the nature and origins of this process.

I. HOW ANCIENT CIVILIZATIONS BEGAN

Precisely what do we mean by the term *civilization*? Anthropologists point to certain characteristics found in ancient civilizations that distinguish them from the preceding tribal Neolithic cultures. They include such characteristics as urban centers, institutionalized political authority in the form of the state, tribute or taxation, writing, social stratification into classes or hierarchies, monumental architecture, and specialized arts and sciences. Not all civilizations have had all these characteristics. The Andean civilization, for example, developed without writing, and the Egyptian and Mayan lacked cities as they are commonly defined. But this cluster of characteristics does serve as a general guide for defining the general nature of the civilizations that emerged at various times in various parts of the world.

The common characteristics of civilizations make clear that this new type of society was altogether different from the preceding egalitarian tribal societies. How was the transition made from the simple Neolithic villages to the complex new civilizations? We can answer that question by tracing the transitional steps in the Middle East, where the first civilizations emerged. In the hills above the Tigris-Euphrates humans had learned to domesticate plants and animals and so brought about the agricultural revolution. There also they now began the next great adventure when they moved down to the river valley and gradually developed a new and more productive irrigation agriculture and new social institutions. The interaction of the new technology and institutions set off a chain reaction that eventually ended in civilization.

The move to the lowlands presented the Neolithic agriculturists with new problems—inadequate rainfall, searing heat, periodic floods, and lack of stone for building. But there were advantages that more than compensated. There were date palms that provided plentiful food and abundant, though poor, wood. There were reedy marshes with wild fowl and game, fish that furnished valuable protein and fat for the diet, and above all, fabulously fertile valley bottom soil. The potential of this new environment was very exciting, but there was one great obstacle. If rainfall was barely sufficient for growing crops in the hilly uplands, in the valleys below it rained even less. Irrigation was necessary to bring the rich alluvial soils under cultivation, so the pioneer farmers dug short canals leading from the river channels to their fields. The resultant crop yields were incredibly large compared to those they had previously wrested from the stony hillsides. Documents dating to 2500 B.C.E. indicate that the average yield on a field of barley was eighty-six times the sowing! Food was now available as never before—more abundant, more varied, and thanks to irrigation, more assured. The increased food supply meant increased population, which in turn made it possible to create more irrigation canals, more new fields, and still more food.

While the technique of irrigation was being worked out, the new craft of metallurgy was also being mastered. It was particularly valuable for the valley settlements, where flint was unavailable. At first the new native metals were treated just like tough and malleable stones, that is, worked cold by hammering and grinding. True metallurgy did not begin until people learned how to reduce metals from their ores by smelting. Copper seems to have been the first metal so treated, for it was discovered that when it was heated it became liquid and assumed the shape of any container or mold. As it cooled it hardened and could be given as good a cutting edge as stone. By 3000 B.C.E. it was widely known in the Middle East and India that a more durable alloy could be produced by adding small quantities of other metals to the copper. Finally they found the ideal combination of copper and tin. The resulting bronze was decidedly superior to stone. Bronze was sought after for making weapons, since stone was too brittle to be dependable in battle. But being expensive because of the scarcity of both copper and tin, bronze wasn't available for general uses, like toolmaking.

Equally significant at this time was the invention of the plow. In the beginning a plow consisted simply of a sapling with one lopped and pointed branch left protruding two-thirds of the way down the trunk. A pair of oxen were yoked to the upper end of the trunk while the

This painting from a royal Egyptian tomb shows a noble family on a boat on a trip to hunt birds in the afterlife, just as they enjoyed doing in their lives on earth.

plowman steered by the lower end as the protruding branch was dragged through the earth. In the light soils of the semiarid Middle East this primitive contrivance was highly functional. By 3000 B.C.E. it was widely used in Mesopotamia and Egypt and was being introduced in India; by 1400 B.C.E. it had reached distant China. The ox-drawn plow is significant because it represents the first time people could use something besides their muscles for motive power. In this sense the plow was the precursor of the steam engine, the internal combustion engine, the electric generator, and the fission reactor.

By 3000 B.C.E. wind also was being har-

nessed to supplement human muscles—in this case to furnish power for water transport. Clumsy square sails were used first in the Persian Gulf and then on the Nile River. They represented the first successful use of inorganic force to provide motive power. Crude though the early sailboats were, they offered a far more economic means for heavy transport than pack asses or oxcarts, so much of the commerce of the ancient civilizations was waterborne.

Another basic invention of this creative millennium was the wheel. In the earliest Mesopotamian models, the wheel and axle were fastened together solidly and the wheels were disks.

By 3000 B.C.E. the axle had been fixed to the cart with the wheel left separate, and shortly thereafter the spoked wheel appeared. Though these early carts were heavy and clumsy, they were preferable to what was available before—human shoulders and the pack animal, usually the ass. The wheel was also used for war chariots, which apparently were driven into the ranks of the enemy until they lost momentum. Then they were used as fighting platforms from which the crew could throw javelins and strike down at the enemy. Another, and more peaceful, use for this invention was the potter's wheel. In its simplest form the early potter's wheel was a pair of disk-shaped cart wheels with axle attached, the axle being set vertically. The operator spun the lower wheel by foot, while with the hands the operator spread and shaped the soft clay on the upper wheel. In this way pottery became the first technical product to be mass-produced.

Far-reaching institutional changes went hand in hand with the far-reaching technological advances. The increase in population enabled some of the villages to grow into towns dominated by a new elite of religious and, later, military and administrative leaders. The increased productivity of agriculture, with its food surpluses, could now support a growing new class of priests, soldiers, and bureaucrats. This development was not a sudden or simple one-way process—although there has been much debate on whether the technological change determined the institutional change or vice versa. This is similar to the debate about the early stages in human evolution: Did development of the human brain come first and then create human culture, including speech and toolmaking? Or did speech and toolmaking cause the brain to develop? It is now agreed that there was interaction back and forth, with speech and toolmaking being both the cause and the effect of brain development. Likewise it appears that technological and social change interacted reciprocally and eventually precipitated the urban revolution and civilization. The Neolithic cultivators did not at some given time agree—nor were they forced—to provide a surplus for a ruling elite and thus to shift over from the status of tribal people to that of peasants. Rather it was a gradual process in which cause and effect were functionally interrelated.

The beginning of the later class differentiation that distinguished civilization may be seen in the modest village shrines that were centers of socioreligious life. But there was not yet a full-time priesthood. When the villages grew to towns, the shrines likewise grew to temples with retinues of priests and attendants—the first persons ever to be freed from direct subsistence labor. We can see why the priests became the first elite group when we realize that they were the successors of the earlier tribal shamans. The shamans had been so influential because of the importance of group agricultural ceremonies, such as rainmaking, for Neolithic farmers. Now the new priesthood bore responsibility not only for the traditional supernatural phenomena but also for the growing managerial functions essential for an increasingly complex society.

The growth of technology and the increasing food surplus had made possible the emergence of the new priestly hierarchies, but the latter in turn contributed to both the technology and the economy. The earliest known examples of writing, which in itself was a priestly invention born of the need for keeping records, tell us that the priests supervised a multitude of economic as well as religious activities. They kept the records necessary for calculating the time of the annual floods. They assumed the vital managerial roles necessary for the proper functioning of the growing irrigation facilities, which included the rationing of water and the construction and maintenance of dams and canals. They also provided the main stimulus for crafts, which were designed mainly for the temples rather than for secular markets.

At this point the growing heterogeneity of society, to which the religious elite had contributed so vitally, began to undermine the position of that elite. The larger and more complex the towns grew, the more ineffective became purely religious sanctions. At the same time warfare was growing in scale and frequency, perhaps because population growth was outstripping agricultural resources, and, paradoxically, the wealth of the temples themselves may have contributed to the disorders by inviting raids. The outcome was a shift of power from the priesthood to a new secular elite.

Previously, the occasional threat of outside attack had been met by the community's adult

Ancient Civilizations of Eurasia, 3500–1500 B.C.E.

males, who assembled and selected a war leader for the duration. But as the intervals of peace became shorter, the tenure of these war leaders became longer, until finally they were ensconced as permanent military chiefs, and eventually as kings. Thus the palaces came to rival the temples, and in time, a working partnership necessarily evolved. The priests normally retained their great landholdings and continued their sacred services, while the palace officials constructed walls around their cities and raised large armies, which they employed against neighboring cities and, eventually, for empire building.

One effect of this rise of secular states and empires was a great increase in the output of nonagricultural commodities. The mass production of pottery and metal utensils, and the hordes of assorted objects found in some of the more substantial houses, all suggest a new and significant middle-class market. Also, luxury commodities in great quantity were absorbed by the growing palace retinues. In addition, increasing militarization required armaments on an unprecedented scale. The armies needed not only metal weapons and armor but also more elaborate equipment such as chariots. All this was a far cry from the relatively limited production of earlier times when crafts were geared mainly to meeting temple needs.

Mass production had important implications for foreign affairs. Most of the crafts were dependent on raw materials brought from the outside, since the lowlands were almost totally devoid of minerals and quality timber. Copper, for example, came from Oman, south of the Persian Gulf; silver and lead from the Taurus Mountains in Asia Minor; and timber from the Zagros Mountains of Iran and from Lebanon on the Mediterranean coast. To pay for such imports, the various crafts had to expand production and provide exports in exchange. The alternative was to conquer the sources of the needed raw materials. That this option was not overlooked is evident from the career of Sargon, king of Akkad in the middle of the third millennium B.C.E. An epic poem, "The King of Battle," describes how Sargon led his army across unknown mountain passes into the heart of Asia Minor in support of Akkadian merchants who were being maltreated by the local ruler. Eventually Sargon's empire extended "from the Lower to the Upper Sea"— from the Persian Gulf to the Mediterranean— and he thereby controlled the crucial sources of metals, stone, and timber. Indeed, a slightly later source relates that Sargon "did not sleep" in his efforts to promote commerce: "Brisk activity dominates the wharf where the ships are docked; all lands live in peace, their inhabitants prosperous . . . without hindrance ships bring their merchandise to Sumer."[1]

The combined cost of the military and palace establishments was so expensive for the early city-states that it undermined the traditional assemblies. They balked against the onerous levies necessary to meet the rising expenditures. As a result, the assemblies were increasingly bypassed and replaced by permanent, hereditary royal authority.

The centralization of political power led to increased class differentiation, the growth of which we can see in the differences in grave offerings. During the early period the disparity was minimal, but the more time passed, the more pronounced it became. The great majority of the graves contained only a few pottery vessels or nothing at all, reflecting the poverty of the commoners. Those of the well-to-do exhibited "conspicuous consumption" in the form of copper vessels and beads of precious metal. The royal tombs, far outdoing the others, were luxuriously furnished with beautifully wrought weapons and precious ornaments and included large numbers of palace attendants—men-at-arms, harem ladies, musicians, charioteers, and general servants—who were sacrificed to accompany the royal occupant and attest to his or her power and wealth.

The royal tombs, whose lavish contents have been unearthed in many civilizations ranging from China to the Andes, point up the dramatic difference between these civilizations and the simple tribal societies they replaced. Our survey of what happened in the Middle East shows that the transition from tribalism to civilization was the end result of technological and social changes that interacted back and forth. Eventually they produced the first Eurasian civilizations that emerged on the banks of the Tigris-Euphrates, the Nile, and the Indus and Yellow rivers. (See map of Ancient Civilizations of Eurasia, 3500–1500 B.C.E. p. 47.)

II. HOW ANCIENT CIVILIZATIONS SPREAD

Once civilization took root in several regions of Eurasia and the New World, it spread out in all directions. Just as the agricultural revolution had replaced hunting societies with tribal ones, so now the tribal societies in turn were replaced by civilizations. They were replaced for precisely the same reason that the hunting bands had been replaced earlier. We noted in the preceding chapter that as the hunters increased in numbers, they had to shift to agriculture because farming was more productive. Many more farmers could live off a unit of land than could hunters. So it was now with the tribal cultivators—they were displaced because of their inferior productivity. The record of the Bemba work-days revealed how comfortable and easygoing life was in that tribe based on kinship relations. But productivity was low because there was no pressure to work more and produce more. Tribal members needed to work only enough to care for their families and for any kin in need.

When tribal populations increased, and the demand for food increased correspondingly, tribal societies could not compete with civilizations that were much more productive. They were more productive because they were class societies with a state structure that squeezed taxes and rents out of the peasants to support the kings, courtiers, bureaucrats, military leaders, ecclesiastics, and scribes. To pay the taxes and rents, the peasants of the civilizations had to work infinitely harder than did the tribal cultivators. Consider the contrast between the daily life of the Bemba and the wretchedness of Egyptian peasants and workers described in the following statement. It was uttered in the third millennium B.C.E. by an Egyptian father taking his son to school and trying to persuade him of the need to study hard by contrasting the misery of the many at the bottom with the blessings of the few at the top.

Put writing in your heart that you may protect yourself from hard labor of any kind and be a magistrate of high repute. The scribe is released from manual tasks; it is he who commands. . . . Do you not hold the scribe's palette? This is what makes the difference between you and the man who handles an oar.

I have seen the metal-worker at his task at the mouth of his furnace, with fingers like a crocodile's. He stank worse than fish-spawn. . . . The stonemason finds his work in every kind of hard stone. When he has finished his labors his arms are worn out, and he sleeps all doubled up until sunrise. His knees and spine are broken. . . . The barber shaves from morning till night; he never sits down except to meals. He hurries from house to house looking for business. He wears out his arms to fill his stomach, like bees eating their own honey. . . . The farmer wears the same clothes for all times. His voice is as raucous as a crow's. His fingers are always busy, his arms are dried up by the wind. He takes his rest—when he does get any rest—in the mud. If he's in good health he shares good health with the beasts; if he is ill his bed is the bare earth in the middle of his beasts. . . .

Apply your heart to learning. In truth there is nothing that can compare with it. If you have profited by a single day at school it is a gain for eternity.[2]

Early Egyptian painting, about 3000 B.C.E., portrays tribes of peasants immigrating to Egypt.

Obviously the Bemba tribal members enjoyed more comfortable and carefree lives than did the wretched farmers, masons, barbers, and metalworkers described by the Egyptian father. But precisely because the tribalists were better off, they were also doomed. They were far less productive than their Egyptian counterparts who were forced to work ever harder to meet the exactions of landlords and tax collectors. Thus, tribal societies were elbowed off the historical stage as inexorably as hunting bands had been shoved off earlier by tribal cultivators.

By the time tribalism had reached the outer fringes of Eurasia, it was being superseded in its core areas in the Middle East. The displacement process continued steadily as civilization spread out of the original river valleys and across adjacent uncivilized regions. By the time of Christ it extended with virtually no interruption from the English Channel to the China Sea. (Compare the map on p. 72–73 with the map on p. 47.)

If 3500 B.C.E. is accepted as the approximate date for the emergence of civilization in Mesopotamia, corresponding dates may be given for the other centers of civilization: in Egypt, about 3000 B.C.E.; in the Indus valley, about 2500 B.C.E.; in the Yellow River valley of China, about 1500 B.C.E.; and in Mesoamerica and Peru, about 500 B.C.E. These dates are rough estimates and are constantly being revised as new findings are made. Indeed radiocarbon dating, on which much prehistoric chronology has been based, has been found recently to be off by several centuries. Hence some scholars now question the traditional assumption that culture spread from the eastern Mediterranean to western Europe.

III. STYLES OF ANCIENT CIVILIZATIONS

We noted in the preceding chapter that the Neolithic cultures differed markedly according to the balance between farming and stockbreeding and the wide variety of plants cultivated and of animals bred. So now there were great differences among the scattered civilizations that emerged around the globe. Each of these civilizations had its distinctive style, which distinguished it from the others. These styles persist to the present day, so that anyone parachuted into the midst of a strange city would immediately recognize, from the architecture and costumes and foods and spoken language, whether the city was Chinese or Indian or Middle Eastern or western European.

Before considering the distinctive features of the various ancient civilizations, we should recognize certain common characteristics that they all shared. Perhaps the two most significant were the new inequity in social relations and the new inequity in gender relations.

The social inequity arose from the fact that all civilizations were based on tributary rather than kin relationships. Day-to-day life was determined not by the mutual aid and obligations of kin to kin but rather by the tribute collected in the form of taxes, rents, and labor services. Consequently the exploitation described by the Egyptian father was the rule rather than the exception. It may seem that the treatment of those peasants and masons and metalworkers on the banks of the Nile was unbelievably harsh, but many surviving accounts depict equally brutal exploitation in all other civilizations. An observer in Han China in the first century C.E. described a peasant with "legs like burnt stumps, back encrusted with salt, skin like leather that cannot be pierced by an awl, hobbling along on misshapen feet and painful legs."[3]

Such inequity persisted to modern times, as in tsarist Russia, where wealthy nobles customarily staffed each of their country estates with 300 to 800 servants. It was common practice for these nobles to sell, mortgage, or exchange their serfs, or "souls." They advertised their souls for sale together with household goods and other commodities. "To be sold: banquet tablecloths and also two trained girls and a peasant." "To be sold: girl of 16 of good behavior and a second-hand slightly used carriage."[4]

This inequity of past civilizations extended even to the dead. Archeologists find in the graves of commoners only a few pottery vessels or nothing at all, while in those of the well-to-do, they have found expensive furniture and jewelry, while royal tombs contain not only lavish personal adornments but also numerous personal attendants, including men-at-arms, harem ladies, eunuchs, musicians, and general servants—all sacrificed so that they might serve the royal personage in afterlife, as well as reflect his affluence and majesty here on earth. In one recently discovered tomb, the great unifying Chinese emperor Chin Shih Huang-ti surrounded himself with an army of 7,500 terra cotta warriors, each life-sized with individually modeled heads representative of the ethnic groups under the emperor's rule 2,000 years ago.

Even the skeletons in the graves reflect the harsh inequality of life in past civilizations. A study of skeletons at Tikal, Guatemala, in the first millennium C.E. disclosed that, while the average Mayan male was a mere five feet one inch in height, those few given elaborate burials had an average stature of five feet seven inches. Their bones also were substantially more robust and their life span clearly had been a longer one. Archeologists conclude that a "nutritional advantage" allowed the Mayan elite to realize their full potential in stature and life expectancy.[5] Such skeletal differentiation on the basis of class persists to the present day. Britain's Health Ministry reported in December 1984 that, "In almost every age group, people from households headed by a manual worker were shorter, on average, than people from non-worker households."[6]

The second common feature of ancient civilizations, in addition to social inequity, was gender inequity. We have seen that in Paleolithic times, women enjoyed equal status because as food gatherers they contributed even more to the food supply than did the male hunters. Likewise during the Neolithic age, when agriculture was simple, women cultivated the land surrounding their camps and continued to gather whatever food they could find. So they remained equal food providers with men and retained their equal status with men.

All this changed with the advent of the plow and of irrigation and of new crafts such as metallurgy. This advanced type of agriculture provided the economic foundations for civilization but at the same time undermined the economic independence of women, and consequently their social independence as well. Women found it difficult to participate in the new agriculture, which required the tending of draft animals, extraction of stumps, maintenance of irrigation ditches, and upkeep of plows and other equipment. This type of work was not suited to women, either because it was too heavy or because it kept them away from the children too long. So women gradually stopped being equal food producers with men. More and more they spent their time at home, taking care of their children and their husbands.

Men gradually dominated the new agriculture and crafts, while women became isolated and dependent. For the first time a distinction was made between the "inside" work of women and the "outside" work of men. Of course the "inside" work was essential for the family and

Diorama showing the city of Ur (Iraq) about 2000 B.C.E.

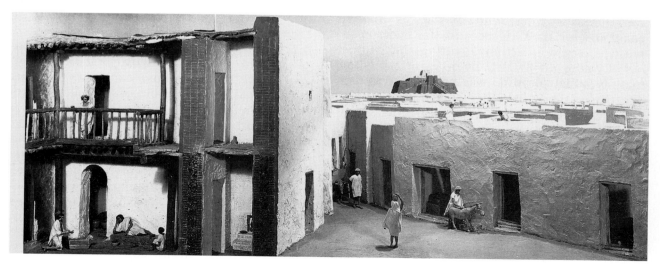

for society. But it was not generally seen to be as important as the work done by men. Since women were thought to be doing less important work, they were also thought to be the less important sex—the "second sex."

Furthermore, since women were tied down by the "inside" work, men gained a monopoly of not only the new agriculture and crafts but also the new positions in the state. They became the leaders in the assemblies, the courts, and the armies. Thus men ended up with a monopoly of economic power, political power, and military power. Women became dependent and submissive—the "weaker sex," as they came to be called. It was not accidental that when the Europeans began their overseas expansion in the fifteenth century, they discovered that women in food-gathering societies such as the Montagnais-Naskapi Indians of Labrador enjoyed a disconcerting degree of equality with men. But in the overseas civilizations, such as those of China, India, and the Middle East, they found women as restricted and submissive as they were in Europe—even more so.

Another reason why women had inferior status in the various civilizations was the new emphasis on inheritable private property. This caused men to go to great lengths to be certain that they were in fact the fathers of their heirs, who were to receive all their wealth. Consequently, the wealthy elite adopted strict regulations and elaborate precautions to control female (though not male) sexual activity. These included chastity belts, bookkeeping devices to record the exact dates of sexual encounters, the castration of men who served as harem guardians for their rulers, and the widespread practice of clitoridectomy (cutting the clitoris out of young girls) which, by decreasing or eliminating sexual pleasure, was believed to be an effective method of keeping women from "straying" with men other than their husbands.

It is well known that there were individual exceptions to this overall pattern of female subordination. Outstanding among them were the ambitious Egyptian Queen Cleopatra, who charmed both Julius Caesar and Mark Antony and sought to use them to restore real power to the Egyptian throne; Aspasia, who was known throughout Greece as the learned, witty, and beautiful mistress of Pericles; the masterful

Empress Irene who dethroned her son and became the first female ruler of the Byzantine Empire (797–802), although in deference to tradition she was referred to in official documents as "Irene, the faithful emperor"; and also Empress Wu Chao, who dethroned her son to become not only the first and only female ruler of China but also one of the most capable and enlightened. These illustrious personalities stand out prominently in the annals of history by virtue of their remarkable talents and achievements. Yet despite their fame, it cannot be said that their careers improved to any significant degree the daily lives of their less exalted sisters, just as in our time the careers of Evita Peron, Indira Gandhi, and Corazon Acquino have not appreciably improved the daily lives of the women of Argentina, India, or the Philippines.

Having surveyed the historic shift from equality to inequality in social and gender relations in all civilizations, we turn now to consider their individual distinctive styles.

Mesopotamia

The style of the pioneer civilization of Mesopotamia was urban. The first center was at Sumer, which by 3000 B.C.E. consisted of twelve separate city-states. The cities fought each other continually, so they were easily conquered by Indo-European invaders from the north and Semitic invaders from the south. Indeed the history of Mesopotamia was in large part a centuries-long struggle between the Indo-European and Semitic invaders for control of the fertile river valley.

The first great empire builder was the aforementioned Semite, Sargon the Great (c. 2276–2221 B.C.E.), whose conquests stretched from Akkad in the middle of the valley to the Persian Gulf in the south and the Mediterranean in the west. Another empire builder was also a Semite, Hammurabi (c. 1704–1662 B.C.E.), who, as we shall see, is most famous for his law code. This pattern of successive invasions continued to modern times, with Hammurabi followed by Hittites, Assyrians, Persians, Macedonians, Romans, Arabs, Mongols, Turks, and Westerners.

Despite the parade of empires, the cities remained the basic units of ancient Mesopotamia.

Most citizens earned their livelihood as farmers, craftmakers, merchants, fishermen, and cattle breeders. Each city had a section reserved for the craftmakers—the masons, smiths, carpenters, potters, and jewelers. They sold their handicrafts in a free town market and were paid in kind or in money that consisted of silver ingots or rings, which were weighed after each transaction.

Outside the city walls were the fields on which the urban inhabitants were dependent. Most of the land was held in the form of large estates that belonged to the king or the priests or other wealthy persons. The workers on these estates were allotted individual plots along with seed, implements, and draft animals. In return they provided the labor and, through a variety of arrangements, gave their surplus produce to the temple or palace or landowner. The basic crops were barley and wheat; the milk animals were goats and cows; sheep supplied the wool that was the chief textile fabric of Mesopotamia. The most common vegetables were beans, peas, garlic, leeks, onions, radishes, lettuce, and cucumbers; the fruits included melons, dates, pomegranates, figs, and apples.

The management of the estates required keeping careful accounts of many details: the rents received from the tenant farmers, the size of the herds, the amount of fodder needed for the animals and of seed for the next planting, and the intricate details regarding irrigation facilities and schedules. Management and accounting records were inscribed with a reed stylus on clay tablets that were then baked to preserve them. This earliest form of writing, known as cuneiform, was clearly invented as an instrument of administration, not for intellectual or literary purposes. As a distinguished scholar has put it, "Writing was not a deliberate invention, but the incidental by-product of a strong sense of private property, always a characteristic of classical Sumerian civilization."[7]

At first the cuneiform consisted of pictographs; the scribe drew simplified pictures of oxen, sheep, grain, fish, or whatever was being recorded. Soon the pictographs became conventionalized and were no longer left to the artistic fancy of each scribe. This ensured uniform writing and reading of records, but a basic problem remained: Pictographs could not be used to depict abstract concepts. Sumerian scribes met

this difficulty by adding marks to the pictographs to denote new meanings, and more important, by selecting signs that represented sounds rather than objects or abstractions. This was the essence of the phonetic alphabet that was evolved centuries later, but the Sumerians failed to apply the phonetic principle systematically and comprehensively. They reduced their signs from an original number of about 2,000 to some 600 by 2900 B.C.E. Although that was a substantial improvement, cuneiform remained far more cumbersome than the alphabet developed later by the Phoenicians and the Greeks. Hence there was a need for those who had mastered the difficult art of writing; scribes alone had this skill and therefore enjoyed high status and privilege.

Although the origins of writing are to be found in the new circumstances arising from the production of economic surplus, it had other far-reaching and fateful effects. It stimulated intellectual development because factual data could now be collected, recorded, and passed along to successive generations. Equally significant, writing helped to define and consolidate individual cultures. It gave permanent written form to religious traditions, which thereby became sacred books; to social customs, which became law codes; and to oral myths and stories, which became classics. Thus writing became the chief means for the cultural integration of the civilizations of mankind.

The Sumerians developed sciences and mathematics, as well as writing, in response to the concrete needs of their increasingly complex society. Their earliest mathematical documents were accounts of flocks, measures of grain, and surveys of fields. Their chief contribution was the development of the first systems for measuring time, distance, area, and quantity. Also, as early as 3000 B.C.E., they were carefully studying and recording the movements of heavenly bodies, their motive again being utilitarian. They believed that the will of the gods determined celestial movements and that knowledge of those movements would enable man to know the divine will and act accordingly. Thus Mesopotamian astrologers over the course of many centuries accumulated an enormous amount of data that later was used to develop scientific astronomy.

Original pictograph	Pictograph in position of later cuneiform	Early Babylonian	Assyrian	Original or derived meaning
				bird
				fish
				donkey
				ox
				sun day
				grain
				orchard
				to plow to till
				boomerang to throw to throw down
				to stand to go

The origin and development of a few cuneiform characters.

The religious beliefs of the Sumerians and their successors were profoundly affected by their physical environment, and particularly by the annual flooding of the Tigris-Euphrates. The coincidence of heavy rains in the northern areas and deep snow in the Zagros and Taurus mountains frequently produced disastrous floods that devastated farmlands instead of filling irrigation canals. Ninurta, the Sumerian god of the flood, was viewed as a malevolent, not a benevolent, god. Sumerian literature is filled with lines like these:

The rampant flood which no man can oppose,

Which shakes the heavens and causes earth to tremble. . . .

And drowns the harvest in its time of ripeness.

Fear of the annual floods, together with the ever-present danger of outside invasion, left the Sumerians with a deep feeling of helplessness in a world of uncontrollable forces. "Mere man— his days are numbered," reads a Sumerian poem, "whatever he may do, he is but wind." The Mesopotamian view of life was tinged with an apprehension and pessimism reflecting the insecurity of the physical environment. Humans, it was felt, had been made only to serve the gods, whose will and acts were unpredictable. Hence a variety of techniques were employed to foresee the uncertain future. One was the interpretation of diverse omens, and especially dreams. Another was hepatoscopy, or divination by inspecting the livers of slaughtered animals. Still another was astrology, which, as already noted, involved the study of planets for their imagined influence

Sumerian statuettes from Tell Asmar. The group, dating from 3000–2500 B.C.E., was found buried beside the altar of a temple at a site near modern Baghdad. The tallest figure in this collection of gods, priests, and worshipers is the god Abu, the "lord of vegetation."

on or predictions about the destinies of men and women. Finally, each person had a personal god as a sort of private mentor. Through this personal god, the person's wishes and needs could be made known to the great gods, who were much too remote for direct communication.

Insecurity also prevailed between people, and the Mesopotamians sought to ease potential conflicts by compiling detailed codes of law. The most outstanding of these was that of Hammurabi, which tried to regulate all social relationships, clearly and for all time. The code sheds as much light on the society as it does on the legal system of ancient Babylon. The following presents some of its typical features:

1. The application of the principle of "an eye for an eye, a tooth for a tooth": "If a man has knocked out the eye of a patrician, his eye shall be knocked out. If he has broken the limb of a patrician, his limb shall be broken." (Laws 196, 197)

2. Class discrimination, so that the lower orders received less compensation: "If a man has smitten the privates of a patrician of his own rank, he shall pay one mina of silver. If the slave of anyone has smitten the privates of a freeborn man, his ear shall be cut off." (Laws 203, 205)

3. The strict requirement of a business society that property be safeguarded: "If a man has stolen goods from a temple, or house, he shall be put to death; and he that has received the stolen property from him shall be put to death." (Law 6)

4. The multitude of "welfare state" provisions, including annual price fixing for basic commodities, limitation of interest rate to 20 percent, minute regulation of family relationships, assurance of honest weights and measures, and responsibility of the city for indemnifying victims of unsolved robbery or murder: "If the highwayman has not been caught, the man that has been robbed shall state on oath what he has lost and the city or district governor in whose territory or district the robbery took place shall restore to him what he has lost." (Law 23)

5. A static view of the past, present, and future, typical of premodern peoples. Thus the code is presented as part of the divine order for the benefit of humankind under its justice, and any later ruler who dares alter the code is colorfully and explicitly cursed with "a reign of sighing, days few in number, years of famine, darkness without light, sudden death . . . the destruction of his city, the dispersion of his people, the transfer of his kingdom, the extinction of his name and memory from the land . . . his ghost [in the underworld] is to thirst for water." (Laws, Epilogue)

Stele with the Hammurabi Code, consisting of some 300 laws meant to regulate society.

Finally, the code of Hammurabi and all other Mesopotamian codes set forth in clear legal terms the superior status of men over women. Matrimony was chiefly a matter of utility—a substitute for nonexistent insurance against illness, disability, or old age. Consequently the choice was made not by the bride and groom, who might be blinded by love, but by the father, or after his death, by the mother or elder brothers. Following marriage, the husband was legally recognized as the undisputed head of the family. His wife and his children

had to show him due respect. As the head of the family, the husband was literally the owner of his wife and children. To honor a debt, he could pawn or sell them as though they were mere objects.

Adultery by the wife was mercilessly punished, usually by death for her and her paramour. For the husband, however, the concept of infidelity was irrelevant because he had the legal right to possess not only a principal wife but also a concubine and slaves "for his desires" and also to ensure descendants. Indeed a childless wife was duty bound to provide a concubine for her husband so that he might have children. Divorce for the husband was easy. He merely had to declare that his wife was barren or a spendthrift or had belittled him. For the wife to seek divorce, however, was a deadly gamble. The code provided that she submit to investigation. "If she has been discreet and has no vice, and her husband has gone out, and has greatly belittled her, she shall take her marriage portion [dowry] and go off to her father's house. . . . But if she has been found indiscreet and has gone out, ruined her house, belittled her husband, she shall be drowned."

Egypt

The style of Egypt's civilization, in contrast to Mesopotamia's, was imperial rather than urban. The main reason for its security and continuity was the geography of the country, a united river valley ruled by long-lasting dynasties. The Nile valley is well protected against foreign invasion by the Libyan Desert on the west, the Arabian Desert in the east, the Nubian Desert and the Nile's cataracts on the south, and the harborless coast of the Delta on the north. The Egyptian people were left free in their sheltered valley to pursue their own destiny without interference from the outside. There was not the constant rise and fall of empires, as there were in Mesopotamia because of foreign invaders. Also the Nile River provided a natural cohesion that held the entire valley together as a stable and functioning unit. Its slow but steady current carried northbound traffic effortlessly, and the prevailing north-to-northwest winds made the return trip almost as easy. Thus the Egyptians were provided with a priceless means for reliable communication and transportation that helped to unify the valley about 3100 B.C.E.

During the 2,500 years between its unification in 3100 B.C.E. and its conquest by the Persians in 525 B.C.E., only three empires ruled Egypt, and the intervening periods between empires were comparatively short. The civilization of Egypt therefore was stable and conservative. It was also a confident and optimistic civilization, partly because the Nile was gentle and predictable, compared to the Tigris-Euphrates with its devastating and unpredictable floods. Whereas the Mesopotamians regarded their flood god as harsh and merciless, the Egyptians viewed theirs as a god "whose coming brings joy to every human being."

A predominant feature of Egyptian religious belief concerned death and the physical preparations for the afterlife, especially that of the king. Since his death was not considered final, his body was embalmed and placed in a gigantic tomb, or pyramid, along with food and other necessities. The greatest of the pyramids was that of the Pharaoh Khufu, or Cheops. It covered thirteen acres, rose to a height of 481 feet, and contained some 2.3 million stone blocks, each weighing an average of 2.5 tons. And this was built with the simplest tools—ramps, rollers, and levers; no pulleys and no iron!

It has been said that the Egyptian peasants worked enthusiastically on these pyramids, believing that they were constructing the dwellings of a god on whom their collective well-being would depend. Whatever the justification for this statement—and it may be assumed that, enthusiastic or not, they had little choice in the matter—it does point up the supposed divinity of Egyptian kingship. From beginning to end the pharaoh was a god-king. No distinction was made between the sacred and the secular; indeed the notion was unthinkable. Thus there was an absence in Egypt of anything corresponding to the Mesopotamian law codes. All law was the expression of the divine authority of the god-king.

Royal authority was enforced by a bureaucracy headed by the vizier—"the steward of the whole land," "the eyes and ears of the king." Other officials included the royal sealbearer, who controlled the Nile traffic, the master of

largesse, who was responsible for all livestock, and the head of the Exchequer, who maintained branch offices and storehouses throughout the kingdom for the collection of taxes. In bad years, the head of the Exchequer probably also took care of the distribution of seeds and livestock. There were governors, or nomarchs, to rule each province, or nome, and below them came the mayors of the towns and villages.

A final distinctive feature of Egyptian civilization was the overwhelming state domination of economic life. Individual property and enterprise were not unknown, but neither were they as common as in Mesopotamia. The state not only controlled most production, both agricultural and handicraft, but also directed distribution. Huge government warehouses and granaries were filled with taxes collected in kind—grains, animals, cloths, and metals. These were used for state expenses and also provided

Queen Nefertari guided by Isis.

Sphinx

reserves for years of scarcity. The king, it was said, was "he who presides over the food supplies of all." In addition to taxes, each community had to provide men for the corvée, or forced labor. The pyramids are the best-known examples of their work, but these laborers were also used for quarrying and mining and for maintaining the irrigation canals.

Egyptian craftmakers were universally recognized for their skills, particularly in luxury products. Their jewelry can scarcely be excelled today; their enamel work and ivory and pearl inlay were superb; they discovered how to make glass in many colors; they were the first to bark-tan leather in the manner still followed in most of the world; and their linen cloth was as fine as has ever been woven. Egyptian technology was very advanced in creating artificial beauty aids. Papyri were written to describe medical procedures for removing wrinkles and darkening gray hair. Among the substances used for cosmetic purposes were kohl for lengthening the eyebrows and lining the outer corners of the eyes; malachite and lead ore for green and gray eye shadow respectively; red ochre for rouge; henna for dyeing the nails, the palms of the hands, and the soles of the feet; and human hair for making wigs, over which melted beeswax was poured.

Crete

The style of the Minoan civilization of the island of Crete is summed up by the Greek word *thalassocracy*, or sea civilization. The prosperity of Crete depended on its trade, which included countries from one end of the Mediterranean to the other. The storms in the landlocked Mediterranean are not as fierce as in the open Atlantic, so Cretan merchants could sail, almost always in sight of land, to all the countries on the Mediterranean Sea. Moreover, the mountains of Crete were covered with forests, which provided timber for building the single-masted trading ships. In these ships, the Minoans carried back and forth the foodstuffs, ivory, and glass of Egypt; the horses and wood of Syria; the silver, pottery, and marble of the Aegean Isles; the copper of Cyprus; and their own olive oil and pottery.

This trade affected all aspects of the Minoan civilization. None of the cities was fortified because Minoan sea power was strong enough to protect the island. Cretan communities seem to have been socially and economically more egalitarian than their counterparts on the mainland. In place of a few great temples and palaces surrounded by relative slums, the pattern on Crete was the open village, with its outdoor shrine as the center for community life.

Minos Palace in Crete, Greece

Families as a rule lived in individual houses built of timber and stucco. Domestic slaves probably were held, though not in large numbers. Archeologists have found no buildings that appear to have been slave quarters, so Cretan galleys presumably were rowed by freemen.

Minoan artists did not try to impress by mere size, nor did they concern themselves with remote and awful deities or divine kings. Instead, on their household utensils, on the walls of their houses, and in their works of art, they reproduced the life about them. They found models everywhere: in natural objects such as birds, flowers, sea shells, and marine life of all types; and in scenes from their own everyday life, such as peasants returning from their fields, athletes wrestling with bulls, and women dancing in honor of the Great Goddess. In architecture the Minoans were more interested in personal comfort than outward appearance. The royal palace at Knossos was a sprawling complex that apparently had grown over several centuries. It included not only a throne room, reception chambers, and living quarters, but also storehouses and workshops that occupied most of the complex, as befitted a trading people. Outstanding was an elaborate plumbing and sanitation system that was not surpassed until modern times.

The freedom from wars and from large military and state establishments enabled the original Neolithic kin system to survive much more in Crete than on the Middle Eastern mainland. Consequently men were not able to gain the monopoly of economic, military, and political power in Crete that they did in Mesopotamia and Egypt. Frescoes, seals, and signet rings show that Cretan women continued to be active in "outside" work as well as "inside" work. They show women working in the fields, dancing in groves, crowding into bleachers at the bull arena, and actually participating in the bull wrestling. Some even took part in war, in contrast to their homebody counterparts in

Mesopotamia and Egypt. Cretan women could own property and could obtain divorce as easily as men. In this way the Cretan civilization stands out as the great exception among the ancient civilizations of Eurasia.

Indus

The style of the civilization in the Indus River valley was conservative, religious, and highly planned. We can see this in the cities, which were carefully built according to a common design. Each city at its height extended over six to seven square miles. Each was laid out on the grid pattern, with wide main streets encompassing large rectangular city blocks some 400 yards in length and 200 yards in width, far larger than the average city blocks of today. The buildings were constructed of bricks hardened in kilns, in contrast to the stone used in Egypt and the sun-dried bricks in Mesopotamia. The bricks everywhere were molded in two standard sizes (11 by 5.5 by 2.5 inches, and 9.2 by 4.5 by 2.2 inches), and weights and measures likewise were uniform throughout the Indus lands. Such orderliness and organization seem to have been all-pervasive in this civilization. After it reached its maturity about 2500 B.C.E., it remained virtually static during the following millennium. Even when cities were destroyed by floods, the new cities were built to duplicate the old. Such undeviating continuity of tradition has had no equal, even in Egypt, and has given rise to the theory that the authority regulating this disciplined society may have been spiritual. This hypothesis is supported also by the absence of military equipment and fortifications.

Like all the other ancient civilizations, that of the Indus was predominantly agricultural. Wheat and barley were the staples, but field peas, melons, sesame, and dates were also grown, as well as cotton, which was first used for cloth making in this valley. There was also considerable trade with the outside world; the exported items included peacocks, apes, pearls, cotton textiles, copper, ivory, and ivory articles such as combs. Combs were fashioned in the same pattern as those still used in India today and are still indispensable for combing lice out

Indus stone stamp seals. Note the familiar humped bull of India.

of the hair. Most foreign trade was with Mesopotamia, and goods were transported with sailing boats that followed the coast to the Persian Gulf. If their ships were driven from sight of land, the sailors released crows that always flew toward the nearest point of coast. According to the Bible, this is precisely the method followed by Noah in the Ark, when he wished to find out where the land lay.

The causes and circumstances of the decline of the Indus civilization remain obscure. Hitherto it was widely believed that Aryan invaders, who came down from central Asia about 1500 B.C.E., were primarily responsible. But it has recently been suggested that the civilization may have been literally drowned in mud. Subterranean volcanic activity, according to this theory, caused a huge upwelling of mud, silt, and sand that dammed the Indus and formed a huge lake, swamping the capital, Mohenjo-daro. After several decades the dam was worn down, the water drained through, and the river resumed its normal course, but in the meantime the city had been ruined. Judging from the multiple layers of silt found in Mohenjo-daro, some such disaster occurred at least five times and perhaps more. The net result was irreparable damage to the heart of the Indus civilization, which left the outlying regions in the north too weak to resist assimilation by native cultures.

Much of this is guesswork and cannot be proven because the Indus script has not yet been deciphered. The script is pictographic and is read from left to right on one line and from right to left on the following line. This is the practice followed in early "Greek and is known as *boustrophedon*—"as the ox plows."

Shang

The style of the Shang civilization on the Yellow River in North China was the most different of all the Eurasian civilizations. To the present day, Chinese civilization remains distinctive and unique, and the main reason is the geographic isolation of the country. China is located at the eastern tip of Eurasia, separated from the rest of the continent by great mountains, deserts, and steppes. To the east China faces the vast Pacific Ocean, and to the north, the frozen Siberian steppes.

Although China was isolated, it was not completely cut off from outside influences. The early Shang civilization emerged north of the Yellow River precisely because that region was a cultural crossroads, influenced by nomadic sheepherding peoples to the northwest, by agricultural peoples to the east, and by forest dwellers to the south. Even the distant Middle East left its imprint on north China, contributing wheat cultivation and also the military technology of bronze weapons and of horse-drawn chariots, which were used by the invaders who established the Shang dynasty about 1500 B.C.E. These invaders became the masters of the scattered Neolithic communities of north China.

The same thing happened to the Shang as to the many other later invaders of China. Because of the great numbers of the Chinese people, the Shang were assimilated, and the general populace remained distinctively Chinese. Although China was enriched by elements from the Middle East such as barley, wheat, sheep, cattle, horses, bronze, and the wheel, these innovations did not change China fundamentally. Whereas the ancient Egyptian civilization has long since disappeared, and likewise those of Mesopotamia and the Indus, by contrast China's civilization has continued uninterrupted. Today China can boast the oldest continuous civilization in the world.

Not only the oldest, China's civilization is also the most unique. It was the first to raise silkworms and to weave their delicate fibers into fine silk cloth. It was the only major civilization that did not use animal milk and milk products for human consumption. Indeed the Chinese had the same reaction toward animal milk as Westerners did toward the eating of worms and ants. Also ancestor worship was a prominent and unique feature of Chinese religion from earliest times. Closely related was the importance attached to one's family name, which always preceded the personal name instead of following it, as in the West. This custom reflected the traditional primary role in Chinese society of the family, instead of the individual, the state, or the church. The familiar Chinese style of archi-

Shang oracle bone, animal bones engraved with written characters which were then heated until they cracked. The cracks were examined in relation to the writing. This practice was the foundation of the Chinese language. The characters are pictographs of classical Chinese.

tecture, with the ornate roof supported by rows of wooden pillars, also dates back to earliest times, as does the use of chopsticks rather than forks and spoons.

Most significant for the later history of China and all east Asia was the complex ideo-graphic script found in Shang remains. This is the direct ancestor of modern Chinese writing, illustrating again the continuity of Chinese civilization. Long ago the ancient hieroglyphics and cuneiform lost all intelligibility to the people of the Middle East, but the Shang script is still recognizable to modern Chinese. Most of the Shang writing surviving today is found on animal bones and turtle shells that were used for divination, another distinctive Chinese custom. Questions about sickness, dreams, hunting, the weather, or the harvest were inscribed on the bone or shell. Incisions were then made at various points and red-hot sticks pressed into them produce cracks. The shape, arrangement, and direction of these cracks were interpreted to yield a "Yes" or "No" answer by the diviner. These bones and shells were carefully buried, so many have survived and have revealed a good deal about Shang daily life, as well as about the Shang script.

As with the other Eurasian civilizations, the peasants were required to yield a portion of their crops to support the nobles, scribes, and officials gathered in the towns. Also they were obliged to serve under their lords in time of war as light-armed warriors. Only the ruling military class could afford the two-horse chariots and the bronze helmets and plate mail that they wore into battle. The elite's monopoly of bronze metallurgy enhanced the sharp class differentiation within Shang society. The gap is reflected in the elaborate palaces and royal tombs, on the one hand, and the crude pit dwellings of the common people, on the other. It shows also in the costly offerings that were placed in the tombs—bronze ritual vessels, fine silks, jades, marbles, musical instruments, and elaborate weapons.

As for relations between the sexes, the same inequity existed in Chinese civilization as in all others. The discrimination began at birth, for baby girls were more likely than baby boys to suffer from infanticide. During childhood, girls were subjected to the practice of footbinding, which left them crippled and kept them from venturing far beyond their households. With marriage, which was an arranged transaction, the trembling bride passed from the rule of her father to that of her husband's mother. In a well-to-do family she might have to accept second wives or concubines, particularly if she did not bear a male heir.

Chinese gender inequity was reflected in the distinctively Chinese view of the world as the product of two interacting, complementary elements, yin and yang. Yin was the attribute of all things female, dark, weak, passive. Yang was the attribute of all things male, bright, strong, and active. Although male and female were both necessary and complementary, one was by nature passive and subordinate. Starting with such philosophical premises, male moralists for thousands of years elaborated behavior patterns by which Chinese women were to be properly obedient and passive.

TRIBESPEOPLE AND PEASANTS

One of the costs of civilization was the division of people into rulers and ruled. This was discovered by Dutch officials in New Guinea. The Papuans there, who had never known civilization, refused to bow and scrape to the Dutch because they considered themselves to be free people. But the Indonesians, who had lived in a class society, were ready to accept the Dutch as masters. The following report by an American correspondent reveals how civilization can affect relations among human beings.*

A Dutch official walked into an office in Hollandia [New Guinea]. Seated at a table were an Indonesian official, still in the Netherlands' service, and two Papuan village headmen. The Indonesian jumped to his feet and stood still. The Papuans looked up, smiled and remained seated.

In the bar of a grimy Government hotel, about 9 o'clock one night, a Dutch official asked the Papuan bartender for a beer. The bartender, after five minutes, produced it. He also produced a pointed look at a wristwatch and asked the Dutchman how long he intended to stay.

A Dutch destroyer pulled into a south New Guinea coastal port. Local Dutch officials thought it would be a good idea to show some people from the jungles, still in the head-hunting stage, some real weapons.

Jungle people trekked down, wandered around the ship, and one of them gave the verdict:

"Yes, you have guns. But see these bows and arrows that we have? We think you are not able to use these fine bows and arrows. We can use them. . . ."

Netherlands officials, who have seen service in Indonesia, have had to do some considerable adjusting in New Guinea.

In Indonesia they came into a society that had its caste and class distinctions, its own ideas of authority and rights of rulers. They were masters and were treated as masters.

In New Guinea there are no masters and no slaves. Papuan life is a free sort of life. There are no village councils, no great lawgivers or authorities. A man's pretty much his own man, except for the influence on life of demons and spirits.

Between the Dutch and the Papuans there is no bowing and scraping. An Indonesian schoolteacher who tried to convince Papuans that the proper way to show respect was to walk hunched over in front of superiors was told:

"We are men, and men walk straight."

*New York Times, December 25, 1957. © 1957 by The New York Times Company. Reprinted by permission.

IV. NOMADS GAIN POWER

During the second millennium B.C.E., all the ancient civilizations collapsed, whether in the Middle East or India or far-off China. Was it internal rot or external force that was primarily responsible for that political and social demolition throughout Eurasia? Such a broad question is hard to answer with certainty and precision. But it is certain that both internal and external factors were important in determining the course of events.

Beginning with the internal weaknesses, there were first the scarcity and costliness of copper and bronze, which prevented their general use in making weapons and tools. Hence monarchs and their political and military allies had a virtual monopoly of armaments and so strengthened their privileged position at the top of the social pyramid. Further, only a small percentage of the total population was armed, a serious weakness when the old centers of civilization had to face the assault of nomads, who were all armed. The high cost of copper and bronze also deprived the peasantry of metal tools, forcing them to rely on stone axes and hoes and on flint knives and sickles. Since stone tools were less efficient and durable than metal, productivity was reduced.

Weakened by this rot inside, the ancient civilizations were easy targets for the nomads outside (for the origins of nomads, see Chapter 2, Section III). Three principal nomadic groups did the work of empire smashing: the Semitic tribespeople in the southern deserts, the Indo-Europeans in the Eurasian steppes to the west, and the Mongol-Turkish peoples to the east.

The Indo-Europeans, a cultural rather than a racial group, appear to have originated in the region of the Caspian Sea, where they tended their herds of cattle and did a little farming on the side. Primarily pastoralists, they were ever ready to pack their belongings into their great oxcarts and move on to more promising lands. Entire tribes participated in these migrations—women and children as well as the warriors. Thus they pushed westward to southern Russia and southeastern Europe and, by 2000 B.C.E., ranged in the broad belt from the Danubian plain to the Oxus and Jaxartes valleys. From this far-flung base they threatened more and more the centers of civilization that were geographically accessible to them—the Middle East, the Balkan peninsula, and the Indus valley.

The original dividing line between the Indo-European peoples in the western part of the steppes and the Mongol-Turkish in the eastern part consisted of the Altai and the Tien Shan mountains. To the east of this line the steppes are higher and drier and the climate generally harsher. The pastures here are not as rich as in the west and can support sheep, camels, and horses, but not cattle. The discrepancy between the relatively poor eastern and the richer western geographic areas created a persistent and powerful east-to-west gradient. The peoples of the eastern steppes were attracted to the west, both as refugees and as conquerors. A succession of tribes followed one after the other—Scythians migrated from the Altai to the Ukraine. Turkish tribes replaced them in central Asia but later followed them westward. Finally, the Mongols kept pushing from the rear until they erupted in the thirteenth century C.E. and overran most of Eurasia. These eastern nomads, because of their geographic location, had access not only to Europe, the Middle East, and India, but also to China, where they broke through periodically when the opportunity presented itself.

Because of the east-to-west gradient, the racial composition of the peoples of the western steppes gradually changed from predominantly Caucasoid to predominantly Mongoloid, at least as far west as the Caspian Sea. The racial shift began late in the first millennium B.C.E. and continued until the end of the medieval period. Then the tide was reversed by the Slavic Russians, who were armed with the weapons and transport of Western technology—muskets and cannon at first, and later machine guns and railroads.

Finally, the Semites occupied roughly the area from the Mediterranean to the Tigris and from the Taurus to Aden. Successive waves have appeared throughout history, emerging apparently from the deserts of Arabia. They used the donkey for transportation until about 1100 B.C.E., when the domestication of the camel transformed their culture as the domestication of the horse did that of the steppe nomads.

With the rise of civilization many Semitic tribes lived on the fringes of the cities, with the urban dwellers, but were always ready to seize any chance for raid and plunder.

The old centers of civilization on the periphery of Eurasia were irresistible magnets for the surrounding tribespeople. The abundant crops, the barns swollen with grain, and the dazzling luxuries of the cities all beckoned to the hungry nomads of steppes and deserts. Hence there were periodic raids and invasions, particularly of the Mesopotamian cities, which were more vulnerable than those of Crete, the Nile, or the Indus. Unsurprisingly, the settled peoples of all the civilizations regarded the nomads as an abomination. An Egyptian official wrote of the Semitic nomads, "Their name reeks more than the stink of bird droppings." At the other end of Eurasia a Chinese imperial secretary likewise reviled the Mongols: "In their breasts beat the hearts of beasts . . . from the most ancient times they have never been regarded as a part of humanity."

It was not until the second millennium B.C.E. that the balance of power throughout Eurasia shifted, and for the first time the nomads threatened the very existence of the great civilizations. The new military capabilities of the nomads rose from two fateful developments—the domestication of the horse and, later, the smelting of iron. As far as is known, the earliest domestication of animals took place in the Middle East, where people first learned to ride animals. Both these events occurred about 5000 B.C.E., but there was little riding then for the simple reason that the only animals available were the ox, which was too slow, and the onager, or wild ass, which was too small. The practice of animal domestication, however, spread northward to southern Russia, where both the onager and the wild horse were to be found. These two animals were domesticated there by 2500 B.C.E., and soon the horse became favored because it was larger, stronger, and faster. Furthermore, with selective breeding the horse gradually increased in size. A wild horse averages thirteen hands (a hand equals four inches), whereas a modern domestic horse averages fifteen to sixteen hands. When allowed to breed indiscriminately for a few generations, domestic horses soon return to a smaller size, as illustrated by the mustang of the American West.

The first military use that the nomads made of their horse was to harness it to a light-bodied chariot with two spoked wheels, which they developed as an improvement on the clumsy Mesopotamian cart, with four solid wheels. The combination of the large horse and easily maneuvered chariot gave the nomads a formidable weapon—the war chariot. The first wave of nomadic invasions in the second millennium B.C.E. were invasions of charioteers. Riding hard into battle, one chariot warrior took charge of the horses while the others in the chariot shot arrows from their powerful compound bows. Few infantrymen could stand up for long to the volleys of arrows, let alone to the massed chariot charges that followed.

Toward the end of the second millennium the nomads further increased their military effectiveness by shifting from chariot to cavalry warfare. Their horses were now large enough and strong enough to bear the direct weight of the rider. The nomads also developed the bridle and bit, for guiding the horse, and the horned saddle and stirrup, which enabled them to ride with both hands free and to launch a shower of arrows at full gallop. Hence the Eurasian nomads, now with unprecedented mobility, were able to outride and outfight armies defending the urban centers. The technology of riding was the basis of nomadic military power throughout the classical and medieval ages, and it culminated in the extraordinary conquests of Genghis Khan in the thirteenth century. The centers of civilization were under constant threat of nomadic invasion until superior Western firearms were brought to bear.

The counterpart of the horse for the desert nomad was the camel. There were two varieties—the one-humped Arabian, which has adapted to hot desert conditions, and the two-humped Bactrian relative, which has adapted to cold desert conditions. Both can live off land where even the ass would starve, and both can go for weeks on fat stored in their humps and on water stored in their multiple stomachs. Where and when the camel was first tamed is not clear, but by 1000 B.C.E. transportation and communication across the deserts of central Asia and the Middle East were dependent on the "ship of the desert."

The discovery of the technique for smelting iron ore also enhanced nomadic military strength. The technique was developed in the middle of the second millennium B.C.E. in northeast Asia Minor. But not until the destruction of the Hittite Empire about 1200 B.C.E., when the local ironsmiths became scattered over wider areas, did their technique become generally known. Iron smelting appeared late because the process differs in basic ways from those used for working copper and its alloys.

In copper smelting, the molten metal collects in the bottom of the furnace, and the slag floats on top. In iron smelting, at least at the temperature possible with ancient furnaces, the iron is never completely liquefied. It forms instead a gray, spongy mass known technically as the bloom. The discovery that wrought iron could be produced by hammering the red-hot bloom was understandably slow in coming. Furthermore the new metal was no improvement over the copper and bronze already available. It was harder to work, required more fuel, and lost its cutting edge more easily. Later it was discovered that iron could be hardened by a process of repeated hammering, heating, plunging into cold water (quenching), and contacting the metal to the charcoal fuel. What had to be discovered, then, was not merely a new metal but a radically new technique of metallurgy, for the early smiths had no past experience to prepare them for the new methods.

Even the improved, harder type of iron was always liable to rust, but the fact that iron ore, in contrast to copper and tin, was very widespread and correspondingly cheap more than made up for rusting. Ordinary peasants could now afford iron tools. Agricultural productivity rose as fields were extended into heavily wooded areas that previously resisted the old stone axe. Equally significant was the effect of the cheap new metal on the Eurasian military balance. Previously the poverty-stricken nomads had not been able to afford as many of the expensive bronze weapons as could the rulers of the urban centers. But now iron ore was available in almost every region, and every village smith could forge new weapons that were both superior to and cheaper than the old. Thus nomadic warriors enjoyed not only superior mobility but also iron weapons that were as good and as plentiful as those of the soldiers guarding the civilized areas.

V. NOMADS DESTROY ANCIENT CIVILIZATIONS

With their horses and iron weapons, the nomads launched two great waves of invasion that overwhelmed the centers of civilization. During the first, between roughly 1700 and 1500 B.C.E., the invaders usually arrived with horse-drawn chariots and bronze weapons; by the second wave, from about 1200 to 1100 B.C.E., they commonly rode on horses and fought with iron weapons. These invasions were not vast incursions of foreign hordes that displaced native stock and completely changed ethnic patterns. Instead there were rather small numbers of invaders who used their superior military technology to establish themselves as military elites, ruling over subject peoples who far outnumbered them.

The end result was the uprooting of civilization everywhere except in the Middle East. Elsewhere empires rose and fell in rapid succession. Although because of its geographic accessibility the Middle East endured the largest number of invasions, civilization there survived, with its cities, palaces, temples, scribes, merchants, and government officials. One reason was that civilization had been established for a longer period and had sunk deeper roots in the Middle East. Moreover, such large expanses of the Middle East had become civilized by 1700 B.C.E. that not all could be overwhelmed and destroyed. Finally, invaders in the Middle East usually were not raw barbarians fresh from the steppes or desert. They were instead semicivilized barbarians who had settled earlier in surrounding lands and who, consequently, were already partially assimilated by the time of conquest.

Middle East

Considering first the Middle East, the invasions began about 2000 B.C.E. when the Indo-European Hittites filtered into Asia Minor. Together with the native peoples, the Hittites organized a large empire, including Asia Minor and much of Syria, though not Mesopotamia. The Hittites were followed by two other Indo-European invaders, the Kassites and the Hurrians. During this period even well-protected Egypt was over-run by a mixed, though mostly Semitic, group of invaders, the Hyksos. By 1500 B.C.E. the first wave of invasions ended, leaving the Middle East controlled by three major powers: the Hittites in the north, the Egyptians in the south, and the Semitic Assyrians in the east.

This triangular balance was upset by the second wave of invasions, which began about 1200 B.C.E. A long series of wars between the Hittites and Egyptians had weakened both empires. Three Semitic invaders moved to fill the vacuum: the Phoenicians into the Mediterranean coast; the Arameans into Syria, Palestine, and northern Mesopotamia; and the Hebrews into Palestine and Syria. About 1100 B.C.E. the powerful Second Assyrian Empire began to expand, with its iron weapons, disciplined army, efficient bureaucracy, and iron battering rams mounted on wheels. By the seventh century the Assyrian Empire, with its capital at Nineveh, included Mesopotamia, Asia Minor, Syria, Palestine, and Egypt. But overextension of the empire and the deep hostility of its subject peoples finally led to disaster. In 612 B.C.E. a coalition of enemies destroyed Nineveh and ended forever the role of the Assyrians in history.

The Assryians were followed by the Persians, who now organized the greatest empire to that date. Under their King Cyrus (550–529 B.C.E.), and using Assyrian military techniques, the Persians conquered all the lands from the Nile River in the west to the Indus River in the east. For the first time the entire Middle East was under one rule, and the barbarian invaders were firmly shut out.

Greece

In contrast to the Middle East, civilization in Greece, India, and China did not survive the barbarian invasions. In these peripheral areas, it lacked depth in time and space, and therefore civilization was plowed under. Thus it was in those regions that new classical civilizations emerged, with new religious, social, and philosophical systems.

In Greece, the first invaders were the Indo-European Achaeans, who came in the twentieth century B.C.E. They were charioteers with bronze weapons, their general level of development far behind that of the Minoan Cretans. But by 1600 B.C.E. the newcomers had absorbed much of the Minoan culture, which had been transplanted to the mainland, and they had established a number of small kingdoms from Thessaly down to the southern tip of the Peloponnesus.

The most advanced settlements were those in the Peloponnesus, which was closest to Crete. Mycenae, the outstanding Achaean center there, gave its name to the emerging civilization. In contrast to the cities of Crete, all settlements in Mycenaean Greece were strongly fortified. Massive hilltop citadels were constructed, where the king and his retainers lived. The commoners

The Lion Gate at Mycenae, Greece.

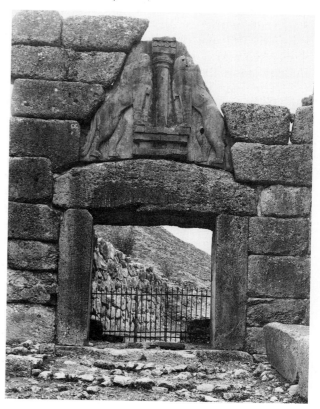

built their dwellings outside the citadel but in time of danger sought refuge within its walls.

Unlike the other Indo-European invaders who had established themselves in the Middle East and the Indus valley, the Mycenaeans took to the sea after the fashion of the Minoans and developed a formidable maritime power. They raided or traded, as opportunities dictated, and they founded overseas colonies in Rhodes, Cyprus, and the west coast of Asia Minor. The Mycenaeans soon undermined the former economic hegemony of Crete in the Mediterranean, and by the fifteenth century B.C.E. they were raiding the great island itself. The unwalled cities, including the capital of Knossos, were taken and destroyed. These disasters, together with a series of devastating earthquakes, led to the virtual extinction of the formerly great Minoan civilization by 1150 B.C.E.

Meanwhile the Mycenaeans were experiencing a similar fate at the hands of new invaders, the Dorians. Appearing about 1200 B.C.E. and armed with superior iron weapons, the Dorians captured the Mycenaean citadels and towns one by one. Administrative systems disintegrated, rural populations scattered, foreign trade withered, and Greece reverted to an agrarian and pastoral economy. A Dark Age descended and obscured Greece until the rise of the city-states about 800 B.C.E.

The main Dorian settlements were again in the Peloponnesus. From there the invaders pushed on overseas to found colonies in Crete, in Rhodes, and on the adjacent coast of Asia Minor. Other Greeks, perhaps Mycenaean refugees, crossed from Athens to the Cyclades Islands and on to the central part of the west coast of Asia Minor. There they established settlements that became known as Ionia, which for a period was the most advanced region of the entire Greek world. Still further north, other bands speaking the Aeolic dialect sailed from Thessaly and central Greece to the island of Lesbos and thence to northern Asia Minor. These new Greek colonies in Asia Minor were never able to expand into the interior because of the resistance of the large local population. Although confined to the coastal areas, they prospered and were destined to play a major role in the general history of the Greek people.

Much more is known of this Dark Age in Greece than of the corresponding postinvasion period in India, largely because of the precious heritage of the four great poems left by the Greeks—Homer's *Iliad* and *Odyssey*, and Hesiod's *Works and Days* and *Birth of the Gods*. Homer wrote of war, adventure, and the life of nobles and kings, whereas Hesiod described the life and lore of the farmer and the genealogies of the gods. Between them they have left a vivid picture of the primitive agricultural and pastoral society of those centuries. Households were largely self-sufficient, growing their own food and making their own cloth with wool from their flocks of sheep. The only full-time traders were foreigners—Phoenicians or Cypriots—who appeared sporadically with trinkets for the commoners and more valuable goods for the nobles. The monotony of the farm work was broken by the occasional visit of a bard who sang of the glories of war and of the exploits of illustrious ancestors.

Each community consisted of the noble families, who governed and led in war, and the commoners, including freehold peasants, tenant farmers, and a few craftmakers, hired laborers, and slaves. At the top was the king, whose authority depended on his prowess in war and his ability to exercise leadership in the meetings of the council of nobles. Occasionally the king called a meeting of the assembly that included all adult males, but the purpose usually was to mobilize popular support for decisions already reached in conjunction with the nobles. These simple institutions, typical of the Indo-European tribes at this level of development, represented the embryo from which the Greek city-state was to develop its organs of government.

India

In India, the Indus valley civilization had the same fate as the Minoan civilization of Crete. About 1500 B.C.E., it was overrun by tribespeople who, with the military advantage of iron weapons and horsedrawn chariots, easily overwhelmed the copper weapons and oxdrawn carts of the natives. The invaders called themselves Aryans and the land in which they settled Aryavarta, or land of the Aryans. They were of the Indo-European family of peoples, of which the western branches had invaded Mesopotamia and Greece. Infiltrating in small groups, the Aryans easily overthrew the decaying Indus valley civilization, so a primitive new society emerged in the latter half of the second millennium B.C.E. Information concerning this society is scanty. Unlike the Indus civilization, which left a wealth of material remains but no decipherable written records, the Aryans left almost no remains, for they used wood or mud for their dwellings and had no large cities, but they did leave a wealth of literature in the form of Vedas. Thus material available for the reconstruction of Aryan life is the direct opposite of that for the Indus civilization.

The word *veda* means knowledge, and for the Hindus the Vedas are a primary source of religious belief, as the Bible is for Christians and the Koran for Muslims. There were originally four Vedas, but the most important is the oldest, the Rigveda. In the course of time other works were added to the four Vedas and acquired a similar sacred status. As Homer's epics are for Mycenaean Greece, the Rigveda is a primary source for study of the early Aryans. It is in essence a collection of 1,028 hymns arranged in ten books, making it as bulky as the *Iliad* and *Odyssey* combined.

The tall, blue-eyed, fair-skinned Aryans were very conscious of their physical features in contrast to those of the conquered indigenous people, who are referred to in the Vedas as short, black, noseless, and as dasas, or slaves. The image of the Aryans that emerges from the Vedic literature is that of a virile people, fond of war, drinking, chariot racing, and gambling. Their god of war, Indra, was the ideal Aryan warrior: He dashed into battle joyously, wore golden armor, and could consume the flesh of 300 buffaloes and drink three lakes of liquor at one time.

When they first arrived in India the Aryans were primarily pastoralists. Their economic life centered around their cattle, and wealth was judged on the basis of the size of the herds. As the newcomers settled in the fertile river valleys, they gradually shifted more to agriculture. They lived in villages consisting of a number of related families. Several villages comprised a clan, and several clans a tribe, at the head of which

was the king. As in Greece, the king's authority depended on his personal prowess and initiative; this authority was limited by the council of nobles and, in some tribes, by the freemen.

The outstanding characteristic of this early Aryan society was its basic difference from later Hinduism: Cows were worshiped but eaten. Intoxicating spirits were not forsaken but joyously consumed. There were classes but no castes, and the priests were subordinate to the nobles rather than dominating the social pyramid. In short, Aryan society resembled much more the other contemporary Indo-European societies than it did the classical Hinduism that was to develop in later centuries.

China

About 1500 B.C.E. charioteers with bronze weapons also invaded the distant valley of the Yellow River in north China. There they found the flourishing Neolithic culture of the Shang, to which they made contributions, but by which they were absorbed. As has always been true in China, these invasions did not create a complete break with the Chinese culture's past, as they did in Greece and India. Hence the distinctively Chinese civilization has continued uninterrupted from the early Shang period to the present, sometimes modified, but never destroyed or transformed.

The pattern of continuity is apparent in the transition from the Shang to the Zhou dynasty in 1027 B.C.E. The Zhou people had for long lived in the Wei valley on the fringes of civilization, so they shared the language and basic culture of the Shang but at the same time borrowed military techniques from the sheepherding "barbarians" to the north and west. Consequently when the Zhou overran north China, they did overthrow the Shang dynasty but did not interrupt the evolution of Chinese civilization. The writing system continued as before, as did ancestor worship, the methods of divination, and the division of society into aristocratic warriors and peasant masses. Political decentralization also persisted and, indeed, became more pronounced as the Zhou rulers assigned the conquered territories to vassal lords. The vassal lords journeyed periodically to the Zhou court for elaborate ceremonies of investiture, but gradually this practice lapsed. So eventually the lords, ensconced in their walled towns, ruled over the surrounding countryside with little control from the capital.

In 771 B.C.E. the Zhou capital was captured by new "barbarians" allied with rebellious lords. The Zhou dynasty resumed its rule from a center further to the east that was not so vulnerable to attacks from the borderlands. Thus the dynastic period before 771 B.C.E. is termed by the Chinese the Western Zhou, and the period thereafter, the Eastern Zhou. During the Eastern Zhou period the kings were rulers in name only. Although accorded certain religious functions and some ceremonial respect, their domains were smaller than those of their nominal vassals, and their power correspondingly weaker. Indeed they managed to survive until 256 B.C.E. only because they provided spiritual leadership. The dynasty was also a royal priesthood and, as such, was preserved as a symbol of national unity.

Although the Eastern Zhou was a period of political instability, it was also a period of cultural flowering. In this dynamic and creative age the great works of literature, philosophy, and social theory were written. This was the period when the classical Chinese civilization was taking form. It corresponded to the classical Greek and Indian civilizations roughly evolving at the same time. The origin and nature of these classical civilizations is the subject of the remaining chapters in Part II.

SUGGESTED READINGS

For the origins of civilizations, see J. Gowlett, *Ascent to Civilization* (Knopf, 1984); P. R. S. Moorey, ed., *The Origins of Civilization* (Clarendon, 1979); C. B. Heiser, Jr., *Seed to Civilization* (W. H. Freeman, 1973); J. E. Pfeiffer, *The Emergence of Society* (McGraw-Hill, 1977); and A. C. Renfrew, *Before Civilization* (Cape, 1973), which challenges the diffusionist theory of civilization.

Surveys of the various civilizations are given in K. C. Chang, *Shang Civilization* (Yale University, 1980); O. R. Gurney, *The Hittites* (Penguin, 1980); C. Y. Hsu, *Western Chou Civilization* (Yale University, 1988); T. Jacobsen, *The Treasures of Darkness: A History of Mesopotamian Religion* (Yale University, 1976); N. Postgate, *The First Empires* (Elsevier, 1977); J. Hawkes and L. Woolley, "Prehistory and the Beginnings of Civilization," in *UNESCO History of Mankind*, Vol. 1 (Harper & Row, 1963); M. Hammond, *The City in the Ancient World* (Harvard University, 1972); J. G. Macqueen, *The Hittites and Their Contemporaries in Asia Minor* (Thames & Hudson, 1975); B. M. Fagan, ed., *Avenues to Antiquity* (W. H. Freeman, 1976); R. F. Willetts, *The Civilization of Ancient Crete* (University of California, 1977); and the lavishly illustrated *The Epic of Man* by the editors of Life (Time Incorporated, 1961), and *The Dawn of Civilization* (McGraw-Hill, 1961).

For the nomadic invaders, see E. D. Phillips, *The Royal Hordes: Nomad Peoples of the Steppes* (Thames & Hudson, 1965); O. Lattimore, *Studies in Frontier History* (Mouton, 1962), and *Inner Frontiers of China* (American Geographical Society, 1940); and A. Guha, ed., *Central Asia: Movement of Peoples and Ideas from Times Prehistoric to Modern* (Harper & Row, 1972). A survey of today's nomads is presented in the well-illustrated volume *Nomads of the World* (National Geographic Society, 1971).

NOTES

1. Cited by N. Bailkey, "Early Mesopotamian Constitutional Development," *American Historical Review* (July 1967), pp. 1, 225.
2. Adapted from J. Hawkes and L. Woolley, *UNESCO History of Mankind*, Vol. 1, *Prehistory and the Beginnings of Civilization* (Harper & Row, 1963), p. 467; and V. Gordon Childe, *Man Makes Himself* (Mentor Books, 1951), p. 149.
3. Cited by A. J. Wright, *Buddhism in Chinese History* (Sanford University, 1959), pp. 19–20.
4. Cited by G. Soloveytchik, *Potemkin* (Butterworth, 1938), p. 25.
5. W. A. Haviland, "Stature of Tikal," *American Antiquity* (July 1967), pp. 316–25.
6. *New York Times*, December 11, 1984.
7. E. A. Speiser, "The Beginnings of Civilization in Mesopotamia," *Supplement to the Journal of the American Oriental Society* (December 1939), p. 27.

4

Classical Civilizations Begin Eurasian Unification, 1000 B.C.E.–500 C.E.

Formerly the things which happened in the world had no connection among themselves. Each action interested only the locality where it happened. But since then all events are united in a common bundle.

Polybius

The most striking feature of the Classical Age was the beginning of the unification of Eurasia. A comparison of the map of Eurasia about 1500 B.C.E. with that of about 200 C.E. makes clear the extent of this unification. (See map on p. 47 and map of Early Eurasian Unification about 200 C.E., pp. 72–73.) The empires of the early period were almost entirely restricted to their respective river valleys and give the appearance of tiny islands in a vast sea of barbarism. By the first century C.E., however, the Roman, Parthian, Kushan, and Han empires spanned the breadth of Eurasia from the Scottish highlands to the China seas. This made possible a modest degree of interaction among empires.

Of course there had always been certain interregional contacts even at the time of the ancient civilizations, as evidenced by the nomadic invasions in all directions. But now in the Classical Age interregional contacts were substantially closer, more varied, and more sustained. And yet—even by the end of the classical period—the Roman and Chinese empires, at opposite ends of Eurasia, had not been able to establish direct, official contact and possessed no specific or reliable knowledge of each other. Thus Eurasian unity remained at the beginning stage throughout those centuries. The origins, nature, and significance of this first stage in the unification process are the subjects of this chapter.

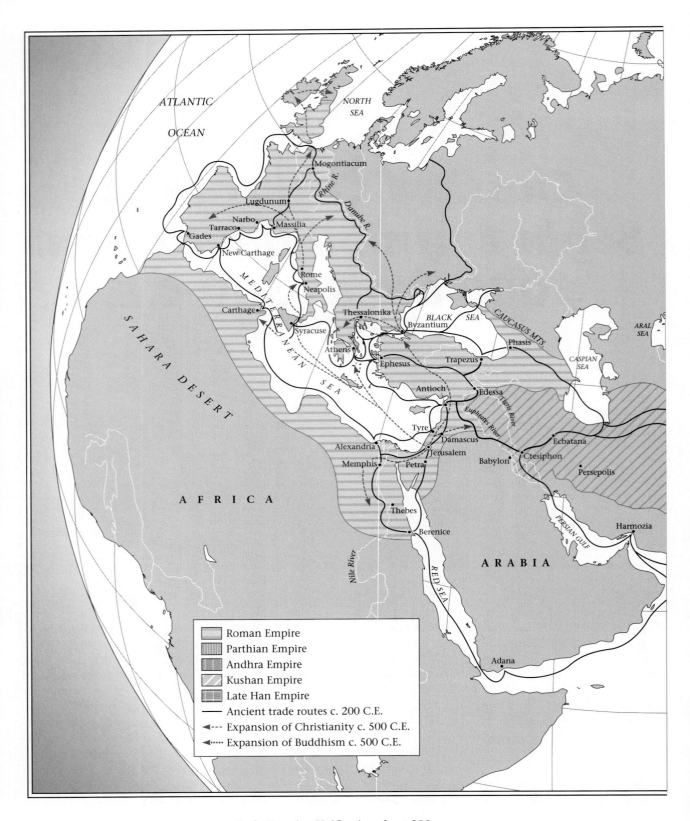

Early Eurasian Unification about 200 C.E.

Lake
Baikal

SEA
OF
JAPAN

EAST
CHINA
SEA

PACIFIC
OCEAN

Lake
Balkash

ARAL
SEA

TIEN SHAN MTS.

Kucha

Hwang Ho

Loyang

Ch'ang-an

Lanchow

CHINA

Bukhara

Samarkand

Kashgar

Yarkand

Khotan

Balkh

Kabul

Taxila

Yangtze River

Indus River

TIBET

SOUTH
CHINA
SEA

Ganges R.

Pataliputra

Baithan

Bay
of
Bengal

ARABIAN

SEA

73

I. ROOTS OF UNIFICATION

Technological advance was at the root of the new Eurasian unity. This was not surprising, since from history's very beginning the territorial range of human activities had always depended on the level of technology. When people were at the food-gathering stage, the range of the individual band was its hunting ground. As people learned agriculture and metallurgy and shipbuilding, their range broadened to encompass, for example, the valley empires of Sargon and of the pharaohs. But now further technological advances allowed for a much greater extension of agriculture and civilization. Regional empires were organized and stretched contiguously across the breadth of Eurasia. The basic technological advance responsible was the discovery and ever more widespread use of iron.

Iron smelting was developed first in Asia Minor in the middle of the second millennium B.C.E., spreading from there after the destruction of the Hittite Empire about 1200 B.C.E. As we have seen, this discovery made possible the second wave of barbarian invasions at the end of the second millennium B.C.E. But some centuries passed before the new metal was available in sufficient quantities for everyday use. When hoes and axes and plows, as well as weapons, could be made of iron, then the economic, social, and political repercussions were immediate and far-reaching.

This stage was reached slowly—about 800 B.C.E. in India, 750 B.C.E. in central Europe, and 600 B.C.E. in China. In these and other regions the use of cheap iron led first and foremost to the cutting down of heavy forests hitherto invulnerable to stone-edged axes and wooden plows. Now farmers were able to use their strong, sharp iron axes and iron-shod plows to extend agriculture from the Middle East eastward across the Iranian plateau and westward across the Mediterranean lands and into central and northern Europe. Likewise in India the Aryan newcomers pushed eastward and cut down the forests of the Ganges valley. At the same time agriculturists in China were extending their operations from the Yellow River valley southward to the great Yangtze basin.

The expansion of the frontiers of agriculture made possible a corresponding expansion of the frontiers of civilization. They grew more in the half millennium from 1000 to 500 B.C.E. than in the preceding three millennia from 4000 to 1000 B.C.E. The basic reason for this was the tremendous increase in productivity that now took place. Not only was agriculture practiced in much larger areas, but also the combination of soils and climate in the newly opened lands of central Europe and of the Ganges and Yangtze monsoon basins was much more productive than were the comparatively arid Middle East, Indus, and Yellow River regions.

The jump in agricultural productivity meant that a surplus was now available for economic development and for state-building purposes. Trade increased in volume, especially along the rivers that constituted ready-made highways. Craftmakers appeared in growing numbers to provide the services needed in the new agricultural communities and the products demanded for the new trade. At first goods and services were exchanged by barter, with obvious inconvenience for both buyer and seller. Then media of exchange were developed, such as measures of grain or, more common, bars of metal. But with every transaction the weight and purity of the metal had to be checked against fraudulent clipping and debasing.

About 700 B.C.E., the Lydians of western Asia Minor began stamping pieces of metal and guaranteeing both their quality and their weight. Various Greek city-states soon improved on this technique by stamping flat, circular, two-sided coins. Thus gold and silver coins now helped large-scale wholesale or interregional trade. Additionally, copper coins enabled farmers to sell rather than barter their produce, and artisans to work for wages rather than foodstuffs. The net effect was a great boost in all kinds of commerce, a corresponding boost in manufacturing and agriculture, and an overall increase in efficiency and productivity. Now for the first time, the manufacturer of cheap goods had a mass market available. The small landholder could turn from subsistence agriculture to specialized farming, whether the specialty was the mulberry and silkworm in China or olive oil and wine in Greece.

The new iron tools also made it possible to build better and larger ships, which in turn led to longer voyages and to more trade and colonization. At the outset overseas expansion was hindered by piracy, which then was thought to be as normal an activity as brigandage on land. *The Odyssey*, which describes the half-piratical, half-commercial expeditions of Menelaus and Odysseus in the Aegean Sea, relates how all the voyagers as a matter of course asked those whom they met if they were pirates. But gradually maritime trade was developed on a regular large-scale basis, with great economic advantage. Transport by sea was many times cheaper than by land and remained so until the development of an efficient horse harness in the Middle Ages and the building of good roads in the eighteenth century.

By the end of the Classical Age, trade routes encircled all of Eurasia. (In contrast, local self-sufficiency was the rule in most regions following the invasions of the second millennium B.C.E.) In addition to the caravan routes across the interior of Eurasia, there were sea routes around its circumference—from the North Sea to the western Mediterranean, from the western Mediterranean to the Levant, from the Red Sea to India, and from India to Southeast Asia and, to a lesser degree, to China. This maritime commerce was accompanied by colonization, especially in the Mediterranean by the Phoenicians and Greeks, and later in Southeast Asia by the Indians.

Side by side with these economic developments came equally significant social and political changes. The military aristocracy, risen to prominence with the invasions of the second millennium B.C.E., was being undermined by the new class of merchants, craftmakers, and mariners. The old tribal society was being transformed by the use of money; personal services and allegiances were being replaced by the demands of the marketplace.

Equally disruptive was the political consolidation made possible by economic growth. Tribal chiefs and their advisory councils and assemblies were replaced by kingdoms and then by empires, whether in Italy, India, or China. Nor was it a one-way process of economic development stimulating political centralization. The reverse also operated, for the great new regional empires spanning the Eurasian land mass enforced order and security, making long-distance trade by land and sea possible. Regional

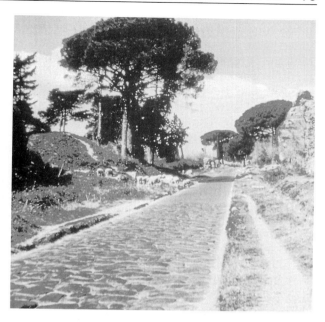

The Appian Way, "queen of roads," connecting Rome with southern Italy, is still in use today.

empires also were able to build and maintain regional road networks that facilitated commerce.

In the Persian Empire, for example, the so-called Royal Road ran 1,677 miles from Susa, located to the north of the Persian Gulf, westward to the Tigris, and thence across Syria and Asia Minor to Ephesus on the Aegean coast. The route was divided into 111 post stations, each with relays of fresh horses for the royal couriers. Caravans took ninety days to travel this road from end to end, whereas the royal couriers traversed it in a week. As the empire was enlarged, branch lines were constructed southwest to Egypt and southeast to the Indus valley. A few centuries later the Romans constructed their well-known system of roads; so well engineered were these that some, along with their bridges, are still in use.

At the other end of Eurasia, the Chinese built an elaborate network of both roads and canals, which enabled them to transport goods from present-day Canton to the Yangtze valley by an all-water route, thereby promoting their overseas trade. To the northwest they built roads that linked up with the long silk route, which, as will be noted in the following section, crossed the whole of central Asia to the Middle East. The main highways were lined with trees and provided with stations and guest houses. Road construction and maintenance was the responsibility of central and local officials who were punished if they did not carry out their duties properly. Likewise in India the Royal Highway ran from the Ganges delta to Taxila in the northwest, near the Khyber Pass, where it connected with the caravan routes west to the Middle East and north to central Asia.

All these developments involved profound changes in social relationships, in political organizations, and in ways of living and working. Such basic and all-inclusive disruption was unsettling and uncomfortable. It led to soul searching—to the posing of new questions and the seeking for new answers. Thinkers had to reconsider their respective traditions and to either abandon them or adapt them to the requirements of an age of transition. People speculated about such questions as the moral basis of ideal government, the functioning of the social order, and the origin and purpose of the universe and life.

About the sixth century B.C.E. such questions were being posed and discussed all over Eurasia. The answers made up the great philosophical, religious, and social systems of the Classical Age. It was not happenstance, then, that the spokespeople for these systems were all contemporaries—Confucius in China, Buddha in India, Zoroaster in Persia, and the rationalist philosophers in Greece. In all these regions the disruption and the challenge were the same, but the answers varied greatly, and the several Eurasian civilizations set off in decidedly different directions. Indeed, it was at this time that these civilizations developed their distinctive philosophical attitudes and social institutions, which have continued to distinguish them through the centuries to the present day.

The attitudes and institutions of each of the classical civilizations will be analyzed in the following chapters. The remainder of this chapter will be devoted to an examination of the interrelationships among these civilizations. Contemporary Eurasians were very much aware of these interrelationships. They were definitely aware that the historical stage was expanding—that life was becoming more complex and that many new domestic and external forces were pressing in on them. Thus the Greek historian Polybius, when starting his history of events from 220 to 145 B.C.E., observed that "during this period history becomes, so to speak, an organic whole. What happens in Italy and in Libya is bound up with what happened in Asia and in Greece, all events culminating in a single result."

Two aspects of this new "organic whole" were particularly clear, even to contemporaries. These were interregional commercial bonds and cultural bonds, the subject of the following two sections.

II. COMMERCIAL BONDS

The principal interregional bonds of a material nature were commercial in character, though not exclusively so. This was a time when not only goods but also people moved about from one region to another, taking with them their technological skills and their plants. We can see how wide-ranging this interchange was by the fact that cotton, sugar cane, and chickens, all first domesticated in India, spread to both China and western Eurasia during this period. Likewise the Chinese during these centuries obtained for the first time the grape vine, alfalfa, chive, cucumber, fig, sesame, pomegranate, and walnut. In return the Chinese gave to the rest of Eurasia the orange, peach, pear, peony, azalea, camellia, and chrysanthemum. There was a similar interchange of technology, as is evident in the case of that fundamental invention, the waterwheel. The first waterwheel to be found in western Asia was that of Mithridates, king of Pontus, and was erected on the south shore of the Black Sea about 65 B.C.E. The first waterwheel in China was built soon after, about 30 B.C.E. The difference between the two dates is much too small for direct diffusion from either source and thus strongly suggests diffusion in both directions from some unknown intermediate source. Such interaction between the various Eurasian regions was the result of a great increase in local and long-distance trade during the centuries of the Classical Age.

Trade was conducted both by land across central Eurasia and by sea around the coasts of the land mass. These two general routes were by

An Athenian silver four-drachma coin (tetradrachm) *from the fifth century B.C.E. (440–430 B.C.E.). On the front (left) is the profile of Athena and on the back (right) is her symbol of wisdom, the owl. The silver from which the coins were struck came chiefly from the state mines at Sunium in southern Attica.*

no means exclusive or independent of each other. A large proportion of the goods were moved along some combination of the two, usually by sea between Egypt and India and by one of several overland routes between India and China. Furthermore, the land and sea routes were competitive; excessively high charges or intolerable lack of security on one route normally shifted the trade to the other.

Maritime trade had first gotten under way at the time of the ancient civilizations. Egyptian traders ventured down the Red Sea to East Africa and along the Levant coast to Lebanon. Likewise, Sumerian merchants sailed down the Persian Gulf, along the Arabian peninsula, while their counterparts from the Indus valley worked their way westward until contact was established, perhaps at the Bahrain Islands in the Persian Gulf. But all these early seafarers were mere landlubbers compared to the Minoans of Crete. The great maritime traders of ancient times, they plied the Mediterranean from end to end as the unrivaled sailors of that inland sea.

With the invasions of the Achaeans and Dorians this far-flung commerce dried up, and the eastern Mediterranean people sank back to an agrarian and isolated existence. The first to resume the mercantile activities of the Cretans were the Phoenicians. A Semitic-speaking people who had settled along the narrow coastal plains of the eastern Mediterranean, they soon developed a flourishing trade as commercial middlemen. Caravans from the east brought in myrrh, spices, and the products of Mesopotamian craftsmanship. From lands overseas came assorted metals, hides, grains, olive oil, and slaves. The Phoenicians themselves manufactured fine furniture, jewelry, metalware, and especially textiles, made from the wool of their own sheep and colored by their famous purple dye obtained from shellfish found in large beds along the coast.

In developing this trade the Phoenicians evolved a type of ship rowed by tiers of oarsmen. It was fast and seaworthy for the long voyages that were made further and further to the west. In the eleventh century B.C.E. the Phoenicians began to spread out over the Aegean, and by the end of the ninth century they had entered the western Mediterranean. They founded trading posts and colonies on the northwest coast of Africa; the south coast of Spain; and on Sicily,

Malta, and the Balearic Islands. They even ventured beyond Gibraltar as far afield as Cornwall, England, where they traded for valuable tin.

From about 1100 B.C.E. until the late eighth century B.C.E. the sailors and merchants of Phoenicia controlled most of the maritime trade of the Mediterranean. Then the Greeks appeared as competitors, spurred on by the same pressure of overpopulation. First they established trading posts, which later developed into agricultural settlements wherever the land resources made this possible. Settlements were quite independent of the mother cities from whence they sprang, even though the colonists established the same institutions and copied the same religious practices they had left behind. So Greek colonization took the form of many independent city-states rather than one centrally controlled empire.

One principal area of Greek settlement was in Sicily and south Italy, where so many colonies were founded that the region came to be known as Magna Graecia, or Greater Greece. On the mainland the Greeks advanced as far north as Naples, where they established contact with Etruscans, who were themselves migrants from Asia Minor. In the western Mediterranean the Greeks established a firm base in northeastern Spain and southern France, where their chief colony was Massilia (Marseilles). Finally, the Greeks found a free field in the Black Sea region, where, at first discouraged by the cold and foggy climate, they eventually settled in large numbers because of the economic opportunities. The Black Sea itself provided the annual run of tunny fish, and the native Scythians, living in what is today southern Russia, exchanged their raw materials for Greek-manufactured goods. By the fifth century B.C.E. the entire Black Sea basin was ringed with flourishing Greek trading posts and settlements.

While the Greeks were prospering on the sea, the Persians were building an empire that eventually extended from the Nile valley to the Indus. Although Persians were a mountain people and had little maritime knowledge, they wanted nevertheless to open sea routes and so facilitate communications between their eastern and western provinces. For this purpose they made use of their subject peoples, the Phoenicians and Asia Minor Greeks, who were experienced seagoers. They appointed a Greek mariner, Scylax, to head an expedition that sailed about 510 B.C.E. from the Indus to Arsino at the head of the Red Sea. The Persians also had plans for cutting a canal from the Nile to the Red Sea and appear to have done considerable work toward that goal. Trade flourished and surpassed anything previously known in volume and in geographic range. Greek, Phoenician, Arab, and Indian mariners sailed back and forth among India, the Persian Gulf, Egypt, and the numerous ports of the Mediterranean.

The empire-builder Alexander and his successors continued the work of the Persians by sending more expeditions, which increased geographic knowledge. They also constructed a series of ports along the Red Sea, through which goods could be transported overland to the Nile and then shipped down the river to Alexandria. The Indian Ocean trade was carried on at this time in two stages. In the first, Indian and Arab traders sailed westward from Indian ports, hugging the coastline until they reached the Arabian peninsula and rounded it to their destination at Aden or Mocha. There they were met by Greco-Egyptian merchants who exchanged their wares for the eastern goods, which they transported via the Red Sea coastal ports to Alexandria.

All this was only the prelude to the great expansion of trade between East and West that blossomed shortly before the Christian era and lasted for about two centuries. One reason for this increase in trade was China's increasing influence in central Asia. The Chinese not only opened overland trade routes but also made it easier to obtain silk, the most important item in interregional commerce. The precise role of China will be considered shortly in the analysis of overland trade. The other main factor behind the trade boom was the consolidation of the Roman Empire, which encompassed the entire Mediterranean basin and much of central and northwestern Europe. The establishment of Pax Romana eliminated brigandage and piracy, which hitherto had hindered trade, and removed almost all tolls and exactions. The wealth of the empire also stimulated trade, particularly since the wealthy Roman ruling class had both the taste and the funds for exotic foreign products.

The Romans carried on a flourishing trade with all neighboring lands—with Scandinavia to the north, Germany across the Rhine, Dacia across the Danube, and Africa south of the Sahara. Most significant in its general Eurasian repercussions was commerce with the East. Eastern commerce was greatly expanded sometime in the first century B.C.E. when a Greek mariner discovered that the monsoon winds could be used to speed the voyage back and forth across the Indian Ocean. (This was more likely a rediscovery, since Arab sailors appear to have preceded the Greeks—monsoon is derived from the Arab word *Mauzim*, or season.) The northeast, or winter, monsoon blows from India toward East Africa from October to April, and the southwest, or summer, monsoon blows in the opposite direction from June to September. No longer was it necessary for the sailors to hug the coasts in a wide, time-consuming arc; now they could scud before the wind directly across the ocean. A merchant could journey from Rome to India in sixteen weeks, including the land stage through Egypt.

"Roman" merchants, mostly Greeks and Syrians, undertook such journeys and also a few settled permanently in Indian cities, as we know from Indian literary sources. They brought with them glass, copper, tin, linen and wool textiles, and, above all, gold coins. In return the Romans wanted pepper and other spices, cotton textiles, precious stones, and, most important, the Chinese silk brought to Indian ports via the overland Silk Road. A few of the more adventurous "Roman" traders made their way further east beyond India. In the second and third centuries C.E. they reached Burma, Malaya, Sumatra, and passed on through the Malacca Strait to Kattigara (Hanoi), from which they at last made direct contact with China.

As far as overland trade was concerned, much depended on the degree to which order and security could be maintained. When large sections of the land routes were under the firm control of some authority, trade could flourish; when anarchy prevailed, trade withered. This pattern is clearly apparent in surveying commercial trends through these centuries. A general upward trend is evident in the volume of trade, the result of the technological advances and the expansion of civilization and of empires. But within this overall trend there are dips and rises as a result of political conditions. For example,

the centuries of the Scythian Empire in western Eurasia, the Chinese empires in eastern Eurasia, and the Mongol Empire embracing most of the continental land mass were all centuries of safe trade routes and increasing commerce.

The Scythians, for example, carried on a lively trade with the Greek cities on the north shore of the Black Sea. They exchanged slaves, cattle, hides, furs, fish, timber, wax, and honey for Greek textiles, wine, olive oil, and various luxury goods. Likewise, the Chinese traded goods back and forth along the famous Silk Road from northwest China across central Asia to the Black Sea and Levant ports. The Chinese exported mostly silk, but they also brought cinnamon, rhubarb, and high-grade iron. In return they received furs, woolens, jade, and livestock from central Asia; amber from the Baltic; and—from the Roman provinces—glass, corals, pearls, linen and wool textiles, and, above all, gold.

This flourishing land trade declined gradually with the growing troubles and anarchy in the Roman and Chinese empires after the second century C.E. The great blow came when the Moslem Arabs conquered the entire Middle East in the seventh century and then pushed into central Asia. After the Arabs defeated the Chinese in the battle of Talas in 751, all central Asia was converted to Islam. The huge Moslem Empire now was a barrier rather than a bridge between China and the West or between China and India. Finally, the overland routes were closed and trade shifted to the surrounding seas, where the Arabs were becoming the leading mariners and merchants. It was not until the thirteenth century, when the Mongols conquered all of Eurasia from the Pacific Ocean to the Baltic and Black seas, that overland routes could be reopened, clearing the way for Marco Polo and his fellow merchants of medieval times.

Despite the various shifts in the direction of trade, one basic fact emerges from this survey—a huge increase occurred in both the range and the volume of commerce during the Classical Age as compared to the preceding ancient period. No longer was the scope of commerce confined to individual regions, whether in the Mediterranean Sea or the Arabian Sea or some segment of the Eurasian steppes. Instead trade now became interregional, with goods being carried from one end of Eurasia to the other by sea and by land.

III. CULTURAL BONDS

Commercial and cultural bonds were neither unconnected nor independent of each other. The Greek merchants who followed Alexander's armies spread their Hellenistic culture throughout the Orient. Likewise the spread of Buddhism from India to China can be traced along the well-known Silk Road. Cultural movements, however, had their own internal force and were by no means entirely caused by merchants and their trade routes. A fundamental factor affecting cultural developments in the classical world, exclusive of China, was the invention of a simple alphabetic script in the late second millennium B.C.E. Prior to that time only a handful of professional scribes had been able to read and write the complicated cuneiform script of Mesopotamia and the hieroglyphics of Egypt. The first alphabetic system was devised by Semitic traders in the Sinai peninsula who adapted the Egyptian signs, with which they had become familiar, to indicate consonantal sounds. But they continued to use many additional symbols for words and syllables and therefore failed to develop a strictly phonetic alphabet. The Phoenicians completed the transition in the thirteenth century B.C.E. by developing an alphabet of twenty-two signs denoting simple consonants. The Greeks improved the Phoenician alphabet by using some of its signs to indicate vowels. This Greek alphabet, with some modifications, was spread by the Romans westward and by the Byzantines eastward.

The alphabet is significant because it extended intelligent communication far beyond the narrow circle of the priests and officials of the old days. The scribes of Egypt and Mesopotamia naturally shunned the new style of writing, continuing to use their traditional scripts almost until the Christian era. Isolated China also maintained its usage of its combination phono-pictographic system, which has continued with modifications to the present day. But elsewhere in Eurasia the alphabet was adopted with slight adjustments to fit the different languages. Everywhere the effect was to reduce somewhat, though by no means entirely, the gap that had developed between urban ruling circles and peasant masses with the appearance of civilization. By challenging the monopoly of

The striding god from Artemisium is a bronze statue dating from about 460 B.C.E. It was found in the sea near Artemisium, the northern tip of the large Greek island of Euboea, and is now on display in the Athens archaeological museum. Exactly whom he represents is not known. Some have thought him to be Poseidon holding a trident; others believe that he is Zeus hurling a thunderbolt. In either case he is a splendid representative of the early classical period of Greek sculpture.

the privileged intellectual cliques who generally supported the status quo, the simplified scripts generated a certain ferment. And the ferment affected both politics and culture. India's famous statesman-historian, Jawaharlal Nehru, recognized the significance of this ferment when he wrote in his *Glimpses of World History,*[1] a series of letters to his teenage daughter, Indira Gandhi:

There must have been a wave of thought going through the world, a wave of discontent with existing conditions and of hope and aspiration for something better. For remember that the great founders of religions were always seeking something better and trying to change their people and improve them and lessen their misery. . . .

The overall cultural pattern noticeable among all Eurasian civilizations during these centuries of the Classical Age was the breakdown of local cultures, which were integrated into new regional civilizations with distinctive languages, religions, and social systems. It was much easier for these civilizations to exchange material goods than cultural traits. Textiles, spices, and luxury products were universally usable and desirable, whereas ancestor worship, the caste system, and the city-state were irrelevant and unacceptable outside their places of origin. Thus the commercial interregional bonds during this period of reorganization were generally more extensive and influential than the cultural.

Cultural bonds did develop, however, and in some cases were of prime historical significance. The first outstanding instance was the spread of Hellenism from the Greek world eastward to the Orient and westward to Europe. Toward the end of the classical period there also rose the great universal religions, especially Christianity and Buddhism, with their claims to the allegiance of all humanity rather than of any one group.

Let us first consider Hellenism, a term derived from the Greek word *Hellas*, meaning Greece. Its diffusion throughout the Middle East was made possible by Alexander's famous conquest eastward to central Asia and the Indus valley. As will be noted in the following chapter, this empire lasted for only a few years during Alexander's lifetime. At his death in 323 B.C.E. the empire was divided among his generals, and later it was partitioned between Rome in the West and the Parthians in the East. During this period of the fourth and third centuries B.C.E. the Greek military dominance paved the way for the hundreds of thousands of Greek merchants, administrators, and professionals who flocked to the numerous cities built by Alexander and his successors (and often named after the great general). From the first and most famous Alexandria in Egypt to the farthest Alexandria, Eschata (Kojand) in Afghanistan, these cities served as centers for the diffusion of Greek culture.

Although the majority of its inhabitants usually were non-Hellenic, the typical city was basically Greek, with elected magistrates, a council, and an assembly of the citizens. A new form of the Greek language, the Koine, or common tongue, was used widely throughout the Middle East. Many of the Greek emigrants married local women. Alexander himself set an example by taking a Persian noblewoman as wife. He then arranged for the mass marriage of 3,000 of his soldiers with Persian women after their return from the Indian campaign. He also enlisted Persian soldiers in his regiments and adopted the costume of the Persian King and the etiquette of his court.

Despite this impressive diffusion, Hellenism did not leave a permanent imprint on the Middle East. The basic reason was that its influence had been restricted to the cities where Greek settlers lived and where Greek dynasties had courts. Some of the native peoples were affected, but they were almost exclusively from the small upper classes. The great majority in the countryside, and even in many of the cities, continued to speak their own languages and worship their own gods. Thus Hellenism did not sink deep roots and was incapable of surviving permanently in its transplanted locales. When the Islamic conquerors appeared during the Middle Ages, they had little difficulty in overwhelming the little islands of Hellenistic culture, and today the Greek language and culture survive only in the Greek homeland on the southern tip of the Balkan peninsula.

Hellenism was slower to take root in the western Mediterranean because the indigenous populations had not yet reached a sufficiently affluent and sophisticated level of civilization. But for that very reason there was less competition from the local culture, and the long-run impact of Hellenism in that region was more durable.

As early as the sixth century B.C.E., the Romans were being influenced by the Greek colonies in southern Italy. But it was not until the third century onward, when the Romans conquered the heartland of Hellenism in the Balkans and the Levant, that they felt the full force of Greek culture. Roman soldiers and officials now came into direct contact with highly educated Greek rulers and administrators, and among the hostages and slaves brought to Rome were many Greeks who served in every capacity—from moral philosopher to acrobat, from laudatory poet to master chef. New intellectual horizons opened for upper-class Romans as they experienced the dazzling rhetoric and high-level discussions of their sophisticated Greek subjects.

Greeks served as tutors for leading Roman families, offering instruction in Greek language, rhetoric, philosophy, and literature. By the first century B.C.E. it was common for young Romans to be sent to Athens or Rhodes for training in the philosophical schools. In the field of literature, the Romans at first translated or imitated Greek originals, though gradually they turned to Roman themes.

Greek influence also was clear in the physical appearance of Rome and the other cities of the empire. All three Greek architectural forms were used—the Doric, Ionic, and Corinthian—though Roman buildings tended to be larger and more ornate. Thus towns and cities in Italy, as in the Middle East, began to take on a uniform physical appearance under the influence of Greek art and architecture. Indeed a basic contribution of the Romans to civilization was their appropriation and adaptation of Greek culture, which they then spread to diverse peoples who had never experienced direct contact with it—Gauls, Germans, Britons, and Iberians.

Much more durable than the impact of Hellenism was that of the two great universal religions, Christianity and Mahayana Buddhism. They began in the late classical period their expansion from their respective places of origin in the Middle East and India. During the course of the following centuries Christianity won over all Europe, and Buddhism, most of Asia. The reason for their success is to be found in certain characteristics that they had in common. One was their emphasis on salvation and the promise of an afterlife of eternal bliss. Another was their egalitarianism; their brotherhood was open to all who sought admittance—women as well as men, rich and poor alike, slave or free. Finally, both religions stressed a high code of ethics, the observance of which was essential for salvation. This requirement, together with efficient ecclesiastical organization, enabled these two religions to have an important influence on the daily lives of the faithful.

The features of these religions were particularly appealing in the later centuries of the Classical Age. These were times of social unrest and moral confusion, especially in the large cities, where the urban multitudes felt uprooted and

drifting. For such people, Christianity and Mahayana Buddhism offered solace, security, and guidance. When Pilate, voicing the despairing mood of the times, asked, "What is truth?" religion provided an answer. It was not accidental that the earliest converts to Christianity were the lowly and dispossessed. Likewise, the greatest triumph of Mahayana Buddhism was in China during the time of troubles following the collapse of the Han dynasty, when there seemed to be no solution to humankind's worldly problems.

Indeed, these satisfying characteristics of the two religions were evolved precisely in response to the needs of the times. They were present neither in the Judaism from which

Fasting Buddha. Before Gautama arrived at the "middle path," he practiced severe austerities for six years. According to a description in an ancient text: "My limbs became like some withered creepers with knotted joints; my buttocks like a buffalo's hoof . . . my ribs like rafters of a dilapidated shed; the pupils of my eyes appeared sunk deep in their sockets as water appears shining at the bottom of a deep well. . . ." This fourth–second century B.C.E. statue of the Buddha from Gandhara (in present-day Pakistan) reflects the Greek influence on early Buddhist sculpture.

Late Roman ivory plaque showing a scene from Christ's Passion—carrying the cross to the crucifixion.

Christianity had emerged nor in the original Buddhism from which developed the later Mahayana variant.

Judaism was the parochial faith of the Jewish people, who about the twelfth century B.C.E. adopted a national god, Jehovah. "I am Jehovah, thy God. . . . Thou shalt have no other gods before me." This first of Jehovah's Ten Commandments did not claim that Jehovah was the only god in the world but, rather, that he was the only god for the children of Israel. Moreover, the Judaistic faith was at this time more social and ethical than mystical and otherworldly. In the words of one Jewish prophet, Jehovah cared nothing for ritual and sacrifice; he cared only that men should "seek justice, relieve the oppressed, judge the fatherless, plead for the widow."

But from the sixth century B.C.E. onward, the Jews changed their religious ideas under the influence of the religious beliefs of the Persians and of their other rulers. They were also affected by the many Jews who lived outside Palestine, where, exposed to the tenets of Hellenism, they sought to interpret Judaism in terms of Greek philosophy. Thus the Jews gradually adopted a belief in the afterlife—obedience to God's will would bring eternal happiness in heaven, and disobedience would bring eternal punishment in hell.

Christianity's appeal to disparate and widespread groups was not immediate; Christianity was a Jewish cult during the lifetime and immediately after the crucifixion of Jesus. But it was universalized by Paul, a Hellenized Jew who lived in the city of Tarsus in Asia Minor. Paul boldly denied that Jesus was sent merely as the redeemer of the Jews. He announced that a loving Father had sent His only Son to atone for the sins of all mankind. Therefore, Christianity was not a sect of Judaism. It was a new church for Gentiles as well as for Jews. Paul's approach meant that Christianity henceforth could appeal not only to a handful of Jews but also to the millions of Gentiles throughout the Roman Empire.

The new religion grew despite steady persecution by Roman officials. Finally, in 313 C.E., Christianity received official toleration through Emperor Constantine's Edict of Milan, and in 399 it was made the official state religion of the Roman Empire. After the fall of the empire, Christian missionaries carried the faith to the English and German peoples between 600 and 800, and to the Scandinavian and Slavic peoples between 800 and 1100. With the expansion of Europe, both missionaries and emigrants spread Christianity to all parts of the globe.

The evolution of Buddhism was somewhat similar in that it began, as will be noted in Chapter 6, as a distinct Indian reaction against the injustice of the caste system and the exploitation by the Brahman priestly class. The founder, Siddhartha (c. 563–483 B.C.E.) of the Gautama clan, was of noble rank, but he became so distressed by the suffering he saw about him that he gave up his family and material comforts for the life of a wandering ascetic. Finally, in a moment of revelation, he achieved enlightenment and thenceforth was known as the Buddha, or the Enlightened One.

At the core of Buddhism are four great truths: (1) Life is sorrow; (2) the cause of sorrow is desire; (3) escape is possible only by stopping desire; and (4) the cessation of desire can only be achieved by the "eight-fold path," which is comprised of right belief, right ambition, right speech, right conduct, right living, right effort, right thoughts, and right pleasures. The objective of all this effort is Nirvana, literally meaning "emptiness," the "blowing out of the flame."

The Buddha had not intended to establish a new religion, but after his death his disciples preached his teachings and founded monastic communities that came to dominate Buddhism. The ideal of these communities was mental and physical discipline culminating in the mystic experience of Nirvana. Satisfying as this was for the monks, it ignored the needs of the everyday life of laypeople; hence the evolution of Mahayana, or the Greater Vehicle, as opposed to Hinayana, or the Lesser Vehicle. The Greater Vehicle was "greater" in the sense of its all-inclusiveness. It incorporated more of the concepts of pre-Buddhist Indian thought as well as the religious ideas of the people it converted. In doing so, it turned somewhat from its original contemplative bent and adopted precepts that were easier to comprehend and observe. Salvation now could be attained through faith, even an unthinking act of faith such as the mouthing of the name of Buddha. Also Nirvana changed—at least for the less-sophisticated believers—to mean an afterlife in Paradise, and Paradise was more attainable through good works that helped others.

This shift of emphasis from monasticism, asceticism, and contemplation to charity, faith, and salvation made Mahayana Buddhism more palatable to non-Indian peoples than the original religion had been, though both forms of the faith won foreign converts. Buddhism spread first to Ceylon and to northwest frontier regions of India in the third century B.C.E. Then in the first century B.C.E. it was carried into central Asia and China, first by traders, then by Indian missionaries, and most effectively by Chinese converts who studied in India and then returned to win over their fellow compatriots. So successful were they that by the late fourth century C.E., nine-tenths of the population of northwest China was said to have been converted, and by the sixth century south China had followed suit. From China, Buddhism spread still further: to Korea in the fourth century C.E., to Japan in the sixth century, and later to Tibet and Mongolia. Meanwhile Buddhism in both its Hinayana and Mahayana forms had been penetrating into Southeast Asia. This did not occur at any particular period; rather, it represented one aspect of the general Indianization of the region that took place over many centuries.

After these successes Buddhism declined in many countries. In China it reached its peak about 700 C.E. but thereafter suffered from internal decay and governmental hostility. Its great landholdings, its vast treasures, and the large numbers of monks and nuns it withdrew from the national economy all aroused official envy and displeasure and brought on persecution. Between 841 and 855, according to official accounts, 4,600 monasteries and 40,000 shrines were destroyed; 260,000 monks and nuns were defrocked and, together with their 150,000 slaves, returned to the tax registers. Buddhism never recovered from this blow, and thereafter it was merely one of "the three religions" (along with Taoism and Confucianism) in which the Chinese were interested. Likewise in India, Buddhism eventually gave way to a revival of Hinduism, so virtually no followers are to be found today in its own birthplace. In Ceylon and in many parts of Southeast Asia, however, Buddhism of the Hinayana variety remains predominant to the present.

Despite this relative decline after its period of greatness, Buddhism in late classical and early medieval times was the predominant religion of Asia. It prevailed in the whole continent except for Siberia and the Middle East, thus giving that vast area a degree of cultural unity unequaled

BUDDHISM IN INDIA AND CHINA

The unification of Eurasia began in classical times, and the bonds were partly commercial and partly cultural. Buddhism was one factor that played an important role in the cultural interaction. This is evident in the following experiences of a Chinese Buddhist monk, Hsüan-tsang, who spent the years from 629 to 645 C.E. visiting monasteries in India. While at the Nalanda monastery he announced his decision to return to China. The reaction of the monks is revealing.*

The monks of Nalanda [monastery], when they heard of it, begged him to remain, saying: "India is the land of Buddha's birth, and though he has left the world, there are still many traces of him. What greater happiness could there be than to visit them in turn, to adore him and chant his praises? Why then do you wish to leave, having come so far? Moreover China is a country of . . . unimportant barbarians, who despise the religious and the [Buddhist] Faith. That is why Buddha was not born there. The mind of the people is narrow, and their coarseness profound, hence neither sages nor saints go there. The climate is cold and the country rugged—you must think again."

The Master of the Law (the Chinese Buddhist) replied, "Buddha established his doctrine so that it might be diffused to all lands. Who would wish to enjoy it alone, and to forget those who are not enlightened? Besides, in my country the magistrates are clothed with dignity, and the laws are everywhere respected. The emperor is virtuous and the subjects loyal, parents are loving and sons obedient, humanity and justice are highly esteemed, and old men and sages are held in honour. Moreover, how deep and mysterious is their knowledge; their wisdom equals that of spirits. They have taken the Heavens as their model, and they know how to calculate the movements of the Seven Luminaries; they have invented all kinds of instruments, fixed the seasons of the year. . . . How then can you say that Buddha did not go to my country because of its insignificance?"

*J. Needham, *Science and Civilization in China* (Cambridge University, 1954), I, pp. 209–210.

before or after. In doing so, it functioned as a great civilizing force in Asia, as Christianity did simultaneously in Europe. To many peoples Buddhism brought not only a religion and a set of ethics, but also a system of writing, a type of architecture, and all the other attributes of the great civilizations of India and China that the missionaries spread together with their religion. In the same way, at the other end of Eurasia, Christian missionaries were bringing to the barbaric Germanic and Slavic peoples the civilizations of Rome and of Constantinople, as well as the teachings of Christ. Such was the impact and historical significance of these powerful "cultural bonds" for the Eurasian peoples.

During the millennia of the ancient civilizations, the Middle East had been the center of initiative. It was the Middle East during that period that had made the fundamental contributions to humankind—contributions such as agriculture, metallurgy, urbanism, and imperial organization. But now in classical times this Middle Eastern predominance faded away, except in one area—that of religion. Not only Judaism but also Zoroastrianism have their roots in the Middle East. The latter religion, although observed today by only a handful of Parsis in India, had considerable influence in the Middle East when the Persian Empire was at its height.

Yet the fact remains that apart from these religions and other related sects, the Middle East no longer was the vital source of innovation during the Classical Age. The new ideas and institutions that took shape in classical times, and which have persisted in many cases to the present, were the products of what formerly had been the peripheral regions of Eurasia. Accordingly, the following three chapters are devoted to the civilizations of these regions: the Greco-Roman, the Indian, and the Chinese. Before considering those civilizations, we should note that the impact of the great Eurasian religions continues to be felt to the present day. Their teachings about war and peace, for example, remain very relevant for peoples of the twentieth and twenty-first centuries. Confucius stated that "Within the four seas, all men are brothers." Likewise, in the Old Testament there is the grand vision of the prophet Micah, which has been the motto of the United Nations: "And they shall beat their swords into plowshares and their spears into pruninghooks; nation shall not lift up a sword against nation, neither shall they learn war anymore." This common relevance of the great religions was strikingly illustrated on October 27, 1986, when their representatives joined Pope John Paul II in a "World Day of Prayer for Peace." The following are excerpts from their prayers, as well as those of other faiths:[2]

Buddhist

May all beings everywhere, plagued with sufferings of body and mind, obtain an ocean of happiness and joy.

Christian

I say to you that hear, love your enemies, do good to those who hate you, bless those who curse you, pray for those who abuse you. To him who strikes you on the cheek, offer the other also; and from him who takes away your cloak do not withhold your coat as well. Give to everyone who begs from you; and of him who takes away your goods do not ask them again. And as you wish that men would do to you, do so to them.

Jewish

Our God in heaven, the Lord of Peace will have compassion and mercy upon us and upon all the peoples of the earth who implore his mercy and his compassion, asking for peace, seeking peace.

African Animist

Almighty God, the Great Thumb we cannot evade to tie any knot, the Roaring Thunder that splits mighty trees, the All-Seeing Lord up on high who sees even the footprints of an antelope on a rock mass here on earth: You are the one who does not hesitate to respond to our call. You are the cornerstone of peace.

American Indian

In smoking the pipe, I invite my family to smoke with me and you, my friends, to pray with me in thanksgiving for this day and for world peace. I will pray that we all may commit ourselves to pray and to work for peace within our families, our tribes, and our nations. I pray for all our brothers and sisters walking our mother earth.

SUGGESTED READINGS

Interregional ties in Eurasia are clearly analyzed in the well-written study by G. F. Hudson, *Europe & China: A Survey of Their Relations from the Earliest Times to 1800* (Edward Arnold, 1931). See also the multivolume study by J. Needham, *Science and Civilization in China* (Cambridge University, 1954), the first volume of which provides an overall survey of China's interaction with the rest of Eurasia, including a theoretical analysis of culture diffusion. Various aspects of the commercial bonds of Eurasia are treated in A. Toussaint, *History of the Indian Ocean* (University of Chicago, 1966); S. Chandra, ed., *The Indian Ocean: Explorations in History, Commerce, and Politics* (Sage, 1987); D. Harden, *The Phoenicians* (Praeger, 1962); E. H. Warmington, *The Commerce Between the Roman Empire and India* (Cambridge University, 1928); Ying-shih Yu, *Trade and Expansion in Han China* (University of California, 1967); J. I. Miller, *The Spice Trade of the Roman Empire, 29 B.C.–A.D. 641* (Oxford University, 1969); C. G. F. Simkin, *The Traditional Trade of Asia* (Oxford University, 1969); and P. D. Curtin, *Cross Cultural Trade in World History* (Cambridge University, 1984).

For the cultural bonds of Eurasia, see H. G. Rawlinson, *Intercourse Between India and the Western World* (Cambridge University, 1916); E. Zürcher, *Buddhism: Its Origin and Spread* (St. Martin's, 1962); R. MacMullen, *Christianizing the Roman Empire, A.D. 100–400* (Yale University, 1984); and J. Pelikan, *Jesus through the Centuries* (Yale University, 1985).

NOTES

1. Jawaharlal Nehru, *Glimpses of World History* (Oxford University, 1982), p. 35.
2. *New York Times*, October 28, 1986.

Greco-Roman Civilization

The pupils of Athens have become teachers of others, and she has made the term Hellene no longer signify a race but a mental outlook.

Isocrates

Of the three chapters dealing with the three classical civilizations—the Greco-Roman, the Indian, and the Chinese—this on the Greco-Roman civilization is the longest. One reason is that two distinct, though related, civilizations are involved. The historical development of the West at this time was basically different from that of the unitary civilizations of India and China. All three civilizations spread out from restricted centers of origin to encompass entire surrounding regions—from the Greek peninsula to the western Mediterranean, from the Indus River valley to south India, and from the Yellow River valley to south China. As noted in Chapter 3, iron tools made this possible because they facilitated the extension of agriculture into forested regions and of commerce and colonization into new coastal areas. But here the common pattern ends. The newly civilized regions in India and China remained generally subservient to the original core areas, whereas in the West, Rome developed a military superiority that enabled it to conquer not only the Greek homeland in the Balkans but also the western portions of the ancient Middle East—Asia Minor, Palestine, Syria, and Egypt. In doing so, Rome began a new phase of history in the West, and launched a new, though related, Western civilization. The history and nature of these two sister civilizations, the Greek and the Roman, are the subjects of this chapter.

I. FORMATIVE AGE, 800–500 B.C.E.

With the Dorian invasions of the twelfth century B.C.E., Greece lapsed into a "Dark Age." (See Chapter 3, Section V.) The Greece of this period was tribal, aristocratic, agricultural, and confined to the Aegean basin. By the end of the sixth century B.C.E. all this had changed. The tribe had given way to the city-state; other social classes had risen to challenge the nobility; industry and commerce had come to play a considerable role; and Greek colonies were scattered on all the Mediterranean shores. These changes transformed the Greek world during its formative period and cleared the way for the Classical Age. (See map of Classical Age Empires in the Middle East and Europe, p. 89.)

A basic factor behind these developments was the geography of the Greek lands. Greece had no rich natural resources—no fertile river valleys or broad plains that, when properly developed and exploited, could support elaborate empires like those of the Middle East, India, and China. In Greece and on the Asia Minor coast there were successive mountain chains that restricted agricultural productivity and divided the countryside into compartments. Consequently, the Greeks had no natural geopolitical center to provide a basis for regional integration. Instead, after the invasions, they settled down in isolated villages, usually located near some easily defended hill or rise that provided both a refuge in time of danger and a location for a shrine to the gods. The settlement as a whole was called the polis and the place of refuge the acropolis—literally, "high town." If the polis was strategically situated near fertile lands or communication routes, it attracted more settlers and became the leading city of the region. In this manner dozens of small city-states emerged, relatively isolated and fiercely independent.

At the outset the city-states depended primarily on subsistence agriculture, herding, and fishing. But by the beginning of the eighth century B.C.E., economic self-sufficiency was undermined by population pressure. Land-hungry peasants were forced to take to the sea, becoming pirates or traders or colonists—or, as often happened, some combination of the three. By the fifth century the entire Mediterranean basin, including the Black Sea, was ringed with prosperous Greek colonies that were overseas replicas of the mother cities. (See Chapter 4, Section II.)

The founding of colonies set off a chain reaction that in the end transformed the Greek world. The colonies shipped raw materials, especially grain, to overpopulated Greece and in return received wine, olive oil, and manufactured goods, such as cloth and pottery. This trade pattern triggered an economic boom in the homeland. The Greek soil was better suited for olive orchards and vineyards than for wheat fields, and now that wheat could be imported, rocky hillsides could be planted with grape vines and olive trees. Hence the amount of land under cultivation increased substantially. The shift to commercial agriculture, therefore, made it possible to support a population three to four times larger than that under the former subsistence agriculture. Likewise manufactures increased, as we can see by the large quantities of Greek pottery unearthed not only around the Mediterranean but also far into the hinterland—into central Russia, southwest Germany, and northeast France. At the same time the Greek merchant marine prospered as it carried these goods back and forth. Indeed, this was the first time in history that bulky commodities, as distinct from luxury items, were traded and transported on such a large scale. All this economic activity was efficiently lubricated by the growing use of coin money, which the Greeks had pioneered.

The commercialization of agriculture meant debts as well as profits, especially for the small landholder. Formerly the nobles had collected rent in the form of a portion of the crop, so that in bad years the people pulled in their belts for the duration. But now the combination of foreign markets, the money economy, and new luxuries left the small farmers vulnerable to mortgages, foreclosures, and even loss of personal freedom. Inevitably this led to bitter class conflict and to popular clamor for debt cancellation and redistribution of land. Likewise in the cities new wealthy families emerged who wanted political recognition equal to their economic strength. They could count on the support of the urban poor, artisans, stevedores, and sailors. All these discontented elements, then, struck out against the traditional political system where all power lay in the hands of the landowning aristocracy.

Change was greatly hastened in the seventh century when the aristocratic cavalryman, once the main figure on the battlefield, was replaced by the heavily armored infantryman,

Classical Age Empires in the Middle East and Europe

The map contains the following labels:

INDIA

ARABIAN SEA

CASPIAN SEA

Aral Sea

PERSIAN GULF

ARABIA

BLACK SEA

Heraclea

Byzantium

PHOENICIA

EGYPT

GREECE

Cyrene

Syracuse

M E D I T E R R A N E A N   S E A

Carthage

Massillia

NORTH SEA

BALTIC SEA

ATLANTIC OCEAN

Gades

500 Miles
500 Kilometers
250
250
0
0

Legend:

Persian Empire c.480 B.C.E.

Alexander's Empire c. 327 B.C.E.

Roman Empire c. 120 C.E.

Greek colonies •

Phoenician colonies +

the hoplite. Massed together in a solid block, or phalanx, with a shield in the left hand and a long spear in the right, the hoplites were trained to act in unison and could make bristling sweeps through the hitherto invincible horsemen. This innovation undermined the military basis of aristocratic political authority. At the same time it raised the status and influence of the independent farmer and artisan who could afford to equip himself for phalanx service.

The combination of economic and military change brought about corresponding political change. The city-states that had started out as monarchies in the Dark Age gradually changed to aristocratic oligarchies. Then, in the seventh century, they came under the rule of dictators, or tyrants as they were called. These ambitious leaders, usually of noble birth, championed popular demands, won mass support, and seized personal power. The word *tyrant* referred to one who ruled without legal right, but the term carried with it no sense of moral reproach. Indeed, tyrants commonly favored the interests of the common people against the privileged classes, and often, though not always, hastened the advent of democracy.

Sparta, in the southern Peloponnesus, was the classic example of the opposite trend—away from democracy. About 1000 B.C.E. the Dorian forefathers of the Spartans had overrun the rich valley of the Eurotas and reduced the native population to the status of helots, or serfs. Later in the eighth century the Spartans conquered the rich plains of neighboring Messenia, so they had no need for overseas expansion. But the price paid for their security was heavy and inevitable. Sparta was deprived of the economic and intellectual stimulus of foreign contacts and condemned to a static rule existence. In addition, the Spartans were forced to organize their state along strict military lines to keep down the large subject population. Everything was subordinated to military needs: Only healthy infants were allowed to live, with the sickly ones left to die of exposure in the wilderness. From the age of seven, boys lived and trained in the barracks. Until age sixty all men remained under military discipline. Private life was all but abolished and luxury was frowned upon. The morning plunge in the cold waters of the Eurotas, the scanty fare on the mess tables, and the rough timbers of the

houses, shaped only with the axe, were famous throughout Greece. Life consisted almost exclusively of organized amusement, communal meals, public business, and military training and duties. This regimen made the Spartans the best infantrymen in all Greece. But it left them no time or inclination for writing plays, carving statues, or formulating philosophy.

Meanwhile the Athenians had been developing an altogether different type of society. Far from being a band of invaders camped amid a hostile population, the Athenians prided themselves on their status as native inhabitants of Attica. Like the Greeks of other city-states, they began with a monarchy, but that gave way to an oligarchy of nine archons who were the chief executive officers and who were invariably aristocrats. In contrast to Sparta, however, the evolution of Athens was toward increasing democracy. The burgeoning trade created a strong middle class that joined forces with the dispossessed peasantry and demanded political reform. In 594 B.C.E. all parties agreed on the appointment of Solon as chief magistrate with full powers for reform. His measures for the alleviation of social distress were simple and drastic. He restored to the debtors full title to their land, freed all citizens who had been enslaved for unpaid debts, and made such enslavement illegal in the future. In the realm of politics he admitted propertyless citizens to the Assembly for the first time, even though this body still possessed little power. He also made wealthy businessmen eligible to become archons and diluted the power of the aristocratic Areopagus, or chief judicial body, by establishing new and more popular courts of justice. In short, Solon's contribution was to create the constitutional base on which the famed Athenian democracy of later times would be built.

The three decades following Solon were filled with strife, for many problems remained unsolved. Enslavement was now illegal, but the poor still found it difficult to earn a living, and the aristocrats, though somewhat curbed, could still block popular legislation. Under these circumstances, Pisistratus established himself as the first tyrant of Athens about 560 B.C.E. During his thirty-year rule he divided the estates of the aristocrats, distributing them among landless peasants, and helped the urban poor with large-scale public works that beautified the city. Pisistratus was succeeded by his sons, but they proved incapable. More strife followed until Cleisthenes gained control about 506 B.C.E. He abolished the old tribes, setting up ten new ones that were based on territorial divisions rather than kinship. This change contributed much to undermining the political power of the aristocrats. Furthermore, he established a new Council of Five Hundred for which all male citizens over thirty years of age were eligible; it had authority to prepare measures for submission to the Assembly, as well as having supreme executive and administrative power. With these reforms of Cleisthenes, Athens by 500 B.C.E. had emerged a democracy, whereas Sparta remained a militarized and regimented society.

II. CLASSICAL AGE, 500–336 B.C.E.

In his famous funeral speech commemorating the Athenian soldiers who had fallen in battle against the Spartans in 431, Pericles declared, "Our city is open to the world. . . . Athens is the school of Hellas." This boast was fully justified. During the fifth century B.C.E. Athens overshadowed Sparta and all other Greek cities. This was the age of Periclean Athens—the Golden Age of classical Greece.

One reason for the dazzling preeminence of Athens was its leading role in the fateful defeat of the great Persian Empire. Shortly before the Persian Wars, the Athenians had the good fortune to discover the Laurium silver lodes. Deciding to use the treasure for naval construction, they built two hundred triremes of latest design. This fleet was decisive in the ensuing struggle.

The root of the war was the Persian conquest of the Greek city-states in Asia Minor during the mid-sixth century B.C.E. Heavy-handed Persian interference in their domestic affairs led the cities to revolt in 499. They appealed to the homeland cities for aid and received a positive response, partly because the Persian Empire at this time was expanding into southeastern Europe and menacing Greece from the north. Despite the naval assistance from across the Aegean, the Asia Minor cities were overwhelmed by 494. The Persian Emperor Darius resolved to

chastise the obstreperous Greeks and sent out an expedition that landed at Marathon, to the northwest of Athens, in 490. Although the Athenians fought almost alone, thanks to rivalries among the Greek cities, their phalanxes inflicted a stunning defeat on the invaders. The effect on Greek morale was enormous. "These were the first Greeks," wrote the historian Herodotus, "who had the courage to face up to Persian dress and the men who wore it, whereas up to that time the very name of the Persians brought terror to a Greek."

Ten years later the Persians came again with much larger forces, and this time by land through Thrace and Thessaly. A mixed force under Spartan command fought gallantly to the

The bronze helmut was dedicated to Zeus by Miltiades to commemorate the Athenian victory over the Persians in 490 B.C.E.

last man at the pass of Thermopylae. The Persians pressed on to Athens, which they sacked, but the Athenian fleet destroyed the Persians in nearby Salamis. An allied Greek fleet followed the retreating Persians across the Aegean and won another naval victory. Soon the Asia Minor cities were freed from Persian rule, and the Greeks emerged as the victors over the great empire that dominated the Middle East.

The repercussions of the Greek triumph were tremendous. First and foremost, it saved the Greeks from being engulfed in an oriental despotism, thereby allowing them to preserve their identity and to make their unique contribution to human civilization. The success of the Greeks, and especially of the Athenian fleet, also furthered the cause of democracy, for the rowers who drove the ships into battle were citizens who could not afford to equip themselves as hoplites. Thus the urban poor now assumed a military role even more important than that of the propertied hoplites. This naturally strengthened the movement for more democracy, which reached its height during the Age of Pericles (461–429 B.C.E.).

Although an aristocrat by birth, Pericles was an earnest democrat who completed the transference of power to the Assembly. All adult male citizens were members of this body, which was the sovereign power in the affairs of Athens. It held forty regular meetings a year and extraordinary sessions as required. It not only settled general questions of policy but also made detailed decisions in every sphere of government—foreign affairs, military operations, finance. Pericles also introduced pay for service in most public offices so that the poor could afford to assume such offices. In addition, he established an array of popular courts in which final decisions were rendered by juries chosen by lot; all citizens could serve on these juries. Pericles was quite justified, then, in his statement that "Athens is the school of Greece."

The prominent role of Athens in the Persian Wars led the city on a course that eventually ended in imperialism. Whereas Sparta was immobilized by its static economy and the constant threat of a helot revolt, Athens took the lead in organizing a confederacy of Asiatic Greeks and islanders. Known as the Delian Confederation because its headquarters was originally on the small island of Delos, its purpose was collective security against possible further Persian attacks. Although theoretically an alliance of equals—for the constitution provided each member with only one vote in the periodic meetings—from the start Athens provided the executive leadership. The generals were Athenians, and Athens also collected tribute from cities unable or unwilling to furnish ships. Step by step Athens tightened its hold: The treasury of the confederation was moved from Delos to Athens; Athenian coinage became the common medium of exchange; and members were denied the right of secession. Thus by 450 B.C.E. the confederation had become an empire, and the power of Athens extended, in the words of Euripides, from Ionia "to the outward Ocean of the West"—that is, to the Atlantic.

Almost inevitably, the sea power of Athens clashed with the land power of Sparta. The fighting dragged on indecisively for ten years. The Spartan armies raided Attica each year but could not penetrate the long walls that joined Athens to the sea and protected its supplies. The Athenians for their part were badly hurt by the great plague of 429 B.C.E., which killed off almost half the population, including Pericles. For a time they could only make random raids on the coast of the Peloponnesus. Then in 415 the fatal decision was made to send the Athenian fleet to capture Sicily and cut off Sparta's grain supply. "Fleet and army," wrote Thucydides, "perished from the face of the earth, nothing was saved." Athens' allies now revolted; the Spartans finally destroyed the long wall; and Athens was starved into capitulation in 404 B.C.E. Athens was left shorn of its fleets, its empire, and even its vaunted democracy, for the Spartan victors imposed a short-lived oligarchic regime.

This ruinous war left the Greek world exhausted and solved none of its problems. Spartan high-handedness caused Thebes and Athens to unite together in a new league for mutual protection. In 371 the Thebans inflicted on the Spartans their first major military defeat in two hundred years. For the next decade Thebes was supreme on the Greek mainland, but then intercity rivalries prevailed again, and the city-states once more were engulfed in a confused anarchy of shifting alliances and petty wars. The stage was set for a foreign power to

PERICLES'S FUNERAL ORATION

The Athenian leader Pericles has left the classic description of the culture of his city during its great Golden Age. He gave the following famous account during his funeral oration commemorating the Athenian soldiers who had fallen in battle against Sparta in 431 B.C.E.*

Our form of government does not enter into rivalry with the institutions of others. We do not copy our neighbours, but are an example to them. It is true that we are called a democracy, for the administration is in the hands of the many and not of the few. But while the law secures equal justice to all alike in their private disputes, the claim of excellence is also recognized, and when a citizen is in any way distinguished, he is preferred to the public service, not as a matter of privilege, but as the reward of merit. Neither is poverty a bar, but a man may benefit his country whatever be the obscurity of his condition. There is no exclusiveness in our public life, and in our private intercourse we are not suspicious of one another, nor angry with our neighbour if he does what he likes. . . . We are lovers of the beautiful, yet simple in our tastes, and we cultivate the mind without loss of manliness. Wealth we employ, not for talk and ostentation, but when there is a real use for it. To avow poverty with us is no disgrace; the true disgrace is in doing nothing to avoid it. An Athenian citizen does not neglect the state because he takes care of his own household; and even those of us who are engaged in business have a very fair idea of politics. We alone regard a man who takes no interest in public affairs, not as a harmless, but as a useless character; and if few of us are originators, we are all sound judges of policy. The great impediment to action is, in our opinion, not discussion, but the want of that knowledge which is gained by discussion preparatory to action. For we have a peculiar power of thinking before we act and of acting too. . . .

To sum up: I say that Athens is the school of Hellas. . . .

I have paid the required tribute, in obedience to the law, making use of such fitting words as I had. The tribute of deeds has been paid in part; for the dead have been honourably interred, and it remains only that their children should be maintained at the public charge until they are grown up: this is the solid prize with which, as with a garland, Athens crowns her sons living and dead, after a struggle like theirs.

*B. Jowett, trans., *The History of Thucydides* (Tandy-Thomas, 1909), book 2, pp. 35–46.

subjugate and forcibly unify Greece. In 338 B.C.E. Philip of Macedon smashed the combined armies of Thebes and Athens at Chaeronea. Philip deprived the Greek cities of most of their autonomy, but before he could proceed further he was assassinated in 336 B.C.E. His successor was his world-famous son, Alexander the Great.

The Classical Age was over; the Hellenistic Age was beginning. Before turning to the latter we shall pause to consider the civilization of the Classical Age, an age that is generally accepted as one of the great triumphs of the human mind and spirit.

III. CIVILIZATION OF THE CLASSICAL AGE

The "Golden Age of Pericles," "the Greek Miracle," "the Glory that was Greece"—these are some of the tributes commonly used in referring to the civilization of fifth-century Greece.

We shall see that this civilization had its shortcomings; nonetheless those extravagant praises are largely deserved. Why is this so? What was the basis of the Greek "genius"? First, it may be safely assumed that it was not literally a matter of genius—that the Indo-Europeans who migrated to the south Balkans did not happen to be genetically superior to those who migrated to the Middle East or India or western Europe. Instead, the answer must be sought through comparison of the historical development of the Greeks with that of the other Indo-Europeans who settled in other regions of Eurasia.

Such a comparison suggests two explanations for the extraordinary achievements of the Greeks. In the first place, they lived near enough to the earliest centers of civilization—Egypt and Mesopotamia—to profit from their pioneering accomplishments. But they were not so close that they lost their individuality. Indeed, the main significance of the outcome of the Persian Wars was precisely that it allowed the Greeks to have their cake and eat it too.

The second factor was the emergence and persistence of the Greek polis, which provided the essential institutional framework for the cultural blossoming. The polis, of course, was not a uniquely Greek institution. In India, for example, the Aryan immigrants in the earlier stage of their development also had what amounted to city-states in certain regions. But these were eventually absorbed by the territorial monarchies that came to dominate the Indian peninsula. It was the Greeks alone who were able to preserve their city-states for several centuries.

One reason for this longevity was the mountainous terrain, which did not afford a geopolitical base for a regional empire. (See Section I, this chapter.) Another was the direct access to the sea enjoyed by most of the Greek city-states, which gave them economic strength as well as intellectual stimulation. It is true that the Greeks paid a heavy price for their polis fragmentation in the form of continual wars. And war led eventually to unification imposed from without, first by Macedon and then by Rome. But in the meantime they enjoyed centuries of freedom within their respective states, and this freedom was a prerequisite for the great creative outburst of the fifth century.

The classical Greek civilization was not purely original. Like all civilizations, it borrowed heavily from what had gone before, in this case the Middle Eastern civilizations. But what the Greeks borrowed, whether art forms from Egypt or mathematics and astronomy from Mesopotamia, they stamped with the distinctive quality of their minds. And this distinctive stamp was, essentially, an open-mindedness, an intellectual curiosity, an eagerness to learn, and a commonsense approach. When the Greeks traveled abroad, as they did very often as traders, soldiers, colonists, and tourists, they did so with a critical eye and skeptical mind. They questioned everything and tested all issues at the bar of reason. In Plato's *Apology*, Socrates maintains that the individual must refuse, at all costs, to be coerced by human authority or by any tribunal to do anything, or think anything, which his own mind condemns as wrong— ". . .the life which is unexamined is not worth living. . . ." Socrates also pointed out the public value of free discussion, on which he based his defense in the famous trial for his own life.

And now, Athenians, I am not going to argue for my own sake, as you may think, but for yours. . . . For if you kill me you will not easily find another like me, who, if I may use such a ludicrous figure of speech, am a sort of gadfly . . . and all day long and in all places am always fastening upon you, arousing and persuading and reproaching you. . . . I would have you know that, if you kill such a one as I am, you will injure yourselves more than you will injure me.[1]

This sort of free thinking was uniquely Greek, at least in such a strong and pervasive form. Unique also was the secular view of life, the conviction that the chief business of existence was the complete expression of human personality here and now. This combination of rationalism and secularism enabled the Greeks to think freely and creatively about human problems and social issues. And they expressed their thoughts and emotions in their great literary, philosophical, and artistic creations, which are relevant and compelling to the present day.

These unique qualities of the Greeks are clearly reflected in their religious thought and practices. The Greeks viewed their gods as similar in nature to themselves, differing only in superior power, longevity, and beauty. By believing in such divinities the Greeks felt secure and at home in a world governed by familiar and comprehensible powers. The relationship between the people and their gods was essentially one of give and take. In return for prayers and sacrifices the gods were expected to demonstrate their good will. The religious tie consisted of "common shrines and sacrifices," as Herodotus stated, rather than of an organized church or a common faith. The Greek religion never formulated a unified body of doctrines or a sacred book, though Homer's *Iliad* and Hesiod's *Theogony* summed up prevailing religious concepts. The quality of Greek religion becomes evident when contrasted with that of the Mesopotamians. According to Mesopotamian explanations of the origins of things, the human race had been specifically created to build temples for the gods and to feed them with offerings. Such duties, in fact, were the whole reason for human existence. How different was the conception of the sixth-century Greek philosopher Xenophanes:

Mortals think that the gods are begotten, and wear clothes like their own, and have a voice and a form. If oxen or horses or lions had hands and could draw with them and make works of art as men do, horses would draw the shapes of gods like horses, oxen like oxen; each kind would represent their bodies just like their own forms. The Ethiopians say their gods are black and flat-nosed; the Thracians, that theirs are blue-eyed and red-haired.[2]

Religion in classical Greece was an integral part of polis life and accordingly affected every aspect of that life. Religion offered an interpretation of the natural world, a consecration of daily work and of social institutions, and was also one of the chief sources of inspiration for poets and artists. Every Greek temple was a focus of local and national culture. Many temples specialized, more or less accidentally, in the development of particular arts. A brotherhood of miracle workers, who grew up around the worship of the legendary Aesculapius on the island of Cos, evolved into the first scientific physicians. Outstanding was the renowned physician Hippocrates, whose medical treatises were resolutely clinical in tone. He diagnosed each case on the basis of objective observation, rejecting magical causes or cures for disease. Regarding the "sacred" disease, epilepsy, he wrote:

It seems to me that the disease called sacred is no more divine than any other. It has a natural cause, just as other diseases have. Men think it divine because they do not understand it. . . . In Nature all things are alike in this, that they can all be traced to preceding causes.[3]

Likewise around the worship of Dionysus, the wine god, there grew a company of actors who evolved from dramatizing the ritual cult of the god to creating profound tragedy and uproarious comedy. This literature cannot be imagined apart from its setting in fifth-century Athens. Plays were produced before the assembled citizens at regularly held religious festivals organized and financed by the state. The close contact and empathy between author and audience were responsible for the balance and normality of Athenian drama. Aeschylus, in his *Persians*, presented a dramatized version of the victory at Salamis before the very citizens who had won that victory. Sophocles referred frequently to the gods in his tragedies yet was not interested primarily in religious problems. Rather he was chiefly concerned with human beings, noble and admirable, confronted with forces beyond their control, committing awful deeds, and suffering terrible retribution. For example, the qualities of heroism and suffering his King Oedipus shows in the face of overwhelming adversity are the essence of tragedy. Sophoclean tragedy expresses something of the meaning of human life and of the problems common to all humanity.

If Sophocles was only mildly interested in conventional religion, Euripides was positively skeptical. Writing plainly and without mincing words, he satirized those who deemed the gods superior to men. Generally critical and a dedicated fighter for unpopular causes, Euripides championed the rights of the slave and the foreigner, urged the emancipation of women, and attacked the glorification of war. The same is even more true of Aristophanes, whose comedies were filled with social satire. Himself a conservative who yearned for the good old days, he ridiculed democratic leaders and policies. In *The Lysistrata* he presented a group of women, who,

The Acropolis was both the religious and civic center of Athens. In its final form it is the work of Pericles and his successors in the late fifth century B.C.E. This photograph shows the Parthenon and to its left the Erechtheum.

appalled by the endless bloodshed, refuse to sleep with their husbands until they stop their wars. In *The Knights*, Aristophanes mocked democratic institutions with the story of a general who tries to persuade a sausage-seller to unseat Cleon, the democratic leader.[4]

Sausage-Seller	Tell me this, how can I, a sausage-seller, be a big man like that?
General	The easiest thing in the world. You've got all the qualifications: low birth, market-place training, insolence.
Sausage-Seller	I don't think I deserve it.
General	Not deserve it? It looks to me as if you've got too good a conscience. Was your father a gentleman?
Sausage-Seller	By the gods, no! My folks were scoundrels.
General	Lucky man! What a good start you've got for public life!
Sausage-Seller	But I can hardly read.
General	The only trouble is that you know anything. To be a leader of the people isn't for learned men, or honest men, but for the ignorant and vile. Don't miss this golden opportunity.

Greek art was another distinctive product of the polis-centered civilization. Art and architecture found their highest expression in the temples, the civic and religious core of polis culture. The temples were the revered dwelling places of the protecting gods and goddesses. A famous example is the Parthenon in Athens, which was built as a shrine to the protecting goddess Athena. Sculpture, the handmaiden of architecture, served to decorate the houses of the gods. Master sculptors, such as Phidias and Praxiteles, worked on temple walls and pediments and also carved statues for the interiors. All of Greek art embodied the basic Greek ideals of balance, harmony, and moderation. This is evident if we compare the Parthenon with an Egyptian pyramid or a Mesopotamian ziggurat or compare a Greek statue with the relatively crude and stilted sculptures of most Middle Eastern peoples of that time.

We find a similar contrast when we compare Greek philosophical speculation with that of other peoples. The sixth-century rationalist philosophers of Ionia on the Asia Minor coast were the first to challenge the traditional supernatural explanations of the nature of the world.

Socrates

They posed the basic question "What is the stuff of which the world is made?" The philosopher Thales speculated that everything originally was water, because this substance is found in liquid, solid, and vapor form. Heraclitus thought fire was the prime element because it was so active and could transform everything. Anaximenes believed it was air, arguing that air became fire when rarefied and became wind, cloud, water, earth, and stone when condensed. In the light of modern science these answers may appear naive, but what is important is that the question was asked and the answers were sought by the free use of reason, not by resorting to explanations based on the intervention of the gods.

As Greek society grew more complex, philosophers about the mid-fifth century B.C.E. turned their attention from the physical universe to human beings and their problems. Protagoras, the outstanding spokesperson of the Sophists, reflected this new interest. "Man is the measure of all things," he maintained, by which he meant that there are no absolute truths since everything is relative to the needs of man himself. The emphasis on man led the Sophists to condemn slavery and war and to espouse most popular causes. On the other hand many Greeks, especially those of conservative persuasion, feared that the relativism of the Sophists

endangered social order and morality. Typical was Socrates, who was profoundly disturbed by the political corruption of his day and by the absence of any unerring guide to correct living. Out of his never-ending conversations with his friends he evolved the science of dialectics. Provisional definitions were tested by questions and answers until universally recognized truths were reached. In this way, Socrates maintained, concepts of absolute truth or absolute good or absolute beauty could be discovered. These would provide enduring guides for personal conduct, in contrast to the relativism of the Sophists, which often provided rationalizations for private and public corruption.

Socrates's disciple Plato (427–347 B.C.E.) was an aristocrat who shared with his friends a great pride in Athens but also a distrust of the Athenian people. Distrust deepened into hatred when Athenian democracy condemned Socrates to death. Plato's goal became a society that preserved aristocratic privileges and yet was acceptable to the poorer classes. Accordingly he divided the citizens of his ideal Republic into four grades: guardians, philosophers, soldiers, and the masses who would do the work. This class differentiation was to be permanent, justified by

Plato

a myth, or "noble lie," that God had created men of four kinds: gold, silver, brass, and iron. Plato had hoped that the ruler of Syracuse would accept and apply his teachings, but when this did not happen he returned to Athens and for the next forty years instructed small groups of disciples.

The other great thinker of this period was Aristotle (384–322 B.C.E.), who began as Plato's disciple but who, following his master's death, founded the Lyceum. Aristotle was a classifier and rational thinker rather than a mystic, a logician and scientist rather than a philosopher. He took all knowledge for his province, so that he ranged more widely than anyone before or since. His outstanding contributions were in logic, physics, biology, and the humanities; indeed, he established these subjects as formal disciplines. As a great encyclopedist, he sought orderliness in every aspect of nature and of human life. Thus he balanced the classes of the human social world with corresponding orders in the natural world, beginning with minerals at the bottom, then vegetables, animals, and finally humans at the top. This gradation justified the division of human beings into born masters and born slaves:

. . . from the hour of their birth some are marked out for subjection, others for rule. . . . The art of war is a natural art of acquisition, for it includes hunting, an art which we ought to practice against wild beasts and against men who, though intended by nature to be governed, will not submit; for war of such a kind is naturally just.[5]

No account of classical Greece would be complete without reference to Herodotus and Thucydides, who related the stirring events of their times and in so doing created a new form of literature: history. Herodotus lived first among the Asia Minor Greeks, who had fallen under Persian rule, and then in Athens, where the Persians had suffered their great defeat. Herodotus wrote that the cause of the Persian defeat was the democratic constitution of the Athenians, making his *History* the first great tribute to democracy. The moral of his tale may be illustrated by the words he attributes to a Greek speaking of his countrymen to the Persian king:

For though they be free men, they are not in all respects free; Law is the master whom they own, and this master they fear more than your subjects fear you. Whatever it commands they do; and its commandment is always the same; it forbids them to flee in battle, whatever the number of their foes, and requires them to stand firm, and either to conquer or die.[6]

Thucydides's history was very different, being of the Peloponnesian War in which Athens, after twenty-seven years of bitter struggle, was finally beaten to its knees. Whereas Herodotus wrote about victory and glory, Thucydides analyzed defeat and suffering. His sympathies were unquestionably with Athens, whose armies he had led as a general. But he sternly suppressed his emotions and set himself the task of determining objectively the causes of the disaster. Although he did not use the phrase, he nevertheless said in effect that he was seeking to create a science of society.

Of the events of the war I have not ventured to speak from any chance information, nor according to any notion of my own; I have described nothing but what I either saw myself or learned from others of whom I made the most careful and particular enquiry. The task was a laborious one, because eye-witnesses of the same occurrences gave different accounts of them, as they remembered or were interested in the actions of one side or the other. And very likely the strictly historical character of my narrative may be disappointing to the ear. But if he who desires to have before his eyes a true picture of the events which had happened, and of the like events which may be expected to happen hereafter in the order of human things, shall pronounce what I have written to be useful, then I shall be satisfied. My history is an ever-lasting possession, not a prize composition which is heard and forgotten.[7]

Now that we have described the remarkable achievements of the Greeks in so many fields, we have also to point out certain failings. One was the presence of slaves, who together with the metics (resident aliens) were denied Athenian citizenship even though they made up the majority of the population. Women also had inferior status in Greece, as in other Mediterranean and Middle Eastern countries. In Athens (which had a worse record than some other city-states), women could not own property and had no political rights, including the right to vote or to serve on juries. Husbands had control of the children, which extended to the infanticide option that was subject exclusively to male decision. Professions such as law, medicine, and theater were all closed to women, as were also the Olympic games. Leading playwrights and philosophers wrote of the innate inferiority of women and warned of dire results if they were given too much authority. To safeguard their respectability, women were expected to remain secluded in their homes. Pericles advised widows that "the greatest glory of a woman is to be least talked about by men." Demosthenes best summed up the blatant gender inequity when he noted that there were three kinds of women in Athens: "We have mistresses [hetaerae] for our enjoyment, concubines or prostitutes to serve our person, and wives for bearing our legitimate offspring."[8]

In the Greek civilization, as in all others of ancient times, the strict rules about female seclusion applied only to upper-class females. Those who were not affluent could not afford to sit at home and hide themselves from the world. They had to get out and work to help support their families. Women from the wealthy families seldom were seen in the streets or in the markets. But working women were busy everywhere, earning wages in workshops or offering wares for sale in marketplaces or working in private houses as servants and nurses and female attendants. Aristotle noted that class determined the nature of women's lives when he wrote that since the poor had no slaves they had to allow their women to go out into the world.

Although these shortcomings were basic, classical Greece should be judged not by what it failed to do but by what it did. If this be the criterion, the contributions and their historical significance stand out clearly and overwhelmingly. The spirit of free inquiry, the theory and practice of democracy, the major forms of art and literature and philosophical thought, and the emphasis on individual freedom and individual responsibility—these are the splendid legacy of Greece to humanity.

IV. HELLENISTIC AGE, 336–31 B.C.E.

The Hellenistic Age derives its name from the new civilization that emerged as classical Greek culture spread throughout the Middle East in the wake of Alexander's conquests. (See Chapter 4, Section III.) On succeeding his father, Philip, in 336 B.C.E., Alexander first crushed a revolt in Thebes with such severity that the other Greek cities were persuaded to accept his rule. Then in 334 B.C.E., he led his Macedonian soldiers eastward against the Persians. Crossing the Hellespont, he overran first Asia Minor, then Syria, Egypt, Mesopotamia, and Persia itself, capturing Darius's capital, Persepolis, in 330 B.C.E. The following year the conqueror pushed on to the Hindu Kush and Bactria, and from there he marched on into India, penetrating as far as the Punjab. Only the refusal of his men to advance any further persuaded Alexander to return to Babylon, where he died of malarial fever in 323 at the age of thirty-three.

Rival generals now fought for control of the great empire until, by the beginning of the third century, three succession states emerged. One of these was Macedon, which now reverted

Alexander the Great

Darius I receiving tribute from a relief on the treasury at Persepolis. Note the incense burners before the king and the noble tribute bringer's gesture of respect. The scepter and lotus blossom held by Darius symbolize his kingship; his son and heir, Xerxes, stands behind him (491–486 B.C.E.)

to a modest, Hellenized, national kingdom. Macedon dominated, but did not directly rule, the Greek city-states to the south. A second was Egypt, ruled by the Ptolemies. It was the most viable of the succession states because of its natural riches and strong sea and desert defenses. The largest state, comprising the Asian provinces of the empire, fell to the Seleucids. Because of their vast holdings they fought a continual and losing battle against a host of surrounding enemies. First they ceded the Indus provinces to the Indian King Chandragupta, followed by Asia Minor to Celtic invaders and Persia and Mesopotamia to the Parthians. Finally in the first century B.C.E., Rome conquered the remaining provinces along the Mediterranean coast, along with Macedon and Egypt, thereby ending the Hellenistic Age and beginning the Roman.

Although Alexander's empire proved short-lived, the succession states survived more or less intact for three centuries, during which time the Middle East became Hellenized. Thousands of Greek merchants, administrators, teachers, professionals, and mercenary soldiers emigrated from their city-states to Egypt and the Asian provinces, attracted by the unprecedented opportunities afforded by those rich lands. Thus the foundations were laid for the new Hellenistic civilization, a hybrid creation that differed from the classical parent stock in virtually every respect.

The political framework changed radically because the polis was undermined and made sterile. The Greek city-states, trying to survive, experimented with federal union. The Achaean League included all the states of the Peloponnesus except Sparta, and the Aetolian Federation, nearly all of central Greece except Athens. Although often described as federal organizations, these leagues actually were confederacies that delegated little power to central authority. The leagues were both too weak and too late, and the city-states were dominated by one or another of the neighboring empires until the coming of the Roman legions.

As for the cities in the far-flung succession states, they never resembled the classical polis of mother Greece. They were divided internally by the distinctions between the Greek immigrants and the native people. Furthermore they were always completely subordinate to one or another imperial structure. If the citizens suffered from tyrannical or weak kings, they could do very little about it. The real decisions were made in the courts or on battlefields, not in meetings of popular assemblies. Thus the citizens understandably concentrated on accumulating wealth and enjoying life, leaving the poor and the slaves to shift for themselves as best they could. The civic spirit and social cohesion of the old polis gave way to self-centeredness and class strife.

Economic conditions and institutions also changed fundamentally. The Greek homeland suffered economic as well as political eclipse. It had depended on the export of wine, oil, and manufactured goods in return for foodstuffs and raw materials from the overseas colonies. But by the fourth century these colonies had taken root and developed their own industries and vineyards and olive orchards.

Although the Greek lands suffered economic decay, many Greeks got rich by emigrating to the Middle East, which was now open to them. They had much to contribute with their enterprising spirit and their advanced commercial and banking methods. They discovered and circulated the huge gold and silver hoard of the Persian dynasty. Also they introduced, or put to wider use, technological inventions such as the suction and piston pumps, the water mill, and the worm screw. The Greeks also directed large-scale public works and state enterprises, including irrigation systems, mines, quarries, salt pans, "royal lands," and workshops for luxury fabrics and ceramics. The net result was increased economic integration, which brought about a corresponding increase in regional commerce and productivity. The proceeds, however, were grossly maldistributed. Speculators took advantage of rising profits to reap great fortunes, while slaves increased in number and free workers declined in status. It was a period, in short, of greater productivity but also of greater economic inequality and social strife.

The average person during the Hellenistic Age was buffeted not only economically but also psychologically. A man—or a woman—felt lost in the large new cities with their teeming multitudes uprooted from their traditional environment. In the old polis, life had been relatively simple. Law, morality, religion, and duties were all clearly defined and generally accepted. Now all this was gone and citizens found themselves in a formless world. Furthermore, the Hellenistic cities frequently were torn by racial and cultural as well as class divisions. The rulers tried to cultivate a mystique of personal loyalty, adopting titles such as "Savior" and "Benefactor." But such expedients offered no lasting solution. Each person remained confronted with the question of how to conduct himself or herself in face of the impersonal and overwhelming forces of the time.

The response of intellectuals tended to be withdrawal from worldly affairs and a turn from reason to mysticism. Their withdrawal was reflected in the vogue for romantic adventure and utopian literature. When authors depicted an ideal society, they described not a city-state on the rocky soil of Hellas but a rainbow-tinted fairyland at the world's end. Especially popular in contemporary fiction were utopian island communities located in the Indian Ocean, blessed with natural riches that satisfied all material needs and inhabited by people who lived "simply and temperately . . . without jealousy and strife." This escapist tendency was reflected also in the philosophies of the day—Cynicism, Skepticism, Epicureanism, and Stoicism—which, though very different in many respects, were generally concerned with the pursuit of personal happiness rather than of social welfare.

Philosophy may have been the religion of the cultivated upper classes, but the religion of the lower classes was very different. They turned to cults of oriental origin—Mithraism, Gnosticism, the Egyptian mother-goddess Isis, and the astral religion of the Chaldeans. All these promised salvation in afterlife. All satisfied the emotional needs of the harried masses with comforting assurances of a paradise to come. Thus the secularism and rationalism of classical Greece now gave way to mysticism and otherworldliness.

In view of these antirational trends in philosophy and religion, it is surprising that more progress was achieved in science in the Hellenistic Age than in any other period prior to the seventeenth century. This gain was due in part to the economic opportunities afforded by Alexander's conquests. The greatly expanded markets provided the incentive to improve technology, which would increase output and thus profit. Also, the continual wars among the succession states, or between them and outside powers, created a demand for more complex war engines. Equally stimulating was the direct contact between Greek science and that of the Middle East—not only of Mesopotamia and Egypt but also, to a certain extent, of India. Finally, the Macedonian rulers of the Hellenistic states, raised as youths to value the prestige of Greek learning, generously supported scientific research, particularly in Egypt, where the Alexandria

This is a Roman copy of one of the masterpieces of Hellenistic sculpture, the Laocoon. *According to legend, Laocoon was a priest who warned the Trojans not to take the Greek's wooden horse within their city. This sculpture depicts his punishment. Great serpents sent by the goddess Athena, who was on the side of the Greeks, devoured Laocoon and his sons before the horrified people of Troy.*

Museum and Library was, in effect, the first state-supported research institute in history. It included astronomical observatories, laboratories and dissecting rooms, botanical and zoological gardens, and a library of from 500,000 to 700,000 volumes. From all over the Mediterranean world, in an early version of the "brain drain," came philosophers, mathematicians, physicians, botanists, zoologists, astronomers, philologists, geographers, artists, and poets—all attracted by the congenial and stimulating atmosphere, by the superb facilities, and by the free meals and lodgings and high salaries.

In mathematics the outstanding name was Euclid, with his *Elements of Geometry*. In astronomy, Hipparchus invented most of the instruments used until modern times and compiled the first star catalog. Ptolemy's compilation of

Hellenistic astronomical knowledge is the best-known work and remained the standard text until the Renaissance. Most original was Aristarchus, who was the first to grasp the enormous size of the universe and to place the sun and not the earth at its center. His views received little support, for they were considered impious as well as contrary to everyday experience. Thus Ptolemy's geocentric system remained generally accepted throughout medieval times. The progress in astronomy facilitated advances in scientific geography. Eratosthenes, the director of the Alexandria Museum, calculated the earth's circumference at 24,700 miles. Only 250 miles off, his calculations were not improved upon until the eighteenth century. He also drew a map of the inhabited world with a grid of latitudes and concluded, from the ebb and flow of tides in the Atlantic and Indian oceans, that the seas were one and that Europe, Asia, and Africa constituted a huge island.

Perhaps the outstanding contributions of Hellenistic science were in medicine and mechanics. The museum encouraged anatomical research, so that physicians now understood for the first time the role of the heart in blood circulation, the significance of the pulse, the functions of sensory and motor nerves, and the convolutions of the brain. Much of this knowledge was passed on by the great encyclopedist of medicine Galen, whose writings were so impressive that doctors dared not question him or strike out in new directions until modern times. In mechanics the outstanding figure was Archimedes, the founder of hydrostatics—the laws of floating bodies—which were used thereafter for testing the purity of metals. He also devised ingenious war machines and formulated the principles of the screw, the pulley, and the lever. It was in connection with the lever that he is supposed to have said, "Give me a place to stand, and I will move the world."

In conclusion, the historical significance of the Hellenistic Age is that it brought the East and West together, breaking the separate molds that had been formed through history. People now for the first time thought of the entire civilized world as a unit. At first the Greeks and Macedonians went to the East as conquerors and rulers and imposed a pattern of Hellenization.

But in the process they themselves were changed, so that the resulting Hellenistic civilization was a blend rather than a transplantation. And in the long run the religions of the East made their way west and contributed substantially to the transformation of the Roman Empire and medieval Europe.

V. EARLY REPUBLIC, TO 264 B.C.E.

Meanwhile the city-states in Greece continued to fight each other as they had in the past. They organized unions such as the Achaean League and the Aetolian Federation, but none proved lasting and effective. Despite many warnings, the divided Greeks ignored the rising power of the Romans. After destroying the Carthaginians, their great rivals in the western Mediterranean, the Romans turned eastward. First they conquered Macedon and the divided Greek cities, and then they overran the entire Hellenistic East.

Why were the Romans able to become the masters of the entire Mediterranean, and eventually of all Europe? Actually there were many similarities between the early histories of the Greeks and the Romans. Both were of the same ethnic stock, for just as the Indo-European Achaeans and Dorians filtered down the Balkan peninsula to Greece, so the Indo-European Latins filtered down the Italian peninsula to the south bank of the Tiber River. Among the Latin

Much of what we know of the Etruscans comes from their funerary art. This sculpture of an Etruscan couple is part of a sarcophagus.

communities formed at the time was Rome, which was located on the Tiber at the lowest point that could be conveniently crossed and at the highest to which small ships could go. This strategic position, similar to that of London on the Thames, made Rome from the very beginning both more mercantile and more open to foreign influences than other Latin settlements.

The chief foreign influences came from two civilized peoples who had come from overseas to settle in Italy—the Etruscans and the Greeks. The Etruscans, who arrived about 800 B.C.E., probably from Asia Minor, settled to the north of the Tiber and then conquered the Latins to the south. Before their rule was overthrown they passed on to the Romans some of their gods and goddesses, a knowledge of the arch and the vault, and the typically Eastern practice of forecasting the future by examining animal entrails. The Greeks, who appeared shortly after the Etruscans, established colonies in southern Italy and Sicily, including Tarentum, Syracuse, and Naples. Among their contributions to the Latins were the alphabet, some art and mythology, and certain religious concepts and practices, including the Greek-borrowed identities of Roman gods. The Greek's Zeus, Hermes, and Artemis became the Roman's Jupiter, Mercury, and Diana.

About 500 B.C.E. Rome expelled its last Etruscan king and began its career as an independent city-state. Within a few years it had conquered the surrounding peoples and controlled the entire Latin plain from the Apennine mountains to the sea coast. Roman institutions during this formative period were similar to those of the early Greek cities. The king originally held the imperium, or sovereign power. He was restrained only by an advisory council of aristocrats and a popular assembly that had power only to approve or disapprove legislation. Then, as in Greece, the monarchy was abolished, and the patricians became the dominant element in society. The sovereign power formerly held by the king was now delegated to two consuls, who were elected for one-year periods and who were always patricians. The Senate, which was the principal legislative body, was also an aristocratic institution and remained so even after a few commoners, or plebeians, were admitted.

Rome's development diverged from that of the Greek city-states when it accomplished what was beyond the capacity of the Greek cities—the conquest and unification of the entire peninsula. Why was it that Rome could master the Italian peninsula whereas no Greek city was able to unify even the Greek lands, let alone the whole of the Balkan peninsula? One reason was the marked difference in terrain. The Balkans are a jumble of mountains; indeed the name Balkan is derived from the Turkish word for mountain. The crisscrossing of ranges is very prevalent in Greece. In Italy, by contrast, there are only the Apennines, which are not as difficult to cross and which run north and south without transverse ranges. Consequently the Italian peninsula, not being so compartmentalized, is easier to unite and keep united. Furthermore, there was never a Balkan counterpart to the system of Roman roads that knitted Italy into one unit. For example, the famous Appian Way stretched all the way from Rome to Brindisium on the heel of the Italian boot. This road is still extant and was used by the British and American troops that landed in southern Italy in 1943.

Another reason for the success of the Romans was their enlightened treatment of the other Italian peoples. Upon its fellow Greeks Athens had levied tribute, and it never extended them citizenship. Rome granted full citizenship to about a fourth of the population of the peninsula. The rest were granted Latin citizenship, which carried substantial but not complete privileges. Autonomy was enjoyed by all. The only restrictions were the loss of control over foreign relations and a compulsory manpower levy for military service. This policy saved Rome, for her Italian allies remained loyal during the critical years when Hannibal was rampaging up and down the length of the peninsula.

Finally, the Romans prevailed because of the superior military force and strategy that they developed. In fighting their neighbors they learned that the traditional phalanx of 8,000 men was too large and unwieldy, especially in mountainous terrain. So they organized their soldiers into "maniples," or "handfuls," of 120 soldiers. Thirty of these, or 3,600 men, constituted a legion, which also had cavalry to protect its flanks. In addition to the traditional helmet, shield, lance, and sword, the Romans equipped the legion with an effective assault weapon—the iron-tipped javelin, which was flung at the enemy from a distance. Then the legionnaires attacked on the run, maneuvering skillfully to take advantage of any breaks in the opposing ranks.

By 295 B.C.E. the Romans had won central Italy and pushed south against Tarentum, the prosperous Greek city in the "instep" of the peninsula. The Tarentines called in the help of the Greek king, Pyrrhus of Epirus, ranked by Hannibal as second only to Alexander in generalship. Pyrrhus won two "Pyrrhic victories." But he could not afford his heavy losses, whereas the Romans, though they lost even more, could draw from a pool of 750,000 Italian fighting men. So Pyrrhus withdrew in 272 B.C.E. with the prophetic observation "What a battleground I am leaving for Rome and Carthage!" Only eight years later, in 264, Rome and Carthage were at war in Sicily.

Before considering the Punic Wars—so named after the Latin word *punicus* for Phoenician—it is necessary to note a certain democratization of Roman institutions. Since the plebeians had provided the manpower for the victorious legions, they were in a position to demand political concessions. When their demands were denied, they resorted to the novel but effective device of a walkout (secessio) and literally withdrew en masse from the city until their demands were met. One of the first gains won in this fashion by the plebeians was the right to choose officials known as tribunes to defend their interests. The tribunes were elected by the new Plebeian Assembly, which also cared for other matters of concern to the masses. Other concessions included the writing down of the laws so that they would be known to all and limitation of the amount of land that could be owned by any one individual.

Thus by 265 B.C.E. Rome, the mistress of Italy, was undergoing a process of democratization. Conceivably this could have culminated in the first democratic national state in the history of the world. But if this were in fact a possibility, it was effectively eliminated by the series of overseas wars in which Rome was now involved. The wars transformed Rome into a great empire, but they also transformed as profoundly its domestic institutions, and one of the many casualties was the trend toward democratization.

VI. LATE REPUBLIC, 265–27 B.C.E.

The transformation of Rome from an Italian republic to a great empire was sudden and spectacular, rather like the conquests of Alexander. Indeed certain common basic factors help to explain the explosive expansions of both Macedon and Rome. Each had evolved superior military instruments and techniques. Each enjoyed the vital advantage of social vigor and cohesion in contrast to the social decrepitude and fragmentation of the Persian Empire and the Hellenistic succession states.

Rome's great rival, Carthage, had started as a Phoenician colony about 850 B.C.E. Thanks to its near monopoly of the transit trade in the western Mediterranean, Carthage had become rich and powerful. With its wide-ranging fleets and mercenary troops, Carthage dominated northwestern Africa, southern Spain, Sardinia, Corsica, and western Sicily. At first there was no direct conflict between Rome and Carthage for the simple reason that one was a land power and the other a sea power. But they finally did clash when the Romans conquered southern Italy. The Romans feared Carthage's growing influence in Sicily, which was all too close to their newly won possessions.

The First Punic War (264–241 B.C.E.) forced the Romans for the first time to turn to the sea. They built a fleet, and by turning naval battles into boarding operations, they doggedly wore down the Carthaginians and conquered Sicily. The struggle to the death between the two great powers was now inevitable. Rome spent the next twenty years subduing the Celtic tribes in the Po Valley, thereby increasing its reserve of peasant soldiers. Carthage, to compensate for the loss of Sicily, consolidated its hold on Spain. From this base the great Carthaginian strategist, Hannibal, launched his daring invasion of Italy, crossing the Alps in 218 and thus beginning the Second Punic War (218–201). He defeated the Romans in battle after battle, particularly in his great triumph of Cannae (216). But the loyalty of Rome's allies robbed him of victory. When a Roman army landed near Carthage, Hannibal, undefeated in Italy, was recalled only to be defeated on his own ground. Once again Rome had exhausted an opponent, and in 201 Carthage was forced to accept a peace leaving it only its small home territory, its walls, and ten ships—enough to chase off pirates. Despite this catastrophic defeat, the Carthaginians made a remarkable economic recovery. But this alarmed the Romans so that they ruthlessly provoked the Third Punic War (149–146). Carthage itself was captured, the city completely destroyed, and the populace enslaved.

With these Punic Wars, Rome was caught in a chain reaction of conquest leading to further conquest. One reason was its overwhelming strength; with Carthage out of the way Rome was now the foremost power in the Mediterranean. Also conquest was manifestly profitable, as booty, slaves, and tribute poured in from each new province. Finally, there were the inevitable commitments and challenges associated with far-flung imperial frontiers. For example, since Philip V of Macedon had aided Hannibal during the Second Punic War, Rome—after having disposed of Carthage—turned on Macedon. The ensuing war proved to be the first of a series in which the Romans skillfully played off against each other the several Middle Eastern powers—Macedon, Seleucid Syria, Ptolemaic Egypt, and the rival Aetolian and Achaean leagues of Greek city-states.

Thus the Romans overran and annexed in quick succession Macedon; Greece; the Asia Minor states of Pergamum, Bithynia, and Cilicia; then Seleucid Syria; and finally Egypt in 31

B.C.E. In this manner the Romans took over the Hellenistic succession states of the East. In Asia though, they acquired only the provinces along the Mediterranean coast. All the interior had fallen to Parthia, which henceforth was to be Rome's chief rival in the East. Meanwhile Julius Caesar had gained fame by conquering (58–49 B.C.E.) all of Gaul between the English Channel and the Mediterranean. Finally the permanent occupation of Britain was begun in the first century of our era and was consolidated with the construction of a line of fortifications between the firths of Clyde and Forth. This marked the limits of Roman rule in northern Europe.

Rome did not treat its newly acquired provinces as generously as it had its earlier Italian allies. The Senate appointed governors who were given a free hand as long as they kept sending home an adequate flow of tribute, taxes, grain, and slaves. The result was shameless exploitation and extortion. The maladministration of Governor Gaius Verres in Sicily (73–71 B.C.E.), described in the following indictment by Cicero, was neither exceptional nor atypical:

Countless sums of money, under a new and unprincipled regulation, were wrung from the purses of the farmers; our most loyal allies were treated as if they were national enemies; Roman citizens were tortured and executed like slaves; the guiltiest criminals bought their legal acquittal, while the most honour-

Busts of a Roman couple from the period of the Republic. Although some people have identified the individuals as Cato the Younger and his daughter Porcia, no solid evidence confirms this claim.

able and honest men would be . . . condemned and banished unheard; strongly fortified harbours, mighty and well-defended cities were left open to the assaults of pirates and buccaneers. Sicilian soldiers and sailors, our allies and our friends, were starved to death; fine fleets, splendidly equipped, were to the great disgrace of our nation destroyed and lost to us. Famous and ancient works of art, some of them the gifts of wealthy kings . . . —this same governor stripped and despoiled every one of them. Nor was it only the civic statues and works of art he treated thus; he also pillaged the holiest and most venerated sanctuaries; in fact, he has not left the people of Sicily a single god whose workmanship he thought at all above the average of antiquity of artistic merit.[9]

These polices affected the Roman homeland almost as adversely as Rome affected the subject territories. Many of the small farmers in Italy had been ruined by the ravages of Hannibal's campaigns and by the long years of overseas service during the following wars. Then came the influx of cheap grain and of droves of slaves from the conquered provinces. The peasants were forced to sell out to the new class of the very rich, who were especially eager to accumulate large estates because agriculture was still considered the only respectable calling for gentlemen. Thus the second century B.C.E. saw the growth in Italy of large plantations (*latifundia*) worked by slaves and owned by absentee landlords. The dispossessed peasantry drifted to the towns, where they lived in squalid tenements and once again had to compete with slaves for such work as was available. The authorities took care to provide them with "bread and circuses" (*panis et circenses*) to keep them quiet. Despite the insecurity and rootlessness, city life at least was exciting and alluring. Poets were loud in their praise of rustic virtues, but the peasants themselves thought otherwise and continued to flock to Rome—the "common cesspool," as the contemporary historian Sallust termed it.

The political fruits of empire were as bitter as the economic. The earlier trend toward democratization was reversed because the Senate had directed the victorious overseas campaigns and gained greatly in prestige and power. Also the new urban mobs offered no basis for popular government since they were always ready to sell their votes or to support any demagogue who promised relief from their troubles. Equally disruptive was the changing character of the armed forces. Imperial obligations required a large standing army. It no longer sufficed to call up property owners for short-term militia service. So the ranks were opened to volunteers, and dispossessed peasants enlisted for long periods. Rome's legions accordingly changed from a citizen army to a professional one. The soldiers' first loyalty now was not to the state but to their commanders, to whom they looked for a share of the booty and of any land that might be available for distribution. The generals increasingly came to regard the legions entrusted to them as their own armies and used them to advance their personal fortunes.

Imperial expansion also disrupted Roman culture. The traditional Roman virtues had been those of poor, hard-working peasants. But when wealth began to pour into the capital, the ancient values of thrift, abstinence, and industry were soon forgotten. The last days of the republic were marked by a wild scramble for money, the sort of ostentatious waste to be expected from the newly rich, and a callous indifference to all human values. "Rome," grumbled a contemporary, "has become a city where paramours fetch a better price than plowlands, and pots of pickled fish than plowmen."

In light of the above, it is understandable that the period from the end of the Punic Wars in 146 B.C.E. to the end of the republic in 27 B.C.E. was one of crisis—of class war, slave revolts, and increasing military intervention in politics. A gallant reform effort was made at the outset by Tiberius Gracchus and his brother Gaius. They sought to use their elective positions as tribunes to push through a moderate program of land distribution. But the oligarchs would have none of it and resorted to violence to gain their ends. Tiberius was murdered in 133 B.C.E. along with three hundred of his followers. Twelve years later Gaius was driven to suicide, and the senatorial class resumed its sway.

The fate of the Gracchi brothers made clear the impossibility of orderly reform. The empire now was torn by generals competing for power at the top and by slave revolts from below. The most serious of the revolts was that of Spartacus, which broke out in 73 B.C.E. For a while the entire imperial system tottered, but in the end

Spartacus was defeated, and the roads to Rome were lined with his crucified followers.

The final victor was Julius Caesar, the conqueror of Gaul, who had built up a powerful and devoted army. In 49 B.C.E. he crossed the river Rubicon, which separated Gaul from Italy, and in a series of brilliant campaigns defeated the forces of the Senate under his rival Pompey. Caesar was now the undisputed master of the empire. Precisely what he would have done with his mastery cannot be known, for he was murdered in 44 B.C.E. by representatives of the old oligarchy.

His death was followed by another thirteen years of political jockeying and armed strife between his adopted son and heir Octavian and the political adventurer Mark Antony. With his naval victory over Antony and Cleopatra at Actium (31 B.C.E.), Octavian was supreme. He was only thirty-three years old at the time, the age at which the great Alexander had died. But Octavian had forty-four years of life ahead of him, during which he laid the foundations for two golden centuries of imperial peace and stability.

VII. EARLY EMPIRE, 27 B.C.E.–284 C.E.

In 27 B.C.E. the Senate conferred upon Octavian the titles of Augustus and Imperator, symbolizing the transformation of Rome from republic to empire. Octavian professed to prefer the republican title of First Citizen (Princeps). But in practice he acted like an emperor and grasped full powers, at the expense of both the Senate and the people. He created a centralized system of courts under his own supervision and assumed direct control over provincial governors, punishing them severely for graft and extortion. He standardized taxes and made their collection a state function rather than a private business operated by greedy tax farmers. He kept close check on the army and saw to it that the soldiers were well provided for and swore allegiance directly to him. He also created a permanent navy that suppressed piracy and safeguarded the transportation of both commodities and troops to all parts of the empire.

By these measures Augustus, as he came to be known, created an efficient administrative system that ensured the Pax Romana that was to prevail for two centuries. The four emperors following Augustus—Tiberius (14–37 C.E.), Caligula (37–41), Claudius (41–54), and Nero (54–68)—were unworthy of their high office. But the empire weathered their misrule and then blossomed under a succession of "five good emperors"—Nerva (96–98 C.E.), Trajan (98–117), Hadrian (117–138), Antoninus Pius (138–161), and Marcus Aurelius (161–180). During these reigns the Roman Empire reached its height, both in geographic extent and in the quality of its civilization.

In the extreme north, the imperial frontier was set by the fortifications built from the Forth to the Clyde. In the northeast, the Rhine and the Danube provided a natural frontier, which further east curved north of the Danube to include Dacia (modern Rumania). Both Asia Minor and Egypt were Roman possessions, but

An example of one of the greatest achievements of the Roman empire, this granite aqueduct was constructed in the time of Trajan and is still in use today.

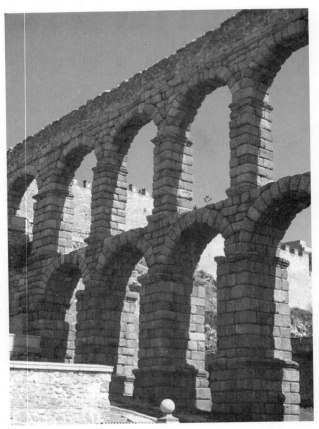

between the two the frontier ran close to the Mediterranean coast, leaving the interior to the Parthians and, after 224 C.E., to the Sassanians. Likewise in North Africa the Romans controlled the coastal territories between Egypt and the Atlantic, with the Sahara as their southern limit.

This huge area, with its strong natural frontiers, constituted a prosperous and virtually self-sufficient economic unit. Various factors contributed to the flourishing imperial economy during these centuries—honest and efficient administration, monetary stability, large-scale public works, and extensive trade, both within and without the empire. Internal free trade ensured unhindered distribution of wheat, papyrus, and glassware from Egypt; linens, woolens, and fruits from Syria; wool, timber, and rugs from Asia Minor; wine, oil, and manufactured goods from Italy; grains, meats, and wool from Gaul; and a variety of minerals from Spain and Britain. The Romans also imported certain goods from the outside: amber, furs, and slaves from the Baltic Sea area; ivory, gold, and slaves from sub-Saharan Africa; and most important, various luxury items from Asia, including perfumes, precious stones, spices, and, above all, silk. (See Chapter 4, Section II.) Thanks to this thriving domestic and foreign trade, staples and luxuries poured into the capital from as near as Gaul and as far as China—enough staples to feed and clothe over a million people, and enough luxuries to satisfy the extravagances of the rulers of the Western world.

In the cultural field, a basic achievement of the Romans was the extension into central and western Europe of urban civilization, with all that that entailed. In this respect their role in the West was similar to that of the Greeks in the Middle East. In the third century B.C.E., after Alexander, the Greeks founded dozens of cities from which Hellenistic culture spread as far as India and Central Asia. So now the Romans founded cities such as London and Colchester in Britain, Autun and Vaison in Gaul, and Trier and Cologne in Germany. These cities, varying from 20 to 500 acres in size, were a distinct improvement on the relatively squalid hilltop forts and villages of the Celts and Germans. Even the slaves' quarters in these cities were more hygienic than the hovels of the contemporary native villagers. Furthermore the cities possessed public

bathhouses for the comfort of the body and public theaters for the pleasures of the mind, as well as residential blocks and public markets and shops. These cities were the basic cells of the imperial culture as well as of the imperial political system.

The great city of the empire, of course, was Rome. It sprawled over 5,000 acres, and its population during the second century C.E. is estimated at a little over 1 million. A visitor would find a complete absence of sanitation facilities in the crowded tenements of the poor but would note that, instead, there were elaborate public latrines with seats of marble and decorated with statues of gods or heroes. An inevitable byproduct of this arrangement was the emptying of chamber pots into the streets—not a rare occurrence as we can see from the many references to this practice in Roman law. Noteworthy also was the total lack of street lighting, so that on moonless nights the capital was plunged in impenetrable darkness. Everyone locked doors and stayed at home; no one dared venture out except for the wealthy with their escort of slaves who carried torches and protected them against robbers. In daytime the streets teemed with life and reverberated with noise. Hawkers bawled their wares, money changers rang their coins, tinkers pounded their hammers, snake charmers played their flutes, and beggars rehearsed their misfortunes to passersby. Night provided no relief. Transport carts were banned from the streets in daytime, so immediately after sunset there appeared a great procession of carts, beasts of burden, and their drivers. This night traffic condemned Romans to perpetual insomnia unless they were wealthy enough to live in isolated villas.

Life under such conditions was made tolerable by the mass entertainment provided by the state. Most popular were the chariot races and gladiatorial contests. A better use of leisure was provided by the sumptuous public baths of Rome. These were so elaborate that those of Diocletian covered thirty-two acres; Caracalla's spread over twenty-seven acres. Such establishments were, of course, much more than simple bathing pools. In addition to hot, tepid, and cold baths, they provided exercise facilities, lounging halls, gardens, and libraries. They were, in short, "athletic clubs" on a grand scale,

A relief from the column of Antonius Pius showing Roman foot soldiers surrounded by cavalry.

and they admirably promoted the ideal of "a healthy mind in a healthy body."

Finally the Rome of these centuries was also the center of imperial culture. This culture, as noted earlier, was essentially Greek-derived, particularly in such fields as literature, art, and philosophy. But in engineering and law, the Romans, with their bent for practicality, had important contributions of their own to make. Typically, the Romans achieved little in abstract science but excelled in the construction of aqueducts, sewer systems, bridges, and roads. The roads were superbly built, with a bottom layer of large stones set in firm soil, a middle layer of gravel, and a top layer of large slabs of stone. They were carefully cambered so that the surface water drained off into the ditches on each side. These famous roads, together with their bridges, were so well engineered that they continued to be used through the Middle Ages, and in some cases even to the present day. Likewise, Roman architecture,

in contrast to the Greek, was concerned primarily with secular structures such as baths, amphitheaters, stadiums, and triumphal arches. And new Roman building materials—concrete, brick, and mortar—made possible vaulting on a grand scale for their large buildings.

Perhaps the most important single intellectual contribution of the Romans was their body of law based on reason rather than custom. Their original laws, as set down in the Twelve Tablets about 450 B.C.E., were simple and conservative, typical of a peasant people. With the growth of commerce and of empire, life became more complicated, and these laws no longer sufficed. Typical was the problem of an alien in Rome who might be arrested and his property seized. What law would be applicable in such a case, particularly in view of the contemporary concept that a people carried their law with them wherever they went? The Romans established a special court to try such cases, and as a result of its operations they realized that among foreign peoples there were many legal systems but only a few almost universal legal principles. Hence the formulation of a new body of law—the *jus gentium*, or law of the people—which they accepted and applied both to themselves and to others.

The Twelve Tablets also defined the subordinate status of the Roman woman, who was subject to the authority of the eldest male ascendant in the family, the pater familias. The legal system included the principle of patriapostestas, by which the husband was the legal head of the household. As such he enjoyed absolute power, including the right of life and death and the right to sell into slavery all the members of his family. But Roman women, unlike the Athenian, did have the right to inherit and acquire real property and could dispose of it without the consent of their guardians. Also Roman women were not so rigidly confined to residential quarters as were their Athenian sisters. Generalizations are risky because of changes during the transition from republic to empire. Yet it is safe to conclude that the women of Rome were better off than those of Athens, though still definitely subordinate to men.

VIII. LATE EMPIRE, 284–476 C.E.

The great days of Rome came to an end with the death of Marcus Aurelius in 180 C.E. For some time his predecessors had passed on the succession to adopted sons of proven talent, a system that had made possible a string of unusually capable rulers. But Marcus Aurelius allowed his true son, Commodus, to succeed him. The results were disastrous. Commodus avoided his duties as head of the empire and spent most of his time at chariot races and gladiatorial contests. After his assassination in 193 he was followed by rulers who were for the most part equally incompetent. The Praetorian Guard, a highly trained and well-paid body created by Augustus to protect the security of the capital, now got out of control. An emperor could remain in power only while he had the support of this body. During the period from 235 to 284 there were almost two dozen emperors, and only one of them died a natural death. Such disintegration at the center

inevitably weakened the frontier defenses. Outlying provinces were overrun by the German tribes in the West and by the revived Persian Empire of the Sassanians in the East.

The imperial decay of the third century was checked with the advent of the strong and capable emperors Diocletian (284–305) and Constantine (312–317). Among the policies they adopted to hold the empire together was a rigid regimentation imposed step by step in response to specific urgent needs. Because agricultural lands were left untilled, villages were required to pay a collective tax on abandoned lands. Because inflation was mounting, the famous Edict of Prices (301) set maximum prices for thousands of commodities and services, with specified variations according to quality. Interest rates were soaring, so they were limited to between 6 and 12 percent, depending on the degree of risk. Shortages of certain products brought on export prohibitions, as in the case of foodstuffs and "strategic products" such as iron, bronze, weapons, army equipment, and horses. These controls were extended to the point where they virtually became a caste system. Constantine required every soldier's son to be a soldier unless unfit for service. Similarly, agricultural

Bust of the Emperor Constantine (306–377 C.E.)

laborers were tied to the land on a permanent and hereditary basis. The tendency was to extend this requirement to all crafts and professions that were deemed indispensable or that had recruitment difficulties.

Another policy during this time of troubles was decentralization, which became necessary as the imperial economy deteriorated. Diocletian divided his realm in two, keeping the eastern half for his own administration and appointing a coemperor for the western. This division was hardened when Constantine built a new capital on the site of the old Greek colony of Byzantium on the Bosphorus. The choice was inspired, for Constantinople, as the new city soon came to be called, was easily defended because of the narrows at each end of the straits. The city also provided ready access to both the vital Danube and Euphrates frontiers. Thus Constantinople became one of the great cities of the world and served as the proud capital of the Eastern Roman, or Byzantine, Empire for centuries after Rome and the Western Empire had passed away.

Another policy of these later centuries that was to affect the future profoundly dealt with relations between Christianity and the imperial government. Constantine made the fateful decision to seek stability and cohesion through cooperation with Christianity rather than its suppression. This was the end of a centuries-old trend in religious attitudes and practices. The hardships of daily life during this later imperial phase caused increasing numbers to turn for solace to salvation religions, as had happened earlier in the Hellenistic East. (See Section IV, this chapter.) Spiritual needs no longer were satisfied by the cult of emperor and the official polytheism. Brotherhoods that celebrated the mysteries of oriental gods now provided satisfying explanations of the world, rules of conduct, and release from evil and from death.

The most successful of the new religions was Christianity. It offered the doctrine of one God, the Father Omnipotent, in place of the polytheism of the Greco-Roman gods and the monotheism of the oriental cults. It brought the solace of a Redeemer, Jesus, who was not an ambiguous figure in a mythological labyrinth but who miraculously lived an earthly life, even though he was the Son of God. "I bring you tidings of great joy which shall be to all people." Christianity also guaranteed salvation to the believer, but instead of a starry eternity, it restored him to life through a personal resurrection foreshadowed by the Resurrection of Christ himself. Perhaps most important of all, Christianity provided fellowship when times were disjointed and common people felt uprooted and

The Arch of Constantine, constructed between 312 and 315 C.E. to honor Constantine as sole emperor of Rome.

forsaken. All Christians were brothers, and their meetings were often called agape, meaning "love" in Greek. They assisted one another, and by their devotion and self-denial they set an aspiring and contagious example. Thus at a time when the laws and philosophy of the old order were becoming irrelevant and unviable, Christianity offered relevance and hope for the meek and the humble.

By the time of the great fire of 64 C.E., the Christians had become so numerous that Nero thought it wise to blame them for the disaster and to begin the first of numerous persecutions. But this merely hallowed the memory of the martyrs and spurred the proselytizing efforts. After a final major persecution early in the fourth century, Emperor Constantine issued the Edict of Milan (313) excusing Christians from pagan rituals and granting their religion the same tolerance accorded to all others. Finally, Emperor Theodosius (379–395) made Christianity in effect the state church. The old Roman aristocracy and the apostate Emperor Julian (361–363) fought a stubborn rearguard action to preserve pagan practices, but by the end of the fourth century Christianity reigned supreme.

Just as the emperors adopted Christianity with the aim of furthering social cohesion, so they adopted the pomp and circumstance of oriental court etiquette. In contrast to Augustus, who had dubbed himself "First Citizen," Diocletian took the name of Jovian, the earthly representative of Jupiter, and Constantine, after his conversion to Christianity, assumed sacred status. The power of the emperor henceforth was considered to be derived from the gods rather than delegated by citizens. Accordingly, court ritual now made the emperor remote and unapproachable. Bedecked in a jeweled diadem and a robe of purple silk interwoven with gold, the emperor forced all subjects to prostrate themselves. Only a privileged few were allowed to kiss the border of the emperor's robe. High imperial officials were correspondingly beatified—the treasurer became "count of the sacred largesses," and the imperial council was known as the "sacred consistory."

With these measures the emperors of the third and fourth centuries strove valiantly to halt the imperial decline. If resolve and effort alone were needed, they would have been spec-

This ivory relief, carved a little after 395 C.E., shows a Vandal warrior, Stilicho, who rose to prominence in the Roman army. From the third century onward, the Roman army was composed increasingly of foreign mercenaries.

tacularly successful. In fact they did stabilize the situation somewhat, but only temporarily. The net effect of their herculean endeavors was to postpone rather than to avert the end. Beginning in 406 the West Roman emperors were powerless to prevent permanent large-scale invasions of Franks, Burgundians, Visigoths, and Vandals in Gaul, Spain, and Africa. Nor could they prevent the ultimate indignity of the sack of Rome by barbarians in 410 and again in 455.

Finally, in 476 Romulus Augustulus, the last of the West Roman emperors, was forced to abdicate by Odoacer, the German, or Hunnic, leader of a band of mercenary soldiers.

Though this incident is generally taken to mark the end of the West Roman Empire, it attracted little attention at the time, for it was merely the culmination of a process of disintegration that had extended over two centuries. To understand the reason for the "fall of Rome," if this traditional cataclysmic phrase may be used, it is necessary to determine the dynamics of the prolonged but inexorable descent to oblivion.

The instrument responsible for the "fall" was, of course, the German barbarians. Thus a French historian has concluded, "Roman civilization did not die a natural death. It was murdered."[10] There is some justification for this verdict, yet it was not a case of irresistible hordes sweeping everything aside by sheer weight of numbers. Historians estimate that only about 100,000 Ostrogoths invaded Italy, and an equal number of Visigoths subjugated Spain and southern France. The Vandal force that crossed the Straits of Gibraltar to North Africa totaled about 80,000 men, or 1 percent of the native population of that province.

So the question still remains—why the "fall"? An American historian has stated that "though war was the apparent cause of death . . . the organic disease of the Empire was economic."[11] In fact, this "organic disease" is discernible not only in the Roman Empire but also in the Hellenistic states, in classical Greece, and even in the earlier ancient civilizations. All were afflicted by the same basic problem of low productivity. It stemmed from the failure to advance technology significantly after the Neolithic age, which had produced such core inventions as metallurgy, the plow, the wheel, the sail, and the solar calendar.

The underlying cause for the technological retardation appears to have been the institution of slavery, which was an integral and universally accepted part of all these civilizations. Even in classical Greece, where slavery never was as rampant as in Rome, Aristotle (as noted earlier) asserted that some men were born to rule and some to be ruled, and if the latter refused to accept their preordained fate, it was "naturally just" that they should be hunted down as though they were "wild beasts."

The repercussions of the institution of slavery were manifold and pernicious. The institution deprived the slave of any incentive to improve on the traditional operations of his or her craft. It also deprived the master of any incentive for technological innovation as long as plenty of slave labor was available. Thus during the reign of Vespasian when an obelisk was to be erected in the present-day Piazza San Pietro in Rome, an inventor of the time suggested an engineering technique that would have made the operation much easier. But the emperor preferred manual slave labor so as not to leave the slaves unemployed. Likewise the water mill, though known in the eastern provinces of the empire as early as the first century B.C.E., was not adopted in Rome until the fourth century, when the supply of slaves had shrunk.

Equally harmful was the natural tendency of a slave-owning society to associate manual labor with slaves and hence to regard such labor as beneath the dignity of free persons. Thus the Greek essayist Plutarch stated that the great Archimedes

. . . did not think the inventing of military engines an object worthy of his serious studies, but only reckoned them among the amusements of geometry. Nor had he gone so far, but at the pressing instances of Hiero of Syracuse, who entreated him to turn his art from abstracted motions to matters of sense, and to make his reasonings more intelligible to the generality of mankind, applying them to the use of common life.

The first to turn their thoughts to mechanics, a branch of knowledge which came afterwards to be so much admired, were Eudoxus and Archytas, who confirmed certain problems, not then soluble on theoretical grounds, by sensible experiments and the use of instruments. But Plato inveighed against them, with great indignation, as corrupting and debasing the excellence of geometry, by making her descend from incorporeal and intellectual, to corporeal and sensible things, and obliging her to make use of matter, which requires much manual labor, and is the object of servile trades. Mechanics were in consequence separated from geometry, and were for a long time despised by philosophers.[12]

In these various ways, then, the institution of slavery tended to inhibit technological innovation during the millennia following the egalitarian Neolithic age. Slavery also depressed the internal economic market because domestic purchasing power was restricted since slaves obviously could not purchase the fruits of their labor.

For some time these basic structural weaknesses were masked by imperial expansion, with the resulting flood of booty, tribute, foodstuffs, and slaves. But there were limits to the expansion of empires at that level of technological development—limits set by logistical and communications requirements. Thus Rome, like China, was able to advance just so far and no further. When that point was reached, the imperial frontiers became fixed, or even began shrinking, and the hitherto hidden structural defects came to light.

The army, which previously had been a profitable source of slaves and material wealth, now became a heavy but inescapable burden. Likewise, the bureaucracy had become swollen during the period of expansion and was impossible to support in a period of contraction. The excessive expenditures led to inflation that eventually reached runaway proportions. In Egypt, for example, a measure of wheat that cost 6 drachmai in the first century C.E. rose to 200 drachmai in 276, 9,000 in 314, 78,000 in 334, and to more than 2 million soon after that. With such inflation, coinage became worthless, and there was some reversion to barter. This trend was hastened by the growing diffusion of industry to the countryside and the provinces. The diffusion occurred for a number of reasons such as the deterioration of imperial communication facilities and the drop in the supply of slaves, which made it necessary to tap new labor pools. The shift of industry from the cities to villages and large country estates meant the agrarianization of the empire. The large estates became increasingly self-sufficient, boasting craftmakers of every kind as well as agricultural laborers. And the more self-sufficient they became, the more the imperial economy disintegrated into autarchic units.

Economic decentralization inevitably was accompanied by political decentralization. With the decline of trade and the shrinkage of state revenues, the imperial edifice no longer could be supported and slowly began to crumble. Diocletian and Constantine made desperate efforts to buttress the structure by imperial fiat. But the disease was "organic" rather than superficial, so all the regimentation, with its propping and bracing, was of no avail in the long run. Regimentation, however, was not the cause of imperial decay but an ineffective remedy that was tried to halt the decay. "Crisis preceded regimentation," as an economic historian has pointed out.[13]

It follows that a major reason why the West Roman Empire "fell" and the East did not was precisely because the economy of the West was less advanced and weaker. Italian agriculture was never as productive as that in the rich river valleys of the Middle East. The grain harvest in Italy was on average no more than four times the sowing. The rich soils of central and northern Europe had to await medieval technological advances for effective exploitation. Likewise industry in the West was of relatively recent origin and generally lagged behind that in the East. Thus although the whole Roman Empire was wracked by "organic disease," the Western part, being the less robust, was the first to succumb. The Eastern part survived to live on for another millennium.

Despite its demise, the West Roman Empire did leave a rich legacy. Most apparent are the material remains—the amphitheaters, arenas, temples, aqueducts, roads, and bridges. Equally obvious is the linguistic bequest in the form of the Romance (or Romanized) languages of Europe. Roman law, as noted before, is very much alive in the legal systems of numerous countries in Europe and the Americas. The organization and ritual of the Catholic church owe much to Roman imperial structure and religious traditions. Finally, the Pax Romana, which had brought two centuries of relative peace and prosperity, left a tradition of imperial unity in place of the city-state particularism of the Greeks. It was this tradition during the following centuries that fired the imagination and ambition of barbarian princes throughout Europe to become imperator or basileus or tsar.

SUGGESTED READINGS

The most recent survey of both Greece and Rome is *The Oxford History of the Classical World*, edited by J. Boardman, J. Griffin, and O. Murray (Oxford University, 1987). For Greece alone, see M. Grant, *The Rise of the Greeks* (Scribner's, 1988); R. Sealey, *A History of the Greek City-States* (University of California, 1977); and R. Meiggs, *The Athenian Empire* (Oxford University, 1972). On specific aspects of Greek history and civilization there are A. R. Burn, *Persia and the Greeks: The Defense of the West* (Edward Arnold, 1963); J. Boardman, *The Greeks Overseas: Their Early Colonies and Trade* (Thames & Hudson, 1982); C. Kerenyi, *The Gods of the Greeks* (Thames & Hudson, 1979); and R. Flaceliére, *Daily Life in Greece at the Time of Pericles* (Macmillan, 1965).

For the Hellenistic world, see the standard history by W. W. Tarn and G. T. Griffith, *Hellenistic Civilization* (Edward Arnold, 1952); the brief survey by M. Grant, *From Alexander to Cleopatra* (Scribner's, 1982); the scholarly biography by N. G. L. Hammond, *Alexander the Great: King, Commander and Statesman* (Chatto & Windus, 1980); and the detailed analysis by M. Rostovzeff, *Social and Economic History of the Hellenistic World*, 3 vols. (Clarendon, 1941).

There are several good one-volume studies of Rome, including A. E. R. Boak and W. G. Sinnigen, *A History of Rome to 565 A.D.*, 5th ed. (Macmillan, 1965); and M. Grant, *History of Rome* (Scribner's, 1978). See M. P. Charlesworth, *The Roman Empire*, (Oxford University, 1951), for the first three centuries; for the later period, see A. H. M. Jones, *The Decline of the Ancient World* (Longmans, 1966). Special topics are treated in J. Carcopino, *Daily Life in Ancient Rome* (Yale University, 1940); R. MacMullen, *Christianizing the Roman Empire, A.D. 100–400* (Yale University, 1984); and M. I. Finley, ed., *Slavery in Classical Antiquity* (Heffer, 1960).

The status of women during the Greco-Roman period is best analyzed in S. B. Pomeroy, *Goddesses, Whores, Wives and Slaves* (Schocken, 1975); in V. Zinserling, *Women in Greece and Rome* (Schram, 1973); in the useful collection of source materials in M. R. Lefkowitz and M. B. Fant, *Women's Life in Greece and Rome* (Johns Hopkins University, 1982); and in the survey by M. W. Bingham and S. H. Gross, *Women in European History and Culture*, Vol. I, *Ancient Greece and Rome* (Glenhurst, 1983).

Finally, the problem of why Rome "fell" is analyzed in the following two convenient collections of readings, which also provide excellent bibliographies on the subject: S. N. Eisenstadt, ed., *The Decline of Empires* (Prentice Hall, 1967); and D. Kagan, ed., *Decline and Fall of the Roman Empire* (D. C. Heath, 1962).

NOTES

1. Plato, *Apology*, trans. B. Jowatt in *Dialogues of Plato*.
2. Cited by F. M. Cornford, *Greek Religious Thought ...* (Dent, 1923), p. 85.
3. Cited by C. J. Singer, *A History of Biology* (Schuman, 1950), p. 4.
4. From *The Greek Mind* by W. R. Agard. © 1957 by Litton Educational Publishing Inc. Reprinted by permission of D. Van Nostrand Company.
5. Aristotle, *Politics*, I, 5, 2.
6. Herodotus, *The Persian Wars*, trans. G. Rawlinson, Book VII, Chap. 104.
7. Thucydides, *The Peloponnesian War*, trans. B. Jowatt, Book I, Chap. 22.
8. Cited by S. Pomeroy, *Women in Classical Antiquity* (Schocken, 1976), p. 8.
9. Cicero, *First Part of the Speech Against Gaius Verres at the First Hearing* (New York, 1928), Chap. 5.
10. A. Piganiol, *L'Empire Chrétien* (Presses Universitaires de France, 1947), p. 422.
11. R. S. Lopez, *The Birth of Europe* (M. Evans, 1967), p. 23.
12. *Life of Marcellus*, from *Plutarch's Lives*, Vol. 3, trans. J. and W. Langhorne (London, 1821), pp. 119ff.
13. J. Lévy, *The Economic Life of the Ancient World*, ed. J. G. Birain (University of Chicago, 1967), p. 99.

CHAPTER
6
Indian Civilization

Government is the science of punishment.

Kautilya

I consider that my duty is the good of the whole world.

Ashoka

Turning from Greece and Rome to India, we enter an altogether different world. The differences are not simply those that might naturally emerge from contrasting physical environments—differences in occupations, diet, habitation, dress, and the like. The differences were much more far-reaching and fundamental. There were nothing in the West remotely resembling basic Indian concepts and institutions such as caste, ahimsa (nonviolence), reincarnation, and karma (the law of moral consequences). These were not just eccentric or abstract ideas. They constituted the bedrock of Indian civilization, molding the thought and daily lives of all Indians. The pattern that resulted was so distinctive and so enduring that Indian civilization to the present day has distin-

guishing characteristics that mark it off from all other Eurasian civilizations.

Distinctiveness also characterizes the civilization of China, as will be noted in the following chapter, but this is natural because of the unparalleled geographic and historical isolation of that country. In India, by contrast, the beginnings appeared to be basically similar to those of the other regions to the west where Aryan invaders had settled—the Iranian plateau and the Balkan and Italian peninsulas. As noted earlier (Chapter 3, Section V), the Aryan tribes that descended on India about 1500 B.C.E. possessed the same physical features, the same pastoral economy, the same social institutions, the same gods, and the same epics as did, for example, the Achaeans and the Dorians. Furthermore, the

Indo-Aryans were not isolated in their subcontinent to anywhere near the degree that the Chinese were on the eastern extremity of Eurasia. The mountain ranges of northwest India are not impassable; armies and merchants and pilgrims crossed back and forth through the centuries. In fact, during much of the time there was more interaction between northern India and the Middle East and central Asia than between north India and the southern part of the peninsula.

The question naturally arises, then, why the Indo-Aryans should have developed a civilization so basically different from those of their kin to the west. The scanty evidence available does not allow for a specific or definitive answer, but the most simple and likely explanation is that the Indo-Aryans were Indianized. In contrast to the Achaeans or Dorians or Latins, who settled in relatively uncivilized areas, the Indo-Aryans encountered in the Indus valley a highly developed civilization with large urban centers and a dense population. (See map of Classical Age Empires in India, p. 119.) The native population, although subjugated and despised, was too numerous and too advanced to be exterminated or pushed aside or assimilated, leaving few traces of the original culture. Instead, as the Aryan pastoralists settled down and took up agriculture, they perforce lived in close proximity with the prior inhabitants of their new land. After some centuries of such coexistence and intermarriage, the inevitable result was a cultural synthesis. The circumstances, nature, and consequences of this synthesis are the subject of this chapter.

I. ARYAN IMPACT

Following their penetration into the Indus valley, the Aryans concentrated in the more rainy parts of the Punjab where the pasture was adequate for their herds. Gradually they began to spread into the heavily forested basin of the Ganges. Their expansion was slow at first, since only stone, bronze, and copper axes were available. But iron was introduced about 800 B.C.E., and the expansion pace quickened. The main occupation shifted from pastoralism to agriculture. The monsoon climate of the Ganges valley was ideal for rice cultivation, which was more productive than the wheat and barley grown in the Punjab. As a result the center of population density shifted from the northwest to the east, which then became the seat of the first powerful kingdoms.

The shift to agriculture stimulated various crafts necessary for the new villages, including carpentry, metallurgy, weaving, and tanning. Agriculture also promoted trade, with the river serving as the natural highway for transporting surplus food. Barter was common practice at first, and the cow was the unit of value in large-scale transactions. When coins appeared, the earliest weight standards, significantly enough, were exactly those of the pre-Aryan Indus civilization. Towns grew out of villages that were strategically located for trade or that had specialized in particular crafts.

This economic growth in turn facilitated political consolidation. Originally, the Indo-Aryans, like their relatives in the West, were organized under tribal chiefs assisted by councils of elders and general assemblies. With economic development the tribes gave way to kingdoms in the Ganges plain and to republics in the Punjab and in the foothills of the Himalayas. Of these early states the kingdom of Magadha in the lower Ganges soon rose to preeminence because of its location on two main trade routes and its control over rich iron-ore deposits. With these advantages Magadha was to serve as the base for the formation of both the Maurya and Gupta empires.

The Nanda dynasty in the fourth century B.C.E. was the first to exploit systematically the resources of Magadha for state-building purposes. They built canals, organized irrigation projects, and established an efficient administrative system for the collection of taxes. The Nandas have been described as the earliest empire builders of India. In fact, they laid the foundations of an empire but were not destined actually to fashion the first imperial structure. This was to be the historic role of Chandragupta Maurya, the young adventurer who usurped the Nanda throne in 321 B.C.E. and went on to build the famous empire named after him.

Economic and political developments were paralleled by fateful changes in social structure. Originally the Indo-Aryans, like other Aryans, were divided into three classes: the warrior nobles, the priests, and the common people. They had none of the restrictions associated with caste,

Classical Age Empires in India

such as hereditary professions, rules limiting marriages to people of the same caste, and taboos about dining companions. But by 500 B.C.E. the caste system was functioning with all its essential features. Although many theories have been advanced concerning its origins, it is generally agreed that color was a basic factor. Indeed the Sanskrit word for caste, varna, means color.

The Aryan newcomers were very conscious of the difference in complexion between themselves and the dark natives, and dubbed them Dasas, or slaves. With their strong sense of racial superiority, the Aryans strove to prevent mixture with their despised subjects. Accordingly they evolved a system of four hereditary castes. The first three comprised their own occupational classes, the priests (Brahmans), the warrior nobles (Kshatriyas), and the farmers (Vaishyas). The fourth caste (Shudras) was reserved for the Dasas, who were excluded from the religious ceremonies and social rights enjoyed by their conquerors.

This arrangement ceased to correspond to racial reality with the passage of time. Aryan tribes frequently made alliances with Dasa tribes to wage war against other Aryan tribes. Also Aryan settlers mingled with the natives, who then adopted Aryan speech and customs. In such cases the Dasas' priests became Brahmans, and their chiefs, Kshatriyas. Thus today black southern Indian Brahmans are no less aristocratic by reason of their dark skin, nor are the light-skinned, grey-eyed untouchables of some northern Indian regions any more elevated because of their pale complexion. In response to these realities, traders and some landowners were classified as Vaishyas, and cultivators and general laborers became Shudras.

A bewildering variety of castes have grown up within these four broad divisions. The castes have four basic features in common. One is characteristic employment, so that bankers and merchants often belong to the Vaishya caste. Another feature of caste is the hereditary principle, expressed in complex marriage regulations and restrictions. Caste also involves further restrictions concerning food, water, touch, and ceremonial purity. Finally, each caste has its dharma, or moral code, which stipulates such duties as maintenance of the family unit and performance of prescribed ceremonies at marriage, birth, and death.

Outside this system are the pariahs, or untouchables, comprising today about a seventh of the Indian population. They are condemned to trades or crafts regarded as unclean because their function involves some ritual defilement or the taking of human or animal life. These occupations include hunters, fishermen, butchers, executioners, gravediggers, undertakers, tanners, leather workers, sweepers, and scavengers. Involvement in these occupations has led in turn to social segregation. Untouchables live in isolated villages or in quarters outside town limits and are required to use their own temples and wells. They have to be most careful to avoid polluting members of the castes by any kind of physical contact or, in extreme cases, by even coming within their sight. For this reason, until recent decades they never moved outside their quarters or villages without striking a pair of clappers together to warn others of their approach.

The untouchables are further subjected to psychological disabilities that are as crippling and degrading as the physical. The doctrine of karma holds that one's status in present life has been determined by the deeds of previous lives.

A Brahman, of India's priestly caste, preaches to the faithful.

The untouchables therefore deserve their low position because of past sins, and their only hope for improved status in future lives is the dutiful performance of their present duties.

This combination of social and religious sanctions has enabled caste to function to the present day. Of course, with its manifold provisions for mutual aid, caste does provide security as long as one follows its rules. So it continues to serve as the steel framework of Hindu society. And although it has been attacked by reformers and undermined by the pressures of modern industrial society, caste nevertheless still operates in rural India, where three-fourths of the total population continues to live.

II. REFORMATION AND COUNTER-REFORMATION

Caste, with its basic tenets of dharma, karma, and reincarnation, is part and parcel of the Hindu religious system. Originally the Aryans had typical tribal gods personifying natural forces, such as Indra, god of thunder and war; Agni, god of fire; and Soma, god of their sacred intoxicant of the same name. Gods of this nature were appropriate for pastoralists, but as the Aryans settled down to agriculture they perforce turned to new deities. Hence the advent of the "great gods" of Hinduism—Brahma, the Creator; Vishnu, the gracious Preserver; and Shiva, the Mighty and the Destroyer. It is not accidental that these new gods, particularly Shiva, bear striking resemblance to finds in the Indus valley sites. At this time, the Aryans naturally appropriated native religious ideas and practices that had evolved through the millennia in the ancient agriculture-based civilization.

With the new gods there came also a growing concentration of power in the hands of the priestly class, or Brahmans. This also was probably derived from pre-Aryan religious tradition. The Brahmans, who in some regions were in contact with native religious leaders, presumably learned of the magical claims and practices of their counterparts in the Indus civilization. Whatever the historic prototypes in the distant past, the Brahmans effectively exploited their mastery of the Vedas, or hymns, that were recited aloud during rituals and sacrifices. These were transmitted orally through the generations and were considered so sacred that they were memorized word for word, sound for sound. As the custodians and transmitters of this precious heritage, the Brahmans were able to assert and enforce their claims as the leaders of Hindu society, superior to the Kshatriya, or secular heads.

The Brahmans enjoyed numerous prerogatives and exemptions because of the sacred nature of their functions. Donors of gifts were assured definite reward in this, as well as in subsequent, lives. A "gift of land" was rated most highly, for it "liberated from all sin." Thus the Brahmans acquired vast estates, including entire villages. Additionally they were exempt from all taxes, since they were deemed to have discharged such debts through "acts of piety." And being sacrosanct, the Brahmans could not be sentenced to death or to any type of corporal punishment. Finally, the doctrines of karma, reincarnation, and dharma provided virtually irresistible means for Brahman control of the mind. There was little chance for individuals to assert themselves when a person's station in life was the inescapable result of one's own past actions, and when hope for a better life in the future depended entirely on one's faithful observance of specific caste duties, regardless of how onerous or degrading they might be.

The Brahman pretensions and exactions were one factor in the religious reformation in India in the sixth and fifth centuries B.C.E. Another was the economic growth previously noted, which created a wealthy merchant, or Vaishya, caste that resented the special privileges enjoyed by the two upper castes. Finally there was the tension between the Brahmans and the non-Aryans who had been admitted to the Hindu fold but who resented the priestly domination. Thus the Shakya tribes in the Nepal hills from which the Buddha came are thought to have been of Mongolian stock. This combination of factors lay behind the ferment in Indian religious and intellectual circles during these centuries. The demand arose for moksha, or freedom—for something more meaningful and satisfying than prescribed rituals and rigid doctrines.

One manifestation of the unrest was a trend toward asceticism. Some of the most active minds, alienated by the society about them, concentrated on pure introspection. They developed techniques for disciplining or "yok-ing" (yoga) the senses to an inward focus, end-ing in a state of trance or ecstasy, which mystics describe as "enlightenment" and skeptics call "self-hypnotism." Out of this inward searching and speculating came many reform movements, of which the most important was Buddhism. The new religion had no place for caste or for Brahmans. It required that the scriptures be understood by all believers and not merely by a few at the top. Buddhism also banned all magic, sacrifices, and obscure writings.

Buddhism became a powerful force not only in India but also in central Asia and East and Southeast Asia. After 600 C.E., however, it lost ground within India. Eventually it existed in only a few localities in the land of its birth. One reason for the decline of Buddhism at home was

A magnificent South Indian bronze of Shiva, one of India's most important Hindu deities. The fluid, balanced image depicts the so-called "dancing Shiva" engaged in his dance of simultaneous destruction and creation of the universe, an artistic-mythical rendering of the eternal flux of all worldly existence (13th century; bronze; 33.5 x 24.8 cm).

that it failed to provide for the usual crises of life. It offered no ceremonies for birth, marriage, death, and other critical turns in the lives of the laity. By contrast the Brahmans were ready with their rites, and their survival was assured despite the attacks of the reformers. More important, the Brahmans themselves embraced reform. In their philosophical texts, the Upanishads, they set forth their own paths to moksha—to free-dom and release.

They taught that the supreme spirit perme-ating the universe was Brahman, a being capable of all knowledge and feeling. He was the univer-sal soul and the all-pervading breath; all else was illusion. The individual soul—Atman—was a spark of the supreme being. By transmigration it passed from state to state until it attained release by reabsorption into Brahman, the Soul of the universe. This identification of the individual soul and the Soul of the universe was the ulti-mate goal that holy men sought to reach by dis-cipline, meditation, and withdrawal from the world of the senses. Seekers after truth could now abandon the world and rest within the fold of Hinduism. Although Buddhism as a practic-ing faith disappeared in India, it has survived to the present because its basic tenets have been incorporated in the Hindu counter-reformation.

III. MAURYAN EMPIRE

Turning from religious movements to political developments, the outstanding political event was the emergence of India's first imperial struc-ture, the Mauryan Empire. As noted earlier in this chapter, the migration of the Aryans to the Ganges valley had shifted the center of gravity to that region, and particularly to the kingdom of Magadha. Meanwhile the northwest prov-inces had been going their own way, isolated from the rest of India because of their close ties with Persian civilization. In fact, Emperor Darius crossed the Hindu Kush mountains about 518 B.C.E. and made the western Punjab the twenti-eth province of his empire. Two centuries later, in 327 B.C.E., Alexander the Great also invaded India from the northwest. But he stayed only two years, and soon after he left, Greek rule in the Punjab ended. Despite his short stay, Alexan-der did have considerable influence on India.

One effect was the growth of the east-west trade from northwest India through Afghanistan and Iran to Asia Minor and Levant ports. The Greek colonies planted throughout the Middle East by Alexander doubtless contributed much to this trade, and the Hellenistic states that followed Alexander promoted it for two centuries.

Most important for Indian history was Alexander's role in creating a political vacuum in northwest India by overthrowing several local kingdoms and republics. Chandragupta Maurya promptly filled the void and founded the empire named after him. In 322 B.C.E., three years after Alexander's departure, Chandragupta, then an ambitious young general, unseated the Nanda dynasty of Magadha and founded his own. In the following years he extended his rule steadily northwestward until his empire extended from the Ganges to the Indus, including the deltas of both rivers. At the same time he organized a powerful army and an efficient administration to sustain his realm. Thus when Seleucus became king of the Middle East as one of the successors to Alexander and attempted to recover Alexander's Indian provinces, Chandragupta easily repelled the Greek forces.

Chandragupta's son conquered the Deccan region in the south, and his grandson, the famous Ashoka (273–232 B.C.E.), conquered Kalinga, or eastern India. Thus the Maurya Empire under Ashoka included the whole Indian peninsula except for the southern tip.

India under the Mauryas was wealthy and well governed, like the Roman Empire at its height. Numerous highways were crowded with merchants, soldiers, and royal messengers. The conquest of Kalinga on the east coast stimulated trade, and an admiralty department maintained waterways and harbors. The capital, Pataliputra, known as the "city of flowers," was famous for its parks, public buildings, and river frontage of over nine miles. Its educational institutions were crowded with students from all parts of the empire and from abroad.

All this was supported by "the king's sixth" of the harvest, which in practice was more commonly raised to a fourth, leaving the peasants with barely enough for existence. Law was severe, and order ruthlessly maintained. The army reputedly numbered 700,000 men, with 9,000 elephants and 10,000 chariots. Spies were

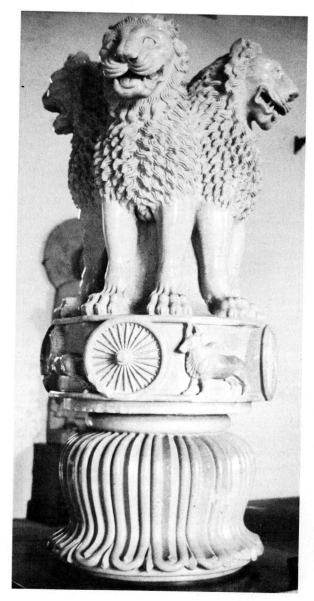

Lion capital from Ashoka column in Sarnath. This work on display in the New Delhi Museum dates from the reign of Ashoka (273–232 B.C.E.) and is one of the many monuments that this ruler of the Maurya Empire ordered erected in honor of the memory of Buddha.

efficient and numerous, sending in a stream of reports to the capital by messenger and carrier pigeon. Torture was frequently used as a means of punishment and to extort confessions. All in all, it was an efficient, harsh, bureaucratic society, based on the principle that "Government is the science of punishment."

Ashoka's reign differed radically from this traditional type of imperial rule. Having conquered the kingdom of Kalinga in a particularly bloody campaign, Ashoka underwent a spiritual experience. He himself described how over 100,000 prisoners were killed and how he felt "profound sorrow and regret." From then on, Ashoka tried to apply the gentle teachings of Buddha. He issued edicts based on Buddhist principles: simplicity, compassion, mutual tolerance, and respect for all forms of life. He ordered many public works that benefited his people rather than his government, including hospitals and medical care at state expense, orchards and resting places on highways, alms that were distributed to all sects, and Buddhist missions to several foreign countries.

Ashoka did not make Buddhism the state faith, nor did he persecute the other sects. To the contrary, he helped the worthy of whatever denomination. It was not a change of religion, then, but of general attitude. He laid most stress on tolerance and nonviolence, not only because they were morally desirable but also because they would promote harmony in his huge and diverse empire. This attitude proved successful during his reign, for Ashoka ruled with great popularity for forty-one years. But within half a century after his death his dynasty was overthrown and his empire destroyed.

This has been the pattern of Indian history to modern times. In contrast to China, where imperial unity was interspersed with short intervals of fragmentation, in India it was precisely the opposite—brief unity and prolonged fragmentation. This is not to say that India had no unity. It did, but it was cultural rather than political. And this culture emphasized loyalty to the social order rather than to the state, as we see by the fact that higher status was accorded to caste than to any political institution. Thus the culture that enhanced unity in one sphere undermined it in another.

IV. INVADERS, TRADERS, AND MISSIONARIES

With the end of the Maurya Empire early in the second century B.C.E. there followed five hundred years of confusion and obscurity. But one constant factor is clear throughout this period. That was the increasing interaction between India and the outside world, with manifold repercussions in all areas—political, economic, and cultural.

First there were the numerous invaders. Beginning with Alexander and his Greeks, there followed the Parthians, the Scythians, and the Kushans, to mention only the most important. The empires of all these peoples were based at least as much in Central Asia or the Middle East as in India. Their linking of India with foreign lands stimulated trade overland and overseas. Roman traders went to southern and western India, whereas Indian traders settled in large numbers in Southeast Asia. Just as the Greeks traded and colonized all through the Mediterranean, so did the Indians all through Southeast Asia.

In the realm of culture, Indian Buddhist missionaries during these centuries were carrying their message to all the surrounding countries. The begging priest could move among hostile or disordered peoples with safety since he was too poor to be worth robbing and also was respected as a man of religion. There was little incentive for robbing or injuring such a man, since the only return was the possibility of retribution from above. Hence there was diffusion of Buddhism and Brahmanism from India to the surrounding countries, with all the culture that went along with such transfer of religions. Nor was the culture flow exclusively one-sided. The succession of invaders from the north brought with them a variety of Greek, Persian, and central Asian influences. And by sea there came to India in the first century C.E. a new religion—Christianity. According to legend, St. Thomas arrived about 52 C.E. on the Malabar coast of southwest India, where he established a number of churches. Thence he traveled overland to the east coast. His preaching, however, was strongly opposed, and he was killed in 68 C.E. near Madras. His work in the Malabar region, however, bore fruit, for considerable Christian communities exist there to the present day.

V. GUPTA CLASSICAL AGE

In the fourth century C.E. the great Gupta Age began—a time when the invaders of the preceding centuries were assimilated and when various cultural trends reached fruition. This was the classical period of Indian civilization, comparable to the Early Empire or Augustan Age in the West. The Gupta Empire, like the Maurya, had as its base the Magadha state in the Ganges valley. This state had managed to preserve its independence following the Maurya collapse, and then, with the end of the Kushans, it began to expand once more into the resulting vacuum.

The Gupta era began with the accession of Chandragupta I, about 320, and reached its height under his grandson, Chandragupta II, who reigned from 375 to 415. He expanded his empire until it stretched from the Indus to the Bay of Bengal, and from the northern mountains to the Narbada River. The Gupta Empire was a north Indian empire and did not include the entire peninsula. Indeed south India at this time was in many ways a world apart, with the Vindhya range still an effective barrier dividing the peninsula in two. The peoples of the south spoke Dravidian or pre-Aryan languages—Tamil, Telugu, and Kanarese—in contrast to the Indo-Aryan speech of the north. On the other hand, the south had accepted the Hindu and Buddhist religions and social customs and used Sanskrit as its language of scripture and learning. Thus a single civilization bound together the diverse peoples despite their disparate ethnic and linguistic backgrounds and the existence in the south of several independent kingdoms.

The Gupta Empire enjoyed much prosperity, especially after Chandragupta II introduced standard gold and silver coins. The volume of trade reached new heights, both within the peninsula and with outside countries. The degree of security under Gupta rule is reflected in the drop of interest rates on loans for overseas trade from 240 percent during the Maurya period to 20 percent at this time. One of the chief industries was textiles—silk, muslin, calico, linen, wool, and cotton—which was produced in large quantities for both domestic and foreign markets. Other important crafts included metallurgy, pottery, carving, and the cutting and polishing of precious stones.

Judging from the reports of Chinese Buddhist pilgrims, Gupta rule was milder than that of the Maurya. Fa-hien, who spent the years 401 to 410 in India, traveling from monastery to mon-

Brahman relief dating from about 600–700 B.C.E.

astery, was impressed by the state services and by the general prosperity. Although the dynasty was Hindu, he found no discrimination against Buddhists. The countryside was peaceful and prosperous, and not overrun by police and spies as under the Maurya. Fa-hien also noted that

The people are numerous and happy; they have not to register their households, or attend to any magistrates and their rules; only those who cultivate the royal land have to pay (a portion of) the gain from it. If they want to go, they go; if they want to stay on, they stay. The king governs without decapitation or

A CHINESE VIEW OF INDIA

*Chinese Buddhist pilgrims have left valuable descriptions of India in the Classical Age. The most famous was Hsüan-tsang, who visited all parts of the country between 629 and 645 C.E., and left the following vivid picture.**

The towns and villages have inner gates; the walls are wide and high; the streets and lanes are tortuous, and the roads winding. The thoroughfares are dirty and the stalls arranged on both sides of the road with appropriate signs. Butchers, fishers, dancers, executioners, and scavengers, and so on, have their abodes without the city. In coming and going these persons are bound to keep on the left side of the road till they arrive at their homes. Their houses are surrounded by low walls, and form the suburbs. The earth being soft and muddy, the walls of the towns are mostly built of brick or tiles. The towers on the walls are constructed of wood or bamboo; the houses have balconies and belvederes, which are made of wood, with a coating of lime or mortar, and covered with tiles. The different buildings have the same form as those in China: rushes, or dry branches, or tiles, or boards are used for covering them. The walls are covered with lime and mud, mixed with cow's dung for purity. At different seasons they scatter flowers about. Such are some of their different customs. . . .

They are very particular in their personal cleanliness, and allow no remissness in this particular. All wash themselves before eating; they never use that which has been left over [from a former meal]; they do not pass the dishes. Wooden and stone

vessels, when used, must be destroyed; vessels of gold, silver, copper, or iron after each meal must be rubbed and polished. After eating they cleanse their teeth with a willow stick, and wash their hands and mouth.

Until these ablutions are finished they do not touch one another. Every time they perform the functions of nature they wash their bodies and use perfumes of sandal-wood or turmeric.

The most usual food is milk, butter, cream, soft sugar, sugar-candy, the oil of the mustard-seed, and all sorts of cakes made of corn are used as food. Fish, mutton, gazelle, and deer they eat generally fresh, sometimes salted; they are forbidden to eat the flesh of the ox, the ass, the elephant, the horse, the pig, the dog, the fox, the wolf, the lion, the monkey, and all the hairy kind. . . .

There is no lack of suitable things for household use. Although they have saucepans and stewpans, yet they do not know the steamer used for cooking rice. They have many vessels made of dried clay; they seldom use red copper vessels: they eat from one vessel, mixing all sorts of condiments together, which they take up with their fingers. They have no spoons or cups, and in short no sort of chopstick.

*Si-Yu-Ki, *Buddhist Records of the Western World*, trans. S. Beal (Kegan Paul, 1884), I. pp. 70–89. Reprinted by Paragon Reprint Corp., New York (1968).

(other) corporal punishments. Criminals are simply fined, lightly or heavily, according to the circumstances. Even in cases of repeated attempts at wicked rebellion, they only have their right hand cut off. The king's body-guards and attendants all have salaries . . . in the markets there are no butchers' shops and no dealers in intoxicating drink.[1]

In linguistics and literature, this was the period of the triumph of Sanskrit. Hitherto the learned and rather archaic language of the Brahmans, Sanskrit now staged a comeback and spread to administration and to secular literature. Poetry and prose flourished with the stimulus of lavish royal patronage. Outstanding were the works of Kalidasa, "the Indian Shakespeare," who rendered ancient legends and popular tales into both dramas and lyrics. His *Sakuntala* was translated into English in the late eighteenth century and has since been widely acclaimed and presented on foreign stages. Perhaps the greatest cultural achievement of the Gupta era was the reduction into final form of the two great national epics, the Mahabharata and the Ramayana. Dating back to many centuries before Christ, the early versions of these works have been entirely lost. Today they are known only in the form left by Gupta writers, in which they have remained the classics of Hindu literature and the repositories of Hindu tradition. Their heroes and heroines are a part of the life of the people; their mine of stories has been used by generations of writers, and their philosophical poem, the *Bhagavad Gita*, is the supreme scripture of the Hindus.

In the field of science the Gupta period was outstanding. Contact with Greeks resulted in mutually beneficial exchanges of ideas. Aryabhata, born in 476 C.E. at Pataliputra, is one of the greatest figures in the history of astronomy. He taught that the earth is a sphere, that it rotates on its own axis, that lunar eclipses are caused by the shadow of the earth falling on the moon, and that the length of the solar year is 365.3586805 days—a calculation with a remarkably slight margin of error.

The greatest achievement doubtless was the formulation of the theory of zero and the consequent evolution of the decimal system. The base could have been any number; the Hindus probably chose ten because they counted on their fingers. With this system, individual numbers were needed only for 0, 1, 2 . . . 9. By contrast, for the ancient Greeks each 8 in 888 was different. And for the Romans, 888 was DCCCLXXXVIII. The difficulty of division and multiplication with these systems is apparent. The simple Hindu numerals were carried westward by Arab merchants and scholars, and so became known as "Arabic numerals." Despite their obvious advantage they were long scorned as pagan and as too vulnerable to forgery; one stroke could turn 0 into 6 or 9. It was not until the late fifteenth century that Hindu-Arabic numerals prevailed in the West and the door was opened to modern mathematics and science. In retrospect, this Indian contribution stands out as comparable to the invention of the wheel, the lever, or the alphabet.

SUGGESTED READINGS

The most useful collections of source materials are by W. T. deBary et al., *Sources of Indian Tradition* (Columbia University, 1958) and by A. T. Embree, ed., *The Hindu Tradition: Readings in Oriental Thought* (Vintage, 1972). An invaluable reference work is J. E. Schwartzberg, ed., *A Historical Atlas of South Asia* (University of Chicago, 1978).

A well-written general history of India is by S. Wolpert, *A New History of India* (Oxford University, 1977). See also P. Spear, *India: A Modern History* (University of Michigan, 1961); R. Thapar, *A History of India* (Penguin, 1961); D. D. Kosambi, *Ancient India: A History of Its Culture and Civilization* (Pantheon, 1965); and H. Kulke and D. Rothermund, *A History of India* (Croom Helm, 1986).

Sociological interpretations of India are given by D. G. Mandelbaum, *Society in India; Continuity and Change*, 2 vols. (University of California, 1970); and by B. S. Cohen, *India, The Social Anthropology of a Civilization* (Prentice Hall, 1971). Much interesting material is to be found in J. Auboyer, *Daily Life in Ancient India from Approximately 200 B.C. to A.D. 700* (Weidenfeld & Nicolson, 1961); and in M. Edwardes, *Everyday Life in Early India* (Batsford, 1969), a beautifully illustrated analysis of life in India between 300 B.C.E. and 700 C.E. Also, see K. W. Morgan, *Asian Religions: An Introduction to the Study of Hinduism, Buddhism, Islam, Confucianism, and Taoism* (Washington, 1964).

NOTE

1. Fa-hien, *A Record of Buddhist Kingdoms*, trans. J. Legge (Clarendon, 1886), pp. 42–43.

Chinese Civilization

When the right men are available, government flourishes. When the right men are
not available, government declines.

Confucius

As compared with the looseness and dis-
continuity of Indian civilization, Chinese
civilization is characterized by cohesion
and continuity. There has been no sharp break
in China's evolution comparable to that caused
in India by the appearance of the Aryans, the
Moslems, or the British. There were, of course,
numerous nomadic invasions of China, and
even a few dynastic takeovers. But it was not the
Chinese who were forced to adopt the language
or the customs or the pastoralism of the invader.
Rather, it was the invader who invariably became Chinese, quickly and completely.

One reason for this was the greater isolation
of China, so that it was invaded only by the
nomads of the northwest. It did not have to cope
with the succession of peoples who invaded India
and who, with their relatively sophisticated cultures, were able to retain in varying degrees their
ethnic group and cultural identity. The Chinese
were all Mongoloids to begin with, as were the
nomadic invaders and the relatively primitive
tribes that they assimilated in the course of their
expansion eastward to the Pacific and southward
to Vietnam. Thus the Chinese enjoyed racial and
cultural homogeneity throughout their history.
During the classical period this homogeneity was
further cemented, as we shall see, by the standardization of the writing system, which enabled
speakers of widely differing dialects to communi-
cate with each other. In India, by contrast, there
are today fourteen "national languages," one of
which, English, serves, in Nehru's words, as "the
link" among the other thirteen.

The remarkable political unity that has persisted through the ages in China has been as

important as its cultural homogeneity. This unity results in large part from the unique secularism of Chinese civilization—the only great civilization that has at no time produced a priestly class. To be sure, the emperor was also a priest who made sacrifices to heaven on behalf of all his subjects, but his religious function was always secondary to the business of governing. Consequently, there was no place in China for the great division between religion and laity, between church and state, which existed in the other Eurasian civilizations. Nor was there any counterpart to India's epics, steeped in metaphysics and concerned with personal salvation. Rather, the Chinese classics emphasized the life of human beings in society, and particularly the relations between the members of a family and between a king and his subjects. This strong secular characteristic provided a firm underlying foundation for political organization and stability. This was further cemented during these centuries by a unique Chinese institution—a civil service recruited on the basis of public competitive examinations. It was 2,000 years before anything comparable appeared in the West, or anywhere else for that matter.

These, then, are some of the background factors that help explain the Chinese civilization and history to be analyzed in this chapter.

I. AGE OF TRANSITION

The period of the Eastern Zhou (771–256 B.C.E.) was on the surface inauspicious, with its powerless dynasty and its feudal lords constantly at war with one another. (See Chapter 3, Section V.) Yet it was also a period of basic socioeconomic change that determined the course of China's evolution decisively and permanently. The root cause for this change here, as in India, was the introduction of iron. Iron came late in China. It was not a significant factor until about 600 B.C.E. But by the fifth and fourth centuries B.C.E. it was making its mark on Chinese society and government.

The pattern of its impact was familiar. New and more efficient iron tools allowed agriculture to spread from the original Yellow River point of origin southward toward the heavily wooded Yangtze basin (corresponding to the spread in India from the Indus to the Ganges). Iron tools also facilitated extensive drainage projects in the valleys, canal building for long-distance hauling of bulky commodities, and well digging for irrigation in the dry northwest lands.

All this meant a very substantial increase in productivity, which in turn stimulated trade and industry, and ended in the use of money in much of the economy. Money had been used earlier, usually in the form of cowrie shells. Now copper coins appeared, and their use grew in all branches of the economy. A new class of free and wealthy merchants and craftmakers were most involved in the increasing use of money. No longer dependent on feudal lords as they had been in the past, they now formed a new monetary aristocracy that soon challenged the leadership of the feudal lords.

With the use of money, land became a form of property that was bought and sold. Wealthy merchants purchased large estates, and nobles sought to increase their revenues by appointing agents to collect more rent. The agents collected the increased rent directly from the peasants instead of in the traditional way, from the village headman.

This economic change was accompanied by political change—by a fundamental shift from feudal decentralization to state centralization. The economic growth and use of money provided the rulers of the various feudal states with the financial resources needed for centralization. Since the newly reclaimed lands could be administered outside feudal relationships, rents were contributed directly to the princes' exchequers. Also the princes set up more and more profitable monopolies to produce and distribute iron and salt. The result was that the princes of the feudal states were able to change fiefs they had formerly parceled out to nobles into administrative units staffed by officials of their own central government. This was a gradual development, but where it did occur, it greatly increased the resources and power of the ruler and correspondingly weakened the Zhou dynasty in the capital. Indeed a basic reason for the success of the rulers of Ch'in in conquering all China was precisely that they pioneered in these measures and reaped the profits. We will discuss this topic in Section III of this chapter.

II. PHILOSOPHERS AND CLASSICS

The disruption and reorganization just described profoundly affected Chinese thinkers. It forced them to take a new look at their traditions and to either abandon them or adapt them to the requirements of a period of transition. Thus the Eastern Zhou period was a time of great intellectual ferment and creativity, reminiscent of the achievements under comparable circumstances of the rationalist philosophers in Greece and of the Buddha and other religious reformers in India.

Because of the secular, this-worldly nature of Chinese civilization, its outstanding thinkers tended to be practical politicians who were mainly interested in winning over to their views the rulers of the various states. In the course of their travels and teachings, they attracted disciples and gradually formed various schools of philosophy. So intense was this intellectual activity that the Chinese refer to this as the period of the "Hundred Schools." Here we shall consider a few of these schools that persisted through the centuries and had an important influence on the evolution of Chinese civilization.

Although the founders of the various schools often were bold innovators, almost all of them looked for inspiration to a supposedly golden age in the distant past. A similar tendency is found in most civilizations, but consciousness and veneration of the past were exceptionally strong among the Chinese. Hence they carefully preserved and studied the writings of earlier ages and considered them indispensable for the conduct of both private and public affairs.

The most important of these ancient works were the *Five Classics*, made up of poems, popular traditions, and historical documents. The *Classics* were studied and used by philosopher-teachers, of which the most outstanding by far was Confucius. His influence has been so overwhelming and lasting that the Chinese way of life during the past 2,000 years can be summarized with one word—Confucianism. Born in 551 B.C.E. to a poor family of the lower aristocracy, Confucius (the Latinized form of K'ung-fu-tzu, or Master Kung) had to make his own way in the world. And the world he faced was harsh. There was runaway feudal anarchy, with no higher power, spiritual or temporal, to attract national loyalty. Confucius was moved by this lack to wander from court to court, seeking a ruler who would adopt his ideas for successful government. He did hold a few minor posts, but his influence in the world of practical politics was slight. So he turned to educating young men who, he hoped, might be more effective in carrying out his ideas.

Confucius at last had found himself. He proved to be a teacher of rare enthusiasm and skill. Surviving records describe him as an attractive and magnetic person—sensible, kindhearted, distressed by the folly of his age, convinced that he could restore tranquility, and blessed with a saving sense of humor. Confucius's teachings were fundamentally conservative. He did not want to tamper with the existing social order: "Let the ruler be a ruler and the subject a subject; let the father be a father and the son a son." But while insisting on the right of the rulers to rule, he was equally insistent that they should do so on the basis of sound ethical principles. Like Plato, he wanted the kings to be sages, and this they could be if they possessed the five virtues of a gentleman—integrity, righteousness, loyalty, altruism, and love, or human-heartedness.

Confucius also was a rationalist in an age of gross superstition and fear of the supernatural. People firmly believed in the prophetic significance of dreams, in the arts of divination, and in the dread power of the spirits of the dead. But Confucius, though he recognized spirits and Heaven, largely ignored them in his teachings. "Recognize," he said, "that you know what you know, and that you are ignorant of what you do not know." And again, "If you do not know about the living, how can you know about the dead?"

Confucius's teachings were far from being generally accepted, let alone applied, during his lifetime. Yet in the end they prevailed and became the official creed of the nation. One reason was his basic conservatism, his acceptance of the status quo, which naturally appealed to those at the top. Another was his emphasis on ethical principles, which he insisted were essential for the proper exercise of authority. Finally, Confucius provided a philosophy for officialdom, for the bureaucrats who became indispensable with the establishment of imperial government 250 years after his death. As a famous

TEACHINGS OF CONFUCIUS

Confucianism was above all a practical moral system concerned with the problems of everyday life. The main emphasis was on propriety and social responsibility, as evident in the following sections.*

The Individual

It is by the rules of propriety that the character is established.

The rules of propriety serve as instruments to form men's characters. They remove from a man all perversity and increase what is beautiful in his nature. They make him correct, when employed in the ordering of himself; they ensure for him free course, when employed toward others.

The Family

The superior man while his parents are alive, reverently nourishes them; and when they are dead, reverently sacrifices to them. His chief thought is how, to the end of life, not to disgrace them.

There are three degrees of filial piety. The highest is being a credit to our parents; the next is not disgracing them; and the lowest is merely being able to support them.

The services of love and reverence to parents when alive, and those of grief and sorrow for them when dead—these completely discharge the duty of living men.

Government

Good government obtains when those who are near are made happy, and those who are far are attracted.

The people are the most important elements . . . the sovereign, least important.

If the people have plenty, their prince will not be left to want alone. If the people are in want, their prince will not be able to enjoy plenty alone.

When rulers love to observe the rules of propriety, these people respond readily to the calls upon them for service.

The ruler must first himself be possessed of the qualities which he requires of the people; and must be free from the qualities which he requires the people to abjure.

Education and Arts

In providing a system of education, one trouble is to secure proper respect for the teacher; when such is assured, what he teaches will also be regarded with respect; when that is done, the people will know how to respect learning.

A scholar should constantly pursue what is virtuous and find recreation in the arts.

Music produces pleasure which human nature cannot be without.

**M. M. Dawson, *The Ethics of Confucius* (Putnam's, 1915), pp. 2–5, 167–68, 255–57.*

Confucianist reminded the founder of the Han dynasty: "You have won the empire on horseback but you cannot rule it from horseback."

In the second century B.C.E. Confucianism was declared the official dogma or faith of the empire. The *Classics* became the principal study of scholars and statesmen. Until the fall of the Manchu dynasty more than 2,000 years later, in 1911, the teachings of Confucius were unchallenged in China. Indeed they persisted even later, for Generalissimo Chiang Kai-shek urged dedication to the principles of Confucianism as the solution for the problems of the Republic. To the present day the Nationalist regime on Taiwan observes Confucius's birthday as Teachers' Day, a national holiday.

After Confucianism, the most influential Chinese philosophy was Taoism. This is understandable, for the two doctrines supplement each other neatly. Between them they satisfy both the intellectual and emotional needs of the Chinese people. Whereas Confucianism emphasized decorum, conformity, and social responsibility, Taoism stressed individual whim and fancy and conformity to the great pattern of nature. This pattern was defined as Tao (the "road" or "way"), and its disciples were known as Taoists. The key to conforming with Tao was abandonment of ambition, rejection of honors and responsibilities, and a meditative return to nature. The ideal subject had big bones, strong muscles, and an empty head, whereas the ideal ruler "keeps the people without knowledge and without desire . . . and fills their stomachs. . . . By non-action nothing is ungoverned."

Altogether different from Confucianism and Taoism were the doctrines of the Legalists. The Legalists were practicing statesmen, not philosophers, and were interested in reorganizing society to strengthen the princes they served and to enable them to wage war and unite the country by force. They viewed the nobility as useless hangovers from the past who could not be depended on by the princes, and who therefore should be replaced by state military forces. The Legalists also believed that the Chinese masses should be forced into productive work. They regarded merchants and scholars as nonessential and therefore not to be tolerated. All aspects of life were to be regulated in detail by laws designed to promote the economic and military power of the state. Rulers were to be guided not by the traditional virtues of humanity and righteousness extolled by the Confucianists but by their need for power and wealth. These Legalist doctrines were used successfully by the Ch'in rulers to conquer other princes and to establish the first empire. They then extended their regimentation ruthlessly to the entire country, but the result, as we shall see, was a reaction that led to the overthrow of the

empire a few years after the death of its founder. Legalism was discredited and Confucianism became the permanent official creed. Henceforth the Confucianists had a monopoly of social respectability and of governmental posts. And so the memory of other schools faded away, while Taoism, absorbing all sorts of popular superstitions and demon lore, became the religion of the uneducated masses and was tolerantly despised by the Confucian teachers and officials.

III. CH'IN EMPIRE

China's long history has been marked by three great revolutions that fundamentally changed its political and social structure. The first in 221 B.C.E. ended the feudal system and created a centralized empire; the second in 1911 C.E. ended the empire and established a republic; and the third in 1949 put the present Communist regime in power.

The first of these revolutions was the work of the leaders of the northwest state of Ch'in in the Wei River valley. This location contributed to the victory, for the valley is largely inaccessible and easy to defend. The Ch'in rulers were able to attack the other states to the east without fear of any enemy action in their rear. The frontier location also helped to keep the Ch'in military forces in fighting trim because of the constant wars against the barbarian nomads. In fact, the Ch'in were among the first Chinese to use iron weapons, in place of bronze, and cavalrymen in place of charioteers. Important also in the Ch'in triumph was the conquest in 318 B.C.E. of the great food-producing plain of Szechwan, which added greatly to the area and strength of Ch'in, placing it in somewhat the same relationship to the other Chinese states as Macedonia had been to the Greek cities. Finally, the Ch'in rulers were able and ambitious realists who pioneered in applying Legalist doctrines and in concentrating all power in their hands. (See map of Classical Age Empires in China, p. 134.)

With these advantages, the Ch'in leaders extended their possessions steadily, overcoming the surrounding states one by one. Contemporaries referred fearfully to the "wild beast of Ch'in" and compared its steady expansion to

The army of life-size terra-cotta soldiers found in the tomb of the first emperor of the Ch'in dynasty (246–210 B.C.E.).

that of a "silkworm devouring a mulberry leaf." By 221 B.C.E. the Ch'in ruler was master of all China, and he adopted the title of Shih Huangti, or "First Emperor." His successor would be "Second Emperor," and so on down the generations for "ten thousand years," meaning forever.

The new emperor applied to all China the Legalist doctrines that had succeeded so brilliantly in his home state. He abolished all feudal states and kingdoms. He reorganized his vast realm into administrative areas, or commanderies, each with a set of officials appointed by and responsible to the central government. Further, he disarmed all soldiers except his own, required the old aristocratic families to reside in his capital where they could be kept under watch, and planted Ch'in garrisons throughout the country. The new emperor also imposed economic centralization by standardizing weights, measures, and coinage.

In the light of future history, one of the most important innovations was the scrapping of the numerous ways of writing the Chinese characters that had been developed in the king-

doms. In their place a standardized script was substituted that was understandable from one end of China to the other. This proved to be a most effective and enduring bond of unity because of the nature of Chinese script. It is not based on a limited number of signs expressing the phonetic elements of a word. Rather, it consists of a large number of symbols or characters, each one of which denotes an object or an abstract concept. The system is precisely that used in the West for figures. All Westerners know what the symbol "5" means, even though they call it five, funf, cinque, or cinq. So it is with Chinese characters, or ideographs, which have meaning but no sound. They are ideas, like numerals, which every reader can sound according to his own dialect. Thus the new Ch'in standardized script, which has continued with modifications to the present, could be read and understood by all educated Chinese, even though they spoke dialects that often were mutually unintelligible. For the same reason, the script was equally comprehensible to foreign peoples, so that educated Japanese, Koreans, or

Classical Age Empires in China

Vietnamese can read Chinese without being able to speak a word of it. The significance of this for future Chinese national unity and for Chinese cultural influence throughout East Asia can well be imagined.

These changes made by the Ch'in dynasty hurt many vested interests and aroused passionate opposition. This was especially true of the scholars, who hated the Legalist doctrines and policies. The first emperor accordingly decided to deprive them of their intellectual props by ordering the "Burning of the Books." All the *Classics* were consigned to the flames, except those dealing with subjects of utilitarian value, such as medicine, agriculture, and divination. The plan failed, for scholars hid their books at great risk or else memorized entire texts before surrendering them. Later, after the fall of the dynasty, the greater part of the traditional literature was recovered from the hidden books and from the memories of old men. The persecution, however, effectively dampened the intellectual ferment that had characterized the Zhou period; the Golden Age of Chinese thought was over.

This intellectual loss should be balanced against the economic progress that was made through more efficient use of human and natural resources. The standardization of weights, measures, and coinage promoted economic growth. Also a network of trunk roads was built, radiating from the capital to the most distant frontiers. To make the roads as useful as possible, the emperor standardized the axle length of the two-wheeled Chinese carts—an essential measure because the wheels cut deep ruts in the sandy soil, so that every cart had to follow the existing ruts or be fitted with new axles. The emperor also used the new national unity and strength to expand the frontiers southward to present-day Vietnam. To the northwest the nomads were beaten back. To keep them out the famous Great Wall was built, running 1,400 miles from Inner Mongolia to the ocean. So great was the loss of life on this stupendous project that even today, more than 2,000 years later, people still speak of the fact that a million workers perished at this task and that every stone cost a human life. Just as the scholars cursed the emperor for the "Burning of

A section of the Great Wall of China, first built in the third century B.C.E. during the Ch'in Dynasty and later restored by the Ming Dynasty.

the Books," so the people cursed him for the building of the Great Wall.

It was this widespread resentment, together with the lack of a competent successor, that explains the popular revolt at the end of the dynasty in 207 B.C.E., only four years after the death of the first emperor. But although Ch'in rule was so short-lived, it left a deep and permanent imprint on China. The country had been transformed from a loose collection of feudal states into a centralized empire, which it remained until the twentieth century. It is only appropriate that the occidental name for China is derived from the Ch'in.

IV. HAN EMPIRE

The first emperor had abolished feudalism in one stroke, but the succeeding Han emperor, more practical and cautious, first restored feudalism a bit and then whittled it away to insignificance. At the outset, he granted fiefs to his sons and close relatives, but these holdings were all smaller than the former feudal states of the Zhou period. Furthermore, they were put under the direct rule of state officials. Then in 127 B.C.E. a decree was issued limiting the inheritance of the oldest son to one-half the fief, the remainder to be distributed among the other sons. Thus the fiefs shrank steadily in size and importance and became merely large estates. The imperial structure erected by the first emperor was gradually restored, though without the original terror and oppression. Thus the Han Empire flourished for four centuries, about the same length of time as the Roman Empire.

The Han Empire also resembled the Roman Empire in its vast size. During the first sixty years the Han rulers concentrated on national recuperation and dynastic consolidation. But under the "Martial Emperor," Wu Ti (141–87 B.C.E.), the imperial frontiers were greatly expanded in all directions. Tribal territories in the south were conquered, though several centuries of Chinese immigration and assimilation of the local peoples were necessary before this part of the empire became predominantly Chinese-speaking. The greatest expansion occurred to the west, where Chinese expeditions drove across central Asia, establishing contact with the Kushan Empire in northwest India and vastly increasing the volume of trade along the Silk Road. (See Chapter 4, Section II.)

The nomadic Hsiung-nu people had the advantage of superior cavalry forces, supported by a limitless supply of horses. In fact, the Chinese had to trade with the nomads for the horses needed by their own cavalry units. But the Chinese had a new weapon that was decisive— the crossbow, which they invented sometime late in the feudal wars. Fitted with a string drawn by a winding mechanism and released by a cocking piece, the crossbow had greater range and penetrating power than the ordinary bow. Because of this weapon and the resources of a great empire, China's frontiers during the Han period began to take on roughly modern lines.

The Han Empire was comparable to the Roman Empire in population as well as territorial extent. A census taken in the year 1 C.E., and believed to be reasonably accurate, showed the empire to have 12.2 million households with a total of 59.6 million people. By contrast the population of the Roman Empire at the time of Augustus (27 B.C.E.–14 C.E.) is estimated at 30 million to 50 million people in Europe, somewhat fewer in Asia, and not quite 20 million in Africa.

At the head of the Han realm stood the emperor, who had full political power and who was responsible for the physical well-being and prosperity of his subjects. The sanctity of the emperor's person was emphasized in his daily activities—in the long ceremonies of court or shrine over which he presided; in the prescribed robes for each occasion; in the army of officials, courtiers, eunuchs, and women who waited on him; in the elegant carriages in which he traveled; and finally in the majestic mausoleum prepared for the time when his mortal remains would be laid to rest with appropriate solemnity.

Below the emperor were two senior officials corresponding to a modern prime minister and a head of civil service. These men were in constant touch with the emperor and were responsible for the actual operation of government. Beneath them were nine ministries entrusted with the following functions: religious ceremonials, security of the palace, care of the imperial stables, punish-

A green glazed pottery model of a Later Han dynasty watchtower (87.6 x 35.6 x 38.1 cm). Note the resemblance to later Chinese Buddhist pagodas.

ment of criminals, receipt of homage and tribute from foreign leaders, maintenance of records of the imperial family, collection of state revenues, and management of the imperial exchequer.

In addition to the central government there was a provincial bureaucracy that administered, in descending order, commanderies, prefectures, districts, and wards. Officials at the grass-roots level were assigned such basic tasks as collection of tax in grain, textiles, or cash; arresting of criminals; maintenance of roads, canals, and granaries; and upkeep of the imperial post, with its horses and chain of stations.

In the first century B.C.E. this bureaucracy is said to have comprised some 130,000 officials, or only one for every 400 or 500 inhabitants. This small number in relation to the total population was typical throughout Chinese history and is to be explained by the restricted role of the imperial government. "Governing a country," according to a Chinese proverb, "is like cooking a small fish: neither should be overdone." Consequently Chinese governments did not assume responsibility for the social services taken for granted in the modern world, as is evident from the ministerial duties just listed. Rather, the main role of government was collection of revenue and defense of the country against external attack and of the dynasty against internal subversion.

The bureaucracy was a privileged, but not hereditary, elite. During the Han period, a unique system was originated for the selection of civil-service personnel by means of competitive public examinations. In 124 B.C.E. a sort of imperial university was established for students destined for government service. This was steadily expanded, so that the student body totaled 3,000 by the second half of the first century B.C.E., and 30,000 before the end of the Han era. In their later, fully developed form, the examinations were on three levels, and each led to the award of one of three degrees that roughly corresponded to those of bachelor, master, and doctor in Western universities. In principle the examinations were open to all, but such prolonged study was needed to become a candidate that only the sons of the well-to-do could qualify. On the other hand, poor boys were quite often given village, clan, or guild endowments so that they could study.

Since the examinations were based on the Confucian *Classics*, the empire in effect was run by Confucianists and according to Confucian principles. Each official was assigned to a post outside his home province to ensure that he would not use his position to build up local family power. The result was an administrative system that was far more efficient and responsive than any other until modern times. Indeed this civil service based on merit was a major factor in the continuity of the Chinese imperial system from the time of the first emperor to the twentieth century. There was another side, however, to this examination system. Since it was based on total acceptance of a single body of doctrine, it produced a rigid orthodoxy and an intellectual arrogance that was to hurt China

centuries later when Western merchants and gunboats appeared.

Although China was to suffer grievously in modern times because it lagged in science and industry, during the Han period it was a very different story. China then caught up technologically with the rest of Eurasia and, in many fields, took a lead that it was to maintain until recent centuries. Some of the more important Chinese inventions of these centuries were the water-powered mill, the shoulder collar for horses—which greatly increased their efficiency—and the techniques for casting iron, making paper, and glazing pottery. Rag paper, dating from about 100 C.E., soon replaced cumbersome wooden and bamboo slips for writing. But paper is not as durable as wood, and since it was developed by the Chinese long before printing, we must, oddly enough, blame the use of paper for the loss of certain books. Pottery glazes, however, which were eventually developed into porcelain, or china, were an undiluted blessing. They not only reached the level of true art, but they also represented a major advance in hygiene, since smooth porcelain was more sanitary than the rough pottery or wooden utensils hitherto available.

The outstanding Han contribution in literature was in the field of historical writing. This was to be expected from a people who looked to the past for guidance in dealing with the present. Their *Five Classics* already contained a good deal of assorted historical materials. But now in the first century B.C.E., a history appeared that was much more comprehensive and sophisticated than any to that date.

This was the *Shih chi*, or *Historical Records*, written by a father-son team, though authorship is commonly attributed to the son, Ssu-ma Ch'ien, who wrote the major part. As court astrologer, he had access to the imperial library and archives. He also had the advantage of extensive traveling throughout the empire, where he used the resources of local libraries. This history, he wrote, was not so much an original work as a compilation of all available historical materials. It was only when dealing with contemporary matters and personalities that he himself expressed personal judgments and wrote original history. As he explained modestly, "My narrative consists of no more than a systematization of the material that has been handed down to us. There is therefore no creation; only faithful representation."

This method had obvious disadvantages, especially the lack of dramatic quality and stylistic unity found in early historians such as Herodotus. On the other hand, it did assemble and preserve for posterity a tremendous quantity of historical material from contemporary books and archives. The *Historical Records* was in effect a universal history. It was equal to a work of approximately 1.5 million words. Its 130 chapters included chronological records and tables of the various dynasties; biographies of Han notables; and essays on varied topics such as rituals, music, astrology, astronomy, economic matters, and foreign peoples and lands. Future Chinese historians paid Ssu-ma Ch'ien the tribute of copying his method. As a result Chinese historiography has transmitted through the millennia a mass of data unequaled by that of any other country over so long a period.

All Chinese historians also shared a belief in the "Mandate of Heaven" concept. They held that a king ruled as the deputy of Heaven only as long as he possessed the virtues of justice, benevolence, and sincerity. When he no longer demonstrated these virtues and misruled his kingdom, he was automatically deprived of the Mandate of Heaven, and rebellion against him was then not a crime but a just punishment from Heaven through the medium of the rebels. Thus Chinese historians, although often aware of the social and economic factors behind dynastic decline, subordinated them to what they considered to be a more basic underlying consideration—the moral qualifications of the ruler. Chinese historiography, then, tended to be more a compilation of sources than the personal analyses of individual historians, and the organizational framework was based on the rise and fall of dynasties interpreted in accordance with the workings of the Mandate of Heaven.

V. IMPERIAL DECLINE

The traditional interpretation of Chinese history views it as a succession of dynastic cycles that repeated each other. But the cyclical facade obscures some fundamental changes. It is true,

Tomb figure of standing attendant from the Former Han dynasty, second century B.C.E.

of course, that dynasties did rise and fall. The founder of a line naturally was a man of ability, drive, and action. But his descendants, after a few generations of living in a court atmosphere, were likely to become effete and debauched.

Sometimes a strong ruler or a capable and devoted minister managed to halt the deterioration. But the overall trend was downhill, until successful revolt removed the dynasty and started the familiar cycle again.

More fundamental than the dynastic cycle, however, was what might be termed the economic-administrative cycle. This began with the security and prosperity common at the outset of every major dynasty. The restoration of peace led to population increase, greater production, correspondingly greater revenues, and full government coffers. But a combination of personal ambitions, family influences, and institutional pressures inevitably led the emperors sooner or later to overextend themselves. They squandered their human and financial resources on roads, canals, fortifications, palaces, court extravagances, and frontier wars. Thus each dynasty began to experience financial difficulties about a century after its founding.

To meet the deficits the government raised taxes. And taxes bore most heavily on the small peasant proprietors who were the backbone of Chinese society. At the beginning of each dynasty small proprietors constituted the majority of the peasantry. But as taxes increased, more and more of them lost their plots to the large landowners and became tenants. The landowners, who had political influence commensurate with their wealth, paid negligible taxes. So the more their holdings increased, the more the government revenues declined, and the more the taxes rose for the diminishing number of small peasants. Thus a vicious circle was set in motion—rising taxes, falling revenues, neglected roads and dikes, and declining productivity. Eventually this development resulted in famines, banditry, and full-scale peasant uprisings. Meanwhile frontier defenses were likely to be neglected, inviting raids across the borders by nomads. Often it was the combination of internal revolt and external invasion that brought down the tottering dynasty and cleared the way for a new beginning.

This was essentially the pattern of the Earlier Han dynasty. The "Martial Emperor," Wu Ti (141–87 B.C.E.), had won great victories and extended China's frontiers deep into central Asia. But in doing so he overstrained the imperial resources. He resorted to a variety of measures to cope with the crisis, including currency debasement; sale of ranks; and reinstitution of government monopolies on salt, iron, and liquor. Although he managed to remain solvent for the duration of his reign, his successors sank deeper into trouble as the number of taxpaying small peasants declined. Large-scale revolts broke out, and even at the court various omens were interpreted as portents from Heaven that the end of the dynasty was drawing near.

In fact the dynasty was briefly ousted (9–25 C.E.) by Wang Mang, a powerful minister who had already dominated the court for some three decades. He boldly tackled the basic economic problem by nationalizing the great private estates and distributing them among the taxpaying peasants. This and other reforms alienated the wealthy families, who opposed the usurper bitterly. At the same time a disastrous change in the lower course of the Yellow River made millions homeless and drove the uprooted peasants into banditry and rebellion. The nomads took advantage of the disorders to invade the country and sack the capital, where Wang Mang died at their hands in 23 C.E. He was succeeded on the throne by a distant cousin of the former Han emperor.

The history of the Later Han (25–222 C.E.) was basically the same as that of its predecessor. During the lengthy wars many of the old aristocrats and landowners had been wiped out. Tax returns, therefore, were adequate at the beginning of the revived dynasty. But again the taxpaying peasantry began to be squeezed out, and the downward spiral once more was under way. Great rebellions broke out, and the situation resembled that of the last days of Rome. The decimation of the small peasants had also destroyed the original peasant draft army. This was replaced by professional troops, whose first loyalty was to their generals. The generals, therefore, could ignore the central government. Great landowners also defied the government by evading taxes and enlarging their holdings by various legal and extralegal means. Helpless peasants, fleeing the barbarian invaders or government tax collectors, became the virtual serfs of these landowners in return for economic and physical security. The great families converted their manors into fortresses, virtually taking over the functions of government in their respective localities. Their estates were largely self-sufficient, so that trade declined and cities shrank correspondingly. Thus in 222 C.E. the Han dynasty disappeared from the stage of history, in a swirl of peasant revolts, warlord coups, and nomadic raids. China then entered a prolonged period of disunity and disorder similar to that in the West following the collapse of the Roman Empire.

SUGGESTED READINGS

The best general histories are by E. O. Reischauer and J. K. Fairbank, *East Asia: The Great Tradition* (Houghton Mifflin, 1978); C. O. Hucker, *China's Imperial Past: An Introduction to Chinese History and Culture* (Stanford University, 1975); and W. Rodzinsi, *The Walled Kingdom: A History of China from Antiquity to the Present* (Free Press, 1985). For more detail, see the ongoing ten-volume *Cambridge History of China* (Cambridge University, 1978).

For a collection of primary materials regarding Chinese intellectual and religious development, see W. T. de Bary et al., *Sources of Chinese Tradition* (Columbia University, 1960). Concerning the greatest figure in Chinese culture, there is H. G. Creel, *Confucius, the Man and the Myth* (John Day, 1949); and A. Waley, *The Analects of Confucius* (Allen & Unwin, 1938). For daily life in premodern China, see M. Loewe, *Everyday Life in Early Imperial China* (Putnam, 1968); and J. Gernet, *Daily Life in China on the Eve of the Mongol Invasion 1250–1276* (Stanford University, 1970). Finally, there is the delightful book by J. Spence, *Emperor of China: Self-Portrait of K'ang-hsi* (Knopf, 1974), consisting of translations from the writings of the emperor of China from 1661 onward.

End of Classical Civilizations

All in all, the invasions gave the coup de gráce to a culture which had come to a standstill after reaching its apogee and seemed doomed to wither away. We are reminded of the cruel bombings in our own day which destroyed ramshackle old buildings and so made possible the reconstruction of towns on more modern lines.

Robert Lopez

The great civilizations of Greece, Rome, India, and China dominated Eurasia in classical times. Yet in the end, the nomads and pastoralists of the frontier regions overran these civilizations and fundamentally altered the course of global history. Beneath the seeming invulnerability of the empires lay roots of decline that brought on decay and eventual disintegration. Because technology was at a standstill, productivity was low. Together these factors made the classical civilizations vulnerable to the barbarian attacks from the third to the sixth centuries.

The effect of the nomadic invasions varied from region to region. Northern China and northern India were overrun but retained their distinctive civilizations. Southern China and southern India escaped invasion because of their distance from the lands of the nomads. Byzantium and Persia proved powerful enough to repel the invaders. The West, however, suffered repeated attacks by Germans, Huns, Moslems, Magyars, and Vikings, so that the old order was uprooted to a degree unequaled anywhere else in Eurasia. Ironically, however, this destruction was a principal reason for the primacy of the West in modern times. A new civilization was able to emerge out of the ashes of the old, a civilization better adapted to the demands of a changing world. The purpose of this chapter is to analyze why the classical civilizations declined, and why the West would be the exception as it started out on a new road leading distantly to world domination.

I. DECLINE OF CLASSICAL CIVILIZATIONS

The basic reason for the decline of the classical civilizations, as just noted, was their relatively stagnant technology, which therefore kept their productivity low. John Maynard Keynes described the technological slowdown:

The absence of important technological inventions between the prehistoric age and comparatively modern times is truly remarkable. Almost everything which really matters and which the world possessed at the commencement of the modern age was already known to man at the dawn of history. . . . At some epoch before the dawn of history . . . there must have been an era of progress and invention comparable to that in which we live today. But through the greater part of recorded history there was nothing of the kind.[1]

Keynes's observation is fully justified. The Neolithic Age preceding civilization had been, in fact, remarkable for its technological progress. It was then that humankind invented the wheeled cart, the sailboat, and the plow; discovered the chemical processes involved in metallurgy; worked out an accurate solar calendar; and learned how to harness the power of animals and of the wind. After the urban revolution, this headlong advance was arrested. During the following millennia only three discoveries were made that compared in significance with those of the earlier period. These were iron, the alphabet, and coinage. All three, significantly enough, were discovered not in the old centers of civilization along the Nile and Tigris-Euphrates, but rather in peripheral and less restricting environs—the Caucasus frontier regions and the Aegean commercial cities.

Apart from these three great inventions, the advances made at this time were based on the earlier discoveries, merely refining the skill with which they were used or applying them on a much larger scale. In many cases even such modest gains were not made, even though they would have yielded rich returns. For example, the ancient harness developed for use with oxen was applied to the horse in such a way that the animal could not pull without choking. As a result at least two-thirds of the power of the horse was wasted. A sensibly functioning harness had to wait for the Middle Ages. Until then horses could pull only the lighter loads. Heavy loads were pulled by human beings. We can see this in the carvings showing thousands of workers engaged in pulling and hauling during the construction of the pyramids and the ziggurats. Another example was the water mill, which made its appearance in Asia Minor and in China in the first century B.C.E. This invention was potentially a great labor saver and could have eliminated many hours of tedious work by women and slaves in grinding corn. Yet water mills were not built in Rome until the fourth century, and even then they were comparatively rare.

Significantly enough, it was only war that could arouse the classical civilizations from their technological lethargy. The Greeks invented ingenious ratchet-equipped catapults and wheeled assault towers pulled by block and tackle. Another first was their so-called "Greek fire" (eighth century C.E.), a petroleum-based incendiary that set fire to enemy ships and siege machinery. But these innovations obviously did not produce wealth nor could they solve the basic economic problem of the old civilizations.

Since labor productivity was not increased by new inventions, wealth could be increased only by bringing new areas under cultivation or by conquest and exploitation. But virgin lands were not limitless. Instead, extensive fertile regions throughout the Mediterranean basin were now being eliminated as food sources because of large-scale erosion, which was becoming a serious problem. Likewise empires could not expand indefinitely; there were strict limits beyond which they stalled because of the level of their military technology. Thus there had to be a point of diminishing returns at which the pressure of military and bureaucratic establishments became too much for productive capacities. A vicious circle then set in, as previously noted. Two good examples on which we have more information are the falls of the Han and Roman empires. Rising taxes and increasing poverty caused uprisings in the cities and countryside, inviting nomadic incursions and ultimately leading to successful internal revolt or invasion from the outside, or a combination of the two, hence the cyclical nature of imperial history in premodern times. One historian, concluding an analysis of the decline of the Roman Empire, emphasized technological backwardness:

The Roman Empire, we must not forget, was technically more backward than the Middle Ages. In agriculture a two-field system of alternate crops and fallow was usually followed, and the potentially richest soils were little exploited. The horse collar had not been invented, so that oxen had to be employed for plowing and for carting. Water mills existed, but seem to have been relatively rare, and corn was generally ground by animals or by human labor in hand querns. Yet with this primitive technique, agriculture had to carry an ambitious superstructure far heavier than that of any medieval state. No medieval kingdom attempted, as did the Roman Empire, to support, as well as a landed aristocracy and the church, a professional standing army, and a salaried bureaucracy.[2]

In retrospect it is clear that the cycle could have been broken only by technological advances that would have provided the economic support necessary for the expensive imperial organizations. But technology was stagnant, and the basic reason was that the ruling establishments everywhere knew how to expropriate existing wealth but did not know how to create more wealth. They were capable of siphoning off astonishingly large surpluses from their peasant subjects, as evident in the stupendous amounts of capital and labor invested in pyramids, ziggurats, cathedrals, and palaces. But technological innovation required something more than efficient organization and coercion, and all the agricultural civilizations failed to achieve this something more—which was why they remained agricultural.

The widespread presence of slavery was one reason for the technological standstill. It was usually simpler and cheaper to put slaves to work than to design and construct new machines. Thus the inventors of the time usually produced gadgets intended not to save labor but to amuse or to carry on religious ritual. Hero of Alexandria in the first century C.E. used his knowledge of steam power to construct a machine that opened temple doors. Likewise, in the same century, Emperor Vespasian in Rome forbade the use of a machine that would erect

A page from an early manuscript of a codification of Roman law made by the Visigothic king Alaric II. This page shows a barbarian king, a bishop, a count, and a duke. Codifications such as this one contributed to the preservation of the principles of Roman law.

columns inexpensively, commenting, "Let me provide food for the common folk." Laudable though this sentiment might be, the fact remains that it made the cities of the classical empires parasites of the countryside rather than centers of productive industry.

Slavery also inhibited technology by fostering a negative attitude toward work. Since labor was the lot of the slaves, it came to be regarded as beneath the dignity of any free citizen. Even in civilizations where slavery was not so widespread, this attitude toward labor existed; witness the cult of the long fingernail in China. Division into sharply distinct social classes pro moted upper-class contempt for work and workers, and slavery accentuated this attitude. As Aristotle wrote in his *Politics*, "in the best-governed polis . . . the citizens may not lead either the life of craftsmen or of traders, for such a life is devoid of nobility and hostile to perfection of character." Likewise the Roman philosopher Seneca, in a letter to Lucilius in 65 C.E., expressed the same scorn for manual labor, which, he said, should be proffered with "bowed body and lowered eyes":

Some things we know to have appeared only within our own memory; the use, for example, of glass windows which let in the full brilliance of day through a transparent pane, or the substructure of our baths and the pipes let into their walls to distribute heat and preserve an equal warmth above and below. . . . Or the shorthand which catches even the quickest speech, the hand keeping pace with the tongue. All these are the inventions of the meanest slaves. Philosophy sits more loftily enthroned: she doesn't train the hand, but is instructress of the spirit. . . . No, she's not, I say, an artisan producing tools for the mere everyday necessities.[3]

It was the isolation of the philosopher from the artisan that blocked the technological growth of the Eurasian civilizations. And it was the interaction between the two—the ordered speculation of the philosopher and the practical experience and traditional lore of the artisan—that enabled the West to achieve its great scientific and industrial revolutions in modern times, and thereby make its unique contribution to human development. Such interaction was impossible in the classical civilizations because of the sharp social cleavages and the resulting social attitudes. The lofty intellectual lacked interest, and the lowly artisan lacked incentive.

Technological stagnation explains the cyclical nature of Eurasian imperial history during the premodern millennia. Empires rose and fell in a basically similar pattern. None was able to break through to a new level of development; hence the repetitive cycles that contrast sharply with the dynamism of modern industrialized societies. W. W. Rostow has described this common feature of agricultural civilizations that was pervasive in the times before Britain erupted in its epochal and pioneering industrial revolution:

The fingernails of a Chinese aristocrat, who allows them to grow in order to prove that he is not a manual worker.

. . . limitations of technology decreed a ceiling beyond which they could not penetrate. They did not lack inventiveness and innovations, some of high productivity. But they did lack a systematic understanding of their physical environment capable of making invention a more or less regular current flow, rather than a stock of ad hoc achievements inherited from the past. . . .

It followed from this productivity ceiling that food production absorbed 75 percent or more of the working force and that a high proportion of income above minimum consumption levels was spent in non-productive or low-productive outlays: religious and other monuments, wars, high living for those who controlled land rents; and for poorer folks there was beggar-thy-neighbor struggle for land or the dissipation of the occasional surplus in an expensive wedding or funeral. Social values were geared to the limited horizons which men could perceive to be open to them; and social structures tended to hierarchy. . . .[4]

II. BARBARIAN INVASIONS

The period from the third to the sixth centuries was one of Eurasia-wide invasions comparable to the bronze and iron invasions of the second millennium B.C.E. And just as the earlier invasions were responsible for the transition from the ancient to the classical civilizations, so these later invasions ended the classical civilizations and cleared the way for the medieval. (See map of Barbarian Invasions in Eurasia, Fourth and Fifth Centuries C.E., p. 146.)

The general direction of nomadic movement was from east to west because of the geographic steppe gradient—the lure that the better-watered and more fertile lands of the western steppes held for the nomads of the east. (See Chapter 4, Section IV.) The main invasion routes followed the corridor of grassland that stretched across central Eurasia, beginning near Peking and ending in the Hungarian plains of central Europe. This is why so many of these nomadic peoples ended their wanderings in present-day Hungary, which became their base for raids into the surrounding European countries.

A basic factor behind the invasions was the constantly increasing interaction between the centers of civilization and the surrounding nomads. In many of the centers, nomads were used as slaves or mercenary soldiers, a practice that was often the initial wedge either for a military coup in the imperial capital or for an invasion by fellow-tribespeople of the barbarian mercenaries. Another factor was the gradual settling down of nomadic peoples, often in regions adjacent to imperial frontiers. This shift from nomadism to agriculture normally led to population growth and to greater economic and military strength. And if imperial weakness was great enough to hold out the promise of success, the new military strength was used. Invasions also were often the end result of a series of shock waves. A defeat before the Great Wall of China or a stumbling block such as the formation of an aggressive tribal confederacy in Mongolia frequently turned the nomads westward. A series of invasions, like a train of shocks moving ever further west, ended finally in nomadic incursions across the Oxus or Danube or Rhine rivers.

Because of the Eurasia-wide scope of the invasions, a great variety of peoples were involved. Han China, Gupta India, and Sassanian Iran usually were assaulted by Turco-Mongols, often referred to as Huns. But the Roman Empire, being at the western end of the invasion route, was the object of attack, at one time or another, of all the peoples along that route, as well as of surrounding barbarians. The procession included assorted Germanic tribes, Iranians, Balto-Slavs, and Vikings, as well as the Turco-Mongols.

The outcome of the invasions varied as much as their personnel. In China, the Han Empire finally succumbed to Turco-Mongol invaders in 222 C.E. Three separate kingdoms emerged: Wei, north of the Yangtze; Wu, in the south; and Shu, in the west. After decades of warfare, Wei defeated its rivals and established in 265 a new dynasty, the Ch'in. This dynasty ruled all China until 316, when a new wave of invaders overran the entire northern half of the country. The Ch'in court fled south to Nanking, whence it ruled the Yangtze valley and those regions of the south settled by the Chinese. China remained divided in two in this manner until finally reunited by the Sui dynasty in 589. It is easy to understand why the Chinese historians called these centuries the "Age of Confusion."

We shall see later that the West Roman Empire, under similar circumstances, was completely changed in its politics, culture, and race. But north China was spared such a complete transformation, primarily because the native Chinese population greatly outnumbered the nomadic invaders. The north at that time was still by far the most populous part of the country and, therefore, was able to absorb the nomads without undergoing radical change. In fact large numbers of Chinese migrated from north to south during these troubled centuries to escape the barbarians, so that not only did the north remain Chinese but also the south became more Chinese. Consequently, the partial barbarization of the north was counterbalanced by the southward expansion of Chinese culture, providing an enormous depth to China from north to south. Thus with reunification of the entire country by the Sui dynasty in 589, China resumed its normal course, as distinctively Chinese as during the Han period.

Turning to India, the invasions there occurred much later, for the Gupta Empire was at its height when China already was beset with

Barbarian Invasions in Eurasia, Fourth and Fifth Centuries C.E.

THE HSIUNG-NU BARBARIANS

Between the third and sixth centuries C.E. the classical civilizations of Eurasia were overthrown by barbarian invaders. The following selection from the Chinese historian Pan Ku describes the Hsiung-nu nomads that overwhelmed the Han Empire.*

The Hsiung-nu live in the north and are a nomadic people. They raise a variety of animals, most of which are horses, cattle, and sheep. Other animals such as camels and donkeys are comparatively small in number. They move constantly to seek water and grass; they have no cities, houses, or crop fields. Land, however, is divided among different tribal groups.

The Hsiung-nu do not have any written language; consequently all agreements or promises are made in oral form. Small children are taught to ride sheep and shoot birds and squirrels. When they grow older, they begin to shoot foxes and rabbits. Meat, instead of grain, is their staple food. All able-bodied men are expert archers and are members of the cavalry in their respective tribes.

Under normal circumstances when life is comparatively easy, the Hsiung-nu earn their livelihood by tending their herds and augment it by hunting. When life becomes difficult, all men are taught the art of warfare, preparing ardently for the launching of attacks. This, you might say, is the nature of the Hsiung-nu. They rely on bows and arrows if the enemy is at a distance and switch to knives and spears in close combat. They attack when they are certain of victory, but are not ashamed to run away from the battlefield if they think that the odds are heavily against them. They go wherever there are profits to be realized; they do not know of such things as righteousness and propriety. . . .

From the king down, all the Hsiung-nu people eat animals' meat, wear their skins, and convert their furs into garments. The young and the strong have priority to the best food; the elderly have to be satisfied with the leftovers. They highly value youth and strength, and look down upon the old and the weak. After the death of his father, a man will marry his step-mother. Likewise he takes his brother's wife as his own when and if his brother dies. . . .

The khan [ruler] worships the rising sun early in the morning and the moon in the evening. In seating arrangement the person who sits on the left and faces the north is the most honored among the group. The dead are buried in coffins, accompanied with gold, silver, and clothing. But the graves are not marked with trees, nor do the mourners wear mourning clothes. Upon the death of a khan approximately one hundred of his favorite ministers and concubines will be put to death so that their spirits will be able to follow his.

During a military campaign the Hsiung-nu watch closely the size of the moon. They attack when the moon is large and bright and withdraw when it becomes small and dim. A Hsiung-nu soldier who kills an enemy will be awarded one goblet of wine plus whatever material goods he has taken from his victim. If he captures a man or woman alive, the latter becomes his slave. Thus on the battlefield all Hsiung-nu soldiers fight valiantly for their own material ends, upon which they converge like hungry vultures. Upon a setback, however, they disintegrate quickly and disperse like flying clouds. Their favorite strategy is to entice their enemy to a pre-arranged place and then encircle him. After a battle, the warrior who brings home the body of a dead comrade will inherit all of the latter's worldly possessions.

---

*From Dun J. Li, *The Essence of Chinese Civilization* (D. Van Nostrand, 1967), pp. 211–13. By permission of the author.

its "Age of Confusion." During the fifth century, however, the eastern branch of the Huns, or the "White Huns" as they are called, crossed the Oxus River and drove south to India, while the western branch advanced over the Russian steppes to Europe. Under the impact of the Hun onslaught the Gupta Empire disintegrated during the first half of the sixth century. Very little is known of events during the following centuries, except that the periodic invasions continued. In addition, there were migrations into India on a large enough scale to form new cultural and social groups. An outstanding example is that of the Rajputs, a sturdy and brave people who gave their name to the area known as Rajputana in northwest India. They were a military aristocracy who were soon absorbed into the Hindu caste of Kshatriyas, or warriors. They became intensely proud of their Hinduism and for some time dominated north and central India. In fact they were still prominent in the nineteenth century, and to some extent even to the present day.

The Rajput experience is significant because it helps explain why India, despite the long centuries of turmoil and invasions, was not fundamentally changed. The newcomers were assimilated into the prevailing caste system. It was much more a case of their adapting to India's civilization than the other way around. Thus India, like China, emerged from its time of troubles with the civilization it had evolved during classical times modified but not transformed.

III. GERMANS AND HUNS IN THE WEST

In Europe, however, the pattern of events was precisely the opposite; there it was transformation rather than modification. The most numerous invaders were the Germans, who occupied the central and east European lands from the Baltic to the Danube and from the Rhine to the Russian plains. Organized in tribes, the more important were the Franks, Vandals, Lombards, and Ostrogoths and Visigoths. All shared the same general religious beliefs and institutions, and all spoke closely related dialects, so that they could understand each other. Fortunately for the Romans, however, they were not united.

They were as ready to fight against each other as against their common foe, thus allowing the Roman Empire to survive as long as it did.

We must pay special attention to the institutions and customs of these Germanic peoples, for they became a basic element in the new civilization that emerged in the West after the fall of Rome. The contemporary Roman historian Tacitus described the Germans as a cattle people who rated their wealth by the number of their animals. Cattle rustling, in fact, was a major cause for strife among them. The social organization of the Germans consisted of three main elements. At the top were the nobles, whose status was usually hereditary and who were the large landholders. Most Germans were freemen who customarily owned their own plots of land. Those who did not were obliged to work for the nobles as sharecroppers. At the bottom was a class of people neither free nor slave. They were bound to the land but could not be sold apart from it. This form of bondage, similar to that of the Roman colonus, was the basis for the institution of serfdom that prevailed in western Europe in medieval times.

The main source of authority in these tribes was the assembly of freemen. It selected the king, if there was one, and also the military leader for each campaign. Tacitus noted that the Germans usually chose their kings on the basis of inheritance. But their war chiefs were selected for their valor and ability on the battlefield. The chief weapon was a long, straight, double-edged sword with a broad point, used for slashing rather than thrusting. Young men were given the right to carry a sword after solemn rites that were the origin of the later medieval ceremony by which a squire was raised to knighthood. Each outstanding warrior leader had a retinue of young followers, or comitatus, who fought beside him in battle and owed him loyalty and obedience. In return the chief provided arms and subsistence as well as a share of the war booty. This institution contributed to the later system of feudalism, which was based on the loyalty of knights to their feudal lords.

Tacitus described the Germans as great eaters, heavy drinkers, and confirmed gamblers. On the other hand he praised their high moral standards, which he held up as a model for his fellow Romans. He also stressed their hospitality as universal and unstinted. During the winter season groups would go from house to house, staying at each until the owner's supplies were exhausted. This is reminiscent of the later medieval arrangement by which a king or noble was entitled, as a part of his feudal dues, to so many days of entertainment for himself and his entourage.

The position of women in the German tribes was much more favorable than that of their sisters in the Roman Empire. Tacitus noted that they inherited and controlled property and took their place beside their husbands both in peace and in war. "Tradition says that [German] armies already wavering and giving way have been rallied by women." Tacitus also noted that German women were active in tribal affairs. "They even believe that the female sex has a certain sanctity and ability to foretell the future and they do not despise their [women's] counsels, or make light of their answers."[5] Thus German tribal women were better off than their Roman contemporaries, who were restricted to their households, and better off also than their medieval successors, who, in accord with Christian doctrine, were required to be pious and submissive.

Such were the people who began to press upon the imperial frontiers as early as the first century B.C.E. At that time the Roman legions were strong enough to hold the line with little difficulty. But with the decline of the empire the army also became weaker, and the Romans were hard pressed to keep control. They resorted to diplomacy, playing off one tribe against another. Also, since they had no choice, they allowed whole bands of German warriors to settle on the Roman side of the border in return for their aid against the tribes on the other side. This policy worked as long as the Romans were able to keep their allies in check. But by the fourth century C.E. they could no longer do so and the floodgates burst.

The onslaught was triggered by dread new invaders that the Europeans had never seen before—the Huns. Their appearance and their deliberate policy of frightfulness terrorized both the Romans and the Germans. The contemporary Roman historian Ammianus Marcellinus described them as "almost glued to their horses" and "so monstrously ugly and misshapen that you might suppose they were two legged animals. . . ."

Terracotta mounted figure from central Asia dating from the Hunnic period. This statue, from a private collection in Paris, possibly represents the Hunnic leader Attila himself.

When provoked they fight, entering battle in wedges and uttering various savage yells. As they are agile and quick they purposely scatter in an irregular line and deal terrible slaughter as they dart about. . . . None has fixed dwelling: without home or law or stable livelihood, they roam about like refugees with the wagons in which they live. . . . None of them can tell you his origin, for he was conceived in one place, born far from there, and brought up still farther away.[6]

Apparently displaced from their original pasture lands in central Asia by other nomads, the Huns headed westward and crossed the Volga in 372 C.E. There on the Russian steppes they quickly defeated the easternmost German tribe, the Ostrogoths, and then terrorized the neighboring Visigoths into seeking refuge across the Danube River on Roman territory. The Visigoths under Alaric marched to Italy and sacked Rome in 410, an event that shocked the imperial world at the time but that soon was to be repeated.

Eventually the Visigoths settled in southern Gaul and northern Spain, where they founded the first German kingdom on Roman territory. Behind the Visigoths came the Huns, who established their base on the Hungarian plains whence they raided both the eastern and western provinces of the empire. Under their feared leader, Attila, they appeared in 452 before the undefended gates of Rome, where, according to an implausible tradition, Pope Leo I persuaded the Hun chieftain to spare the capital. In any case, Attila turned northward without sacking the capital, and a year later he was found dead one morning, of a burst artery, lying beside his new bride, a German princess whom he had married the day before. His empire collapsed with his death, and the Huns disappeared from European history.

The Hunnic devastations, however, shattered Roman control over the western provinces, and German tribes now migrated across the frontiers virtually at will. The Vandals crossed the Rhine, pushed their way through Gaul and Spain, and crossed the Straits of Gibraltar to North Africa, where they established a kingdom. From their new base they turned to sea raiding, and in 455 one of their expeditions sacked Rome. Meanwhile the Burgundians were occupying the Rhone Valley; the Franks were spreading out and sinking deep roots in northern Gaul; and the Angles, Saxons, and Jutes promptly invaded England when the last Roman soldiers departed in 407. The local Celtic population fled to the mountains of Scotland and Wales, so that Anglo-Saxon stock now became the dominant ethnic strain in England. Thus it was that the West Roman Empire passed under the control of new German succession kingdoms, a passing symbolized by the deposing of the last emperor, Romulus Augustulus, by the German Odoacer, in 476.

To this point the course of events in Europe was familiar. The West Roman Empire had succumbed to the barbarians as had the Han and Gupta empires in China and India. Furthermore it appeared in the sixth century that the aftermath of imperial disintegration in the West would be the same as that in China. Just as the Sui dynasty had finally united China in 589, so Europe at about the same time seemed to be on the road to reunification by the Frankish kings and the East Roman emperors.

The Franks had originated in the lower Rhine valley, whence they had emigrated in the fifth century to northern Gaul. There they

One of the reasons the Byzantyines were able to repulse the Arab attack on Constantinople in 717–718 was a secret weapon: Greek fire, a highly flammable mixture of petroleum, sulphur, and pitch that would burn even on water. In this fourteenth-century manuscript, the Byzantine navy is spraying Greek fire from a copper tube onto an enemy vessel.

A sixth-century ivory panel depicting the Byzantine emperor Justinian as the champion of the Christian faith. From 500 to 1100, the Byzantine Empire was the center of Christian civilization.

played a modest role in the turbulent history of the times until, under the leadership of the Merovingian kings, they became the most powerful people in the West. The most outstanding of the Merovingians was Clovis (481–511), who united the Frankish tribes; defeated the Romans, Byzantines, and Visigoths; and organized a kingdom stretching from the Pyrenees across Gaul and well into Germany. A principal reason for Clovis's success was his conversion to Catholicism, which won him the support not only of the pope but also of the local Gallo-Roman population. It appeared that the Merovingians might be able to re-create the West Roman Empire, enlarged by the addition of the Frankish lands on the eastern bank of the Rhine.

This imperial ambition was shared by the rulers at Constantinople. While the West Roman Empire had been falling apart, the East Roman Empire remained intact, thanks to its naval power, its superior financial resources, and the natural strength of its capital located on the straits between Europe and Asia. Thus Constantinople survived the barbarian invasions that overwhelmed Rome, and, in fact, endured another millennium before falling to the Turks in 1453. During those centuries the empire developed a distinctive civilization, a mixture of

Greek, Roman, Christian, and Eastern elements. To emphasize this distinctiveness, the empire is commonly referred to as the Byzantine Empire, so named after the original Greek colony on the site of Constantinople.

After the western provinces had become German kingdoms, the rule of the Byzantine emperors was restricted to the eastern half of the original empire—that is, to the Balkan peninsula, Asia Minor, Syria, and Egypt. This contraction was unacceptable to Justinian the Great (527–565), who was an Illyrian by birth and a westerner at heart. He spoke and thought in Latin and was determined to recover the western lands and to restore the original Roman Empire. One of his generals, Belisarius, with a small number of heavily armed troops, conquered the Vandal kingdoms in North Africa in one year. Southeast Spain also was recovered from the Visigoths, but eighteen years of bitter fighting was needed to subdue the Ostrogoths in Italy. Thus within two decades almost all the Mediterranean had become once more a Roman lake, and Justinian expressed the hope "that God will grant us the remainder of the empire that the Romans lost through indolence."

IV. CONTINUED INVASIONS IN THE WEST

But this was not to be. The West did not follow the path of China. Instead a new wave of invasions smashed the fragile new imperial structures of the Franks and the Byzantines, and it left the West once more in confusion and disunity. Again it was turmoil in Mongolia that pushed hordes of refugees westward along the invasion route to Europe. Like their Hunnic predecessors, these Avars, as they came to be known in the West, used the Hungarian plains as a base from which they launched raids in all directions. They forced the Germanic Lombards into Italy (568), where the Lombards in turn drove out the Byzantines from most of the peninsula, thus blasting Justinian's hopes for an imperial restoration. The Avars also pushed Slavic tribes southward into the Balkan peninsula, where they occupied a broad band from the Adriatic to the Black seas.

In the eighth century hopes were rearoused for Western imperial unity by the spectacular successes of the Carolingian dynasty, which had replaced the Merovingians. The successors of Clovis were weak rulers, being known as "do-nothing kings." The kingdom was held together, however, by the strong-willed ministers who held the office of "mayor of the palace." The most outstanding of these was Charles Martel, the Hammer, who was the power behind the throne from 714 to 741. His greatest achievement was the defeat at the Battle of Tours (732) of the Moslems who had overrun North Africa and Spain and had advanced into southern France.

Martel's son, Pepin the Short, was not content to remain the minister of "do-nothing" kings and in 751 deposed the last Merovingian and established what came to be known as the Carolingian dynasty. The name is derived from Charlemagne, the son of Pepin, and the most famous of the line. During his long reign from 768 to 814, Charlemagne campaigned ceaselessly

Charlemagne: King of the Franks (768–814) and emperor of the West (800–814).

to extend his frontiers. He conquered the Saxons in northwest Germany, dispersed the Avars in Hungary, annexed the Lombard kingdom in Italy, and forced the Moslems back over the Pyrenees. By the end of the eighth century he was the undisputed master of the West, his empire extending from the North Sea to the Pyrenees and from the Atlantic Ocean to the Slavic lands in eastern Europe. In recognition of his supremacy, Pope Leo III crowned him emperor on Christmas Day in the year 800. And the assembled multitude, according to Charlemagne's secretary and biographer, shouted, "To Charles Augustus, crowned of God the great and pacific Emperor of the Romans, life and victory!"

The scene shows that the dream of imperial unity had not yet died. But it was destined to remain a dream, for soon after Charlemagne's death Europe was swamped by new waves of attacks from the south, the east, and the north. In the south, Moslem pirates and adventurers conquered the islands of Crete and Sicily and also raided all the Mediterranean coasts with devastating effect on maritime trade. In the east, still another nomadic force from central Asia, the Magyars, reached the Hungarian plains in 895 and followed the example of the preceding Huns and Avars in raiding the surrounding lands.

Most wide-ranging were the raids of the Norsemen, or Vikings. They were the equivalent on sea of the nomads on land. In place of horses they built fast ships with shallow draught that gave them unrivaled speed and mobility. The Vikings from Norway sailed westward to Iceland, Greenland, and North America. With their comrades from Denmark they raided the British Isles and the west coast of Europe and even forced their way through the Straits of Gibraltar to ravage both shores of the Mediterranean. Since Sweden faces eastward, the Vikings from that country crossed the Baltic Sea to Russian rivers and followed them to their outlets in the Caspian and Black seas.

Thus the whole of Europe was overrun by these daring raiders. At first, in the late eighth and ninth centuries, they were interested only in plunder, and they destroyed countless monasteries and towns. Few regions were safe, for the Norsemen with their shallow-draught ships were able to penetrate the rivers far into the interior. In the churches of the time was heard the prayer,

The Oseberg longship, excavated in 1904, is the best-preserved Viking ship in the world and is on display in the Viking Ship Museum in Oslo, Norway.

"From the wrath of the Northmen, O Lord, deliver us." In the tenth and eleventh centuries the Vikings began to settle in the overseas territories, thus occupying and ruling large parts of northern France and the British Isles. But wherever they settled they were eventually absorbed into the existing Christian state. The king of France, for example, in the hope of forestalling further depredations by the Vikings, recognized their leader in 911 and gave him the title of duke of what came to be known as Normandy, a name derived from the Norsemen who settled there. One of the descendants of this Duke Rollo of Normandy was William the Conqueror, who successfully invaded England in 1066.

The triple assault of Moslems, Magyars, and Vikings destroyed the Carolingian Empire. Western Europe once more was in a shambles. The

Continued Barbarian Invasions in the West, Ninth and Tenth Centuries lowest point was reached in the tenth century. At no time since the end of the Roman Empire did the present seem so wretched and the future so bleak. (See map of Continued Barbarian Invasions in the West, Ninth and Tenth Centuries, p. 154.)

V. THE GREAT WESTERN EXCEPTION

From this survey of the invasions marking the transition from the classical to the medieval eras, it is apparent that the various regions of Eurasia were affected quite differently. South China and south India were unscathed because they were geographically too remote to be reached by the invaders. Through the centuries, the Byzantine Empire, with its resourceful diplomacy and its financial and naval strength, successfully repelled a long succession of assailants—Germans, Huns, Avars, Slavs, Persians, and Arabs. Persia was equally successful under its Sassanian dynasty, which replaced the Parthian in 226 C.E. The Sassanians united the country by appealing to Persian pride, by reviving Zoroastrianism as a state religion, and by organizing a force of heavily armored cavalrymen. Thus Persia was able to repel waves of nomads along the Oxus River while fighting Byzantium to an exhausting standstill that left both empires easy prey for the oncoming Moslem Arabs.

China and India, as noted earlier, did not fare so well in their northern regions. Both were overrun by barbarians, yet both were able to preserve the distinctive civilizations that they had developed during the Classical Age. Thus the Chinese of the first-century-B.C.E. Han period would have felt quite at home had they been resurrected in the early eighth century C.E. They would have found the contemporary T'ang dynasty essentially the same as the Han, and they would have noted the same language, the same Confucianism and ancestor worship and imperial administration, and so forth.

This points up the uniqueness of the historical experience of the West. If the Romans of the first century B.C.E. had been resurrected in the Europe of 1000 or 1500 or 1800, they would have been astonished by the German peoples in many parts of the old empire and by the strange new ways of life. They would have found the Latin language replaced by several new Germanic and Romance languages; the Roman togas replaced by blouses and trousers; the ancient Roman gods cast aside for the new Christianity; the Roman imperial structure superseded by a conglomeration of new nation-states; and the old ways of earning a living rivaled by new agricultural techniques, by commerce with hitherto unknown parts of the globe, and by new crafts with strange machines that saved labor and that ran without the traditional human or animal power.

The explanation, of course, is that only in the West was a classical civilization permanently submerged and succeeded by something fundamentally new. Everywhere else in Eurasia the various regional civilizations escaped the invaders (south China and south India), repelled them (Byzantium and Persia), or endured and survived them (north China and north India). Only in the West was the classical civilization shattered beyond recall despite repeated attempts at restoration over several centuries.

Since it was precisely this uniqueness that made it possible for the West to attain worldwide supremacy in modern times, we must pay special attention to its origins. As noted in Section I of this chapter, technological stagnation was a basic structural weakness of the classical civilizations. But since this was true of all of them, why did only the west European civilization founder?

A comparison of the west European institutions and experiences with those of the rest of Eurasia leads to certain conclusions. In the first place western Europe was not as productive in classical times as, for example, China. The monsoon winds provide most of east Asia with plentiful rainfall during the summer growing months, in contrast to Europe where most of the rain comes in the sterile winter months. This, together with the greater solar heat in the lower latitudes, allows more intensive and prolonged cultivation in east Asia, including two crops per year in many localities. Furthermore, rice, the principal crop of east Asia, produces a much larger yield per acre than wheat, rye, and the other cereals grown in the West. According to one estimate, rice on a given plot of land yields caloric value that is five times as great as that of wheat on the same land. The net result was a far greater productivity in China than in the West, which led to the correspondingly denser population found in China from the beginnings of agriculture to modern times. This superiority in productivity and in population in turn made China more capable of supporting its empire's bureaucratic and military establishments and of resisting, or, if necessary, absorbing, barbarian invaders.

Another was the absence in the West of anything comparable to the Chinese writing system, which provided lasting cultural homogeneity, and to the Chinese examination system, which provided administrative efficiency and stability. Finally, the Roman Empire had to cope with more formidable enemies on its frontiers. Being located on the western receiving end of the steppe invasion route, Europe bore the brunt of attacks by virtually all the nomadic peoples. Furthermore, the Roman Empire's Germanic neighbors were more numerous than the nomads on China's northwestern frontier. Also the neighboring Persians and Arabs were more advanced, and a more serious and lasting military threat, than were China's nomadic neighbors. For all these reasons the invasions in the West dragged on centuries longer than in the rest of Eurasia. Hence the unique denouement in the West—the absolute and final dissolution of the Roman imperial structure and of its classical civilization.

This outcome is of such significance that it can fairly be described as a major turning point in world history. It was so fateful because the wholesale destruction cleared the way for innovation that was long overdue. One historian has presented the following conclusion concerning the end of the Roman Empire:

> All in all, the invasions gave the coup de gráce to a culture which had come to a standstill after reaching its apogee and seemed doomed to wither away. We are reminded of the cruel bombings in our own day which destroyed ramshackle old buildings and so made possible the reconstruction of towns on more modern lines.[7]

But this "culture" was no different from all the others of Eurasia that were also at a "standstill." Those others, however, managed to survive the invasions and to gain a new lease on life. But it was the old life that was prolonged, whereas the West, with the death of the Roman Empire, was able to start a new life—to make a new beginning.

The significance of this new beginning becomes clear if it is recalled that during the ancient period the Middle East had been the center of initiative from which had diffused the fundamental innovations of those millennia. But during the classical period it was Europe, India, and China that generated most of the innovations, while the Middle East lagged

This late-Roman ivory plaque shows a scene from Christ's Passion. The art of the late empire was transitional between the classical past and the medieval future.

behind. And the reason was precisely that the ancient civilization of the Middle East had survived the invasions of the second millennium B.C.E., whereas the ancient civilizations of the peripheral regions had gone under, leaving the way clear for a fresh start—for the emergence of the new classical civilizations.

So it was during the transition from the classical to the medieval civilizations. But this time the existing classical civilizations survived everywhere except in the West. For this reason the West alone was free to strike out in new directions and to evolve, during the Medieval Age, a new technology, new institutions, and new ideas—in short, a new civilization. And in modern times this new civilization proved its superiority over the "standstill" civilizations of the rest of Eurasia—indeed of the entire world—as inevitably and completely as the agricultural civilizations had triumphed over tribal cultures at an earlier time.

SUGGESTED READINGS

The problem of the rise and fall of empires is considered in the following collection of readings: S. W. Eisentadt, ed., *The Decline of Empires* (Prentice Hall, 1967); and C. M. Cipolla, ed., *The Economic Decline of Empires* (Methuen, 1979). Various viewpoints regarding the decline of Rome are presented by P. Brown, *The World of Late Antiquity* (Harcourt, 1971); S. Magzarino, *The End of the Ancient World* (Faber and Faber, 1966); and F. W. Walbank, *The Awful Revolution* (University of Liverpool, 1969).

The invaders of the Roman Empire are considered by R. MacMullen, *Enemies of the Roman Order*

(Oxford University, 1967); E. A. Thompson, *A History of Attila and the Huns* (Clarendon, 1948); O. J. Maenchen-Helfen, *The World of the Huns* (University of California, 1973); T. S. Burns, *A History of the Ostrogoths* (Indiana University, 1984); and G. Jones, *A History of the Vikings* (Oxford University, 1968). The developments following the invasions are analyzed in J. D. Randers-Pherson, *Barbarians and Romans: The Birth and Struggle of Europe, A.D. 400–700* (University of Oklahoma, 1983); in W. C. Bark, *Origins of the Medieval World* (Stanford University, 1958), which stresses the creativity of the early Middle Ages in the West; and in R. S. Hoyt, ed., *Life and Thought in Early Middle Ages* (University of Minnesota, 1967), which also interprets this period as one of transition and transformation. This thesis has been presented more recently by M. Grant, *Dawn of the Middle Ages* (McGraw-Hill, 1981).

NOTES

1. J. M. Keynes, *Essays in Persuasion* (Harcourt, 1932), pp. 360–361.
2. A. H. M. Jones, "The Decline and Fall of the Roman Empire," *History*, XL (October 1955), p. 220.
3. Cited by F. Klemm, *A History of Western Technology* (Allen & Unwin, 1959), p. 23.
4. W. W. Rostow, *The Process of Economic Growth*, 2nd ed. (Norton, 1962), pp. 311–312.
5. Cited by S. H. Gross and M. W. Bingham, *Women in Medieval-Renaissance Europe* (Glenhurst, 1983), p. 11.
6. Cited by M. Hadas, *A History of Rome* (Doubleday, 1956), pp. 204–205.
7. R. Lopez, *The Birth of Europe* (M. Evans, 1967), p. 58.

What It Means for Us Today

CIVILIZATION: CURSE OR BLESSING?

In all civilizations there have been poets and thinkers who have looked to the past with longing. They have regarded the prehistoric human as the "noble savage," untainted by the corrupting influence of civilization. Long ago, "in the beginning," during that wonderful first chapter of human existence, there was paradise on earth. In the Hindu epics there are passages extolling an idyllic past in which castes were absent and humans could enjoy life in freedom and security. Likewise Hesiod, an eighth-century-B.C.E. Greek poet, described a Golden Age of long ago and then traced humanity's declining fortunes through the Silver and Iron ages to the deplorable present in which the author lived.

This concept of original bliss had some basis in historical fact. As far as economic and social relationships were concerned, the tribal peoples before the advent of civilization had enjoyed free and equal access to the natural resources necessary for livelihood. Economic equality and social homogeneity had been the hallmark of their Neolithic villages. But when the tribal peoples became peasants they no longer had free access to land and they no longer enjoyed the full product of their labor. Their specific obligations varied from region to region, but the result everywhere was the same. After making the payments required by the state, the church, the landlord, and the money-lender, the peasants were left with half or less of what they produced. They were left with only enough for sheer existence. Historians estimate that in the civilizations around the world, the ruling elites comprised only 1 to 2 percent of the total population. Yet everywhere they extorted half to two-thirds of the entire national income. This fact explains why a peasant uprising occurred almost every year during the millennia of China's history, and why tsarist Russia was wracked by 1,467 revolts between 1801 and 1861, when the serfs at last were emancipated.

The coming of civilization brought drastic change in political as well as economic relationships. The Neolithic villagers had been subject to only a few controls, whether internal or external. But tribal chiefs and elders now were replaced by a king or emperor and by an ever-present bureaucracy, including palace functionaries, provincial and district officials, judges, clerks, and accountants. Working closely with this imperial administration was the ecclesiastical hierarchy that was also an essential feature of civilization. In place of the former shaman, who had been a "leisure-time specialist," there was the priest, a "full-time specialist." Now it was possible to develop an official theology and a priestly hierarchy. Both the theology and the hierarchy served to buttress the existing social order. They gave political institutions and leaders divine sanction and attributes. For example, the Egyptian pharaoh was not only the ruler of his country but also the "living god." This coupling of divine and secular authority provided most powerful support for the status quo. It was a rare individual who dared risk both swift punishment in this life and everlasting punishment in the afterlife.

The transformation of culture wrought by civilization was fundamental and enduring. The culture of a Neolithic village had been autonomous and homogeneous. All members had shared common knowledge, customs, and attitudes and had not depended on outside sources for the maintenance of their way of life. But with civilization, a new and more complex society emerged. In addition to the traditional culture of village agricultural people, there was now the new culture of the scribes, who knew the mysterious art of writing; of the priests, who knew the secrets of the heavens; of the artists, who knew how to paint and carve; and of the merchants, who exchanged goods with lands beyond deserts and seas. So there was no longer a single culture. Instead there developed what has been called high culture and low culture. The high culture was to be found in the schools, temples, and palaces of the cities; the low culture was in the villages. The high culture was passed on in writing by philosophers, theologians, and literary people; the low culture was passed on by word of mouth among illiterate peasants.

The high and low cultures of the various civilizations differed in details but were all similar in essentials. They were all based on "sacred books," such as the Indian Vedas, the Buddhist Canon, the Chinese Classics, and the Christian Old and New Testaments. Since these texts were the basis of knowledge, they dominated education. Anyone who wished to get ahead had to memorize large portions of them. The sacred books also were used to enforce loyalty and obedience. Repudiation of official teachings or challenge to the social order were branded as crimes punishable in this world and in the next. The "hells" that were so prominent in all high cultures were eternal concentration camps for those who dared resist their secular or religious leaders.

The low cultures of all civilizations also were essentially the same. Peasants everywhere had a considerable body of factual information concerning the care of animals and plants. They all regarded hard work as a virtue and looked down on town people as weaklings who tired easily. All peasants also had a common passion to own a plot of land, a few animals, and the simple tools of field and shop. These meant independence and security, and to attain them all peasantries stubbornly resisted, and still resist, intervention, whether by a landlord or by today's government-run collective. The "rugged individualism" of the peasant was balanced, however, by the communal life and relationships of the village. The good neighbor was always ready to offer aid and sympathy when needed, as well as to participate in house-raisings, housewarmings, harvest festivals, and other community affairs.

Relations between the high and low cultures usually were strained. On the one hand, the peasants felt superior, regarding country life and agricultural work as morally "good," in contrast to urban life and professions. On the other hand, the peasants were economically and politically subject to the city. The landlords, the tax collectors, the church officials, and the soldiers all came from the city. Their arrogance and arbitrariness made it crystal clear who were the rulers and who the ruled. Whereas the elite viewed their rich life as the product of their own superior mental and moral qualities, their good life was actually made possible by the exploitation of the peasantry. Inevitably, in the course of millennia, the peasants internalized the attitudes of the elite toward them and became servile and obsequious.

It is clear that the coming of civilization was a setback for equality among human beings. Yet civilization also brought great gains and achievements. Viewed in the light of historical perspective, it was a major step forward despite all the injustice and exploitation. In this respect it resembled the industrial revolution, which at first caused painful social disruption and human suffering, but which in the long run decisively advanced human productivity and well-being. So it was with the coming of civilization. The average Neolithic tribal member probably led a more rounded and satisfying life than the average peasant or urban worker. But precisely because tribal culture was comfortable and tension-free, it was also relatively unproductive. The demands of the tax collector, the priest, and the landowner were harsh, but they were also effective in stimulating output. Positive proof of this enhanced productivity can be seen in the enormous population increase in the agrarian river valleys. Living standards also rose along with population figures. Certainly the monarchs and the top officials, both secular and ecclesiastical, enjoyed a variety of food and drink, along with richness in clothing and housing, that no tribal chieftain could ever have imagined. The new middle classes—merchants, scribes, lower officials, and clergy—also were able to lead lives that probably were as pleasant and refined as those enjoyed by their counterparts today. Even the masses may in some cases have been better off in the material sense, if not the psychosocial.

Civilization, with the new art of writing, made it possible to accumulate more and more knowledge and transmit it to successive generations. Various sciences, including mathematics, astronomy, and medicine, were able to take root and to flourish. Also the appearance of wealthy upper classes gave opportunities for the creativity of architects, sculptors, painters, musicians, and poets. The results of this creativity we can see today in masterpieces such as the Parthenon, the Taj Mahal, and Notre Dame Cathedral.

These precious gains benefited the few much more than the many, who in the final analysis bore the costs of the high culture. But the important point insofar as the whole history of humanity is concerned is that the advances were made. And it was these advances, accumulating through the millennia, that finally allowed us to gain such mastery over nature and to attain such productivity through science and technology which today benefit the many along with the few.

It is true that many millions of people are still illiterate, diseased, and hungry. But that condition is very different from the mid-fourteenth century, when a third to a half of Europe's total population was wiped out by the Black Death. It is different also from 1846, when a million Irish died of hunger because of the potato blight, and from 1876, when 5 million Indians starved to death when their crops failed. These victims of plague and famine could not possibly have been saved because the people of those times lacked the necessary knowledge.

Today we have that knowledge, and therefore we have the potential to free ourselves from millennia-old scourges. It is tragic that the potential has not yet been realized, but the fact remains that it does exist. And it exists because of the advances made possible in the past by the different civilizations of the human race. Therefore, to answer the question, has civilization been a curse or a blessing?—in the past it has been both. What it will be in the future depends on whether the knowledge accumulated from past civilizations is used for destructive or constructive purposes.

SUGGESTED READINGS

Archeologists and anthropologists have written thought-provoking books on the relative merits of civilization: Chang Kwang-Chih, *Early Chinese Civilization: Anthropological Perspectives* (Harvard University, 1972); V. Gordon Childe, *Man Makes Himself* (Mentor, 1951); R. Redfield, *Peasant Society and Culture: An Anthropological View to Civilization* (University of Chicago, 1956); L. A. White, *The Evolution of Culture; The Development of Civilization to the Fall of Rome* (McGraw-Hill, 1959); and W. Goldschmidt, *Man's Way* (Holt, 1959). Also noteworthy are the views of the distinguished philosopher K. Jaspers in his *The Origin and Goal of History* (Yale University, 1953), and *Man in the Modern Age* (Doubleday Anchor, 1957). Other viewpoints are presented by W. W. Wagar, *Building the City of Man* (Grossman, 1971); and H. Baudet, *Paradise on Earth: Some Thoughts on European Images of Non-European Man* (Yale University, 1965).

PART III

Medieval Civilizations of Eurasia, 500–1500

Like the Classical Age, the Medieval Age was heralded by invasions—by the Dorians, Aryans, and Zhou in the first case, and by the Germans, Huns, and Turks in the second. There the parallel ends, however, for the medieval centuries, unlike the classical, suffered continued invasions that affected virtually all regions of Eurasia. Beginning in the seventh century there were the invasions of the Islamic warriors, who overran not only the entire Middle East, where they originated, but eventually North Africa, Spain, the Balkans, India, Southeast Asia, and much of central Asia. Even more extensive were the conquests of the Turks and the Mongols during the half-millennium between 1000 and 1500. They encompassed the great bulk of the Eurasian landmass from the Baltic Sea to the Pacific Ocean.

Despite their fury and range, these great conquests did not uproot civilization in most of Eurasia as did the earlier incursions of the Dorians, Aryans, and Zhou. By medieval times most civilizations had sunk roots too deep to be pulled up so easily. Thus the traditional civilizations everywhere survived. In China, for example, the native Ming dynasty replaced the Mongol Yüan, and the country returned with a vengeance to age-old ways. In the sprawling Moslem world the indigenous Greco-Roman, Iranian, Semitic, and Egyptian traditions were not wiped out but rather were fused into the civilization of Islam. Likewise the East Roman Empire continued without interruption for a full millennium as the Byzantine Empire, so that its inhabitants referred to themselves in modern times as "Romaioi," or Romans.

The one exception to this general pattern, as noted in the preceding chapter, was in the West. There, and there alone, the prevailing classical civilization was torn up root and branch. Only in the West, therefore, was the ground sufficiently cleared for a new civilization to emerge. In contrast to the traditional civilizations of the rest of Eurasia, the new civilization was free to develop along fresh lines.

It was this unique feature of the West that enabled it to develop the economic vigor, the technological skills, and the social dynamism to expand overseas and to gain control of the sea routes of the world. With this fateful development the Medieval Age came to an end. But it should be noted that it ended not with land invasions by Eurasian nomads, as did the ancient and classical periods, but rather with the maritime enterprise of the West. The overseas activities of Western explorers, merchants, missionaries, and settlers marked the transition from medieval to modern times, and from the Eurasian to the global phase of world history.

Medieval Civilizations Complete Eurasian Unification

> What has emerged is a sense of the remarkable complexity of the interplay between the Occident and East Asia from Roman and Han times onward. This involved a two-way traffic, in many items, along many routes, and of varying density in different periods. . . . Despite difficult communication, mankind in the Old World at least has long lived in a more unified realm of discourse than we have been prepared to admit.
>
> *Lynn White, Jr.*

Just as an emerging Eurasian unity differentiated the Classical Age from the Ancient Age, so now a full-fledged Eurasian unity differentiated the Medieval Age from the Classical Age. The early stage had been attained as a result of improved technology, particularly the large-scale production of iron, with its manifold repercussions in all aspects of life. (See Chapter 4.) Likewise full unity was now made possible by further technological advances, especially in shipbuilding and navigation. But more significant during these centuries was a political consideration—the existence for the first time of tremendous empires. These empires did not comprise merely river valleys as in the Ancient Age, nor did they encompass merely regions as

in the Classical Age. Now they reached across several regions at once to embrace a large proportion of the entire Eurasian landmass.

As we have seen, the great Alexander knew nothing of the Ganges valley or of China. And virtually no direct relations existed between the later Roman and Han empires at the opposite ends of Eurasia. Alexander's empire was primarily confined to the Middle East, and the Roman and Han empires were for all practical purposes restricted to the western and eastern tips of Eurasia. In striking contrast, during the medieval period the Islamic Empire by the mid-eighth century stretched from the Pyrenees to the Indian Ocean, and from Morocco to the borders of China. In later centuries Islam expanded much further into central Asia, Southeast Asia, and Africa's interior. Even more impressive was the thirteenth-century Mongol Empire that included Korea, China, all of central Asia, Russia, and most of the Middle East—the greatest empire of all time.

Empires of such unprecedented size eliminated the age-old regional isolation. Direct contact and interaction among the various parts of the landmass were now possible. This chapter will consider the nature of the resulting new bonds—commercial, technological, religious, and intellectual.

I. COMMERCIAL BONDS

In classical times, the existence of the large Roman and Han empires at the opposite ends of the Eurasian trade routes stimulated commerce at all points between them. Conversely, the disintegration of these empires undermined and reduced this commerce. It revived, however, and reached new heights during medieval times with the appearance of the Islamic and later the Mongol empires.

The Moslem conquests unified the entire Middle East, through which ran all the trans-Eurasian trade routes—both the land routes that terminated at various Black Sea and Syrian ports, and the sea routes that ran through the Red Sea and the Persian Gulf. Particularly flourishing was the trade across the Arabian Sea with the Malabar coast of southwest India. Sizable settlements of Moslem merchants, mostly Arabs and Persians, grew up in the ports of India and Ceylon. Horses; silver; wrought-iron objects; and linen, cotton, and woolen fabrics were shipped from west to east, where they were exchanged for silks, precious stones, teak, and assorted spices.

Moslem merchants went on from India and Ceylon to Kalah Bar (Kedah) on the Malay coast. From there, some sailed on to Sumatra and Java, and others went through the Malacca Straits and then north to Kanfu (Canton) in south China. The customary schedule was to leave the Persian Gulf in September or October, sail with the northeast monsoon to India and Malaya, and arrive in the China Sea in time for the southern monsoon to Canton. There the Moslem merchants spent the summer, and then they returned with the northeast monsoon to the Malacca Straits and across the Bay of Bengal, arriving back in the Persian Gulf in the early summer—making a round trip of a year and a half.

After the first Moslem reached Canton in 671, considerable numbers settled there as they had in the various Indian Ocean ports. Granted autonomy by the local authorities, they selected their own headman, who was responsible for maintaining order in their section of the city. The descendants of some of these Moslem families later entered the Chinese civil service, as Marco Polo was also to do. By 758 the Moslems were numerous enough to attack Canton, and as a result the Chinese closed the port to foreign trade. Reopened in 792, Canton continued to be a center for Moslem traders until 878, when they were massacred by rebellious Chinese bands. Thereafter Moslem and Chinese merchants met at Kalah Bar in Malaya to exchange their commodities.

With the advent of the Sung dynasty (960–1127), the Chinese ports again were reopened to foreigners. During the Sung period the Chinese made considerable progress in ship-building and navigation. By the end of the twelfth century they were replacing the Moslems in the waters of east and Southeast Asia. When the Mongols conquered China and founded the Yüan dynasty (1279–1368), Chinese ships were the largest and best-equipped, and Chinese merchants were settling in various ports in Southeast Asia and India. Marco Polo, who in 1291 accompanied a Mongol princess around Southeast Asia to Iran, witnessed and described the vigor of Chinese maritime enterprise. So did the Arab traveler Ibn Battuta, who fifty years later chose to make his way from India to China on a Chinese junk. Noteworthy also is the nature of China's imports and exports, which reflected its leading position in the world's economy during this period. Apart from fine cotton textiles, the imports were raw materials such as hides and horses from central Asia, and fine woods, gems, spices, and ivory from south Asia. Conversely, Chinese exports, apart from some minerals, were manufactured goods such as books, paintings, and especially porcelains and silks.

During the Ming dynasty (1368–1644), Chinese maritime activity reached its height,

Seventeeth-century leather wall hanging of bustling seaports during the Sung dynasty.

ending in a remarkable but short-lived naval domination of the Pacific and Indian oceans in the early fifteenth century. For example, a series of seven expeditions was sent out between 1405 and 1433 under the superintendency of the chief court eunuch, a certain Cheng Ho. These expeditions were unprecedented in their magnitude and in their achievements. The first, made up of sixty-two ships and 28,000 men, sailed as far as Java, Ceylon, and Calicut. On the return a flotilla of Sumatran pirates tried to block the way, but they were completely annihilated. The later expeditions pressed on further, reaching as far as the east coast of Africa and the entrances to the Persian Gulf and the Red Sea. More than thirty ports in the Indian Ocean were visited by the Chinese, and everywhere they persuaded or compelled the local rulers to recognize the suzerainty of the Ming emperor. And all this at a time when the Portuguese were just beginning to feel their way down the coast of Africa, where they did not reach Cape Verde until 1455! (See map of Early Fifteenth-Century Chinese and Portuguese Voyages, p. 168.)

These extraordinary Chinese expeditions were suddenly halted by imperial order in 1433. The reasons for their beginning as well as for their ending remain a mystery. It is believed that the expeditions may have been launched to compensate for the loss of foreign trade over the land routes when the Mongol Empire disintegrated. Or they may have been sent to enhance the prestige of the imperial court or to find the emperor's predecessor, who had disappeared underground as a Buddhist monk. Some think that the expeditions may have been halted because of their excessive cost or because of the traditional rivalry between court eunuchs and

Early Fifteenth-Century Chinese and Portuguese Voyages

Confucian bureaucrats. In any case, the withdrawal of the Chinese left a power vacuum in the waters of east and south Asia. Japanese pirates harried the coasts of China, and in the Indian Ocean the Moslem Arabs regained their former primacy. But adept though they were as merchants, the Arabs lacked the unity and the resources to develop naval power as had the Chinese. Thus when the Portuguese sailed around Africa into the Indian Ocean in 1498, they encountered no effective resistance and proceeded to establish their domination.

Meanwhile a great revolution in land trade had occurred with the rise of the Mongol Empire. For the first and only time in history one political authority extended across the breadth of Eurasia—from the Baltic Sea to the Pacific, and from Siberia to the Persian Gulf. A mid-fourteenth-century Italian handbook summarized the commercial significance of this Pax Mongolica in describing a trade route running across central Asia from its beginning point at Tana at the mouth of the Don River:

The road you travel from Tana to Cathay [China] is perfectly safe, whether by day or by night, according to what the merchants say who have used it. . . . You may reckon that from Tana to Sarai [on the Volga] the road is less safe than on any other part of the journey; and yet even when this part of the road is at its worst, if you are some sixty men in the company you will go as safely as if you were in your own house.[1]

When Kublai Khan in 1264 moved his capital from Karakorum in Mongolia to Peking, China was automatically opened to the European merchants trading along the trans-Eurasian routes. The first Europeans to arrive at Kublai's new court were not diplomatic emissaries but two Venetian merchants, Nicolo and Maffeo Polo. Of greater economic importance than access to China was access for the first time to the source of spices in India and the East Indies. Hitherto spices had reached Europe via two routes: through the Red Sea and Egypt, or to the Persian Gulf and then by caravan routes to ports on the Black Sea or the eastern Mediterranean. The first route was controlled by Arabs, who shipped the spices to Egypt, and by the Venetians, who loaded cargoes at Alexandria for distribution in Europe. The second route was dominated by the Mongol ruler (Ilkhanate) of Persia and Mesopotamia, and by the Genoese who awaited the spices at the port terminals.

The Genoese, however, were not content to sail only the Black Sea. They ascended the Don River from the Azov Sea in small, light vessels, which they transported, probably on ox-wagons, across the narrow neck of land to the Volga and thence to the Caspian Sea and to Persia. Thus the Genoese were able to reach the Persian Gulf and to go directly to India and the East Indies, where they discovered how cheap the spices were in their places of origin and what fabulous profits had been made during the past centuries by the

Marco Polo in the court of Kublai Khan.

succession of middlemen between the producers in Southeast Asia and the consumers in Europe.

This revival of overland trade during the Pax Mongolica proved short-lived. One reason was the expulsion of the Mongols from China in 1368 and the general disintegration of the Mongol Empire, which led to fragmentation in central Asia and hence to the disruption of trans-Eurasian trade. More important was the conversion of Ilkhan Ghazan (1295–1304) to Islam, which automatically barred to European merchants the transit route to the spice islands. Almost all spices henceforth were shipped along the Red Sea–Nile route, with golden profits for the Arab and Venetian middlemen. But other Europeans were unwilling to continue paying exorbitant prices, particularly since they now knew from where the spices came and at what cost; hence the search for a new sea route around the Moslem barrier—a search that was to end with da Gama's great voyage around Africa.

II. TECHNOLOGICAL BONDS

The great Moslem and Mongol empires quickened not only the flow of trade within Eurasia but also the diffusion of technology. An outstanding example is the lateen sail, a tall, triangular, fore-and-aft sail that has always been used on Arab craft. In the Mediterranean, by contrast, the Egyptians, Phoenicians, Greeks, and Romans had used a square sail, which is easier to handle in bad weather. But the Arab sail is much more maneuverable, being able to keep closer to the wind and to tack on rivers and narrow waters. For this reason it soon replaced the square sail in the Levant, and by the eleventh century it had become the normal rig throughout the Mediterranean. Today this triangular sail is known as the "Latin," or "lateen," sail, though it was the Arabs who, with the Moslem invasions, introduced it into the Mediterranean. And from there it spread to the Atlantic, where, during the fifteenth century, Portuguese and Spanish ship designers combined the square sail on the foremast with the lateen on the main and mizzen. The resulting hybrid three-masters were capable of sailing in all reasonable weathers and thus made possible the long ocean voyages of Columbus and da Gama.

The English philosopher Francis Bacon wrote in 1620:

It is well to observe the force and virtue and consequences of discoveries. These are to be seen nowhere more conspicuously than in those three which were unknown to the ancients, and of which the origin, though recent, is obscure and inglorious; namely, printing, gunpowder, and the magnet. For these three have changed the whole face and state of things throughout the world, the first in literature, the second in warfare, the third in navigation; whence have followed innumerable changes; insomuch that no empire, no sect, no star, seems to have exerted greater power and influence in human affairs than these mechanical discoveries.[2]

All three of these inventions, whose historical significance Bacon correctly noted, were of Chinese origin. The oldest existing example of block printing—printing in which a single block of wood is engraved for each page printed—is a Chinese Buddhist sacred text from the year 868. The first invention of separate movable type also is Chinese, the work of a simple artisan who between 1041 and 1049 made movable type of baked clay. In later centuries the Chinese substituted wood and various metals for the clay. The diffusion of these inventions has been traced from China to the Middle East and thence to Europe, where the first example of block printing dates back to 1423, followed in 1456 by the first book printed with movable type—Gutenberg's Bible.

Gunpowder was used in China for fireworks as early as the T'ang dynasty (618–906). By 1120 the Chinese had evolved a weapon known as the "firelance" comprising a stout bamboo tube filled with gunpowder. This was almost certainly the precursor of the metal-barrel gun, which appeared about 1280, though it is not known whether it was first constructed by Chinese or Arabs or Europeans.

The earliest definite reference to magnetism is found in a Chinese book of about 240 B.C.E., but for centuries thereafter the compass was used only for magical purposes. By 1125, however, it was used in navigation, and apparently the Arab merchants who came to China learned of this instrument and introduced it into Europe.

In addition to these three basic inventions, the Chinese gave much more to their Eurasian neighbors. In 105 C.E. they invented paper, the prerequisite for printing. Chinese prisoners of war who were taken to Samarkand in 751 introduced the paper-making process to the Arabs, who in turn spread it to Syria, Egypt, Morocco, and, in 1150, to Spain. From there it passed on to France and the rest of Europe, displacing parchment as it went. Its value is evident in the fact that to produce one copy of the Bible on parchment, the skins of no fewer than three hundred sheep would be required.

Other Chinese inventions that spread throughout Eurasia with profound repercussions were the stern-post rudder, which appeared in Europe about 1180 at the same time as the compass; the foot-stirrup, which made possible the heavily armored feudal knights of medieval Europe; and the breast-strap harness, which rests on the horse's shoulders and allows it to pull with full force without choking as had been the case with the old throat harness. Finally the Chinese domesticated numerous fruits and plants, which were spread throughout Eurasia, usually by the Arabs. These include the chrysanthemum, the camellia, the azalea, the tea rose, the Chinese aster, the lemon, and the orange. The orange is still called "Chinese apple" in Holland and Germany.

III. RELIGIOUS BONDS

The medieval period was characterized not only by an unprecedented trans-Eurasian exchange of goods and technologies, but also by an unprecedented diffusion of religious creeds. In the case of Christianity and Buddhism, this began toward the end of the classical period and continued during the medieval. (See Chapter 4, Section III.) But by all odds the outstanding religious change during the medieval centuries was the appearance of Islam. Apart from its teachings, which will be noted in the following chapter, the new religion profoundly affected extensive regions of Eurasia and Africa as it burst out from the Arabian peninsula following the death of Mohammed in 632 C.E.

The spread of Islam (the details of which will be noted later) occurred in two stages. During the first, from 632 to 750, it flooded over the Middle East and then west to the Pyrenees and east to central Asia. The net effect was the virtual transformation of the Mediterranean into a Moslem lake. But the second stage of expansion between 1000 and 1500 made the Indian Ocean also a Moslem preserve, for during these centuries Islam expanded much further—into India, Southeast Asia, and Africa.

The vast extension of the domains of Islam naturally alarmed the rulers of Christendom,

Movable Chinese wood types: Four types carved with characters representing words and syllables.

who were now isolated on the western tip of Eurasia. This explains their ambivalent reaction to the appearance of the Mongols in the thirteenth century. They were terrified by the slaughter inflicted by the Mongol horsemen. But the picture was not all black, because the Mongols also crushed the Moslems in Persia and Mesopotamia. The Christian rulers therefore hoped they might be able to convert the pagan Mongols to Christianity, as they had earlier converted the pagan Magyars and Vikings.

The pope sent two missions to the court of the grand khan in Karakorum in northern Mongolia. They tried to persuade the khan to adopt Christianity and to join the pope in a crusade against the Moslems. But the traditional magicians or shamans were very influential at the court, and the missions failed to win any converts. They were successful, however, in gathering the first reliable information about Mongol customs and military tactics. They also learned that twenty days' journey east from Karakorum was the mysterious land of Cathay, or China. It was known to be not only wealthy but also non-Islamic and, therefore, a possible ally against the Moslems.

Since China was a part of the great Mongol Empire, Kublai Khan moved his capital in 1264 from Karakorum to Cambaluc, or modern Peking. The first Europeans to arrive in the capital were the two aforementioned Venetian merchants, Nicolo and Maffeo Polo. Kublai welcomed them warmly, questioned them about Europe, and gave them letters to deliver to the pope. In these letters he asked for a hundred missionary-scholars to come to his court to instruct his people and to dispute with representatives of other religions.

In making this request it is doubtful that Kublai was motivated by zeal for Christianity. More likely he wanted trained men for his bureaucracy, since he had only recently conquered China and did not wish to risk the appointment of too many Chinese to higher offices. In fact he did employ large numbers of foreigners in his service, and he was careful to maintain a balance among the various elements in order to safeguard his authority.

Fifteenth-century Arab manuscript from the collection of the National Library, Paris, showing Mohammed and his daughter Fatima.

IV. EXPANDING HORIZONS

The great breakthrough in European knowledge of the world came with the Mongol Empire. Its existence brought about the transition from a Mediterranean to a Eurasian perspective, just as the voyages of Columbus and da Gama later brought about a transition from a Eurasian to a global perspective. The travels of merchants, missionaries, and prisoners of war revealed the existence of a great empire in the Far East that not only equaled but surpassed Europe in population, wealth, and level of civilization. Nor was this a one-way process, for the East now became aware of the West as well. Marco Polo, who opened the eyes of the West to Cathay, had his counterparts in China and the Middle East.

MARCO POLO'S NEW WORLD

Medieval Eurasia was united primarily by merchants who traveled back and forth from the Mediterranean Sea to China and Southeast Asia. The following excerpts from Marco Polo's great travel account make clear how much the horizons of the medieval world were opening up.*

As regards the size of this city [Cambaluc, or modern Beijing], you must know that it has a compass of 24 miles, for each side of it hath a length of 6 miles. . . . There are 12 gates, and over each gate there is a great and handsome palace. . . . The streets are so straight and wide that you can see right along them from end to end and from one gate to the other. And up and down the city there are beautiful palaces, and many great and fine hostelries, and fine houses in great numbers. . . .

And first let us speak of the [Chinese] ships in which merchants go to and fro amongst the Isles of India. These ships, you must know, are of fir timber. They have but one deck, though each of them contains some 50 or 60 cabins, wherein the merchants abide greatly at their ease, every man having one to himself. The ship hath but one rudder, but it hath four masts; and sometimes they have two additional masts, which they ship and unship at pleasure. . . . Each of their great ships requires at least 200 mariners [some of them 300]. They are indeed of great size, for one ship shall carry 5000 to 6000 baskets of pepper.

Chipangu [Japan] is an Island towards the east in the high seas 1500 miles distant from the Conti-

nent; and a very great Island it is. The people are white, civilized, and well-favoured. They are Idolaters, and are dependent on nobody. And I can tell you the quantity of gold they have is endless.

When you sail from Chamba [Indochina], 1500 miles in a course between south and south-east, you come to a great Island called Java. And the experienced mariners of those Islands who know the matter well, say that it is the greatest Island in the world, and has a compass of more than 3000 miles. It is subject to a great King and tributary to no one else in the world. The people are Idolaters. The Island is of surpassing wealth, producing black pepper, nutmegs, spikenard, galingale, cubebs, cloves, and all other kinds of spices. . . .

When you leave the Island of Seilan [Ceylon] and sail westward about 60 miles, you come to the great province of Maabar which is styled India the Greater; it is best of all the Indies and is on the mainland. . . . The people are Idolaters, and many of them worship the ox [sacred cow], because it is a creature of such excellence. They would not eat beef for anything in the world, nor would they on any account kill an ox.

**H. Yule, ed. and trans., *The Book of Ser Marco Polo* (Scribner's, 1903), vol. 1, pp. 423–426; vol. 2, pp. 249–250, 253–254.*

We know of Chinese trading colonies in Moscow, Tabriz, and Novgorod during this period. Chinese engineers were employed on irrigation projects in Mesopotamia. Also there are records of Chinese bureaucrats who accompanied Genghis Khan on his campaigns and inspection tours from one end of Eurasia to the other. In addition there was the Christian Nestorian monk Rabban Bar Sauma, who was born in Peking and who traveled in 1278 to the Moslem court in Baghdad. From there he was sent by the Mongols to Europe to seek Christian help against Islam. Starting out in 1287, he traveled to Constantinople, Naples, Rome, Paris, and London, meeting en route both Philip IV of France and Edward I of England. The most wide-ranging of these medieval travelers was the Moslem Ibn Battuta (1304–1378). Starting from his native Morocco, he made the pilgrimage to Mecca and journeyed on through Samarkand to

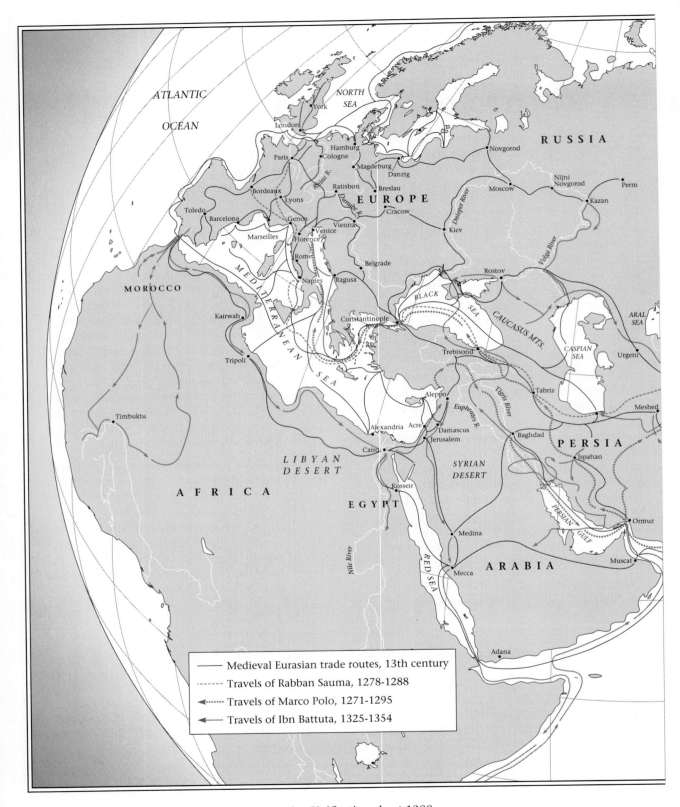

ATLANTIC
OCEAN

NORTH
SEA

RUSSIA

York

London

Hamburg
Cologne

Paris

Magdeburg
Danzig

Novgorod

Nijni
Novgorod

Perm

Bordeaux

Lyons

Ratisbon

Moscow

Kazan

EUROPE

Toledo

Genoa

Vienna

Cracow

Kiev

Barcelona

Marseilles

Florence

Venice

Rome

Belgrade

Rostov

MOROCCO

Naples

Ragusa

BLACK

SEA

CAUCASUS MTS.

CASPIAN
SEA

ARAL
SEA

Kairwah

Constantinople

Trebisond

Urgenj

MEDITERRANEAN SEA

Tabriz

Meshed

Tripoli

Aleppo

Tigris River

Euphrates R.

Baghdad

PERSIA

Timbuktu

Alexandria

Acre

Damascus

Jerusalem

Ispahan

Cairo

LIBYAN
DESERT

SYRIAN
DESERT

Ormuz

AFRICA

Kosseir

Muscat

EGYPT

Medina

Nile River

RED SEA

Mecca

ARABIA

Adana

	Medieval Eurasian trade routes, 13th century
	Travels of Rabban Sauma, 1278-1288
	Travels of Marco Polo, 1271-1295
	Travels of Ibn Battuta, 1325-1354

Eurasian Unification about 1300

Lake Baikal

A S I A

Karakorum

Great Wall

KOREA

JAPAN

Changanor

Peking

GOBI DESERT

ALTAI MTS.

Lake Balkash

ARAL SEA

TIEN SHAN MTS.

Turfan

Hwang Ho

Nanking

Kinsai

PACIFIC OCEAN

Bukhara

Samarkand

PAMIR

Yarkand

ALTYN TAGH

KUN LUN MTS.

C H I N A

Zaitun

FORMOSA

Balkh

Kabul

Peshawar

Yangtze River

Herat

Multan

HIMALAYA MTS.

Ganges R.

PHILIPPINE ISLANDS

Lahari

Indus River

Chittagong

SIAM

INDIA

Pulicat

Calicut

Jafnapatam

Bay of Bengal

BORNEO

EAST INDIES

ARABIAN SEA

SUMATRA

INDIAN OCEAN

India, where he served as judge and also as ambassador to China. Returning later to Morocco, he resumed his travels, crossing north to Spain and then south to the interior of Africa, where he reached Timbuktu. When he finally returned to Morocco and settled down, he had traveled no fewer than 75,000 miles.

By all odds the most important traveler for the Western world was the famous Marco Polo. Accompanying his father and his uncle on their second journey to China, he arrived at Kublai Khan's court in 1275. He favorably impressed the khan and served him for seventeen years in various ways that required him to travel throughout the country. As an official he carefully observed the inhabitants and resources of the lands through which he journeyed, noting such things as "a kind of black stone, which is dug out of the mountains like any other kind of stone and burns like wood." In 1292 he escorted a Mongol princess on a voyage around Southeast Asia and across the Indian Ocean to Persia where she was to be the bride of the Moslem ruler. Marco Polo then continued westward to his native Venice, arriving there in 1295 after an absence of twenty-five years. Shortly afterward he was captured in a battle with the Genoese, and while in prison he dictated his account of his travels.

He told of the grand khan's palace with its gardens and artificial lakes and its elephants with harnesses of silver and precious stones. He told also of roads that were paved and raised above the surrounding ground so that they might drain easily; of the Grand Canal through which merchant vessels passed each year; of ports with ships larger than any known in Europe; and of lands that produced spices, silk, ginger, sugar, camphor, cotton, salt, saffron, sandalwood, and porcelain. Marco also described all the fabulous countries he visited and heard about while escorting the Chinese princess to Persia—Singapore, Java, Sumatra, Ceylon, India, Socotra, Madagascar, Arabia, Zanzibar, and Abyssinia.

It all seemed so fantastic and exaggerated that he was dubbed Il millione, "the man who talks in millions." Actually he had provided Europeans with the most comprehensive and authoritative account of China available until the mid-sixteenth century. The title of his book is significant—*The Description of the World*. In fact this work had suddenly doubled the size of the known world for Westerners (as shown in the map of Eurasian Unification about 1300, pp. 174–75.) Marco Polo opened up new vistas for his contemporaries fully as much as Columbus was to do two centuries later. Indeed it was his tantalizing picture of Cathay and the Spice Islands that beckoned the great explorers onward as they sought a direct sea passage after the Moslems had blocked the overland routes.

SUGGESTED READINGS

The most important works dealing with all types of interaction within Eurasia are the first volume of J. Needham, *Science and Civilisation in China* (Cambridge University, 1954); J. H. Bentley, *Old World Encounters* (Oxford University, 1993); and J. L. Abu-Lughod, *Before European Hegemony: The World System, A.D. 1250-1350* (Oxford University, 1989). The maritime trade is described by G. F. Hourani, *Arab Seafaring in the Indian Ocean in Ancient and Early Medieval Times* (Princeton University, 1951); P. D. Curtin, *Cross-Cultural Trade in World History* (Cambridge University, 1984); K. N. Chaudhuri, *Trade and Civilization in the Indian Ocean* (Cambridge University, 1985); and Vol. 4, Part III of the Needham study, which deals with Chinese maritime enterprise, including the Ming voyages. The overland trade is analyzed by G. F. Hudson, *Europe and China: A Survey of Their Relations from the Earliest Times to 1800* (Beacon, 1961); and by P. Yung, *The Silk Road: Islam's Overland Route to China* (Oxford University, 1986). An analysis of Eurasian trade in general is given in C. G. F. Simkin, *The Traditional Trade of Asia* (Oxford University, 1969). For technological exchange, the basic work is the multivolume study by Needham, just listed.

For the experiences of Marco Polo and other travelers, see *The Travels of Marco Polo*, trans. R. E. Latham (Penguin, 1958); L. Olschki, *Marco Polo's Precursors* (Johns Hopkins Press, 1943); I. de Rachewiltz, *Papal Envoys to the Great Khans* (Stanford University, 1971); and R. Dunn, *The Adventures of Ibn Battuta: A Muslim Traveller of the Fourteenth Century* (University of California, 1986), which provides a fascinating panorama of the entire Moslem world.

NOTES

1. H. Yule, ed., *Cathay and the Way Thither*, Hakluyt Society, Series 2, XXXVIII (London, 1914), pp. 152, 154.
2. Francis Bacon, *Novum Organum*, Book I, aphorism, p. 129.

Rise of Islam

The burden of the desert of the sea. As whirlwinds in the south pass through; so it cometh from the desert, from a terrible land.

Isaiah 21:1

We have revealed to thee an Arabic Koran, that thou mayest warn Mecca, the Mother of Cities, and those who are about her; that thou mayest give warning of the Day of Judgement, of which is no doubt—when part shall be in Paradise and part in the flame.

Koran, Sura XLII

The centuries between 600 and 1000 saw the emergence of Islam, a major turning point in Eurasian and world history. The spectacular conquests of the Moslem warriors united the entire Middle East as Alexander the Great had done almost a millennium earlier. The Islamic conquests of the seventh and eighth centuries united under the star and crescent all the territories from the Pyrenees to India and from Morocco to central Asia.

More remarkable than these military exploits were the cultural achievements of Islam. Although the conquered territories were the centers of humanity's most ancient civilizations, nevertheless, by the eleventh century, the Arabs had affected both their languages and their cultures. Arabic became the language of everyday use from Persia to the Atlantic. And a new Islamic civilization emerged that was an original synthesis of the preceding Judaic, Perso-Mesopotamian, and Greco-Roman civilizations. This transformation has lasted to the present day, so that Iraqis and Moroccans now have linguistic and cultural ties as strong as those of the English and the Australians.

I. MOHAMMED

Mohammed, the most influential historical personality of the Medieval Age, was born in 569. Since his father died before he was born, and his mother when he was six, Mohammed was brought up first by his grandmother and subsequently by his uncle. Little is known of his youth, though tradition has it that at the age of twelve he was taken by his uncle on a caravan to Syria. In the course of that journey he may have picked up some Jewish and Christian lore. At the age of twenty-five he married a wealthy widow, who bore him several daughters and two sons who died in infancy.

About his fortieth year Mohammed went through a period of intense spiritual tension, in the course of which he became convinced that God had chosen him to be a prophet, a successor to Abraham, Moses, and Jesus. Asked to describe the process of revelation, he answered that the entire text of the Koran existed in Heaven and that one fragment at a time was communicated to him, usually by the archangel Gabriel, who made him repeat every word. Mohammed now believed that he had received a divine call to teach of the unity and supreme power of Allah, to warn his people of the Day of Judgment, and to tell them of the rewards for the faithful in Paradise and the punishment of the wicked in Hell.

His teachings were written down soon after his death and became the sacred scripture of the new religion known as Islam, meaning "submission to God's will." Mohammed did not establish an organized priesthood nor did he prescribe specific sacraments essential for salvation. But he did call on his followers to perform certain rituals known as the Five Pillars of Islam:

1. Once in their lives believers must say with full understanding and absolute acceptance, "There is no God but Allah; Mohammed is the Messenger of Allah."
2. Five times daily they must pray—at dawn, at noon, in midafternoon, at dusk, and after it has become dark. Facing in the direction of Mecca, worshipers pray on a carpet, with their shoes removed and heads covered.
3. Moslems must give alms generously, as an offering to Allah and an act of piety.
4. Moslems must fast from daybreak to sunset during the whole month of Ramadan.
5. Once in their lives Moslems, if they can, must make the pilgrimage, or Hadj, to Mecca.

These rituals provided the believers with an extraordinarily powerful social cement. They prayed and fasted together, they assumed responsibility for their less fortunate fellow believers, and they journeyed to Mecca together—rich and poor, yellow, white, brown, and black. Furthermore, the Koran provided guidance for all phases of the life of the faithful—for manners and hygiene, marriage and divorce, commerce and politics, crime and punishment,

Page from an eighth- or ninth-century Qur'an in Kufic script (23.8 x 35.5 cm). Because of the Muslim aversion to images, calligraphy early became a major Islamic art form. The Arabic script developed primarily to render the Qur'anic text as exactly as possible, and the calligraphic art developed along with it. The horizontally elongated Kufic script was the earliest and dominated Qur'anic calligraphy for three centuries.

peace and war. Thus Islam was not only a religion but also a social code and a political system. It offered to its followers both religious commandments and specific guidance for private and public life. There was no split between the secular life and the religious, between the temporal and the spiritual, as there was in the Christian world. What is Caesar's, in Islam, is God's, and what is God's is also Caesar's. The Shari'a, or Holy Law, was until recently the law of the land throughout the Moslem world, and it is still the basic law in individual countries.

Mohammed slowly won converts to these teachings. The first were members of his immediate family and personal friends, who later enjoyed great prestige as "Companions of the Prophet." As the little band of converts grew, the wealthy merchants of Mecca became alarmed for fear that Mohammed's teachings would undermine the older religious beliefs and discourage pilgrims from coming to worship at the shrine of the Black Stone in their city. Because of the growing opposition, Mohammed accepted an invitation to go to Medina, an oasis town on the trade route nearly three hundred miles north of Mecca. There was a mixed population of Arab and Jewish tribes, so Mohammed was welcomed as an arbitrator. His emigration to Medina, known as the hegira, took place in 622, and the Moslem calendar is dated from the beginning of that year.

Since his teachings were based largely on Judaic doctrines, tales, and themes, Mohammed expected the Medina Jews to welcome him as the successor of their own prophets. Instead they ridiculed his claims, so Mohammed turned against them, eventually driving them out of the town and dividing their property among his followers. Gradually Mohammed persuaded the Medina Arabs to accept his religion, and he organized a theocratic state based on his teachings.

From his base in Medina, Mohammed organized attacks on the Mecca caravans. Such raiding was an accepted and popular economic activity among Arab nomads, who now flocked to the banner of the Prophet in the hope of winning booty, and incidentally salvation. By 630 the Moslems were strong enough to capture Mecca, whereupon Mohammed made the Black Stone, housed in the Ka'ba, the chief shrine of his religion. Thus he effected a compromise by which he preserved the basic tenets of his faith and yet rooted it in traditional Arab custom. By the time of his death in 632, most—though by no means all—of the Arab tribes had recognized his overlordship and paid him tribute.

Mohammed had found his native land divided with many local idolatrous practices. He left it with a religion and a book of revelation, and with a community and a state sufficiently well organized and armed to dominate the entire peninsula. Within a century his followers were to march from victory to victory, building an imposing empire across the breadth of Eurasia and spreading his creed, which today boasts half a billion followers, throughout the world.

II. AGE OF CONQUESTS

Precisely because the Moslem community was the product of Mohammed's genius, it now seemed likely with his death to break up into its component elements. The tribal sheikhs, who considered their submission to him ended with his death, stopped their tribute and resumed their freedom of action. This withdrawal, known in Islamic history as the Ridda, or apostasy, was answered with a series of well-planned campaigns that overwhelmed the "apostate" tribes and forced them back into the community of Islam. But the subdued tribes, sullen and resentful, obviously were ready to seize the first opportunity to break away again. The ideal distraction from this disaffection, the Moslem leaders knew, would be to initiate some foreign raids that would promise the booty beloved by every Bedouin. The resultant raids, then, did not begin as religious crusades to propagate the faith. Mohammed did not think of Islam as a universal faith and did not believe that God had chosen him to preach to any other people than his own Arabs. So the Arab raids grew out of the need to keep the turbulent Bedouins preoccupied and loyal to Medina.

The leader of the raids was the caliph, or deputy, who was chosen to represent the Prophet in his secular role. There was no possibility, of course, of a successor to Mohammed as Prophet, but a secular chief of the community was essential. Thus when Abu Bakr, Mohammed's father-in-law, was selected as caliph, it meant that he

The ritual worship, or prayer. These illustrations show the sequence of movement prescribed for the ritual prayers that each Muslim should perform five times a day. Various words of praise, prayer, and recitation from the Qur'an accompany each position and movement. The ritual symbolizes the Muslim's complete obedience to God and recognition of God as the one, eternal, omnipotent Lord of the universe.

was the defender of the faith rather than religious leader. It was under Abu Bakr that the apostate tribes were forced back to the fold and the earliest foreign raids begun.

Under Caliph Omar, who succeeded Abu Bakr in 634, the early raids blossomed into full-fledged campaigns of conquest. They did so because the outwardly powerful Byzantine and Persian empires were soon found to be hollow shells. They had been weakened by the series of wars between them, and their subjects were highly dissatisfied because of heavy taxation and religious persecution. Furthermore the Moslem forces now were growing from raiding parties into large-scale armies as entire tribes from all Arabia migrated northward, attracted by reports of dazzling riches. Any attempt to turn them back to their barren homeland would have provoked a new and possibly fatal Ridda, so the Moslem leaders crossed over into Syria at the head of their Bedouin forces. Thus the great conquests that followed represented the expansion not of Islam but of the Arab tribes, who on many occasions in earlier centuries had pushed northward into the Fertile Crescent. The unprecedented magnitude of the expansion at this time can be explained by the exceptional

weakness of the two empires and by unity and élan engendered by the new Islamic faith.

Once the invasions were under way the Arabs made good use of their experience in desert warfare. Mounted on camels, instead of horses like the Byzantines and Persians, they were able to attack at will and, if necessary, to retreat back to the safety of the desert. Just as the Vikings later were capable of ravaging the coasts of Europe because of their command of the sea, so now the Arabs used their "ships of the desert" to attack the wealthy empires. It was not accidental that in the provinces they conquered, the Arabs established their main bases in towns on the edge of the desert. They used existing cities like Damascus when they were suitably located and when necessary created new ones. These garrison towns met the same need for the emerging Arab Empire that Gibraltar, Malta, and Singapore later did for the British sea empire.

In 636 the Arabs won a decisive victory over the Byzantines in the ravines of the Yarmuk River, a tributary of the Jordan. Attacking in the midst of a blinding sandstorm they almost annihilated a mixed force of Greek, Armenian, and Syrian Christians. Emperor Heraclius fled to Constantinople, abandoning all of Syria to the

CHRISTIAN-MOSLEM MUTUAL SLANDER

Christians and Moslems were mortal enemies in the Middle Ages, fighting on battlefields in Europe, the Middle East, and overseas. They also had a low opinion of each other, as evident in the following two statements. The first is by a Moslem judge of Toledo, Spain, who placed northern Europeans at the bottom of his category of nations.* The second is by a Christian bishop who expressed the common Western belief in Moslem moral degeneracy.**

Judge Sa'id al-Andalusi: . . . As for the rest of this category which cultivated no sciences, they are more like animals than human beings. Those of them who live deep in the north have been so affected by the extreme distance from the sun from the Zenith above their heads, resulting in cold climate and thick atmosphere, that their temperaments have become chilly and their humors rude. Consequently their bodies are huge, their color pale and their hair long. For the same reason they lack keenness in intelligence and perspicacity, are characterized by ignorance and stupidity. Folly and mental blindness prevail among them as among Slavs, Bulgars and other neighboring peoples.

William of Adam, Bishop of Sultaniyah: In the Muslim sect any sexual act at all is not only not forbidden, but allowed and praised. So, as well as the innumerable prostitutes that there are among them, there are many effeminate men who shave the beard, paint their own face, put on women's dress, wear bracelets on the arms and feet. . . . The Muslims, therefore, forgetful of human dignity, are shamelessly attracted by those effeminates, and live together with them as with us husband and wife live together publicly.

*From Islam and the West *by P. K. Hitti © 1962 by Litton Educational Publishing Inc.*
**N. Daniel, Islam and the West *(Edinburgh University Press, 1960), p. 144.*

victors. Caliph Omar now turned against the neighboring rich province of Iraq. Its Semitic, partly Christian, population was alienated from its Persian and Zoroastrian masters. This split contributed to the great victory won by the Arabs in the summer of 637 at Qadisiya. The Persian emperor hastily evacuated his nearby capital, Ctesiphon, and fled eastward.

The astonishing triumphs at Yarmuk and Qadisiya left the Moslems with unheard-of riches, which further swelled the flood of Bedouin tribes from the southwestern deserts. Their pressure on the frontiers was irresistible, and the Arab armies rolled onward, westward into Egypt and eastward into Persia. Omar's successors in the caliphate bore the banners of Islam still further afield, driven on by the momentum of victory, of religious enthusiasm, and of nomadic greed. In North Africa the Arab forces, supplemented by native Berber converts, fought their way clear across to Morocco and then crossed the Straits of Gibraltar into Spain. In 711 they defeated Roderick, the last Visigothic king of Spain, and advanced to the Pyrenees and on into France. There, however, they were defeated by Charles Martel at Tours in 732.

At the same time other Moslem forces were expanding eastward into the province of Sind in northwest India. Then they turned northward, advancing as far as Talas in central Asia. Thus what had started out as a simple desert religion had grown quickly into a great Eurasian empire. By 750 Islam ruled over the vast territories stretching from the Pyrenees to Sind, and from Morocco to central Asia. (See map, Expansion of Islam to 1500, p. 182.)

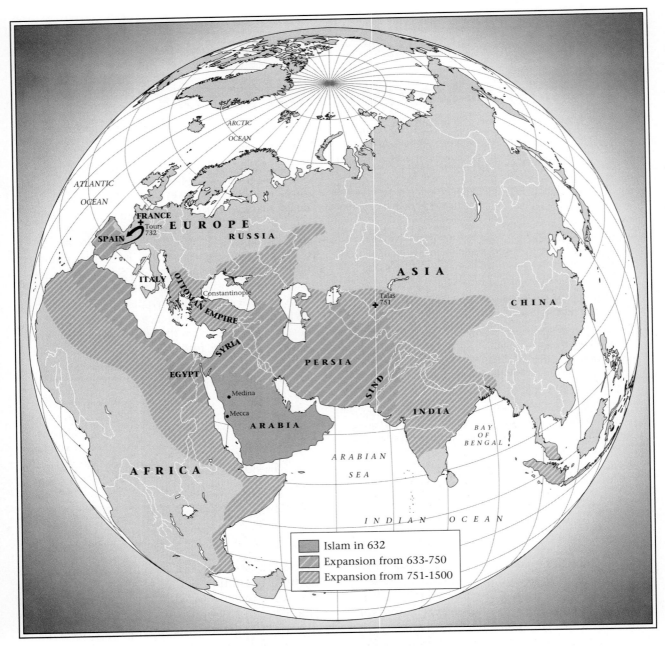

Expansion of Islam to 1500

III. ARAB KINGDOM TO ISLAMIC EMPIRE

With the first phase of expansion completed, the Arabs now settled down to enjoy the fruits of victory. Virtually an army of occupation in their subject lands, they lived mostly in strategically located camp cities, from where they controlled the surrounding countryside. Since Caliph Omar had decided at the outset that his followers should not be given fiefs in the conquered provinces, they now were supported by government pensions. The funds for these pensions were obtained from lands confiscated by the Islamic state and from taxes that were levied at a higher rate on non-Moslems than on Moslems. Apart from this discriminatory taxation, the non-Moslems were left virtually undisturbed. No effort was made to convert them;

indeed conversion was not at all welcomed for it involved, under the circumstances, a decline in revenue. Thus Islam was in effect a privilege of the Arab warrior-aristocracy who ruled over the much more numerous subject peoples.

This arrangement was soon disturbed by the appearance in increasing numbers of the Mawali, or non-Arab Moslems. These converts flocked to the cities, where they served the needs of the Arab aristocracy as servants, artisans, shopkeepers, and merchants. Being Moslems they claimed equality with the Arabs, but it was not granted. Although the Mawali fought in the armies of Islam, they were usually restricted to the infantry, which received a lower rate of pay and less booty than the Arab cavalry.

As the empire expanded and wealth poured into the cities from the subject provinces, the Mawali increased in numbers and wealth. But they were still excluded from the ruling circles, so they became a disaffected urban element, determined to gain status equal to their economic power. Thus the Arab Umayyad dynasty of caliphs, which had moved the capital from Medina to Damascus in 661, came to be regarded with much justification as a parasitic clique that had outlived its usefulness once the conquests were completed. The opposition to the Arab aristocracy, therefore, was both a national and a social movement of protest.

A disputed accession to the throne set off a decade of civil strife that ended in the accession of the Abbasid Caliphate in 750. This represented much more than a mere change of dynasty. The Mawali, and particularly the Persians, now replaced the old aristocracy. The Arabs no longer were a privileged salaried soldiery but were replaced by a royal standing army that was at first largely Persian. The former garrison cities became great commercial centers under Mawali control. Some of the Arabs became absorbed into the mass of townspeople and peasants, whereas others reverted to nomadism.

The imperial structure also changed radically, especially with the shift of the capital from Damascus eastward to Baghdad in 762. In effect this meant that the Abbasid caliphate was turning its back on the Mediterranean and looking to Persia for traditions and support. The caliph no longer was an Arab sheikh but a divinely ordained autocrat—the "Shadow of God upon Earth." His authority rested not on tribal support but on the salaried bureaucracy and standing army. Thus the caliphate became an oriental monarchy similar to the many that had preceded it in Ctesiphon and Perespolis and Babylon. Under the order and security imposed by this monarchy, a syncretic civilization that was a mixture of Judaic, Greco-Roman, and Perso-Mesopotamian traditions evolved during the following centuries. Islam ceased to be merely the creed of a ruling warrior-aristocracy and became instead a new and distinctive civilization.

IV. ISLAMIC CIVILIZATION

Caliph Mansur, who selected Baghdad as the site for the Abbasid capital, foresaw a glorious future for his choice:

This island between the Tigris in the East and the Euphrates in the West is a market place for the world. All the ships that come up the Tigris . . . will go up and anchor here; wares brought on ships down the Tigris and along the Euphrates will be brought and unloaded here. It will be the highway for the people of the Jabal, Isfahan and the districts of Khurasan. Praise be to God who preserved it for me and caused all those who came before me to neglect it. By God, I shall build it. Then I shall dwell in it as long as I live and my descendants shall dwell in it after me. It will surely be the most flourishing city in the world.[1]

Mansur's expectations were quickly realized. Within a century Baghdad numbered about a million people. In the center was a citadel some two miles in diameter in which were the caliph's residence and the quarters of his officials and guards. Beyond the citadel walls a great commercial metropolis sprang up, supported by the plentiful produce of the fertile Mesopotamian valley. The main crops were wheat, barley, rice, dates, and olives. The provinces contributed rich supplies of metals— silver from the Hindu Kush; gold from Nubia and the Sudan; copper from Isfahan; and iron from Persia, central Asia, and Sicily. Precious stones came from many regions of the empire, while the waters of the Persian Gulf yielded pearls. Industry also flourished, textiles being the most important in the number of workers employed and the value of the output. The art of paper making, learned from Chinese prisoners, spread rapidly across the Islamic world, reaching Spain by 900.

Such a rich economy, stretching across the breadth of the far-flung Abbasid Empire, greatly increased interregional trade. Moslem merchants, as noted in the preceding chapter, traded overland through central Asia and overseas with India, Ceylon, Southeast Asia, and China. A flourishing trade was carried on also with Africa, whence were obtained gold, ivory, ebony, and slaves. We know about commerce with the northern countries from the discovery in Scandinavia of large hoards of Moslem coins dating from the seventh to the eleventh centuries. Such large-scale trade stimulated a highly developed banking system with branches in all leading cities, so that a check could be drawn in Baghdad and cashed in Morocco.

With this solid economic base, the Abbasid caliphs were able to enjoy themselves in their dazzlingly luxurious palaces. *The Thousand and One Nights* describes Harun al-Rashid (786–809), the best known of these caliphs, as a cultured ruler surrounded by poets, musicians, singers, dancers, scholars, and wits. Among the popular indoor games were chess, dice, and backgammon, and outdoor sports included hunting, falconry, hawking, polo, archery, fencing, javelin throwing, and horse racing. Harun was contemporary with Charlemagne, but their respective capitals, Baghdad and Aix-la-Chapelle, were quite incomparable—as incomparable as Baghdad and Paris today, but in the reverse sense.

The Abbasid Caliphate was noted not only for its affluence and splendor but also for its relative tolerance in religious matters in an age when this quality was markedly absent in the West. The explanation is to be found partly in the religious law of Islam. The sacred law recognized the Christians and Jews as being, like the Moslems, People of the Book. Both had a scripture—a written word of revelation. Their faith was accepted as true, though incomplete, since Mohammed had superseded Moses and Jesus Christ. Islam therefore tolerated the Christians and Jews. It permitted them to practice their faith, with certain restrictions and penalties.

The Abbasid Caliphate also was noteworthy for its achievements in the field of science, although the tendency here was to preserve and to pass on rather than to create something new. One of its greatest scientists, al-Biruni (973–

The Dome of the Rock in Jerusalem. An early example of Islamic architecture (but not a mosque), it dates from the seventh century and the first wave of Arab expansion. It is built on the rock from which Muslims believe Muhammad ascended into heaven and on which Jews believe Abraham prepared to sacrifice Isaac.

1048), stated, "We ought to confine ourselves to what the Ancients have dealt with and to perfect what can be perfected."[2] On the other hand, the sheer size of the empire, its contacts with literally all regions of Eurasia, and its rich legacy from the several great centers of civilization that it encompassed all contributed to the very real achievements of Islamic science. Baghdad, for example, boasted a "House of Wisdom" consisting of a school of translators, a library, an observatory, and an academy. The scholars associated with it translated and studied the works of Greek scientists and philosophers, as well as scientific treatises from Persia and India.

In astronomy the Moslems generally accepted the basic tenets of their Greek predecessors and made no significant advances in theory. But they did continue without interruption the astronomical observations of the ancients, so that the later Renaissance astronomers had available some nine hundred years of records, which provided the basis for their crucial discoveries.

In geography, as in astronomy, the Moslems made little theoretical progress, but the extent of their empire and of their commerce enabled them to accumulate reliable and systematic data concerning the Eurasian land mass. Al-Biruni's famous book on India, for example, described not only the physical features of the country but also the social system, religious beliefs, and scientific attainments of the Hindus in a manner that was not to be equaled until the eighteenth century. The Moslems also prepared charts and maps in which they naturally located Mecca in the center, as the contemporary Christian cartographers did for Jerusalem.

In addition to their own original achievements, the Moslems made an invaluable contribution in translating and transmitting ancient works. The Umayyad caliphs had distrusted all non-Arabs and were uninterested in their civilizations. The Abbasids, by contrast, had been strongly supported by Christians, Jews, and Zoroastrian Persians and were much more tolerant and broadminded. The "House of Wisdom" in Baghdad included a large staff of translators, one of the outstanding ones being a Christian, Hunain ibn-Ishaq (809–873). He visited Greek-speaking lands to collect manuscripts, and with his assistants he translated a large number of them, including works of Hippocrates, Galen,

Fourteenth-century manuscript showing Avicenna and scholars. This page is taken from "The Canon" of Avicenna and is in the collection of the Bologna University Library.

Euclid, Ptolemy, Plato, and Aristotle. Another great translation center was in the city of Toledo in Moslem Spain, where the translators during the twelfth and thirteenth centuries included Jews, Spaniards, and foreign scholars from all over Europe. This activity was of utmost significance, for western Europeans had lost direct acquaintance with Greek learning and for long were unaware even of its existence. Thus Moslem scholarship preserved the Greek works until western Europe was ready once more to resume its study.

In conclusion, it should be emphasized that two basic bonds held together the diverse peoples of the sprawling caliphate: the Arabic language and the Islamic religion. Much more remarkable than the Arab conquests was the diffusion of the Arabic language. By the eleventh century Arabic had superseded the old Greek, Latin, Coptic, and Aramaic languages and prevailed from Morocco to Persia, as it does to the

Leaf from the manuscript of Dioscorides: a recipe for cough medicine and a doctor preparing it. Arab conributions to the field of medicine were substantial, and drugs in great quantities were carried to Europe in Italian ships.

lization evolved during the centuries following the conquests as a fusion of Christian, Jewish, Zoroastrian, and Arab religious elements, and Greco-Roman and Perso-Mesopotamian administrative, cultural, and scientific elements. The end product was not a mere mosaic or agglomeration of previous cultures but rather a fusion that represented a new and original civilization. It was diverse in its origins and strands yet uniquely molded by the distinctive imprint of Arabic Islam.

To the present day, Islam remains a major force, being the world's second-largest religion. It has nearly 1 billion followers, or about 18 percent of the world's population. By contrast, Christianity has about 1.7 billion, or 33 percent of the world's population. Moslems (literally, "submitters" to the will of God) range from the Atlantic coast of Africa, across North Africa, through the Middle East and south Asia, to Indonesia. Consequently many ethnic groups fill the ranks of the faithful; Arabs, the originators of Islam, now are a minority in their religion.

present day. This common language explains the feeling of common identity prevailing in this region, even though it includes Negroid Sudanese as well as the prevailing Semites, and Christian Lebanese and Coptic Egyptians as well as the prevailing Moslems. Even beyond this vast area that was permanently Arabized, Arabic exerted a profound influence on other Moslem languages. Arabic words are as common in these other languages as Greek and Latin words in English, and some of these languages (Urdu, Malay, Swahili, and Turkish until World War I) are written in Arabic script.

The Islamic religion also is a powerful bond—much more powerful than Christianity in this respect because it is not only a religion but also a social and political system and a general way of life. Religion thus provides the basis for Islamic civilization as language does for the Arabic world. We have seen that the Islamic civi-

V. DECLINE OF THE CALIPHATE

The Abbasid Caliphate reached its height during the reign of Harun al-Rashid and then declined in much the same way as did the Roman Empire. There was first the matter of sheer size—a very real problem in an age when communications were dependent on horse and sail. The outlying provinces were 3,000 miles distant from the capital, so it is unsurprising that they should have been the first to break away: Spain in 756, Morocco in 788, and Tunisia in 800.

Further, as in the case of Rome, there was the problem of imperial expenditures, which were excessive and unsupportable by the prevailing economy and technology. The rampant luxury of the Baghdad court and the heavy weight of the inflated bureaucracy were not matched by technological progress. The resulting financial crisis forced the caliphs to appoint provincial governors as tax farmers in the areas they administered. With the revenues they collected, these governors maintained the local soldiery and officials and remitted an agreed sum to the central treasury. This arrangement left the governors-farmers the real rulers of the provinces, together with the army commanders with whom they soon reached working agreements. By the mid-ninth century the caliphs were losing both military and administrative control and were being appointed and deposed at will by Turkish mercenaries.

Imperial weakness, as usual, invited barbarian attacks. Just as the Roman Empire had been invaded across the Rhine and the Danube, so the caliphate now was assaulted from the north, south, and east. From the north came the Crusaders who overran Spain, Sicily, and Syria, aided by Moslem discord in all three areas. In Sicily the end of the local dynasty in 1040 was followed by civil war, which facilitated the invasion of the island by the Normans from southern Italy. By 1091 the whole of Sicily had been conquered, and the mixed Christian-Moslem population came under the rule of Norman kings.

Likewise in Spain the Umayyad dynasty was deposed in 1031 and the country was split up into numerous petty states ruled by "parties" or factions reflecting diverse ethnic groups. These included the Arabs, the Berbers, the indigenous pre-Moslem Iberian stock, and the "Slavs," or European slaves. This fragmentation of Moslem Spain enabled the Christian states of the north to expand southward. By 1085 they captured the important city of Toledo, and by the end of the thirteenth century only Granada on the southern tip of the peninsula was left to the Moslems.

The loss of Sicily and Spain to Christendom proved permanent, but such was not the case with Syria. Here also the warring of the several Moslem states enabled the Crusaders from 1096 onward to advance rapidly down the Syrian coast into Palestine. They established four states—Edessa (1098), Antioch (1098), Jerusalem (1099), and Tripoli (1109)—all organized along Western feudal lines. But these states lacked roots. They never assimilated their Moslem Arab subjects. Their existence depended on the sporadic arrival of recruits from Europe. Also they were all confined to the coastal areas and hence vulnerable to resistance movements organized in the interior. These states could exist only as long as the surrounding Moslem world remained divided. The disunity was ended by Salah ad-Din, better known in the West as Saladin. By uniting Moslem Syria and Egypt he sur-

rounded the Crusader principalities and began the counterattack in 1187. By the time of his death in 1193 he had recaptured Jerusalem and expelled the westerners from all but a narrow coastal strip. During the following century this also was overrun and the Moslem reconquest was completed.

In addition to these Crusader onslaughts from the north, the caliphate was attacked by Berbers from southern Morocco and the Senegal-Niger area and by the two Arab Bedouin tribes of Hilal and Sulaim from Upper Egypt. These tribes swept across Libya and Tunisia, wreaking havoc and devastation. It was this attack rather than the earlier seventh-century Arab invasion that ruined civilization in North Africa.

Finally, the third group of invaders were the Turks and Mongols from the East. Their incursions, lasting for several centuries and taking in virtually the entire Eurasian landmass, constitute a major chapter of world history. The Turco-Mongol invasions are comparable to the Arab-Islamic conquests in scope and impact. Indeed the two are intimately related, for many of the Turco-Mongols were converted to Islam, and they then extended the frontiers of their faith into distant new regions. The course and significance of these Turco-Mongol invasions is the subject of the following chapter.

SUGGESTED READINGS

For Mohammed and his teachings, see T. Andrae, *Mohammed* (Scribner's, 1936); E. Dermenghem, *The Life of Mahomet* (Dial, 1930); H. A. R. Gibb, *Mohammedanism: An Historical Survey* (Oxford University, 1953); and the convenient edition of the translation of the Koran by M. M. Pickthall (New American Library, 1953).

The Arabs and their general history are described authoritatively by A. Hourani, *A History of the Arab Peoples* (Harvard University, 1991); by P. Hitti, *History of the Arabs from the Earliest Times to the Present*, 5th ed. (St. Martin's, 1951); and B. Lewis, *The Arabs in History* (Home University Library, 1966). For the Arab conquests and early Islamic history, see M. A. Shaban, *Islamic History A.D. 600–750* (Cambridge University, 1972); and F. M. Donner, *The Early Islamic Conquests* (Princeton University, 1981). After the initial conquests, Islam continued to expand through quiet missionary work, as described by T. W. Arnold,

The Preaching of Islam: A History of the Propagation of the Muslim Faith (Constable, 1913).

Various aspects of Islamic civilization are considered by T. Arnold and A. Guillaume, eds., *The Legacy of Islam* (Clarendon, 1931); W. Montgomery Watt and P. Cachia, *A History of Islamic Spain* (Doubleday, 1967); A. G. Chejne, *The Arabic Language: Its Role in History* (University of Minnesota, 1969); R. A. Nicholson, *A Literary History of the Arabs* (Cambridge University, 1969); and A. Lewis, ed., *The Islamic World and the West, 622–1492 A.D.* (Wiley, 1970).

NOTES

1. Cited by B. Lewis, *The Arabs in History* (Hutchinson's University Library, 1950), p. 82.
2. Cited by A. Mieli, *La Science Arabe* (Brill, 1939), p. 376.

11

Turco-Mongol Invasions

> Nay, it is unlikely that mankind will see the like of this calamity, until the world comes to an end and perishes. . . . These [Tartars] spared none, slaying women and men and children, ripping open pregnant women and killing unborn babes.
>
> *Ibn al-Athir (Moslem historian, 1160–1233)*

By all odds the most spectacular development during the half-millennium from 1000 to 1500 C.E. was the great eruption of Turco-Mongol peoples from the vast racial hive of central Asia. The historic achievement of the Turco-Mongols was that they jointly altered the traditional relationship between nomads and civilizations. For millennia the nomads had been on the outside, eyeing covetously the riches of civilized peoples. But with the Turco-Mongol conquests the balance shifted dramatically. The nomads became the unifiers and masters of most of the Eurasian landmass, rather than mere tenders of steppe animals.

During their centuries of glory the Turco-Mongols overran all Eurasia except for distant extremities such as Japan, Southeast Asia, southern India, and western Europe. These stunning conquests occurred in three stages. The first (1000–1200) marked the emergence of the Turks,

initially as mercenaries and then as masters of the Abbasid Caliphate. They infused vigor and aggressiveness into the now sickly world of Islam, extending its frontiers into Asia Minor at the expense of Byzantium and into northern India at the expense of Hindustan. The second stage, during the thirteenth century, saw the Mongols overrun not only central Asia, east Asia, and Russia, but also the Moslem Middle East, thereby halting the expansion of the Moslem Turks. The final stage (1300–1500) involved the disintegration of the Mongol Empire, which cleared the way for the resurgence of the Turks and the resumption of the Turkish-Islamic advance into Christian Europe and Hindustan.

This chapter will consider in turn each of these stages and their implications for general world history.

I. TURKISH INVASIONS

The Turks are a linguistic rather than an ethnic group. Their common bond is that they all speak one form or another of a Turkish family of languages. Although an ethnically mixed people, they are generally Caucasoid in appearance rather than Mongoloid. By the mid-sixth century they dominated the extensive steppe lands from Mongolia to the Oxus, or Amu Darya. From the eighth century onward they came increasingly under Islamic influence as a result of the Arab conquest of Persia and defeat of the Chinese at Talas (751).

The response of the Turkish tribes to the brilliant Abbasid Caliphate across the Oxus River was very similar to that of the Germans to the Roman Empire across the Rhine. First there was the cultural impact, as the primitive Turkish pagans succumbed to the teachings of Islam and to the lures of a sophisticated civilization. At the same time the tribes' warriors were entering the military service of the caliphate, as the Germans earlier had entered that of Rome. As mounted archers of great mobility, they soon demonstrated their superior military qualities and increasingly replaced the Arabs and Persians in the caliph's armed forces.

As the caliphs became weaker, the Turkish mercenaries, like their German counterparts, became masters rather than servants. They made and unmade successive caliphs in Baghdad. About 970 a branch of the Turkish people known as the Seljuks were crossing over unhindered into Moslem territory and soon had gathered power into their hands. This was formally recognized in 1055, when the caliph proclaimed the Seljuk leader, Tughril Beg, the "sultan," or "he who had authority." Although the caliphs remained the nominal heads of the empire, the real rulers henceforth were the Turkish sultans. Under their aggressive leadership, the frontiers of Islam now were further extended into two regions.

One was Asia Minor, which had remained for centuries a center of Christian Byzantine power against repeated attacks by Arabic Islam. But in 1071 the Seljuks won a crushing victory at Manzikert in eastern Asia Minor, taking prisoner the Byzantine Emperor Romanus IV. This proved to be a turning point in Middle Eastern history. The Asia Minor peasants, who had been exploit-

ed by corrupt Byzantine officials, now welcomed the Turks with relief. Thus between the eleventh and the thirteenth centuries the larger part of Asia Minor was transformed from a Greek and Christian to a Turkish and Moslem region, and it remains so to the present day. Furthermore, Byzantium was gutted by the loss of Asia Minor, a province that hitherto had provided the bulk of the imperial revenue and army manpower. Constantinople now was like a huge head atop a shriveled body. Thus the roots of the fall of Constantinople in 1453 extend back to 1071.

While the Seljuks had been pushing westward into Asia Minor, other Turks had been fighting their way southward toward the vast treasure house of India. Outstanding was a certain Mahmud (997–1030), who from his base at Ghazni in Afghanistan raided the Indian lands almost annually and finally annexed the Punjab, which has ever since remained Moslem. Mahmud's zeal in destroying Hindu temples and smashing their idols, a zeal that was based on the Islamic tenet that any visible representation of the deity was sinful, earned him the epithet "the image breaker." Fired by the fierce monotheism of Islam, Mahmud and his followers came to India not only in search of plunder but also to convert the infidels, or to exterminate them. There was also a social conflict involved—the clash between two different societies, one believing that all men are brothers and the other based on caste, which presupposes inequality. It was at this time, then, that the struggle of two fundamentally different cultures began. After World War II this struggle ended in the division of the peninsula into Hindu India and Moslem Pakistan.

Mahmud was followed by other Turkish invaders from Afghanistan. They advanced southward to Gujarat and eastward into the Ganges valley. In 1192 they captured Delhi and made it the capital of the Turkish Sultanate in India. During these campaigns, Buddhist monasteries were destroyed and Buddhist monks were slaughtered on such a scale that Buddhism never recovered in its place of origin.

The relative ease with which the Turks conquered a land in which they were hopelessly outnumbered was due partly to the outdated Indian military tactics. They were the same as those that had proven inadequate against

Alexander 1,500 years earlier. The infantry was usually an undisciplined rabble, and their vaunted elephants were useless against the Moslem cavalry. Equally damaging, and a more fundamental weakness, was the Hindu caste system, which left the fighting to only the Kshatriya, or warrior caste. The rest of the population was untrained and largely indifferent, particularly because class differentiation separated oppressive landlords from their peasants and so added to the fragmentation of the caste system. Thus the masses either remained neutral or else welcomed the invaders and embraced their faith. This pattern was to be repeated frequently in the future and explains why in modern times the British were able to rule from Delhi just as the Turkish sultans had before.

II. GENGHIS KHAN'S CONQUESTS

While the Turks were becoming the masters of the Moslem world, an obscure chieftain in far-off Mongolia was beginning his career of conquest that was to culminate in the greatest empire of history. Genghis Khan (spelled also Chinggis, Chingis, Jenghiz, etc.), whose personal name was Temujin, was born about 1167, the son of a minor clan leader. When Temujin was twelve years old his father was poisoned, and as a result the future Khan spent a childhood of misery. He was able to overcome these humble beginnings by mastering the complicated art of tribal politics, which called for a mixture of loyalty, cunning, and ruthless treachery, as well as physical prowess. After turning against his overlord and eliminating various rivals, he finally was able to combine the various Mongol-speaking tribes into a single unit. An assembly of Mongol chieftains, held in 1206, proclaimed him the supreme head of his people with the title Genghis Khan, signifying "ruler of the universe."

He was now in a position to satisfy his nomadic impulse for conquest and booty. "Man's highest joy," he reportedly said, "is in victory: to conquer one's enemies, to pursue them, to deprive them of their possessions, to make their beloved weep, to ride on their horses, and to embrace their wives and daughters." In this respect Genghis Khan was no different from the long line of steppe conquerors who had gone before him. Why then was he alone destined to become the master of the greater part of Eurasia? This question is particularly intriguing

Fifteenth-century Chinese painting showing Genghis Khan hunting.

Mongol Empire at the Death of Kublai Khan, 1294

because, as a Mongol, Genghis Khan did not have the manpower resources of other nomad conquerors, who were almost invariably Turks. All the Mongol tribes together numbered about 1 million men, women, and children, which gave Genghis Khan a maximum of 125,000 warriors. With such limited resources, how was he able to come so close to becoming literally the "ruler of the universe"?

Genghis Khan began with the built-in advantage enjoyed by all nomad warriors—the fact that their daily life was a continuous rehearsal of campaign operations. Clad in leather and furs, leading extra horses as remounts, and capable of riding several days and nights in succession with a minimum of rest and food, these warriors introduced blitzkrieg into the world of the thirteenth century. During their campaigning on the plains of Hungary, they are said to have covered 270 miles in three days. They carried leather bags for water, which when empty could be inflated for swimming across rivers. Normally they lived off the countryside, but if necessary they drank the blood of their horses and the milk of their mares. Their skills in the hunt, acquired from boyhood, enabled them to coordinate the operations of flying horse columns over long distances. Their favorite tactic was feigned flight, during which the enemy might pursue the fleeing Mongols for days, only to be lured to ambush and destruction. Other tactical maneuvers included the tying of branches to the tails of horses to stir up dust in order to give the impression of large forces on the march, and also the mounting of dummies on spare horses for the same purpose.

The basic Mongol weapon was the compound large bow, more powerful than the English longbow and capable of killing at 600 feet with its armor-piercing arrows. This was a fearful weapon in the hands of Mongol horsemen, who were able to carry a supply of thirty arrows and shoot them all at full gallop. Other equipment included a steel helmet, light body armor made of hide, a saber, and sometimes a lance with a hook and a mace. The Mongol horses grazed only on the open range, with no shelter during the long, bitter winter and no hay or grain for supplementary feed. This made them somewhat stunted in size but very tough and adaptable. Genghis Khan further strengthened his forces by adding new skills and equipment learned mostly from the Chinese. Thus Genghis Khan supplemented his incomparable mounted archers with the siege weapons necessary for capturing fortified cities.

The Mongols were also masters of espionage and psychological warfare. Before undertaking a campaign they collected all possible intelligence regarding the enemy's roads, rivers, fortifications, and political and economic conditions. They also used agents to spread demoralizing stories about the size of the Mongol forces and the uselessness of resistance. In the course of the campaigning they used terror tactics to undermine enemy morale. Prisoners of war were forced to lead the assault against their own people, and entire populations were put to the sword when any resistance was offered.

Even with his military genius and superb fighting machine, Genghis Khan could not have become a world conqueror had he not appeared at the right historical moment. A strong and united China, such as had existed under the Han and the T'ang, could have stopped him with ease. So also could the Moslem Arabs have done so at the height of their power. But the Eurasian balance of power was quite different in the early thirteenth century. China was divided then into three fragments: the Ch'in dynasty ruling the north, the Sung the south, and the Tibetan Tanguts controlling the northwest with their kingdom of Hsi Hsia. To the west was the state of Kara-Khitai based on oasis cities such as Bokhara and Samarkand. Beyond that, on the Oxus River, was the Moslem kingdom of Khorezm, and still further west the Abbasid Caliphate at Baghdad, both far past their prime.

Genghis Khan first subjugated the Hsi Hsia state between 1205 and 1209 and forced it into a tributary status. In 1211 he attacked north China, first overrunning the region north of the Great Wall and then in 1213 piercing the wall and penetrating to the Yellow River plain. By 1215 he had captured and pillaged Peking and also gained the services of Chinese who knew how to besiege cities and others who knew how to administer and exploit agricultural societies. In accordance with his overall strategy, Genghis Khan now turned to the surrounding nomadic territories. Manchuria fell in 1216, Korea in 1218, Kara-Khitai in the following year. These conquests brought him to the frontiers of Khorezm, which he overran between 1219 and 1221. Rich and ancient cities such as Bokhara, Samarkand, and Balkh were pillaged and their inhabitants massacred. The only exceptions were the skilled artisans, who were sent to Mongolia.

Meanwhile, Genghis Khan had returned to Mongolia to direct another victorious campaign against the Hsi Hsia kingdom, which had revolted against his rule. This was his final exploit, for he died soon after in 1227. In accordance with his expressed wish, he was buried in his homeland beneath a large tree he had selected. The escort that had brought the corpse to the site were all slaughtered to ensure that the location of the grave should remain secret. (See map of Mongol Empire at the Death of Kublai Khan, 1294, p. 192.)

III. MONGOL EMPIRE

After a two-year interval, Genghis Khan's son Ogodai was selected as successor. During his reign from 1229 to 1241 the campaigning was resumed in the two extremities of Eurasia—China and Europe—some 5,000 miles apart. In China the remnants of the Ch'in state in the north were liquidated by 1234, and then the Sung in the south were immediately attacked. They resisted stoutly, but the war, which lasted forty-five years, ended in their complete destruction. At the same time Genghis Khan's grandson Batu was sent with a force of 150,000 Mongols and Turks to the European West. Crossing the middle Volga in the fall of 1237 he fell upon the principalities of central Russia. Town after town was captured, including the then comparatively unimportant town of Moscow. By March 1238 Batu was approaching Novgorod near the Baltic Sea, but fearing that the spring thaw would mire his horsemen in mud, he withdrew suddenly to the south.

Two years later, in the summer of 1240, the Mongols attacked southern Russia again, this time from their bases in the Caucasus. By December they had captured the ancient Russian capital of Kiev. Such was Mongol frightfulness that a contemporary monk recorded that the few survivors "envied the dead." The following year the Mongols pressed on into Poland and Hungary, defeated a German army of 30,000 at Liegnitz in Silesia, crossed the frozen Danube, captured Zagreb, and reached the Adriatic coast. Thus Mongol armies now were operating across the breadth of Eurasia from the Adriatic to the Sea of Japan. In the spring of 1242 came news of the death of Ogodai Khan in Mongolia, so Batu withdrew through the Balkans to the lower Volga valley, where he laid the foundations of the khanate known as the Golden Horde, a name derived from the golden tent of its khan.

Ogodai's successors decided to complete the conquest of south China and to take over the Abbasid Caliphate of Baghdad. In China, the Mongols were bogged down in decades of fighting before finally capturing the great southern port of Canton in 1277. The new khan, Kublai, moved his capital from Karakorum to Peking in north China. Kublai then launched new cam-

This illustration from a thirteenth-century Persian history of the Mongols shows the court of Genghis Khan. The Khan himself is seated on his throne, and his three sons stand at the left. One of these sons, Ogodai, succeeded his father in 1229.

paigns: on land against Indochina and Burma, and overseas against Java and Japan.

Meanwhile, other Mongol armies had been rampaging through the Middle East, capturing in 1258 the Abbasid capital, Baghdad. Most of its 800,000 inhabitants are reported to have been massacred, with the exception of a few skilled artisans who were sent to Kublai's court. It seemed that nothing could prevent the Mongols from advancing on Egypt and North Africa and from completing the conquest of the entire Moslem world. In 1260, however, the Egyptian Mamelukes unexpectedly defeated the advancing Mongols in Palestine. The defeat marked the high-water mark of the Mongol Empire in the Middle East, just as similar defeats in Japan and

Java marked its high point in the Far East. Unable to expand further, the Mongol Empire fell apart almost as rapidly as it had been built up.

IV. MONGOL DECLINE

The basic reason for the decline of the Mongols was that they were too few in number and too primitive in relation to their subject peoples. The Mongols, as Pushkin put it, were "Arabs without Aristotle and algebra." This left them vulnerable to assimilation as soon as they dismounted from their horses and settled down to enjoy their conquests. In this respect they differed fundamentally from the Arabs, who had both a language and a religion that their subjects were willing to adopt and which served as strong bonds for imperial unity. The Mongols, being less advanced than the Arabs, enjoyed no such advantage. Rather, the opposite was the case with them, for they adopted the languages, religions, and cultures of their more-advanced subjects and thereby lost their identity. This was the root reason why their empire dissolved so soon after its creation.

Indicative of the assimilation process was Kublai Khan's decision to move the Mongol capital from Karakorum to Peking. Inevitably he became a Chinese-style emperor, ruling from a palace of Chinese design, conducting elaborate Confucian ceremonies, and building new Confucian temples. As the Grand Khan, he was nominally the suzerain of all the Mongol khanates. Actually his authority did not extend beyond China. His brother Arikboga had contested his election as Grand Khan. Kublai Khan had prevailed only after a four-year struggle. Then he was challenged by his cousin, Kaidu, who controlled Turkestan, and the ensuing forty-year civil war ended in stalemate. Thus the Mongol Empire was shattered by internal dynastic rivalries as well as by cultural assimilation.

While Kublai Khan was becoming a Chinese emperor, Hulagu was becoming a Persian ruler. With Tabriz as his capital he established the so-called Ilkhanate. (The term *Ilkhan* means "subject Khan" and was applied to the Mongol rulers of Persia as subordinates to the Grand Khan.) His successor's adoption of Islam in 1295 as the official religion both reflected and accelerated the Mongols' assimilation into their Iranian-Islamic milieu. Likewise the Golden Horde across the Caucasus went its own way, influenced by the native Christian Orthodox culture and by the official Islamic creed. Before long the only remaining pure Mongols were those in ancestral Mongolia, where they came under the influence of Buddhism and sank into impotent obscurity.

It is a tribute to Marco Polo's keen insight that he foresaw Mongol decline even when he was serving under the great Kublai Khan. In his account of his travels, Marco Polo made the following significant analysis of the assimilation of the Mongols by the people they conquered.

All this that I have been telling you is true of the manners and customs of the genuine Tatars [Mongols]. But I must add also that in these days they are greatly degenerated; for those who are settled in Cathay have taken up the practices of the Idolaters of the country, and have abandoned their own institutions; whilst those who have settled in the Levant have adopted the customs of the Saracens.[1]

V. TURKISH REVIVAL

Since the Mongols were so few in number, they had taken an ever-increasing proportion of Turks into their armies. Then with the breakup of the empire these Moslem Turks quickly came to the fore, as they had earlier in the caliphate before the Mongol onslaught. A succession of military adventurers now rose and fell in the struggle for control of the central Eurasian steppes. The most remarkable of these was Timur, known to Europe as Tamerlane. He seized Samarkand in 1369, and from there he struck out in all directions. First he destroyed the Ilkhanate in Persia and Mesopotamia, then defeated the Golden Horde in Russia and the Ottoman Turks in Asia Minor, and he even invaded India and sacked Delhi. He was determined to make his capital, Samarkand, the finest city in the world, and after each campaign he sent back caravans loaded with booty, together with craftmakers, artists, astrologers, and scholars. At its height, his empire extended from the Mediterranean to China, and Timur was preparing to invade the latter country when he died in 1405. His empire then disintegrated even more rapidly than that of the Mongols.

After Timur, the outstanding development was the extension of Moslem Turkish power in India and in Byzantium. During the thirteenth century the Turkish sultans of Delhi, under the pressure of the Mongol threat, had confined themselves to strengthening their position in north India. In the fourteenth century, with the threat removed, they expanded two-thirds of the way down the peninsula to the Kistna River. Then in the aftermath of Timur's raid, north and central India were reduced to a few small Turkish-ruled states, with none strong enough to revive the Delhi sultanate. Meanwhile the expansion of Islamic power over a large part of India had provoked a reaction from the Hindus. They set up the large Hindu state of Vijanagar, comprising the whole of India south of the Kistna River. Such was the fragmented condition of the Indian peninsula when unity was imposed from without during the sixteenth century by another Moslem Turkish dynasty, the Mughal.

Meanwhile in the Middle East the frontiers of Islam were being extended at the expense of Byzantium by the Ottoman Turks. These newcomers from central Asia had entered the Seljuk Empire in its decline and settled in the northwest corner of Asia Minor, less than fifty miles from the strategic straits separating Asia from Europe. In 1299 the leader of these Turks, Uthman, declared his independence from his Seljuk overlord, and from these humble beginnings grew the great Ottoman Empire, named after the obscure Uthman.

The first step was the conquest of the remaining Byzantine portion of Asia Minor. This was accomplished by 1340, thanks to the disaffection of the Christian peasantry and the plentiful supply of ghazis, or warriors of the faith, who flocked in from all parts of the Middle East to battle against the Christian infidels. Next the Turks crossed the straits, winning their first foothold in Europe by building a fort at Gallipoli in 1354. They hardly could have selected a more favorable moment for their advance into Europe. The Balkan peninsula was divided by the strife of rival Christian churches and by the rivalries of the Byzantine, Serbian, and Bulgarian states, all past their prime. Also the Christian peasants of the Balkans were as disaffected as their counterparts in Asia Minor. And Western Christendom was too divided to go to the aid of the Balkans even if there was the will to do so, which there was not, because of the ancient antipathy between Catholic and Orthodox Christians. Thus the way was clear for the Ottoman Turks, and they took full advantage of the opportunity.

They surrounded Constantinople by taking Adrianople in 1362 and Sofia in 1384. Then they were diverted for some decades when their sultan was defeated and captured by Timur in 1402. But Timur was a flash in the pan, and his death in 1405 left the Ottomans free to rebuild and to resume their advance. Finally, in 1453 they took Constantinople by assault, and the Ottomans were the masters of the entire Balkan peninsula to the Danube River, with the exception of a few Venetian-held coastal fortresses. (For details, see Chapter 12, Section IV.)

VI. SIGNIFICANCE OF TURCO-MONGOL INVASIONS

One result of the Turco-Mongol invasions between 1000 and 1500 was the emergence of a new Eurasian balance of power in which Islam was the central and decisive force. When the West began its overseas expansion in the late fifteenth century, Islam already was expanding overland in all directions. The Ottomans were crossing the Danube into central Europe; central Asia was completely won over, with the exception of the eastern fringes; and the Mughals were about to begin their conquest of virtually the entire Indian peninsula. Beyond Eurasia, Islam was spreading steadily into the interior of the continent of Africa from two centers. From the North African coast it advanced across the Sahara to West Africa, where a succession of large Negro Moslem kingdoms flourished. Likewise from the Arab colonies on the East African coast, Islam spread inward over lands that included the Christian kingdom of Nubia, which was conquered and converted.

Islam was also carried by Arab and Indian merchants to Southeast Asia. Here, as in Africa and other regions, conversion was easy because of the simplicity and adaptability of the new faith. All one had to do to become a Moslem

The Alhambra, palace of the Moorish kings at Granada, built between 1248 and 1354. Masterpieces of Islamic architecture throughout Eurasia are indications of the vast diffusion of the Moselm faith between 1000 and 1500.

was to repeat the words "I bear witness that there is no God but Allah and that Mohammed is the Messenger of Allah." Local practices and traditions usually were accepted and made holy simply by the addition of Islamic ritual. Thus the faith was spread, not by the sword, but by the unobtrusive work of traders who won over the populace by learning their language, adopting their customs, marrying their women, and converting their new relatives and business associates. By the end of the fifteenth century, Islam had spread as far east as Mindanao in the Philippines. Taking Southeast Asia as a whole, the main Moslem centers, as might be expected, were those areas with the most active trade contacts: the Malay peninsula and the Indonesian archipelago.

This diffusion of Islam throughout Eurasia during these five centuries almost tripled the area that accepted the Moslem faith, with important repercussions on the course of world history. The initial stage of Islamic expansion in the seventh and eighth centuries had made the Mediterranean a Moslem lake; this later stage of expansion made the entire Indian Ocean a Moslem lake. This meant that virtually all the goods reaching Europe from Asia now were carried along Moslem-controlled land or sea routes, especially after the Persian Ilkhanate embraced Islam in 1295. Thus the several decades after 1240 during which the Mongol Empire permit-

ted safe travel and trade across Eurasia were only an interlude between earlier and later eras when Arab-Turkish control of central Asia and the Middle East raised a barrier between China and the West. The continued expansion of the Moslem faith also served to make Islam by 1500 a world force rather than simply a Middle Eastern power. This has affected profoundly the course of world affairs to the present day. It explains why today the Indian peninsula is divided into two parts, why Moslem political parties are so influential in Southeast Asia, why Islam is a powerful and rapidly growing force in Africa, and why it is now the faith of 18 percent of the people of the world.

The Turco-Mongol invasions are significant also because of the cross-fertilization that they stimulated within Eurasia. In the technological field, we have seen that Pax Mongolica was responsible for the transmission of a cluster of Chinese inventions, including gunpowder, silk, machinery, printing, and the blast furnace for cast iron. (See Chapter 9, Section II.) Another example of cross-fertilization is the case of Ilkhanid Persia, which by its location was exposed to influences from both East and West. We know of Chinese artillerymen who reached Persia in the service of the Mongol armies. We also know of one Fu Meng-chi, who spread the principles of Chinese astronomy; of Chinese physicians at the Ilkhan's court; and of Chinese artists who left an indelible impression on Persian miniature painting. From the opposite direction, European influence was mostly in the field of trade and diplomacy. A colony of Italian merchants flourished in the capital of Tabriz, and from their numbers the Ilkhans recruited the ambassadors and interpreters for their various missions to Europe. And then there was, of course, Marco Polo, who escorted from China to Persia a Mongol princess to be the Ilkhan's bride and then proceeded to Venice.

Thus the Turco-Mongol invasions served to integrate the Eurasian landmass more tightly than ever before. This was noted at the time by a Chinese observer, Wang Li (1314–1389), who left the following remarkable account of the unprecedented integration unfolding before his eyes:

. . . the land within the Four Seas had become the territory of one family, civilization had spread everywhere, and no more barriers existed. . . . many [newcomers to China] forgot the region of their birth, and took delight in living among our rivers and lakes. As they settled down in China for a long time, some became advanced in years, their families grew, and being far from home, they had no desire to be buried in their fatherland. Brotherhood among peoples has certainly reached a new plane.[2]

Finally, the opportunities offered by this cross-fertilization were fully exploited only by the new civilization developing in Europe—a profoundly significant fact that was to mold the course of world history to the present day. All the other Eurasian civilizations were too set in their ways. At first it seemed as though the Islamic world would have no difficulty in adapting and changing. Despite the primitive background of Arabia from which it had emerged, Islam had proven itself remarkably adept at borrowing from the great established civilizations and creating something new and impressive. But there was too great a gulf between the dogma of the Islamic faith and the rationalist philosophy and science of the Greeks. In the early years the Caliph al-Mamun (813–833) had generously supported the translation of the ancient classics and had accepted the rationalist doctrine that the Koran was created and not eternal. But his successors were quite different. They supported conservative theologians who rejected all scientific and philosophical speculation as heresy and atheism.

This was the triumph of scholasticism, in the sense that seeking God was more important than understanding nature. Such scholasticism had prevailed also in the early medieval West following the barbarian invasions. The papacy had then dominated the intellectual life of the age, and theology was the accepted queen of the sciences. The same development occurred now in the Islamic world following its series of barbarian invasions—Crusaders, Berbers, Bedouins, Seljuks, and Mongols. Here, as in the West, people turned to religion for succor and consolation in the face of material disaster. But whereas in the West scholasticism eventually was challenged and replaced, in the Moslem world it remained dominant through the nineteenth century.

In his *Incoherence of Philosophy*, the outstanding theologian of Islam, al-Ghazzali (1058–1111), strongly attacked the whole secular school. He argued that the ultimate source of truth is divine revelation and that the intellect should be used to understand that self-trust must be destroyed and replaced by trust in the divine. The extent of orthodox reaction is reflected in the work of the great historian and father of sociology, Ibn Khaldun (1332–1406). He was the first to view history not as the conventional chronicling of events or episodes—the view in his time—but as the science of the origin and development of civilizations. And yet this learned and creative thinker rejected philosophy and science as useless and dangerous:

It should be known that the opinion the philosophers hold is wrong in all its aspects. . . . The problems of physics are of no more importance to us in our religious affairs or our livelihoods. Therefore we must leave them alone. . . . Whoever studies it [logic] should do so only after he is saturated with the religious law and has studied the interpretation of the Koran and jurisprudence. No one who has no knowledge of the Moslem religious sciences should apply himself to it. Without that knowledge, he can hardly be safe from its pernicious aspects.[3]

Thus intellectual growth and innovation in the Moslem world ceased, and at a time when

Europe's universities were in full ferment, the Islamic madrasas were content with rote memorization of authoritative texts. Whereas the Moslem world had been far ahead of the West between 800 and 1200, by the sixteenth century the gap had disappeared, and thereafter it was the West that boomed ahead while Islam stood still and even went backward.

A similar disparity developed between the West and the other Eurasian civilizations, for the simple reason that only the West made the fateful transition to modernism. Both India and Byzantium were conquered by Islam and affected by its stagnation. China, reacting against the Mongols, who were expelled in 1368, developed a strong ethnocentrism—an almost instinctive hostility and scorn for all things alien and hence barbarian. Russia also succeeded in 1480 in throwing off the Mongol yoke, but permanent scars remained. The country had been closed to fresh winds from the West for 250 years, and Mongol ideas and usages had paved the way for the absolutism of the Muscovite state and of the Orthodox church.

The West alone was the exception to this general pattern. Only there occurred the great mutation—the emergence of modern civilization with a new technological base that quickly proved its superiority and diffused throughout not only Eurasia but the entire globe. This uniqueness of the West stems, as noted earlier (Chapter 8, Section V), from the shattering impact of the barbarian invasions, which plowed under the classical civilizations and allowed new concepts and institutions to take root and flourish. The following chapters first will consider the traditional Byzantine and Confucian civilizations that flanked the Islamic world on each side, and then will analyze the contrasting revolutionary civilization of the West.

SUGGESTED READINGS

For the Turkish invasions in various regions, see T. T. Rice, *The Seljuks* (Thames & Hudson, 1961); C. Cahen, *Pre-Ottoman Turkey* (Sidgwick & Jackson, 1968); S. Vryonis, Jr., *The Decline of Medieval Hellenism in Asia Minor and the Process of Islamization from the Eleventh through the Fifteenth Century* (University of California, 1971); H. Inalcik, *The Ottoman Empire: The Classical Age 1300–1600* (Weidenfeld & Nicolson, 1972); *The Cambridge History of Iran*, Vol. 5, *The Seljuk and Mongol Periods*, ed. J. A. Boyle (Cambridge University, 1931); M. Nazim, *Life and Times of Sultan Mahmud of Ghazna* (Cambridge University, 1931), for a discussion of the Turks in India; and H. Lamb, *Tamberlane the Earth Shaker* (McBride, 1928). An excellent collection of readings is presented by J. J. Saunders, ed., *The Muslim World on the Eve of Europe's Expansion* (Prentice Hall, 1966).

For the dynamics of Mongol expansionism, see various essays in O. Lattimore, *Studies in Frontier History* (Mouton, 1962), and his article "Chingis Khan and the Mongol Conquests," *Scientific American*, August 1963, pp. 55–68. Several biographies of Genghis Khan are available, including a popular account by R. Grousset, *Conqueror of the World: The Life of Chingis-Khan* (Viking, 1972); a scholarly study by B. Y. Vladimirtsov, *The Life of Chingis-Khan* (Houghton Mifflin, 1930); and H. D. Martin, *The Rise of Chingis Khan and His Conquest of North China* (Johns Hopkins Press, 1950), which is strong on Mongol military organization. Broader studies of the Mongol Empire as a whole are available in J. J. Saunders, *The History of the Mongol Conquests* (Harper & Row, 1972); J. A. Boyle, *The Successors of Genghis Khan* (Columbia University, 1971); and the authoritative evaluation by B. Spuler, *The Mongol Period* (Princeton University, 1995).

NOTES

1. R. Latham, trans., *Travels of Marco Polo* (Penguin, 1958), p. 71.
2. Cited by J. H. Bentley, *Old World Encounters* (Oxford University, 1993), p. 145.
3. Ibn Khaldun, *Muqaddimah*, trans. F. Rosenthal (Pantheon, 1958), pp. 250–258.

Traditional Byzantine Civilization

> A thousand years of Byzantium produced extinction; a thousand years of medieval effort [in the West] produced the Renaissance, the modern state, and ultimately the free world.
>
> *William Carroll Bark*

Byzantium was one of the traditional Eurasian civilizations that survived the barbarian invasions and continued without interruption from the Classical Age to modern times. But this unbroken, 1,000-year sweep of history eventually meant *obsolescence* and extinction, especially in the political sense. Because it was the most vulnerable, the Byzantine civilization was the first to suffer this fate. China, for example, faced nomadic invasions only from the northwest and was so far out of the way on Eurasia's eastern tip that the aggressive West was not able to break in until the mid-nineteenth century. While Byzantium faced a succession of barbarian invasions from across the Danube, comparable to those menacing China, it also had to bear the onslaught of the expanding West in the form of Venetian mer-chants and Norman knights. At the same time a resurgent East assaulted Byzantium. First came the Sassanian Persian attack and then the Moslem Arab and Turkish invasions. Thus, whereas the traditional Chinese civilization endured to 1912, the Byzantine collapsed first in 1204, was partially revived in 1261, and survived in a crippled state until the death blow in 1453. (See map of Decline of the Byzantine Empire, p. 201.)

I. EMERGENCE OF BYZANTIUM

No Western capital approaches the proud record of the Byzantine capital, Constantinople, either in continuity or in the scope of its imperial rule. It was already an old city when rebuilt by Con-

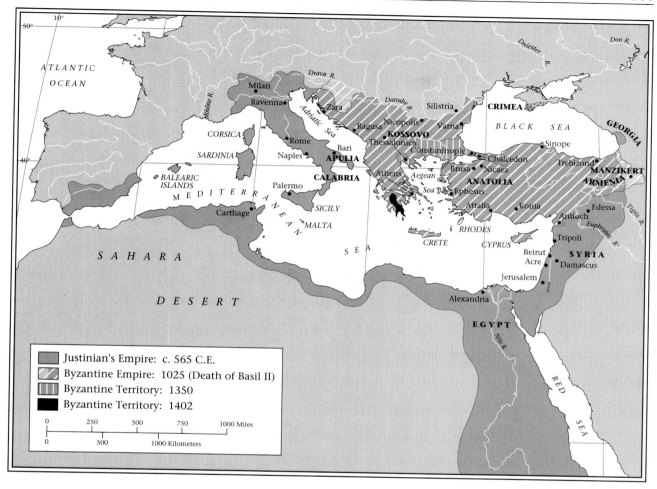

Decline of the Byzantine Empire

stantine in 330 C.E. to be the new Rome. Its origins go back to the seventh century B.C.E., when it was founded as the colony Byzantion by emigrants from the Greek city-state Megara. Despite its magnificent location, Byzantium, to use the common Latin form of its name, remained a second-class commercial city during the next thousand years. It was unable to rise to a rank worthy of its position as long as it was menaced and cut off from its hinterland by the barbarous Thracians. The conquests of Trajan and his successors brought the interior lands under Roman imperial control and ended this disadvantage. Thus when Byzantium became Constantinople, or the city of Constantine, it was secure by land as well as by sea, and in the following centuries it stood impregnable before

the barbarian assaults to which the first Rome succumbed.

For 1,000 years Constantinople was the capital of Byzantium, until it fell to the Ottoman Turks in 1453. Then it became the capital of a new empire. And as the Ottoman warriors pressed their conquests, the rule of Constantinople spread to new frontiers, reaching from Morocco to Persia and from Vienna to the Indian Ocean. Constantinople presided over this vast region up to modern times, when the Ottoman Empire gave way to the Turkish Republic. Then Kemal Ataturk moved his capital from Constantinople on the shores of the Bosphorus to the safety of Ankara on the Anatolian plateau.

The remarkable history of Constantinople is due in large part to its commanding position on the straits between Europe and Asia. To the south is the Sea of Marmora and to the north the bay of Bosphorus, forming the magnificent harbor known as the Golden Horn. Constantinople also has, on both north and south, a long, narrow, but navigable sea channel. The city is therefore protected by two marine gates that can be closed to hostile ships from either the Aegean or the Black sea. The Byzantine emperors supplemented these natural defenses with two great walls on the land side, the first four miles long, and the second—some thirty miles further west—forty miles long and twenty feet wide. These double ramparts, together with the natural bulwark of the Balkan Mountains, protected the land approaches to Constantinople. Thus the city was able to hold out during the thousand-year existence of Byzantium, although it was a besieged fortress for much of this period.

After the overthrow of Romulus Augustulus in Rome in 476 C.E., the Eastern emperors in Constantinople continued to regard themselves as the heirs of the Caesars. Justinian tried to make this imperial myth a reality by winning back from the barbarians North Africa, Italy, and a part of Spain. (See Chapter 8, Section IV.) But the revived empire proved short-lived. Soon after Justinian's death, a new barbarian tribe, the Lombards, overran most of Italy. Likewise on the Danube frontier, the Avars and Slavs were pouring southward into the Balkans, while in the East the Persians overran Syria, Palestine, and Egypt and camped on the shores of the Bosphorus opposite Constantinople.

Under the great Emperor Heraclius (610–641) Byzantium took the offensive against the surrounding enemies. In 627 Heraclius defeated the Persians and forced them to return all their conquests. Turning to the Danube frontier, Heraclius discovered that in the meantime the Slavs had occupied and sunk roots in large parts of the northern Balkans. Making a virtue of necessity, he assigned definite areas to them, and in return, they acknowledged his suzerainty and agreed to pay annual tribute. Thus the Slavic newcomers changed gradually from invaders into settlers. With the passing of a few centuries these widely scattered Balkan Slavs had developed along different lines and crystallized into four major groups: the Slovenes at the head of

the Adriatic; the Croatians between the Drave River and the Adriatic; the Serbs in the central Balkans between the Adriatic and the Danube; and the Slavs, who shortly were to adopt the name of their Bulgarian conquerors, in the remaining territory to the Black Sea.

Later in the seventh century the Byzantine Empire again was threatened, this time by the combination of Moslem sea raids and Bulgar land attacks. The Arabs developed a naval power with which they conquered Cyprus and Rhodes and then besieged Constantinople on several occasions, beginning in 669. At the same time Byzantium was threatened from the north by the Bulgars, who had occupied the territory between the Danube and the Balkan Mountains.

Once more Byzantium was saved by inspired imperial leadership, this time in the person of Leo III the Isaurian (717–741). A military commander of Syrian origin, he seized power when Constantinople was under siege by the Arabs. He not only lifted the siege but drove the Arabs back out of Asia Minor. By the end of his reign the imperial frontiers were secure, but they were drastically shrunken frontiers compared to those of Justinian. Italy had been lost to the Lombards; the northern Balkans to the Slavs and the Bulgars; and Syria, Palestine, Egypt, and North Africa to the Arabs.

This reduced empire, however, was a more homogeneous territory. It was strengthened rather than weakened by withdrawal to the Taurus Mountains, which separated Greek Asia Minor from what was now becoming the heartland of the Islamic world. This separation was reinforced by internal convulsions in the Moslem world that culminated in the accession of the Abbasid Caliphate (750). The Islamic capital was moved from Damascus to Baghdad so that the orientation of Islam now was to the East rather than toward the Mediterranean. In this way the Byzantine and Moslem empires were able to coexist peacefully until the appearance of the militant Turks in the eleventh century.

The emerging Byzantine Empire of the eighth century was much smaller than Justinian's short-lived creation but, as we have noted, was also much more homogeneous. It had shed the diverse racial, cultural, and religious elements of the eastern and western provinces, and the remaining core was basically, though not

Justinian and Retinue, *mosaic from San Vitale, Ravenna.*

exclusively, Greek. In this manner, then, the transition was made from the East Roman Empire of the sixth century to the Byzantine Empire of the eighth—an empire with a culture clearly distinct from both that of Islam to the east and that of the new Europe to the west.

II. BYZANTIUM'S GOLDEN AGE

The Byzantine Empire reached its height during the period between the early ninth and early eleventh centuries. Imperial administration was soundly based on the *themes*, or provinces, each headed by a *strategos*, or general. The general was in charge of both civil and military affairs. Heraclius had militarized the administration so that he could act quickly at a time of imminent foreign danger. Imperial lands in the themes

were divided among the peasants in return for military service. Under strong emperors, this theme arrangement provided good administration, a reliable military reserve, and a well-filled treasury since the peasants assumed much of the tax burden.

Byzantium's economy also was solidly based on free peasant communities that functioned alongside the estates of the great landowners. In the urban centers that had survived since Greco-Roman classical times, craftmakers worked at a high level of competence. Arab writers described the quality of Byzantine handicrafts, especially the luxury products, as being equaled only by those of China. Equally important was the great volume of goods that passed through Constantinople from all regions of Eurasia—slaves and salt from the Black Sea lands; spices, perfumes, and precious stones

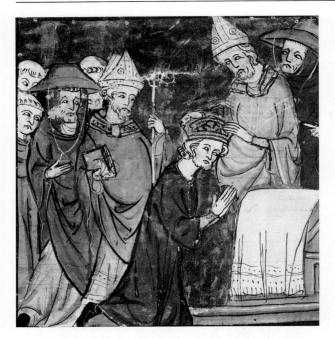

Fourteenth-century French illuminated manuscript depicting the papal coronation of Charlemagne in 800. This event caused Constantinople to recognize the political independence of the West in 812 with the granting of the title Basileus *to Charlemagne.*

from India; papyrus and foodstuffs from Egypt; silk and porcelain from China; and silver, wrought iron objects, and linen, cotton, and woolen fabrics from the West.

This political, economic, and military strength allowed the Byzantine emperors to launch reconquest campaigns that were more realistic than Justianian's, if not as ambitious. Crete and Cyprus were recovered, thereby curbing Arab naval raids in the Aegean waters. The imperial frontiers were extended also into northern Syria, Armenia, and Georgia. In the northern Balkans, where the Bulgars were a constant threat to the empire, Basil II won such a crushing victory in 1014 that he was known thereafter as *Bulgaroktonos*, or "the Bulgar-Slayer."

In cultural matters this was a period of stability and homogeneity. The Byzantines still called themselves *Romaioi*, or Romans, but Greek, in either its literary or popular forms, was the universal language of the empire. Religious homogeneity also had been promoted with the conversion of the Moslems on reconquered Crete and of the Slavs in the northern Balkans. In 865 the Bulgarian Khan Boris accepted Chris-

tianity from Constantinople in return for imperial recognition of his conquests. In the following years Byzantine missionaries provided the Bulgarians with an alphabet, translated the Scriptures into their language, and prepared a Slavonic liturgy. About the same time the Serbian tribes were converted to Orthodoxy, as were the Russians of the Kievan state.

Imperial stability was strengthened by the intimate, mutually supporting relationship between emperor and patriarch. The principle of a subservient state church was traditional and accepted. The emperor called himself not only *autokrator,* but also *isapostolos*, or the equal of the apostles. The tenth-century book of ceremony for the election of the patriarch of Constantinople spelled out the subservient relationship. The metropolitans of the church were to meet in the great Hagia Sophia church in Constantinople on the command of the emperor and submit to him three candidates for the patriarchate. The emperor was free to select any of the three or to reject all and to nominate his own candidate. The metropolitans then had to agree that the candidate was worthy of the post. In the installation ceremony the new head of the church was pronounced patriarch "by the will of God and Emperor."

In conclusion, Byzantium during these centuries was stable, powerful, wealthy, self-satisfied, and rather inward-looking now that a reasonable coexistence had evolved with both the Western and Moslem worlds. These characteristics are reminiscent of China under the Ming dynasty, as will be noted in the following chapter.

III. BYZANTIUM'S DECLINE

When Basil "the Bulgar-Slayer" died in 1025 the Byzantine Empire seemed secure and unchallenged in its splendid eminence. The northern frontier rested solidly on the Danube. Arabic Islam, now divided, was no longer a threat. And whatever was emerging in the West was patently primitive and insignificant in comparison to the second Rome on the Bosphorus. Yet within half a century after Basil's death the empire was in serious trouble, and less than two centuries later, in 1204, its capital had fallen to the despised Western barbarians.

LATIN CONQUEST OF CONSTANTINOPLE

A major event in the decline of Byzantium was the capture of Constantinople by the Latins of the Fourth Crusade in 1261. The following description by the contemporary Byzantine historian Nicetas Choniates reveals as much about Greek hatred for the Latins as it does about what actually happened.*

. . . How shall I begin to tell of the deeds wrought by these nefarious men! Alas, the images, which ought to have been adored, were trodden under foot! Alas, the relics of the holy martyrs were thrown into unclean places! Then was seen what one shudders to hear, namely, the divine body and blood of Christ was spilled upon the ground or thrown about. They snatched the precious reliquaries, thrust into their bosoms the ornaments which these contained, and used the broken remnants for pans and drinking cups. . . .

Nor can the violation of the Great Church [Santa Sophia] be listened to with equanimity. For the sacred altar, formed of all kinds of precious materials and admired by the whole world, was broken into bits and distributed among the soldiers, as was all the other sacred wealth of so great and infinite splendor.

When the sacred vases and utensils of unsurpassable art and grace and rare material, and the fine silver, wrought with gold, which encircled the screen of the tribunal and the ambo, of admirable workmanship, and the door and many other ornaments, were to be borne away as booty, mules and saddled horses were led to the very sanctuary of the temple. Some of these which were unable to keep their footing on the splendid and slippery pavement, were stabbed when they fell, so that the sacred pavement was polluted with blood and filth. . . .

Nothing was more difficult and laborious than to soften by prayers, to render benevolent, these wrathful barbarians, vomiting forth bile at every unpleasing word, so that nothing failed to inflame their fury. Whoever attempted it was derided as insane and a man of intemperate language. Often they drew their daggers against any one who opposed them at all or hindered their demands.

No one was without a share in the grief. In the alleys, in the streets, in the temples, complaints, weeping, lamentations, grief, the groaning of men, the shrieks of women, wounds, rape, captivity, the separation of those most closely united. Nobles wandered about ignominiously, those of venerable age in tears, the rich in poverty. Thus it was in the streets, on the corners, in the temple, in the dens, for no place remained unassailed or defended the suppliants. All places everywhere were filled full of all kinds of crime. Oh, immortal God, how great the afflictions of the men, how great the distress!

*D. C. Munro, trans., *Translations and Reprints from the Original Sources of European History*, rev. ed., series 1, vol. 1, number III (University of Pennsylvania Press, 1912), pp. 15, 16.

One reason for the dramatic reversal was the undermining of the imperial military system by the growing insubordination of the *strategoi*, or generals, in charge of the *themes*, or provinces. Basil II had been strong enough to keep the military in check, but his weak successors were unable to do so, especially when the *strategoi* joined forces with the great provincial landowners.

The empire was plagued also by serious economic ailments. The large private and monastic estates reduced imperial revenues, especially when Basil's successors relieved the large landowners of most taxes. At the same time imperial expenditures were rising because of court extravagances and the cost of the mercenary army. Equally serious were the mounting raids of Patzinaks and Seljuk Turks, which left

In the spring of 1204, Crusaders under the command of Baldwin of Flanders subjected the city of Constantinople to three days of looting and slaughter. The scene is illustrated here in a nineteenth-century painting by Eugène Delacroix.

certain regions devastated and unproductive. The Byzantine gold *solidus*, which had remained stable for seven centuries, now went through a series of devaluations.

In Byzantium, as in many other empires, internal weakness attracted external aggression. The Norman adventurers from the West, who originally had served as Byzantine mercenaries, now turned against the weakened empire and overran its possessions in southern Italy, which had survived since the time of Justinian's conquests. Likewise in the east were the Seljuk Turks who had infiltrated from their central Asian homeland into the Islamic Empire. There they were employed as mercenaries by the Baghdad caliphs. Gradually the mercenaries became masters, and in 1055 they captured Baghdad and founded the Seljuk Empire. These Turks brought new life into the moribund Islamic world, reuniting the lands between India and the Mediterranean and pressing on the Taurus Mountain frontier that for centuries had separated the Byzantine and Islamic worlds.

This was the background of the two disasters that befell Byzantium in 1071, marking the beginning of centuries of decline. The first occurred at Bari in southern Italy, where the Normans conquered the sole surviving Byzantine foothold. The second and much more decisive setback was at Manzikert in Asia Minor. There the Seljuks defeated the Byzantine emperor in a fateful battle that began the transformation of Asia Minor from a Greek to a Turkish stronghold. Following this battle two rival emperors fought for the Byzantine throne, using Turkish forces against each other. Thus Turkish tribes were able to enter at will, gradually changing Asia Minor from the bedrock of Greek Byzantine power to the heartland of the Turkish nation.

The Byzantine Empire was saved from what appeared to be imminent dissolution by the shrewdness and tenacity of Emperor Comnenus (1081–1118). He granted valuable commercial concessions to the Venetians in return for their support against the Normans who were threatening to attack Constantinople. He also appealed to Western Christendom for assistance against the Moslem Seljuks. Instead of the few mercenaries he had hoped for, he received hordes of undisciplined Crusaders. Some were led by the Normans that Alexius had excellent reason to distrust. The contact between Eastern and Western Christendom resulted in mutual suspicion and open hostility. Greeks and Latins disliked each other's languages, religions, politics, and ways of life.

Such was the background of the Fourth Crusade, appropriately nicknamed the "businessmen's crusade." Characterized by the economic scheming of Venetian merchants, the quest for loot and lands by Western adventurers, the blandishments of a Byzantine pretender, and the long pent-up grievances harbored by Latins against what they considered to be the cunning, effeminate, grasping, and heretical Greeks, the Fourth Crusade was deflected by greed and revenge from its original goal of liberating Jerusalem. Instead the crusaders attacked Constantinople. A mixed force of French, Venetians, Flemings, and Germans stormed the capital in the spring of 1204 and subjected it to three days of merciless looting and slaughter. "Even the Saracens," observed a Byzantine chronicler, "would have been more merciful." Paradoxically, the end result of the Fourth Crusade was to pave the way for Islamic domination of the entire Middle East. Although the Byzantine Empire was restored in 1261, it never recovered from the traumatic shock of the Latin conquest, remaining in helpless impotence until the Ottoman capture of Constantinople in 1453.

IV. END OF BYZANTIUM

The victorious Latins set up their feudal states on the ruins of Byzantium. They established a Latin empire at Constantinople, a Latin kingdom at Thessaloniki, and several Latin states in Greece. The commercially minded Venetians occupied a whole quarter of Constantinople and annexed numerous islands and ports strategical-ly located on their route to the Levant. These new states, however, were doomed from the outset. The native Greek Orthodox populations were bitterly hostile to the end. Furthermore, the Latin conquerors had won only a few isolated toeholds on the fringes of the Balkan peninsula and were surrounded on all sides by enemies. They faced not only the Serbian and Bulgarian kingdoms in the Balkan interior, but also three Greek succession states located at Arta in Epirus, at Trebizond on the southern shore of the Black Sea, and at Nicaea in western Asia Minor. The first of these Greek states was too poor to provide effective leadership, and the second was too isolated. So it was Nicaea, with its strategic location, adequate resources, and able leadership, that organized Greek resistance to Latin rule.

By skillful diplomacy and force of arms the Nicaean rulers steadily reduced the Latin Empire until only the city of Constantinople itself remained. Finally, in 1261 the Latin emperor and the Venetian settlers fled from Constantinople without offering resistance. The Nicaean emperor, Michael Palaeologus, then made his solemn entry into the capital and, amid popular acclamation, took up his residence in the imperial palace.

The final phase of Byzantine history took place in the period between 1261, when Michael Palaeologus recovered Constantinople, and 1453, when his successor, Constantinople Palaeologus, was killed at a gate of the capital fighting the Turks. During these two centuries the restored empire consisted merely of the cities of Constantinople and Thessaloniki, with small fluctuating areas around each, and two separate appendages: Mistra, in the Peloponnesus, and Trebizond, in northern Asia Minor.

The outlook for this pitiful remnant of empire was scarcely more promising than that of its Latin predecessors. In Asia it faced the formidable Turks, and in Europe it was surrounded by small Latin states that remained in Greece and by the Serbians and Bulgarians to the north. To these external dangers were added internal difficulties. Economically the empire was bankrupt. The Italian stranglehold on commerce continued unbroken, so that in the mid-fourteenth century the Genoese quarter in Constantinople was collecting seven times as much as the imperial government in customs revenues. The emperors were reduced to debasing their currency and pawning their crown jewels with Venetian bankers. Increased taxes commonly were avoided by the politically influential rich. The poor rose in revolt against the aristocracy of birth and wealth, so that cities were torn by social strife.

Between 1342 and 1349 the city Thessaloniki was ruled by revolutionary leaders known as the Zealots. They reduced taxes on the poor, canceled their debts, confiscated and distributed monastery lands, and introduced participatory democracy with mass rallies and popularly elected officials. Their political program appears to have been influenced by the example of the republican city-states in Italy. But a dying Byzantine Empire could not support the political and social innovations then emerging naturally in the vigorous and expanding West. With Serbian and Turkish aid the emperor suppressed the Zealots and ended their republic. The episode was symptomatic, however, of the deep and widespread discord, as is evident in the following contemporary account:

. . . the rising spread through the Empire like a terrible and cruel epidemic, attacking many who formerly were quiet and moderate. . . . And so all the cities rose against the aristocracy. . . . The whole empire was in the throes of the most cruel and desperate struggle. . . . The people were ready to rise in arms under the slightest provocation, and committed the most violent deeds because they hated the rich. . . .[1]

The empire was weakened also by religious dissension. Hoping to obtain Western aid against the approaching Turks, the emperors on three separate occasions had agreed to the submission of the Orthodox church to the papacy (Unions of Lyons, 1274; Rome, 1369; and Florence, 1439). These agreements proved meaningless, for the West gave insignificant aid, and Byzantium was further torn by the bitter popular opposition to granting any concessions to the hated Latins. "Better Islam than the pope" was the defiant popular response to the barbarities of the Fourth Crusade and to the exploitation by Italian merchants.

The cry of preference for the Turks had been heard frequently in the past, but in the mid-fifteenth century the situation was unique because the Turks then were in a position to accept the invitation. As noted in Chapter 11, Section V, the Ottoman Turks had taken over from the Seljuks, conquered the remaining Byzantine enclaves in Asia Minor, crossed the straits to Europe, defeated the Bulgars and Serbs, and finally by 1453 were ready to close in on the beleaguered Byzantine capital.

Constantinople's population by this time had shrunk to between 50,000 and 70,000. The total force available for the defense of the city, including a small number from the West, amounted to no more than 9,000. This was totally inadequate to man the extensive series of walls and to repair the breaches pounded by the enemy cannon. The Ottoman army, led by the capable Sultan Mohammed II, numbered at least 80,000. Yet the defenders, under the courageous leadership of Emperor Constantine, repulsed the attackers from April 2, when the siege began, to May 29, when the final assault prevailed. The city was then given over to the soldiery for the promised three-day sack. The contemporary Byzantine historian Ducas describes as follows this ending of a thousand years of Byzantium:

Three days after the fall of the city he [Mohammed] released the ships so that each might sail off to its own province and city, each carrying such a load that it seemed each would sink. And what sort of a cargo? Luxurious cloths and textiles, objects and vessels of gold, silver, bronze and brass, books beyond all counting and number, prisoners including priests and lay persons, nuns and monks. All the ships were full of cargos, and the tents of the army camps were full of captives and of the above enumerated items and goods.[2]

V. BYZANTIUM'S LEGACY

In retrospect Byzantium obviously made significant contributions in various fields. One was in its role as a protective shield behind which the West was left free to develop its own civilization. The full meaning of this advantage became clear when, after the fall of Constantinople in 1453, the Turks within barely half a century reached the heart of Europe and besieged Vienna. Equally important was Byzantium's stimulus to trade and general economic development. For centuries Byzantium was the economic dynamo for the entire Mediterranean basin, and its currency served as the standard international medium of exchange. Its merchants and its commodities did much to lift western Europe out of its feudalized self-sufficiency and to start the Italian city-states on the road to commercial domination of the Mediterranean. In the realm of culture, Byzantium salvaged the intellectual and artistic treasures of antiquity and transmitted them to posterity along with its own legacy. From Byzantium came Roman law codified by Justinian; a religious art that only recently has been properly understood and appreciated; and the literary and scholarly masterpieces of classical and Hellenistic times as compiled, annotated, and preserved by conscientious scholars.

Finally, Byzantium was for the eastern Slavs what Rome had been for the Germans—the great educator and the source of both religion and civilization. The early Russian principalities strung out along river routes carried on a flourishing commerce with Byzantium. Through Kiev were funneled raw materials gathered from the Russian countryside—furs, hides, grains, timber, and slaves—and in return the Byzantine traders delivered luxury goods such as fine cloths, glassware, spices, jewelry, and wine.

With Greek material goods came Greek cultural institutions. Most important to the eastern Slavs was *Orthodox Christianity*, adopted by Prince Vladimir about 988. This involved much more than a mere change of religion. An ecclesiastical hierarchy based on the Byzantine model was now organized. The head was the metropolitan of Kiev, appointed by and subject to the jurisdiction of the patriarch of Constantinople. Orthodox Christianity also brought with it a new religious and legal literature, including translations of the Bible, Byzantine collections of the writings of the church fathers, lives of saints, and law books. Byzantine art also was now introduced in the form of stone churches, mosaics, frescoes, paintings, and particularly icons, in which the Russians excelled and developed their distinctive Russo-Byzantine style. The Orthodox church also brought with it Byzantine ecclesiastical law and established ecclesiastical courts. As in western Europe, these courts had very wide jurisdiction, including all cases involv-

The Russian Orthodox cathedral of St. Basil in Red Square, Moscow.

ing morals, beliefs, inheritance, and matrimonial matters.

In the realm of politics the new church served to strengthen the authority of the prince. Just as in western Europe the papacy had transformed the Frankish kings from tribal chieftains to the Lord's anointed, so now Russian Orthodoxy transformed the heads of the principalities from mere leaders of bands of personal followers to "servants of the lord" and hence rulers by divine right. Furthermore, the Russian church, in accordance with Byzantine tradition, accepted secular authority and control. There was no counterpart in Moscow, as there had been none in Constantinople, of Gregory VII or Innocent III in Rome, demanding and exacting obedience from emperors and kings alike.

This tradition continued after the disappearance of Byzantium. The Russian Orthodox church transferred its loyalty and subservience to the Russian emperor, until the tsarist empire followed the Byzantine to extinction.

In conclusion, Byzantine civilization stands out for its historic role and achievements. Yet Byzantium did lack the freshness and luster of classical Athens, even though, by comparison, Athens was insignificant in size and in time. The reason is that the role of Byzantium was, in the proper sense of the word, conservative. This is not to say that Byzantium was static. From beginning to end it was adjusting itself to changing times and circumstances. But the fact remains that its destiny was to conserve rather than to create. It was born already an aged state within the Roman Empire. It lived in the shadow of past power and glory, which it sought to maintain or recover. It produced a remarkable succession of outstanding leaders—administrators, generals, scholars, and theologians—but because of the context in which they worked very few of them were genuinely creative.

The fact that the East Roman Empire survived that of the West by a full millennium constituted a great advantage at the outset. Between the fifth and eleventh centuries the West was primitive and insignificant in comparison to the second Rome on the Bosphorus. But these were centuries when the West, precisely because it had to start fresh, was laying the foundations for a new civilization, while Byzantium was living on its splendid but overpowering patrimony. This is why from the eleventh century onward the West was able to forge ahead with its booming economy, rising national monarchies, new intellectual horizons, and a dynamic expansionism that manifested itself first in local crusades and then in an overseas thrust that was to lead within a few centuries to global hegemony. And in pitiful contrast, during these later centuries Byzantium was incapable of breaking the bonds to the past and thus became an obsolete *anachronism* that fought a gallant but doomed holding action to the ignominious and inevitable end in 1453.

SUGGESTED READINGS

The best full-scale study is by G. Ostrogorsky, *History of the Byzantine State* (Rutgers University, 1957); and the best short study is by S. Vryonis, Jr., *Byzantium and Europe* (Harcourt, 1967). The latter author also has written an authoritative study of a decisive turning point in Byzantine history entitled *The Decline of Medieval Hellenism in Asia Minor and the Process of Islamization from the Eleventh through the Fifteenth Century* (University of California, 1971). One of the best sources of information on almost every aspect of Byzantium, the south Slavs, and relations with Kiev and Islam is the *Cambridge Medieval History*, Vol. 4 (Cambridge University, 1966). Another standard work that considers cultural as well as political matters is by A. A. Vasiliev, *History of the Byzantium Empire*, 2 vols. (University of Wisconsin, 1958). A short survey that concentrates on the state, on Christianity, and on the Byzantine mind is by D. A. Miller, *The Byzantine Tradition* (Harper & Row, 1966). For other phases of Byzantine culture, see D. T. Rice, *Byzantine Art* (Penguin, 1961) and A. Grabar, *Byzantine Painting* (World, 1953). Finally, a source for primary materials is provided by D. J. Geanakoplos, *Byzantium: Church, Society and Civilization, Seen Through Contemporary Eyes* (University of Chicago, 1985).

NOTES

1. Cited by G. L. Seidler, *The Emergence of the Eastern World* (Pergamon Press, 1968), pp. 116–117.
2. S. Vryonis, Jr., *Byzantium and Europe* (Harcourt Brace Jovanovich, 1967), pp. 190–192.

CHAPTER 13

Traditional Confucian Civilization

I am happy because I am a human and not an animal; a male, and not a female; a Chinese, and not a barbarian; and because I live in Loyang, the most wonderful city in all the world.

Shao Yung (Neo-Confucianist, 1011–1077)

The fact that the Han dynasty eventually was succeeded by the Sui and T'ang dynasties ensured that civilization in China was to continue along traditional lines. Hence the course of China's civilization contrasts sharply with the unique change that was taking form in the West following Rome's collapse. (See Chapter 8, Sections III–V.) The ensuing millennium was a great Golden Age for the Chinese people. During the Han period China had succeeded in catching up to the other Eurasian civilizations, but now, during the medieval period, China forged ahead. China remained the richest, most populous, and in many ways most culturally advanced country in the world.

The millennium between the sixth century, when the Sui dynasty restored imperial unity, and the sixteenth, when the Westerners began their intrusion by sea, was for China an era of unparalleled political, social, and cultural stability. But this stability paradoxically proved to be a curse as well as a blessing. It was a blessing because Chinese society during this millennium provided more material advantages and more psychological security for more people than any other society in the world. But the stability was also a curse because China was so successful and comfortable that it remained relatively unchanged, though not completely static. At the same time, however, as we shall see in the following chapter, the West was being transformed by its technological achievements, its economic vitality, and its social and political *pluralism*. All this engendered a dynamism that culminated in the West's domination of the entire globe. The end result, then, was the disruption of the beautifully balanced but conservative Chinese society by the irresistible expansionism of the West.

Despite this outcome, we should not overlook the fact that for a full millennium the civilization of China led the world by its sheer viability and by its contributions to the human heritage.

I. SUI AND T'ANG DYNASTIES

The Sui dynasty (589–618) played the same role in Chinese history as the Ch'in dynasty had some eight centuries earlier. Both dynasties reunited China after long periods of disorder, and both then proceeded to make fundamental contributions to the development of the country. But in doing so they drove their people so hard and antagonized so many vested interests that both scarcely survived their founders.

The great contribution of the Ch'in rulers was the imperial unity they forced on China through road and canal building; construction of the Great Wall; standardization of weights, measures, and script; and extension and strengthening of the frontiers. The efforts of the Sui emperors were very similar and equally exhausting. They reconstructed the Great Wall, parts of which had fallen into disrepair. They built the main sections of the gigantic canal system that came to be known as the Grand Canal. This met a pressing need by linking the Yangtze valley, which had become the economic center of the country, with the north, which remained the political center. But so heavy was the cost in treasure and lives that the Sui emperor responsible for the undertaking lost popular support and undermined his dynasty.

Equally exhausting were the series of campaigns that extended the imperial frontiers to include the island of Formosa (Taiwan), Annam and Champa in Indochina, and Kansu in the northwest. But the attempts to conquer the most northern of the three kingdoms into which Korea was then divided proved disastrous. Four successive invasions were repulsed by the resolute Korean defenders. The disaffected soldiers mutinied, and overtaxed Chinese peasants rose in rebellion in various parts of the country. The emperor fled to south China, where he was assassinated in 618. The victor in the ensuing struggle among several pretenders established the T'ang dynasty, regarded by many Chinese and Western historians as the most outstanding of them all.

The most striking accomplishment of the T'ang dynasty was its expansion of the empire. In a series of great campaigns, it extended the frontiers even beyond those of the Han emperors. In central Asia it established Chinese *suzerainty* over the Tarim basin and beyond the Pamirs to the states of the Oxus valley and even to the headwaters of the Indus in modern Afghanistan. Other vast territories that now were forced to accept Chinese suzerainty were Tibet in the south, Mongolia in the northwest, and Korea and Manchuria in the northeast. The only other comparable empire in the world at the time was that of the Moslem Arabs in the Middle East.

China's foreign conquests were made possible by the reestablishment of strong central government at home. The Han dynasty had been undermined by powerful local families that had accumulated huge, self-sufficient, and tax-free estates. They built fortresslike manor houses on these estates and so could successfully defy central authority. Disintegration was also furthered by the appearance of Buddhist monasteries, which, with their extensive and growing landholdings, offered another challenge to the imperial government. The Sui and T'ang dynasties developed an antidote to this political fragmentation. It consisted of the *equal-field system* by which the central government assigned plots of about nineteen acres to all able-bodied peasants. This did not deprive the powerful families of their holdings, for the land assigned to the peasants was obtained from other sources, such as reclamation projects and fields that had been abandoned during the wars. Moreover, only the free peasants received the land grants, and in actual practice, by no means all of them got land. Nevertheless, the equal-field system did help somewhat to loosen the grip of the great families and to strengthen the T'ang regime. It halted for some time the growth of the large semifeudal estates. It increased government revenues, since the small peasants paid taxes whereas the politically powerful great landholders did not. Furthermore, the peasants were given military training and organized into a regular militia, thereby strengthening the military position of the imperial government.

The T'ang dynasty strengthened its authority also by developing a competent bureaucracy to administer the empire. The Sui earlier had reinstated the Han system of civil service based on competitive public examinations. The T'ang continued and expanded this system, following the basic Confucian tenet that matters of state are best resolved by recruiting people of talent. It rejected the typical Western practice of handling state affairs by changing laws and institutions. When fully developed, the Chinese system consisted of a series of examinations held amid elaborate ritual. The first, in the district and prefectural cities, occurred every two or three years, and approximately 2 percent of the candidates who passed these took the prefectural exams a few weeks later. Prefecture-examination survivors (about half the candidates) became eligible for appointment to minor posts and for further examinations held every three years in the provincial capitals. Success here entitled one to take the imperial examinations at the capital. Only 6 percent passed this hurdle and became eligible for appointment to high office; and only a third of these normally passed the final palace examination in the presence of the emperor himself. They were then admitted to membership in the most exalted fraternity of Chinese scholarship, the Hanlin Academy. Historiographers and other high literary officers were selected from the academy.

At first the examinations were fairly comprehensive, emphasizing the Confucian classics but including also subjects like law, mathematics, and political affairs. Gradually, however, they came to concentrate on literary style and Confucian orthodoxy. The net result was a system that theoretically opened offices to all talented males but in practice favored the classes with enough wealth to afford the years of study and preparation. This did not mean that a hereditary aristocracy ruled China; rather, it was a hierarchy of the learned, a "literocracy." On the one hand, it provided China with an efficient and stable administration that won the respect and admiration of Europeans. But on the other, it was a system that stifled originality and bred conformity. As long as China remained relatively isolated in east Asia, it made for stability and continuity. But with the intrusion of the dynamic West it prevented effective adjustment

A standing Buddha on a lotus pedestal from the early Sui dynasty (589–618). The work is carved from sandstone and has traces of pigment. (From Tianlongshan, Shanxi, China; 68.6 x 17.8 x 15.24 cm)

Sixth-century Chinese stoneware figure from the collection of the Victoria and Albert Museum, London.

and response. It was finally abolished altogether in 1905.

The capital of the T'ang Empire was Ch'ang-an, a magnificent city of probably over 1 million people. Its broad thoroughfares, criss-crossing in checkerboard fashion, often were crowded with Persians, Indians, Jews, Armenians, and assorted central Asians. They came as merchants, missionaries, and mercenary soldiers, for China under the T'ang was more open to foreigners than at any other time except for the short-lived Mongol Yüan interlude.

Freedom of thought was most apparent in matters of religion. The extension of imperial frontiers and the reopening of land and sea trade routes brought in many foreign religious ideas and missionaries. This was the case with Buddhism, which first entered China from India during the Han dynasty, and which began to seriously challenge the official Confucianism during the chaos following the collapse of the Han. In that time of trouble Confucianism was increasingly questioned because its emphasis on filial piety and family loyalty appeared to weaken an already weak state. Consequently Buddhism gained rapidly and reached the height of its influence during the early T'ang, which is sometimes called the "Buddhist period" of Chinese history.

Although Buddhism attained great wealth and influence in China, it became thoroughly sinicized in the process. It also contributed fundamentally to Neo-Confucianism. Since there was considerable religious toleration and freedom of thought in China, various Buddhist sects evolved, outstanding being Ch'an, which later appeared in Japan as Zen. This sect emphasized meditation and self-reliance and was the only one to continue a vigorous intellectual life after the T'ang. Another feature of *sinicization* was the government's attempt to control and even subsidize the monasteries and temples, following the typically Chinese concept that a religion should serve the interests of the state and function as its spiritual organ.

In the long run the attempts at control failed, and eventually the government resorted to outright persecution. The Buddhist emphasis on the salvation of the individual rather than on one's obligation to the family was too contrary to basic Chinese traditions. The complete with-

Seated Buddha from the T'ang Dynasty, dated 618–907 C.E.

drawal from society of monks and nuns not only was contrary to tradition but also was considered unnatural and antisocial. Most important, the government coveted the vast treasures and estates that the monasteries had accumulated through the centuries—hence the series of persecutions that crippled Buddhism in China, though it did not disappear altogether as it did in India. The persecution, restricted to the institutions and their clergy, did not include the rank-and-file believers, as happened in comparable situations in the West. The end result of this Buddhist interlude was minimal as far as the overall evolution of Chinese civilization was concerned. Buddhism made significant contributions to Chinese philosophy, metaphysics, art, and literature. But it did not remold Chinese society as a whole, as Christianity had remolded the European.

During the last century and a half of their reign, the T'ang rulers were faced with the usual problems of a dynasty in decline. Imperial expenses outstripped revenues. Population growth likewise outstripped land supply, so that peasant families no longer could be provided with individual plots. The equal-field system broke down, and the wealthy families once more enlarged their estates at the expense of the peasants. Since the revenue system was based on per-capita taxes, the burden of paying for the mounting imperial expenses fell on the peasants at a time when their holdings were shrinking.

The T'ang emperors managed to hang on for about another 150 years, but it was a period of steady deterioration. Incompetence and provocative luxury in the capital along with successive droughts and widespread famine provoked rebellions in many provinces. The dynasty enlisted the support of local military leaders and assorted "barbarian" border peoples. But these soon were out of control. They disregarded court orders and fought among themselves for the succession to the obviously doomed dynasty. The end came in 907, when one of the rebel leaders deposed the last T'ang ruler and sacked Ch'ang-an. The empire now broke into fragments, and the ensuing half-century is known as the period of the "Five Dynasties." An able general finally was able to restore unity and to found a new dynasty, the Sung, which, like its predecessor, endured for about three centuries (960–1279).

II. SUNG GOLDEN AGE

The Sung emperors were much more passive in their external relations than their Han and T'ang predecessors. Instead of beginning with great campaigns reestablishing imperial frontiers in the heart of Eurasia, the second Sung emperor merely tried to regain from nomad control the territory between Peking and the Great Wall. But he was disastrously defeated, and his successor gave up claim to this region. He even paid the nomads an annual "gift," which in fact was thinly veiled tribute. Thus the Sung never recovered the northeast territories in Manchuria, nor the northwest territories that provided access to the overland routes to the West.

This was a grave weakness for the Sung dynasty, leaving it vulnerable to nomadic invasions. The policy of paying "gifts" worked well for a century and a half, but disaster came when a Sung emperor made a rash attempt to recover the northeastern lands. Instead of easy victory he suffered a crushing defeat that was followed by massive invasion of north China. The Sung defenses crumbled, and the dynasty was left with only the Yangtze valley in central China and the lands to the south. Consequently the second half of the dynasty (1127–1279) is

Relief from the tomb of the T'ang Emperor T'ai Tsung (597–649) showing a chestnut bay battle charger.

Blockprinted page from Han Shu *(History of the Han Dynasty). Printed between 1208 and 1224, this book is one of the finest examples of Sung printing.*

known as the Southern Sung, and the first half (960–1127) is called the Northern Sung.

The Southern Sung dynasty was much berated by later Chinese historians for failing at the outset to regain the outlying provinces and then suffering the loss of the entire northern half of the country. Although this criticism is undeniable, it is also true that in many respects Chinese civilization reached its height during the centuries of the T'ang and the Sung, particularly in the cultural fields. During these centuries the vast encyclopedias of Buddhist texts and Confucian classics appeared, as well as the comprehensive dynastic histories written by teams of scholars; this period also saw the appearance of the masterpieces of many great poets and artists; the art of calligraphy, depicted on scrolls prized as highly as paintings; the beautiful porcelain as thin as glass and almost as transparent; the priceless invention of printing, which was utilized for the mass duplication and distribution of Buddhist scriptures; and the extraordinary advances in science and technology that are only now being adequately understood. (See Chapter 9, Section II.)

In addition to its cultural attainments, the Sung period is noteworthy for a commercial revolution with much significance for all Eurasia. The roots are to be found in a marked increase in the productivity of China's economy. Steady technological improvements raised the output of the traditional industries. Agriculture likewise was stimulated by the introduction of a quickly maturing strain of rice that allowed two crops to be grown each season where only one had been possible before. Also new water-control projects undertaken by the Sung greatly expanded the acreage of irrigated paddy fields. Thus it is estimated that the rice crop doubled between the eleventh and twelfth centuries.

Increasing productivity made possible a corresponding increase in population, which in turn further stimulated production, in circular fashion. The volume of trade also rose with the quickening tempo of economic activity. For the first time there appeared in China large cities that were primarily commercial rather than administrative centers.

Even more marked than this spurt in domestic trade was the increase in foreign trade. Considerable overseas commerce had been carried on since Han times, but during the T'ang, and more especially during the Sung, the volume of foreign trade far surpassed all previous records. The basis for this burgeoning trade was, of course, the unprecedented productivity of China's economy. Important also were the improvements in maritime technology, including the use of the compass, of the adjustable centerboard keel, and of cotton sails in place of bamboo slats. Finally, overseas trade was stimulated by the initiative of Moslem merchants and mariners who were the great entrepreneurs in Asian seas at this period.

The end result was that for the first time the seaports rather than the old overland routes became China's principal contact with the outside world. Indicative of China's economic leadership at this time is the fact that its exports were mostly manufactured goods such as silk, porcelain, books, and paintings, whereas the imports were mostly raw materials such as spices, minerals, and horses. Finally, it should be noted that during the Sung the Chinese themselves for the first time engaged in overseas trade on a large scale. They no longer depended on foreign intermediaries. In conclusion, China during the Sung was well on its way to becoming a great maritime power. However, the all-important fact—for world history as well as for Chinese—is that this potentiality was never realized. And equally significant, this commercial revolution of the Sung era had none of the explosive repercussions on Chinese society that a corresponding commercial revolution had on Western society. (See Section IV, this chapter.)

III. YÜAN MONGOL RULE

The rule of the Southern Sung, though confined to only half the century, was exceptionally peaceful and prosperous. Meanwhile, north China was under the Ch'in, a people of Manchurian origin. About 1215 they appealed to the Southern Sung for help against the formidable Mongols, who had driven them out of Peking. The Sung, not aware of their deadly power, supported the Mongols instead by sending infantry skilled in siege warfare, and by 1234 the Ch'in were overwhelmed. Then the Sung emperor rashly attempted to secure north China for his own empire. The Mongols retaliated by promptly invading south China. Because the Mongols were preoccupied elsewhere, the war dragged on for decades, but the end came in 1279 when the last Sung ruler perished in a naval battle. A new Mongol dynasty that took

the name Yüan now began its rule, which was to last until 1368.

This was the first and only time that China was ruled by full nomads who had not already been partly sinicized by earlier contact with the empire. The first reaction of the rude conquerors was to level the cities and to incorporate their new subjects into the traditional Mongol tribal society. But they soon learned this was impossible and that a more lucrative alternative was feasible. A Chinese adviser described that alternative:

Now that you have conquered everywhere under Heaven and all the riches of the four seas, you can have everything you want, but you have not yet organized it. You should set up taxation on land and merchants, and should make profits on wine, salt, iron, and the produce of the mountains and marshes. In this way in a single year you will obtain 500,000 ounces of silver, 80,000 rolls of silk and 400,000 piculs of grain. How can you say that the Chinese people are of no use to you?[1]

The Mongols acted on this advice and established an administrative apparatus essentially similar to that of their Chinese predecessors. At the same time they were able to preserve their identity because their nomadic background separated them from their subjects in language, customs, and laws. They also took care to employ many foreigners in their service to counterbalance the Chinese majority, whom they did not trust. Marco Polo is the best known of these foreign-born bureaucrats, though most of them were central Asian Moslems.

Kublai Khan, who moved the Mongol capital from Karakorum to Peking and became essentially a Chinese emperor, dutifully performed the traditional Confucian imperial rites. He also sought to appease the Confucian literati by exempting them from taxation, but they remained largely alienated. They resented the large number of foreigners who had turned their civil service into an international bureaucracy. They also resented the Mongol toleration and patronage of various foreign religions, including Islam and Nestorian Christianity. (See Chapter 12, Section IV.)

Because of its nature and relatively short duration, Mongol rule in China did not leave a

Kublai Khan, wearing ermine coat, with Mongol warriors at the hunt. Note the camel caravan in the hills at rear.

duced by the Sung but developed further by the Mongols. Marco Polo repeatedly expressed his astonishment at the use of paper money, as did a fellow Italian merchant in the following words:

Whatever silver the merchants carry with them to Cathay the lord of Cathay takes from them and puts in his treasury and gives that paper money of theirs in exchange . . . and with this money you can readily buy silk and whatever other merchandise you desire to buy, and all of the people of the country are bound to receive it, and you shall not pay a higher price for your goods because your money is of paper.[2]

The able Kublai Khan died in 1294 at the age of eighty and was succeeded by his equally able grandson, Timur. But Timur died young, and the following khans were incompetent and debauched by palace life. Fratricidal conflicts broke out within the dynasty, and frequent flooding of the Yellow River produced widespread famine in north China. Rebellions broke out in most of the provinces, and only the rivalry among the rebel leaders enabled the Mongols to hold out as long as they did. Finally, the turmoil was ended by an able commoner who, like the founder of the Han, rose through sheer ability in time of crisis and opportunity to become the "Son of Heaven." Thus the Chinese Ming dynasty was established in 1368 and remained in power to 1644.

IV. MING ETHNOCENTRISM AND WITHDRAWAL

Two dynasties, the Ming (1368–1644) and the Ch'ing (1644–1912), ruled China during the more than half-millennium between the overthrow of the Mongols and the advent of the republic. These centuries comprise one of the great eras of orderly government and social stability in human history. A main reason for this unusual durability was the complete primacy of a new Confucian metaphysics known as *Neo-Confucianism*. This renaissance of Confucian thought took place mostly during the time of troubles following the collapse of the T'ang dynasty, when the needs of the age clearly called for something more than the mere memoriza-

deep imprint on the country. Perhaps the most lasting contribution was the selection of Peking (modern Beijing) as the capital. Situated in the north China plain on the routes leading westward to central Asia and eastward to Manchuria, (Beijing) has remained an important military, economic, and administrative center to the present day. Mongol rule also brought about a sharp rise in overland trade, since China now was part of a huge empire encompassing most of Eurasia. Commerce was facilitated by the widespread use of paper money, which was introtion of Confucian classics. Accordingly, a number of scholars undertook a searching reappraisal of the problems of humankind and of the universe.

A leader in this undertaking was Chu Hsi (1129–1200), who in his youth had studied both Buddhism and Taoism. Satisfied with neither, he turned to the Confucian classics, and with his remarkable talent for synthesis he worked out an interpretation that combined elements of Buddhism and Taoism with Confucianism and that was more satisfying and relevant for his time. His approach—essentially that of the empirical rationalist—taught that the universe is governed by natural law, which should be understood and respected. He also believed in the goodness of people and in their ability to become more perfect. He compared the individual to a mirror covered with dust, which if cleaned will be as bright as ever. Evil, therefore, was the result of neglect and of defective education, and hence could be corrected.

Chu Hsi's influence in the Confucian world was comparable to that of Thomas Aquinas in Western Christendom. Just as Aquinas soon was to weave Aristotle and St. Paul into the official scholastic philosophy, so Chu Hsi now integrated contemporary Chinese thought into Neo-Confucianism. And by his very comprehensive and persuasive ideas Chu Hsi, like Aquinas, discouraged further philosophical development. This was particularly true during the Ming period, when, as a reaction against the preceding foreign Mongol domination, there was a pronounced ethnocentrism and a looking backward to past traditions. In such an atmosphere, Chu Hsi came to be regarded as the absolute and final authority. "Ever since the time of the philosopher Chu," declared a Ming scholar, "the Truth has been made manifest to the world. No more writing is needed: what is left to us is practice."[3]

Since the Confucian classics, with Chu Hsi's commentaries, became the basis of the civil-service examinations, this Neo-Confucianism became the official orthodox view of the empire until the late nineteenth century. Its effect was to provide the growing social rigidity with an intellectual reason for its existence. It contributed fundamentally to the unique and long-lasting continuity of Chinese civilization, but the cost was stultifying conformity that quashed all originality or new ideas from the outside.

Chinese society owed its stability not only to Neo-Confucianism, but also to the entrenched power of the so-called gentry ruling class, whose power rested on their combined possession of land and office in an agrarian-based bureaucratic empire. As landlords and as money-lenders the gentry dominated the economic life of the villages and towns. Shortage of land and of capital enabled them to impose extortionate rents and interest rates. Frequent natural disasters bankrupted people with mortgages, who then virtually became serfs under contract to local gentry families. It was common for these families by late Ming times to have several thousand indentured peasant households of this sort.

The gentry also were degree holders; indeed, this is what the Chinese term for "gentry" literally means. Landowning was almost a necessity for financing the years of study necessary to become a degree holder, and hence to be eligible for a post in the bureaucracy. Thus the association between the local gentry and the imperial bureaucracy was intimate and mutually supporting. Frequently a government official arriving at a new provincial post found the native dialect quite incomprehensible and so was completely dependent on the local gentry for orientation and guidance.

Ming and Ch'ing China were ruled by the bureaucracy and the gentry together, if a meaningful distinction can be made between the two. Both the imperial establishment and the local gentry were interested in preserving the mutually beneficial status quo, and they cooperated to that end. Whereas earlier dynasties occasionally had attempted to force through land redistribution and other such reforms, the Ming and the Ch'ing carefully avoided any challenges to the gentry's control of the countryside.

By contrast, it is revealing and significant that the Ming government took the initiative in controlling and repressing the merchant class. This was a basic and most meaningful difference between the Western and Chinese societies. In the West, as will be noted in the following chapter, the bourgeoisie from the start enjoyed considerable autonomy and was able to increase it

ROOTS OF CHINESE STABILITY

Foreign observers invariably were impressed by the antiquity and stability of Chinese civilization. T. T. Meadows, a British consular officer who served in China in the mid-nineteenth century, gave the following explanation based on first-hand observation.*

The real causes of the unequalled duration and constant increase of the Chinese people, as one and the same nation . . . consists of three doctrines, together with an institution. . . . *The doctrines are*

I. That the nation must be governed by moral agency in preference to physical force.

II. That the services of the wisest and ablest men in the nation are indispensable to its good government.

III. That the people have the right to depose a sovereign who, either from active wickedness or vicious indulgence, gives cause to oppressive and tyrannical rule.

The institution is

The system of public service competitive examinations. . . .

The institution of Public Service Examinations (which have long been strictly competitive) is the cause of the continued duration of the Chinese nation: it is that which preserves the other causes and gives efficacy to their operation. By it all parents throughout the country, who can compass the means, are induced to impart to their sons an intimate knowledge of the literature which con-

tains the three doctrines above cited, together with many others conducive to a high mental cultivation. By it all the ability of the country is enlisted on the side of that Government which takes care to preserve it in purity. By it, with its impartiality, the poorest man in the country is constrained to say, that if his lot in life is a low one it is so in virtue of the "will of Heaven," and that no unjust barriers created by his fellow men prevent him from elevating himself. . . .

The normal Chinese government is essentially based on moral force: it is not a despotism. A military and police is maintained sufficient to crush merely factious risings, but totally inadequate, both in numbers and in nature, to put down a disgusted and indignant people. But though no despotism, this same government is in form and machinery a pure autocracy. In his district the magistrate is absolute; in his province, the governor; in the empire, the Emperor. The Chinese people have no right of legislation, they have no right of self-taxation, they have not the power of voting out their rulers or of limiting or stopping supplies. They have therefore the right of rebellion. Rebellion is in China the old, often exercised, legitimate, and constitutional means of stopping arbitrary and vicious legislation and administration.

*T. T. Meadows, *The Chinese and Their Rebellions* (Smith, Elder, 1856), pp. 23, 24, 401–403.

with the passage of time. In China there was a corresponding merchant class, which during the Sung enjoyed a real commercial revolution. Furthermore, China made most of the basic technological inventions of medieval times. Yet the commercial revolution and the technological advances together were not enough to cause the revolutionary repercussions in China that completely transformed society in the West. The

basic reason for this, as noted in Chapter 8, Section V, was the continuity of Chinese history—the fact that the Han dynasty was continued in essentials by the Sui, and the Sui in turn by the T'ang and the Sung, and so on in unbroken succession until the end of imperial history in 1912. Thus the traditional bureaucracy–gentry ruling establishment, propped up by the ideas of Neo-Confucianism, was able to absorb and blunt

Chinese general, one of the guardian figures along the road to the Ming tombs outside of Peking.

the effects of new technology and of economic growth. But in the West, Rome came to an end with no imperial successor. Instead, a new pluralistic civilization emerged in which gunpowder, the compass, the printing press, and the oceangoing ship were not muffled but rather exploited to their full potential with explosive consequences, first for Europe and then for the entire world, including China.

Explosive repercussions were impossible in China because the imperial establishment there was too enveloping and restricting. For example,

Chinese merchants and industrialists customarily organized themselves into local guilds headed by chiefs. But guild chiefs were certified by the government, which held them responsible for the conduct of individual members. Boat traders were organized under harbor chiefs who were also responsible to the government. More important were the government monopolies in the production and distribution of many commodities that the court and the administration consumed, including arms, textiles, pottery, leather goods, apparel, and wine. The government also completely controlled the production and distribution of basic commodities, such as salt and iron, that were necessities for the entire population. Such restraints deprived Chinese merchants of the opportunity for free enterprise and restricted economic growth. The restraints also promoted official corruption, for members of the imperial court used their privileged positions to manipulate the state monopolies for personal gain.

Another example of the restrictive, inward-looking policies of China's ruling establishment was its active opposition to overseas enterprise. Chinese emigrants had trickled down to Southeast Asia before the arrival of the Europeans. Probably at no time were there as many Spaniards as Chinese in the Philippines. In 1603, thirty-two years after the founding of Manila as a Spanish settlement, the Chinese population there was about 20,000 compared with perhaps 1,000 Spaniards. And these Chinese, who virtually controlled the economic life of the settlement, were extending their control to the other islands of the archipelago. When in that year, 1603, the Manila Chinese suffered one of the massacres that they and their compatriots in Southeast Asia have periodically endured to the present day, an official of the nearby mainland province of Fukien condoned the massacre and denounced all overseas Chinese as deserters of the tombs of their ancestors and people who were unworthy of the emperor's concern. Likewise an imperial edict of 1712 forbade Chinese to trade and reside in Southeast Asia. Five years later another edict allowed those already abroad to come home without fear of punishment, and in 1729 still another edict set a deadline after which those overseas could not be allowed to return. What a striking contrast between this

Chinese policy and that of the West. The Western states would soon be actively promoting overseas settlements and trading companies and would be ready to take up arms against any threats to these enterprises.

The bizarre history of the early fifteenth-century Ming voyages provides the most dramatic example of the negative official Chinese attitude toward overseas activities. These voyages had an astonishing range and showed a technological superiority that proved conclusively China's world leadership in maritime undertakings. Then came the imperial order forbidding further overseas expeditions and the immediate enforcement of that order. (See Chapter 9, Section I.)

Although the precise motives behind this edict are unknown, the significant fact is that it was possible to issue it only because Chinese merchants lacked the political power and social status of their Western counterparts. This fundamental difference in institutional structure and outward-thrusting dynamism deflected Chinese energies inward at this fateful turning point in world history and left the oceans of the globe open to Western enterprise. The inevitable result was the eclipse within a few centuries of the great "Celestial Kingdom." The barbarians of the West now came to the fore.

V. CHINESE CIVILIZATION IN JAPAN

Since the Chinese civilization and Chinese empires persisted in unbroken continuity to modern times, they have dominated east Asia in a way that no Western country has dominated the West. Consequently there did not develop in east Asia the political and cultural diversity that has characterized the West since the fall of Rome. The only exception has been in the steppes and deserts of the far north and west, where agriculture is climatically impossible and where the nomads accordingly developed a distinctive, non-Chinese, pastoral way of life. By contrast, in the neighboring Vietnamese, Korean, and Japanese lands, there was no climatic obstacle to the development of agriculture and hence to the spread of Chinese civilization. Of these three lands, Japan was able to remain the most independent of the Chinese colossus, both

politically and culturally, and hence played a correspondingly more significant role in both east Asian and world history. The remainder of this chapter, therefore, will concentrate on the evolution of Japan to the eve of the Western penetration.

Japanese history has been shaped to a considerable degree by the influence of geographic location. In this respect there is a close parallel with the British Isles at the other end of the Eurasian landmass. The Japanese islands, however, are more isolated than the British Isles; 115 miles separate them from the mainland, compared with the 21-mile width of the English Channel. Thus, before their defeat in World War

A clay statue of a warrior in armor from an ancient tomb.

II by the United States, the Japanese had been seriously threatened by foreign invasion only in the thirteenth century by the Mongols. The Japanese, therefore, have been close enough to the mainland to benefit from the great Chinese civilization but distant enough to be able to select and reject as they wished. In fact, the Japanese have been unusually sensitive and alert to what they have imported from abroad. Although popularly regarded as a nation of borrowers, they have independently evolved, because of their isolation, a larger proportion of their own culture than have any other people of comparable numbers and level of development.

The Japanese are basically a Mongoloid people who migrated from northeast Asia, but the hairy Caucasoid Ainu who originally inhabited their islands contributed to their racial composition. Malayan and Polynesian migrants from the south probably did also. Early Japan was organized into a large number of clans, each ruled by a hereditary priest-chieftain. Toward the end of the first century after Christ, the Yamato clan established a loose political and religious domination over the others. Its chief was the emperor, and its clan god was made the national god.

This clan organization was undermined by the importation of Chinese civilization, which began on a large scale in the sixth century. Buddhism, introduced from Korea, was the medium for cultural change, playing the same role here as Christianity did in Europe among the Germans and Slavs. Students, teachers, craftmakers, and monks crossed over from the mainland, bringing with them a new way of life as well as a new religion. More significant was the role of those Japanese who went to the "Celestial Kingdom" and returned as ardent converts. The forces for change produced the Taika Reform, which began in 645 and sought to change Japan into a centralized state on the model of T'ang dynasty China. In accordance with the Chinese model, the country was divided into provinces and districts ruled by governors and magistrates who received their power from the emperor and his council of state. Also, all land was nationalized in the name of the emperor and given to peasant households. The new owner-cultivators were responsible for paying to the central government a land tax in the form of rice and a labor tax that sometimes included military service.

These and other changes were designed to strengthen imperial authority, and they did so in comparison with the earlier clan structure. But in practice, the Japanese emperor was far from being the undisputed head of a highly centralized state. The powerful hereditary aristocracy forced certain changes in this Chinese-type administration that finally brought about its downfall. Although officials supposedly were appointed, as in China, on the basis of merit through examination, actually the old aristocracy succeeded in obtaining positions of status and power. Likewise, they kept many of their large landholdings, which were usually tax exempt and became manors outside the governmental administrative system. During this period the Fujiwara family perfected the *dyarchy*, or dual system of government. They did the actual work of ruling, furnishing the consorts for the emperor and filling the high civil and military posts. Meanwhile, the emperor passed his life in luxurious seclusion, not bothered by affairs of state or by contacts with commoners. His chief responsibility was to guarantee that his dynasty would continue forever. This dyarchical system of government, which had no parallel in China, remained the pattern in Japan until the country was opened up by the Europeans in the nineteenth century.

In cultural matters there was the same adaptation of Chinese models. The Japanese borrowed Chinese ideographs but developed their own system of writing. They borrowed Confucianism but modified its ethics and changed its political doctrines to suit their social structure. They accepted Buddhism but adapted it to satisfy their own spiritual needs, while keeping their native Shintoism. They built new imperial capitals, first at Nara and then at Kyoto, that were modeled after the T'ang capital, Ch'ang-an. But there was no mistaking the Japanese quality of the temples, pavilions, shrines, and gardens. The imperial court became the center of highly developed intellectual and artistic activity. Court life is delightfully described in Lady Murasaki's famous eleventh-century novel, *The Tale of Genji*. But this novel also reflects a society grown effeminate and devoted almost exclusively to aesthetic and sensual pleasures. This degeneration, which worsened in the next century, contributed to the coming of the new age of feudalism, when political power shifted from the imperial court to virile rural warriors.

VI. JAPANESE FEUDALISM

The Chinese system of imperial organization introduced by the Taika Reform of 645 worked effectively for a long period. By the twelfth century, however, it had been undermined and replaced by a Japanese variety of feudalism. One reason was the tendency of provincial governors, who were too fond of the entertainments of Kyoto, to give their powers and responsibilities to local subordinates. Another was that powerful local families and Buddhist communities were always hungry for land and often able to seize it by force. They were willing to bring new land under cultivation as long as the incentive of tax exemption was maintained. These trends reduced the amount of tax-paying land, which meant an increased tax load for the peasant owner-cultivators. They in turn either fled to the northern frontier areas, where the Ainu were being pushed back by force of arms, or else commended themselves and their lands to lords of manors. This freed them of taxes and provided them with protection, but at the cost of becoming serfs. The net result of this process was that by the end of the twelfth century, tax-paying land amounted to 10 percent or less of the total cultivated area, and local power had been taken over by the new rural aristocracy.

At the same time, the aristocracy had become the dominant military force because of the disintegration of the imperial armed forces. The Taika Reform had made all males between the ages of twenty and sixty subject to military service. But the conscripts were required to furnish their own weapons and food and were given no relief from the regular tax burden. This arrangement proved unworkable and was abandoned in 739. Government military posts usually were filled by effeminate court aristocrats. As a result, the campaigns against the Ainu were fought by the rural aristocrats. They became mounted warriors and gradually increased their military effectiveness until they completely overshadowed the imperial forces. A feudal relationship now developed between these rural lords and their retainers, or *samurai* (literally, "one who serves"). This relationship was based on an idealized ethic that was known as *bushido*, or "way of the warrior." The samurai enjoyed special legal and ceremonial rights, and in return were expected to give unquestioning service to their lords.

By the twelfth century, Japan was controlled by competing groups of feudal lords, who struggled to gain control of as much land as possible. The outcome was the rise of great territorial magnates known as *daimyo* ("great name"). At the beginning of the sixteenth century there were several hundred of these daimyo, each seeking to attain hegemony over all Japan.

One of the many lovely gardens of Kyoto, capital of the Ashikaga Shogunate.

VII. JAPAN'S WITHDRAWAL AND ISOLATION

The period of daimyo control was one of rapid economic growth, with important repercussions for Japanese society. Important technological advances were made in agriculture as well as in handicrafts. Production per acre apparently doubled or even tripled in some parts of the country. The increased productivity stimulated more trade and a shift from a barter to a money economy. Towns gradually developed in the fifteenth and sixteenth centuries at strategic crossroads or coastal harbors or major temples. In these towns appeared the Japanese guilds, or *za*, which, like their Western counterparts, sought to gain monopoly rights in the production or transportation of certain goods or in the exercise of certain trades or professions. They obtained these monopoly rights by paying fees to certain local authorities, thereby gaining greater freedom and higher status for their members.

Foreign and domestic trade quickened with the rising productivity of the Japanese economy. As early as the twelfth century enterprising Japanese had crossed overseas to Korea and then to China, prepared both for trade and for piracy. Gradually they extended their operations, so that by the late fourteenth century these pirate-traders were active throughout Southeast Asia. Japanese settlers and soldiers of fortune also were widely scattered, especially in Indochina, Siam, and the Philippines.

These socioeconomic developments began to undermine feudalism in Japan, as they had done earlier under similar circumstances in the West. If this trend had continued without interruption, Japan presumably would have followed the west European example and developed into a modern unified nation-state with an overseas empire. But Japan did not do so; instead it withdrew into seclusion.

A prime reason for this withdrawal appears to have been the penetration of the Western powers into the waters of Southeast and east Asia. This blocked the natural course of Japanese expansionism. If the Westerners had not appeared, the Japanese probably would have won footholds in Formosa and in various parts of Southeast Asia. But now the Japanese were alarmed by the obvious superiority of Western military technology on the seas, as well as by the surprising effectiveness of Western missionaries within Japan. The Japanese response was to withdraw into the almost complete seclusion adopted in the early seventeenth century by the Tokugawa Shogunate.

All missionaries were forced to leave and their converts required to renounce their faith. Eventually all foreigners had to depart, with the exception of a few Chinese and Dutch who were allowed to trade under restricted conditions on the Deshima islet in Nagasaki harbor. In addition, Japanese subjects were forbidden to go abroad on penalty of death. Thus began over two centuries of seclusion for Japan.

The end result, then, was not a modern expansionist nation-state. Rather, Japanese feudalism was preserved and shielded from outside influences by the Tokugawa walls of seclusion. In their search for stability, the Tokugawa imported Confucian ideas and institutions from China. They adopted the Confucian hierarchy of four classes—the warrior administrator, the peasant, the artisan, and the merchant. They also borrowed Confucian philosophy, with its emphasis on proper relationships between rulers and ruled. An influential school of Confucianism was established at Edo, and gradually the Japanese people were influenced by the ethical and moral standards of Chinese philosophy. Buddhism remained the dominant religion of the masses, but Confucianism slowly became the strongest intellectual force in Japan.

The cost for Japan, as for China, was institutional rigidity and obsolescence. Yet there was a fundamental difference between the two countries. Japan was not saddled with a monolithic, overpowering imperial structure, as was the case in China. Rather, the Tokugawas had merely papered over the cracks, so that when the West intruded in the nineteenth century, Japan, unlike China, was able to respond positively and creatively.

SUGGESTED READINGS

The basic works for China are listed in the bibliography for Chapter 8. To that list should be added the interpretative bibliographical essay published by the American Historical Association's Service Center for

Teachers of History: J. K. Fairbanks, *New Views of China's Tradition and Modernization* (Washington, 1968). This bibliography describes recent works on subjects such as the rise of the bureaucratic state, the role of the merchants, and class structure and mobility.

Some of the more important studies on the period from 220 to 1644 are W. Bingham, *The Founding of the T'ang Dynasty* (Waverly Press, 1941); E. A. Kracke, *Civil Service in Early Sung China, 960–1067* (Harvard University, 1953); J. T. C. Liu, *Reform in Sung China* (Harvard University, 1959); C. O. Hucker, *The Traditional Chinese State in Ming Times, 1368–1644* (University of Arizona, 1961); and E. Balazs, *Chinese Civilization and Bureaucracy: Variations on a Theme* (Yale University, 1964). Intellectual trends are analyzed in the following two volumes presenting assorted symposia papers: A. F. Wright, ed., *Studies in Chinese Thought* (University of Chicago, 1953); and J. K. Fairbank, ed., *Chinese Thought and Institutions* (University of Chicago, 1957). Another useful collection is by J. M. Menzel, ed., *The Chinese Civil Service: Career Open to Talent?* (Heath, 1963). Finally, there is M. Elvin, *The Pattern of the Chinese Past* (Stanford University, 1973), which analyzes why medieval China's flair for technology did not lead to an industrial revolution, as does also J. Needham, *The Grand Titration: Science and Society in East and West* (George Allen & Unwin, 1969). For those who find Needham's monumental volumes too massive, a more accessible yet reliable account is available in R. Temple, *The Genius of China: 3,000 Years of Science, Discovery and Invention* (Simon & Schuster, 1987). On a related subject, another readable work is by P. Snow, *The Star Raft: China's Encounter with Africa* (Weidenfeld & Nicolson, 1988). Finally, China's achievements during these centuries are analyzed in a global context by W. H. McNeill, *The Pursuit of Power* (University of Chicago, 1982).

On Japan, the American Historical Association's Service Center for Teachers of History has published a convenient general bibliography by J. W. Hall, *Japanese History: New Dimensions of Approach and Understanding*, 2nd ed. (Washington, 1961). The standard annotated bibliography is by B. Silberstein, *Japan and Korea: A Critical Bibliography* (University of Arizona, 1962). Invaluable source materials on Japanese political, moral, and philosophical thought are provided in R. Tsunoda et al., *Sources of the Japanese Tradition* (Columbia University, 1958). Standard general histories have been written by the British scholar G. B. Sansom, *Japan: A Short Cultural History*, rev. ed. (Appleton, 1944), and his definitive three-volume *A History of Japan* (Stanford University, 1958–64). The best introductory survey is by E. O. Reischauer, *Japan Past and Present*, rev. ed. (Knopf, 1953).

NOTES

1. Cited by J. Needham, *Science and Civilization in China* (Cambridge University, 1954), pp. 1, 140.
2. H. Yule, ed., *Cathay and the Way Thither*, Hakluyt Society, Series 2, XXXVII (London, 1914), p. 154.
3. Cited by L. C. Goodrich, *A Short History of the Chinese People* (Harper & Row, 1943), p. 200.

CHAPTER

14

Revolutionary Western Civilization

The chief glory of the later Middle Ages was not its cathedrals or its epics or its scholasticism: it was the building for the first time in history of a complex civilization which rested not on the backs of sweating slaves or coolies but primarily on non-human power.

Lynn White, Jr.

"We should note the force, effort, and consequences of inventions which are nowhere more conspicuous than in those three which were unknown to the ancients, namely, printing, gunpowder, and the compass. For these three have changed the appearance and state of the whole world."[1] This statement by the British philosopher-scientist Francis Bacon (1561–1626) is especially significant because all three of the inventions that he so wisely selected originated in China. Yet they had little effect on that country in comparison with their explosive repercussions in the West. Chinese civilization was too deeply rooted and Chinese imperial organization too all-embracing to allow such inventions to disrupt traditional institutions and practices. Thus printing was used to disseminate old ideas rather than new; gunpowder reinforced the position of the emperor rather than of emerging national monarchs; and the compass, despite the remarkable expeditions of Cheng Ho, was not used for world trade and exploration and empire building as in the West.

The root of this fateful difference is to be found in the unique characteristics of the new Western civilization—pluralistic, adaptable, and free of the shackles of tradition that bound all the other Eurasian civilizations. The new civilization brought about historic change not only for the West but also, as Bacon foresaw, for the entire globe as it came under the influence of the revolutionary new society.

I. PLURALISM IN THE WEST

"In order to escape the evils which they saw coming, the people divided themselves into three parts. One was to pray God; for trading and ploughing the second; and later, to guard these two parts from wrongs and injuries, knights were created."[2] This analysis by the secretary to Phillip VI of France describes simply but accurately the basic division of medieval Western society into priests, workers, and warriors. Although these three classes were to be found in all Eurasian civilizations, their status and interrelationships were unique in the West because of the disintegration of the Roman Empire and the failure to reconstruct it. Precisely how the classes functioned under these circumstances will be considered now in relation to the three institutions they represented: feudalism, manorialism, and the church.

Feudalism was a system of government in which those who possessed landed estates also possessed political power. State authority was replaced by contractual agreements between lords and vassals. Feudalism appeared when the German kings—who had taken over Roman imperial authority but lacked the funds to maintain a bureaucracy, a judiciary, and armed forces—found that their only alternative was to grant estates as reward for service. But the recipients, or vassals, tended to rule them as private realms. Charlemagne was strong enough to exact and enforce oaths of loyalty from his vassals. But under his weak successors political power shifted to the vassals, and their estates, or *fiefs*, became virtually private property. These powerful lords in turn subdivided their holdings into lesser fiefs, which they allocated to followers who were dependent on them rather than on the king. The feudal contract between these lords and vassals specified certain mutual obligations. The most important were that the lord should provide protection in addition to granting the estate, and the vassal rendered military service for as long a time each year as local custom required—usually about forty days.

This process of feudalization proceeded rapidly within each of the feudal kingdoms that took form following the disintegration of Charlemagne's empire. Since the legal justification for the fiefs of the great lords was supposed

The successor to feudalism, manorialism relied on the self-sufficiency of the serfs.

to come from royal authority, the lords were careful to select a suitable king even though they had no intention of respecting his sovereignty. But as western Europe settled down after 1000 and the foreign invasions ceased, the kings gradually were able to assert their feudal rights and to begin the building of strong monarchies. The ensuing struggle between kings and nobles was the essence of Western political history during the following centuries.

Just as feudalism emerged when large-scale political organization collapsed, so also manorialism emerged with the collapse of large-scale economic organization. Responding to this economic disintegration, the manor became a self-sufficient village worked by serfs who were not free to leave and who, by dint of their labor, supported a hierarchy of lay and clerical lords. The size of the manors varied considerably; inhabitants might number in the scores or the hundreds. Unlike slaves, serfs had recognized rights as well as responsibilities. They were entitled to protection, were assured a plot of land for the support of themselves and family, and enjoyed many religious holidays and harvest festivals that gave them relief from toil. In return they were required to till strips of land in the cultivated fields that were reserved for the lord, to perform other domestic and farm chores for the lord, and to give him a portion of any income from any source.

The *manor* had to fill almost all its own needs because of the virtual disappearance of long-distance trade, of centralized handicraft production, of imperial currencies, and the like. Despite, or perhaps because of, this self-sufficiency, manorial technology was not at all primitive compared to that of Roman times. When the economy of the empire disintegrated, there was a loss of luxury crafts, irrigation works, aqueducts, and road systems. But the self-sufficient villages, just because they were self-sufficient, had no need for imperial organization. They functioned—and with steadily improving efficiency—on a local, village-to-village basis. The manors kept and improved the mills and smithies and used more iron than ever before since it could be produced locally. Thus agricultural technology in the medieval West (as will be noted in Section III of this chapter) advanced substantially beyond Greco-Roman standards and had far-reaching effects on all aspects of life.

Turning to the Roman Catholic church, we find a similarly paradoxical development; that is, the pope emerged with more power precisely because of the fall of Rome. He did not have to fight against imperial domination, as did the bishops of Constantinople, Alexandria, and Antioch, who had to contend with the dictates of the Byzantine emperor. When one of these emperors sought to control the church in the West, Pope Gelasius (492–496) sent him a famous letter in which he asserted that "bishops, not the secular power, should be responsible for the administration of the church." Furthermore, the Byzantine emperors were distracted by the attacks of the Moslems and of other enemies. The popes were left free to strengthen their position in the West, and they did this in two ways. First, they made an alliance with the rising Franks, which culminated in the crowning of Charlemagne by Pope Leo III in 800. Second, the papacy sent out missions to convert the pagans in northern Europe. They succeeded in organizing new churches that accepted the pope's authority—such as the English church in 597, the Lombard and Frisian in the seventh century, and the German in the eighth.

Such, then, were the components of the new pluralistic society emerging in the West: an independent church instead of one subject to dictation by the emperor; feudal kings and lords in place of imperial authority; autonomous manors working individually to tame the wilderness instead of the slave plantations of Roman times; and, before long, a rising merchant class operating effectively from its urban bases against nobles, prelates, and, ultimately, against monarchs. How this society, alone in all Eurasia, evolved and adapted during the half-millennium after 1000 and how it eventually developed the strength and dynamism for overseas expansion is the subject of the following sections.

II. GEOGRAPHIC BACKGROUND

Geographic considerations are a significant factor in Europe's thrust forward ahead of other regions during the medieval period. One of these considerations was an advantageous location. Being on the western tip of the Eurasian landmass, Europe escaped most of the great invasions after the year 1000. The importance of the remote location of western Europe is evident when we look at events in the rest of Eurasia—the disastrous Mongol conquest of Russia in the thirteenth century, the Ottoman Turkish conquest of the Balkan peninsula in the fifteenth and sixteenth centuries, and the repeated Berber assaults in North Africa. Spared such ravages, western Europe certainly had a substantial advantage over the more vulnerable regions to the east.

Equally important were Europe's exceptionally good natural resources. A large part of northern Europe is a great plain that begins at the western end of the Pyrenees and flares out to the north and east, becoming wider as it progresses until eventually it extends without interruption from the Black Sea to the Baltic. The prevailing westerly winds from the Atlantic sweep unhindered over these plains, across all Europe and deep into Russia. Hence Europe north of the Mediterranean basin enjoys a relatively moderate climate and constant rainfall, which along with fertile soils provide an ideal combination for productive agriculture. Rivers usually run ice-free and full-depth, providing convenient means of transportation and communication. The deeply indented coastline gives inland regions relatively easy access to coastal outlets.

These natural resources had always been available, of course, but they could not be effectively exploited until a certain level of technological competence had been reached. This need for adequate skills has existed everywhere and at all times. The United States, for example, has profited tremendously during the past century from the vast iron-ore deposits in the Mesabi Range of northern Minnesota. But for thousands of years Indians had fished and hunted in that area without exploiting the ore, or even being aware of its existence. The same is true currently of the rich oil fields now being tapped in the Middle East, in northern Alaska, and on various ocean floors. And so it was in medieval western Europe where, for the first time, advancing technology made it possible to exploit local resources effectively. The resulting increase in productivity had profound effects, including the shift of the economic and political center of Europe northward from its traditional site in the Mediterranean basin.

III. TECHNOLOGICAL PROGRESS

More technological progress was made during the period of medieval western Europe than had been made during the entire history of classical Greece and Rome. One reason for this was the absence of slavery, a practice that tended to inhibit new technology. Another was that the frontier conditions, which existed in many areas, called for labor-saving devices. The manorial system of the medieval West also contributed to technological progress. Under this system the social scale ranged not from a "divine" emperor to a subhuman slave but from a serf—with very definite rights and duties—to a manorial lord—who kept in touch with his serfs and had some real knowledge of the processes of

production. Accordingly, manual labor acquired a status and respect that were unknown in the old slave-based civilizations.

Finally, technology in the West was stimulated by the humanitarian ethic of Christianity, which itself began as a revolt against the inhumanity of the old imperial society. The monks in the monasteries insisted that manual labor was part of spiritual life. Or, as they put it, "to work is to pray"—*laborare est orare*. These monks have gone down in history as the first intellectuals to get dirt under their fingernails. They were the first to combine brainpower and sweat, and in doing so they aided technological advance. In their monasteries they pushed the frontiers of settlement into the forests of northern and eastern Europe, and they also introduced advanced methods of agriculture.

The specific technological achievements of the West included basic inventions in the primary occupation of agriculture. One was the "three-field" rotation system of farming. Gradually adopted from the eighth century onward, this system raised productivity because only a third of the land lay fallow at any one time instead of the half left by the former "two-field" system. Another was the development of a heavy-wheeled plow with a sharp iron point that could cut under the sod six to eight inches or even more. Behind the plowshare was the mold board, so placed that it heaved over the cut sod. It was a very different implement from the primitive scratch-plow traditionally used in the light, thin soils of the Mediterranean basin. The new plow made it possible to cultivate the rich but heavy soils of central and northern Europe.

More effective use of horsepower also aided agriculture. In ancient times the horse had been of little use on the farm because the yoke then in use encircled the belly and neck of the animal. Consequently the horse strangled itself when it pulled too hard. By the tenth century, however, a harness had been developed that rested on the horse's shoulders. The horse could then pull without choking, increasing its pulling capacity four to five times. Hence the horse—fast and efficient compared to the ox, which had been used formerly—became an essential source of power in farming operations. The invention of horseshoes was also significant because it increased the usefulness of the horse for hauling as well as for plowing.

Finally, a brief look should be taken at the all-important water mill and windmill. Both of these were known in Greco-Roman times but were little used because of the abundance of slave labor and the scarcity of streams dependable the year around. These obstacles were absent in the northern lands, so the mill and the miller soon were to be found in almost every manor. And whereas the water wheel had been employed in the Mediterranean basin as a specialized device for grinding grain, in the course of the Middle Ages it was developed into a generalized prime mover. Thus water power came to be used for forge hammers and forge bellows; for sawmills and lathes; and for fulling mills making cloth, pulping mills making paper, and stamping mills crushing ore. Indeed, 5,000 mills were listed in England's *Domesday Book* of 1086. This represented one for every fifty households, certainly enough to affect living standards substantially.

IV. DEVELOPING ECONOMY

Technological advance was matched by corresponding economic advance. There was steady economic growth from 900 to 1300. Then came the fourteenth-century slump, brought on by a combination of factors: First there was a series of crop failures and famines, especially during 1315 and 1316; then came the Black Death, which carried off between one-third and two-thirds of the urban populations when it first struck in 1349, and which recurred periodically thereafter for generations; finally, there were the Hundred Years' War between England and France and other conflicts in Germany and Italy. Shortly after 1400, however, a revival set in, and the trend from then on was generally upward.

Europe's economic development was evident in all fields. New mining methods led to rising outputs of salt, silver, lead, zinc, copper, tin, and iron ore in central and northern Europe. Likewise, the rich timber and naval stores of Britain, Scandinavia, and the Baltic now were exploited more extensively than ever before. The same was true of the northern fisheries, particularly the cod of Iceland and Norway and the herring of the Baltic. Most important, of course, was

the rise in the productivity of agriculture, in which most of the population was engaged. Peasants first began to cultivate the wastelands around their own villages. It is startling but true that in the twelfth century only about half the land in France, a third in Germany, and a fifth in England was under cultivation. The rest was forest, swamp, and waste. All around the edges of the small, tilled regions were larger, untilled areas open for colonization. Into these vacant spaces the European peasants streamed, preparing the way for the plow and hoe by clearing forests, burning brushwood, and draining swamps.

Peasants not only cultivated nearby unused lands but also with population growth emigrated to the vast underpopulated frontier regions. Just as the United States had its westward movement to the Pacific Ocean, so Europe had its eastward movement to the Russian border. By 1350 in Silesia, for example, there were 1,500 new settlements farmed by 150,000 to 200,000 colonists. Not only were there German colonists moving beyond the Elbe at the expense of the Slavic and Baltic peoples of eastern Europe, but also other colonists were pushing into Moslem Spain and Anglo-Saxon colonists were advancing into the Celtic lands of Wales, Scotland, and Ireland.

The combination of population increase and rising output in agriculture, mining, fishing, and forestry stimulated a corresponding growth of commerce and of cities. In the tenth century, merchants were to be found in Europe, but they traded mostly in luxuries. By the fourteenth century, however, commerce had advanced from the periphery to the center of everyday life. Goods exchanged included raw wool from England, woolen cloth from Flanders made from English wool, iron and timber from Germany, furs from Slavic areas, leather and steel from Spain, and luxury goods from the East. Although this commerce never engaged more than a small minority of the total population, nevertheless its great expansion in late medieval times had important repercussions for the whole society. Starting out as centers of local trade and local administration, towns slowly appeared. Urban progress came first in Italy, where the inhabitants of such centers as Venice, Amalfi, and Naples were cut off from their hinterland by the Lombard invaders and so took to the sea for a living. Later other cities appeared along inland

A fifteenth-century rendering of an eleventh- or twelfth-century marketplace. Medieval women were active in all trades, but especially in the food and clothing industries.

trade routes and the Baltic coast. The great fairs that developed along inland trade routes were also important for the distribution of goods. The most outstanding of the fairs were held in the county of Champagne, strategically located equidistant from Flanders, Italy, and Germany.

Western European cities were insignificant in medieval times compared to those of China, India, or the Middle East, both in population and in volume of trade. But they were quite unique because of their growing autonomy and political power. Precisely because they were starting fresh—and within the framework of a politically fragmented Europe rather than a monolithic empire—the burghers from the beginning exhibited a self-confidence and independence that had no parallel anywhere else in Eurasia.

As they acquired power and financial resources, the townspeople could usually get the king to give them a royal charter licensing them to unite in a single commune. The commune had the right to act as a corporation; to make agreements under its corporate seal; and to have its own town hall, court of law, and dependent territory outside the walls. The charter also permitted merchants and craftmakers to organize into guilds, which were voluntary associations designed for protection and mutual aid, including the regulation of manufacturing standards, prices, and working hours. Thus towns gradually came to be recognized as a new element in society, with inhabitants who were outside feudal law. For example, the custom was that if a serf escaped to a town and lived there for a year and a day without being apprehended, that person became free. A saying at that time was "Town air makes a man free."

In certain regions, groups of cities banded together to form leagues, which became powerful political as well as economic entities. When the Hohenstaufen emperors attempted to force the wealthy cities of northern Italy—Milan, Brescia, Parma, Verona, and others—to pay taxes and accept imperial administration, they organized themselves into the Lombard League. Aided by the pope, the league successfully waged war against the emperors. Likewise, various Baltic towns—Bremen, Lubeck, Stettin,

Italian bank at the end of the fourteenth century.

Danzig, and others comprising a total of ninety—organized themselves in 1350 into the Hanseatic League, which fought against pirates, pressed for trading privileges in foreign countries, and virtually monopolized the trade of northern Europe.

This evolution gave the European merchant status and power that were unique in Eurasia. Outside Europe, merchants had no chance to rise to positions of authority. In China, government was carried on by scholars; in Japan, by soldiers; in the Malay lands and in the Rajput states of India, by the local nobility; but nowhere by merchants. Nowhere, that is, except in Europe, where they were steadily gaining in political as well as economic power. There they were becoming lord mayors in London, senators in the German Imperial Free Cities, and grand pensioners in Holland. Such social status and political connections meant more consideration and more consistent state support for mercantile interests and, later on, for overseas ventures.

V. RISE OF NEW MONARCHIES

Western Europe by the tenth century had become a mosaic of petty feudal states that had gradually acquired the land and authority of the defunct Carolingian Empire. During the following centuries several traditions and interests operated at cross purposes. There were feudal kings engaged in continual conflict with their feudal vassals, who often held larger fiefs and wielded more power. There were city-states that sometimes combined in powerful organizations such as the Lombard and Hanseatic leagues. And in opposition to the particularist interests of these groups, there was the striving for a united Latin Christendom headed by the pope in Rome, or by a "Roman" emperor as the successor to Charlemagne and his predecessors. This complex of conflicting interests produced an infinite variety of constantly changing alliances and alignments at all levels of political life.

In very broad terms, the political evolution of western Europe after Charlemagne may be divided into three stages. Between the ninth and eleventh centuries, popes and emperors generally cooperated. The popes helped the emperors against the German secular lords, and in return they were supported in preference to the Byzantine opponents of papal authority. In 1073 a period of papal supremacy began with the accession of Pope Gregory VII. By the thirteenth century Pope Innocent III was involved in the affairs of virtually every European state, making and breaking kings and emperors. "Nothing in the world," he declared, "should escape the attention and control of the Sovereign Pontiff." For over two centuries, the papacy generally was recognized as the head of Latin Christendom.

The period of papal supremacy ended suddenly and dramatically when Pope Boniface VIII issued the bull *Unam sanctum* (1302), in which he set forth uncompromisingly the doctrine of papal authority: ". . . We declare, state, define and pronounce that it is altogether necessary to salvation for every human creature to be subject to the Roman pontiff." But what had been acceptable in previous centuries was no longer so. The monarchs and their councilors now were placing the welfare of their kingdoms ahead of the wishes of popes. Boniface was subjected to threats and mistreatment by an agent of the French king, and he died soon after his humiliation. In 1305 a French archbishop was elected pope as Clement V, and instead of going to Rome he took up residence at Avignon in southeastern France. During the next seventy years the Avignonese popes were the pawns of the French monarchy and lost their predecessors' commanding position in Latin Christendom.

The new power of the European kings was derived in large part from their informal alliance with the rising merchant class. The burghers provided financial support to the monarchs. They also supplied managerial talent in the form of chamberlains, overseers, keepers of the king's accounts, managers of the royal mint, and so forth. In return, the new monarchs provided the burghers with protection against the frequent wars and arbitrary demands of the feudal lords and bishops. They also served merchant interests by doing away with some of the crazy-quilt pattern of autonomous local authorities, each with its own customs, laws, weights, and currencies. With the removal of such encumbrances and the enforcement of royal law and order, the new monarchies emerged. By the fifteenth century, they encompassed roughly the territories of modern England, France, Portugal, and also, after the marriage of Ferdinand and Isabella, Spain.

These large new political entities proved to be essential for the mobilization of the human and material resources needed for overseas enterprise. Although most of the early explorers were Italian navigators, it was not accidental that their sponsors were the new national monarchies rather than their minuscule home city-states. The Spanish and Portuguese courts provided the backing for Columbus and da Gama, and the English and French courts quickly and eagerly followed up with backing for Cabot, Verrazano, and many others.

VI. RENAISSANCE FERMENT

The medieval West experienced cultural and intellectual developments that were as innovative and significant as the economic and political events. The centuries from the fall of Rome to about the year 1000 constituted a "Dark Age" in the sense that there was little cultural creativity. The weight of poverty, insecurity, and isola-

The University of Bologna in central Italy was distinguished as the center for the revival of Roman law. This carving on the tomb of a Bologna professor of law shows students attending one of his lectures.

tion was too great to permit the production of literary, artistic, or scholarly masterpieces. It is true that the monks in the monasteries did manage to preserve certain parts of classical culture, but they naturally concentrated on what conformed to their own religious convictions and ignored things that were more secular. The result was a "Christianized" or "clericized" culture that was supplementary to and dependent on the church.

In the eleventh century, cathedral schools were established by the bishops for the education of the priests of their dioceses. A century later the first universities evolved out of the cathedral schools. A distinctive feature of these universities was that they were self-governing corporations with a legal identity of their own. And rather than consisting simply of a liberal arts faculty, as did the cathedral schools, in addition they usually had faculties of canon law, civil law, medicine, and theology. The liberal arts curriculum was made up of the *trivium* (Latin grammar, logic, and rhetoric) and the *quadrivium* (geometry, arithmetic, music, and astronomy). The first universities appeared in the twelfth century at Bologna, Paris, and Oxford. In the following century others were

founded at Padua, Naples, and Salamanca; and in the fourteenth century they spread to central Europe—to Prague, Cracow, and Vienna. All these universities were primarily institutions for training the clergy. This emphasis was natural and proper at a time when the clergy had a monopoly of literate occupations and administrative positions.

The educational and intellectual environment changed with the *Renaissance* ferment of the period from roughly 1350 to 1600. The Renaissance got under way first in Italy and hence reflected the conditions and values of contemporary Italian society. This was a bustling urban society based on flourishing industries and on the profitable commerce between western Europe and the wealthy Byzantine and Islamic empires. Prosperous cities such as Venice, Genoa, Florence, Milan, and Pisa were dominated by the great merchant families, who controlled politics as well as trade and crafts. It was these families that were the patrons of Renaissance artists and writers. Their needs, interests, and tastes colored the Renaissance cultural revival, even though the patrons included ducal families such as the Sforza of Milan, as well as popes such as Nicholas V, Pius II, Julius

THE RENAISSANCE GENIUS

The supremely talented Leonardo da Vinci was an outstanding Renaissance figure. He personified his age, not only because of his achievements in so many fields, but also because of his readiness to advertise his genius. At the age of thirty he wrote the following letter to the Duke of Milan, who was sufficiently impressed to hire the young man.*

1. I have plans for bridges, very light and strong and suitable for carrying very easily, with which to pursue and at times defeat the enemy; and others solid and indestructible by fire or assault, easy and convenient to carry away and place in position. And plans for burning and destroying those of the enemy.

2. When a place is besieged I know how to cut off water from the trenches, and how to construct an infinite number of bridges, mantlets, scaling ladders, and other instruments which have to do with the same enterprise. . . .

4. I have also plans for making cannon, very convenient and easy of transport, with which to hurl small stones in the manner almost of hail, causing great terror to the enemy from their smoke, and great loss and confusion.

5. Also I have ways of arriving at a certain fixed spot by caverns and secret winding passages, made without any noise, even though it may be necessary to pass underneath trenches or a river.

6. Also I can make armored carts, safe and unassailable, which will enter the serried ranks of the enemy with their artillery, and there is no company of men at arms so great that they will not break it. And behind these infantry will be able to follow quite unharmed and without any opposition. . . .

9. And if it should happen that the engagement is at sea, I have plans for constructing many engines most suitable either for attack or defense, and ships which can resist the fire of all the heaviest cannon, and powder and smoke.

10. In time of peace I believe that I can give you as complete satisfaction as anyone else in architecture in the construction of buildings both pubic and private, and in conducting water from one place to another. . . .

And if any of the aforesaid things should seem impossible or impracticable to anyone, I offer myself as ready to make trial of them in your park or in whatever place shall please Your Excellency, to whom I commend myself with all possible humility.

*J. P. and I. A. Richter, eds. *The Literary Works of Leonardo da Vinci* (Oxford University Press, 1939), pp. 92, 93.

II, and Leo X; hence the secularism and humanism of the Renaissance—its concern with this world rather than the hereafter, and its focus on pagan classics rather than Christian theology.

The secularism and individualism of the Renaissance were reflected in its scholarship and education. The so-called father of Renaissance literature, Francesco Petrarca, or Petrarch (1304–1374), stressed the value of the classics as a means for self-improvement and a guide to social action. Likewise the new boarding schools of the Renaissance trained not priests but the sons of merchants. The curriculum emphasized classical studies and physical exercise and was designed to educate the students to live well and happily and to function as responsible citizens.

The Renaissance spirit is most strikingly expressed in its art. Since the church no longer was the sole patron of the arts, artists were encouraged to turn to subjects other than the traditional biblical themes. Religious themes continued to appear quite commonly, but in the

Commissioned in 1501, when the artist was 26, Michelangelo's David *became the symbol of the Florentine republic and was displayed in front of the Palazzo Vecchio. The detail shown here highlights the restrained emotion and dignity for which the statue is famous. [Michelangelo (1475–1564) David-p. (testa di profilo).]*

works of such masters as Leonardo da Vinci, Michelangeo, Raphael, and Titian, the emphasis shifted more and more to portraits designed to reveal the hidden mysteries of the soul, to paintings intended to delight the eye with striking colors and forms.

The Renaissance, not an exclusively Italian phenomenon, spread its innovations to northern Europe in the sixteenth century. Two factors responsible for this were the Italian diplomats and generals who were employed by northern monarchs and the printing press, which accelerated the circulation of books and ideas. Printing was particularly influential in northern Europe because literacy was more widespread there than in Europe's southern and eastern regions. The flood of printed matter fomented popular agita-

tion concerning political and religious issues and so contributed substantially to the Reformation and ensuing religious and dynastic wars.

In conclusion, what is the significance of the Renaissance in the perspective of world history? It is obvious that the new emphasis on human beings and on what they could accomplish was more conducive to overseas expansion than the preceding medieval outlook. The fact remains that there was an intellectual ferment in western Europe and that it had no counterpart in the rest of Eurasia. This is a fundamental difference of enormous import.

In China, Confucianism continued to dominate society. Its esteem for age over youth, for the past over the present, for established authority over innovation made it a perfect instrument for the preservation of the status quo in all its aspects. This atmosphere of conformity and orthodoxy prevented continued intellectual development and helps to explain why China fell behind the West in technology, despite its brilliant initial achievements in developing paper, printing, gunpowder, and the compass. These early inventions were not followed by the formulation of a body of scientific principles.

The situation was basically the same in the other Eurasian lands. In the Ottoman Empire, for example, the Moslem *medressehs*, or colleges, emphasized theology, jurisprudence, and rhetoric at the expense of astronomy, mathematics, and medicine. The graduates of these schools knew nothing about what was being done in the West and were not interested in finding out. No Moslem Turk believed that a Christian infidel could teach anything of value. Now and then, a rare, far-sighted individual warned of the dangers of this intellectual iron curtain separating the Ottoman Empire from neighboring Christendom. One of these voices was Katib Chelebi, the famous Turkish bibliographer, encyclopedist, and historian who lived in the first half of the seventeenth century. Coming from a poor family, he was unable to obtain a formal higher education. But this was a blessing in disguise. He was spared the superficial, hair-splitting concentration on Moslem sacred studies that was typical of Ottoman education at this time. The fact that he was self-taught explains in large part his open-mindedness toward Western learning.

One of Chelebi's works was a short naval handbook that he wrote following a disastrous defeat of the Ottoman fleet in 1656. In the preface of this work, Chelebi emphasized the need for mastering the science of geography and map making:

For men who are in charge of affairs of state, the science of geography is a matter of which knowledge is necessary. They may not be familiar with what the entire globe is like, but they ought at least to know the map of the Ottoman State and of those states adjoining it. Then, when they have to send forces on campaign, they can proceed on the basis of knowledge, and so the invasion of the enemy's land and also the protection and defense of the frontiers becomes an easier task. Taking counsel with individuals who are ignorant of that science is no satisfactory substitute, not even when such men are local veterans. Most such veterans are entirely unable to sketch the map of their own home region.

Sufficient and convincing proof of the necessity for learning this science is the fact that the heathen, by their application to and their esteem for those branches of learning, have discovered the New World and have overrun the markets of India.[3]

Chelebi saw the connection between Europe's intellectual advance and its overseas expansion. In his last work before his death in 1657, Chelebi warned his countrymen that if they did not abandon their dogmatism they would soon "be looking at the universe with the eyes of oxen." His prediction proved prophetic. The Turks continued to be steeped in their religious obscurantism, and like other non-Western peoples, they paid a high price. The Christian infidels with their new learning eventually became the masters not only of the New World but also of the ancient empires of Islam and of Confucianism.

VII. WESTERN EUROPE'S EXPANSIONISM

Between the fourth and tenth centuries Europe was invaded by Germans, Huns, Magyars, Vikings, and Moslems. But from the tenth to the fourteenth centuries this situation was dramatically reversed as Europe took the offensive on all fronts. (See map of Expansionism of the Medieval West, Eleventh to Fifteenth Centuries, p. 240.) Assorted crusaders pushed back the Moslems in Spain, southern Italy, Sicily, and the Holy Land, and even overran the Christian Byzantine Empire. Meanwhile in northeast Europe, German frontier lords were winning lands east of the Elbe. As German expansion continued east of the Oder it was carried on as a *Crusade* by the Teutonic Knights against the pagan Prussians. The Knights built strongholds and around them settled Germans, who provided the supplies and people for further expansion. German merchants soon appeared and founded towns at strategic points along the coasts and along river routes. Thus by the end of the fifteenth century large areas formerly occupied by Slavic and Baltic peoples had become thoroughly German from top to bottom: lords, bishops, townspeople, and peasants.

These Crusades were considered at one time to have been responsible for starting virtually every constructive development in the later Middle Ages, including the growth of trade and towns and the advances in culture. This interpretation is no longer accepted. Instead it is generally agreed that the Crusades were the consequence rather than the cause of this progress. Without the preceding technological advances, commercial revival, demographic upsurge, and general exuberance of spirit, the Crusades would have been quite impossible. This dynamism continued and picked up speed after the fourteenth-century slump. The result was to extend the expansionist drive of the crusaders to overseas territories.

A significant factor in the overseas drive was the Christian religion, with its belief that Christianity is universal, its zeal to make converts, and its crusading militancy. The early explorers and their backers were motivated partly by religious considerations. They wanted to reach the great countries of India and China, whose existence had been known to Europeans since the thirteenth-century travels of Marco Polo. These countries were known to be non-Moslem, and so it was hoped that they might join forces with the Christians. Also there was the enduring medieval legend of Prester (or Priest) John, reputed to be a powerful Christian ruler somewhere out in the vague East. For centuries, Christian leaders had dreamed of estab-

Expansionism of the Medieval West, Eleventh to Fifteenth Centuries

Map labels and legend:

SARACENS

THE HOLY LAND

Infidels defeated temporarily and the Latin States were created 1099-1244

SULTANATE OF ROUM

Edessa
Antioch
Tripoli
Acre
Jerusalem
Alexandria

CYPRUS

Tigris R.
Euphrates R.

BLACK SEA

Constantinople

BYZANTINE EMPIRE

CRETE

MEDITERRANEAN SEA

MALTA

RUSSIA

Moscow
Novgorod
Kiev
Astrakhan

Volga R.
Dniester R.
Danube R.

Swedes convert the Finns, c. 1150

SWEDES

BALTIC SEA

Danzig
Lübeck
Bremen

HOLY ROMAN EMPIRE

Ratisbon
Vienna
Metz
Véselay
Milan
Venice
Zara
Genoa
Lyons
Marseilles

Odder R.
Elbe R.
Rhine R.
Rhône R.

ITALY

Pisa
Rome
Naples
CORSICA
SARDINIA
SICILY
Tunis

SARACENS

Normans to Italy
Normans from Normandy

NORTH SEA

ENGLAND

London

NORMANY

FRANCE

Clermont-Ferrand
Toulouse

Loire R.

IBERIA

Toledo
Granada
Lisbon
Ceuta

ATLANTIC OCEAN

Conquests and Reconquests by Christendom
Reconquest of Iberia from the Moors, 1000-1492
Norman Conquest of South Italy and Sicily, 1042-1147
Major routes of the Crusaders to The Holy Land, 1097-1250
Teutonic Order, 1100-1250

1029-1096
1097-1186
After 1200

0 50 100 Miles
0 100 Kilometers

240

lishing contact with him and launching a great assault on the Moslem world from both east and west. The Europeans did not find Prester John, but they did stumble on strange new peoples in Africa and the Americas—peoples who were barbarians and heathens and, therefore, fit subjects for conquest, conversion, and redemption.

God, along with gold, was perhaps the most compelling of the many motives that led Europeans to begin their overseas enterprises. Vasco da Gama explained to the surprised Indians that he had come to their land in search of Christians and spices. Likewise, the conquistador Bernal Diaz wrote in his memoirs that he and his comrades went to the New World "to serve God and His Majesty, to give light to those who were in darkness, and to grow rich, as all men desire to do."[4]

The continued technological advances of the West also contributed directly to overseas expansion. Particularly significant was the progress made in shipbuilding, in the instruments and techniques of navigation, and in naval armaments. Between 1200 and 1500 the

This Jesuit missionary, wearing his distinctive Catholic vestments, is baptizing an Indian in New France. French Jesuits proved to be more tolerant than most European missionaries in allowing Indian converts to retain at least some of their own customs.

tonnage of the average European ship doubled or trebled. Slender galleys with a burden of 150 to 200 tons gave way to round-hulled sailing ships of 600 to 800 tons. The stern rudder, adopted in the thirteenth century, rapidly displaced the older and less efficient lateral steering devices. Equally important was the Portuguese adaptation in the fourteenth century of the Arab lateen rig, which allowed vessels to sail more directly into the wind. Such advantages in the construction and rigging of ships represented a combining of innovations originally developed in northern Europe, in the Mediterranean, or in the Middle East. The result was a ship that was larger, speedier, and more maneuverable. It was also more economical because the elimination of 100 to 200 oarsmen with their food and equipment greatly increased the cargo space.

Hand in hand with these advances in shipbuilding went advances in the art of navigation. Particularly important were the increasingly effective use of the compass, the astrolabe, and the new maps now drawn with accurate compass bearings and explicit details concerning coastlines and harbors. At the same time the Europeans were taking a decisive and significant lead in naval armaments. Sea battles traditionally had consisted of boarding and hand-to-hand fighting on decks. This changed in the first two decades of the sixteenth century when Flemish and German metallurgists developed new techniques for casting guns. The new guns could shoot balls capable of damaging a hull at 300 yards. Naval tactics now shifted from boarding to broadside gunfire, enabling Europeans to seize and control the oceans of the world for four centuries. Their supremacy finally ended with the epochal Japanese naval victory over the Russians at Tsushima in 1905.

Along with advances in shipbuilding, navigation, and naval armaments came important new techniques for conducting business affairs. The invention in Italy of double-entry bookkeeping made it possible to see the financial state of a business at a glance. Also, the growing use of money and the minting of standard coins acceptable by everyone made it easier to conduct business. The development of banks and credit instruments, and the gradual ending of medieval Christianity's ban on interest charges or loans, also helped business. Finally, after European

Before Europeans could safely navigate the Atlantic, they needed larger and more maneuverable ships. This drawing illustrates the evolution of sailing vessels from the late Middle Ages to the fifteenth century. Technological improvements included larger hulls, more masts, and new arrangements of sails.

overseas expansion got under way, business was greatly strengthened by the development of *joint stock companies*. By providing a medium for investment with limited liability, these companies mobilized vast amounts of European capital for overseas enterprise. Eastern merchants, limited to their own resources or those of their partners, were unable to compete successfully in the long run with the several East India and Levant companies, the Muscovy Company, and the still extant Hudson's Bay Company.

In conclusion, the combination of all these factors imbued Europe with an impelling and unique dynamism. We can see how unique it was when we look at the variety of Eurasian responses to the expansion of the Moslem world in the fifteenth century. As noted in Chapter 11, Section V, Islam at that time was fanning out from the Middle East in all directions. The Turks, after capturing Constantinople, overran the Balkan peninsula and then crossed the Danube and pushed through Hungary to the walls of Vienna. Likewise in the East, the Turks under the colorful Babur were striking southward from Afghanistan, to begin the founding of the great Mogul Empire that would rule India until the British takeover in the nineteenth century. In Africa also, Islam was spreading steadily into the interior from its bases on the northern and eastern coasts of the continent. Finally, Moslem merchants dominated the Eurasian sea routes running from the Red Sea and the Persian Gulf across the Indian Ocean and around Southeast Asia to the China seas.

With these advances by its soldiers, merchants, and preachers, the world of Islam had become the heartland of Eurasia. It occupied the strategic center of the great landmass, and the more it expanded, the more it isolated the Chinese at the eastern end of Eurasia and the Europeans at the western. The completely different responses of the Chinese and the Europeans to this encirclement have deeply influenced the course of world history from that time to the present.

The Chinese, as noted before, withdrew voluntarily, even though their earlier expeditions under Cheng Ho had clearly shown that they possessed both the technology and the resources to dominate the oceans. But during the Ming period, after the interlude of Mongol domination, the Chinese were turning their backs to the outside world. And their merchant class, which lacked the political power and social status of its Western counterpart, was unable to challenge imperial orders that banned overseas enterprise. Thus the Chinese turned their formidable talents and energies inward and deliberately relinquished a lead role in Eurasian and, ultimately, world affairs.

The response of Europeans was precisely the opposite. The geographic horizons and commercial ambitions of the Europeans had been broadened by *Pax Mongolica*, so that the sudden disintegration of the Mongol Empire left them with acute frustration and yearning. Likewise, the loss of the crusaders' outposts in the Levant, the Islamization of the Ilkhanate in Persia, and the Turkish conquest of the Balkans all served to deprive the Europeans of access to the Black Sea, the Persian Gulf, and the Indian Ocean. Thus the Europeans were effectively fenced in on the western tip of Eurasia. The all-important spice trade still flourished, as Italian merchants continued to meet Arab traders in the ports of the Levant and pick up cargoes for transshipment to the West. But though the arrangement was satisfactory for the Italians and the Arabs, who reaped the golden profits of the middleman, other Europeans were not so happy. They sought earnestly for some means to reach the Orient and to share the prize.

Their search was bound to succeed, given their technical skills, their economic strength, their intellectual exuberance, and the rivalry of their competing monarchies. There was no emperor in Europe to issue restraining orders; instead there were national monarchies competing strenuously in overseas enterprises. Also, there was in Europe a genuine need and strong demand for foreign products, and the merchants were sufficiently powerful to satisfy the need. Thus if Columbus had not discovered America and if da Gama had not rounded the Cape, assuredly others would have done so within the next few decades. In short, Western society had reached the takeoff point. It was ready to burst out. And when it did, it found the ocean ways clear, and it spread irresistibly over the entire globe.

VIII. WOMEN IN THE NEW WESTERN CIVILIZATION

In view of the current controversy about the status of women in various societies throughout the world, it is instructive to see how women were affected by the emergence of the new civilization in medieval Europe. We have seen that during the long millennia of the Paleolithic era, relations between the sexes were more equitable

Florentine women are shown doing needlework, spinning, and weaving. These activities took up much of a woman's time and contributed to the elegance of dress for which Florentine men and women were famed.

than at any time since. With the advent of agriculture and then of civilizations, women lost their equal status and became the subordinate and dependent sex. The degree of inequity varied from one region to another (as between the various Greek city-states) and from one period to another (as between republican and imperial Rome). But in all early civilizations, women definitely were the "second sex." They were restricted to the "inside" work, which was considered less important, whereas men were free to engage in the "outside" work, which was regarded as significant and creative.

This pattern continued during the thousand years of the medieval period, when a revolutionary new civilization gradually emerged in the West. But there were certain modifications that deserve attention and that are of some significance for women today.

The status of women in the new Western civilization was determined largely by two institutions—the Catholic church and feudalism. In theory the church championed equality in sex relations, as it did also in race and class. "For ye are all the children of God by faith in Christ Jesus," wrote Saint Paul. "There is neither Jew nor Greek, there is neither bond nor free, there is neither male nor female; for ye are all one in Christ Jesus."[5] In practice, however, the church was profoundly *ambivalent* on the sex issue. It viewed woman as Eve, the wife of Adam, and therefore the supreme temptress and the great obstacle in the way of salvation. But the church also viewed woman as the blessed Mary, the Holy Mother, the queen of virgins, and the mediator between God and humankind. Consequently the medieval woman found herself oscillating between the pit and the pedestal. Within the church itself she could not be ordained a priest and she was denied the right to preach.

The church did provide, however, one important institution designed specifically for the medieval woman, namely, the nunnery. This has been described as a "class institution,"[6] because would-be nuns were required, in practice though not in strict canon law, to bring with them a *dowry*. Though this dowry was not as much as a husband would expect, the nunneries nevertheless were open mostly to wealthy females from the nobility and, in the later Middle Ages, from the merchant families. Almost all medieval females married, and did so at a very young age. A small minority did not find a husband, either because of illegitimate birth or physical deformity or lack of adequate dowry, or because of a preference for a life as a bride of Christ rather than a bride of some man.

For these exceptional cases the nunnery offered an alternative to married life. Furthermore the cloister did provide certain advantages to life on the outside. The nuns usually could obtain a better education than was available to their secular brothers or sisters. If a nun was exceptionally ambitious and capable, she could rise to the office of abbess, managing large estates and assuming responsibility for as many as eighty nuns. Some of these nuns experienced the intense satisfaction of the contemplative life in the service of the Holy Father, and a few are remembered as great monastic saints. Others found in the cloisters self-respect and the respect of society, as well as the freedom from male authority that only the nunnery afforded. On the other hand, there were some who viewed themselves bitterly as the rejects of society: "I was not good enough for man and so am given to God."[7]

The second institution that most affected medieval women was feudalism. Since this was a system by which a lord granted land to a vassal in return for military service, feudalism created a male-dominated world. Feudal estates were passed on, with their military obligations, to a single male heir. A woman could inherit only in the absence of male heirs. Throughout her life the medieval woman was under the guardianship of a man—first her father and then her husband. If widowed, she became the *ward* of the feudal lord, who pocketed the income of the ward's estate until she remarried. The lord determined whom she should marry, so it was by no means uncommon for him to "sell" his ward's marriage to the highest bidder, or conversely, to exact payments from a widow who did not wish to marry or who wished to choose her own mate. Noblewomen also had to bear the cross of an idle and aimless existence. The management of their households and the care of their children were entrusted to stewards and nurses. Therefore there was little for them to do unless their husbands were absent on military service or court attendance. In essence, the unhappy lot of these noblewomen was to serve as pawns in the forging of political and economic alliances and then to produce heirs for the family into which they married.

This dependent and peripheral existence was escaped, to a large degree, by the working women in the villages and towns; hence the paradox that the status of medieval women "varied roughly in inverse ratio to wealth and social standing."[8] The great majority of village girls married and took their place beside their husbands in performing virtually every type of agricultural work. The few who did not marry were usually from the poorest families. So they supported themselves by leaving their village to work as serving girls in towns or as hired agricultural workers in neighboring villages. How laborious was the day-to-day life of peasant women is reflected in the following medieval proverb:

Some respite to husbands the weather may send,
But housewives' affairs have never an end.[9]

Likewise in the towns, women were active in almost all the trades. This is evident in the thirteenth-century *Book of Trades* (*Livre des Métiers*) by Etienne Boileau, which listed the rules of all the guilds in Paris. Of the 100 guilds enumerated, women were working in eighty-six. How important this female role was is evident in the use of the suffix *ess* or *ster* with medieval

English words to describe an occupation held by women.

Webster:	woman weaver
Brewster:	woman beer maker
Baxter:	woman baker
Laundress:	woman washer of clothes
Seamstress:	woman sewer
Spinster:	woman spinner
Governess:	woman teacher

Equal burdens and equal responsibilities did not win equal rights for medieval women. In the villages the housewives' labors never ended, yet they were excluded from all decision-making bodies. They could not serve as village notary or as parish priest or as scribe of the manorial court. The meetings of village landowners were attended only by men, except for unmarried or widowed female landowners. Married women who owned land were represented at all village meetings by their husbands. Likewise in towns, women enjoyed economic rights such as owning property, joining guilds, and engaging in commerce, but they had no corresponding political rights. Thus they could not elect or be elected to the governmental institutions of the towns.

The underlying inequity in sex relations is evident in various practices that were common in medieval Europe. One was the prevalence of wife beating. "A good woman and a bad one equally require the stick," ran a Florentine saying. A thirteenth-century French law code stated: "In a number of cases men may be excused for the injuries they inflict on their wives. . . . Provided he neither kills nor maims her, it is legal for a man to beat his wife when she wrongs him."[10] Sex inequity was manifest also in the persistence of the traditional double standard regarding adultery. Kings, noblemen, and merchants openly kept mistresses and spawned illegitimate children. But erring wives were disgraced and severely punished and their lovers castrated or killed. Also it was taken for granted that upper-class men should have access to lower-class women. A twelfth-century tract, *The Art of Courtly Love*, encouraged a knight who desired a peasant girl "not to hesitate to take what you seek and to embrace her by force."

Equally indicative of the pervasive sex inequity was the common assumption that women should be content with "little feminine trifles," while men occupied themselves with "high achievements." Leon Battista Alberti, a leading figure of the Italian Renaissance, wrote in the 1430s that men should "leave the care of minor matters" to their wives, so that the husbands could be free for "all manly and honorable concerns."[11]

All this harks back to the fateful shift in sex relations following the agricultural revolution, when women lost their equal status and a distinction began to be made between the unimportant "inside" work of females and the important "outside" work of males. Once this distinction was accepted, it became deeply rooted in civilizations throughout the world. What is significant here is that the distinction persisted not only in the successive ancient civilizations but also in the new civilization that emerged in western Europe. Despite the technological advances, the economic dynamism, and the political innovations, the customs of the past continued to weigh heavily on European women at the end of the Middle Ages. Built-in sex discrimination persisted even during centuries of technological, economic, and political transition. This triumph of the past over the present is noteworthy because the same pattern is discernible today, in our time, as is evident in the following "Rules of Conduct for Teachers," published in the Cabell County (West Virginia) Board of Education's school bulletin in 1915.

1. You will not marry during the term of your contract.
2. You are not to keep company with men.
3. You must be home between the hours of 8 P.M. and 6 A.M. unless attending a school function.
4. You may not loiter downtown in ice cream stores.
5. You may not travel beyond the city limits unless you have the permission of the chairman of the board.
6. You may not ride in a carriage or automobile with any man unless he is your father or brother.
7. You may not smoke cigarettes.
8. You may not dress in bright colors.
9. You may under no circumstances dye your hair.
10. You must wear at least two petticoats.

11. Your dresses must not be any shorter than two inches above the ankle.

12. To keep the schoolroom neat and clean, you must sweep the floor at least once daily; scrub the floor at once a week with hot, soapy water; clean the blackboards at least once a day, and start the fire at 7 A.M. so the room will be warm by 8 A.M.[12]

SUGGESTED READINGS

For works on the early medieval period following the invasions, see the bibliography for Chapter 12. A significant and stimulating study of medieval Europe in a global context is by R. L. Reynolds, *Europe Emerges: Transition Toward an Industrial World-Wide Society 600–1750* (University of Wisconsin, 1961). An excellent general history of the medieval West is by R. S. Lopez, *The Birth of Europe* (Lippincott, 1966).

The best introduction to feudal institutions is provided by J. R. Strayer, *Feudalism* (Van Nostrand, 1965); and by M. Bloch, *Feudal Society*, 2 vols. (University of Chicago, 1961). On social and economic developments there is J. LeGoff, *Your Money or Your Life: Economy and Religion in the Middle Ages* (MIT Press, 1988); R. H. Bautier, *The Economic Development of Medieval Europe* (Harcourt, 1971); R. S. Lopez, *The Commercial Revolution of the Middle Ages, 950–1350* (Prentice Hall, 1971); B. H. Slicher van Bath, *The Agrarian History of Western Europe, 500–1850* (Arnold, 1963); L. White, Jr., *Medieval Technology and Social Changes* (Clarendon, 1962). On the rise of the monarchies, see B. Guenée, *States and Rulers in Later Medieval Europe* (Blackwell, 1984). An excellent general introduction to the Renaissance is by W. K. Ferguson, *The Renaissance* (Torchbook, 1940). See also P. Kristeller, *Renaissance Thought*, 2 vols. (Torchbook, 1961–65); and W. Pater, *The Renaissance* (Meridian, 1961). Finally, the key question of why the West rather than some other region of Eurasia took the lead in overseas expansion is considered in J. R. Levenson, ed., *European Expansion and the Counter-Example of Asia, 1300–1600* (Prentice Hall, 1967); D. L. Jensen, ed., *The Expansion of Europe* (Heath, 1967); E. L. Jones, *The European Miracle: Environments, Economics and Geopolitics in the History of Europe and Asia* (Cambridge University, 1981). The latest analysis of why Europe bolted ahead of other continents is by A. W. Crosby, *The Measure of Reality: Quantification and Western Society, 1250–1600* (Cambridge University, 1996), which stresses the new technology and the new mentality viewing the universe in quantitative terms.

The pioneer study of medieval women is the still valuable survey by E. Power, "The Position of Women," in C. G. Crump and E. F. Jacob, eds., *The Legacy of the Middle Ages* (Clarendon, 1926), pp. 401–434. Important recent works are by S. Shahar, *The Fourth Estate: A History of Women in the Middle Ages* (Methuen, 1983); F. and J. Gies, *Women in the Middle Ages* (Crowell, 1978); S. M. Stuard, *Women in Medieval Society* (University of Pennsylvania, 1976); and S. H. Gross and M. W. Bingham, *Women in Medieval-Renaissance Europe* (Glenhurst, 1983).

NOTES

1. Francis Bacon, *Novum Organum*, aphorism, p. 129.
2. Cited by R. S. Lopez, *The Birth of Europe* (Lippincott, 1967), p. 146.
3. Cited in manuscript by L. V. Thomas, *Ottoman Awareness of Europe, 1629–1800*.
4. Cited by J. H. Parry, *The Age of Reconnaissance* (Weidenfeld & Nicolson, 1963), p. 19.
5. Galatians 3:28.
6. Eileen Power, "The Position of Women," in C. G. Crump and E. F. Jacob, eds., *The Legacy of the Middle Ages* (Clarendon, 1926), p. 413.
7. Eileen Power, *Medieval English Nunneries, c. 1275–1535* (Cambridge University, 1922), p. 31.
8. F. and J. Gies, *Women in the Middle Ages* (Crowell, 1978), p. 232.
9. S. H. Gross and M. W. Bingham, *Women in Medieval-Renaissance Europe* (Glenhurst, 1983), p. 84.
10. Ibid., p. 46.
11. Ibid., p. 228.
12. Republished in "Dear Abby" column by Abigail Van Buren, *Los Angeles Times*, June 17, 1979.

What It Means for Us Today

DEVELOPING SOCIETIES AND THE "RETARDING LEAD"

The most surprising and significant development during the thousand years of Eurasian medieval history was the rise of western Europe from poverty and obscurity. During most of this period from roughly 500 to 1500, the West was the underdeveloped region of Eurasia. We have seen that this underdevelopment proved an advantage in contrast to the development of China, which acted as a brake on that country. The Chinese enjoyed a sophisticated culture, advanced crafts, large-scale commerce, an efficient bureaucracy based on merit, and the creed of Confucianism that provided social cohesion and intellectual rationale. Very naturally, the Chinese considered their civilization to be superior to any other and regarded foreigners as "barbarians." When the first Westerners appeared on their coasts, the Chinese assumed there was nothing important they could learn from those peculiar "long-nosed barbarians."

This attitude, understandable though it was, left the Chinese unchanging during a time of great change. By contrast, the western Europeans, precisely because of their relative backwardness, were ready and eager to learn and to adapt. They took Chinese inventions, developed them to their full potential, and used them for overseas expansion. This expansion, in turn, triggered more technological advances and institutional changes. The end result was the transition from medieval to modern civilization, with the Europeans serving as the pioneers and the beneficiaries.

This was not the first time that a backward, peripheral region had led in the transition from one historical era to another. During the period of the ancient civilizations (3500–1000 B.C.E.), the Middle East had functioned as the developed core that made the basic innovations in agriculture, metallurgy, writing, and urban life. But this highly developed center fell behind during the transition from the ancient to the classical civilizations. It was the peripheral and comparatively backward regions of China, India, and Europe that pioneered in the creative innovations of the Classical Age, including effective exploitation of iron metallurgy, coinage, and the alphabet, as well as the new religions of Confucianism, Hinduism, and Christianity.

This pattern suggests that in history, nothing fails like success. Anthropologists refer to this as the *Law of Retarding Lead*, which holds that the best adapted and most successful societies have the most difficulty in changing and retaining their lead in a period of transition. And conversely, the backward and less successful societies are more likely to be able to adapt and to forge ahead.

The significance of this law is obvious for us today, when the West—the heir of medieval western Europe—no longer represents an underdeveloped region of Eurasia but rather the most highly developed part of the globe. Furthermore, we are living in an age of transition when the tempo of history has speeded up immensely in comparison with the Middle Ages. The speed-up is evident today in what has happened in the few years since World War II: the meteoric economic recovery of Japan and Germany since their devastation during the war, and the equally sudden political collapse of the Soviet Union from a superpower to a blank on the world map. In such a period of constantly accelerating change, adaptability is the key to personal and national success—or perhaps we should say, personal and national survival. President Lyndon B. Johnson summarized it best with this warning to his fellow Americans: "We must change to master change."

SUGGESTED READINGS

The full implications of the "retarding lead" concept are set forth in M. D. Sahlins and E. R. Service, eds., *Evolution and Culture* (University of Michigan, 1960); and E. R. Service, *Cultural Evolutionism: Theory in Practice* (Holt, Rinehart & Winston, 1971).

PART IV

Non-Eurasian World to 1500

Thus far we have dealt exclusively with Eurasian history. Now we turn to the history of the non-Eurasian part of the globe. The reason for this separate treatment is that the histories of the peoples involved were in fact largely separate. Before 1500, there was little interaction between the Eurasian and non-Eurasian segments of the world. Human history during those millennia was essentially regional, not global, in scope. Once human beings scattered to all the continents, they lost contact with each other and lived for thousands of years in isolation on their respective continents. Here we note the paradox that advances in human technology were responsible both for the early dispersal and isolation of human beings, and then for their later interaction and reunification.

We noted earlier (Chapter 1, Section III) that when our Paleolithic ancestors learned to use tools, to make clothing, and to control fire, they were able to leave what is commonly believed to be their original African homeland and to spread out and occupy all the continents except Antarctica. But once they settled down in their new homes, they did not keep contact with the relatives they had left behind because their technology was too primitive to allow voyages back and forth across the oceans separating the continents. This was especially true after the melting of the glaciers raised ocean levels and submerged the land bridge between Siberia and Alaska, and also the island stepping stones between Southeast Asia and Australia. For this reason, human settlements necessarily existed for millennia in regional isolation. They continued to do so until advances in shipbuilding and navigation technology enabled the Chinese to sail around Southeast Asia and across the Indian Ocean, and likewise the western Europeans to sail around the southern tips of Africa and South America and across the Atlantic, the Pacific, and the Indian oceans. In this way the peoples of the world reestablished direct contact with each other, thus beginning a new global phase of their history.

Because the Europeans took the lead in overseas exploration, history textbooks have focused on Columbus, da Gama, and Magellan, on their discoveries, and on the repercussions that followed. Such an approach is inadequate for global history. A global perspective requires consideration not only of the expanding West but also of the regions into which the West expanded. The peoples of these regions, after all, made up a considerable proportion of the human race, and their evolution must not be ignored. Moreover, the lands, peoples, and institutions of the non-Eurasian world were as significant in determining the outcome of Western expansionism as were the Westerners themselves. For these reasons, then, the following two chapters are devoted to Africa, to the Americas, and to Australia.

15

Africa

On the woody vales of the Niger,
And the meandering plains of the Volta,
On the shoulders of Kilimanjaro
Carpeted with the icy sheen of snow,
There breathes the vast elusive Africa,
That Africa of long ago.

Michael Dei-Anang (Ghanaian poet)

A glance at a world map reveals that Africa is centrally located. To the north, Africa is separated from Europe by the Mediterranean Sea, a body of water that is narrow, is easy to cross, and historically has functioned as a highway. To the east the Sinai Peninsula provides a bridge to Asia, and the Red Sea is even narrower and easier to cross than the Mediterranean. Finally, the great expanses of the Indian Ocean are neutralized by the monsoon winds, which facilitate communication back and forth between East Africa and southern Asia.

Yet historically Africa was wrongly viewed as cut off from Eurasia and the rest of the world. Africa was viewed as isolated from other regions, and this perceived isolation affected the histori-cal experiences of the continent. At the same time that historians emphasized the continent's isolation, they stressed the fact that Africa borrowed much from the outside world during this period; however, exchange is a two-way street that works only when there is meaningful contact and interaction. This chapter will examine the internal developments in Africa, and the continent's contacts with the outside world.

I. GEOGRAPHY

Viewed as a whole, the continent of Africa begins with small, fertile strips at its extreme northern and southern tips. These soon yield to the great desert expanses of the Kalahari in the south and the Sahara in the north. Next come the rolling grasslands, or savannas, known in the north as the Sudan, the Arab term meaning "the country of the black people." Then come the tropical rain forests, which in their densest parts are more difficult for outsiders to penetrate than the deserts.

The African continent is immense and diverse. Its geographical diversity has always posed a challenge to Africans, but it was never regarded as a barrier. What emerges clearly from historical developments is that even in the most geographically unfavored parts of Africa, the indigenous peoples created important civilizations and cultures.

Africa has often been artificially divided into North Africa and Africa south of the Sahara. But the Sahara Desert was never a divider or a barrier in the history of the continent. The perceived barriers provided a hindrance to outsiders and made Africa difficult to penetrate and conquer during the early period of the continent's history. Africa was not isolated from the rest of the world, however; it was criss-crossed with numerous trade routes that linked African communities, and trade routes also linked Africa with the outside world via the Red Sea, the Mediterranean Sea, and the Indian Ocean. Africa achieved at an early stage a high social, political, and economic organization, which effectively controlled trade, trade routes, and markets and for the most part kept potential invaders at bay.

In viewing political organizations on the continent, African historians have often given great emphasis to centralized kingdoms, states, and empires. Besides organized states, there were many African groups that remained decentralized but evolved appropriate structures of government that functioned and served them well. The Igbos of modern Nigeria, for example, who numbered in the millions, never developed centralized states.

II. AGRICULTURE AND IRON

Africa has often been seen as a borrower of technology and agriculture from Eurasia. Recent archeological research is changing our views of these developments in Africa, revealing that iron workings and knowledge existed in many parts

Iron tools were used in Africa long before the coming of the Europeans. This illustration, taken from David Livingstone's Last Journals, *shows Africans forging hoes.*

of Africa prior to the Christian era. There were iron workings in the lakeland regions of modern Tanzania by the seventh century B.C.E., in Meroe by the fifth century B.C.E., in Nok in West Africa by the fourth century B.C.E., and in the northern lake regions of East Africa by the third century B.C.E. What this suggests is that there were probably many areas that independently evolved the use of iron rather than importing it from the outside. These early users of iron probably kept their use of iron a secret. However, between the second and fifth centuries C.E. iron technology spread to most places in central, eastern, and southern Africa through Bantu farmers who had acquired the use of iron by this time.

The movement of the Bantu peoples from West Africa to central, eastern, and southern Africa has often been described as a migration, but it was a gradual movement of small numbers of peoples who often intermarried with the people in the areas they infiltrated. The Bantu were in the area of modern Zaire by the fifth century B.C.E., but the widespread use of iron between the second and fifth centuries C.E. allowed the Bantu to move more quickly to the rest of the southern portion of the continent.

The appearance of iron had repercussions in Africa as wide as those we noted in Eurasia. Iron-tipped hoes and iron-shod axes made it possible to extend agriculture into the forests of Africa, just as the earlier use of iron brought agriculture into the forests of central Europe and of the Ganges and Yangtze valleys. The resulting increase in agricultural output left a surplus available for trading purposes. As in Eurasia, this in turn led to social differentiation—to the division of peoples into rulers and ruled in place of simple kinship relationships; hence the appearance about the ninth century C.E. of definite state structures with military and administrative services and with the revenue sources necessary for their support.

Technological advances in Africa affected the ethnic composition of the continent. It was the accessible Negroes rather than the inaccessible Pygmies and San who adopted and profited from agriculture and iron metallurgy. Consequently, it was also they who increased disproportionately in number and who were able, with their iron tools and weapons, to push southward at the expense of the San and Pygmies. Their expansionism was particularly marked in the case of the Bantu, a predominantly Negroid linguistic group. Starting from their original center in the Cameroon highlands, the Bantu infiltrated in the early Christian era into the Congo basin, where they developed a symbiotic relationship with the sparse San hunters. From there they pushed southeast to the fertile, open Great Lakes country between 600 and 900 C.E. They then continued southward across the savanna at the expense of the San. These migrations explain why the Negroes were the predominant ethnic group by the time the Europeans arrived, whereas a millennium earlier they had shared the continent fairly evenly with the Caucasoids, San, and Pygmies.

African Agriculture

Before its desiccation 7,000 years ago, the Sahara supported a pastoral society that had flocks of sheep, goats, and cattle. These people also fished

Traditional African farming methods as painted by a modern African artist. The women in the left foreground are grinding grain in a large mortar, while the men beyond are hoeing and harvesting.

and herded flocks using sickles and blades which have been found in ruins.

It is not known precisely when these people began to grow food, but we do know that agricultural systems evolved in this area which supported extensive village populations with far-flung market and trading centers. These centers helped to give rise to African cultures such as the Nok, Benin, Ghana, Mali, and other Sudanic and East African kingdoms.

There was an intimate association between plants and African peoples, as was the case with other humans extending back to the roots of human origin. Although agriculture emerged in Egypt around 6500 B.C.E., tool kits associated with intensive gathering and the use of food crops go back as early as 18,000 years ago. The evidence indicates that these tool kits were African and not Near Eastern. The archeological evidence in Egypt suggests that the first farmers in that area 6,500 years ago also had sheep, goats, and cattle; cool seasons yielded crops such as barley, emmer, flax, lentil, and chickpea.

In the area of the West African forests there is also early evidence of the domestication of crops such as the oil palm, cowpea, and guinea yam. This domestication does not indicate borrowing from elsewhere. In the area of the savanna, for example, the rice cultivated is believed to be of savanna origin. Furthermore, in the area of Ethiopia most of the crops cultivated there are native to Africa, and there is no evidence that borrowing took place.

III. ISLAM

Africa was influenced by the impact of Moslem Arabs who overran all of North Africa in the seventh century C.E. and later extended their control down the east coast as merchants and colonists. From these coastal bases Islam had a profound influence on the African peoples. The impact of Islam was most obvious in the externals of life—names, dress, household equipment, architectural styles, festivals, and the like. It was evident also in the agricultural and technological progress that resulted from wider contact with the outside world; in East Africa, for example, the Arabs introduced rice and sugar cane from India.

Islam also stimulated commerce linking the African economy to the far-flung network of Eurasian trade routes controlled by Moslem merchants. From their bases in North Africa the Moslems used the camel much more than had the Romans, and they increased the number of trans-Saharan trade routes and the volume of trade. Southward they transported cloth, jewelry, cowrie beads, and, above all, salt, which was in urgent demand throughout the Sudan. In return the Africans provided ivory, slaves, ostrich feathers, civet for perfumes, and, most important, gold from the upper Niger, Senegal,

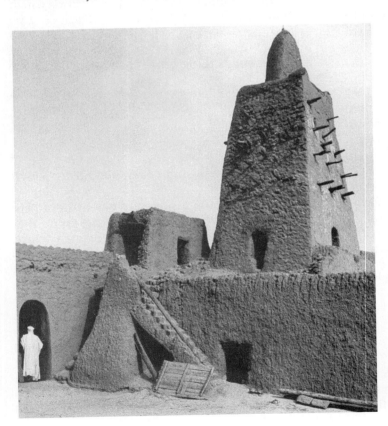

The Djinguereber mosque in Timbuktu. The mud and wood building is typical of western Sudanese mosques. The distinctive tower of the mosque was a symbol of the presence of Islam, which came to places like Timbuktu in central and West Africa by way of overland trade routes.

and Volta rivers. Much of this gold ultimately found its way to Europe—in such large quantities, in fact, that it became important for off-setting medieval Europe's unfavorable balance of trade with the East. The trade between the Sudan and North Africa was so profitable for both sides that by 1400 the whole of West Africa was criss-crossed with trading trails and dotted with market centers.

Meanwhile a similar trading pattern had been developing in East Africa. Moslem middlemen on the coast sent agents into the interior who brought ivory, slaves, gold from present-day Zimbabwe and copper from Katanga. These commodities then were exported through Indian Ocean trade channels, controlled at the time by Moslem merchants. In later centuries iron ore also was obtained from the interior, shipped to southern India, and made into the so-called Damascus blades. In return for these products, Africans received Chinese and Indian cloth and various luxury goods, especially Chinese porcelain, remains of which still can be found along the coast. This trade was the basis for the string of thriving ports and city-states along the East African coast. Thus we see that just as the Mediterranean Sea had made possible centuries-old interaction between North Africa and the peoples of Europe and the Middle East, so the Indian Ocean made possible similar interaction between East Africa and the peoples of the Middle East, India, Southeast Asia, and even the Far East.

To return to the role of Islam in Africa, it served also to stimulate the intellectual life of the Sudan. Literacy spread with the establishment of Koranic schools. Scholars could pursue higher learning at various Sudanese universities, of which the University of Sankore at Timbuktu was the most outstanding. This institution was modeled after other Moslem universities at Fez, Tunis, and Cairo. It was the custom for scholars to move about freely among these universities and others in the Moslem world in order to study at the feet of particular masters.

The adoption of Islam also strengthened the political organization of the Sudanic kingdoms. Traditionally Sudanic rulers could claim the allegiance only of their own kinship units or clans and of such other related kinship units that recognized descent from a great founding ancestor. But when the kingdoms were enlarged into great empires, the kinship relationship obviously became inadequate as the basis for imperial organization. The greater the extent of an empire, the more alien its emperor appeared to a large proportion of the subjects. Local chiefs could not be depended on to serve as faithful vassals; they tended instead to lead their own people in resistance to imperial rule. Islam helped to solve this institutional problem by strengthening the imperial administration. Moslem schools and colleges turned out a class of educated men who could organize an effective imperial bureaucracy. These men were not dominated by their kinship alliances; their own interests were tied to imperial authority, and they normally could be counted on to serve that authority loyally.

IV. TRADE AND SUDANESE EMPIRES

The Islamic conquest gave trans-Saharan trade new impetus and linked it to the Moslem world, whose monetary system depended upon gold. The earliest kingdom associated with the growth of trade across the Sahara is the Ghana Empire (400–1200). (See map of African Empires and Trade Routes, p. 256.) This empire was founded by Soninke-speaking Africans who lived in the area of the grassland south of the Sahara. Although we do not know the precise date for the founding of the kingdom, it was in existence by the fifth century C.E. Ghana's fame reached far beyond the Sahara and as far as Baghdad. The Arabic writer Al-Fazari, who lived at the court of the Abbasid caliph in that city, described Ghana as the "land of gold."

Moslems played a key role in trade and administration of the empire, but the king controlled the trade of the empire and administered justice in the kingdom. Despite the Moslem presence, the king clung to the religion of his ancestors.

The Ghana Empire reached its peak during the middle of the eleventh century and then began to decline. Religious conflict and destructive wars disrupted trading activities of the empire. Ghana also lost control of the gold-mining regions toward the end of the twelfth century. Furthermore, environmental factors such as desertification and overgrazing in the region

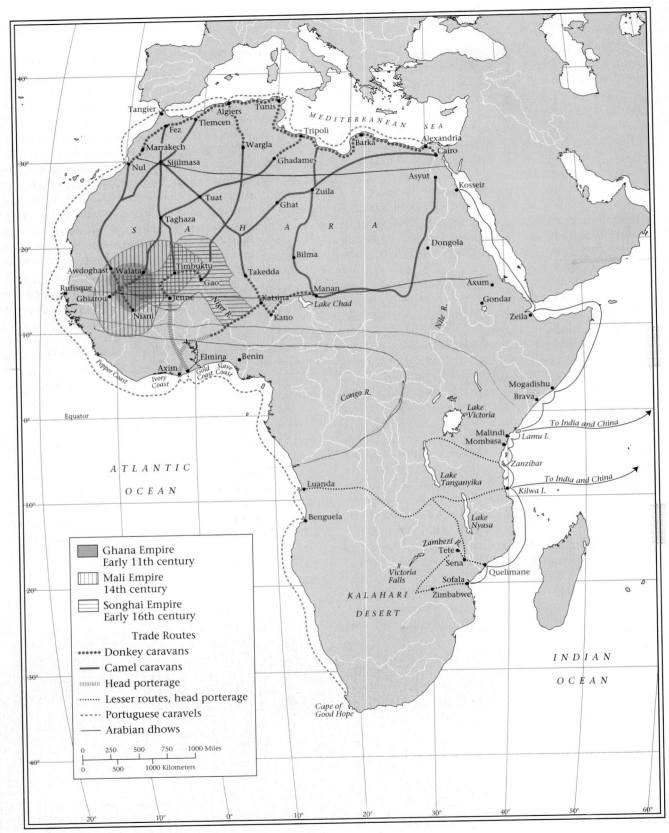

Legend

Ghana Empire
Early 11th century

Mali Empire
14th century

Songhai Empire
Early 16th century

Trade Routes

••••• Donkey caravans

——— Camel caravans

▥▥▥ Head porterage

········· Lesser routes, head porterage

‒ ‒ ‒ Portuguese caravels

——— Arabian dhows

| 0 | 250 | 500 | 750 | 1000 Miles |

| 0 | 500 | 1000 Kilometers |

African Empires and Trade Routes

forced farmers and traders to disperse and move to more favorable regions.

As the empire of Ghana declined, it gave way to the Mali Empire (1200–1500). The expansion and fame of Mali during this period depended on two able rulers: Mansa Musa (1312–1337) and Mansa Sulayaman (1341–1360). Islam became well established at Mansa Musa's court. The fame of Mali spread following Mansa Musa's pilgrimage to Mecca in 1324. Mansa Musa distributed gold and lavish gifts on his pilgrimage. In Egypt he distributed so much gold that his visit was noted by Arab historians as the most significant event in Egypt in 1324. On his return from his pilgrimage Mansa Musa brought back with him religious scholars and missionaries. The major commercial areas thus became major centers for education. Mansa Musa purified Islam on his return by stricter adherence to the Moslem religion.

Despite its commercial and political attainments, Mali began to decline as a result of internal political problems and outside attacks. The last of the great empires of the western Sudan was Songhay (1350–1600). Its origins go back to at least the eighth century. Trans-Saharan trade as well as its location in the fertile Sudan savanna area contributed to the rise of the kingdom. The location of the kingdom on the banks of the Niger River also afforded opportunities for fishing. When Songhay emerged as an empire, people were divided into three professional classes: the Sorko (mostly fishermen), the Do (mostly farmers), and the Gow or Gabibi (mostly hunters).

Songhay remained a small kingdom until it regained its independence from Mali in the late fourteenth century and began to expand. As an empire it enjoyed only about a century of brilliance, from the second half of the fifteenth century until the early decades of the sixteenth century.

The expansion of Songhay and the consolidation of the empire can be attributed to two monarchs: Sunni Ali (1464–1492) and Askia Mohammed (1492–1528). The latter exploited the strategic location of Timbuktu and revived the trade that was so vital to the empire. Realizing the importance of Islam, Askia reached out to the Moslem community. He made contact with notable Muslim scholars and encouraged education. In Timbuktu, his university in the mosque of Sankore produced many distinguished scholars. One of these has left us a description of the intellectual life of Timbuktu:

In those days Timbuktu did not have its equal . . .
from the province of Mali to the extreme limits of the

Examples of iron coins found in Equatorial Africa.

region of the Maghrib for the solidity of its institutions, its political liberties, the purity of its morals, the security of persons, its consideration and compassion towards foreigners, its courtesy towards students and men of learning.

Leo Africanus, the Moorish historian who traveled in the region, also wrote:

Here are great stores of doctors, judges, priests and other learned men that are bountifully maintained at the king's cost and charges, and hither are brought divers manuscripts or written books of Barbary, which are sold for more money than any other merchandise.

Despite its wealth and learning, the empire fell because of internal tensions and raids from Morocco. By the end of the sixteenth century Songhay was a shadow of its former self.

These empires had certain fundamental characteristics in common. They all were based primarily on trade, so that each extended its authority northward to control the import of salt and southward to control the purchase of gold. Each derived most of its revenues from levies on the buying and selling of these and other commodities. The revenues from these duties allowed for progressively greater sophistication in imperial administration. Thus the Songhay Empire was more complex than its two predecessors. It was divided into definite provinces, each with a governor on long-term appointment. It also boasted the beginnings of a professional army and even a number of ministries—for finance, justice, home affairs, agriculture, and forests, as well as for the Arabs and Berbers on the Saharan frontiers of the empire.

The Mali and Songhay empires owed much to Islam for furthering trade, providing a trained bureaucracy, and stimulating intellectual life. Islam also transformed the Sudan from an isolated African region to an integral part of the Moslem world. Thus the fourteenth-century Arab traveler Ibn Battuta included Mali in his journeys, which ranged as far east as China. Arriving at the Mali capital in June 1353, he was favorably impressed by the imperial administration and by the habits of the people:

The negroes possess some admirable qualities. They are seldom unjust, and have a greater abhorrence of

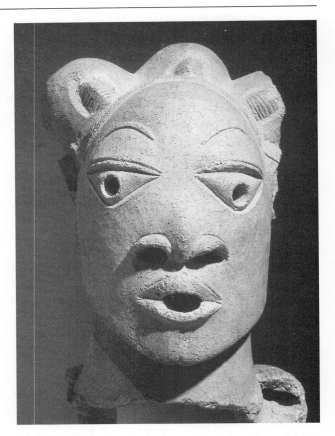

West African terra-cotta sculpture (36 cms high) from the Nok culture, which flourished in the Western Sudan from about 900 B.C.E. to about 200 C.E. The style of terra-cotta castings like this one suggests that they may have had wooden prototypes.

injustice than any other people. Their sultan shows no mercy to anyone who is guilty of the least act of it. There is complete security in their country. Neither traveler nor inhabitant in it has anything to fear from robbers or men of violence. They do not confiscate the property of any white man who dies in their country, even if it be uncounted wealth. On the contrary, they give it into the charge of some trustworthy person among the whites, until the rightful heir takes possession of it. They are careful to observe the hours of prayer, and assiduous in attending them in congregations, and in bringing up their children to them. On Fridays, if a man does not go early to the mosque, he cannot find a corner to pray in, on account of the crowd.[1]

Although Islam played a key role in the formation and functioning of the Sudanic empires, it should be noted that it was primarily an urban faith. It was the merchants and townspeople who became Moslems, whereas the country folk by and large remained loyal to their traditional pagan gods and beliefs. Thus the reliance of many of the emperors and of their imperial establishments on Islam was a source of weakness as well as strength. Islam, as we have seen, had much to contribute, but its base was narrower than it seemed to contemporary observers, who naturally visited urban centers and traveled along trade routes. Thus in times of crisis the town-centered empires proved unexpectedly fragile and quickly fell apart.

Another weakness of the Sudanic empires was their vulnerability to attack from the north by Berbers looking for the source of African gold or seeking to impose their particular version of the true faith. The fanatical Almarovids were responsible for the overthrow of Ghana in 1076, and likewise an invasion from Morocco destroyed Songhay in 1591. The latter catastrophe marked the end of the Sudanic imperial era. In the words of a seventeenth-century Timbuktu historian: "From that moment everything changed. Danger took the place of security; poverty of wealth. Peace gave way to distress, disasters, and violence. . . ."[2]

V. KINGDOMS AND STATES

The three empires noted above are the best-known African medieval political creations. In the rest of the continent, however, there existed a great variety of other political structures. In southeast Africa, for example, there were certain similarities to the situation in the Sudan. Just as the Sudan was famous for its gold exports, so southeast Africa was famous for the same reason in the Indian Ocean basin. And just as the Sudanic empires and North African states were nourished by the one trade pattern, so by the fifteenth century the Monomotapa Empire in the interior and the Kilwa city-state on the coast were supported by the other.

Monomotapa, a word adapted by the Portuguese from the royal title Mwenemutapa, included much of Zimbabwe and Mozambique. It controlled the sources of gold and the routes to the coast, after the fashion of the Sudanic

empires. The monarchs of Monomotapa raised the Great Temple of Zimbabwe, a massive enclosure with walls thirty-two feet high, constructed to provide an appropriate setting for the conduct of royal ceremonial rites. On the coast, the merchant rulers of the port of Kilwa controlled the flow of goods from Monomotapa to the Moslem trading ships that ranged the Indian Ocean and even beyond to the China seas. "Kilwa is one of the most beautiful and well-constructed towns in the world. The whole of it is elegantly built," wrote Ibn Battuta—the same traveler impressed also by Mali.[3]

Just as the Sudanic kingdoms were ravaged by Berber invaders from the north, so Monomotapa and Kilwa were destroyed by Portuguese intruders from overseas. Within a decade after Vasco da Gama's rounding of the Cape of Good Hope in 1497, the Portuguese had plundered many of the coastal cities of southeast Africa and were carrying on in the Indian Ocean as though it were a Portuguese lake. Da Gama had missed Kilwa on his first voyage, but a Portuguese fleet was provided shelter there in 1500. Five years later another fleet responded to this

Benin King and Attendants, *from Nigeria, circa 1550– 1680 B.C.E.*

9 *Copper crucifix of sixteenth or seventeenth century from the Kipangue Province of the Lower Congo*

10 *Head of Christ carved in wood in East Africa. The Arabic features and Assyrian beard are in sharp contrast with the Negro faces of the other side of the continent*

A sixteenth or seventeenth century copper crucifix from Kipangue Province, Lower Congo.

CONCLUSION

Contrary to popular belief, Africa during the period before European expansion was never isolated. External contact and internal relationships increased from the seventh century onwards with the dynamism brought by Islam. Interregional trade grew because of more effective means of communication. The camel was already in use in North Africa, but from the seventh century on its use became widespread. Cross-breeding of the two-humped camel of central Asia with the Arabian or one-humped dromedary produced two kinds of camels: One had a slow gait and was capable of carrying heavy loads for long distances; the other was faster and was used as a courier.

The increase in trade also gave impetus to navigation and allowed the Arabs to build up powerful fleets in the trade between East Africa and the countries of the Indian Ocean, the Red Sea, and the Mediterranean. There was also a spectacular growth of commercial towns all over the continent: Sidjimasa was a staging post for trans-Saharan trade; Cairo was central to the trade of the Moslem east and the Moslem west and the savanna area; and Awdaghust was the central market that linked North Africa with the savanna. On the East African coast, Moslem merchants settled in the commercial towns of Mogadishu, Malindi, Mombasa, Kilwa, and Sofala.

A variety of products were traded, including raw materials such as iron, flax, cotton, gum, and indigo; subsistence products such as sorghum, rice, shear-butter, millet, olive oil, salt, and fish; and also luxury goods such as gold and ivory.

The pre-1500 centuries saw significant economic, social and political developments. After 1500 other parts of the world would pull ahead of Africa in terms of development. The reasons for this divergence lie in Africa's internal developments and destructive external contacts after 1500, as we shall note in the next volume.

The British Africanist Thomas Hodgkin wrote that

Allowing for the difference between the Moslem and the Christian intellectual climates, a citizen of fourteenth-century Timbuktu would have found himself reasonably at home in fourteenth-century Oxford. In

hospitality with ruthless looting. A member of the expedition recounts that they captured this city of "many strong houses several stories high" without opposition from the surprised inhabitants. Then "the Vicar-General and some of the Franciscan fathers came ashore carrying two crosses in procession and singing the Te Deum. They went to the palace, and there the cross was put down and the Admiral prayed. Then everyone started to plunder the town of all its merchandise and provisions."[4]

Later the Portuguese made their way up the Zambezi River and similarly undermined the Monomotapa Empire. They settled in various strategic locations along the river and extended their influence in all directions until the inevitable showdown in 1628. With their firearms the Portuguese easily defeated two Monomotapa armies, but several substantial kingdoms survived on the ruins of the former empire.

the sixteenth century he would still have found many points in common between the two university cities. By the nineteenth century the gulf had grown very deep.[5]

Hodgkin's point describes a process that is certainly not unique to Africa. It is clear from the preceding chapters that divergence is a worldwide phenomenon for the simple reason that the West pioneered in modernization and consequently pulled ahead of all other societies. Yet the fact remains that the gap between the West and Africa opened much wider than that between the West and other Eurasian regions. Constantinople, Delhi, and Peking did decline in relation to London, Paris, and Berlin, but they did not decline to virtual extinction, as did Timbuktu.

SUGGESTED READINGS

A useful introduction to Africa is by J. F. A. Ajayi and M. Crowder, eds., *Historical Atlas of Africa* (Longman, 1985). On geography, see W. A. Hance, *The Geography of Modern Africa*, 2nd ed. (Columbia University, 1975); and G. W. Hartwig and K. D. Patterson, eds., *Disease in African History* (Duke University, 1978). Collections of source materials are provided by B. Davidson, *The African Past: Chronicles from Antiquity to Modern Times* (Little, Brown, 1964); and P. J. M. McEwan, ed., *Africa from Early Times to 1800* (Oxford University, 1968). The pre-Western history of Africa is presented as authoritatively as current knowledge permits by P. D.

Curtin, et al., *African History* (Little, Brown, 1978); J. D. Fage, *A History of Africa* (Knopf, 1978); and in more detail in R. Oliver and J. D. Fage, eds., *The Cambridge History of Africa*, 8 vols. (Cambridge University, 1975 ff.); *UNESCO General History of Africa* (University of California, 1981 ff.); and P. J. C. Dark, *An Introduction to Benin Art and Technology* (Oxford: Clarendon Press, 1973).

For African arts, see M. Posnansky, ed., *Prelude to East African History* (Oxford University, 1966); J. F. A. Ajayi and M. Crowder, eds., *History of West Africa*, vol. 1, 3rd ed. (Longman, 1985); B. Davidson, *The Prehistory of Africa* (Thames and Hudson, 1970); B. Davidson, *The African Genius* (Little, Brown, 1969); and B. H. Dietz and M. B. Olantunji, *Musical Instruments of Africa* (John Day, 1965). On the role of Islam in African history, see volumes II and III of *The Cambridge History of Africa* above; and N. Levtzion, *Ancient Ghana and Mali* (Methuen, 1973), a thorough study of what is known.

NOTES

1. Cited by C.M. Cipolla, *European Culture and Overseas Expansion* (Pelican, 1970), p. 105.
2. Ibn Battuta, *Travels in Asia and Africa, 1325–1354*, trans. H. A. R. Gibb (Routledge & Kegan Paul, 1929), pp. 329–330.
3. Cited by T. Hodgkin, "Kingdoms of the Western Sudan," in *The Dawn of African history*, ed. R. Oliver (Oxford University, 1961), p. 43.
4. Cited by B. Davidson, *Africa in History* (Macmillan, 1968), p. 63.
5. Ibid., p. 168.

CHAPTER
16

Americas and Australia

To the nations, however, both of the East and West Indies, all the commercial benefits which can have resulted from these events [the expansion of Europe] have been sunk and lost in the dreadful misfortunes which they have occasioned.

Adam Smith

The Vikings, who stumbled on North America in the eleventh century, tried for about one hundred years to maintain settlements there, but without success. In the fifteenth century Columbus likewise stumbled on the New World, but this time the sequel was altogether different. Instead of failure and withdrawal, Columbus's discovery was followed by massive and overwhelming penetration of both North and South America. The contrast shows how much European power and dynamism had increased during the intervening half-millennium.

Equally striking was the contrast between the rapid European penetration and exploitation of the Americas and the centuries that elapsed before the same could take place in Africa. One reason was geography; the New World was physically more accessible and inviting. The other reason was that the overall nature of the Indian cultures was such that effective resistance was impossible. And if this was true of the American Indians, it was much more so of the Australian aborigines who were still at the food-gathering stage. In this chapter we shall consider the physical setting and the cultural background of the fateful developments that followed the landing of Columbus in the West Indies and of Captain James Cook in New South Wales.

I. LAND AND PEOPLE

The Americas, in contrast to Africa, were exceptionally open to newcomers from Europe. No sandbars obstructed the approaches to the coasts. There were many more harbors available along the indented coastline of the Americas than along the unbroken coastline of Africa. Also, the Americas had a well-developed pattern of waterways that were relatively free of impediments and offered easy access to the interior. There is no counterpart in Africa to the majestic and smooth-flowing Amazon, Plata, Mississippi, and St. Lawrence rivers. The explorers soon learned the use of the native birchbark canoe, and they discovered that with comparatively few portages they could paddle from the Atlantic up the St. Lawrence, along the Great Lakes, and thence south down the Mississippi to the Gulf of Mexico. Or they could paddle north down the Mackenzie to the Arctic Ocean, or west down the Columbia or the Fraser to the Pacific Ocean.

The climate of the Americas, too, is generally more attractive than that of Africa. The Amazon basin, it is true, is hot and humid, and the polar extremities of both continents are bitterly cold. But the British and French settlers flourished in the lands they colonized north of the Rio Grande, and the Spaniards likewise felt at home in Mexico and Peru, which became their two principal centers. The climate there is not much different from that of Spain, and certainly a welcome contrast to the sweltering and disease-ridden Gold and Ivory coasts of Africa.

The Indians that the Europeans found in the Americas were the descendants of the bands that had crossed the Bering Sea from Siberia to Alaska. Until recently it was believed that the Indians first began crossing to the Americas about 10,000 years ago. New archeological findings, together with the use of carbon-14 dating, have forced a drastic revision of this estimate. It is now generally agreed that humans were in the New World roughly 30,000 years ago. The last major migration of Indians took place about 3,000 years ago. Then came the Eskimos, who continued to travel back and forth across the straits until modern political conditions forced them to remain on one side or the other. In any case, by this time the parts of America closest to Asia were densely enough populated to discourage further migration.

The actual crossing to the New World presented little difficulty to these early newcomers. The last Ice Age had locked up vast quantities of sea water, lowering the ocean level by 460 feet and thus exposing a 1,300-mile-wide land bridge connecting Siberia and Alaska. A "bridge" of such proportions was, in effect, a vast new subcontinent, which allowed ample scope for the transfer of plants and animals that now took place. Furthermore, this area, because of low rainfall, was covered not with ice but with lakes, mosses, grasses, and assorted shrubs typical of the tundra. This vegetation offered pasturage for the large mammals of the time: mastodon, mammoth, musk oxen, bison, moose, elk, mountain sheep and goats, camels, foxes, bears, wolves, and horses. As these herds of game crossed to the New World they were followed by the hunters who depended on them for food.

Even after rising temperatures lifted the sea level and submerged the connecting lands, the resulting narrow straits could easily have been crossed in crude boats without even losing sight of shore. Later and more advanced migrants probably traveled by boat from Asia to America and then continued along the northwest coast until they finally landed and settled in what is now British Columbia.

Most who crossed to Alaska moved on into the heart of North America through a gap in the ice sheet in the central Yukon plateau. They pressed forward because of the same forces that led them to migrate to Alaska—the search for new hunting grounds and the continual pressure of tribes from the rear. In this manner, both the continents were soon peopled by scattered tribes of hunters.

Regarding racial traits, all Indians may be classified as Mongoloids. They have the characteristic high cheekbones, straight black hair, but sparse hair on the face and body. Not all Indians, however, look alike. Those on North America's northwest coast have flatter faces and noses and narrower eyes (Mongolian fold) than do those of the southwest. The explanation for this difference is twofold: First, the earliest immigrants were much less Mongoloid in appearance because they left the East before the Asian Mongoloids—as we know them today—had fully evolved. Second, the immigrants at once spread out and settled in small, inbred groups in a variety of climates. This led to the evolution of a great variety of physical types, even though they are all of the same Mongoloid family.

II. CULTURES

The migrants to the New World brought little cultural baggage with them since they came from northeast Siberia, one of the least developed regions of Eurasia. They were, of course, all hunters, organized in small bands, possessing only crude stone tools, no pottery, and no domesticated animals, except perhaps the dog. Since they were entering an uninhabited continent, they were completely free to develop their own institutions without the influences from native populations that affected the Aryans when they migrated to the Indus valley, or the Achaeans and Dorians when they reached Greece.

During the ensuing millennia the American Indians did indeed develop an extraordinarily rich variety of cultures, which were adapted to one another as well as to the wide range of physical environments they encountered. Some remained at the hunting-band stage, whereas others developed kingdoms and empires. Their

Olmec Head. This colossal head, now in the Museo Nacional de Antropologia in Mexico City, was excavated at San Lorenzo. Carved of Basalt, it may be a portrait of an Olmec ruler. Olmec civilization thrived between 1500 and 800 B.C.E.

religions encompassed all known categories, including monotheism. They spoke perhaps 2,000 distinct languages, some as different from one another as Chinese and English. This number represents almost as much variation in speech as found in the entire Old World, where about 3,000 languages are known to have existed in 1500 C.E. Nor were these languages primitive, either in vocabulary or in any other respect. Whereas Shakespeare used about 24,000 words, and the King James Bible about 7,000, the Nahuatl of Mexico used 27,000 words, and the Yahgans of Tierra del Fuego, considered to be one of the world's most culturally retarded peoples, possess a vocabulary of at least 30,000 words.

Taking all types of institutions and practices into account, anthropologists have defined some twenty-two culture areas in the New World—the Great Plains area, the Eastern Woodlands, the Northwest Coast area, and so forth. A simpler classification, on the basis of how food was obtained, involves three categories: hunting, gathering, and fishing cultures; intermediate farming cultures; and advanced farming cultures. This scheme not only is simpler but is also meaningful from the viewpoint of world history, for it helps to explain the varied responses of the Indians to the European invaders.

The advanced farming cultures were located in Mesoamerica (central and southern Mexico, Guatemala, and Honduras) and the Andean highland area (Ecuador, Peru, Bolivia, and northern Chile). The intermediate farming cultures were generally in the adjacent regions, and the food-gathering cultures were in the more remote regions—the southern part of South America and the western and northern part of North America. It is significant that agriculture was first developed in the Americas in regions that were strikingly similar to the Middle East, where agriculture originated in Eurasia—that is, highland regions not requiring extensive clearing of forests to prepare the fields for crops, with enough rainfall to allow the crops to mature, and with a supply of potentially high-yielding native plants available for domestication.

The Indians domesticated over one hundred plants, or as many as were domesticated in all Eurasia, a truly extraordinary achievement. More than 50 percent of the farm products of the United States today are derived from crops grown by the Indians. Furthermore, we are realizing the superior food value of certain plants grown by the Indians but neglected by the European newcomers. One example is the grain amaranth, which had been as important as corn and beans to the Aztecs. They mixed the amaranth with human blood to form cakelike replicas of their gods and fed those replicas to the faithful. The Spaniards regarded this ritual as barbaric and as a mockery of Christian communion. Therefore, the Spaniards forbade the ritual by condemning to death anyone found growing or possessing amaranth. Yet this plant survives to the present day. A confection made of popped amaranth and honey is still popular in Mexico. Meanwhile, scientists are beginning to recognize the value of this grain, which can be ground into flour or popped like corn and can be used to make bread, crackers, cookies, soups, porridge, dumplings, and beverages. In addition to this versatility, a recent report of the National Academy of Sciences notes that amaranth is superior to other grains as a source of protein, vitamins, and minerals. Like the raised field agriculture noted above (Chapter 2, Section III), the current recognition of amaranth as "the grain of the future" points up the fact that lessons can be learned from our prehistoric ancestors, even in our age of "high technology."

Maize, which was the staple in almost all regions, was originally a weed with ears no larger than a person's thumbnail. The Indians bred it into a plant with rows of seeds on long cobs. So completely did they domesticate maize that it became completely dependent on humans for survival; it would become extinct if humans stopped planting it, for in its domesticated form it cannot disperse its seeds, the kernels. Also impressive was the skill of the Indians in utilizing large numbers of poisonous plants. One of these is manioc, known in the United States as tapioca. The Indians removed a deadly poison from manioc, leaving the starch. Other important plants grown by the Indians were squashes, potatoes, tomatoes, peanuts, chocolate, tobacco, and beans, a major source of protein. Among the medicinal plants bequeathed by the Indians were cascara, cocaine, arnica, ipecac, and quinine. The fact that none of the plants grown in America were cultivated in the Old World before its discovery of the New proves conclusively that the origins of agriculture were independent in the two hemispheres.

The regions where the Indians began agriculture were also the regions where they first developed it further and gradually evolved advanced farming cultures. This in turn profoundly changed the Indians' way of life. In general, the result was, as in Eurasia, a greatly increased sedentary population and the development of cultural activities not directly connected with bare subsistence. In other words, it was in these advanced farming cultures that it became possible to develop large empires and sophisticated civilizations comparable in certain respects to those in West Africa. Unfortunately, these indigenous American civilizations were suddenly overwhelmed by the Spaniards. Thus they left behind them little but their precious domesticated plants.

III. CIVILIZATIONS

The three major Amerindian civilizations were the Mayan, in present-day Yucatan, Guatemala, and Belize; the Aztec, in present-day Mexico; and the Inca, stretching for 3,000 miles from mid-Ecuador to mid-Chile. (See map of Amerindian Empires, p. 267.) The Mayas created the oldest civilization in the Americas and were outstanding for their remarkable development of the arts and sciences. They alone evolved an ideographic form of writing in which characters or signs were used as conventional symbols for ideas. They also studied the movements of the heavenly bodies in order to measure time, predict the future, and set favorable dates for sacrifices and major undertakings. So extensive was the astronomical knowledge compiled by highly trained priests that it is believed to have been at least equal to that of Europe at that time. The intricate sacred calendar of the Mayas was based on concurrent cycles merging into greater cycles as their multiples coincided in time. Some of their calendrical computations spanned millions of years, a particularly impressive concept of the dimension of time when we remember how recently in Europe the creation of the world was still fixed at 4004 B.C.E.

Mayan cities, if they may be so called, were ceremonial centers rather than fortresses, dwell-

Mayan figure of a dignitary or priest.

have been soil exhaustion or epidemic disease or peasant revolutions against the burden of supporting the religious centers and their priestly hierarchies. In any case, the great stone structures were abandoned to decay and were swallowed by the surrounding forest. They have been unearthed only in recent decades by archeological excavations.

The Aztecs were brusque and warlike compared to the artistic and intellectual Mayas—a contrast reminiscent of that between the Romans and the Greeks in the Old World. The Aztecs actually were latecomers to Mexico, where a series of highly developed societies had succeeded one another through the centuries. They were vulnerable to attacks by barbarians from the arid north who naturally moved down in response to the lure of fertile lands. The last of these invaders were the Aztecs, who had settled on some islands on Lake Texcoco, which then filled much of the floor of the valley of Anáhuac. As their numbers grew and the islands became overcrowded, the Aztecs increased their arable land by making chinampas—floating islands of matted weeds, covered with mud dredged from the lake floor, and anchored to the bottom by growing weeds. To the present day, this mode of cultivation is carried on in certain regions. Before each planting the farmers scoop up fresh mud and spread it over the chinampa, whose level steadily rises with the succession of crops. The farmers then excavate the top layers of mud, which they use to build a new chinampa, thus beginning a new cycle.

The chinampas enabled the Aztecs to boom in numbers and wealth. Early in the fifteenth century they made alliances with towns on the lake shore, and from that foothold they quickly extended their influence in all directions. Raiding expeditions went out regularly, forcing other peoples to pay tribute in kind and in services. By the time the Spaniards appeared on the scene, Aztec domination extended to the Pacific on the west, to the Gulf of Mexico on the east, almost to the Yucatan on the south, and to the Rio Grande on the north. The capital, Tenochtitlán, was by then a magnificent city of 200,000 to 300,000 people, linked to the shore by causeways. The conqueror Cortes compared the capital to Venice and judged it to be "the most beautiful city in the world."

ing places, or administrative capitals. This was so because the Mayas practiced slash-and-burn agriculture, which exhausted the soil within two or three years, requiring constant moving of the village settlements. To balance this transitory mode of life, the Maya cultivators expressed their social unity by erecting large stone buildings in centers that were devoted primarily to religious ceremonies. These buildings were large temple pyramids and also community houses in which the priests and novices probably lived. The architecture, produced entirely with stone tools, was decorated with sculpture that was unsurpassed in the Americas and that ranks as one of the world's great arts.

The Maya civilization flourished between the fourth and tenth centuries, but it then declined for reasons that remain obscure. It may

GULF
OF
MEXICO

ATLANTIC

OCEAN

Oxitipan
Tuxpan
Tenochtitlán
TLAXCALA
Coatza-
coalco
Querétaro
Petlatlán
Acapulco
Oaxaca
Mitla
Chiapa
Comitán
Ayotlán
*Indefinite
Eastern
Frontier*

TARASCANS

MAYAS

Chichén Itzá
Uxmal

Tikal

Copan

CARIBBEAN SEA

THE
CHIBCHAS

Orinoco R.

Pasto
Quito
Manta
Tumbez
Moyobamba
Cajamarca
Chimu
Huanuco
INCAS
Machu Picchu
CHINCHAS
Cuzco
*Lake
Titicaca*
Tiahuanaco
Arequipa
Cochabamba

Amazon R.

Equator

PACIFIC

OCEAN

Iquique
Tarija
Atacama
Tucumán
Copiapó
Coquimpu
Catamarca

A R A U C A N I A N S

Maule R.

Aztec Empire (approximate area)

Inca Empire (approximate area)

0   500   1000 Miles

0   500   1000 Kilometers

Amerindian Empires on the Eve of the Spanish Conquest

267

A turquoise mosaic of a double-headed serpent of the Aztec culture.

Aztec power was based on constant war preparedness. All men were expected to bear arms, and state arsenals were always stocked and ready for immediate use. With their efficient military machine the Aztecs were able to extract a staggering amount of tribute from their subjects. According to their own records, they collected in one year 14 million pounds of maize, 8 million pounds each of beans and amaranth, and 2 million cotton cloaks in addition to assorted other items such as war costumes, shields, and precious stones.

The splendor of the capital and the volume of tribute pouring into it naturally led the Spaniards to conclude that Montezuma was the ruler of a great empire. Actually this was not so. The vassal states remained quite separate, practicing full self-government. Their only tie to Tenochtitlán was the tribute, which they paid out of fear of the Aztec expeditions. None of the Amerindian states, except for that of the Incas in Peru, was organized on any concept wider than that of the city-state. The Aztecs, in contrast to the Incas, made no attempt to adapt their subjects to the Aztec way of life in preparation for full citizenship.

The Spaniards were not only dazzled by the wealth and magnificence of the Aztec state but also horrified by the wholesale ritual massacre of a continual procession of human victims. These were slaughtered at the top of the ceremonial pyramids that abounded everywhere, and the Spaniards soon realized that the pyramids functioned as altars for human sacrifice. Sacrificial cults were common in Mesoamerica, but nowhere did they lead to the obsessive slaughtering practiced by the Aztecs. Indeed, the reasons for Aztec expeditions were not only to collect tribute for their capital but to take captives for sacrifice as well.

They considered the taking of captives as even more important than getting tribute, for their priests taught that the world was in constant danger of cataclysm, especially the extinguishing of the sun—hence the need for offering human victims to appease the heavenly deities. But this practice trapped the Aztecs in a truly vicious circle: Sacrificial victims were needed to forestall universal disaster; victims could be obtained only through war; successful war could be waged only by sacrificing victims, but these in turn could be secured only through war. Bernal Diaz was an eyewitness to the end result:

One certain spot in this township [Xocotlan] I shall never forget, situated near the temple. Here a vast number of human skulls were piled up in the best order imaginable,—there must have been more than 100,000; I repeat, more than 100,000. In like manner you saw the remaining human bones piled up in order in another corner of the square; these it would have been impossible to count. Besides these, there were human heads hanging suspended from beams on both sides. . . . Similar horrible sights we saw towards the interior of the country in every township. . . .[1]

Turning finally to the Incas of Peru, it should be noted that Inca was the title of their king of kings, so that it is technically incorrect, though common usage, to refer to them as the Inca Indians. Actually they were one of the numerous tribes of Quechua stock and language who raised llamas and grew potatoes. In the twelfth century they established themselves in the Cuzco valley, which they soon dominated. At this early stage they built up a dynasty made up of their war chiefs, with their tribespeople constituting an aristocracy among the other tribal peoples. The combination of a hereditary dynasty and an aristocracy was unique in the New World, and it was an effective empire-building instrument. Their empires were particularly strong because of the outstanding ability of the Incas, or heads of state, for generation after generation. The Inca's only legitimate wife was his own full sister, so that each Inca was the son of a sister and a brother. This full inbreeding had

continued for some eight generations, and the original stock must have been exceptionally sound because the royal princes, as the Spaniards observed, were all handsome and vigorous men.

From their imperial city of Cuzco in the Peruvian highlands, the Incas sent forth armies and ambassadors west to the coastal lands and north and south along the great mountain valleys. By the time of the Spanish intrusion they had extended their frontiers some 2,500 miles from Ecuador to central Chile. Thus they ruled much more territory than did the Aztecs, and furthermore they ruled it as a genuine empire.

This empire was held together physically by a road system, which can still be traced for hundreds of miles and which included cable bridges of plaited aloe fiber and floating bridges on pontoons of buoyant reeds. Equally important was an extensive irrigation system, parts of which are still in use and which made the Inca

The Inca city of Machu Picchu perches on a saddle between two peaks on the eastern slopes of the Andes.

Empire a flourishing agricultural unit. Communications were maintained by a comprehensive system of post stations and relays of runners who conveyed messages swiftly to all parts of the empire.

Imperial unity was furthered also by elaborate court ritual and by a state religion based on worship of the sun. The Inca was held to be a descendant of the sun; he played an essential role in its ceremonial worship. Other techniques of imperial rule included state ownership of land, mineral wealth, and herds; careful census compilations for tax and military purposes; the deposing of local hereditary chieftains; forced population resettlement in order to assimilate conquered peoples; and mass marriages under state auspices. Not surprisingly, the Inca Empire is considered to be one of the most successful totalitarian states the world has ever seen.

IV. AMERINDIANS IN HISTORY

Impressive as were these attainments of the American Indians, the fact remains that a handful of Spanish adventurers were able easily to overthrow and completely uproot all three of the great New World civilizations—and this despite the fact that these civilizations had dense populations numbering into the tens of millions. The explanation for the one-sided Spanish triumph is to be found ultimately in the isolation of the Americas. Not only were the American Indian civilizations cut off from stimulating interaction with civilizations on other continents, but also they were largely isolated from each other:

With respect to interrelations between Peru and Mesoamerica [reports an archeologist], it is sufficient to state that not a single object or record of influence or contact between these areas had been accepted as authentic from the long time span between the Formative period [about 1000 B.C.E.] and the coming of the Spaniards. . . .[2]

In other words, there is no reliable evidence of interaction between the Mesoamerican and Peruvian civilizations over a span of 2,500 years. And during those millennia, as we have seen, the various regions of Eurasia, and to a lesser extent sub-Saharan Africa, were in continual contact. The end result was that the American Indians—even those of the Andes and Mesoamerica—lagged far behind the Eurasians and especially behind the technologically precocious Europeans. By 1500 C.E. the New World had reached the stage of civilization that Egypt and Mesopotamia had attained about 2500 B.C.E.

Precisely what did this mean when the Spaniards arrived and confrontation occurred? It meant, in the first place, that the Indians found themselves economically and technologically far behind the invader's civilization. The highly developed art, science, and religion of the Indians should not be allowed to obscure the fact that they lagged seriously in more material fields. The disparity was most extreme in Mesoamerica, but it also prevailed in the Andean area. In agriculture, the Indians were brilliantly successful in domesticating plants but much less effective in actual production. Their cultivation techniques never advanced beyond the bare minimum necessary to feed populations that rarely reached the numbers of those of the Old World. Their tools were made only of stone, wood, or bone. They were incapable of smelting ores, and though they did work with metal, it was almost exclusively for ornamental purposes. The only ships they constructed were canoes and seagoing rafts. For land transportation they made no use of the wheel, which they knew but used only as a toy. With the exception of the llama and the alpaca, which were used in the Andes but could not carry heavy loads, only the human back was available for transportation.

The immediate significance of this technological lag should not be exaggerated. The Indians obviously were at a grave disadvantage with their spears and arrows against the Spaniards' horses and guns. But after the initial shock, the Indians became accustomed to firearms and cavalry. Furthermore, the Spaniards soon discovered that the Indian weapons were sharp and durable, and they came to prefer the Indian armor of quilted cotton to their own. One of the conquistadors related that the Aztecs had

. . . two arsenals filled with arms of every description, of which many were ornamented with gold and precious stones. These arms consisted in shields of different sizes, sabres, and a species of broadsword,

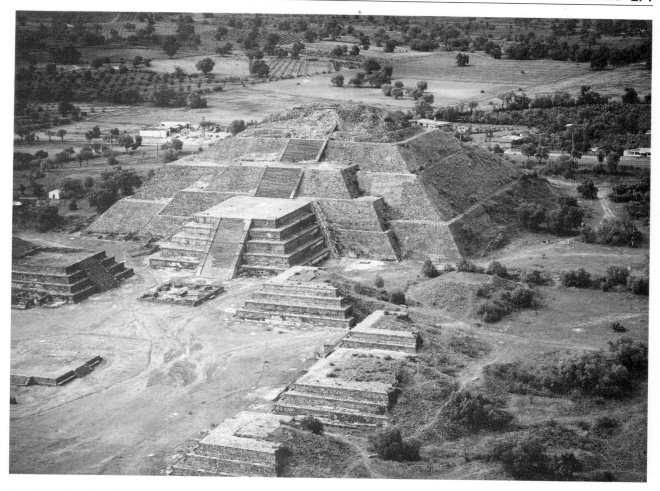

The Pyramid of the Moon stands at the southern end of Teotihuacán's great central thoroughfare, the Avenue of the Dead.

which is wielded with both hands, the edge furnished with flint stones, so extremely sharp that they cut much better than our Spanish swords: further, lances of greater length than ours, with spikes at their end, full one fathom in length, likewise furnished with several sharp flint stones. The pikes are so very sharp and hard that they will pierce the strongest shield, and cut like a razor; so that the Mexicans even shave themselves with these stones. Then there were excellent bows and arrows, pikes with single and double points, and the proper thongs to throw them with; slings with round stones purposely made for them; also a species of large shield, so ingeniously constructed that it could be rolled up when not wanted; they are only unrolled on the field of battle, and completely cover the whole body from the head to the feet.[3]

This observation suggests that technological disparity was not the only factor that lay behind the Spanish victories. Another was the lack of unity among the Indian peoples. In both Mexico and Peru the Spaniards were able to use disaffected subject tribes who had been alienated by the oppressive rule of Cuzco and Tenochtitlán. The Indians were also weakened by overregimentation and overdependency. They had been so indoctrinated and were so accustomed to carrying out orders without question that when their leaders were overthrown they were incapable of organizing resistance on their own. Once the kings Montezuma and Atahuallpa had fallen into Spanish hands, the Aztec and Inca empires became bodies without heads, and resistance was paralyzed.

This passivity was increased by religious inhibitions. The natives thought that both Cortes in Mexico and Pizzaro in Peru were gods returning in fulfillment of ancient prophecies. This explains the suicidal vacillations of Atahuallpa in Cuzco and of Montezuma in Tenochtitlán. To Atahuallpa the Spaniards were the creator-god Viracocha and his followers, and for this reason, the ruler waited meekly for Pizzaro, who with his 180 men quickly seized control of the great empire. Likewise, to Montezuma, Cortes was the god Quetzalcoatl who was returning to claim his rightful throne, so that again the ruler waited listlessly for the Spaniards to ensconce themselves in his capital.

Equally disastrous for the Aztecs was their concept of war as a short-term ritual endeavor. Their main interest in war was to capture prisoners, whose hearts they offered to their gods. Accordingly their campaigns frequently were ceremonial contests during which prisoners were taken with minimal dislocation and destruction. This type of military tradition obviously was a serious handicap. The Spaniards killed to win; the Aztecs simply tried to take prisoners.

If the American Indians lacked the technology and the cohesion to repel the Europeans, even more serious was their lack of immunity against the diseases brought by the Europeans. Because the Indians had no contacts with peoples of other continents after crossing the Bering Sea tens of thousands of years earlier, they became biologically vulnerable to smallpox, measles, typhus, yellow fever, and other diseases carried by the Europeans and their African slaves.

Estimates of New World native populations before 1492 have been revised sharply upward in recent years. A total of 43 million to 72 million are now believed to have lived in North and South America. As might be expected, the large majority lived in the three great civilizations of Mesoamerica. Regardless of where they lived, all Indians died at an appalling rate on first contact with the Europeans. This is why the newcomers often found abandoned fields and deserted villages, which they simply took over. Mexico's population in 1492 is estimated at 25 million. By 1608, it had shrunk to about one million. The decline was equally precipitous in other

A sixteenth-century Aztec drawing depicts a battle in the Spanish conquest of Mexico.

regions. The island of Hispaniola (today Haiti and the Dominican Republic) had 60,000 Amerindians in 1508, 30,000 in 1554, and 500 in 1570. The magnitude and horror of this holocaust is evident in the following 1586 report from Peru:

Influenza does not shine like the steel sword, but no Indian can dodge it. Tetanus and typhus kill more people than a thousand greyhounds with fiery eyes and foaming jaws . . . smallpox annihilates more Indians than all the guns. The winds of pestilence are devastating these regions. Anyone they strike, they blow down: they devour the body, eat the eyes, close the throat. All smells of decay.[4]

Later, when the full flood of immigration from Europe was under way, the Indians were hopelessly overwhelmed. First came the traders, who penetrated throughout the Americas with little competition or resistance, for the Americas, unlike Africa, had no native merchant class. Then appeared the settlers who, attracted by the combination of healthful climate and fertile land, came in ever-increasing numbers and inundated the hapless Indians. When the latter occasionally took up arms in desperation, they were foredoomed to failure because they lacked both unity and the basic human and material resources. This was especially true north of the Rio Grande, where the Indian population had been sparse to begin with. Consequently there were few survivors, and these were herded into reservations. In the lands of the Aztecs, Incas, and Mayas, which had been more densely populated, a large number survived the European flood. Gradually these survivors staged a comeback as they developed immunity to the diseases of the Europeans and of the Africans. Today Indians comprise a majority of the population in countries such as Bolivia and Guatemala. In the United States, the U.S. Census Bureau reported in 1990 a total Indian population of 1.9 million, of which the largest number (308,132) are Cherokee, followed by Navajo (219,138), by Chippewa (103,826), and by Sioux (103,255).

It is apparent that the balance of forces was quite different in America than it was in Africa. Geography, relatively small population, and a comparatively low level of economic, political, and social organization all worked against the

Indian and made it possible for the Europeans to take over the Americas at a time when they were still confined to a few toeholds on the coasts of Africa. Although the Amerindians were unable to offer much resistance against the European invaders, the fact remains that they made outstanding contributions to human development. By far the most significant of these contributions was their domestication of numerous plants that have become mainstays of daily diet throughout the world. Outstanding were maize, potatoes, beans (the major source of proteins), squashes, tomatoes, and chocolate. In all, about as many plants were domesticated in the Americas as in the entire Old World—a truly extraordinary achievement. More than 50 percent of the farm products of the United States today are derived from plants originally domesticated by the Indians. Since the United States is a major exporter of foodstuffs to the world markets, it follows that the world's total population would be substantially smaller today were it not for the Amerindian pioneers.

Finally it should be noted that ongoing archeological investigations necessitate constant revision of our understanding of Amerindian cultures. For example, recent excavations suggest that in addition to the Mayan, Aztec and Inca cultures, there may have been a fourth one in the Amazon jungle of South America. This finding is intriguing because hitherto it has been believed that early food gatherers lacked the skills and technology to survive in a tropical rain forest. Now, however, archeologists are finding and analyzing thousands of artifacts and charred food remains found in caves near the mouth of the Amazon that were occupied some 11,000 years ago. This was a distinctive culture because it was dependent primarily not upon big game hunting, as were the other Amerindian cultures, but rather on river and forest foraging—its people subsisting mostly on fish, mollusks, turtles and birds.

V. AUSTRALIA

Australia is the most isolated large landmass in the world. It is so isolated that archaic forms of life have survived to modern times, including plants such as the eucalyptus family, and mammals such as the monotremes and the marsupials. In Australia archaic human types also survived that were still in the Paleolithic stage when the first British settlers arrived in the late eighteenth century. As in the case of the American Indians, the date of the first aboriginal appearance in Australia has not been determined precisely. The latest findings indicate an arrival about 50,000 years ago. This means that the ancestors of the aborigines probably were the world's first mariners, since they had to cross about forty miles of open water at that time to reach the island continent from Southeast Asia.

Three different ethnic groups crossed to Australia, and they still can be detected in the present-day aboriginal population. The majority are slender, long-limbed people with brown skin, wavy to curly hair and beards, and little body hair. They have survived in substantial numbers because they live in desert areas that are of little use to the modern white settlers. In the cool and fertile southeastern corner of the continent, there are a few survivors of a very different native stock—thick set, with light brown skin, heavy body hair, and luxuriant beards. Along the northeastern coast, in the only part of Australia covered with dense tropical rain forest, lives the third ethnic group. Part of the Negroid family, they are small, of slight build, and with woolly hair and black skins.

The culture of these peoples was by no means uniform. The most advanced were those in the southeast, where rainfall was adequate for permanent settlements. But throughout the continent, the aborigines, thanks to their complete isolation, had remained Paleolithic food gatherers. Their retardation was particularly evident in their technology and in their political organization. They wore no clothing except for decorative purposes. Their housing consisted, in dry country, of simple, open windbreaks, and in wet country, of low, domed huts thrown together out of any available material. Their principal weapons were spears, spear throwers, and boomerangs, all made of wood. They were ignorant of pottery, their utensils consisting merely of a few twined bags and baskets and occasional bowls made of bark or wood. As food gatherers and hunters they were highly skilled and ingenious. They had a wide range of vegetable, as well as animal, foods and an intimate knowledge of the varieties, habits, and properties of these foods. They did all in their power to keep up the rate of reproduction of the plants and animals on which they depended. But since they were not food producers, their method of ensuring an adequate food supply was one of ritual rather than of cultivation. A typical ceremony was the mixing of blood with earth in places where the increase of game and plants were desired.

The poverty of Australian technology was matched by an almost equal poverty of political organization. Like most food-gathering peoples, the aborigines lived in bands, groups of families who normally camped together and roamed over a well-defined territory. They had no real tribes but only territorial divisions characterized by differences in language and culture. Consequently, they did not have chiefs, courts, or other formal agencies of government. Yet these same aborigines had an extraordinarily complex social organization and ceremonial life. The hunter who brought in game or the woman who returned from a day of root digging was required to divide his or her take with all kin according to strict regulations. Among the northern Queensland natives, when a person sneezed, all those within hearing slapped themselves on their bodies, the place varying according to their precise relationship to the sneezer.

So involved were these nonmaterial aspects of Australian society that they have been a delight to students of primitive institutions. But precociousness in these matters was of little help to the aborigines when the Europeans appeared in the late eighteenth century. If the American Indians with their flowering civilizations and widespread agricultural communities were unable to stand up to the whites, the Paleolithic Australians obviously had no chance. They were few in numbers, totaling about 300,000 when the Europeans arrived. This meant one or two persons per square mile in favorable coastal or river valley environments, and only one person every thirty to forty square miles in the arid interior. In addition to this numerical weakness, the aborigines lacked both the arms and the organization necessary for effective resistance. And unlike the American Indians and the African Negroes, they showed little inclination to secure and use the white man's "fire stick."

Thus the unfortunate aborigines were brutally decimated by the British immigrants, many of whom were lawless convicts shipped out from overcrowded jails. The combination of disease, alcoholism, outright slaughter, and wholesale land confiscation has reduced the native population to 45,000 today, together with some 80,000 mixed breeds. The treatment accorded to the Australians is suggested by the following typical observation of a Victorian settler in 1853: "The Australian aboriginal race seems doomed by Providence, like the Mohican and many other well known tribes, to disappear from their native soil before the progress of civilization."[5]

SUGGESTED READINGS

The most recent information on the peopling of the Americas is given in R. Shutler, Jr., ed., *Early Man in the New World* (Sage, 1973), which also contains a selection on the parallel peopling of Australia. A stimulating analysis of the European impact on the American Indians is given by F. Jennings, *The Invasion of America: Indians, Colonialism, and the Cant of Conquest* (University of North Carolina, 1975). The latest estimates on the numbers of American Indians are given in M. Denevan, ed., *The Native Population of the Americas in 1492* (University of Wisconsin, 1976). The lethal biological repercussions of European expansion are analyzed in A. W. Crosby, *Ecological Imperialism: The Biological Expansion of Europe, 900–1900* (Cambridge University, 1986).

A lavishly illustrated volume on the American Indians from their early migrations to the present day is *America's Fascinating Indian Heritage* (Reader's Digest Press, 1978). A stimulating interpretation is by P. Farb, *Man's Rise to Civilization as Shown by the Indians of North America . . .* (Dutton, 1968), which includes an analysis of the significance for modern people of the experiences of the Indians. Other noteworthy studies are by A. M. Josephy, Jr., *The Indian Heritage of America* (Knopf, 1968); C. Beals, *Nomads and Empire Builders: Native Peoples and Cultures of South America* (Chilton, 1961); and the excellent collection of readings by H. E. Driver, ed., *The Americas on the Eve of Discovery* (Prentice Hall, 1964). V. W. Von Hagen has readable accounts of all three of the leading American civilizations: *The Aztec: Man and Tribe* (New American Library, 1958), *The Incas: People of the Sun* (World, 1961), and *World of the Maya* (New American Library, 1960). The best general study of the Eskimos is by K. Birket-Smith, *The Eskimos* (Crown, 1971). Interesting details of recent archeological discoveries of early Indians in Chile, and how they got there, are given in *Science*, September 18, 1998, pp. 1775–76, 1830–35.

For the Australia aborigines the standard works are A. P. Elkins, *The Australia Aborigines*, 3rd ed. (Angus, 1954); W. E. Harney, *Life Among the Aborigines* (Hale, 1957); R. M. and C. H. Berndt, *The World of the First Australians: An Introduction to the Traditional Life of the Australia Aborigines* (University of Chicago, 1964); A. A. Abbie, *The Original Australians* (Muller, 1969); and G. Blainey, *Triumph of the Nomads: A History of Aboriginal Australia* (Overlook Press, 1976).

NOTES

1. J. J. Lockhart, trans., *The Memoirs of the Conquistador Bernal del Castillo* (London, 1844), I, 238.
2. R. M. Adams, "Early Civilizations, Subsistence and Environment," in *City Invincible*, eds., R. M. Adams and C. H. Kraeling (University of Chicago, 1960), p. 270.
3. Lockhart, *op. cit.*, I, 231–232.
4. Citd in E. Galeano, *Memory of Fire: Genesis* (Pantheon, 1985), p. 158.
5. Cited by A. G. Price, *White Settlers and Native Peoples* (Melbourne University, 1949), p. 121.

CHAPTER 1

The World on the Eve of Europe's Expansion

> . . . A technological revolution by which the West made its fortune, got the better of all the other living civilizations, and forcibly united them into a single society of literally worldwide range. The revolutionary Western invention was the substitution of the Ocean for the Steppe as the principal medium for world communication. This use of the Ocean, first by sailing ships and then by steamship, enabled the West to unify the whole inhabited and habitable world, including the Americas.
>
> *A. J. Toynbee*

During the medieval millennium between 500 and 1500 C.E., profound changes occurred in the world balance of power. At the outset the West was a turbulent outpost of Eurasia, wracked by the disintegration of empires and recurring invasions. As late as the twelfth century, the English chronicler William of Malmesbury voiced a sense of isolation and insecurity:

The world is not evenly divided. Of its three parts, our enemies hold Asia as their hereditary home—a part of the world which our forefathers rightly considered equal to the other two put together. Yet here formerly our Faith put out its branches; here all the Apostles save two met their deaths. But now the Christians of those parts, if there are any left, squeeze a bare subsistence from the soil and pay tribute to their enemies, looking to us with silent longings for the liberty they have lost. Africa too, the second part of the world, has been held by our enemies by force of arms for two hundred years and more, a danger to Christendom all the greater because it formerly sustained the highest spirits—men whose works will keep the rust of age from Holy Writ as long as the Latin tongue survives. Thirdly, there is Europe, the remaining region of the world. Of this region we Christians inhabit only a part, for who will give the name of Christians to those barbarians who live in the remote islands and seek their living on the icy ocean as if they were whales? This little portion of the world which is ours is pressed upon by warlike Turks and Saracens: for three hundred years they have held Spain and the Balearic Islands, and they live in hope of devouring the rest.[1]

But already by the twelfth century the tide had begun to turn. The West was developing the internal resources and the dynamism that found expression first in the long-drawn-out and successful Crusades against Moslems and pagans and, later, in overseas expansion to all parts of the globe. By contrast, Ming China was withdrawing into seclusion, and the Ottoman Turks, after futile efforts to expel the Portuguese from the Indian Ocean, sadly concluded, "God has given the land to us, but the sea to the Christians." Equally revealing is the fact that in his famous Memoirs, Babur, the founder of the Mogul Empire, never once mentioned the Portuguese, nor did any Mogul navy ever attempt to restore Moslem primacy in the Indian Ocean. The seas of the world were thus left wide open for the Westerners, who took prompt advantage of the opportunity. The significance for world affairs is apparent in the following comment by an Ottoman observer in 1625:

Now the Europeans have learnt to know the whole world; they send their ships everywhere and seize important ports. Formerly, the goods of India, Sind, and China used to come to Suez, and were distributed by Muslims to all the world. But now these goods are carried on Portuguese, Dutch, and English ships to Frangistan [Western Christendom], and are spread all over the world from there. What they do not need themselves they bring to Istanbul and other Islamic lands, and sell it for five times the price, thus earning much money. For this reason gold and silver are becoming scarce in the lands of Islam. The Ottoman Empire must seize the shores of Yemen and the trade passing that way; otherwise before very long, the Europeans will rule over the lands of Islam.[2]

If this perceptive analysis is compared with that of William of Malmesbury half a millennium earlier, the basic change in the global balance of power becomes evident. Indeed, so basic was this change that it marked the beginning of the modern age of Western predominance.

Heralding the earlier classical and medieval ages had been land invasions by nomads who used their superior mobility to break into the centers of civilization when imperial weakness gave them the opportunity. Ushering in the Modern Age, by contrast, were sea invasions by the Westerners, who functioned with equal

This portrait of Katharina, by Albrecht Dürer, provides edvidence of African slavery in Europe during the sixteenth century. Katharina was in the service of João Bradao a Portuguese economic minister living in Antwerp, then the financial center of Europe. Dürer became friends with Bradao during a stay in the Low Countries in 1520–1521.

mobility on the world's oceans and thus were free to operate on a global scale.

In addition to their unchallenged maritime superiority, the Westerners had the more important advantage of overall technological superiority, which increased steadily during the following centuries. Thus whereas the sixteenth-century Europeans with their ocean-sailing ships and naval artillery enjoyed an advantage comparable to that of iron weapons over bronze, by the nineteenth century their steamships, factory industries, and machine guns gave them an advantage more like that of the agriculturist over the hunter. Thus the Europeans established their global domination as inexorably as the Bantu displaced the Bushmen. Hence the Europeans brought all continents into direct contact with each other, therby ending the Eurasian phase of world history and beginning the global. (See map of Culture Areas of the World About 1500, p. 278.)

NOTES

1. Cited by W. Clark, "New Europe and the New Nations," *Daedalus* (Winter 1964), p. 136.
2. Cited by B. Lewis, *The Emergence of Modern Turkey* (Oxford University, 1961), p. 28.

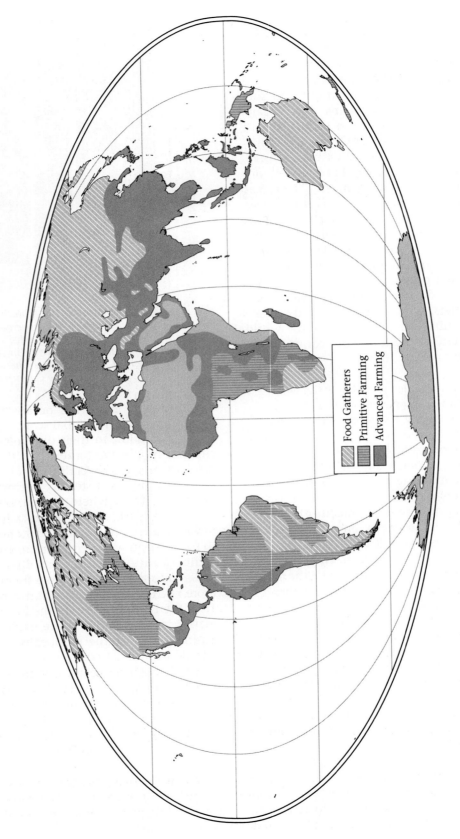

Culture Areas of the World about 1500

Food Gatherers
Primitive Farming
Advanced Farming

What It Means for Us Today

RACES IN HISTORY

When the western Europeans began their voyages of exploration, they found peoples scattered around the world and living at very different levels of development. The Chinese, for example, had a civilization that was so wealthy, sophisticated, and well governed that many of the early European visitors considered it superior to their own. Other overseas people were naked, nomadic food gatherers whom the Europeans looked down on as barely human. So they pushed them aside into deserts or jungles or enslaved them or hunted them down and exterminated them. In doing these things, the Europeans justified their actions on the ground that they were a superior people bringing the light of their superior civilization to the inferior (and therefore backward) peoples of the world.

This argument raises a question that is still a matter of dispute today. Are the various human races genetically equal, or are some inherently superior and others inferior? The great majority of scientists, though not all, agree that races are generally equal. Typical is the statement issued at an international conference of physical anthropologists and geneticists in September 1952:

> Available scientific knowledge provides no basis for believing that the groups of mankind differ in their innate capacity for intellectual and emotional development. . . . Genetic differences are of little significance in determining the social and cultural differences between different groups of men.[1]

279

If genes do not explain the great differences that European explorers found overseas, then what does? This is a burning question in today's world. It raises the controversial issue of racism, or belief in the biologically determined superiority of one race over another. Pope John II was sufficiently concerned about this issue to ask the Pontifical Commission, Iustitia et Pax, to "help and awaken consciences . . . about the reciprocal respect between ethnic and racial groups." The Commission reported in 1988 that racism is a modern phenomenon that did not exist in ancient times; Greeks and Romans were convinced of their cultural superiority over barbarians, but they did not consider the so-called barbarians to be inferior because of innate biological reasons. In premodern times, genetically based racism was not an urgent issue for the simple reason that the various races lived in regional isolation and therefore did not need to face this issue. But with Europe's overseas expansion and subsequent conquest and enslavement of Amerindians and Africans, racism became a convenient rationalization for justifying these actions. Pope Paul II denounced in 1537 those who held that "the inhabitants of the West Indies and the southern continents . . . should be treated like irrational animals and used exclusively for our profit and our service. . . . We hereby decide and declare that the said Indians, as well as any other peoples which Christianity will come to know in the future, must not be deprived of their freedom and their possessions . . . even if they are not Christians and that, on the contrary, they must be left to enjoy their freedom and their possessions. . . . The message she [the Church] proposes to everyone, and which she tries to live, is: 'Every person is my brother or sister.'"[2]

Returning to the above question about why European explorers found such extreme variations in the development of overseas peoples, the distinguished anthropologist Franz Boas has offered a theory that seems to mesh with actual historical experience:

> The history of mankind proves that advances of culture depend upon the opportunities presented to a social group to learn from the experience of their neighbors. The discoveries of the group spread to others and, the more varied the contacts, the greater the opportunities to learn. The tribes of simplest culture are on the whole those that have been isolated for very long periods and hence could not profit from the cultural achievements of their neighbors.[3]

In other words, the key to different levels of human development has been accessibility. Those with the most opportunity to interact with other people have been the most likely to forge ahead. Indeed, they were driven to do so, for there was selective pressure as well as opportunity. Accessibility involved the constant threat of assimilation or elimination if opportunity was not grasped. By contrast, those who were isolated received neither stimulus nor threat, were free from selective pressure, and thus could remain relatively unchanged through the millennia without jeopardizing their existence.

If this hypothesis is applied on a global scale, the remote Australian aborigines should have been the most culturally retarded of all major groups; next, the American Indians in the New World; then the Negroes of sub-Saharan Africa; and finally—the least retarded, or the most advanced—the various peoples of Eurasia, who were in constant and generally increasing contact with each other. This, of course, is precisely the gradation of culture levels found by the European discoverers after 1500. The Australian aborigines were still at the Paleolithic food-gathering stage; the American Indians varied from the Paleolithic tribes of California to the impressive civilizations of Mexico, Central America, and Peru; the African Negroes presented comparable diversity, though their overall level of development was higher; and finally, at quite another level, there were the highly advanced and sophisticated civilizations found in Eurasia—the Moslem in the Middle East, the Hindu in south Asia, and the Confucian in east Asia.

We may conclude, then, that the Western domination of the globe after 1500 did not mean Western genetic superiority. It meant only that, at that period of history, the western Europeans were in the right place at the right time. At other periods of history the situation was very different. For example, at the time of the classical civilizations it was the people of the Mediterranean who were in the center of things and who, therefore, were the most accessible and most developed. By contrast, the northern Europeans were then on the periphery, and were therefore isolated and underdeveloped. Thus we find Cicero writing to a friend in Athens in the first century B.C.E.: "Do not obtain your slaves from Britain because they are so stupid and so utterly incapable of being taught that they are not fit to form a part of the household of Athens."[4]

Likewise, during the period of the medieval civilizations, the Mediterranean was still the center, and northern Europe still an isolated region of backward peoples. Thus a Moslem in Toledo, Spain, wrote in the eleventh century: "Races north of the Pyrenees are of cold temperament and never reach maturity; they are of great stature and of a white color. But they lack all sharpness of wit and penetration of intellect."

Both Cicero and the Toledo Moslem seemed in their times to have been justified in looking down on northern Europeans as "stupid" and lacking in "wit" and "intellect." But Nordic "backwardness" in classical and medieval times had no more to do with genes than did the "backwardness" of Africans or American Indians or Australian aborigines in the times of the discoveries—or than does the "backwardness" of the underdeveloped peoples of the world today.

Regardless of the period, "backwardness" means vulnerability, because "backward" people lag behind others in numbers and in technology. This is especially true in today's world of six billion people and runaway technology. Consequently it is estimated that since 1500, at least one-third of the world's human cultures have disappeared—either overwhelmed or assimilated. Therefore the American Anthropological Association has established a "Committee for Human Rights," and likewise in 1972 a body entitled "Cultural Survival" was created. Seeking to protect existing cultures, it has spoken up, for example, in behalf of the Yanomami Indians imperilled by a gold rush in the Amazon basin, the Tibetan people pressured by the adjacent 1 billion Chinese, the Ogoni tribe in Nigeria disrupted by the operations of oil companies, and the Maya Indians harried by the Guatemalan army. Despite their precarious status, the "indigenous" peoples, as these members of endangered communities are commonly known, still comprise 5 percent of the world's population.[5]

SUGGESTED READINGS

The most useful book on the nature, significance, and results of race is by P. Mason, *Race Relations* (Oxford University, 1970). UNESCO has a collection of essays by an international group of scientists: *The Race Question in Modern Science* (Morrow, 1956). All these contributors agreed that race achievement is determined by historical and social backgrounds, not by genes. The opposite view has been set forth by A. R. Jensen, in *Genetics and Education* (Harper & Row, 1972), and in his *Bias in Mental Testing* (Free Press, 1980). Jensen's findings have been rejected by L. J. Kamin, *The Science and Politics of IQ* (John Wiley, 1974); and most entertainingly and authoritatively by S. J. Gould, *Ever Since Darwin* (Norton, 1981). An important analysis of the role of race during World War II in the Pacific is provided by J. Dower, *War Without Mercy* (Pantheon, 1986).

NOTES

1. Cited by UNESCO, *What Is Race?* (Paris, 1952), pp. 85, 86.
2. F. Boas, "Racial Purity," *Asia*, XL (May, 1940), p. 231.
3. Cited by R. Benedict, *Race: Science and Politics*, rev. ed. (Viking Press, 1943), p. 7.
4. Ibid., p. 8.
5. *New York Times*, March 19, 1996.

PART V

World of Isolated Regions, to 1500

Part V is concerned with two basic questions: Why should a study of world history begin with the year 1500, and why was it that Westerners took a primary role in carrying out the fantastic discoveries and explorations of the late fifteenth and early sixteenth centuries? The first question will be answered in Chapter 18; the second will be the subject of the remaining chapters of Part V.

We usually take it for granted that only Westerners could have made the historic discoveries that would change the course of humanity and begin a new era in world history. This assumption is quite unjustified, particularly in view of the great seafaring traditions of the Moslems in the Middle East and the Chinese in east Asia. Why then did the West take the initiative in overseas enterprise with repercussions that are still felt today? Chapters 18 and 19 will analyze the traditional societies in the Moslem and Confucian worlds, and Chapters 20 and 21 will offer an examination of the contrasting dynamism of Western society.

CHAPTER
18
Moslem World at the Time of the West's Expansion

He who would behold these times in their greatest glory, could not find a better scene than in Turkey.

H. Blount, 1634

To answer the question of why Columbus was not Chinese or Arabic, it is necessary to see what was going on in the Confucian and Moslem worlds at that time. In this chapter, and the following one, we shall analyze why China and the Middle East lacked the expansionism of western Europe, even though they were highly developed and wealthy regions. We shall see that paradoxically, it was their wealth and high level of development that left them smug and self-satisfied, and therefore unable to adapt to their changing world.

I. RISE OF MODERN MOSLEM EMPIRES

An observer on the moon looking at this globe about 1500 would have been more impressed by the Moslem than by the Christian world. The mythical observer would have been impressed first by the extent of the Moslem world and then by its unceasing expansion. The earliest Moslems were the Arabs of the Arabian peninsula who were united for the first time under their religious leader, Mohammed. Believing that he had received a divine call, Mohammed warned his people of the Day of Judgment and told them of the rewards for the faithful in Paradise and the punishment of the wicked in Hell. He called on his followers to perform certain rituals known as the Five Pillars of Islam (including daily prayers, alms giving, fasting, and a pilgrimage to Mecca). These rituals, together with the precepts in the Koran, provided not only a religion but also a social code and a political system. The converts felt a sense of brotherhood and common mission, which served to unite the hitherto scattered Arab peoples.

After the death of Mohammed in 632 C.E., the Arabs burst out of their peninsula and quickly overran the Byzantine and Sassanian empires in the Middle East. Then they expanded eastward toward China and westward across North Africa and into Spain. By 750, the end of this first phase of Islamic expansion, there existed a huge Moslem Empire that stretched from the Pyrenees to India and from Morocco to China (see map of Expansion of Islam to 1500, p. 287). The Moslems carried out the second phase of their expansion between 750 and 1500, during which time they penetrated westward to central Europe, northward to central Asia, eastward to India and Southeast Asia, and southward into the interior of Africa. Thus, the Moslem world doubled in size. It far surpassed in area both the Christian world on the western tip of Eurasia and the Confucian world on the eastern tip.

Not only was the Moslem world the most extensive about 1500, but it also continued to expand vigorously after that date. Contrary to common assumption, western Europe was not the only part of the world that was extending its frontiers at that time. The Moslem world was still expanding, but by overland routes, whereas the Christian world was reaching out overseas. The Portuguese in the early sixteenth century were gaining footholds in India and the East Indies, and the Spaniards were conquering an empire in the New World. But at the same time, the Ottoman Turks, a central Asian people who had converted to Islam, were pushing into central Europe. They overran Hungary, and in 1529 they besieged Vienna, the Hapsburg capital in the heart of Europe. Likewise, in India the great Mogul emperors were steadily extending their empire southward until they became the masters of almost the entire peninsula. Elsewhere the Moslem faith continued to spread into Africa, central Asia, and Southeast Asia.

The steady expansion of Islam was due partly to the forceful conversion of nonbelievers, though compulsion was not employed so commonly by Moslems as by Christians. But much more effective than these measures was the quiet missionary work of Moslem traders and preachers, who were particularly successful among the less civilized peoples. Frequently, the trader appeared first, combing proselytism with the sale of merchandise. His profession gave the trader close and constant contact with the people he wanted to convert. Also, there was no color bar, for if the trader were not of the same race as the villagers, he probably would marry a native woman. Such a marriage often led to the adoption of Islam by members of the woman's family. Soon religious instruction was needed for the children, so schools were established and frequented by pagan as well as Moslem children. The children were taught to read the Koran and were instructed in the doctrines and ceremonies of Islam. This explains why Islam, from the time of its appearance, was far more successful in gaining converts than any other religion. Even today, Islam is more than holding its own against Christianity in Africa, thanks to its unique adaptability to indigenous cultures as well as to the popular identification of Christianity with the foreign white master.

Apart from this ceaseless extension of frontiers, the Moslem world about 1500 was distinguished by its three great empires: the Ottoman in the Middle East, North Africa, and the Balkans; the Safavid in Persia; and the Mogul in India. These empires had all risen to prominence at this time and now dominated the heartland of Islam.

Their appearance was due in part to the invention of gunpowder and its use in firearms and cannon. The new weapons strengthened central power in the Moslem world, as they did at the same time in Christian Europe. Firearms, however, were by no means the only factor explaining the rise of the three Moslem empires. Equally significant were the appearance of capable leaders who founded dynasties and the existence of especially advantageous circumstances that enabled these leaders to conquer their empires. Let us consider now the particular combination of factors that made possible the growth of each of the three Moslem empires.

Ottoman Empire

The Ottoman Turks, who founded the empire named after them, were a branch of widely scattered Turkish people who came originally from central Asia (in contrast to the Semitic Arabs, who came originally from the Arabian peninsula). Over the centuries, successive waves of Turkish tribespeople had penetrated into the rich lands of the Middle East. They had appeared as

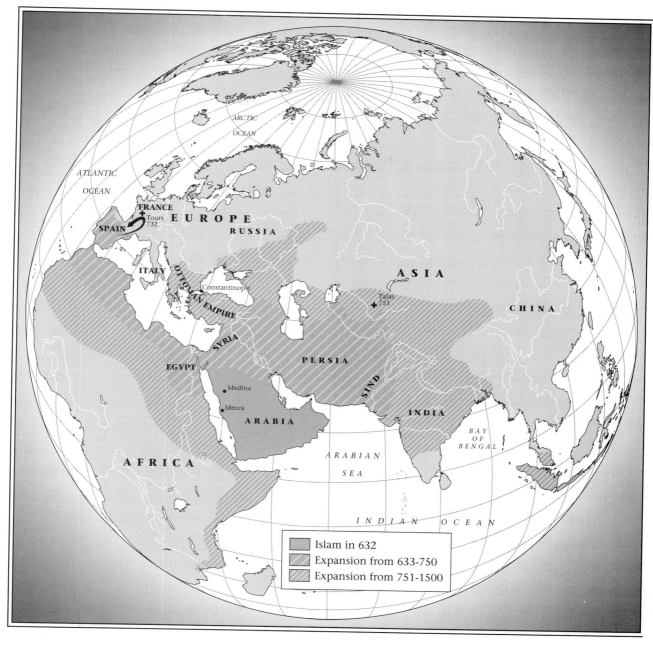

Expansion of Islam to 1500

early as the eighth century and infiltrated into the Islamic Empire, where they were employed first as mercenaries. In the tenth century, Mongol pressure from the rear forced more Turkish tribes, including a group known as the Seljuk Turks, to move into the Middle East. These newcomers broke the traditional frontier of Asia Minor along the Taurus Mountains—the frontier that had sheltered Rome and Byzantium for

1,400 years—by defeating the Byzantine army in the fateful battle of Manzikert in 1071. The victory made most of Asia Minor a part of the Seljuk Empire, leaving only the northwest corner to the Byzantines.

The Seljuk Empire, however, experienced a decline, disintegrating into a patchwork of independent principalities, or sultanates. In the late thirteenth century, the disorder was heightened by new bands of Turkish immigrants. One of these bands settled down on the extreme northwestern fringe of Seljuk territory, fewer than fifty miles from the strategic straits separating Asia from Europe. In 1299 the leader of this band, a certain Uthman, declared his independence from his Seljuk overlord. From these humble beginnings grew the great Ottoman Empire, named after the obscure Uthman.

The Süleiman mosque, named after its founder, Süleiman the Lawgiver, is one of the finest mosques in Istanbul. Completed in 1557 by the architect Sinan, who is buried in the mosque, it rises above the Golden Horn on Istanbul's third hill. Sinan was a slave-soldier recruit who rose through the ranks to his high position.

The first step in this dazzling success story was the conquest of the remaining Byzantine portion of Asia minor. By 1340 all of Asia Minor had fallen to the star and crescent. In 1354 the Turks crossed the straits and won their first foothold in Europe by building a fortress at Gallipoli. They hardly could have selected a more advantageous moment for their assault on Europe. The whole of Christendom in that century was weakened and divided. The terrible plague, the Black Death, had carried off whole sections of the populations of many Christian nations. The ruinous Hundred Years' War immobilized England and France. (The dates of this conflict are significant. It began in 1338, when the Turks were rounding out their conquest of Asia Minor, and it ended in 1453, when they captured Constantinople.) The Italian states also could do little against the Turks because of the long feud between Venice and Genoa. And the Balkan peninsula was hopelessly divided by the religious strife of Catholic and Orthodox Christians and heretic Bogomils, as well as by the rivalries of the Byzantine, Serbian, and Bulgarian empires, all long past their prime. And in the Balkans, as in Asia Minor, the Christian peasants frequently were so discontented that they offered little or no resistance to the Turkish onslaught.

These circumstances explain the extraordinary success of the Ottomans as they spread out from their base in Asia Minor. In 1384 they captured Sofia, and soon after they had control of all Bulgaria. Five years later they destroyed a south Slav army at the historic battle of Kossovo, which spelled the end of the Serbian Empire. These victories left Constantinople surrounded on all sides by Turkish territory. In 1453 the beleaguered capital was taken by assault, ending a thousand years of imperial history.

The Turks next turned southward against the rich Moslem states of Syria and Egypt. In a whirlwind campaign, they overran Syria in 1516 and Egypt the following year. The final phase of Ottoman conquest took place in central Europe. Under their famous Sultan Suleiman the Magnificent, the Turks crossed the Danube River and in one stroke crushed the Hungarian state in the Mohacs Battle in 1526. Three years later, Suleiman laid siege to Vienna but was repulsed, partly because of torrential rains that prevented him from bringing up his heavy artillery. Despite this setback, the Turks continued to make minor gains: Cyprus in 1570, Crete in 1669, and the Polish Ukraine in the following decade.

At its height, the Ottoman Empire was indeed a great imperial structure. Its heartland was Turkish Asia Minor, but the majority of the population consisted of Moslem Arabs to the south and Balkan Christians to the west. The empire sprawled over three continents and comprised some 50 million people, compared to the 5 million of contemporary England. Little wonder that Christians of the time looked on the ever-expanding Ottoman Empire with awe and described it as "a daily increasing flame, catching hold of whatsoever comes next, still to proceed further."[1]

Safavid Empire

The second great Moslem empire of this period was the Safavid in Persia. That country had fallen under the Seljuk Turks, as had Asia Minor. But whereas Asia Minor had become Turkified, Persia remained Persian—or Iranian—in race and culture. Probably the explanation for this different outcome is that Persia had already become Moslem during the first stage of Islamic expansion in the seventh century, in contrast to Asia Minor, which had formerly been a part of the Christian Byzantine Empire. For this reason, Persia was not swamped by Moslem warriors as Asia Minor had been, and Persian society was left basically unchanged by the comparatively small ruling class of Turkish administrators and soldiers.

Persia remained under the Seljuk Turks from approximately 1000 C.E. to the Mongol invasion in 1258. The new Mongol rulers, known as the Il-Khans, were at first Buddhists or Christians, but about 1300 they became Moslems. Persia suffered considerable permanent damage from the Mongols, who destroyed many cities and irrigation systems, but this setback was overcome when the Il-Khan dynasty was replaced by the Safavid in 1500.

Shah Ismail I founded the new dynasty of Safavid monarchs, the first native Persian rulers in several centuries. In the twenty-four years of Ismail's reign, his military abilities and religious policy enabled him to unite the country. By his proclamation, the Shiite sect of Islam became the state religion, and through his ruthlessness,

The Sultan, Suleiman the Magnificent, battling the Hungarians.

the rival Sunnite sect was crushed. Persians identified themselves with Shiism, differentiating them from the Turks and other surrounding Moslem peoples who were mostly Sunnites.

The greatest of the Safavid rulers was Abbas I, the shah from 1587 to 1629. It was he who modernized the Persian army by building up its artillery units. Under his rule, Persia became an internationally recognized great power, as seen by the constant stream of envoys from European countries who sought an alliance with Persia against the Ottoman Empire. In fact, both these Moslem states figured prominently in European diplomacy during these years. Francis I of France, for example, cooperated with Suleiman the Magnificent in fighting against the Hapsburg Emperor Charles V. And the Hapsburgs, in turn, cooperated with the Persians against their two common foes. These relationships between Christian and Moslem states were denounced at the time as "impious" and "sacrilegious," but the fact was that the Ottoman and Safavid empires had become world powers that no European diplomat could afford to overlook.

Mogul Empire

Just as two outstanding Safavid rulers founded a "national" dynasty in Persia, so two outstanding Mogul rulers—Babur and Akbar—founded a "national" dynasty in India, a very remarkable achievement for Moslem rulers in a predominantly Hindu country.

The Moslems came to India in three waves, widely separated in time. The first consisted of Arab Moslems who invaded the Sind region near the mouth of the Indus in 712 C.E. These Arabs were unable to push far inland, so their influence on India was limited.

The second wave came in about 1000, when Turkish Moslems began raiding India from bases in Afghanistan. These raids continued intermittently for four centuries, with much loss of life and property. The net result was that numerous Moslem kingdoms were established in northern India, whereas southern India remained a conglomeration of Hindu states. But even in northern India the mass of the people continued to be Indians in race and Hindu in religion. They did not become Islamicized and Turkified, as did the people of Asia Minor. The explanation again is that Turks who came down from the north were an insignificant minority compared to India's teeming millions. They could fill only the top positions in the government and the armed forces. Their Hindu subjects were the ones who tilled the land, worked in the bazaars, and comprised most of the bureaucracy. In certain regions, it is true, large sections of the population did turn to Islam, especially some depressed castes who sought relief from their exploitation in the new religion. Yet the fact remains that India was an overwhelmingly Hindu country when the third Moslem wave struck in 1500 with the appearance of the Moguls.

The newcomers again were Turks, their leader being the colorful Babur, a direct descendent of the great Turkish conqueror Timur, or Tamerlane. In 1524 Babur, with a small force of 12,000 men armed with matchlock muskets and artillery, defeated an Indian army of 100,000. After his victory, Babur occupied Delhi, his new capital. Four years later he died, but his sons followed his path, and the empire grew rapidly. It reached its height during the reign of Babur's grandson, the famous Akbar, who ruled from 1556 to 1605.

Akbar was by far the most outstanding of the Mogul emperors. He rounded out his Indian possessions by conquering Rajputana and Gujarat in the west, Bengal in the east, and several small states in the Deccan peninsula in the south. Mogul rule now extended from Kabul and Kashmir to the Deccan, and later under Aurangzeb (1658–1707) it extended still further—almost to the southern tip of the peninsula. In addition to his military exploits, Akbar was a remarkable personality of great versatility and a wide range of interests. Although illiterate, he had a keen and inquiring mind that won the grudging admiration of Jesuits who knew him well. The astonishing range of his activities is reminiscent of Peter the Great. Like his Russian counterpart, Akbar had a strong mechanical bent, as evidenced in his metallurgical work and in his designs for a gun with increased firepower. He learned to draw, loved music, was an expert polo player, and played various instruments, the kettledrum being his favorite. Akbar even evolved an entirely new religion of his own, the Din Ilahi, or "Divine Faith." It was eclectic, with borrowings from many sources, especially from the Parsees, the Jains, and the Hindus. Akbar hoped that a common faith would unite his Hindu and Moslem subjects. But in practice, it had little impact on the country. It was too intellectual to appeal to the masses, and even at court there were few converts.

What Akbar failed to achieve by his synthetic faith, he did by ending discriminatory practices against Hindus and establishing their equality with Moslems. He abolished the pilgrim tax that Hindus had been required to pay when traveling to their sacred shrines. He ended the poll tax on Hindus, a standard levy on nonbelievers in all Moslem countries. Akbar also opened the top state positions to Hindus, who now ceased to look on the Mogul Empire as an

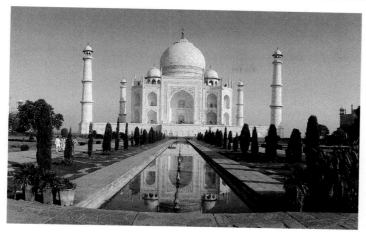

The Taj Mahal. Probably the most beautiful tomb in the world, the Taj was built from 1631 to 1653 by Shah Jahan for his beloved wife, Mumtaz Mahal. Located on the south bank of the Yamuna River at Agra, the Mughal capital, the Taj Mahal remains the jewel of Mughal architecture.

enemy organization. A new India was beginning to emerge, as Akbar had dreamed—a national state rather than a divided land of Moslem masters and a Hindu subject majority.

II. SPLENDOR OF MOSLEM EMPIRES

Military Strength

All three of the Moslem empires were first-class military powers. Eloquent proof is to be found in the appeal sent in December 1525 by the king of France, Francis I, to the Ottoman sultan, Suleiman the Magnificent. The appeal was for a Turkish attack on the Holy Roman emperor and head of the House of Hapsburg, Charles V. Suleiman responded in 1526 by crossing the Danube, overrunning Hungary, and easing the pressure on Francis. This was only one of many Ottoman expeditions that not only aided the French—and incidentally provided the Turks with additional territories and booty—but also saved the Lutheran heretics by distracting Hapsburg attention from Germany to the threatened Danubian frontiers. It is paradoxical that Moslem military power should have contributed substantially to the cause of Protestantism in its critical formative stage.

Moslem military forces generally lagged behind those of Europe in artillery equipment. They depended on the Europeans for the most advanced weapons and for the most experienced gunners. The discrepancy, however, was one of degree only. It was not a case of the Moslem

empires being defenseless because of lack of artillery. Plenty of equipment was available, though it was not as efficient and as well-manned as were the best contemporary European armies. The Moslems, and especially the Turks, were shrewd enough to pay for both Western artillery and artillerymen, but they lacked the technology and the industries to keep up with the rapid progress of Western armaments.

On the other hand, European observers were impressed by the vast military manpower of the Moslem world. It is estimated that the permanent regular forces of the whole of India at the time of Akbar totaled well over 1 million men, or more than double the size of the Indian armies in 1914. Furthermore, these huge military establishments were well trained and disciplined when the Moslem empires were at their height. For obvious geographic reasons, Europeans were most familiar with the Ottoman armed forces, with whom they had a good deal of firsthand experience. After this experience the Europeans were very impressed and respectful. Typical were the reports of Ogier Ghiselin de Busbecq, Hapsburg ambassador to Constantinople during the reign of Suleiman the Magnificent. After Busbecq inspected an Ottoman army camp in 1555, he wrote home as follows:

It makes me shudder to think of what the result of a struggle between such different systems [as the Hapsburg and the Ottoman] must be. . . . On their side is the vast wealth of their empire, unimpaired resources, experience and practice in arms, a veteran soldiery, an uninterrupted series of victories, readiness to endure hardships, union, order, discipline, thrift, and watchfulness. On ours are found an empty exchequer, luxurious habits, exhausted resources, broken spirits, a raw and insubordinate soldiery, and greedy generals; there is no regard for discipline, license runs riot, the men indulge in drunkenness and debauchery, and, worst of all, the enemy are accustomed to victory, we, to defeat. Can we doubt what the result must be? The only obstacle is Persia, whose position on his rear forces the invader to take precautions. The fear of Persia gives a respite, but it is only for a time.[2]

Administrative Efficiency

All heads of Moslem states had absolute power over their subjects. Accordingly, the quality of the administration depended on the quality of the imperial heads. In the sixteenth century, they were men of extraordinary abilities. Certainly Suleiman and Abbas and Akbar were the equals of any monarchs anywhere in the world. Akbar had a well-organized bureaucracy whose ranks were expressed in terms of cavalry commands. Excellent pay and the promise of rapid advance in the Mogul service attracted the best men in India and from abroad. It is estimated that 70 percent of the bureaucracy consisted of foreigners such as Persians and Afghans. The rest were Indian Moslems and Hindus. Upon the death of an official, his wealth was inherited by the emperor, and his rank became vacant. This practice lessened the evils of corruption and hereditary tenure that plagued Western countries at the time.

Since Akbar opened his bureaucracy to all his subjects, ability rather than religion became the criterion for appointment and advancement. Busbecq in Constantinople made precisely the same point about the Ottoman administrative system:

In making his appointments the Sultan pays no regard to any pretensions on the score of wealth or rank. . . . He considers each case on its own merits, and examines carefully into the character, ability, and disposition of the man whose promotion is in question. It is by merit than men rise in the service, a system which ensures that posts should only be assigned to the competent. . . . Among the Turks, therefore, honours, high posts, and judgeships are the rewards of great ability and good service. If a man be dishonest, or lazy, or careless, he remains at the bottom of the ladder, an object of contempt. . . . These are not our ideas, with us there is no opening left for merit; birth is the standard for everything; the prestige of birth is the sole key to advancement in the public service.[3]

Economic Development

As far as economic standards were concerned, the Moslem states in early modern times were, in current phraseology, developed lands. Certainly they were so regarded by western Europeans, who were ready to face any hardships or perils to reach fabled India and the Spice Islands beyond. Closer to home, the Ottoman Empire was an impressive economic unit. Its vast extent assured it of virtual self-sufficiency. For most Europeans, more dazzling than the Ottoman Empire was far-off, exotic India, the weaver of fabulous textiles, especially fine cotton fabrics unequaled anywhere in the world. India was the country that, since the early days of the Roman Empire, had drained gold and silver away from Europe.

As significant as the wealth of the Moslem empires was the control of south Asian commerce by Moslem merchants. Particularly important was the trade in spices, which were eagerly sought after in a world that knew so little of the art of conserving foodstuffs apart from salting. For centuries the spices, together with many other goods such as silk from China and cotton fabrics from India, were transported back and forth along two sets of trade routes. The northern land routes extended from the Far East through central Asia to ports on the Black Sea and Asia Minor; the southern sea routes, from the East Indies and India along the Indian Ocean and up the Persian Gulf or the Red Sea to ports in Syria and Egypt. With the collapse of the Mongol Empire, conditions in central Asia became so anarchical that the northern routes were virtually closed after 1340. Henceforth, most of the products were funneled along the southern sea routes, which by that time were dominated by Moslem merchants.

This commerce contributed substantially to the prosperity of the Moslem world. It provided not only government revenue in the form of customs duties but also a source of livelihood for thousands of merchants, clerks, sailors, shipbuilders, camel drivers, and stevedores, who were connected directly or indirectly with the trade. The extent of the profits is indicated by the fact that articles from India were sold to Italian middlemen in Alexandria at a markup of over 2,000 percent.

When the Portuguese broke into the Indian Ocean in 1498, they quickly gained control of much of this lucrative commerce. But they did so because their ships and guns, rather than their goods or business techniques, were superior. In fact, we shall find that the Portuguese at first were embarrassed because they had little to offer in return for the commodities they coveted. They were rescued from this predicament only by the flood of bullion that soon was to pour in from the mines of Mexico and Peru.

III. DECLINE OF MOSLEM EMPIRES

The Moslem world of the sixteenth century was most impressive. Suleiman, Akbar, and Abbas ruled empires that were at least the equals of those in other parts of the globe, and yet these empires began to go downhill during the seventeenth century. By the following century they

were far behind western Europe, and they have remained behind to the present day.

One explanation is the deterioration of the ruling dynasties. Suleiman the Magnificent was succeeded in 1566 by Selim II, who was lazy, fat, dissipated, and so addicted to wine that he was known to his subjects as Selim the Sot. The same thing happened in Persia after Abbas, and in India after Akbar. Dynastic decline, however, was not the only factor responsible for the blight of the Moslem lands. All the European royal families had their share of incapable and irresponsible rulers, yet their countries did not go down with them.

A more basic explanation for the misfortunes of the Moslem world was that it lacked the dynamism of Europe. It did not have those far-reaching changes that were revolutionizing European society during these centuries (as we shall see in Chapters 22 and 23). In the Moslem economic field, for example, there were no basic changes in agriculture, in industry, in financial methods, or in commercial organization. A traveler in the Moslem lands in the seventeenth or eighteenth centuries would have observed essentially the same economic practices and institu-

The battle of Lepanto occurred off the coast of Greece on October 7, 1571. In the largest naval engagement of the sixteenth century, the Spanish and their Italian allies under Don John of Austria smashed the Turkish fleet and ended the Ottoman threat in the western Mediterranean.

OTTOMAN EMPIRE IN DECLINE

The British consul and merchant William Eton lived in the Ottoman Empire for many years at the end of the eighteenth century. His colorful report on Ottoman conditions and institutions reflects how far the empire had declined since its days of glory.*

General knowledge is, from these causes, little if at all cultivated; every man is supposed to know his own business or profession, with which it is esteemed foolish and improper for any other person to interfere. The man of general science, a character so frequent and so useful in Christian Europe, is unknown; and any one, but a mere artificer, who should concern himself with the founding of cannon, the building of ships, or the like, would be esteemed little better than a madman. The natural consequence of these narrow views is, that the professors of any art or science are themselves profoundly ignorant, and that the greatest absurdities are mixed with all their speculations. . . .

From the mufti to the peasant it is generally believed, that there are seven heavens, from which the earth is immovably suspended by a large chain; that the sun is an immense ball of fire, at least as big as the whole Ottoman province, formed for the sole purpose of giving light and heat to the earth; that eclipses of the moon are occasioned by a great dragon attempting to devour that luminary; that the fixed stars hang by chains from the highest heaven &c. &c. . . .

They distinguish different Christian states by different appellations of contempt. Epithets which the Turks apply to those who are not Osmanlis, and which they often use to denominate their nation:

Albanians	gut-sellers
Armenians	t-rd-eaters, dirt-eaters, also pack-carriers
Bosniaks and Bulgarians	vagabonds
Christians	idolaters
Dutch	cheese-mongers
English	atheists
Flemmings	panders
French	faithless
Georgians	louse-eaters
Germans	infidel blasphemers
Greeks of the islands	hares
Italians or Franks	many-coloured
Jews	mangy dogs
Moldavians	drones
Poles	insolent infidels
Russians	mad infidels
Spaniards	lazy
Tatars	carrion-eaters
Walachians	gypsies

It is a certain fact, that a few years ago a learned man of the law having lost an eye, and being informed that there was then at Constantinople an European who made false eyes, not to be distinguished from the natural, he immediately procured one; but when it was placed in the socket, he flew into a violent passion with the eye-maker, abusing him as an impostor, because he could not see with it. The man, fearing he should lose his pay, assured him that in time he would see as well with that eye as with the other. The effendi was appeased, and the artist liberally rewarded, who having soon disposed of the remainder of his eyes, left the Turks in expectation of seeing with them. . . .

*W. Eton, *A Survey of the Turkish Empire*, 4th ed. (London, 1809), pp. 190–93.

tions as the Crusaders had seen five hundred years earlier. As long as the rulers were strong and enlightened, the autocratic empires functioned smoothly and effectively, as Busbecq reported. But when central authority weakened, the courtiers, bureaucratic officials, and army officers all combined to fleece the productive classes of society, whether peasants or artisans or merchants. Their uncontrollable extortions stifled private enterprise and incentive. Any subject who showed signs of wealth was fair game for arbitrary confiscation. Consequently, merchants hid their wealth rather than openly invest it to expand their operations.

Another cause and symptom of decline was the blind superiority complex of the Moslems, with their attitude of invincibility vis-à-vis the West. It never occurred to them at this time that they might conceivably learn anything from giaours, or nonbelievers. Their attitude stemmed partly from religious prejudice and partly from the spectacular successes of Islam in the past. Islam had grown from an obscure sect to the world's largest and most rapidly growing religion. Consequently, Moslem officials and scholars looked down with arrogance on anything relating to Christian Europe. As late as 1756, when the French ambassador in Constantinople announced the alliance between France and Austria that marked a turning point in the diplomatic history of Europe, he was curtly informed that the Ottoman government did not concern itself "about the union of one hog with another."[4] This attitude was perhaps understandable in the sixteenth century; in the eighteenth it was suicidal.

One of the most damaging results of this self-centeredness was that it let down an intellectual iron curtain between the Moslem world and the West, especially in the increasingly important field of science. Moslem scholars knew virtually nothing of the epoch-making achievements of Paracelsus in medicine; Vesalius and Harvey in anatomy; and Copernicus, Kepler, and Galileo in astronomy. Not only were they ignorant of these scientific advances, but also Moslem science itself had stagnated, with little impetus for new discoveries in the future.

A final factor explaining Moslem decline is that the three great Moslem empires were all land empires. They were built by the Turks, the Persians, and the Moguls, all peoples with no seafaring traditions. Their empires faced inward toward central Asia rather than outward toward the oceans. The rulers of these empires were not vitally interested in overseas trade. Therefore they responded feebly, if at all, when Portugal seized control of the Indian Ocean trade routes.

This situation was significant, because it allowed the Europeans to become the masters of the world trade routes with little opposition from the Moslems, who hitherto had controlled most of the trade between Asia and Europe. The repercussions were far-reaching. The control of world trade enriched the Europeans tremendously and further stimulated their economic, social, and political development. Thus a vicious circle developed, with worldwide trade making western Europe increasingly wealthy, productive, dynamic, and expansionist, while the once-formidable Moslem empires, taking little part in the new world economy, remained static and fell further and further behind.

SUGGESTED READINGS

Directly relevant to this chapter is the excellent collection of sources by J. J. Saunders, ed., *The Moslem World on the Eve of Europe's Expansion* (Prentice Hall, 1966). The spread of Islam from the time of Mohammed to the end of the nineteenth century is well described by T. W. Arnold, *The Preaching of Islam*, rev. ed. (Constable, 1913).

For the various Islam empires, see H. A. R. Gibb and H. Bowen, *Islamic Society and the West*, Parts 1 and 2 (Oxford University, 1950, 1957); H. Inalcik, *The Ottoman Empire: The Classical Age, 1300–1600* (Weidenfeld and Nicolson, 1972); the multivolume *Cambridge History of Iran* (Cambridge, 1968ff.); N. Itkowitz, *Ottoman Empire and Islamic Tradition* (University of Chicago, 1980); the sprightly written S. Wolpert, *A New History of India* (Oxford University, 1977); and R. Dunn, *The Adventures of Ibn Battuta: A Muslim Traveller of the Fourteenth Century* (University of California, 1986), which presents a revealing overview of the Moslem world.

Finally, on the decline of the Moslem Empires, see J. J. Saunders, "The Problem of Islamic Decadence," *Journal of World History*, 7 (1963), 701–720; T. Stoianovich, "Factors in the Decline of Ottoman Society in the Balkans," *Slavic Review*, 21 (December 1962), 623–632; and B. Lewis, "Some Reflections on the Decline of the Ottoman Empire," in C. M. Cipolla, ed., *The Economic Decline of Empires* (Methuen, 1970), pp. 215–234.

NOTES

1. Mehmed Pasha, *Ottoman Statecraft: The Book of Counsel for Vezirs and Govenors*, W. L. Wright, ed. and trans. (Princeton University, 1935), p. 21.
2. C. T. Foster and F. H. B. Daniell, eds., *The Life and Letters of Ogier Ghiselin de Busbecq* (London, 1881), pp. 221, 222.
3. Ibid., pp. 154, 155.
4. Cited by W. Eton, *A Survey of the Turkish Empire* (London, 1809), p. 10.

Confucian World at the Time of the West's Expansion

One need not be obsessed with the merits of the Chinese to recognize that the organization of their empire is in truth the best that the world has ever seen.

Voltaire, 1764

Corresponding to the Moslem world in the Middle East and south Asia was the Confucian world in east Asia. Just as the Moslem world was dominated by the Ottoman, Safavid, and Mogul empires, so the Confucian world was dominated by China, with Korea and Japan on the periphery. The two worlds were similar in one fundamental respect: They were both agrarian-based and inward-looking societies. Their tempo of change was slow and within the framework inherited from earlier times. On the other hand, the Confucian world differed substantially from the Moslem because of its much greater unity. China had no indigestible minority blocs comparable to the various Balkan Christians in the Ottoman Empire, and no religious divisions comparable to the Hindus and Moslems in the Mogul Empire. This cohesiveness of China was not a recent phe-

nomenon. It dated back for millennia to the beginnings of Chinese civilization and has persisted to the present day. Indeed, the Chinese civilization is the oldest continuous civilization in the world.

I. CONTINUITY OF CHINESE CIVILIZATION

One reason for the longevity of the Chinese civilization is geographic, for China is isolated from the world's other great civilizations to an unprecedented degree. China has nothing comparable to the Mediterranean, which linked Mesopotamia, Egypt, Greece, and Rome, or the Indian Ocean, which allowed India to interact with the Middle East, Africa, and south Asia. Instead, during most of its history, China was effectively cut off on all sides by mountains, deserts, and the vast Pacific Ocean. The significance of this isolation is that it allowed the Chinese to develop their civilization with fewer intrusions from the outside than the peoples of the Middle East or India had to face. Consequently, their civilization was both more continuous and also more distinctive. It has more fundamental differences from the other great Eurasian civilizations than any of them have from each other.

The unique size of China's population has also contributed to the continuity of civilization. From the beginning China has been able to support a huge population because of a favorable combination of soil and climate. The monsoon rains come during the warm months of the year, so that two crops per year are possible in some areas south of the Yangtze River, in contrast to the average one-crop yields of the Middle East and Europe. Furthermore, rice produces a much larger yield per acre than the wheat or barley grown in most parts of Eurasia. Thus the census of 2 C.E. showed that Han China had a population of 59.5 million—more than that of the Roman Empire at its greatest extent. By the early sixteenth century, when the Portuguese first arrived, China's population was over 100 million, more than that of all Europe. By the mid-nineteenth century, when China was being forced open by Western gunboats, its population had spurted upward to over 400 million, partly because of the introduction of such New World food crops as peanuts, maize, and sweet potatoes.

Such an unequaled population made it possible for the Chinese to retain their identity regardless of the course of events. They had been conquered and ruled by the Mongols and Manchus, as well as battered and undermined by the West. But in the end their superiority in numbers together with their superiority in civilization always enabled them to assimilate or expel the intruders and to adapt selected aspects of foreign cultures to their traditional civilization. Never has wholesale transformation been imposed from the outside, as it was in Europe with the Germanic invasions, or in the Middle East and in India with the Moslem ones.

Another important factor in China's cohesiveness is the existence of a single written language that goes back several millennia to the earliest Shang dynasty. This written language is of special significance because it is understood by Chinese from all regions, speaking dialects as different from each other as Italian is from German or Swedish from Spanish. The reason it is understandable to all is that it consists of characters representing ideas or objects. These characters are pronounced in different ways in different parts of China, but the meaning of any character is the same no matter how it is pronounced. A Western parallel would be the arabic number system: For example, the word for the number 8 is pronounced differently in Italian, in Swedish, or in English, but the meaning of the symbol 8 remains the same in all three tongues. This common written language has been an important force in providing unity and historic continuity to China. In fact, it has done so to all of east Asia, for the Chinese method of writing has been adopted in whole or in part by most of the surrounding peoples, including the Japanese, Koreans, and some of the Southeast Asians.

Related to the common written language is the extraordinary system of public examinations which formed the basis of the merit system by which for nearly two millennia China staffed its civil service. "When the right men are available, government flourishes. When the right men are not available, government declines." This Confucian maxim expresses the fundamental Chinese doctrine that problems of state are better met by recruiting people of talent than by depending on laws and institutions, as was done in the West. When fully evolved, the Chinese system consisted of a series of examinations held, in ascending order, in district and prefectural cities, provincial capitals, and finally the imperial capital.

At first the examinations were fairly comprehensive, emphasizing the Confucian classics but including also subjects like law, mathematics, and political affairs. Gradually, however, they came to concentrate on literary style and Confucian orthodoxy. The net result was a system providing China with an efficient and stable administration that won the respect and admiration of Europeans. On the other hand, it was a system that stifled originality and bred conformity. As long as China remained relatively isolated in east Asia, it provided stability and continuity. But with the intrusion of the dynamic West the system prevented effective reaction and adjustment. It was finally abolished altogether in 1905.

Perhaps the most important factor contributing to the cohesiveness of Chinese civilization was the moral code and the literary and intellectual heritage known as Confucianism. This was made up of the teachings of Confucius (551–479 B.C.E.), the name being a Latinized form of K'ung-fu-tzu, or "Master Kung." Like most Chinese thinkers, Confucius was concerned primarily with the establishment of a happy and well-organized society in this world. His first principle was "every man in his place": "Let the ruler be a ruler and the subject a subject; let the father be a father and the son be a son."

Confucius also provided China with a philosophy of government. Just as the individual should be subordinate to the family, so the family should be subordinate to the emperor. But the emperor in turn should set an example of benevolent fatherhood, and this was to be done by following the ethics of Confucianism rather than a system of law. Confucius thus was the founder of a great ethical tradition in a civilization that, more than any other, came to concentrate on ethical values.

All these factors are necessary to explain the continuity of Chinese civilization since its beginnings about 1500 B.C.E. The history of the Middle East presents a sharp contrast: Alexander's conquests spread the new Hellenistic culture; the Moslem conquests brought radical changes in race, language, and culture, as well as religion. India, likewise, was transformed fundamentally with the Aryan invasions about 1500 B.C.E. and the Moslem invasions after 1000 C.E. The historical evolution of China was never jarred by such violent upheavals. There were many invasions, and on two occasions foreign dynasties ruled the entire country, but these intrusions disturbed rather than transformed. Instead of massive breaks and new beginnings, China throughout its history experienced merely the rise and fall of dynasties within the traditional framework.

II. DYNASTIC CYCLES

The cyclical rise and fall of dynasties can be explained by certain recurring trends in Chinese history. Each new dynasty normally began by ruling the country efficiently and starting a period of comparative peace and prosperity. It stimulated intellectual and cultural life and protected the country by sending military expeditions against the nomads and extending the imperial frontiers. But gradually the dynasty was weakened by the personal degeneration of individual rulers and by court struggles between cliques of gentry and palace eunuchs. This deterioration and factionalism undermined central authority and promoted corruption in the bureaucracy. Together with the increasing luxuriousness of court life, the corruption meant heavier taxes on the peasantry, who ultimately had to produce the surplus that supported the entire imperial structure. Taxes tended to increase also because of the costly foreign wars and the practice of the emperors of granting tax exemption to many of the gentry and to Buddhist temples and monasteries. As the government became lax, the irrigation systems and other public works essential for agriculture tended to be neglected.

Thus an increasingly impoverished peasantry had to bear the burden of a mounting tax load. When the inevitable crop failures and famines were added to the burden, the explosion came, and revolts broke out against the government tax collectors and landlord rent agents. In time, local uprisings broadened into general insurrections. These in turn were an invitation to

Confucius instructing his disciples in the precepts of living in a happy and organized society.

the nomads to invade, especially since the imperial armies by this stage were poorly maintained. The combination of internal rebellion and external invasion usually heralded the beginning of a new cycle—the approaching end of the old dynasty and the coming of a new one.

The first dynasty, the Shang (1523–1028 B.C.E.), arose in the north in the Yellow River valley. Already the Chinese had learned to make silk, had devised their distinctive writing system, had mastered the art of creating beautiful earthenware and bronze vessels, and had begun to make a clear distinction between "Chinese" and "barbarians" based on a sense of cultural rather than racial superiority.

The succeeding Zhou dynasty (1028–221 B.C.E.), although long lived, was unable to establish a stable central government. The Zhou political structure was somewhat similar to that of medieval Europe, with a large number of warring feudal states that disregarded the nominal Zhou overlord. But this troubled political scene led to anxious soul searching among Chinese intellectuals. Their speculations on the nature of humanity and society culminated in the great philosophical systems and literary classics of Chinese civilization. Both Confucianism and Taoism evolved, so that the Zhou centuries, spanning a period as long as the entire European Middle Ages, stand out as the era when the cultural foundations of China were laid.

The following Ch'in dynasty (221–206 B.C.E.), despite its short duration, was responsible for replacing Zhou feudalism with a tightly organized imperial structure that lasted, with occasional lapses, until the fall of the last dynasty in 1912. This structure included an all-powerful emperor, an efficient and disciplined bureaucracy, a network of military roads and the Great Wall in the north, all of which gave China the most stable and lasting government in the world.

The Ch'in dynasty was succeeded by the Han (206 B.C.E.–220 C.E.), which is noted for its expansion of China's frontiers in all directions—west into central Asia, north into Manchuria, and south into Indochina. The Han Empire was at least the equal of the contemporary Roman Empire in size, population, wealth, and cultural achievement. The Han dynasty was followed, after an intervening period of disorder, by the T'ang and Sung dynasties (618–907 and 960–1279), which represented a continuation of the traditional civilization, although with certain refinements and modifications.

The Yüan dynasty that followed (1279–1368) was unique in that it was Mongol rather than Chinese. The Mongols, in fact, had overrun most of Eurasia, so that China was now part of a huge empire extending from the Pacific to the Black Sea. But these Mongol rulers were few in number compared to their millions of Chinese subjects, and they failed to win the support of the Chinese gentry and peasants. They ruled as conquerors, making few concessions to Chinese institutions or to the Chinese way of life. When their military power declined, their regime was swept away by rebellious peasants and hostile scholar-bureaucrats.

Following the expulsion of the Mongols, China was ruled by two more dynasties, the Chinese Ming (1368–1644) and Manchu Ch'ing (1644–1911). Although the Manchus were foreigners like the Mongols, they were successful in ruling China because they gave prestige and opportunity to Chinese scholar-bureaucrats while maintaining administrative control. The traditional institutions and practices continued smoothly and satisfyingly—the agricultural economy, the Confucian way of life, the examination system for the selection of public officials, and the revered rule of the Son of Heaven in Peking.

In ordinary times such order and permanence would be considered a blessing. But these were the centuries that witnessed the rise of a new and dynamic Europe—the centuries of the Renaissance, the Reformation, the commercial and industrial revolutions, the French Revolution, and the rise of powerful national states that quickly extended their domination over the entire globe. In such a period, stability became a curse rather than a blessing. China appeared, and in fact was, relatively static and backward. The idea of continual change and "progress," which now was taken for granted in the West, remained alien to the Chinese mind. The basic difference between Chinese and European attitudes toward the world about them was manifested in the Chinese decision to discontinue the spectacular overseas expeditions of the Ming dynasty (see Chapter 21, Section V).

III. EARLY RELATIONS WITH THE WEST

Relations between China and the West did not become continuous until the expansion of Europe following the voyages of Columbus and the Portuguese navigators. China began to feel the direct impact of the dynamic new Europe when Portuguese merchants opened trade with Canton in 1514 and established a permanent commercial base at Macao in 1557. The Portuguese purchased Chinese silks, wood carvings, porcelain, lacquerware, and gold, and in return they sold nutmeg, cloves, and mace from the East Indies; sandalwood from Timor; drugs and dyes from Java; and cinnamon, pepper, and ginger from India. No European goods were involved for the simple reason that there was no market for them in China. The Portuguese were functioning as carriers and middlemen for a purely intra-Asian trade.

The Dutch and the British arrived in the early seventeenth century to challenge Portugal's monopoly in the China trade. Neither was given official permission to trade, so for decades the Dutch and English preyed on Portuguese shipping and conducted an irregular trade along the south China coast. By the mid-eighteenth century the Chinese opened up the trade to all countries, though confining it to Canton and Macao. The English soon won the lion's share of this trade, partly because of their growing commercial and industrial superiority and also because of their convenient base of operations in India.

Meanwhile, the Russians in Siberia had been trying to open trade relations with China, and the Chinese had reacted by restricting and regulating the commerce closely. The treaties of Nerchinsk (1689) and Kiakhta (1727) allowed the Russians to trade at three border points and to send commercial caravans every three years to Peking. There they were permitted to build a church and maintain a priest and three curates, though their community in the Chinese capital was limited in numbers to 300. Under these terms a few goods were exchanged—Russian furs, leather goods, textiles, cattle, horses, and glassware for Chinese silks, tea, lacquerware, and porcelain.

Cultural interaction between China and the West during these early centuries was con-

Russians traveled through Siberia and set up forts along the Amur River, attempting to open trade relations with China. With Jesuit priests acting as interpreters and advisers, the treaty of Nerchinsk was signed in 1689.

fined to the efforts of the Jesuits to propagate their faith. The net result of centuries of Jesuit enterprise was negligible. Indeed, Europe had been much more impressed by China's examination system and Confucian ethics, than China had been by Europe's science and mathematics. The Chinese remained supremely self-confident and self-contained. They had kept Western merchants confined to few seaports and frontier trading posts; they had accepted with a few exceptions only tributary relations in their conduct of international affairs; and they had shown only a passing interest in Jesuit teachings about science and theology. Rarely in history had a people faced the future with so much self-assurance and with so little understanding of the storms that awaited them.

IV. JAPAN ABSORBS CHINESE CIVILIZATION

Compared to China, Japan was on the periphery in the sixteenth century when the Europeans first appeared. This does not mean that the Japanese were primitive; indeed, they had evolved a complex and dynamic society. Although their first reaction to the appearance of the Europeans was positive—many of them embraced Christianity—soon they reacted against the "insolent barbarians" and severed virtually all ties with them. But the Japanese eventually came to realize that a policy of withdrawal was not realistic. They proceeded to study the ways of the West and adapt elements of Western culture to their needs. Thanks to their unique historical and cultural background, the Japanese were extraordinarily successful and quickly outdistanced the Chinese, who for so long had been their teachers.

The importance of geographic location is particularly apparent in the case of Japanese history. In this respect there is a close parallel with the British Isles at the other end of the Eurasian landmass. The Japanese islands, however, are more isolated than the British. One hundred and fifteen miles separate them from the mainland, compared to the twenty-one miles of the English Channel. Thus until their World War II defeat by the United States, the Japanese had only once before been seriously threatened by foreign invasion, and that was in the thirteenth century by the Mongols. The Japanese, therefore, have been close enough to the mainland to benefit from the great Chinese civilization, but distant enough to be able to select and reject as they wished.

The Japanese are basically a Mongoloid people who migrated from northeast Asia. But the hairy Caucasoid Ainu who originally inhabited the Japanese islands contributed to their racial composition, and Malayan and Polynesian migrants from the south probably did also. Early Japan was organized in a large number of clans, each ruled by a hereditary priest-chieftain. Toward the end of the first century C.E., the Yamato clan established a loose political and religious control over the others. Its chief was the emperor, and its clan goddess, the Sun Goddess, was made the national deity.

This clan organization was undermined by the importation of Chinese civilization, which began on a large scale in the sixth century. Buddhism, introduced from Korea, was the medium for cultural change, fulfilling the same function here as Christianity did among the Germans and Slavs in Europe. Students, teachers, craftsmen, and monks crossed over from the mainland, bringing with them a new way of life as well as a new religion. The impetus for change culminated in the Taika Reform, which began in 645 and

Yoritomo (1147–1198), first Minamoto Shogun of Japan and founder of the Kamakura Shogunate. He was the first founder of a long line of actual rulers of Japan.

sought to transform Japan into a centralized state on the model of the T'ang dynasty in China. In accordance with the Chinese model, the country was divided into provinces and districts ruled by governors and magistrates who derived their power from the emperor and his council of state.

These and other changes were designed to strengthen imperial authority, and they did so in comparison with the preceding clan structure. But in practice, the Japanese changed and adapted everything they borrowed from China. They limited the power of their emperor by allowing the hereditary aristocracy to keep their large landholdings. They borrowed Chinese ideographs but developed their own system of writing. They borrowed Confucianism, but modified its ethics and adjusted its political doctrines to satisfy their own spiritual needs, while retaining their native Shintoism. They built new imperial capitals, first at Nara and then at Kyoto, that were modeled after the T'ang capital, Ch'ang-an. But there was no mistaking the Japanese quality of the temples, pavilions, shrines, and gardens.

V. TOKUGAWA SHOGUNATE

The Chinese system of imperial organization introduced by the Taika Reform of 645 worked effectively for a long period. By the twelfth century, however, it had been undermined and replaced by a Japanese variety of feudalism. One reason for this was the tendency of provincial governors, who were too fond of the pleasures of Kyoto, to delegate their powers and responsibilities to local subordinates. Another was that powerful local families and Buddhist communities were always hungry for land and often able to seize it by force. These trends reduced the amount of taxpaying land, which meant an increased tax load for the peasant owner-cultivators. The latter in turn either fled to the northern frontier areas where the Ainu were being pushed back by force of arms, or else they commended themselves and their lands to lords of manors. This relieved them of taxes and provided them with protection, but at the cost of becoming serfs. The net result of this process was that by the end of the twelfth century, taxpaying land amounted to 10 percent or less of the total cultivated area, and local power had been taken over by the new rural aristocracy.

At the same time, this aristocracy had become the dominant military force because of the disintegration of the imperial armed forces. The Taika Reform had made all males between the ages of twenty and sixty subject to military service. But the conscripts were required to furnish their own weapons and food and were given no relief from the regular tax burden. This arrangement proved unworkable and was abandoned in 739. Government military posts became sinecures generally filled by effeminate court aristocrats. As a result, the campaigns against the Ainu were conducted by the rural aristocrats. They became mounted warriors and gradually increased their military effectiveness until they completely overshadowed the imperial forces. A feudal relationship now developed between these rural lords and their retainers, or samurai (literally, "one who serves"). This relationship was based on an idealized ethic, known as bushido, or "way of the warrior." The samurai enjoyed special legal and ceremonial rights, and in return they were expected to give unquestioning service to their lords.

By the twelfth century, Japan was controlled by the competing groups of feudal lords. In the end, one of these lords emerged victorious, and he was appointed by the emperor to the position of Seii-Tai-Shogun (Barbarian-Subduing-Generalissimo), with the right to nominate his own successor. Henceforth Japan was controlled by a succession of shogun families, or shogunates. They commanded the military forces while the emperor lived in seclusion in Kyoto. The most important of these families was the Tokugawa Shogunate, founded by Tokugawa Ieyasu in 1603. It ruled the country until the restoration of imperial rule and the beginning of modernization in 1868. Ieyasu and his immediate successors formulated policies designed to perpetuate their family dominance. The material basis of their power lay in the Shogunal domain, which comprised between a fourth and a third of the total arable land and consisted of estates scattered strategically throughout the country. These estates provided control points against potentially hostile daimyo, or local landholding families. Top government posts were filled by members of the Tokugawa family or personal retainers. The emperor was provided with revenues for his own support as well as that of a small group of court nobles, but he had no political function or authority.

As part of their effort to prevent any change that might undermine their rule, the Tokugawa perpetuated a rigid, hereditary class structure. At the top was the aristocracy, comprising about 6 percent of the population. The vast majority of Japanese were farmers, the second-ranking class, which included landless tenants as well as landholders with plots ranging from an acre and a quarter to as many as eighty-five acres. Whatever their status, these peasants produced the rice that, in the final analysis, supported the aristocracy. The latter, in fact, measured their income in terms of rice.

The last two classes recognized by the Tokugawa were, in order of rank, the artisans and the merchants. The long period of peace and security during this shogunate allowed these townspeople to grow enormously in numbers and wealth. The Tokugawa created an ideological basis for their regime by sponsoring the Chu Hsi school of Confucianism, which stressed the virtues of filial piety and of loyalty to one's superior in any social grouping. Paternal power was absolute and unquestioned in the ideal Japanese family, and even more specifically spelled out than in China. Particularly appealing to the Tokugawa was the Confucian emphasis on the moral basis of political legitimacy and on all the conservative virtues. One effect of this ideology was that the Japanese family system, especially that of the samurai, was closely integrated into Tokugawan society because of its subordination to the interests of the shogun or the daimyo. This harmony between the family and the state, much stronger than in China, facilitated the modernization of Japan in the nineteenth century by providing a grass-roots basis for national unity and action.

VI. EARLY RELATIONS WITH THE WEST

For a while the Tokugawa policy of preserving the status quo was threatened by the intrusion of western Europeans. The first to appear were Portuguese traders in the mid-sixteenth century, who discovered that rich profits could be made in commerce between China and Japan. Because of raids by Japanese pirates, the Ming emperors had banned all trade with Japan. The Portuguese quickly stepped into the void and prospered handsomely, exchanging Chinese gold and silk for Japanese silver and copper. These merchants combined missionary enterprise with their commercial activities. Francis Xavier and other Jesuit fathers landed in 1549 and were allowed to preach among the masses of the people. They were unusually successful, apparently because their revivalist methods of proselytism satisfied the emotional needs of the downtrodden peasantry.

With the advent of the Tokugawa in 1603, Dutch traders, and a few British, were active in Japan alongside the Portuguese. The intense rivalry among these Europeans gave the Japanese a new freedom of action. They could now move against the missionaries without fear of losing the commerce. And they did want to curb the missionaries, whose success they feared was undermining the traditional Japanese society. Accordingly, Ieyasu decreed in 1614 that all missionaries must leave, and their converts, who by now numbered 300,000, must renounce their faith. This order was ruthlessly enforced. As a control measure, converts were forced to belong to a Buddhist temple, and many were executed for refusing. Missionaries also were martyred, but it was often difficult to distinguish between commercial and religious activities. The Japanese therefore went a step further and in 1624 banned all Spaniards, since they had been the most aggressive and defiant. In 1637 all Portuguese also were forced to depart, leaving only the Dutch, who had never shown any interest in propagating Christianity. Henceforth the Dutch were the only Europeans allowed to carry on trade, but only under severely restricted conditions on the Deshima islet in Nagasaki harbor. The isolationist policy was extended in 1636 to Japanese subjects, who were prohibited from going abroad on penalty of death. Over two centuries of seclusion had begun for Japan.

The policy of excluding all foreign influences and freezing the internal status quo was designed to perpetuate the Tokugawa dominance. In practice it proved extraordinarily effective. Japan was reunified and subjected to a centralized political control as thorough and as efficient as in any European state before the French Revolution. But a heavy price was paid for this security and stability. Japan did not have the transformation and rejuvenation of historical movements that western Europe did during this period. There was no ending of feudalism, no Renaissance or Reformation—or Counter-Reformation—and no overseas expansion. For the Japanese, as for the Chinese, the price of two centuries of comforting seclusion was institutional and technological backwardness. This became apparent, more quickly to the Japanese than to the Chinese, when the Europeans forcibly broke into the hermit world of east Asia in the mid-nineteenth century.

SUGGESTED READINGS

Useful annotated bibliographies are provided by the Service Center for Teachers of History of the American Historical Association: J. W. Hall, *Japanese History* (1961); C. O. Hucker, *Some Approaches to China's Past* (1973); and J. K. Fairbank, *New Views of China's Tradition and Modernization* (1968). Source materials on the culture of east Asia are available in W. T. de Bary et al., *Source of Chinese Tradition* (Columbia University, 1960); and R. Tsunoda et al., *Sources of the Japanese Tradition* (Columbia University, 1958).

An authoritative study of all east Asia is by E. O. Reischauer and J. K. Fairbank, *East Asia: Tradition and Civilization*, rev. ed. (Houghton Mifflin, 1978). Standard general histories of China are by W. Rodzinski, *The Walled Kingdom: A History of China from Antiquity to the Present* (Free Press, 1984); and C. O. Hucker, *China's Imperial Past: An Introduction to Chinese History and Culture* (Stanford University, 1975). Noteworthy is M. Elvin, *The Pattern of the Chinese Past* (Stanford University, 1973), which analyzes why medieval China's flair for technology did not lead to an industrial revolution. Comparable histories of Japan are by E. O. Reischauer, *Japan: The Story of a Nation*, rev. ed. (Knopf, 1970); G. B. Sansom, *Japan, A Short Cultural History*, rev. ed. (Prentice Hall, 1944), and the same author's definitive *A History of Japan*, 3 vols. (Stanford University, 1958–1964).

Finally, for the initial contact between east Asia and the West, see the multivolume work by D. F. Lach, *Asia in the Making of Europe* (University of Chicago, 1965 ff.); W. Franke, *China and the West* (Blackwell, 1967); G. F. Hudson, *Europe and China: A Study of Their Relations from Earliest Times to 1800* (Beacon, 1961); C. R. Boxer, *Fidalgos in the Far East, 1550–1770* (Martinus Nijhoff, 1948); C. R. Boxer, *The Christian Century in Japan, 1549–1650* (University of California, 1951); and J. D. Spence, *The Memory Palace of Matteo Ricci* (Viking, 1984), which provides a fascinating juxtaposition of two cultures, through the experiences of Ricci.

Expanding Civilization of the West: Renaissance and Reformation

Men can do all things if they will.

Leon Battista Alberti

For the work of God cannot be received and honored by any works, but by faith alone.

Martin Luther

. . . by an eternal and immutable counsel God has once and for all determined both whom He would admit to salvation, and whom He would condemn to destruction.

John Calvin

In the late Middle Ages, a curious and fateful development occurred in the Eurasian world. On the one hand, Islamic and Confucian empires were becoming increasingly ossified and were withdrawing into themselves. On the other hand, the western tip of Eurasia was experiencing an unprecedented and thoroughgoing transformation. Far-reaching changes were taking place in almost all phases of west European life. The end result was the emergence of a new type of dynamic, expansionist civilization—modern civilization, which was qualitatively different from the traditional agrarian-based civilizations of the rest of Eurasia and, for that matter, of the rest of the globe. Thus began what is now termed the process of modernization, which has persisted at an accelerating tempo to the present day and which has determined the course of modern world history.

I. MODERNIZATION

Economists define modernization as the process by which humans have increased their control over their physical environment as a means to increasing per capita output. Sociologists and anthropologists point out other features of modernization, including the awakening and activation of the masses, more interest in the present

305

and the future than in the past, a tendency to view human affairs as understandable rather than as manipulated by supernatural forces, and, until recent years, a faith in the beneficence of science and technology.

From the viewpoint of world history the significance of this modernization process is that it led inexorably to European domination of the globe. The reason is that modernization provided the Europeans not only with superior economic and military power but also with superior sociopolitical cohesion and dynamism. For example, a handful of British merchants and soldiers were able to conquer and rule the great Indian subcontinent more because of its sociopolitical fragility than because of British military technology. Conversely, it is significant that there never has been any speculation about the possibility of a reverse course of events—the landing in England of Indian soldiers and merchants with the designs for trade and booty that had motivated the English nabobs. The notion that Indians might have been able to do in England what Robert Clive and Warren Hastings did in India seems so preposterous as never to be considered even as a remote possibility. But it is preposterous precisely because of the difference between English and Indian societies—the latter hopelessly fragmented, with an infinitely greater gulf between rulers and ruled than in the former. Whereas Clive and Hastings had been able to play off Moslems against Hindus, prince against prince, and local potentates against imperial officials, while the peasant masses remained inert in their villages, any Indian counterpart of Clive and Hastings doubtless would have encountered a united front of Protestants and Catholics and of government and citizens, including the gentry, the townspeople, and the peasants.

Such was the chasm, so fateful for world history, separating traditional societies from those that had undergone modernization. Furthermore, this modernization was not a one-shot affair. It continues to the present day and at an ever faster pace. In late medieval and early modern times, as we shall note in this chapter and the following one, modernization comprised the Renaissance and Reformation, economic expansion, emerging capitalism, state building, and overseas enterprise. These devel-

opments set off a chain reaction in the form of the great scientific, industrial, and successive political revolutions (Chapters 26 and 27) that have molded human history from the seventeenth century to the present.

II. RENAISSANCE

The term *Renaissance* is polemical. It means new birth or revival and was coined by fifteenth-century intellectuals who believed that their age represented the rebirth of classical culture following an intervening "age of darkness," as they termed the medieval period. This interpretation was accepted through the nineteenth century, but historians today no longer consider it to have been a case of medieval pitch darkness against Renaissance dazzling light. The fact is that interest in the classics was by no means completely absent during the Middle Ages, and conversely, certain characteristics associated with medievalism were very much in evidence during the Renaissance. So modern historians, although not discarding the familiar term, now define the Renaissance as connoting not a sharp break or turning point but rather an age of transition from medieval to modern civilization— roughly from 1350 to 1600.

The Renaissance began first in Italy and hence reflected the conditions and values of contemporary Italian society. This was a bustling urban society based on flourishing industries and on the profitable commerce between western Europe and the wealthy Byzantine and Islamic empires. The Italians were the middlemen in this commerce and prospered accordingly. By about 1400 the Venetian merchant fleet was made up of 300 "large ships," 3,000 ships of less than 100 tons, and 45 galleys, manned in all by some 28,000 men. Venetian shipyards employed an additional 6,000 carpenters and other workers. Comparable activity was to be found in other Italian cities such as Florence, Genoa, Pisa, and Rome. These cities were dominated by the great merchant families who controlled politics as well as trade and crafts. These families were the patrons of Renaissance artists and writers. Their needs, interests, and tastes colored the Renaissance cultural revival even though the patrons also included ducal families

The true "Renaissance man"—Leonardo da Vinci. Painter, sculptor, inventor, Leonardo demonstrated how far ahead of his time he truly was with his Study of the Human Body, *1492.*

such as the Sforza of Milan, as well as popes such as Nicholas V, Pius II, Julius II, and Leo X. This explains the secularism and humanism of the Renaissance—its concern with this world rather than the hereafter and its focus on pagan classics rather than Christian theology.

At the center of most Renaissance art and literature was the person—the new Renaissance person who was the molder of his or her own destiny rather than the plaything of supernatural forces. People did not need to be preoccupied with supernatural forces; rather, the purpose of life was to develop one's innate potentialities. "Men can do all things if they will," wrote Leon Battista Alberti (1404–1472), and his own attainments abundantly validated this maxim. This Florentine patrician was an architect, mathe-

matician, and archeologist, as well as playwright; poet; art critic; organist; singer; and, in his youth, a well-known runner, wrestler, and mountain climber.

The secularism and individualism of the Renaissance were reflected in its scholarship and education. The so-called father of Renaissance literature, Francesco Petrarca, or Petrarch (1304–1374), stressed the value of the classics as a means for self-improvement and a guide to social action. Likewise, the new boarding schools of the Renaissance trained not priests but the sons of merchants. The curriculum emphasized classical studies and physical exercise and was designed to educate the students to live well and happily and to function as responsible citizens.

The Renaissance spirit is most strikingly expressed in its art. Since the church no longer was the sole patron, artists were encouraged to turn to subjects other than the traditional biblical themes. Giotto (1276—1337) marked the transition in painting to naturalism. This trend was carried much further by Masaccio (1401–1428), who mastered the distinctive Renaissance invention of perspective. In contrast to medieval painting, that of the Renaissance projected light and shadow and gave the appearance of depth to figures and scenes.

By the mid-fifteenth century Italian Renaissance painting attained its maturity. In Florence, Masaccio was followed by Sandro Botticelli (1444–1510) and by the versatile genius Leonardo da Vinci (1452–1519), who was a sculptor, musician, architect, and engineer as well as painter. As such, da Vinci was the personification of the "new Renaissance person." His seventy-two-page notebook, known as the Codex Hammer, was sold in London on November 15, 1994, for $30.8 million. In this manuscript he speculated on why the sky is blue and why fossils are found on mountaintops. He also predicted the invention of the submarine and the steam engine.

About 1550, after two centuries of sparkling achievement, the Italian Renaissance began to wane. One reason for the decline was the French invasion of 1494, which precipitated decades of war that involved the various European powers and left the Italian peninsula devastated. More basic in the long run was the economic blow suffered when Vasco da Gama sailed into Calicut Harbor, India, on May 22, 1498. This ended the profitable monopoly that the Italians had enjoyed as the middlemen in the trade between western Europe and the East. In four years (1502–1505), the Venetians were able to obtain an average of only 1 million English pounds of spices a year at Alexandria, whereas in the last years of the fifteenth century they had averaged 3.5 million pounds. Conversely, Portuguese spice imports rose from 224,000 pounds in 1501 to an average of 2,300,000 in the four years from 1503 to 1506.

More serious than this commercial decline was the industrial. For centuries Italy had exported manufactured goods, especially textiles, to northern Europe and the Near East, and also had derived substantial revenues from banking and shipping services. But by the late sixteenth century the British, French, and Dutch had surpassed the Italians, who were hampered by restricting guild regulations, high taxes and labor costs, and failure to adapt goods to changing tastes. Thus the average annual production of woolens in Florence was 30,000 cloths between 1560 and 1580, but only 13,000 between 1590 and 1600, and 6,000 by 1650. Likewise, Venice was producing an average of 20,000 to 30,000 cloths about 1600, but only 2,000 by 1700. This gap between Italy and the northern European countries was further widened by the growing importance of colonial trade, from which the Italian cities, lacking overseas possessions, were excluded.

To use modern terminology, Italy, which had been the developed part of Europe during the Middle Ages, now became the underdeveloped. It was Italy that henceforth exported raw materials (oil, wine, grain, wool, and raw silk) to northern Europe in return for manufactured goods. This meant that cities and their grandi no longer were dominant in Italy, their primacy being replaced by that of landed proprietors of a feudal character. Thus the economic foundations of the Renaissance crumbled.

III. RENAISSANCE LEGACY

The Renaissance was not an exclusively Italian phenomenon. Its innovations spread to northern Europe in the sixteenth century. The instruments of diffusion were Italian diplomats and generals employed by northern monarchs and the printing press, which speeded up the circulation of books and ideas. In the process of transmission northward the Renaissance changed somewhat in character. Whereas in Italy it had manifested itself primarily in art and literature, in the north it found expression more in religion and morals. But this was by no means exclusively so, as evident in the works of German painters such as Albrecht Dürer (1471–1528) and Hans Holbein the Younger (1497–1543), and of Flemish painters such as the Van Eycks and Peter Breughel. Breughel was the most unorthodox and socially conscious of the northern artists. Turning away from the tradi-

The printing press made possible the diffusion of Renaissance learning. But no book stimulated thought more at this time than did the Bible. *With Gutenberg's publication of a printed* Bible *in 1454, scholars gained access to a dependable, standardized text, so that Scripture could be discussed and debated as never before.*

tional themes of his predecessors—religious subjects and portraits of merchant families amid their luxurious surroundings—he focused on scenes from everyday peasant life. He also used his art to combat Spanish rule in the Netherlands, as in his painting *The Massacre of the Innocents*, depicting Spanish soldiers slaughtering women and children.

Printing was particularly influential in northern Europe because literacy was more widespread there than in the southern and eastern regions of Europe. The flood of printed matter certainly fomented popular agitation concerning political and religious issues, thereby contributing substantially to the Reformation and the ensuing religious and dynastic wars. Printing also stimulated the development of national schools of literature during this early modern period. Luther's translation of the Bible provided the basis for modern literary German. Likewise, the King James Bible and the plays of Shakespeare (1564–1616) laid the foundation for modern English literature. In Spain, Miguel de Cervantes (1547–1616) made the same contribution to the national language with his novel *Don Quixote*. And in France, this was the role of François Rabelais (c. 1490–1553) and Michel de Montaigne (1533–1592). The significance of

such literary endeavors was implicitly recognized in 1635 when the Académie Française was established for the purpose of officially defining the vocabulary and grammar of the national language.

In conclusion, what is the significance of the Renaissance in the perspective of world history? It is apparent that new emphasis on persons and on what they could accomplish obviously was more conducive to overseas expansion than the preceding medieval outlook. On the other hand, this point can easily be exaggerated and needs serious modification. The fact is that Renaissance Europe was not science-oriented. The leading figures tended to be more aesthetic and philosophical than objective and skeptical. They retained in various degrees certain medieval patterns of thought. They persisted in admiring and believing the incredible and the fantastic. They continued to seek the philosopher's stone that would convert other metals into gold. They still believed in astrology and confused it with astronomy.

The Iberian pioneers of overseas expansion definitely were not "Renaissance men." Prince Henry the Navigator, for example, was described by his contemporaries as a rigid, pious, and chivalrous ascetic rather than as a humanist.

Although a generous patron of sailors and cartographers, he was not interested in learning and the arts. The story of a school of astronomy and mathematics that he allegedly supported at Sagres is a myth. Thus the stimulation of rapidly widening "new intellectual horizons" explains less about the origins of European expansion before 1500 than it does about the impetus and irresistible power that that explosion of knowledge provided after 1600. Indeed, European expansion was vastly important in its own right. The fact remains that there was an intellectual ferment in western Europe and that it had no counterpart in the rest of Eurasia. This is a fundamental difference of enormous significance.

In the Ottoman Empire, for example, the Moslem medressehs, or colleges, emphasized theology, jurisprudence, and rhetoric at the expense of astronomy, mathematics, and medicine. The graduates of these schools were uninformed about what was being done in the West and quite uninterested in finding out. No Moslem Turk could believe that a Christian infidel could teach him anything of value. Now and then, a rare, far-sighted individual warned of the dangers of the intellectual iron curtain that separated the Ottoman Empire from neighboring Christendom. One of the voices was Katib Chelebi, the famous Turkish bibliographer, encyclopedist, and historian who lived in the first half of the seventeenth century. Coming from a poor family, he was unable to obtain a formal higher education. This was to be a blessing in disguise. He was spared the superficial, hairsplitting specialization on Moslem sacred studies that characterized Ottoman education at this time. The fact that he was self-taught explains in large part his open-mindedness toward Western learning.

One of Chelebi's works was a short naval handbook that he compiled following a disastrous defeat of the Ottoman fleet in 1656. In the preface of this work, Chelebi emphasized the need for mastering the science of geography and map making.

For men who are in charge of affairs of state, the science of geography is a matter of which knowledge is necessary. They may not be familiar with what the entire globe is like, but they ought at least to know the map of the Ottoman State and of those states adjoining it. Then, when they have to send forces on campaign, they can proceed on the basis of knowledge, and so the invasion of the enemy's land and also the protection and defense of the frontiers becomes an easier task. Taking counsel with individuals who are ignorant of that science is no satisfactory substitute, not even when such men are local veterans. Most such veterans are entirely unable to sketch the map of their own home regions.

Sufficient and convincing proof of the necessity for learning this science is the fact that the heathen, by their application to and their esteem for those branches of learning, have discovered the New World and have over-run the markets of India.[1]

Chelebi grasped the connection between Europe's intellectual advance and its overseas expansion. In his last work before his death in 1657, Chelebi warned his fellow citizens that if they did not abandon their dogmatism they would soon "be looking at the universe with the eyes of oxen." His prediction proved prophetic. The Turks remained steeped in their religious obscurantism, and like other non-Western peoples, they paid a high price. The Christian infidels with their new learning eventually became the masters not only of the New World but also of the ancient empires of Islam and Confucianism.

IV. REFORMATION IN GERMANY

The term *Reformation* is as misleading as the term *Renaissance*. Luther began as a reformer but ended as a revolutionary, driven by the logic of his basic convictions to challenge and reject the foundations of the Roman Church. Superficially, the Reformation can be interpreted as the reaction to certain abuses within the Church, including the illiteracy of many of the priests; the dissolute lives of some of the clergy, including popes; and the sale of religious offices, of dispensations (exemptions from church laws), and of indulgences (pardons for sins). Provocative as these abuses were, the fact is that they were more the pretext than the root cause of the Protestant Reformation. Indeed, at the time when the Reformation was getting under way, pious Catholics within the Church were beginning their own reform efforts to correct these conditions. To explain a basic upheaval that shattered the age-old unity of Western Christendom, it is necessary to go beyond abuses and to consider certain background historical forces that had been building up for centuries.

One was the undermining of the prestige of the papacy during the fourteenth-century "Babylonian Captivity," when soldiers of King Philip IV of France arrested Pope Boniface VIII. The arrest was followed by the transference of the papal capital to Avignon, where the popes perforce were subservient to French interests. Even more ruinous to papal prestige was the Great Schism at the end of the fourteenth century. Two popes, one in Rome and one in Avignon, each claimed to be the legitimate successor of St. Peter and excommunicated the other. Another factor behind the Reformation was the legacy of earlier heresies such as those of John Wycliffe in England and John Hus in Bohemia. The latter was burned at the stake at the Council of Constance in 1415, but his followers were still alive when Luther began preaching essentially similar doctrines a century later.

Political factors also were involved in the Reformation, namely the growth of national feeling in northern Europe and the related rise of the "New Monarchs" in various states. Both monarchs and subjects increasingly viewed the popes as foreigners with no right to meddle in national affairs or to raise revenues within national frontiers. This led to the final force behind the Reformation—the popular resentment against the taxes collected by the Church and against its great landed properties scattered throughout western Europe. The economic dispute, together with the preceding political factor, will be considered in more detail in the following chapter. Here it should be noted that the interests of the growing middle class and of the national monarchs led both to eye greedily the vast landholdings of the Church and its enormous movable wealth in the form of jewels, bullion, art objects, and luxurious furnishings.

A portrayal of Jan Hus as he was led to the stake at Constance. After his execution, his bones and ashes were scattered in the Rhine River to prevent his followers from claiming them as relics. This pen-and-ink drawing is from Ulrich von Richenthal's Chronicle of the Council of Constance *(ca. 1450).*

Martin Luther and the Wittenberg Reformers *with Elector John Frederick of Saxony (1532–1547), painted about 1543. Luther is on the far left, Philip Melanchthon in the front on the far right. [Lucas Cranach the Younger, German, 1515–1586, oil on panel, 27-5/8 x 15-5/8 in.]*

rulers were too weak to resist the powerful Church in cases of excessive exactions. One of these cases was the decision of the pope in 1517 to sell a large number of indulgences throughout Europe to pay for the repair of St. Peter's Church in Rome. The indulgence in Germany that triggered the Reformation promised absolution "from all thy sins, transgressions, and excesses, how enormous soever they may be . . . so that when you die the gates of punishment shall be shut, and the gates of the paradise of delight shall be opened. . . ." It was in protest against this "unbridled preaching of pardons" that Luther, then a priest at the University of Wittenburg, posted his ninety-five theses on the church door. Most of his propositions were not revolutionary, but he did argue that the "word of God" lay not in the doctrine of the Church but in the Bible, thereby undercutting Church authority.

Pope Leo X dismissed the incident as a "squabble among monks," but the theses were quickly translated into German and widely circulated in print. The enthusiastic popular response demonstrated that Luther had given voice to deeply felt national grievances. The ensuing public debate led Luther to spell out the revolutionary implications of his basic doctrine of justification by faith—that is, that the priestly offices and ministrations of the Church were unnecessary intermediaries between the individual and God. By the end of 1520 Luther had broken irrevocably with the Church and embraced the earlier heresies of Wycliffe and Hus as "most Christian." In October 1520 Luther burned a papal bull of excommunication, and the following year he was summoned to appear before the Imperial Diet meeting at Worms. Called on to recant, Luther refused "unless I am convinced by the testimony of the Scriptures or by clear reason." The emperor secured passage of an edict condemning the obstinate friar as a heretic, but the sympathetic Elector Fredrick of Saxony provided refuge in his castle and saved Luther from the fate of Hus.

In this place of exile Luther busied himself in the following years translating the Bible into German and building an independent German church. Emperor Charles V was unable to move decisively against the spreading heresy because he was involved in wars with the French and the

Equally coveted were the revenues flowing from the states to Rome in the form of the tithe; the funds from the sale of offices; and the innumerable fees for appeals, dispensations, and indulgences.

This combination of historical forces reached the explosion point first in Germany because that land was then a collection of over a hundred principalities—fiefs, ecclesiastical city-states, free cities, counties, and duchies—whose

Turks. By 1546 he was free of these distractions so he set out to crush the Lutheran princes and restore the unity of the church. He was encouraged in this by the pope, who provided money and troops. But the Lutherans banded together in the Schmalkaldic League and won support from the Catholic French king, who was more concerned with dynastic than religious considerations. The fighting dragged on inconclusively until the signing of the Peace of Augsburg (1555), which granted each German prince the right to select either the Catholic or Lutheran faith and to impose it on his subjects. Thus the end result of the Reformation in Germany was the roughly equal division of the country into Lutheran and Catholic states.

V. REFORMATION BEYOND GERMANY

The Peace of Augsburg opened the gates to the rising flood of heresy, or rather heresies. The settlement at Augsburg had recognized only Lutheranism as a possible alternative to the Catholic faith. But Protestantism by its very nature lent itself to a continual proliferation of new sects. Luther's fundamental doctrine of individual interpretation of the Scriptures led inevitably to different interpretations and hence to new varieties of Protestantism. In Switzerland, for example, John Calvin joined Luther in rejecting salvation by "works" but also rejected his doctrine of salvation by "faith." Instead Calvin preached predestination—each individual's fate was decreed by God before birth. "In conformity, therefore, to the clear doctrine of Scripture, we assert that by an eternal and immutable counsel God has once for all determined both whom He would admit to salvation, and whom He would condemn to destruction." Calvin differed from Luther also in requiring that the Church should actively intervene in community affairs to ensure the elimination of heresy, blasphemy, and wickedness. During his ascendancy in Geneva (1541–1564), his Consistory of Elders transformed that city into a Christian community whose austerity and holiness astonished visitors. Furthermore, the availability of printing presses enabled Calvin to make Geneva the headquarters of a proselytizing drive that profoundly affected such countries as

Bohemia, Hungary, the Netherlands, Scotland, England, and the thirteen American colonies overseas.

An entirely different form of Protestantism was that of the Anabaptists, whose religious and social radicalism earned them persecution by Catholics, Lutherans, and Calvinists alike. Carrying to its logical conclusion Luther's doctrine that every man should follow the dictates of his conscience, they demanded full religious liberty, including separation of church and state. Equally radical were their social teachings—their opposition to individual accumulation of wealth, to class or status differentiation, to military service, and to payment of taxes for war-making purposes. It is not surprising that these tenets, undermining the authority of all religious and political establishments, led to the persecution and wholesale massacre of Anabaptists throughout Europe. The Hutterites and Mennonites are their survivors who have managed to hold out to the present day.

The prevailing factor determining the religion of a state almost invariably was the decision of its prince. If he favored a break with Rome, the Reformation triumphed; if he opposed a break, the Reformation was doomed. Very substantial benefits awaited the prince who opted in favor of Protestantism. His political power increased for he became the head of his national church rather than having to accept the ecclesiastical suzerainty of the international papacy. His economic position also improved because he could confiscate Church lands and movable wealth and also check the flow of revenue to Rome. Despite these advantages of turning against the pope, as many princes remained loyal as chose to break away. One reason was the threat of attack by the imperial forces of Charles V supported by the pope. Also many princes found they could extract as many political and economic concessions from the papacy by remaining Catholic as they were likely to obtain as Protestant princes—hence the hodge-podge religious map of Europe that evolved after Luther's death.

This religious map eventually showed almost half the German states Lutheran, along with the Baltic lands of the Teutonic order and the Scandinavian kingdoms of Denmark-Norway and Sweden-Finland. In England, Henry VIII was a good Catholic in doctrinal matters and enjoyed as much control over the Catholic clergy as did the French king across the Channel. Yet Henry eventually established the independent Church of England (1534) because he was determined to divorce his wife, Catherine of Aragon. The pope could not oblige him because Catherine was the aunt of Emperor Charles V, whose army had sacked Rome a few years earlier. So Henry now became the head of the new Anglican church, and to ensure the support of his gentry, he gave them the expropriated monastery lands. But as long as he was alive, the new church remained staunchly Catholic in doctrine and ritual, the only innovation being the translation of the Bible into English. Henry's successors introduced changes in accord with their individual inclinations—Edward VI (1547–1553) moving far toward Protestantism, Mary (1553–1558) reverting to Catholicism, and Elizabeth (1558–1603) settling on a moderate Protestantism.

In the Netherlands (present-day Holland and Belgium), a combination of religious and political issues led to protracted war. The majority of the population in the northern Dutch provinces had become Calvinistic, which caused friction with the devout Catholic sovereign, Philip II of Spain. Political differences also were involved, the Netherlands challenging Philip's interference in what they considered to be their domestic affairs, and resenting also his heavy taxes and commercial restrictions. In 1566 Dutch resistance flared into what became the first modern revolution for national independence. The revolution in turn became an international war when Queen Elizabeth of England went to the aid of the Dutch rebels. Philip responded by sending his Invincible Armada of 132 ships northward in 1588. But the more maneuverable English ships forced the armada northward around Scotland and southward back to Spain—a defeated and battered remnant of the original expedition. The war continued its bloody course until a compromise settlement in 1609 recognized the independence of the northern provinces as the Dutch Republic, whereas the southern Belgian provinces remained under Spanish rule.

Meanwhile Calvinism had been spreading in France, where its adherents were known as Huguenots. The dynasty was not tempted to

The Saint Bartholemew's Day Massacre, as depicted by the contemporary Protestant painter François Dubois. In this notorious event, 3,000 Protestants were slaughtered in Paris and an estimated 20,000 others died throughout France. The massacre transformed the religious struggle in France from a contest for political power into a war for survival between Protestants and Catholics.

join its Protestant subjects because Francis I had obtained, by the Concordat of Bologna (1516), almost complete control over the Church offices and revenues in his realm. His successor, Henry II (1547–1559), severely persecuted the Huguenots. Mere ownership of a Bible was enough to condemn a subject as a heretic. Henry's death gave the Huguenots an opportunity, as neither the Queen Mother, Catherine de Medici nor her weak sons enjoyed the popular support that Elizabeth did in England. Despite Catherine's efforts for a compromise, the country was polarized between the growing, dynamic Huguenots and the large Catholic majority. The ensuing religious war culminated in the St. Bartholomew's Day Massacre (August 24, 1572), when thousands of Huguenots were massacred throughout the country. Even this slaughter did not subdue the new faith, the struggle dragging on with the Huguenots receiving help from Protestant groups in England, Holland, and Germany, whereas the Catholics received men and money from King Philip of Spain. Peace was not restored until 1598, when Henry IV issued the Edict of Nantes guaranteeing freedom of conscience to the Huguenots. By granting legal recognition and status to two religions in the same state, this settlement represented a turning point in European religious history comparable to the Augsburg Treaty that allowed a prince to choose between two religions.

VI. CATHOLIC REFORMATION

The Catholic Reformation formerly was known as the Counter-Reformation, but historians now recognize it as being more than simply an anti-Protestant movement. Its roots go back to pre-Luther times, so that the Catholic Reformation was a religious reform movement similar to the Protestant Reformation. In the late fifteenth and early sixteenth centuries, Catholic leaders in various countries had sought to correct abuses and regenerate spiritual values. In the process they organized new religious orders, such as the Capuchins, to revive Catholic piety and promote social service. But these early reformers, who tended to be contemplative and aristocratic, failed to arouse the masses or to win support in high Church circles in Rome. The Catholic

Reformation did not become a dynamic and effective movement until the seriousness of Luther's challenge in Germany became clear. The reformers within the Church had hesitated to launch a counter movement against the Protestants for fear of irrevocably splitting Western Christendom. And the popes for long ignored Luther, viewing him as another of the long line of critics and heretics who in the past had always been suppressed or won back to the fold. Not until Pope Paul III (1534–1549) and his three successors who presided in Rome until the end of the sixteenth century did the papacy appreciate the significance of Protestantism and take appropriate steps.

The two measures of Paul III that proved the most significant in shaping the course and character of the Catholic Reformation were his summoning of the Council of Trent, which met intermittently from 1545 to 1563, and his approval of the founding of the Jesuit order, the Society of Jesus, in 1540. The main achievements of the Council of Trent were the reaffirmation of traditional Catholic doctrine in firmly anti-Protestant terms and the adoption of practical measures to eliminate abuses and restore Church discipline. These measures included a ban on the sale of indulgences, the prohibition of any bishop from holding more than one benefice, the stipulation that every diocese should establish a seminary to train priests, and the publication of an *Index* of books that Catholics would be forbidden to read.

The Jesuit order was the creation of the Spanish Basque nobleman Ignatius Loyola (1491– 1556). While convalescing from a serious war wound he read various religious tracts that induced a profound spiritual crisis. He resolved to turn his back on his past life of philandering and brawling and to devote himself to serving the Lord. With a group of like-minded young men he organized the Society of Jesus along military lines. Its members did not lead the contemplative lives of earlier Catholic reformers. Rather, they viewed themselves as soldiers of Christ, and they strictly followed Loyola's first rule in his Spiritual Exercises, requiring unquestioning obedience to the "Hierarchical Church."

It was the discipline and militancy of these Jesuits that ensured implementation of the reforms of the Council of Trent. Many members served as agents of the Inquisition, which had been founded in 1542 to root out heresy wherever it was discovered. Others established schools that trained a new generation of priests and laymen with the theological certainty and confidence that had made the Protestant heretics so formidable. Jesuit schoolmen and diplomats were largely responsible for the stamping out of Protestantism in countries such as Austria, Bavaria, and Poland, where it had gained many converts. In addition to combating Christian heretics in Europe, the Jesuits extended their operations all over the world to spread the gospel among the heathen in Asia, Africa, and the Americas. The nature and extent of their activities are indicated by the careers of such men as St. Francis Xavier in Japan, Matteo Ricci in China, Robert de Nobili in India, and Father Jacques Marquette in America.

VII. REFORMATION LEGACY

The legacy of the Reformation is ambiguous. It engendered doctrinal dissension and intolerance, which culminated in a succession of bloody religious wars. But the resulting fragmentation of Western Christendom compelled the contending sects to accept the fact that the hegemony of any universal church was not feasible—hence the gradual acceptance and implementation of religious toleration, a process so slow and contested that it is not yet fully complete. The Reformation was equally ambiguous concerning the status of the individual. Luther championed individual interpretation of the Scriptures, but when this led to the radicalism of the Anabaptists and to peasant revolts, he called on the civil authorities to destroy the "murdering, thieving hordes." Yet the emphasis on the reading of the Bible did lead to greater literacy, which opened doors to books and ideas other than religious.

The Reformation was ambiguous also in its effect on the status of women. In certain respects the Reformation enabled women to move forward. Protestant leaders rejected the medieval Catholic belief in the moral superiority of celibacy. Instead they considered married life desirable for three reasons: procreation of children, sexual satisfaction, and mutual help and comfort between partners. This attitude toward marriage and family encouraged the new idea of a single standard of morality for men and women, and also the equally novel idea of the right of a prospective bride or groom to veto a proposed marriage. Of course the transition from the old to the new was slow and erratic. Protestant theologians railed against adultery by men as well as women, but practice lagged far and long behind theory. Also young men were considered to be foolish "poor greenheads" if they did not select a wife who was not only compatible but "fit," a concept that encompassed the practical considerations usually emphasized by parents.

The principal Protestant leaders never considered or undertook a systematic reappraisal of the status of women. They stressed mutual love and respect between husband and wife, but they also took for granted the husband's primacy in the family. Luther made this quite clear: "Men have broad and large chests, and small narrow hips, and more understanding than the women, who have but small and narrow breasts, and broad hips, to the end they should remain at home, sit still, keep house, and bear and bring up children."[2]

Very different from mainline Protestantism were the radical sects such as the Lollards, Anabaptists, and Levellers. They favored free divorce and allowed women to participate in church government and to preach, and some even championed sexual freedom for both women and men. These sectarians were ahead of their time, for not only political but also technological reasons. The English Leveller leader, Gerrard Winstanley, conceded that sexual freedom outside the family left the mother and children vulnerable, "for the man will be gone and leave them, and regard them no more than other women . . . after he hath had his pleasure. Therefore you women beware. . . . By seeking their own freedom they embondage others."[3] Winstanley was acknowledging the fact that before the advent of effective birth control, sexual freedom amounted to freedom only for men.

Finally, as far as the immediate legacy of the Reformation was concerned, it shattered the universal medieval Church into a large number of local territorial churches—some national, some princely, some provincial, and some confined to a single city. The common feature of all these local churches was their control by secular rulers. Regardless of whether the church remained Catholic in doctrine or adhered to one of the Protestant faiths, it was the secular authority that controlled ecclesiastical appointments and church finances. The immediate and decisive legacy of the Reformation was the transfer of power from church to state. In this sense, the Reformation represents a stage in the evolution of the modern nation-state—the subject of the following chapter.

World (Beacon Press, 1966); and E. I. Eisentein, *The Printing Press as an Agent of Change: Communications and Cultural Transformations in Early Modern Europe*, 2 vols. (Columbia University, 1979).

The status of European women during these centuries is summarized in S. M. Wyntjes, "Women in the Reformation Era," in R. Bridenthal and C. Koonz, eds., *Becoming Visible: Women in European History* (Houghton Mifflin, 1977), pp. 165–191; and analyzed in detail in the two studies by R. Bainton, *Women of the Reformation in Germany and Italy* and *Women of the Reformation in France and England* (Augsburg Publishing House, 1971 and 1973).

SUGGESTED READINGS

Standard general histories of this period are W. K. Ferguson, *Europe in Transition: 1300–1500* (Houghton Mifflin, 1962); E. Breisach, *Renaissance Europe 1300–1517* (Macmillan, 1973); and for a global perspective: J. L. Abu-Lughod, *Before European Hegemony: The World System A.D. 1250–1350* (Oxford University, 1989). E. Troeltsch, *Protestantism and Progress: A Historical Study of the Relation of Protestantism to the Modern*

NOTES

1. Cited in manuscript by L. V. Thomas, "Ottoman Awareness of Europe, 1650–1800."
2. Cited by S. M. Wyntjes, "Women in the Reformation Era," in R. Bridenthal and C. Koonz, eds., *Becoming Visible: Women in European History* (Houghton Mifflin, 1977), p. 174.
3. Cited by C. Hill, *The World Turned Upside Down* (Viking, 1972), p. 257.

Expanding Civilization of the West: Economic Growth and State Building

. . . the chief glory of the later Middle Ages was not its cathedrals or its epics or its scholasticism: it was the building for the first time in history of a complex civilization which rested not on the backs of sweating slaves or coolies but primarily on non-human power.

Lynn White, Jr.

Therefore it is necessary for a prince, who wishes to maintain himself, to learn how not to be good, and to use this knowledge and not use it, according to the necessity of the case.

Niccolo Machiavelli

The Renaissance and Reformation, as we saw in the preceding chapter, contributed to the modernizing of western European civilization. During these times literacy increased and there was much intellectual ferment. There was a mass awakening and a degree of participation unequaled in other regions of Eurasia. A more direct contribution to the modernizing process was made by the concurrent economic expansion and state building. These provided Europe with the resources and dynamism necessary for the fateful expansion overseas. This expansion, which has molded world history to the present day, did not occur simply because Columbus sailed westward and

stumbled on the new world. The Vikings also had stumbled on North America in the eleventh century and for about a hundred years had unsuccessfully tried to maintain settlements there. By contrast, Columbus was followed by people from all countries of Europe in a massive and overwhelming penetration of both North and South America. The difference in the reaction between the eleventh and fifteenth centuries suggests that certain developments had occurred in the intervening half-millennium that made Europe able and anxious to expand overseas. These developments included economic expansion and state building.

I. EXPANDING ECONOMY

Europe's economy did not grow uninterrupted during the medieval period. There was a steady rise from 900 to 1300, but then came the four-teenth-century slump, brought on by a combi-nation of factors: a series of crop failures and famines, especially during 1315 and 1316; the Black Death, which carried off between one-third and two-thirds of the urban populations when it first struck in 1348 and 1349 and which recurred periodically thereafter for generations; and the Hundred Years' War between England and France and other conflicts in Germany and Italy. Shortly after 1400, however, a revival set in, and the trend from then on was generally upward.

Apart from the fourteenth-century decline, then, western Europe had fairly steady economic growth after the early medieval centuries. One reason for the advance was the cessation of inva-sions after 1000, with the ending of the Magyar and Viking attacks. Freedom from invasion was most significant, for it saved western Europe from the devastation suffered in eastern Europe from the series of onslaughts that lasted until the defeat of the Turks at the end of the seven-teenth century. This also explains in part the marked increase of population in central and western Europe between the tenth and four-teenth centuries. Population in those regions grew about 50 percent, a rate of increase that seems insignificant today but that was unmatched at the time in any equivalent world area. The demographic spurt stimulated improvements in agriculture to support the growth of population, and the increased food supply in turn made possible further population increase.

Europe's rising agricultural output was obtained in two ways. One was through inten-sive development—through improved methods of cultivation. One outstanding improvement was the gradual adoption from the eighth centu-ry onward of the three-field system of farming. The three-field system raised productivity sub-stantially, since only a third of the land was allowed to lie fallow instead of half. More effec-tive use of horsepower also helped increase agri-cultural output. In antiquity the horse had been of little use on the farm because the yoke then

The three-field system of farming improved efficiency and increased production from the eighth century onward.

used strangled the horse if it pulled too hard. Moreover, without nailed shoes the horse often injured its hoofs and became useless. By the tenth century, however, Europe had developed the horse collar, which rests on the horse's shoulders and does not choke the neck. In addi-tion, the horseshoe was invented and also the tandem harness, which allows more than one pair of horses to pull a load. The net result was that the horse, faster and more efficient com-pared to the ox, became an essential source of power in farming operations.

Europe's agricultural output was also raised through extensive development. Areas were opened up that had not been farmed before. It is startling but true that in the twelfth century only about half the land of France, a third of the land of Germany, and a fifth of the land of England were under cultivation. The rest was forest, swamp, waste. All around the edges of the small, tilled regions were larger, untilled areas open for settlement. Into these vacant spaces the European peasants streamed, preparing the way for the plow and hoe by clearing forests, burning brushwood, and draining swamps. The peasants not only cultivated the unused lands in their midst but also migrated eastward into the vast underpopulated areas of eastern and southern Europe. Just as the United States had its westward movement to the Pacific Ocean, so Europe had its eastward movement to the Russian border (see map of Expansionism of the Medieval West, p. 240.)

The growth of population and of agriculture stimulated a corresponding growth of commerce and cities. From new farm lands, surplus food was shipped back to more densely populated western areas, which in return provided the tools and the manufactured goods needed by frontier regions. Thus commerce flourished and towns grew up, especially along the Baltic coast. This economic growth is very important. It represents the beginning of the rise of northwestern Europe, a trend that later helped the British and the Dutch to overshadow the Spaniards and the Portuguese throughout the world.

Commerce was growing not only within Europe but also between Europe and the outside world. Here, again, growth began when the Viking raids stopped, ending the terror that had dominated European coasts from the Arctic to Sicily in the ninth and tenth centuries. Another impetus from the eleventh century onward was provided by the Crusades. The tens of thousands of Europeans who had participated in the expeditions returned with an appetite for the strange and luxurious commodities they had seen and enjoyed abroad. Also, the Crusades enabled the Europeans to snatch the Mediterranean from the Moslems and to make it a great trade route between East and West, as it had been in ancient times. A third reason for the growth of international trade was the establishment in the thirteenth century of the Mongol Empire, which imposed unity on most of the vast Eurasian landmass. European traders, especially the Italians, took advantage of the peace, security, and well-serviced routes, and traded almost directly with the Orient.

The extension and intensification of commercial relations had important repercussions. Europe's economy became much more geared to international trade than did the economies of the more self-sufficient empires of the East. Both the consumer and the producer in Europe became accustomed to, and dependent on, foreign commodities and foreign markets. As populations increased, the scale of operations also increased. The demographic pressure, together with the spur of competition between nations and city-states, drove merchants to seek new sources, new routes, new markets. Their competitive attitude was very different from that of the contemporary Chinese, who voyaged several thousand miles for completely noneconomic reasons (see Section V, this chapter). Since the Chinese were quite uninterested in trade, they brought back to their self-contained homeland such curiosities as giraffes for the pleasure of their emperor. For obvious geographic reasons, Europe was far from self-contained. It had urgent need for spices and other foreign products, which, together with the burgeoning economic activity and vitality, eventually put European ships on every ocean and European merchants in every port.

II. DEVELOPMENT OF TECHNOLOGY

While its economy expanded, Europe's technology also developed and provided the materials and techniques necessary for expansion. It would have been physically impossible for Europeans to reach India or the Americas without adequate ships and navigational instruments. The basis for their technological success in these areas is the steady, unspectacular, but immensely significant progress in improving tools and techniques that was made during the medieval period.

As Lynn White, Jr., has observed, the "chief glory of the later Middle Ages" was its unprecedented development of "non-human power." Examples were the water mills and windmills that were developed and used for grinding cereal, cutting wood, and draining swamps and

NGRAVING BY THEODORE DE BRY, 1594, LIBRARY OF CONGRESS

Shipbuilding in 1500—an example of the technological advances that increased European expansion.

mines. Other useful inventions included the carpenter's plane, the crank, the wheelbarrow, the spinning wheel, and the canal lock. Indeed, the Greeks and the Romans, despite their lofty achievements in philosophy and art, did less in a thousand years to relieve human toil through machine power than the medieval Europeans did in a few centuries.

An interesting illustration of the technological progress made by the western Europeans during the medieval period is found in a letter written in 1444 by a Greek scholar, Cardinal Bessarion. Bessarion, who had lived many years in Rome, was impressed by the advanced state of handicrafts in Italy. So he wrote to Constantine Paleologos, then ruler of the autonomous Byzantine province of Morea, and suggested that "four or eight young men" should be sent surreptitiously to Italy to learn Italian craft skills. They should also learn Italian "so as to be conversant with what is said." Bessarion was particularly impressed by the waterdriven sawmills that eliminated hand labor. He wrote about "wood cut by automatic saws, millwheels moved as

quickly and as neatly as can be." He referred to water-driven bellows when he mentioned that "in the smelting and separation of metals they have leather bellows which are distended and relaxed untouched by any hand, and separate the metal from the useless and earthy matter that may be present." Bessarion also reported that in Italy "one may easily acquire knowledge of the making of iron, which is so useful and necessary to Man." The significance of this testimony is obvious. The technological advances made by medieval western Europe had been of such magnitude that now, for the first time, an Easterner was recommending that pupils should be sent to the West to learn the "practical arts."[1]

As far as the overseas expansion of Europe was concerned, the most significant technological advances were those in shipbuilding, in the instruments and techniques of navigation, and in naval armaments. Hand in hand with these advances went advances in the art of navigation. The most important contributions in this field came from the Mediterranean. The Chinese appear to have possessed a magnetic compass, but it is not certain that the Europeans acquired it from them or from Arab intermediaries. In any case, the compass was the most useful single instrument for navigators, but it was supplemented by several others. The astrolabe, a graduated brass circle for estimating the altitude of heavenly bodies, was known before 800 but was first used in Western navigation by the Portuguese about 1485. It was an expensive instrument and was soon replaced by the simpler and cheaper quadrant. The determination of longitude presented more of a problem. A rough estimate could be gained by means of an hourglass, but precise reckoning had to await Galileo's discovery of the principles of the pendulum in the seventeenth century. Navigators were also aided by compilations of nautical information and by maps. The portolani of the Mediterranean seamen were the first true maps, furnished with accurate compass bearings and explicit details concerning coastlines and harbors.

When the Europeans reached the highly developed and militarily powerful countries of south and east Asia, their one decisive advantage was the superiority of their naval armament. In the first two decades of the sixteenth century the metallurgists of Flanders and Germany, and later of England, developed techniques for casting guns that were light enough to mount on ships and yet had great firing power. These new pieces, five to twelve feet long, could shoot round stones—and later cast-iron balls—that weighed five to sixty pounds and could damage a hull at a range of 300 yards. Naval tactics now shifted from boarding to broadside gunfire, and warships were redesigned so that soon they were able to carry an average of forty guns.

These developments gave the Europeans a decisive advantage and enabled them to seize and retain control of the oceans of the world. Eastern rulers hastened to arm their own ships, but their vessels were neither designed nor built for mounting guns. Before they could redesign their vessels, European naval armaments developed so rapidly that the designs of the Easterners were already obsolete. Hence the gap increased rather than narrowed, and the Westerners remained the unchallenged masters of the

Skilled workers were an integral component of the commerce of medieval towns. This scene shows the manufacture of cannons in a foundry in Florence.

seas until the epochal victory of the Japanese over the Russians at Tsushima in 1905.

As important as the European advances in marine technology was their discovery of the world wind systems. Thanks to Portuguese mariners, Columbus knew he could sail west with the trade winds, confident that further north he would find westerlies to bring him back home. Likewise, Vasco da Gama learned the basic pattern of Indian Ocean monsoons from local pilots. By 1522, when Magellan's ships returned to Spain after the first European voyage around the world, the wind system of the Pacific as well as of the Atlantic was known to the Europeans. Now they could sail all oceans with confidence.

Having made these advances in shipbuilding and in knowledge of world wind systems, the Europeans were able to exploit their advantages because of their favorable geographic location for crossing the Atlantic and reaching the treasures of the New World. Of course, West Africa also juts out into the Atlantic, as does the Iberian peninsula. But West African commerce for centuries had been directed northward across the Sahara to the Mediterranean. In East Africa the port of Sofala was engaged in overseas trade, but that trade naturally was conducted eastward across the adjacent Indian Ocean. Sofala is 3,000 miles farther away from the Americas than the Canary Islands (Columbus's jumping-off point), and China was still much more distant. So geographic location was an important factor, along with several others, in determining that Columbus should have been a European rather than an African or Asian.

III. EMERGENCE OF CAPITALISM

Because Columbus for various reasons turned out to be a European, it was Europe that experienced a powerful economic stimulus from the gold and silver that poured in from the Americas. The flow was so large that it tripled Europe's silver stock during the sixteenth century and increased the gold stock by 20 percent. In addition to this bullion windfall from the New World, Europe was further enriched by numerous overseas enterprises, so that profits poured in from the slave trade, from the spice trade, from exports to the colonies and imports from the colonies, and even from piracy. This external economic boost, combined with the internal commercial revival and technological progress noted above, led to greatly increased use of money in Europe's economy.

This monetarization undermined the feudal order that had developed after the fall of Rome. The bonds of serfdom could not be preserved indefinitely when it became known that freedom could be gained by flight to the growing towns or to the frontier lands opening eastward. The lords had to modify their demands or risk the loss of their labor supply. Serfs in western Europe increasingly paid for their land with money rather than labor, so that feudal lords became landlords and serfs became free peasants. The weakening of serfdom was a prerequisite to the expansion of Europe. It created a more fluid society that could accumulate the capital; provide the organization; and free the population needed for the work of exploration, conquest, and settlement. It is not accidental that among the European nations the degree of success in overseas enterprise was in direct ratio to the degree of liberation from the bonds of feudalism.

Likewise, use of money undermined the feudal craft and merchant guilds in the towns. The guilds, with their strict regulation of workmanship and of pricing and trading practices, were geared not to making profit but to preserving a traditional way of life. Guild members were committed to the concept of a "just price," and profiteering at the expense of a neighbor was considered unethical and definitely un-Christian. But these concepts and practices broke down with the appearance of entrepreneurs. They avoided the guilds by purchasing raw material and taking it to underemployed artisans in the countryside, who labored on a piece-work basis. The rationale of this "putting-out" system was profit rather than "just price." The entrepreneurs paid as little as possible for the material and labor, and they sold the finished product as dearly as possible to secure the maximum return on their capital investment.

Europe's economy was changed not only by the growing use of money but also by the minting of standardized coins that were acceptable everywhere and by the development of

Cosimo dé Medici (1389–1464), Florentine banker and statesman, in his lifetime the city's wealthiest man and most successful politician. This portrait is by Pontormo.

banks and of credit instruments. Florence led the way in 1252 with the gold florin, and other cities and states soon followed. Simple bills of exchange also appeared in Italy as early as the twelfth century. Gradually, mighty banking families appeared, first in Italy and later in northern Europe.

What was happening to Europe, then, was a historic shift to a fundamentally different type of economic system, the type known today as capitalism. Capitalism has been defined as "... [a] system in which the desire for profits is the driving motive and in which large accumulations of capital are employed to make profits by various elaborate and often indirect methods."[2]

The emergence of capitalism was epoch making. It affected not merely the economy but all aspects of life. Whereas in the early Middle Ages money had been peripheral and little used, by the late Middle Ages it provided energy that was responsible for Europe's future meteoric rise. No earlier societies or economic systems had been based on the notion of growth. Their aim had been only to maintain the material well-being of the past rather than to enhance it. But henceforth, with capitalism, the precise opposite was the case. Profits now were plowed back to increase the quantity of capital available for production. "Capitalizing" of profits, in the sense that surplus was converted into more capital, is the rationale behind the term *capitalism*. The new "capitalists" were not content with making a living but were driven by the urge to enlarge their assets. They did not cease their efforts when their needs for consumption were satisfied. The new "capitalist spirit" is epitomized by the statement of Jacob Fugger, the wealthiest banker of the sixteenth century, who said, "Let me earn as long as I am able."

In order to "earn," Fugger and his fellow bankers needed to be free to charge interest on money they loaned. But the medieval Church for long had denounced interest as constituting usury, a mortal sin and "a vice most odious and detestable in the sight of God." By 1548, however, some Church members were pleading for the acceptance of "moderate and acceptable usury." This modification soon gave way to the cynical attitude: "He who takes usury goes to hell; he who does not goes to the poorhouse." Given the choice of hell in afterlife, or poorhouse in the present, it is not surprising that usury won out. So it was the affluent European bankers who organized the numerous joint stock companies that won control of commerce on all oceans, garnering the ensuing profits.

These joint stock companies were the counterpart in early modern times of the multinational corporations of today. These new organizations were most effective instruments for economic mobilization and penetration. Anyone who wished to speculate with a little money could do so without risking one's whole future. The individual risked only the amount invested in company shares, and that person could not be held further liable for whatever losses the company might incur. Furthermore, there was no need for the individual investors to know or trust each other or to concern themselves with the specific conditions of the market and the policies of the company. These details of management were entrusted to directors selected for their responsibility and experience, and these directors in turn could choose dependable individuals to manage company affairs in the field. This arrangement made it attractive for all sorts of scattered individuals—a London wool merchant, a Paris storekeeper, a Harlem herring fisher, an Antwerp banker, or a Yorkshire landowner—to invest their savings in individual ventures. In this way it was possible to mobilize European capital easily and simply, and vast amounts were invested in various overseas undertakings. No Eastern merchants, limited to their own resources or those of their partners, and choosing their managers from their family

or circle of acquaintances, could hope to compete with the powerful and impersonal joint stock company. It became the instrument for the operation of European capitalism on a global scale. World commerce fell under the control of the various East India and Levant companies, the Muscovy Company, and the still-operating Hudson's Bay Company.

Thus we can see why an American historian has concluded that the most important figures in Europe's overseas expansion were not Columbus and da Gama and Magellan. Rather, they were the new entrepreneurs with capital. They were the merchants who stayed in the home ports but who were "responsible for the foundation of many of the colonies . . . who kept the colonies supplied . . . who opened new markets, sought new lands, and enriched all of Europe. . . ."[3]

The new capitalist economic system not only dominated the world economy in early modern times but it also continues to do so to the present day. The basic reason is to be found in its ruling principle: profit or perish. To avoid perishing, capitalist entrepreneurs through the centuries have maximized profit in two ways: by reducing the wages they pay their workers or by increasing their workers' productivity through improved technology. The first strategy has been much used but it can be carried only so far because workers obviously have to be paid a certain minimum amount if they are to be kept alive, healthy, and productive. The second strategy—improving technology—can be continued indefinitely. In fact, this is precisely what happened, as indicated by the constantly accelerating pace of technological innovation, strikingly evident in today's high technology. This built-in technological dynamism explains why Europe's capitalist entrepreneurs in early modern times won control of the global economy with their unceasing technological innovations and their joint stock companies, and also why today's capitalists continue to control the world economy with their biotechnology, their computers, and their multinational corporations. Just as Europe's joint stock companies a few centuries ago planted colonies in the Americas and penetrated irresistibly the markets of the Middle East and the Far East, so today the same inherent dynamism drives multinational corporations to move factories from continent to continent, to erect golden arches in scores of countries, and even to establish a 500-seat Kentucky Fried Chicken in Beijing's historic Tienanmen Square with a view of the Gate of Heavenly Peace and of Mao Tse-tung's mausoleum. The new enterprise retains its familiar slogan in Chinese—*Haodao shun shouzhi* ("So good you suck your fingers").

IV. RISE OF THE NEW MONARCHS

The emergence of capitalists in Europe was paralleled by the concurrent emergence of the "New Monarchs" who were building cohesive political structures. By the end of the fifteenth century, the trend toward national monarchies was apparent in the powerful political structures presided over by Ferdinand and Isabella in Spain (1479–1516), by Henry VIII in England (1509--1547), and by Francis I in France (1515–1547). One reason for the success of these rulers was the revolution in military technology that came with the advent of artillery. Feudal lords no longer could defy royal authority from behind their castle walls. Only national monarchs possessed the financial resources and administrative organization necessary to purchase the guns, powder, and shot and to provide the required logistical support.

Another source of power for the new monarchs was their informal alliance with the growing merchant class. From this class the monarchs obtained essential financial support and also competent and subservient officials to staff the growing state bureaucracies. In return, the consolidation of royal power aided the burghers by ending the incessant feudal wars and doing away with the crazyquilt pattern of local feudal authorities, in which each had had its own customs, laws, weights, and currencies. As late as the end of the fourteenth century there were thirty-five toll stations on the Elbe, over sixty on the Rhine, and so many on the Seine that the cost of shipping grain 200 miles down the river was half its selling price. The elimination of such domestic barriers obviously was a great boon to entrepreneurs. So was the patronage of the increasingly elaborate royal courts, which supported craftspeople and sometimes whole industries, as in the case of Gobelin tapestry and Sévres porcelain in France.

The new monarchs naturally had their own defenders and rationalizers, as do all political establishments. The best known of these was Niccolo Machiavelli (1459–1527). A product of the ruthless struggle for survival among the competing city-states of Renaissance Italy, Machiavelli viewed politics as a struggle for power in which the end justifies the means. In his book, *The Prince*, he set forth guidelines for the ruler who aspired to unite the fragmented Italian peninsula and to rid it of the French and Spanish invaders. With cool and relentless realism he rejected moral restraints and spelled out the difference between politics and religion or philosophy.

Niccolo Machiavelli

National monarchs pursuing strategies based on the precepts of *The Prince* were bound to clash with the two universal institutions of Europe, the papacy and the empire. The conflict was sharpened by the sensational rise of the Spanish dynasty through marriage ties. Ferdinand and Isabella married their daughter Joanna to Philip of Hapsburg. Charles, the offspring of this union, inherited the united Spanish kingdom together with the Spanish possessions in the New World and in Italy (Sardinia, Sicily, Naples). He also held the hereditary Hapsburg lands in central Europe (the duchies of Austria, Styria, Carinthia, Carniola, and the county of Tirol). In addition, Charles's grandmother, Mary of Burgundy, left him Burgundian territories, Franche-Comté, Luxembourg, and the wealthy Netherlands. And to crown this imposing edifice, Charles was elected in 1519 Holy Roman Emperor in spite of the opposition of the French and English monarchs, Francis I and Henry VIII, respectively. Thus Charles V, at the age of nineteen, became the ruler of a larger territory than had been collected under one monarch since the breakup of Charlemagne's empire seven centuries earlier.

For a time it appeared that western Europe would be united once more in a vast international organization. But the other European dynasties, and especially the Valois of France, were determined to prevent Hapsburg hegemony. The result was the long series of wars, partly religious, partly dynastic. This violence was followed by the even more disastrous Thirty Years' War (1618–1648) — a struggle between the Bourbon and Hapsburg dynasties for control of the continent of Europe. The principal victims of the three decades of fighting were the civilians who suffered at the hands of undisciplined mercenaries, especially when their pay was not forthcoming, as often happened. About a third of the population of Germany and Bohemia perished, and wholesale devastation ensued in the cities and the countryside.

The territorial provisions of the Treaty of Westphalia (1648) did not last, but their overall significance is clear. Henceforth the individual sovereign state was recognized as the basic unit in European politics, and relations between the states were conducted according to generally accepted tenets of diplomatic practice. Thus began the international anarchy of a world composed of states with unlimited sovereignty—a world that has persisted from the Westphalia conference to the present day.

V. WESTERN EUROPE ON THE EVE OF EXPANSION

Modern world history had been dominated by European expansion overseas and then by the disintegration of European empires during the twentieth century. The fateful expansion of Europe was largely the product of the historical forces analyzed in this chapter: the technological progress, the population increase, the resulting growth in economic productivity and resources, the emergence of dynamic capitalism, and the rise of the new monarchs. It was the European monarchs who issued charters to joint stock companies and backed them up, if necessary, with their royal navies. The Spanish and Portuguese courts, for example, provided the backing necessary for the achievements of Columbus and da Gama.

The significance of the unique western European complex of interests, institutions, and traditions is pointed up by the remarkable history of the famous maritime expeditions sent out from China during the Ming period (see map of Early Fifteenth-Century Chinese and Portuguese Voyages, p. 329). Between 1405 and 1433, seven ventures were made under the superintendency of the chief court eunuch, a certain Cheng Ho. The expeditions were startling in their magnitude and in their achievements. The first, comprised of sixty-two ships, carried 28,000 men. The average ship had a beam of 150 feet and a length of 370 feet, but the largest were 180 feet wide and 444 feet long. They were veritable floating palaces compared to Columbus's little flagship, the *Santa Maria*, which was 120 feet long and 25 feet wide. And the Santa Maria was twice as large as Columbus's two other ships, the Pinta and the Niña. The Chinese expeditions were impressive in performance as well as in size. They sailed around Southeast Asia to India; some went on to Aden and the head of the Persian Gulf; and individual ships entered ports on the east coast of Africa. During this time, it should be recalled, the Portuguese were only

Early Fifteenth-Century Chinese and Portuguese Voyages

beginning to feel their way down the coast of Africa, and they did not reach Cape Verde until 1445.

Yet these remarkable Chinese expeditions were suddenly halted by imperial order in 1433. Why they were halted remains as much a mystery as why they were started in the first place. But the significant point here is that an order to stop would have been utterly inconceivable in Europe. There was no European counterpart to the Chinese emperor, who could and did issue orders binding on his entire realm. Instead, there were rival national monarchies that were competing in overseas ventures, and no imperial authority existed to prevent them from doing so. The political power and social prestige of the merchants in northwestern Europe, in contrast to the merchants' inferior position in China, made it quite impossible to enforce any decree banning overseas enterprise. Furthermore, Europe had a tradition of trade with the outside world. Its genuine need and strong demand for foreign products was altogether lacking in China.

In short, there was an impelling dynamism in Europe—a lust and an opportunity for profit. The uniqueness of western Europe is reflected in contemporary European and Chinese writings. "Coming into contact with barbarian peoples," wrote Chang Hsieh in 1618, "you have nothing more to fear than touching the left horn of a snail. The only things one should really be anxious about are the means to mastery of the waves of the seas—and, worst of all dangers, the minds of those avid for profit and greedy of gain."[4] By contrast, the Portuguese Captain João Ribeiro boasted in 1685, "From the Cape of Good Hope onwards we were unwilling to leave anything outside of our control; we were anxious to lay hands on everything in that huge stretch of over 5,000 leagues from Sofala to Japan . . . there was not a corner which we did not occupy or desire to have subject to ourselves."[5]

During the Middle Ages, a combination of developments isolated and fenced in the western Europeans, and so further stimulated their natural tendency to look overseas. The loss of the Crusaders' outposts in the Levant, the breakup of the Mongol Empire, and the expansion of the Ottoman Turks into central Europe up to the walls of Vienna served to restrict the Europeans. European merchants could no longer penetrate into central Asia, because chaos reigned where once the Mongols had enforced order. The Black Sea also became closed to Christian merchants when the Turks transformed it into a Moslem preserve. The all-important spice trade was little affected. Italian merchants continued to meet Arab traders in various ports in the Levant to pick up the commodities demanded by the European public. But though this arrangement was satisfactory for the Italians and Arabs, who reaped the golden profits of the middleman, other Europeans were not so happy. They sought earnestly for some means to reach the Orient directly, in order to share the prize. This explains why there were numerous plans in late medieval times for breaking through or getting around the Moslem barrier that confined Europeans to the Mediterranean. Europe at this time, as one author has put it, was like a "giant fed through the chinks of a wall."[6] But the giant was growing in strength and in knowledge, and the prison walls were not to contain him for long.

SUGGESTED READINGS

General interpretations of why European society became expansionist are given by E. L. Jones, *The European Miracle* (Cambridge University, 1981); E. R. Wolf, *Europe and the People Without History* (University of California, 1982); M. Beaud, *A History of Capitalism, 1500–1980* (Monthly Review Press, 1983); L. S. Stavrianos, *Global Rift: The Third World Comes of Age* (William Morrow, 1981); J. Baechlev, J. A. Hall, and M. Mann, eds., *Europe and the Rise of Capitalism* (Basil Blackwell, 1987); and the important three-volume study of F. Braudel, *Civilization and Capitalism, 15th–18th Century* (Harper and Row, 1981–84).

The development of Europe's economy in early modern times is analyzed in the first three volumes of the *Cambridge Economic History* (Cambridge University, 1941–1963); B. H. S. van Bath, *The Agrarian History of Western Europe, 500–1850* (Edward Arnold, 1963); F. Braudel, *Capitalism and Material Life, 1400–1800* (Harper & Row, 1973); and H. I. Miskimin, *The Economy of Early Renaissance Europe, 1300–1460* (Prentice Hall, 1969). European technological progress of this period is analyzed in the studies by L. White, Jr., *Medieval Technology and Social Change* (Oxford University, 1962), *and Machina Ex Deo: Essays in the Dynamism of Western Culture* (MIT, 1968); and also in the works of C. M. Cipolla, *Literacy and Development in the West* (Pelican, 1969), and *European Culture and Overseas Expansion* (Pelican, 1970), the latter dealing with guns, sails, and clocks. Provocative interpretations of the economic and technological changes in Europe are presented in the classics by R. H. Tawney, *Religion and the Rise of Capitalism* (Mentor, 1926); M. Weber, *The Protestant Ethic and the Spirit of Capitalism* (Scribner's, 1948); and, more recently, A. O. Hirschman, *The Passions and the Interests: Political Arguments for Capitalism Before Its Triumph* (Princeton University, 1977).

The question of why the West rather than some other region of Eurasia took the lead in overseas expansion is considered by J. Needham, *Science and Civilization in China* (Cambridge University, 1956ff.), especially Vol. 4, Part 3, which deals with Chinese nautical technology, including the Ming voyages. Other works on this subject are by C. G. F. Simkin, *The Traditional Trade of Asia* (Oxford University, 1968); J. R. Levenson, ed., *European Expansion and the Counter-Example of Asia, 1300–1600* (Prentice Hall, 1967); and J. M. Blaut, *The Colonizer's Model of the*

World (Guilford Press, 1993). The latter book is unique in challenging the concept of a "European miracle," and emphasizing the role of overseas lands in stimulating Europe to global primacy.

NOTES

1. A. G. Keller, "A Byzantine Admirer of 'Western' Progress: Cardinal Bessarion," *Cambridge Historical Journal*, XI (1955), pp. 343–348.
2. S. B. Clough and C. W. Cole, *Economic History of Europe* (D. C. Heath, 1952), p. 66.
3. T. K. Rabb, "The Expansion of Europe and the Spirit of Capitalism," *Historical Journal*, XVII (1974), p. 676.
4. Cited by J. Needham, *Science and Civilization in China: IV, Civil Engineering and Nautics* (Cambridge University, 1971), p. 533.
5. Ibid., p. 534.
6. R. H. Tawney, *Religion and the Growth of Capitalism* (Murray, 1925), p. 68.

What It Means for Us Today

HISTORY AND FADS

Five centuries ago, Christopher Columbus set foot on San Salvador, a tiny island in the Bahamas. He assumed he had reached Southeast Asia, so he referred to the native islanders as Indians—a name that has stuck ever since. Soon after Columbus died, his assumption was proven wrong when Balboa reached the Pacific Ocean in 1513 and when Magellan's expedition sailed around the world from 1519 to 1522.

The realization that the Americas were a "new world" led to speculation about the origins of the Indians. Either they had originated in the New World, or they had arrived there from somewhere else. The idea of independent origin in the Americas was unthinkable heresy, for that would imply a dual creation—a duplicate Adam and Eve in a transatlantic Garden of Eden—a belief that clashed too much with the teachings of the Old Testament. So it was agreed that the Indians must be the descendants of Adam and Eve. A new question now arose: How did these descendants make their way from the Old World to the New? A great debate has raged over this question, with dozens of theories being advanced during the past four centuries and new ones still popping up in the present day.

Most of the theories are false, based more on faith than on reason. Various fads have gone through popularity cycles, each reflecting the knowledge and prejudices of their times. One of the earliest was the Lost Tribes of Israel hypothesis, for in those days, ancient Hebrew ethnology as described in the Old Testament was almost the only known example of the "primitive" way

333

of life. So the early theorists were convinced that the Indians were the descendants of the Hebrew tribes conquered and carried away from Samaria by the king of Assyria in 721 B.C.E. Some supporters of the Lost Tribes theory believed that the Hebrews reached the New World by crossing the mythical continent of Atlantis, but most preferred a route across Persia and China to the Bering Strait.

In the eighteenth century Europeans were impressed by the achievements of the ancient Mediterranean peoples, and especially the Phoenicians, who were famous for their seafaring skills. The Phoenicians were believed to have rounded Africa's Cape of Good Hope and also to have crossed the Atlantic to the Americas. However, with the advent of nineteenth-century archeological discoveries in Egypt, that country came to be considered the origin of American Indian civilizations. This theory was widely accepted as fact because of the existence of pyramids in Mesoamerica that seemed similar to those of Egypt. Many other fads about the origins of the American Indians have come and gone. Thus our "redskins" have been traced back to Greeks, Trojans, Romans, Etruscans, Scythians, Mongols, Chinese Buddhists, Mandingoes or other Africans, early Irish, Welsh, Norse, Basques, Portuguese, French, Spaniards, and even survivors of the "lost continents" of Mu and Atlantis, which allegedly sank 11,000 years ago beneath the Pacific and Atlantic oceans, respectively.

All of these claims have been disproven, or at least found to be questionable, with a single exception: A late tenth-century Norse settlement in Newfoundland has been scientifically confirmed. One reason why so many believed, and still believe, in so many groundless theories is that they wrongly assume that common customs mean a common origin. On the contrary, one can go to the human relations area files in any major university and ask for an inventory of all the peoples of the world who practice some particular custom—say, preferred-cousin marriage. One will quickly be given dozens of examples from peoples all over the world who could not possibly have borrowed that marriage practice from one common source. But early writers, unfamiliar with modern anthropological science, very naturally assumed historical connection between similar customs in the distant past.

Also, apparently similar institutions or structures have proven on close examination to be quite different. Pyramids have been found in both Egypt and Mesoamerica, but those of Mesoamerica were primarily centers of religious ritual, whereas those of Egypt were vast tombs. Equally important is the fact that recent excavations reveal the gradual evolution of Mesoamerican pyramids over thousands of years. This long development period demolishes the theory that the technique of pyramid building had been transplanted full-blown across the Atlantic. Likewise, in the native California language known as Yuki, the word *ko* means "go," and *kom* means "come," yet no one could conclude from this example that Yuki and English are historically related.

Even if small numbers of ancient Old World seafarers had reached the New World, the claim that their cultures would have instantly dominated New World customs is highly questionable. Those who assume that small groups of Hebrews, Greeks, Romans, Phoenicians, or others could have arrived in the New World and spread their culture among natives over vast areas should consider the experience of eighteen Spaniards (sixteen men and two women) who were shipwrecked on the coast of Yucatan six years before

Cortes arrived. All were sacrificed and ritually eaten, except for two men who were enslaved by local chieftains. One of these survivors went so completely native that he wore the elaborate nose plug and earrings of his adopted tribe and refused to give up his new life to rejoin Cortes. Likewise, the Vikings, who we know did actually land in Newfoundland, were forced to give up their attempt to establish a colony because of the hostility of the local Indians. Thus until the appearance of modern repeating rifles and machine guns, small landing parties were either wiped out or assimilated into the local culture.

These are some of the reasons why a 1968 symposium held in Santa Fe, New Mexico, concluded that "there are to date—excluding the Viking contacts (that is, Newfoundland)—no verified archaeological finds of artifacts from one hemisphere in pre-Columbian context to the other." The symposium likewise agreed that "there is no hard and fast evidence for any pre-Columbian human introduction of any single plant or animal across the ocean from the Old World to the New World or vice-versa. This is emphatically not to say that it could not have occurred."[1]

What is the significance of this discussion for the student of history? In the first place, it points up the basic question of how human civilizations have developed—whether by diffusion from one or a few early centers or by independent inventions in various parts of the world. This question probes not only the origins of the American Indian civilizations but also the origins of civilizations throughout the globe. Did civilization spread from the Middle East to northwest Europe, North Africa, south Asia, and east Asia, or was it independently developed in these various regions? The controversy between the diffusionists and the independent inventionists has been long standing.

Increasingly we are realizing that it is not a case of either/or but rather of varying degrees of diffusion and independent invention. These varying degrees can be determined not by romantic speculations based on preconceived notions but rather by painstaking research and objective evaluation of the results. The more archeologists unearth human prehistory, the more they are realizing that all branches of the human race have been inventive in responding to their environments. The nature and the extent of their responses and achievements have varied greatly, depending on their historical and geographical backgrounds, especially the degree of accessibility to outside stimulation, as has been noted before.

Equally significant for students of history is the fact that many laypersons still cherish the vision of assorted Europeans, Asians, or Africans landing on the shores of the pre-Columbian New World, bearing aloft the torch of civilization. The fact is that humans today, as in earliest Paleolithic times, are mesmerized by the cult of the mysterious. They cling to romantic and simplistic explanations, even when they do not square with known facts. Our food-gathering ancestors depended on their totems and shamans or medicine men. Modern humans have similar faith in UFOs, numerology, tarot cards, intelligent plants, and astrology. Readers of this text will appreciate the significance of the following report by George Abell, professor of astronomy at the University of California, Los Angeles:

> I have polled the general university students taking my survey astronomy courses and find that about a third have an interest and belief in astrology.

From discussions with my colleagues in other parts of the country I gather that about the same ratio holds everywhere and that it probably fairly well represents the fraction of Americans who believe in astrology. It is estimated that there are more than 5,000 astrologers making a living in the subject in the United States. More than 1,200 daily newspapers carry astrology columns.[2]

Professor Abell's report was made in 1975. Polls since that date indicate that faith in astrology is steadily increasing. Between 1980 and 1985 the proportion of American teenagers who believe in astrology has grown from 40 to 55 percent.[3] This resurgence of astrology today is especially noteworthy in view of the fact that it largely disappeared when modern astronomy began in the sixteenth century.

Similarly a 1996 *Newsweek* poll disclosed that 48 percent of Americans believe UFOs (Unidentified Foreign Objects) are real, and 29 percent think we've made contact with aliens, while another 48 percent believe there is a government plot to cover it all up. More specifically, some stargazers claim to have seen Elvis eating fried chicken on Uranus. Nor are Americans unique in this respect. In France, nearly 50,000 taxpayers in 1995 declared income from their work as stargazers, healers, mediums, and similar occupations. By contrast, France has 36,000 Roman Catholic priests and 6,000 psychiatrists.[4]

SUGGESTED READINGS

An interesting analysis of science and irrationality is given by M. Gardner, *Fads and Fallacies in the Name of Science* (Dover, 1957). A recent and fascinating survey of this subject is by the late space scientist, Carl Sagan, *The Demon-Haunted World: Science as a Candle in the Dark* (Random House, 1997). A similar survey focused on the United States, is by J. Gilbert, *Redeeming Culture: American Religion in an Age of Science* (University of Chicago Press, 1997).

NOTES

1. C. L. Riley et al., *Man Across the Sea: Problems in Pre-Columbian Contacts* (University of Texas, 1975), pp. 448, 452–53.
2. *Los Angeles Times*, September 14, 1975.
3. Ibid., April 21, 1985.
4. *Newsweek*, July 8, 1996, p. 50; *New York Times*, April 30, 1996.

PART VI

World of the Emerging West, 1500–1763

During much of the medieval period the western Europeans felt isolated and threatened on the western tip of Eurasia. Situated as they were at the terminal of the classic invasion route—the endless expanse of steppes stretching from north China across the length of Eurasia to the Danube valley in central Europe—they had been traditionally vulnerable to attack from the east. A long succession of nomadic invaders—Huns, Germans, Avars, Magyars, Mongols, and Turks—had used their unmatched mobility to break into the centers of civilization whenever imperial weakness gave them the opportunity.

The age-old pattern was reversed in early modern times by the emergence of a dynamic new West with superior technology, particularly in armaments and naval shipbuilding. This gave the western Europeans the same mobility and superiority on the oceans of the world that had been enjoyed hitherto by the nomads on the steppes of Eurasia. The result was a fundamental alteration in the configuration of world affairs. All Eurasia now was enveloped by two gigantic European pincers. One arm was the Russian thrust overland across Siberia to the Pacific, and the other, the west European expansion around Africa to India, Southeast Asia, and China. At the same time other Westerners, beginning with Columbus, ventured westward across the Atlantic, discovering the New World and circumnavigating the globe.

It is true that during these same decades Turkish janissaries, like many of their Asian predecessors, were pressing up the Danube valley and besieging Vienna in the heart of Europe. But in the context of the new global historical stage, this was only a minor operation of local importance. What was truly significant in the perspective of world history was the initial Iberian expansion overseas, the later overseas activities of the northwest Europeans, and the simultaneous overland expansion of the Russians to the Pacific.

22

West European Expansion: Iberian Phase, 1500–1600

The discovery of America, and that of passage to the East Indies by the Cape of Good Hope, are the greatest and most important events recorded in the history of mankind.

Adam Smith

The two countries of the Iberian peninsula, Spain and Portugal, took the lead in the expansion of Europe in the sixteenth century. For several reasons this seems paradoxical on first thought: The Iberian peninsula for centuries had been a Moslem stronghold. A large number of Moors and Jews were left behind in the country, creating ethnic and religious divisions. And it is well known that after the sixteenth century the Iberian countries declined rapidly, and that throughout modern times they have been insignificant. What, then, is the explanation for the short-lived but brilliant expansion of Spain and Portugal during the sixteenth century? This chapter is concerned, first, with the roots of Iberian expansionism; second, with the process of empire building in the East and in the New World; and, finally, with the causes and results of Iberian decline at the end of the sixteenth century.

I. ROOTS OF IBERIAN EXPANSIONISM

Religion was an important factor in European overseas expansion, but nowhere was it so important as in the Iberian peninsula. Both the Spaniards and the Portuguese were urged on by memories of their long anti-Moslem crusade. To other peoples of Europe, Islam was a distant menace, but for the Iberians it represented a traditional and ever-present enemy. Most of the peninsula at one time had been under Moslem rule, and now, in the fifteenth century, Granada in the south was still a Moslem stronghold. Furthermore, the Moslems were in control of the nearby North African coast, and the growing Turkish seapower was making itself felt throughout the Mediterranean. Other Europeans were crusaders by fits and starts, but for the devout and patriotic Iberian, the struggle against Islam combined religious duty and patriotic necessity

(see map of Expansionism of the Medieval West, p. 341.)

Prince Henry the Navigator first won fame in 1415 for his gallant role in the capture of the North African fortress and town of Ceuta, across the Straits of Gibraltar. Likewise, Queen Isabella, moved by intense religious conviction, was determined to wipe out Moslem Granada and also to carry the war into the enemy's territory in North Africa, as the Portuguese had done at Ceuta. Isabella began her crusade against Granada in 1482 and pressed on, village by village, until final victory in 1492. Immediately thereafter, the Spaniards crossed the straits and captured the city of Melilla. Again in 1492, a royal decree was promulgated requiring all Jews in Spain to accept the Catholic faith or leave the realm. Ten years later a similar decree was issued against the Moslems remaining in Castile. At the time of their oceanic discoveries, the Iberians took their crusading spirit with them across the oceans, where they found more Moslems to exterminate and new heathens to save from idolatry.

The Iberians were lured overseas also by four island groups—the Canaries, the Madeira, the Azores, and the Cape Verde—stretching westward across the Atlantic and southward down the coast of Africa. These were highly attractive, in part because they were fertile and productive, but also because they provided strategic bases and ports of call. After much local fighting and several appeals to the pope, the Canaries were recognized as Spanish and the other three island groups as Portuguese. Throughout the fifteenth century, progressively more adventurous Spanish and Portuguese sailors had been discovering these islands stretching a quarter of the way across the Atlantic. It was natural that they should assume there were more islands awaiting discovery and exploitation. The agreement that Columbus reached with Isabella in 1492 stated that he should head an expedition "to discover and acquire islands and mainland in the Ocean Sea."

It was Portugal, however, not Spain, that took the lead in overseas enterprise during the fifteenth century. Spain moved belatedly, and usually in reaction to Portuguese initiative. There were two reasons for Portugal's head start. One was its small size and its location on the Atlantic coast, where it was surrounded on three sides by Spanish territory. This position effectively saved the Portuguese from the temptation to squander their resources in European wars. Thanks to the leadership of Prince Henry, they turned instead to seafaring projects. The other advantage was Portugal's superior knowledge of navigation, gained primarily from the Italians. Lisbon was on the route of the Genoese and Venetian sea traffic with Flanders that sailed through the Straits of Gibraltar. The Portuguese took advantage of this to lure Italian captains and pilots into the royal navy. Prince Henry followed up by employing talented seamen, including Italians, Catalans, and even a Dane. Furthermore, Henry's work was continued by the crown following his death, so that the Portuguese became the most knowledgeable of all Europeans in seamanship and geography.

Portugal's interest in exploration quickened following the capture of Ceuta in 1415. Moslem prisoners gave information about the ancient and profitable trade across the Sahara with the Negro kingdoms of the Sudan. For centuries the Sudan had provided ivory, slaves, and gold in return for various manufactured goods and salt. Since western Europe in general and Portugal in particular were then suffering from a serious shortage of bullion, Prince Henry was intrigued by the possibility of sending his captains down the African coast and tapping the gold trade. In short, Henry's original objective was confined to Africa and did not extend to the East.

A major step forward in early Portuguese exploration was taken when Prince Henry's captains passed south of Africa's desert coast in 1445 and found below it a fertile, green land. By the time of Henry's death, the coast had been explored down to Sierra Leone and a number of coastal stations had been established, so that the Portuguese were able to exploit at least part of the African caravan trade that they had sought.

Meanwhile, even before Henry's death, Portuguese aspirations had come to include India as well as Africa. Europe at this time was blocked from access to the East by the Moslems, who controlled all of North Africa and the Middle East. The Mediterranean was for the Europeans a prison rather than a highway. Therefore, with the exception of the Venetians, who profited as middlemen, the Europeans eagerly sought a new

Expansionism of the Medieval West

route "to the Indies where the spices grow." Prince Henry had not thought of India when he first began his operations, but as his ships crept further and further down the African coast, it was natural that his horizon should expand from the African caravan trade to the Indies spice trade. From then on, the discovery and domination of the spice route was the prime objective of Portuguese policy.

II. COLUMBUS DISCOVERS AMERICA

In view of Portugal's pioneering work in the theory and practice of maritime navigation, it is paradoxical that the first great discovery—that of the New World—was made under Spanish auspices. It is even more paradoxical that the reason for this outcome is that the Portuguese were more advanced in their geographical knowledge than the Spaniards and realized that Columbus was wrong in his calculations. By the fifteenth century, informed people knew that the world was round. The question was not the shape of the world but its size and what precise relationship its continents bore to the oceans. Columbus had based his calculations on several sources. By combining (1) Marco Polo's estimate of the east-west extent of Asia, which was an overestimate; (2) Polo's report of the distance of Japan from the Asian mainland—1,500 miles, an extreme overestimate; and (3) Ptolemy's estimate of the circumference of the globe, which was an underestimate, Columbus concluded that fewer than 3,000 miles of ocean separated Europe from Japan. Accordingly, he believed that the shortest and easiest route to Asia was by a short voyage across the Atlantic, and this was the project that he proposed before various courts. The Portuguese, thanks to Prince Henry, had more practical experience and were better informed of the most advanced knowledge of the day. They were convinced that the globe was larger than Columbus held, that the oceans were wider, and that the shortest route to the Orient was around Africa rather than across the Atlantic. For this reason the Portuguese king turned Columbus down when he applied for financial assistance in 1484. Two years later Columbus was at the Spanish court, where, after

This woodcut, which first appeared on the cover of a pamphlet in 1493, may be the first European drawing of Columbus's arrival in America. King Ferdinand of Spain sits on the left, directing Columbus and his three ships to an island. The nearly naked native peoples (depicted as being larger than the Europeans) appear to flee from the ships.

a preliminary rejection, he finally won the support of Queen Isabella.

On August 2, 1492, Columbus set sail from Palos with three small ships manned by reliable crews with capable and seasoned officers. By mid-October he had landed at one of the Bahaman Islands, which Columbus named San Salvador. One of the supreme ironies of world history is that Columbus was convinced until the end of his life that he had reached Asia. He was certain that San Salvador was very near to where Japan ought to be, and the next step was to find Japan itself. When he sailed southwest to the mainland of the New World, he believed that he was somewhere near the Malacca Straits. The fact that Columbus persisted in his delusion had momentous consequences: It spurred on further exploration of the Americas until the great prizes in Mexico and Peru were discovered.

The Spanish monarchs loyally supported Columbus and invested large sums in outfitting him for three additional expeditions. But not until 1519 did the Spaniards stumble on the rich

COLUMBUS DISCOVERS THE NEW WORLD

On his return from his first voyage, Columbus described his discoveries in a letter to Gabriel Sanchez (March 1493). The letter shows how anxious Columbus was to convince people that he had discovered valuable lands, and that he was ready to strip those lands of their riches and to make their "honest" and affectionate people into slaves.*

As I know that it will afford you pleasure that I have brought my undertaking to a successful result, I have determined to write you this letter to inform you of everything that has been done and discovered in this voyage of mine.

On the thirty-third day after leaving Cadiz I came into the Indian Sea, where I discovered many islands inhabited by numerous people. I took possession of all of them for our most fortunate King by making public proclamation and unfurling his standard, no one making any resistance. . . . The inhabitants of both sexes of this and of all the other islands I have seen, or of which I have any knowledge, always go as naked as they came into the world, except that some of the women cover parts of their bodies with leaves or branches, or a veil of cotton, which they prepare themselves for this purpose. They are all, as I said before, unprovided with any sort of iron, and they are destitute of arms, which are entirely unknown to them, and for which they are not adapted; not on account of any bodily deformity, for they are well made, but because they are timid and full of terror. They carry, however, canes dried in the sun in place of weapons, upon whose roots they fix a wooden shaft, dried and sharpened to a point. But they never dare to make use of these, for it has often happened, when I have sent two or three of my men to some of their villages to speak with the inhabitants, that a crowd of Indians has sallied forth; but when they saw our men approaching, they speedily took to flight, parents abandoning their children, and children their parents. This happened not because any loss or injury had been inflicted upon any of them. On the contrary, I gave whatever I had, cloth and many other things, to whomsoever I approached, or with whom I could get speech, without any return being made to me; but they are by nature fearful and timid. But, when they see that they are safe, and all fear is banished, they are very guileless and honest, and very liberal of all they have. No one refuses the asker anything that he possesses; on the contrary, they themselves invite us to ask for it. They manifest the greatest affection toward all of us, exchanging valuable things for trifles, content with the very least thing or nothing at all. . . .

Finally, to sum up in a few words the chief results and advantages of our departure and speedy return, I make this promise to our most invincible Sovereigns, that, if I am supported by some little assistance from them, I will give them as much gold as they have need of, and in addition spices, cotton, and mastic, which is found only in Chios, and as much aloes-wood, and as many heathen slaves as their Majesties may choose to demand.

. . .

As these things have been accomplished, so have they been briefly narrated. Farewell.

CHRISTOPHER COLOM,

Lisbon, March 14th.

Admiral of the Ocean Fleet.

*Reprinted from *Old South Pamphlets*, Vol. 2, No. 33 (Directors of the Old South Work, 1897).

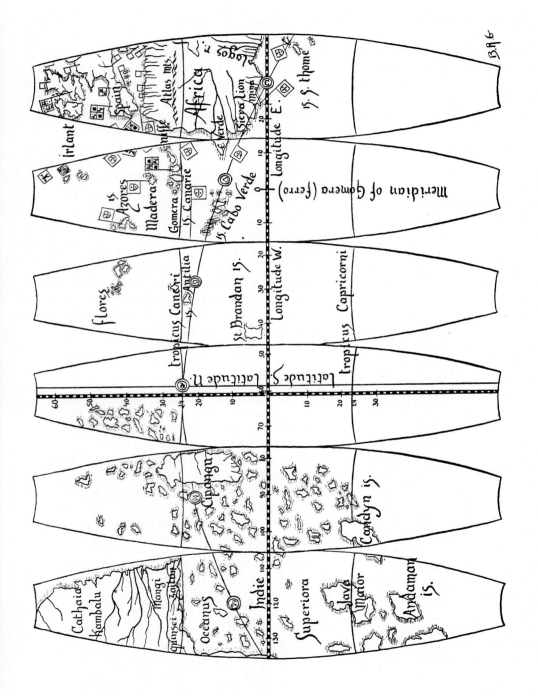

What Columbus knew of the world in 1492 was contained in this map by the Nuremberg geographer Martin Behaim, creator of the first spherical globe of the Earth. The ocean section of Behaim's globe is reproduced here. Departing the Canary Islands (in the second section from the right), Columbus expected his first major landfall to be Japan (Cipangu, in the second section from the left). When he landed at San Salvador, he thought he was on the outer island of Japan. And when he arrived in Cuba, he thought he was in Japan.

Aztec empire in Mexico. During the quarter-century between this windfall and Columbus's first expedition, disappointment followed disappointment as the Spaniards explored the innumerable and unpromising islands of the West Indies. Columbus's great discovery appeared to be a grand failure. Several thousand adventurers had flocked to the West Indies and found disappointingly small quantities of gold. But there was an immediate reaction to the discovery of the New World that was very important. It prodded the Portuguese to circumnavigate Africa and reach India directly by sea.

III. PORTUGAL IN ASIA

The Portuguese in the meantime had been making considerable profit from their trade along the African Guinea coast. Coarse pepper, gold, ivory, cotton, sugar, and slaves now entered European commerce through Portugal. Prince Henry's successors continued his work of opening up the West African coast. A breakthrough occurred in 1487 when Bartholomeu Dias, while sailing along the coast, was caught by a gale that blew his ships south for thirteen days out of sight of land. When the wind moderated, Dias steered for the West African coast but discovered that he had already passed the Cape without knowing it. He landed at Mossel Bay on the Indian Ocean and wanted to explore further, but his weary and frightened men forced him to return. On the homeward passage he first sighted the great cape, and named it the Cape of Storms. It was the Portuguese king who, upon Dias's return, renamed it the Cape of Good Hope. But the king did not follow up on this rounding of the Cape because of political and financial complications. The result, as noted, was that Columbus was the first to reach the New World, which he insisted in claiming as the Orient.

The more knowledgeable Portuguese were dubious from the beginning, but they now hastened to open and secure the Cape route to India. On July 8, 1497, Vasco da Gama sailed from Portugal with four ships, and at the end of May 1498, he entered Calicut harbor. Da Gama did not receive a warm welcome in Calicut. The resident Arab merchants were naturally alarmed by the threat to their traditional monopoly and did their best to throw obstacles in the way of the European intruders. Furthermore, the Portuguese trade goods—mostly trinkets and woolen cloth—were unsuitable for the Indian market. The fact is that the Portuguese had completely underestimated the level and sophistication of Indian civilization. Thus, da Gama had difficulty trading in Calicut not only because of the hostility of the resident Arab traders but also, and more important, because Portugal (and all Europe) produced little at this time that was of interest to the Eastern peoples. European manufactures were generally inferior in quality and higher in price than the goods produced in the East.

With much effort da Gama collected a cargo of pepper and cinnamon and cleared for home, arriving in September 1499. The cargo proved to be worth sixty times the cost of the entire expedition. Dazzling horizons opened up before the delighted Portuguese, and King Manuel assumed the titles "Lord of the Con-

Vasco da Gama

quest, Navigation, and Commerce of Ethiopia, Arabia, Persia, and India." These titles were taken quite seriously. The Portuguese were determined to monopolize the trade along the new route and to exclude not only other Europeans, but also the Arabs and other Eastern peoples who had traded in the Indian Ocean for centuries. To enforce their claims, the Portuguese resorted to ruthless terrorism, particularly when they encountered the hated Moslems. Da Gama, on a later voyage, found some unarmed vessels returning from Mecca. He captured the vessels and, in the words of a fellow Portuguese, "after making the ships empty of goods, prohibited anyone from taking out of it any Moor and then ordered them to set fire to it."[1]

Such was the nature of the epoch-making meeting of two Eurasian cultures when they came face to face for the first time after millennia of regional isolation. The Europeans were the aggressive intruders. They were the ones who seized the initiative and retained it until gradually but inexorably they emerged the masters in every quarter of the globe. This unprecedented domination of the world is at first difficult to understand. Why was Portugal, with a population of approximately 2 million, able to encroach on highly civilized Asiatic countries with much greater human and natural resources?

First, the Portuguese had the great advantage of being ready to use the vast bullion supply that was soon to start pouring in from the New World. The flood of bullion from the treasures of the Aztec and Inca empires and from the Mexican and Peruvian silver mines came just in time to finance Portugal's trade with the East. Without this windfall the Portuguese would have been very seriously restricted, because they had neither natural resources nor manufactured goods that were of interest to the Eastern peoples.

Second, the Portuguese triumphed because of the disunity of the Indian subcontinent. When the Portuguese arrived on the scene, northern India was controlled by the new Mogul invaders, who were interested in conquest rather than trade, and southern India, and especially the Malabar coast, was under the control of petty Hindu rulers who were fighting one another. By contrast, the Portuguese and their European successors had a singleness and continuity of purpose that more than counterbalanced

their inferiority in resources. The Europeans obviously were not united; they were riddled with political and religious dissension. But on one point they were all agreed—the need to expand eastward to reap profits and to outflank Islam. In pursuit of this objective the Europeans demonstrated a determination to succeed that was stronger than the will of the Asiatic peoples to resist. When da Gama returned from his historic voyage, the Portuguese court was prepared to follow up promptly. It had a detailed plan for organized trade, involving the establishment of trading posts in the Malabar ports and the sending of annual fleets under royal charter.

Da Gama's flagship, the São Gabriel

The Portuguese were successful also because of the superiority of their naval power. They had developed efficient new naval artillery that enabled them to use ships as floating batteries rather than as transports for boarding parties. The gun, not the foot soldier, was now the main instrument of naval warfare, and the guns were employed against the enemy's ships rather than against its men. It was these new developments that made it possible for the Portuguese to smash Moslem naval power in the Indian Ocean and to win a profitable Asiatic empire.

The architect of this empire was the great Alfonso de Alburquerque, governor general from 1509 to 1515. His policy was to smash the Arab trade network by capturing control of the narrow sea passage leading to and from the Indian Ocean. He seized the islands of Socotra and Hormuz, which were the keys to the Red Sea and the Persian Gulf, respectively. In India he took the city of Goa, located in the middle of the Malabar coast. He made Goa his main naval base and general headquarters, and it remained a Portuguese possession until 1961. Further to the east he captured Malacca, commanding the strait through which all commerce with the Far East had to pass. Two years later, in 1513, the first Portuguese ship to reach a Chinese port put into Canton. This was the first recorded European visit to China since Marco Polo's day. The Portuguese obtained the right to establish a warehouse and a settlement in Macao, a little downstream from Canton, and from there they carried on their Far Eastern operations.

The Portuguese Empire in Asia was small in actual extent, made up of only a few islands and coastal posts. But these possessions were so strategically located that they gave the Portuguese command of trade routes spanning half the globe. Each year Portuguese fleets sailed down the African coast, which was dotted with stations for provisioning and refitting the ships. After they rounded the Cape, they put in at Mozambique in East Africa, another Portuguese possession. Then they sailed with the monsoon across to Cochin and Ceylon, where they loaded the spices that had been brought in from the surrounding territories. Further east was Malacca, which gave them access to the trade of east Asia and for which they served as middlemen and carriers. Thus, the Portuguese profited from purely Asian trade—between China and Japan and the Philippines, for example—as well as from the trade between Europe and the East.

With this network of trading stations and strong points, Albuquerque had broken the traditional monopoly of the Arab merchants in the Indian Ocean. In doing so he was competing with the Venetian merchants for the "spiceries" that they had customarily obtained in the ports of the Levant. The Venetians no longer found the spices they had bought for centuries in Alexandria and other Levant ports. Instead, the spices were now being shipped on the longer but cheaper ocean route to Lisbon. This explains why in 1508 the Egyptians, with full Venetian support, sent a naval expedition to help the

Fort Jesus at Mombasa, built by the Portuguese as a major stronghold for their domination of the East African coast.

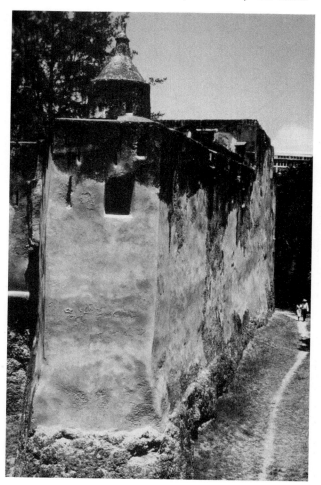

Indian rajas drive the Portuguese interlopers out of the Indian Ocean. The effort failed, but the Turks, who conquered Egypt in 1517, continued the campaign against the Portuguese and sent several fleets during the following decades. They were all unsuccessful, and the spices continued to flow around the Cape to Europe.

Yet it should not be assumed that the old routes through the Middle East fell into complete disuse. In fact, after the initial dislocation, the old routes regained much of the lost trade for a variety of reasons. One reason was that there were some corrupt Portuguese officials who were willing, when bribed, to allow Arab shipping to enter the Red Sea and the Persian Gulf. The Arabs and Venetians thus were able to compete successfully with the Portuguese throughout the sixteenth century. It was not until the following century, with the appearance in the Indian Ocean of the more efficient and economically powerful Dutch and English, that the old Italian and Arab middlemen were completely displaced. The traditional Middle Eastern trade routes then gave way to oceanic routes.

IV. DIVISION OF THE WORLD

When the Europeans began to expand overseas, they adopted the convenient doctrine that they had the right to take the lands of non-Christians without regard for the native peoples concerned. Another doctrine, adopted at least by Portugal and Spain, was the right of the pope to give sovereignty to any lands not possessed by a Christian ruler. As early as 1454, Pope Nicholas V issued a decision granting to the Portuguese title over territories they were discovering along the African coast toward India. When Columbus returned from his voyage convinced that he had reached the Indies, the Spanish court feared Portuguese counterclaims and therefore pressed Pope Alexander VI for recognition of Spanish sovereignty. On May 4, 1493, Pope Alexander defined a dividing line running 100 leagues west of the Azores and Cape Verde Islands; to the west of this line he granted all lands to Spain, and to the east all lands went to Portugal. On June 7, 1494, Spain and Portugal negotiated an agreement, the Treaty of Tordesillas, moving the line 270 leagues further west. This change gave Portugal a claim to Brazil in the New World.

The riches that Portugal reaped from the spice trade after da Gama's voyage goaded the other European countries into a frantic search for another route to the Indies. The successive failures of Columbus to find Cathay did not kill the hope of reaching Asia by sailing west. It might still be possible to thread a way between the various masses of inhospitable land so far discovered. This was the aim of a new class of professional explorers that appeared in the early sixteenth century. Mostly Italians and Portuguese—the best-informed and the most experienced explorers at that time—they were ready to carry on explorations for any monarch willing to finance them. The Italians included Amerigo Vespucci, who sailed for Portugal and Spain; John Verrazano, who sailed for France; and the two Cabots, father and son, who sailed for England. The Portuguese included Juan Diaz de Solis, Juan Fernandez, and Ferdinand Magellan, all of whom sailed for Spain.

Magellan was the only one who found the passage to Asia. Spain sent him to find it because, with regular spice cargoes arriving in Lisbon, the Spanish realized that they were being beaten in the race for the Spice Islands. Since they claimed that the line of demarcation defined by the Tordesillas Treaty ran around the globe, they sent Magellan west to find Asia, hoping that at least some of the Spice Islands were on the Spanish side of the line.

In one of the great epics of seafaring, Magellan set out from Seville on September 10, 1519, with a fleet of five ships, each about 100 tons. By October he reached the straits that bear his name, but the seas were so rough that it took well over a month to cross into the Pacific. Meanwhile one ship had been wrecked and another had deserted, so with the remaining three he sailed up the Chilean coast to the fiftieth latitude and then veered to the northwest.

During the next eighty days only two uninhabited islands were sighted. Magellan and his men ran short of food and water and suffered terribly from scurvy. On March 6 they reached an island, perhaps Guam, where they were able to obtain provisions. On the sixteenth of the same month they arrived at the Philippines, where Magellan and forty of his crew were killed in a local war. With the aid of native pilots, the surviving Spaniards sailed to Borneo and thence to their destination, the Moluccas or Spice Islands, which they finally reached in November 1520. The Portuguese, who were already there, did not hesitate to attack the two remaining Spanish ships (one had been abandoned in the Philippines). Despite all obstacles the Spaniards were able to obtain cargoes of cloves and then set off on the journey home by different routes. The ship that tried to recross the Pacific was turned back by head winds and captured by the Portuguese. The other successfully completed a fantastic voyage through the Macassar Strait, across the Indian Ocean, around the Cape of Good Hope, and up the entire length of Africa. On September 3, 1522, this last surviving ship, the *Victoria*, leaking badly and with a decimated crew, limped into the harbor of Seville. Yet the single cargo of spices was valuable enough to pay the expense of the entire expedition.

The Spaniards sent out another expedition, which reached the Spice Islands in 1524. But it was a disastrous failure because the Portuguese were too firmly established to be challenged profitably. Furthermore, the Spanish king was desperately in need of money at this time to finance his war with France. So in 1529 he signed the Treaty of Saragossa with Portugal. In return for 350,000 ducats, he gave up all claims to the Spice Islands and accepted a demarcation line fifteen degrees east of them. This treaty marked the end of a chapter in the history of discovery (see map of Western Knowledge of the Globe, 1 to 1800 C.E., p. 350). The Portuguese held on to the Spice Islands until they lost them to the Dutch in 1605, whereas the Spaniards continued to show interest in the Philippines and eventually conquered them in 1571, even though the islands were east of the line stipulated by the Saragossa Treaty. Long before this, however, Spain shifted her attention to the New World, where great treasures had been found equal in value to the spices of the East.

V. CONQUISTADORS AND NEW SPAIN

The year 1519, in which Magellan left Seville on his famous voyage around the world, was also the year Hernando Cortes left Cuba on his equally famous expedition against the Aztec Empire. In doing so, Cortes began what might be termed the age of the conquistadors. The preceding decades, from 1500 to 1520, had been the age of the explorers, when numerous navigators under various flags probed the entire length of the Americas in search of a passageway. In the thirty years that followed, a few thousand Spanish adventurers won the first great European overseas empire.

One of these soldiers of fortune, a typical product of the Iberian crusading tradition, was Hernando Cortes, an unsuccessful law student and the son of a respectable family. In 1504 he arrived in Hispaniola, and six years later he participated in the conquest of Cuba. Distinguishing himself during this campaign, he was selected to head an expedition to Yucatan to investigate reports of civilized city dwellers living in the interior. In March 1519 Cortes landed on the mainland coast near present-day Veracruz. He had only 600 men, a few small cannon, thirteen muskets, and sixteen horses. Yet with this insignificant force he was to win fabulous riches and become master of an exotic, highly advanced empire.

Cortes began by scuttling his ships to show his men that they had no hope of returning to Cuba in case of setbacks. Then, after some fighting, he reached agreements with various tribes that were hostile to their Aztec overlords. Without the food, the porters, and the fighting men provided by these tribes, Cortes could not have won the victories he did. By playing on the superstitions of Montezuma, the Aztec war chief, Cortes was able to march peacefully into the capital, Tenochtitlan. He was graciously received by Montezuma, whom he treacherously took prisoner and kept as a hostage. But the Indians were vastly superior in numbers, and their priests stirred them to rebellion. The Spanish policy of destroying native temples provoked an uprising during which Montezuma was killed. Cortes fought his way out of the capital by night, losing a third of his men and most of his baggage in the process. He recovered from this setback because his Indian allies remained loyal and reinforcements arrived from Cuba. A few months later Cortes returned and laid siege to the capital with a force of 800 Spanish soldiers and at least 25,000 Indians. The fighting was bit-

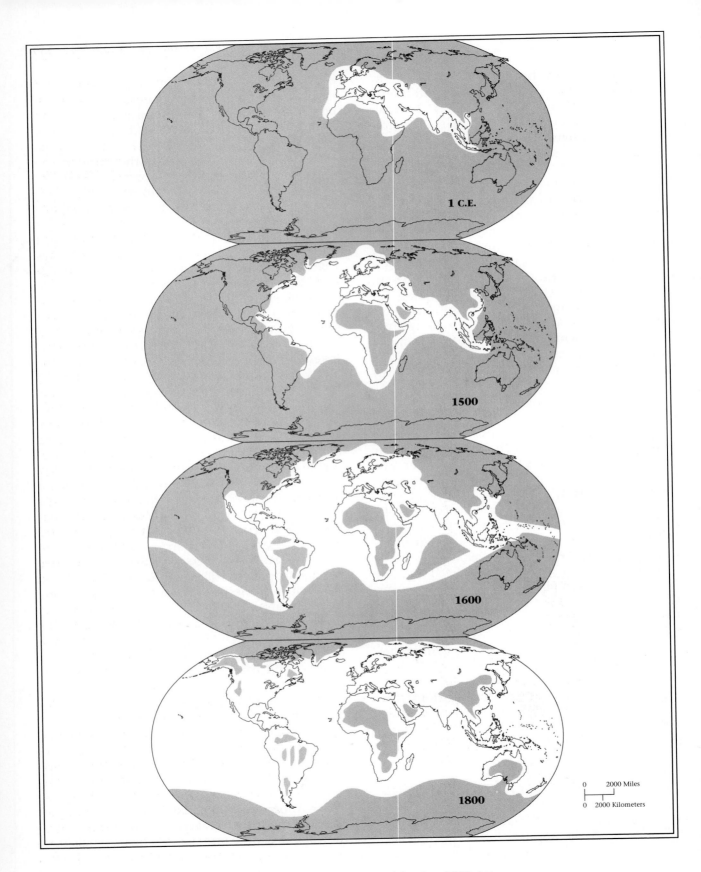

Western Knowledge of the Globe, 1 to 1800 C.E.

ter and dragged on for four months. Finally, in August 1521 the surviving defenders surrendered their city, which was almost entirely reduced to rubble. Today, Mexico City stands in its place, with hardly a trace left of the original Aztec capital.

Even more audacious was the conquest of the Inca Empire by a Spanish expedition comprising 180 men, twenty-seven horses, and two cannons. The leader was Francisco Pizarro, an illiterate drifter who was the illegitimate son of a Spanish officer. After preliminary explorations from which he learned the general location of the Incas, he set forth in 1531, with his four brothers, on his great adventure. After a long delay in crossing the Andes, Pizarro reached the deserted city of Cajamarca on November 15, 1532. The following day the Inca ruler, Atahualpa, who was curious about these strange "men with beards," paid a formal visit to Pizarro. In

A sixteenth-century Aztec drawing depicts a battle in the Spanish conquest of Mexico.

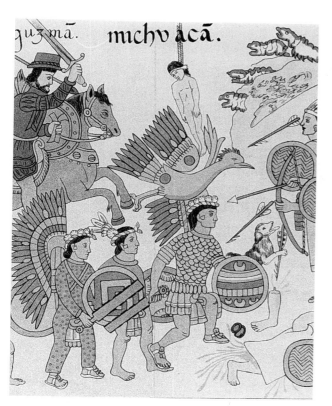

imitation of Cortes, Pizarro captured the unarmed and unsuspecting emperor and massacred many of his followers. The emperor paid an enormous ransom for his freedom—a room twenty-two feet by seventeen feet piled seven feet deep with gold and silver articles. Pizarro seized the booty, and with customary treachery and bigotry, executed Atahualpa. The Inca Empire now was left leaderless, and the population, used to paternalistic regimentation, offered little resistance. A few weeks later Pizarro entered and looted the capital, Cuzco. The next year, 1535, he left for the coast, where he founded Lima, still the capital of Peru.

The triumphs of Cortes and Pizarro inspired other conquistadors to march through vast areas of both the American continents in search of more booty. They found nothing comparable to the Aztec and Inca treasures, but they did determine the major configuration of all of South America and of a large part of North America. By the middle of the sixteenth century they had followed the Amazon from Peru to its mouth. By the end of the century they were familiar with the entire coastline of South America, from the Gulf of California south to Tierra del Fuego and north to the West Indies. Likewise in North America, Francisco de Coronado, in his search for the fabled Seven Cities of Cibola, traversed thousands of miles and discovered the Grand Canyon and the Colorado River. Hernando de Soto, who had been prominent in the conquest of Peru, explored widely in the southeast of what was to become the United States. He landed in Florida in 1539, made his way north to the Carolinas and west to the Mississippi, and followed that river from its junction with the Arkansas River to its mouth. These men, and many others like them, opened the New World for the Spaniards in the same way that La Salle and Lewis and Clark opened it for the French- and English-speaking peoples.

By 1550 the conquistadors had completed their work. The way was now clear for the Spaniards to proceed with the development of their overseas possessions. Since the native populations were not so dense or so highly organized as those of Africa and Asia, it was possible for the Iberians to settle in considerable numbers in the New World and to impose their cultures. Thus they built Europe's first true colonial empire—something quite different from the purely commercial empires in Africa and Asia.

The swashbuckling conquistadors were effective as empire builders but quite ineffective as empire administrators. Incapable of settling down, they fell into fighting among themselves, and their ranks were decimated by feuding and warfare. The Spanish crown replaced the conquistadors with bureaucrats who imposed royal authority and royal justice.

At the top of the imperial administrative structure was the Council of the Indies, located in Spain and closely supervised by the crown. It made all important appointments and exercised general jurisdiction over colonial affairs. Supreme authority in the New World was entrusted to two viceroys who sat in Mexico City and Lima. The official in Mexico City headed the viceroyalty of New Spain, which was made up of all the Spanish territories in North America together with the West Indies, Venezuela, and the Philippines. The Lima official presided over the viceroyalty of Peru, which was made up of the remaining Spanish possessions in South America. These two vast viceroyalties were subdivided into smaller units ruled by audiencias, or courts. Audiencias were staffed by professional lawyers who usually had no excessive family pride or military ambition and therefore made ideal royal servants. In the sixteenth century there were ten such audiencias in the New World.

A basic problem of Spanish administration in the Americas was the treatment of the Indians. The crown granted to deserving conquistadors, known as "protectors," or encomenderos,

Bartolomé de Las Casas was a Spanish priest who defended native Americans against the harsh treatment of the Spaniards. His writings described the cruel and inhumane treatment of native Americans in the West Indies.

the right to draw specified tribute from assigned Indian villages and also to levy forced labor. In return, the encomenderos were required to give military service and to pay the salaries of the parish clergy. The provision for forced labor obviously opened the door to abuse, so it was modified in the mid-sixteenth century. The natives still could be made to work, but by public officials rather than private encomenderos, and official wage rates had to be paid to the laborers so recruited. Needless to say, these safeguards were not always enforced. The colonies were too far from Madrid and too isolated from each other. Yet the fact remains that the Spaniards discussed seriously and conscientiously the problem of exploitation, for which there were no precedents.

The all-important fact for the economy of the Spanish colonial empire is that with the work of native labor a great flood of gold and silver poured in from the mines of Mexico and Bolivia. The law required that all precious metals be taken to the royal offices to be stamped and taxed at the rate of one-fifth their value, the royal quinto. Between 1503 and 1660 Spain received from America a total of 18,600 registered tons of silver and 200 registered tons of gold. Unregistered bullion smuggled into Spain has been variously estimated at from 10 to 50 percent of the total.

Apart from mining, the principal occupations in Latin America were agriculture and stock raising in the haciendas and plantation monoculture in the tropical coastlands. The haciendas employed Indian labor and produced foodstuffs for their own use and for sale to nearby cities and mining settlements. The plantations were quite different, employing mostly imported African slaves and producing only one crop for the European market. The first plantations were evolved for the growing of sugar on the Atlantic islands—the Azores, Madeiras, Cape Verdes, and Canaries. Later this institution was further developed, first in the sugar plantations of Brazil and the West Indies, and later in the tobacco, cotton, and coffee plantations of North and South America. The plant and animal products from haciendas and plantations steadily increased in value, so that by the early seventeenth century their value had exceeded even that of the legendary gold and silver exports.

VI. IBERIAN DECLINE

During the sixteenth century the Iberian countries led Europe in overseas enterprise and won vast riches from the Eastern spice trade and from the New World mines and haciendas and plantations. But by the end of the century they were rapidly slipping back from their respective positions of primacy. The French, Dutch, and English were poaching with increasing success in Portugal's Eastern Empire and in Spain's American colonies. One reason for the Iberian decline was their involvement in the religious and dynastic wars of the sixteenth and seventeenth centuries. Spanish manpower and treasure were squandered by Charles V and Philip II in fighting the religious wars against the Protestants; the recurring campaigns against the formidable Turks; and the dynastic struggles against rival royal houses, especially the French. In waging these campaigns the rulers of Spain fatally overextended themselves. They attempted to play the leading role on land as well as on sea. Their actions were in striking contrast to the successful strategy pursued later by England of remaining on the periphery of continental affairs and intervening only in case the balance of power were seriously threatened. British strategy enabled them to concentrate their efforts on the defense and development of their colonies. But Spain, like France, focused on the European continent and was continually involved in its wars. The end result was that the British were able to build a great worldwide empire, whereas the Spaniards lost economic, and then political, control of their empire.

Although the Iberian states definitely were weakened by foreign entanglements, a more important cause for their continued decline was the fact that they had become economic dependencies of northwest Europe. They had been so before they began their overseas expansion and they remained so afterward. As a result they were unable to exploit the economic opportunities offered by their newly won empires, and their empires, like the mother countries, fell under the domination of the northwest European states and became their colonies or semicolonies.

The economic dependence of the Iberian countries was a part of the general shift of the economic center of Europe in the late Middle Ages from the Mediterranean basin to the north. The reason for the shift was the accelerating productivity of northern Europe (see Chapter 21, Sections I–III), which enabled the new mass trade of the Baltic—North Sea area (grain, lumber, fish, and coarse cloth) to surpass the traditional luxury trade of the Mediterranean (spices, silks, perfumes, and jewelry). As the European economy grew and living standards rose, the mass trade catering to the general population increased much more rapidly than the luxury trade for the wealthy few.

Northern commerce was controlled by the Hanseatic League, which played the same role in the Baltic and North seas as Venice and Genoa did in the Mediterranean. In the sixteenth century the Hansa was dislodged by the Dutch, who built such a large and efficient merchant marine that they soon dominated the Atlantic seaboard. Formerly the Atlantic trade had been controlled by the Venetians and Genoese sailing northward with luxury commodities. But now it was controlled by the Dutch sailing southward with bulk cargoes. In this new trade pattern, the dependent economic status of the Iberian states was evident in their exports, which were almost exclusively raw materials—wine, wool, and iron ore from Spain, and African gold and salt from Portugal. In return the Iberians received back their own wool, which had been manufactured abroad into cloth, as well as metallurgical products, salt, and fish. Thus the Iberian states, like the Italian, were declining at this time from the status of developed to underdeveloped societies relative to the burgeoning capitalist economies of northern Europe (see Chapter 20, Section II, for the similar decline of Italy).

The economically backward Iberian states were able to take the lead in overseas expansion only because of a fortunate combination of favorable geographic location, maritime technology, and religious drive. But their expansion was not based on economic strength and dynamism, which explains why the Iberian states could not exploit their new empires effectively. They lacked the shipping necessary for imperial trade and also the industries to supply the manufactured goods needed in the Spanish American colonies. It is true that Spanish indus-

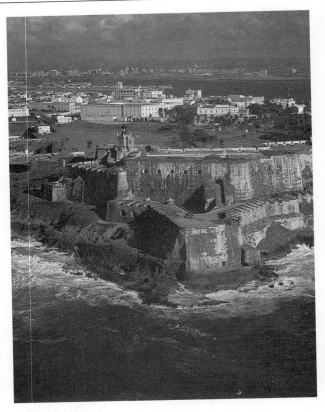

The fortress of El Morro in the harbor of San Juan, Puerto Rico. This massive citadel protected the Spanish treasure fleets that carried gold and silver each year to Spain from the mines of Mexico and Peru.

try for a few decades was stimulated by the expanding overseas market for manufacturers. But the industrial growth stopped about 1560, and chronic decline then set in.

Paradoxically enough, one reason for the decline was the great inflow of treasure, which produced a sharp inflation. Prices rose approximately twice as high in Spain as in northern Europe, and Spanish wages lagged only slightly behind the soaring prices, whereas wages in the rest of Europe were much lower. The inflation penalized Spanish industry, making its products too expensive to compete in the international market.

At least as important as the price and wage inflation was the ruinous influence of the Spanish aristocrat, or hidalgo, on the national economy and on national values. Although the aristocrats, together with the higher churchmen, comprised less than 2 percent of the population, they owned 95 to 97 percent of the land. It follows that the peasants, about 95 percent of all Spaniards, were almost all landless. The remaining 3 percent—clerics, merchants, and professional people, many of whom were Jews—were not a middle class in any economic or social sense. They were completely overshadowed by the nobility who had social status and prestige. And because the nobility looked down on careers in commerce or industry as demeaning, this prejudice became the national norm. Nor was this mere empty vanity, for the hidalgo had all the advantages—honors, exemption from taxation, and territorial wealth, which was more secure than commercial or industrial riches. Consequently, the ambition of successful merchants was to acquire estates; buy titles, which were sold by the impoverished crown; and thus abandon their class and become hidalgos. The blighting influence of this hidalgo spirit was felt in all branches of the economy—in the favoritism shown toward sheep farming as opposed to agriculture, in the expulsion of the industrious Jews and Moslems, and in the negative attitude of the Cortes assembly toward commercial and industrial interests. As a result of these attitudes, the economic spurt that occurred in Spain in the first half of the sixteenth century ended in failure.

This failure made it impossible to overcome the traditional Iberian economic backwardness and subservience to northwest Europe. It also doomed the Iberian colonial possessions to a corresponding backwardness and subservience. First the Dutch and then the British controlled most of the carrying trade with the Spanish and Portuguese colonies. The northwest Europeans also were soon supplying up to 90 percent of the manufactured goods imported by Brazil and Spanish America, as well as a high proportion of similar goods consumed in the Iberian peninsula itself. The merchant guild of Seville enjoyed a monopoly of all trade with the colonies, in which foreigners were forbidden by law to participate. But it was the foreigners who possessed the shipping and the manufactured goods needed in the colonies. Inevitably the Spanish merchants exported under their own name goods that belonged to foreign firms and were of for-

eign manufacture. Also through an elaborate set of pretenses, foreign merchants and financiers became members by proxy of the Seville guild. Thus the legal members conducted a vast commission business for foreigners that soon surpassed their own legitimate trade. The end result is apparent in the following complaint of a contemporary Spaniard: "All that the Spaniards bring from the Indies after long, prolix, and hazardous navigations, and all that they harvest with blood and labour, foreigners carry off to their homelands with ease and comfort."[2]

It is ironic that the net effect of Spanish overseas enterprise was to fuel the booming capitalist economy of northwest Europe, whereas in the Iberian peninsula it provided just enough wealth to forestall the basic institutional reforms that were long overdue. This is the root cause for the sudden and irreversible decline that followed so soon after the few decades of imperial glory.

Today's parallel to the boomerang effect of New World bullion on the Iberian peninsula is to be found in the Gulf oil states, where huge oil revenues are being squandered for foreign luxuries and consequently are ending up in foreign industrialized countries. When the Persian Gulf oil fields are exhausted, the flow of oil revenues will cease, as did the earlier flow of American bullion. The Gulf states then will find themselves in an even worse position than the Iberian states because after the oil is gone, the Gulf region will be left with little more than sand and dry holes.

SUGGESTED READINGS

The best overall survey of Europe expansion is provided by J. H. Parry, *The Age of Reconnaissance: Discovery, Exploration and Settlement 1450–1650* (New American Library, 1963), and his *European Reconnaissance: Selected Documents* (Harper & Row, 1968). See also G. V. Scammell, *The World Encompassed: The First European Maritime Empires, c. 800–1650* (University of California, 1981). The following interpretations of European expansion reflect an Indian viewpoint: K. M. Panikkar, *Asia and Western Dominance* (Harper & Row, 1954); and K. N. Chaudhuri, *Trade and Civilization in the Indian Ocean* (Cambridge University, 1985). The lethal biological repercussions of European expansion are analyzed by A. W. Crosby, *Ecological Imperialism: The Biological Expansion of Europe, 900–1900* (Cambridge University, 1986). The religious factor in European expansion is presented by C. R. Boxer, *The Church Militant and Iberian Expansion 1440–1770* (Johns Hopkins University, 1978).

For Portuguese maritime and colonial enterprise, see B. W. Diffie, *Prelude to Empire: Portugal Overseas Before Henry the Navigator* (University of Nebraska, 1963); E. Bradford, *Southward the Caravels: The Story of Henry the Navigator* (Hutchinson, 1961); C. R. Boxer, *The Portuguese Seaborne Empire, 1415–1825* (Knopf, 1969); and G. R. Crone, *The Discovery of the East* (St. Martin's, 1972). The best general analyses of the Spanish colonial system are C. H. Haring, *The Spanish Empire in America* (Oxford University, 1947); and J. Lockhart and S. B. Schwartz, *Early Latin America* (Cambridge University, 1983). See also C. Gibson, *The Aztecs Under Spanish Rule: A History of the Indians of the Valley of Mexico, 1519–1810* (Stanford University, 1964); J. Descola, *Daily Life in Colonial Peru 1710–1820* (Allen & Unwin, 1968); and J. H. Parry, *The Spanish Seaborne Empire* (Knopf, 1966). For the Portuguese

efforts in America there are G. Freyre, *Brazil, an Interpretation* (Knopf, 1945); and C. R. Boxer, *The Golden Age of Brazil, 1695–1750: Growing Pains of a Colonial Society* (University of California, 1963).

Finally, the roots and course of Iberian decline are presented in J. Lynch, *Spain Under the Hapsburgs*, Vol. I, *Empire and Absolutism, 1516–1598* (Oxford University, 1964); in J. H. Elliott, *Imperial Spain 1469–1716* (New American Library, 1966); in the two excellent studies by R. T. Davies, *The Golden Century of Spain, 1501–1621* (Macmillan, 1954), and *Spain in Decline, 1621–1700* (Macmillan, 1957); and in the stimulating analysis by S. J. and B. H. Stein, *The Colonial Heritage of Latin America* (Oxford University, 1970).

NOTES

1. Cited by K. M. Panikkar, *Asia and Western Dominance* (Day, 1953), p. 42.
2. Cited by *The New Cambridge Economic History,* I (Cambridge University, 1957), p. 454.

CHAPTER

23

West European Expansion: Dutch, French, British Phase, 1600–1763

I should like to see Adam's will, wherein he divided the earth between Spain and Portugal.

King Francis I

In the period between 1600 and 1763 Spain and Portugal were overtaken and surpassed by the powers of northwestern Europe—Holland, France, and Britain. This development was of great significance for the entire world. It made northwestern Europe the most influential and dynamic region of the globe. And the countries of northwestern Europe were to dominate the world—politically, militarily, economically, and, to a certain degree, culturally—until 1914. Their practices and institutions became the models for peoples everywhere.

The domination of the world by northwestern Europe did not actually materialize until after 1763. But it was between 1600 and 1763 that the basis for domination was laid. These were the years when the British gained their first foothold in India, when the Dutch drove the Portuguese out of the East Indies, when all the northwestern powers set up stations on the coasts of Africa, and when the British and the French became the masters of North America above the Rio Grande and came to control much of the commerce of the Iberian colonies south of it.

This chapter will analyze the roots of northwest European primacy, and the struggles of Holland, France, and Britain for leadership, culminating in 1763 with the emergence of Britain as the dominant colonial power of the world.

I. EARLY NORTHWEST EUROPEAN EXPANSION

Northwestern Europe did not rise from utter obscurity to the leading position in continental commerce and overseas enterprise. As noted in the preceding chapter, the foundation was laid during the late Middle Ages when the economic center of Europe shifted from the Mediterranean basin northward, and when the principal trade routes likewise shifted from the Mediterranean to the Atlantic. In addition to economic superiority, northwestern Europe possessed a social structure and a cultural climate that were particularly responsive to economic interests. Far from regarding business enterprise with disdain, the patricians of Holland and the nobility of England, and even of France, were always ready to participate in any business venture that promised profit. Not only did the gentry take part in commerce, but there was also much greater class mobility in the north, where merchants and financiers often entered the ranks of the nobility. This favored a positive attitude toward economic enterprise, in contrast to the short-sighted hidalgo spirit that contributed so much to Iberian decadence.

Finally, northwestern Europe was aided by a price-wage-rent differential. Prices rose 256 percent in England during the sixteenth and seventeenth centuries, whereas wages rose only 145 percent. Rents also lagged badly behind prices in northwestern Europe. This meant that of the three main elements of society—the laborers, landlords, and entrepreneurs—the entrepreneurs were the ones who reaped golden profits during these centuries of inflation. Profits were plowed back into mining ventures, industrial establishments, and commercial enterprises, with the result that the economy of northwestern Europe boomed ahead at an unprecedented rate. The famous British economist John Maynard Keynes has described the period from 1550 to 1650 as follows: "Never in the annals of the modern world has there existed so prolonged and so rich an opportunity for the business man, the speculator, and the profiteer. In these golden years modern capitalism was born."[1] That it was born in northwestern Europe explains why the northwestern countries forged ahead of Spain and Portugal and attained a predominant position in world affairs, a position they were to retain until the outbreak of World War I.

The countries of northwestern Europe were naturally envious of the lucrative empires of Spain and Portugal. But for a long time they refrained from poaching on these imperial preserves for fear of Iberian power. Accordingly, the English, the Dutch, and the French turned to the North Atlantic, which was beyond the limits of Iberian activity. Henry VII of England sent John Cabot out into the North Atlantic in 1496, the year of Columbus's second return. And Cabot discovered a resource that turned out in the long run to be even more valuable than the silver mines of the Spaniards: He found fish. The sea off Newfoundland was teeming with fish—probably the most important article of trade in fifteenth- and sixteenth-century Europe. Fish was the winter staple of the people and their diet on fast days throughout the year. The regular supply of immense quantities of cod was a great windfall for a continent where many people at that time lived near starvation level for part of every year. And the Newfoundland fisheries bred successive generations of mariners who were trained and fitted for ocean navigation. The ships that later probed the Arctic for a northeast or a northwest passage, the expeditions that began the settlement of North America, the English and the Dutch fleets that fought the armadas of Spain and Portugal—all these were largely manned by seamen trained in the hard school of the Banks fisheries.

The maritime states of northwestern Europe were by no means satisfied with cod. They still hankered after spices, but they were not yet prepared to challenge Portugal's mastery of the Cape route. So they began their long and fruitless series of expeditions in search of a northeast or northwest passage to the Orient. They reasoned that since the tropics had proved passable, contrary to all expectations, the Arctic should be passable too. Hence the 1553 English expedition under Sir Hugh Willoughby and Richard Chancellor sought a northeast passage to China, only to be blocked by a wall of ice. This expedition, however, did succeed in making a landing on the shores of the White Sea, where it established contact with the court of Tsar Ivan IV. This contact led to the founding of the Muscovy Company (1555) for the purpose of direct trade between England and Russia. Other attempts to find a northeast passage proved futile. Several expeditions seeking a northwest passage (John Davis, 1585–1587; Henry Hudson, 1607–1611; William Baffin, 1615–1616) had no better luck. But just as the efforts in the northeast brought about trade with Russia, so the

Landing of Richard Chancellor at Holmogory in the White Sea, 1553.

northwest ventures discovered the Hudson Strait and Hudson Bay. Together they provided a back entrance to the richest fur-producing region of the New World.

The failure of the northern Europeans to find new routes to the East drove them to encroach on the preserves of the Iberian powers. Since Portugal's eastern possessions were still too strongly guarded, the northerners struck first at the more vulnerable Spanish colonies in the Americas. English interlopers showing up in Spanish America at this time tried to carry on trade on a peaceful, commercial basis. They wanted not to plunder but to take advantage of the opportunities offered by the inability of the weak Spanish industry to meet the needs of the colonies. Of the two commodities most in

demand in the Spanish colonies—cloth and slaves—the English produced the first and could purchase the second in West Africa. Because he was shrewd enough to see the possibilities of the situation and bold enough to act without regard for legal niceties, Sir John Hawkins won fame and fortune as the founder of the English slave trade. In 1562 he made his first voyage. He picked up slaves in Sierra Leone and exchanged them in Hispaniola (Haiti) for hides and sugar. The profits were so spectacular that Queen Elizabeth and several of her Privy Councilors secretly invested in his second voyage. He followed the same procedure as before and returned with a cargo of silver that made him the richest man in England.

The Spanish ambassador in London made strong protests against this contraband trade. Even though Hawkins had peacefully exchanged slaves for colonial commodities, the fact remained that it was illegal for foreigners to trade with the Spanish colonies. Although not piracy, it definitely was poaching. Hawkins nevertheless sailed out for a third time in 1567. This venture ended in disaster, with three of Hawkins's five ships sunk or captured. The other two, one commanded by Hawkins and the other by his cousin Francis Drake, reached England in 1569 in disabled condition.

If the commerce could not be conducted peacefully and legally, it was bound to be carried on by other means. The opportunities for profit were too great for the English and the other northerners to refrain and forget. During the following decades, the Protestant sea captains visited the Spanish Indies as pirates and privateers rather than as peaceful, though illegal, traders. When King Philip of Spain sent his armada against England in 1588, two of its most formidable adversaries were John Hawkins and Francis Drake. The defeat they inflicted on the armada was, for them, sweet revenge for what they had suffered in the West Indies.

Formal war with Spain (which at this time had absorbed Portugal) removed any inhibitions that may have restrained the Protestant powers. They broke boldly and openly into the Iberian imperial preserves—into the Portuguese East as well as into Spanish America. And the more they penetrated, the more they were encouraged to

In 1588 Philip II sent a massive naval armada to invade England. The English, however, with the help of the weather and the Dutch, dispersed and destroyed the Spanish fleet. Spain never fully recovered from this defeat.

go further as they found out how weak the Iberians were. The Dutch were the first to exploit the opportunity afforded by Iberian decline. The seventeenth century was to be for Holland *Het Gouden Eeuw*— "the Golden Century."

II. HOLLAND'S GOLDEN CENTURY

The remarkable rise of Holland to power and prosperity in the seventeenth century was in part a result of its favorable geographic location. Backed by the great hinterland of Germany, Holland was strategically located along the ancient trade routes of Europe running north-south from Bergen to Gibraltar, and east-west from the Gulf of Finland to Britain. Basic trade commodities were transported along these routes: herring and salt from Biscay; wine from the Mediterranean; cloth from Britain and Flanders; copper and iron from Sweden; and cereals, flax, hemp, timber, and wood products from the Baltic.

The Dutch began their rise to greatness by serving as the carriers of these commodities. Their merchant marine owed its start to the local coastal fisheries. The Dutch devised new methods of preserving, salting, and smoking, and they exported their catch to all parts of Europe in return for corn, timber, and salt. With the building of the Spanish and Portuguese overseas empire, the Dutch picked up cargoes of the new colonial products in Seville and Lisbon and distributed them throughout Europe. In return, they supplied the Iberian countries with Baltic grain and naval stores. The Dutch transported these commodities in their *fluyt*, or flyboat, an inexpensive general carrier with enormous capacity. Hitherto the typical merchantman had been built with heavy timbering and galleried transom so that it could mount cannon and serve, when necessary, as a man-of-war. The

Dutch were the first to take the risk of building a merchant packet deliberately designed to carry only goods and no guns. The fluyt's broad beam, flattened bottom, and restricted cabin accommodations gave it maximum hold space and unusual economy of building material. This slow and ugly but cheap and capacious boat was the mainstay of the Dutch merchant marine that came to dominate the seas of the world.

At the end of the sixteenth century the Dutch began to challenge Portugal's empire in the East. The first task was to collect reliable data to guide the navigators around the long Cape route. The Portuguese had taken the greatest precautions to keep such information from their rivals, but their navigation secrets gradually leaked out. The Dutch swarmed into the Eastern waters. No fewer than five fleets made up of twenty-two ships sailed in the year 1598 alone. From the beginning they outmatched the Portuguese. They were better sailors, they could transport spices more cheaply in their fluyten, and their trade goods were cheaper and better constructed because their home industry was superior to that of the Iberian states.

By 1602 the Dutch amalgamated their various private trading companies into one great national concern, the Dutch East India Company. The English had organized their own East India Company two years earlier, in 1600, but they were no match for the Dutch. The sub-scribed capital of the English company was small, and in later years, the Dutch Company established a network of fortified posts in the East Indies. The posts made it necessary to have treaties with local rulers. Treaties led to alliances, and alliances, to protectorates. By the end of the seventeenth century the Dutch were actually administering only a small area, but numerous states making up a much greater area had become protectorates. Then during the eighteenth and nineteenth centuries the Dutch annexed these protectorates outright and built up a great territorial empire.

The export of spices to Europe diminished in value after about 1700, but the Dutch developed a new economic resource at about that time when they introduced coffee bushes into the East Indies. Modestly beginning in 1711 with a harvest of 100 pounds of coffee, by 1723 they were marketing 12 million pounds. Thus, as Europe acquired a taste for coffee, the Dutch became the principal suppliers of this exotic beverage. Through these various means the Dutch East India Company managed to average annual dividends of 18 percent throughout the seventeenth and eighteenth centuries.

Dutch overseas activities were not confined to the East Indies, however. In the Arctic waters around Spitzbergen the Dutch virtually monopolized the whaling industry. In Russia they badly outdistanced the English Muscovy Company.

By the 1600s, the Dutch were seriously challenging Spain's superiority on the seas. Here the Dutch are shown capturing Spanish ships.

They also dominated the rich Baltic trade so that they became the chief provisioners in western Europe of all-important naval stores—timber, pitch, tar, hemp for rope, and flax for canvas sailcloth.

Their merchant marine was by far the largest of the world, numbering 10,000 ships as early as 1600. Dutch shipyards were highly mechanized and could produce almost a vessel a day. Furthermore, the ships were economical to build and to operate, so that Dutch shipowners undercut their competitors. Thus, they served as the carriers among Spain, France, England, and the Baltic. Not until the eighteenth century were the English able to compete with the Dutch in merchant shipping.

In the New World, the Dutch founded the profitable but short-lived colony of New Amsterdam on Manhattan Island in 1612 and also briefly held various islands and coastal strips in the West Indies. But the Dutch colony that proved to be the most durable of all was the small settlement established in 1652 on the Cape of Good Hope in South Africa. This was not a trading station but a true colony founded to provide fuel, water, and fresh provisions for the ships en route to the East. The colony soon proved its value. The fresh meat and vegetables it provided to Dutch and other ships helped keep down scurvy and saved the lives of thousands of seamen. Today the descendants of these Dutch peasants, or Boers, comprise three-fifths of the 3 million Europeans residing in South Africa.

During the eighteenth century Holland fell behind Britain and France in economic development and overseas activity. One reason for this decline was the persistent efforts of the French and British governments to build up their merchant marines with the help of discriminatory decrees against the Dutch. The Dutch were weakened also by a series of exhausting wars—with Britain from 1652 to 1674 over mercantile disputes, and with France from 1667 to 1713 over the territorial ambitions of Louis XIV.

Perhaps the chief reason for the decline of the Dutch was that they lacked the resources of their rivals. The French had a large population, a flourishing agriculture, and a rich homeland with outlets on both the Atlantic and the Mediterranean. The English also had much greater natural resources than the Dutch and enjoyed the great boon of an insular location, which spared them the cost of periodic invasions. Furthermore, the English had behind them the rapidly growing wealth and strength of their overseas colonies, whereas the Dutch were backed by only one small and isolated settlement on the tip of South Africa. Thus the value of British exports rose from £8 million in

This earliest known depiction of New Amsterdam (published 1651) on the tip of Manhattan island testifies to the town's slow growth. It contained only a few dozen houses and a windmill located outside a fort. The European ships in the background, as well as the Indian canoes in front, indicate the importance of trade to the Dutch colony.

1720 to £19 million in 1763, and the French exports increased from 120 million livres in 1716 to 500 million in 1789. The Dutch, who has already reached their peak, were simply incapable of matching such growth. In the final analysis, Holland gave way to Britain and France in the eighteenth century for the same reason that Britain and France were to give way to the United States and the Soviet Union in the twentieth.

III. ANGLO-FRENCH RIVALRY

The eighteenth century was marked by a struggle between Britain and France for colonial supremacy. The two countries were in face-to-face rivalry throughout the globe—in North America, in Africa, and in India.

In North America, the British and French possessions had many characteristics in common. They were settled at about the same time. They were located on the Atlantic seaboard and in the West Indian islands. The native populations were relatively sparse and primitive so that the British and the French, unlike the Spanish, could not hope to live off native labor, although they did depend on Negro slave labor in the sugar islands. Since the British and French found no precious metals, they had to support themselves by agriculture, fishing, lumbering, commerce, and fur trading.

The English colonies fell roughly into three groups: Virginia and its immediate neighbors, which produced mostly tobacco; New England with its little groups of nonconformist settlements, which engaged in fishing, lumbering, commerce, and the fur trade; and the British West Indies, by far the most highly prized because of their extremely profitable sugar plantations. One characteristic of the English colonies, taken as a whole, was their large populations, which were much greater than those of the French. Their other chief characteristic was their political independence. Every colony had a governor, an executive council, and a judiciary, all appointed from England. Nearly every colony also had an elective legislative assembly, and as a rule it was at loggerheads with the appointed officials. Its most common quarrel with the London government was the insistence of the latter

This eighteenth-century label for Virginia tobacco depicts an Indian smoker on the right. To the left is an African slave. For most of the seventeenth century, white indentured servants predominated among Virginia's laborers, but a transition to African slaves began to occur in the 1680s.

that all colonial products be sent to England in English ships. This seemed to the royal officers a reasonable requirement, since they in turn gave the colonies a monopoly of the home market for their products. But the colonial merchants and planters protested bitterly when they were prohibited from using the cheaper Dutch shipping and from exporting their products to more profitable non-English markets.

The French settlements in North America were outstanding because of their strategic location. The first French posts were established in Acadia, or Nova Scotia, in 1605; in Quebec in 1608; and in Montreal in 1642. Using the St. Lawrence River valley as their main base of colonization, the French took advantage of the incomparable inland water system to push westward to Lake Superior and southward to the Ohio River. In 1682 a French nobleman, La Salle, paddled down the Mississippi and laid claim to the whole basin, which he named Louisiana in honor of Louis XIV. This raised complications, for most of the colonial charters issued by the English crown in the seventeenth century included clauses granting lands "from sea to sea"—that is, from the Atlantic to the Pacific. It was clear that whenever the English colonists reached and crossed the Appalachian Mountains, the rival French and English claims would clash head-on. At the outset, however, the French had the great advantage of posses-sion. Their explorers had been the first to open up these regions, after which their officials had planted numerous forts along the route from the St. Lawrence to Louisiana. The English colonies along the Atlantic seaboard were effectively encircled by a great arc running from the Gulf of St. Lawrence to the Gulf of Mexico.

The French not only possessed the com-manding positions in North America, but they also had the great advantage of discipline and cohesion. There were no uncontrollable elective bodies in the French colonies. Paris appointed the governors, who were responsible for the defense of each colony, and the intendants, who handled financial and economic affairs. This arrangement was quicker and more efficient than the creaking English representative system. The governors of the English colonies could only request and urge their assemblies to take a certain course of action. They could scarcely command, especially since the assemblies voted the funds for their salaries. In the French colonies the governors and intendants gave the orders, and their subordinates carried them out.

The French and English were neighbors also in the West Indies. The chief French posses-sions in this region were Martinique and Guade-loupe; the English were Jamaica, Barbados, and the Bahamas. These colonies were valuable as stations for trade with the Spanish and Por-tuguese colonies to the south, but their greatest asset was their tropical produce—sugar, tobacco, and indigo—which supplemented the economies of France and Britain.

India also was the scene of sharp Anglo-French conflicts, paralleling those in North America. The British had fallen back on the Indi-

an subcontinent when they were driven out of the East Indies by the Dutch in the early seven-teenth century. By the end of the century they had four major footholds in India: Calcutta and Madras on the eastern coast, and Surat and Bombay on the western. The French had orga-nized an East India Company of their own in 1604, but it soon became inactive. It was revived in 1664, and by the end of the century the French were ensconced in two major posts—Chandarnagar, near Calcutta, and Pondichéry, near Madras.

During the seventeenth century all Euro-peans who resided and traded in India did so on the sufferance of the powerful Mogul emperors. The Moguls could easily have driven the Euro-peans into the sea had they not behaved them-selves and humbly submitted petitions for the privilege of carrying on their commercial opera-tions. During the eighteenth century the situa-tion was completely reversed because of the dis-integration of the Mogul empire. Emperor Akbar's successors persecuted the Hindu majori-ty, which led to disaffection and turmoil. Provincial governors began to assert their inde-pendence and to establish hereditary local dynasties. The Marathas, who represented Hindu nationalism in a vague and incipient sense, expanded from their capital of Satara, about a hundred miles south of Bombay on the west coast to within two hundred miles of Cal-cutta on the east. This disintegration of central authority gave the British and the French East India companies the opportunity to transform themselves from mere commercial organizations to territorial overlords and tribute collectors. They built forts, maintained soldiers, coined money, and entered into treaties with surround-ing Indian potentates. No central authority in India was able to stop this spread of British and French influence.

IV. ENGLAND'S TRIUMPH

Such, then, was the lineup of the rival British and French empires in India and the Americas. The duel between the two empires during the seventeenth and eighteenth centuries ended in an overwhelming British triumph. One reason was that France was less interested in overseas

A view of the taking of Quebec by the English forces commanded by General Wolfe, September 13, 1759.

possessions than in European hegemony. Since the sixteenth century, the French Bourbons had concentrated primarily on gaining ground in Italy and on combating the Hapsburgs in Austria and Spain.

Another reason for Britain's triumph was that many more Englishmen than Frenchmen emigrated to the colonies. By 1688 there were 300,000 English settlers concentrated in the narrow region along the Atlantic coast compared to a mere 20,000 French scattered over the vast areas of Canada and the Mississippi valley. At the time of the American Revolution the population of the English colonies amounted to no fewer than 2 million. The mass transplantation explains in large part why Britain was victorious over France in 1763 and why the American Republic defeated Britain two decades later.

The colonial and commercial rivalry between Britain and France was fought out in a series of four wars that dragged on for almost a century until England's great victory in 1763. All these wars had two phases: one European and the other overseas. The European revolved about dynastic ambitions, especially those of Louis

XIV of France and Frederick the Great of Prussia. The overseas operations were fought over diverse issues—the balance of power in India, conflicting territorial claims in America, terms of trade in the Spanish colonies, and control of the world trade routes. The dichotomy between the European and overseas aspects of these wars was sufficiently marked so that each one was known by one name in Europe and another in America. Hence the wars have come down in history as the War of the League of Augsburg, or King William's War (1689–1697); the War of the Spanish Succession, or Queen Anne's War (1701–1713); the War of the Austrian Succession, or King George's War (1740–1748); and the Seven Years' War, or the French and Indian War (1756–1763).

The net result of the first three of these wars was that the British acquired Nova Scotia, Newfoundland, and the Hudson Bay territories. But these conquests did not settle the basic question of whether the French would retain Canada and the Mississippi Valley, and thereby restrict the English to the Atlantic seaboard. This question was finally answered conclusively by the fourth war, which also settled the future of India.

This fateful struggle is known as the Seven Years' War because it was waged for seven years—between 1756 and 1763. The turning point of the war came in 1757, largely because of William Pitt (the Elder), who then entered the British cabinet. Pitt concentrated his resources on the navy and the colonies, while subsidizing his ally, Frederick of Prussia, to fight on in Europe. His strategy was, as he put it, to win an empire on the plains of Germany, and he succeeded brilliantly. His reinforced navies swept the French off the seas, and the American colonists, stirred by his leadership, joined the British regulars to form a force of about 50,000 men. This huge army overwhelmed one French fort after another. The climax came with the siege of Quebec, the heart of French Canada and a great natural stronghold on the banks of the St. Lawrence. In the ensuing battle, the British and the French commanders, General James Wolfe and the Marquis de Montcalm, were killed. But the British veterans prevailed, and Quebec surrendered in September 1759. The fall of Montreal the following year spelled the end of the French colonial empire in America.

In India the success of the English was no less complete. Again naval superiority was the deciding factor. Britain was able to transport troops, money, and supplies from Europe while preventing France from doing likewise. The British, too, had the inspired leadership of Robert Clive, a company official who had come out years before as a clerk. Clive possessed both outstanding military talents and an ability to understand Indian politics. In 1756, on hearing of the war in Europe, he marched on Bengal. With the support of Indian merchants who had become wealthy in the trade with Europe, Clive defeated the pro-French Moslem ruler at the Battle of Plassey in 1757. He put his own puppet on the throne and extorted huge reparations both for himself and for his company. During the rest of the war, thanks to the strong British navy, Clive was able to shift his forces at will from one part of India to another. At the same time he severed the communications of the French posts with each other and with France. The end came with the surrender in 1761 of the main French base at Pondichéry.

The overseas phase of the Seven Years' War was decided by the fall of Quebec in America and of Pondichéry in India. But the war dragged on in Europe until 1763, when the belligerents concluded the Peace of Paris. Of its American possessions, France retained only Guiana in South America; the insignificant islands of St. Pierre and Miquelon on the Newfoundland coast; and a few islands in the West Indies,

The Dutch established a major trading base at Batavia in the East Indies. The city they called Batavia is now Djakarta, Indonesia.

including Guadeloupe and Martinique. Britain therefore received from France the whole of the St. Lawrence valley and all the territory east of the Mississippi. Spain had entered the war late on the side of France and was, therefore, compelled to cede Florida to Britain. As compensation, France gave Spain western Louisiana; that is, the territory west of the Mississippi River. In India the French retained possession of their commercial installations—offices, warehouses, and docks—at Pondichéry and other towns. But they were forbidden to build fortifications or make political alliances with the Indian princes. In other words, the French returned to India as traders and not as empire builders.

When the Treaty of Paris was signed, the British political leader Horace Walpole remarked, "Burn your Greek and Roman books, histories of little people." This far-seeing observation points up the long-range, worldwide implications of the peace settlements. As far as Europe was concerned, the treaty allowed Prussia to keep Silesia and to become Austria's rival for the leadership of the Germanies. But of much more significance for world history was France's loss of North America and India, which meant that America north of the Rio Grande was to develop in the future as a part of the English-speaking world.

France's expulsion from India was also a historical event of global significance, for it meant that the British were to take the place of the Moguls there. Once installed in Delhi, the British were well on their way to world empire and world primacy. It was the incomparable base offered by the vast and populous subcontinent of India that enabled the British in the nineteenth century to expand into the rest of south Asia and then beyond to east Asia. For these reasons the 1763 settlement has profoundly affected the course of world history to the present day.

SUGGESTED READINGS

For works on general European overseas expansion, see the bibliography for Chapter 24. On the eighteenth-century period, see J. H. Parry, *Trade and Dominion: The Overseas European Empires in the Eighteenth Century* (Praeger, 1971); and W. L. Dorn, *Competition for Empire, 1740–1763* (Harper & Row, 1940). For Holland's overseas activities, see C. R. Boxer, *The Dutch Seaborne Empire, 1600–1800* (Knopf, 1965); D. W. Davies, *A Primer of Dutch Seventeenth Century Overseas Trade* (Nijhoff, 1961); and G. Musselman, *The Cradle of Colonialism* (Yale University, 1963). The reasons why the Dutch displaced the Portuguese in Asia are analyzed in N. Steensgaard, *The Asian Trade Revolution of the Seventeenth Century* (University of Chicago, 1974); and H. Furber, *Rival Empires of Trade in the Orient 1600–1800* (University of Minnesota, 1976).

A general survey of French overseas activity is available in H. I. Priestly, *France Overseas Through the Old Regime: A Study of European Expansion* (Prentice Hall, 1939). More specialized studies are the two works of N. M. Crouse, *French Pioneers in the West Indies, 1624–1664* (Columbia University, 1940), and *The French Struggle for the West Indies, 1665–1713* (Columbia University, 1943); G. M. Wrong, *The Rise and Fall of New France*, 2 vols. (Macmillan, 1928); and S. P. Sen, *The French in India* (Mukhopadhyay, 1958).

Two excellent general surveys of Britain overseas are C. E. Carrington's *The British Overseas: Exploits of a Nation of Shopkeepers* (Cambridge University, 1950); and W. B. Willcox's *Star of Empire: A Study of Britain as a World Power, 1485–1945* (Knopf, 1950). The colonial wars are described by E. P. Hamilton, *The French and Indian Wars: The Story of Battles and Forts in the Wilderness* (Doubleday, 1962). The classic history of the most dramatic phase of the Seven Years' War in America is by F. Parkman, *Montcalm and Wolfe*, 2 vols. (Boston, 1884).

NOTE

1. Cited by L. Huberman, *Man's Worldly Goods* (Harper & Row, 1936), p. 103.

CHAPTER
24

Russian Expansion in Asia

Throughout Russian history one dominating theme has been the frontier; the theme of the struggle for the mastering of the natural resources of an untamed country, expanded into a continent by the ever-shifting movement of the Russian people and their conquest of and intermingling with other peoples.

B. H. Sumner,
A Short History of Russia

At the same time that western Europeans were expanding overseas to all corners of the globe, the Russians were expanding overland across the entire length of Eurasia. The mastering of the continental expanses of Siberia is an epic story comparable to that of westward expansion across the United States to the Pacific. In fact, the ever-advancing frontier has left as indelible a stamp on the Russian character and Russian institutions as it has on the American. The Russians were not the only European peoples who were affected by a frontier. During the medieval period, large parts of central and eastern Europe were lightly populated (see Chapter 21, Section I). For centuries, various European peoples, and particularly the Germans, pressed a line of settlement eastward along the Baltic coast and down the Danube valley. But by the end of the Middle Ages, internal colonization no longer was a dominant movement. Overseas colonization took its place, and the peoples of western Europe concentrated their energies on opening and exploring new frontiers in new worlds. The

Russian people, by contrast, continued to expand overland into the vast Eurasian plain stretching out from their doorstep. This was a stupendous undertaking, which continued for several centuries until the last of the Moslem khanates in central Asia was subdued in 1895. It is not surprising, then, that the frontier has been a major factor throughout the course of Russian history, as it has been throughout American history. In this chapter we shall examine the nature and the course of Russian expansion into Siberia and the Ukraine.

I. GEOGRAPHY OF RUSSIAN EXPANSION

To understand the remarkable Russian expansion across the plains of Eurasia we must first understand the geography of those plains. A glance at the map shows their staggering proportions (see map of Russian Expansion in Europe and Asia, p. 369). Russia encompasses a sixth of the land surface of the globe and is larger than

Russian Expansion in Europe and Asia

Legend:
- Russia in 1533
- Russia in 1598
- Russia in 1689
- Acquired by 1914
- 1970 boundary

1000 Miles
1000 Kilometers
500
500

ARCTIC OCEAN

BERING SEA

PACIFIC OCEAN

SEA OF OKHOTSK

SIBERIA

KAMCHATKA

Petropavlovsk

Magadan

Okhotsk

Yakutsk

Albazin

Khabarovsk

Vladivostok

JAPAN

NORTH KOREA

SOUTH KOREA

CHINA

MONGOLIA

Lake Baikal

Irkutsk

Krasnoyarsk

Yenisei R.

Tomsk

Tobolsk

Ob R.

Itlysh R.

Omsk

Karaganda

Lake Balkhash

ARAL SEA

Syr Darya

Tashkent

Amu Darya

Khiva

Geok Tepe

Merv

AFGHANISTAN

IRAN

CASPIAN SEA

Sverdlovsk

Kazan

Stalingrad

Volga R.

Don R.

Dnieper R.

Kiev

Moscow

Leningrad

Murmansk

Archangel

FINLAND

SWEDEN

NORWAY

BALTIC SEA

POLAND

GERMANY

RUMANIA

TURKEY

BLACK SEA

369

the United States, Canada, and Central America combined. Another prominent characteristic of the Russian landmass is its remarkable topographical uniformity. It is in very large part a flat plains area. The Ural Mountains do run across the plains in a north-south direction, and they are commonly thought of as dividing the country into two separate parts—European Russia and Asiatic Russia. But the fact is that the Urals are a single, narrow, worn-down chain of mountains with an average altitude of only 2,000 feet. Furthermore, they do not extend further south than the fifty-first parallel, leaving a wide gap of flat desert country stretching down to the Caspian Sea. This topographic uniformity helps to explain why the Russians were able to spread so rapidly from the Baltic to the Pacific.

The Eurasian plains that make up most of present-day Russia are surrounded by a natural southern boundary stretching from the Black Sea to the Pacific Ocean. This boundary consists of an uninterrupted chain of mountains, deserts, and inland seas; beginning in the west and moving eastward, they are the Caucasus Mountains; the Caspian Sea; the Ust Urt Desert; the Aral Sea; the Kizil-Kum Desert; the Hindu Kush, Pamir, and Tien Shan ranges; the Gobi Desert; and the Great Khingan Mountains, which extend east to the Pacific Ocean. The ring of mountains surrounding the Eurasian plains keeps out the moisture-laden winds from the Pacific and the warm monsoons from the Indian Ocean and explains both the desert climate of central Asia and the cold, dry climate of Siberia. The whole expanse of Siberia, from the Baltic to the Pacific, has essentially the same continental type of climate, with short, hot summers and long, cold winters. The uniformity of climate, like that of topography, facilitated Russia's eastward expansion, for the frontierspeople felt equally at home throughout the 5,000-mile expanse of plains. The central Asian deserts, on the other hand, seemed strange and forbidding. Moreover, they were held by militarily powerful Moslem khanates in contrast to the weak tribes in Siberia. As a result, the Russians did not master the central Asian deserts until 250 years after they had reached the Pacific further north.

Russian expansion was affected by river systems as well as by topography and climate. Because of the flat terrain, Russian rivers are generally long, wide, and unencumbered by rapids. Consequently they are invaluable as routes for commerce, colonization, and conquest. West of the Urals there are a number of outstanding rivers: the Western Dvina flowing into the Baltic; the Dniester, the Dnieper, and the Don flowing south to the Black Sea; and the Volga flowing first east and then south to the Caspian. East of the Urals the Siberian plains are watered by four vast river systems: the Ob in the west, the Yenisei in the center, the Lena in the northeast, and the Amur in the southeast. Since the whole of Siberia tilts downward from the massive Tibetan ranges, the first three of these rivers flow northward into the Arctic, whereas the fourth makes its way eastward to the Pacific. These rivers, together with their numerous tributaries, provide a natural network of highways across the plains. Thus the Russian fur traders were able to make their way eastward with few portages to the Pacific Ocean, just as French and English fur traders in the New World made their way westward along similar riverways to the same ocean.

A final geographic factor in the pace and course of Russian expansion is the combination of soil and vegetation prevailing in various parts of the country. Four major soil-vegetation zones run in east-west layers across Russia. (See map of Soil and Vegetation Zones of Eurasia, p. 371.) In the far north, along the Arctic coast, is the barren tundra, frozen the year round except for a six- to eight-week growing period in the summer. To the south of the tundra is the taiga, or forest belt. The largest of the four zones, it is 600 to 1,300 miles wide and 4,600 miles long. It includes a fifth of the total forest area of the world. The Russians felt at home in the forests, and they were able to cross the whole of Eurasia without ever losing the familiar protective covering.

On their southern edges the forests thin out, and the trees grow smaller until they give way completely to the open, treeless steppe. Here there is fertile black earth formed by millennia of decayed grass. Today it is the breadbasket of Russia, but for centuries it was a source of misery and woe. The steppe was the home of the marauding horse nomads of central Eurasia. When these nomads were sufficiently strong, they struck out along the line of least resis-

Soil and Vegetation Zones of Eurasia

tance—sometimes westward into central Europe or eastward into China. More frequently they attacked the vulnerable Russians in eastern Europe. A major theme of Russian history is this continued conflict between the Slavic peasants of the forest zone and the Asiatic nomads of the steppe. At first the nomads prevailed, and the result was two centuries of Mongol rule over Russia. But in the end the Slavic woodspeople became stronger, and they were able not only to win their independence but also to expand over the Eurasian plains.

The fourth zone, the desert, is the smallest in area, starting in China but extending westward only to the Caspian Sea. We have seen that for various reasons—inaccessibility, severe climate, and the military power of the native peoples—the desert zone was not engulfed by the Russian tidal wave until the late nineteenth century.

II. EARLY RUSSIAN EXPANSION

About 1,500 years ago, the Russians began their advance eastward from their place of origin in the upper reaches of the Dniester, Dnieper, Neman, and Dvina rivers. From there they fanned out in a great arc. The broad plains beckoned them on to the Arctic shores in the north, to the Black Sea in the south, and to the Urals and beyond in the east. Their subsistence type of agriculture could not support a dense population, so they lived in scattered homesteads and small hamlets rather than in compact villages or towns. The few towns that did appear grew up as trade centers along main river routes. This was the case with Kiev on the Dnieper River, which carried the north-south traffic, and with Novgorod on Lake Ilmen, which commanded the east-west commerce. This long-distance trade provided the basis for the first Russian state, which developed in the ninth century C.E. The center was Kiev, but the state remained a loose federation of principalities strung out along the river routes. Kiev itself was extremely vulnerable to invasion because it was located at the point where the forest zone gave way to the steppe. Consequently, it was forced to wage a continual struggle for existence against the nomad peoples. Russian colonists were unable to settle

more than 150 miles south and east of Kiev, for the threat of invasion by the nomads hung over their heads like the sword of Damocles.

The sword descended in 1237 when the Mongols swept over the Russian lands as they did over most of Eurasia. The Mongols continued their devastating inroads into central Europe, to the gates of Italy and France. Then they withdrew voluntarily, retaining only the Russian lands in Europe. Their sprawling empire did not survive long as an entity. It broke up into regional fragments. One fragment, the so-called Golden Horde, included the Russian territories. The capital of the Golden Horde, and of Russia also for the next two centuries, was Sarai, near present-day Volgograd. The age-old struggle between the forest and the steppe had been settled decisively with the victory of the steppe and its nomad peoples.

The Russians now surrendered their small enclaves on the steppe and withdrew into their forest fastnesses. There they were left alone as long as they recognized the suzerainty of the khan and paid him annual tribute. Gradually the

Ivan the Terrible

Russians recovered their strength and developed a new national center—the principality of Moscow, located deep in the forest zone away from the dangerous steppe. Moscow had advantages other than its relative inaccessibility to the nomads. A number of rivers flowing in various directions came closest to each other in the Moscow region, so Moscow could profit from an inland water system. The principality also enjoyed the advantage of a line of rulers who were peaceful, frugal, and calculating. The rulers added to their possessions patiently and ruthlessly, until Moscow became the new national nucleus. Whereas at the opening of the fourteenth century the principality was made up of only about 500 square miles, by the mid-fifteenth century it had grown to 15,000 square miles. And a century later, during the reign of Ivan the Terrible (1533–1584), all the Russian principalities were brought together under Moscow's rule.

This "gathering of the Russian lands" reversed the balance of power between the Russians and the Mongols or Tatars, as they were now more commonly known. Originally the Tatars had triumphed because they were united, in contrast to the strife-ridden Kievan state, and also because they were militarily more advanced with their fast-moving cavalries. But by the sixteenth century it was the Russians who were united under Moscow, whereas the Golden Horde had split into the three rival khanates of Kazan, Astrakhan, and the Crimea, as well as the khanate of the Siberian Tatars to the east of the Urals. Furthermore, the Russians were also pulling ahead in military techniques, because they were able to profit from the great advances being made in western Europe, especially in firearms and artillery. Thanks to this military advantage, the Russians were able to overrun the whole Kazan Khanate. They swept down the Volga valley and in 1556 captured Astrakhan. To consolidate their gains, the Russians built a series of fortified posts along the banks of the Volga to its mouth at Astrakhan. Thus the Russians became the masters of the great Volga basin and reached the Caspian Sea in the south and the Urals in the east. The way now was open for limitless Russian expansion beyond the Volga and the Urals (see map of Russian Expansion in Europe and Asia, p. 369).

III. CONQUEST OF SIBERIA

The Russian victories had eliminated the Kazan and Astrakhan khanates. But the Tatars in the Crimea and across the Urals remained independent and continued to harass the Russian colonists with frequent raids. For various reasons discussed later in this chapter, the Russians had to suffer the attacks of the Crimean Tatars until the late eighteenth century. But they were able to destroy the Siberian Khanate with little difficulty, and in doing so they began their epic march to the Pacific.

The crossing of the Urals and the conquest of Siberia were largely the work of the rough-and-ready frontierspeople known as the Cossacks. In many respects they resembled the frontierspeople of the American West. Most of them were former peasants who had fled from Russia or Poland to escape the bonds of serfdom. Their refuge was the wild steppe country to the south, where they became hunters, fishers, and pastoralists. Just as their counterparts in America became half-Indian, so they became half-Tatar. They were a liberty-loving and equalitarian, but unruly and marauding, element, ever ready to turn bandit or freebooter if it seemed profitable to do so.

A typical product of this frontier environment was Yermak Timofeevich. At the age of twenty-one he was condemned to death for stealing horses, so he fled to the Volga where he became the leader of a band of river pirates. He preyed indiscriminately on Russian shipping and Persian caravans until government troops began to close in.

Yermak the robber now showed that he had in him the stuff of a great empire builder. He did for Russia in Siberia what Pizarro and Cortes had done for Spain in America. With the audacity of the conquistador, Yermak decided that the best defense was the offense. On September 1, 1581, he set out at the head of 840 men to attack Khan Kuchum on his own territory. Yermak, like his Spanish counterparts, had the great advantage of superior weapons. He was well equipped with firearms and cannon, and after stiff fighting, he captured the Khanak's capital, Sibir. The Russians now gave the name of the city to the entire trans-Ural area, which became known as Sibir, or, in its Anglicized form, Siberia. The road to the Pacific lay open.

The Russian conquest of Siberia was a remarkable achievement. Like the Spaniards in America, the Russians in Siberia won a great empire in a few years with incredibly small forces. The pace of the Russian advance was staggering. Yermak campaigned between 1581 and 1584, at the same time (1584) that Sir Walter Raleigh landed on Roanoke Island in North Carolina. Within half a century, by 1637, the Russians reached Okhotsk on the Pacific Ocean, covering a distance half as much again as that between the Atlantic and the Pacific coasts of the United States. During that same period the English colonists had not crossed to the other side of the Allegheny Mountains.

Various factors explain the rapidity of the Russian advance. The climate, the terrain, the vegetation, and the river systems were, as we have seen, all favorable to the invaders. The native peoples were handicapped by small numbers, inferior armaments, and lack of unity and organization. We must give credit also to the stamina and courage of the Cossacks, who—like the coureurs des bois, or fur traders, of French Canada—endured fantastic hardships and dangers in the wilderness. And the reason they did so may be summed up with one word—fur. The sable lured them ever eastward, from river to portage and on to new rivers.

As the Cossacks advanced, they secured their communications by building fortified posts, or ostrogs, which were like the blockhouses of the American frontier. Thus they advanced from Sibir to the Ob River, to the Yenisei, and to the Lena, which they followed down to the Arctic coast in 1645. Two years later they reached the shores of the Pacific, where they built Okhotsk.

The type of Russian horseman who conquered Russia's eastern lands.

Siberian tribesmen, traveling by reindeer and skis. In the background is a Russian fort.

Up to this point the Russians had not encountered any power capable of stopping them. But when they pushed down into the Amur valley they more than met their match. There they came up against the outposts of the mighty Chinese Empire, which then was at the height of its strength (see Chapter 19, Section III). It was hunger that drove the Russians to the Amur basin. The frozen north yielded furs but no food, and the distant granaries of European Russia might as well have been on another planet. So the Russians hopefully turned southward where, according to native lore, there existed a fabulous country with fertile soil and golden grain.

The Cossack Vasily Poyarkov led the way down the Amur valley in 1643–1644. He was followed by a series of adventurers who captured the town of Albazin, built a string of ostrogs, and killed and pillaged in typical Cossack fashion. The Chinese emperor finally was sufficiently exasperated by these outrages on the fringe of

his empire to send an expedition northward in 1658. The Chinese recaptured Albazin and cleared the Russians out of the whole Amur basin. After more skirmishes the two governments negotiated the Treaty of Nerchinsk (August 27, 1689). The frontier was fixed along the Stanovoi mountain range north of the Amur River, so that the Russians were forced to withdraw completely from the disputed river valley. In return, the Russians were given commercial privileges allowing subjects of both empires to travel freely across the frontier and buy and sell without hindrance. The trade that grew up in the following years, carried on by caravan, consisted of gold and furs which the Russians exchanged for tea. It was from the Chinese that the Russians obtained what was to become their national drink. The Russians soon became greater tea drinkers than even the English.

With the signing of the Nerchinsk Treaty, the first stage of the Russian expansion in Asia came to a halt. For the next 170 years the Rus-

One of the few remaining Siberian trappers after the effects of Russian expansion were felt, 1706.

acquired furs by various means: It collected tribute, or tax, from the natives in furs, and it took a 10 percent tax in the best furs from the Russian trappers and traders. In addition, it reserved the right to buy the best furs obtained by both the natives and the Russians. By 1586, the state treasury was receiving annually from these various sources 200,000 sables, 10,000 black foxes, and 50,000 squirrels, besides beavers and ermines. Furthermore, the government had a lucrative monopoly of the foreign trade in furs. Estimates of the revenue derived from Siberian furs in the mid-seventeenth century vary from 7 to 30 percent of the total income of the state. A leading student of this subject has concluded that "The government paid the administrative expenses in Siberia out of the fur trade, retained a large surplus, and added an immense region to the state."[1]

In the eighteenth century, the traders and trappers began to give way to permanent colonists who emigrated from European Russia to escape creditors, military service, religious persecution, and, above all else, the bonds of serfdom. Whereas serfdom had developed and spread through European Russia in the sixteenth and seventeenth centuries, it did not take root in Siberia at any time. The explanation seems to be that serfdom existed primarily to satisfy the needs of the nobility, who were essential for the functioning of the state. But the nobles did not migrate to Siberia, which offered no attractions comparable to those of Moscow and St. Petersburg. Consequently, Siberia escaped the nobility and thus also escaped serfdom. The growth of population in Siberia to 1763 is given in Table 24.1.

sians observed the provisions of the treaty and stayed out of the Amur basin. They did not resume their advance southward until the mid-nineteenth century, when they were much stronger than in the days of Vasily Poyarkov, and the Chinese were relatively weaker.

IV. ADMINISTRATION AND DEVELOPMENT OF SIBERIA

The fur trade dominated Siberia throughout the seventeenth century. The government was the chief fur trader; indeed, fur was one of its most important sources of revenue. The government

Table 24.1	Siberian Population Growth to 1763*		
	Natives	**Russians and Foreigners**	**Total**
1622	173,000	23,000	196,000
1662	288,000	105,000	393,000
1709	200,000	229,227	429,227
1763	260,000	420,000	680,000

The Great Siberian Migration: Government and Peasant in Resettlement from Emancipation to the First World War, by Donald W. Treadgold (copyright © 1957, 1985 renewed by Princeton University Press): part of Table 1, p. 32. Reprinted with permission of Princeton University Press.

It is significant that whereas only 420,000 Russians were living in Siberia by 1763, the population of the thirteen colonies in North America had risen by the same date to between 1,500,000 and 2 million, or about four times as many. In other words, the Russians, who had been much faster in exploring and conquering, were now much slower in colonizing. One reason was that Siberia could draw only on Russia for immigrants, whereas the American colonies were receiving immigrants from several European countries. Even more important was the greater attractiveness of America for would-be colonists. Climatic conditions in Siberia were akin to those prevailing in Canada. It is no accident that by 1914 the populations of Canada and Siberia were about the same—8 million for Canada and 9 million for Siberia. By that same

REFLECTIONS ON CROSSING SIBERIA

*In 1908 a young Russian diplomat crossed Siberia by railway en route to the embassy in Peking. His thoughts are revealing of Siberia as a country and as a class-divided society.**

On my way to Peking I had to cross the whole of Siberia, Manchuria, and North China. No one can fail to be impressed by the journey through Siberia, especially the first time. The dimensions of Russia are staggering. You travel a day, you travel a week, you travel ten days, and you are still in Russia. Except for the Ural Mountains and a stretch near Lake Baikal, the country is absolutely flat.

After you leave European Russia the population becomes very scarce; you pass hours and hours without seeing any village or habitation. Near the stations there are a few houses. Usually, when the express train arrives at the station, the entire local population comes to stare at the travelers. Especially in the evenings, when the train is brilliantly illuminated by electricity and the elegant figures of some inhabitants of Shanghai or other Far Eastern ports are visible inside, the travelers must appear to the local residents like men from another planet. What envy and dissatisfaction the exotic creatures in furs must provoke in the hearts of those doomed to spend their entire life in some miserable station!

I imagine a young girl who has not yet lost the capacity to dream waiting on the station platform. She hears the express approaching and sees it all illuminated. The train stops for five minutes. The passengers, looking like people from a fairy land, jump on the platform; they laugh and joke. There is a whistle, the train with its passengers disappears, and darkness, emptiness, and dullness reign again.

It is unjust that some should move from place to place in luxury, while others must remain in some forsaken place in misery. Small wonder that this should cause irritation and discontent. I am convinced that the Siberian express played an important part in the awakening of the population of Siberia and thereby hastened the coming of the revolution.

The sight of unlimited space and the absence of life begins to affect you, and the passengers prefer to pass their time in the diner, drinking endless glasses of tea and playing cards....

*The Memoirs of Dmitrii Ivanovich Abrikossow, MS, 1, 191–194, as edited and translated by G. A. Lensen. Published with permission of the Archive of Russian and East European History and Culture, Columbia University.

year the United States, smaller in area than either Canada or Siberia, had grown to a population of 100 million.

V. CONQUEST OF THE UKRAINE

We noted earlier that Ivan the Terrible's conquest of Kazan and Astrakhan in the mid-sixteenth century left two independent khanates—that of the Crimean Tatars in the south and of the Tatars across the Urals. The latter were subdued in a few years by Yermak and his successors, but the Crimean Tatars held out until the end of the eighteenth century. One reason for their survival is that they enjoyed the powerful support of the Ottoman Empire. But the Ottoman Turks were defeated by Catherine the Great, who forced them to accept the Treaty of Jassy (1792). This gave to Russia the entire north shore of the Black Sea from the Kuban River in the east to the Dniester River in the west.

The whole of the Ukraine now was under Russian rule. The forest at last had triumphed over the steppe. The desert zone of central Asia still held out, but it also was destined to fall under Muscovy's sway during the following century. In this manner a small duchy in eastern Europe expanded through the centuries to become the world's largest state with dozens of minority peoples in addition to the original Slavs. Until 1917, this state was known as the

1 Ukraine — 73%, 21% Russian, 1% Jewish, 5% Other

2 Belorussia — 80%, 12% Russian, 4% Polish, 4% Other

3 Estonia — 66%, 28 Russian, 3% Ukrainian, 4% Other

4 Latvia — 38 Russian, 49%, 5% Belorussian, 8% Other

5 Lithuania — 80%, 9% Russian, 8% Polish, 3% Other

6 Russian Rep. — 84%, 4% Ukrainian, 12% Other

7 Moldavia — 64%, 13% Russian, 14% Ukrainian, 9% Other

8 Georgia — 69%, 8% Russian, 9% Armenian, 14% Other

9 Turkmenistan — 69%, 13% Russian, 9% Uzbek, 9% Other

10 Azerbaijan — 78%, 8% Russian, 8% Armenian, 6% Other

11 Uzbekistan — 69%, 11% Russian, 4% Tajiks, 16% Other

12 Kazakhstan — 40, 40%, Russian, 6% Ukrainian, 14% Other

13 Tajikistan — 58%, 11% Russian, 23% Uzbek, 7% Other

14 Armenia — 90%, 3% Russian, 6% Azerbaijanis, 1% Other

15 Kirgizia — 48%, 26% Russian, 12% Uzbek, 14% Other

Note: numbers may not equal one hundred due to rounding

ETHNIC COMPOSITION OF SOVIET REPUBLICS. This chart of the fifteen constituent republics that comprised the USSR shows how ethnic groups retained their numerical predominance within each republic. Consequently they were able to demand and win independent statehood when the USSR was replaced by the Commonwealth of Independent States. (Los Angeles Times, January 28, 1990. Used by permission.)

Tsarist Empire; after the 1917 Bolshevik Revolution it became the Union of Soviet Socialist Republics (USSR). This existed until its disintegration in 1991, when it was replaced by the Commonwealth of Independent States, as we shall see in Chapter 44, Section III.

The dozens of minority peoples in the USSR preserved their sense of identity, despite the centuries they spent under Tsarist and then Soviet rule. Therefore they were able to establish independent states when the USSR fell apart in 1991. By contrast, the equally large number of ethnic elements comprising the United States have not demanded an independent existence. Why the basically different situation in the two countries?

One explanation is that the USSR was a mosaic of nationalities, while the United States is a melting pot of nationalities. The USSR was a mosaic because centuries ago, as we noted above, the Russians began conquering their neighbors all the way to the Pacific Ocean and then combined them into one empire, like a mosaic holding together many different-colored pieces of glass. Just as each piece of glass in a mosaic retains its color, so the various nationalities in the Tsarist-Soviet mosaic retained their identity. In 1991 those broke off and became independent states.

The Americans also conquered the various Indian tribes all the way to the Pacific Ocean, just as the Russians conquered the Eurasian peoples all the way to the Pacific Ocean. But the number of Indians between the Atlantic and Pacific oceans was much smaller than the number of Eurasians between the Ural Mountains and the Pacific Ocean. So the Americans were able to push all the Indians into a few reservations. That cleared the ground for the immigration of millions of people from all over the world into the relatively empty lands of the United States. In those lands the immigrants "mixed up" so that today descendants of many different peoples often live side by side as neighbors in one American city block or in one apartment building, instead of a whole republic consisting entirely, or largely, of one people or another, as is the case with the fifteen Soviet Socialist Republics (SSRs) that comprised the USSR. That is one reason why the many elements in the melting pot (Mexicans, Koreans, Chinese, Germans, African-Americans, and so on) are not demanding autonomy or independence in the United States, as did the Baltics, Armenians, Ukrainians, and various Moslem ethnic groups in the USSR. The illustration, "Ethnic Composition of Soviet Republic," on page 378 provides statistics that demonstrate why the USSR disintegrated as a mosaic, in contrast to the melting pot that has survived as the United States.

SUGGESTED READINGS

The best general surveys of the Russian expansion into Siberia are by F. A. Golder, *Russian Expansion on the Pacific, 1641–1850* (Clark, 1914); R. J. Kerner, *The Urge to the Sea: The Course of Russian History* (University of California, 1942); the volume of readings by G. A. Lensen, ed., *Russia's Eastward Expansion* (Prentice Hall, 1964); T. Armstrong, *Russian Expansion in the North* (Cambridge University, 1965); and L. H. Neatby, *Discovery in Russian and Siberian Waters* (Ohio University, 1973).

Special phases of Siberian history are treated in D. W. Treadgold, *The Great Siberian Migration* (Princeton University, 1957); R. H. Fisher, *The Russian Fur Trade, 1550–1700* (University of California, 1943); G. V. Lantzeff, *Siberia in the Seventeenth Century* (University of California, 1943); V. Chen, *Sino-Russian Relations in the Seventeenth Century* (Nijhoff, 1966); A. S. Donnelly, *The Conquest of Bashkiria, 1552–1740* (Yale University, 1968); and J. R. Gibson, *Feeding the Russian Fur Trade: Provisionment of the Okhotsk Seaboard and the Kamchatka Peninsula* (University of Wisconsin, 1969).

NOTE

1. R. J. Kerner, *The Urge to the Sea* (University of California, 1942), p. 86.

Beginning of Global Unity

> The discovery of America . . . certainly made a most essential [change]. By opening a new and inexhaustible market to all the commodities of Europe, it gave occasion to new divisions of labour and improvements of art, which in the narrow sphere of ancient commerce, could never have taken place. . . . The silver of the new continent seems in this manner to be one of the principal commodities by which the commerce between the two extremities of the old one is carried on, and it is by means of it, in great measure, that those distant parts of the world are connected with one another.
>
> *Adam Smith*

The early modern period from 1500 to 1763 was one of the more critical periods in human history. It was at this time that European explorers made the great discoveries that disclosed new continents and thereby heralded the global phase of world history. During this period also the Europeans began their rise to world primacy because of their leadership in overseas activities. Certain global interrelationships that developed during these centuries naturally became stronger with the passage of time. Hence the years from 1500 to 1763 are the period when global unity got under way—the period of transition from the regional isolationism of the pre-1500 era to the European global hegemony of the nineteenth century. The purpose of this chapter is to analyze the precise nature and extent of the global ties that developed in various fields (see map of World of the Emerging West, 1763, p. 382).

I. NEW GLOBAL HORIZONS

The first and most obvious result of Europe's expansion overseas and overland was an unprecedented widening of horizons. No longer was geographic knowledge limited to one region or continent or hemisphere. For the first time, the shape of the globe as a whole was known and charted (see map of Western Knowledge of the Globe, 1 to 1800 C.E., p. 350). This was largely the work of the western Europeans, who had taken the lead in transoceanic exploration. Before the Portuguese began feeling their way down the coast of Africa in the early fifteenth century, Europeans had accurate information only of North Africa and the Middle East. Their knowledge concerning India was vague. It was still vaguer regarding central Asia, east Asia, and sub-Saharan Africa. The very existence of the

A depiction of the inhabitants of the Andaman Islands, based on a report given Marco Polo that these people had heads, eyes, and teeth "like those of dogs."

Americas and of Australia—let alone Antarctica—was, of course, unsuspected.

By 1763 the picture was altogether different. The main coastlines of most of the world had become known in varying degrees of detail, including the Atlantic coast of the Americas, the Pacific coast of South America, the whole outline of Africa, and the coasts of south and east Asia. In certain areas European knowledge went beyond the coastlines. The Russians were reasonably familiar with Siberia, and the Spaniards and Portuguese with Mexico, Central America, and parts of South America. North of the Rio Grande the Spaniards had explored considerable areas in their futile search for gold and fabled cities, and further north the French and English ranged widely, using the canoes and the river-lake routes known to the Indians.

On the other hand, the Pacific coast of North America was largely unknown, and Australia, though sighted on its west coast by Dutch navigators, was almost wholly uncharted. Likewise, the interior of sub-Saharan Africa was almost completely blank, and so was central Asia, about which the main source of information still was the thirteenth-century account of Marco Polo. In general, then, the Europeans had gained knowledge of most of the coastlines of the world during the period to 1763. In the following period they were to penetrate into the interior of continents and also to explore the polar regions.

II. GLOBAL DIFFUSION OF HUMANS, ANIMALS, AND PLANTS

The European discoveries led not only to new global horizons but also to a new global distribution of races. Prior to 1500 there existed, in effect, worldwide racial segregation. The Negroids were concentrated in sub-Saharan Africa and a few Pacific islands; the Mongoloids in central Asia, Siberia, east Asia, and the Americas; and the Caucasoids in Europe, North Africa, the Middle East, and India. Today this pattern has been fundamentally altered to the point where half the people of African descent live outside of Africa. By 1763 this radically different race distribution was clearly discernible. The Russians had begun their slow migration across the Urals into Siberia. Much more substantial was the mass migration to the Americas—voluntary in the case of the Europeans, involuntary for the Africans.

The influx changed the Americas from purely Mongoloid continents to the most racially mixed regions of the globe. Immigration of Africans continued to the mid-nineteenth century, reaching a total of 10 million slaves. Euro-

World of the Emerging West, 1763

pean immigration also steadily increased, reaching a high point at the beginning of the twentieth century when nearly 1 million arrived each year. The net result is that the New World today is peopled by a majority of whites, with substantial minorities of blacks, Indians, mestizos, and mulattoes, in that order (see Chapter 35, Section I, and map of Racial Distribution in the World, p. 384).

The new global pattern that resulted from these depopulations and migrations has become so familiar that it is now taken for granted and its extraordinary significance generally overlooked. What happened in the period to 1763 is that the Europeans staked out claims to vast new regions, and in the following century they peopled those territories—not only the Americas but also Siberia and, eventually, Australia. We can see the vital importance of the redrawing of the world racial map if we imagined that the Chinese rather than the Europeans first reached and settled the underpopulated continents. In that case the proportion of Chinese to the total world population would probably be closer to three out of six rather than one out of six, as it is now.

The intermixture of human races was accompanied inevitably by a corresponding intermixture of plants and animals. With a few insignificant exceptions, all plants and animals being utilized today were domesticated by prehistoric humans in various parts of the world. Their diffusion from their places of origin had proceeded slowly until 1500, when globe-spanning Homo sapiens began transplanting them back and forth among continents. An important contribution of the Old World were the various domesticated animals, especially horses, cattle, and sheep. The New World had nothing comparable. The llama and alpaca were of relatively little value. Of course the New World did have huge bison herds, estimated to have totaled 40 to 60 million animals. The Indians had hunted them for food and hides but had killed only about 300,000 a year, well below the natural replacement rate. Europeans began killing them at first for meat, and after 1871 for hides to be made into commercial leather. The slaughter rose to 3 million a year, which decimated the herds to the point of extinction by the end of the nineteenth century. Now bison survive in a few carefully managed herds, which are beginning to compete with cattle as a meat source for the American consumer.

The Amerindians also contributed their remarkable store of food plants, particularly corn and potatoes, but also cassava, tomatoes, avocados, sweet potatoes, peanuts, and certain varieties of beans, pumpkins, and squashes. So important are these Indian plants that today they are responsible for about one-half of the world's total plant-food production. In addition to these food plants, the American Indians were responsible for two major cash crops: tobacco and cotton, as well as several native American drugs that are prominent in modern pharmacology. They contributed coca for cocaine and novocaine, curare used in anesthetics, cinchona bark (the source of quinine), datura used in pain relievers, and cascara for laxatives.

The interchange of animals and plants was not, of course, confined to Eurasia and the Americas. The entire globe was involved, as is illustrated strikingly in the case of Australia. Australia is now a leading world exporter of pri-

Indian artists recorded the arrival of mounted Spanish soldiers with this painting on a rock wall in Canyon del Muerto, Arizona. Horses were just one of several domesticated animals brought by the Spanish to the Americas.

15th Century

||||| Mongoloid	▨	Australoid
⣿	Caucasoid	☰	Negroid

20th Century

Racial Distribution in the World

mary products such as wool, mutton, beef, and wheat, all commodities derived from species that were transplanted from elsewhere. The same is true of Indonesia with its great rubber, coffee, tea, and tobacco production, and of Hawaii with its sugar and pineapples.

Today the global intermixture of humans, plants, and animals continues, though at an accelerating pace as steamships and jet planes replace canoes and sailboats. Frequently the mixing occurs accidentally, and with repercussions that sometimes are disastrous. For example, marine creatures of all types are being transferred routinely every day from one end of the world to another in the ballast tanks of ships. Dumped into new habitats when the ships make port, billions of organisms spread out, sometimes replacing native species. Scientists sampling the ballast tanks of 159 Japanese cargo ships arriving at Coos Bay, Oregon, discovered in their ballast waters 367 different types of plants and animals, mostly in larval form. "We found shrimps, crabs, fish, barnacles, sea urchins, starfish, worms, jellyfish, clams, snails, really the complete spectrum of marine life. . . . Perhaps 5 to 10 percent of species introduced to a new environment become established there."[1]

Ballasts are by no means the only problem in controlling species diffusion. The rapidly increasing volume of global trade and travel probably is the most important diffusion force today. Species are spreading everywhere along with live animals, plants, and seeds, and also with the ships, planes, and trucks on which they are transported. The diffusion, of course, is a two-way process—outward from the United States as well as the reverse. The slipper limpet was inadvertently exported from the United States to Europe in the 1880s with a shipment of oysters; a North American moth currently is defoliating trees in a large area in central China; and a pinewood nematode from the southeastern United States is killing black pines in Japan.

III. GLOBAL ECONOMIC RELATIONS

By the latter part of the eighteenth century a large intercontinental trade had developed for the first time in history. Before 1500, Arab and Italian merchants transported mostly luxuries from one part of Eurasia to another—goods such as spices, silk, precious stones, and perfumes. By the late eighteenth century the limited luxury trade had been transformed into a mass trade based on the exchange of new, bulky necessities. Atlantic commerce especially became enormous since the New World plantations produced huge quantities of tobacco, sugar, and, later, coffee, cotton, and other commodities that were sold in Europe. Because the plantations practiced monoculture, they had to import all necessities such as grain, fish, cloth, and metal products. They also had to import their labor. This led to the flourishing triangle trade: rum, cloth, guns, and other metal products from Europe to Africa; slaves from Africa to the New World; and sugar, tobacco, and bullion from the New World to Europe.

Another important aspect of the new mass global trade of this era was the exchange of products between western and eastern Europe. Here again western Europe received raw materials,

By the 1600s, the Dutch were seriously challenging Spain's superiority on the seas. Here the Dutch are shown capturing Spanish ships.

especially bread grains, which were in great demand because of population increase and because much arable land had been converted into pasture. At Danzig, chief port for the Baltic grain trade, rye prices between 1550 and 1600 rose 247 percent, barley 187 percent, and oats 185 percent. This stimulated a great increase in the export of grains and other raw materials, so that the value of Polish and Hungarian exports to the West during these decades usually was double that of imports. Poland, Hungary, Russia, and ultimately the Balkans received textiles, arms, metal products, and colonial goods, and in return provided grain, cattle, hides, ship stores, and flax. They also provided furs, which were obtained by the Russians in Siberia in the same way that the Spaniards obtained bullion in the New World; namely, by exploiting native labor.

Europe's trade with Asia was not equal to the trade with the Americas or eastern Europe for two principal reasons. The first was that the European textile industries opposed the importation of cotton goods from various Asiatic countries. Foreign cottons were immensely popular in Europe because they were light, bright, inexpensive, and above all, washable, and they began to be imported in large quantities. Soon objections were raised by native textile interests and by those who feared that national security was endangered by the loss of the bullion that was drained away to pay for the textiles. These interests brought sufficient pressure to bear on their respective governments to secure the passage of laws forbidding or reducing the importation of Indian cottons.

The second factor limiting European commerce with Asia was the difficulty of finding something that would sell in the Asiatic market. This problem dated back to classical times, when the Roman Empire was drained of its gold to pay for Chinese silk and Indian textiles. Likewise in the sixteenth, seventeenth, and eighteenth centuries, Asia remained uninterested in European goods, and Europe was reluctant to send bullion to pay for the Asiatic produce it wanted. Europe did not solve this problem of trade with Asia until it developed power machinery at the end of the eighteenth century. Then the situation was reversed, for it was Europe that was able to flood Asia with cheap, machine-made textiles. But until that time, East-West trade was hampered by the fact that Asia was willing to accept little else but bullion from Europe.

What was the significance of the new worldwide economic ties? First and foremost, international division of labor for the first time

The Imperial Court of Peking receiving Pieter Van Hoorn's Dutch Trade Delegation (1668).

ADAM SMITH ON THE EXPANSION OF EUROPE

In his world-famous Wealth of Nations *(1776), Adam Smith paid considerable attention to the effect of colonies. He noted that they added to the wealth of the European countries except Spain and Portugal, which owned the colonies.*

The discovery of America, and that of a passage to the East Indies by the Cape of Good Hope, are the two greatest and most important events recorded in the history of mankind. Their consequences have already been very great: but, in the short period of between two and three centuries which has elapsed since these discoveries were made, it is impossible that the whole extent of their consequences can have been seen. What benefits or what misfortunes to mankind may hereafter result from those great events, no human wisdom can foresee. By uniting, in some measure, the most distant parts of the world, by enabling them to relieve one another's wants, to increase one another's enjoyments, and to encourage one another's industry, their general tendency would seem to be beneficial.

In the meantime, one of the principal effects of those discoveries has been to raise the mercantile system to a degree of splendour and glory which it could never otherwise have attained to. It is the object of that system to enrich a great nation rather by trade and manufactures than by the improvement and cultivation of land, rather by the industry of the towns than by that of the country. But, in consequence of those discoveries, the commercial towns of Europe, instead of being the manufacturers and carriers for but a very small part of the world (that part of Europe which is washed by the Atlantic ocean, and the countries which lie round the Baltic and Mediterranean seas), have now become the manufacturers for the numerous and thriving cultivators of America, and the carriers, and in some respects the manufacturers too, for almost all the different nations of Asia, Africa, and America. Two new worlds have been opened to their industry, each of them much greater and more extensive than the old one, and the market of one of them growing still greater and greater every day.

The countries which possess the colonies of America, and which trade directly to the East Indies, enjoy, indeed, the whole show and splendour of this great commerce. Other countries, however, notwithstanding all the invidious restraints by which it is meant to exclude them, frequently enjoy a greater share of the real benefit of it. The colonies of Spain and Portugal, for example, give more real encouragement to the industry of other countries than to that of Spain and Portugal. In the single article of linen alone the consumption of those colonies amounts, it is said, but I do not pretend to warrant the quantity, to more than three millions sterling a year. But this great consumption is almost entirely supplied by France, Flanders, Holland, and Germany. Spain and Portugal furnish but a small part of it. The capital which supplies the colonies with this great quantity of linen is annually distributed among, and furnishes a revenue to, the inhabitants of those other countries.

*Adam Smith, *Wealth of Nations* (Edinburgh, 1838), p. 282.

had been achieved on a significant scale. The world was on the way to becoming an economic unit. The Americas and eastern Europe (with Siberia) produced raw materials, Africa provided labor, Asia an assortment of luxury commodities, and western Europe directed these global operations and concentrated more and more on industrial output.

The requirements of the new global economy raised the question of how to get a big enough labor supply in the regions producing raw materials. The New World plantations met this need by importing African slaves on a large scale. Hence African populations are most numerous today in precisely those areas that had formerly been devoted to plantation agriculture—northern Brazil, the West Indies, and the southern United States. The early Europeans' solution to their labor needs was to leave a bitter legacy. These areas to the present day are wracked by basic problems dating back to the colonial period—the problems of race discrimination and of underdevelopment. The current racial conflict in American ghettos and on Caribbean islands is the end result of over four centuries of transatlantic slave trade. Likewise, the underdevelopment of all Latin America is simply a continuation of the economic dependency on northwestern Europe of the Spanish and Portuguese colonies (and of Spain and Portugal themselves).

Whereas the price for the participation of the Americas in the new global economy was slavery, the price for eastern Europe was serfdom. The basic reason was the same—namely, the need for a plentiful and reliable supply of cheap labor to produce goods for the lucrative west European market. Heretofore the nobles in Poland and Hungary had required minimal labor from the peasants—three to six days a year—for there was no incentive to increase output. But when production for market became profitable, the nobles responded by drastically raising the labor obligations to one day a week, and by the end of the sixteenth century to six days a week. To make sure that the peasants would remain to perform this labor, laws were passed limiting their freedom of movement more and more strictly. Eventually they were completely bound to the soil, thereby becoming serfs, denied freedom of movement and subject to the exactions of the nobles.

Africa also was vitally affected by the new global economy, serving as the source of slave labor for the American plantations. Slavery existed in Africa before the transatlantic trade, with slaves being used as soldiers and farmers. Slaves also were exported, along with gold, over ancient trade routes across the Sahara to the Mediterranean coast, whence they were shipped mostly to the Middle East. An estimated 3.5 million to 10 million Africans were sold in this fashion prior to the Atlantic slave trade.

The Portuguese, who were the pioneers in the transatlantic trade, began by selling Africans in Spain, Italy, and Portugal, where they were used for domestic and farm labor. Their numbers were small, however, compared to the multitudes that soon were being shipped to work on New World plantations. Local Indians could not be used for that purpose because they were disappearing—victims of European diseases. The plantation owners at first tried to get along with the indentured European workers, but they proved to be too expensive and undisciplined. So African slaves were substituted, the first ones being shipped soon after Columbus's first voyage. Their numbers rose sharply after the discovery of silver in Peru in the 1520s and the establishment of sugar plantations in Brazil in the 1540s and soared still more as new plantations were established in Mexico and the Caribbean islands for other crops such as tobacco, rice, and coffee. Estimates of the total number of slaves vary widely; the most recent studies indicate between 12 million and 20 million being forcibly shipped from Africa between 1500 and 1867. Consequently, by 1850 there were three or four enslaved Africans in the Americas for every white person.

The effect of the slave trade varied greatly from one part of Africa to the other. Angola and East Africa suffered severely because their populations were relatively sparse to begin with and their economies were often close to the subsistence level. For them, even a small population loss was devastating. By contrast, West Africa was more advanced economically and hence more populous, so that the devastations of the slavers were not so ruinous. Considering the continent as a whole, the effect on the population was not as great as might be expected, because the slaves were taken over a period stretching from 1450 to 1870 and from a total sub-Saharan population estimated at 70 million to 80 million. Nevertheless, the slave trade had a corrosive and unsettling effect on the entire African coast from Senegal to Angola and for 400 to 500 miles inland. The appearance of the European slavers with their cargoes of rum,

The sugar plantations of Brazil and the West Indies were a major source of the demand for slave labor. Slaves are here shown grinding sugar cane and refining sugar, which was then exported to the consumer markets in Europe.

guns, and hardware set off a chain reaction of slave-hunting raids into the interior. Wars broke out among various groups for control of the lucrative and militarily decisive trade. Some, like the Ashanti Confederacy and the Dahomey Kingdom, rose to ascendancy, whereas others, like the Yoruba and Benin civilizations and the Congo Kingdom, declined. The overall effect was definitely disruptive.

And yet the slave trade did involve trade as well as slavery. In return for their fellow native people, whom the Africans themselves sold to the Europeans, they received not only alcohol and firearms, but also certain useful and economically productive commodities, including textiles, tools, and raw materials for local smithies and workshops. A more important positive influence in the long run was the introduction of new food plants from the Americas. Corn, cassava, sweet potatoes, peppers, pineap-ples, and tobacco were brought in by the Portuguese and spread very rapidly from tribe to tribe. Therefore it has been argued that the substantially larger number of people that could be supported with these new foods probably outweighed the population lost to the slave trade. On the other hand, the slave trade was not essential for the introduction of the new food plants. They were spreading rapidly during these centuries all over the globe. Slavery or no slavery, they doubtless would have reached the interior of Africa as they did the interior of China.

Of the various continents, Asia was the least affected, because it was sufficiently strong militarily, politically, and economically to avoid direct or indirect subjugation. Most of Asia was quite unaware of the persistent and annoying European merchants who were appearing in the coastal regions. Only a few coastal areas in India, and some of the islands in the East Indies, felt the impact of Europe's early economic expansion. As far as Asia as a whole was concerned, its attitude was best expressed by the emperor of China, Ch'ien-lung. He replied as follows to a 1793 message from King George III of Britain asking for the establishment of diplomatic and commercial relations:

Swaying the wide world, I have but one aim in view, namely, to maintain a perfect governance and to fulfill the duties of the State: strange and costly objects do not interest me.... As your Ambassador can see for himself, we possess all things. I set no value on objects strange or ingenious, and have no use for your country's manufactures.[2]

Europe also was affected by the new global economy, but the effects in this case were all positive. The Europeans were the pioneer middlemen of world trade. They had opened the new oceanic routes and supplied the necessary capital, shipping, and technical skills. So it was natural that they should have profited most from the slave trade, the sugar and tobacco plantations, and the Eastern commerce. Some of the benefits trickled down to the European masses, as is indicated by the fact that tea cost about £10 a pound when introduced in England about 1650 but had become an article of common consumption a century later. More important than the effect on living standards was the effect the new global commerce had in stimulating Europe's economy. As we will see later, the industrial revolution that got under way in the late eighteenth century owed much to the capital earned from overseas enterprises and to the growing demand for European manufacturers in overseas markets.

It was during this period, then, that Europe forged ahead in the great ascent to global economic primacy. The overall results were positive because global division of labor led to increased global productivity. The world of 1763 was richer than that of 1500, and the economic growth has continued to the present day. But from the beginning, northwestern Europe, as the world's entrepreneur, received most of the benefits at the expense of the other regions. What this expense involved is apparent in the current conflict of races, in the discrepancy between rich and poor nations, and in the scars left by serf-dom throughout eastern Europe and by slavery throughout the world.

IV. GLOBAL POLITICAL RELATIONS

Global political relations changed as fundamentally during the period to 1763 as did economic ones. The western Europeans were no longer fenced in on the western tip of Eurasia by an expanding Islam. Instead, they had outflanked the Moslem world in the south by winning control of the Indian Ocean. Meanwhile, the Russians had outflanked the Moslems in the north by their conquest of Siberia. At the same time, western Europeans by their discovery of the New World had opened up vast territories for economic exploitation and colonization. In doing so, they built up a tremendous reservoir of resources and power.

All this represented a basic and fateful change in the global balance of power—a change comparable to that which had occurred in the demographic balance. Hitherto the Moslem world had been the center of initiative, probing and pushing in all directions—into southeast Europe, into sub-Saharan Africa, into central and Southeast Asia. Now a new center had arisen that was able to operate on a global, rather than merely Eurasian, scale. From this new center, first in the Iberian peninsula and later in northwest Europe, the routes of trade and of political influence radiated outward to envelop the entire world—westward to the Americas, south around Africa, and east to India and around Southeast Asia.

All these territories were not actually controlled by 1763. But there was effective domination of the underpopulated lands—the Americas, Siberia, and later Australia—even though their actual peopling on a continental scale had to wait until the nineteenth century. In Africa and Asia the western Europeans obtained only coastal footholds during this period, but with one exception: The Dutch penetrated the Cape and the East Indies. Elsewhere the native peoples were too strong and highly organized to allow a repetition of what had happened in the Americas and Siberia.

In West Africa, for example, the Europeans could not penetrate inland because of climatic

The trade and empires of the eighteenth century were held together and protected by navies. These navies patrolled sea lanes to protect ships from pirates and smugglers and from attacks by hostile forces. In this painting (1735) by Peter Monamy, ships from the British sailing fleet rest in Lisbon harbor where they may well have stopped to take on supplies. Britain and Portugal were major trading partners, with British wool being exchanged for Portuguese wine.

difficulties. They were prevented also by the coastal chiefs, who jealously guarded their profitable position as middlemen between the interior tribes and the Europeans. In India the Europeans were kept at arm's length for 250 years following the arrival of Vasco da Gama in 1498. During those centuries they were allowed to trade in a few ports, but clearly and explicitly only on the sufferance of the native rulers. In China and Japan there was no chance at all of European territorial encroachment, as the Russians discovered when they entered the Amur valley.

We may conclude that in the political field, as in the economic, Europe in 1763 was at a halfway point. It was no longer a relatively isolated and unimportant peninsula of the Eurasian landmass. It had expanded overseas and overland, establishing its control over the relatively empty and militarily weak Americas and Siberia. But in Africa, the Middle East, and south and east Asia, the Europeans had to wait until the nineteenth century to assert their dominance.

V. GLOBAL CULTURAL RELATIONS

The imposition of European culture, like that of European political rule, depended on the state of the native societies. In the Americas, for example, European culture was transported bodily because the native peoples were either wiped out or pushed aside. Yet even the casual traveler in Latin America cannot fail to notice evidence of Indian cultural survivals. There is, for example, the use of adobe for building purposes and of unmilled pine logs as beams, or *vigas*. Likewise, the blanket, or serape, that is draped over the shoulders is of Indian origin, as is also the poncho, consisting of two blankets sewn together with a slit for the head. The Roman Catholicism currently practiced in much of Latin America is a blend of Christian and Indian beliefs and practices. Although the names of native gods have been dropped, the Indians assign the attributes of these gods to the Virgin Mary and to the saints, expecting the images of the Catholic gods

Western ship arriving in Tientsin.

to cure disease, control the weather, and keep them from harm, as they believed their former gods had done. Perhaps the most conspicuous evidence of Indian influence is to be found in the Latin American cuisine. Tamales, tortillas, and the various chili dishes are based on the two great Indian staples, beans and corn.

European influence on the native cultures of Africa and Eurasia was slight in the period prior to 1763, except for the diffusion of new food plants, which, as noted, was of primary importance. In West Africa the native chiefs confined the European traders largely to their coastal posts. In the old Middle Eastern, Indian, and Chinese centers of civilization, the native peoples, as might be expected, were not at all impressed by the culture of the European intruders. The Moslem Turks, who had the closest ties with the Christian Europeans, looked down on them with the utmost contempt. Even in the seventeenth and eighteenth centuries, when the

Turks were themselves on the downgrade, they did not hesitate to express their disdain for the Christian infidels. "Do I not know you," burst out the grand vizier to the French ambassador in 1666, "that you are a Giaour [nonbeliever], that you are a hogge, a dogge, a turde eater?"[3]

Likewise, the native peoples on the mainland of India reacted very negatively when the Portuguese, who were ensconced at Goa, introduced the Inquisition in 1560. Between 1600 and 1773, seventy-three victims were consigned to the flames because of their heretical views. The Indian population could not fail to see the inconsistency in a religion that imprisoned, tortured, and condemned to the flames people whose only crime was unorthodoxy. But at the same time it prevented widows from being burnt of their own free will, a sublimely virtuous act by Hindu standards of the period. Furthermore, the lawless and boisterous behavior of European adventurers in India further lowered the Indian people's opinion of the Western Christians. An English clergyman, Mr. Terry, was told in 1616, "Christian religion devil religion; Christian much drink; Christian much do wrong; Christian much beat; Christian much abuse others."[4]

The Chinese reaction to the Europeans was relatively favorable at the outset (as noted in Chapter 19, Section III) because of the exceptional ability and intellectual attainments of the Jesuit missionaries. The Jesuits succeeded in winning some converts, including a few scholars and some members of the imperial family. But even the capable Jesuits, with their knowledge of astronomy, mathematics, and geography, did not make much of an impression on most Chinese scholars, who rejected both Western science and religion. As far as the popular Chinese attitude toward the Europeans at that time is concerned, it probably was reflected accurately in the proverb that Chinese alone possessed two eyes, the Europeans were one-eyed, and all the other inhabitants of the earth were blind. Given this attitude, it is not surprising that with the exception of certain specialized fields of learning such as astronomy, European influence on Chinese civilization before 1763 was very slight.

Although the Chinese, the Indians, and the Turks were unimpressed by European culture during this period, the Europeans, by contrast, were very much impressed by what they saw in Constantinople, in Delhi, and in Peking. They became familiar first with the Ottoman Empire, and their reaction was one of respect, admiration, and apprehension. As late as 1634, after the decline of the empire had set in, a thoughtful English traveler concluded that the Turks were "the only modern people great in action" and that "he who would behold these times in their greatest glory, could not find a better scene than Turkey."[5] During the seventeenth century the Ottoman Empire lost prestige among Europeans. But at the same time European intellectuals were becoming fascinated with numerous detailed accounts of the fabulous civilization of far-off Cathay. They were entranced as they learned of China's history, art, philosophy, and government. China came to be held up as a model civilization because of its Confucian system of morals; its examination system for government service; its respect for learning rather than for military prowess; and its exquisite

handicrafts, including porcelain, silk, and lacquer work. Voltaire (1694–1778), for example, adorned the wall of his library with a portrait of Confucius, and the German philosopher Leibniz (1646–1716) extolled the Chinese emperor K'ang-hsi as "the monarch . . . who almost exceeds human heights of greatness, being a god-like mortal, ruling all by a nod of his head, who, however, is educated to virtue and wisdom . . . thereby earning the right to rule."[6]

In the late eighteenth century European admiration for China began to wane, partly because the Catholic missionaries were now being persecuted and also because the Europeans were beginning to be more interested in China's natural resources than in its culture. The shift in

Conflicts among native peoples became deadlier once Indians acquired European arms. This 1657 engraving depicts a Huron warrior carrying a gun and wearing a type of armor made of tightly laced sticks–which would have provided little protection from a musket ball.

attitude is reflected in the sixteen volumes of the *Memoirs on the History, Sciences, Arts, etc., of the Chinese*, published in Paris between 1776 and 1814. The eleventh volume, which appeared in 1786, contained little but reports on resources that might interest traders—borax, lignite, quicksilver, ammoniac, horses, bamboo, and wool-bearing animals.

Just as European interest had shifted in the seventeenth century from the Ottoman Empire to China, so now in the late eighteenth century it shifted to Greece and, to a lesser extent, India. The classical Greeks became the great favorites among educated Europeans. "How can you believe," wrote a German scholar in 1778, "that uncultivated Oriental peoples produced annals and poetry and possessed a complete religion and morality, before the Greeks, who were the teachers of Europe, were able to read?"[7] A few European intellectuals became engrossed in Indian culture. The Hindu pandits, or learned men, were unwilling to impart their sacred lore to foreigners, but a few Europeans, mostly Jesuit fathers, acquired a knowledge of Sanskrit language, literature, and philosophy. The German philosopher Schopenhauer (1788–1860) fell as much under the spell of Hindu philosophy as Leibniz had under the Chinese. An English scholar, Sir William Jones, proclaimed before the Asiatic Society of Bengal in 1786 that "the Sanskrit Language, whatever be its antiquity, is of wonderful structure; more perfect than the Greek, more copious than the Latin, and more exquisitely refined than either."[8]

VI. EARLY MODERN PERIOD IN HISTORICAL PERSPECTIVE

The early modern period from 1500 to 1763 represents a halfway point between the regional isolationism of the preceding ages and the European world domination of the nineteenth century. Economically, it was a time when the Europeans extended their trading operations to virtually all corners of the globe, though they were not yet able to exploit the interiors of the great landmasses. Intercontinental trade reached unprecedented proportions, though still far below the volume it was to reach in the following centuries.

Politically, the world was still far from being a single unit. The great Seven Years' War, which convulsed Europe, did not affect the Americas west of the Mississippi nor the interior of Africa nor most of the Middle East nor any of East Asia. The Europeans had secured a firm grip on Siberia, South America, and the eastern portion of North America, but they had as yet only a few territorial enclaves in Africa, India, and the East Indies. In the Far East they could venture only as merchants, and even in that capacity

A Jesuit attempt to reproduce ancient Chinese characters.

they had to submit to the most restrictive and arbitrary regulations.

Culturally, it was a period of widening horizons. Throughout the globe peoples were becoming aware of other peoples and other cultures. By and large, the Europeans were more impressed and affected by the ancient civilizations of Eurasia than vice versa. They felt a sense of wide-eyed wonder as they discovered new oceans and continents and civilizations. At the same time they were scrambling greedily for booty and for trade, they exhibited a certain humility. They even underwent an occasional anxious searching of conscience, as in the case of the treatment of the Indians in Spanish America. But before this period had passed, Europe's attitude toward the rest of the world was noticeably changing. It was becoming coarser and harder and more intolerant. In the mid-nineteenth century the French sinologist Guillaume Pauthier complained that the Chinese civilization, which in the time of Leibniz had keenly interested European intellectuals, "now scarcely attracted the attention of a select few. . . . These people, whom we daily treat as barbarians, and who, nevertheless, had attained to a very high state of culture several centuries before our ancestors inhabited the forests of Gaul and Germany, now inspire in us only a deep contempt." The following chapters will be concerned with why the Europeans came to feel themselves superior to the "lesser breeds" and how they were able to impose their rule on them.

SUGGESTED READINGS

The general effect of Europe's expansion during the early modern period is analyzed in the multivolume work of I. Wallerstein, *The Modern World System* (Academic Press, 1974ff.); W. P. Webb, *The Great Frontier* (Houghton Mifflin, 1952); P. D. Curtin, *Cross Cultural Trade in World History* (Cambridge University, 1984); E. F. Frazier, *Race and Culture Contacts in the Modern World* (Knopf, 1957); L. S. Stavrianos, *Global Rift: The Third World Comes of Age* (William Morrow, 1981);

and for the ecological repercussions: C. Ponting, *A Green History of the World* (St. Martin's Press, 1991).

More specialized studies of Europe's impact are by E. Reynolds, *Stand the Storm: A History of the Atlantic Slave Trade* (Schocken, 1985); S. J. and B. H. Stein, *The Colonial Heritage of Latin America* (Oxford University, 1970); S. W. Mintz, *Sweetness and Power: The Place of Sugar in Modern History* (Viking, 1985); A. W. Crosby, Jr., *The Columbian Exchange: Biological and Cultural Consequences of 1492* (Greenwood Publishing Co., 1972); and A. G. Price, *The Western Invasion of the Pacific and Its Continents: A Study of Moving Frontiers and Changing Landscapes 1513–1958* (Clarendon, 1963).

The opposite process—the effect of overseas expansion on Europe—is analyzed in the multivolume study by F. D. Lach, *Asia in the Making of Europe* (University of Chicago, 1965ff.); J. E. Gillespie, *The Influence of Overseas Expansion on England to 1700* (Vol. 91 in Columbia University Studies in History, Economics and Public Law, 1920); A. I. Hallowell, "The Impact of the American Indian on American Culture," *American Anthropologist*, LIX (1957), pp. 210–217; L. S. S. O'Malley, ed., *Modern India and the West* (Oxford University, 1941); A. Reichwein, *China and Europe: Intellectual and Artistic Contacts in the Eighteenth Century* (Knopf, 1925); and P. J. Marshall and G. Williams, *The Great Map of Mankind: Perceptions of New Worlds in the Age of Enlightenment* (Harvard University, 1982).

NOTES

1. Cited by F. Whyte, *China and Foreign Powers* (Oxford University, 1927), p. 38.
2. Cited by A. C. Wood, *A History of the Levant Company* (Oxford University, 1935), p. 230.
3. Cited by L. S. S. O'Malley, ed., *Modern India and the West* (Oxford University, 1941), p. 51.
4. H. Blount, "A Voyage into the Levant," in J. Pinkerton, ed., *A General Collection of the Best and Most Interesting Voyages . . . X* (London, 1808–1814), p. 222.
5. Cited by D. Lach, "Leibniz and China," *Journal of the History of Ideas*, VI (October 1945), p. 440.
6. Cited by A. Reichwein, *China and Europe: Intellectual and Artistic Contacts in the Eighteenth Century* (Knopf, 1925), p. 152.
7. Cited by O'Malley, *Modern India*, p. 546.
8. Cited by Reichwein, *China and Europe*, p. 151.

What It Means for Us Today

REGIONAL AUTONOMY VERSUS GLOBAL UNITY

The period after 1500 is significant because it marked the beginning of the clash between regional autonomy and global unity. Before that date there was no conflict because there were few global contacts, let alone global unity. For tens of thousands of years, human beings had lived in regional isolation. When the first humans fanned out from their ancestral birthplace, presumably in Africa, they lost contact with their original neighbors. They repeated this endlessly as they spread in all directions, until they inhabited all continents except Antarctica. For example, when the first Mongoloids crossed from northeast Siberia to Alaska, they pressed on throughout North and South America. They settled down in new communities in relative isolation. Over thousands of years they developed distinctive local languages and cultures and even physical types. This process went on all over the globe, so that until 1500, racial segregation existed on a global scale. All blacks, or Negroids, lived in Africa; all whites, or Caucasoids, lived in Europe and the Middle East; all Mongoloids, in east Asia and the Americas; and all Australoids, in Australia.

This traditional regional autonomy began to yield to global unity when Western overseas expansion began about 1500. Races no longer were isolated because millions of people moved, willingly or unwillingly, to new continents. Since the Europeans took the lead in this global activity, it was they who dominated the newly united world. By the nineteenth century they controlled the globe politically with their great empires and economically with their joint-stock companies and corporations. They also enjoyed cultural domination, so that Western culture became the global model. It was equated with civilization, and non-Western cultures came to be regarded as inherently inferior. This Western hegemony was taken for granted in the nineteenth century, not only by Europeans but also by non-Europeans. It was assumed to be almost divinely ordained—a part of the natural order of things.

Now in the twentieth century, the pendulum has begun to swing once more toward regional autonomy. Europe needed four centuries (1500–1900) to build up its worldwide dominance. It has only taken five decades for that dominance to disintegrate. The disintegration began after World War I and picked up speed after World War II. Political disintegration took the form of the end of empires. Cultural disintegration is even more widespread. Western culture no longer is regarded as synonymous with civilization, nor are non-Western cultures equated with barbarism.

Western culture today is being directly challenged, and even rejected, throughout the world. In November 1979, when American embassy personnel in Teheran were taken hostage, Western reporters submitted a number of written questions to the youthful captors. The latter replied as a group, and their answer included the following: "Western culture is a splendid means for the colonialists, a tool that alienates the nation from itself. By making a nation accept Western and American values, they make it submit to their domination." The captors also expressed distrust of Western-trained or -influenced Iranian intellectuals. "What need do we have for these decaying brains. Let them go where they want. These decaying brains are those intellectuals molded on Western models and they have no role in our movement and our revolution."[1]

Such views are not limited to young radicals. They are now shared by many non-Westerners of all political beliefs. In his influential work *Beyond Marxism: Towards an Alternative Perspective*, Indian political theorist Vrajenda Raj Mehta argues that neither Western democracy nor Soviet communism offers appropriate guidelines for India's development. He rejects liberal democracy because he believes it reduces humans to producers and consumers and results in a selfish, atomistic society. Likewise, he rejects communism because it emphasizes economic concerns and state activities, so that it leaves little to individual choice and destroys life's richness and diversity. Mehta therefore concludes that "Each national community has its own law of development, its own way to fulfill itself. . . . The broken mosaic of Indian society cannot be re-created in the image of the West. India must find its own strategy of development and nation-building suited to its own peculiar conditions."[2]

Rejection of Western global domination is not surprising. Such domination was a historical aberration, produced by a peculiar combination of circumstances and therefore bound to be temporary. But what is surprising is that the forces of regional autonomy are also awakening today within the leading Western states. National groups or subgroups, which have been asleep for decades or for centuries, are now stirring and demanding autonomy. In the United States, there are the minority groups: blacks, Hispanics, and native Americans. In neighboring Canada, the unity of the dominion is threatened by the separatist demands of the French Quebecois. Britain likewise is coping with would-be secessionists in Scotland, Ireland, and Wales. France is facing the same challenge from Corsican, Breton, and Basque liberation fronts.

The demand for regional autonomy is not directed only against central authority in the West. In Iran, the popular revolt against Western influences is paralleled by regional uprisings against Teheran—uprisings by minorities such as the Kurds, Arabs, Baluchis, and Turkomen. Since these minorities comprise almost half of the total population of that country, Iran is far more threatened by regional autonomy demands than is any Western country. The same was true of the USSR, where dozens of ethnic groups demanded self-rule as soon as Gorbachev loosened controls with his *glasnost* or openness—hence the unexpected end of the USSR in the 1990s and its replacement by the Commonwealth of Independent States.

Much of the turmoil of our age arises from the clash of two great contradictory forces. On the one hand, modern technology is uniting the globe as never before, thanks to modern communication media, multinational corporations, and world-encircling spaceships. On the other hand, the globe is being torn apart by the awakening of hitherto dormant masses who are determined to create their own futures. The roots of this historic modern conflict go back to the centuries after 1500 when Western explorers and merchants for the first time brought together all the peoples of the world. The fateful repercussions, both positive and negative, confront us to the present day. "Encircled nationalisms," writes the Egyptian journalist Mohammed Heikel, "have fortified themselves for a last ditch stand in the battle for their future, not their past."[3]

The outcome of this ongoing battle is becoming more uncertain with the passage of time. Issues no longer are as simple and clearcut as they seemed to be only a few decades ago. It cannot be merely a case of East versus West at a time when various Asian people are adopting and applying Western science and technology successfully. Likewise, it cannot be merely a case of socialism versus capitalism when the socialist countries are abandoning their planned economies and their one-party political systems. In the Third World, there is growing disillusionment with all foreign models, but the disillusionment has left a vacuum with no agreed-upon goals and no agreed-upon strategies. China's Premier Chou En-lai best described our times as an age of "great disorder under heaven."

SUGGESTED READINGS

The revolt against Western domination is best summarized by E. Fischer, *The Passing of the European Age*, rev. ed. (Harvard University, 1948). Various aspects of the world-wide challenge to central authority are analyzed in L. Kohr, *The Breakdown of Nations* (Routledge & Kegan Paul, 1957); D. Morris and K. Hess, *Neighborhood Power: The New Localism* (Beacon, 1975); C. Bezold, ed., *Anticipatory Democracy* (Random House, 1978); A. Amalrik, *Will the Soviet Union Survive Until 1984?* (Harper & Row, 1979); H. C. d'Encausse, "Decline of an Empire: The Soviet Socialist Republics in Revolt" (*Newsweek*, 1979); and T. G. Verhelst, *No Life Without Roots: Culture and Development* (Zed Books, 1990), which summarizes global alternatives to the Western development model. The most recent survey of the "great disorder under heaven" is by Z. Brzezinski, *Out of Control: Global Turmoil on the Eve of the 21st Century* (Scribner's, 1993). The turmoil in the vast area of central Asia is analyzed in A. Rashid, *The Resurgence of Central Asia. Islam or Nationalism?* (Zed Books, 1994).

NOTES

1. *New York Times*, November 30, 1979. © 1979 by The New York Times Company. Reprinted by Permission.
2. V. R. Mehta, *Beyond Marxism: Towards an Alternative Perspective* (New Delhi: Manohar, 1978), p. 92.
3. *New York Times*, February 4, 1980.

PART VII

World of Western Dominance, 1763–1914

BASIS OF DOMINANCE

The century and a half between 1763 and 1914 stands out in the course of world history as the period of European domination over a large part of the globe. In 1763 Europe was still far from being the master of the world. It had only coastal footholds in Africa and in Asia. But by 1914 the European powers had annexed the whole of Africa, and they had effectively established their control over Asia: either directly, as in India and Southeast Asia, or indirectly, as in the Chinese and Ottoman empires. The unprecedented expansion of Europe was made possible by the continuation and acceleration of the modernization process. This process was set in motion earlier by the Renaissance, Reformation, technological development, capitalist enterprise, state building, and overseas expansion (see Chapter 20, Section I). These triggered a chain reaction in the form of the three great revolutions—scientific, industrial, and political—which gave Europe irresistible dynamism and power.

Two features of these revolutions might be noted at this point. One is that they were well under way before 1763. The English Civil War, a major phase of the political revolution, occurred in the 1640s. The scientific revolution took place primarily during the century and a half between the publication of Copernicus's *De revolutionibus orbium coelestium* (1543) and of Newton's *Principia* (1687). Likewise, the roots of the industrial revolution were planted in the sixteenth and seventeenth centuries, when the countries of northwestern Europe "were seething with such genuinely capitalistic phenomena as systematic mechanical invention, company formation, and speculation in the shares of financial and trading concerns."[1] But the worldwide impact of none of these revolutions was fully felt until the nineteenth century. That is why we are considering them here rather than earlier in this text.

The other point to note about the three great revolutions is that they did not run in parallel or independent lines. Scientific, industrial, and technological events were interdependent and reacted continuously upon each other. Newton's discovery of the laws governing the movements of heavenly bodies and Darwin's theories of biological evolution both had profound effects on political ideas. Likewise, we could not conceive of modern nationalism without technological innovations such as printing and the telegraph. Conversely, politics affected science, as in the case of the French Revolution, which provided a powerful stimulus to scientific advancement. Politics also affected economics, as was made clear by the English manufacturer John Wilkinson, who stated bluntly, "manufacture and commerce will always flourish most where Church and King interfere least."[2]

After analyzing the nature and the unfolding of these three European revolutions, we shall then, in the following chapters of Part VII of this volume, trace their effect on various parts of the globe. We shall see how they made possible the Europeanization of the Americas and of Australia, the partitioning of Africa, and the domination of Asia and Oceania.

NOTES

1. E. J. Hamilton, "American Treasure and the Rise of Capitalism (1500–1700)," *Economica* (November, 1929), p. 356.
2. Cited by C. E. Robinson, "The English Philosophies and the French Revolution," *History Today*, VI (February, 1956), p. 121.

26

Europe's Scientific and Industrial Revolutions

The so-called scientific revolution ... outshines everything since the rise of Christianity and reduces the Renaissance and Reformation to the rank of mere episodes, mere internal displacements within the system of medieval Christendom.... It looms so large as the real origin both of the modern world and of the modern mentality that our customary periodisation of European history has become an anachronism and an encumbrance.

Herbert Butterfield

The manufacturing system as it exists in Great Britain, and the inconceivably rapid creation of immense towns under it, are without previous parallel in the history of the world.

Manchester Guardian
November 17, 1832

The material culture of the human race has changed more in the past two hundred years than it did in the preceding five thousand. In the eighteenth century people were living essentially in the same way as the ancient Egyptians and Mesopotamians. They were still using the same materials to erect their buildings, the same animals to transport themselves and their belongings, the same sails and oars to propel their ships, the same textiles to make their clothes, and the same candles and torches to provide light. But today metals and plastics supplement stone and wood; the rail-road, the automobile, and the airplane have replaced the oxen, the horse, and the donkey; steam, diesel, and atomic power drive ships in place of wind and labor; many synthetic fabrics compete with the traditional cottons, woolens, and linens; and electricity has replaced the candle and become a source of power for many tasks at the flick of a switch.

The origins of this great transformation are to be found in the scientific and industrial revolutions, the outstanding contributions of Western civilization to human development. In the light of historical retrospect it appears that these two revolutions are of even greater significance than the agricultural revolution of Neolithic times. The agricultural revolution made civilization possible, but once this great step forward was taken, agriculture had no further contribution to make. Scientific technology, on the other hand, is cumulative by its very methodology. It contains within itself the possibilities of infinite advance. If we bear in mind its achievements in the past few centuries and its present accelerating pace of development, we may appreciate, if not comprehend, its staggering potential and significance. Scientific technology, furthermore, is universal. Based as it is on an objective methodology, it has obtained general assent to its propositions. It is the one product of Western civilization that non-Western peoples generally respect and seek. In fact, it was science and its related technology that made it possible for Europe to dominate the world in the nineteenth century. And today the formerly subject peoples are striving to redress the imbalance by learning the mysteries of the West's great and unique contribution to humanity.

It is easy to see why the scientific and industrial revolutions are of basic significance for the study of world history. This chapter will trace the unfolding of these revolutions from their beginnings in early modern times until World War I.

I. ROOTS OF THE SCIENTIFIC REVOLUTION

The roots of science may be traced to ancient Mesopotamia, Egypt, and China; to classical Greece; and to the medieval Moslem world. Yet the scientific revolution is a unique product of Western civilization. The reason seems to be that only in the West did science become part and parcel of general society. Or, to put it another way, only in the West were the philosopher-scientist and the artisan united so that they stimulated each other. And it was this union of science and society, of scientist and artisan, that contributed greatly to the unprecedented blossoming of science in the Western world.

In all human societies the artisans developed certain skills in hunting, fishing, and farming and in working with wood, stone, metal, grasses, fibers, roots, and hides. Through their observations and experiments they gradually improved their techniques and sometimes reached very high levels, as in the case of the Eskimos. Yet the degree of progress achieved by all premodern societies was sharply restricted because the artisans were interested only in making pots or building houses or constructing boats; they did not bother with underlying chemical or mechanical principles. They did not ask about the relationship between causes and their effects. In short, the artisans by definition concerned themselves with technological know-how rather than with scientific know-why.

The philosophers and the artisans undoubtedly did work together at certain times to produce the elaborate calendars, the navigation aids, and the everyday rituals of antiquity. But the fact remains that until recent times the tendency was toward compartmentalization— toward the isolation of the thinker from the worker. The great achievement of the West was to bring the two together. This fusion of know-how and know-why gave science the grounding and the impetus that was to make it the dominant force that it is today.

Why did this epochal development take place in the West? One reason was the humanistic scholarship of the Renaissance. Scholars and artists had access not only to Plato and Aristotle but also to Euclid and Archimedes, who stimulated the study of physics and mathematics. Even more important was the impetus for the biological sciences. Medical students studied the complete works of Hippocrates and Galen, and naturalists those of Aristotle, Dioscorides, and Theophrastus. However, the fruits of human scholarship could not have brought about the scientific revolution without the favorable social atmosphere in western Europe. In this atmosphere the gulf between artisans and scholars was narrowed. Artisans were not so despised during the Renaissance as they had been in classical and medieval times. Respect was given to the practical arts of spinning, weaving, ceramics, glass making, and, most of all, the increasingly important arts of mining and metallurgy. All these crafts in Renaissance Europe were in the hands of free people rather than of slaves, as in classical times. And the people were not so far removed, socially and economically, from the ruling circles as were the artisans of the Middle Ages. The higher status of the Renaissance craftsman allowed him to strengthen his ties with the scholar. Each had an important contribution to make. The craftsman had the old techniques of antiquity and added the new devices evolving during the Middle Ages. The scholars likewise provided the facts, speculations, and procedures of rediscovered antiquity and of medieval science. The two approaches fused slowly, but in the end they produced an explosive combination.

Closely connected with this union of the craftsperson and scholar was the corresponding union of labor and thought that was brought about by individual scholars or scientists. A strong prejudice existed in ancient times against combining creative learning and manual work. This prejudice, which presumably arose out of the ancient association of manual labor with slavery, persisted in medieval Europe even after slavery had almost disappeared. Medieval scholastic philosophers drew a distinction between the liberal and the servile arts, between work done with the mind alone and work that involved a change in matter. Poets, logicians and mathematicians, for example belonged to the first category, and sculptors, glaziers, and ironworkers to the second. This attitude held back progress, as was clearly evident in the field of medicine. Because the work of a physician did not change matter, it was regarded as "liberal," whereas that of a surgeon, by the same criterion, was considered "servile." Accordingly, experimentation was looked down on, and vivisection was deemed illegal and repulsive.

When William Harvey (1578–1657) made his great discovery concerning the movements of the heart and blood, he did so because he resolutely turned his back on this scorn for manual work. Instead, for decades he carried on painstaking experiments of all types. He cut the arteries and veins of living things, from large animals to tiny insects, observing and recording with care and patience the flow of the blood and the motions of the heart. He also utilized the new magnifying glass to observe wasps, hornets, and flies. Today this procedure seems sensible and obvious, but in Harvey's time it definitely was not. It took much courage for Harvey to use in his time what is considered today to be normal scientific method.

Science was stimulated also by the discoveries of explorers and the opening up of overseas lands. New plants, new animals, new stars, even new human beings and new human societies were found, and all these challenged traditional ideas and assumptions. Similarly, the growth of commerce and industry led to technological advances, which in turn stimulated, and were stimulated by, science. Oceanic commerce created an enormous demand for shipbuilding and navigation. A new class of mathematically trained craftsmen made compasses, maps, and instruments. Navigation schools were founded in Portugal, Spain, Holland, and France, and astronomy was studied seriously because of its obvious utilitarian value. Likewise, the needs of the mining industry brought about advances in power transmission and pumps. This was the beginning of a new interest in mechanical and hydraulic principles. In the same way, metallurgy was responsible for notable progress in chemistry. As mining operations expanded, new ores and even new metals, like bismuth, zinc, and cobalt, were discovered. Techniques for separating and handling these had to be found and refined by painful experience. But in doing so, a general theory of chemistry began to take form, involving oxidations and reductions, distillations and amalgamations. Finally, the new knowledge in all these fields was both stimulated and circulated by the universities and the printing press. The latter was especially important in promoting literacy and spreading new ideas.

These achievements gave the scientists, or philosophers, a self-assurance and a confidence that they were the signs of a new age. In 1662 Charles II of England granted a charter for the establishment of "The Royal Society of London for Promoting Natural Knowledge." Its members, seeing the advantage of cooperation between technicians and scientists, coordinated the efforts in every occupation throughout the country to gather data that might advance scientific knowledge.

All Places and Corners are now busy and warm about this Work: and we find many noble Rarities to be every Day given in [to the Society] not only by the Hands of learned and professed Philosophers; but from the Shops of Mechanicks; from the Voyages of Merchants; from the Ploughs of Husbandmen, from the Sports, The Fishponds, The Parks, The Gardens of Gentlemen. . . .[1]

At first, science received much more from the mine and the workshop than science itself could give back. During this early period science was not an integral part of economic life and was used sparingly and sporadically. This was true even in the early phase of the industrial revolution in the late eighteenth and early nineteenth centuries. But by the end of the nineteenth century the situation changed. Science no longer was in a subordinate position: It had begun to transform old industries and even to create entirely new ones.

II. COURSE OF THE SCIENTIFIC REVOLUTION

As we might expect, the first major advance of modern science occurred in the field of astronomy, which was closely related to geography and to navigation. This advance was achieved in the sixteenth and seventeenth centuries, and the great names were Minolaj Kopernik, or Copernicus (1473–1543); Galileo Galilei (1564–1642); and Isaac Newton (1642–1727). Copernicus took up the idea of some ancient philosophers that the sun, rather than the earth, was the center of the universe, and he demonstrated that this provided a simpler explanation of the movement of the heavenly bodies than did the traditional Ptolemaic system. Galileo supported Copernicus empirically by using the recently discovered telescope to see what actually was in the heavens. "By the aid of a telescope," he reported, "anyone may behold that. . . the Galaxy is nothing else but a mass of innumerable stars planted together in clusters. Upon whatever part of it you direct the telescope straightaway a vast crowd of stars presents itself to view. . . ."[2]

By far the most outstanding figure of early science was Newton, a towering genius comparable to Euclid and Einstein. In addition to his pioneering work in optics, hydrodynamics, and

The telescope with which Galileo worked after 1609. He observed Earth's moon and the cyclical phases of the planet Venus and discovered the most prominent moons of Jupiter. These observations had revolutionary intellectual and theological implications in the seventeenth century.

mathematics, he discovered the law of gravitation: "Every particle of matter in the universe attracts every other particle with a force varying inversely as the square of the distance between them and directly proportional to the product of their masses."

Here was a sensational and revolutionary explanation that tore the veils from the heavens. Newton had discovered a fundamental, cosmic law that could be proved mathematically and applied to all matter, from the minutest object to the universe at large. Nature indeed appeared to be a gigantic mechanical object operating according to certain natural laws that could be found by observation, experiment, and calculation. All branches of human knowledge could be broken down into a few, simple, uniform laws that rational persons could discover. People began to apply the analytical method of Newtonian physics to the entire field of thought and knowledge, to human society as well as to the physical universe.

Sir Isaac Newton discovered the mathematical and physical laws governing the force of gravity. Newton believed that religion and science were compatible and mutually supportive, and that the study of nature gave one a better understanding of the Creator. This portrait of Newton is by Sir Godfrey Kneller.

As the industrial revolution got under way in the late eighteenth century, it affected, and in return was affected by, the scientific revolution. An example is the development of the steam engine. It provided sorely needed power to operate machines and locomotives and, at the outset, to pump water out of mines. James Watt combined technical ingenuity and scientific knowledge to improve the steam engines to a reasonable level of efficiency. In 1769 Watt began to use a separate condensing cylinder, and soon after he converted linear into rotary motion by means of a crankshaft. If the relatively unlimited power of the steam engine had not been available, the industrial revolution might well have petered out. It might have amounted to a mere speedup in textile manufacturing, as happened in China, where analogous technical advances had been made centuries earlier.

The science that made the most progress during the first half of the nineteenth century was chemistry—partly because of its close association with the textile industry, which experienced such rapid growth during those decades. The Newton of chemistry was Antoine Lavoisier (1743–1794), whose law of the conservation of matter is comparable to the law of gravitation: "...although matter may alter its state in a series of chemical actions, it does not change in amount; the quantity of matter is the same at the end as at the beginning of every operation, and can be traced by its weight." Lavoisier's successors in the nineteenth century made discovery after discovery that had important practical applications: Justus von Liebeg for chemical fertilizers; W. H. Perkin for synthetic dyes; and Louis Pasteur for his germ theory of disease, which led to the adoption of sanitary precautions and so brought under control old scourges like typhoid, diphtheria, cholera, and malaria.

As Newton dominated seventeenth-century science with his discovery of the laws governing the bodies of the universe, so Darwin dominated nineteenth-century science, for he discovered the laws governing the evolution of humanity itself. His doctrine of evolution holds that animal and vegetable species in their present diverse forms are not the fixed and unchangeable results

In two works of seminal importance, The Origin of Species *(1859) and* The Descent of Man *(1871), Charles Darwin articulated the theory of evolution by natural selection and applied that theory to human beings. The result was a storm of controversy that affected not only biology but also religion, philosophy, sociology, and even politics.*

of separate special acts of creation. They are different. They are capable of change. And they are the natural outcomes of a common original source. Darwin believed that the chief manner in which variation took place was by natural selection. He defined this process as follows:

As many more individuals of each species are born than can possibly survive, and as, consequently, there is a frequently recurring struggle for existence, it follows that any being, if it vary however slightly in any manner profitable to itself, under the complex and sometimes varying conditions of life, will have a better chance of surviving, and thus be naturally selected. From the strong principle of inheritance, any selected variety will tend to propagate its new and modified form.[3]

It may be hard to conceive of all the variety in nature as being the product of such an appar-

ently slow process of change as that afforded by natural selection. Yet statistical calculations show that even if a mutation resulted in only a 1 percent better chance of survival, the change would establish itself in half the individuals of a species in a hundred generations. In other words, if 101 individuals with a particular mutation survived for every 100 without it, it would spread through the species in what is, biologically speaking, a short time. The details of Darwin's theories have been modified by later research, but virtually all scientists now accept the essentials of the doctrine. There was bitter opposition in certain quarters, particularly among the clergy. This was understandable, because Darwin was denying the act of divine creation. Just as the Copernican system of astronomy had deposed the earth from its central place in the universe, so Darwinism seemed to dethrone human beings from their central place in the history of the earth.

Despite the hostile reception in religious and other circles, Darwinism had profound repercussions on Western society. Its emphasis on survival of the fittest and struggle for survival fitted in admirably with the temper of the times. In politics, during this period, Bismarck was unifying Germany by blood and iron. Nationalistic admirers in all countries believed that Darwinism offered them support and justification. They held that in politics, as in nature, the strongest are victorious and that warlike qualities decide who will win in the international "struggle for survival." In economic life this was the period of free enterprise and rugged individualism. The upper and middle classes, comfortable and contented, stoutly opposed any state intervention for the promotion of greater social equality. They argued that they deserved their blessings and prosperity because they had proven themselves "fitter" than the shiftless poor. Furthermore, the absorption of smaller concerns by big business was a part of the "struggle for survival." The late nineteenth century was also the golden age of colonial expansion, and Darwinism was used to justify imperialism. The argument was that colonies were necessary for the prosperity and survival of a great power. Moreover, native peoples, judged in terms of worldly success, were weak, inferior, and in need of the protection and guidance of the superior and stronger Europeans.

The application of Darwin's theories to the social scene is known as Social Darwinism. Darwin himself had never dreamed, let alone intended, that his findings would be exploited in this fashion. But the fact remains that they were, for the simple reason that they seemed to offer scientific support for the materialism that was spreading over Europe at this time. Darwinism, in short, fitted in conveniently with Kipling's dictum:

That they should take who have the power
And they should keep who can.

III. SIGNIFICANCE OF THE SCIENTIFIC REVOLUTION

As the nineteenth century passed, science became an increasingly important part of Western society. At the beginning of the century science was still on the periphery of economic and social life. But by the end it was making basic contributions to the old, established industries; it was creating entirely new industries; and it was profoundly affecting the way of thinking as well as the way of living of Western society. Furthermore, the metamorphosis wrought by the scientific revolution affected the entire world in many ways, direct and indirect. It made Europe's domination of the globe technologically possible, and it determined to a large extent the nature and effects of this domination. Also it provided the basis for the West's intellectual predominance in the nineteenth century. European art or religion or philosophy did not affect non-Western peoples very much because they had made comparable contributions in these fields. But there was no such equality in science and technology. Only the West had mastered the secrets of nature and had exploited them for material advancement. This was an undeniable and persuasive fact. Non-Westerners no longer looked down on Europeans as uncouth barbarians who happened to have a certain superiority in sailing ships and firearms. Reluctantly they recognized the importance of Europe's scientific revolution. And today the primary aim of former colonial peoples is to experience this unique revolution themselves. For all these reasons, the distinguished British historian Herbert Butterfield concludes that the scientific revolution:

. . . proved to be so capable of growth, and so many-sided in its operations, that it consciously assumed a directing role from the very first, and, so to speak, began to take control of the other factors —just as Christianity in the middle ages had come to preside over everything else, percolating into every corner of life and thought. And when we speak of Western civilization being carried to an oriental country, like Japan in recent generations, we do not mean Graeco-Roman philosophy and humanist ideals, we do not mean the Christianising of Japan, we mean the science, the modes of thought and all that apparatus of civilization which were beginning to change the face of the West in the latter half of the seventeenth century.[4]

IV. ROOTS OF THE INDUSTRIAL REVOLUTION

The term industrial revolution is frequently challenged because it is used to describe, not a rapid overnight change, but a "revolution" that began before the eighteenth century and, for all practical purposes, has continued to the present day. Obviously, then, this was not a revolution in the sense of a spectacular change that began and ended suddenly.

Yet the fact remains that during the 1780s a breakthrough did occur in productivity, or as economists now put it, there was "a takeoff into self-sustained growth." More specifically, a mechanized factory system was created that produced goods in vast quantities and at rapidly diminishing costs, so it was no longer dependent on existing demand but could create its own demand. An example of this now common but hitherto unknown phenomenon is the automobile industry. It was not the demand for automobiles that existed at the turn of the century that created the giant automobile industry of today. Rather, the capacity to build the cheap Model-T Ford, in large quantities, stimulated the modern mass demand for them.

The first question that arises in considering the industrial revolution has to do with its timing. Why did it occur in the late eighteenth cen-

A RIDE ON AN EARLY RAILWAY

*The world's first railway was opened in 1825 and the second in 1830
between Liverpool and Manchester. A description of the second railway has been
left by the actress Frances (Fanny) Kimble, who rode on it as a young girl
in the year of its opening.* *

My father knew several of the gentlemen most deeply interested in the undertaking [the Liverpool-Manchester railway], and Stephenson having proposed a trial trip as far as the fifteen mile viaduct, they, with infinite kindness, invited him and permitted me to accompany them; allowing me, moreover, the place which I felt to be one of supreme honour, by the side of Stephenson. . . . He was a rather stern-featured man, with a dark and deeply marked countenance. . . .

We were introduced to the little engine which was to drag us along the rails. . . . This snorting little animal, which I felt rather inclined to pat, was then harnessed to our carriage, and, Mr. Stephenson having taken me on the bench of the engine with him, we started at about ten miles an hour. The steam-horse being ill-adapted for going up and down hill, the road was kept at a certain level, and appeared sometimes to sink below the surface of the earth, and sometimes to rise above it. Almost at starting it was cut through the solid rock, which formed a wall on either side of it, about sixty feet high. You can't imagine how strange it seemed to be journeying on thus, without any visible cause of progress other than the magical machine, with its flying white breath and rhythmical, unvarying pace. . . . We were to go only fifteen miles, that distance being sufficient to show the speed of the engine. . . . After proceeding through this rocky defile, we presently found ourselves raised upon embankments ten or twelve feet high; we then came to a moss, or swamp, of considerable extent, on which no human foot could tread without sinking, and yet it bore the road which bore us. . . .

We had now come fifteen miles, and stopped where the road traversed a wide and deep valley. Stephenson made me alight and led me down to the bottom of this ravine, over which, in order to keep his road level, he has thrown a magnificent viaduct of nine arches, the middle one of which is seventy feet high, through which we saw the whole of this beautiful little valley.... We then rejoined the rest of the party, and the engine having received its supply of water, the carriage was placed behind it, for it cannot turn, and was set off at its utmost speed, thirty-five miles an hour, swifter than a bird flies (for they tried the experiment with a snipe). You cannot conceive what that sensation of cutting the air was; the motion is as smooth as possible, too.

*F. A. Kimble, *Record of a Girlhood*, 3rd ed. (Richard Bentley, 1879), pp. 158–160.

---

tury rather than a hundred or a thousand years earlier? The answer in large part lies in the remarkable economic growth of Europe following the great expansion overseas. This growth was so pronounced that it is commonly referred to as the "commercial revolution."

The commercial revolution was characterized in the first place by a change in the articles of world trade. Before the sixteenth century the most important items were spices traded from East to West and bullion traded in the opposite direction. But gradually new overseas products became staples of consumption in Europe and grew in commercial importance. These included new beverages (cocoa, tea, and coffee), new dyes (indigo, cochineal, and brazilwood), new flavors (allspice and vanilla), and new foodstuffs (guinea fowl and turkeys and a greatly increased supply of Newfoundland cod). The other main feature of the commercial revolution was the marked increase in the volume of trade. Between 1715 and 1787 French imports from overseas territories increased tenfold, and exports increased between seven- and eightfold. England's trade grew almost as spectacularly—in the period from 1698 to 1775 both imports and exports rose between 500 and 600 percent. Europe's general trade was growing, but colonial trade was accounting for a larger and larger portion of it. In 1698, for example, about 15 percent of England's seaborne trade was with its colonies, but by 1775 this figure had risen to 33 percent. Furthermore, the reexport of colonial goods was responsible for much of the increase of France's and England's trade with other European countries.

The commercial revolution contributed to the industrial revolution in several important respects. First, it provided large and expanding markets for European industries, particularly those producing textiles; firearms; hardware; ships; and ship accessories, including lumber, rope, sails, anchors, pulleys, and nautical instruments. To meet the demands of these new markets, industries had to improve their organiza-

tion and technology. The commercial revolution also contributed the large amounts of capital necessary to finance the construction of factories and machines for the industrial revolution. The capital, in the form of profits, poured into Europe from all parts of the world—from the fur trade in Siberia and North America; from the silver mines of Mexico and Peru; from the African slave trade; and from the profits of the several East India companies, West India companies, Levant companies, Africa companies, and assorted others, including the Muscovy Company, the Hudson Bay Company, and the various land settlement companies in the Americas. It is estimated that the amount of capital extracted from India and from the West Indian sugar colonies during the eighteenth century was about equal to the amount of capital invested in British industry in 1800.

Profitable commercial enterprise, together with the accompanying technological growth and institutional change, explains why the industrial revolution reached the "takeoff" stage in the late eighteenth century. This raises the question of why the "takeoff" occurred first in England. One important advantage Britain enjoyed is that it had taken an early lead in the basic coal and iron industries. Because its forest reserves were being depleted, Britain early began using coal for fuel and for smelting iron. By the time of the French Revolution (1789), Britain was producing about 10 million tons of coal per

This painting shows the pithead of an eighteenth-century coal mine in England. The machinery on the left includes a steam engine that powered equipment to bring mined coal to the surface or to pump water from the mine. Britain's rich veins of coal were one of the factors contributing to its early industrialization.

year, whereas France was producing 700,000 tons. England also pioneered in the development of the blast furnace, which, in contrast to the old forges, could mass-produce iron. In 1780 Britain's iron output had been a third that of France; by 1840, it was three times more. All this meant that Britain was pushing ahead in the production of goods for mass consumption. And there was a large and steady demand for these goods. France, on the other hand, specialized more in luxury commodities of limited and fluctuating demand.

England also had more fluid capital available for the financing of the industrial revolution. More profits from commerce poured into England than into any other country. English court and military expenditures were less than the French costs, so that English taxation was lighter and English government finances were in better condition. Furthermore, banking developed earlier and more efficiently in England, providing pooled funds for individual and corporate enterprise.

Noteworthy also is the impressive concentration of managerial talent in England. This is to be explained in part by the outstanding contributions of Nonconformists like the Darbys in the iron industry, Cookworthy in pottery, the Brights in cotton milling and in politics, and Dalton and Eddington in science. Freedom from convention and stress on personal responsibility produced a disproportionate quota of experiments and inventors among the Nonconformists, and their frugality led them to plow profits back into business rather than to squander them in luxurious living. The influence of the Nonconformists in England was enhanced by the influx of coreligionists from the continent. With the revocation of the Edict of Nantes in 1685, for example, France lost considerable managerial talent to England, especially in the textile industry.

Britain also had the advantage of a mobile and plentiful supply of labor. The great supply was made available by the earlier disintegration of the guilds and by the enclosing of the traditional strips of farmland. The end of the guilds, with their manifold restrictions, made it easier to introduce the putting-out system and to equip the factories with power machinery. The land enclosures began in the 1500s and continued for three centuries, reaching their height in the late eighteenth and early nineteenth centuries. The yeomen frequently were forced to sell out, because the enclosing of common and of waste lands left them no land for grazing and for fuel. The earlier enclosures were caused by the rising price of wool, so that the land was used mostly for grazing. In the later period the need to grow foodstuffs for the burgeoning cities was more important, so the enclosed land was cultivated according to the most up-to-date and efficient methods. Crop rotation replaced the wasteful old system of allowing fields to lie fallow. Superior seeds were developed and cattle were improved by scientific breeding. Some agricultural machinery, such as a horse-driven hoeing machine and an automatic drill for planting seeds, was developed.

Between 1714 and 1820, over 6 million acres of land were enclosed in England. This meant serious dislocation and distress. The poor peasants lost part or all of their land and were forced to become tenants or day laborers or else seek employment in the cities. Socially minded people were appalled by this wholesale uprooting of England's yeomanry and spoke up against it. The process of enclosing the land was unsettling and unpleasant, but as far as the industrial revolution was concerned, it fulfilled two essential functions—it provided labor for the factories and food for the cities. For this reason the enclosures may be considered a prerequisite to England's industrial supremacy in the nineteenth century. Enclosures did occur in certain other European countries, but to a much lesser extent. In France, for example, the French Revolution provided the peasants with more land and thereby increased their attachment to their birthplaces and their unwillingness to pack up and move.

V. COURSE OF THE INDUSTRIAL REVOLUTION

Inventors seldom invent except under the stimulus of strong demand. Many of the principles that the new inventions of the industrial revolution were based on were known long before the eighteenth century but were not applied to industry because the incentive was lacking. This was the case, for example, with steam power. Although known in Hellenistic Egypt, it was used merely to open and close temple doors. In England, however, a new source of power was urgently needed to pump water out of mines and to turn the wheels of the new machinery. This need stimulated a series of inventions and improvements that finally resulted in the development of a commercially practical steam engine.

The pattern of demand leading to invention is plainly evident in the course of the industrial revolution. Inventions in one field created an imbalance and stimulated counterinventions in other fields to redress the balance. For example, the cotton industry was the first to be mechanized because cotton goods, which were originally imported from India, had become exceedingly popular with the British public. In fact, cotton was used so widely that the old and powerful woolen interests secured the passage of a law in 1700 prohibiting the importation of cotton cloth or goods. The law, however, did not ban the manufacture of cotton cloth. This created a unique opportunity for local industry, and enterprising middlemen soon were exploiting it. The problem was how to speed up the spinning and weaving enough to meet the demand of the large and protected home market. Prizes were offered for inventions that would increase output, and by 1830 a series of such inventions had completely mechanized the cotton industry.

Outstanding were John Kay's flying shuttle (1733), which speeded up weaving; Richard Arkwright's water frame (1769), which spun fine, strong yarn between rollers; James Hargreave's spinning jenny (1770), on which one person could spin eight, then sixteen, then finally over a hundred threads of yarn at once; and Samuel Crompton's spinning mule (1779) so called because it combined features of the water frame and the jenny. All these new spinning machines soon were producing far more thread than could be handled by the weavers. A clergyman, Edmund Cartwright, sought to redress the balance by patenting in 1785 a power loom operated first by horses and after 1789 by steam. At first the contraption was clumsy and commercially unprofitable, but after two decades of improvement the most serious defects were remedied. By the 1820's the power loom had largely supplanted the handweavers in the cotton industry.

Just as inventions in spinning led to related inventions in weaving, so inventions in one

The spinning jenny.

industry encouraged people to invent machinery so that other industries could keep up. For example, the new cotton machines created a demand for more plentiful and reliable power than that provided by the traditional water-wheels and horses. The response was James Watt's multiple improvements on a primitive engine built by Thomas Newcomen about 1702. By 1800 some 500 Watt engines were in service, 38 percent being engaged in pumping water and the remainder in supplying rotary power for textile mills, iron furnaces, flour mills, and other industries.

The historical significance of the steam engine can scarcely be exaggerated. It provided a means for harnessing and utilizing heat energy to furnish driving power for machines. Thus, it ended the age-old dependence on animal, wind, and water power. A vast new source of energy now was available. Before long it was possible to tap the fossil fuels locked up in the earth—namely, oil and gas. In this way began the trend that has led to the enormous energy sources available to modern-day industrialized nations. For example, in 1975 western Europe had 11.5 times and North America had 29 times as much energy available per capita as did less industrialized Asia. The meaning of these figures is obvious in a world where economic and military strength depends directly on the energy resources available. Indeed, it may be said that Europe's domination of the globe in the nineteenth century was based more on the steam engine than on any other single device or force.

The new cotton machines and steam engines required an increased supply of iron, steel, and coal. The need was met by a series of improvements in mining and metallurgy—Abra-

English power-loom weaving in the early nineteeth century.

ham Darby's substitution of coal for coke in smelting iron ore, Henry Cort's "puddling" process for removing impurities in smelted iron, and the use of the Watt steam engine for operating the bellows and hammers and for rolling and splitting. As a result of these various developments, by 1800 Britain was producing more coal and iron than the rest of the world combined. Britain's coal output rose from 6 million tons in 1770 to 12 million tons in 1800 to 57 million tons in 1861. Likewise, its iron output increased from 50,000 tons in 1770 to 130,000 tons in 1800 to 3,800,000 tons in 1861. Iron had become plentiful and cheap enough to be used for general construction, and human society had entered the Age of Iron as well as the Age of Steam.

The expansion of the textile, mining, and metallurgical industries created a need for improved transportation facilities to move the bulky shipments of coal and ore. This started a canal-building boom that gave England 2,500 miles of canals by 1830. The canal era was paralleled by a great period of road building. After 1750 a group of road engineers—John Metcalf, Thomas Telford, and John McAdam—developed methods of building hard-surfaced roads that would bear traffic all through the year. Travel by coach increased from four miles an hour to six, eight, or even ten. After 1830 both roads and waterways were challenged by the railroad. The chief figure here was a mining engineer, George Stephenson. In 1830 his steam engine *Rocket* pulled a train thirty-one miles from Liverpool to Manchester at an average speed of fourteen miles per hour. Within a few years the railroad dominated long-distance traffic, for it could move passengers and freight faster and more cheaply than was possible by road or canal. By 1838 Britain had 500 miles of railroad; by 1850, 6,600; and by 1870, 15,500.

The steam engine was also applied to water transportation. The pioneer was Robert Fulton, who in 1807 launched his *Clermont* on America's Hudson River. By 1833 the *Royal William* steamed from Nova Scotia to England, and five years later the *Sirius* and the *Great Western* crossed the Atlantic in the opposite direction. They took sixteen and one-half and thirteen and one-half days, respectively, or about half the time required by the fastest sailships. In 1840

Samuel Cunard established a regular transatlantic service, announcing beforehand dates of arrival and departure.

The industrial revolution was a revolution in communication as well as transportation. Hitherto a message could be sent to a distant place only by wagon, postrider, or boat. But in the middle of the nineteenth century the electric telegraph was invented. In 1866 a transatlantic cable was laid, establishing instant communication between the old and new worlds.

The industrial revolution did not end with the rise of railroads or transatlantic steamships or telegraphic communication. It continues to the present day, with certain stages discernible in its evolution. The first stage lasted to the mid-nineteenth century and included, as noted, the mechanization of the cotton industry, of mining, and of metallurgy and the development of the steam engine and its application to industry and transportation. The second stage lasted through the latter part of the nineteenth century and was characterized by the more direct application of science to industry and by the development of mass-production techniques. Whereas science at the outset had little effect on industry, it gradually became an integral part of all large industrial enterprises. A spectacular example of the practical applications of industrial research laboratories are the many coal derivatives that have been developed. Coal not only yielded coke and a valuable gas that was used for illumination. It also gave a liquid, or coal tar. Chemists discovered a veritable treasure trove in coal tar: hundreds of dyes, aspirin, saccharin, wintergreen, disinfectants, laxatives, perfumes, photographic chemicals, high explosives, and essence of orange blossom.

Whereas Germany led the world in the nineteenth century in applying science to industry, the United States was the pioneer in developing mass-production techniques. These were of two varieties. One was the making of standard interchangeable parts and the assembling of these parts into the completed unit with a minimum of handicraft labor. The classic example is Henry Ford's endless conveyor belt. Car parts traveled along the belt and were assembled into the Model T by workers who were transformed into cogs of the machines. The other

THE WONDER of the AGE ! !
INSTANTANEOUS COMMUNICATION.

Under the special Patronage of Her Majesty & H.R.II. Prince Albert.

THE GALVANIC AND ELECTRO-MAGNETIC
TELEGRAPHS,
ON THE
GT. WESTERN RAILWAY.

May be seen in constant operation, daily, (Sundays excepted) from 9 till 8, at the
TELEGRAPH OFFICE, LONDON TERMINUS, PADDINGTON
AND TELEGRAPH COTTAGE, SLOUGH STATION.

An Exhibition admitted by its numerous Visitors to be the most interesting and ATTRACTIVE of any in this great Metropolis. In the list of visitors are the illustrious names of several of the Crowned Heads of Europe, and nearly the whole of the Nobility of England.

"*This Exhibition, which has so much excited Public attention of late, is well worthy a visit from all who love to see the wonders of science.*"—MORNING POST.

The Electric Telegraph is unlimited in the nature and extent of its communications; by its extraordinary agency a person in London could converse with another at New York, or at any other place however distant, as easily and nearly as rapidly as if both parties were in the same room. Questions proposed by Visitors will be asked by means of this Apparatus, and answers thereto will instantaneously be returned by a person 20 Miles off, who will also, at their request, ring a bell or fire a cannon, in an incredibly short space of time, after the signal for his doing so has been given.

The Electric Fluid travels at the rate of 280,000 Miles per Second.

By its powerful agency Murderers have been apprehended, (as in the late case of Tawell,)—Thieves detected; and lastly, which is of no little importance, the timely assistance of Medical aid has been procured in cases which otherwise would have proved fatal.

The great national importance of this wonderful invention is so well known that any further allusion here to its merits would be superfluous.

N.B. Despatches sent to and fro with the most confiding secrecy. Messengers in constant attendance, so that communications received by Telegraph, would be forwarded, if required, to any part of London, Windsor, Eton, &c.

ADMISSION ONE SHILLING.
T HOME, *Licensee.*

Nurton, Printer. 48, Church St. Portman Market.

An English handbill, 1845.

production technique was the manipulation of large masses of material by means of advanced mechanical devices. The prime example of this method is the steel industry, whose productivity was described in justifiably boastful terms by the industrial tycoon Andrew Carnegie:

Two pounds of ironstone mined upon Lake Superior and transported nine-hundred miles to Pittsburgh; one pound and one-half of coal, mined and manufactured into coke, and transported to Pittsburgh; one-half pound of lime, mined and transported to Pittsburgh; a small amount of manganese ore mined in Virginia and brought to Pittsburgh—and these four pounds of materials manufactured into one pound of steel, for which the consumer pays one cent.[5]

VI. EFFECT OF THE INDUSTRIAL REVOLUTION ON EUROPE

Diffusion of Industrialization

During the nineteenth century the industrial revolution spread gradually from England to the continent of Europe. The pattern of diffusion depended on various factors, such as supply of natural resources and the existence of a free and mobile working population, unencumbered by guild restrictions or feudal obligations. Belgium was the first country to be industrialized, so that by 1870 the majority of its population lived in cities and were directly dependent on trade or industry. After Belgium followed France, Germany, Austria-Hungary, Italy, and Russia. Meanwhile, non-European countries were being industrialized—first the United States and then the British dominions and Japan. Latecomers

enjoyed the advantage of new and more efficient factories, so that Britain lost its original status as the "industrial workshop of the world."

Table 26.1, listing the powers in the order of their industrial production, demonstrates the changes that have occurred in the world's industrial balance.

Changes in the balance of the world's economy have persisted in the 1990s. In 1995 the world economy grew by 3.7 percent, but most of the growth was outside Europe. The growth of the American and European economies in 1995 was between 2.6 and 3.0 percent, compared to 8.7 percent for Asia. Within Asia the 1995 growth rates were 10.2 percent for China, 9.7 percent for South Korea, 9 percent for Vietnam, and 7.5 percent for Indochina.[6]

Increase of Population

Another effect of the industrial revolution on Europe was further increase in population, which had started earlier with the increased productivity in agriculture. In spite of the emigration overseas of millions of Europeans during the nineteenth century, the population of the continent in 1914 was well over three times that of 1750. The reasons for this population explosion were, first, economic and, second, medical. Most mortality in earlier centuries had been due to infectious diseases, and the incidence of infection had depended mostly on the level of living standards. With the increased cultivation of the potato during the nineteenth century, nutritional levels rose, natural resistance to disease rose correspondingly, and mortality rates dropped correspondingly. Famine in most parts of Europe west of Russia became a memory of

---

TABLE 26.1 Changing World Industrial Balance, 1860–1980

1860	1880	1900	1980
Great Britain	United States	United States	United States
France	Great Britain	Germany	Japan
United States	Germany	Great Britain	Soviet Union
Germany	France	France	Germany

the past. Even if crops failed, the new railway networks ensured adequate supplies from the outside. At the same time the industrial revolution made possible improved sewage systems and safer water supplies, which further lowered mortality rates. Thus mortality statistics reveal that deaths from major infectious diseases declined about thirty years before the major chemotherapy discoveries.

Then the application of new medical science through vaccination and segregation of infected persons further reduced death rates in western Europe. By 1914 they had fallen from at least 30 per 1,000 persons in 1800 to about fifteen in 1914. Thus Europe's population climbed steeply from 140 million in 1750 to 188 million in 1800, 266 million in 1850, 401 million in 1900, and 463 million in 1914. This rate of increase in Europe was so much higher than in the other regions of the world that it altered the global population balance (see Table 26.2).

Urbanization

The industrial revolution led also to an unprecedented urbanization of world society. The size of cities traditionally had depended on the amount of food that the surrounding land could produce. Thus the most populous cities were in the valleys and flood plains, like the Nile, the Fertile Crescent, the Indus, and the Hwang Ho. With the industrial revolution and the factory system, a mass influx flooded the new centers of industry. The large new urban populations could be fed because food supplies were available from all parts of the world. Technological and medical advances eliminated the plagues that previously had decimated cities and even made city living relatively endurable and pleasant. The most important of these advances were plenty of pure water, the perfecting of centralized sewerage and waste disposal systems, insurance of an adequate food supply, and prevention and control of con-

---

TABLE 26.2 Estimated Population of the World*

	1650	1750	1850	1900	1950	1990
Millions						
Europe	100	140	266	401	572	787
United States and Canada	1	1	26	81	166	276
Latin America	12	11	33	63	164	448
Oceania	2	2	2	6	13	27
Africa	100	95	95	120	219	642
Asia	330	479	749	937	1,368	3,113
TOTAL	545	728	1,171	1,608	2,502	5,293
Percentages						
Europe	18.3	19.2	22.7	24.9	23.0	15.0
United States and Canada	0.2	0.1	2.3	5.1	6.7	5.0
Latin America	2.2	1.5	2.8	3.9	6.3	8.5
Oceania	0.4	0.3	0.2	0.4	0.5	0.5
Africa	18.3	13.1	8.1	7.4	8.8	12.0
Asia	60.6	65.8	63.9	58.3	54.7	59.0
TOTAL	100.0	100.0	100.0	100.0	100.0	100.0

*These figures show that Europe's percentage of the total world population rose from 18.3 percent in 1650 to a high of 24.9 percent in 1900 to 18 percent in 1977. But by the twentieth century most of the population of the United States, Canada, and Oceania was of European origin, and at least half the population of Latin America was also. Accordingly, it is more meaningful to say that through the twentieth century the percentage of Europeans and people of European origin had risen to about one-third of the world total. Adapted from A. M. Carr-Saunders, *World Population* (Clarendon, 1936), p. 42, and *United Nations Demographic Yearbooks*.

tagious diseases. Cities all over the world grew at such a rate that by 1930 they included 415 million people, or one-fifth of the human race. This represents one of the great social transformations in human history, for city dwelling meant an entirely new way of life. By 1914 many Western countries, such as Britain, Belgium, Germany, and the United States, had a substantial majority of their people living in cities.

Increase of Wealth

The industrial revolution, with its efficient exploitation of human and natural resources on a worldwide scale, brought about an increase in productivity that is without precedent in all history. Great Britain, which was the first affected, increased its capital from 500 million pounds sterling in 1750 to 1,500 million pounds in 1800, to 2,500 million pounds in 1833, and to 6,000 million in 1865. In the latter part of the nineteenth century the entire world felt the impact of the increasing productivity. The wool of New Zealand, the wheat of Canada, the rice of Burma, the rubber of Malaya, the jute of Bengal, and the humming factories of western Europe and the eastern United States—all these resources were enmeshed in a dynamic and constantly expanding global economy. The figures in Table 26.3 indicate the rate at which industrial production rose, both in Europe and throughout the world, in the second half of the nineteenth century.

There has been much difference of opinion among authorities in recent years concerning the distribution of the wealth created during the industrial revolution. One group holds that all classes benefited to a greater or lesser extent, whereas the other maintains that a few made huge fortunes while the many were ruthlessly exploited and suffered declining standards of living.

There is no doubt that there was much exploitation and social disruption in the early days of industrialization. The tenant farmers were dispossessed, and the weavers and other craftspeople were wiped out by the irresistible competition of the new machine-made goods. These people, and others like them, faced the strain of moving to the city, finding employment, and adjusting to an unfamiliar environment and to strange ways of living and working. They were completely dependent on their employers, for they had no land, no cottage, no tools, and no capital. In short, they had become mere wage earners and had nothing to offer but their labor.

When they found employment, they discovered that the hours were long. A sixteen-hour day was by no means rare. When the workers finally won the right to divide their work into two twelve-hour shifts, they looked on the change as a blessing. The long hours alone would have been tolerable, since they were no worse than the hours worked at home under the putting-out system. But the real hardship came in getting used to the discipline and monotony of tending machines in a factory. The workers came and went at the sound of the factory whistle. They had to keep pace with the movements of the machine, always under the strict supervi-

---

TABLE 26.3   Rise of Industrial Production (1913 = 100)*

	1860	1870	1880	1890	1900	1910	1913
Germany	14	18	25	40	65	89	100
Great Britain	34	44	53	62	79	85	100
France	26	34	43	56	66	89	100
Russia	8	13	17	27	61	84	100
Italy	—	17	23	40	56	99	100
United States	8	11	17	39	54	89	100
World	14	19	26	43	60	88	100

*F. Sternberg, *Capitalism and Socialism on Trial* (Day, 1951), p. 21. Translated by Edward Fitzgerald. Copyright 1950 by Fritz Sternberg. Copyright renewed. Reprinted by permission of HarperCollins Publishers, Inc.

sion of an ever-present overseer. The work was monotonous—pulling a lever, brushing away dirt, mending broken threads. Employers naturally regarded their wage bill as an expense that should be kept as low as possible. Consequently, many of them, particularly in the textile industries, preferred to employ women and children, who were willing to accept lower wages and were more willing to follow orders. Exploitation of female and child labor reached such proportions that a number of parliamentary committees who conducted investigations found shocking conditions.

There is, however, another side to this question of the effect of the industrial revolution on the working class. In the first place, the parliamentary committees investigated only industries such as mining and textiles where conditions were worst. The shocking testimony of the witnesses who appeared before the committees were based on facts, but those facts were by no means applicable to English industry as a whole. Furthermore, the plight of the worker in early nineteenth-century England must be viewed in the light of contemporary rather than present-day standards. The fact is that the villages from which these workers came were in many respects as squalid as the cities. In the typical rural dwelling, rats and vermin infested the straw bedding, and the wind whistled through the thinly thatched roof and the poorly plastered walls. Day laborers in the countryside were so poorly paid that they kept crowding into the new industrial cities. Thousands of Irish also crossed over to fill the jobs opening up in the new factories. Furthermore, the population of

England soared during these early days of the industrial revolution, a fact that does not jibe with the usual picture of the unrelieved and debilitating misery. It is quite possible that most of the workers in these early factories enjoyed higher real incomes than their forebears.

Although we cannot be sure of the effect of the industrial revolution on working-class living standards in the late eighteenth and early nineteenth centuries, we are quite certain that the standards rose substantially in the second half of the nineteenth century. The great increases in productivity together with the profits made from the huge overseas investments gradually benefited even the lower classes in western Europe. After the "Hungry Forties," when there was much suffering from unemployment, the workers of western Europe enjoyed general prosperity and rising living standards until World War I. The figures in Table 26.4 show that between 1850 and 1913, real wages in Britain and France almost doubled.

New Consumerism

The increased income for the many at the bottom as well as for the few at the top made possible the emergence in England for the first time in human history of a consumer society. The desire to consume was not unique, for Shakespeare had noted in *Much Ado About Nothing* that "fashion wears out more apparel than the man." So what was unique in eighteenth-century England was not the desire to consume but the ability of many to do so. In all past human

TABLE 26.4   Rise in Real Wages, 1850–1913 (1913 = 100)*

	Great Britain	France
1850	57	59.5
1860	64	63
1870	70	69
1880	81	74.5
1890	90	89.5
1900	100	100

*F. Sternberg, *Capitalism and Socialism on Trial* (Day, 1951), p. 27. Translated by Edward Fitzgerald. Copyright 1950 by Fritz Sternberg. Copyright renewed. Reprinted by permission of HarperCollins Publishers, Inc.

societies the income of the masses had been so meager that half to three-quarters of it was needed for food alone. The little that was left had to be spent on other necessities, so nothing remained for passing whims or fashions. This explains why fashions did not come and go with each season as they do today. It explains why for centuries the kimono remained unchanged in Japan, the dhoti in India, the pyjama in some Moslem countries, and the poncho in Latin America.

Eighteenth-century England was the first country to break with this traditional pattern. The break occurred because of the increase in national income, thanks to the agricultural revo-lution after the enclosures, the profits flowing in from overseas enterprises, and the productivity jump with the industrial revolution. Some of the swollen national income trickled down to the masses, so that a domestic market developed that was much greater than any in the past, when only the tiny elite at the top had any purchasing power.

Businesspersons soon developed techniques for tapping the rich, new domestic market. As early as the eighteenth century they were using the full range of what are now considered modern selling techniques, including market research, credit, discount schemes, handbills, catalogues, newspaper and magazine advertis-

Consumption of all forms of consumer goods increased greatly in the eighteenth century. This engraving illustrates a shop, probably in Paris. Here women, working apparently for a woman manager, are making dresses and hats to meet the demands of the fashion trade.

ing, and money-back-if-not-satisfied sale offers. A pioneer in this mass merchandising was the potter Josiah Wedgwood, who states candidly that "Fashion is superior to merit." Accordingly he conducted sales campaigns that made his pottery the best known and most desired in the world, even though it often was neither the best nor the cheapest.

A student of this new consumerism has concluded that it "brought goods within the reach of classes never before offered such opportunities for buying, and made available a greater range of goods than ever before. . . the manipulation of social emulation made men pursue 'luxuries' where they had previously bought 'decencies,' and 'decencies' where they had previously bought only 'necessities'. . . in fact, fashion and its exploiters raised men's levels of 'pecuniary decency.'"[7] In this manner appeared in eighteenth-century England the mass consumerism that has become the hallmark of twentieth-century societies throughout the globe.

New Roles for Women

The industrial revolution was responsible not only for the new consumerism but also for new roles for women. The revolution had as profound an impact on women as did the agricultural revolution several millennia earlier. The general effect was to force women out of the family economy in which they had lived and worked into a new wage economy outside the household.

The family economy that existed in preindustrial times was based on the home, where the wife, husband, and even very small children worked together. This suggests pleasant and wholesome family activity, but usually it was far from that. Women had plenty of monotonous and repetitive work, such as spinning, tatting, and setting up looms. Their work often was auxiliary or preparatory to that of their fathers or husbands, so they normally worked long hours along with the men. Moreover, women had to combine this labor with other onerous tasks, namely, housekeeping and child care.

With the industrial revolution, the primary work place shifted from the home to factories and workshops, and female workers became a part of the money economy as wage earners. This had certain advantages, such as more steady work, since the industrialists had much capital invested in their plant and machinery and therefore closed down operations as little as possible. In addition to higher yearly incomes from year-round employment, factory women received substantially higher wages than they previously had earned with piecework in their family quarters. In the Manchester cotton factories, for example, working wives in 1914 were earning weekly sums more than twice as high as the wives who hemmed handkerchiefs at home.

The new factory jobs, on the other hand, did have certain negative features, which both male and female workers intensely disliked. As noted, these features included long hours; unhealthy working conditions; and myriad rules, regulations, and penalties. Women were especially vulnerable to abuse and exploitation because they tended to be docile and less likely to be organized into unions. The male leaders of the unions did little to encourage and much to discourage female membership. Also women usually lacked both the time and the money needed for participation in unions. Thus the average wage for women at the end of the nineteenth century was less than half of that for their male counterparts.

Most women workers gave up their factory jobs after marriage and the birth of children. But their husbands' wages usually were inadequate to cover all family expenses so the mothers took on as much home work as they could handle. This type of temporary work included taking in boarders, sewing clothes, making artificial flowers, washing laundry, and taking care of the children of working mothers.

In the late nineteenth century the status of middle-class women changed because infant mortality was declining sharply in western Europe. The birthrate dropped correspondingly, so wives were relieved of the burden of interminable pregnancies. Also new labor-saving devices now appeared, which eased the burden of household chores. This combination of circumstances theoretically should have lightened substantially the responsibilities and workloads of housewives. In practice the outcome was quite different. The labor-saving gadgets did not

Women working at a telephone exchange. The invention of the telephone opened new employment opportunities for women.

actually relieve the housewives as much as expected because the supply of cheap servants was drying up. So mothers discovered that in operating the new washing machines and electric irons, they were working more than in the old days when laundresses were in charge.

Equally important was the growing expectation that the primary responsibility of the middle-class wife was not housework but mothering. Books, magazines, and sermons all promoted the concept that mothers should be concerned with the emotional as well as the physical well-being of their families. Experts expounded new "scientific" techniques for successful modern mothers. At the same time these mothers were expected to uphold traditional values and to preserve their femininity. Little wonder that many middle-class women felt anxious and inadequate. Some began to question the assumption that marriage required their subordination to husband and children—hence the emergence of the feminist movement demanding equality and more opportunities for women, both inside the home and out.

Meanwhile, working-class women lacked the time, money, and energy to fret over middle-class concerns about housework versus motherhood. They could not realistically aspire to the role of perfect wife, perfect mother, and perfect housekeeper. Rather, they had to cope with the immediate daily crises precipitated by unemployment, desertion, sickness, and the chronic gap between wages and family expenses. For such hard-pressed working-class women, who always comprised a substantial percentage of the total, life boiled down to a never-ending struggle to keep the family afloat between paychecks.

VII. EFFECT OF THE INDUSTRIAL REVOLUTION ON THE NON-EUROPEAN WORLD

Europeanization of the Earlier Empires

In the period before 1763 the European powers had only a few footholds in Asia and Africa. Their major holdings were in the Americas. After

Family was central to the middle-class conception of a stable and respectable social life. This portrait of the Bellelli family is by Degas. Notice that the husband and father sits at his desk, suggesting his association with business and the world outside the home, whereas the wife and mother stands with the children, suggesting her domestic role.

1763 they established their political control over large parts of Asia and almost all of Africa. In the Americas and the British dominions, they were able to do much more. Taking advantage of the sparse populations in those regions, millions of Europeans emigrated and filled up those relatively empty spaces.

The industrial revolution was largely responsible for the mass migrations. We have seen that increased productivity together with the advances of medical science led to a sharp increase in Europe's population in the nineteenth century. This created a population pressure that found an outlet in overseas migration.

Railways and steamships were available to transport masses of people across oceans and continents, and persecution of one sort or another stimulated further emigration, as did disasters such as Ireland's potato famine. These various factors combined to produce a mass migration unequaled in human history to that date. With every decade the tide of population movement increased in volume. In the 1820s a total of 145,000 left Europe; in the 1850s about 2.6 million; and between 1900 and 1910 the crest was reached with 9 million emigrants, or almost 1 million per year (see map of Racial Distribution in the World, p. 384).

Before 1885 most of the emigrants came from northern and western Europe; after that date the majority were from southern and eastern Europe. By and large, the British emigrants went to the dominions and the United States; the Italians, to the United States and Latin America; the Spaniards and Portuguese, to Latin America; and the Germans, to the United States and, in smaller numbers, to Argentina and Brazil. From the perspective of world history, this extraordinary migration is significant because it was all directed to the New World and Oceania, with the exception of the large flow to Asiatic Russia and the trickle to South Africa. The result has been the almost complete ethnic Europeanization of Siberia, the British dominions excepting South Africa, and the Americas. The Indian population in Latin America managed to survive but was left a minority.

The ethnic Europeanization of overseas territories led inevitably also to political, economic, and cultural Europeanization. This process is described in Chapter 35.

New Imperialism Conquers New Empires

The industrial revolution was largely responsible not only for the Europeanization of overseas territories, but also for the creation of huge European colonial structures in Asia and Africa. The great wave of empire building after 1870 was known as the new imperialism. It made a large part of the earth's surface into an appendage of a few European powers. The interrelationship of the new imperialism and the industrial revolution was manifested in a growing desire to obtain colonies that might serve as markets for the rising volume of manufactured goods. The several European and overseas countries that became industrialized during the nineteenth century were soon competing with each other for markets. In the process they raised tariffs to keep out each other's products. Soon it was being argued that each industrialized country must have colonies to provide "sheltered markets" for its manufactures.

The industrial revolution also produced surplus capital, which again led the great powers to seek colonies as investment outlets. The more capital piled up at home, the lower the profits fell and the greater the need to find better investment markets abroad. Vast amounts of capital were, in fact, invested in foreign countries, especially by Britain, France, and Germany. For example, Britain by 1914 had invested £4 billion abroad, a sum amounting to one-fourth of its total national wealth. Europe by 1914 had become the banker of the world. In the first half of the nineteenth century most overseas investments were made in the Americas and Australia —in the white man's world. But in the century's

European immigrants on their way to the United States, 1906. Between 1846 and 1932, more than fifty million Europeans immigrated to the United States, Canada, South America, Australia, and South Africa.

second half they were made mostly in the non-white and relatively unstable countries of Asia and Africa. The thousands of small private investors and the large banking combinations that provided the capital naturally were anxious about their investments' safety. They preferred "civilized" administration, preferably by their own respective governments, in the regions in which their investments were situated. This is how the need to invest surplus capital safely promoted the new imperialism.

The industrial revolution also created a demand for raw materials to feed the machines. Many of these materials—jute, rubber, petroleum, and various metals—came from the "uncivilized" portions of the globe. In most cases heavy capital outlays were needed to secure adequate production of these commodities. Such investments, as we have seen, usually led to the imposition of political control.

The new imperialism was not entirely economic in its origins; it was not related exclusively to the industrial revolution. A variety of other factors also were operative at this time. One was the desire to strengthen national security with strategic naval bases such as at Malta and Singapore. Another was the need to secure additional sources of labor, as the French did in North Africa. Still another factor was the influence of the missionaries, who were particularly active during the nineteenth century. Sometimes these missionaries were maltreated, or even killed, by the natives they were seeking to convert. Even though the missionaries themselves might be willing to tolerate such risks for the sake of their cause, public opinion frequently demanded action, and it was not unknown for governments to use such incidents as pretexts for military intervention. Finally, the vogue of Social Darwinism, with its doctrines of struggle for existence and survival of the fittest, led naturally to ideas of racial superiority. The white man's "burden" was to rule over the "inferior" colored peoples of the earth. The great empire builder Cecil Rhodes was quite outspoken on this matter. "I contend that we are the first race in the world, and that the more of the world we inhabit the better it is for the human race. . . If there be a God, I think what He would like me to do is to paint as much of the map of Africa British red as possible."[8]

The net result of these economic, political, and intellectual psychological factors was the greatest land-grab in the history of the world, unequaled even by the conquests of Genghis Khan. In the generation between 1871 and 1900 Britain added 4.25 million square miles and 66 million people to its empire; France added 3.5 million square miles and 26 million people; Russia in Asia added half a million square miles and 6.5 million people; and Germany added 1 million square miles and 13 million people. Even little Belgium managed to acquire 900,000 square miles and 8.5 million inhabitants. In this manner most of the earth's surface and most of the world's population had by 1914 come under the direct or indirect domination of a few European countries, including Russia, and of the United States. This was a development without precedent in human history. Today, in the late twentieth century, much of the global turmoil represents the inevitable reaction to this European domination.

Impact of the New Imperialism

Why should we label the great European expansion of the late nineteenth century the new imperialism? Imperialism, after all, was not something new. If it is defined as "the rule or control, political or economic, direct or indirect, of one state, nation or people over similar groups," then imperialism is as old as human civilization.[9] Certainly the Romans were imperialistic, having conquered and for centuries ruled large parts of Europe and the Near East. And many other empires in all parts of the globe, both before and after the Romans, were conquered by all types of peoples.

Yet the term new imperialism is justified, because the late-nineteenth—century European expansion was quite unique in its impact on the colonial and dependent territories. Rome exploited its possessions simply and directly by plundering and by collecting tribute, chiefly in the form of foodstuffs, but its exploitation did not particularly affect the economic life and structure of the colonies. They continued to produce pretty much the same foodstuffs and handicrafts in the same ways as in the past. To compare this imperialism with the later version that overran and remade entire continents is like comparing a spade to a steam shovel. The traditional imperialism involved exploitation but no basic economic and social change. The tribute merely went to one ruling clique rather than another. The new imperialism, by contrast, forced a thorough transformation of the conquered countries. This was not so much deliberate policy as it was the inevitable impact of the dynamic industrialism of western Europe on the static, self-contained agrarian regimes of Africa and Asia. In other words, Europe's industrial capitalism was far too complex and expansionistic to stop with a simple tribute relationship with the colonies.

At the outset, the European conquerors certainly did not hesitate to plunder and to levy tribute. The British did so in India, as the Spaniards had earlier in Mexico and Peru. But after this initial phase, Europe's dynamic economy began in various ways to enfold and refashion the colonial economic and social structures. This happened because, as we have seen, industrialized Europe needed sources of raw materials and markets for its surplus capital and manufactures. Thus the historic role of the new imperialism was to carry the industrial revolution to its logical conclusion—to enable the industrial

nations, or industrial capitalism, to operate on a worldwide scale. The global operation of industrial capitalism resulted in much more extensive, coordinated, and efficient use of the material and human resources of the globe. Certainly world productivity rose greatly when European capital and skills were combined with the raw materials and labor of the underdeveloped regions. The combination produced, for the first time, an integrated global economy. In fact, world industrial production increased threefold between 1860 and 1890 and sevenfold between 1860 and 1913. The value of world trade grew from £641 million in 1851, to £3,024 million in 1880, to £4,025 million in 1900, and to £7,840 million in 1913.

Everyone agrees that this increase in the size of the economic cake has been a great advantage. But there is much dispute over the question of how the cake has been sliced. Colonial peoples feel that in the past they have had less than their due share. The total amount that they have received obviously has increased; otherwise their rising populations could not have been supported. For example, a British economist has shown that in 1949 European companies engaged in mining in mineral-rich northern Rhodesia (Zimbabwe) sold their output for a

European exploitation of Africa. Photograph of white foremen and black laborers in a gold-mining company of South Africa (undated).

total of £36.7 million. Of this, they spent only £12.5 million in northern Rhodesia, which meant that two-thirds of the money was transferred abroad. Moreover, of the £12.5 million spent in northern Rhodesia, £4.1 million was paid to Europeans living and working there. Only £2 million out of the £36.7 million went to the Africans working in the mines. And yet these workers were receiving an average of £41 a year compared to an average income of £27 a year per adult African male in the colony.[10]

Under these circumstances it is understandable that colonial peoples are not very impressed by increased productivity or by the wages paid by foreign companies. They are more impressed by the wretched level at which they subsist, especially in comparison with Western levels. They also resent being cast in the role of hewers of wood and drawers of water, even in regions where there are human and material resources for industrial development.

There is an obvious parallel here between the reaction of Western workers to industrial capitalism and of colonial peoples to the new imperialism. Both have been dissatisfied with their lot, and both have supported movements designed to bring about radical change. But a basic difference is that the colonial peoples are ranged not against employers of their own nationality but rather against foreign rulers. Accordingly, their movement of protest, at least in the first stage, was not socialism but rather a range of Western political doctrines—liberalism, democracy, and, above all, nationalism.

We turn now to consider those "isms" that have made up Europe's political revolution. An understanding of that revolution is as essential for world history as an understanding of the industrial revolution. Because of Europe's political revolution, the world, as we shall see, was affected by Western political ideas, slogans, and institutions as well as by Western cottons, railways, and banks.

paperback surveys of the entire history of science are available, especially W. C. Dampier, *A Shorter History of Science* (Harcourt Brace Jovanovich, 1957); A. R. and M. B. Hall, *A Brief History of Science* (New American Library, 1964); and F. S. Taylor, *A Short History of Science and Scientific Thought* (W. W. Norton, 1949). See also the useful collection by W. C. Dampier Whetham and M. Dampier, *Cambridge Readings in the Literature of Science* (Cambridge University, 1928).

A convenient analysis of the interpretations and literature of the industrial revolution is provided by E. E. Lampard, *Industrial Revolution: Interpretations and Perspectives* (Service Center for Teachers of History, 1957), No. 4. The best overall survey is by D. S. Landes, *The Unbound Prometheus: Technological Change and Industrial Development in Western Europe from 1750 to the Present* (Cambridge University, 1969). See also the stimulating interpretation by A. Thompson, *The Dynamics of the Industrial Revolution* (Edward Arnold, 1973). For the diffusion of the industrial revolution from England, see W. D. Henderson, *The Industrial Revolution on the Continent* (Cass, 1961). For the social and political repercussions of the industrial revolution, see E. J. Hobshawn, *The Age of Revolution: Europe, 1789–1848* (Weidenfeld, 1962); E. P. Thompson, *The Making of the English Working Class* (Gollancz, 1963); T. McKeowan, *The Modern Rise of Population* (Academic Press, 1977); N. McKendrick et al., *The Birth of a Consumer Society: The Commercialization of Eighteenth-Century England* (Indiana University, 1982); L. Brockway, *Science and Colonial Expansion* (Academic Press, 1979); D. R. Headrick, *The Tools of Empire: Technology and European Imperialism in the 19th Century* (Oxford University, 1981); and H. Magdoff, *Imperialism from the Colonial Age to the Present* (Monthly Review Press, 1978).

The impact of the industrial revolution on women is summarized in R. Bridenthal and C. Koonz, eds., *Becoming Visible: Women in European History* (Houghton Mifflin, 1977), Chaps. 11–14. For more detailed works, see L. A. Tilly and J. W. Scott, *Women Work and Family* (Holt, Rinehart and Winston, 1978); E. S. Riemer and J. C. Fout, eds., *European Women: A Documentary History, 1789–1945* (Schocken, 1980); and J. Rendall, *The Origins of Modern Feminism: Women in Britain, France and the United States, 1780–1860* (Macmillan, 1985).

SUGGESTED READINGS

An excellent bibliography of the scientific revolution is provided by M. Boas, *History of Science* (Service Center for Teachers of History, 1958), No. 13. Excellent

NOTES

1. T. Sprat, *The History of the Royal Society of London, for Improving of General Knowledge* (London, 1734), p.72.

2. *Siderius nuncius*, trans. E. S. Carolos (1880). Cited by M. Nicolson, *Science and Imagination* (Cornell University, 1956), p. 15.

3. Charles Darwin, *Origin of Species*, Vol. I (New York, 1872), p. 3

4. H. Butterfield, *The Origins of Modern Science, 1300–1800* (Bell, 1957), p. 179.

5. Cited by L. Huberman, *We, the People*, rev. ed. (Harper &Row, 1947), p. 218.

6. L. R. Brown, *Vital Signs 1996* (W. W. Norton, 1996), p. 74.

7. Cited by N. McKendrick, *The Birth of a Consumer Society* (Indiana University, 1982), p. 98.

8. Cited by Huberman, *We, the People*, p. 263.

9. Definition from W. L. Langer, *Diplomacy of Imperialism 1890–1902*, 2nd ed. (Knopf, 1935), p. 67.

10. P. Deane, *Colonial Social Accounting* (Cambridge University, 1953), p. 37.

Europe's Political Revolutions

> When individuals and nations have once got in their heads the abstract concept of full-blown liberty, there is nothing like it in its uncontrollable strength.
>
> G. W. F. Hegel

Europe's domination of the world in the nineteenth century was based not only on its industrial and scientific revolutions but also on its political revolution. The essence of the political revolution was the end of the concept of a divinely ordained division of people into rulers and ruled. Government was no longer regarded as something above the people and the people as something below the government. Instead, the political revolution for the first time in history, at least on a scale larger than the city-state, called for the identification of government with people. The masses were awakened and activized so that they not only participated in government but also considered it their inherent right to do so. In this chapter we shall consider the general pattern of this political revolution, its origins in the English, American, and French revolutions, and its varied manifestations and worldwide impact during the nineteenth century.

I. PATTERN OF THE POLITICAL REVOLUTION

The political revolution, like the economic, developed in several stages. We noted that the economic revolution began in England, spread to the Continent and to the United States, and later to other parts of the globe. Likewise, the political revolution got under way with the English Revolution in the seventeenth century, developed much further with the American and

French revolutions that followed, next affected the whole of Europe during the nineteenth century, and finally engulfed the entire globe during the twentieth.

The parallel course in the spread of the two revolutions was not accidental; indeed, the two were intimately related. The economic revolution was in large degree responsible for the political because it created new classes with new interests and with new ideologies that rationalized those interests. We will see this more clearly as we trace briefly the general course of the economic and political revolutions.

During the early medieval period, there were three well-defined social groups in western Europe: the nobility, who constituted a military aristocracy; the clergy, who formed an ecclesiastical and intellectual elite; and the peasants, who labored to support the two upper classes. With the development of commerce, the profile of the medieval social order began gradually to change with the appearance of a new element, the urban bourgeoisie. As this class grew in wealth and numbers, it became more and more discontented with the special privileges of the feudal orders and with the numerous restrictions that hampered the development of a free-market economy. Accordingly, the bourgeoisie made a mutually beneficial alliance with the national monarchies. The kings obtained financial support from the bourgeoisie and so were able to assert their authority over the feudal orders. The bourgeoisie in return profited from the establishment of law and order throughout the royal domains. The alliance lasted until it became irksome for the constantly growing middle class. Then the middle class turned against the kings to free itself from royal restrictions on commerce, from a growing burden of taxation, and from restraints on religious freedom. These objectives were important factors in the English, American, and French revolutions. The success of these revolutions also meant the success of classical liberalism—the new ideology that provided a rationalization for bourgeois interests and objectives. In this sense, liberalism may be defined as the particular program by which the growing middle class proposed to get for itself the benefits and control it was aiming for.

The middle class, with its creed of liberalism, was challenged in turn by the urban work-ers, or proletariat. With the industrial revolution of the late eighteenth century, the workers in the crowded cities became increasingly class conscious. More and more they felt that their interests were not identical to those of their employers, and that their situation could be improved only by combined action on their part. So the workers, or rather the intellectuals who led them, developed a new ideology, socialism. Socialism directly challenged the liberalism of the bourgeoisie, calling for social and economic change as well as for political reform. We shall see that socialism was to become a major force in European affairs in the late nineteenth century and in world affairs in the twentieth.

Europe's political revolution was powered not only by the dynamic creeds of liberalism and socialism, but also by nationalism—an ideology that cut across classes and activated great masses of people. Traditionally the first allegiance of these people had been to region or to church. In early modern times it had extended to the new national monarchs. But beginning with the English Revolution, and particularly during the French Revolution, increasing numbers of Europeans gave their loyalty to the new cause of the nation. The rise of national churches, national dynasties, national armies, and national educational systems all combined to transform former ducal subjects, feudal serfs, and town burghers into all-inclusive nations. The new national ideology spread during the nineteenth century from western Europe, where it originated, to all parts of the Continent. Today, in the twentieth century, it is the driving force behind the awakening of formerly subject colonial peoples throughout the world.

These three creeds—liberalism, socialism, and nationalism—are the principal components of Europe's political revolution. Together they galvanized into action broader and broader strata of the peoples of Europe, giving them a dynamism and a cohesiveness unequaled in any other portion of the globe. In this way the political revolution, like the scientific and the economic revolutions, contributed vitally to Europe's world domination. When the Europeans began to expand overseas, they encountered societies where there was little rapport between rulers and ruled. The apathy of the masses—their lack of identification with their governments—explains why in region after region the Europeans were able to establish and to maintain their rule with little difficulty. India is perhaps the leading example of the extent to which lack of rapport between rulers and ruled made societies vulnerable. India was a society that had remained a disparate collection of peoples, religions, and conflicting provincial loyalties, and so it was easy prey. For over a century and a half, the great Indian subcontinent, with its teeming millions, its splendid civilization, and its ancient historical traditions, was ruled with little difficulty by a comparative handful of British officers and officials. When the mutiny against British rule broke out in 1857, it was put down not only by British troops, but also by Indian troops. The correspondent of the *London Times* reported this fact with astonishment: "I looked with ever-growing wonder on the vast tributary of the tide of war which was running around and before me. All these men, women and children, with high delight were pouring towards Lucknow to aid the Feringhee [Europeans] to overcome their brethren."[1]

But European political and economic domination inevitably meant the diffusion of European political ideas. Just as the entire globe felt the impact of Stephenson's locomotive, of Fulton's steamship, and of Gatling's machine gun, so it felt the impact of the Declaration of Independence, the Declaration of the Rights of Man and Citizen, and the Communist Manifesto. The worldwide convulsions that are the hallmark of our present age are the direct outcome of these heady documents.

II. ENGLISH REVOLUTION

The first phase of Europe's political revolution was the English Revolution of the seventeenth century. The roots of the upheaval in England rest in the conflict between Parliament and the Stuart dynasty. The conflict degenerated into an open civil war from which Parliament emerged victorious. The Tudor dynasty, which preceded the Stuart, was generally popular, particularly with the middle class and the gentry. It brought the warring noble families under central control. It severed the ecclesiastical ties with Rome by

establishing a national Anglican church, and in the process distributed extensive lands and other properties that had belonged to Catholic institutions. It also built up the navy and pursued an anti-Catholic foreign policy that met with popular approval.

The first Stuart king, James I (reigned 1603–1625), and his son and successor Charles I (1625–1649) soon dissipated this fund of goodwill. They tried to impose the doctrines and ritual of the Anglican church on all the people, thereby alienating their Nonconformist, or Puritan, subjects. They also tried to rule without Parliament but ran into difficulties, because Parliament controlled the national purse. They tried to get around this obstacle by selling monopolies in the export and import trades, in domestic commerce, and in many fields of manufacturing. This produced considerable revenue, but it also antagonized the bourgeoisie, which demanded that "all free subjects be inheritable to the free exercise of their industry."[2]

The crisis came when the Scots rose in rebellion against Charles's attempt to impose Anglican religion on them. To get funds to suppress the uprising, Charles was forced to call on Parliament, and this "Long Parliament," which met in 1640, ignored his requests for money and instead made a number of far-reaching demands. They called for the execution of the chief royal advisers and the complete reorganization of the Anglican church. Charles refused to submit, and in 1642 fighting broke out between the royalist Cavaliers and the Puritan Roundheads.

England did not settle down again for almost half a century, not until the so-called Glorious Revolution in 1688. The stirring events of those decades made up the English Revolution, which went through five stages. The first, from 1642 to 1645, was the civil war. The royalists were routed by the famous New Model Army that Oliver Cromwell had organized. During the second stage, from 1645 to 1649, a situation developed that was to be repeated with certain variations during the French Revolution in 1792 and the Russian Revolution in 1917. A split occurred between the moderate and radical elements among the victorious Puritans. The moderates led by Cromwell, prevailed over the radicals, led by John Lilburne. When Charles was executed in 1649, Cromwell emerged as the head of an English republic, which was known as the Commonwealth.

Cromwell and his Puritan followers ruled England with great efficiency and much godliness during the third stage, from 1649 to 1660. During this time, the various feudal rights were suppressed and the religious question settled. Cromwell died in 1658 and was succeeded as lord protector of the Commonwealth by his son Richard. The latter was a nonentity, and furthermore the country was weary of the restricted and austere life under the Puritans. Accordingly, the Stuarts were placed back on the throne, and from 1660 to 1668 England went through the fourth stage, which is known as the Restoration.

The restored Stuart kings, Charles II (1660–1685) and James II (1685–1688), did not and could not undo the reforms of the republic. But they did try to revive personal rule. This effort, together with their subservience to the French crown and their encouragement of Catholicism, made them increasingly unpopular. Finally, James II was overthrown in the Glorious Revolution of 1688, which marks the fifth and last stage of the English Revolution. The new ruler was William of Orange, son-in-law of James II. In 1689 William accepted a Bill of Rights, which expressed the essential principles of parliamentary supremacy. The bill provided that no law could be suspended by the king, no taxes raised or army maintained except by Parliament's consent, and no subject arrested and detained without legal process. Such provisions did not mean that England had become a democracy. It was not until the establishment of universal suffrage in the late nineteenth century that this goal was attained. But the settlement in 1689 did establish once and for all the supreme authority of Parliament, and in doing so it ended the English Revolution that had begun almost a half-century earlier.

From the viewpoint of world history, the major significance of the English Revolution is that it defined the principles of liberalism and put them to work. This was natural, because the English Revolution was essentially a middle-class affair. The merchants and the lesser gentry who supported Parliament had two principal ends in view—religious toleration and security of person

Oliver Cromwell's New Model Army defeated the royalists in the English Civil War. After the execution of Charles I in 1649, Cromwell dominated the short-lived English republic, conquered Ireland and Scotland, and ruled as Lord Protector from 1653 until his death in 1658.

and property. But there was no unanimity of opinion on the Puritan side concerning these matters. Many conflicting views were expressed and passionately debated. In the case of religion, for example, a veritable flood of new sects appeared, including the Congregationalists, the Baptists, and the Quakers. At the same time, the Presbyterians strove to establish their church as a national organization that could exercise its discipline on all citizens. These religious differences obviously had to be reconciled or else Parliament's victory would be undone and the state itself might founder. It was under these circumstances that the basic liberal doctrine of religious toleration was worked out and established. On grounds of principle as well as of expediency, it came to be generally agreed that it was both immoral and ineffective to coerce people into belief. It is true that the Anglican church remained the official, state-supported church and that its members were favored in the filling of government posts and in other respects. But by and large, the principle was established that liberty of conscience should be granted to all Christians who did not threaten public order or interfere with other people's worship.

The question of the rights of person and of property also aroused fierce controversy. This question divided the right- and left-wing elements among the Puritans even more sharply than did the religious issue. The split occurred gradually, as the common soldiers of the New Model Army came to feel that their interests were being ignored by their officers and by Parliament. Their feelings were articulated by the Levellers, a name of opprobrium given to a mass movement drawn chiefly from the lower-middle class and from agricultural tenants. It is true that legislation passed by the House of Commons for the establishment of the Commonwealth included basic Leveller doctrine: "The Peoples are, under God, the Original of all just Power," and the Commons "being chosen by, and representing the Peoples, have the supreme Power in this Nation."[3]

If Parliament was thus willing to accept the principle of the sovereignty of the people, what was the issue dividing Parliament and the Levellers? The answer is in the definition of the word people. Cromwell and his followers held that the "people" who should participate in the election of the Commons were those with a "real or permanent interest in the kingdom"— that is, property owners—whereas the Levellers maintained that "any man that is born in England ought. . . to have his voice in election of burgesses [members of Parliament]."[4] Thus, the issue was between constitutional parliamentary government and democratic government. Many of those who favored democratic government did so with the intention of using their votes to bring about social reform. And fear of such

reform motivated Cromwell and his followers in their resolute opposition to the Levellers.

The fact is that there were two revolutions under way in seventeenth-century England. The first was the political revolution of the lesser gentry and the bourgeoisie, who were interested in winning the civil and religious freedom necessary to make their way in the world. The second was the social revolution of the lower-middle class and the tenant farmers, who had a vision of a community of small-property owners, with complete religious and political equality and with generous provisions for the poor. The social revolution failed in England in the seventeenth century, as it was to fail in France in the eighteenth. In both cases the protagonists lacked the numbers, the organization, and the maturity necessary for victory. Their time was to come in the late nineteenth century, when the industrial revolution had spawned a large and class-conscious urban proletariat. The proletariat was to evolve its own ideology—socialism—distinct from, and in opposition to, the liberalism of bourgeoisie.

III. ENLIGHTENMENT

The next stage in Europe's political revolution, following the upheaval in seventeenth-century England, was the so-called Enlightenment that manifested itself during the century before the French Revolution of 1789. The term Enlightenment owes its origin to the fact that the leaders of this movement believed that they lived in an enlightened age. They viewed the past largely as a time of superstition and ignorance, and they thought that only in their day were human beings at last emerging from darkness into sunlight. Thus, one basic characteristic of this Age of Enlightenment was the idea of progress, an idea that was to persist into the twentieth century. With the Enlightenment, it began to be generally assumed that the condition of humanity would steadily improve, so that each generation would be better off than that which came before.

How was this unceasing progress to be maintained? The answer was simple and confident: by the use of humankind's reasoning powers. Faith in reason was the other basic feature of

The following images were detected

the Enlightenment. Indeed, the two key concepts were progress and reason, and the exponents of these concepts were a highly articulate group known as the philosophes. Not to be confused with formal philosophers, the philosophes were not profound or systematic thinkers in any particular field. They were mostly literary men or popularizers—more journalists than philosophers. They were generally opposed to the existing order, and they wrote plays, novels, essays, and histories to popularize their ideas and to show the need for change.

Much influenced by the law of gravitation that Newton had demonstrated, the philosophes believed in the existence of natural laws that

John Locke (1632–1704), defender of the rights of the people against rulers who think their power absolute.

regulated, not only the physical universe, but also human society. Acting on this assumption, they proceeded to apply reason to all fields in order to discover the natural laws that operated in each. They subjected everything—all persons, all institutions, all traditions—to the test of reason. What would be a rigorous ordeal for any society in any period was particularly unsettling for France's ancien régime, past its prime and creaking in many joints. Thus the philosophes subjected the old regime in France, and throughout Europe, to a barrage of devastating criticism. More important, they evolved a set of revolutionary principles by which they proposed to effect a wholesale reorganization of society. Of particular interest to us are their specific proposals in three area—economics, religion, and government.

Their key slogan in economics was laissez-faire—let the people do what they will, let nature takes its course. The opposition to government intervention was a reaction to the rigid regulation of economic life generally known as mercantilism. In the early period of state building, mercantilism had been accepted as necessary for national security. But by the eighteenth century it seemed superfluous and damaging. The classic account of laissez-faire was made by the Scotsman Adam Smith in his famous work *An Inquiry into the Nature and Causes of the Wealth of Nations* (1776). He argued that individuals are motivated by self-interest as far as their economic activities are concerned, that the national welfare is simply the sum of the individual interests operating in a nation, and that each man knows his own interest better than does any statesman.

In religion the key slogan was *Écrasez l'infame!*—"crush the infamous thing," or stamp out religious fanaticism and intolerance. The philosophes rejected the traditional belief that God controls the universe and arbitrarily determines the fate of humanity. Instead, they sought a natural religion that followed the dictates of reason. The outcome was a variety of radical departures from religious orthodoxy. Some became outright atheists, denying the existence of God and denouncing religion as a tool of priests and politicians. Others became agnostics, who neither affirmed nor denied the existence of God. The majority were deists, willing to go along with the proposition that God existed and had created the universe but insisting that, after the act of creation, God allowed the universe to function according to certain natural laws and refrained from intervention. Thus the deists were able to have their cake and eat it too. They could accept God and the teaching of Christianity and at the same time reject supernatural features such as the virgin birth, the resurrection, the divinity of Christ, and the divine inspiration of the Bible. The important point to note is that all these new dogmas—atheism, agnosticism, deism—reflected the unprecedented growth of

Jean-Jacques Rousseau (1712-1778) raised some of the most profound social and ethical questions of the Enlightenment.

skepticism regarding "revealed" or "supernatural" religion. For the first time since the triumph of Christianity in Europe, a definite break had occurred with the Christian tradition.

In government, also, the philosophes had a key phrase—"the social contract." The contract theory of government was not new. The English political theorist John Locke had formulated it in his *Essay on Civil Government* (1690), in which he defined government as a political contract between rulers and ruled. But the French philosopher Jean-Jacques Rousseau transformed it into a social rather than a political contract. For him it involved an agreement among the people themselves. In his major political work, *The Social Contract* (1762), Rousseau viewed government as simply a "commission," by which he justified revolution as a restoration to the sovereign people of its rightful power.

This brief survey suggests the significance of the Enlightenment for Europe's political revolution. The slogans "écrasez l'infame," "laissez-faire," and "social contract" were subversive of traditional institutions and practices. Furthermore, they represented a challenge to the status quo, not only in France but also throughout Europe and even in overseas lands. In fact, the philosophes thought of themselves not as Frenchmen or Europeans but as members of the human race. They thought and acted in global rather than Western terms. They sought to discover social laws that had universal application, like Newton's laws of the physical world.

If the philosophes did not discover fixed laws governing all humankind, their writings did influence thinking people in many parts of the world. Their greatest immediate success was in persuading a number of European monarchs to accept at least some of their doctrines. These monarchs still held to the theory that they ruled by divine right, but they changed their ideas about the purpose of their rule. Governmental authority was still to be the prerogative of the kings, but now it was to be used for the benefit of the people. Hence these rulers were known as benevolent despots.

The best known of these benevolent despots were Frederick the Great of Prussia (1740–1786), Catherine the Great of Russia (1762–1796), and Joseph II of the Hapsburg Empire (1765–1790). Catherine was perhaps the most articulate, frequently using typical slogans of the Enlightenment such as "All citizens ought to be equal before the law," "Sovereigns are made to serve their people," and "It is dangerous for a country to be divided into a few large estates." But Catherine and her fellow sovereigns did not merely talk about reform. Catherine improved the administrative and educational systems of her country substantially; Frederick did much to advance agriculture in Prussia; and Joseph II, the most sincere and conscientious of the enlightened despots, wore himself out during his reign trying to remold his empire in accord with the new principles. Yet in spite of their royal authority, these rulers had a very modest impact. Their successors frequently undid their work, and the clergy and the aristocrats were relentless in their fight against the reforms that menaced their vested interests.

IV. AMERICAN REVOLUTION

We should not overrate the role of the benevolent despots in putting the doctrines of the Enlightenment to work, for the Enlightenment did not have much effect on the masses of the people in Europe until the outbreak of the French Revolution in 1789. But before then a revolution had broken out in England's thirteen colonies, and this revolution was to offer a laboratory demonstration of the new doctrines in action.

We noted earlier (Chapter 25, Section III) that a leading characteristic of the colonies was their political independence. Their elective assemblies were continually at loggerheads with the governors and the other officials sent from London. We also noted that Britain decisively defeated France in the Seven Years' War and, by the Treaty of Paris of 1763, acquired France's colonies north to the Arctic and west to the Mississippi. Both the British and the Americans felt considerable pride in the magnitude of their joint victory. But at the same time that it settled old ones, the victory created new problems. One was the growing spirit of defiance in the colonies now that the danger of a French attack had been removed. Another was the decision of the British government, following its acquisition of vast new colonial territories, to tighten its imperial organization. This tightening might have been feasible at an earlier date, but now, after the elimination of the French danger, the colonists were convinced that they were able to take care of themselves and had every right to do so. Thus the American Revolution arose primarily out of the conflicting claims of British imperial authority and American colonial self-government.

Not all, or even most, of the American colonists favored violent revolution. In fact, they were split into two antagonistic camps. The conservatives wanted only to return to the loose relations between the mother country and the colonies that prevailed before 1763. The radicals,

In response to the Coercive Acts of 1774, the First Continental Congress called upon Americans to join in a Continental Association that pledged them to cut off commercial dealings with Britain. This print, published in London the following year, suggests what might happen to Virginians who failed to sign up. A bag of feathers and barrel of tar hang from the gallows in the background.

THOMAS PAINE ON THE AMERICAN REVOLUTION

Thomas Paine's Rights of Man *(1791) is an eloquent appraisal of the American Revolution. It was written as a reply to Edmund Burke's negative* Reflections *on the French Revolution. Paine was typical of this time in looking forward to more revolutions that would open "A new era to the human race."*

What Archimedes said of the mechanical powers, may be applied to Reason and Liberty: "Had we," said he, "a place to stand upon, we might raise the world."

The revolution of America presented in politics what was only theory in mechanics. So deeply rooted were all the governments of the old world, and so effectually had the tyranny and the antiquity of habit established itself over the mind, that no beginning could be made in Asia, Africa, or Europe, to reform the political condition of man. Freedom had been hunted round the globe; reason was considered as rebellion; and the slavery of fear had made men afraid to think.

But such is the irresistible nature of truth, that all it asks, and all it wants, is the liberty of appearing. The sun needs no inscription to distinguish him from darkness; and no sooner did the American governments display themselves to the world, than despotism felt a shock, and man begin to contemplate redress.

The independence of America, considered merely as a separation from England, would have been a matter but of little importance, had it not been accompanied by a revolution in the principles and practices of governments. . . .

If universal peace, civilization, and commerce, are ever to be the happy lot of man, it cannot be accomplished but by a revolution in the system of governments. All the monarchical governments are military. War is their trade, plunder and revenue their objects. While such governments continue, peace has not the absolute security of a day. What is the history of all monarchical governments, but a disgustful picture of human wretchedness, and the accidental respite of a few years' repose? Wearied with war, and tired with human butchery, they sat down to rest, and called it peace. This certainly is not the condition that Heaven intended for man. . . .

The revolutions which formerly took place in the world, had nothing in them that interested the bulk of mankind. They extended only to a change of persons and measures, but not of principles, and rose or fell among the common transactions of the moment. What we now behold, may not improperly be called a "counter revolution." Conquest and tyranny, at some early period, dispossessed man of his rights, and he is now recovering them. And as the tide of all human affairs has its ebb and flow in directions contrary to each other, so also is it in this. Government founded in a moral theory, on a system of universal peace, on the indefeasible hereditary Rights of Man, is now revolving from west to east, by a stronger impulse than the government of the sword revolved from east to west. It interests not particular individuals, but nations, in its progress, and promises a new era to the human race.

*Thomas Paine, *Rights of Man* (London, 1792), pp. 1–5.

on the other hand, wanted a change in their relations with the British Empire that would give the colonies complete control of their own affairs. They also wanted a shift of political power inside the colonies in favor of the common people. On this point the conservatives were violently opposed. They had no desire for democracy. Rather, they wished to retain upper-class leadership after the fashion of the Glorious Revolution of 1688 in England. In the end the radicals had their way, thanks to the blunders of inept officials in Britain.

The steps leading to the revolution are well known and need not be related in detail. First there was the Proclamation of 1763 prohibiting settlement west of a line drawn along the crests of the Appalachians. This was intended as a temporary measure to preserve peace until an orderly land policy could be worked out, but the prospective settlers and speculators assumed that they were to be excluded forever for the benefit of a few British fur traders. Then there was a series of financial measures—the Sugar Act, Quartering Act, Stamp Act, and Townshend Duties—designed to shift a part of Britain's heavy tax load to the American colonists. These levies seemed reasonable to the British, especially since they had spent a great deal of money to defeat the French in the recent war, and since they estimated that they would have to spend

even more to protect the American frontiers in the future. But the colonists were all affected by these imposts and unanimously opposed them. They called a continental congress, which organized a boycott of British goods to last until the financial measures were repealed. But then another series of ill-considered measures by the British government started a fresh storm that was to lead to revolution.

The sequence of the dramatic events is familiar—the East India Company's tea monopoly, the Boston Tea Party, and the Coercive, or Intolerable, Acts intended as punishment for the vandalism in Boston harbor. At the same time, in 1774, Parliament passed the Quebec Act, providing a governmental system for the conquered French Canadians and drawing the boundaries of Quebec to include all the territories north of the Ohio River—that is, the present states of Wisconsin, Michigan, Illinois, Indiana, and Ohio. Much can be said in defense of the Quebec Act, but the American colonists denounced it as another Intolerable Act that blocked their westward expansion for the benefit of the Catholic French Canadians. The First Continental Congress met in Philadelphia in September 1774 and organized another boycott against British goods. Fighting began the next year when British troops set out from Boston to seize unauthorized stores of weapons at Concord. It

The Boston Tea Party, December 16, 1773. To prevent payment of the tax on tea shipped to America by the British East India Company in 1773, the Sons of Liberty disguised themselves as Indians and threw the tea overboard.

was during this operation that someone fired at Lexington Green the "shot heard round the world." The outcome was that the British troops found themselves besieged in Boston. When the Second Continental Congress met the following month, in May 1775, it had a full-fledged war on its hands and proceeded to raise an American army.

Congress was still reluctant to make the final break with the mother country, but sentiment for independence grew with the spread of the fighting. In January 1776, Thomas Paine published his incendiary pamphlet, *Common Sense*. It was read everywhere in the colonies, and it contributed substantially to Congress's decision on July 4, 1776, to adopt the Declaration of Independence. Once military operations got fully under way, the decisive factor proved to be France's aid to the revolutionaries. During the first two years of the war, France, although not officially involved, poured large amounts of munitions into the colonies. Ninety percent of the arms used by the Americans in the crucial battle of Saratoga in 1777 were of French origin. The following year France signed an alliance with the insurgents and declared war on Britain. Holland and Spain joined France, and most of the other European powers formed an Armed Neutrality to protect their commerce from Britain's naval power. The help of the French navy and of a French expeditionary force of 6,000 men contributed substantially to the victories of George Washington's forces and to the final British surrender at Yorktown in 1781. The peace treaty signed at Paris in 1783 recognized the independence of the American republic, whose frontiers were to extend west to the Mississippi.

From the viewpoint of world history, the American Revolution is significant not because

Cartoon from 1779 pictorializing the end result of the American Revolution.

THE HORSE AMERICA, *throwing his Master.*

it created an independent state but because it created a new and different type of state. The Declaration of Independence proclaimed, "We hold these truths to be self-evident: that all men are created equal." Now the American people, both during and after the revolution, passed laws to make this declaration true in real life as well as on paper. They seized and distributed the large estates owned by the Tories. They extended the franchise until all men (but not women) had the right to vote. Many state governments passed laws forbidding the importation of slaves. Established churches were abolished, and freedom of religion became the law of the land. All thirteen states adopted constitutions that included bills of rights, which guaranteed the natural rights of citizens.

These changes were not so far-reaching and fundamental as those that were brought about later by the French and Russian revolutions. These later revolutions, and particularly the Russian, involved far more extensive social and economic reorganization. Nevertheless, the American Revolution had a profound impact in its time. The establishment of an independent republic in the New World was widely interpreted in Europe as meaning that the ideas of the Enlightenment were practicable—that it was possible for people to establish a state and a workable system of government based on the rights of the individual. Thus America became a symbol of freedom and of opportunity, envied as a new land, free from the burdens and chains of the past.

V. FRENCH REVOLUTION

Roots of Revolution

The French Revolution looms much larger on the stage of world history than the English or the American revolutions. It brought about more economic and social change and influenced a larger portion of the globe than did the earlier upheavals. The French Revolution marked not only the triumph of the bourgeoisie, but also the full awakening of the masses. Middle-class liberalism came to the fore, but so did nationalism with its appeal to the people in all sections of society. And indeed, "the people," long in the wings, now strode out to the front of the stage, to remain there ever since.

Why did this great change take place in France? The basic reason is that France, the home of the Enlightenment, was not ruled by an enlightened despot until the advent of Napoleon. Consequently, France was a country of such gross inefficiency and inequality that the machinery of government creaked to a standstill. The breakdown of government gave the ambitious and dissatisfied bourgeoisie a chance to make its successful bid for power.

The old regime in France was aristocratic in its organization. All French people belonged legally to an "estate," or order of society, and this membership determined their legal rights and privileges. The First Estate comprised the clergy, who numbered about 100,000 out of a total population of 24.5 million. The Second Estate was made up of the nobility, who totaled about 400,000. The Third Estate included everyone else—over 20 million peasants and about 4 million urban merchants and artisans. Thus, the first two estates made up only about 2 percent of the total population. Yet they owned about 35 percent of the land and enjoyed most of the benefits of government patronage. Despite these disproportionate advantages, they were exempted from almost all taxes, which indeed they thought were beneath their station.

The burden of taxation consequently fell on the Third Estate, and especially on the peasants. The peasants accounted for over 80 percent of the population but owned only 30 percent of the land. Furthermore, the peasants were required to pay a tithe to the church; an assortment of feudal dues to the nobles; and a land tax, an income tax, a poll tax, and various other imposts to the state. This tax load was particularly heavy because the across-the-board price level for general goods had risen 65 percent between 1720 and 1789, while the prices of farm goods (the source of peasant income) lagged far behind.

The artisans in the cities were also discontented, because their wages had risen only 22 percent during those same decades. The bourgeoisie, by contrast, were not so badly off in the matter of taxes because they could protect them-

This late-eighteenth century cartoon satarizes the French social structure. It shows a poor man in chains, who represents the vast majority of the population, supporting an aristrocrat, a bishop, and a noble of the robe. The aristocrat is claiming feudal rights, the bishop holds papers associating the church with religious persecution and clerical privileges, and the noble of the robe holds a document listing the rights of the noble-dominated parliaments.

selves better than the artisans and the peasants. Furthermore, most businessmen profited from the rising prices and from the fivefold increase in French trade between 1713 and 1789. Yet the bourgeoisie were thoroughly dissatisfied with the old regime. They resented being snubbed by the nobility; treated as second-class subjects by the crown; and excluded from the higher posts in the bureaucracy, church, and army. In short, the bourgeoisie wanted political power and social prestige to match their growing economic importance.

Aristocratic Revolution

Such was the nature of the old regime in France when the great upheaval began. The French Rev-

olution, like others before and after, started moderately and became progressively more radical. In fact, it began, not in 1789 as a bourgeois revolution but in 1787 as an aristocratic revolution. Then it moved to the left through bourgeois and mass phases until a reaction occurred that brought Napoleon to power.

The aristocrats began the revolution because they wanted to regain the political power they had lost to the crown during the sixteenth and seventeenth centuries. The king's special commissioners, or intendants, had replaced the noble governors, and the king's bureaucracy controlled all levels of government throughout the country. The power of the monarchs was reflected in the fact that they had not bothered to call the Estates-General, or national parliament, since 1614. It is understandable then that when Louis XVI found himself in financial straits after the heavy expenses incurred in supporting the American Revolution, the nobles tried to seize the opportunity to regain power.

The nobility and the clergy forced the issue in 1787 when Louis attempted to levy a uniform tax on all landed property without regard to the social status of the holder. The privileged orders branded the new tax illegal and said that only the nation as a whole sitting in the Estates-General could institute so sweeping a change. The pinch for money became so acute that the king finally gave way and summoned the Estates-General to meet in the spring of 1789. The nobility assumed that they would be able to control this body and thereby regain a dominant position in the government. But their assumption proved completely wrong. The meeting of the Estates-General led, not to the triumph of the nobility, but rather to the unleashing of an elemental revolutionary wave that was to sweep away established institutions and ruling classes in France and in much of Europe.

Bourgeois Revolution

The Estates-General that met in Versailles on May 5, 1789, did not represent the people of France. Rather, it represented the three estates into which they traditionally had been divided. From the beginning the Third Estate was the most dynamic and decisive. It had the advantage of numbers. There were 600 representatives in the Third Estate as against 300 each in the other two. Actually, the Third Estate outnumbered the other two combined because a certain number of clergy were ready to throw in their lot with the lower orders. There were also a few liberal-minded nobles, like the Marquis de Lafayette, who already had fought for the revolutionary cause in America and sided with the Third Estate. The middle-class representatives also had some reformist ideas. Knowing that they wanted to change the old regime, and—from their reading in the works of the philosophes—having at least a general idea of how they should bring about the change, the middle-class representatives also had the ready cash that the government needed so desperately,

and they did not hesitate to use this potent weapon to get the concessions they wanted.

The commoners won their first victory by pressuring King Louis to transform the Estates-General into a National Assembly. This was a vital change because, as long as decisions were made on the basis of estates, the Third Estate would be in a perpetual minority of one among three. But as soon as the representatives of all three estates combined to form a National Assembly, the commoners, with their allies in the other two camps, would have a majority. King Louis, who was a rather stupid and unimaginative man, at first vacillated on this critical issue. But when the commoners boldly defied him and proclaimed themselves the National Assembly, Louis capitulated and, on June 23, instructed the three estates to merge.

The king's concession did not represent a change of heart. He continued to heed the counsels of the so-called "Queen's party"—the reactionary advisers of Marie Antoinette. The king's real intentions became apparent when, on July 11, he dismissed Jacques Necker, the minister who was regarded as most favorable to reform. At the same time several regiments of loyal troops were quietly transferred to Versailles. The rumor spread that the king was preparing to dissolve the National Assembly by force. Furthermore, it seemed that nothing could prevent him from doing so. He had the bayonets, whereas the commoners had only words and resolutions. But at this critical point the commoners in the National Assembly were saved by an uprising of the common people in Paris. The masses intervened decisively, initiating the third, or mass, phase of the revolution.

Mass Revolution

The masses who now saved the revolution in France were not the riffraff of the streets. In fact, they were the lesser bourgeoisie, made up of shopkeepers and heads of workshops. They were the ones who circulated news and organized demonstrations, and their illiterate journeymen and clerks followed their leadership. In the revolutionary outburst that followed the dismissal of Necker, mobs roamed the streets, demanding

On July 14, 1789, crowds stormed the Bastille, a prison in Paris. This event, whose only practical effect was to free a few prisoners, marked the first time the populace of Paris redirected the course of the revolution.

cheaper bread and parading busts of Necker draped in mourning. On July 14 they stormed and razed the Bastille, an ancient royal castle in Paris used as a prison. The event was of little practical significance since the Bastille by this time was little used. Nevertheless, it stood in the eyes of the populace as a symbol of oppression, and now this symbol was destroyed. That is why Bastille Day continues to be celebrated in France as Independence Day is in the United States.

The fall of the Bastille marks the appearance of the masses on the historical stage. Their intervention had saved the bourgeoisie, and the middle class was forced henceforth to rely on the street mobs to supply a "dose of revolution" at crucial moments. There were to be a good many such moments in the years to come, as the bourgeoisie waged its struggle for power against the king, against the privileged orders, and, eventually, against the old order in all Europe.

Mass revolution occurred in the countryside as well as in Paris. The peasants took up arms, incited by their long-standing grievances and by the stirring news of the storming of the Bastille. In many parts of the countryside they tore down fences, seized lands, and burned manor houses. Faced with this revolutionary situation, the nobles and the clergy in the National Assembly made a virtue of necessity and voted with the commoners to abolish feudalism. During the famous "August Days" of 1789, legislation was passed that ended all feudal dues, the privilege of tax exemption, the right of the church to collect tithes, and the exclusive right of the nobility to hold office. Outstanding among the numerous other important measures decreed by the National Assembly were the confiscation of church lands, the reorganization of the judicial and administrative systems, and the adoption of the Declaration of the Rights of Man and Citizen.

The declaration set forth certain fundamental principles concerning liberty, property, and security—"Men are born, and always continue, free and equal, in respect of their right. . . . The Nation is essentially the source of all sovereignty. . . law is an expression of the will of the community. . . liberty consists in the power of doing whatever does not injure another. . . ." The final clause showed that the bourgeoisie had not lost control of the direction of the revolution: "The right to property being inviolable and sacred, no one ought to be deprived of it, except in cases of evident public necessity, legally ascertained, and on condition of a previous just indemnity." This declaration was the essential message of the revolution. Printed in thousands of leaflets, pamphlets, and books, and translated into other languages, the declaration carried the revolutionary slogan of "Liberty, Equality, Fraternity" throughout Europe, and eventually to all the world.

King Louis was by no means willing to accept either the sweeping reforms of the Fourth of August or the revolutionary principles of the declaration. Once more it was the Paris mob who overcame the royal opposition. Early in October a hungry crowd, composed chiefly of women, raided bread stores in Paris and then marched on the royal palace in Versailles. Under the pressure of the mob, Louis agreed to move the court to Paris. The royal family took up residence in the Tuileries (a palace in Paris), where they became virtual prisoners, and the National Assembly settled down in a nearby riding school. These turbulent October days ensured the ratification of the decrees of August. They also increased the influence of the Paris mob tremendously. Both the royal family and the

National Assembly were now vulnerable to mass action.

War and Terror

Although the king in Paris was virtually powerless, many of the clergy and nobles were determined to regain their lost estates and privileges. Some of them fled abroad, where they worked to enlist the aid of foreign powers in a war against the revolutionary regime in France. Their efforts were successful. The radical, or Girondist, group in the National Assembly also favored war because they believed that thereby a republic could be established in France and revolutionary doctrines disseminated throughout Europe. War began in April 1792, with Austria and Prussia ranged against France. At first the poorly prepared French were routed, but thousands of volunteers flocked to the colors in a wave of national patriotism. At the same time the Paris mob swung into action against the unpopular Louis and his hated Austrian queen, Marie Antoinette. Under pressure from the mob, the National Assembly suspended the king on August 10 and called for the election of a National Convention.

The convention, elected by universal male franchise, met on September 21, 1792, and was brilliantly successful in meeting its most pressing problem—the defense of the country against the Austrian-Prussian invaders. The combination of revolutionary élan and popular support proved irresistible. The Prussians and the Austrians were driven back across the frontier. In 1793 Britain, Holland, and Spain joined the coalition against France. The revolutionaries responded with their famous levée en masse. The people rose to the defense of their country. Fourteen armies were put into the field, under the command of young generals who had risen from the ranks. Inspired by the revolutionary slogan "Liberty, Equality, Fraternity," the French citizen armies swept everything before them. By 1795 the enemy coalition had been smashed.

Meanwhile, the National Convention was shifting more and more to the left, partly because it had been elected by universal franchise and also because of the revolutionary fervor engendered by the war effort. By June 1793, the Girondists had been displaced by the more radical Jacobins. The dominant organ of government now was the Committee of Public Safety. With revolutionary zeal and passionate patriotism, this committee appointed and discharged generals, spurred the masses to heroic action, conducted foreign policy, legislated on countless matters, and crushed the opposition by means of a ruthless Reign of Terror. Thousands were charged with treason, or merely with insufficient patriotism, and were subjected to the "national razor," as the guillotine was called.

But the terror got out of control, and the revolution began "devouring its own children." In the unceasing struggle for power, one after another of the revolutionary leaders followed Louis and Marie Antoinette to the guillotine. Equally disturbing for the bourgeoisie was the growing social radicalism of the revolution. The sans-culottes (literally, those who lacked the knee breeches of genteel society) were pressing hard for a more egalitarian state. Corresponding to the Levellers of the English Revolution, they demanded a more equitable division of the land, government regulation of prices and wages, and a social security system. Such measures were quite beyond the plans of the French bourgeoisie. So like their counterparts in England, they worked to halt the leftward course of the revolution. In England, the outcome was the defeat of the Levellers and rule by Cromwell. In

Louis XVI was executed on January 21, 1793.

France, the sans-culottes were brought under control, first by a Directory of five in 1795, and then by Napoleon Bonaparte in 1799.

Napoleon

Napoleon won fame as a brilliantly successful general in Italy and used his reputation and popularity to overthrow the Directory. He governed France as First Consul from 1799 to 1804 and as Emperor from 1804 to 1814. Two features of his fifteen-year rule of France are noteworthy for our purposes: his domestic reforms, which consolidated the gains of the revolution, and his military campaigns, which provoked a nationalist reaction in neighboring countries and eventually brought about his downfall.

As far as domestic policies are concerned, Napoleon may be compared to the enlightened despots. He was interested in technical efficiency rather than abstract ideas. He ruled the country autocratically but efficiently. He codified the laws, centralized the administration, organized a system of national education, established the Bank of France, and reached an agreement with the papacy concerning church-state relations in France. These solid achievements of Napoleon made him generally popular. There were diehards who hankered for the restoration of the old regime or who thought that Napoleon had betrayed the revolution. But the majority hailed him for ending the disturbance and instituting an honest and energetic government.

Napoleon squandered this goodwill by waging war unceasingly. Since he was a military genius, he was fabulously successful. By 1810 he reached the height of his fortunes. He had extended France's frontiers across the Rhine to Lubeck and across the Alps to Rome. The rest of Europe consisted of dependent satellites or allies. Britain alone remained independent and implacably hostile.

In all his conquered territories Napoleon put into practice some of the basic principles of the French Revolution. He abolished feudalism and serfdom, recognized the equality of all citizens, and instituted his famous law codes. These innovations disturbed and alienated vested interests everywhere, but there was also widespread support for them in many quarters. The bourgeoisie and many intellectuals responded favorably to them, but the facts remain that it was foreign rule and that, where necessary, it was imposed by force. Napoleon's non-French subjects eventually grew tired of the requisitioning, the taxes, the conscription, and the wars and rumors of wars. French rule usually meant a higher quality of administration, but the time came when people were more impressed by the Frenchness of the administration than by its quality.

In other words, people had become nationalistic, and their nationalism had developed as a movement of resistance against Napoleon's domination. This explains the unrest in Italy, the armed resistance in Spain, and the growing national unity in Germany. Most fatal for Napoleon was the bitter resistance of Russians of all classes when he invaded that country in 1812. Resistance, as much as ice and snow, was responsible for the catastrophic destruction of his Grand Army. From the frozen plains of Russia, the course of Napoleon's career ended precipitously and inevitably on the island of Elba. Thus the ideology of the French Revolution backfired on its originators. The people Napoleon had "offended" were people who had first been awakened and enthused by the slogan "Liberty, Equality, Fraternity." Then they had turned against their teacher when the very principles he had espoused were betrayed by him.

The Congress of Vienna, which met from September 1814 to June 1815 to redraw the map of Europe after Napoleon's downfall, was guided by three principles—legitimacy, containment, and compensation. By the principle of legitimacy, the monarchs of France, Spain, Holland, and the Italian states were restored to their thrones. By the principle of containment, the states bordering France were made as strong as possible. Holland was given Belgium; Austria received Lombardy and Venetia; and Prussia received lands along the Rhine as well as part of Saxony. The victorious allies compensated themselves by taking various territories—Norway went to Sweden; Malta, Ceylon, and the Cape of Good Hope to Britain; Finland, Bessarabia, and most of Poland to Russia; and Dalmatia and Galicia (as well as Lombardy and Venetia) to Austria. In anticipation of later events it should be noted that Germany and Italy remained disunited. Germany consisted of the loose Germanic Confederation of thirty-nine states. Italy was simply a "geographic expression." It was made up of nine states, all of them dominated by Austria because of its commanding position in Lombardy and Venetia.

VI. NATIONALISM

What is the significance for world history of the three great revolutions we have studied—the English, the American, and the French? The best answer to this question was given by an illiterate Greek guerrilla chieftain who led his fellow citizens in revolt against their Turkish overlord in 1821:

According to my judgment, the French Revolution and the doings of Napoleon opened the eyes of the world. The nations knew nothing before, and the people thought that kings were gods upon the earth and that they were bound to say that whatever they did was well done. Through this present change it is more difficult to rule the people.[5]

In this simple language the guerrilla leader summarized, too, the essence of the English and the American, as well as the French, revolutions. We have seen how the eyes of the world were opened by the Levellers and the Minutemen and the sans-culottes. This political awakening represented a profound social revolution. It marked the beginning for the first time in history of active and institutionalized mass participation in government. The revolution expressed itself in numerous "isms," which flourished during the nineteenth century. In the remainder of this chapter we shall concern ourselves with three of them—nationalism, liberalism, and socialism—the three that have since exerted the most influence on the course of European and world history.

Nationalism is a phenomenon of modern European history. It did not exist in recognizable form in the Middle Ages. At that time the universalism of the Roman Empire lived on in the Catholic Church, to which all Western Christians belonged; in the Latin language, which all educated people used; and in the Holy Roman Empire, ramshackle structure though it was. Consequently, mass allegiance to a nation was, during those centuries, unknown. Instead, most people considered themselves to be first of all Christians; second, residents of a certain region, such as Burgundy or Cornwall; and only last, if at all, French or English.

Three developments gradually modified this scale of allegiances. One was the rise of vernacular languages and the use of these languages for literary expression. Another was the breakaway from the Catholic Church of several national churches. Finally, the western European dynasties built and consolidated several large, homogeneous, independent states—England, France, Spain, Portugal, and Denmark. These developments laid the basis for the rise of nationalism, though until the late eighteenth century a nation was identified with the person of the sovereign. Luther, for example, regarded "the bishops and princes" as "Germany," and Louis XIV stated that the French nation "resided wholly in the person of the king."

Nationalism did not assume its modern form until the eighteenth century, when the western European bourgeoisie came to share or obtain full power. They did so in the name of the nation, so that the nation no longer was the king, his territory, and his subjects. Rather, it was now comprised of citizens (only propertied citizens until the late nineteenth century) "who inhabited a common territory, possessed a voice in their common government, and were conscious of their common (imagined or real) heritage and their common interests."[6]

This modern form of nationalism received its greatest boost during the French Revolution and the Napoleonic period. To survive the onslaught of the old regimes of Europe, the revolutionary leaders were forced to mobilize national armies—armies of politically conscious citizens ready and eager to fight for their fatherland. The French Revolution contributed to the development of nationalism in several other ways. It required all French citizens to speak French—"the central or national language"—in place of the numerous regional dialects. It established a network of public elementary schools for the purpose of teaching French and love of country. The French Revolution also stimulated the publication of newspapers, pamphlets, and

LE CONGRES.

In this political cartoon of the Congress of Vienna, Tallyrand simply watches which way the wind is blowing. Castlereagh hesitates, while the monarchs of Russia, Prussia, and Austria form the dance of the Holy Alliance. The king of Saxony holds onto his crown and the republic of Geneva pays homage to the Kingdom of Sardinia.

periodicals that were cheap and popularly written, and therefore effective in leaving their imprint on the whole nation. And it inaugurated such nationalist rites and symbols as the national flag, the national anthem, and national holidays. All these developments enabled nationalism to overcome the people's traditional commitments to religion and to region.

We noted earlier that this passionate identification with one's nation spread from France to neighboring countries. It did so by the natural diffusion of nationalist ideology. Its spread was also a reaction to French aggression and domination. Nationalism was further stimulated by the industrial revolution, which, with its new media (cheap newspapers, books, and leaflets) for mass communication, brought about a more effective and all—embracing indoctrination of citizens. Thus nationalism became a prime factor in European history in the nineteenth century and in world history in the twentieth. But nationalism changed in character as the nineteenth century passed. It began as a humane and tolerant creed, based on the concept of the brotherhood rather than the rivalry of the various nationalist movements. But in the latter part of the century it became increasingly chauvinistic and militaristic because of the influence of Social Darwinism and the success of Bismarck in uniting Germany by Machiavellian diplomacy and war, or, as he put it, by "blood and iron."

Nationalism manifested itself strongly immediately after 1815 because the territorial settlement of that year left millions of peoples either disunited or under foreign rule. This was the case with the Germans, the Italians, the Belgians, the Norwegians, and the numerous nationalities of the Hapsburg and Ottoman empires. The inevitable result was a series of nationalist revolts that broke out in all parts of

Europe after 1815. The Greeks revolted success-fully in 1821, winning their independence from Turkish rule. The Belgians did likewise in 1830, breaking away from Dutch domination. The Italians, after futile uprisings in 1820, 1830, and 1848, established an independent and united state between 1859 and 1871. The Germans, under the leadership of Prussia, built their German Empire after defeating Austria in 1866 and France in 1870–1871.

The principle of nationalism had triumphed in western Europe by 1871. But in central and eastern Europe the Hapsburg, Tsarist, and Ottoman empires remained "prison of nationalities." The inmates of these prisons, however, were becoming increasingly ungovernable as nationalist movements succeeded all around them. The rulers of the three empires were aware of the consequences of nationalism for their multinational states, and they tried to check it by various restrictive measures and by deliberately playing one subject nationality against another. These measures were successful at first but could not prevail indefinitely. The first breaches in the imperial structures were made by the Balkan subjects of the Turks. By 1878 the Serbs, the Rumanians, and the Montenegrins had gained their independence, and in 1908 the Bulgarians did likewise. Much more significant was the assassination in June 1914 of the Hapsburg Archduke Francis Ferdinand by a young Serbian patriot, Gavrilo Princip. This was the fateful event that precipitated World War I, whose outcome was the destruction of all the empires of central and eastern Europe—the German, Austro-Hungarian, Russian, and Turkish. The peace treaties that terminated the war (discussed in Chapter 36, Section VI) were generally based on the principle of nationalism, so that several new states appeared—Poland, Czechoslovakia, Yugoslavia, and Albania—that expressed the independent existence of hitherto subject peoples. For better or for worse, nationalism had triumphed throughout Europe with the conclusion of World War I. And in the following decades, as we shall see in later chapters, the idea of nationalism began to awaken and spur to action the hundreds of millions of subject peoples in Europe's overseas possessions.

VII. LIBERALISM

Liberalism, whose central feature is the emancipation of the individual from class, corporate, or governmental restraint, was the second great European doctrine to affect the globe. Its rise was intimately related to the rise of the middle class, although in central and eastern Europe, where that class was weak, liberalism was espoused by enlightened members of the nobility. Still, liberalism developed in its classic form in western Europe, and it has remained essentially a middle-class movement in its theory and source of support.

Liberal doctrines were first clearly formulated and implemented during the English Revolution. At that time, these doctrines were primarily those of religious toleration and of security of person and of property against the arbitrariness of the crown. Specifically, carrying out these doctrines involved parliamentary control of government, the existence of independent political parties, and the recognition of the need for, and the rights of, opposition parties. On the other hand, the franchise was limited by property qualifications, so that the lower-middle class and the workers, who made up most of the population, were left voteless. Thus, liberalism in seventeenth-century England advanced middle-class interests.

Liberalism was further defined and applied as the American Revolution brought about substantial advances in restricting slavery, extending religious toleration, broadening the franchise, and establishing constitutional government. The federal Constitution adopted in 1791 was based on the principle of the separation of powers in order to prevent tyranny—by having the executive, legislative, and judicial powers check and balance each other. The Bill of Rights guaranteed freedom of religion, speech, press, and assembly. And the U.S. Constitution, like the English settlement, carefully safeguarded the interests of the propertied classes: by limiting the franchise and by providing for the indirect election of the president and the senators and for the election of the various branches of the government for different periods of time. These arrangements were designed to prevent a radical popular movement from getting control of the entire government at any one time and introducing dangerous changes.

Even more advanced in its liberal tenets than the American Revolution was the French. Its Declaration of the Rights of Man and Citizen is the classic statement of eighteenth-century liberalism, proclaiming in ringing phrases the liberties of the individual. But French liberalism, too, was primarily a bourgeois movement. The Declaration, like all the several constitutions adopted by the French revolutionaries, stressed the rights of property as "inviolable and sacred." And Napoleon's famous codes, which proved to be the most durable and influential, specifically forbade the organization of trade unions and the waging of strikes.

We may conclude that the liberalism that emerged from the English, American, and French revolutions took the institutional form of constitutional parliamentary government and was concerned about equal civil rights, though not equal political and social rights. As the nineteenth century passed, liberalism, like other historical movements, changed appreciably in character. It could not continue to concern itself mainly with bourgeois interests at a time when the masses were becoming more assertive as a result of increasing education and trade-union organization. Consequently, there was a shift from the early classical liberalism to a more democratic variety. Equality before the law was supplemented by equality before the ballot box. By the end of the nineteenth century male suffrage had been adopted in most of the western European countries. Even the hallowed principle of laissez-faire was gradually modified. Hitherto intervention by the government in economic and social matters had been regarded as mischievous and futile meddling with the operation of natural laws. This theoretical proposition, however, did not jibe with the facts of life as far as the workers were concerned. Civil liberties and the right to vote did not relieve them from the poverty and insecurity produced by unemployment, sickness, disability, and old age. So they used their voting power and union organization to press for social reforms. Under this pressure a new democratic liberalism developed that recognized the responsibility of the state for the welfare of all its citizens. Thus the western Euro-

pean countries, led by Germany, adopted social-reform programs, including old-age pensions; minimum-wage laws; sickness, accident, and unemployment insurance; and regulation of hours and conditions of work. These reforms of democratic liberalism were the prelude to the welfare state that has become the hallmark of our own age.

VIII. SOCIALISM

Socialism is the antithesis of the classical liberalism of the eighteenth and early nineteenth centuries. Liberalism emphasizes the individual and his or her rights; socialism, the community and

Civic equality was one of the hallmarks of the revolutionary era. This figure of Equality holds in her hand a copy of the Declaration of the Rights of Man and Citizen.

its collective welfare. Liberalism represents society as the product of natural laws and is skeptical of advancing human welfare artificially by legislation. Socialism, by contrast, holds that people, by rational thought and action, can determine their own social system and social relationships. Furthermore, it maintains that human nature is primarily the product of social environment. Accordingly, contemporary evils may be eliminated by establishing a society specifically designed to promote collective well-being rather than individual profit and to instill cooperative social attitudes and patterns of behavior rather than competitive ones. In short, socialism stresses the collective society and planned social change rather than the individual and laissez-faire.

Plans for the reorganization of society are by no means peculiar to our modern age. Ever since the rise of civilization, political and economic power has been concentrated in the hands of a few. This has led prophets and reformers of all periods to advocate plans promoting social justice and equality. In the classical world, for example, Plato in his *Republic* called for an aristocratic communism, a dictatorship of communistic philosophers. In the medieval period the English peasant leader John Ball declared to his followers, "My good people,—things cannot go well in England, nor ever will, until all goods are held in common, and until there will be neither serfs nor gentlemen, and we shall all be equal."[7] The turmoil and the passions of the English and French revolutions naturally stimulated more schemes for the promotion of the common welfare, but the final outcome, as we have seen, was the triumph of the relatively conservative Cromwell and of Napoleon.

A vigorous new school of social reformers—the Utopian Socialists—appeared in the early nineteenth century. Outstanding were two Frenchmen, Henri de Saint-Simon (1760–1825) and Charles Fourier (1772–1837), and the English industrialist Robert Owen (1771–1858). Their proposals varied widely but had one basic characteristic in common. Although they paid much attention to the principles and to the precise workings of their projected model communities, they never seriously faced the problem of

how these were to take the place of the existing society. Saint-Simon, for example, tried to enlist the support of the pope and of Louis XVIII. Fourier sat in his room at noon every day for twelve years waiting in vain for responses to his newspaper appeals for support. These reformers definitely did not think in terms of revolution or of class warfare. In fact, they scarcely thought at all about how their elaborate blueprints might be put into practice. It is for this reason that they are known as "Utopian" Socialists.

Karl Marx (1818–1883), the father of modern socialism, differed fundamentally from the Utopian Socialists in almost every respect. He was as materialistic in his outlook as they were idealistic. He spent most of his life studying the historical evolution and the precise functioning of the existing capitalist society, whereas utopians prepared blueprints of model communities. Marx was convinced from his study of history that capitalism would be overthrown by class struggle and would be replaced by a new type of socialist society. He reached this conclusion because he believed that the wages paid to workers were insufficient for them to buy what they produced. This inadequate purchasing power eventually must lead to the closing of factories, unemployment, a further decline of purchasing power, and, at length, a full-scale depression. Furthermore, Marx believed that these depressions would become increasingly frequent and severe until finally the unemployed proletariat would be driven in desperation to revolution. In this way capitalism would be replaced by socialism, as feudalism earlier had been by capitalism. And the new socialistic society would be depression-proof because, with government ownership of the means of production, there could be no private employers, no profits, and hence no lack of purchasing power.

Marx did not limit himself to theorizing and writing. Throughout his life he combined intellectual activity with efforts to organize and activize workers. The last sentence of his 1848 *Communist Manifesto* reads, "Workers of the world, unite." Marx played an important role in the establishment in 1864 of the International Workingmen's Association or, as it is commonly called, the First International. This body was committed to Marx's program of the workers'

Karl Marx's socialist philosophy eventually triumphed over most alternative versions of socialism in Europe, but his monumental work has been subject to varying interpretations, criticisms, and revisions that continue to this day.

seizure of power in order to reorganize society along socialistic lines. It attracted considerable attention with its propaganda and its participation in various strikes. But it disintegrated in 1873, largely because its membership included an undisciplined and constantly feuding assortment of romanticists, nationalists, and anarchists, as well as Socialists.

In 1884 the Socialist, or Second, International was established in Paris. This was a loosely knit organization affiliated with the numerous Socialist parties that had appeared by this time in various countries. The Second International grew rapidly, so that by 1914 it included the Socialist parties of twenty-seven countries with a total membership of 12 million workers. The Second International was much more moderate in its doctrines and its actions than the

First. The reason for the shift in emphasis was that the major constituent parties were themselves turning away from simon-pure Marxism to what was termed revisionism. A number of factors explain this shift in emphasis. One was the gradual extension of the franchise in the western European countries, which meant workers could use ballots rather than bullets to attain their objectives. Another was the steady rise after 1850 in European living standards, which tended to make workers more willing to accept capitalism. The German revisionist leader Eduard Bernstein expressed the new viewpoint when he declared that Socialists should "work less for the better future and more for the better present." The new strategy, in other words, was to make immediate gains by gradual reform measures rather than to strive for a socialistic society by revolution. Not all Socialists were willing to go along with this revisionism.

Some of them remained true to what they considered to be the teachings of Marx, so that most Socialist parties split into "orthodox" and "revisionist" factions. The revisionists, however, were more in tune with the temper of the times and usually controlled their respective parties. Indeed, they were able to organize powerful trade union movements and to win millions of votes in electoral contests. In fact, the German, the French, and the Italian Socialist parties had by 1914 a larger number of seats in their respective national assemblies than any other political parties.

When World War I began in 1914, the Second International paid the price for its revisionism: The majority of its members proved to be nationalists first and socialists second. They responded to the exhortations of their respective national governments, with the result that millions of workers died fighting on both sides of the trenches. Thus the Second International was torn asunder, and although it was revived after the war, it never attained its former strength and prestige.

Socialism, however, did not peter out with the disintegration of the Second International. In fact, it was during World War I that the Russian Socialists, or Bolsheviks, as they were called, succeeded in seizing power and establishing the first proletarian government in history. Furthermore, the Bolsheviks organized the Third, or Communist, International to challenge the Second, or Socialist, International. Because peasants and workers in the underdeveloped countries have not enjoyed the prosperity and freedoms of workers in developed countries, Marxism won many followers in former colonial lands. This was especially true after the bloodshed and suffering of the two world wars. In recent years, Marxism has lost much of its appeal because, as we shall see below, the Marxist societies that have emerged in various parts of the world have proved to be very different from the shining ideals set forth by Marx in the nineteenth century.

IX. WOMEN IN POLITICAL REVOLUTIONS

Women played an active role in all the political revolutions, but with very mixed results. The basic reason is that women did not insist that their demands be formally accepted and incorporated in the revolutionary programs. Rather, they were content to serve as auxiliaries in male-controlled political movements. Their support naturally was welcomed during the struggle for power, but after victory was won, they were ignored and forced to return to their prerevolutionary subordinate status. This pattern is evident in all modern revolutions, from the English in the seventeenth century to the Russian and Chinese in the twentieth.

The various stages of the French Revolution show clearly how this pattern evolved. Before the revolution French women, like women throughout Europe, accepted the authority of father before marriage and of husband after. The Marquis de Condorcet was one of the very few leaders of the French Revolution who publicly urged that women be allowed to own property, to vote, to hold office, and to receive the same free public education as males. But the Marquis was far ahead of his time. Much more acceptable were the views of Rousseau, who expounded advanced political ideas in his *Social Contract* but in his novel *Emile* (1761) advised women to "Be simple in your dress, hard working in your homes, never go to the popular assemblies wanting to speak. . . . Is there a sight in this world

The women of Paris marched to Versailles on October 5, 1789. The following day the royal family was forced to return to Paris with them. Henceforth, the French government would function under the constant threat of mob violence.

a Versaille a Versaille du 5 Octobre 1789.

so touching, so respectable as that of a mother surrounded by her children, directing the work of her domestics, procuring a happy life for her husband, and wisely governing the home?"

When the revolution began, middle-class women set forth their demands in their cahiers (notebooks) to the Estates General. They asked for safeguarding of women's dowries from profligate husbands, protection for wives against abuse, state jobs for women who were being forced to prostitution by economic necessity, and a public education system to widen employment opportunities for women. But the women did not press home their demands, so the Declaration of the Rights of Man adopted by the National Assembly on August 26, 1789, was silent on the rights of women. Working-class women were more forceful because there was no bread in Paris and they were hungry. In October 1789 they marched to the palace at Versailles and brought back with them the royal family, referring to them as "the baker, the baker's wife, and the baker's little boy."

By 1790 women were publishing their own newspapers in which they demanded the right to vote, to participate in assemblies, to serve on juries, and to obtain divorce. These demands were included in the Declaration of the Rights of Women, proclaimed by female leaders in 1791. Women became most active in the spring of 1793 when the king was executed for treason and France was invaded by five foreign armies. The hard-pressed Paris government called on French women to join in the defense of their country. They responded enthusiastically, rolling bandages in hospitals and making shirts, trousers, hats, stockings, and gloves for their soldiers. Some even volunteered and fought in the revolutionary armies.

The republican government showed its appreciation by passing laws legalizing divorce, making marriage a civil contract, granting wives a share of family property, and providing free and compulsory primary schools for both girls and boys. At the height of their activism, members of the Republican Revolutionary Women patrolled streets, wearing trousers with pistols in their belts and red caps on their heads.

A year later, when the danger of foreign invasion had passed, the reaction against female revolutionaries began. A specific issue was the ending of price controls and the reduction of the bread ration. Workers' families suffered while profiteers flaunted their new riches. When thousands of desperate men and women took up arms, the convention called out the regular army and surrounded the rebellious neighborhoods. The democratic constitution of 1793 was scrapped, as were most of the women's rights recently granted. Napoleon consolidated the reaction by including laws in his code that restored the absolute authority of father and husband.

The basic reason for the setback was that the cause of women's rights lacked mass support among the women themselves. During the revolution they had responded primarily to the needs of their class rather than of their sex. They had taken to the streets primarily for social reform and economic relief rather than for female rights. When the French Revolution, like the English before it, rejected social restructuring and turned conservative, the gains of the women as females were swept away along with their gains as workers. Apart from Condorcet, the top leaders of the revolution agreed wholeheartedly with Rousseau that women's place was in the home. They recognized and applauded the contributions that women had made during the revolution. But after the revolution the political leaders made speeches about the future contributions that women could make within the family, not outside it.

The feminist themes developed during the French Revolution were not forgotten in the postrevolution years. They were resurrected by middle- and upper-class European women throughout the nineteenth century. Feminist leaders published books and periodicals and established a network of national and international women's associations. These organizations promoted education for women, opposed state-regulated prostitution, supported aid for abandoned children and unwed mothers, agitated against alcoholism, and mounted peace movements that branded war as the ultimate expression of male politics. Progress was modest, and activist women concluded by the late nineteenth century that they could not gain their goals unless they shared political power with men on an equal basis. Henceforth the vote became the dominant issue for suffragists in all countries. Rapid progress was made in the twen-

Member of one of the earliest feminist movements—an early twentieth-century suffragette.

tieth century, so that the number of countries that enfranchised women rose from 1 in 1900 to 3 in 1910, 15 in 1920, 21 in 1930, 30 in 1940, 69 in 1950, 92 in 1960, 127 in 1970, and 129 in 1975.

The right to vote did not prove to be the cure-all for women's problems, as had been expected. Casting a ballot on election day did not automatically confer political power. Few women were elected to representative bodies, and still fewer ended up in positions with executive authority. In fact, the international women's movement lost much of its vigor after the franchise had been won. The doldrums persisted until World War II, when a combination of several new and decisive factors emerged to ener-

gize the feminist movement. The origins and nature of these new factors and their impact on women throughout the globe will be analyzed in the concluding chapter.

SUGGESTED READINGS

For a comparison and interpretation of the English, French, and Russian revolutions, see C. Brinton, *The Anatomy of Revolution* (Random House, 1958); and the collection of readings by R. W. Postgate, *Revolution from 1789 to 1906* (Harper & Row, 1962.)

On the English Revolution, see P. Zagorin, *A History of Political Thought in the English Revolution* (Routledge & Kegan Paul, 1954); and the studies by C. Hill,

Intellectual Origins of the English Revolution (Clarendon, 1962), and *The World Turned Upside Down: Radical Ideas During the English Revolution* (Viking, 1972). For the Enlightenment, see the surveys of R. B. Mowat, *The Age of Reason* (Houghton Mifflin, 1934); E. Cassirer, *The Philosophy of the Enlightenment* (Princeton University, 1951); and also the documentary collection of F. E. Manuel, ed., *The Enlightenment* (Prentice Hall, 1965).

Studies of the American Revolution are by P. Maier, *From Resistance to Revolution* (Routledge & Kegan Paul, 1973); L. H. Gipson, *The Coming of the Revolution, 1763–1775*, and J. R. Alden, *The American Revolution, 1775–1783*, the latter two in the "New American Nation" series (Harper & Row, 1954). For the impact of the American Revolution on Europe, see M. Kraus, *The North Atlantic Civilization* (D. Van Nostrand, 1957); and G. D. Lillibridge, ed., *The American Image Past and Present* (D. C. Heath, 1968).

Of the thousands of books on the French Revolution, noteworthy is J. M. Thompson, 2nd ed., *The French Revolution* (Blackwell, 1966); and the collection of readings by J. H. Stewart, *A Documentary Survey of the French Revolution* (Macmillan, 1951). Of particular significance for the analysis of the revolutionary movement in the Western world between 1760 and 1800 is R. R. Palmer, *The Age of the Democratic Revolution: A Political History of Europe and America, 1760–1800*, 2 vols. (Princeton University, 1959, 1964). More recent studies are O. Connelly, *French Revolution–Napoleonic Era* (Holt, Rinehart & Winston, 1979); L. Hunt, *Politics, Culture and Class in the French Revolution* (University of California, 1986); and G. Rude, *The Crowd in History: Popular Disturbances in France and England* (Lawrence and Wishart, 1981).

A voluminous literature on nationalism now exists, some comprehensive surveys being B. C. Shafer, *Nationalism: Myth and Reality* (Harcourt Brace Jovanovich, 1955); and K. R. Minogue, *Nationalism* (Basic Books, 1967). The bibliography on liberalism also is tremendous, though there are few comprehensive studies. Outstanding among these are H. J. Laski, *The Rise of Liberalism* (Harper & Row, 1936); J. R. Pennock, *Liberal Democracy: Its Merits and Prospects* (Holt, Rinehart & Winston, 1950); J. Sigmann, *1848: The Romantic and Democratic Revolutions in Europe* (Harper & Row, 1973); and the brief survey, with appended readings, in J. S. Schapiro, *Liberalism: Its Meaning and History* (D. Van Nostrand, 1958).

On socialism, there is no end of literature, much of it controversial. Most recent is the appraisal of Marx's influence in D. McLellan, ed., *Marx: The First Hundred Years* (St. Martin's Press, 1983); A. S. Lindemann, *A History of European Socialism* (Yale University, 1983); the useful reference work by T. Bottomore, *A Dictionary of Marxist Thought* (Harvard University, 1983); and the paperback collection of relevant readings by C. Wright Mills, *The Marxists* (Dell, 1982).

Finally, for an overview of the role of women, see the relevant chapters in R. Bridenthal and C. Koonz, *Becoming Visible: Women in European History* (Houghton Mifflin, 1977). More detailed accounts are available in R. J. Evans, *The Feminists: Women's Emancipation Movements in Europe, America and Australia 1840–1920* (Barnes & Noble, 1978); P. Stock, *Better Than Rubies: A History of Women's Education* (Putnam's, 1978); C. Banks, *Faces of Feminism: A Study of Feminism as a Social Movement* (Oxford University, 1981); and J. Kelly, *Women, History and Theory* (University of Chicago, 1985).

NOTES

1. Cited by G. Wint, *The British in Asia* (Institute of Pacific Relations, 1954), p. 18.
2. Sir Edwin Sandys, in a speech in Parliament. Cited by J. L. Laski, *The Rise of Liberalism* (Harper & Row, 1936), p. 117.
3. P. Zagorin, "The English Revolution, 1640–1660," *Journal of World History*, II (1955), p. 903.
4. A. S. P. Woodhouse, *Puritanism and Liberty* (Dent, 1938), p. 55.
5. T. Kolokotrones and E. M. Edmonds, *Kolokotrones, Klepht and Warrior* (London, 1892), pp. 127–28.
6. B. C. Shafer, *Nationalism: Myth and Reality* (Harcourt Brace Jovanovich, 1955), p. 105.
7. Cited by D. W. Morris, *The Chrstian Origins of Social Revolt* (George Allen & Unwin, 1949), p. 34.

For three hundred years Russia has aspired to consort with Occidental Europe; for three hundred years she has taken her most serious ideas, her most fruitful teachings, and her most vivid delights from there.

Peter Y. Chaadayev

In a sense, it is paradoxical to consider Europe's impact on Russia; Russia, after all, is a part of Europe, and the Russian people are a European people. But Russia lies on the fringe of Europe and provides a great buffer zone between that continent and Asia. Because of this location the historical experience of the Russian people has been quite different from that of other Europeans, and the culture they have developed is correspondingly different. As a result, Russian thinkers have tormented themselves generation after generation with the basic issue of national orientation and national goals.

Russia's relationship with the West has generally been that of passive recipient. Only in the past century and a half has Russia been able to repay the West, at first with the creations of its great writers and composers, and later with the social stimuli generated by the Bolshevik Revolution. But until the twentieth century Europe's impact on Russia was much greater than was the reverse, and this influence has been a central factor in the development of the country.

I. RUSSIA AND EUROPE TO 1856

The first Russian state developed about the principality of Kiev in the ninth century after Christ (see Chapter 24, Section II). This early Russian state had numerous ties with the rest of Europe. It conducted a very considerable trade across the Black Sea with Byzantium and across the Baltic with northwest Europe. It is significant that Prince Yaroslav in the eleventh century had marriage connections with the leading dynasties of Europe. His sister was married to Casimir I of Poland, his son to a princess of Byzantium, and his two daughters to Henry I of France and to Harald II of Norway.

During the following centuries two crucial developments combined to isolate Russia. One was Prince Vladimir's decision about 990 C.E. to adopt the Byzantine Orthodox form of Christianity rather than the Roman Catholic. Although the differences between the two religions were not very substantial at the time, during the following decades the development of the doctrine of papal supremacy and its increasing practice finally led in 1054 to a schism between the two churches. Russia inevitably became involved in this Catholic and Orthodox feuding. This was particularly so after the fall of Constantinople to the Turks (1453), which left Russia as the only independent citadel of Orthodoxy. These events made the Russians self-satisfied, self-righteous, and self-isolated, and they ignored and scorned the great changes that were transforming the rest of Europe.

The other development that cut Russia off from the West was the Mongol invasion in 1237. The Mongols did not interfere with the affairs of their Russian subjects as long as the latter accepted the domination of the khan and paid him annual tribute. Nevertheless, Mongol domination severed most of the remaining ties between Russia and the rest of Europe. This rupture, which persisted during the two centuries of Mongol rule, came at a time when the West was experiencing the Renaissance, the Reformation, overseas expansion, and the commercial revolution. But isolated Russia remained largely unaffected by these profound economic and cultural movements. Furthermore, the Mongols left their own imprint on Russian society. Their ideas and administrative usages paved the way for the establishment of the semi-oriental absolutism of the later Muscovite tsars. And their ethnic contribution was also significant—for example, approximately 17 percent of the Moscow upper class at the end of the seventeenth century was of non-Russian, or Eastern, origin.

When the Russians rid themselves of Mongol rule in the fifteenth century, the Muscovite civilization that came to light was quite different from anything in western Europe. It was a homogeneous civilization in the sense that the Orthodox religion shaped and colored people's outlook and actions. But it was also a civilization largely devoid of the commerce, the industry, and the science that had made the West so dynamic and expansionist. More emancipated and far-seeing Russian leaders soon perceived that their economic and technological backwardness represented a threat to their national security. Thus it was that the Russians in the sixteenth century, like the Turks, the Japanese, and the Chinese in later centuries, began to borrow from the West as a measure of self-defense. And

what they were primarily interested in borrowing was military technology.

Tsar Peter the Great (1682– 1725) accelerated the borrowing process tremendously. With his iron will and herculean energy he issued over 3,000 decrees, many in his own hand, and almost all inspired by him. He reorganized his administration and armed forces along Western lines; established industries to support his armies; imported thousands of foreign experts of various types; sent droves of young Russians to study abroad; and set up a number of schools, all of them utilitarian in character. He founded schools of mathematics and navigation, admiralty schools, war-department schools, ciphering schools, and, at the summit, the Academy of Sciences. Peter also shattered all precedent by traveling through western Europe to study foreign institutions and practices at first hand.

In all these various ways Peter succeeded in large part in reaching his goal of opening a "window to the West." Furthermore, he opened this window in a literal sense by defeating Sweden

Tsar Peter the Great.

PETER the GREAT.

and acquiring frontage on the Baltic Sea. Here he built his new capital, St. Petersburg—the symbol of the new Russia, as Moscow was of the old. These changes, however, were not brought about without bitter opposition from wide segments of the population. Peter had to fight against the overt and covert opposition of conservative boyars and churchmen, as well as against the apathy and suspicion of the masses. Even the changes that he did introduce were limited in two important respects: They were largely military, economic, and technical in character, and they affected only the sympathetic members of the thin upper crust of the population.

Peter's work was continued by the gifted and colorful Catherine the Great (1762–1796). Catherine regarded herself and her court as a medium for the Europeanization of Russia. She was much more intellectual than the pragmatic Peter and energetically patronized literature, art, theater, and the press. She was not an original thinker, but she readily absorbed the ideas of others, especially the philosophes. In fact, she prided herself on being an enlightened despot and often quoted the maxims of the Enlightenment. During her reign the higher Russian nobility became Europeanized. They had worn beards and flowing oriental robes during Peter's reign, but under Catherine they aped the court of Versailles in their speech, clothes, dwellings, and social functions. Their children were brought up by French governesses, learned French as their mother tongue, and then picked up only enough Russian to manage the servants. Thus the Europeanization of Russia was no longer confined to technical matters, yet it was also still limited to the upper class. Indeed, the gulf between the Europeanized upper crust and the peasant masses who were bound to the estates as serfs was becoming wider and more ominous.

The seriousness of the gulf became clear after the great Russian victory over Napoleon's Grand Army. Between 1815 and 1818 a Russian army of occupation had been stationed in France. Many of the officers were much impressed by the relatively free Western society in which they had lived for four years. There they had absorbed the liberal and radical ideas in contemporary France and had been profoundly influenced by them. When they returned to Russia in 1818, they found the tsarist autocracy stifling.

Sentiments such as these explain the so-called Decembrist Revolt that broke out in December 1825, upon the death of Alexander I. The leaders were mostly army officers who wished to westernize Russia by abolishing serfdom and the autocracy. The revolt failed miserably because there was no mass support. The Russians at this time lived under conditions so utterly different from those prevailing in western Europe that they simply were not ready for Western political ideas and institutions. More

St. Petersburg—Tsar Peter's "Window to the West."

specifically, Russia lacked the commerce, the industry, and the middle class that had played so decisive a role in the political evolution of the West. Instead, there were at the bottom the bound and inert serf masses—the "dark people," as they were called—and at the top the nobility and the court. Consequently, there was no mass support for the reforms and for the Western type of society desired by the Decembrists.

The meaning of these basic differences between Russia and the West divided Russian thinkers into two groups, the Westerners and the Slavophils. The Westerners deplored the differences, interpreting them as a product of Russia's slower rate of development. Accordingly, their hero was Peter the Great, and they urged that other rulers match Peter's heroic efforts to catch up with the West. The Slavophils, on the other hand, rejected the Westerner's basic assumption of the unity of human civilization. They held that the differences between Russia and the West were fundamental and inherent and reflected profound dissimilarities in national spirit rather than degrees of advance. Accordingly these Slavophils idealized the homogeneous Muscovite society of the period before Peter, and they regarded him as the archenemy of Russian civilization and national unity. Far from considering Western society superior, they rejected it as materialistic, irreligious, and torn by dissension and revolution.

II. RUSSIA AND EUROPE, 1856–1905

The issues between the Slavophils and the Westerners were settled, but not by persuasion of one side by the other, but by the irresistible pressure of the rapidly developing and expanding Western society. This pressure was dramatically illustrated by the Crimean War (1854–1856) between Russia and a number of Western powers, of which the most important were Britain and France. The war was fought on Russian soil—in the Crimean peninsula—and yet Russia was defeated and forced to accept the humiliating Treaty of Paris. This treaty required Russia to scrap its naval units in the Black Sea and its fortifications along the Black Sea coast.

The Crimean defeat was a severe shock for the Russian nationalists and Slavophils. Unlike

many Westerners, who had warned of Russia's impending defeat because it had not kept up with the West, the Slavophils had predicted that the superiority of Russia's autocratic institutions would lead to a victory comparable to that of 1812 over Napoleon. Actually, the Crimean defeat unveiled the corruption and backwardness of the old regime. Russia's soldiers had fought as gallantly in 1855 as in 1812, but the odds were hopelessly against them. They had rifles that shot only a third as far as those of the Western armies. They had only sailing ships to use against the steamships of the British and the French. They had no medical or food-supply services that were worthy of the name.

The revelation of the old regime's bankruptcy led to its modification. The first change was the emancipation of the serfs, who had been intensely restless even before the war. In fact, over five hundred peasant disturbances had broken out during the three decades of Nicholas I's reign between 1825 and 1855. With the disas-

Tsar Alexander I (r. 1801–1825). A mild reformer when he succeeded to the throne, Alexander became increasingly reactionary after 1815.

ter in the Crimea, the mounting pressure of the serfs became irresistible, and Nicholas's successor, Alexander II, accepted emancipation as the only alternative to revolution. His Emancipation Decree (March 1, 1861) freed the serfs and divided the land that they tilled between themselves and the noble proprietors. This was a great turning point in Russian history, even greater than the 1863 Emancipation Proclamation in American history. Emancipation in the United States concerned only the black minority, whereas in Russia it involved the overwhelming majority of the population. The repercussions of the freeing of the serfs were so far reaching that a series of other reforms were unavoidable. These included the reorganization of the judiciary and of the local government.

During the decades following the Crimean War, western Europe further undermined the old regime in Russia by contributing decisively to the industrialization of the country. Of the total of £500 million invested in Russian industry in 1917, just over one-third was made up of foreign investments. The number of factory workers rose from 381,000 in 1865, to 1,620,000 in 1890, and to 3 million in 1898. By 1913, Russia was producing as much iron and three-fourths as much coal as France.

These developments meant that the Russia of 1914 was much more similar to Europe than the Russia of the Decembrists of 1825. But as the Slavophils had warned, the increasing similarity brought about certain divisions and conflicts within Russian society. One of these was the growing unrest and rising political consciousness among the peasants. The peasants had been far from satisfied with the terms of the Emancipation Decree, which they felt had left too large a proportion of the land to the nobles. During the following decades, as the peasants grew rapidly in numbers, their land hunger grew correspondingly, and they became increasingly dissatisfied. Another source of grievance for the peasants was the intolerably heavy tax load. They paid not only redemption dues for the land they had received in 1861, but also an assortment of local taxes. In addition, they bore much of the cost of Russia's industrialization, because high protective tariffs forced up the cost of the manufactured goods they bought. The extent and the intensity of peasant discontent were shown by the increasing frequency of violent peasant outbreaks against landlords and unpopular government officials.

Peasant disaffection found political expression in the Socialist Revolutionary party, which was organized in 1901. The main plank of its platform was the distribution of state and noble lands among the peasantry. The unrest of the peasants was matched by that of the urban proletariat, who had appeared with the growth of industry. The early days of industrialization in Russia, as elsewhere in Europe, involved gross exploitation of labor: sixteen-hour working days, low wages, child labor, and abominable working and living conditions. Under these circumstances the Russian workers, like those of central and western Europe, came under the influence of Marxist doctrines. Thus a Social Democratic party was organized in 1898 just as similar Socialist parties had been established elsewhere in Europe. And like the other Socialist parties, the Russian party split into revisionist and orthodox factions—or, as they were called in this instance, the Mensheviks and the Bolsheviks.

In addition to the peasants and the urban workers, there was in Russia at the turn of the century a middle class that also was becoming increasingly discontented with the tsarist regime. The political organization reflecting the views of this group was the Constitutional Democratic party, commonly known under the abbreviated title of Cadets. The program of this party, founded in 1905, resembled that of the English Liberals: a constitutional monarchy balanced by a parliamentary body similar to Britain's House of Commons. The Cadets included many of Russia's outstanding intellectuals and businesspersons. When the tsar was forced to accept an elected assembly (Duma) following the 1905 revolution, the Cadets played a leading role in its deliberations because of their knowledge of parliamentary procedures. And yet the Cadets never won a mass following comparable to that of the Social Democrats or the Socialist Revolutionaries. One reason was that the middle class was relatively small in Russia because of the retarded development of commerce and industry. The middle class was further weakened because so much of the national economy was controlled by foreign interests. And the Cadets were peculiarly vulnerable to the pressures of the tsarist autocracy

Life in Russian villages during the 1870s was very difficult. Tsar Alexander II abolished serfdom in 1861, but peasants were required to pay compensation to the government for forty-nine years and living standards remained dismal. This painting shows peasants waiting patiently outside a government office while officials inside take their time over lunch.

because, with their middle-class background, they were less willing to meet force with force.

Such, then, was the West's impact on Russia by the turn of the century. The intrusion of the West had undermined a distinctive and homogeneous society; and the repercussions of the resulting stresses and dissensions were to culminate in the great revolutions of 1905 and 1917. Before considering these upheavals, we shall survey Russian policies in Asia up to the time of the Russo-Japanese War, which set the stage for the 1905 revolution.

III. RUSSIA AND ASIA TO 1905

Just as the relations between Russia and Europe were determined largely by the economic and technological superiority of Europe, so the relations between Russia and Asia were determined by the superiority of Russia. This superiority had enabled Russia between the sixteenth and eighteenth centuries to overcome the tribespeople of Siberia and to expand eastward to the Pacific. But in the southeast the Russians had been halted by the strong Chinese Empire and forced to accept the Nerchinsk Treaty (1689) confining them to the territory north of the Amur valley (see Chapter 24, Section III).

During the eighteenth and nineteenth centuries the Russians resumed their advance to the east and the south, rounding out their empire by acquiring Alaska, the Amur valley, and central Asia. The addition of Alaska involved simply a continuation of the earlier trans-Siberian push into relatively empty territories. But in the Amur valley the Russians prevailed over the Chinese Empire, and in central Asia they imposed their rule on ancient Moslem khanates. These successes were made possible by Russia's steady technological progress. Russia's technology, though inadequate vis-á-vis the West, and indeed, derived from the West, was nonetheless sufficient to give Russians a decisive advantage in their relations with the Chinese in east Asia and with the Moslems in central Asia. Thus, the Russians continued to extend their imperial frontiers until they were stopped by powers that were technologically equal or superior—that is, by the Americans in Alaska, by the British in India and Persia, and by the Japanese in Manchuria.

Alaska

The Russian advance to Alaska began during the reign of Peter the Great. The westernizing tsar was as much interested in the Far East as in Europe, so he selected Captain Vitus Bering, a naval officer of Danish extraction, to lead expeditions to the American continent in 1728 and 1740. Bering sailed eastward across the sea that bears his name, explored the Aleutian Islands, and landed on the coast of Alaska. The main achievement of the Bering expeditions is that they discovered that North America and Asia were joined in the North Pacific waters.

Russian merchants followed on the heels of the explorers, attracted by the profitable trade in

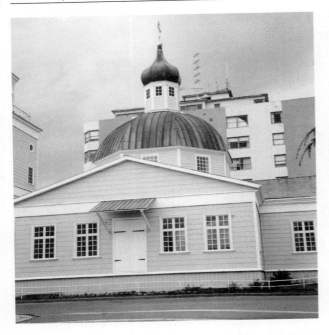

St. Michael's Orthodox Cathedral in Sitka, former capital of Russian Alaska.

to establish settlements where fresh supplies could be grown for the Alaskan posts. In November 1811, Fort Ross was established on the Russian River north of San Francisco, and by 1819 the Russians had a chain of nineteen settlements on the American coast.

This expansion led to friction with Spain and with the United States. In fact, the presence of the Russians in the northwest Pacific was partly responsible for the proclamation of the Monroe Doctrine in 1823. In the end, the Russians decided to give up their American holdings. The decline in the fur trade had brought the Russo-American Company to the point of bankruptcy, and the Russians feared that Alaska was too distant to be defended against American expansionism. Anticipating that they would lose the territory sooner or later, they sold it to the United States in 1867 for $7.2 million, or less than two cents per acre—the greatest real estate bargain of all time.

Amur Valley

Meanwhile, the Russian activity in North America had reawakened Russian interest in the Amur valley. The Russians needed an outlet on the Pacific Ocean to serve as a base for supplying their American settlements. They had the port of Okhotsk, but this was altogether inadequate. It was frozen every year until June and almost continually fogbound. Consequently, the Russians once more looked longingly toward the broad and navigable Amur River, from which they had been ousted by the Nerchinsk Treaty in 1689.

Russian interest was further sharpened by the so-called Opium War of 1839–1842 between Britain and China (see Chapter 31, Section I). As a result of the war, Britain annexed Hong Kong and acquired a predominant influence in the Yangtze valley. The Russians now resolved to establish themselves in the Amur valley lest the British next gain control of the mouth of the river and block their natural outlet to the Pacific. In little more than a decade, the Russians gained all their objectives in this vital region. One reason for their success was the ambition and energy of young Count Nikolai Muraviev, who was appointed governor general of eastern Siberia in 1847 at the age of thirty-eight. Another reason was the weakness of China, by that

sea otter furs. The merchants first exploited the Aleut islanders and then established posts along the Alaskan coast. Since the Aleuts had no firearms, they were vulnerable and were mercilessly exploited. In 1761 the enraged inhabitants of Umnak island turned on the Russian traders, killing many and forcing the survivors to flee. The Aleuts won five years of independence, during which they returned to their subsistence level hunting and fishing. But in 1766 the Russians retaliated with mercenary troops that destroyed the Aleut villages, killing over 3,000 inhabitants. Forced by their overlords, the Aleuts resumed the hunting of sea otters, whose furs the Russians requisitioned insatiably, since they could be sold in China for four times the purchase price. The spoliation continued until both Aleuts and otters were decimated.

In 1799 the various private trading companies combined to form the Russo-American Company. The outstanding Russian leader in Alaska was Alexander Baranov, who directed operations energetically and autocratically for a generation. His chief problem was transporting supplies from Siberia across one of the world's stormiest and foggiest seas. Accordingly, Baranov sent expeditions down the American coast

Japanese troops take the fort at Port Arthur in 1904 in a major battle of the Russo-Japanese War. Fifteen thousand Japanese were killed in this battle, ten times the losses of the Russians.

time a hollow shell compared to the powerful Chinese Empire that had expelled the Russians from the Amur valley in the seventeenth century.

Count Muraviev was given extensive vice-regal powers, but he went beyond them and sent out exploratory expeditions that planted the Russian flag on foreign soil. One of his officers, Captain (later Admiral) Nevelskoi, established the fortress of Petropavlovsk on the Kamchatka peninsula. He explored and occupied Sakhalin Island after ousting Japanese settlers, launched steamships on the Amur River, encouraged Russian colonists to settle in the Amur valley, and founded a number of posts along the coast between the mouth of the Amur and the Korean frontier. The Russians were able to expand so easily because the entire region was a no man's land over which the Chinese had only a vague suzerainty and no control whatsoever. In fact, the Chinese court was quite unaware of the Russian measures, and it was the Russian government itself that, in May 1851, informed the Chinese of what had taken place.

Five years later, in 1856, hostilities broke out once more between China and Britain. The Chinese again were badly beaten and forced by the Tientsin Treaties (1858) to open more ports to Western merchants and to make other concessions. Muraviev seized the opportunity to warn the Chinese of the danger of British control of the Amur and to propose joint Russo-Chinese defense of the region. The outcome was the Aigun Treaty (1858) by which Russia obtained the left bank of the Amur to the Ussuri River. Beyond the Ussuri Russia and China were to exercise joint sovereignty over both banks of the river to the ocean.

Muraviev now explored carefully the newly won territories and discovered that the formation of ice on the lower Amur was such that control of both banks was essential for navigation. He also found a magnificent harbor on the coast near the Korean frontier. Despite the provisions of the Aigun Treaty, he founded a city there (1860), which he significantly named Vladivostok, or Lord of the East. Meanwhile, China had become embroiled in further trouble with the Western powers, and in 1860 Peking was occupied by Anglo-French forces. The Russian minister in Peking, Count Nikolai Ignatiev, offered his services as an intermediary and succeeded in getting the allies to evacuate the capital under conditions that were not too unfavorable for China. In return for this service the Chinese government negotiated the Treaty of Peking (1860), giving Russia both banks of the Amur from the Ussuri to the sea and the entire coastal area from the mouth of the Amur to the Korean border. With the winning of these new farflung frontiers (which exist to the present day), Russian expansion in the Far East came to a halt. It was not resumed again until the beginning of the twentieth century, when Tsar Nicholas II attempted to penetrate south into Korea and Manchuria and thereby started a disastrous war with Japan.

Central Asia

In the meantime, the Russians had also been penetrating into central Asia, although their advance in this region did not begin until the second quarter of the nineteenth century. The delay was partly because of the lack of economic incentives comparable to the profitable fur trade in the north. But there were other reasons: The climate and vegetation of central Asia were quite different from that to which the Russians were accustomed. Immediately to the south of Siberia was the steppe country where the Kazakh nomads lived. Still further south began the great desert, dotted with rich oases that supported the ancient Moslem khanates of Bukhara, Khiva, and Kokand. Much stronger militarily than the scattered Siberian tribes, these khanates were able to keep the Russians at arm's length until the late nineteenth century.

During the three decades between 1827 and 1854 the Russians made their first advance into central Asia by conquering the Kazakh steppes to the Syr Darya River. They hoped that the river would serve as a permanent natural frontier, but this was not to be. The ambition of local commanders, far away from the capital and eager for glory and promotion, frequently forced the government's hand and presented it with a fait accompli. The constant harassment of marauding bands also led the Russians to press further in spite of misgivings in St. Petersburg and protests from Britain.

One after another, the legendary centers of central Asian Moslem civilization fell to the advancing Russians—Tashkent in 1865, Bukhara in 1868, Khiva in 1873, Geok-Tepe in 1881, and Merv in 1884. These thrusts greatly alarmed the British in India, and there were recurring crises and rumors of war. But the century passed without open conflict, primarily because the distances were so great and the means of transport so limited. Instead of going to war, the British and the Russians struggled to control intervening states, particularly Persia and Afghanistan.

Russian rule changed central Asia significantly. On the positive side the Russians abolished the widespread slavery and slave trade, freeing 10,000 slaves in Samarkand and its environs alone. The Russians also built railways—notably the Orenburg-Tashkent line—which

helped them both to subjugate and to modernize the area. Thanks to the cheap transportation and the growing demands of the Russian textile industry, cotton cultivation increased spectacularly. In 1884, 300 desiatinas (1 desiatina = 2.7 acres) were planted in cotton on Russian initiative; by 1899, cotton acreage had jumped to 90,000 desiatinas. The Russians also introduced certain agrarian reforms, including a reduction of peasants' taxes and labor obligations to the state and to the landlords.

On the other hand, the Russians' systematic expropriation of Kazakh grazing lands led to a decrease in the size of herds and to widespread famine. The Russians did nothing for the education of the natives, leaving this task almost entirely to the Moslem mullahs. In other areas, such as the judiciary and local government, they were less active than the British were in India. The net result was that prior to the Bolshevik Revolution, which brought as many changes to central Asia as to other regions of the tsarist empire, the mass of Kazakhs, Kirghizes, Turkomans, Uzbeks, and Tajiks were little affected by the coming of the Russians. Despite the railway building and the spreading cotton cultivation, conquerors and conquered lived in different worlds, separated by barriers of language, religion, and customs.

Manchuria and the Russo-Japanese War

In the 1890s Russian interest was shifting from central Asia to the Far East. The Trans-Siberian railway, which was slowly nearing completion, presented new opportunities for Russian economic and political expansion. Count Sergei Witte, the newly appointed minister of finance, presented a report to Tsar Alexander III (November 6, 1892), in which he stated that the Trans-Siberian line would supersede the Suez Canal as the principal trade route to China. He foresaw Russia in the position of arbiter between Asia and the Western world and advocated a Russo-Chinese alliance as the best means for attaining that position.

The outbreak of the Sino-Japanese War in 1895 (see Chapter 31, Section I) paved the way for the alliance that Witte favored. China again was easily defeated, and it repeatedly requested Britain and the United States to mediate. Their refusal forced China to accept the Treaty of Shimonoseki (April 17, 1895), by which it ceded to Japan the Formosa and Pescadores Islands and the Liaotung Peninsula. But Russia, together with Germany and France, now intervened and compelled the Japanese to restore the peninsula.

This assistance impressed the Chinese, who, in the following year, signed a secret treaty with Russia. It provided for mutual assistance in case of Japanese aggression, and it also granted to a joint Russo-Chinese Bank a concession for the construction of the Chinese Eastern Railway across Manchuria to Vladivostok. The bank, nominally a private concern, was actually owned and operated by the Russian government. By the outbreak of the Russo-Japanese War in 1904, it had built a total of 1,596 miles of railway in Manchuria.

Russia's next advance in the Far East was in 1898, with the negotiation of a twenty-five-year lease of the Liaotung peninsula, including strategic Port Arthur. Two years later the Russians took advantage of the disturbances during the Boxer Rebellion to occupy the entire province of Manchuria. This steady Russian encroachment alarmed the Japanese, who had ambitions of their own on the mainland of Asia. Since they were in no position to stop the Russians single-handed, they decided to strengthen themselves by securing an ally. On January 30, 1902, they concluded a military alliance with Britain (details in Chapter 31, Section IV), and, with this backing, they resolved to settle accounts with Russia. In July 1903, the Japanese proposed that Russia should recognize their "preponderant interests" in Korea, and in return they would recognize Russia's "special interests in railway enterprises in Manchuria."

The Russians were divided concerning the Japanese offer. The finance minister, Count Witte, favored acceptance because he was interested in economic penetration rather than in political annexation with its dangers of war. But influential Russian adventurers with vast timber concessions in northern Korea wished to involve their government to advance their personal fortunes. Russian military circles wanted to obtain a base along the Korean coast because of the great distance between their existing bases at Port Arthur and Vladivostok. And certain Russian politicians, concerned by the mounting revolutionary wave in the country, favored a "little victorious war" that would serve as a lightning rod for the popular unrest. There was no doubt in their minds, or in those of the military, that Russia would win in a war with Japan.

This group of adventurers, militarists, and politicians had its way. It secured the dismissal of Witte and virtually rejected the Japanese offer. Assured by their alliance with the British, and apprehensive about the near completion of the Trans-Siberian railway, the Japanese struck promptly and decisively. On February 5, 1904, they broke off negotiations, and three days later they attacked the Russian fleet at Fort Arthur without a formal declaration of war.

In the campaigns that followed, the Japanese David consistently defeated the Russian Goliath. The single-track Trans-Siberian railway proved quite inadequate to supply Russian armies fighting several thousand miles from their industrial centers in European Russia. In the first stage of the war, the Japanese surrounded Port Arthur and, after a siege of 148 days, captured the fortress on December 19, 1904. The second stage consisted of a series of battles on the plains of Manchuria. The Japanese were victorious here also, driving the Russians north of Mukden. These campaigns, however, were not decisive because the Russian armies remained intact and were reinforced and strengthened as communications improved. But on the sea the Japanese won an overwhelming triumph that led to the beginning of peace negotiations. On May 27, 1905, the Russian Baltic fleet arrived at the Tsushima Straits between Japan and Korea after sailing a distance equivalent to more than two-thirds the circumference of the globe. It was attacked at once by a Japanese fleet that was superior both in numbers and in efficiency. Within a few hours virtually all the Russian units had been sunk or captured. The Japanese merely lost a few destroyers.

With this debacle the Russians were ready to discuss peace, especially since the war was very unpopular at home and the 1905 revolution had started. The Japanese also wanted peace negotiations because, although they had won the victories, their still meager resources had been strained by the burden of the war. On September 5, 1905, the Treaty of Portsmouth was signed, by which Russia acknowledged Japan's "paramount political, military, and economic interests" in Korea; surrendered all preferential or exclusive concessions in Manchuria; and ceded to Japan the southern half of Sakhalin Island and the lease of the Liaotung peninsula. In this way the Japanese halted Russia's expansion in the Far East. Not until four decades later, when the Japanese were disastrously defeated in World War II, was Russia able to recover the territories lost at Portsmouth.

IV. FIRST RUSSIAN REVOLUTION AND AFTERMATH, 1905–1914

While the Russo-Japanese War was being fought in the Far East, revolution was spreading behind the lines within Russia. The revolution had its roots in the chronic disaffection of the peasants, the urban workers, and the middle class. This disaffection was aggravated by the war with Japan, which was unpopular to begin with and became increasingly so after the string of defeats. Finally there occurred the so-called "Bloody Sunday" of January 22, 1905. The Imperial Guard fired on an unarmed crowd of several thousand persons who were peacefully carrying a petition to the Winter Palace in St. Petersburg.

Bloody Sunday irreparably smashed the benevolent "Little Father" image of the tsar that so many Russians had traditionally cherished. Citizens throughout the empire turned against the regime, setting off the great Russian Revolution of 1905. This upheaval passed through three stages before the imperial government was able to reassert its authority. The first, between January and October 1905, was the rising wave of revolution. All classes and interests came out against the autocracy. The subject nationalities demanded autonomy, peasants pillaged houses and seized estates, city workers organized councils or "soviets" for revolutionary action, university students everywhere walked out of their classrooms, and the sailors of the Black Sea fleet mutinied and seized their ships. The tsar had no alternative but to yield, so he issued his famous October Manifesto (October 30). It promised freedom of speech, press, and assembly and also granted Russia a constitution and an elective national assembly, or Duma.

During the second stage of the revolution, between October 1905 and January 1906, the uprising continued at high pitch, but the revolutionaries no longer were united. The moderates, consisting mostly of middle-class elements, accepted the October Manifesto, whereas the radicals, including the Social Democrats and the Socialist Revolutionaries, demanded that a constituent assembly, not the tsar's ministers, should prepare the new constitution. To gain their ends the radicals tried to prolong the revolution by organizing more strikes and disturbances. By this time, however, the government was getting stronger and was able to hit back. The signing of the Portsmouth Treaty with Japan on September 5, 1905, freed many troops, and they were sent home to restore order. A timely loan of $400 million from Paris and London greatly strengthened the faltering tsarist government. Consequently, it was able to crush a dangerous workers' revolt that raged in Moscow between December 22 and January 1. Meanwhile, the moderates, alienated by the prolonged violence, were swinging over to the government's side. Thus by the beginning of 1906 the crest of the revolutionary wave had passed.

The third stage of the revolution, from January to July 21, 1906, was that of tsarist consolidation of power. Government forces hunted down radicals and rebellious peasants, in some cases burning whole villages. On May 6 the government issued the so-called Fundamental Laws by which the tsar was proclaimed autocrat and retained complete control over the executive, the armed forces, and foreign policy. The elective Duma was to share legislative power with an upper chamber, and its budgetary power was closely restricted. When the Duma did meet on May 10, it refused to accept the Fundamental Laws and criticized the government violently. A deadlock ensued, and the tsar dissolved the Duma on July 21. The liberal Duma members retaliated by calling on the country to refuse to pay taxes. But the response was feeble. The fact is that by this time the revolutionary tide had ebbed and the First Russian Revolution had run its course.

Although the revolution failed, it left its imprint on the course of Russia's history. Russia now had a constitutional regime, even though the Duma had little power. A second Duma was elected in February 1907, but it proved to be even more defiant than the first. The govern-

On Bloody Sunday, January 22, 1905, troops of Tsar Nicholas II fired on a peaceful procession of workers who sought to present a petition at the Winter Palace in Saint Petersburg. After this event, there was little chance of reconciliation between the Tsarist government and the Russian working class.

ment then restricted the franchise so drastically that the third and fourth Dumas elected in 1907 and 1912 were acceptably conservative and subservient. Nevertheless, the absolutist tsarist autocracy ended with the October Manifesto, and after World War I began, the Duma came increasingly into its own until it was swept away by the Bolshevik Revolution.

The events of 1905 are important also because of their contribution to Russian revolutionary experience and tradition. Soviets were organized in the cities and proved their value as organs for revolutionary action. It is true that after 1906 a lull seemed to set in, but it was only a brief respite. The number of workers on strike declined from 1 million in 1905 to 4,000 in 1910. But by 1912, the number had risen again to 1 million and it remained at that level during the next two years. Then all discord ceased abruptly with the outbreak of World War I. But with the catastrophic defeats at the front, new storm clouds gathered, and the tsarist regime entered a new time of troubles from which it never emerged. Thus, the Russian Revolution of 1905 stands out as a dress rehearsal for the world-shaking revolution of 1917.

SUGGESTED READINGS

Aspects of the relations between Russia and the West are treated by D. W. Treadgold, *The West in Russia and China*, Vol. I, *Russia 1472–1917* (Cambridge University, 1973); W. L. Blackwell, *The Beginnings of Russian Industrialization, 1800–1860* (Princeton University, 1968); T. H. Von Laue, *Sergei Witte and the Industrialization of Russia* (Columbia University, 1963); M. Malia, *Russia Under Western Eyes: From Peter the Great to Khrushchev* (Wiley, 1964); and most recently, the study by L. Hughes, *Russia in the Age of Peter the Great* (Yale University, 1998).

For Russian expansion in central Asia, see G. V. Lantzeff and R. A Pierce, *Eastward to Empire: Exploration and Conquest on the Russian Open Frontier to 1750* (McGill University, 1973); E. E. Bacon, *Central Asia Under Russian Rule: A Study in Culture Change* (Cornell University, 1966); and S. Becker, *Russia's Protectorates in Central Asia: Bukhara and Khiva, 1865–1924* (Harvard University, 1968).

CHAPTER
29

The Middle East

It is not open to question that all social changes in the Near East during the past century or so have arisen, directly or indirectly, from the impact of our Western society and the penetration of Western techniques and ideas.

H. A. R. Gibb

The West's influence on the Middle East was quite different from its influence on Russia, and the response of the Middle Eastern peoples was just as different. A new group of peoples, religions, and cultures was involved, to be sure, but there was also a different political and social organization. The Ottoman Empire, which embraced most of the Middle East during the nineteenth century, remained a hodgepodge of peoples, religions, and conflicting loyalties. We noted in Chapter 18 that the empire was organized as a theocracy on the basis of ecclesiastical communities rather than ethnic groups. These communities, the most important of which were the Greek Orthodox, Roman Catholic, and Jewish, were allowed considerable autonomy under their respective ecclesiastical leaders. Thus for centuries the various Moslem peoples (for example, Turks, Arabs, Albanians, and Kurds) and the various Christian peoples (for example, Serbs, Greeks, Bulgars, and Ruma-nians) lived side by side in semiautonomous and self-sufficient communities. Individual non-Moslems did suffer discrimination regarding dress, behavior, living areas, and higher taxes. Yet each community was allowed its own church, language, schools, and local government, as long as it accepted the sultan's authority and paid taxes to the imperial treasury.

The significance of this loose imperial organization is that Western ideas and pressures encountered a variety of cultures and conditions. Consequently, the West did not have a uniform impact on the Ottoman lands. Therefore, in analyzing the nature of that impact, it is essential to take into account the marked variations in regional conditions and responses. For this reason we shall now consider, not the Ottoman Empire as a whole, but rather its three main regions in turn—the Balkan peninsula, with its predominantly Christian population; Asia Minor, with its ruling Moslem Turkish population; and the provinces south of Asia Minor, with their Moslem Arab peoples.

I. BALKAN CHRISTIANS

The Balkan peoples were under Turkish rule for four centuries or more. It is often assumed that these were centuries of unrelieved tyranny, that the oppressed Christians only yearned for freedom and waited impatiently for an opportunity to revolt. This interpretation does not fit the actual course of events. The various Balkan peoples greatly outnumbered the few Turks living in their midst. They lived in compact groups and retained their languages and religions. If they had been eager to revolt, they could have caused more trouble for the Turks than they actually did. Yet during the early centuries, the Turks had no more trouble ruling their Christian subjects in the Balkans than their Moslem subjects in Asia.

The explanation is that the Turkish conquerors were efficient and benevolent compared to the Byzantine emperors, Frankish nobles, Venetian signors, and Bulgarian and Serbian princes who formerly had ruled the Balkan lands. Ottoman administration was stern but just, taxation was light, and the non-Moslems enjoyed a degree of tolerance unparalleled in Christian Europe. During the eighteenth and nineteenth centuries, however, this situation changed drastically. The decline in Ottoman power and efficiency during this period led to widespread corruption and extortion, which in turn drove the now oppressed and embittered Balkan Christians to take up arms in self-defense. At the same time the Balkan peoples, for a number of reasons, were being affected and aroused by a variety of influences from the West.

The Balkan peoples were affected earlier and more profoundly by the West than any of the other ethnic groups of the Ottoman Empire. Mostly Christians, they were more receptive to the Christian West than were the Moslem Turks and Arabs. The territorial contiguity of the Balkan lands to the rest of Europe made it easier for persons and goods and ideas to converge on the Balkan peninsula from across the Danube and the Adriatic, Mediterranean, and Black seas. The increasing demand for food imports in western Europe stimulated agriculture in the Balkans, especially the cultivation of the new colonial products, cotton and maize. The export of these commodities in turn contributed to the growth of a class of native Balkan merchants and mariners. The expansion of trade also stimulated the demand and output of handicraft products. Important manufacturing centers appeared in various parts of the peninsula, frequently in isolated mountain areas where the artisans could practice their crafts with a minimum of Turkish interference. Finally, the rise of commerce and industry promoted the growth of a merchant marine along the Adriatic coast and among the Aegean Islands. The new Balkan marine exported products such as cotton, maize, dyeing materials, wine, oil, and fruits, and it brought back mostly colonial products and manufactured goods—spices, sugar, woolens, glass, watches, guns, and gunpowder.

The significance of this economic renaissance is that it created a middle class of merchants, artisans, shipowners, and mariners that was particularly susceptible and sympathetic to Western ideas and institutions. These people, by their very nature, were dissatisfied with Ottoman rule, which by this time had become ineffective and corrupt. Merchants and seamen who journeyed to foreign lands, and who frequently resided there, could not help contrasting the security and enlightenment they witnessed abroad with the deplorable conditions at home. Very naturally, many concluded that their own future, and that of their fellow Balkan citizens, depended on the earliest possible removal of Turkish rule.

Serbian merchants in southern Hungary, Bulgarian merchants in southern Russia, and Greek merchants scattered widely in the main cities of Europe all contributed to the intellectual awakening of their fellow compatriots. They did so by publishing books and newspapers in their native languages, by establishing schools and libraries in their home towns and villages, and by financing the education of their young men in foreign universities. All this meant not only more education but a new type of education. It was no longer primarily religious. Instead, it was profoundly influenced by the current Enlightenment in western Europe.

Western influence in the Balkans became more directly political and inflammatory during the French revolutionary and Napoleonic era. Politically conscious elements were much impressed by the uprisings in Paris; by the slogan "Liberty, Equality, Fraternity"; and by the spectacle of Napoleon toppling over one dynasty after another. A contemporary Greek revolutionary testified, "The French Revolution in general awakened the minds of all men.... All the Christians of the Near East prayed to God that France should wage war against the Turks, and they believed that they would be freed.... But when Napoleon made no move, they began to take measures for freeing themselves."[1]

The tempo of national awakening varied greatly from one Balkan people to another. The Greeks came first because of certain favorable circumstances: the numerous contacts with the West; their glorious classical and Byzantine heritage, which stimulated national pride; and their Greek Orthodox Church, which embodied and preserved national consciousness. After the Greeks came the Serbs, who enjoyed a high degree of local self-government as well as the stimulating influence of the large Serbian settlements in southern Hungary. These advantages of the Greeks and the Serbs suggest the reasons for the slower rate of national revival among the other Balkan peoples. The Bulgars had no direct ties with the West and were located near the Ottoman capital and the solid Turkish settlements in Thrace and eastern Macedonia. The Rumanians suffered from a sharp social stratification that was unique in the Balkans and that produced a cultivated upper class and an inert peasant mass. The Albanians were the worst off, with their primitive tribal organization and their division among three creeds, Orthodoxy, Catholicism, and Islam.

These factors explain why in place of a common Balkan revolution against Ottoman rule, there were separate uprisings ranging from the early nineteenth century to the early twentieth. The Greeks won complete independence from the Turks following a protracted War of Independence between 1821 and 1829. The Serbs had revolted earlier in 1804 but only gained an autonomous status within the Ottoman Empire in 1815. It was not until 1878 that the Serbian Principality gained full independence and became the Kingdom of Serbia. The Rumanians came next, winning autonomy in 1859 and full independence in 1878. The Bulgarians followed later, gaining autonomy in 1878 and independence in 1908. Three of

Russo-Turkish wars. This nineteenth-century line engraving shows the Cossack Imperial Guard on horses.

The Christianity of the Balkans is portrayed here as the garrison of Belgrade pledges its allegiance to King Milan I.

these Balkan peoples, the Serbs, Greeks, and Bulgarians, combined forces in 1912 to drive the Turks completely out of the peninsula. They were successful on the battlefield, and despite a fratricidal war amongst the victors, the Turks were compelled in 1913 to surrender all their remaining territories in the Balkans with the exception of an enclave stretching around the straits from Constantinople to Adrianople.

In this manner the imperial Ottoman frontiers shrank from the walls of Vienna in 1683 to the Danube in 1815, to the mid-Balkans in 1878, and to the environs of Constantinople in 1913. As the empire receded, independent Balkan states took its place—Greece, Serbia, Rumania, Bulgaria, and, in 1912, Albania. The West contributed decisively to this resurgence of the Balkan peoples by providing a revolutionary nationalist ideology, and by stimulating the growth of a middle class that was ready to act on the basis of that ideology.

II. TURKS

The West affected the Turks much less and much later than it did the Balkan Christians. Various factors explain this difference. The most important of these probably were the Turks' Moslem religion and their lack of a native middle class.

If the Christian faith of the Balkan peoples constituted a bond with the West, the Moslem faith of the Turks was a barrier—and a most formidable one because of the long history of antagonism and conflict between Christianity and Islam. The Turks also were little affected by the West because they never developed their own middle class. They had no interest in or respect for commercial pursuits, so that the Ottoman bourgeoisie was largely Greek, Armenian, and Jewish. By contrast, the Turks were either peasants, who were generally apathetic, or teachers and judges in the Moslem ecclesiastical organization—which almost always meant that they were bitterly anti-Western—or else they were officeholders in the imperial bureaucracy—in which case they usually were interested only in retaining their posts and advancing in rank. When we think of the vital role played by Greek, Serbian, and Bulgarian merchants in their respective countries, the significance of the Turkish situation is obvious. With no comparable group of Turkish merchants, the rare advocates of reform among the Turks found themselves without any following. They found themselves, in other words, in the same plight as did the Decembrists in Russia in 1825, and for the same reason.

Yet during the course of the nineteenth century the Ottoman Empire, like the Russian, was penetrated, influenced, and controlled by

THE SICK MAN OF EUROPE

*During the nineteenth century the Ottoman Empire was known as the "sick man of Europe." Why it was sick is evident in the following account by the British merchant and diplomat Sir Charles Eliot. He describes his efforts to interest the vali (governor) of Karakeui in development projects and the vali's negative response.**

I suppose I might be described as a concession hunter or a commission agent. The essence of my trade is to make Orientals buy what they don't want—anything from matches to railroads. I bribe them to purchase my wares and they bribe me to put down in the bill (which the Ottoman Government pays) a much larger sum than I have actually received. So we both make money. . . .

"If you would only develop," [I told him,] "the commercial and material resources of your Empire, Christians and Turks would have a common interest. The Christians would want to support your Empire as the source of their prosperity.

"We Turks [replied the Vali,] don't know how to make money; we only know how to take it. You want to introduce a system in which Christians will be able to squeeze all the money out of us and our country and keep it. Who profit by all these concessions for railways, harbours, and quays? Franks, Jews, Greeks, and Armenians, but never a Moslim. Do you remember that railway I helped you to build from Durograd to Moropolis? Franks travel by it, Greeks and Armenians sell the tickets, and in

the end all the money goes to the Jews. But what Turk wants the railway, and how much has any Turk made out of it?"

I might have said, "Exactly as much as passed into your Highness's pockets when the concession was arranged," but I forbore from this obvious retort and let the Vali go on. "This country is a dish of soup," he said, "and no one has any real intention except to eat it. We eat it in the good old-fashioned way with a big spoon. You bore little holes in the bottom of the soup-bowl and drain it off with pipes. Then you propose that the practice of eating soup with spoons should be abolished as uncivilised, because you know we have no gimlets and don't understand this trick of drinking through pipes."

"But surely your Highness has had experience yourself of the advantages which Osmanlis may obtain from commercial enterprises and—"

"Oh, I have had a suck at the pipe," said the Vali, "but, after all, I prefer eating with the spoon."

*Charles Eliot, *Turkey in Europe*, 2nd ed. (Edward Arnold, 1908), pp. 94–97.

the West in numerous direct and indirect ways. Of the several channels of penetration, the earliest, and in some respects the most effective, was the military. Like the Russians, the Turks found it necessary to adopt European military techniques for self-preservation. During the latter half of the nineteenth century the Western pow-

ers actively encouraged the Turks to modernize their military forces in order to block Russian expansion into the Middle East. But of the many young men who were sent abroad to study in foreign military academies, some inevitably learned about Western ideologies as well as Western military techniques. Thus it is not sur-

The first Ottoman parliament in session 1877, from the Illustrated London News of April 14, 1877.

prising that when the old Ottoman regime was finally overthrown in 1908, the coup was executed, not by a political party or a mass movement, but by an army clique.

In the field of religion, also, the West affected the Moslem Middle East. Missionaries were preaching and founding schools throughout the empire. By 1875 the American missionaries alone had 240 schools with 8,000 pupils. Most of the latter were Armenians and other Christians, since proselytism among Moslems was forbidden. But a fair number of Turkish students were to be found in the foreign colleges scattered throughout the empire.

At least as significant as this cultural impact was the West's economic penetration of the Ottoman Empire. In 1869, after ten years of construction by a European syndicate headed by the French diplomat and promoter Ferdinand de Lesseps, the Suez Canal was opened. The effect of the canal was to place the Ottoman Empire once more on the main trade route between Europe and Asia. At the same time the Ottoman government was falling hopelessly into debt to European governments and to private financiers. They contracted their first loan in 1854, and by 1875 their debts totaled £200 million sterling. Some £12 million sterling a year was required to meet annuities, interest,

and sinking fund, a sum that amounted to a little more than half the total revenues of the empire. In addition to this hold over Ottoman public finances, foreign interests had control over the Turkish banking and railway systems, irrigation works, mining enterprises, and municipal public utilities.

The effect of all these Western pressures and controls cannot be measured precisely, but there can be no doubt that they gradually cracked the hitherto impregnable and monolithic Islamic structure. The actual cracking was done by Turkish army officers who had studied in the West, where they realized that Sultan Abdul Hamid's opposition to all change was obsolete and dangerous. In July 1908 these officers threatened to march on Constantinople unless the Sultan accepted a constitution, which he did.

During the few years before the outbreak of World War I in 1914, the Turkish military leaders tried to strengthen their empire, but with little success. They tried to promote loyalty to the Ottoman Empire and the Ottoman Sultan, but the more they persisted, the greater the opposition. It was too late to deny the inexorable awakening of Albanians, Arabs, Greeks, Bulgars and other subject peoples. The result was a vicious circle of revolt and repres-

The construction of the Suez Canal.

sion, which left the Ottoman Empire in turmoil until 1914, when the Turks made their fateful decision to join the Central Powers, a decision that doomed the Ottoman Empire to extinction.

III. ARABS

The West's impact on the modern Arab world may be said to begin on the day in 1798 when Napoleon landed in Egypt with his army of invasion. Napoleon's real objective was to strike at Britain's position in the East, but after Admiral Nelson destroyed his fleet near Alexandria, Napoleon gave up his objective and returned home. Yet his expedition had a lasting effect on Egypt, for it was more than a military affair. It was also a cultural incursion by the West into the heart of the Arab world. Napoleon brought with him the first printing press to reach Egypt, and he was accompanied by scientists, who deciphered the ancient hieroglyphic writing, and by engineers, who prepared plans for joining the Mediterranean and Red seas.

Napoleon also smashed the power of the established ruling class in Egypt during his brief campaign in that country. This paved the way for the rise to power of an Albanian adventurer of genius, Mehemet Ali. Mehemet Ali is historically significant because he was the first Middle Eastern potentate who sensed the significance of Western technology and used it efficiently to serve his purposes. His achievements were numerous and revolutionary. He started Egypt's modern system of irrigation; introduced the cultivation of cotton, which quickly became the country's greatest resource; reopened the harbor of Alexandria; encouraged foreign trade; sent students to study abroad; opened schools of all

Muhammad Ali (1769–1849). The famous viceroy of Egypt is depicted as an equestrian in this portrait.

varieties, though he himself was illiterate; and established a School of Translation, which translated into Arabic about two thousand European books between 1835 and 1848. Mehemet Ali also engaged foreign experts who helped him build the first modern army and navy in the Middle East. He even tried valiantly to build a modern industrial structure in Egypt, and he did erect a considerable number of factories in Cairo and Alexandria. These enterprises, however, eventually failed because of domestic deficiencies and the opposition of the European powers to Egyptian expansionism and industrialization.

Yet for a time these accomplishments transformed Egypt into a formidable power. Mehemet easily overran Arabia, the Sudan, the island of Crete, and the entire Levant coast that today includes Israel, Lebanon, and Syria. His plan was to create an Arab Empire out of the Ottoman provinces south of Asia Minor. But this was not acceptable to Britain, which preferred the weak Ottoman Empire rather than a strong Arab Empire dominating the routes to India. Mehemet was forcefully compelled to surrender all his possessions except Egypt, where he remained the hereditary and autonomous ruler. Great power interests had postponed the realization of Arab unity and independence and would continue to do so for over a century.

SUGGESTED READINGS

Bibliographical guides are available in R. H. Davison, *The Near and Middle East: An Introduction to History and Bibliography* (Service Center for Teachers of History, 1959); and B. Lewis and P. M. Holt, *Historians of the Middle East* (Oxford University, 1962).

General histories of the Balkans and the Near East include L. S. Stavrianos, *The Balkans Since 1453* (Holt, Rinehart and Winston, 1958); B. Jelavich, 2 vols., *History of the Balkans* (Cambridge University, 1983); and B. Lewis, *The Middle East: A Brief History of the Last 2000 Years* (Scribner, 1996). For the West's cultural impact on the Middle East, see D. Lerner, *The Passing of Traditional Society: Modernizing the Middle East* (Free Press, 1958); B. Lewis, *The Middle East and the West* (University of Indiana, 1964), and his *Muslim Discovery of Europe* (Norton, 1982). For the West's economic impact, see C. Issawi, ed., *The Economic History of the Middle East, 1800–1914* (University of Chicago, 1966); and J. R. Lampe and M. R. Jackson, *Balkan Economic History: 1550–1950* (Indiana University, 1982).

NOTE

1. Ch.Photios, *Apomnemoneumata peri tes Hellenikes Epanastaseos* [Memoirs on the Greek Revolution], Vol. I (Athens, 1899), p. 1.

CHAPTER

30

India

India is the one great non-Western society that has been, not merely attacked and hit, but overrun and conquered outright by Western arms, and not merely conquered by Western arms but ruled, after that, by Western administrators. ...India's experience of the West has thus been more painful and more humiliating than China's or Turkey's, and much more so than Russia's or Japan's.

Arnold J. Toynbee

Prior to the appearance of the British, India had been invaded time and time again—by the Aryans, Greeks, Scythians, Turks, and Moguls. Each of these invaders left its mark on the great subcontinent, contributing in varying degrees to the evolution of India's traditional society. The historical role of the British was to disrupt and remold this traditional society. The other invaders wrought changes mostly at the top, but the British impact was felt down to the level of the village. The reason for this difference between the British and their predecessors is to be found in the dynamic and expansive nature of British society, which consequently undermined the comparatively static and self-sufficient society of India. To understand this process of penetration and transformation, it is necessary first to study the character of the traditional Indian society. Then we shall consider the nature of the British impact and the Indian reaction to it.

I. INDIA'S TRADITIONAL SOCIETY

The basic unit of traditional Indian society was the village, as it was in most of the rest of the world, including Europe, in the preindustrial period. Within the village it was not the individual that mattered but rather the joint family and the caste. This group form of organization was a source of social stability but also of national weakness. Loyalty to the family, to the caste, and to the village was the primary consideration, and this prevented the formation of a national spirit.

The land was regarded by immemorial custom as the property of the sovereign, who was entitled to a share of the gross produce or its equivalent. This constituted the land tax that was the main source of state revenue and the main burden of the cultivator. The share paid to the state varied from period to period, ranging from a sixth, to a third, or even to a half. Usually the responsibility for making this payment, whether in produce or in money, was collective, resting on the village as a unit. The peasant family had hereditary right to the use of the land as long as they paid their share of the taxes.

Transportation and communication facilities were primitive, so the villages tended to become economically and socially self-sufficient. Each village had its potter, who turned out on a wheel the simple utensils needed by the peasants; its carpenter, who constructed and repaired the buildings and plows; its blacksmith, who made axes and other necessary tools; its clerk, who attended to legal documents and wrote correspondence between people of different villages; its town herdsman, who looked after the cattle and returned them at night to the various owners; its priest and its teacher, who frequently were combined in the same person; and its astrologer, who indicated the auspicious time for planting, for harvesting, for marriages, and other important events. These artisans and pro-

fessional men served their villages on something akin to a barter basis. They were paid for their services with grain from the cultivating households or with tax-free village land for their own use. These hereditary and traditional divisions of occupation and function were turned into obligations by the caste system.

The political structure of the village consisted of an annually elected council of five or more, known to this day as the Panchayat (pancha meaning "five"). The Panchayat, which normally consisted of caste leaders and village elders, met periodically to dispense local justice; to collect taxes; to keep in repair the village wells, roads, and irrigation systems; to see that the craftsworkers and other professionals were provided for; and to extend hospitality to travelers passing through the village and to furnish them with guides. The village had little contact with the outside world apart from the payment of the land tax and the irregular demand for forced labor. The combination of agriculture and hand industry made each village largely independent of the rest of the country except for a few indispensables like salt and iron. Consequently, the towns that existed in traditional India were not industrial in character. Rather, they were religious centers such as Benares, Puri,

A group of men of the Banjara tribal community in India engaged in a discussion with village elders.

and Allahabad; political centers such as Poona, Tanjore, and Delhi; or commercial centers such as Mirzapur on the trade route from central India to Bengal.

Some Indian writers have romanticized this traditional society, painting an idyllic picture of village life, continuing peacefully generation after generation in its slow and satisfying rhythm. It is true that the existence of group organizations such as the joint family, the caste, and the village council provided the peasants with both psychological and economic security. Each individual had recognized duties, rights, and status in his or her native village. If the central government was sufficiently strong to maintain order and to keep the land tax down to the customary sixth of the harvest, then the peasant masses did lead a peaceful and contented existence. But as often as not the central government was too weak to keep order, and the villagers were mercilessly fleeced by greedy tax collectors and by robber bands. This was the case in the seventeenth century when the Mogul imperial structure was disintegrating. Yet even in such trying periods the Indian village was not transformed in any basic respect. Individual regions were ravaged, but eventually the cultivators returned to resume their traditional institutions and their traditional ways of life.

II. BRITISH CONQUEST

The Indian village, then, remained relatively unchanging and self-sufficient until the coming of the British. But before examining the impact of these Western intruders, we shall consider why they were able with comparatively little difficulty to conquer the whole of India during the late eighteenth and nineteenth centuries. This is a significant question because for 250 years after the Portuguese Albuquerque had captured Goa early in the sixteenth century, the Europeans had been able to cling only to a few stations along the coasts. Then within a few decades the balance of power shifted decisively, and the whole of the Indian subcontinent fell under British rule.

One reason for this outcome was the decline of Mogul power and authority (see Chapter 18, Section III). This enabled Moslem warlords and provincial governors to declare their independence and establish personal dynasties in various regions. At the same time the Hindus asserted themselves by organizing the powerful Maratha confederacy, with its center in the city of Poona. The Marathas won control of the entire Deccan peninsula and then, about 1740, began to invade northern India with the intention of displacing the declining Moguls. Thus India was in an anarchical state in the eighteenth century, with various officials seeking to convert their posts into hereditary princedoms and plotting with any power, whether Indian or foreign, if it would serve to realize their ambitions. The British consequently were able to play off one Indian prince against another until they became the masters of the entire peninsula. This was altogether different from China, where the Manchu imperial structure remained intact and compelled all foreigners to deal directly with the emperor in Peking.

Another important factor that contributed substantially to the vulnerability of India was the rise of a powerful merchant class whose economic interests were bound up with those of the Western companies. These companies were allowed to trade relatively freely in India (they were almost entirely excluded in China). During the sixteenth century India's economy was little affected by the trade because it was confined largely to spices and textiles. But in the seventeenth century various commercial crops such as indigo, mustard seed, and hemp, as well as saltpeter, were exported in large quantities. Bengal was the center of this trade, and in that province there now arose wealthy native merchants who dominated the local economy and who were becoming increasingly restless under the corrupt and inefficient rule of the Mogul officials. One of these merchants, Jagat Seth, bought the allegiance of the generals who supposedly were under the orders of the nawab, or governor, of Bengal. At the Battle of Plassey (1757) these generals refrained from fighting against the British, who lost only sixty-five men in that fateful encounter. As one Indian historian has put it, Plassey was "a transaction, not a battle."

The British now were the actual rulers of Bengal, though they continued to recognize puppet nawabs as a matter of form. In 1764, after defeating the Mogul's forces, the East India

An Indian artist's painting of James Todd (c. 1880) riding in a ceremonial procession on a royal elephant.

Company was granted the Diwani, or the right of tax collection, in the rich provinces of Bengal, Bihar, and Orissa. This opened up many opportunities for profit making and outright extortion, and the English agents exploited them to the full. By raising the taxes, controlling the trade, and accepting numerous "gifts" from native officials, they amassed fortunes for themselves and their superiors in London.

The foothold in Bengal gave the British the base and the resources necessary for further expansion in India. They began pushing northward in a search for natural frontiers. To the northeast, in Himalayan Nepal, they defeated the Gurkhas, who henceforth fought on the side of the British. Likewise to the northwest they finally defeated the proud Sikhs of the Punjab. Thus by the middle of the nineteenth century the British were the masters of all India.

III. BRITISH RULE

We have seen that the East India Company was at first very exploitive in its administration of the Indian territories it controlled. The excesses aroused public opinion in Britain and prompted Parliament to pass acts in 1773 and 1784 that placed the company under the supervision of the London government. The company continued to trade, and its servants and soldiers continued to govern and fight in India, but it functioned under the watchful eye of Parliament and the British government. This arrangement continued, with various modifications, until the Indian Mutiny of 1857.

The mutiny was not the national movement or war of independence that some Indian writers have called it. Rather, it was primarily a military outbreak that was exploited by certain discontented princes and landlords whose interests had been harmed by the British. Lord Dalhousie, the governor-general between 1848 and 1856, had dispossessed many princes and aroused uneasiness and suspicion among those who remained. Other groups, too, were dissatisfied: Conservative elements of the Indian population were deeply disturbed by the introduction of the railway and telegraph; the opening of Western-type schools; the aggressive activities of certain Christian missionaries; the legalization of remarriage by widows; and the abolition of practices such as infanticide and suttee, or the self-cremation of widows on their husband's funeral pyres. The Sepoys, as the Indian soldiers serving in the British forces were called, were disaffected because of prolonged campaigning in distant lands and the refusal of extra allowances for such service. The spark that set off the uprising was the introduction of cartridges that were greased with cow and pig fat, obnoxious to both the Hindus and the Moslems. All these factors combined

A tea planter on his estate. One of the symbols of the raj, the great tea plantations of Sri Lanka and northeastern India—especially those of Assam—were major sources of wealth for the British overlords. They were also partly responsible for the deforestation of much of the subcontinent that occurred under British colonial rule in the nineteenth century.

to make the mutiny assume proportions of a popular uprising in certain scattered regions.

When the mutiny began on May 10, 1857, the British were caught by surprise and forced to go on the defensive. But the revolt did not spread throughout the country. It was confined largely to the north. Even there most of the important native states remained loyal to the British and gave invaluable assistance. Thus after about four months the British were able to counterattack, and by July 1858 the mutiny had been crushed. Both sides were guilty of brutality. The Indians murdered many captives, and the English burned down villages and indiscriminately killed the inhabitants.

A month after the suppression of the mutiny, Parliament passed the India Act, ending the rule of the East India Company and substituting that of the Crown. Henceforth India was ruled by a vast hierarchy with its base in India and its apex in London in the person of the secretary of state for India. The efficiency of British rule in India is reflected in the composition of the Indian bureaucracy; in 1900 there were a total of 4,000 British civilian administrators in the country compared to 500,000 Indians. And in 1910, the Indian army comprised 69,000 Britishers and 130,000 Indians. This small number of British soldiers and bureaucrats ruled a vast subcontinent with a vast population.

IV. BRITISH IMPACT

The British impact on India was felt first in the economic field, and naturally so since the British arrived in India in search of markets and commodities. There was a strong demand in the nineteenth century for Indian raw materials such as jute, oilseeds, wheat, and cotton. These commodities were transported to the seaports by a newly built railroad network totalling 4,000 miles by 1870 and 41,000 miles by 1939. The opening of the Suez Canal also facilitated the export of Indian raw materials by reducing the distance traversed by freighters between London and Karachi from 10,800 to 6,100 miles. Thus India became one of the world's important

Faces of the raj. *A tennis party at the Residency, Kapurkala, Panjab, ca. 1894.*

sources of raw materials. And because of the high prices commanded by these materials, India was left with a favorable balance of trade throughout the nineteenth century.

The resulting capital surplus could have been used to develop modern industry. The fact that this was not done doomed India to its present critical state of underdevelopment. Britain made no attempt to encourage manufacturing in India, and in certain crucial areas, such as textiles, actively discouraged it. Thus there was no chance to erect tariffs to protect Indian infant industries against the tidal wave of cheap machine-made products from British factories. Indian economic historians describe this as a case of "aborted modernization." India had entered the world market and earned large sums of capital with no structural change in its outmoded national economy. In place of the economic modernization that had occurred in Europe, the British and their associates "skimmed cash crops off the surface of an immobilized agrarian society."[1]

Meanwhile, thanks to Western medical science, health measures, and famine-relief arrangements, India's population rose from 255 million in 1872 to 305 million in 1921. Similar population growth had occurred earlier in Europe but had been absorbed by new factories in the cities. Since no such industrialization

occurred in India, the new extra millions could only fall back on agriculture. They naturally put a terrible overpressure on the land. And this remains to the present day one of the most acute problems of the Indian economy—and indeed of most Third World economies since they also suffer from "aborted modernization," and for the same reasons.

British rule affected India profoundly in intellectual matters as well as economic. The impact began in 1823 when the British appointed a Committee on Public Instruction to determine educational policy. During the following decades a national system of education was worked out. It was made up of universities, training colleges for teachers, high schools, and vernacular elementary schools designed for the masses. Between 1885 and 1900 the number of students in colleges and universities rose from 11,000 to 23,000, and those in secondary schools from 429,000 to 633,000. At the same time the introduction of the printing press greatly stimulated intellectual life in India. Sanskrit works became public property rather than the jealously guarded monopoly of Brahmins, and newspapers appeared in the various modern Indian languages as well as in English.

These developments affected the intellectual climate of India profoundly. They did not touch the masses, who remained completely

Cotton weaving in India in the early nineteenth century.

illiterate. Nor, at first, did they reach the Moslems, who remained generally hostile to the new schools and books. Thus, English education became almost the exclusive possession of a small Hindu upper class. But this was enough to start off a chain reaction that has continued to the present day. English education created a new class of Indians familiar with foreign languages and cultures and committed to liberal and rational ideologies. This Western-educated class used European ideology to attack British domination and to organize a nationalist movement that eventually culminated in an independent India.

V. INDIAN NATIONALISM

Britain's intellectual impact stimulated an upsurge and a creativity in Indian thought and culture that is commonly known as the Indian Renaissance. To appreciate the significance of this movement, we should note that when the British arrived on the scene, Hinduism was in a rather depressed and demoralized state. During the preceding seven hundred years of Moslem domination, Hinduism had been looked down on as the idolatrous religion of a subject race. It lacked prestige, organization, and active leadership. But when the British overthrew Mogul rule, Hinduism for the first time in seven centuries was on a par with Islam. And when the British opened their schools, the Hindus, unlike the Moslems, flocked to them eagerly. By so doing, they benefited in two ways: They filled the posts in the new bureaucracy, and they experienced an intellectual revival because of their Western contacts.

The stimulus of the West provoked three types of reaction or three schools of thought among the Hindus, although the lines were by no means clear-cut, and there was much overlapping. The first was wholeheartedly and uncritically pro-Western and antitraditional: Everything Western was accepted as superior and preferable.

The second reaction was one of complete rejection. The West was admittedly stronger, but its ideas were subversive and its customs repugnant. No true Indians, Hindus, or Moslems should compromise with the evil West. Rather, they should withdraw as far as possible from contact with the foreigner and live their own lives in the traditional way. Proponents of this view regarded caste rule as unchangeable, accepted the authority of the Hindu classics without reservations, and opposed such reforms as the abolition of suttee or of infanticide.

The third and most common reaction to the West represented a compromise between worship and outright rejection. It accepted the essence of Western secularism and learning, but it also sought to reform Hinduism from within and to preserve its basic truths while ridding it of corruptions and grossly unhuman practices. The outstanding leader of this school of thought was Ram Mohan Roy, widely venerated as the "father of modern India." Born in 1772 in a devout Brahman family of Bengal, he broke with his parents over the spectacle of his sister's torture on the funeral pyre of her husband. An insatiable student, he mastered Persian, Arabic,

INDIA FOR THE INDIANS

B. G. Tilak was an early Indian nationalist who demanded that the British get out and who raised the slogan "India for the Indians." This nationalist feeling is clear in the following selection from a speech by Tilak in 1906.*

One fact is that this alien government has ruined the country. In the beginning, all of us were taken by surprise. We were almost dazed. We thought that everything that the rulers did was for our good and that this English government has descended from the clouds to save us from the invasions of Tamerlane and Chingis Khan, and, as they say, not only from foreign invasions but from internecine [civil] warfare. We felt happy for a time, but it soon came to light that the peace which was established in this country did this. . .—that we were prevented from going at each other's throats, so that a foreigner might go at the throat of us all. Pax Britannica [British peace or rule] has been established in this country in order that a foreign government may exploit the country. That this is the effect of this Pax Britannica is being gradually realized in these days. It was an unhappy circumstance that it was not realized sooner. . . . English education, growing poverty, and better familiarity with our rulers, opened our eyes and our leaders. . . . Your industries are ruined utterly, ruined by foreign rule; your wealth is going out of the country

and you are reduced to the lowest level which no human being can occupy. In this state of things, is there any other remedy by which you can help yourself? The remedy is not petitioning but boycott. We say prepare your forces, organize your power, and then go to work so that they cannot refuse you what you demand. . . . Every Englishman knows that they are a mere handful in this country and it is the business of every one of them to befool you in believing that you are weak and they are strong. This is politics. We have been deceived by such policy so long. What the new party wants you to do is realize the fact that your future rests entirely in your own hands. . . . We shall not give them assistance to collect revenue and keep peace. We shall not assist them in fighting beyond the frontiers or outside India with Indian blood and money. We shall not assist them in carrying on the administration of justice. We shall have our own courts, and when time comes we shall not pay taxes. Can you do that by your united efforts? If you can, you are free from tomorrow. . . .

*B. G. Tilak, *His Writings and Speeches* (Ganesh and Co., 1923), pp. 55–67.

and Sanskrit and then learned English and entered the service of the government. He was fascinated by Western thought and religions, and he studied Greek and Hebrew in order to read the Scriptures in the original. Roy rejected formal doctrinal Christianity but accepted its humanitarian message. He also reinterpreted Hinduism in his Brahmo Samaj, or Society of God, a new reformed sect of Hinduism that he founded. The Samaj was a synthesis of the doc-trines of the European Enlightenment with the philosophical views of the Upanishads.

Ram Mohan Roy was the pioneer leader not only of India's religious renaissance but also of its political awakening, or nationalist movement. This was a new phenomenon in India. Hitherto there had been cultural unity and regional loyalties but no all-Indian feeling of patriotism. Nationalism developed under British rule for several reasons. One was the "superiority complex" of the English—their conviction that they were a racial elite and divinely ordained to rule India permanently. This racism, which was particularly strong following the Indian mutiny, manifested itself in all fields—in the army and the bureaucracy, where Indians could not rise above certain ranks regardless of their qualifications, and in social life, where Indians were excluded from certain hotels, clubs, and parks. Under these circumstances it was inevitable that the Indians should counter with the gradual development of a sense of cultural and national consciousness.

The British also stimulated nationalism by imposing an unprecedented unity on the Indian peninsula. For the first time the whole of India was under one rule. The British also forged a physical unity with their railways and telegraph and postal services. Equally important was the linguistic unity that followed the adoption of English as the common speech of the educated.

The British system of education introduced the whole body of Western literature and political thought into the country and thereby furthered Indian nationalism. The principles of liberalism and nationalism, of personal freedom and self-determination, inevitably were turned against the foreign British rule. The Indian leaders used not only Western political principles but also Western political techniques. Newspapers, platform oratory, pamphleteering, mass meetings, and monster petitions—all were used as grist for the nationalist mill.

Ram Mohan Roy laid the foundations of Indian nationalism with his agitation for political and social reform. The first generation of Indian nationalists, then, were admirers of Great Britain and apostles of cooperation. But after 1890 these "moderates" were challenged by the extremists led by Bal Gangadhar Tilak (1856–1920), the "father of Indian unrest." Tilak was a militant crusader who sought to transform the nationalist cause from an upper-class to a popular mass movement. This may explain his dogmatic support of many Hindu social customs. He even went so far as to organize a cow-protection society and to support child marriage. Yet at the same time he fought for a minimum wage for labor, freedom for trade union organization, creation of a citizen army, universal franchise, and free and compulsory education without distinction as to sex. Tilak won followers throughout the country with slogans such as "Educate, Agitate, and Organize"; "Militancy, not mendicancy"; and "Freedom is my birthright and I will have it."

Tilak was aided in his crusade by a series of famines and plagues in the 1890s that gave impetus to the growing sense of grievance. Indian militancy was also aroused by the revolution in Russia in 1905 and by Japan's defeat of Russia in the same year. The latter event was particularly exciting because it was taken as a refutation of the claim of Western superiority. Widespread though it was, this nationalist movement was almost exclusively a middle-class movement of lawyers, journalists, teachers, and merchants. These people were more familiar with John Stuart Mill, Herbert Spencer, and Charles Darwin than with the misery, grievances, and aspirations of the masses of their own Indian people in the villages. Not unnaturally, there was little rapport between the nationalist leaders and the illiterate peasants. The gulf persisted until bridged by Mohandas Gandhi in the postwar period. And Gandhi succeeded because he sensed the essentially religious outlook of his people and preached, not political abstractions, but religious concepts to which he gave a political meaning (see Chapter 38, Section IV).

In conclusion, the impact of the West on India was quite different from its impact on Russia or the Middle East. In the case of Russia, the West exerted decisive cultural and economic influence, but Russia remained politically and militarily strong and independent. The Near East, on the other hand, was dominated economically and militarily by the West, yet because of strategic considerations, the Ottoman Empire managed to retain its independence until World War I. India, by contrast, was conquered outright by Britain during the late eighteenth and nineteenth centuries. British rule lasted for nearly two centuries in Bengal and for more than a century in the Punjab. Consequently India never had the privilege of picking and choosing those features of European civilization that were most appealing. It was subjected to the impact of Western power and culture more indiscriminately than any other major region of Asia.

SUGGESTED READINGS

A survey of the historical literature on India is provided in the pamphlet by R. I. Crane, *The History of India: Its Study and Interpretation* (Service Center for Teachers of History, 1958). A collection of primary materials is provided by W. T. de Bary, ed., *Sources of Indian Tradition* (Columbia University, 1950). An invaluable reference work is by J. E. Schwartzberg, ed., *A Historical Atlas of South Asia* (University of Chicago, 1978).

Good general histories of India are available in P. Spear, *A History of India* (Penguin, 1965); and the sprightly written S. Wolpert, *A New History of India* (Oxford University, 1982). General studies of British rule in India are provided by R. P. Masani, *Britain in India* (Oxford University, 1961); P. Woodruff, *The Men Who Ruled India*, 2 vols. (Jonathan Cape, 1954–1955); H. Furber, *John Company at Work* (Harvard University, 1951); and the collection of readings reflecting various viewpoints in M. D. Lewis, ed., *The British in India: Imperialism or Trusteeship* (D.C. Heath, 1962).

The most thorough study of Europe's impact on India is by L. S. S. O'Malley, *Modern India and the West* (Oxford University, 1941). For the intellectual and nationalist trends in India, see A. Seal, *The Emergence of Indian Nationalism* (Cambridge University, 1968); B. T. McCully, *English Education and the Origins of Indian Nationalism* (Columbia University, 1940); A. Ward, *Our Bones Are Scattered: The Cawnpore Massacres and the Indian Mutiny of 1857* (Henry Holt, 1997); J. R. McLane, *Indian Nationalism and Early Congress* (Princeton University, 1977); and the same author's collection of documents on *The Political Awakening in India* (Prentice Hall, 1970).

NOTE

1. Cited by E. Stokes, "The First Century of British Colonial Rule in India: Social Revolution or Social Stagnation," *Past & Present* (February, 1973), p. 153.

CHAPTER
31

China and Japan

The historian who grasps the true secret of Japan's success in rapid Westernization has a key to modern Far Eastern history.

John K. Fairbank

The Far East was the last major region of Eurasia to feel the impact of expanding Europe. Various factors explain why China and Japan followed behind Russia, the Near East, and India in this respect. First, and most obvious, the Far East, by definition, is that portion of the Eurasian continent that is farthest removed from Europe. China and Japan do not touch upon Europe, as did the Russian and Ottoman empires, and they are much further to the east and north than India. Probably more significant than geographic isolation was the political unity of the two Far Eastern countries. In China and Japan the European intruders were not able to employ the divide-and-rule policy that had proven so effective in India. There were no independent local potentates who could be enlisted against the central governments in Peking and Tokyo. And because of the rigid seclusion poli-

cies of both these governments, there were no native merchants ready to collaborate with the Europeans.

Consequently, the Far Eastern countries were able to limit their contact with Europe to a mere trickle of closely supervised trade. But in the mid-nineteenth century the situation changed suddenly and drastically. First China and then Japan were forced to open their doors and to accept Western merchants, missionaries, consuls, and gunboats. Both of the Far Eastern countries were fundamentally affected, though in very different ways. Japan adopted and used the instruments of Western power. It was able to exploit them for self-defense and, later, for aggrandizement. China, by contrast, was unable to reorganize itself to meet the Western challenge. Yet, being too large and cohesive to be conquered outright like India and the other

FIRESHIPS AND MONKEYS

During the 1839 Opium War, the Chinese with their old-fashioned weapons had no chance against the British with their steam warships and artillery. This was proven when the Chinese tried to recapture the city of Ningpo. The resulting fiasco is described by the British historian Arthur Waley, who uses contemporary Chinese sources.*

There were a great many literary men on the [Chinese] General's staff, and ten days before the attack commenced (January 31st) he ordered them to compose announcements of victory. Thirty of these were sent in, and the General arranged them in order of merit. The first place went to Miu Chia-ku who had composed a detailed and vivid account of the exploits of the various heroes. Second on the list was Ho Shih-ch'i (a fairly well-known calligrapher) who sent in a vast composition, full of classical tropes and brilliant felicities.

The signal for the general attack was to be the setting alight of the fire-rafts which were to be let loose upon the English ships and, drifting against them, would set fire to them before they could weigh anchor. . . . The English ships' boats put out long before the blazing rafts arrived, took them in tow—a ticklish operation during which several sailors were badly burnt—and beached them. A second contingent of fire-rafts at a point some miles away was also prematurely ignited as soon as the flames were seen rising from the other rafts; but when less than half of this second contingent had been launched the Chinese irregulars in charge were attacked by boats put out from English warships, and fled.

Someone suggested that fire-crackers should be tied to the backs of a number of monkeys, who would then be flung on board the English ships. The flames would spread rapidly in every direction and might with luck reach the powder-magazine, in which case the whole ship would blow up. Nineteen monkeys were bought, and at the time of the advance were brought in litters to the advanced base. After the failure of the Chinese attack they accompanied the retreating armies to Tz'u-ch'i. "The fact is," says Pei, "that no one ever dared go near enough to the foreign ships to fling them on board, so that the plan was never put into effect." During the panic that ensued after the defeat of the remaining Chinese troops on the heights behind Tz'u-ch'i, the people fled from the town, including a Mr. Feng in whose charge the monkeys had been put. There was no one to care for them, and they eventually died of starvation in Mr. Feng's deserted front lodge.

*A. Waley, *The Opium War Through Chinese Eyes* (George Allen & Unwin, 1958), pp. 165, 169, 170.

---

countries of Southeast Asia, China was never to succumb entirely. So China remained in an uncomfortable and unstable state until World War I, and even for some decades thereafter.

I. OPENING OF CHINA

Over a period of four thousand years the Chinese people developed a unique and self-contained society at the extreme eastern end of the Eurasian landmass. This society, like others in Asia, was based on agriculture rather than trade and was governed by landlords and bureaucrats rather than by merchants and politicians. A distinctly self-centered and self-assured society, it regarded the rest of the world as inferior and subordinate.

The Chinese first came into direct contact with the West when the Portuguese appeared off the southeast coast in 1514. After the Portuguese came the Dutch and the British, who also arrived by sea. The Russians came from the north overland to the Amur valley. The Chinese resolutely kept all these intruders at arm's length (see Chapter 19, Section III). They restricted commercial relations to a few ports and refused to establish diplomatic relations on a full and equal basis.

The Chinese were forcefully jarred out of their seclusion and complacency by three disastrous wars: the first with Britain in 1839–1842, the second with Britain and France in 1856–1858, and the third with Japan in 1895. The humiliating defeats suffered in these wars compelled the Chinese to throw open the gates, to end their condescending attitude toward the West, and to reappraise their own traditional civilization. The outcome was a chain reaction of intrusion and response that produced a new China, with repercussions that are still felt in the Far East and in the entire globe.

Britain was able to take the lead in opening up China because it had a powerful base in India as well as control of the seas. Britain's main objective was to remove the many obstacles that the Chinese had placed in the way of trading operations. Triggering the start of hostilities between Britain and China was the immediate issue of trade in opium. European sailors had introduced opium smoking in China in the sev-

enteenth century, and the habit had spread rapidly from the ports. The demand for opium solved the British problem of paying for Chinese products. Hitherto the British had been forced to pay mostly in gold and silver, because the Chinese were little interested in Western goods. But now the market for opium reversed the balance of trade in favor of the British. The Peking government issued decrees in 1729 and 1799 prohibiting the importation of opium, but the trade was so profitable that Chinese officials could be bribed to permit smuggling.

The first Anglo-Chinese War, or the Opium War as it is frequently called, broke out when the Chinese attempted to enforce their prohibition of the opium traffic. The emperor appointed as special imperial commissioner a man of proven integrity and firmness, Lin Tse-hsu. Lin seized 20,000 chests of opium worth $6 million and destroyed them at a public ceremony. Complications following this action led to a clash between Chinese war junks and British frigates, and war began in November 1839. During the hostilities that followed the hopeless military inferiority of the Chinese became obvious. The odds against the Chinese were even worse now than they had been between the conquistadors and the Aztecs. European warships and artillery had improved immeasurably between the sixteenth and nineteenth centuries, whereas Chinese military technology had stagnated at a

The Opium War, 1840. Armed Chinese junks were no match for British warships. The war ended in 1842 with the Treaty of Nanking.

level little above that of Aztec capabilities. In 1842, the Peking government capitulated and accepted the Treaty of Nanking, the first of a long series of unequal treaties that were to nibble away much of China's sovereignty.

By the Nanking Treaty China ceded the island of Hong Kong and opened five ports to foreign trade. The Nanking Treaty did not end the friction between the Chinese and the Europeans. The later wanted more concessions in order to increase trade, whereas the Chinese felt that the treaties already had granted too many privileges to the Europeans. It is not surprising, then, that hostilities began again in 1856. The occasion this time was the imprisonment by Chinese officials of the Chinese crew on board a Chinese ship flying the British flag. When the Peking government refused to release the crew, the British bombarded Canton. The French also entered the war, using the murder of a French priest as a pretext. The Anglo-French forces proved irresistible, and in 1858 and 1860 China was forced to sign more "unequal treaties."

The third defeat suffered by China was the most humiliating, for it was at the hands of the small neighboring kingdom of Japan. We shall see later in this chapter that the Japanese, in contrast to the Chinese, had been able to adapt Western technology to their needs and to build an efficient military establishment. Thus they accomplished what no other oriental state had been able to achieve thus far. Japan now pressed certain shadowy claims in Korea, where China also had claims. The two forces clashed, and war was formally declared by China and Japan in August 1894. The Chinese armies again were easily routed, and, in April 1895, Peking was forced to accept the Treaty of Shimonoseki. Its terms required China to pay an indemnity; to recognize the independence of Korea; to cede to Japan certain territories.

The Japanese war was a shattering blow to the pride and complacency of China. The great empire had been shown to be completely helpless at the hands of a despised neighbor equipped with modern instruments of war. Furthermore, the European powers during the preceding years had been taking advantage of China's weakness and annexing outlying territories that traditionally had recognized Peking's suzerainty. In addition to the territorial acquisitions, the Western states divided up China proper. They set up "spheres of influence" in which the political and economic primacy of each respective power was recognized. Thus Yunnan and the area bordering on Indochina became a French sphere, Canton and the Yangtze valley and the large area in between was a British sphere, Manchuria was Russian, Shantung was German, and Fukien Japanese.

These humiliations and disasters that China experienced in the latter half of the nineteenth century forced the traditionally self-centered Middle Kingdom to undertake a painful self-assessment and reorganization. We will now trace the course of this process, noting how the Chinese slowly and grudgingly underwent reform and then revolution.

The empress dowager Tz'u-hsi (1835-1908), who manipulated the levers of power at the Manchu court in Peking.

II. REFORM AND REVOLUTION IN CHINA

Japan's defeat of China won the attention of the young emperor, Kuang-hsu, who recognized the need for thorough reform. In the summer of 1898 he issued a series of reform decrees known collectively as the Hundred Days Reform. They centralized the provincial governments under Peking, established new schools based on European learning, encouraged Western-style production methods, and organized a new conscript army along Western lines. These measures never got beyond the paper stage because the military supported the old empress dowager who had always defended the old order. Now she deposed the young emperor, declared herself regent, rescinded all reform decrees, and executed six of the reform leaders.

The collapse of the Hundred Days Reform gave the reactionaries full power. In their zeal they actively channeled social and political discontent against the foreigners. Antiforeign secret societies, incited by court reactionaries and provincial governors, organized local militias to combat foreign aggression. Chief among these societies was the I Ho T'uan or "Righteous Harmony Fists," popularly termed *Boxers*. With official connivance the Boxers began to attack foreigners, and by 1900 numerous Chinese Christians and foreigners had been killed in north China. When European naval detachments began to land at Tientsin, the Boxers declared war on all foreigners and besieged the

Boxers awaiting execution in Canton Prison, Canton, China.

foreign legations in Peking. Within a few months, international armies relieved the legations, and the imperial court fled from the capital. Once more China was forced to accept a peace with humiliating terms, including further commercial concessions and payment of an indemnity of $333 million.

The fiascos of the Hundred Days Reform and of the Boxer Rebellion dramatically demonstrated the futility of trying to modernize China by reform from above. The alternative was revolution from below, and this did take place in 1911, when the Manchu dynasty finally was overthrown and its place taken by a republic.

The leader and ideologist of the revolutionaries was Dr. Sun Yat-sen (1866–1925). Compared to the reform leaders who had hitherto been prominent, Sun was a strange and anomalous figure. He was not one of the upper-class literati; in fact, his training was as much Western as Chinese. He was born in the Canton Delta, which had been subject to foreign influence longer than any other area in China. At the age of thirteen he joined his brother in Honolulu, where he remained five years and completed a high school course in a Church of England boarding school. Then he went to Queen's College in Hong Kong, and after graduation he enrolled in the Hong Kong Medical College, where he received his medical degree in 1892. Thus Sun acquired an excellent scientific education that he could have used to win wealth and status. Instead he identified with the poor and always felt a passionate concern for their welfare.

With such sentiments, he did not remain long in professional practice. The defeat by Japan in 1895 convinced him that the government of his country was rotten to the core and that nothing short of a revolution would provide the remedy. Sun Yat-sen derived his main support from Chinese merchants overseas. Within the country only a few students and merchants were influenced by his ideas, and the mass of the population remained illiterate and apathetic. A small-scale republican uprising in Canton was suppressed, but on October 10, 1911, an accidental explosion in a bomb factory at Hankow led to mutiny among nearby imperial troops. Despite lack of coordination, the revolutionary movement spread rapidly throughout

Sun Yat-sen (1866–1925), father of China's 1911 republican revolution.

the country. Sun Yat-sen, who was in the United States at the time, hurried back, and on December 30, 1911, a provisional revolutionary assembly elected him president of the United Provinces of China.

Sun was unable to control the country even though he was the nominal leader. He organized a new political party, the *Kuomintang* or National Peoples' party, which won a majority of seats in the National Assembly elected in April 1913. But real power was held by the bureaucracy and army leaders who ignored the republican government that nominally ruled from Peking. Instead, they pillaged the countryside mercilessly and dragged China down to a brutalizing anarchy. These early years of the republic until 1926 marked one of the worst periods in the history of China.

Several factors account for this wretched outcome of the reform effort in China. First there is the sheer size of China, which for many years left the interior of the country unaffected by Western contact. The interior functioned as a vast reservoir, out of which tradition-minded civil-service candidates continued to appear for several decades. The bureaucracy that they formed consisted of intellectuals who were steeped in the Confucian classics and who consequently placed much greater emphasis on ethical principles than on the manual arts or the technology of warfare. This ruling class was further inhibited by the fact that, apart from Buddhism, China had little or no tradition for borrowing from abroad. Thus it is not surprising that although China did change in the second half of the nineteenth century, the tempo of its change was far slower than that of the other countries responding to the West. Finally, the young Western-trained Chinese also were partly to blame. Some of them played leading roles in the early days of the republic, but they tried to set up in China carbon copies of the institutions they had observed abroad, especially in the United States. What they established naturally had no meaning for the Chinese people and quickly crumbled before the realities of Chinese politics.

III. MODERNIZATION OF JAPAN

Historians have presented several explanations for the difference between the Chinese and the Japanese response to the challenge of the West. The physical compactness of the Japanese Islands facilitated both the forging of national unity and the spread of new values and new learning throughout the country. It also made the country vulnerable to, and aware of, foreign pressures, unlike the vast interior provinces of China, which for long were inaccessible to Western influences. Furthermore, Japan's long tradition of borrowing from the great Chinese cultural world made similar borrowing from the Western world in the nineteenth century less jarring and painful. Japan had adapted selected aspects of Chinese culture with the slogan "Japanese spirit and Chinese knowledge." Now it borrowed what it wished from the West with the slogan "Eastern morale and Western arts." Also, Japanese government and society were pluralistic in structure in comparison with the monolithic features of the Chinese Empire. The clan tradition and regional particularism of Japan were reinforced by geographic separation due to the broken mountainous terrain. The merchant class in Japan had more autonomy and economic strength, and, as we shall see, it

was rapidly extending its power at the critical moment of the West's intrusion. The military elements in Japan were at the top of the social ladder, rather than at the bottom, as was the case in China. This meant that Japan had a ruling class that was much more sensitive and responsive to Western military technology than were the Chinese literati. In sum, geography, cultural traditions, and pluralistic organization combined to make Japan more vulnerable to Western intrusion than China, and quicker to respond to that intrusion.

Despite these basic differences, Japan, like China, remained in seclusion until the mid-nineteenth century. The Tokugawa shoguns severed one by one the ties between Japan and the Western world. By the mid-seventeenth century the sole remaining contact was the handful of Dutch traders who were confined to the islet of Deshima (see Chapter 19, Section VI). The aim of the Tokugawa leaders was to keep Japan isolated and unchanging in order to perpetuate their regime. But despite their efforts, certain developments did occur that gradually altered the balance of forces in the country and undermined the status quo. The long peace enforced by Tokugawa rule stimulated population growth, economic expansion, and the strengthening of the merchant class. The population jumped from 18 million in 1600 to 26 million in 1725. Cities grew disproportionately, Edo (later Tokyo) approaching the million mark by 1700, and Osaka and Kyoto each reaching 300,000. The population spurt increased the demand for commodities and encouraged merchants and rich peasants to invest surplus capital in new forms of production, including the domestic, or putting-out, system. They provided materials and equipment for peasants and craftspeople, and marketed the finished products. Rising production led to wide-scale exchange of goods, which in turn led to the development of a money economy.

Thus Japanese society was in a state of transition. It was experiencing profound economic and social change, which gave rise to political tensions. These tensions were reaching the breaking point when Commodore Perry forced Japan's doors open to trade. One reason the Japanese proved so ready to reorganize their

After delivering President Fillmore's letter in 1853, Commodore Perry confers with bakufu *officials.*

society under the impact of the West was precisely because many of them were all too aware that their society needed reorganizing.

On July 8, 1853, Commodore Matthew Perry cast anchor in Edo Bay and delivered a letter from President Fillmore asking for trading privileges, coaling stations, and protection for shipwrecked Americans. Within a week he sailed away after warning that he would be back for an answer the following spring. When he returned in February 1854, he made it clear that the alternative to a treaty was war. The Japanese yielded and on March 31 signed the Treaty of Kanagawa. Its terms opened ports for the repair and provisioning of American ships, provided for proper treatment and repatriation of shipwrecked Americans, permitted the appointment of consular representatives if either nation considered it necessary, and promised most-favored-nation treatment for the United States.

In accordance with the provisions of this treaty, the United States sent Townsend Harris, an unusually able man, as the first consul to Japan. With his extraordinary tact and patience, Harris gradually won the confidence of the Japanese and secured the Commercial Treaty of 1858. This opened four more ports to trade, provided for mutual diplomatic representation, gave to Americans both civil and criminal extraterritoriality, prohibited the opium trade, and gave freedom of religion to foreigners. Soon after signing these two treaties with the United States, Japan concluded similar pacts with Holland, Russia, Britain, and France. Thus Japan, like China before it, now had to suffer the intrusion of the West. But its response to that intrusion was altogether different from that of the Middle Kingdom.

The first effect of the Western encroachment was to produce a crisis that precipitated the downfall of the Tokugawa Shogunate. With the signing of the treaties the shogun was subject to conflicting pressures: on the one hand from the foreign powers, which were demanding implementation of all the provisions, and on the other from the Japanese population, which was strongly antiforeign. The popular sentiment was exploited by the anti-Tokugawa clans, often referred to as the Satcho Hito group. Between 1858 and 1865 attacks were made on Europeans and their employees with the slogan "Honor the Emperor! Expel the barbarians!" With the death in 1867 of both the emperor and the Tokugawa shogun, the way was clear for the so-called Meiji Restoration. The Tokugawa clanspeople were shorn of their power and fiefs, and their place was taken by the Satcho Hito clans, which henceforth controlled the government in the name of the new Meiji emperor. It was the young samurai in the service of these clans who now provided Japan with the extraordinary leadership that made possible successful modernization. In contrast to China's literati, Japan's new leaders realized that they were retarded in certain fields, and they were willing and able to do something about it.

This is not altogether surprising if we note that even during their centuries of seclusion the Japanese leaders had gone out of their way to keep informed of developments in Europe. In fact, the Dutch were allowed to continue trading primarily so that they could be questioned concerning the outside world. Both the shogunate and the clans promoted military industry and maintained schools for the study of foreign languages and foreign texts. The general level of knowledge rose to the point where, in the natural sciences, physics was separated from chemistry, and in medicine, students were trained in special fields such as surgery, pediatrics, obstetrics, and internal medicine. In the Nagasaki naval school, instruction was given in navigation and gunnery only after a solid base had been laid in mathematics, astronomy, and physics. In other words, the Japanese all along had been much more appreciative of and responsive to Western culture. In the light of this background, it is understandable why the Japanese acted quite differently from the Chinese once the Westerners forced their way in.

Japan's new leaders were interested only in those features of Western civilization that enhanced national power. In the field of religion, for example, the Meiji leaders supported Shinto as the state cult because it identified the national character with the emperor, who it held was descended from the Sun Goddess. In other words, Shinto stimulated national unity and patriotism, and these attributes were deemed necessary if Japan were to hold its own in the modern world. In education, it was explicitly stated that the objective was the furtherance of state interests rather than the development of the individual. Compulsory elementary education was required because the state needed a literate citizenry. Large numbers of foreign educa-

The first Diet opened in 1890 during the ministry of Yamagata Aritomo. The Emperor Meiji, with sword, sits on the right under a canopy. The empress, with her ladies-in-waiting, can be seen at the upper left. This two-story building, located at the western corner of Hibiya Park, burned down in January 1891. A new Diet building was built by October of the same year.

tors were brought to Japan to found schools and universities, and thousands of Japanese studied abroad and returned to teach in the new institutions. But the entire educational system was kept under close state supervision to ensure uniformity of thought as well as of administration.

In military affairs the Japanese abolished the old feudal levies and organized modern armed forces based on the latest European models. They built a conscript army with the aid of a German military mission and a small navy under the guidance of the British. The Meiji leaders foresaw that the new military forces required a modern economy to supply their needs. Accordingly, they secured the establishment of the needed industries by granting subsidies, purchasing stock, or forming government corporations. The government leaders were careful to support not only light industries such as textiles but also heavy industries such as mining, steel, and shipbuilding, which were necessary to fill military needs. Once these enterprises were founded, the government generally sold them to various favored private interests at extremely low prices. In this way a few wealthy families, collectively known as the Zaibatsu, gained a stranglehold on the national economy that has persisted to the present.

The Japanese also overhauled their legal system. At the same time various political innovations were made to provide Japan with at least the trappings of parliamentary government. A cabinet and a privy council were first established, and then, in 1889, a constitution was adopted. This document promised citizens freedom from arbitrary arrest; protection of property rights; and freedom of religion, speech, and association. But in each instance the government was given authority to curb these rights when it so desired. The constitution provided Japan with a parliamentary facade while preserving oligarchic rule and emperor worship. Indeed, the first article of the constitution provided that "The Empire of Japan shall be reigned over and governed by a line of Emperors unbroken for ages eternal," and the third article likewise stipulated that "The Emperor is sacred and inviolable."

With the adoption of the constitution and of the legal reforms, the Japanese were in a position to press for the abolition of the unequal treaties. They could fairly argue that Japan now had taken its place in the ranks of civilized nations and that there was no longer any need for extraterritoriality and for the other infringements on their sovereignty. After prolonged diplomatic efforts they were able in 1894 to persuade Britain and the United States to end extraterritoriality and consular jurisdiction in five years. In the same year the Japanese won their unexpected and spectacular victory over the Chinese Empire. Henceforth there could be no more question of treating Japan as an inferior country, and the other powers soon followed Britain and the United States in yielding their special privileges. By 1899 Japan had gained legal jurisdiction over all foreigners on its soil, and in doing so, it became the first Asian nation to break the chains of Western control.

IV. EXPANSION OF JAPAN

After its self-modernization, Japan embarked on a career of expansion on the mainland. This is not surprising in view of Japan's warlike tradition and the immense prestige that its military leaders enjoyed from earliest times. Furthermore, the Far East was then a hotbed of international rivalry, and the practical-minded leaders of Japan drew the obvious conclusion: Each people must grab for themselves. Their first expansionist move was in Korea where, as noted earlier in this chapter, the Japanese defeated the Chinese and then annexed Korea in 1910.

After their victory over China, the Japanese were faced by the much more powerful Russians, who were advancing southward into Manchuria and Korea. Described earlier (Chapter 28, Section III) was Japan's offer for a compromise settlement, Russia's refusal of the offer, Japan's attack and victory over Russia, and the Portsmouth Treaty (September 5, 1905) by which Japan won the southern half of Sakhalin Island and Russia's Liaotung leasehold, as well as recognition of Japan's special interests in Korea.

In retrospect this war stands out as a major turning point in the history of the Far East, and even of the world. Certainly it established Japan as a major power and altered the balance of forces in the Far East. But much more significant is the fact that for the first time an Asian state defeated a European state, and a great empire at that. This had an electrifying effect on all Asia. It demonstrated to millions of colonial peoples that European domination was not divinely ordained. For the first time since the days of the conquistadors, the white race had been beaten, and a thrill of hope ran through the nonwhite races of the globe. In this sense the Russo-Japanese War stands out as a landmark in modern history; it represents the prelude to the great awakening of the non-European peoples.

SUGGESTED READINGS

For background references, see the bibliography for Chapter 21. The best overall survey of the impact of the West on East Asia is by E. O. Reischauer, J. K. Fairbank, and A. M. Craig, *East Asia: Tradition and Civilization*, rev. ed. (Houghton Mifflin, 1978); and J. K. Fairbank, *China, a New History* (Harvard, 1992). See also the excellent study by G. M. Beckmann, *The Modernization of China and Japan* (Harper & Row, 1962); and J. K. Fairbank, *The Great Chinese Revolution, 1800–1985* (Harper & Row, 1986). The most important work on the West's impact on China is the following collection of documents with explanatory essays: Ssu-ye Teng and J. K. Fairbank, *China's Response to the West: A Documentary Survey, 1839–1923* (Harvard University, 1954).

The outstanding works on the West's impact on Japan are the documentary collection by R. Tsunoda, *Sources of the Japanese Tradition* (Columbia University, 1958); and the analysis by G. B. Sansom, *The Western World and Japan* (Knopf, 1950). Also noteworthy are E. O. Reischauer, *Japan: The Story of a Nation*, rev. ed. (Knopf, 1970); J. Halliday, *A Political History of Japanese Capitalism* (Pantheon, 1975); and W. W. Lockwood, *The Economic Development of Japan: Growth and Structural Change, 1868–1938* (Princeton University, 1954).

For Western diplomacy in the Far East, see W. L. Langer, *The Diplomacy of Imperialism, 1890–1902*, rev. ed. (Knopf, 1956). The problem of the contrasting response to China and Japan to the Western intrusion is considered in N. Jacobs, *The Origin of Modern Capitalism and Eastern Asia* (Hong Kong University, 1958); and in F. V. Maulder, *Japan, China and the Modern World Economy* (Cambridge University, 1977).

32

Africa

For better or for worse the old Africa is gone and the white races must face the new situation which they have themselves created.

Jan Christiaan Smuts

Europe's impact on sub-Saharan Africa was felt considerably later than that on Eurasia. The European powers fastened their rule on India, the East Indies, and much of North Africa before they expanded south of the Sahara. France acquired Algeria in 1830 and Tunisia in 1881, and England occupied Egypt in 1882. European penetration southward generally came later because of various reasons, including adverse climate, prevalence of disease, geographic inaccessibility, and the superior organization and resistance of the Africans compared to the American Indians or the Australian aborigines. Also, unlike the bullion of Mexico and Peru, there was a lack of exploitable riches to lure Europeans into the interior. Thus sub-Saharan Africa, apart from certain coastal regions, remained largely unaffected by Europe until the late nineteenth century. In the last two decades of that century, however, the European powers made up for lost time. They partitioned virtually the entire continent and exploited its material and human resources. By 1914 the African peoples had, in many respects, come under European influence even more than had the Asians, though many villagers in the interior regions continued to live as before and to be little influenced by the European intruder.

I. SLAVE TRADE

For centuries the most valuable of African resources for Europeans were the slaves, but these could be obtained at coastal ports, without any need for penetration inland. Slavery had been an established and accepted institution in Africa. Prisoners of war had been enslaved, as

This late eighteenth-century engraving, showing European slave traders on the coast of Africa, graphically illustrates the first step in the wrenching and dehumanizing process of enslavement.

were also debtors and individuals guilty of serious crimes. But these slaves usually were treated as part of the family. They had clearly defined rights, and their slave status was not necessarily hereditary. Therefore it is commonly argued that Africa's traditional slavery was benign compared to the transatlantic slave trade organized by the Europeans. This argument, however, can be carried too far. Professor Edward Reynolds warns against the illusion that "cruel and dehumanizing enslavement was a monopoly of the West. Slavery in its extreme forms, including the taking of life, was common to both Africa and the West. . . the fact that African slavery had different origins and consequences should not lead us to deny what it was—the exploitation and subjugation of human beings."[1] Neither can it be denied that the wholesale shipment of Africans to the slave plantations of the Americas was made possible by the participation of African chiefs who rounded up their fellow Africans and sold them at a handsome profit to European ship captains waiting along the coasts.

Granting all this, the fact remains that the transatlantic slave trade conducted by the Europeans was entirely different in quantity and quality from the traditional type of slavery that had existed within Africa. From the beginning the European variety was primarily an economic institution rather than social, as it had been in Africa. Western slave traders and slave owners were motivated by purely economic considerations and were quite ready to work their slaves to death if it was more profitable to do so than to treat them more leniently. This impersonalism was reinforced by racism when the Europeans became involved in the African slave trade on a large scale. Perhaps as a subconscious rationalization they gradually came to look down on Negroes as inherently inferior and therefore preordained to serve their white masters. Rationalization also may have been involved in the Europeans' use of religion to justify the traffic in human beings. Enslavement, it was argued, ensured the conversion of the African heathen to the true faith as well as to civilization.

In this self-satisfied spirit the Portuguese shipped thousands of African slaves to their homeland. This was but a petty prelude to the new and fateful phase of the slave trade that began in 1510 when the first shipload of African slaves was shipped to the New World. The venture was highly successful, for there was urgent need for labor in the Americas, especially on the sugar plantations. The market for slaves was almost limitless, and several other countries entered the slave trade to share in the rich profits. Portugal dominated the trade in the sixteenth century, Holland during most of the seventeenth, and Britain in the eighteenth. The West African coast was dotted with about forty European forts that were used for defense against the rival trading nations and for storing the slaves while awaiting shipment across the Atlantic.

The typical voyage of the slave traders was triangular. The first leg was from the home port to Africa, with a cargo including salt, cloth, firearms, hardware, beads, and rum. These goods were bartered for slaves brought by fellow Africans from the interior to the coast. The unfortunate victims were packed under atrocious conditions in the vessels and shipped across the Atlantic on the so-called "middle passage." At their New World destinations the slaves were either sold at once or held in stock-

ades to be retailed on demand. The final lap was the voyage home with plantation produce such as sugar, molasses, tobacco, or rice.

Thanks to the prevailing trade winds the "middle passage" was normally swift and brief, the average being sixty days. Nevertheless, the death rate during the trip ranged from 10 to 55 percent, depending on the length of the voyage, the chance occurrence of epidemics, and the treatment accorded the slaves. This treatment almost invariably involved inhuman crowding, stifling heat, and poor food. Even greater casualties were suffered earlier, during the overland march to the coast. Raiding parties plundered villages and broke up families in their search for strong young men and women. The captives were then driven from dawn to dusk in the blazing heat and pouring rain, through thick jungles

Lithograph depicting a slave ship plying between Africa and America before the Civil War.

or over dry plains. The survivors who reached the coast were driven naked into the market like cattle. Then they were branded with the name of the company or buyer and herded into the forts to await shipment across the ocean. It is not surprising that in supplying American plantations with between 12 and 20 million slaves, Africa suffered an estimated loss in casualties of about four times that number of people (see Chapter 25, Section III, for the overall effects on Africa).

Despite these horrors, Europeans continued to buy and sell Africans for over four centuries. The profits were so great that powerful vested interests strongly opposed any proposals for control or abolition. There were first of all the African chiefs, who received as much as £20 to £36 for a single able-bodied slave. These African leaders played a vital role in the slave-trade operations. Their participation was essential for the Europeans, who were confined to the coastal areas and who suffered mortality rates of 25 to 50 percent. Not only did the African middlemen reap handsome profits from the trade but they also were violently opposed to all abolition proposals. Indeed, riots against Europeans were organized on African soil in defiance of the abolition movement! It is true that a few chiefs did try to stop the abhorrent trade in their fellow Africans, but they had no chance because those who continued trading received firearms and threatened the existence of the few who tried to abstain. Thus the chiefs were caught in a trap from which the few dissenters could not escape.

The plantation owners in the Americas likewise supported the slave trade, especially the Barbados planters, who held an important bloc of seats in the eighteenth-century British Parliament. There were European vested interests also that championed the slave trade, both among the traders and the various merchants at home who provided the rum and the manufactured goods. According to one estimate, Britain shipped to Africa manufactures valued at £1 million a year, and the other European countries sent an equal amount for the same purpose. The return on this outlay was so extraordinarily high that in the eighteenth century the prosperity of cities such as Liverpool and Bristol depended

heavily on this traffic. The famous abolitionist leader William Wilberforce properly observed that "Interest can draw a film over the eyes so thick that blindness itself could do no more."[2]

Despite these formidable obstacles, a small group of reformers campaigned vigorously for abolition. In 1787 they established in England the Society for the Abolition of the Slave Trade. In 1823 they founded the Anti-Slavery Society to end the institution of slavery as well as the slave trade. These abolitionists were aided by the progress of the industrial revolution, which was rendering slavery obsolete. Advancing technology called for overseas markets rather than for a cheap supply of human power. In fact, the abolitionists argued that the slave trade was inefficient and insisted that a more profitable "legitimate" trade could be developed in Africa.

In 1833 Parliament passed a decree that completely abolished slavery on British territory and provided 20 million pounds as compensation for the slaveholders. The British government went further and persuaded other European countries to follow its example in allowing British warships to seize slave ships flying other flags. At one period, a fourth of the whole British navy was patrolling the coasts of Africa, Cuba, and Brazil with a force of fifty-six vessels manned by 9,000 sailors. Complete success was not possible until the various countries in the New World gradually abolished slavery as an institution—as did Haiti in 1803, the United States in 1863, Brazil in 1888, Cuba at about the same time, and so forth.

While the slave trade was being stamped out on the west coast of Africa, it continued to be carried on by the Arabs in central and East Africa, though on a much smaller scale. The Arabs had been engaged in this trade long before the appearance of the Europeans, and they continued through the nineteenth century and even into the twentieth. The captives were marched across the Sahara to North African fairs, or they were taken to east coast ports and then shipped to Zanzibar, Madagascar, Arabia, Turkey, Persia, and even India. Many of these slaves worked in clove and sugar plantations on various Indian Ocean islands. This traffic was much more difficult to suppress than that on

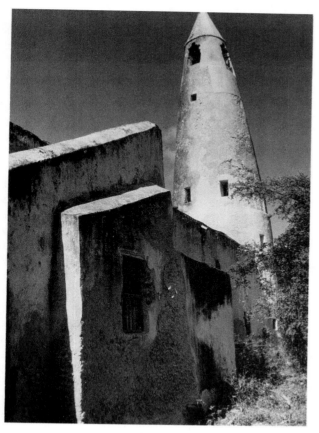

The Friday mosque at Shela on the southeastern coast of Lamu Island, Kenya. This fine example of late Swahili architecture dates to the early nineteenth century. It is the only surviving pre-twentieth-century mosque in the region with a minaret. Swahili settlements on Lamu Island date to about the fifteenth century and enjoyed a period of substantial wealth that reached its zenith in the nineteenth century.

the west coast. Despite British naval patrols in the Red Sea and the Indian Ocean, it persisted until World War I and later.

II. AGE OF EXPLORATION

The agitation for the abolition of slavery contributed directly to the exploration and opening up of the "Dark Continent." The abolitionists hoped to curtail the slave trade by pushing into the interior where the slaves were captured.

There they hoped to develop "legitimate" or regular commerce that would replace the traffic in slaves. At the same time, a growing fad for geography made Europeans intensely curious about unexplored lands. These factors all combined to bring to Africa in the nineteenth century a number of remarkable and colorful explorers.

The systematic exploration of the continent began with the founding of the African Association in 1788. It was headed by the noted British scientist Joseph Banks, and its purpose was "to promote the cause of science and humanity, to explore the mysterious geography, to ascertain the resources, and to improve the conditions of that ill-fated continent." The association's attention was directed first to exploring the Niger basin and West Africa.

Interest shifted to East Africa after a disastrous trading expedition up the Niger proved that commercial opportunities were scanty there. The big question in East Africa was the whereabouts of the source of the Nile. Hostile natives, vast marshes, and innumerable rapids had defeated all attempts to follow the river upstream to its headwaters. In 1856 two Englishmen, John Speke and Richard Burton, started inland from the African east coast. They discovered Lake Tanganyika, Lake Victoria, and eventually followed the Nile through Egypt to the Mediterranean.

Outstanding amongst the explorers was David Livingstone who criss-crossed the continent, and also the correspondent Henry Stanley who in 1877 reached the mouth of the Congo River on the west coast. Two years later, Stanley was again on the Congo River, but this time he was functioning as the agent for King Leopold of Belgium rather than as an explorer. The age of African exploration had given way to the age of African partition.

III. PARTITION OF AFRICA

Prior to 1870 the European powers had insignificant holdings in Africa. They consisted mostly of seaports and fortified trading stations, together with bits of adjacent territory acquired as adjuncts to trade rather than as bases for territorial expansion. With the termination of the European slave trade, most of these coastal footholds were virtually abandoned since the legitimate trade was not great enough to support them. European leaders during this early period repeatedly stated their opposition to the acquisition of colonies.

After 1870 a combination of factors (see Chapter 26, Section VII) produced a reversal of this anticolonial attitude. Colonies now were regarded as assets for the mother country, and the continent of Africa, being unoccupied and defenseless, became the focus of imperialist aspirations. The leader of the imperialist drive in Africa was King Leopold of Belgium. At the outset he was interested primarily in East Africa. But with Stanley's exploration of the Congo Basin from 1876 to 1877, Leopold at once saw the potential of this great central region. In fact, it had been Stanley himself who had seen the opportunity, but, unable to enlist support in England, in 1878 Stanley entered Leopold's service, returning in the following year to the Congo. Between 1879 and 1880 Stanley signed numerous treaties with chiefs, handing over no fewer than 900,000 square miles to the International Association of the Congo, a new organization set up under Leopold's direction. The chiefs had no way of knowing that signing the pieces of paper and accepting token payments meant permanent loss of their tribal lands. An African chief traditionally was entrusted with his people's land. His selling was like a mayor's selling "his" city hall. Yet this was the standard European procedure all over the continent, and repercussions are being felt to the present day.

The immediate effect of Leopold's machinations was the holding of an international conference in Berlin (1884–1885) to prepare rules for the further acquisition of African territories. It was agreed that no power should annex land or establish a protectorate without first giving notice of intent; that recognition of territorial claims must depend on effective occupation; and that disputes were to be settled by arbitration. Now that an international code for territorial aggrandizement was agreed on, the entire continent was partitioned in less than two decades. In the Congo, Leopold bought out in 1887 all non-Belgian interests in order to eliminate possible criticism of his enterprise. So unbe-

lievably brutal were his various methods of forced labor that the population of the Congo declined by one-half (from 20 million to 10 million) between 1885 and 1908 during its rule by Leopold. News of these atrocities leaked out, and Leopold was forced to turn over his Congo possessions to the Belgian government in 1908. What had been private property now became a Belgian colony. The government took measures to end the atrocities, though a modified form of forced labor did continue.

In the rest of West Africa the French were the most active. Starting from their old trading posts on the Ivory Coast, in Dahomey, and on the north bank of the Congo, they conceived a grand plan for pushing inward and founding a French West African Empire that would stretch from Algeria to the Congo and from the Senegal to the Nile or even to the Red Sea. Since the Germans and the British also had footholds along the west coast, the French had to outflank their rivals in a race for the hinterland. By and large they were successful. Only the British in Nigeria and the Germans in the Cameroons were able to expand significantly into the interior. All the rest of West Africa, together with the vast Sahara, became a great French domain ruled from Paris.

In 1886 and 1890 the British and the Germans signed agreements settling their claims in East Africa. The Germans retained the huge area known as the German East Africa Protectorate, to be named Tanganyika after 1919. The British kept their East Africa Protectorate, later to be known as Kenya Colony, together with a protectorate over Uganda.

Meanwhile, the Italians had belatedly joined the scramble for African territory. They managed to obtain two barren colonies on the Red Sea coast, Eritrea and Somaliland, and later, in 1896, they gambled for higher stakes by sending an army to conquer the kingdom of Ethiopia. The Christian Ethiopians were able to resist more effectively than the people in most other parts of Africa. Their Emperor Menelik had an army of 80,000 men trained by French officers and armed with French weapons. Able to defeat the small Italian army of 10,000, his kingdom remained free from European rule. But except for the small republic of Liberia on the west coast, by 1914 Ethiopia was the only independent state on the whole continent. Even Liberia, set up in 1822 as a settlement for freed American Negroes (named from the Latin *liber*, meaning "free"), became a virtual U.S. protectorate in 1911 because of bankruptcy and internal disorders.

The net result of this unprecedented territorial aggrandizement was the partitioning of the entire continent of Africa among the European powers, the only exceptions being the fragile states of Liberia and Ethiopia. One reason why the Europeans carved up Africa so easily was that they were able to pit Africans against Africans (just as they had used Indians against Indians in conquering the Americas). Another reason was that the Africans waged frontal, head-on warfare, which left them sitting ducks

Mosheshwe, king and founder of Lesotho. Not all of the Bantu peoples followed the militaristic example of Shaka. Mosheshwe, prince of a subtribe of the Sotho Bantus, fought off Zulu attacks and led his people to a mountain stronghold in southern Africa, where, through diplomacy and determination, he founded a small nation that has endured to the present. The kingdom became the British protectorate of Basutoland in 1868. In 1966 it achieved independence as the kingdom of Lesotho under Mosheswe's great-grandson, King Mosheshwe II.

to the murderous European firepower. After being defeated in the field, they usually retreated to walled cities where they were vulnerable to European artillery. If they had waged guerrilla warfare, their knowledge of the terrain and their assurance of mass support might have enabled them to hold out long enough to make conquest prohibitively expensive. As it was, they could not stand up to river gunboats, coastal warships, and Gatling and Maxim machine guns firing over ten shots per second.

Despite the overwhelming odds, the Africans were by no means passive pawns. In certain regions they put up enough resistance to slow down the "European" forces seriously. The conquest of West Africa took twenty-five years, and parts of the Ivory Coast, Mali, Niger, Eastern and Northern Nigeria, and Mauritania were not pacified till the second decade of the twentieth century. The leaders of this African resistance today serve as national heroes for the newly independent states of Africa.

IV. EUROPE'S IMPACT

Economic

Since economic motives were prominent in the partitioning of Africa, it is not surprising that drastic economic changes followed in its wake. Europe no longer was content with boatloads of slaves at the coastal ports. The industrialized West no longer needed human slaves; technology had replaced them with an abundance of machines. Instead the West had need for the raw materials found in the interior of Africa, and it now had the technological means to extract these materials.

The first important step in the exploitation of Africa's resources came with the discovery of diamonds in Kimberly (1867) and gold in the Witwatersrand (1884). Equally great mineral wealth was discovered in the Rhodesias (gold and copper) and in the Congo (gold, copper, and diamonds). Many portions of the west coast yielded rich supplies of such tropical forest products as palm oil, rubber, and ivory. From explorers' reports it was known that some of the interi-

MEDICAL DOCTOR AND RAIN DOCTOR

Western missionaries in Africa brought a new culture as well as a new religion.
The clash between old and new is illustrated in the following argument between
*David Livingstone (medical doctor) and a native rain doctor.**

R. D. You ought not to despise our little knowledge, though you are ignorant of it.

M. D. I don't despise what I am ignorant of; I only think you are mistaken in saying that you have medicines which can influence the rain at all.

R. D. That's just the way people speak when they talk on a subject of which they have no knowledge. When we first opened our eyes, we found our forefathers making rain, and we follow in their footsteps. You, who send to Kuruman for corn, and irrigate your garden, may do without rain; we cannot manage in that way. If we had no rain, the cattle would have no pasture, the cows give no milk, our children become lean and die, our wives run away to other tribes who do make rain, and have corn, and the whole tribe become dispersed and lost; our fire would go out.

M. D. I quite agree with you as to the value of the rain; but you cannot charm the clouds by medicines. You wait till you see the clouds come, then you use your medicines, and take the credit which belongs to God only.

R. D. I use my medicines, and you employ yours; we are both doctors, and doctors are not deceivers. You give a patient medicine. Sometimes God is pleased to heal him by means of your medicine; sometimes not—he dies. When he is cured, you take the credit of what God does. I do the same. Sometimes God grants us rain, sometimes not. When he does, we take the credit of the charm. When a patient dies, you don't give up trust in your medicine, neither do I when rain falls. If you wish me to leave off my medicines, why continue your own?

M. D. I give medicines to living creatures within my reach, and can see the effects though no cure follows; you pretend to charm the clouds which are so far above us that your medicines never reach them. The clouds usually lie in one direction, and your smoke goes in another. God alone can command the clouds. Only try and wait patiently; God will give us rain without your medicines.

R. D. Mahala-ma-kapa-a-a! ! Well, I always thought white men were wise till this morning. Who ever thought of making trial of starvation? Is death pleasant then?

M. D. Could you make it rain on one spot and not on another?

R. D. I wouldn't think of trying. I like to see the whole country green, and all the people glad; the women clapping their hands and giving me their ornaments for thankfulness, and lullilooing for joy.

M. D. I think you deceive both them and yourself.

R. D. Well, then, there is a pair of us (meaning both are rogues).

The above is only a specimen of their way of reasoning, in which, when the language is well understood, they are perceived to be remarkably acute. These arguments are generally known, and I never succeeded in convincing a single individual of their fallacy, though I tried to do so in every way I could think of. Their faith in medicines as charms is unbounded. The general effect of argument is to produce the impression that you are not anxious for rain at all; and it is very undesirable to allow the idea to spread that you do not take a generous interest in their welfare.

*D. Livingstone, *Missionary Travels and Researches in South Africa* (J. Murray, 1857), pp. 22–25.

or plateaus had fertile soil as well as a pleasant climate. Consequently, European settlers flocked in, particularly to Southern Rhodesia and East Africa. Before long they had gained possession of the most desirable agricultural properties in these regions.

To transport the minerals and the agricultural commodities now being produced, the Europeans proceeded to build a network of railways in Africa, as they already had done in Asia. These railways were designed to facilitate the export of produce rather than to stimulate general economic development. The expansion of production and the construction of transportation facilities stimulated trade to the point where the traditional barter gave way to a monetary system. No longer did the Africans exchange slaves, gold dust, feathers, and ivory for the Europeans' salt, glassware, cloth, rum, and gin. By the end of the nineteenth century there was fairly widespread use of English silver coins and of Austrian and American dollars.

All of these economic developments naturally had profound effects on the native peoples. The inhabitants of the temperate plateau areas were affected most by the loss of the lands taken by white settlers. In some cases whole districts were reserved for exclusive white use, and the land could not be tilled by the Africans, even though it sometimes lay fallow. Consequently, the Africans were forced to work for wages on the white man's plantations, and some even "squatted" on the land of the white farmers for whom they worked to gain the privilege of tilling a small plot for themselves. In other regions the Africans found it necessary to leave their families and go to work in the mines. If the Africans refused to provide the labor needed for the plantations and mines, various types of forced labor were used. The most common was the levying of a head tax compelling the African to work in order to earn the money to pay the tax. These various developments reduced the traditional economic self-sufficiency of the African. No longer did he or she work simply to feed self and family. Africans were involved more and more in a money economy and so were affected by world economic conditions. Thus the effect of Europe's economic impact was twofold: to entangle the Africans in a worldwide money economy and to subordinate them,

directly or indirectly, to the whites who were everywhere the "boss."

Cultural

Together with the European traders, investors, and settlers came the European missionaries. They had a profound effect on African culture because they were the first Europeans who consciously sought to change it. The others affected it only indirectly and incidentally, as when they forced Africans to leave their ancestral villages to work in cities or mines. But missionaries came with the avowed purpose of changing the African way of life. They used three instruments to carry this out: education, medicine, and religion.

Schools offering a Western education and Western ideals were an integral part of every mission station. These schools were particularly influential since most colonial governments left the job of educating to the missionaries. In many respects the mission schools were constructive in their influence: Often they taught the pupils how to build better houses, improve their agricultural methods, and observe the rudi-

A missionary visit to a Zulu Kraal. The nineteenth-century European-American enthusiasm for working toward "The evangelization of the world in our time" found one of its major outlets in missionary efforts in Africa.

ments of hygiene and sanitation. They also taught reading and writing in African as well as European languages. The missionaries converted the African languages to writing and so laid the foundations for native African literature. The great majority of those Africans who chose literary careers were educated in missionary schools.

On the other hand, these schools inevitably had a subversive influence on the African people; they often taught that the traditional way of life was primitive and wrong. In time the students listened less to their parents and elders and more to their European teachers, whom they learned to respect. In addition, the mission schools used European books that taught more about Europe than about Africa. In fact, the beginning lessons in early history textbooks used in the French colonies dealt with "our ancestors the Gauls." Missionary education encouraged individualism, which was contrary to the communal African way of life. It is not surprising that Africans subjected to several years of this type of education were usually loath to return to their villages. Instead they looked for jobs with the colonial governments, missions, or private business, and so moved further away from their traditional culture.

The missions also brought medical knowledge and facilities that saved the lives of many Africans. But besides saving lives, medicine also forced Africans to question their traditional ideas of what caused illness and death. Whites had the power to make people well even after the proper petitioning of spirits had not worked. So traditional religion no longer could be counted on to meet all emergencies and to provide all the answers. Even though the majority of Africans clung to their old faiths, traditional religion was no longer as effective as it previously had been in holding together the African's whole way of life.

Political

The most serious and direct challenge to the traditional tribal authorities came from the class of Western-educated Africans that gradually developed in almost all the colonies. They tended to challenge not only the native chiefs but also the European officials. They did so because they imbibed in Western schools certain political ideas such as individual liberty and political freedom, and they saw no reason why the principles of liberalism and nationalism should apply in Europe but not in Africa. They were also goaded into political agitation by the discrimination they frequently encountered in government and private employment. Usually they were not allowed to be more than poorly paid clerks in European firms or very minor officials in the colonial administration. Again they could not see why, when they had the required education and experience, they should be kept in subordinate positions simply because their skins were dark. The Christian religion, and especially Protestantism, stimulated nationalism because it emphasized individual judgment and initiative. This point was made by a writer in an Angolan journal who said, "To tell a person he is able to interpret the Bible freely is to insinuate in him an undue autonomy and turn him into a rebel. . . . A Protestant native is already disposed towards—not to say an active agent in—the revolt against civilized peoples."[3]

SUGGESTED READINGS

For general histories of Africa, see the bibliography for Chapter 22 and also the comprehensive survey of historical literature on this area by P. D. Curtin, *African History*, No. 56 (Service Center for Teachers of History, 1964). The most recent survey of the slave trade is the judicious study by E. Reynolds, *Stand the Storm: A History of the Atlantic Slave Trade* (Shocken, 1985), which provides a full annotated bibliography. A more recent study is the special section in the *Journal of African History*, 1989, Vol. 30, No. 1, devoted to the subject "Atlantic Slave Trade: Scale, Structure and Supply." How 10 million Africans left their homelands since 1500 and how they responded to their new environments are analyzed in M. L. Kilson and R. I. Rotberg, eds., *The African Diaspora: Interpretative Essays* (Harvard University, 1976); and also in G. W. Irwin, *Africans Abroad: A Documentary History of the Black Diaspora in Asia, Latin America, and the Caribbean During the Age of Slavery* (Columbia University, 1977). For the abolition movement, see E. Williams, *Capitalism and Slavery* (University of North Carolina, 1944); R. Anstey, *The Atlantic Slave Trade and British Abolition, 1760–1810* (Humanities Press, 1975); and S. Miers, *Britain and the Ending of the Slave Trade* (Longman, 1975).

The accounts of the explorers provide colorful material on the opening up of the continent. A convenient collection is provided by M. Perham and J. Simmons, *African Discovery: An Anthology of Exploration* (Faber & Faber, 1942). A readable survey of the history of African exploration is available in C. Hibbert, *Africa Explored: Europeans in the Dark Continent* (Penguin, 1985).

A survey of the partitioning of Africa is available in A. Boahen, *African Perspectives on Colonialism* (Johns Hopkins University, 1987); and T. Pakenham, *The Scramble for Africa* (Random House, 1991). Finally, for the impact of the West on Africa there are P. D. Curtin, ed., *Africa and the West: Intellectual Responses to European Culture* (University of Wisconsin, 1972); R. W. July, *The Origins of Modern African Thought* (Praeger, 1968); and A. D. Roberts, ed., *The Colonial Movement in Africa* (Cambridge University, 1986).

NOTES

1. E. Reynolds, *Stand the Storm: A History of the Atlantic Slave Trade* (Schocken, 1985), p. 13.
2. Cited by H. Russell, *Human Cargoes* (Longman, 1948), p. 36.
3. Cited by T. Hodgkin, *Nationalism in Colonial Africa* (New York University, 1957), p. 98.

The Americas and the British Dominions

> Afterwards the Spaniards resolved to go and hunt the Indians who were in the mountains [of Cuba], where they perpetrated marvellous massacres. Thus they ruined and depopulated all this island which we beheld not long ago; and it excites pity, and great anguish to see it deserted, and reduced to a solitude.
>
> *Bartolome De Las Casas, 1552*

> The disappearance of these people [Australian aborigines] before the white invaders is just as certain as the disappearance of wolves in a country becoming civilized and populous.
>
> *James Stephen, 1841*

Even more far reaching than Europe's impact on Asia and Africa during the nineteenth century were its effects on the Americas and the British Dominions. In fact, this "impact" was so extensive and dramatic that it is more appropriate to refer to it as outright Europeanization.

Europeanization involves more than just political domination or cultural penetration. It involves actual biological replacement, the physical substitution of one people by another—as happened in the relatively empty territories of the Western Hemisphere and the South Pacific. The scanty indigenous populations were either wiped out or pushed aside, and tens of millions of European emigrants swarmed in and occupied the lands of the native peoples. With them the Europeans brought their political institutions, their ways of earning a living, and their cultural traditions. Thus the ethnic Europeanization of overseas territories was followed inevitably by political, economic, and cultural Europeanization.

I. ETHNIC EUROPEANIZATION

In Chapter 26, Section VII, we explained why Europe was able to supply so many emigrants, and why these millions of people were willing to leave their ancestral homes and brave unknown dangers in far-off continents. The thin ribbons of European settlement that existed in 1763 had stretched by 1914 to cover entire continents, including Australia and New Zealand, which had still been untouched at the earlier date.

The majority of European emigrants went to the Americas. This is natural, since the earliest European colonies were established in the Americas. Also, those continents offered much greater natural resources and economic opportunities. However, since the first European settlements were in Central and South America, it is surprising that so many more of these emigrants settled in North America.

The fundamentally different character of the Spanish and Portuguese colonies, compared to the English, explains the greater immigrant population in North America. The Spaniards and the Portuguese settled in territories with relatively dense Indian populations. Although estimates of the number of Indians in the Americas before the coming of the Europeans vary tremendously, it is agreed that the Indian populations were concentrated in what came to be Latin America. These native peoples supplied all the labor that was needed, so European settlers were not required for that purpose. Accordingly emigrants to the Spanish and Portuguese colonies in the Americas were mostly soldiers, members of the clergy, government officials, and a few necessary craftspeople.

North of the Rio Grande, by contrast, the Indian population was relatively sparse and provided no reservoir of labor. The English along the Atlantic seaboard and the French on the banks of the St. Lawrence had to do their own work, whether it was cutting the forests, plowing the cleared land, or fishing the coastal waters. Under these circumstances North America wanted all the settlers it could get, and so the British North American colonies were opened to immigrants of all races, languages, and faiths. By 1835 there were 4.8 million European settlers in all of Central and South America as against 13.8 million in North America.

In the second half of the nineteenth century European emigration steadily increased, reaching its height between 1900 and 1910 when almost 1 million people left each year. This unprecedented flood poured into every continent, so that Australia, South Africa, and South America now were peopled by substantial numbers of Europeans, although North America continued to be the main beneficiary.

The migration of millions to the Americas resulted in the displacement of corresponding millions of native Amerindians. The extent of this displacement is being realized only now, when demographers and historians are discovering how wrong was the long-held assumption that the New World was largely empty, available for colonists from other continents. Recent research discloses that about 1500 the old and new worlds were roughly comparable in population density[1], with some 100 million in China, and 60 to 70 million in the Mediterranean region, compared to about 80 million in the Americas (untouched by the Black Death and

Table 33.1   Racial Distribution in the Americas (in millions)

	White		Negro		Indian
	1835	*1935*	*1835*	*1935*	*1935*
North America	13.8	124.3	2.6	12.4	1.8
Central America	1.9	6.9	2.7	8.4	21.4
South America	2.9	40.9	4.5	18.7	29.2
Total	18.6	172.1	9.8	39.5	52.4

Italian immigrants on Ellis Island, New York around 1900. The faces of these new arrivals from southern Italy reflect the anxiety and hope inspired by the move to a new land. By 1900, Italy was supplying more immigrants to the Western Hemisphere than any other country in Europe.

responsible for the most devastating holocaust in human history. The lists include smallpox, measles, diphtheria, trachoma, whooping cough, chicken pox, bubonic plague, malaria, typhoid fever, cholera, yellow fever, dengue fever, scarlet fever, amoebic dysentery, influenza, and certain varieties of tuberculosis.

It may well be asked why the Amerindians, who originally also were immigrants from Eurasia, did not arrive in the Americas already immunized against those diseases. The offered explanation is that in those distant times the early immigrants were still in the food gathering stage, when those diseases had not yet appeared. Moreover, they had come from Siberia, where the scanty population and frigid climate was not conducive to epidemics. So the immigrants arrived without a built-in immunity, which they could not acquire after reaching the empty lands of the New World—hence their genocidal vulnerability when the Europeans arrived with their native diseases and those of their African slaves.

As far as the specific sources of immigration were concerned, the Latin American countries were peopled, as might be expected, mostly by emigrants from the Iberian peninsula, although considerable numbers also came in the late nineteenth century from Italy and Germany. The great majority of the emigrants to North America were, until 1890, from northwestern Europe. After that date, approximately one-third came from northwestern Europe, and the remaining two-thirds came from eastern and southern Europe. In the case of the British dominions, immigration restrictions limited the supply largely to the British Isles. After World War I, and especially after World War II, the dominions liberalized their immigration policies in order to attract more people to fill their wide open spaces.

The net result of these migrations has been the ethnic Europeanization of the Americas and the British dominions. These areas have become largely European in population, although there are certain important exceptions such as the native Indian strain remaining predominant in Central America (58 percent of the total population) and highly significant in South America (33 percent). The substantial Negro element

other current Eurasian epidemics). The Americas definitely were not empty when Columbus arrived, but the estimated 5 million Amerindians who lived in the present-day United States in 1492 had declined to 600,000 by 1809.

Some of the deaths were due to violence and overwork, but the chief cause was the combination of Eurasian and African diseases that the immigrants unwittingly introduced to the New World. Scientists have assembled lists of these diseases, which proved as lethal for the vulnerable Amerindians as the fourteenth-century Black Death had been for Eurasians. The lists comprise an intimidating array of afflictions that were largely, though not exclusively,

Smallpox wreaked havoc among Native Americans who lacked biological resistance to European diseases. This drawing by Aztec illustrators shows Aztec victims of a smallpox epidemic that struck Tenochtitlán in 1520. Historians estimate that up to forty percent of the population of central Mexico died within a year. This catastrophic decline weakened the Aztecs' ability to resist the Spanish conquest of their land.

introduced into the Americas as a result of the slave trade is another exception to ethnic Europeanization. As observed earlier, it is estimated that between 12 million and 20 million slaves survived the transatlantic passage and reached the New World. Their descendants today comprise about 10 percent of the total population in North America, 30 percent in Central America, and 21 percent in South America. South Africa represents another exception to ethnic Europeanization; there the native Africans outnumber the whites (whether of Boer or British origin) by more than three to one.

Finally, the European Schools of Tropical Medicine that developed in the nineteenth century facilitated overseas ethnic Europeanization by reducing European mortality rates in the tropics. The Schools based their work on the research of Robert Koch, Louis Pasteur and other microbiologists, and also on the observations of medical officers responsible for the health of military personnel in tropical areas. Through trial and error they learned the importance of providing pure water for the troops, of discarding sewage hygienically, and of using mosquito netting against tropical insects. Americans pio-

neered with these measures in Cuba and Panama, successfully curbing the ravages of malaria and yellow fever.

II. POLITICAL EUROPEANIZATION

Ethnic Europeanization was accompanied by political Europeanization. This took many forms, reflecting original differences in the European mother countries, as well as different conditions existing in the overseas lands. For example, Latin America and Britain's thirteen colonies won their political independence through armed revolution in the late eighteenth and early nineteenth centuries. By contrast, the British dominions gained self-government in the late nineteenth century by acts of the British Parliament. Therefore, they have remained with the British Commonwealth of Nations to the present day, recognizing the sovereignty of the British Crown, and at the same time enjoying full self-rule.

Another example of diversity within political Europeanization is the successful unification of the thirteen colonies and their eventual

OKLAHOMA LAND RUSH

*A vivid example of how the Indian lands were flooded by Europeans is found in the opening for settlement of the Oklahoma Cherokee Strip in 1893. The following description is from one of the participants, Billy McGinty.**

I had already slipped over into the Strip and picked out the place I aimed to file on. A hundred and sixty acres on the bank of Camp Creek; land sloping down so pretty you could run furrows smooth and straight as ribbons. Dig up the brush and you could set out enough peach trees to keep a whole country in fruit. I'd sow seed and reap money. Then I'd find me a spry girl and raise myself a crop of kids on that stretch. . . .

Day of the Run, I beat the roosters up. . . . By eight o'clock, four hours till starting time, men and horses were packed in so close lightning couldn't have cut them loose.

Men cursed and snarled at each other like dogs, as they tried to cut in their wagons ahead of others. Fist fights broke out along with dog fights.

Eleven fifty. Ten minutes until hell would break, and every minute like a year of your life. Eleven fifty-five, but the soldiers on guard not noticing that my horse's front hoofs were already two inches across the line.

Eleven-fifty-nine. And now the talk was like the buzz of wild bees starting to swarm, as the official starter stepped on the line. He had his watch in one hand and his gun in the other. He looked at the watch and lifted the gun.

He fired one shot in the air. Wheels cracked! Whips popped! Hoofs thundered! The Run was on. . . .

All around me, wheel matched distance with saddle and man with man. Wagon was crashing against wagon. Horse's hides were raw red from being whipped to make them run faster. Drivers were standing up in wagons and buggies, lashing their own teams and those of other men when they crowded too close....

Just before we reached the creek, I jumped off at the stretch I had picked out.

I grabbed rocks and sticks to mark off my hundred and sixty. . . . When I had put down the last marker, I cut a branch from a cottonwood and stuck my bandanna on it. For the law said you had to put up some kind of a banner when you had finished staking a place.

Then I stood up and looked out over that first piece of ground I had ever called my own. My heart was pounding as loud as the hoofs I had left behind.

"You're somebody now, Bill," I said to myself. "You got the finest horse, and you staked the finest claim. You outrode 'em all and, by thunder, you'll outfarm 'em all."

*Billy McGinty, "Plow Fever," in Harold Preece, *Living Pioneers* (Thomas Y. Crowell, 1952), pp. 190–201.

expansion from the Atlantic to the Pacific as the United States of America. Latin America, by contrast, experienced political fragmentation. A final example of the variety of political Europeanization is the political stability of the United States and the British dominions as against the never-ending coups in Latin America.

Whereas the United States has kept its 1787 Constitution to the present day, the Latin American states have adopted an average of ten different constitutions each.

In conclusion, political Europeanization involved the transplanting of European political institutions to overseas lands. But in the process

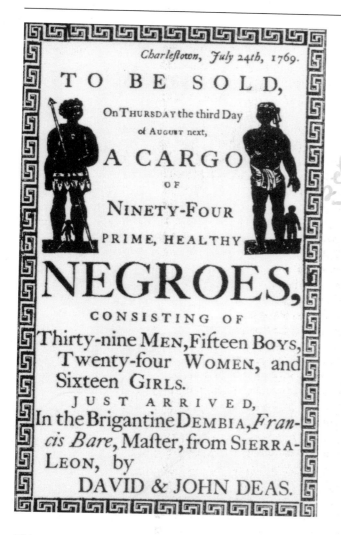

This 1769 Broadside advertised the arrival of a cargo of West African slaves in Charleston, South Carolina. By that date, slaves made up over two-thirds of the colony's settlers. Note that nearly equal numbers of men and women have been imported. This practice would eventually contribute to the formation of slave families and communities.

of transplanting there were adaptation and change. A Canadian or Australian political leader would be quite lost today if he found himself at the head of an American political party with its precarious balance of sectional interests, nationality blocs, and big-city machines. He would have been even more bewildered by Latin American politics and their unceasing succession of constitutions and caudillos.

III. ECONOMIC AND CULTURAL EUROPEANIZATION

Europeanization prevailed as much in the economic as in the political field. Europe provided much of the labor, the capital, the technology, and the markets for the economic development of the overseas lands. Between 1820 and 1830, 36 percent of all American exports went to Britain, and 43 percent of all American imports came from Britain. European capital—mostly British, Dutch, and German—poured into the United States during the nineteenth century, especially in the building of railways. By 1914, foreign investments in the United States totaled $7.2 billion. And in the comparatively underdeveloped Latin American countries, European investments dominated the national economies to a much greater degree than they did the American.

Cultural Europeanization inevitably accompanied the ethnic, political, and economic Europeanization, and this was true almost as much of the regions that won independence as of those that remained with the British Commonwealth. In Latin America the predominant cultural pattern is Spanish, with the exception of Portuguese Brazil; this pattern is evident in the Spanish language spoken by the majority of the people and in the Roman Catholicism they profess. One sees it also in architectural forms such as the patio or courtyard, the barred window, and the house front that is flush with the sidewalk. Town planning, based on the central plaza rather than on the main street, is equally revealing. Much of the clothing is Spanish, including the men's broad-rimmed hats of felt or straw and the women's cloth head coverings—mantilla, head shawl, or decorative scarf. In family organization the typical Spanish pattern of male dominance and close supervision of young women has been followed, as has the tendency to regard physical labor as undignified and unsuitable for gentlemen.

Although Latin American culture is basically Spanish or Portuguese, a strong Indian influence prevails, especially in Mexico, Central America, and the northwestern part of South America, where the Indians make up a large percentage of the total population. This influence (see Chapter 25, Section V) is evident in cook-

The framing of the United States Constitution in 1787 by the Constitutional Convention and its acceptance in 1789 by the states—with the understanding that it would be amended immediately to include a Bill of Rights—began a bold political experiment in republican government across a large nation.

ing, clothing, building materials, and religious practices. Latin American culture also has a considerable African element, brought over by the millions of slaves imported to work on plantations. This African influence is strongest in the Caribbean area, where most of the slaves settled, although examples of their influence can be found in most parts of Latin America.

The culture that developed in the United States was less influenced by the native Indian population than was Latin American culture. The main reason is that the Indians were fewer in number and less advanced. Nevertheless, Indian influence was not altogether negligible: twenty-five states bear Indian names; at least 300 Indian words are now part of the English language; and many Indian inventions, such as moccasins, canoes, toboggans, and snowshoes, are in common use. Likewise, the United States

has been less influenced by African culture than have certain Caribbean states. Still, the influence here has been considerable; blacks make up nearly 12 percent of the total U.S. population, compared to the one-half of 1 percent that is Indian. Despite these Indian and African populations, American culture is overwhelmingly European in origin, even though its European characteristics were drastically modified during the process of transplantation and adaptation.

SUGGESTED READINGS

General surveys of the process of Europeanization are E. Fischer, *The Passing of the European Age* (Harvard University, 1948); L. Hartz, *The Founding of New Societies* (Harcourt Brace Jovanovich, 1964); W. B. Hamilton, ed., *The Transfer of Institutions* (Duke University,

The forces of Emiliano Zapata march on Xochimilco in 1914. Women fought alongside men and played other prominent roles during the Mexican Revolution.

1964); P.D. Curtin, *Death by Migration: Europe's Encounter with the Tropical World in the Nineteenth Century* (Cambridge University, 1989) which analyzes the medical obstacles to ethnic Europeanization; and A.W. Crosby, *Germs, Seeds and Animals: Studies in Ecological History* (M.E. Sharpe, 1994), a fascinating ecological approach to the Europeanization process.

NOTE

1. M. Lunenfeld, *1492: Discovery, Invasion, Encounter* (D.C. Heath, 1991), pp 321–326.

CHAPTER

34

Polynesia

I. ISLANDS AND VOYAGERS

Beyond the American continents that the Europeans stumbled upon by accident in the fifteenth century is the vast realm of the Pacific known as Oceania, and also as Polynesia because of its multitude of islands. It extends for thousands of miles from the Western coasts of the Americas to the continent of Asia. Since the Pacific realm is the farthest removed from Europe, it remained unknown to Europeans until long after they had discovered and explored the more accessible Americas and Africa.

Europeans remained ignorant of Polynesia for so long not only because it was on the other side of the world, but also because it lacked the many riches that attracted Europeans to other regions. Nowhere in the Pacific are there spacious prairie lands or luxuriant river valleys of the sort that generated the magnificent civilizations of Mesopotamia, Egypt, India, and China. Instead the Pacific world is an immense oceania, dotted with thousands of islets. So minuscule are these scattered fragments that, excluding the large islands of New Guinea and New Zealand, the combined area of all the islets total only that of England or of the state of New York.

Although the Pacific islands lacked the massive resources of the Eurasian landmass, nevertheless they did yield certain staples that, according to an Australian authority, enabled the native peoples to be "better fed than many of their cash-cropping descendants who eat largely out of tins."[1]

The major staples were two tree crops and two root crops. The tree crops were coconuts and breadfruit. Without coconuts, human life hardly could have been sustained on many of

The expansion of Western multinational corporations has altered patterns of consumption throughout the world, undermining countless traditional ways of life.

the small islands, where to the present day the daily consumption per person is at least five nuts. These provided both food and drink, while the trunk of the coconut tree provided timber for houses, canoes and spears, and likewise the leaves supplied thatch, fans and mats. Equally essential was the breadfruit, produced by a prolific tree yielding annually about 150 large fruits weighing two to five kilograms each. The fruits were baked, or fermented in covered pits to form a dough which kept for months.

The root crops were the yam and the taro. The first is a starch tuber, often weighing thirty pounds or more, that was boiled, baked, or ground into flour. The taro also is a starchy tuber, served as a vegetable, or a pudding, or ground into flour. Noteworthy also are bananas, both wild and cultivated, which served as a staple on some of the islands.

These foodstuffs were introduced to the scattered islands by colonists who fanned out over the Pacific from Southeast Asia, goaded by population pressure. By 1100–1000 B.C.E. they were settled in the Tonga-Samoa area; by 300 C.E. they had reached the Marquesas; and a century or two later they had sailed as far north as Hawaii and as far east as 2,000 miles from the South American coast, where on Easter Island they erected the remarkable mono-

lithic stone heads, from thirty to forty feet tall. The southernmost reach of these intrepid "Vikings of the Pacific," as they have been called, was New Zealand, where they arrived by 800 C.E. Despite the immense area colonized, the Pacific colonists retained an impressive cultural homogeneity. The great explorer James Cook was astonished to find in the eighteenth century that his men could trade in the same language at Hawaii as in New Zealand in the distant south.

II. COMMERCE AND COLONIES

Europe's first contact with Oceania was episodic, in contrast to the sustained and systematic exploration and colonization of Africa and the Americas. The Pacific basin was viewed as a passageway rather than as a destination. The passageway was used sporadically for such purposes as conducting the lucrative trade between Acapulco and Asia (exchanging Mexican silver for Chinese products such as silk and porcelain) and searching for a water passage from the North Pacific across the North American Arctic to Hudson's Bay.

In the late eighteenth century, Europeans began to reappraise the Pacific basin as an intrinsically valuable region. They were attracted by oceanic commodities that were of value in the world markets. Whale and seal oil were treasured in the days before the large-scale production of vegetable oils, and the location and extraction of petroleum. Likewise whale-bone or baleen, being light, tough, and flexible, was used in corsets and in the hoops of crinolines, as well as for many other purposes now met by plastic. The furs of sea animals also were prized, especially the sea otter whose luxurious pelt was particularly coveted in China. Other Pacific products included sweet-smelling sandalwood popular in China for ceremonial burning as incense, live pigs and salt pork valued for ship rations and for export to Europe where it cost substantially less than local pork, and minor products of reef and lagoon, such as pearl shell, tortoise shell, and bêche-de-mer, or sea slug, a delicacy relished in China.

In Polynesia, as in other regions, the economic penetration of European commerce was followed or paralleled by the political intrusion of European colonialism. This was the case in the North Pacific where the Russians had been active since the early eighteenth century when Peter the Great sent Vitus Bering to the Far East to determine the precise nature of the connection, if any, between Asia and North America. During that expedition the Russians discovered that otter and seal pelts afforded riches comparable to the bullion garnered by the Spaniards in the Aztec and Inca empires. To exploit the opportunity, Moscow chartered in 1799 the Russian-America Company, which soon fulfilled its mission. By 1818 it had shipped out 80,000 otter and 1,495,000 seal pelts, in the process decimating those animals in the North Pacific waters, as well as the native Eskimos and Indians who were grossly exploited. Under aggressive directors, the Russian-America Company sought to establish settlements as well as trading posts. By 1820 some fifteen Russian settlements dotted the coast between the Bering Strait and Fort Ross, only 100 kilometers north of San Francisco.

These settlements, however, did not make the Pacific coast Russian, as the Atlantic coast had become Spanish, English and French. The basic reason was the lack of any mass Russian migration to the North Pacific, comparable to the massive West European settlement of the entire Atlantic seaboard from Newfoundland to Tierra del Fuego. In that pre-jet era, it was much easier to cross oceans in sailing ships than to traverse the thousands of miles of Siberian wilderness separating the Russian heartland from the Pacific coast. So those fifteen Russian settlements reaching down to California remained isolated and thinly held toeholds. The largest at Novo-Arkhangel'sk (presently Sitka) had only 222 inhabitants.

The other settlements were even smaller, so none had the resources to sink enduring roots. They remained wretched hutments along the coasts, where free-wheeling Western entrepreneurs showed up periodically to buy cheap from the Russians and sell dear in Canton. Consequently Moscow had no real alternative in 1867 when it sold Alaska for a pittance to the Americans, whose Yankee clippers were so prominent in Pacific waters, and whose frontiersmen were advancing irresistibly in their covered wagons overland to the West coast.

In contrast to the abortive efforts of the Russians, the Western Europeans quickly dominated the Pacific basin as they already had the Atlantic. They had far superior commercial and naval resources, enabling them to focus on the most productive and strategic islands, which they then proceeded to annex one by one. For example, Britain annexed Fiji in 1874, and France likewise annexed Tahiti in 1880. The United States in 1898, following the Spanish-American War, annexed Hawaii, Guam and the Philippines. With the outbreak of the First World War in 1914, New Zealand forces occupied Samoa, and an Australian force took German New Guinea and parts of the Bismarck Archipelago. Thus by 1914 Oceania, like Africa, had been partitioned and absorbed into the worldwide European empires.

III. EUROPE'S IMPACT

Europe's impact on Polynesia was far greater than on Africa or Eurasia. The clear reason was that the small and lightly peopled Pacific islands could not possibly muster the resistance of mil-

A Polynesian canoe similar to the great double canoes that once criss-crossed the Pacific.

lennia-old civilizations backed by populations of hundreds of millions rather than a few thousands. So those few thousands soon were overwhelmed by immigrants from all countries, attracted by the lure of what were popularly regarded as the "paradise islands of the Pacific." The attractiveness of those islands was enhanced by the fact that they were free of most of the tropical diseases that decimated Europeans who tried to settle in Africa or the Caribbean. This was especially true of the lethal malaria affliction. Most of the Pacific islands are malaria free, simply because they have no anopheline mosquitos.

As in other regions, population diffusion in Oceania also involved disease diffusion and cultural disruption. Native crafts were discarded with the importation of European tools and machine-woven cloth. Forgotten was the skill for making cloth from the bark of a tree and for building the great double canoes with which their ancestors had criss-crossed the Pacific. Even the sport of surf riding became too burdensome and was abandoned. Those perfect Polynesian teeth that the early explorers had so admired began to decay with the consumption of European foods.

More serious than decaying teeth were new ailments such as tuberculosis, smallpox, dysentery, and venereal disease, which now were being passed on from one generation to the next. Thus depopulation ravaged the Polynesians as cruelly as it had the Amerindians earlier. On the island of Tahiti, for example, the inhabitants totaled about 40,000 when Captain Cook arrived in 1769. By the end of the century, missionaries were reporting that wars and disease had shrunk this number to 15,000. By the 1830s the number was down to 9,000 and eventually dropped further to 6,000.

Cook repeatedly expressed a nagging sense of responsibility for what was happening to the Tahitians.

I cannot avoid expressing it as my real opinion that it would have been far better for these poor people never to have known our superiority in the accommodations and arts that make life comfortable. . . . it may be too late to go back to their old, less perfect, contrivances, which they now despise, and have discontinued since the introduction of ours. For, by the time the iron tools, of which they are now possessed, are worn out, they will have almost lost the knowledge of their own. A stone hatchet is, at present, as rare a thing amongst them, as an iron one was eight years ago, and a chisel of bone or stone is not to be seen.[2]

It is noteworthy that Captain Cook was appalled not only by the miseries inflicted on the Pacific Islanders. He also recognized that they were part and parcel of a world wide process.

. . . we debauch their morals already prone to vice and we introduce among them wants and perhaps diseases which they never before knew and which serve only to disturb that happy tranquillity they and their forefathers had enjoyed. If any one denies the truth of this assertion let him tell what the natives of the whole extent of America have gained by the commerce they had had with Europeans.[3]

Noteworthy also is the fact that Cook felt empathy not only for the attractive inhabitants of favored islands such as Tahiti, but also for the comparatively underdeveloped aborigines on the relatively inhospitable continent of Australia. His first impression of the aborigines was that "they may appear to some to be the most wretched people on earth but in reality they are

Sloops lie at anchor in Kealakakua Bay during the visit of Captain James Cook. Hawaiians paddle in outrigger canoes out to the ships through choppy waves.

far happier than we Europeans." Cook's botanist, Joseph Banks, concurred: "Thus live these I had almost said, happy people, content with little, nay almost nothing."[4]

These appraisals presented Europeans with a disturbing anomaly. On the one hand they were confident and smug about the technological superiority of their culture and the material comforts it provided. On the other hand the Pacific islanders and other native peoples, with an obviously inferior technology, and lacking the "contrivances" enjoyed by Europeans, nevertheless appeared to be content and even "happier." Searching for an explanation, some Europeans developed the idea of the "noble savage," living happily close to nature, and free from the stresses and restraints of civilization. Those Europeans who, for one reason or another, were unhappy with the society in which they lived, were especially attracted to the "noble savage" concept. For them, the enemy was civilization itself, and therefore they romanticized Polynesia as a paradise of idyllic island communities.

The romanticization involved considerable envy, as evident in Joseph Banks' observation that in Tahiti, "Love is the Chief Occupation." This pleasurable condition, he noted, was possible because on the islands, a man could support his family with minimal work, leaving ample time for amorous pursuits. A man, "by planting 4 breadfruit trees, a work which cannot last more than an hour, does as much for his generation as a European who with yearly returning toil cultivat[es] corn for his family, and this Leisure is given up to Love."[5]

Inevitably the "noble savage" concept gave way to a more realistic appraisal as Europeans came to know better the Pacific islanders. Then they became aware of a grim underside to oceanic culture, including social ailments such as warfare, infanticide, oppressive taboos, human sacrifice, and slavery, as well as natural disasters such as hurricanes and tsunami that periodically devastated the islands.

Europe's ambivalence towards Polynesia was most evident in the contrasting reactions of missionaries and artists and intellectuals. Missionaries were repelled by the Polynesian predilection for extramarital sex, for dancing with scanty clothing, and for Sunday game playing. They campaigned vigorously against such behavior, with results by no means as beneficial as they had assumed.

More positive was the reaction of European artists and intellectuals, as evident in Herman Melville's novels (notably *Moby Dick*); in Paul Gaugin's art, inspired by his experiences in Tahiti; and in the life of Robert Louis Stevenson,

In response to the accelerated pace of change in the late nineteenth century, Paul Gauguin (1848–1903) left his native France for the South Seas where he was captivated by a simpler and seemingly timeless way of life. He romanticized this environment in his 1894 painting The Day of the God *(Mahana no Atua).*

who took his family, his household trappings, and his chronic sickliness to Hawaii, Tahiti, the Marquesas, and finally to remote Samoa.

These early admirers of Polynesia and its inhabitants have their modern-day counterparts in the swarms of tourists who flock to the islands each year, seeking a brief respite from the pressures of everyday life. This appears to be a mutually satisfying arrangement, with tourists enjoying the respite, and the locals welcoming the abundant tourist-derived revenues. On the other hand, even a brief sojourn in Polynesia reveals that Captain Cook's apprehension about long-term disruption of Polynesian culture is as relevant and worrisome today as it was in the sixteenth century. Not only is there ongoing cultural disruption, but also undermining of personal health and obliteration of ancestral birthplace islands.

As regards culture, the Polynesians on remote Easter Island have felt sufficiently threatened to organize a "Corporation for Cultural Protection." The founder of the corporation has defined clearly its rationale: "If I want to sleep, I sleep. If I want to eat, I eat. I can spend a week without spending any money. If we are not careful, people will turn this island into another Hawaii or Tahiti, where the only important thing is money."[6]

As regards personal health, Captain Cook wrote in his journal about Polynesians who had perfect teeth and "walk gracefully and run nimbly." Very different are the descendants of those Polynesians, who are the least healthy people in today's multiethnic Hawaiian state. Their death rates are 44 percent higher than the average for heart disease, 39 percent higher for cancer, 31 percent higher for strokes, and 196 percent higher for diabetes.[7]

More alarming than cultural and physical deterioration is the threat of literal extinction under rising ocean levels. The rising is linked to the "greenhouse" warming that is melting glaciers and ice caps and causing oceans to expand as they warm. Although there is disagreement about the scale and tempo of this drift, there is no question about unprecedented and unpredictable "surges" now sweeping over Polynesian islets. "These aren't storms, they're surges," states Giff Johnson, editor of the newspaper of the Marshall Islands near New Guinea. "Its nice weather, and all of a sudden water is pouring into your living room. Its very clear that something is happening in the Pacific, and these islands are feeling it. Its so close to the heart here, because you're talking about people's very existence. It scares the hell out of people to think that their country might just be gone."[8]

Seven immense solemn moai statues stand in a row atop a stone base at the altar of ahu Akivi. The Moai were built by the Rapa Nui natives of Easter Island. Over six hundred statues were cut from the volcanic rock at Rano Raraku "the nursery" and they all face west.

The Marshall Islands editor is not alone in expressing concern about the security of his homeland. The president of the United States voiced equal concern about the entire globe in a statement to the United Nations environmental conference (June 26, 1997):

Concentrations of greenhouse gases in the atmosphere are at their highest levels in more than 200,000 years and climbing sharply. If the trend does not change, scientists expect the seas to rise two feet or more over the next century. In America, Louisiana and other coastal areas will be flooded; in Asia 17 percent of Bangladesh, land on which six million people now live, will be lost; island chains such as the Maldives will disappear from the map unless we reverse the predictions.[9]

NOTES

1. D. H. K. Spate, *Paradise Found and Lost* (Australian National University Press, 1988), p. 34.
2. Cited by A. Moorehead, *The Fatal Impact: An Account of the Invasion of the South Pacific 1767–1840* (Harper & Row, 1966), p. 70.
3. Ibid., pp. 55, 56.
4. Ibid., p. 117.
5. Cited by Spate, *Paradise Found*, p. 35.
6. *New York Times*, February 6, 1993.
7. Kathryn True, "Reclaiming Tradition," *In Context*, No. 39, p. 54.
8. *New York Times*, March 2, 1997.
9. *New York Times*, June 27, 1997.

CHAPTER
35

Consolidation of Global Unity

Above all I wish to urge upon you once again the immense vista of difficulty and possibility of danger opened up by the newly awakened ambitions and aspirations of the Eastern races. What may be the final outcome of the collision ... it is impossible to foretell. This, however, is certain—that contact with Western thought and Western ideas has exercised a revivifying influence upon all the races of the East. Those that have come into sharpest contact with it have exhibited most markedly its effects.

Lord Ronaldshay, 1909

The period between 1763 and 1914 stands out in world history as the period when Europe became master of the entire globe, whether directly or indirectly. Europe's domination was evident not only in the political sphere—in the form of great colonial empires—but also in the economic and cultural spheres. On the other hand, the decade before 1914 also witnessed the first serious challenges to Europe's predominance. The most significant challenge was Japan's defeat of Russia. The contemporary revolutions in Turkey and Persia and the underground rumblings in various colonial or semi-colonial regions were also noteworthy. Let us first consider Europe's political, economic, and cultural global predominance, to be followed by a look at the early challenges to this predominance.

I. EUROPE'S POLITICAL DOMINANCE

Between 1500 and 1763 Europe had emerged from its obscurity and gained control of the oceans and the relatively empty spaces of Siberia and the Americas. But as far as Asia and Africa were concerned, Europe's impact was still negligible at the end of the eighteenth century. In Africa there were only a string of slave-trading stations along the coasts and an insignificant settlement of Boers on the southern tip of the continent. Likewise, in India the Europeans were confined to their few coastal trading posts and had not yet begun to have a substantial effect on the vast hinterland. In east Asia the Westerners were rigidly restricted to Canton and Deshima despite their pleas for further contacts. If by some miracle the relations between Europe on the one hand and Africa and Asia on the other had been suddenly severed in the late eighteenth century, there would have been little left to show for the three centuries of interaction. A few ruined forts and churches would have been almost the only reminders of the intruders who had come across the sea. Everyday life would have continued along traditional lines as in the past millennia.

By 1914 this situation had changed fundamentally. Europe's impact had grown immeasurably, both in extent and in depth. Vast portions of the globe—the United States, Latin America, Siberia, and the British dominions—had been Europeanized. Europeans had migrated to those territories in droves, displacing to a greater or lesser degree the native peoples. It is true that by 1914 the United States and Latin America had won political independence, and the British dominions were self-governing. Nevertheless, as we have seen, the dominions had become Europeanized. They were intimately related to Europe as regards ethnic composition, economic ties, and cultural institutions.

Vast territories, including the entire continent of Africa, with the exception of Liberia and Ethiopia, and the greater part of Asia, had become outright colonial possessions of the European powers. Of the 16,819,000 square miles in Asia, no fewer than 9,443,000 square miles were under European rule. These included 6,496,000 square miles under Russia, 1,998,000 under Britain, 587,000 under Holland, 248,000 under France, 114,000 under the United States, and a paltry 193 for Germany. In contrast to these tremendous colonial territories, Japan, the only truly independent Asian nation in 1914, accounted for a mere 161,000 square miles.

The remaining portion of the globe, apart from these colonial possessions and the Europeanized territories, consisted of countries that were nominally independent but were actually semicolonial. These semicolonial countries included the great Chinese and Ottoman empires as well as such smaller states as Iran, Afghanistan, and Nepal. All these countries were dominated by European economic and military power. They were allowed to retain a nominal political independence simply because the European powers could not agree on the details of their dismemberment.

In this way the entire globe had come under Europe's domination by 1914. It was the extraordinary climax of the long process started a half-millennium earlier when Portuguese captains began to feel their way down the coast of Africa. One peninsula of the Eurasian landmass was now the center of the world, with a concentration of power altogether unprecedented in past history (see map of World of Western Dominance, 1914, p. 525).

II. EUROPE'S ECONOMIC DOMINANCE

The fact that by 1914 Europe's domination was unprecedented not only in extent but also in depth was evident in the economic control that Europe exercised. Europe had become the banker of the world, providing the capital needed for building transcontinental railroads, digging interoceanic canals, opening mines, and establishing plantations. Europe had become not only the banker but also the industrial workshop of the world. By 1870 Europe was responsible for 64.7 percent of the world's total industrial output. The only rival was the United States, with 23.3 percent. Even though the United States had forged ahead by 1913 to 35.8 percent, Europe's factories in that year still turned out 47.7 percent of the world's total production.

The effect of Europe's great outpouring of capital and technology was an unprecedented global economic unity. By 1914 over 516,000 kilometers of cables had been laid on ocean beds, as well as a vast network of telegraph and telephone lines on the land surface of the globe. By 1914 over 30,000 ships with a total tonnage of 50 million carried goods from one part of the world to another. Several canals were built to facilitate world commerce. The most important were the Suez (1869), which shortened the route between western Europe and India by 4,000 miles, and the Panama (1914), which reduced the distance between New York and San Francisco by almost 8,000 miles. Continents were opened for economic exploitation by the construction of several transcontinental railroads. The first in the United States was completed in 1869, the first in Canada in 1885, the trans-Siberian in 1905. The Berlin to Baghdad and the Cape to Cairo railroads were almost completed by 1914.

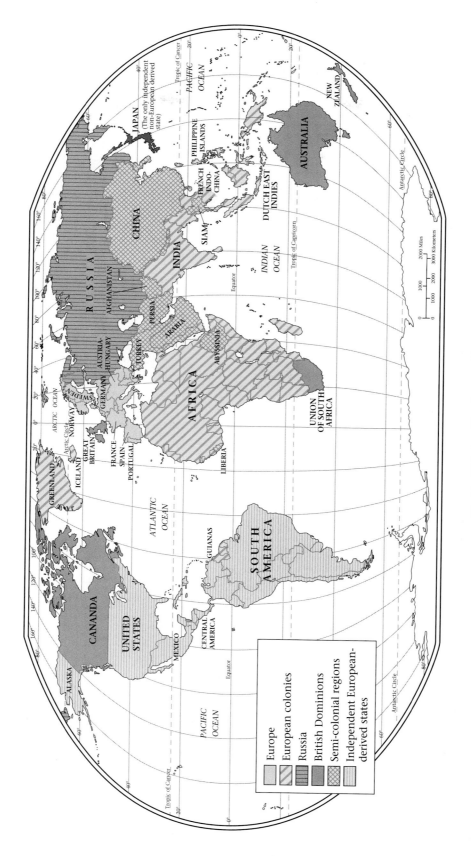

World of Western Dominance, 1914

JAPAN (The only independent non-European derived state)

PACIFIC OCEAN

NEW ZEALAND

AUSTRALIA

PHILIPPINE ISLANDS

FRENCH INDO-CHINA

DUTCH EAST INDIES

CHINA

SIAM

INDIA

INDIAN OCEAN

RUSSIA

AFGHANISTAN

PERSIA

ARABIA

ABYSSINIA

AUSTRIA-HUNGARY

TURKEY

GERMANY

SWEDEN

NORWAY

ICELAND

GREAT BRITAIN

FRANCE

SPAIN

PORTUGAL

LIBERIA

UNION OF SOUTH AFRICA

ARCTIC OCEAN

Arctic Circle

GREENLAND

ATLANTIC OCEAN

GUIANAS

SOUTH AMERICA

CANANDA

UNITED STATES

MEXICO

CENTRAL AMERICA

ALASKA

PACIFIC OCEAN

Tropic of Cancer

Equator

Tropic of Capricorn

Antarctic Circle

Tropic of Capricorn

0   1000   2000 Miles
0   1000   2000   3000 Kilometers

Europe
European colonies
Russia
British Dominions
Semi-colonial regions
Independent European-derived states

525

On May 10, 1869, the last rails of the Union Pacific and Central pacific (now the Southern Pacific) were joined at Promontory, Utah. A memorable scene was enacted as a spike of pure California gold was driven, signaling the completion of the first chain of railroads to span the American continent

The economic integration of the continents led to a spectacular increase in overall global productivity. World industrial production multiplied no fewer than six times between 1860 and 1913, and the value of world trade increased twelve times between 1851 and 1913. Europe, as might be expected, benefited the most from this economic leap forward. Statistics are not available for conditions all over the globe, but it is estimated that the difference in per capita income between colonial or semicolonial regions and the European metropolitan countries was roughly three to one in 1800. By 1914 it had increased to about seven to one.

III. EUROPE'S CULTURAL DOMINANCE

The everyday life of the peasant masses in colonial territories had been drastically affected by the shift from a traditional natural economy to a money economy. Money had been used in the earlier period but only in a peripheral manner, and production had been carried on by the peasant households primarily to satisfy family needs. A few commodities might have been sold in the local market, but not for the purpose of making a profit. Rather, the aim was to get a little money to meet tax obligations and to buy a few essentials such as salt and a little iron. Frequently the transactions and obligations were met by simple barter, and no money changed hands. But a new market economy was introduced when the Europeans appeared with their railroads, their machine-made goods, and their insatiable demands for foodstuffs and industrial raw materials. Before long the peasants found themselves producing for an international market rather than for themselves and their neighbors, which in turn meant that they became subject to global economic fluctuations. And they were at the mercies of merchants and moneylenders, who now flourished in the new economy. The transition from a closed and static natural economy to a dynamic money and market economy was beneficial as far as productive capacity was concerned, but certainly its initial effects were disruptive and uncomfortable.

The way of thinking as well as the way of life was affected by Europe's intrusion. However, this intellectual change primarily involved the smaller upper class in the colonial world rather than the peasant masses. It was the few members of the thin upper crust who knew some Western language, who read Western newspapers and books, and who were familiar with European history and current politics. The initial response to this exposure to the alien culture was often an enthusiastic, uncritical admiration of everything Western. But it was usually followed by a reaction against the West and an attempt to preserve and foster at least some elements of the traditional culture. The ambivalent response to Western culture is clearly expressed in the following reminiscence written in 1925 by a prominent Indian:

Our fore fathers, the firstfruits of English education, were violently pro-British. They could see no flaw in the civilization or the culture of the West. They were charmed by its novelty and its strangeness. The enfranchisement of the individual, the substitution of the right of private judgement in the place of traditional authority, the exaltation of duty over custom, all came with a force and suddenness of a revelation to an Oriental people who knew no more binding obligation than the mandate of immemorial usage and of venerable tradition. . . . Everything English was good—even the drinking of brandy was a virtue; everything not English was to be viewed with suspicion. . . . In due time came the reaction, and with a sudden rush. And from the adoration of all things Western, we are now in a whirlpool that would recall us back to our ancient civilization and our time-honored ways and customs. . . .[1]

IV. WHITE MAN'S BURDEN

The political, economic, and cultural dominance of Europe at the turn of the century naturally led Europeans to assume that their primacy arose from the superiority of their civilization and that this in turn reflected their superiority as a race. It was confidently believed that God had created people unequal. He had made the whites more intelligent so that they could direct the labor and guide the development of the inferior races, who had broad backs and weak minds. Hence arose the concept of the white man's burden—a preaching that cloaked the imperialism of the times with a mantle of idealistic devotion to duty. In the well-known lines of Rudyard Kipling, written appropriately at the end of the century (1899):

Take up the White Man's Burden—
Send forth the best ye breed—
Go bind your sons to exile
To serve your captives' need. . . .[2]

Whereas a British poet was writing in 1899 with complete self-assurance about the "white man's burden," a distinguished British historian Basil Davidson wrote in 1992 a book entitled *Black Man's Burden*. He was referring to certain institutions and practices that the Europeans had imposed on their colonial subjects, but that have since proven to be unsuitable and unworkable—a "burden" for the "black man" rather than the "white."

In contrast to today's soul searching, Europeans in the time of Kipling were regarded almost as divinely ordained rulers. In India they were addressed respectfully as sahib, in the Middle East as effendi, in Africa as bwana, and in Latin America as patron. Under these circumstances it is scarcely surprising that Europeans came to view the world with a myopia and a self-centeredness that today seems incredible. Americans also shared this attitude. President Theodore Roosevelt in a message to Congress in 1904 warned Latin America that ". . . chronic wrongdoing, or an impotency which results in a general loosening of the ties of civilized society, may in America, as elsewhere, ultimately require intervention by some civilized nation."[3] Likewise, an American missionary, Henry W. Luce, father of the well-known publisher, reported from China in 1904 that conditions were favorable for their activities and that "We may work together for God, for China, and for Yale."[4] Most spectacular was the supreme self-confidence and

The Indian Mutiny of 1857 is an example of a weaker society, threatened by one more vigorous and aggressive, reacting with retreat and escapism.

aggressiveness of Cecil Rhodes, who was ahead of his time in dreaming of other planets to conquer:

The world is nearly parcelled out, and what there is left of it is being divided up, conquered, and colonized. To think of these stars that you see overhead at night, these vast worlds which we can never reach. I would annex the planets if I could; I often think of that. It makes me sad to see them so clear and yet so far.[5]

Cecil Rhodes may sound overconfident, but it was a confidence based solidly on the West's technological superiority. Since Western technology has continued to grow at an ever-accelerating pace, Rhodes's present-day successors in the business world are even more self-assured. Former Citicorp Chairman George Moore stated in 1987 that in twenty-five years the world would be dominated by a handful of large financial institutions that would have their headquarters on space platforms to avoid government regulations. Whereas Rhodes was saddened that the planets were inaccessible to him, his counterparts now assume those planets not only will become accessible but will also serve as their private launching pads.

V. FIRST CHALLENGES TO EUROPE'S DOMINANCE

In 1914 Europe's global domination seemed to be unassailable and eternal. But in the clearer light of retrospect one can easily perceive the lurking threat of a colonial world slowly awakening and striking the first blows against Western domination.

Throughout history, whenever a weaker society has been threatened by one more vigorous and aggressive, there have been two contradictory types of reactions: The first is to sever all contact with the intruding forces, withdraw into isolation, and seek refuge in traditional beliefs and practices. The second reaction is to try instead to adopt as many features of the alien society as are necessary to meet it on equal terms and thus to resist it effectively. The first reaction represents retreat and escapism; the other, adjustment and adaptation. The slogan of the first is "Back to the good old days"; that of the second, "Learn from the West in order to fight the West."

There were many examples during the nineteenth century of both types of reaction to the Western intrusion. Classic examples of the escapist variety were the Indian mutiny in 1857–1858 and the Boxer Rebellion in 1900 (see

The second type of reaction to vigorous and aggressive threat to a weaker society is an example of the women textile workers at a turn-of-the-century silk-weaving mill in Japan. Their product, made from mechanically reeled silk thread, was superior. Women constituted more than half of Japan's industrial labor force well into the twentieth century. They worked a span of years after leaving primary school and before marrying. Their hours were long, their dormitories crowded, and they often contracted tuberculosis.

Chapter 30, Section III, and Chapter 31, Section II, for details). Both the mutiny and the rebellion were bitter, bloody affairs, yet neither of them seriously challenged Europe's supremacy because they were essentially negative revolts, seeking to oust the hated Europeans by force in order to restore the good old days. But the power of Western arms and the dynamism of Western economic enterprise were irresistible. It was an entirely different matter, however, when native peoples began to adopt Western ideas and technology to use them against the West.

The Japanese were the first Asian people to succeed in carrying out the policy of resistance by adaptation. They defeated the weak Chinese Empire in 1894–1895 and then the mighty Russian Empire in 1904–1905 (see Chapter 31, Sections III and IV, for details). The triumph of a small Asian kingdom over a giant European power marks a turning point in recent world history. It was an event that sent a tremor of hope and excitement throughout the colonial world. Just as influential as the outcome of the Russo-Japanese War was the great Russian Revolution, stimulated in part by the war (see Chapter 28, Section IV). The news that the tsarist autocracy was on the verge of downfall was as exciting to oppressed peoples everywhere as the reports from the battlefields of Manchuria. A Britisher who was in Persia at this time sensed an undercurrent of aroused emotions and expectations in all the colonial lands. In a letter of August 1906 he reported:

It seems to me that a change must be coming over the East. The victory of Japan has, it would appear, had a remarkable influence all over the East. Even here in Persia it has not been without effect.... Moreover, the Russian Revolution has had a most astounding effect here. Events in Russia have been watched with great attention, and a new spirit would seem to have come over the people. They are tired of their rulers, and, taking example of Russia, have come to think that it is possible to have another and better form of government ... it almost seems that the East is stirring in its sleep. In China there is a marked movement against the foreigners, and a tendency towards the ideal of "China for the Chinese." In Persia, owing to its proximity to Russia, the awakening would appear to take the form of a movement towards democratic reform. In Egypt and North Africa it is signalized by a

remarkable increase in fanaticism, coupled with the spread of the Pan-Islamic movement. The simultaneousness of these symptoms of unrest is too remarkable to be attributed solely to coincidence. Who knows? Perhaps the East is really awakening from its secular slumber, and we are about to witness the rising of these patient millions against the exploitation of an unscrupulous West.[6]

This analysis proved prophetic. It was borne out by the 1905 Persian Revolution, the 1908 Young Turk Revolution, the 1911 Chinese Revolution, and the heightened unrest and terrorism in India. We may conclude that although Europe's global hegemony in 1914 seemed irresistible and everlasting, it was actually being challenged at many points and in many ways. In the pre-1914 period the European powers were able to suppress the opposition. Yet this early opposition did represent a beginning—the birth of the nationalist movements that after World War I, and especially after World War II, were to sweep everything before them.

SUGGESTED READINGS

The most important studies of the pre-1914 challenges to Europe's global hegemony are by E. R. Wolf, *Peasant Wars of the Twentieth Century* (Harper & Row, 1969); J. Romein, *The Watershed of Two Eras: Europe in 1900* (Wesleyan University, 1978); L. S. Stavrianos, *Global Rift: The Third World Comes of Age* (William Morrow, 1981); and R. Storry, *Japan and the Decline of the West in Asia* (St. Martin's Press, 1979).

NOTES

1. S. Banerjea, cited in L. S. S. O'Malley, *Modern India and the West* (Oxford University, 1941), p. 766.
2. From "The White Man's Burden," in *Rudyard Kipling's Verse: Definitive Edition* (Doubleday),
3. Cited by R. Emerson, *From Empire to Nation* (Harvard University, 1960), p. 403.
4. Cited by J. Israel, "'For God, for China and for Yale'—The Open Door in Action," *American Historical Review* (February, 1970), p. 801.
5. W. T. Stead, *The Last Will and Testament of Cecil Joyn Rhodes* (London, 1902), p. 190.
6. E. G. Browne, *The Persian Revolution of 1905–1909* (Cambridge University, 1910), pp. 120–23.

What It Means for Us Today

MARX TURNED UPSIDE DOWN

Karl Marx assumed that revolution would occur in the industrialized countries before it did in the colonies. He noted that Western capitalists were investing their surplus money in the colonies where higher profits could be made. Like all the socialists of his time, Marx assumed that these investments would continue and that the colonies would become industrialized capitalist countries like their mother countries in western Europe. Marx wrote in his famous work *Das Kapital* (1867), "The industrialized developed country only shows the less-developed country the picture of its own future."

Marx also expected that as the colonies became industrialized and prosperous, the old manufacturing centers of the West would fall behind and suffer unemployment. This in turn would eventually force the suffering Western workers to rise in revolt and establish socialistic societies. Marx therefore concluded that revolution would come first in the West. In fact, in a letter to his friend Friedrich Engels (October 8, 1858), he expressed the fear that when Europe became socialist, the prosperous colonies would remain capitalist and would attack and "crush" the newly born Western socialistic societies. Today, more than a century later, we see that what has happened is the exact opposite of what Marx had feared. Revolution has come, not in the West, but in the former colonies, now known as the Third World. Thus history has turned Marx upside down. Why has it done so?

One reason is that Western workers won the right to vote and the right to organize in unions. They used these rights to increase their wages and to organize the welfare state, which provided help in case of accident, illness, or unemployment. Western workers therefore were relatively satisfied and became reformers rather than revolutionaries. A second reason is that the colonies of the Third World, did not become industrialized. Western manufacturers did not want competition from overseas, so they actively opposed the establishment of industries in the colonies. As a result, the colonies remained producers of raw materials for Western factories and importers of manufactured goods made in Western factories. The trouble with this arrangement is that after 1880 world prices for raw materials fell steadily while the prices of manufactured goods rose steadily. Between 1880 and 1938, the amount of manufactured goods that Third World countries received for a set quantity of raw materials fell by over 40 percent.

This unfavorable trend in the "terms of trade," as the economists call it, is partly responsible for the serious economic problems of the Third World today. Other factors also have contributed to these problems (see Chapter 27, Section VIII). The end result has been the widening gap between rich countries and poor—between the developed First World and the underdeveloped Third World. The ratio of per capita income between these two worlds has increased as follows: from 3:1 in 1800, to 7:1 in 1914, to 12:1 in 1975.

These figures explain why history has turned out the exact opposite of what Marx had expected. Before Marx, all the great revolutions had occurred in the West—the English, American, and French revolutions. But in the twentieth century, all the great revolutions have been in the Third World: 1917—Russia; 1949—China; 1975— Indochina; 1976—Portuguese Africa; 1979—Iran and Nicaragua; 1980— Zimbabwe. In the 1990s still another surprise occurred, turning Marx upside down once more. The new revolutionary regimes established in the Third World since 1917 have been collapsing one after another because of the failure of their planned economies. So the Socialist regimes in the USSR, eastern Europe, and elsewhere have disintegrated, with ongoing frantic searching for alternative social systems, as we shall note in the concluding chapter.

SUGGESTED READINGS

Many studies of current global trends consider the unexpected interaction between the First and Third worlds. Noteworthy are J. Hough, *The Struggle for the Third World* (Brookings Institution, 1985); L. S. Stavrianos, *Global Rift: The Third World Comes of Age* (William Morrow, 1981); P. Worsley, *The Three Worlds: Culture and World Development* (University of Chicago, 1984); and G. Chaliand, *Revolution in the Third World: Myths and Prospects* (Viking, 1977).

PART VIII

World of Western Decline and Triumph, 1914–Present

The decades since 1914 have witnessed at one and the same time both the decline and the triumph of the West. Indeed these two seemingly contradictory trends reinforced each other. The unprecedented integration of the globe led to the proliferation of Western technology, ideas, and institutions at an accelerating pace. But it was precisely this proliferation that undermined the global hegemony of the West that had appeared so invulnerable prior to 1914. Colonial peoples were selectively adopting Western civilization to better resist the West. For this reason, world history since 1914 is the history of the West's decline as well as of its triumph.

The combination of these two trends explains the turmoil of the world in which we live today. A glance at newspaper headlines or television screens shows that Beijing and Cairo and New Delhi are now as prominent in international affairs as Paris and London and Washington. And everywhere, the hitherto silent masses are taking over the historical stage and shouting demands that would have been inconceivable a few decades ago.

36

World War I: Global Repercussions

The Great War of 1914–1918 was from the Asian point of view a civil war within the European community of nations.

K. M. Panikkar
Indian diplomat and historian

In the autumn of 1914, as one European country after another was being dragged into the holocaust of World War I, the British foreign secretary, Earl Grey, remarked, "The lamps are going out all over Europe." His comment was indeed fully justified, and to a much greater degree than he could have foreseen. World War I was destined to bring down in ruins the Europe that Earl Grey was familiar with. It wiped out the centuries-old Hapsburg, Hohenzollern, Romanoff, and Ottoman dynasties. In their places there appeared new leaders, new institutions, and new ideologies that aristocrats such as Earl Grey only dimly understood. The Europe of 1918 was as different from that of 1914 as the Europe of 1815 had been different from that of 1789.

World War I also marked the end of the Europe that had dominated the globe so completely and abnormally during the nineteenth century. By the end of the war Europe's control had manifestly weakened and was everywhere being challenged. In one way or another the challenges were successfully resisted in most parts of the world. But the respite lasted only two decades, for the Second World War completed the undermining process begun by the first and left the European empires everywhere in shambles.

From the viewpoint of world history as well as European history, World War I stands out as a historic turning point. The purpose of this chapter is to analyze the roots, the course, and the global repercussions of this fateful event.

I. ROOTS OF WAR

The Versailles Treaty terminating World War I included an article specifically stating that the war was provoked "by the aggression of Germany and her allies." This "war guilt" clause was of more than academic interest, for it was used by the Allies to justify their claim for reparation payments from the defeated Central Powers. Consequently, it stimulated a passionate and prolonged controversy that led to the publication of great collections of documents, totaling over 60,000, as well as thousands of articles and books, all of which championed one side or another in the continuing debate over who was responsible for the war. By the mid-1930s the polemics had quieted down, and relatively scholarly studies appeared that paid less attention to "war guilt" and more to historical conditions and forces that produced the war. Most historians now distinguish between background causes that had been operative for some decades and the immediate causes that came into play during the hectic weeks following the assassination of the Archduke Francis Ferdinand on June 28, 1914. The five most important background factors were economic rivalries, colonial disputes, conflicting alliance systems, irreconcilable nationalist aspirations, and irreversible military timetables.

Economic Rivalries

Considering first the economic rivalries, most of the major European powers became involved in tariff wars and in competition for foreign markets. For example, Italy and France waged a tariff war between 1888 and 1899, Russia and Germany between 1879 and 1894, and Austria and Serbia between 1906 and 1910. The most serious economic rivalry developed between Britain and Germany because of the latter's extraordinarily rapid rate of industrialization in the late nineteenth century. In 1870 Britain produced 31.8 percent of the world's total industrial output, compared to Germany's 13.2 percent. By 1914 Britain's share had dropped to 14 percent, whereas Germany's had risen slightly to 14.3 percent, or a shade greater than that of Britain.

Germany's upgraded naval strength at the start of World War I is typified by the battleship Tann, *here shown in dock.*

This German spurt meant stiff competition for Britain in overseas markets. It is impossible to define precisely all the political repercussions of this economic rivalry, but it did strain the relations between the two countries. It further contributed to international tension by stimulating competition in naval armaments. In both countries it was argued vociferously that building up naval strength was essential to safeguard trade routes and merchant shipping. Germany's new building program launched under Admiral von Tirpitz in 1897 embittered relations between Britain and Germany without basically changing the balance of power. The kaiser's determination to have a big navy, as well as the most powerful army, contributed significantly to the final outbreak of war.

Colonial Disputes

Economic rivalries and domestic difficulties fomented colonial disputes, for additional colonies were eagerly sought after to ensure protected overseas markets for surplus capital and manufactures. Since the Germans did not enter the colonial race until after their national unification in 1871, they were particularly aggressive in their demands for an empire equal to their growing economic strength. The Pan-German League pointed to the substantial colonial possessions of small countries like Portugal, Holland, and Belgium, and insisted that Germany also must have its "place in the sun." But in almost every part of the globe the Germans found themselves blocked by the far-flung possessions of the British, whom they bitterly accused of "dog in the manger" selfishness.

The competition for colonies, however, was by no means restricted to Britain and Germany. Almost all the major powers were involved in the scramble for empire in the late nineteenth century, so they repeatedly clashed in one region or another: Britain and Germany clashed in East Africa and Southwest Africa; Britain and France, in Siam and the Nile valley; Britain and Russia, in Persia and Afghanistan; and Germany and France, in Morocco and West Africa. These colonial disputes created an atmosphere of rising tension during the three decades preceding World War I.

Admiral Alfred von Tirpitz (1849-1930) was responsible for building the German navy into a force capable of challenging the Royal Navy of Great Britain, reflecting Kaiser William II's desire to increase Germany's prominence among the great powers of Europe

Conflicting Alliance Systems

The colonial rivalries in turn contributed to the forging of conflicting alliance systems that were in large part responsible for the coming of war. These systems began in 1879 when the German chancellor, Otto von Bismarck, concluded the Dual Alliance with Austria-Hungary. This was a defensive pact designed to protect Germany against the French, who aspired to recover the Alsace-Lorraine provinces lost in 1871. It was also meant to protect Austria-Hungary against the Russians, with whom they continually clashed in the Balkans. In 1882 the Dual

Alliance became the Triple Alliance with the addition of Italy. Again the objective was defensive: to protect Italy against France because of sharp conflict over Tunis. The Triple Alliance, then, was definitely not aggressive in intention or in its provisions. Germany and Austria-Hungary were both satisfied powers interested primarily in preserving the existing state of affairs on the Continent.

But from the other side of the fence the Triple Alliance seemed quite different. For France and Russia it was an overwhelming bloc that dominated Europe and left them isolated and vulnerable. Furthermore, France and Russia both had serious difficulties with Britain over colonial issues in several regions. The result was the Franco-Russian Alliance, concluded in 1894, with the double purpose of countering the Triple Alliance and resisting Britain in colonial disputes. The Franco-Russian Alliance became the Triple Entente with the signing of the Anglo-French Entente in 1904 and the Anglo-Russian Entente in 1907. Both of these arrangements were essentially colonial in nature. Britain and France, for example, agreed to recognize their respective interests in the Nile valley and Morocco, and Britain and Russia likewise agreed to divide Persia into spheres of influence. (See map of Europe, 1914, p. 539)

Thus all the major powers now were aligned in rival alliance systems, with disastrous results for international relations. Whenever any dispute of consequence arose, the members of both blocs felt compelled to support their respective allies who were directly involved, even if they were doubtful about the issues. Otherwise they feared that their alliances would disintegrate, leaving them alone and exposed. Each dispute consequently was magnified into a major crisis involving, willy-nilly, all the members of both alliances.

Irreconcilable Nationalist Aspirations

Another background factor was the rising nationalist aspirations of Europe's subject minorities. This pressure was volatile enough in Alsace-Lorraine, where the ethnic French remained unreconciled to German rule. But it was a nightmare in central and eastern Europe, where the multinational empires were in danger of being literally torn to pieces by the growing demand for self-determination. In the Hapsburg Empire, for example, the ruling Austrians and Hungarians were confronted by the awakening Italians and Rumanians, as well as by the many Slavic peoples: Czechs, Slovaks, Ruthenians, Poles, Slovenes, Croats, and Serbs. Very understandably, the Hapsburg officials decided that firm measures were necessary if the empire was to survive. This was especially true regarding the militant Serbs, who were clamoring for unification with the independent Serbia across the Danube—hence the stiff terms sent to Belgrade when the archduke was murdered by a Serb patriot at Sarajevo. But behind Serbia was Russia, and behind Russia were France and Britain. Austria-Hungary, likewise, was backed by Germany and, theoretically, by Italy. Thus the combination of national self-determination and conflicting alliance systems drove the European powers to the holocaust.

Irreversible Military Timetables

The final background factor, irreversible military timetables, made it extremely difficult to reverse the drift to war following the Sarajevo assassinations. The late nineteenth century was a time when European military technology was making a great leap forward by integrating science and the military. Old weapons were being improved and new ones introduced, including submarines and airplanes. Private armament companies such as Armstrong in Britain, Krupp in Germany, and Schneider-Creusot in France, fomented a worldwide arms race by selling arms to one country, which aroused fears and stimulated sales to neighboring countries. The military leaders of the major powers played safe by ordering huge quantities of the latest weapons. Then they coordinated their bulging arsenals with their railway networks to prepare detailed mobilizations plans by which huge quantities of military supplies and millions of conscripted soldiers were to be moved to war fronts against any conceivable combination of enemies.

Once a button was pressed for activating Mobilization Plan A or B or C or whatever, men and supplies were programmed to move like

Europe, 1914

clockwork and on a massive scale. No counter-manding order could be tolerated because the flow of men and materials would be jammed, leaving the country defenseless in the resulting bedlam. Consequently, no major mobilization order could be reversed by any authority, whether emperor or prime minister. This "exigency of the military timetable," as historians have dubbed it, proved to be a major obstacle for those seeking a peaceful settlement following the Sarajevo assassinations on June 28, 1914. It is sobering to note that the diplomats of that era had a grace period of several weeks before guns actually began firing on August 4. Today the

grace period has virtually vanished, with modern weapons-delivery technology able to span continents in minutes, and with thousands of autonomous combat systems, each with its own decision-making computers, leaving almost no time for human participation in the unleashing of nuclear Armageddon.

II. SARAJEVO

On June 28, 1914, Archduke Francis Ferdinand and his wife were assassinated in Sarajevo, the capital of the recently annexed province of

Bosnia. The murder was committed by a young Bosnian Serb student named Gavrilo Princip. He was not alone in carrying out the murder. He was backed by the secret Serbian organization Ujedinjenje ili Smrt, or "Union or Death," popularly known as the Black Hand. Founded in Belgrade in 1911, the Black Hand had as its avowed aim the realization of "the national ideal: the union of all Serbs." The Serbian government was not behind this society, which indeed was regarded as dangerously radical and militant. But this did not prevent the Black Hand from building an underground revolutionary organization that conducted an effective campaign of agitation and terrorism.

The unfortunate Francis Ferdinand played into the hands of these Serb revolutionaries by agreeing to pay an official visit to the Bosnian capital. When the archduke and his duchess began their procession on the radiant Sunday morning of June 28, no fewer than six assassins, armed with bombs and revolvers, were waiting along the designated route. As fate would have it, the procession stopped at the very corner where Princip was stationed. He drew his revolver and fired two shots, one at Francis Ferdinand and the other at General Potiorek, the governor of Bosnia. The second shot went wild and hit the duchess instead. Before medical aid arrived both the archduke and his wife were dead.

On July 23, Austria presented Serbia with a stiff ultimatum that included several demands. The Serbian reply on July 25 accepted nearly all of the terms but refused the demand that Hapsburg officials participate within Serbian territory in the investigation of the crime. Austria promptly broke off diplomatic relations and, on July 28, declared war on Serbia.

Russia now retaliated and ordered full mobilization on July 30. The next day Germany sent a twelve-hour ultimatum to Russia demanding that the mobilization be stopped. When no reply was received, Germany declared war against Russia on August 1 and against Russia's ally, France, on August 3. On the same day Germany began actual hostilities by invading Belgium. After Germany's involvement the British intervened, but not openly on the justification

The Austrian Archduke Francis Ferdinand and his wife in Sarajevo on June 28, 1914. Later in the day the royal couple were assassinated by young revolutionaries trained and supplied in Serbia, igniting the crisis that led to World War I. Moments after the assassination the Austrian police captured one of the assassins.

of their secret military commitment to France. Instead, they justified their entry as a reaction to the German invasion of Belgium, which was more palatable for the British public. Thus the great powers of Europe were at each other's throats five weeks after the murders at Sarajevo.

III. EUROPEAN PHASE OF THE WAR, 1914–1917

1914: War of Attrition in the West

World War I began with peoples on both sides confidently expecting a brief and victorious war. Instead, they soon found themselves embroiled in a prolonged and brutalizing ordeal that took unprecedented toll of material wealth and human lives. The reason for the bloody deadlock was that from the beginning of the war defensive weapons proved superior over offensive. The traditional mode of attack was the massed infantry charge supported by a preliminary artillery barrage. But this was of no avail against the combination of deep trenches, barbed-wire entanglements, ingenious land mines, and machine-gun nests. Thus the casualties on the western front during the first four months were 700,000 Germans, 850,000 French, and 90,000 British. Contrary to the plans of all general staffs, the struggle in the west now became a war of position and attrition.

This was not the case on the Russian and Balkan fronts, where vast distances and scanty transportation facilities necessitated a fluid war of movement. The Russians led off with a surprisingly fast and powerful offensive into east Prussia, designed to relieve the pressure on the French in the west. The strategy worked, for the Germans transferred four divisions from Belgium to the east. Before they reached their destination, the issue had been decided by smashing victories over two Russian armies advancing into east Prussia. The German commanders, Hindenburg and Ludendorff, used their superior railway network to concentrate their forces against first one Russian army and then the other. By the middle of September, east Prussia was cleared of its invaders.

On the Balkan front the Austrians meanwhile were suffering humiliating setbacks. General Potiorek, who had barely escaped Princip's bullet in Sarajevo, was impatient to destroy "the viper's nest." On August 12 he crossed the Drina River into Serbia with 250,000 men. But he was met by a Serbian army of 350,000, of whom 90 percent were seasoned veterans of the Balkan

Wars of 1912–1913. In less than two weeks the Serbs had forced the Austrians back across the river with a loss of one-third of their numbers. Potiorek returned to the attack in September and succeeded in taking Belgrade on December 2. But again the Serbians counterattacked, and by the end of the same month the Serb commander triumphantly announced, "On the territory of Serbia there remains not one free enemy soldier."[1]

1915: Russian Retreat in the East

The 1915 campaigns were dominated by the new German commander-in-chief, Erich von Falkenhayn. In view of the stalemate on the western front he concentrated his forces on the east in an effort to knock out the Russians. Combined German and Austrian armies attacked with stunning effect on May 1, advancing by the end of the summer an average of 200 miles. In addition to military casualties totaling 2,500,000 men, Russia lost 15 percent of its territories, 10 percent of its railways, 30 percent of its industries, and 20 percent of its civilian population. The tsarist regime suffered a blow from which it never was able to recover.

On the western front the war of attrition continued. The French General Joffre clung to his belief that intensive artillery bombardment plus massed frontal attack would bring victory. But repeated offensives left the lines unchanged and resulted only in appalling loss of life.

Turkey's entry into World War I on November 2, 1914, precipitated the famous Dardanelles campaign. When Turkey joined the Central Powers, the straits were automatically closed to the Allies, thus making it difficult to ship much-needed supplies to Russia. Accordingly, on March 18, 1915, a squadron of fourteen British and four French battleships steamed into the straits with guns blazing. Heavy losses from mines and coastal artillery forced the Allied ships to withdraw. An attempt then was made to take the straits by landings on the Gallipoli beaches, but only shallow footholds were secured in the face of withering machine-gun fire. The Turks held the heights above the beaches until the Allies finally faced facts and withdrew permanently in January 1916.

The failure at the straits together with the disaster on the Russian front persuaded Bulgaria to join the Central Powers on October 14, 1915. This intervention spelled the end for the Serbs. An overwhelming number of German, Austrian, and Bulgarian divisions attacked Serbia on October 6 from three sides. By the end of the year the entire country was occupied.

To counterbalance these setbacks in the Balkans, the Allies were strengthened by the decision of Italy to join their cause. Although the Italians technically had been allies of the Central Powers, they decided at the outset of the war to remain neutral. The bulk of the Italian people favored this course, especially since it was Austria that held the "unredeemed" lands across the Adriatic. The Allies now freely offered these lands to Italy, together with additional territories at the expense of Turkey. The bait was effective, and on April 29 Italy signed the Treaty of London, agreeing to enter the war in one month in return for these territorial promises.

1916: Verdun and the Somme

By 1916 the Central Powers had reached the height of their military fortunes. They controlled the continent of Europe from Hamburg to the Persian Gulf, yet they were not able to force a peace settlement on the Allies. To secure such a settlement, the Germans in February 1916 launched an all-out attack on the key French fortress of Verdun. The British counterattacked with an offensive to the northwest at the Somme. But the defense again proved superior to the offense. The two 1916 drives cost about 850,000 German casualties and about 950,000 British and French. Yet neither side was able to advance more than seven miles.

Meanwhile the Russians, under General Brusilov, made a successful offensive on the eastern front. The failure of the Germans at Verdun and the unexpected success of the Brusilov offensive encouraged Rumania to intervene in the war on the side of the Allies on August 27, 1916. The Central Powers now decided to make an object lesson of Rumania as

French troops, advancing on the western front. This scene of trench warfare characterizes the twentieth century's first great international conflict. The trenches were protected by barbed wire and machine guns, which gave defenders the advantage.

a warning to other neutrals who might be thinking of following its course. German, Austrian, Bulgarian, and Turkish forces descended in overwhelming force. By the end of the year the Rumanians had lost two-thirds of their country, including their capital.

The involvement of Rumania in the war left Greece as the only neutral in the Balkans. But on June 27, 1917, Greece entered the war on the Allied side and so paved the way for the 1918 offensives in Macedonia that knocked Bulgaria out of the war.

1917: Bloodletting and Defeatism

Meanwhile, the terrible bloodletting was continuing unabated on the western front. Whereas in 1916 the Germans had assumed the offensive at Verdun, now in 1917 the Allies took the lead. The cautious General Joffre was replaced by the audacious General Nivelle, who preached with persuasive fervor of a new type of lightning offensive that would bring victory with few casualties. Despite the opposition of many military leaders, both French and British, Nivelle's aggressive strategy was accepted.

The Germans at the same time had replaced Falkenhayn with their eastern front team of Hindenburg and Ludendorff. After the shattering experience of the previous year at Verdun and the Somme, they decided to go on the defensive on the western front and to open unrestricted submarine warfare at sea. They hoped thereby to starve England into submission, leaving France isolated on the Continent. They were all aware that submarine warfare involved the risk of American intervention, but they gambled that England would be broken before American aid could become effective.

We shall see shortly that this gamble came within an ace of being won, though in the end it brought disaster. But the defensive strategy on land paid off handsomely. To consolidate and strengthen his front lines, Hindenburg withdrew his forces to a new fortified position (the Hindenburg Line) that was straighter, shorter, and more heavily fortified. The withdrawal badly upset Nivelle's offensive plans, but he persisted

in going through with them. French, British, and Canadian troops went over the top as scheduled, but they suffered one of the bloodiest defeats of the war. Hindenburg's defensive strategy had served the Germans well. They inflicted 400,000 casualties on the Allies, while incurring only 250,000 themselves.

By this time the peoples of Europe were enduring the fourth year of the most devastating and murderous war in history. Despite all the sacrifices and grief, no end was yet in sight. War weariness and defeatism appeared not only in the trenches but also among the civilians in both camps. One of the most spectacular manifestations was the passage of a Peace Resolution by the German Reichstag on July 19, 1917, by a vote of 212 to 126. In Austria-Hungary the death of the respected old Emperor Francis Joseph on November 21 brought to the throne the young Emperor Charles, who began secret peace overtures. Likewise in England, a former foreign secretary, Lord Lansdowne, wrote an open letter prophesying the collapse of Western civilization unless some way was found to end the conflict.

IV. GLOBAL PHASE OF THE WAR: 1917 RUSSIAN REVOLUTION

Nineteen hundred seventeen proved to be the year of decision because of two fateful developments—the Russian Revolution and the intervention of the United States. These events changed the character of the war—from an essentially European affair fought over primarily European issues to a war of global proportions. It is true that Japan had entered the war on August 21, 1914, but it had done little more than help itself to scattered German colonial possessions in the Pacific. But now the entry of the United States involved a great non-European power that quickly decided the outcome of the war.

The American intervention and the Russian Revolution also introduced a new ideological element that immediately had worldwide effects. Wilson's Fourteen Points and Lenin's revolutionary slogans were universal and disruptive in their impact, unlike limited European issues such as the fate of Alsace-Lorraine or of the Hapsburg subject nationalities. It was in 1917, then, that the transition occurred from the European to the global phase of World War I.

March 1917 Revolution

Two revolutions occurred in Russia in 1917: The first, in March, ended tsarism and created a Provisional Government; the second, in November, toppled the Provisional Government and substituted Soviet rule. The first revolution was an unplanned affair that took everyone by surprise. Strikes and riots broke out in Petrograd on March 8 because of the desperate shortage of food and fuel due to poor transportation facilities. The authorities ordered the army to restore order, but instead the soldiers mutinied and sided with the demonstrators. The tsar, always distrustful of the Duma, suspected it of complicity and ordered its dissolution on March 11. The Duma leaders refused to obey the order, and the tsar discovered that he no longer could enforce obedience. The realization of powerlessness was to all intents and purposes the revolution itself. Russia no longer had a functioning government. This became the situation legally as well as factually when Tsar Nicholas abdicated on March 15 in favor of his brother Michael, and when Michael in turn gave up the throne the following day.

Some new structure had to be erected quickly lest the radical elements in the streets take over. On March 12 a Provisional Government was organized to administer the country until a Constituent Assembly could be elected. The new government was headed by the Liberal Prince Georgi Lvov and included the Cadet leader Professor Paul Miliukov, as minister for foreign affairs, and Alexander Kerensky, the only socialist, as minister of justice. This was a bourgeois, liberal, middle-of-the-road cabinet, which favored reform up to a certain point. In fact, it did proclaim freedom of speech, press, and assembly; it declared an amnesty for political and religious offenses; recognized the legal equality of all citizens without social, religious, or racial discrimination; and passed labor legislation, including the eight-hour day. However,

despite its record of reform, the Provisional Government never sank roots in the country. For eight months it strove desperately but in vain to provide an adequate administration. At the end of that time the new government was not overthrown; rather, it collapsed as helplessly as the tsarist regime had in March.

Between Revolutions

The period between March and November 1917 was one of struggle for power between the Provisional Government and populist revolutionary bodies or soviets. In this struggle the Provisional Government was fatally handicapped because from the beginning it refused to consider the two things that most Russians wanted—peace and land. Prince Lvov and his ministers insisted that such a fundamental reform as redistribution of land must wait for a Constituent Assembly that would be truly representative of the people and would have the authority to decide on such a basic issue. Likewise, the government refused to end the war because Russia had certain commitments to its allies that could not be denied. These arguments were sensible and understandable, but politically they were suicidal. While the government was pleading for patience, soviets were winning over the masses by demanding immediate peace and immediate distribution of land.

The origin of the soviets goes back to the 1905 Revolution, when the workers elected councils, or soviets, to coordinate their struggle against tsarism. Although suppressed at that time, the soviets had proven their value as organs for agitation and direct action. They had precisely that quality that the Provisional Government conspicuously lacked—intimate rapport with the masses.

Very naturally, soviets reappeared with the crisis precipitated by the war. Because of their origin and composition, they had none of the Provisional Government's squeamishness about waiting for elections before proceeding with peace negotiations and land distribution. Without hesitation or reservations they gave voice to popular needs, and in doing so they attracted more and more mass support. Soviets soon were

General view of the flags on the burial day of the victims of the Russian Revolution—Petrograd, March 23, 1917.

appearing in the villages and in military units as well as in the cities. Thus the soviet movement mushroomed throughout the country, developing virtually into a grass-roots government that continually challenged that in Petrograd (formerly St. Petersburg, and soon to be known as Leningrad). Village soviets were organizing seizures of nobles' estates; city soviets were behind the unceasing demonstrations and riots in the streets; and the soldiers' soviets were gradually usurping the authority of the officers to the point where the soviets had control of all weapons and countersigned all orders before they could be executed.

At the beginning, the delegates elected to the soviets were predominantly Socialist Revolutionaries and Mensheviks. The Bolsheviks remained relatively insignificant until the return of their leaders from Switzerland. On April 16, Lenin arrived in Petrograd and issued his famous "April Theses" demanding immediate peace, land to the peasants, and all power to the soviets. In the light of what was to come,

Lenin's demands may seem natural and logical. Actually they aroused much opposition within the soviets among the Socialist Revolutionaries and Mensheviks, and even some of the Bolsheviks. Especially controversial was the demand for "all power to the soviets." This seemed at the time preposterous and irresponsible. Time, however, was on Lenin's side, for the longer the war continued, the more the public discontent mounted, and the more popular his demands became. Slogans that seemed bizarre in April were to sound perfectly reasonable six months later. By late 1917 many were ready to fight for "all power to the soviets" if that would rid them of the Provisional Government, which stood in the way of the much-desired peace and land.

An early indication of shifting public opinion was the forced resignation of Foreign Minister Miliukov on May 17. His insistence that Russia remain in the war made him so unpopular that he was dropped, and a new Provisional Government was formed under Lvov and Kerensky. It remained in office until July 20, when

Kerensky, who had been steadily emerging as the strongman, organized a new government with himself as premier. By this time the temper of the country had swung so far to the left that the new ministers were mostly Socialist Revolutionaries and Mensheviks. Gone were the days when the Cadets were regarded as the radicals of Russian politics. Now Kerensky was cooperating with the Mensheviks and the Socialist Revolutionaries in order to withstand Lenin and his Bolsheviks.

1917 Bolshevik Revolution

Kerensky declared that his main objective was "to save the revolution from the extremists." In an effort to halt the growing seizure of estates he warned that the future Constituent Assembly would not recognize land transfers made after July 25. He also tried to restore some discipline in the armed forces by reintroducing the death penalty for certain offenses. These measures naturally made Kerensky very unpopular with the Bolsheviks and other radicals. Furthermore, by this time the Bolsheviks were becoming increasingly influential within the soviets as public opinion veered more and more to the left. By October the Bolsheviks had

a majority in both the Petrograd and Moscow soviets. Lenin now decided that the time had come to overthrow Kerensky and bring about the socialist revolution. The date was set for November 7.

The actual revolution was anticlimactic. With almost no resistance the Bolshevik forces seized key positions in Petrograd—railway stations, bridges, banks, and government buildings. There was no fighting because Kerensky had as few dedicated supporters in November as Nicholas had had in March. The easy victory of the Bolsheviks did not mean that they commanded the support of all the Russian people, or even the majority. This was demonstrated by the composition of the Constituent Assembly, which was finally elected on November 25: Socialist Revolutionaries, 370; Bolsheviks, 175; Left Socialist Revolutionaries, 40; Cadets, 17; Mensheviks, 16; national groups, 86. The Constituent Assembly met in Petrograd on January 18, 1918, and, after holding one session, was dispersed by the Bolsheviks, who now had military power. Nevertheless, its makeup reveals the relative following of the various parties at that time.

One of the first measures of the new Bolshevik government was to fulfill the promise of peace. On March 3, 1918, it signed the Brest-

Lenin and Trotsky (saluting) in Red Square in Moscow in 1919, from a documentary film made by Herman Axelbank. Trotsky's organizational skill was largely responsible for the Red Army's victory in the Russian civil war of 1918-1920. By 1921, as a result of war, revolution, and civil war, the Russian economy had all but collapsed.

Litovsk Treaty with Germany. The treaty's severe terms required the surrender by Russia of Poland, the Baltic provinces, Finland, the Ukraine, and parts of the Caucasus. The areas surrendered involved 62 million people and 1,250,000 million square miles of territory where, disastrously, three-fourths of Russia's iron and coal were produced. They also included half of its industrial plants and a third of its crop area. (see map of Russia in Revolution, 1917–1921, p. 548.)

In this manner Russia dropped out of World War I, and the new Bolshevik rulers proceeded to organize the Union of Soviet Socialist Republics.

V. GLOBAL PHASE OF THE WAR: AMERICAN INTERVENTION

When World War I began, President Wilson immediately called on his fellow citizens to be strictly neutral. This met with general approval, for the great majority of Americans wished to stay out of the war. And yet, by 1917, Wilson himself was leading the country into war. One reason for the shift from neutrality to intervention was the government's campaign for military preparedness culminating in the National Defense Act of June 3, 1916. The militaristic propaganda during the campaign helped to prepare the nation psychologically for intervention in the war. Another factor was the American armed intervention in Mexico (March 1916–February 1917) precipitated by Pancho Villa's raid on New Mexico. Nothing came of the intervention, but it provided the thrills of military action without much grief or sacrifice. Also favoring intervention were the American financiers and industrialists who had been supplying Britain and France with war materials on credit, and who would have been ruined if their customers were defeated. The drift to war was speeded up by Germany's unrestricted submarine warfare during which American lives and American ships were lost. Finally, the overthrow of the tsarist regime in March 1917 enabled the United States to join a league of democratic powers battling the autocracies of central Europe.

This combination of factors led President Wilson to declare war on Germany in April 1917. In his Fourteen Points he set forth specific and detailed war aims, including the end of secret diplomacy and the drafting of "open

President Woodrow Wilson reads his war message to Congress, April 2, 1917. He predicted "many months of fiery trial and sacrifice ahead of us."

Russia in Revolution, 1917–1921

TABLE 36.1 Production of the Belligerent Powers (in millions of tons)

	August 1, 1914		September 15, 1914		1917	
	Allies	Central Powers	Allies	Central Powers	Allies	Central Powers
Pig Iron	22	22	16	25	50	15
Steel	19	21	16	25	58	16
Coal	394	331	346	355	851	340

F. Sternberg, *Capitalism and Socialism on Trial* (Day, 1951), pp. 166–167. Translated by Edward Fitzgerald. Copyright 1950 by Fritz Sternberg. Copyright renewed. Reprinted by permission of HarperCollins Publishers, Inc.

covenants of Peace," freedom of the seas, removal of barriers to international trade, reduction of armaments, impartial arbitration of all colonial claims on the principle that the interests of the colonial peoples must have equal weight with the claims of colonial powers, and the application of the principle of self-determination in dealing with the various subject minorities in central and eastern Europe.

How decisive was the American intervention is made clear in the statistics shown in Table 36.1 concerning the productivity of the belligerents. The intervention of the United States gave the Allies decisive superiority in manpower as well as in war supplies. In the month of March 1918, a total of 84,889 American soldiers reached the western front, and in July the number rose to 306,350. Thus a fresh new army was made available to the Allied commanders each month. It is not surprising that during 1918 the Central Powers surrendered one by one.

Thus ended World War I—a war that lasted four years and three months, involved thirty sovereign states, overthrew four empires, gave birth to seven new nations, took approximately 8.5 million combatant and 10 million noncombatant lives, and cost $180.5 billion directly and $151.6 billion indirectly.

VI. PEACE SETTLEMENT

Separate peace treaties were signed with each of the Central Powers: the Versailles Treaty with Germany, June 28, 1919; the St. Germain Treaty

One of the last British soldiers killed on the western front in November 1918. The carnage of World War I was one of the main causes of European weakness and instability in the 1920s and 1930s.

with Austria, September 10, 1919; the Trianon Treaty with Hungary, March 22, 1919; the Neuilly Treaty with Bulgaria, November 27, 1919; and the Sévres Treaty with Turkey, August 20, 1920. Three features of this overall peace settlement are significant for world history: the establishment of the League of Nations, the application of the principle of self-determination in Europe, and the failure to apply this principle outside of Europe.

The League of Nations was organized to attain two basic objectives. The most important was to preserve the peace. Its members were to give each other mutual protection against aggression, to submit disputes to arbitration or inquiry, and to abstain from war until three months after arbitration. The secondary purpose of the league was to concern itself with health, social, economic, and humanitarian problems of international scope. For this purpose there were established specialized league bodies such as the Health Organization, the Committee on Intellectual Cooperation, and the International Labor Organization. By and large, the league succeeded in its secondary functions. It proved invaluable in improving international labor conditions,

The Allies promoted Arab efforts to secure independence from Turkey in an effort to remove Turkey from the war. Delegates to the peace conference of 1919 in Paris included British Colonel T.E. Lawrence, who helped lead the rebellion, and representatives from the Middle Eastern region. Pictured are: Prince Feisal, the third son of King Hussein, standing in the foreground; Colonel T.E. Lawrence in the middle row, second from the right; and Brigadier General Nuri Pasha Said of Baghdad second from the left.

promoting world health, combating the narcotic and slave traffics, and coping with economic crises. But we shall see that the league was not able to keep the peace, and since this was its chief aim, that failure spelled the end of the entire organization.

The post-World War I settlement was characterized also by the redrawing of European frontiers on the basis of the principle of self-determination. This, stated explicitly in the Fourteen Points, was officially implemented in the various peace treaties. The net result was a drastic revision of the map of Europe. Alsace-Lorraine was returned to France without question. Russia was deprived of most of its Baltic coastline by the establishment of the independent states of Finland, Latvia, Estonia, and Lithuania. An independent Poland was created, carved out of former Russian, German, and Hapsburg provinces; Czechoslovakia emerged from the former Hapsburg Empire. Yugoslavia also appeared, comprising prewar Serbia and Montenegro and various former Hapsburg territories inhabited by south Slavs. Rumania more than doubled in size as a result of its acquisitions from Austria-Hungary, Russia, and Bulgaria. Finally, from the remains of the old Hapsburg Empire, there emerged the two rump states of Austria and Hungary.

The principle of self-determination was not respected in every instance in drawing the new frontiers. Indeed, there were bitter protests concerning the sizable German minorities in Poland and Czechoslovakia; the Hungarian minorities in Yugoslavia, Rumania, and Czechoslovakia; and the Russian minorities in Poland, Czechoslovakia, and Rumania. Yet despite these deviations, the new frontiers were more in accord with nationalist aspirations than the old. And the number of minority peoples was much smaller after World War I than before. (See map of Europe after World War I, 1923, p. 552.)

Although the peacemakers generally applied self-determination in Europe, they definitely did not do so outside of Europe. This discrimination was clearly evident in Wilson's Fourteen Points, which specifically spelled out how the aspirations of the various European minorities were to be satisfied. By contrast, Point 5 declared that in the colonies "the interests of the populations concerned must have equal weight with the equitable claims of the government whose title is to be determined." The significant point here is the reference to the "interests" rather than to the "wishes" of the colonial peoples. Needless to say, it was the Europeans themselves who decided what these "interests" were, and the outcome was a modified form of imperial rule known as the mandate system.

Article 22 of the League Covenant referred to the inhabitants of the colonies taken from the Central Powers as "peoples not yet able to stand by themselves under the strenuous conditions of the modern world." The article accordingly provided that the "tutelage of such peoples should be entrusted to advanced nations who, by reason of their resources, their experience, or their geographical position, can best undertake this responsibility. . . and that this tutelage should be exercised by them as Mandatories on behalf of the League." It is significant that this provision for "tutelage" under "Mandatories" was not extended to the colonies of the victorious Allies, whose inhabitants in many cases were at a similar level of development or lack of development.

VII. WORLD WAR I IN WORLD HISTORY

A glance at the globe before and after World War I reveals comparatively few changes. Europe's frontiers were different because of the disappearance of four empires, but as far as the world as a whole was concerned, European dominance appeared undiminished. Britain, France, and the other imperial powers still ruled as many overseas colonies as before 1914. Indeed, their possessions were even greater, for they now controlled territories in the Middle East that formerly had been under the sultan. Thus, Europe's global hegemony appeared to be more complete after World War I than before.

Beneath the surface, however, the situation was entirely different. In fact, the overriding significance of World War I from a global viewpoint is precisely that it began the undermining of Europe's supremacy—a process that was completed following World War II. The undermining was evident in at least three regards: the economic decline, the political crisis, and the weakening hold over the colonies.

Europe after World War I, 1923

Before 1914, Europe's economy was dependent to a considerable degree on massive overseas investments, yielding massive annual returns. During World War I, however, Britain lost a quarter of its foreign investments, France a third, and Germany lost all. The reverse of this trend may be seen in the new financial strength of the United States. In 1914 the United States owed about $4 billion to European investors, but by 1919 it had become a creditor nation to the tune of $3.7 billion; by 1930 this sum had risen to $8.8 billion. The same pattern is evident in industry, for many European industrial areas were devastated whereas American factories mushroomed spectacularly under the impetus of unlimited wartime demand. By 1929 the United States was responsible for no less than 42.2 percent of world industrial output, an amount greater than that of all the countries of Europe, including Russia. Thus, the economic relationships between Europe and the United States were reversed as a result of World War I. Europe no longer was the banker and the workshop of the world, as it had been during the nineteenth century. Leadership in both areas had crossed the Atlantic.

The war gutted Europe politically as well as economically. Prior to 1914 Europe had been the source of the basic political ideas and institutions of modern times. Their impact, as we have seen, had been felt in all corners of the globe. The holocaust of war, however, left Europeans demoralized and unbelieving. In all parts of the Continent the old order was being questioned and challenged. In a confidential memorandum of March 1919, the British premier, David Lloyd George, wrote, "There is a deep sense not only of discontent, but of anger and revolt, amongst the workmen against pre-war conditions. The whole existing order in its political, social and economic aspects is questioned by the masses of the people from one end of Europe to the other."[2]

In this revolutionary crisis, many Europeans looked for guidance to two non-Europeans, the American Wilson and the Russian Lenin. Wilson's Fourteen Points had stirred up a ferment of democratic hope and expectancy. When he stepped on the blood-soaked soil of Europe in December 1918, huge crowds greeted Wilson with delirious enthusiasm as "King of Humanity," "Savior," "Prince of Peace." They listened avidly to his plans for a future of peace and security.

At the same time another gospel of salvation was coming from the East. The millions of dead and wounded, the smoking ruins of cities and villages, made large masses receptive to the call for revolution and for a new social order. In imitation of the Bolshevik Revolution, soviets were set up in Berlin, Hamburg, and Budapest. Demonstrations were staged in the streets of London, Paris, and Rome. Wilson's confidant, Colonel House, wrote in his diary on March 22, 1919, "Rumblings of discontent every day. The people want peace. Bolshevism is gaining ground everywhere. Hungary has just succumbed. We are sitting upon an open powder magazine and some day a spark may ignite it."[3]

Finally, Europe's domination was undermined by World War I because of the repercussions in the overseas colonies. The spectacle of one bloc of European powers fighting another to the bitter end damaged the prestige of the white masters irreparably. No longer were they regarded as almost divinely ordained to rule over colored subjects. Equally disruptive was the participation in the war of millions of colonials as soldiers or as laborers. Indian divisions fought on the western front and in Mesopotamia; many Africans in French uniform fought in northern France; and large numbers of Chinese and Indochinese served in labor battalions behind the lines. Needless to say, the colonials who returned home after such experiences were not likely to be as obedient to European overlords as before.

Revolutionary ideas in the colonies were also spread by propaganda associated with the conduct of the war. It is true that Wilson's Fourteen Points had referred only to the "interest" rather than to the desires of the colonial peoples. But this was an overfine distinction in a time of war. The revolutionary phrase "self-determination of peoples" left its imprint on the colonial world as well as on Europe. Equally influential were the ideologies of socialism and communism. Before World War I, Asian intellectuals had been inspired by Western liberalism and nationalism. They had quoted Voltaire, Mazzini, and John Stuart Mill. But their sons now were likely to quote Marx and Lenin. Dr. Sun Yat-sen, on July 25, 1919, gave evidence of this shift when he declared, "If the people of China wish to be free. . . its only ally and brother in the struggle for national freedom are the Russian workers and peasants of the Red Army."[4]

All these repercussions of World War I on the colonial world inevitably had profound political consequences. One of the few who saw this clearly was the African-American leader W. E. B. Du Bois, who in 1918 wrote the following remarkable forecast of the world to come:

This war is an end and also a beginning. Never again will darker people of the world occupy just the place they had before. Out of this place will rise, soon or late, an independent China, a self-governing India, an Egypt with representative institutions, an Africa for the Africans, and not merely for business exploitation. Out of this war will rise, too, an American Negro with the right to vote and the right to work and the right to live without insult.[5]

SUGGESTED READINGS

The most recent of the numerous studies of the origins of World War I are G. F. Kennan, *The Fateful Alliance: France, Russia and the Coming of the First World War* (Pantheon, 1984); J. Joll, *The Origins of the First World War* (Longman, 1985); and G. Barraclough,

From Agadir to Armageddon: Anatomy of a Crisis (Holmes and Meier, 1981), the latter stressing the domino effect of Agadir leading to Sarajevo and suggesting implications for the post–World War II cold war. For the broader significance of World War I, see H. Holborn, *The Political Collapse of Europe* (Knopf, 1951); M. Ferro, *The Great War 1914–1918* (Routledge & Kegan Paul, 1973); and J. Winter, *Sites of Memory, Sites of Mourning: The Great War in European Cultural History* (Cambridge University, 1995).

The most thorough study of the Russian Revolution is by E. H. Carr, *The Bolshevik Revolution, 1917–1923*, 3 vols. (Macmillan, 1953). See also the interpretation by H. Salisbury, *Black Night, White Snow: Russia's Revolutions 1905–1917* (Doubleday, 1978.) Documentary materials are provided by J. Bunyan and H. H. Fisher, *The Bolshevik Revolution, 1917–1918* (Stanford University, 1934); and R. P. Browder and A. F. Kerensky, *The Russian Provisional Government, 1917*, 3 vols. (Stanford University, 1961). See also J. Bradley, *Allied Intervention in Russia 1917–1920* (Basic Books, 1968.) The global impact of the Russian Revolution is analyzed by P. Dukes, *October and the World: Perspectives on the Russian Revolution* (St. Martin's Press, 1979).

For the Versailles settlement, see the definitive study by A. J. Mayer, *Politics and Diplomacy of Peacemaking: Containment and Counterrevolution at Versailles 1918–1919* (Knopf, 1967); the revealing analysis of the role of the United States by N. G. Levin, Jr., *Woodrow Wilson and World Politics: America's Response to War and Revolution* (Oxford University, 1968); and A. Walworth, *Wilson and His Peacemakers* (W. W. Norton, 1986).

NOTES

1. Cited by J. C. Adams, *Flight in Winter* (Princeton University, 1942), p. 29.
2. Cited by R. S. Baker, *Woodrow Wilson and World Settlement*, Vol. 3 (Doubleday, 1922), p. 451.
3. C. Seymour, ed., *The Intimate Papers of Colonel House*, Vol. 4 (Houghton Mifflin, 1928), p. 389.
4. Cited by K. M. Panikkar, *Asia and Western Dominance* (Day, 1953), p. 364.
5. Cited by R. Emerson and M. Kilson, "The American Dilemma in a Changing World: The Rise of Africa and Negro America," *Daedalus*, Vol. 94 (Fall 1965), p. 1057.

37

Nationalist Uprisings in the Colonial World

Since the day of Japan's victory over Russia, the peoples of Asia have cherished the hope of shaking off the yoke of European oppression, a hope which has given rise to a series of independence movements—in Egypt, Persia, Turkey, Afghanistan, and finally in India. . . . If we want to regain our rights, we must resort to force.

Sun Yat-sen, 1924

World War I was followed by a wave of revolutions in the colonial territories. The roots of these revolutions go back to the pre–1914 years, but it was the war itself that provided the immediate stimulus. The final outcomes varied, with the Turks winning most of their objectives, whereas the Egyptians, Iraqis, Indians, and others won only modest constitutional concessions. These uprisings represent the prelude to the great upheavals that finally ended the European empires during the two decades following World War II.

I. TURKEY

The most spectacular and successful of all the post–World War I colonial revolts against Euro-

pean domination was that of the Turks. They had suffered disastrous defeat during the war and had then been compelled to accept humiliating armistice and peace terms. Yet they bounced back, defeating their enemies in armed conflict and winning a new treaty with more favorable terms. Thus, of all the Central Powers, only primitive and despised Turkey was capable of turning on the victorious Allies and forcing them to accept a revision of the peace settlement. To understand this extraordinary outcome it is necessary to review the tangled wartime diplomacy concerning the Ottoman Empire. Britain was the prime mover behind most of the diplomacy involving the Middle East during the war years. It was responsible for three sets of often conflicting agreements—with its own allies, with Arab representatives, and with the Zionists.

The agreements among the Allies consisted of four secret treaties: the Constantinople Agreement of March-April 1915; the Treaty of London of April 26, 1915; the Sykes-Picot Agreement of April 26, 1916; and the Saint-Jean-de-Maurienne Treaty of April 1917. These treaties allotted to Russia Constantinople, the Straits, and a considerable portion of northeast Asia Minor; to Italy southwest Asia Minor; to Britain Mesopotamia and an enclave about Haifa and Acre; and to France the Syrian coast with the hinterland eastward to the Russian sphere. These secret treaties marked the death warrant of the Ottoman Empire, leaving to the Turks only 20,000 square miles in the northern section of their homeland. More important, these secret treaties were in direct conflict with certain agreements that Britain was concluding at this time with Arab and Jewish representatives.

When Turkey joined the Central Powers in November 1914, the British negotiated a military alliance with the Arab leader Emir Hussein, Prince of Mecca. In return for an Arab revolt against the Turks, the British agreed to recognize the postwar independence of all Arab lands. This commitment conflicted with another that the British made to Lord Rothschild of the World Zionist Organization. Zionism was a nationalist movement that had developed among European Jews in the late nineteenth century as a reaction against mounting anti-Semitism. The World Zionist Organization, established in Basel in 1897, had repeatedly but vainly sought permission from the Ottoman government to establish a Jewish settlement in Palestine, the Jewish biblical homeland. With Turkey's involvement in World War I, Zionist leaders in England and the United States seized the opportunity to press for an Allied commitment to create a Jewish commonwealth in Palestine after the end of the Ottoman Empire. They succeeded when on November 2, 1917, Lord Balfour wrote to Lord Rothschild that the British Government favored the establishment in Palestine of a "national home for the Jewish people. . . it being clearly understood that nothing shall be done which may prejudice the civil and religious rights of existing non-Jewish communities

Washington Naval Disarmament Conference, 1922—(left to right) L. Gonyo, Japanese Secretary of Foreign Affairs; S, Yada, Japanese Defense Consul; U.S. Secretary of State Hughes; General K. Tanaka; Vice-Admiral Kato; and assistant to Kato, E. R. Schipp.

in Palestine. . . . "It is evident that this Balfour Declaration conflicted with the commitment to Hussein, as well as with the secret treaties for the division of the Ottoman provinces among the Allies.

The final outcome was the Sévres Treaty (August 10, 1920), by which France obtained Syria as a mandate, and Britain got Mesopotamia and Palestine, in addition to a protectorate over Egypt. The Dodecanese Islands were ceded to Italy, and Greece, thanks to the skillful diplomacy of its Premier Venizelos, obtained several Aegean islands, eastern Thrace, and the right to administer the Smyrna region for five years. After that its final disposition was to be determined by a plebiscite. Armenia and the Kingdom of Hejaz were recognized as independent. Finally, Soviet Russia, which was now in armed conflict with Allied interventionist forces and which had published and repudiated the secret treaties signed by the tsarist ministers, did not obtain Constantinople and the Straits. Instead, this strategic territory was left under Turkish sovereignty, though the Straits were to be demilitarized and placed under international control.

These provisions, so contrary to the promises made to the Arabs and to the professed Allied principle of self-determination, aroused a wave of armed resistance throughout the Middle East. A combination of factors enabled the Turks to scrap the Sévres Treaty altogether, and the Arabs won piecemeal concessions after ten years of stubborn struggle.

A prime factor in the Turkish success was the personality of Mustafa Kemal, later known as Ataturk or Foremost Turk. He first won fame for his successful defense of the Dardanelles against the Allies. After the war he led the resistance against the Sévres Treaty. He was willing to surrender the Arab provinces of the old empire, but he refused to accept the partition of Asia Minor and the loss of Constantinople and the Straits. In the elections of October 1919 Kemal's followers won a majority. When Parliament met in January 1920 it adopted a National Pact based on Kemal's program. In April 1920 Parliament dethroned the sultan, who was a virtual Allied prisoner in Constantinople, and established a republic headed by Kemal as president.

The young republic had to struggle against not only the sultan but also the victorious Allies.

Photo of Mustafa Kemal taken at the window of his special train as he leaves Istanbul for Angora (presently Ankara).

It succeeded against such odds because of Kemal's inspired leadership and because the Turkish people united behind him, especially after the landing of Greek troops at Smyrna in the spring of 1919. Kemal skillfully exploited differences among the Allies to conclude separate treaties with them, thereby isolating the Greeks in Smyrna. By September 1922 Kemal was riding triumphantly into Smyrna. Before him fled not only the Greek army but also Greek civilians who had lived in that coastal region since ancient times.

Kemal now was in a position to demand revisions of the Sévres Treaty, which he obtained after long negotiations in the Lausanne Treaty signed on July 24, 1923. Having created a new Turkey, Kemal turned to the equally difficult task of creating new Turks. He ruthlessly swept away outdated institutions as reform followed reform in a great torrent. The capital was moved from vulnerable Constantinople to Ankara in the interior of Asia Minor. The caliphate was abolished; all religious orders and houses suppressed; a constitution adopted along with new civil, criminal, and commercial codes; and women given the right to vote and sit in the assembly. By the time of Kemal's death on November 10, 1938, the new Turkey was securely established.

II. ARAB MIDDLE EAST

While the Turks were successfully scrapping the Sévres Treaty, the Arabs were stubbornly resisting the Mandatory Powers to which they had been assigned. Contrary to the Hussein Agreement, Syria-Lebanon had been given as a mandate to France, Mesopotamia and Palestine had been made British mandates, and full British control had been established in Egypt. This high-handed parceling out of Arab lands was bound to lead to trouble because the war itself had stimulated tremendous national sentiment among the Arabs.

A common pattern developed in the postwar struggle for independence. First, an explosion of defiance and armed revolt occurred during the years immediately following the peace treaties. Then Britain and France gradually restored order and reasserted their authority. Finally, they granted varying degrees of autono-

my, which did not entirely satisfy the nationalists but which did preserve an uneasy peace until World War II.

In Palestine the situation was unique because it quickly deteriorated into a bitter three-way struggle involving Britain, Arabs, and Jews. The Arabs maintained that the Balfour Declaration concerning a Jewish "national home" was in violation of prior commitments made to the Arabs. In 1921, Britain tried to appease the Arabs by setting apart the interior portion of the country as the independent state of Transjordan. This was exempt from all the clauses of the mandate concerning the establishment of a Jewish home.

In Palestine proper, however, the triangle conflict became increasingly fierce as Jewish immigrants poured in and the apprehensive Arabs struck back against both the Jews and the British. Article 6 of the mandate required Britain to "facilitate" Jewish immigration and to "encourage close settlement by Jews on the land." But the same article also provided that "the rights and position of other sections of the population" were to be safeguarded. The British apparently felt at the time that the two orders

Jewish colonists enroute to a settlement in Palestine, 1920.

were not necessarily contradictory. They expected that Jewish immigration would never reach such proportions as to threaten "the rights and positions" of the Arabs. They could not have foreseen the repercussions of Hitler's rise to power in 1933. Jewish immigration jumped from 9,553 in 1932 to 61,854 in 1935 and the total Jewish population in Palestine rose from 65,000 in 1919 to 450,000 in 1939.

As long as the Jewish influx had been modest, the Arabs had not raised serious objections. In fact they had welcomed the Jews with their money and energy and skills. The Arabs themselves had benefited substantially from the success of the Jews in restoring exhausted land, founding industries, and checking diseases. But when the stream of immigration became a torrent, the Arabs reacted violently. They pointed out that there was no reason why they should lose their country because of western anti-Semitism. "Anti-Semitism is a deplorable Western disease. . . . We aren't anti-Semites; we are also Semites. Yet this Western problem is being smoothed over at our expense. Is that your idea of right?"[1]

Arab attacks against the Jews became increasingly frequent and serious. The British response was to send Royal Commissions following the major outbreaks. By the time of World War II several commissions had investigated the situation and had vacillated in their recommendations as they sought to satisfy three distinct and conflicting interests—the Jewish Zionist aspirations, Arab nationalist demands, and British imperial interests. The White Paper of May 1939, for example, proposed that Palestine become an independent state in ten years and that definite limits be placed on Jewish immigration and land purchases. Both Arabs and Jews rejected the British proposals, and the Palestine controversy remained as far from settlement as ever when World War II began.

III. INDIA

At the turn of the century British rule in India seemed perfectly secure for the foreseeable future. In 1912, a great imperial durbar was held in Delhi to celebrate the coronation of King George V. Amid pageantry and splendor, King George received the homage of India's princes and potentates without a voice being raised in dissent. In 1914, India rallied solidly behind Britain at war. The princes contributed generous financial aid, and no fewer than 900,000 Indians served in the British army as combatants and another 300,000 as laborers.

Yet only three decades after World War I, British rule in India came to an end. One reason for this extraordinary outcome was the impact of the war itself—the influence of slogans about self-determination and the unsettling effect of overseas service on hundreds of thousands of soldiers who returned with new ideas and attitudes. Unrest was stimulated also by a series of disasters in the immediate postwar years. The failure of the monsoon in 1918 brought famine to many parts of India. The influenza epidemic of 1918–1919 killed no fewer than 13 million people! Another factor contributing to unrest was the repressive policy followed by Britain after the war.

The "Great Soul," "Mahatma" Mohandas K. Gandhi, father of the modern state of India.

Gandhi was by all odds the outstanding figure in this postwar anti-British movement. The Indian Congress, organized in 1885, did not seriously threaten the British before 1914 (see Chapter 30, Section V). It had remained essentially a middle-class movement with little support from village masses. Gandhi's great contribution was that he managed to break through to the villagers, establish rapport with them, and involve them in the struggle for independence. His message was simple and appealing. He pointed out that in 1914 the British were ruling 300 million Indians with a mere 4,000 administrators and 69,000 soldiers. This was possible only because all classes of the population were cooperating with the British in one way or another. If this cooperation were withdrawn, British rule inevitably would collapse. The task, then, was to educate and prepare the people for satyagraha, or nonviolent passive resistance. Gandhi also called on the people to practice hartal, or to boycott British goods. In place of imported machine-made goods, Gandhi preached the wearing of homespun cloth. This would undermine the economic basis of British rule and also revive village industries. He himself wore a loin cloth of homespun material and publicly worked at his spinning wheel. The combination of satyagraha and hartal, Gandhi taught, would make possible the realization of swaraj, or home rule. Once India's villagers understood these teachings and acted on them, the days of British rule would be numbered.

Another nationalist leader, Jawaharlal Nehru, was now coming to the fore alongside Gandhi. The son of a wealthy lawyer, Nehru had been educated at Harrow and Cambridge and had been admitted to the bar in 1912. On his return, he plunged into the nationalist struggle for freedom and became a follower and admirer of Gandhi. Nehru, however, was very different from his mystical and ascetic leader. He was a socialist and a firm believer in science and technology as the means for liberating humanity from its age-old misery and ignorance.

Indian nationalists were divided not only between Gandhi and Nehru, but also between warring Hindu and Moslem blocs. The All-India Moslem League was founded as early as 1919 but was of little significance until after 1935, when it came under the leadership of a Bombay lawyer, Mohammed Ali Jinnah. He appealed to the Moslem masses with the cry "Islam is in danger." The response was enthusiastic, for many Indian Moslems felt they had more in common with the rest of the Moslem world than with their Hindu neighbors. Jinnah's electoral success made possible the future establishment of the independent Moslem Pakistan.

IV. CHINA

In China, Dr. Sun Yat-sen had established a republic in 1911, and had organized his Kuomintang political party. (See Chapter 31, Section II). Although Sun was the president and nominal head of his country, real power was held by bureaucratic and military leaders who controlled the country as warlords. On the death of Sun in 1925, General Chiang Kai-shek became the head of the Kuomintang and of China. Under his guidance, considerable progress was made in building railways, roads, and industries and in improving public health and education.

But there were serious gaps in Chiang's reform program, and these ultimately proved fatal. Badly needed land reform was neglected because the Kuomintang party in the rural areas was dominated by landlords who opposed any change. And Chiang's authoritarian, one-party government prevented the growth of democracy, so that opposition groups could not assert themselves by constitutional means; revolution was the sole alternative. These weaknesses of the Kuomintang regime might have been gradually overcome if it had been given a long period of peace. But it did not have this opportunity because of two mortal enemies, the Communists at home and the Japanese abroad.

The Chinese Communist party was organized in Shanghai in 1921 and attracted many students and intellectuals with its program for a more equitable society. Sun Yat-sen had worked closely with the Communists, but not Chiang Kai-shek who strongly opposed their social radicalism. He launched five "bandit extermination campaigns," as they were called, but the Communists survived because they won over the peasants by seizing and distributing the estates of the large landowners. The outstanding Communist leader was Mao Tse-tung, who evolved a

Mao Tse-tung, leading figure of the Chinese Communists, speaking in Shensi Province, northwest China, 1937.

new revolutionary strategy in defiance of the Communist International in Moscow. He rejected the traditional Marxist doctrine that only the urban proletariat could be depended on to carry through a revolution. From firsthand observation in the countryside he concluded that the poor peasants, who made up 70 percent of the population, were "the vanguard of the revolution. . . . Without the poor peasant there can be no revolution." This was pure heresy in Moscow, but Mao went his way, organizing the peasants and building up a separate army and government.

After years of struggle against Chiang's "extermination" campaigns, Mao finally fought his way to the northwest provinces, where he dug in and established a base. Gradually he extended his base, thanks to his land-reform policies and to Japanese attacks along the eastern coast, which were weakening Chiang's government. Finally the combination of Communist subversion and Japanese aggression forced

Chiang to flee to Taiwan, leaving Mao the ruler of the Chinese mainland.

SUGGESTED READINGS

General surveys of the post–World War I colonial uprising are available in the relevant sections of H. Kohn, *The Age of Nationalism: The First Era of Global History* (Harper & Row, 1962); M. Edwardes, *Asia in the European Age, 1498–1955* (Thames & Hudson, 1961); and J. Romein, *The Asian Century* (George Allen & Unwin, 1962).

World War I diplomacy involving the Middle East is analyzed in M. Kent, ed., *The Great Powers and the End of the Ottoman Empire* (George Allen & Unwin, 1984). For Turkey's revival under Kemal, see S. R. Sonyel, *Turkish Diplomacy, 1918–1923: Mustafa Kemal and the Turkish National Movement* (Sage, 1975).

For the Arab nationalist awakening, see N. Safran, *Egypt in Search of Political Community* (Harvard University, 1961); Z. N. Zeine, *The Struggle for Arab Independence: Western Diplomacy and the Rise and Fall of Feisal's Kingdom in Syria* (Khayat, 1960); A. Hourani, *Arabic Thought in the Liberal Age 1798–1939* (Oxford University, 1962); and S. G. Haim, ed., *Arab Nationalism: An Anthology* (University of California, 1964).

On the outstanding figures in India, there are M. K. Gandhi, *An Autobiography: The Story of My Experiments with Truth* (Beacon Press, 1957); *All Men Are Brothers: Life and Thoughts of Mahatma Gandhi as Told in His Own Words* (UNESCO, 1958); E. Erikson, *Gandhi's Truth* (W. W. Norton, 1970); and *Toward Freedom: The Autobiography of Jawaharlal Nehru* (Harper & Row, 1941).

On the outstanding figures in China, there is H. Z. Schiffrin, *Sun Yat-Sen and the Origins of the 1911 Revolution* (University of California, 1969); E. Hahn, *Chiang Kai-shek: An Unauthorized Biography* (Doubleday, 1955); and M. Meisner, *Mao's China* (Free Press, 1977). The most useful works on the interwar period are by L. Bianco, *Origins of the Chinese Revolution 1915–1949* (Stanford University, 1971); H. R. Isaacs, *The Tragedy of the Chinese Revolution*, 2nd rev. ed. (Atheneum, 1968); and J. E. Sheridan, *China in Disintegration: The Republican Era in Chinese History, 1912–1949* (Free Press, 1975).

NOTE

1. Cited by W. R. Polk, "What the Arabs Think," *Headline Series*, No. 96, p. 38.

Revolution and Settlement in Europe to 1929

The failure to strangle Bolshevism at its birth and to bring Russia, then prostrate, by one means or another, into the general democratic system, lies heavy upon us today.

Winston Churchill
April 1, 1949

At the same time that the colonial world was in the throes of national revolution, Europe itself was seething with social revolution. All over the Continent the old order was being questioned, partly because of the trauma of the world war, and partly because of the impact of the Russian Revolution. Thus, European history during the decade to 1929 was largely a history of struggle between revolutionary and counterrevolutionary forces. In Russia, communism emerged triumphant after years of civil war and intervention. In central Europe the revolutionary forces were crushed and a variety of non-Communist regimes appeared, ranging from the liberal Weimar Republic in Germany to the rightist Horthy government in Hungary and to the fascist Mus-

solini state in Italy. Western Europe was spared such violent upheavals, but even here, the authority of traditional parliamentary institutions was being strained by economic difficulties, mass unemployment, and cabinet instability. By the late 1920s, some measure of order seemed to be returning to Europe. Prosperity was growing, unemployment was on the decline, and various international issues appeared to be resolved by the Dawes Plan, the Locarno Pacts, the Kellogg-Briand Pact, and the commitment of the Soviet Union to Five-Year Plans rather than to world revolution. Europe was returning to a normal state, or so it seemed, until the Great Depression precipitated the series of domestic and international crises that were to culminate in World War II.

I. COMMUNISM TRIUMPHS IN RUSSIA

By signing the harsh Brest-Litovsk Treaty on March 3, 1918 (see Chapter 36, Section IV), the Bolsheviks hoped that at last they would be able to turn from war to the more congenial task of building a new social order. Instead, they were destined to fight for three more years against counterrevolution and foreign intervention. The counterrevolution was in part the work of members of the propertied classes—army officers, government officials, landowners, and businessmen—who, for obvious reasons, wished to be rid of the Bolsheviks. Equally ardent in their counterrevolutionary activities, however, were the various elements of the non-Bolshevik Left. Of these the Socialist Revolutionaries were by far the most numerous. They agreed with the Bolsheviks on the need for social revolution, but they bitterly resented the fact that the Bolsheviks had monopolized the revolution when it finally came. They regarded the Bolshevik coup of November 7, 1917, as a gross betrayal, particularly because the Constituent Assembly elected on November 25, 1917, included only 175 Bolsheviks as opposed to 370 Socialist Revolutionaries and 159 other assorted representatives. Accordingly, the non-Bolshevik Left took the lead in organizing an underground opposition, while the elements of the right led armed forces in open revolt, beginning in the Cossack territories.

These anti-Bolshevik groups were encouraged and assisted by the Western powers, who were motivated by various considerations, such as the strident Bolshevik campaign for world revolution. Also the Bolshevik nationalization of foreign properties and refusal to pay foreign debts naturally alienated powerful vested interests, and these interests used their influence to help the forces of intervention and counterrevolution.

Under these circumstances several counterrevolutionary governments were set up all along the borders of Russia soon after the signing of the Brest-Litovsk Treaty—in the northern Archangel-Murmansk region, the Baltic provinces, the Ukraine, the Don territories, Transcaucasia, and Siberia. The Western powers provided these governments generously with funds and war materials, as well as with military advisers and small detachments of troops on certain fronts. At first the Bolsheviks suffered one reverse after another, simply because the old Russian army had disintegrated, and there was nothing else to take its place. The commissar for defense, Leon Trotsky, gradually built up a new Red Army, which numbered about 500,000 men by the end of 1918. At times this force had to fight on two dozen different fronts, as revolts broke out in all parts of the country and Allied forces landed in coastal areas.

During the civil war in the Soviet Union, hunger and starvation haunted the countryside. Here a group of malnourished children posed for a photograph.

(See map of Russia in Revolution, 1917–1921, p. 548.)

The combination of civil wars and foreign aggressions ravaged Russia until 1921. In the end the Red Army unexpectedly prevailed for various reasons. Probably the most important was that the Bolsheviks were generally more successful in winning the support of the peasant masses. This does not mean that the Russian peasants were won over to Marxist ideology; indeed, most of them were fed up with both the Reds and the Whites and would rather have been left alone. But when forced to make a choice, they more frequently decided in favor of the Reds, who, they thought, would allow them to keep the plots they seized from the landlords.

In retrospect, the protracted civil war and intervention were a disaster for all parties concerned. It left the Russian countryside devastated from the Baltic to the Pacific and the Russian people decimated by casualties, starvation, and disease. Equally serious was the poisoning of relations between the new Soviet state and the Western world. The Soviet leaders were confirmed in their Marxist fears of "capitalist encirclement," and Western statesmen took all too seriously the futile manifestos of the Communist International established in 1919. So deep and lasting was this mutual distrust that it poisoned international relations during the following decade and contributed significantly to the coming of World War II.

II. COMMUNISM FAILS IN CENTRAL EUROPE

Weimar Republic in Germany

While civil war was raging in Russia, the crucial question for Europe was whether communism would spread westward. Lenin and his fellow Bolsheviks assumed that if this did not occur, their cause would be doomed. In line with Marxist ideology, they could not conceive that their revolution might survive and take root in a single country, least of all in predominantly agrarian Russia. Accordingly, they followed closely and hopefully the course of events in central Europe—especially Germany, which was clearly the key country. If it went communist, the combination of German industrial strength and Russian natural resources would be unbeatable, and the future of the revolution would be assured.

At first it appeared that these Bolshevik hopes might be realized. Workers' and Soldiers' Councils, similar to the Russian soviets, appeared in European cities, including Berlin. So strong was the revolutionary movement that it seemed possible that communism would engulf the Continent, at least to the Rhine. The final outcome, however, was not a Soviet Germany but the bourgeois Weimar Republic.

Several factors that escaped attention at the time explain this fateful outcome. One was the prosperity of prewar Germany, which left the working class relatively contented and in no mood for revolution. It is true that the German Social Democratic party in 1914 was the strongest party in Europe, but it was conservative, committed to social reform rather than to revolution. Equally important was the prosperity of the German peasants, so that the Bolshevik slogan "Land to the Peasants," which had been so effective in Russia, made very little impact on Germany. Also, the war had already ended at the time of the German Revolution, again in contrast to the situation in Russia. The demand for peace, which probably helped the Bolsheviks more than anything else, was irrelevant in Germany. Furthermore, although the German army was defeated, it was far from being as demoralized and mutinous as the Russian army of 1917. The opponents of revolution in Germany were able to call on reliable military forces when the showdown came.

A final factor of major significance was the split in the ranks of the German socialists, between the radicals who wanted a revolution and a Soviet Germany, and the conservatives who opposed both revolution and soviets. The conservatives had their way, so the elections held in Germany on January 19, 1919 were for a National Assembly rather than for a Soviet Congress. Thus the new German state that emerged was the democratic Weimar Republic—not a Soviet Germany.

PEASANTS AND BOLSHEVIKS

C. R. Buxton, secretary to the British Labour party, visited Russia in June 1920. His report on the attitude of the Russian peasants explains why the Bolsheviks won, even though they were a small minority of the total population.*

My host's name was Alexander Petrovich Emilianov. He was of the "middle" type of peasant, which formed the great majority of the village. About one-fifth of its people were considered "poor" peasants. Of "rich" peasants there were only four or five, I was told . . .

Before the Revolution my host had had eight acres—about the average holding in that region. He had now no less than eighty-five. This was the tremendous fact that I had turned over and over in my mind as we bumped along. Tremendous, surely; for my host's case was a type, not only of thousands, but of millions of others. . . .

"Look there," said Emilianov, pointing out from the edge of the village field over the limitless rolling steppe. "All that was the land of the landlords (barin)." . . .

"Who owned all this land?" I asked.

"All sorts of landlords. One was a Cossack. Two were Samara merchants. One was a German, Schmidt, who bought his from the Crown. Some was held by the Monks. One was an estate of Maria Feodorovna, the Tsaritsa."

"What has happened to them?"

"They are mostly gone," he replied in a matter-of-fact tone. "Some are in Samara. Most of them have left Russia, I suppose." . . .

"And what do the peasants think of it all now?" I asked Emilianov.

"It's a fine thing, the Revolution. Every one is in favour of it. They don't like the Communist Party, but they like the Revolution."

"Why don't they like the Communist Party?"

"Because they are always worrying us. They are people from the towns and don't understand the country. Commissars—powerful persons—are continually coming. We don't know what to do with them. New orders (prikazi) are always coming out. People are puzzled. As soon as you understand one of them, a different one comes along."

"What party do most people belong to here?"

"None at all. They are non-party (bezpartini)." . . .

The general attitude of the peasants, so far as I could judge, was that they owed much to the Soviet Government in the matter of the land; they approved of the "principle of everybody being equal"; they often talked of the "true" Communist as being an ideal sort of person. But they complained bitterly of the absence of necessities, of the compulsory contributions, and the worry of perpetual orders and appeals, often hard to understand. They considered that the Government was responsible for all these evils alike, and that the peasant was somehow in a position of inferiority to the townsman.

And yet, in spite of all these complaints, when the opportunity was offered them to choose between Kolchak on the one side and the Soviet Government on the other, the peasants do not seem to have had much hesitation. . . .

They were for the Revolution; and for the moment the Soviet power was the embodiment of the Revolution. They grumbled and cursed at it; but when the opportunity was offered to overthrow it, they said "No."

*C. R. Buxton, *In a Russian Village* (Labour Publishing Co., 1922), pp. 14–15, 19, 21, 26–27, 47–48.

Revolution and Reaction in Central Europe

The establishment of the Weimar Republic ensured that the rest of central Europe would not go communist. Nevertheless, for a number of years this part of Europe seethed with unrest and revolt. The peasant masses between the Baltic and the Aegean were politically awake and active to an unprecedented degree. One reason for the unrest was that millions of peasant army recruits had widened their horizons immeasurably as a result of their war experiences. They had observed not only the differences between city and village life but also the differences in living standards and social institutions among various countries. The peasants were also profoundly affected by the overthrow of the Hapsburg, Hohenzollern, and Romanoff dynasties. In the light of centuries-old traditions, this was a shock that aroused nationalist aspirations and class consciousness. Finally, the unprecedented destruction and suffering that took place during the long years of war aggravated the revolutionary situation, especially in the countries that had suffered defeat.

The precise manifestation of this revolutionary ferment varied from country to country according to local circumstances. The Communist parties did not play an outstanding role except in the case of Hungary, where in March 1919 a Soviet republic was established under the leadership of Bela Kun. It lasted less than a year because of the hostility of the peasants and the invasion of the country by Rumanian troops. When the Rumanians departed in February 1920, a right-wing government headed by Admiral Miklós Horthy was established with Allied support. Horthy remained in power for the whole interwar period, during which time Hungary was unique in central Europe for the almost complete absence of agrarian or other reforms.

In most of the other central European countries, agrarian or peasant parties were giving voice to popular discontent. The following peasant leaders assumed office in the postwar years: Aleksandr Stamboliski in Bulgaria in 1919, Stefan Radich in Yugoslavia in 1925, Wincenty Witos in Poland in 1926, and Iuliu Maniu in Rumania in 1928. Owing to their pacifism and distaste for violence, however, none of them was able to retain power for long. They were vulnerable to the entrenched military and bureaucratic elements that did not hesitate to seize power by force when their interests were threatened. Another reason for their failure was the increasing control that lawyers and urban intellectuals gained over the peasant parties. Under this leadership, the parties usually represented the interests of the wealthy peasants and had little contact with the great mass of poor peasants.

One after another the peasant leaders were ousted from office. Stamboliski was assassinated in 1923, and a dictatorship was established by King Boris. Radich was assassinated in 1928, and the following year King Alexander set up his dictatorship. In Poland, Witos lasted only a few days before he was removed by General Joseph Pilsudski, who dominated the country until his death in 1935. Maniu was eased out of office in 1930 by King Carol II, who made and unmade governments until forced to flee Rumania a decade later.

Thomas Masaryk was the first president of the Czechoslovak Republic, which was the only successful democratic state in eastern Europe during the interwar period.

The same pattern prevailed in Austria and Greece where, for various reasons, agrarian parties never took hold. Yet Austria ended up with an authoritarian government under Chancellor Dollfuss in 1934, and Greece with an avowedly fascist regime under General Metaxas in 1936. Thus, by World War II, the whole of central Europe was under dictatorial rule, with one exception—Czechoslovakia. This country possessed certain advantages that explain its uniqueness: a high level of literacy, a trained bureaucracy inherited from the Hapsburgs, the capable leadership of Jan Masaryk and Eduard Benes, and a balanced economy that provided higher living standards and greater security than was possible in the predominantly agrarian countries to the east.

III. ITALY GOES FASCIST

While bolshevism, agrarianism, and traditional parliamentarianism battled for primacy in eastern and central Europe, an entirely new "ism" was coming to the fore in Italy—fascism, the outstanding political innovation in Europe in the postwar years. Bolshevism had a history going back at least to the Communist Manifesto of 1848, and agrarianism was taking political form with the appearance of peasant parties at the turn of the century. Fascism, by contrast, appeared unexpectedly and dramatically with Mussolini's march on Rome in October 1922.

Postwar conditions in Italy provided fertile soil for a violent, melodramatic, and antiintellectual movement such as fascism. The Italy of 1919 had behind it only two generations of national independence and unity. Parliamentary government was, in practice, a morass of corruption in which party "bosses" manipulated short-lived coalition blocs. This unstable political structure was further weakened in the postwar years by serious economic dislocation. Many of the demobilized millions were unable to find jobs. Foreign trade and tourist traffic were declining in the aftermath of war. Emigration, which for decades had served as a safety valve and a source of overseas remittances, now petered out because of restrictive legislation in the United States and other countries. The popular unrest caused by this economic stress was aggravated by the slighting of Italian claims at the Paris peace conference. The resulting frustration and injured pride produced an inflammable situation.

Ready to exploit this situation was Benito Mussolini, the son of a Socialist blacksmith. He first attracted attention during the Tripolitan War of 1911 by his inflammatory speeches in which he referred to the Italian flag as "a rag fit only to be planted on a dung heap." The following year he became editor of the official Socialist paper, *Avanti!* When World War I began in August 1914, he was still a revolutionary and a pacifist, but the following month his great transformation took place, helped along by funds from the French government, which was anxious to secure Italy as an ally. Mussolini was enabled to start his own newspaper, *Il Popolo d'Italia,* in which he conducted a passionate interventionist campaign.

Called to battle in September 1915, Mussolini fought in the trenches for a few weeks until he was wounded and invalided out of the

Premier Benito Mussolini of Italy, 1939.

army. He languished in obscurity until 1919, when he formed his first "combat troops," and organized the Fascist party. Unity and authority were his watchwords against the political anarchy and social strife of the period. At the outset he attracted the support of only a handful of frustrated students and demobilized soldiers. But in the early 1920s he forged rapidly ahead, partly because the passivity of the Socialists had created a vacuum that Mussolini promptly filled. Equally important was the substantial support that Mussolini was now receiving from industrialists, landowners, and other members of the propertied classes. Terrified by the widespread seizure of factories and estates, they now looked hopefully to the Fascist squadristi, or armed bands, as a bulwark against the dreaded social revolution. The government and the wealthy elements of society not only tolerated squadristi violence and terrorism but even secretly gave it their aid and support.

In the fall of 1922, Mussolini prepared for a coup by winning over both the monarchy and the Church with specific assurance that their interests would be respected. Since the regular army and the police already had shown their benevolent neutrality, Mussolini proceeded with assurance to mobilize his Blackshirts for a widely publicized march on Rome. Only a token march on Rome by the Blackshirts was necessary, and Mussolini arrived anticlimactically in Rome on October 27 in a sleeping car.

Mussolini had become premier by technically constitutional methods, but it soon became apparent that he had no intention of respecting constitutional procedures. The showdown came with the elections of April 6, 1924. Through liberal use of the squadristi, the Fascist party polled 65 percent of the votes and won 375 seats, compared to the 35 they had previously held. Two months later Mussolini faced a major crisis with the murder of a prominent Socialist deputy, Giacomo Matteoti. It was widely suspected, and later proven, that Matteoti had been killed on orders from Mussolini himself. Thanks to the indecisiveness of the opposition and the unwavering support of the king, Mussolini weathered the storm and, by the fall of 1926, felt strong enough to take the offensive. He disbanded the old political parties, tightened censorship of the press, and established an orga-

nization of secret police. Italy had become a one-party state, with the Chamber functioning as a rubber-stamp body for passing Fascist bills.

The new Fascist regime gradually evolved certain distinctive features. One was the corporative state in which deputies were elected as representatives not of geographical constituencies but rather of trades and professions. Theoretically it eliminated class conflict by bringing capital and labor together under the benevolent auspices of the state. Another feature of Mussolini's Italy was the elaborate public works program designed to provide employment and to erect impressive structures for the glorification of fascism. Monuments of the past were restored, and many cities were adorned with large new buildings, workers' tenements, and stadiums. Tourists were particularly impressed by the trains that "ran on time" and by the extensive new highways, or autostrade.

IV. PROBLEMS OF DEMOCRACY IN WESTERN EUROPE

In western Europe there were no upheavals comparable to the civil war in Russia or to the bitter clash between right and left in central Europe. Democratic institutions had deeper roots in the West, and the prevailing social structures were healthier and enjoyed more popular support. In addition, the Western powers had been the victors rather than the losers in the war, a fact that further contributed to political and social stability. It does not follow, however, that western Europe had no difficulties in the postwar years. There were many problems. The most serious were economic in nature, though with far-reaching social and political repercussions. The experiences of the two leading Western countries, Great Britain and France, illustrate this point.

The chief problem in Britain was, by all odds, the severe and chronic unemployment. There was a short-lived boom immediately after the war when factories operated overtime to meet long-pent-up consumer demands. But the bust came in 1920, and by March 1921, over 2 million people were out of work. Unemployment persisted through the 1920s, and the situation grew worse in the 1930s. Thus the Depression actually began in Britain in 1920 rather than in 1929 and continued without interruption to World War II. Millions of families subsisted on state relief, or the "dole" as it was popularly called. A whole generation grew up without an opportunity to work. Such a situation was as unhealthy psychologically as it was economically. Eventually the unemployed became demoralized, depending on the dole without hope for the future.

These conditions inevitably caused political repercussions. Most important was the decline of the Liberal party as the workers turned increasingly to the Labour party in the hope of finding relief. Thus the economic crisis tended to polarize British politics, with the propertied classes generally voting Conservative, the workers supporting Labour, and the middle class fluctuating between the two. Each party had its panacea for the country's ills: The Conservatives called for protection; the declining Liberals, for free trade; and Labour, for a capital levy and for the nationalization of heavy industry. The net result was a succession of alternating Conservative and Labour ministries under Stanley Baldwin and Ramsay MacDonald, respectively. None was able to improve significantly the national fortunes.

France, too, was plagued by economic difficulties in the postwar years, although in certain respects it was better off than most of its neighbors. France had a well-balanced economy, so that it was not as vulnerable as the predominantly agrarian or industrial countries. The peace settlement strengthened its economy by adding the Saar Basin, with its coal mines, and the Alsace-Lorraine region, with its textile industry and rich potash and iron-ore deposits. In contrast to Britain's two or three major parties, France had five or six, so that a government's life depended on its ability to organize a bloc of these parties to secure majority support. This explains the relatively rapid turnover of governments in France compared to that in Britain. The leading parties, from left to right, were the Communists and Socialists, who represented mostly urban and rural workers; the Radical Socialists, who were in the center and were supported by the lower-middle class; and various parties on the right, such as the Republican Democratic Union and the Democratic Alliance,

Stanley Baldwin was the Conservative Party prime minister during the general strike of 1926. His solid, calm appearance suggested to many voters the qualities most needed in their government.

which were usually strongly Catholic and represented big business and high finance.

For five years after the end of the war, France was ruled by National Bloc ministries based mostly on the parties of the right. The dominant personality during this period was Raymond Poincaré, who was determined to make the Germans pay the costs of reconstruction. His policy culminated in the French occupation of the Ruhr in 1923, an expensive operation that yielded little revenue. By early 1924 the franc had fallen from its prewar value of 19.3 cents to little more than 3 cents. In July 1926 Poincaré formed a National Union ministry of all parties except the Socialist and Communist. Poincaré adopted orthodox but stringent measures to reduce expenditures and increase revenues. By the end of 1926, the franc stood at four cents and was stabilized at that level. Since this was only one-fifth of its prewar value, the government had relieved itself of four-fifths of its debts. The devaluation attracted many tourists, especially the Americans, and also facilitated the exportation of French goods. Poincaré's success enabled him to remain premier for three years, an interwar record.

V. STABILIZATION AND SETTLEMENT IN EUROPE

European diplomacy in the years immediately following the war was dominated by France and its allies in central and eastern Europe. Owing to the disappearance of Austria-Hungary and the prostration of Germany and Russia, France was now the first power on the Continent. Because sooner or later both Germany and Russia would obviously seek to reassert themselves, the aim of French diplomacy was to organize some dependable and lasting basis for national security.

Theoretically, the League of Nations provided general security with Article 10 of the Covenant, which required member states "to respect and preserve against external aggression the territorial integrity and existing political independence of all members of the League." The difficulty was that the league lacked the power necessary to enforce this article. It possessed no weapons and no armed force. Having experienced two German invasions in fewer than fifty years, France refused to entrust its security to a league without authority. France turned to the smaller European states that shared its interest in supporting the peace settlement and opposing treaty revision. It negotiated a formal military alliance with Belgium in September 1920, with Poland in 1921, and with Czechoslovakia in 1924.

This alliance system was basically anti-German, its primary purpose being to protect France and its allies by isolating Germany. About 1925, however, Franco-German relations improved, thanks to the temporarily successful operation of the Dawes Plan, and also to the foreign ministers of the two countries, Aristide Briand of France and Gustav Stresemann of Germany. The two foreign ministers decided that the security of their respective countries could be enhanced by direct negotiations and agreements. They were encouraged by British Foreign Minister Sir Austen Chamberlain, who also brought the Italians around to this view. The outcome was a series of agreements known as the Locarno Pacts, signed in October 1925.

These provided that Germany should enter the League of Nations and become a permanent Council member. In return, Germany agreed not

In 1923 Germany suffered from cataclysmic inflation. Paper money became worthless and children used packets of it as building blocks.

to seek treaty revision by force and to settle peacefully every dispute with France, Belgium, Czechoslovakia, and Poland. Germany did reserve the right to seek modifications of its eastern frontiers by peaceful means, but it recognized the permanence of its western frontiers. Germany, France, and Belgium undertook to respect for all time their mutual borders, and Britain and Italy guaranteed observance of this provision.

The Locarno Pacts made a deep impression at the time. Chamberlain expressed the prevailing view when he declared that they marked "the real dividing line between the years of peace and the years of war." Likewise, Briand made eloquent speeches about "the Locarno spirit," which banned war and substituted "conciliation, arbitration, and peace." In the afterglow of this optimism, the American secretary of state, Frank Kellogg, acting on a suggestion of

Briand, proposed that nations pledge themselves to renounce war as "an instrument of national policy." The proposal was implemented, and on August 27, 1928, the Kellogg-Briand Pact was signed. Since the pact only involved renunciation of war and made no provision for sanctions, it was quickly signed by more than sixty countries. Although it depended exclusively on the moral pressure of world public opinion, the mere fact that so many countries signed contributed to a further lessening of international tension.

Equally promising were the improved relations with Germany. That country was admitted into the League of Nations in 1926 and was made a permanent member of the Council. Also, a settlement was reached with Germany concerning the payment of reparations. The 1924 Dawes Plan had begun the negotiations for reparations payments by Germany to the Allies for World War I damages. The negotiations were completed with the 1930 Young Plan requiring Germany to pay $8 billion over 58 years.

There was a general feeling in the late 1920s that Europe had at last returned to normalcy: Germany and its former enemies appeared to be reconciled; the Germans were in the League of Nations; the problem of reparations appeared to be finally resolved; over sixty nations had renounced war "as an instrument of national policy"; prosperity was on the rise, and unemployment was correspondingly declining. Even the news from the Soviet Union was encouraging, for that country had launched in 1928 a novel and grandiose Five-Year Plan (see Chapter 39, Section I). Most authorities in the West regarded the plan as impractical and doomed to failure, but at least it diverted the Russians from international adventures to internal economic development. Thus the "Locarno spirit" appeared to have meaning and substance, and it was assumed that Europe now could settle back to enjoy decades of peace and prosperity as it had in the nineteenth century.

SUGGESTED READINGS

The standard accounts of the civil war and intervention in Russia are the three-volume work by E. H. Carr, *The Bolshevik Revolution, 1917–1923* (Macmillan, 1951–1953); J. Bradley, Allied *Intervention in Russia 1917–1920* (Basic Books, 1968); G. F. Kennan, *Russia and the West Under Lenin and Stalin* (Little, Brown, 1961); and D. Footman, *Civil War in Russia* (Praeger, 1962). The most recent and critical study of the Russian Revolution and of the subsequent Soviet regime is by R. Pipes, *Russia Under the Bolshevik Regime* (Knopf, 1993).

Several books deal with the critical developments in Germany in 1918 and after, including R. G. L. White, *Vanguard of Nazisms: The Free Corps Movement in Post War Germany, 1918–1923* (Harvard University, 1952); R. Coper, *Failure of a Revolution: Germany in 1918–1919* (Cambridge University, 1955); W. T. Angress, *Stillborn Revolution: The Communist Bid for Power in Germany, 1921–1923* (Princeton University, 1964); and the collection of documents by C. B. Burdick and R. H. Lutz, eds., *The Political Institutions of the German Revolution 1918–19* (Praeger, 1966).

The best surveys of the forces molding central and eastern Europe in these years are by H. Seton-Watson, *Eastern Europe Between the Wars, 1918–1941* (Cambridge University, 1946); L. S. Stavrianos, *The Balkans Since 1453* (Holt, Rinehart & Winston, 1959); and W. E. Moore, *Economic Demography of Eastern and Southern Europe* (League of Nations, 1945).

The standard works on Mussolini and fascism are by C. Seton-Watson, *Italy from Liberation to Fascism 1870–1925* (Methuen, 1967); I. Kirkpatrick, *Mussolini: A Study in Power* (Hawthorne, 1964); E. Wiskemann, *Fascism in Italy: Its Development and Influence* (Macmillan, 1969); M. Gallo, *Mussolini's Italy* (Macmillan, 1973); D. M. Smith, *Mussolini's Roman Empire* (Viking, 1976); and E. R. Tannenbaum, *The Fascist Experience: Italian Society and Culture, 1922–1945* (Basic Books, 1972).

Various aspects of Britain's development are analyzed in the general but meticulous survey by C. L. Mowat, *Britain Between the Wars, 1918–1940* (University of Chicago, 1955); and in the lively account by A. J. P. Taylor, *English History 1914–1945* (Oxford University, 1965). On France, see the detailed presentation by D. W. Brogan, *France Under the Republic*, 1870–1939 (Harper & Row, 1940); the more lucid account by D. Thompson, *Democracy in France* (Oxford University, 1952); and the various works by the well-informed journalist A. Werth, especially *France in Ferment* (Jarrolds, 1935).

The Five-Year Plans and the Great Depression

The year 1931 was distinguished from previous years in the "post-war" and in the "pre-war" age alike—by one outstanding feature. In 1931, men and women all over the world were seriously contemplating and frankly discussing the possibility that the Western system of Society might break down and cease to work.

Arnold J. Toynbee

As the 1920s drew to a close, Europe seemed to be settling down to an era of peace, security, and relative prosperity. This comfortable prospect was, however, destroyed completely by the onset of the Great Depression. The resulting economic dislocation and mass unemployment undermined the foundations of the settlement that had been reached in the preceding years. Everywhere governments rose and fell under the pressure of mounting distress and discontent. Such political instability affected directly—and disastrously—the international situation. Some governments resorted to foreign adventures as a means for diverting domestic tension, whereas others ignored the acts of aggression because of their own pressing problems at home. Thus the Depression represents the "Great Divide" of the interwar period. The years before 1929 were years of hope, as

Europe gradually resolved the various issues created by World War I. By contrast, the years after 1929 were filled with anxiety and disillusionment, as crisis followed crisis, culminating finally in World War II.

The impact and significance of the Great Depression were heightened by Russia's Five-Year Plans. At the same time that the West's economy was a veritable shambles, the Soviet Union was proceeding with its unique experiment in economic development. Although they were accompanied by rigid repression and mass privation, the Five-Year Plans did enable the Soviet Union to rise rapidly from a predominantly agrarian state to the second-greatest industrial power in the world. This unprecedented achievement had international repercussions, particularly because of the economic difficulties besetting the West at the time.

And so the Five-Year Plans and the Great Depression stand out in the interwar period, the one accentuating the other, and each having effects that are being felt to the present day.

I. FIVE-YEAR PLANS

War Communism

As soon as the Bolsheviks found themselves the masters of Russia, they faced the challenge of creating the new socialist society about which they had preached for so long. They soon discovered that it was a challenge they were unprepared to meet. There was no model in history to follow. Lenin himself admitted, "We knew when we took power into our hands, that there were no ready forms of concrete reorganization of the capitalist system into a socialist one. . . . I do not know of any socialist who has dealt with these problems. . . . We must go by experiments."[1]

At first there was little opportunity for experimenting because the struggle for survival took precedence over everything else. The so-called "War Communism" that prevailed between 1917 and 1921 evolved out of the desperate measures taken to supply the battlefront with needed materials and manpower. One feature of War Communism was the nationalization of land, banks, foreign trade, and heavy industry. Another was the forcible requisitioning of surplus agricultural produce needed to feed the soldiers and the city dwellers. The original plan was to compensate the peasants with manufactured goods, but this proved impossible because almost all factories were producing for the front.

The ending of the civil war meant that the stopgap system of War Communism was no longer needed, so it was promptly dropped. The peasants were up in arms against confiscation without compensation. At the same time, the economy of the country was paralyzed, owing largely to the uninterrupted fighting between 1914 and 1921. Industry had fallen to 10 percent of prewar levels, and the grain crop declined from 74 million tons in 1916 to 30 million tons in 1919. The crowning disaster was the widespread drought of 1920 and 1921, which contributed to the worst famine in Russia's history. Millions of people died of starvation, and millions more were kept alive only by the shipments of the American Relief Administration.

NEP

The practical-minded Lenin realized that concessions were unavoidable—hence the adoption in 1921 of *New Economic Policy*, or NEP, as it was commonly known, which allowed a partial restoration of capitalism. Peasants were permitted to sell their produce on the open market and private individuals were allowed to operate small stores and factories. Both the peasants and the new businesspeople could employ labor and retain what profits they made from their operations. Lenin, however, saw to it that the state kept control of title to the land and of what he termed "the commanding heights" (banking, foreign trade, heavy industry, and transportation). As far as Lenin was concerned, the NEP did not mean the end of socialism in Russia; rather, it was a temporary retreat, "one step backward in order to take two steps forward."

NEP did cope successfully with the immediate crisis left by the years of war. By 1926, industrial and agricultural production had reached pre-1914 levels. But the population had increased by 8 million since 1914, so the prewar per capita standards had not been reached. The Bolshevik leaders faced the basic problem of how to take the "two steps forward" that they had planned. Shortly before his death in 1925, Lenin appears to have decided that continuation of NEP offered the best road to socialism. Following Lenin's death, Nikolai Bukharin was the outstanding champion of the NEP. A warm and enthusiastic personality, with interests in sports, science, and the arts, as well as politics, Bukharin believed that NEP market relations could "grow into socialism." He favored such a course because it would require little coercion and would respect his favorite principle that "our economy exists for the consumer, not the consumer for the economy."[2]

Although Bukharin was Lenin's favorite and the most popular of the Bolshevik leaders, his views did not prevail. He was no match for Joseph Stalin, "the master builder of bureaucratic structures."[3] Stalin saw clearly that the Communist party was the only real power in the country, and he used his position as general secretary of the party to become the master of the party and of the country. After considerable wavering, Stalin decided to abandon the NEP in favor of a centralized economy in which both agriculture and industry would be managed and directed from Moscow. This meant not only continued government operation of factories, as had been the case under War Communism, but also government control of agriculture through collectivization of peasant plots.

Soviet Planned Economy

In 1928 Stalin launched the first of a series of Five-Year Plans, prepared by the Gosplan or State Planning Commission. The Gosplan members, appointed by the government, drafted each plan on the basis of general directives from Moscow and of statistical data received from all parts of the country. The first of these Five-Year Plans, though primitive when compared with the later computer-prepared ones, comprised a three-volume text of 1,600 pages.

In agriculture the Plans called for collectivization of the land. Many peasants, especially the kulaks, opposed the collective farms for they had to enter on the same terms as the poor peasants who brought little with them. In some cases, the kulaks burned the buildings of the collectives, poisoned the cattle, and spread rumors to frighten away other peasants. The Soviet government retaliated by uprooting hundreds of thousands of kulak families from their villages, putting them in prisons and in Siberian labor camps. Finally, the government had its way, though at a cost of many lives. By 1938 almost all peasant holdings had been amalgamated into 242,400 collective farms, or kolkhozy, and 4,000 state farms, or sovkhozy.

Although the Soviet government was successful in eliminating almost all private farms, the output of its collectivized agriculture proved very disappointing. With 50 percent more land being farmed, and with ten times more people working on it, the Soviet Union produced only three-fourths of the U.S. farm output. One reason for this difference was that the climate of

Lenin's successor, Joseph Stalin.

the Soviet Union is much less favorable for agriculture than that of the United States. Another reason was that the Soviet government was more interested in developing industry and therefore starved agriculture. Soviet farmers used only half as much machinery and fertilizer per acre as did Americans. But the chief difficulty with Soviet agriculture was excessive control from Moscow. Soviet bureaucrats told the farmers what to plant, when to plant, when to cultivate, how much fertilizer to apply, and when to harvest. The farmers preferred to work hard on their own private plots, where they could farm as they thought best and then sell any produce on the open market for as high a price as they could get, rather than for a low, government-set price, as was the case with produce from the collective fields. Thus the private plots, which com-

Russian farmers attend a rally to celebrate the arrival of new tractors at their collective farm.

prised only 3 to 5 percent of the farmlands, yielded 25 to 30 percent of Soviet agricultural output.

Unlike the farms, most of the factories under Stalin's planned economy were not run as cooperatives but were mostly owned and operated by the government. Besides providing industry with the necessary capital, the government also employed a combination of the "carrot" and the "stick" to stimulate maximum production. Both workers and managers were required to meet certain quotas on pain of fine or dismissal. On the other hand, if they surpassed their quotas, they were rewarded with bonuses.

Trade unions were allowed and recognized but were denied the basic right to strike. Soviet industry grew rapidly because the government withdrew about one-third of the national income for reinvestment; in comparison, the United States withdrew about half that proportion. Furthermore, in a planned economy the government is able to allocate investment capital as it wishes. Thus about 70 percent of the total Soviet industrial output was made up of capital goods and 30 percent of consumer goods, whereas in the United States the ratio was roughly the reverse. By the end of the first Five-Year Plan, in 1932, the Soviet Union had risen in industrial output from fifth to second place in the world. This extraordinary spurt was due not only to the increase of productivity in the Soviet Union but also to the decline of productivity in the West that was brought about by the Depression. Nevertheless, Soviet Gross National Product (GNP), which included the lagging agricultural as well as the industrial output, increased three-and-a-half times during the quarter-century between 1928 and 1952—a rate of growth surpassing that of any other country during this period. From the viewpoint of world balance of power, which was Stalin's main concern, the Soviet share of total global industrial output rose from 1.5 percent in 1921 to 10 percent in 1939 to 20 percent in 1966.

We should emphasize that Soviet economic growth was achieved at the expense of the Soviet citizens, who were forced to work hard for the future and to endure privation in the present, regardless of their wishes. Consumer goods were scarce, expensive, and of poor quality. The GNP of the Soviet Union remained at 46 to 48 percent of the GNP of the United States. And in per capita terms, the Soviet GNP was only about two-fifths that of the United States, because the Soviet work force was about one-fourth larger than the American.

Significance for World History

For the Russian people the Five-Year Plans were a mixed blessing. On the positive side they made the country strong economically and militarily so that it was able to contribute substantially to the defeat of Hitler in World War II. The Five-Year Plans also transformed Russia from a primitive to a modern society. They increased literacy from 28.4 percent in 1897 to 56.6 percent in 1926, 87.4 percent in 1939, and 98.5 percent in 1959. In medical care, between 1913 and 1961, the number of physicians increased from 23,200 to 425,700; life expectancy rose from thirty-two to sixty-nine years; and infant mortality declined from 273 to 32 per thousand. Likewise in social services, the Five-Year Plans provided Soviet citizens with free medical care, old-age pensions, sickness and disability benefits, maternity leaves, paid vacations, and children's aid.

But the Russian people also endured negative experiences as a result of the Five-Year Plans. Most damaging was the ending of the alliance between the Bolsheviks and the peasants, which had made possible the 1917 revolution. The savage repression during the collectivization of the land was not soon forgotten. The peasants thereafter dragged their feet, regarding the kolkhozy as something alien that had been imposed on them—hence the contrast between their high productivity in their own small plots and their low productivity in the collective fields. The low productivity in agriculture in turn hurt the performance of Soviet industry. Since agriculture did not produce as much as was needed to finance the cost of industrialization, the factory workers also were squeezed to pay for the high cost of the successive Five-Year Plans. When the Soviet government withdrew one-third of the national income each year for reinvestment, it meant low wages and scarce consumer goods. The reaction of one Soviet worker was typical: "They pretend they are paying us, so we pretend we are working."

The Five-Year Plans had a mixed impact not only on the Soviet Union but also on the world. The impact was different on the Western world from what it was on the underdeveloped countries. Westerners at first were skeptical about Soviet plans for a new society, many assuming that they were bound to fail. As the successive Five-Year Plans unfolded, skepticism gave way to genuine interest. But those Westerners who were sufficiently interested to visit the Soviet Union were usually unimpressed, if not disillusioned. They were struck by the shabby clothing, the monotonous diet, the wretched housing, and the scarcity of consumer goods. They were also appalled by the lack of individual freedom as reflected in the one-party political structure, the hobbling of trade unions, the regimentation of education, and the rigid control of all communication media. Soviet society, despite the achievements of the Five-Year Plans, did not seem to most Westerners a socialist paradise worth copying. On the other hand, most Westerners conceded that without the industrial growth under the Five-Year Plans, the Soviet Union would not have been able to contribute so much to Hitler's defeat in World War II.

Former colonial peoples in the underdeveloped world reacted differently. To them, the Soviet Union was the country that succeeded in transforming itself within a generation from a backward agrarian state into the second-greatest industrial and military power in the world. The institutions and the techniques that made this dramatic change possible were of vital concern to these peoples. Also noteworthy is the fact that the Soviet Union was a great Asian as well as European state. Its frontiers stretched from Korea, past Mongolia, Sinkiang, Afghanistan, and Iran, to Turkey. The other side of the long frontier has had few counterparts to the substantial advances made in the Soviet central Asian republics, including irrigation works, textile mills, machinery plants, health services, and educational programs that raised literacy rates from about 2 percent in 1914 to 75 percent in 1940 to over 90 percent in 1960.

This mixed impact of the Soviet experiment changed after World War II to an almost totally negative impact. We shall see (Chapter 44, Section III) that in recent decades the Soviet planned economy fell steadily behind the Western market economy, while personal rights and freedoms remained conspicuous by their absence. Hence

the disintegration and disappearance of the Soviet superpower, replaced in the 1990s by the Commonwealth of Independent States.

II. THE GREAT DEPRESSION

Origins of the Crash

In the beginning of 1929, the United States appeared to be flourishing. The index of industrial production in that country averaged only 67 in 1921 (1923–1925 = 100) but rose to 110 by July 1928 and to 126 by June 1929. Even more impressive was the performance of the American stock market. During the three summer months of 1929, Westinghouse stock rose from 151 to 286; General Electric, from 268 to 391; and U. S. Steel, from 165 to 258. Businesspeople, academic economists, and government leaders were all expressing confidence in the future. The secretary of the treasury, Andrew W. Mellon, assured the public in September 1929, "There is no cause for worry. The high tide of prosperity will continue."[4]

This confidence proved unjustified; in the fall of 1929, the bottom fell out of the stock

Crowds gathered on Wall Street in New York on October 29, 1929, the day the stock market crashed. The Great Depression in the United States dried up American capital previously available for investment in Europe.

POVERTY AMID PLENTY IN THE UNITED STATES

The Great Depression was unprecedented in its intensity, scope, and longevity. Its effect on the United States is described in the following testimony before a congressional committee in February 1932.*

During the last three months I [Oscar Ameringer of Oklahoma City] have visited, as I have said, some 20 states of this wonderfully rich and beautiful country. Here are some of the things I heard and saw: In the State of Washington I was told that the forest fires raging in that region all summer and fall were caused by unemployed timber workers and bankrupt farmers in an endeavor to earn a few honest dollars as fire fighters. The last thing I saw on the night I left Seattle was numbers of women searching for scraps of food in the refuse piles of the principal market of that city. A number of Montana citizens told me of thousands of bushels of wheat left in the fields uncut on account of its low price that hardly paid for the harvesting. In Oregon I saw thousands of bushels of apples rotting in the orchards. Only absolutely flawless apples were still salable, at from 40 to 50 cents a box containing 200 apples. At the same time, there are millions of children who, on account of the poverty of their parents, will not eat one apple this winter.

While I was in Oregon the Portland Oregonian bemoaned the fact that thousands of ewes were killed by the sheep raisers because they did not bring enough in the market to pay the freight on them. And while Oregon sheep raisers fed mutton to the buzzards, I saw men picking for meat scraps in the garbage cans in the cities of New York and Chicago. I talked to one man in a restaurant in Chicago. He told me of his experience in raising sheep. He said that he had killed 3,000 sheep this fall and thrown them down the canyon, because it cost $1.10 to ship a sheep, and then he would get less than a dollar for it. He said he could not afford to feed the sheep, and he would not let them starve, so he just cut their throats and threw them down the canyon.

The roads of the West and Southwest teem with hungry hitchhikers. The camp fires of the homeless are seen along every railroad track. I saw men, women, and children walking over the hard roads. Most of them were tenant farmers who had lost their all in the late slump in wheat and cotton. Between Clarksville and Russellville, Ark., I picked up a family. The woman was hugging a dead chicken under a ragged coat. When I asked her where she had procured the fowl, first she told me she had found it dead in the road, and then added in grim humor, "They promised me a chicken in the pot, and now I got mine. . . ."

The farmers are being pauperized by the poverty of industrial populations and the industrial populations are being pauperized by the poverty of the farmers. Neither has the money to buy the product of the other; hence we have overproduction and underconsumption at the same time and in the same country.

**Unemployment in the United States. . . Hearings before a subcommittee of the Committee on Labor, House of Representatives, 72nd Congress, 1st Session (Government Printing Office, 1932), pp. 98–99.*

market, and a worldwide depression, unprecedented in its intensity and longevity, followed. The serious international economic imbalance that developed when the United States became a creditor nation on a large scale (following World War I) seems to have been one reason for this unexpected denouement. Britain had been a creditor nation before the war, but it had used the proceeds from its overseas investments and loans to pay for its chronic excess of imports over exports. The United States, by contrast, normally had a favorable trade balance, accentuated by tariffs that were kept at high levels for reasons of domestic politics. In addition, money poured into the country in the 1920s in payment of war debts, and the American gold hoard rose between 1913 and 1924 from $1.924 to $4.499 billion, or half the world's total gold supply.

This imbalance was neutralized for several years by large-scale American loans and investments abroad: Between 1925 and 1928, the average annual total for American foreign investments amounted to $1.1 billion. In the long run, this, of course, intensified the imbalance and could not be continued indefinitely. As payments came due, debtor countries were forced to curtail imports from the United States, and certain branches of the American economy, especially agriculture, were hurt. In addition, some countries found it necessary to default on their debts, which shook certain financial firms in the United States.

As serious as the imbalance of the international economy, was that of the American economy; the basic reason being that wages lagged behind the rising productivity. Between 1920 and 1929, hourly industrial wages rose only 2 percent, whereas the productivity of workers in factories jumped 55 percent. At the same time, the real income of the farmers was shrinking because agricultural prices were falling while taxes and living costs were rising. Whereas in 1910 the income per farm worker had been slightly less than 40 percent that of the nonfarm worker, by 1930, it was just under 30 percent. Such poverty in the countryside was a serious matter, because the rural population at the time was one-fifth of the total population.

The weakness of the American banking system was a final factor contributing to the crash

of 1929. A great number of independent banking firms were operating, and some of these lacked sufficient resources to weather financial storms. When one closed its doors, panic spread, and depositors rushed to withdraw their savings from other banks, thus setting in motion a chain reaction that undermined the entire banking structure.

Worldwide Depression

The stock market crash in the United States began in September 1929. Within one month, stock values dropped 40 percent, and apart from a few brief recoveries, the decline continued for three years. During that period, U. S. Steel stock fell from 262 to 22; General Motors, from 73 to 8. By 1933, both general industrial production and national income had slumped by nearly one-half; wholesale prices, by almost one-third; and merchandise trade, by more than two-thirds.

The Great Depression was unique not only in its intensity but also in its worldwide impact. American financial houses were forced to call in their short-term loans abroad; naturally, there were repercussions. In September 1931, Britain went off the gold standard, to be followed two years later by the United States and nearly all the major countries. The breakdown of the financial world had its counterpart in industry and commerce: The index of world industrial production, excluding the Soviet Union, fell from 100 in 1929 to 86.5 in 1930, 74.8 in 1931, and 63.8 in 1932, a drop of 36.2 percent. The maximum decline in previous crises had been 7 percent. Even more drastic was the shrinking of world international trade, from $68.6 billion in 1929 to $55.6 in 1930, $39.7 in 1931, $26.9 in 1932, and $24.2 in 1933. Again it might be noted that the maximum drop in international trade in the past had been 7 percent, during the 1907–1908 crisis.

Social and Political Repercussions

These economic catastrophes gave rise to social problems of corresponding magnitude. Most serious was the mass unemployment, which reached tragic proportions. In March 1933, the number of people out of work in the United States was estimated conservatively at over 14 million, or a fourth of the total labor force. In Britain, the jobless were numbered at nearly 3 million, representing about the same proportion of the workers as in the United States. Germany was the worst off, with more than two-fifths of trade-unionists unemployed and another fifth on part-time work.

Unemployment on this scale drastically lowered living standards in all countries. Even in the wealthy United States there was wholesale misery and privation, especially in the beginning, when relief was left to private and local agencies with inadequate funds. In Germany, with its higher percentage of jobless people, the frustrations and tensions were more acute. Eventually they made it possible for Hitler to triumph, for social dislocation on such a large scale inevitably had profound political repercussions.

The son of a minor Austrian customs official, Adolf Hitler went to Vienna early in life, aspiring to be a painter. According to his own account—which seems to be greatly exaggerated—he spent five miserable years working at the most menial jobs to keep body and soul together. From Vienna, Hitler drifted to Munich, where in 1914 he enlisted in a Bavarian regiment. At the end of the war, Hitler joined a struggling group called the National Socialist German Workers' party, of which he soon became the leader, or Führer. After making rabble-rousing speeches on nationalist and anti-Semitic themes, in 1923 he joined Field Marshal Ludendorff in an uprising in Munich. It was easily put down by the police, and Hitler was imprisoned for nine months. There, at the age of thirty-five, he wrote *Mein Kampf*—"My Battle"—a long and turgid autobiographical reflection into which he poured his hatred of democracy, Marxism, and Jews.

Upon release from prison, Hitler resumed his agitation but with disappointing results. In the December 1924 elections, his Nazi party won only fourteen seats and a mere 908,000 votes, and in May 1928 won even fewer—twelve seats and 810,000 votes, or 2.6 percent of the total number. The turning point came with the September 1930 elections, when the Nazis won 107 seats and 6,407,000 votes, or 18.3 percent of the total. Hitler attracted this support by promising relief from unemployment, and from the

During a Nazi Party rally in Nuremberg in 1927, Adolf Hitler stops his motorcade to receive the applause of the surrounding crowd. In the late 1920s the Nazi movement was only one of many bringing strife to the Weimar Republic.

Soon after seizing power, the Nazi government began harassing German Jewish businesses. Non-Jewish German citizens were urged not to buy merchandise fromn shops owned by Jews.

chains of the Versailles Treaty and also by branding the Jews as being both exploiting financiers and materialistic Communists. Hitler had been campaigning on this platform for years, with little response. But now the Depression provided him with an eager audience that greeted him as the Fuhrer who supplied scapegoats for misery and a program for individual and national fulfillment. Hence the steady rise in Hitler's fortunes. In the July 1932 elections he won 13,799,000 votes and 230 seats. In January 1933 he became Chancellor, and proceeded like Mussolini, to dominate Germany with propaganda and terrorism.

The Depression had made Hitler's triumph possible, though by no means inevitable. The possibility was translated into actuality by a combination of other factors, including Hitler's own demagogic talents, the support afforded by assorted vested interests, and the myopia of his opponents, who underestimated him and failed to unite in opposition. On August 2, 1934 President Hindenburg conveniently died, enabling Hitler to combine the offices of president and chancellor in his own person. The following month the Nazi Party Congress assembled in Nuremberg, and Hitler proclaimed, "The German form of life is definitely determined for the next thousand years."

International Repercussions

The British foreign minister, Sir Austen Chamberlain, comparing the international situation in 1932 with that of the Lacarno era, observed, for some reason or other, owing to something upon which it is difficult to put one's finger, in these last two years the world is moving backward. Instead of approaching nearer to one another, instead of increasing the measure of goodwill, instead of progressing to a stable peace, it has fallen into an attitude of suspicion, of fear, of danger, which imperils the peace of the world.[5]

That "something" that Chamberlain could not identify was the Depression and its manifold repercussions, international as well as national. Various international agreements of the Locarno era became unworkable, particularly those concerning reparations and war debts. It soon became obvious that governments, pushed to the brink of bankruptcy by their slumping economies and mounting unemployment, would not be able to meet commitments undertaken a few years earlier.

Another effect of the Depression was to accentuate the ever-present economic nationalism to the point where it disturbed international relations. Self-protective measures by individual nations took such forms as higher tariffs, more rigid import quotas, clearing agreements, currency-control regulations, and bilateral-trade pacts. These measures inevitably brought economic friction and political tensions among states. Various attempts were made to reverse the trend, but without success. The World Economic Conference that met in London in 1933 was a dismal fiasco. "Autarchy," or economic self-sufficiency, gradually became a commonly accepted national goal.

Closely related was the petering out of disarmament efforts, which gave way to massive rearmament programs. The Disarmament Conference that met intermittently for twenty months, beginning in February 1932, was as futile as the Economic Conference. As the 1930s progressed, countries devoted more and more of their energies to rearming. The trend was impossible to stop because armament manufacturing provided jobs as well as imagined security. Unemployment in the United States, for example, was not substantially reduced until the country began to rearm on the eve of World War II. Likewise, Hitler quickly disposed of the unprecedented unemployment he faced by launching a gigantic rearmament program.

The armaments now being accumulated were bound sooner or later to be used, and their use required some justification. The most obvious was that of lebensraum, or living space. This was the term coined by Hitler, but similar expressions and arguments were employed by Mussolini in Italy and by the military leaders in Japan. The unemployment and general misery, according to this doctrine, arose from the lack of lebensraum. The few fortunate countries had seized all the colonies and underpopulated lands overseas, leaving the other nations without the natural resources needed to support their people. The obvious way out was to expand, by force if necessary, to remedy the injustices inflicted by the past. Such were the arguments used by the so-called "have-not" countries against the "haves."

The reasoning was obviously false in view of the fact that the Depression had devastated equally and impartially the United States, Canada, and Britain, along with Germany, Italy, and Japan. Nevertheless, the lebensraum ideology served to unite the people of the "have-not" countries in support of the expansionist policies of their respective governments. It also gave a superficial moral justification to aggression committed for the avowed purpose of providing food for the needy and work for the jobless.

Such, then, was the combination of forces behind the "suspicion," the "fear," and the "moving backward" that Chamberlain had observed in 1932. During the following years, these forces undermined completely the settlement that had been reached in the 1920s and precipitated one crisis after another, culminating finally in World War II.

SUGGESTED READINGS

A good brief summary of the Five-Year Plans from their beginning to their end is available in R. Munting, *The Economic Development of the USSR* (St. Martin's Press, 1982). Reappraising of the NEP and the plans is reflected in S. Cohen, *Rethinking the Soviet System* (Oxford University, 1985); M. Lewin, *The Making of the Soviet System* (Pantheon, 1985); C. Bettelheim, *Class Struggles in the USSR*, 2 vols. (Monthly Review Press, 1976, 1978); and S. Brucan, *The Post-Brezhnev Era: An Insider's View* (Praeger, 1983). The global impact of the plans is analyzed by E. H. Carr, *The Sovi-*

et *Impact on the Western World* (Macmillan, 1954); by
C. K. Wilber, *The Soviet Model and Underdeveloped
Countries* (University of North Carolina, 1970); and
more critically, by R. Pipes, *Communism: The Vanished
Spectre* (Oxford University, 1994).

Analyses of the Depression are available in J. K.
Galbraith, *The Great Crash, 1929* (Houghton Mifflin,
1955); G. Rees, *The Great Slump: Capitalism in Crisis*
(Harper & Row, 1971); C. P. Kindleberger, *The World in
Depression 1929–1939* (University of California, 1975);
and J. A. Garrity, *The Great Depression* (Harcourt Brace
Jovanovich, 1986). On Hitler's rise to power there is
the spirited account by W. L. Shirer, *The Rise and Fall
of the Third Reich* (Simon & Schuster, 1960); and the
competent biographies by A. Bullock, *Hitler: A Study in
Tyranny* (Harper & Row, 1952); and J. Toland, *Adolf
Hitler* (Doubleday, 1976). Conflicting views on the circumstances of Hitler's rise to power are presented by
R. F. Hamilton, *Who Voted for Hitler?* (Princeton Uni-

versity, 1982); H. A. Turner, Jr., *German Big Business
and the Rise of Hitler* (Oxford University, 1985); and D.
Abraham, *The Collapse of the Weimar Republic: Political
Economy and Crisis* (Princeton University, 1981).

NOTES

1. Cited by S. and B. Webb, *Soviet Communism: A New Civilization*, Vol. 2 (Gollanez, 1937), p. 605.
2. Cited by S. F. Cohen, *Rethinking the Soviet Experience* (Oxford University, 1985), p. 77
3. M. Lewin, *Russian Peasants and Soviet Power* (W. W. Norton, 1968), p. 517.
4. H. E. Salisbury, *New York Times*, September 29, 1953.
5. Cited by J. K. Galbraith, *The Great Crash, 1929* (Houghton Mifflin, 1955), pp. 20, 75.

40

Drift to War, 1929–1939

This is not Peace. It is an Armistice for twenty years.
Marshal Foch, 1919

The late 1920s were years of prosperity, stabilization, and settlement; the 1930s were years of depression, crises, and war. New leaders appeared in the thirties in Germany and Japan who were determined to revise the territorial settlement of World War I and who possessed the means and the will to do so. Their massive rearming programs and their breathtaking aggressions drastically altered the balance of power. No longer was the relatively weak Italy the only revisionist state attempting ineffectually to challenge the status quo. The Third Reich and Imperial Japan also gave strength to the revisionist drive, resulting in an entirely new balance of power. A triangle situation developed, with Britain, France, and their Continental allies supporting the status quo; Germany, Italy, and Japan driving for revision; and the Soviet Union, strengthened by the Five-Year Plans, playing an

increasingly important role. The interplay of these three forces explains the recurring crises of the 1930s and the final outbreak of World War II.

I. JAPAN INVADES MANCHURIA

The first major act of aggression was made by Japan, in pursuit of long-cherished territorial ambitions on the mainland. Japanese economic and military leaders had been preaching "lebensraum" for years. They argued that Japan should conquer an empire in order to become prosperous and economically independent of the rest of the world. The ravages of the Depression made "lebensraum" persuasive in Japan, as had happened with Hitler in Germany. The Japanese expansionists were not only motivated by economic considerations. They were also concerned about the growing strength of the Soviet Union and the increasing success of Chiang Kai-shek in unifying China. In addition, they were fully aware of the unemployment situation and other problems that were then engrossing the attention of Western statesmen. These calculations figured in the Japanese decision to attack the Chinese province of Manchuria in 1931.

It was not accidental that Manchuria was the first objective of Japanese expansionism. This province in the northeast corner of China had the double advantage of being loosely connected with the central Nanking government and possessing abundant natural resources, including iron, coal, and extensive fertile plains. Furthermore, Japan had obtained through past treaty arrangements certain special privileges in Manchuria. These could be used to find pretexts for justifying aggressive measures.

On the evening of September 18, 1931, an explosion wrecked a small section of track on the Japanese-controlled South Manchuria railway to the north of Mukden. Baron Shidehara, who was foreign minister in 1931, testified before the International War Crimes Tribunal in June 1946 that the incident had been staged by army officers whom he had tried vainly to stop. His testimony is supported by the speed and precision with which the Japanese army swung immediately into action. Without declaring war, it captured Mukden and Changchun in the space of twenty-four hours and then fanned out in all directions. The taking of Harbin in late January 1932 signified the end of all organized resistance in Manchuria. In March 1932, the victors renamed their conquest Manchukuo, the "State of Manchu."

Meanwhile, the Chinese government had appealed to the League of Nations which appointed a commission that submitted its report in October 1932. It proposed a settlement making Manchuria an autonomous state under Chinese sovereignty, but with Japan in control.

Germany rearms in staggering numbers, as it renounces the Versailles Treaty and gears up for war. SS troops at a Nazi Party rally in 1938.

Germany in 1930
German aggression
Italian Empire in 1930
Italian aggression
Japanese Empire in 1930
Japanese aggression

German, Italian, and Japanese Aggression, 1930–1939

Hitler and Mussolini both justified their conquests by claiming the need for lebensraum, or living space. They blamed their national problems on the lack of empires with resources and markets. This argument was made in the following statements by the two leaders.*

Hitler, 1930: If the German people does not solve the problem of its lack of space, and if it does not open up the domestic market for its industry, then 2,000 years have been in vain. Germany will then make its exit from the world stage and peoples with more vigor will come into our heritage. . . .

Space must be fought for and maintained. People who are lazy have no right to the soil. Soil is for him who tills it and protects it. If a people disclaims soil, it disclaims life. If a nation loses in the defense of its soil, then the individual loses. There is no higher justice that decrees that a people must starve. There is only power, which creates justice. . . .

Parliaments do not create all of the rights on this earth; force also creates rights. The question is whether we wish to live or die. We have more right to soil than all the other nations because we are so thickly populated. I am of the opinion that in this

respect too the principle can be applied: God helps him who helps himself.

Mussolini, 1933: . . . Fascism, the more it considers and observes the future and the development of humanity quite apart from political considerations of the moment, believes neither in the possibility nor the utility of perpetual peace. It thus repudiates the doctrine of Pacifism—born of a renunciation of the struggle and an act of cowardice in the face of sacrifice. War alone brings up to its highest tension all human energy and puts the stamp of nobility upon the peoples who have the courage to meet it. . . .

For Fascism, the growth of empire, that is to say the expansion of the nation, is an essential manifestation of vitality, and its opposite a sign of decadence. Peoples which are rising, or rising again after a period of decadence, are always imperialist.

*Voelkischer Beobachter, May 7, 1930; and Benito Mussolini, "The Political and Social Doctrines of Fascism," *Political Quarterly* (July–September 1933), p. 356.

The League adopted the report in February 1933, and the next month Japan left that body, with Manchuria a puppet client state.

In retrospect, the Manchurian affair stands out as the first serious blow leveled at the League of Nations and at the entire diplomatic structure designed to maintain the status quo. The ease with which Japan had acquired its rich new possession was not lost on the revisionist leaders of Italy and Germany; Manchuria set off a chain reaction of aggressions that ultimately led to

World War II. (See map of German, Italian, and Japanese Aggression, 1930–1939, p. 586).

II. ITALY CONQUERS ETHIOPIA

The Japanese conquest of Manchuria was a rude challenge to the status quo in the Far East, but even more upsetting was the demolition of the status quo in Europe by Hitler and Mussolini. For several years, France had buttressed the

European status quo by forging an alliance network with neighboring countries such as Czechoslovakia, Poland, and Yugoslavia. This comfortable situation changed radically when Hitler became chancellor in Germany, demanded revision of the Versailles Treaty provisions, and together with Mussolini, proceeded to dismantle the entire Versailles edifice.

On March 16, 1935, Hitler renounced the Versailles clauses requiring the disarmament of Germany and simultaneously launched a massive rearmament program. The Western powers responded by calling for common action against the German menace. But no action followed the rhetoric, so Germany once again became a major military power. This altered fundamentally the European balance of power because German armies and fortifications now separated France from her allies in Central and Eastern Europe.

Just as Japan's successful aggression in Manchuria encouraged aggression in Europe, so Hitler's unchallenged rearmament encouraged Italian aggression in Ethiopia. On October 3, 1935, Mussolini's legions invaded the independent African kingdom of Ethiopia. Behind this aggression were several motives, including Mussolini's yen for restoring Roman imperial glory, and his hope that colonial expansion would relieve economic distress at home. The League of Nations responded by declaring Italy the aggressor and voting for economic sanctions.

Again there was fatal disparity between rhetoric and action. This time the disparity was caused by controversy over the economic sanctions. League supporters wanted to make them effective by including key materials, especially oil. But some British and French ministers were opposed, fearing that if oil were included, Mussolini would leave the League, as Japan had done, and join forces with Hitler. The appeasers had their way, thus dooming the hapless Ethiopians, who were crumbling before the Italian legions.

The Ethiopian tribal leaders, in their suicidal pride and ignorance, scorned guerrilla warfare as unworthy and demeaning. Instead, attempting to wage a war of position, they were mercilessly bombarded, strafed, and even sprayed with mustard gas. After a campaign of

seven months, the Italians triumphantly entered Addis Ababa on May 5, 1936. The same day, Mussolini proclaimed "a Roman peace, which is expressed in this simple, irrevocable, definite phrase—'Ethiopia is Italian.'" And so, at a cost of 3,000 men and $1 billion, Mussolini had won an empire of 350,000 square miles, 10 million inhabitants, and rich natural resources.

During the next three years, Mussolini and Hitler scored triumph after triumph, beginning with their successful intervention in the Spanish Civil War.

Mussolini was determined to make Italy a self-sufficient food producer. In July 1938, he stood on a threshing platform at a farm rally, stripped to the waist in the hot sun, to declare that Italy would never turn to other nations for grain.

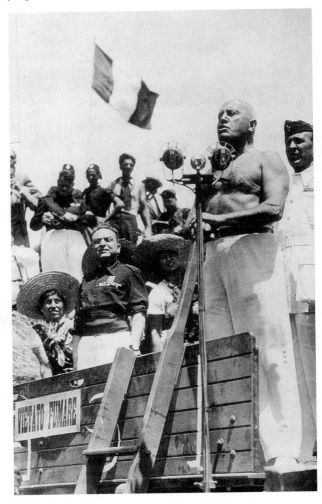

III. SPANISH CIVIL WAR

The Spanish Civil War was of more than ordinary significance because it was essentially two wars in one—a deep-rooted social conflict generated by the decay and tensions of Spanish society, and a dress rehearsal for World War II arising from the clash of ideologies and of great power interests.

Spain in the twentieth century was very different from what it had been in the sixteenth, when that country was the most powerful and feared nation in Europe. Symbolic of the decline during the intervening centuries was the Spanish-American War of 1898. With humiliating ease, the United States stripped Spain of most of its remaining colonial possessions. The war exposed not only the military weakness of Spain but also the corruption and inefficiency of the entrenched oligarchy that ruled the country. Three principal elements made this oligarchy: the large landowners, the army, and the church.

The landowners, comprising about 35,000 families, possessed about 50 percent of the total arable land. They contributed nothing to the national economy, being absentee owners who squandered their incomes in Madrid or foreign capitals. The army was noteworthy for only two reasons: the extraordinarily large number of officers in proportion to the number of rank and file, and its constant intervention in the politics of the country. Finally, the Roman Catholic church in Spain was a wealthy and powerful institution. It controlled the educational system and exerted much influence through certain newspapers, labor groups, and various lay organizations. The Church's power engendered much anticlericalism, and the attacks on priests, nuns, and Church property during the Civil War were by no means unique in Spanish history.

Such was the Spain that Alfonso XIII was called on to rule when he ascended the throne in 1902. His reign was marked by cabinet instability and numerous strikes, mutinies, and assassinations. The Depression made the situation still more unstable, until at last Alfonso decided to restore the constitution and to hold municipal elections in April 1931. The vote went heavily against the regime, the Republicans carrying forty-six of the fifty provincial capitals. The state of public opinion was evident, and Alfonso prudently left the country, as four of his predecessors had done since 1789.

A republic was proclaimed on April 14, 1931, and elections were held for a Constituent Assembly, or Cortes. When this body assembled in July, its members fell into three broad groupings: a conservative right, a republican center, and a left comprised of Socialists, Stalinist and Trotskyite Communists, and Anarcho-Syndical-

General Francisco Franco led an uprising against the duly elected government of Spain in 1936, producing a bloody civil war. Here he marches through the city of Burgos, in northern Spain.

ists. The center and the left, which together constituted a large majority, combined to adopt a liberal constitution that provided universal suffrage for both sexes, complete religious freedom, the separation of church and state, secularized education, and nationalized church property.

This drift to the left alarmed the powerful vested interests of Spain. At this juncture, the Spanish rightists, with the connivance of Germany and Italy, and under the leadership of General Francisco Franco, began a counterrevolution. On July 17, 1936, the army in Morocco revolted, and the next day a number of mainland generals took up arms. The rebels, or self-styled Nationalists, quickly overran the southern and the western regions. The Loyalists lost about one-half the country in the first weeks of the revolt, but they then rallied and managed to retain control of Madrid in the center, the Basque provinces in the north, and the highly developed east coast with the large cities of Barcelona and Valencia. The Loyalists were now in a strong position. They had behind them the industrial centers, the most densely populated regions, and the capital, with its exceptionally large gold reserve. Despite these advantages, the Loyalists were eventually beaten, mainly because they were unable to obtain arms from abroad in quantities approaching those received by the Nationalists from Germany and Italy.

For two years there was a stalemate, with the Nationalists controlling the agrarian western and southern regions, and the Loyalists, the more developed northern and eastern sections. But in mid-1938, the Soviet government which had been the main source of arms for the Loyalists, decided to stop further arms shipments. The Soviet withdrawal enabled Franco's armies to break the stalemate. By late December 1938, they had taken Barcelona, and by March, they were in Madrid, and the Civil War had ended.

For Spain, the long ordeal involved 750,000 casualties out of a population of 25 million, and one of every seven of the uninjured was left without shelter. For the Western powers, the Civil War represented another stunning defeat. As in the case of Ethiopia, they had again shown themselves to be weak and vacillating in the face of Axis aggression. The same pattern was to appear again during the German annexation of Austria and Czechoslovakia.

IV. END OF AUSTRIA AND CZECHOSLOVAKIA

Nineteen thirty-eight was the year of the great bloodless victories of the Axis powers. On February 12, 1938, Hitler invited Austria's Chancellor Kurt von Schuschnigg to his Bavarian mountain

On September 29?30, 1938, Hitler met with the leaders of Britain and France at Munich to decide the fate of Czechoslovakia. The Allied leaders abandoned the small democratic nation in a vain attempt to appease Hitler and avoid war. Hitler sits in the center of the picture. To his right is British Prime Minister Neville Chamberlain.

retreat at Berchtesgaden. There the Führer demanded various concessions that would have seriously violated Austrian independence. Schuschnigg resisted by scheduling a plebiscite on March 13 on the following question: "Are you for a free and independent, German and Christian Austria?"

In the ensuing crisis, no great power went to the aid of Austria. Chamberlain informed the House of Commons on February 22 that "... we must not try to delude small weak nations into thinking that they will be protected by the League against aggression and acting accordingly when we know that nothing of the kind can be expected."[1] On March 13, decrees from Berlin and Vienna declared Austria a part of Germany, and the next day Hitler made his triumphant entry into the land of his birth. Thus Austria was taken over by telephone. The event was not mentioned in the League of Nations.

With Austria safely annexed, Hitler turned against the neighboring state of Czechoslovakia, a larger and much stronger country with an efficient modern army and a considerable industrial establishment. But the presence of a German minority of 3 million in the Sudeten borderlands made Czechoslovakia vulnerable to Nazi propaganda and subversion.

With the disappearance of Austria, the Sudeten problem became a serious menace for Czechoslovakia. The country was now surrounded on three sides by the enlarged Reich. Even more serious were certain indications that the British and French governments were ready to abandon Czechoslovakia as they had Austria. The abandonment occurred in September 1938 at Munich, where Britain and France agreed that Germany should acquire large border regions of Czechoslovakia.

V. COMING OF WAR

With Austria and Czechoslovakia taken, and with Hitler making stiff new demands on Poland, the Western powers were faced by the prospect of limitless German expansion. So Britain and France on March 31, 1939, pledged aid to the Poles in case of "any action which clearly threatened Polish independence." Axis aggression now shifted to Albania, which Italy invaded and conquered in April. Britain and France countered by pledging full support to neighboring Greece and Rumania if Italy pushed further into the Balkans.

These commitments to various East European countries were worthless unless the Western Powers acted in concert with the Soviet Union. As Churchill declared in the House of Commons on May 19, "Without an effective eastern front, there can be no satisfactory defence of our interests in the West, and without Russia there can be no effective eastern front."[2] Both sides obviously had a common interest in forming a "Peace Front." But they were unable to do so, because of deep mutual distrust. Britain and France feared that the Soviet Union would exploit a Western pact to expand into Eastern Europe, while the Soviets feared that Britain and France would not honor a commitment to aid Russia in case of German aggression, leaving Russia alone to face Hitler.

This distrust escalated disastrously when British officials broached to a German representative in London the possibility of a British-German nonaggression pact that would enable Britain to rid itself of its commitments to Poland. The suspicious Russians foresaw a repetition of this strategy, but directed against them. Hence Stalin's fateful decision to turn to his hitherto mortal Axis enemies. On August 23 Russia and Germany signed a nonaggression pact and agreed to remain neutral if either were attacked by a third power. Significantly enough, the pact did not contain the so-called "escape clause," characteristic of Soviet nonaggression pacts with other countries, that would render the agreement inoperative if either party committed aggression against a third state. Perhaps this omission was related to a secret protocol in the pact stipulating that in the event of a "territorial or political rearrangement," Lithuania and western Poland were to come under the German sphere of influence, and the remainder of Poland, together with Finland, Estonia, Latvia, and Bessarabia, were to fall to the Russian sphere.

Now that he was protected on his eastern flank, Hitler felt free to strike. Early in the morning of September 1, 1939, without a declaration of war, German troops, tanks, and planes crossed Poland's frontier all along the line. On September 3, both Britain and France declared war on Germany. Mussolini, despite his oratory about the Axis "pact of steel," remained neutral. World War II had begun.

SUGGESTED READINGS

Conflicting interpretations of the diplomacy of the 1930s are presented by G. L. Weinberg, *Diplomatic Revolution in Europe 1933–1936*, and *The Foreign Policy of Hitler's Germany: Starting World War II, 1937–1939* (University of Chicago, 1970, 1980), who holds Hitler responsible for the war because of his demand for a free hand in central and eastern Europe; and A. J. P. Taylor, *The Origins of the Second World War* (Hamilton, 1961), who holds that war resulted primarily from Anglo-French blundering. A convenient brief survey of the steps to war is available in J. Remak, *The Origins of the Second World War* (Prentice Hall, 1975).

For the background to Japanese expansionism, see A. Iriye, *After Imperialism: The Search for a New Order in the Far East, 1921–1931* (Harvard University, 1965); D. M. Brown, *Nationalism in Japan* (University of California, 1955); Y. C. Maxon, *Control of Japanese Foreign Policy: A Study of Civil-Military Rivalry, 1930–1945* (University of California, 1957); and J. B. Crowley, *Japan's Quest for Autonomy* (Princeton University, 1966). Details concerning the actual expansion are available in D. Bergamini, *Japan's Imperial Conspiracy* (Morrow, 1971); J. M. Maki, *Conflict and Tension in the Far East: Key Documents, 1894–1960* (University of Washington, 1961); D. Borg, *The United States and the Far Eastern Crisis of 1933–38* (Harvard University, 1964); and F. C. Jones, *Japan's New Order in East Asia: Its Rise and Fall, 1937–1945* (Oxford University, 1954).

The Italian invasion of Ethiopia is considered in G. W. Baer, *The Coming of the Italo-Ethiopian War* (Harvard University, 1961); A. Mockler, *Haile Selassie's War: The Italo-Ethiopian Campaign* (Random House, 1985); G. W. Baer, *Test Case: Italy, Ethiopia and the League of Nations* (Hoover Institution, 1976); and A.

Sbacchi, *Ethiopia Under Mussolini: Fascism and the Colonial Experience* (Zed Press, 1985).

For the background of the Spanish Civil War, see E. E. Malefakis, *Agrarian Reform and Peasant Revolution in Spain: Origins of the Civil War* (Yale University, 1970); and P. Preston, ed., *Revolution and War in Spain 1931–1939* (Methuen, 1985). The war itself is studied from various viewpoints in D. A. Puzzo, *Spain and the Great Powers, 1936–1941* (Columbia University, 1962); H. Thomas, *The Spanish Civil War* (Harper & Row, 1961); G. Jackson, *The Spanish Republic and the Civil War 1931–1939* (Princeton University, 1965); B. Bolloten, *The Grand Camouflage* (Hollis and Carter, 1961); and the two books by S. G. Payne, *Politics and the Military in Modern Spain* (Stanford University, 1967), and *The Spanish Revolution* (W. W. Norton, 1970).

The rapid drift to war after the Ethiopian invasion and the outbreak of the Spanish Civil War are described from various viewpoints by F. W. Deakin, *The Brutal Friendship: Mussolini, Hitler and the Fall of Italian Fascism* (Weidenfeld and Nicolson, 1962); G. F. Kennan, *Russia and the West* (Little, Brown, 1960); E. H. Carr, *German-Soviet Relations Between the Two World Wars* (Hopkins, 1951); M. George, *The Warped Vision: British Foreign Policy 1933–1939* (University of Pittsburgh, 1965); A. A. Offner, *American Appeasement: United States Foreign Policy and Germany 1933–1938* (Harvard University, 1969); and T. Taylor, *Munich: The Price of Peace* (Doubleday, 1979). The most recent study of the drift to World War II is D. C. Watt, *How War Came: The Immediate Origins of the Second World War, 1938–1939* (Pantheon, 1989), which uses effectively the captured archives of the German foreign ministry and includes revealing appraisals of the leading personalities on both sides.

NOTES

1. *Bulletin of International News*, XV (March 5, 1938), p. 9.
2. W. S. Churchill, *The Second World War: The Gathering Storm* (Houghton Mifflin, 1948), p. 376.

World War II: Global Repercussions

The next World War will be fought with stones.

Albert Einstein

In signing the pact with Stalin, Hitler's aim was to secure Russia's neutrality while he disposed of Poland. Then he could, and did, marshal his armed forces against Britain and France. He declared privately at the time, "Let us think of the pact as securing our rear." As for Russia, that country also was on his list of future victims. "At present she is not dangerous," he stated. "We can oppose Russia only when we are free in the West. For the next year or two, the present situation will remain."[1] Thus, Hitler from the beginning had charted his schedule of conquest: first Poland, then the West, and finally Russia. He adhered to this schedule and in doing so determined the course of World War II until Russia and the West became strong enough to seize the initiative.

World War II, like World War I, began as a European conflict precipitated by the issue of minorities in eastern Europe. During the first two years the campaigns were waged on European battlefields. Then Japan's attack on Pearl Harbor in 1941 transformed war into a global struggle, just as America's intervention in 1917 had transformed World War I. At this point, however, the similarity between the two wars ends. With Japan's lightning conquest of the entire East and Southeast Asia, World War II came to involve much more of the globe than did the preceding war. Moreover, the two wars differed fundamentally in the strategy and weapons employed. During the first war defense, based on trenches and machine-gun nests, proved superior to offense. During the second war offense, based on tanks and planes, proved stronger than defense. This explains the extraordinary fluidity of battle lines that characterized the later struggle. Whole countries, and even continents, changed hands back and forth in striking contrast to the bloody stalemate on the western front between 1914 and 1918.

I. EUROPEAN PHASE OF THE WAR

Partitioning of Poland

In Poland the Germans demonstrated for the first time the deadly effectiveness of their new type of blitzkrieg, or "lightning war." First came waves of dive bombers, or Stukas, blasting communication lines and spreading terror and confusion. Then followed the armored tank divisions, or Panzers, smashing holes in the enemy lines, penetrating deeply into the rear, destroying transportation and communication facilities, and cutting the opposing forces into ribbons. Finally, the lighter motorized divisions and the infantry moved in for the "mopping up" of the splintered and battered enemy forces, supported where necessary by air and artillery cover.

Unfortunate Poland, with its flat plains and obsolete army, was a "setup" for this type of warfare. Within ten days the campaign had been virtually decided. The German tank and plane teams raced through the Polish countryside against declining resistance. The speed of the German advance forced Stalin to move in order to take over the territories he had staked out in his pact with Hitler. On September 17, the Red Army crossed into eastern Poland, and two days later it established contact with the triumphant Germans. On September 27, Warsaw fell. The Polish government leaders fled to Rumania and thence to France. Their country was partitioned two days later. The Germans took 37,000 square miles with 22 million people, and the Russians took 77,000 square miles with a population of 13 million. Within less than a month, one of the largest countries of Europe had disappeared completely from the map. (See map of World War II: Axis Conquests, 1939–1943, p. 595)

The Soviet government now took advantage of the secret protocol of the Moscow Pact to strengthen its strategic position in the Baltic area. In September and October 1939, it compelled Estonia, Latvia, and Lithuania to accept Russian military bases on their territories. Lithuania, by way of compensation, received the long-desired district and city of Vilna, hitherto a part of Poland. The Soviets next demanded from

A motorized German cavalry sweeps into Poland in the early days of the German invasion.

World War II: Axis Conquests, 1939–1943

Finland certain territories in the Karelian Isthmus and around Petsamo on the Arctic Ocean. The Finns refused, and on November 30 the Red Army attacked.

Finland appealed to the League of Nations, and that body expelled the Soviet Union from membership. The Finns resisted the Russian onslaught with unexpected success, repulsing repeated attacks on their Mannerheim Line. The Russians, who had grossly underestimated Finnish strength, brought up their regular forces with heavy artillery. By mid-March they cracked the Mannerheim Line and forced the Finns to sue for peace. The ensuing treaty gave the Russians somewhat more territory than they originally demanded, including the Petsamo region, the port of Viipuri, several islands in the Gulf of Finland, and a naval base at Hanko.

Perhaps the chief significance of these Russian moves against Finland and the other Baltic states was that they reflected the rivalry and distrust that existed behind the façade of Russo-German cooperation. This was demonstrated by Russia's insistence on the evacuation to Germany of the Baltic Germans who for centuries had dominated urban centers such as Memel and Riga.

Poland to France

Meanwhile, the western front had been discertingly quiet. The British and the French had stood helplessly by while Poland was being partitioned. They could not enter the Baltic Sea, which the Germans had sealed tight; their air forces were unable to operate across the breadth of the Reich; and their ground troops were confronted by the elaborate fortifications built by Hitler following his 1936 occupation of the Rhineland. Thus the French were forced to sit behind their Maginot Line, while the Germans made no move from behind their Siegfried Line or West Wall.

This surface calm proved deceptive. On April 9, 1940, the Wehrmacht suddenly erupted into action, sweeping through Denmark and making landings on the coast of Norway. The main objective was to gain control of the Norwegian fiords, which could provide invaluable bases for German submarines and also safeguard the shipment of Swedish iron ore down the coast to Germany. The Danes could offer no resistance, but the Norwegians, with British support, fought back stubbornly. But by early June France itself was in mortal peril, so the Allied expeditionary forces sailed away, accompanied by the Norwegian government, which took refuge in London.

The Allied setback in Norway was soon dwarfed by the stunning blitzkrieg that overran France and the Low Countries in seven weeks. On May 10 the Germans attacked Holland and Belgium, and two days later France. The Dutch defense collapsed in five days. The Belgians held out longer, but by May 28 King Leopold surrendered in person and the Belgian army capitulated. Meanwhile the Germans had skirted the northern end of the Maginot Line, which had never been extended to the sea, and drove through the Ardennes Forest, smashing a fifty-mile breach in the French lines at Sedan. The Panzer divisions now raced westward to the English Channel, reaching it on May 21. The German breakthrough left the British, French, and Belgian forces in the north cut off from the main French armies. The Allied armies in Flanders, mostly British, retreated to Dunkirk, whence they were evacuated to Britain.

With the completion of the Dunkirk evacuation the German forces resumed their advance southward, occupying Paris on June 13. A demoralized French government accepted the severe German armistice terms, which included release of all German prisoners of war; disbandment of French military forces; surrender of French warships; and occupation by Germany of slightly over half of France.

The staggering impact of the German blitzkrieg is reflected in the incredibly low casualty figures. During the entire campaign the French lost about 100,000 men, the other Allies 20,000, and the Germans 45,000. These losses were less than half those sustained in single offensives during World War I. The speedy collapse by what was considered to be the strongest Western power came as a most painful shock. Charges of treason and cowardice were leveled in explanation for the great disaster. Though these charges were not altogether unwarranted, other factors seem to have been more decisive. One was the effect of the Russo-German pact, which enabled Hitler to concentrate his forces on a single front. Perhaps most important was the German superiority in several fields, especially in the development of the new blitzkrieg technique.

Battle of Britain

After Dunkirk and the fall of France, Hitler assumed that Britain would see reason and would come to terms. But he failed to reckon with the British people and with their new prime minister, Winston Churchill. With characteristic resoluteness and audacity Churchill told his people—and the world—"We shall fight on the beaches. We shall fight on the landing grounds. We shall fight on the fields and in the streets. We shall fight in the hills; we shall never surrender."

Meanwhile, Hitler was marking time, unsure what the next step should be. The unexpectedly rapid fall of France had caught him by surprise. First he tried to make a deal with the British. When his overtures were ignored, he unleashed his Luftwaffe, confident that it could subdue Britain by air attack alone, without resort to a hazardous sea crossing.

The ensuing air assault developed into the critical Battle of Britain, one of the major turning points of World War II. In this epic struggle in the skies, the Luftwaffe had the advantage of numbers—2,670 planes against the Royal Air Force's 1,475. But the RAF Spitfires and Hurricanes were more advanced, because Britain had gone into mass production of planes several years later than Germany. The British also had

German troops march down the Champs-Elysées in Paris in September, 1940, after the rapid collapse of French defenses.

the use of radar, a new invention that enabled enemy aircraft to be "sighted" fifty to a hundred miles before reaching their targets. With these advantages, a few thousand British and dominion fighter pilots, with a scattering of Poles, Czechs, French, and Belgians, were able to repulse the Luftwaffe and thus end Hitler's chance for invading Britain.

Conquest of the Balkans

Because of his failure in the Battle for Britain, Hitler decided to invade Russia the following spring. Preparing for the projected invasion, Hitler sent troops into Rumania to ready the Rumanian army, which was to participate in the attack on the Soviet Union. At this point, Mussolini launched his blundering invasion of Greece. What Mussolini assumed would be an effortless occupation proved in fact to be a humiliating fiasco. On October 28, 1940, Italian troops crossed from Albania into Greece, expecting a triumphal procession to Athens. But after pushing some distance across the Greek-Albanian frontier, they suffered a decisive defeat at the battle of Metsovo on November 11. Taking advantage of the difficulties of the ponderous Italian armored divisions in the mountains of Epirus, the Greeks invariably made for the high ground and from there cut off and surrounded the enemy below. By mid-November they had driven the Italians back across the frontier into Albania. In the following weeks the Greeks captured several large Albanian towns. For a while it appeared that Mussolini might even have to endure a Dunkirk in the Adriatic.

Hitler could not sit back and watch the Italians flounder, particularly because the British were landing air units in Greece, which could prove troublesome once his invasion of Russia was under way. So on April 6 he launched his Operation Marita for the conquest of both Yugoslavia and Greece. As in Poland and France, the Panzer divisions and the Luftwaffe swept everything before them. The mountainous terrain of the Balkan peninsula did not prove an effective obstacle, as had been hoped, and the British ground and air units were too weak to halt the tide. By April 13, the Germans had entered Belgrade, and ten days later the British were evacuating their forces from southern Greece to Crete. The Germans then launched an airborne invasion of Crete, surprising the British who did not expect an air attack from the Greek mainland 180 miles to the north. Though they suffered heavy losses, the Germans finally gained complete control of the island by the beginning of June.

In addition to the triumph in the Balkans, Hitler's armies had won an equally impressive victory in North Africa under the able and energetic General Erwin Rommel. With the Balkans and North Africa under his control, Hitler ordered his Wehrmacht across the Soviet frontier on June 22, 1941. (See map of World War II: Axis Conquests, 1939–1943, p. 595.)

II. GLOBAL PHASE OF THE WAR

Invasion of Russia

Stalin signed the August 1939 nonaggression pact with Hitler for a variety of reasons. He was deeply distrustful of the Western leaders and wanted to gain time to strengthen his military and industrial establishments. He also calculated that sooner or later Germany and the Western powers would clash in a war of attrition, whereas Russia, thanks to the pact, would be free to remain aloof until it was profitable to intervene. "If war begins," he told his comrades, "we cannot simply sit back. We will have to get into the fighting, but we must be the last to join in. And we shall join so as to cast the decisive weight onto the scales, the weight that will tip the balance."[2] This strategy was shrewd, yet it boomeranged and came very close to destroying the Soviet state. It was based on the assumption that the German and Western forces were evenly matched and would decimate each other, leaving the Red Army the dominant force on the Continent. Instead, the Wehrmacht crushed all opposition with incredible ease, leaving Germany the master of the Continent and the Soviet Union isolated and imperiled.

At first, it seemed that Russia would collapse as quickly as had Poland and France. The Panzer divisions, in their now familiar fashion, smashed through the frontier defenses and drove deeply into the rear, encircling entire Soviet armies and taking hundreds of thousands of prisoners. By the end of the year the Wehrmacht had penetrated 600 miles eastward, overrunning the most industrialized and populous regions of the Soviet Union.

One reason for the German triumph, apart from the important factor of surprise, was numerical preponderance at the outset. Hitler struck with an army of about 3 million as against approximately 2 million on the other side. The Russians, of course, had huge reserves to draw on, but the Luftwaffe's bombing made it difficult to utilize them promptly and efficiently. The German forces also had the telling advantage of battle experience under varied conditions in Poland, France, and the Balkans. In addition, Stalin had refused to take seriously many warnings of the imminent Nazi invasion, so a large part of his air force was destroyed on the ground the very first day. It should also be recalled that this was not a struggle between the Soviet Union and Germany but rather between the Soviet Union and the European continent. This meant that the Red Army had to cope with substantial Finnish, Rumanian, and Hungarian forces as well as German, and that Soviet armament plants were in competition with those of France and Czechoslovakia as well as Germany. Thus, whereas Soviet steel output in 1941 was almost equal to Germany's, it was considerably less than half that of Germany and the rest of the Continent. Finally, the invading German armies were assisted by very large numbers of Soviet citizens. Some of them were disaffected non-Russian minorities, and others were peasants who still resented Stalin's forced collectivization of their plots, and the ensuing mass deportations to Siberia. Consequently, many Soviet citizens collaborated with the Germans as the lesser of two evils.

Thanks to the above factors, the Germans advanced far into the Soviet Union, almost completely surrounding Moscow and Leningrad. Nevertheless the Red Army remained intact, even launching a counteroffensive in December 1941. One reason for Hitler's failure to win complete victory was that he lost the support of most of the people in the countries he had overrun, partly because many had been forced to work as slave laborers in German industries and agriculture. Also many had been antagonized by Hitler's racist policy of classifying and treating Eastern Europeans as inferior subhumans (*Untermenschen*) who were to be swept away and replaced by the superior Nordic Germans. His plans for a New Order in eastern Europe called

These are some of the dead at the Nordhausen concentration camp, which was liberated by the American Army in April 1945. The Nazis set up their first concentration camps in Germany in 1933 to hold opponents of their regime. After the conquest of Poland, new camps were established there as part of the "final solution," the extermination of the Jews. About six million Jews were murdered in these camps. Even in those camps not dedicated to extermination—in which political prisoners and "undesirables" such as Gypsies, homosexuals, and Jehovah's Witnesses were held— conditions were brutal in the extreme, and tens of thousands died. The crimes of the Nazi regime have no precedent in human history.

for elimination of 30 million Slavs. Even worse was Hitler's decision for a "final solution" of the "Jewish problem" by the literal extermination of all Jews within his reach. Victory in Poland brought him between 2 million and 3 million Jews; victory in the West added a half-million more; and his invasion of Russia increased the figure by another 3 million. Special "action teams" (Einsatzgruppen) followed on the heels of the advancing German armies as extermination squads. Mobile gas vans began to be used in late 1941. They could not keep up with the growing number of victims, so five large extermination centers were constructed. Auschwitz achieved a grim record for efficiency in production-line murder—12,000 per day.

Thus perished an estimated 6 million Jews—three-fourths of Europe's Jews and two-fifths of the world's. But Jews were not the only victims. Five million Protestants and 3 million Catholics also disappeared in the extermination camps, along with half a million gypsies. This holocaust was so unique in the annals of world history that a new word was coined to define it. The word is genocide, from the Greek genos (race or nation) and the Latin cide (killing). Wholesale massacres of course are not peculiar

to the twentieth century. Historian Arnold J. Toynbee has noted, however, that twentieth-century genocide is unique in "that it is committed in cold blood by the deliberate fiat of holders of despotic political power, and that the perpetrators of genocide employ all the resources of present-day technology and organization to make their planned massacres systematic and complete."[3]

The Nazis systematically used their prisoners as a source of labor while they were alive and as a source of "raw materials" after death. They ordered the ashes in the ovens carted off to be used as fertilizer, the hair from the corpses used for mattresses, the bones crushed for phosphates, the fat used to make soap, and the gold and silver fillings from teeth deposited in the vaults of the Reichsbank.

As far as the course of World War II was concerned, the unspeakable atrocities associated with genocide were as short-sighted as they were criminal. Millions who had been alienated in the interwar years by the excesses of Stalinism and of the assorted discredited regimes of the Continent would have supported Hitler's New Order had they not been even more cruelly oppressed by the German racists. The end result was that only a handful of compromised collaborators stood by the Nazis to the end. The great majority in the occupied lands supported in varying degrees the resistance forces and contributed significantly to Hitler's eventual defeat.

Japan Attacks Pearl Harbor

World War II was transformed from a European to a global conflict with the Japanese attack on Pearl Harbor on December 7, 1941. At the beginning of the war, almost all Americans were determined to remain neutral. But Hitler's unexpected victories, and particularly the fall of France, compelled American policy makers to question whether neutrality automatically afforded protection against involvement. If Hitler were to conquer England and then gain control of the Atlantic, might not the New World be next on the schedule of conquest?

These considerations led Washington to conclude that the best way to avoid involvement in the war was to give all aid short of war to those still fighting Germany. This explains the steady drift of the United States from neutrality to nonbelligerency with the Destroyers-Bases Agreement (September 2, 1940) and from nonbelligerence to undeclared war with the Lend-Lease Act (March 11, 1941), and the signing of the Atlantic Charter (August 12, 1941).

While striving to limit Axis expansion in the West, President Roosevelt also attempted to restrain Japan from aggression in the Pacific. Successive Tokyo governments, however, became increasingly bellicose in response to what appeared to be golden opportunities provided by the course of events in Europe. Hitler's victories had left almost undefended the rich French, British, and Dutch possessions in east and Southeast Asia. The entire region appeared ripe for plucking if only the United States would not intervene.

Japan's leaders were divided on the question of relations with the United States. The army was ready to challenge Britain, France, and the United States directly, but the navy, the diplomats, and the industrialists mostly held back. The turning point came with the resignation in October 1941 of the premier, Prince Fumimaro Konoye, who favored a settlement with the United States. He was succeeded by General Hideki Tojo, at the head of a cabinet of army and navy officers. Tojo decided to settle accounts with the United States. Just as the Japanese forced the issue against the Russians in

Pearl Harbor, Hawaii—
December 7, 1941.

1904 by attacking Port Arthur without a declaration of war, so now on December 7, 1941, they struck at Pearl Harbor. Within a few hours five of the eight battleships in Pearl Harbor had been destroyed, as well as three cruisers and three destroyers. At the same time another Japanese task force destroyed most of the U.S. army's planes in the Philippines, and Germany and Italy declared war on the United States. Thus America was fully involved in the war, both in Europe and in Asia.

1942: Year of Axis Triumphs

During the year 1942, Germany, Italy, and Japan were almost everywhere victorious. Great offensives overran large parts of Russia, North Africa, and the Pacific, like a huge three-taloned claw grasping the Eurasian hemisphere. The most spectacular triumphs were won by the Japanese, who quickly conquered a vast Pacific empire, stretching from the Aleutians to Australia and from Guam to India. The Japanese were successful for several reasons. One was right timing: They struck when France and Holland were occupied, when Britain was struggling to survive, and when the United States was only starting to convert from a peace to a war economy. The Japanese were successful also because during the years of fighting against Chinese guerrillas they had trained their men to infiltrate around enemy positions and to attack on the flanks and rear. These tactics worked well in the fighting against Western forces in the jungles of Southeast Asia. Finally, the Japanese benefited from the resentment of colonial peoples against their past exploitation by Western imperial powers. The Japanese invaders encouraged this sentiment with slogans such as "Asia for the Asians."

These factors explain the unbelievably swift Japanese advance from victory to victory—from Hong Kong to Guam to Singapore, and then around Southeast Asia to the Philippines, Malaya, Indonesia, and Burma, thus reaching the frontiers of India. In five months, at a cost of only 15,000 killed and wounded, the Japanese had won an empire that had a population of over 100 million and that supplied 95 percent of the world's raw rubber, 90 percent of the hemp, and two-thirds of the tin.

Meanwhile, on the Russian front, Hitler had launched another massive offensive in June 1942. Since Moscow and Leningrad had proven impregnable the previous year, he now directed his armies southward. His objective was to reach the Volga and the Caspian, thereby cutting the Soviet Union in two and depriving the Red Army of its oil supplies from the Caucasus. As in 1941, the Panzer divisions at first rolled swiftly across the flat steppe country. The main tank forces then drove through to the Volga slightly to the north of Stalingrad.

In North Africa also, 1942 was a year of victory for the Germans. Under the dashing General Rommel, the Afrika Korps in March 1941 had driven the British across Libya to the Egyptian border. In May 1942 Rommel resumed the attack, crossed into Egypt, and reached El Alamein, a scant fifty miles from Alexandria. So confident was Rommel of complete victory that he selected a white stallion for his triumphal entry into Cairo.

On every front the Axis powers were at the height of their fortunes. In North Africa Rommel was preparing to strike for Cairo, in Russia the Wehrmacht had reached the Volga, and in the Pacific the Japanese appeared to be ready to spring on Australia and India.

1943: The Turning Tide

During the first three years of the war the Axis powers had everything their own way. The turning point began at the end of 1942 with the Russian victory at Stalingrad, the British breakthrough in Egypt, and the Allied landings in French North Africa, and it continued in 1943 with the fall of Mussolini, the mounting aerial bombardment of Germany, and the defeat of Japanese fleets in the Pacific.

At Stalingrad the Russians had dug in with orders to defend the city to the last man. The battle for the city began on August 22. By mid-September the Germans had fought their way into the center, and there they bogged down. While the soldiers were fighting hand to hand in cellars, on rooftops, and in sewers, two Russian armies crossed the Volga from the east, one attacking to the north of Stalingrad and the other to the south. With this gigantic pincers

Russian soldiers, in their heroic defense of Stalingrad, dug trenches from building to building in the city. The German defeat at Stalingrad in February 1943 marked the turning point of the Russian campaign. Thereafter, the Russians advanced inexorably westward.

operation the besiegers became the besieged. The Germans on the banks of the Volga were hopelessly stranded. On February 3, 1943, the Russians accepted the surrender of 120,000 men, the frozen survivors of the original army of 334,000. Thereafter the Russians were on the offensive all along the front, forcing the Germans to fight defensive actions to prevent their retreat from becoming a rout. (See map of World War II: Axis Defeat, 1942–1945, p. 603.)

While the Germans were being forced out of Russia, they and their Italian allies were being driven out of North Africa. A new British commander, Sir Bernard Montgomery, attacked from Egypt and drove the Germans and Italians back along the coastal road, reaching Tripoli by January 1943. At the same time Anglo-American troops landed on the other end of North Africa, in Morocco and Algeria. They advanced eastward to Tunis and then invaded Sicily in July 1943. By the following month they were attacking across the Messina Straits to the Italian mainland.

Mussolini paid for these disasters with his office and eventually with his life. King Victor Emmanuel III was persuaded by monarchists and Fascist dissidents to dismiss and imprison Mussolini. A new government was formed, headed by Marshal Pietro Badoglio, the con-

queror of Ethiopia. The latter concluded an armistice with the Allies on September 3, 1943. The Germans responded by seizing Rome and occupying the central and northern parts of the country. In a bold raid, Nazi parachutists rescued Mussolini from prison. The shopworn Duce established a "Fascist Republic" in northern Italy and proclaimed his intention of fighting to the bitter end. For the next year and a half Italy was to be a divided and war-wracked country—the Germans with their puppet Mussolini in the North, and the Allies with Badoglio's government in the south.

Meanwhile, the soil of the Third Reich itself was being subjected to steadily increasing aerial bombardment. By 1943, round-the-clock bombing became possible, the British raiding by night and the Americans by day. More explosives were now dropped on German cities in one hour than had been loosed during the entire Battle of Britain.

At the same time, the Japanese were suffering reverses comparable to those of their Axis partners in Europe. After their spectacular victories in the first six months, the Japanese finally were stopped and then pushed back at an accelerating pace. The basic reason for this shift in the course of the war was the overwhelming superiority of American resources and productiv-

World War II: Axis Defeat, 1942–1945

U.S. manufacture of warplanes increased by an astonishing number, as seen in this factory in Inglewood, California, 1942.

ity. Once the American economy was converted to a war footing, it simply swamped the Japanese, despite their fanatic courage. For example, the disasters during the early part of the war left the United States with only three first-line aircraft carriers, but within two years of Pearl Harbor the number jumped to fifty. Likewise, the number of navy planes rose from 3,638 in 1941 to 30,070 in 1944; the construction of submarines increased from 11 in 1941 to 77 in 1944; and the production of landing craft, from 123 in 1941 to 54,206 in 1945.

The Japanese could not even begin to match this flood from American factories. The first step on the long road to Tokyo was taken at Guadalcanal, where U.S. Marines landed on August 7, 1942. Slowly, and at heavy cost, American forces captured other enemy bases in the South Pacific. By mid-1944 Saipan and Guam in the Marianas were taken, bringing the Japanese home islands within range of the new B-29

superfortresses. It was the beginning of the end of Japan's brief hour of glory.

Liberation of Europe

Europe was liberated in 1944–1945 primarily by the Red Army advancing from the east and by Anglo-American forces invading from the Normandy landing beaches in the west. Normandy was invaded on June 6 by an armada from England comprising 4,000 merchant vessels and 700 warships. With invaluable assistance from the French underground *maquis*, the Allied forces consolidated their coastal beachheads. By early August General George Patton was racing across northern France toward Paris, and on August 19 resistance forces began open insurrection in the French capital. By the end of the month, American-French forces had liberated the city, and General de Gaule, now recognized as the leader

Allied troops landed in Normandy on D-Day, June 6, 1944. This photograph, taken two days later, shows long lines of men and equipment moving inland from the beach to reinforce the troops leading the invasion.

of the French people, drove in triumph to Notre Dame.

While the Western powers were liberating France, the Red Army was advancing rapidly from the east. Having driven the Wehrmacht from the Crimea and the Ukraine by the spring of 1944, it then began a general offensive. In the north the Russians knocked Finland out of the war by September. In the center they crossed both the old and new frontiers of Poland and drove to the gates of Warsaw. In the south they reached the mouth of the Danube in the heart of Rumania. Young King Michael of Rumania seized the opportunity to pull his country out of the war in September, thus opening the Balkan peninsula to the Red Army. Bulgaria followed this example by suing for peace and reentering the war on the side of the Soviet Union. The German armies in the Balkans were now in danger of being trapped and began to pull out as fast as possible. As they did so, the Communist-led resistance forces in Yugoslavia and Greece descended from the mountains and took over control of their respective countries—a development that was to contribute to the forthcoming cold war between Russia and the Western powers. Aided by the local Communist-led guerrillas and by an exceptionally mild winter, the Red Army continued its westward drive to the frontiers of Austria and Germany. By April 1945 they had taken Vienna and were crossing the Oder, forty miles from Berlin. Meanwhile, American, British, and French armies were making corresponding progress on the western front. They were temporarily thrown off balance by a German offensive in December 1944 in the

Ardennes in Belgium. After recovering from this setback, the Allies fought their way to the Rhine. There they discovered to their astonishment that the retreating Germans had neglected to blow up the Ludendorff railway bridge at Remagen, south of Bonn. The Allies swarmed over, and within a month they had conquered the Rhineland and taken a quarter-million prisoners. Seven allied armies raced through the collapsing Reich. They could have taken Berlin, since the Red Army still was on the Oder and since the Germans had concentrated their defenses against the Russians on the east, leaving the western approaches to their capital almost defenseless. General Eisenhower, the supreme Allied commander, decided against taking the prize for strategic and diplomatic reasons.

The Allied armies stood aside while Zhukov opened his final offensive against Berlin on April 16. Nine days later he had the capital surrounded. At the same time, on April 25, an American patrol linked up with the Soviet vanguard at the village of Torgau on the Elbe, cutting Germany in two. On the last day of April, Hitler and his companion, Eva Braun, committed suicide in a concrete bunker with shells thudding on all sides. On May 2, Berlin surrendered to the Russians. During the next week Nazi emissaries surrendered unconditionally to the Western powers at Rheims and to the Soviet Union in Berlin. At the same time German commanders in Italy signed terms of unconditional surrender. Mussolini tried to escape to Switzerland but was apprehended by guerrillas and summarily shot. His body and that of his mistress were hung up on display in Milan.

Surrender of Japan

The surrender of Germany and Italy made even bleaker the prospects for the Japanese in the Pacific. Already by mid-1944 their home islands were being bombarded by superfortresses based on Iwo Jima and Okinawa. Using these two islands as bases, American airmen subjected Japan's crowded cities to the same storm of explosives that had wracked Germany. The Japanese were even more vulnerable, for their flimsy wood and paper structures went up in flames like so much kindling.

The militarists who had been responsible for Japan's intervention in the war were loath to acknowledge their error and to begin serious peace negotiations. While they were hesitating, a series of unprecedented cataclysms abruptly ended their indecision. On August 6, 1945, an American superfortress dropped an atomic bomb on Hiroshima, demolishing three-fifths of the city and killing 140,000 inhabitants. Two days later, Russia declared war on Japan, and the Red Army promptly drove across the frontier into Manchuria. The final blow was the dropping of a second atomic bomb on August 9 on the city of Nagasaki, resulting in 70,000 deaths. The extreme Japanese militarists still opposed a general surrender, and it seemed at one point that the war would deteriorate into a struggle of individual guerrilla groups led by diehard officers. But the emperor, on the advice of the cabinet and the elder statesmen, decided to capitulate, and on August 14 the Allied ultimatum was accepted. The formal ceremony of surrender took place on board the USS Missouri in Tokyo Bay on September 2.

Thus ended World War II—a war even more destructive and savage than the first. In contrast to the 28.4 million casualties in World War I, the cost now was 50 million, including 20 million Russians, 15 million Chinese, 5 million Germans, 2.5 million Japanese, 1 million British and French, and 300,000 Americans. Most appalling was that of the 50 million deaths, no less than one-fifth represented cold-blooded murder. Those 10 million victims had been "exterminated" as "undesirables" for racial, religious, political, or other reasons.

III. WORLD WAR II IN WORLD HISTORY

World War II completed the undermining of Europe's global hegemony that had been started by World War I. Thus, the two wars had a similar significance for world history. There were significant differences, however, that are of prime importance for the contemporary scene.

The formal Japanese surrender being signed aboard the USS Missouri, *as General MacArthur looks on.*

The Nazis and the Japanese militarists were infinitely more destructive of the old orders in Europe and Asia than the Hohenzollerns and the Hapsburgs had ever been. The Germans had overrun the entire continent of Europe; and the Japanese, the whole of east and Southeast Asia. But these vast empires were short-lived. They disappeared in 1945, leaving behind two great power vacuums embracing territories of great economic and strategic significance. It was the existence of these vacuums, as much as any ideological considerations, that was responsible for the outbreak of the cold war and the inability to conclude a general peace settlement immediately after 1945.

Another difference between the two postwar periods was the successful upsurge of colonial subjects after 1945, in contrast to the enforcement of imperial authority after 1918. Within a period of two decades the farflung European empires had all but disappeared. Thus the two outstanding global developments in the immediate postwar years were the worldwide colonial revolutions and the cold war. These are the topics of the following two chapters.

SUGGESTED READINGS

The most fascinating and revealing introduction to the Second World War is by S. Terkel, *"The Good War": An Oral History of World War II* (Pantheon, 1984). A useful bibliographical guide is provided by L. Morton, *Writings on World War II* (Service Center for Teachers of History, 1967). The best general histories are by B.

H. Liddell Hart, *History of the Second World War* (Putnam's, 1970); G. Wright, *The Ordeal of Total War 1939–1945* (Harper & Row, 1969); M. B. Hoyle, *A World in Flames: A History of World War II* (Atheneum, 1970); and R. A. Divine, *Causes and Consequences of World War II* (Quadrangle Books, 1969).

A fascinating account of the fall of France is provided by W. L. Shirer, *The Collapse of the Third Republic* (Simon & Schuster, 1969). The German-Russian war in its various phases is treated by B. Whaley, *Codeword Barbarossa* (MIT, 1973); G. I. Zhukov, *Marshal Zhukov's Greatest Battles* (Harper & Row, 1969); A. Werth, *Russia at War, 1941—1945* (E. P. Dutton, 1964); W. Craig, *Enemy at the Gates: The Battle for Stalingrad* (E. P. Dutton, 1973); and H. E. Salisbury, *The 900 Days: The Siege of Leningrad* (Harper & Row, 1969). Hitler's extermination policies and actions in eastern Europe are set forth in M. Gilbert, *The Holocaust* (Holt, Rinehart and Winston, 1985); G. Fleming, *Hitler and the Final Solution* (University of California, 1984); and D. J. Goldhagen, *Hitler's Willing Executioners* (Knopf, 1996), which holds that many Germans were not obeying orders in killing Jews but believed they were doing the "right thing."

The diplomacy leading to Japan's intervention is analyzed by H. Feis, *The Road to Pearl Harbor* (Princeton University, 1950); and J. M. Meskill, *Hitler and Japan: The Hollow Alliance* (Atherton, 1966). The circumstances of the attack are authoritatively analyzed by R. Wohlsetter, *Pearl Harbor: Warning and Decision* (Stanford University, 1964). An excellent anthology of the Pacific War, edited by D. Congdon and published as a Dell paperback, is *Combat: The Pacific Theater: World War II* (1959). The war from the Japanese viewpoint is described by J. Toland, *The Rising Sun: The Decline and Fall of the Japanese Empire* (Bantam Books, 1970). American use of the A-bomb is defended by H. Feis, *The Atomic Bomb and the End of World War II* (Princeton University, 1970) and attacked as an anti-Soviet move by G. Alperowitz, *Atomic Diplomacy: Hiroshima and Potsdam* (Random House, 1965); and his *Decision to Use the Atomic Bomb* (Knopf, 1995). For the human implications of the A-bomb, see R. J. Lifton, *Death in Life: Survivors of Hiroshima* (Random House, 1968). An important contribution is by J. Dower, *War without Mercy* (Pantheon, 1986), which reveals the prevalence of racism in both the American and Japanese camps during the Pacific war. R. Overy, *Why the Allies Won* (Norton, 1996) argues that the war was a close contest to the end, with Allied victory not preordained.

Finally, the entire August 1985 issue of the *Bulletin of the Atomic Scientists* is worth reading for the collection of important articles interpreting the nature and consequences of World War II and the current prospects for the human race.

NOTES

1. Cited by A. Dallin, "The Fateful Pact: Prelude to World War II," *New York Times Magazine* (August 21, 1948), p. 40.
2. Cited by Dallin, "Fateful Pact," p. 163.
3. A. J. Toynbee, *Experiences* (Oxford University, 1969), p. 241.

CHAPTER
42

End of Empires

Hereafter, perhaps, the natives of those [overseas] countries may grow stronger, or those of Europe may grow weaker, and the inhabitants of all the different quarters of the world may arrive at that equality of courage and force which, by inspiring mutual fear, can alone overawe the injustice of independent nations into some sort of respect for the rights of one another. But nothing seems more likely to establish this equality of force than that mutual communication of knowledge and of all sorts of improvements which an extensive commerce from all countries to all countries naturally, or rather necessarily, carries along with it.

Adam Smith

A major difference between the First and Second World Wars lay in their colonial aftermaths. Europe's hold over the colonial empires was weakened but not broken by World War I; indeed, the colonial holdings were expanded by the acquisition of Arab lands as mandates. After World War II, by contrast, an irrepressible revolutionary wave swept the colonial empires and ended European domination with dramatic speed. Just as most of Europe's colonies had been swiftly acquired in the last two decades of the nineteenth century, so most of them now were lost in an equally short period following World War II. Between 1944 and 1985, a total of ninety-six countries had won their

independence. These included about a third of the world's total population (see Table 42.1). After so many epoch-making triumphs and achievements overseas, the Europeans appeared in the mid-twentieth century to be retreating back to the small Eurasian peninsula whence they had set forth half a millennium earlier (see map of World of New Global Relationships, 1985, p. 612). Table 42.1 also reveals that the breakaway of overseas Afro-Asian colonies was followed by the breakup of multiethnic European states into several ethnic succession states. The table shows that in 1991 and 1992, the USSR was replaced by thirteen succession states, Yugoslavia by three, and Czechoslovakia by two.

Table 42.1 March to Independence

Country	Became Independent of	Year
Syria	France	1944
Lebanon	France	1944
Jordan	Britain	1946
Philippines	United States	1946
India	Britain	1947
Pakistan	Britain	1947
Burma	Britain	1948
North Korea	Japan	1948
South Korea	Japan	1948
Israel	Britain	1948
Sri Lanka (Ceylon)	Britain	1948
Indonesia	Netherlands	1949
Libya	Italy	1952
Cambodia	France	1954
Laos	France	1954
North Vietnam	France	1954
South Vietnam	France	1954
Sudan	Britain-Egypt	1956
Morocco	France	1956
Tunisia	France	1956
Ghana	Britain	1957
Malaya[a]	Britain	1957
Guinea	France	1958
Republic of the Congo	Belgium	1960
Somalia	Italy	1960
Nigeria	Britain	1960
Cameroon	France	1960
Mali	France	1960
Senegal	France	1960
Malagasy	France	1960
Togo	France	1960
Cyprus	Britain	1960
Ivory Coast	France	1960
Upper Volta	France	1960
Niger	France	1960
Dahomey	France	1960
Congo Republic	France	1960
Central African Republic	France	1960
Chad	France	1960
Gabon	France	1960
Mauritania	France	1960
Sierra Leone	Britain	1961
Tanganyika[b]	Britain	1961
Algeria	France	1962
Burundi	Belgium	1962
Jamaica	Britain	1962
Rwanda	Belgium	1962
Trinidad and Tobago	Britain	1962
Uganda	Britain	1962
Western Samoa	New Zealand	1962
Kenya	Britain	1963
Zanzibar[b]	Britain	1963
Malta	Britain	1964
Malawi	Britain	1964
Zambia	Britain	1964
Gambia	Britain	1965
Maldive Islands	Britain	1965
Singapore	Britain	1965
Guyana	Britain	1966
Botswana	Britain	1966
Lesotho	Britain	1966
Barbados	Britain	1966
South Yemen	Britain	1967
Mauritius	Britain	1968
Swaziland	Britain	1968
Equatorial Guinea	Spain	1968
Nauru	Australia	1968
Fiji	Britain	1970
Tonga	Britain	1970
Bangladesh	Pakistan	1971
Bahrain	Britain	1971
Bhutan	Britain	1971
Oman	Britain	1971
Qatar	Britain	1971
United Arab Emirates	Britain	1971
Bahamas	Britain	1973
Grenada	Britain	1974
Guinea-Bissau	Portugal	1974
Sao Tomé and Principe	Portugal	1975
Mozambique	Portugal	1975
Cape Verde Islands	Portugal	1975
Comoro Islands	France	1975
Seychelles	Britain	1976
Djibouti	France	1977
Solomon Islands	Britain	1978
Tuvalu	Britain	1978
Saint Lucia	Britain	1979
Kiribati	Britain	1979
Zimbabwe (Rhodesia)	Britain	1980
St. Vincent and Grenadines	Britain	1980
Antigua and Barbudo	Britain	1981
Belize	Britain	1981
Vanuatu	Anglo-French condominium	1981
St. Christopher and Nevis	Britain	1983
Brunei	Britain	1984
Namibia	South Africa	1990
Marshall Islands	U.S. Trust Territory	1991
Russian Federation	USSR	1991
Estonia	USSR	1991
Latvia	USSR	1991
Lithuania	USSR	1991
Moldova	USSR	1992
Kazakhstan	USSR	1992
Kyrgyzstan	USSR	1992
Uzbekistan	USSR	1992
Armenia	USSR	1992
Tajikistan	USSR	1992
Turkmenistan	USSR	1992
Azerbaijan	USSR	1992
Georgia	USSR	1992
Slovenia	Yugoslavia	1992
Bosnia and Herzegovina	Yugoslavia	1992
Croatia	Yugoslavia	1992
Czech Republic	Czechoslovakia	1992 (Dissolved on December 31, 1992)
Slovak Republic	Czechoslovakia	1992 (Dissolved on December 31, 1992)

[a] Combined in 1963 with Singapore, Sarawak, and Sabah (British North Borneo) to form the state of Malaysia with a population of 10 million.

[b] Tanganyika and Zanzibar combined in 1964 to form the United Republic of Tanganyika and Zanzibar, or Tanzania.

I. ROOTS OF COLONIAL REVOLUTION

During the course of World War II, the leaders of the imperial nations made it clear that they were determined to hold on to their colonies. Yet despite their statements, virtually all the Asian colonies were free within a decade after the war, and virtually all the African colonies, within two decades after the war. One reason for this unexpected outcome was the unprecedented weakening of the foremost colonial powers during World War II. France and Holland were overrun and occupied, and Britain was debilitated economically and militarily. Equally important was the growth of democratic, anti-imperialistic sentiment within the imperial countries themselves. Gone were the days when whites in the colonies confidently asserted, "We are here because we are superior." Now their presence was questioned, not only by their subjects but also by their own fellow Europeans. Mussolini's attack on Ethiopia in 1935 was widely regarded in western Europe as a deplorable throwback. The end of the Western empires was due as much to the lack of will to rule as it was to the lack of strength.

The short-lived Japanese Empire in Asia also contributed substantially to the colonial revolution. Western military prestige was shattered by the ease with which the Japanese drove the British out of Malaya and Burma, the French out of Indochina, the Dutch out of Indonesia, and the Americans out of the Philippines. The political foundations of Western imperialism were undermined by Japanese propaganda based on the slogan "Asia for the Asians." When the Japanese were at last forced to surrender their conquests, they deliberately made the restoration of Western rule as difficult as possible by leaving arms with local nationalist organizations and by recognizing these organizations as independent governments—as in the case of Ho Chi Minh's Viet Minh in Indochina and Sukarno's Putera in Indonesia.

We should note, however, that the Africans who escaped Japanese invasion also won freedom along with the Asians, thus pointing up the fact that important as the Japanese impact was, it merely strengthened the great unrest and awakening that had been gathering momentum since the beginning of the century. The series of colonial uprisings following World War I reflected this growing movement (see Chapter 37). In the intervening years it had gained strength and purpose with the growth of a Western-educated native intelligentsia. It was not accidental that the successful nationalist leaders were people who had studied in Western universities and observed Western institutions in operation—for instance, Gandhi, Nehru, Sukarno, Nkrumah, Azikwe, and Bourguiba.

The worldwide colonial awakening was further stimulated during World War II with the service of millions of colonials in both Allied and Japanese armies and labor battalions. Many Africans fought under the British, French, and Italian flags. Over 2 million Indians volunteered for the British forces, and an additional 40,000 Indian prisoners captured in Hong Kong, Singapore, and Burma signed up for the Japanese-sponsored Indian National Army. When all these men returned to their homes, they inevitably regarded in a new light the local colonial officials and native leaders. Finally, the civilian populations were affected at this time, as during World War I, by the Allied propaganda regarding freedom and self-determination.

II. INDIA AND PAKISTAN

By far the most important single event in the colonial revolution was the winning of independence by India and Pakistan. When Britain declared war on Germany on September 3, 1939, the viceroy, the Marquis of Linlithgow, on the same day proclaimed India also to be at war. Leaders of Congress protested bitterly that they were not consulted on this momentous decision, and on August 7, 1942, passed a "Quit India Resolution" demanding immediate freedom, "both for the sake of India and for the success of the cause of the UN." Britain replied with wholesale repression. Over 60,000 people were arrested—including all the Congress leaders. During the remaining years of the war, the British stood firm in refusing to release the Congress leaders unless they modified their "Quit India" demand.

A new and decisive turn in Indian affairs was taken with the Labour party victory in the British elections of July 1945. Labour traditionally had championed Indian freedom, and now

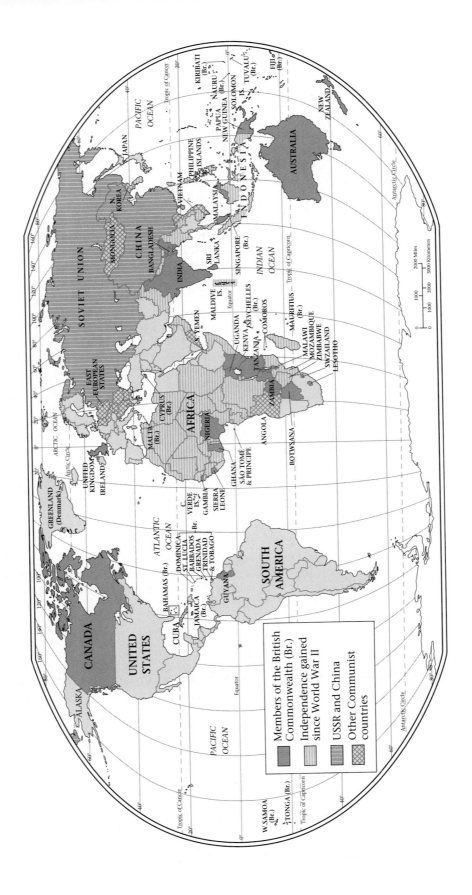

World of New Global Relationships, 1985.

A veiled woman votes in an Indian village.

Prime Minister Attlee acted swiftly to carry out his party's promises. Actually apart from his party's commitments and sympathies, the fact is that Attlee had little choice but to accept independence. The truth was that Britain could no longer rule the country against the wishes of its people. Nor was there much desire any longer to try to do so. The Indian Civil Service had become even more Indianized during the war, and British investments in India had shrunk drastically. Also the British public had become weary of the never-ending Indian problem. Thus Attlee was now able to sever ties with the former "jewel of the empire" with relatively little opposition at home.

Hurried conferences with the feuding leaders of the Congress Party and the Moslem League revealed that an independent India could not be a united India. So in July 1947, the British Parliament passed the Indian Independence Act, and on August 15, both Pakistan and the Union of India became free nations in the British Commonwealth.

III. SOUTHEAST ASIA

Southeast Asia, in contrast to India, was occupied by the Japanese during the war. A common pattern is discernible throughout the area during this brief occupation period between 1942 and 1945. In almost every country, widespread disaffection against Western rule had contributed substantially to the swift conquests of the Japanese (see Chapter 41, Section II). The latter then proclaimed, like the Germans, that their conquests inaugurated the beginning of a "New Order." The watchwords of this New Order were "Asia for the Asians," "Greater East Asia Co-Prosperity Sphere," and "no conquests, no oppression and no exploitation."

If these principles had been applied, the Japanese could have mobilized solid popular support in most of Southeast Asia. The Japanese military, however, had other plans, so that the principles remained propagandist slogans that soon sounded hollow and unconvincing. These military leaders viewed Greater East Asia not as a "Co-Prosperity Sphere" but as a region consisting of satellite states under varying degrees of control. The Japanese armed forces everywhere lived off the land as much as possible, frequently creating severe local shortages of food and supplies. Also, they ruthlessly expropriated whatever foodstuffs and industrial raw materials were needed for the home islands. In return, the Japanese were able to offer little, since their economy was not strong enough to produce war materials and consumer goods.

After the initial honeymoon period, relations between the Japanese and the local nationalists rapidly deteriorated. If the occupation had been prolonged, the Japanese undoubtedly would have been faced with serious uprisings. Fortunately for them, they were forced to pull out during 1945. In doing so, they did every-

The last British troops leave India.

thing possible to create obstacles in the way of a restoration of Western rule. In Indochina they overthrew the Vichy regime and recognized Ho Chi Minh's provisional government; in Indonesia they handed over the administration to the nationalist leader Sukarno; and in many regions they distributed arms to local revolutionary groups.

It is not surprising that within ten years of the Japanese withdrawal, all Southeast Asia was independent. The manner in which the various countries won their freedom varied, depending on the imperial rulers involved. The British, having been forced to face facts in India, were the most realistic in coping with Southeast Asian nationalism. In January 1948 they recognized Burma as an independent republic outside the Commonwealth, and in the next month they granted Ceylon (now Sri Lanka) full dominion status within the Commonwealth. Malayan independence, however, was delayed until February 1957. One reason for the delay was the country's mosaiclike ethnic composition. It included Malayans and Chinese—each a little over 40 percent of the total population—as well as Indians, Pakistanis, and a few Europeans.

The French and the Dutch, whose subjects also demanded independence, were less adjustable and fared much worse. The Dutch were willing to grant Sukarno's nationalists some measure of self-government but not enough to

satisfy their demand. The negotiations broke down, and the Dutch resorted to armed force to reassert their authority. The war dragged on until 1947, when the Dutch finally recognized the independent United States of Indonesia. This legacy of armed conflict embittered the future relations between the two countries. Although a Dutch-Indonesian Union with a common crown existed for a few years, it ended when Sukarno withdrew in 1954. Relations became more strained in the following years because the Dutch refused to yield Netherlands New Guinea to the new republic. In 1957, in retaliation, Indonesia seized more than $1 billion worth of Dutch assets, and, in 1960, it severed diplomatic relations with The Hague. Three years later Sukarno gained control over West Irian, thus liquidating the last remnant of an empire older than most of the British Empire.

The French in Indochina fought longer to retain their colony, but in the end they, too, were forced out. Indochina consisted of three nations: Vietnam, Laos, and Cambodia. Resistance against the restoration of French rule was led by the Viet Minh, or the League for the Independence of Vietnam. Though comprising many elements, the Viet Minh was led by a Communist, Ho Chi Minh, who had lived in Paris, Moscow, and China. In 1945, after war's end, Ho Chi Minh proclaimed the provisional Republic of Vietnam. The French refused to recognize the new regime, and war ensued. Laos and Cambodia were easily reoccupied by the French, but an exhausting struggle dragged on in Vietnam.

With the advent of the cold war, the United States backed up the French financially as a part of the policy of "containment." By 1954, most of northern Vietnam was in the hands of the Viet Minh, and in the same year, the French suffered a major defeat at Dien Bien Phu. The ensuing Geneva settlement recognized the independence of all Vietnam, divided the country temporarily at the seventeenth parallel, and called for supervised elections to be held in 1956 to reunify the country. This settlement in effect gave Ho Chi Minh half the country and the expectation of the other half within two years, since his resistance record had made him a national hero.

To avert this outcome the United States supported in the south the anti-Communist Catholic leader Ngo Dinh Diem. His policies aroused such fierce opposition among the peasants and the powerful Buddhist monks that in 1963 his regime was overthrown and a succession of coups followed until the rise to power, with Washington's support, of Nguyen Cao Ky and then of Nguyen Van Thieu. They were able to hold out in Saigon only because of accelerating American intervention, beginning with money and arms and progressing to "advisers," combat troops, and bombing. Although the bombing far surpassed World War II levels, and although over a half-million American troops were committed, victory remained elusive. The longer the war dragged on, the stronger became an antiwar movement within the United States.

President Nixon sought to neutralize this opposition by conducting secret diplomacy with China and the Soviet Union, culminating in his well-publicized 1972 visits to Peking and Moscow. Finally, a ceasefire was signed in Paris on January 27, 1973, with terms essentially similar to those of the 1954 Geneva accords. Both agreements called for a temporary partition of Vietnam into a Communist North and a non-Communist South, for the determination of the future of South Vietnam by an election, for the neutralization of Laos and Cambodia, for the withdrawal from all Indochina of all foreign troops—French in 1954, American in 1973—and for the supervision of both settlements by a small and largely powerless international committee.

The cost of obtaining in 1973 what the United States had opposed in 1954 was the longest war in American history, 46,000 American deaths, 600,000 civilian and military deaths in South Vietnam, and an estimated 900,000

Ho Chi Minh (1892–1969), center, and advisors meet during the war against the French in 1954.

deaths in North Vietnam. Also, there was incalculable damage to the American social fabric, including G.I. drug addiction, bitter domestic discord, and festering national problems neglected with the financial drain of war expenditures totaling $146 billion. Nor did the 1973 Paris agreement finally end the fighting. The war dragged on until April 1975, when the demoralized Thieu regime collapsed like a house of cards before a North Vietnamese offensive.

IV. TROPICAL AFRICA

In Africa the colonial revolution was even more dramatic than it was in Asia. The triumph of nationalism in the latter area was not altogether unexpected, given ancient cultures and local political organizations that had been agitating for some decades. In Africa, by contrast, the nationalist movements were much younger and weaker. Also the continent had not been jarred and aroused by Japanese occupation. And yet, just as the first postwar decade witnessed the liberation of Asia, so the second witnessed the liberation of Africa. During that decade, no fewer than thirty-one African countries won their independence. The few remaining colonies in turn got rid of foreign rule during the following years. The course of this nationalist awakening differed fundamentally from region to region because of the varying historical backgrounds. Accordingly, the colonial revolution will be considered not on a continentwide basis but individually in tropical Africa, in South Africa, and the Middle East.

Even within tropical Africa alone, there were wide variations. For example, in West Africa a basic factor was the hot and humid climate, which discouraged large-scale European settlement. This made it easier for the home governments to grant independence since there were few European settlers insisting on preserving imperial bonds. This happened on the Gold Coast where the outstanding African political leader was Kwame Nkrumah, who had studied in American and English universities. Returning home, he organized the Convention People's party, which was unique in having a genuine mass basis. So it won a large majority in the 1951 election, and the British government responded by giving Nkrumah an expanding role in the administration of the Gold Coast. By 1957 the colony became the independent Commonwealth country of Ghana.

Once the colonial dam was broken in Ghana, it quickly broke also in the rest of tropical Africa. Most important was the winning of independence in 1960 by Nigeria, the most populous country in Africa. The surrounding colonies of France were also infected with decolonization fever. By the end of 1960 all the for-

Accra, Ghana, with corrugated iron shanties. These are quite a contrast to the city's modern buildings.

Mutesa of Buganda and his court. Noted for his cunning and diplomatic skill and for his autocratic and often cruel conduct, Mutesa was one of the few African rulers who was able to maintain a powerful and successful army and court, which enabled him to deal effectively with Egyptian and British efforts to encroach on his sphere of influence.

mer colonies of French West Africa and French Equatorial Africa had been transformed into independent African countries.

Very different was the course of events in East Africa, commonly referred to as "White Man's Country" because its salubrious climate had attracted numerous European colonists. They soon appropriated the best farming land, causing the landless Africans to organize the *Mau Mau*, a secret terrorist society. In the ensuing war, the colonists strongly supported the government in the campaigns against the *Mau Mau*. The war dragged on with heavy losses on both sides, until the British had to recognize the futility of pursuing simultaneously conciliation in West Africa and bellicosity in the East.

Accordingly the British released from prison the outstanding East African leader, Jomo Kenyatta. Educated in London and author of an anthropological study of his people, Kenyatta had been imprisoned for suspected sympathies with the Mau Mau, though actual collaboration was never proven. Now he was released and, like Nkrumah, he won a majority vote in an election, and became premier of Kenya in 1963. In the same year, Kenya became an independent state amid wild rejoicing in Nairobi for the cherished emancipation.

V. SOUTH AFRICA

Turning from East Africa to South Africa, we find the same pattern of turmoil and violence, and for the same reason: the presence of large numbers of European settlers. Indeed South Africa began as a colony when the Dutch landed settlers at the Cape of Good Hope in 1652. Their purpose was to gather provisions (water, meat and vegetables) needed by Dutch ships on their long voyages around the Cape to the East Indies. With the decline of Holland, the British were able in 1814 to take over the isolated Dutch outpost on the Cape. But the Dutch settlers, or *Boers*, refused to accept the new imperial authority. Instead they trekked northward, where they established the independent republics of the Transvaal and the Orange Free State. With the discovery in these republics of diamonds in 1871 and gold in 1886, the British made moves to annex them. The resulting Boer War (1899–1902) ended with the Boers accepting British sovereignty, but in return they were promised self-rule. This promise was fulfilled in 1909, when South Africa became a self-governing dominion in the British Commonwealth.

A little more than half a century later, in May 1961, South Africa left the Commonwealth to become an independent republic. The main reason for the separation was the clash between South Africa and new African and Asian Commonwealth members, such as Nigeria and India, over the issue of apartheid. Apartheid involved two basic policies: the exclusion of all non-whites from any share in political life; and the confinement of the Africans to separate areas known as Bantustans, or preserves for the "Bantu," as the Africans have been known. These Bantustans comprised only 14 percent of South Africa's land, whereas the Africans made up 73.8 percent of South Africa's total population of 31.7 million (in 1984). The whites, by contrast, made up only 14.8 percent, and the Afrikaners comprised three-fifths of the white minority. The other ethnic elements are the Coloreds, or mixed race (9.3 percent), and the Asians (2.9 percent).

The Afrikaner minority controlled South Africa partly because parliamentary representation was weighted in favor of the predominantly Afrikaner rural areas, and also because many English-speaking whites supported apartheid for economic reasons. This was especially true of white labor, which feared competition in employment from nonwhites if the latter were given equal opportunities. In fact, the first Afrikaner (Nationalist) government was able to take office in 1924 because of support from the South African Labour party.

It is generally agreed that apartheid was not a viable program, either economically or politically. If the Africans were in fact segregated on the proposed Bantustans, the entire economy of South Africa would collapse. Their labor, as well as that of the Coloreds and the Indians, has been essential for agriculture and commerce as well as mining and other industries. In addition, Bantustans had not been able to support the African population, and the government was unwilling to spend the large sums needed to increase their absorptive capacity. Most important of all, the great majority of Africans had no desire to be isolated as separate "tribal" entities. Instead, they demanded a fair share in the united South Africa of which they were an integral part. In this demand they were backed by the growing power of African nationalism in the rest of the continent.

Apartheid was long preserved in South Africa primarily because the government possessed by far the most powerful military forces on the continent of Africa and did not hesitate to use them, as demonstrated in the mass killing of black demonstrators in Sharpeville (1960) and Soweto (1976). This strategy proved workable until the 1980s. Then it was hit by a veritable tidal wave of opposition, external as well as internal, which for the first time threatened the future of apartheid. The opposition consisted of several elements. Most important was the "angry generation"—young Africans who were completely alienated, and who were determined to destroy apartheid whatever the cost. Another important opposition element was the black trade unions, which were given the right to bargain with their employers but which used their organizational strength in the political struggle against apartheid. The resulting turmoil prompted leading businesspeople in South Africa to call publicly for the abolition of apartheid and even to meet with leaders of the banned African National Congress. Likewise, leading South African clergy, such as Nobel Laureate Archbishop Desmond Tutu, rejected apartheid and criticized the government's use of "law and order" and the specter of communism to justify its campaign to crush black political aspirations.

Finally, the Pretoria government for the first time encountered powerful opposition in foreign countries, especially in church, student, and trade union circles. This movement was strong enough to persuade the American government in September 1985 to adopt certain economic sanctions against South Africa, including a ban on loans, on the sale of computers, and on the importation of the Krugerrand gold coin. These pressures proved too much for President Pieter W. Botha, who resigned in 1989.

Whereas Botha's strategy had been to rely on the government's overwhelming military power to impose "grand" apartheid by force on the disfranchised African majority, Botha's successor, Frederick W. de Klerk, stated by contrast that some way must be found to reconcile the African demand for "one person, one vote" with the Afrikaner response of "never." De Klerk began his search dramatically in February 1990 by legalizing the African National Congress and by releasing its leader, Nelson Mandela, from prison where he had been incarcerated for twenty-eight years. De Klerk went further by stating publicly that in the South Africa of the future, all adults must have the vote, though he added that this enfranchisement must be balanced by "checks and balances" to protect minorities, including the hitherto dominant whites.

Despite the powerful ideological and economic forces buttressing apartheid society, it proved possible to achieve a peaceful transition to a new nonracial, democratic South Africa through four-day free elections based on universal suffrage. Held in late April 1994, these elections gave Mandela's African National Congress 62.7 percent of the votes (252 seats in the new parliament); de Klerk's National party received 30.4 percent of the votes (82 seats); Mangosuthu Buthelezi's Zulu-based Inkatha Freedom party got 5.8 percent of the votes; and the Freedom Front led by former army chief Constand Viljoen, which favors a white homeland, received 2.8 percent of the votes. As leader of the largest party, Mandela became the president of South Africa in place of de Klerk, who, as

On May 10, 1994 Nelson Mandela was sworn in as President of South Africa, bringing an end to the apartheid, white minority government that had imprisoned him for twenty-eight years.

leader of the second-ranking party, became deputy president.

The contrast between the new South African state and its apartheid predecessor is evident in its constitution, which states forthrightly, "there is a need to create a new order in which all South Africans will be entitled to a common South African citizenship in a sovereign and democratic constitutional state in which there is equality between men and women and people of all races so that all citizens shall be able to enjoy and exercise their fundamental rights and freedoms."

The significance of this statement is apparent if it is recalled that the apartheid system was constructed by Afrikaners using as their model the Jim Crow segregation laws of the American South. South Africa's citizens transcended this heritage of segregation-apartheid, and they did so at the time when in the United States Rodney King, following his beating and the ensuing rioting and looting in Los Angeles, asked his agonized question, "Can we all get along?"

South Africans cannot claim to have answered that question at this writing, but thanks to inspired leadership from both sides, they have taken a first step toward an answer. Many more steps remain to be taken, because the new South Africa has inherited the most inequitable society in the world. In 1990 the whites controlled 87 percent of the land, and 95 percent of the means of production. Government expenditures for white social needs were in 1990 five to six times higher per capita than the expenditures for the Africans.[1] Not surprisingly, those who are benefiting from such a cozy arrangement are not likely to give it up without fierce resistance.

VI. MIDDLE EAST

Turmoil and violence have been even more prominent in the Middle East than in Africa. However, the basic reason here is not the intrusion of foreign settlers. Rather it is the persistence and clash of millennia—old religions with conflicting claims.

The hostility is especially evident in Palestine which, as noted above, became after World

War I, a cockpit of three conflicting interests: Jewish Zionist aspirations, Arab nationalist demands, and British imperial concerns. The clash of these interests intensified during World War II and Hitler's mass execution of Jews in Europe. The genocide created strong pressures for opening up Palestine to the desperate Jewish survivors. President Truman responded by proposing in August 1945 that 100,000 Jews be allowed to enter the mandate. The Arabs immediately proclaimed their opposition, but the United Nations General Assembly went along by voting on November 29, 1947 in favor of partitioning the mandate. The Jews followed up by proclaiming the establishment the following year of a Jewish state to be called Israel. Truman promptly recognized the new state, but the Arabs equally promptly sent their armies across the borders of Israel.

The course of the war went contrary to general expectations. The Israelis repulsed the invading Arab armies, and then advanced and occupied more territory than had been allotted to them by the United Nations. The Arabs demanded the return of this extra territory, but the Israelis refused, arguing that they had won the land in a war that the Arabs had started, and also that the extra land was needed for Jewish immigrants already pouring in from all over the world.

This issue resulted in deadlock and a long series of attacks and counterattacks. The downward spiral continued until it was checked, at least temporarily, by the signing of an agreement on September 13, 1993, by Prime Minister Yitzhak Rabin of Israel and Yasir Arafat, Chairman of the Palestine Liberation Organization (PLO). The agreement called for the establishment of an elected interim Palestinian council representing Gaza and the West Bank "for a transitional period not exceeding five years, leading to a permanent settlement."

Emotional rallies were staged by opponents and supporters of the agreement. Typical was the impassioned rhetoric of Binyamin Netanyahu, leader of the Likud coalition opposing the pact: "Mr. Rabin, you speak dismissively of 400 Jews in Hebron. I tell you it's not only 400 Jews in Hebron, it's 4,000 years of history that ties us to this land. You say the Bible is not a property deed. But I say the opposite—the Bible is our mandate, the Bible is our deed."[2]

This presentation of political precepts as religious commandments was replicated on the

In 1993 the leaders of Israel and the Palestine Liberation Organization signed a peace accord in Washington, D. C. Here, Prime Minister Yitzhak Rabin of Israel and PLO Chairman Yasir Arafat shake hands as President Bill Clinton of the United States looks on.

other side by assorted fundamentalist Islamic organizations such as the Islamic Resistance Movement or Hamas, the Islamic Holy War, and the Party of God. These groups are more militant than the secular PLO because they reject on religious principle the PLO's willingness to accept the existence of the state of Israel. Hamas states in its charter: "The soil of all Palestine is a wakf (Muslim property) that belongs to the Muslims forever." — a manifest Islamic version of Netanyahu's view of the Bible as "our mandate" "our deed."

The full implication of such blurring of religion and politics was demonstrated on November 4, 1995, when Yigal Amir, a Jewish religion student, shot and killed Prime Minister Rabin in Tel Aviv. Amir repeatedly explained that his objective was to stop Rabin from endangering Israel by implementing the accord with the PLO. "Everything I did was for the God of Israel. . . . The damage that was going to be caused [by the PLO accord] would have been irreversible . . . . I acted alone on God's orders, and I have no regrets."[3]

"No regrets" also was the response of Abir al-Wehaidi, acclaimed as a Palestinian heroine for her participation in an attack that killed a Jewish settler. When asked, following her release from prison, whether she had regrets, she replied: "Of course not. He is a settler and this is occupied land. Their existence here is illegal and this was legal resistance to occupation. There was no other way."[4]

SUGGESTED READINGS

The post–World War II colonial revolutions are analyzed from various viewpoints by R. Emerson, *From Empire to Nation: The Rise to Self Assertion of Asian and African Peoples* (Harvard University, 1960); D. Horowitz, *Imperialism and Revolution* (Penguin, 1969); L. Kaplan, ed., *Revolutions: A Comparative Study* (Vin-tage, 1973); and R. J. Barnet, *Intervention and Revolution* (World, 1968).

For the winning of independence by India, see M. J. Akbar, *Nehru: The Making of India* (Viking, 1989); and V. P. Menon, *The Transfer of Power in India* (Princeton University, 1957). The long Vietnam struggle has stimulated many studies, of which the following are the most recent and noteworthy: General B. Palmer, Jr., *The 25-Year War: America's Role in Vietnam* (Simon & Schuster, 1985); G. M. Kahin, *Intervention: How America Became Involved in Vietnam* (Knopf, 1986); and G. Kolko, *Anatomy of a War: Vietnam, the United States and the Modern Historical Experience* (Pantheon, 1986).

For general surveys of Africa's awakening, see I. Wallerstein, *Africa: The Politics of Independence* (Random House, 1963); P. Gifford and W. R. Louis, eds., *The Transfer of Power in Africa: Decolonization, 1940–1960* (Yale University, 1982); R. Emerson and M. Kilson, eds., *The Political Awakening of Africa* (Prentice Hall, 1965); and R. I. Rotberg and A. A. Mazrui, *Protest and Power in Black Africa* (Oxford University, 1972).

For the rise of nationalism in the Middle East, see G. Lenczowski, ed., *The Political Awakening in the Middle East* (Prentice Hall, 1970); A. Home, *A Savage War of Peace: Algeria 1954–1962* (Viking, 1977); P. J. Vatikiotis, *Nasser and His Generation* (St. Martin's Press, 1978); and A. Hourani, *A History of the Arab Peoples* (Harvard University, 1991). Differing interpretations of the Arab-Israeli conflict are given in T. Draper, *Israel and World Politics* (Viking, 1967); *The Israeli-Arab Reader* (Bantam Books, 1969); E. W. Said, *The Question of Palestine* (Times Books, 1980); M. Benvenisti, *Conflicts and Contradictions* (Villard, 1986); D. K. Shipler, *Arab and Jew: Wounded Spirits in a Promised Land* (Times Books, 1986); Y. Harkabi, *Israel's Fateful Hour* (Harper & Row, 1988); and T. L. Friedman, *From Beirut to Jerusalem* (Farrar, Straus and Giroux, 1989).

NOTES

1. *Los Angeles Times*, July 1, 1990.
2. *New York Times*, October 6, 1995.
3. *New York Times*, November 6, 1995; March 28, 1996.
4. *New York Times*, February 13, 1997.

CHAPTER
43

Grand Alliance, Cold War, and Aftermath

It is not so difficult to keep unity in time of war since there is a joint aim to defeat the common enemy, which is clear to everyone. The difficult task will come after the war when the diverse interests tend to divide the Allies.

Stalin, at Yalta

World War I was followed by revolution in central and eastern Europe and by the threat of revolution in western Europe. World War II stimulated no comparable disturbances. Revolutions did not convulse the Continent, despite the fact that the second war inflicted greater material damage and political dislocation than the first. One reason was the sheer fatigue of the civilian populations. For six years they had been subjected to constant bombardment from the air; to wide-ranging ground operations; and to mass uprooting through flight, forced labor, or imprisonment. More than 15 million soldiers were killed, as well as 10 million civilians, including 6 million Jews. This was approximately twice the casualties and thirteen times the material damage of World War I.

Those who survived had experienced unprecedented privation and dislocation. In the first three-and-a-half years of the war alone, 30 million Europeans had fled or were driven from their original homes. At the end of the hostilities, Allied armies and international relief agencies returned more than 12 million "displaced persons" to their homes, yet there still remained a hard core of more than a million—mostly anti-Communists from eastern Europe—who refused to go home. The wholesale reshuffling of peoples, together with cold, hunger, and disease, left most Europeans too exhausted and dispirited to think of revolution.

Equally decisive was the occupation of all Europe by the forces of the victorious Allies. The Red Army, no less than the British and the American, stamped out opposition and disorder. A revolution in the social structure did occur in eastern Europe, but it was an imposed revolution directed from Moscow. The Communist parties throughout Europe were obedient instruments of Soviet foreign policy rather than fomenters of indigenous revolutions. Thus, the Soviet Union, Britain, and the United States effectively controlled developments in Europe after the downfall of Hitler. It was these powers that were responsible for the policies and events that gradually disrupted the wartime Grand Alliance and brought on the cold war.

I. WARTIME UNITY

During the war years, the Western powers and the Soviet Union were forced to present a common front against the menace of a mortal enemy. On the very day of Hitler's invasion of Russia, Churchill proclaimed, "The Russian danger is. . . our danger, and the danger of the United States, just as the cause of any Russian fighting for his hearth and home is the cause of free men and free peoples in every quarter of the globe."[1]

Two months later, on August 14, 1941, Churchill and Roosevelt issued their Atlantic Charter, in which they set forth in idealistic terms their common aims and principles. More specific expressions of Allied cooperation were the twenty-year mutual-aid pact signed by Great Britain and the Soviet Union in May 1942 and the American-Russian Lend-Lease Agreement of the following month. Another manifestation of cooperation was the decision of the Soviets in May 1943 to abolish the Communist International, which they had established in 1919 to overthrow world capitalism. In view of their friendly relations with the Western powers, the Soviets now decided that the Comintern had outlived its usefulness. However, this decision meant little in practice because the top Comintern officials had been transferred to the Party Secretariat, where they continued to function. Still another result of Allied wartime cooperation was the establishment in November 1943 of the UN Relief and Rehabilitation Administration (UNRRA). UNRRA followed in the wake of the armed forces and provided relief of all kinds to the liberated countries until the new national administrations could assume responsibility. It began work in the spring of 1944, and, by the time of its dissolution in September 1948, it had

distributed 22 million tons of supplies including food, clothing, and medicines, mostly of American origin. Its main operations were in Greece, Yugoslavia, Poland, Czechoslovakia, Austria, and Italy. Without its contributions the deprivation and distress in postwar Europe would have been substantially worse than it was.

As the war neared its end, the cooperation forced by mutual danger began to falter. The partners were more and more inclined to sacrifice unity for what they considered to be their postwar national interests. Thus with peace, the Grand Alliance was rent by discord and, within two or three years, was replaced by a cold war that constantly threatened to become hot.

The breakup of the Grand Alliance was hastened by the failure of the Allied leaders during the war years to make serious plans for the postwar settlement. By the fall of 1944, political issues no longer could be evaded. The advance of the Red Army up the Danube valley was forcing the Germans to evacuate the Balkan peninsula, and the Communist-led resistance fighters were filling in the vacuum. The prospect of a Communist-dominated Balkans caused Churchill, in October 1944, to meet with Stalin in Moscow. These two leaders quickly agreed on spheres of influence in the disputed peninsula. Bulgaria and Rumania were to be in the Soviet sphere, Greece in the British, and Yugoslavia a buffer zone under joint British-Soviet influence. Thus Churchill was forced, by the unfavorable strategic situation, to accept Soviet predominance in the northern Balkans in order to preserve Britain's traditional primacy in Greece.

At the same time that Churchill was bargaining with Stalin in Moscow, British troops were beginning to land in Greece. They advanced northward on the heels of the retreating Germans but found the Greek resistance forces preceding them in all the towns and cities. No opposition was offered by these forces, led by disciplined Communists who obediently followed the current Kremlin line. They welcomed the small British units, although, had they wished, they could have easily barred them at that time just as the nationalist-minded Tito was doing in Yugoslavia.

Despite the compliance of the Greek resistance forces, the fact remained that they were the preponderant military power in the country

CHURCHILL AND STALIN DIVIDE THE BALKANS

*Prime Minister Winston Churchill and Communist Party Secretary Joseph Stalin met in Moscow the evening of October 9, 1944. Churchill has left the following colorful account of how the two men divided the Balkan peninsula between them into British and Russian spheres of influence.**

The moment was apt for business, so I said, "Let us settle about our affairs in the Balkans. Your armies are in Rumania and Bulgaria. We have interests, missions and agents there. Don't let us get at cross-purposes in small ways. So far as Britain and Russia are concerned, how would it do for you to have ninety per cent predominance in Rumania, for us to have ninety per cent of the say in Greece, and go fifty-fifty about Yugoslavia?" While this was being translated I wrote out on a half-sheet of paper:

Rumania

  Russia 90%

  The others   10%

Greece

  Great Britain   90%

    (in accord with U.S.A.)

  Russia 10%

Yugoslavia	50–50%
Hungary	50–50%
Bulgaria	
Russia	75%
The others	25%

I pushed this across to Stalin who had by then heard the translation. There was a slight pause. Then he took his blue pencil and made a large tick upon it, and passed it back to us. It was all settled in no more time than it takes to set it down. . . .

After this there was a long silence. The pencilled paper lay in the centre of the table. At length I said, "Might it not be thought rather cynical if it seemed we had disposed of these issues, so fateful to millions of people, in such an off-hand manner? Let us burn the paper." "No, you keep it," said Stalin.

*W.S. Churchill, *The Second World War: Triumph and Tragedy* (Houghton Mifflin, 1953), pp.227–228.

as the Germans withdrew. This was an intolerable situation for Churchill. To ensure the British dominance in Greece that he and Stalin had agreed on in Moscow, it was essential to disarm the resistance forces and transfer state power to the royal Greek government-in-exile that he favored. Various disarmament formulas were proposed, but none satisfied both sides. This dispute precipitated an armed clash that developed into the bitter and bloody Battle of Athens. British and Indian troops were rushed in from Italy, and after a month of fighting the resistance forces withdrew from the Athens area.

On February 12, a peace agreement (the Varkiza Pact) was signed by which the resistance troops surrendered their arms in return for a promise of elections and a plebiscite on the question of the return of the king. Thus

Churchill secured the sphere allotted to him in Moscow: Greece was to be on the side of the West during the postwar years. Equally significant was Stalin's eloquent silence while Churchill was dispersing the leftist resistance fighters. The British-Soviet deal on the Balkans was in operation and was working.

The fighting in Athens had barely ceased when, in February 1945, Roosevelt, Churchill, and Stalin met at Yalta for the last of their wartime conferences. With the Allied armies converging on Germany from all sides, the problems of a postwar settlement now had to be considered specifically and realistically. Little difficulty was encountered in reaching an agreement on the Far East. Stalin agreed to declare war against Japan within sixty days after the end of hostilities in Europe. In return, the USSR was to regain the Kuril Islands and also the concessions and territories lost to Japan in 1905. On Germany, the conference postponed decisions about most issues, including reparations and frontiers.

It was agreed, however, that the country should be divided into four occupation zones (including one for France) under an Allied Control Council. Berlin, located within the Soviet zone, was to be occupied and administered jointly.

Most of the negotiating at Yalta had to do with the newly liberated countries in eastern Europe. Stalin was in a strong position in this area, for his armies had done the liberating and were in actual occupation. Given this context, the agreements that were made on eastern Europe were, on paper, satisfactory from the Western viewpoint. The USSR was to receive the Polish territory east of a modified Curzon Line, which had been drawn after World War I but subsequently ignored. Poland was to be compensated with territory in east Germany. Concerning the Polish and Yugoslav governments, Stalin agreed that the Communist regimes already established under Soviet auspices should be broadened by the admission of representatives from the West-oriented governments-in-

"The Big Three"—Stalin, Roosevelt, and Churchill—meet for the last time at Yalta, 1945.

exile. The latter were understandably apprehensive about this arrangement, which left the Red Army and the Communist governments in physical and legal control. Their doubts were met, in theory, by a broad statement of policy known as the Yalta Declaration on Liberated Europe. This committed the three powers to assist the liberated peoples of Europe "to form interim governmental authorities broadly representative of all democratic elements in the population and pledged to the earliest possible establishment through free elections of governments responsive to the will of the people. . . ."

Taken at face value, this declaration represented a substantial concession on the part of Stalin. Despite his domination of eastern Europe, he had consented to free elections that might well bring anti-Soviet governments to office. The substance of this concession, however, was negligible. The declaration turned out to be meaningless and was a constant source of friction, because it was interpreted very differently by the various signatories. The United States interpreted it literally—that is, free elections and no spheres of influence in eastern Europe. The United States was free to take this position because it was not bound by the agreement reached by Churchill and Stalin in Moscow the previous October.

Stalin, by contrast, clung to the Moscow agreement and regarded the declaration as mere window dressing. He had scrupulously kept quiet while the British crushed the Greek resistance forces. In return, Stalin expected the Western powers to respect his primacy in the northern Balkans. He was surprised and outraged when the British gradually joined the Americans in demanding strict enforcement of the declaration. Stalin refused to budge on this point, regarding "friendly" governments in eastern Europe as prerequisite for Soviet security. He made this clear at the next three-power conference at Potsdam (July–August 1945), where the American secretary of state, James Byrnes, demanded freely elected governments in eastern Europe. "A freely elected government in any of these countries," responded Stalin, "would be anti-Soviet and that we cannot allow."[2] The contradiction between "friendly" and "freely elected" governments was one of the main causes for the disruption of the Grand Alliance in the months to come.

Despite the seeds of discord at Yalta, the conference was generally welcomed and interpreted as the climax of the wartime cooperation of the allies. Cooperation was shown again with the organization of the United Nations (UN). The final charter was signed by the representa-

*The United Nations
Security Council in session.*

tives of fifty nations at the conclusion of a conference held in San Francisco from April to June 1945. By 1990 UN membership had more than tripled. Some of the newcomers were wartime enemies or neutrals, but the majority were newly independent states in Asia and Africa. The UN, like its predecessor, the League of Nations, was set up to accomplish two basic tasks: to preserve peace and security and to cope with international economic, social, and cultural problems. Also like the league, the UN was established as an association of sovereign states. The charter specified that the organization might not "intervene in matters which are essentially within the domestic jurisdiction of any state."

The task of maintaining peace was entrusted primarily to a Security Council made up of five permanent members—the United States, the Soviet Union, Britain, France, and China—and six other members elected for two-year terms by the General Assembly on the recommendation of the council. In all substantive matters the unanimous vote of the permanent members was required (together with the vote of two of the nonpermanent members), for it was recognized that peace could be maintained only if the great powers were in agreement.

The second task of the UN—the fight against hunger and disease and ignorance—was entrusted to the Economic and Social Council. It established programs designed to provide more food for the half of the world's people who were hungry, cure the one-eighth of the world's population that had malaria, save the 40 percent of the children who died before the end of their first year, and teach the 50 percent of the world's adults who were illiterate to read and write.

Like the League of Nations, the UN has been quite successful in these various nonpolitical activities. But again like the League, the UN has had a spotty record in its main job of keeping the peace. It has helped to prevent all-out war between the great powers by providing a medium for maintaining rapport. It has stopped fighting in areas such as Indonesia and Kashmir, where vital interests of the major powers were not involved. But it was not able to forestall a series of local, or "brush-fire," wars in Korea, Algeria, the Middle East, and Vietnam. Nor was there any consultation of the UN during the highly dangerous Cuban crisis of 1962 or the prolonged Vietnam agony. The basic difficulty of the UN, as of the League, is that in a world of sovereign states it can provide machinery for settling disputes but cannot compel use of that machinery.

Two months after the establishment of the UN, Japan surrendered and the war in the Far East was over. The victorious Allies could now devote full attention to the making of peace. Their foreign ministers on February 10, 1947, signed peace treaties with Italy, Rumania, Hungary, Bulgaria, and Finland. All the treaties imposed reparations on the defeated countries, limited their armed forces, and redrew their frontiers.

II. COLD WAR IN EUROPE

The peace treaties were followed by growing dissension between East and West. This, in turn, may be explained to a large degree by the immense power vacuums in Europe and Asia following the collapse of the German and Japanese empires. These vacuums required some fundamental readjustments of power relationships. Under the best of circumstances such readjustments are difficult to arrange, as evidenced by the crises following the Napoleonic Wars and World War I. Now, after World War II, the process of readjustment was made even more complicated and perilous by the addition of ideological issues to the traditional power struggle. The most dramatic manifestation of the oncoming cold war was President Truman's intervention in the Greek Civil War in March 1947. Communist-led guerrillas had appeared the preceding fall in the mountains of northern Greece. One reason for the renewed civil strife was the wretched economic condition that drove many impoverished peasants to the rebel ranks. Another was the deteriorating international situation, which led the Soviet bloc to incite and aid the guerrillas against the British-supported Athens government.

These circumstances engendered considerable popular support for the insurrection, which spread from the northern mountains to the Peloponnesus and the larger islands. The likelihood for suppressing the revolt appeared bleak, so that Greece faced the prospect of prolonged civil war with the possibility of an eventual Communist victory. President Truman met the emergency by proclaiming the doctrine named after him. Stating that "the very existence of the Greek state is today threatened," he requested Congress to appropriate $400 million for aid to Greece and Turkey. Thus Britain surrendered its century-old primacy in Greece. The United States assumed the responsibility for preventing the extension of Communist influence in the eastern Mediterranean.

The task proved more expensive than anticipated. The United States between March 1947 and June 1949 spent approximately $400 million for military purposes and $300 million for economic aid. Even with this lavish support, both the 1947 and 1948 campaigns were inconclusive. In 1949 the balance shifted decisively in favor of the Athens government. The Tito-Stalin split led Marshal Tito to close the Yugoslav border and stop all aid to the guerrillas who had sided with Stalin. At the same time the Athens armies were being retrained by American officers to fight a mobile offensive war instead of garrisoning key towns and communication routes. Thus, in the fall of 1949 the national armies were able to drive the guerrillas from their mountain strongholds and to reach and seal the northern frontiers.

The counterpart to the Truman Doctrine in the economic sphere was the European Recovery Program, commonly known as the Marshall Plan. By the time of its termination on December 31, 1951, a total of $12.5 billion had been spent in support of Marshall Plan operations. This extraordinary investment, together with the human and material resources of Europe, brought about a rapid recovery that raised production and living standards to above prewar levels. But from the viewpoint of East-West relations, the Marshall Plan marked the final step toward the cold war. In January 1949, Moscow established the Council for Mutual Economic Assistance (Molotov Plan) as the Eastern counterpart to the Marshall Plan.

Thus the line was drawn between the Communist and Western worlds. The cold war now was in full sway, and for the next half-decade one crisis followed closely on another. The moves and countermoves culminated in the establishment of the two confrontational military alliances: the North Atlantic Treaty Organization, or NATO (April 4, 1949), which included the United States, Canada, and western European states, and the Warsaw Pact (May, 1955), comprising the Soviet Union and its eastern European allies. Thus Europe, as well as Germany, was cut in two by the cold war.

President Harry Truman greets Secretary of State George Marshall returning from Europe. Truman and Marshall were the architects of American foreign policy during the early years of the Cold War.

III. COLD WAR IN THE FAR EAST

In 1950, the focus of the cold war shifted from Europe to the Far East. By this time a balance had been reached in Europe between East and West. But in the Far East the balance was upset by the triumph of the Communists in China. Just as the Bolshevik Revolution was the outstanding byproduct of World War I, so the Chinese Communist Revolution was the outstanding byproduct of World War II.

Chiang Kai-shek had become the head of the Chinese government in 1928, but from the outset his Kuomintang regime was threatened by two mortal enemies, the Communists within and the Japanese without. During World War II his position became particularly difficult.

Japan's surrender in August 1945 set off a wild scramble by the Nationalists and Commu-

Chiang Kai-shek (1887–1975) as a young revolutionary officer.

nists to take over the Japanese-occupied parts of China. The Communists issued orders to their troops to take over the areas held by the Japanese. Chiang Kai-shek promptly canceled these orders and insisted that the Communists make no move without instructions from him. He was ignored, and clashes occurred between Communist and Kuomintang forces. The Communists occupied the countryside around the major cities. They were helped by the Russians, who turned over to them the arms the Japanese had surrendered in Manchuria. The Nationalists, aided by the transportation services of the U.S. Navy and Air Force, won all the main cities.

The Communist armies swept down from Manchuria through the major cities of North China. By April 1949 they were crossing the Yangtze and fanning out over south China. The Communist steamroller advanced even more rapidly in the south than in the north. By the end of 1949 it had overrun all of mainland China. Chiang fled to the island of Taiwan, and on October 1, 1949, in Peking, the Communist leader, Mao Tse-tung, proclaimed the People's Republic of China.

In the Far East, as in Europe, World War II was followed by the cold war. But in the Far East the cold war became hot when in 1950 fighting broke out in Korea, with North Korean troops invading the South.

The course of the Korean War fell into two phases—the first before, and the second after, the Chinese intervention. The first phase began with the headlong rush of the North Korean forces down the length of the peninsula to within fifty miles of the port of Pusan at the southern tip. Then on September 14, 1950, an American army landed at Inchon, far up the coast near the thirty-eighth parallel, and in twelve days retook the South Korean capital, Seoul. The North Koreans, their communications severed, fell back as precipitously as they had advanced. By the end of September the UN forces had reached the thirty-eighth parallel.

The question now was whether to cross or not to cross. The issue was transferred to the General Assembly, because the Soviet Union, with its veto power, had returned to the Security Council. On October 7, 1950, the assembly

United Nations forces in Korea fought the weather as well as communist North Koreans and Chinese. Baking summer heat alternated with fierce winters. Snow and cold were a major help to the Chinese when they surprised United States troops in November 1950 and drove the American forces southward.

resolved that "all constituent acts be taken. . . for the establishment of a unified, independent, and democratic government in the sovereign state of Korea." The next day American forces crossed the thirty-eighth parallel and quickly occupied Pyongyang, the North Korean capital. By November 22 they reached the Yalu River, the boundary line between Korea and the Chinese province of Manchuria.

At this point the second phase of the Korean War began with a massive attack by Chinese "volunteers" supported by Soviet-made jets. The Chinese drove southward rapidly in what looked like a repetition of the first phase of the war. Early in January 1951 they retook Seoul, but the UN forces now recovered and held their ground.

In March, Seoul once more changed hands, and by June the battle line ran roughly along the thirty-eighth parallel.

By mid-1951 it was apparent that a stalemate prevailed at the front. After two years of stormy and often-interrupted negotiations, an armistice agreement was concluded on July 27, 1953. The terms reflected the military stalemate. The line of partition between North and South Korea remained roughly where it had been before the war. The Western powers had successfully contained communism in Korea and had vindicated the authority of the United Nations. The Chinese had secured North Korea as a Communist buffer state between Manchuria and Western influences. And meanwhile, most of the

Korean countryside had been laid waste and about 10 percent of the Korean people had been killed.

IV. END OF THE COLD WAR

At the end of World War II, both western and eastern Europe were forced to turn for support to the two new superpowers, the United States and the Soviet Union. In military affairs western Europe depended on the American-organized NATO, and eastern Europe depended on the Soviet-organized Warsaw Pact. In economic matters western Europe relied on the Marshall Plan financed by the United States, and eastern Europe depended on the Council for Mutual Economic Assistance, which theoretically funneled in Soviet aid, though in practice it did the opposite.

The primacy of Washington and Moscow was accepted because their support was needed in the face of the pressures produced by the cold war. But after building up for several years, the cold war began to subside in 1953. One reason was the death in April 1953 of Joseph Stalin, who had become increasingly paranoid and inflexible in his later years. The younger men who succeeded him were ready for a relaxation of both the cold war abroad and the dictatorship at home. At the same time, the new Eisenhower administration was replacing that of Truman in the United States. This also contributed to the international "thaw," for Eisenhower was able to make a compromise peace in Korea, whereas domestic political considerations would have made this extremely difficult for Truman. Thus the Korean War was ended in July 1953, eliminating the most serious single source of international tension.

The following month the Soviet government announced that it also possessed the secret of the hydrogen bomb. Paradoxically, this strengthened the movement for a settlement. It was known that the hydrogen bomb exploded by the United States at Bikini was 750 times more powerful than the Hiroshima atomic bomb, which had killed 78,000 people. All but the most fanatic cold warriors sensed that war

After the discovery of Soviet missiles in Cuba, President Kennedy and his advisors held long, agonizing meetings to consider possible responses. This picture shows the president bending over the table (second from the right) and his brother, Attorney General Robert Kennedy, pacing on the left.

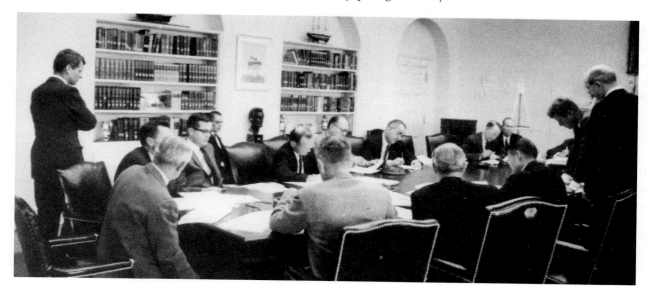

was no longer a feasible instrument of national policy.

The deterring effect of the H-bomb was manifested during the 1962 Cuban crisis, precipitated when American air reconnaissance revealed that Soviet missile bases were under construction in Cuba and that a large part of the United States soon would be within range. In a dramatic broadcast on October 22, 1962, President Kennedy proclaimed a "quarantine" to halt ships carrying offensive weapons to Cuba and demanded the removal of the Soviet strategic missiles. But he did not demand the removal of the Castro regime or even of the Cuban defense missiles. It was clear that neither country wanted war when Soviet vessels bound for Cuba altered course and the United States permitted a Soviet tanker to proceed when satisfied that it carried no offensive weapons. Finally, on October 28, Khrushchev announced that he had ordered Soviet missiles withdrawn and all Soviet bases in Cuba dismantled under UN inspection. In return, the United States ended its blockade and pledged not to invade Cuba.

Although the Cuban crisis ended peaceably, it was a very near thing—so near that it stimulated several agreements for the limitation of nuclear weapons: controls on tests of nuclear weapons (1963), prohibition of nuclear weapons in space (1967), a nonnuclear zone in Latin America (1967), nonproliferation of nuclear weapons beyond the nations already possessing them (1968), prohibition of nuclear weapons on the seabed (1971), prohibition of the use of biological weapons (1971), and the first Western-Soviet Strategic Arms Limitation Treaty (1972). These agreements together helped to lessen substantially the international tensions of the cold war.

The Cuban missile crisis was a narrow squeak, narrower than a scared world realized at the time. This became clear to American and Soviet officials who met in Moscow a quarter-century later, in January 1989, to review and reflect on what had happened. Robert S. McNamara, secretary of defense at the time of the crisis, reached this conclusion from the Moscow discussions:

The missile crisis is replete with examples of misinformation, misjudgment, miscalculation. . . .

This must lead to the conclusion that, insofar as it is achievable, we must seek to return to a nonnuclear world.[3]

During the 1960s and 1970s the cold war slowly and painfully thawed. During the 1980s, the cold war suddenly and unexpectedly ended. The reason was simple and dramatic. It takes two to wage a cold war, and the two after the second world war were the American and Soviet superpowers. But in the 1980s the Soviet superpower weakened rapidly to the point of actual disintegration. An astonished world witnessed the disappearance of the USSR from our world map, replaced by the Commonwealth of Independent States (CIS). How and why the Soviet Union gave way to the Commonwealth will be analyzed in the following chapter.

As startling as the breakup of the Soviet Union was the breakup of the Soviet-Chinese alliance. When the victorious Chinese Communists established the People's Republic in 1949, they were promptly recognized by the Soviet Union. A score of other countries, including Britain and India, did likewise. The United States, however, continued to treat Chiang Kai-shek's exiled regime in Taiwan as the legal government of China. Peking therefore turned to

Mao Tse-tung chatting with Soviet premier Nikita Krushchev in Moscow in 1958. By this time the Sino-Soviet alliance was already beginning to fray.

Moscow and, in 1950, signed a thirty-year treaty of "friendship, alliance, and mutual assistance." Under the terms of the treaty, the Soviet Union helped China to build a large modern army and to begin an ambitious program of industrialization.

The Soviet-Chinese alliance began to show signs of disruption in the late 1950s. The roots of this dramatic and fateful rift in the Communist world appear to be partly a conflict of national interests and partly a conflict of ideologies. The national issues arose from traditional material considerations such as frontier demarcation. The 2,000-mile frontier separating the two countries has been drawn in precise detail in Soviet maps. On Chinese maps certain sections have been depicted as "undemarcated," including the eastern margins of the Pamir highlands, some islands at the confluence of the Amur and Ussuri rivers, and almost the entire frontier with Mongolia. These territories, formerly a part of the Chinese Empire, were annexed by tsarist Russia during the nineteenth century and now are claimed by Communist China. Many armed clashes have occurred along these disputed frontiers.

At the outset of the Soviet-Chinese dispute it appeared that ideological issues were more important than frontier lines. Years of revolutionary struggle in China had stimulated a new vision of human and social relations—a vision of an egalitarian Communist order in which the individual is motivated by the desire for social service rather than personal gain. Thus, although the Soviet-type Five-Year Plans were successful in furthering industrialization and raising productivity, Mao was unwilling to accept the increasing income differentiation and bureaucratic elitism on which these plans were based. This explains the Great Leap Forward of 1958 and the Cultural Revolution of 1966, with their slogans such as "organization without bureaucracy" and "serve the people." The Soviets regarded this as utopian romanticism doomed to failure, which was one reason why they stopped their aid to Mao.

Since Mao's death in 1976 the ideological differences between China and the Soviet Union (now the Commonwealth of Independent States —CIS) have become blurred. Mao's successors launched a "modernization" drive, which not only included measures hitherto denounced as "revisionist" but also went much further down the revisionist path toward "market socialism." These measures included restoring family farms in place of communes; substituting individual managers for revolutionary committees in factories; rewarding good workers and penalizing poor ones; and moving away from industrial self-reliance and toward mass importation of factories and technologies.

This post-Mao program has changed fundamentally the cold war world. No longer are the Russian and Chinese Communist giants close allies in a global feud with the capitalist West. Rather, they are competing with each other in a search for practical economic strategies to satisfy the rising consumer expectations of their respective peoples. In this way the cold war world is giving way to a very different world that is taking shape gradually in the 1990s and into the twenty-first century.

SUGGESTED READINGS

World War II diplomacy and the ensuing cold war have been the subject of vigorous debate by historians. The traditional view, holding the Soviet Union primarily responsible for the cold war, is set forth by H. Thomas, *Armed Truce: The Beginnings of the Cold War 1945–6* (Atheneum, 1987); R. J. Maddox, *The New Left and the Origins of the Cold War* (Princeton University, 1973); and J. L. Gaddis, *The United States and the Origins of the Cold War, 1941–1947* (Columbia University, 1973). The revisionist interpretation that holds the West responsible, or more so, than the Soviet Union, was first propounded in detail by D. F. Fleming, *The Cold War and Its Origins, 1917–1960*, 2 vols. (George Allen & Unwin, 1961). This thesis has been elaborated by other writers such as G. Kolko, *The Politics of War: The World and U.S. Foreign Policy 1943–1945* (Random House, 1969); W. La Feber, *America, Russia and the Cold War* (John Wiley, 1968); T. G. Paterson, ed., *Cold War Critics: Alternatives to American Policy in the Truman Years* (Quadrangle Books, 1972); N. D. Houghton, ed., *Struggle against History: U.S. Foreign Policy in an Age of Revolution* (Simon & Schuster, 1972); and B. A. Weisberger, *Cold War, Cold Peace: The United States and Russia since 1945* (Houghton Mifflin, 1984). For the Truman Doctrine and the Near East, see B. Kuniholm, *The Origins of the Cold*

War in the Near East (Princeton University, 1980); and L. S. Wittner, *American Intervention in Greece* (Columbia University, 1982). Finally, American-Soviet relations since 1966 are examined by R. L. Garthoff, *Detente and Confrontation: American Soviet Relations from Nixon to Reagan* (Brookings, 1985).

Varying interpretations are available also concerning Far Eastern diplomacy in works such as Y. Nagai and A. Iriye, *The Origins of the Cold War in Asia* (Columbia University, 1977); Tang Tsou, *America's Failure in China 1941–50* (University of Chicago, 1964); W. I. Cohen, *America's Response to China* (John Wiley, 1971); B. Cumings, *The Origins of the Korean War* (Princeton University, 1984); and J. Halliday and B. Cumings, *Korea: The Unknown War* (Pantheon, 1988).

On the ending of global bipolarism, see W. S. Vucinich, ed., *At the Brink of War and Peace: The Tito-Stalin Split in a Historic Perspective* (Columbia University, 1982); W. G. Rosenberg and M. B. Young, *Transforming Russia and China: Revolutionary Struggle in the Twentieth Century* (Oxford University, 1982); and R. J. Barnet, *The Alliance: America, Europe and Japan* (Simon & Schuster, 1983).

NOTES

1. W. S. Churchill, *The Second World War: The Grand Alliance* (Houghton Mifflin, 1950), p. 373.
2. P. E. Mosely, "Face to Face with Russia," *Headline Series*, No. 70 (July-August 1948), p. 23.
3. *New York Times*, October 26, 1989.

CHAPTER 4

Second Industrial Revolution: Global Repercussions

We are amidst the biggest technological revolution men have known, far more intimate in the tone of our daily lives, and of course far quicker, either than the agricultural transformation in Neolithic times, or the early industrial revolution. . .

C. P. Snow, 1966

The major problems of our day confront all human beings in all societies. In 1985, about $1 trillion was invested in armaments in a desperate search for security. Yet the more money spent, the greater the insecurity. By far the largest hoards of arms were accumulated by the two superpowers of the time, yet Americans and Soviets were no more secure than the peoples of tiny Switzerland or Sri Lanka. Likewise, unemployment and poverty are scourges usually associated with underdeveloped Third World countries, but today they are afflicting millions in western Europe and North America as well as in Asia, Africa, and Latin America. Ecological deterioration is normally attributed to shortsighted policies of Third World countries that allow their tropical forests to be denuded and their deserts to advance into arable lands. Yet the topsoils of the American Midwest continue to erode as in dust-bowl days; parts of Cal-

ifornia's fertile Central Valley are becoming salt deserts; and in the northeastern United States, eastern Canada, and northern Europe, acid rain is turning forests brown and lakes a lifeless blue, not to mention the corrosion of famous monuments in London, Paris, and Cologne.

What is responsible for these afflictions ravaging all societies in all parts of the globe? Many forces are at work, but probably most basic is the second industrial revolution that began during World War II. We noted in Chapter 26 how decisive was the impact of the first industrial revolution on both European and non-European lands. Much deeper, swifter, and all-pervasive is the impact of today's second industrial revolution. In this chapter we shall examine the origin and nature of the new industrial revolution and then analyze its impact on various regions of the world, and on various aspects of our lives.

I. SECOND INDUSTRIAL REVOLUTION: ORIGINS AND NATURE

World War II stimulated several technical break-throughs of such magnitude and significance that they warrant classification as the second industrial revolution.

Example: Nuclear Energy. The first industrial revolution created new energy sources such as steam power, electricity, and the gasoline engine. During World War II an explosion on the desert floor of New Mexico marked the harnessing of the power of the atom. This power was used first for military purposes with the dropping of atom bombs on Hiroshima and Nagasaki. Today it is used for numerous other purposes, such as nuclear powered ships, biomedical research, medical diagnosis and therapy, and nuclear power plants.

Example: Labor-Replacing Machines. Whereas the first industrial revolution created labor-saving machines, the second is creating labor-replacing machines. The roots of these new machines go back to Britain's World War II anti-aircraft batteries, which were filled with computers—a combination of electric memory and programs that told the machine how to process the stored data. Thanks to microconductors, or silicon chips, computers now are much smaller and faster. They have become the backbone of modern economies, being used in power stations, business offices, supermarket checkout stands, textile mills, telephone switching systems, and factory production lines. They are the "brains" in robots, which are used today for welding and painting and moving materials and which will be used tomorrow for chores in homes.

Example: Space Science. When the Germans bombarded London with their V-2 rockets, they were using arms that led to the space age a few years later. On October 4, 1957, the Soviets shot Sputnik I into orbit around the earth. For the first time human beings had burst the bonds of gravity and were free to explore outer space. No one can foresee precisely what the repercussions will be. Outer space offers many advantages for manufacturers because of the absence of gravity and the limitless supply of vacuum and of super-high and super-low temperatures. Hence projects are now under way for automated pharmaceutical space factories producing vaccines and pure tissue cultures for enzymes, automated space factories creating near-perfect crystals for use in electronic circuits, and giant solar collectors bearing energy from the sun to earth stations via microwave. More futuristic are the speculations of scientists such as American physicist Gerald K. O'Neill and Soviet astrophysicist Iosif S. Shklovsky, who foresee the construction in outer space of huge platforms or islands where eventually more humans might live than on earth.

Example: Genetic Engineering. Scientists discovered in 1953 the structure of DNA (deoxyribonucleic acid), the chemical that carries the genetic code of all living things. Since learning how to read the messages of genes through DNA, scientists have also learned how to write their own genetic messages by cutting apart and splicing the genes, by making animal and human genes grow in bacteria, and even by manufacturing totally new and artificial genes in the test tube. Thus scientists now can read genetic codes, modify them, and create new ones. Humans have been tampering with genes since they began domesticating plants and animals about ten thousand years ago. But now the tampering is direct and instantaneous. Instead of choosing among plants and animals through many generations, scientists now choose among individual genes and manipulate them. Such genetic engineering opens up possibilities for a new agricultural revolution. In the field of medicine, genetic engineering already has created insulin and growth hormone as well as several new vaccines, including one against the highly infectious hoof-and-mouth disease of cattle.

Example: Information Revolution. This is a revolution of two parts—accumulating information and distributing information. The rate at which knowledge is being accumulated today is unprecedented and explosive. The amount of scientific information alone that is being published around the world every twenty-four hours would fill seven complete twenty-four-volume sets of the *Encyclopaedia Britannica.* Equally unprecedented and explosive is the rate at

Scientists are learning more and more about the genetic factors that prompt the eventual development of serious diseases. If offered the opportunity, would you want to undergo a genetic screening that would predict the long-term future of your own health?

which information can be stored and retrieved by computers and also distributed throughout the world at the speed of light, especially via satellites. Any person, in any country, can receive this information through a newspaper, magazine, radio, television set, or computer.

Example: New Agricultural Revolution. The first industrial revolution was accompanied by an agricultural revolution (Chapter 27, Section IV) characterized by enclosures, improved seeds, scientific stock breeding, and new agricultural machinery. The second industrial revolution also has been accompanied by an agricultural revolution ("green revolution") stimulated by the steep rise in the demand and prices for farm products during World War II. New hybrid varieties of major cereals greatly increased crop yields when used in conjunction with irrigation, fertilizers, and pesticides. Because of genetic engineering the first "green revolution" is being followed in the 1990s by a second, in which scientists are mixing and matching genetic materials from different organisms. Just as this technique has yielded useful substances such as human insulin and interferon, so it is also being applied to agriculture to produce plants that can grow in salty or dry soils; that will make their own nitrogen fertilizers; that are less susceptible to diseases caused by viruses, bacteria, fungi, and worms;

and that will yield larger and more nutritious crops. This is one reason why food output in the Third World since World War II has increased more than has the population growth.

The first industrial revolution had a profound impact on the European continent, where it originated, and also on the rest of the globe. So it is now with the second industrial revolution. But since this revolution is infinitely more powerful and dynamic, its impact everywhere is correspondingly more disruptive and encompassing.

II. IMPACT ON THE DEVELOPED FIRST WORLD

Postwar Prosperity and Recession

The quarter-century after World War II was the golden age of capitalism. World industry during those years grew at the unprecedented annual rate of 5.6 percent, and world trade at 7.3 percent. The prolonged boom was caused by several factors, including the need to make up for wartime damage, the enormous pent-up demand for goods and services neglected during the war, civilian spinoffs from military technology in fields such as electronics and jet transport, and the large military purchases during the Korean and Vietnam wars and throughout the cold war years.

Multinational corporations spearheaded the global economic expansion during this boom. They now had available for the first time the technology necessary for global operations because of certain innovations of the second industrial revolution, including containerized shipping, satellite communications, and computerized cash management systems. Such facilities have made it possible for the median multinational corporation of this period to produce twenty-two products in eleven different countries. Corporations now can export not only their manufactured goods but also their plants to Third World countries, where daily wages often are no more, and sometimes less, than hourly wages at home. Thus the multinationals during the quarter-century boom grew at an average rate of 10 percent a year, as opposed to 4 percent for noninternational corporations.

The global prosperity filtered down to the working classes, at least in the industrialized countries. Real wages rose substantially, providing enough money for weekend outings; annual vacation trips; and the purchasing on credit of private homes, cars, and other durable goods. Many economists were persuaded that their monetary and fiscal policies created the necessary purchasing power to avoid the boom-slump business cycles of the past. Their optimism proved as unfounded as that of earlier economists on the eve of the 1929 crash.

In the mid-1970s the boom gave way to "stagflation"—a disconcerting combination of stagnation in the economy and inflation in prices. The wartime damages had been repaired, the consumer needs deferred during the war had been satisfied, and expanding industrial capacity had ended up by creating overcapacity. The overcapacity resulted in surpluses because the majority of the human race living in the Third World had not been included in the global boom, at least not as consumers. The low wages paid in overseas plants put a cap on local purchasing power. World Bank statistics show that in 1950, per capita income in the industrialized countries was ten times that of the underdeveloped countries. By 1965 the ratio was fifteen to one, and by the end of the century the World Bank predicts it will be thirty to one.

A basic structural weakness of the post–World War II boom was that it rested on integrated global production, but it lacked global consumption. The imbalance was worsened by the disproportionate drop in prices of raw materials exported by Third World countries and by their heavy external debts. By 1986 the debts neared $1 trillion, and interest payments for the debts absorbed between one-quarter and one-half of the export earnings of the Third World countries. To meet the interest payments, Third World governments reduced their social expenditures and their imports. But one-third of all industrial countries' exports have gone to the Third World, so reduction of Third World imports promptly increased First World unemployment. Among fifteen members of the Organization for Economic Cooperation and Development, unemployment averaged 3.4 percent in 1973, 5 percent in 1979, 8.3 percent in 1983, and 11.3 percent in 1995. Unemployment in turn triggered demands for protective tariffs, which revived memories of the 1920s protectionism that contributed to the onset of the Great Depression.

These economic attacks dispelled post–World War II confidence and euphoria. Economists who believed that at last they had exorcised the boom and bust cycle now expressed bewilderment and apprehension. Scholars from fifteen countries agreed during a meeting of the International Federation of Institutes for Advanced Study (June 1983) that neither capitalist nor socialist economies were functioning satisfactorily. "We are living in a disjointed planet which is based on economic concepts

In January 1954 Life *magazine profiled some pioneers of the suburban frontier. In a reflection of segregated housing patterns, all of the profiled families were white. The family shown here enjoyed "a pleasant secure life on what to many Americans seems like the ultimate economic goal—a five-figure income." An annual income of $12,291 supported payments on their six-room house in Denver with do-it-yourself additions and allowed one great splurge—a $389 television set.*

which have nothing to do with present-day reality. . . We want to question the basic tenets to see if they can be modified or adjusted."[1] The need for modifying or adjusting was evident in the 1996 UN International Labor Organization report stating that 30 percent of the world's total labor force was either unemployed or underemployed.

Social Repercussions

The economic setbacks after the mid-1970s were intellectually unsettling for economists, but they were much more disruptive for the many who had become accustomed to relative affluence. American farmers had been encouraged by the federal government during the 1970s to increase their output for overseas markets to counterbalance growing trade deficits. The farmers responded enthusiastically, so that agricultural exports jumped from $8 billion in 1971 to $43.8 billion in 1981. Then the foreign market suddenly shrank because of Washington's embargo on exports to the Soviet Union after its invasion of Afghanistan; the overvalued dollar, which in effect imposed in 1984 a 32 percent surcharge on all American exports; and the cutback on all imports by financially strapped Third World governments. American agricultur-

al exports between 1981 and 1983 dropped 21 percent in price level and 20 percent in volume.

American farmers found themselves caught in a squeeze, especially because many had borrowed heavily at high interest rates to buy more land and equipment to meet the government appeal for more output. Bankrupt farmers were dispossessed, and the number of family farms dropped from a peak of 6.8 million in the mid-1930s to 2.8 million in 1980 to 1.9 million in 1994. The U.S. Census Bureau found that farm family incomes in 1985 were only three-fourths that of nonfarm families, and that the poverty rate among those living on farms was 24 percent, compared with 15 percent for nonfarm residents. The resulting emotional and social disruption was reflected in suicide rates, which in 1984 were twice as high in rural Iowa counties as the national average.

Disruption has been evident in urban communities as well as rural because of high unemployment. Although the unemployment rate in the 1980s and 1990s has been far below that of the Great Depression, many urban workers consider themselves to be worse off now. During the 1930s the unemployment was assumed to be typically cyclical and therefore bound to end with the transition from bust to boom. Today it is realized that this assumption cannot be made, for several reasons. First, with factories being

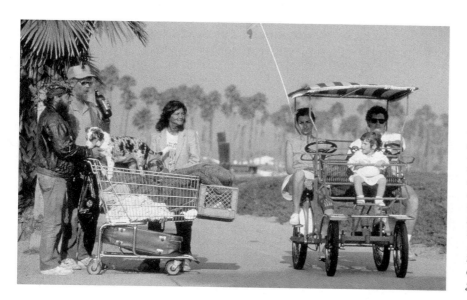

An affluent family pedals by a group of homeless people in Santa Barbara, California. In the 1980s a combination of rising housing prices and the closure of most mental hospitals pushed increasing numbers of Americans onto the streets. Estimates of the number of homeless Americans in the late 1980s ranged from 300,000 to 3 million, depending on the definition of homelessness and the political goals of the estimator.

transplanted from expensive-labor to cheap-labor countries, Western workers no longer can demand and receive the high wages to which they have become accustomed. Second, the spread of automation and robots is displacing white-collar workers in offices along with blue-collar workers in factories. The number of unemployed in the entire Western world rose from 10 million in January 1970 to 31 million in January 1983. It is true that although factory jobs are decreasing, service jobs (for instance, bank tellers, fast-food workers, hotel clerks, recreation and health attendants) are increasing rapidly. But wages in the service sector are substantially lower than in manufacturing.

The human implications of these statistics have been spelled out in the 1985 report of the twenty-two-member Physician Task Force on Hunger in America, headed by J. Larry Brown, chair of the Harvard School of Public Health. The task force interviewed governors, teachers, ministers, and social workers, as well as the hungry people themselves, in the search for "the human face of hunger." The investigators concluded that about 20 million American citizens were suffering from hunger, meaning specifically that they were unable to purchase an adequate diet and periodically ran out of food altogether. "Hunger in America," stated the physicians, "is a national health epidemic. It is our judgment that the problem of hunger in the United States is more widespread and serious than at any time in the last ten to fifteen years. . . . We believe that today hunger and malnutrition are serious problems in every region of the nation. We have, in fact, returned from no city and no state where we did not find extensive hunger."[2]

As revealing as this report on hunger in the United States was an October 1993 report from Fordham University, where social scientists issue an annual "Index of Social Health." This monitors the well-being of American society by examining reports from the Census Bureau on sixteen major social problems, including unemployment, teenage suicide, high school dropout rates, and supply of affordable housing. The nation's best year, as measured by the report, was 1973, when the index stood at 77.5. But in 1993, the most recent year for which complete data were available, the index was down to 38.8,

which the director of the study described as "awful."[3]

III. IMPACT ON THE SOCIALIST WORLD

The second industrial revolution has had a profound impact on the socialist world as well as the capitalist, so much so that the socialist world disintegrated. We noted (Chapter 40, Section I) that Stalin's Five-Year Plans had accelerated the economic development of the Soviet Union, making that country the second-greatest industrial power by 1932. Then the Soviet economy suffered a grievous setback with the staggering human and material losses sustained during World War II. But recovery was swift, with sharp gains achieved during the 1950s and 1960s. This success encouraged Khrushchev to boast in 1961 that Soviet industrial output would surpass that of the United States by 1980. In fact, the opposite happened. The Soviet rate of growth slowed during the 1970s, so that the Soviet economy fell further behind the American economy, rather than catching up to it and surpassing it.

One reason for the Soviet slowdown was a shrinking supply of labor and natural resources, in contrast to the Stalin period, when both were plentiful. Another reason was the growing size and complexity of the economy, which made it increasingly difficult and inefficient to direct everything from the center. Perhaps the chief reason for the Soviet economic slowdown was political—the unwillingness of Soviet workers, technicians, and scientists merely to carry out orders from above with no role in decision making. Such a one-sided arrangement was feasible during the early years, when Stalin was dealing mostly with illiterate muzhiks fresh from the villages. But today the Soviet labor force includes many highly educated engineers, managers, and professionals, whose creative energies need to be tapped if the former Soviet Union is to participate actively in the ongoing second industrial revolution. This has not been done, and the consequences have been disastrous, as noted most perceptively by the famous Soviet physicist and dissenter Andrei Sakharov. In March 1970 Sakharov, along with a fellow physicist and historian, addressed an *Appeal of Soviet Scientists to the Party-Government Leaders of the U.S.S.R.* Its penetrating analysis of Soviet ailments merits quotation:

Why have we not only failed to become the pioneers of the second industrial revolution but, as it transpires, are we even incapable of keeping abreast of the developed capitalist countries in this revolution? Can it be that the socialist system does not present the same opportunities as the capitalist system for the development of productive forces and that in the economic competition between capitalism and socialism, capitalism will emerge victorious?

Of course not. The source of our difficulties does not lie in the socialist system at all, but, on the contrary, in those features and circumstances in our life which run counter to socialism and are alien to it. This source lies in the anti-democratic tradition and norms of public conduct which were laid down during the Stalinist period and which have not been eradicated even to this day. . . .

The obstacles blocking the development of our economy lie in the sociopolitical sphere, and all measures which fail to remove these obstacles are doomed to inefficacy. . . .

From our friends abroad we sometimes hear the U.S.S.R. compared to a huge truck, whose driver presses one foot hard down on the accelerator and the other on the brake. The time has come to make more intelligent use of the brake!. . .

What has our country to expect if a course leading towards democratization is not taken? It can expect to lag behind the capitalist countries in the second industrial revolution and to gradually revert to the status of a second-rate provincial power.[4]

During Leonid Brezhnev's long stewardship from 1964 to 1982, Sakharov's plea for "more intelligent use of the brake" was ignored. Instead, the brake continued to be pressed down hard. The Soviet bureaucracy squelched periodic proposals to decentralize the Soviet economy and allow some initiative to local factories and administrative bodies. Even copiers were viewed as potential instruments of subversion and were kept under lock and key, with access to them strictly regulated and recorded.

The repercussions of brake-slamming have been precisely what Sakharov foretold. Regimentation and ossification have proven incompati-

ble with participation in the second industrial revolution. Today's global economy is characterized by a fast tempo of technological innovation, constantly changing consumer tastes, and keen competition in an integrated world market. All this demands flexibility, efficiency, and adaptability—qualities notably lacking in the multilayered party and state bureaucracies of the former Soviet Union. Hence the average annual growth of the Soviet GNP declined from 5 to 6 percent between 1950 and 1970, 3.7 percent between 1971 and 1975, and 2.7 percent between 1976 and 1980. Instead of the USSR surpassing America, as Khrushchev expected, Japan now has surpassed the former Soviet Union and has become the world's second-greatest industrial power.

With the death of Brezhnev and of his short-lived successors (Yuri Andropov and Konstantin Chernenko), the founding generation of Soviet leaders departed from the historical stage. Mikhail Gorbachev assumed power in 1985 as the first of a younger generation, which realizes that in this age of the second industrial revolution, the Soviet "truck" will be left behind as long as one foot presses on the brake and the other on the accelerator. At the Twenty-seventh Congress of the Communist Party, which opened on February 25, 1986, Gorbachev criticized the failings of the Brezhnev years in terms that recalled and validated Sakharov's warning in 1970:

The inertness and stillness of our administration, the decline of dynamism in our work and an escalation of bureaucracy—all this has done no small damage. . . Difficulties began to build up in the economy in the 1970s, with the rates of economic growth declining visibly. . . . A lag ensued in the material base of science and education, health protection, culture and everyday services. . . . Unfortunately, there was a widespread view that any change in the economic mechanism should be regarded as being practically a retreat from the principles of socialism. . . . The situation called for a change, but a peculiar psychology—How to improve things without changing anything?—took the upper hand.[5]

Once in power, Gorbachev proceeded to reverse the policies of his predecessors with a gusto reminiscent of Tsar Peter the Great. In June

After the failed coup in August 1991, Boris Yeltsin soon displaced Mikhail Gorbachev as leader of the new Commonwealth of Independent States. Here they appeared jointly before the parliament of the collapsing Soviet Union.

1987, he spoke frankly to the Communist Party Central Committee about his determination to make a clean break with the past: "Ours is a rapidly changing society. . . . We are in for new problems, considerable complexities. We are not insured against mistakes. . .. Yet I am confident that the greatest mistake is fearing to err."[6]

Gorbachev's phrase, "fearing to err," is strikingly similar to President Roosevelt's phrase, "nothing to fear but fear itself." In fact, a parallel may be drawn between Roosevelt's New Deal in the 1930s and Gorbachev's perestroika, or restructuring, in the 1980s. Both programs were designed in response to traumatic crises— Hoover's Great Depression in the United States and Brezhnev's great stagnation in the Soviet Union. Both programs were headed by leaders who came not from below but from above— from the national elites. Both Roosevelt and Gorbachev were interested not in a revolution that would overthrow their social systems, but in reform substantial enough to rejuvenate and preserve those systems. Despite the conservative objective of their reform programs, both leaders were strenuously opposed by conservatives who feared an uncertain future, and by radicals who demanded societal surgery rather than first aid. Thus, FDR was excoriated from the right as a traitor to his class, and from the left by radicals such as Louisiana's Huey Long, with his "Share-Our-Wealth" program.

In the end, FDR and his New Deal were rescued by World War II, which opened factories, created jobs, and thus ended the nightmare of the Great Depression. Fortunately for the world but perhaps unfortunately for Gorbachev, no World War III occurred to rescue him from his predicament. So he had no alternative but to struggle directly with a host of problems even more formidable than those that confronted FDR. These problems included the restive minorities living in the sixteen republics that comprised the Union of Soviet Socialist Republics (USSR). Their hostility increased because of an economic crisis at least as severe as the American Great Depression of the 1930s. Gorbachev's perestroika program for economic restructuring raised expectations for improved economic conditions. Instead, there was economic deterioration. Because inefficient enterprises were forced to trim payrolls or even to close down, unemployment increased sharply. The resulting social distress heightened ethnic unrest and conflicts, as it has in the United States and western Europe, where minority immigrants have been blamed for lost jobs and low wages.

These mounting problems proved too much for Gorbachev. By 1991 he had been replaced as leader by Boris N. Yeltsin, and the USSR itself had disintegrated, being replaced by a looser political structure known as the Commonwealth of Independent States. Another sign

Lithuanians demonstrate for independence in 1990. As the Gorbachev reform era came to a close, the various republics of the former Soviet Union began to demand independence.

of the popular dissatisfaction with the old Communist order was the decision of the citizens of Leningrad to restore the old tsarist name of their city, St. Petersburg.

Yeltsin tried to give the Commonwealth a fresh start by making changes that dismantled the old Communist system much more than Gorbachev had been willing to do. In agriculture, he abolished the state-owned and collective farms. In industry, he turned over by 1993 one-third of formerly state-owned enterprises to private ownership. Another change that was unplanned and unwelcome was the mass emigration of highly trained scientists who had been left unemployed and unpaid during the economic crisis in their country. With the lifting of restrictions on emigration, 39,000 citizens left in 1987; 600,000 in 1991; and 1 million in 1992.

In the past, most emigrants had been disaffected minorities such as Jews, Volga Germans, and Armenians. Now so many of the top scientists are leaving that it is feared that not enough will remain to train the next generation of scientists.

Just as alarming for many Russians is the ideological vacuum they are now facing. In the past, the official Stalinist ideology had answers for all their questions. True socialism, they were taught from childhood, required government ownership of the means of production and a central planning board to prepare plans for the economy and to supervise its functioning. At first, this strategy seemed to work satisfactorily. But by the 1990s the Russians had to face up to the fact that their country, as Sakharov had warned back in 1970, seemed to be sinking down to "the status of a second-rate provincial power." So despite their past bragging about "surpassing" the United States, Russians now were confronted by a devastating economic slump and an embarrassing ideological predicament.

At a time when the second industrial revolution is unfolding at breakneck speed, millions throughout the world must cope with the task of devising social systems suitable for this age of high technology. It is a difficult and uncomfortable task requiring careful sorting out of the good from the bad in the numerous contending social systems. This brings us back to a key problem that has plagued humans from their beginnings (as noted in Chapter 1, Section I)—the problem of the chronic time lag between technological and social change. We defined that problem as one of balancing our expanding knowledge with wisdom in how we use that knowledge.

With luck, this task can be fulfilled, in which case the twentieth century, which has witnessed so much barbarism, may yet close in a blaze of creative innovation. On the other hand, if the twentieth century closes with ill luck rather than good, then the end result of the second industrial revolution might well prove grim, as indicated by the savagery now rampant from Northern Ireland to Rwanda to Bosnia to the Commonwealth emerging from the wreckage of the former Soviet Union.

IV. IMPACT ON THE UNDERDEVELOPED THIRD WORLD

Third World history since World War II has been made up of a combination of political triumphs and economic disasters. The political triumphs culminated in the dismantling of colonial empires and the creation of new independent states on the imperial ruins (see Chapter 43). But the accompanying economic disasters culminated in a decline of living standards in Third World countries. One important cause for economic deterioration has been the impact of the second industrial revolution on the daily lives of Third World peoples.

In agriculture, the new seeds and new techniques of the green revolution resulted in greater productivity. But this did not benefit most of the peasants, who lacked the capital required for the hybrid seeds, fertilizers, and irrigation equipment. Only medium- and large-scale farmers were able to participate in the Green Revolution, and they tended to shift from domestic staple food crops to the more profitable export crops. Also, they were likely to

In recent years, the former Soviet Union has moved towards a market economy. Thus economic reforms have made some people quite wealthy, while others have been reduced to selling household goods in order to buy food.

introduce labor-saving machines, which forced the already underemployed peasants to flee to city slums, where they usually found themselves as superfluous as they had been in the countryside. This pattern is clear in Mexico, where the most efficient farms are now producing winter fruits and vegetables for the American market while corn and bean staples are imported from the United States, and where millions of uprooted peasants are crossing the frontier in search of work. Meanwhile, the capital, Mexico City, grew by 1980 to an almost unmanageable population of 14 million, with an increase of another 14 million expected in the next two decades.

Runaway urbanization is under way on all continents, so that by the year 2000 there will be an estimated forty metropolitan areas in the Third World with populations of 5 million or more, but only twelve of that size in the First World. In 1900 the largest metropolitan areas in descending order were London, New York, Paris, Berlin, Chicago, Vienna, Tokyo, St. Petersburg, Philadelphia, and Manchester. In 2000 they are expected to be Mexico City, Sao Paulo, Tokyo, New York, Shanghai, Beijing, Rio de Janeiro, Bombay, Calcutta, and Jakarta. The important point about this global urbanization is that there is no accompanying industrialization. Therefore the newcomers to the cities are forced into the kind of marginal employment that saves them from outright starvation but that contributes little to the national economies. They spend their lives in such work as street vending, shining shoes, running errands, and pushing a cart or pedaling a rickshaw.

V. IMPACT ON THE GLOBE

The second industrial revolution is having not only a specific impact on the societies of the First, Second, and Third worlds but also a profound general impact on all peoples of all societies. We have seen that throughout human history, technological change has deeply affected daily life. The shift from hunting-gathering to agriculture necessitated a shift from nomadic band life to sedentary village life. Equally far-reaching was the effect on human existence of the first industrial revolution. More pervasive and disruptive is the impact of the ongoing sec-

ond industrial revolution, corresponding to the unprecedented power of its new technology. We shall analyze four of the most important aspects of this global impact: on ecology, on race relations, on gender relations, and on war.

A. Impact on Ecology

So powerful is the second industrial revolution that it is leaving its imprint on planet Earth as well as on its inhabitants. This is an ecological impact, since the planet is the oikos, or home of the human species. All peoples in all ages have affected their environment, simply by virtue of being human with human needs and with human technology, even if it consisted only of stone tools and fire. But today their impact is infinitely greater because of their combined technological and population explosions.

The contrast between past and present ecology is illustrated clearly in the livelihood of the Semang, a group of 2,000 to 3,000 nomadic forest foragers in Malaysia. They appear to be ecologically irresponsible in their everyday life, using their river as a bath, laundry, toilet, fishing ground, and source of drinking water. Likewise, they freely set fire to the surrounding forest in the course of their slash-and-burn cultivation. They plant seeds in the fire-cleared ground, then resume their nomadic foraging, returning only to collect whatever the animals have left in the unprotected plots.

With this mode of life, the average per capita daily consumption of energy by the Semangs is under 5,000 kilocalories (40 percent from human labor and 60 percent from burning firewood) in contrast to the 250,000 kilocalories used by the typical U.S. citizen. So the Semang, living on such a modest scale, have no appreciable impact on their river and on the surrounding forest, despite activities that would be catastrophic in our world with its proliferating machines and its billions of inhabitants rather than a few thousand.[7]

Since both machines and inhabitants are increasing at an accelerating pace, the ecological situation may well deteriorate. World population has been growing rapidly because it could be supported by increasingly productive agriculture and industry, and because advances in med-

The Aral Sea, which straddles Kazakhstan and Uzbekistan in the southwest region of the former Soviet Union, was once a plentiful source of water and fish. Today, due to policies that overly exploited this resource, the sea has all but vanished.

ical science and in public health measures reduced death rates. So whereas the human race required millions of years to reach its first billion in 1830, it needed only one century to reach its second billion, only thirty years to reach its third billion, a mere fifteen its fourth billion, and eleven years its fifth.

These new billions of human beings crowding the planet were provided with numerous new machines produced during the first and second industrial revolutions. The inevitable result has been infinitely greater stress on our oikos than that exerted by our ancestors. Even in the United States, which is relatively underpopulated and richly endowed, evidence of the stress can be seen everywhere—in the depletion of the great Ogallala Aquifer, which supplies irrigation water to the Great Plains from Nebraska to the Texas Panhandle; in the conversion of California's orchards and Long Island's potato fields into housing developments; in the clear-cutting of remnant primeval forests in the northwest; and in the 99 percent of known toxic dumps that have not been cleaned up and that are contaminating water supplies throughout the country.

The ecological impasse is not confined to the United States. It has become a worldwide problem with the spread of the second industrial revolution. China offers a good example, as it is now the second-largest industrial power and is growing the fastest. Its headlong industrialization is powered mostly by the country's huge reserves of coal. But coal is the dirtiest of fuels in carbon emissions, so that China now ranks second in such emissions and may well be the first by 2025. Chinese consumers (of whom there are over 1 billion) doubtless will behave like consumers everywhere in striving for an ever-higher living standard with more cars, more refrigerators, more home heating, and more consumer goods, all requiring more energy to produce and to operate. Some environmentalists have questioned the escalating expectations of the "have-nots," but Norway's former prime minister, G.H. Brundtland notes that Western Europeans who initiated the Industrial Revolution and the ensuing ecological problems, cannot now condemn "have-nots" to the status of "never-will-haves."[8]

B. Impact on Race Relations

All through history, technology has affected race relations profoundly by determining population growth and population movements. For example, when our earliest ancestors in Africa's savannas developed their technology to the point where they could make fire, fashion clothes, and build shelters, they were able to expand from their African base and strike out across Europe and Asia, ultimately reaching the Americas and Australia. Likewise, the first industrial revolution, with its advances in agriculture and industry, triggered a jump in Europe's population from 100 million in 1650 to 463 million in 1914. This made possible during the eighteenth and nineteenth centuries a great emigration of Europeans to the underpopulated lands of Siberia and the Americas. Today, with the second industrial revolution, a similar emigration flood is occurring, though in reverse—from underdeveloped to developed lands. Increased food production and improved health technology (mass immunization, DDT, and oral rehydration therapy) have reduced sharply the death rates in underdeveloped countries, while birthrates have remained high. Consequently, between 1950 and 1970, annual population growth rates in developed and underdeveloped

Poor countries affect the natural environment primarily by the size of their populations; rich nations tax the environment because of their high standard of living. Today, most people in China use muscle power rather than fossil fuels to move about. But what are the likely environmental consequences of future posperity in this nation of more than 1 billion people?

countries were 1.1 percent and 2.2 percent, respectively. Third World population growth now is twice that of the developed world, and this new pattern will be hard to change because Third World populations are predominantly young. What this means for the future is evident in Table 44.1, which shows total world population is increasing at a constantly accelerating pace, and how most of the population growth is in underdeveloped countries.

The rapidly growing populations in the Third World are finding it hard to support themselves because most Third World economies have bogged down, as noted above. Therefore, these hard-pressed people have migrated, whenever possible, from their poverty-stricken countries and taken any jobs available in the developed lands. During the post–World War II boom years, many jobs were open, so approximately 15 million to 20 million workers flocked to northwestern Europe—to Germany, Britain, France, and the Scandinavian states. Many of the immigrants came from southern European countries: Spain, Portugal, Italy, Greece, Yugoslavia, and Turkey. The remainder came from overseas countries, chiefly from North Africa, Pakistan, India, and the West Indies.

The Europeans at first welcomed the immigrants as "guest workers," assuming that after a few years they would return to their homelands with their savings. But the newcomers did not act as expected. As the years passed, they sank roots in their adopted countries and naturally were unwilling to relocate again. Their children, born in the new countries, regarded themselves as Germans or French or Swedes rather than as Turks or Pakistanis or West Indians. Nevertheless, when the postwar economic boom ended, unemployment became a serious problem for Europeans, and former "guest workers" found themselves no longer welcomed as "guests." Instead, they were now resented, and sometimes even attacked, by the unemployed. Some governments tried to resolve the dilemma by offering to pay the fares for immigrants willing to go back home, but few accepted the offer.

Gradually and reluctantly, Europeans are being forced to recognize that they face not a temporary problem of foreign minorities, but the permanent fact of a new multiethnic, multicultural, and multireligious continent. It is a jarring experience for hitherto insulated Europeans to see the minarets of new mosques rising amidst their cities, to hear calls to prayer issuing

TABLE 44.1 Population Projections: 1950–2100 (population in millions)

	1950[a]	1980[a]	2000[b]	2025[b]	2050[b]	2100[b]
Underdeveloped countries	1,670	3,284	4,922	7,061	8,548	9,741
Developed countries	834	1,140	1,284	1,393	1,425	1,454
Total world	2,504	4,424	6,206	8,454	9,973	11,195

[a]Estimated.
[b]Projected.
Source: UN and World Bank estimates and projections.

loudly from those mosques several times each day, to have television and radio stations broadcasting full-time in foreign languages, and to receive protests when Moslem children are taught in state schools to sing "Onward Christian Soldiers."

Similar discord is occurring in the United States, where a 1995 Census Bureau study disclosed that 8.7 percent of the population (or 22.6 million people) had been born elsewhere. In California, 25 percent of the population is foreign born, and in New York 16 percent. Indeed, an expert on the subject has concluded that if the present pace of ethnic intermixture continues, the complexion of most Americans will change from white to brown in a few generations. the number of children in interracial families in the United States rose from 500,000 in 1970 to 2 million in 1990.

Ethnic changes of such magnitude have repercussions in the United States as elsewhere. A 1994 Louis Harris poll in the United States disclosed that non-whites believe that they have fewer opportunities than whites. But in that poll, the non-whites expressed nearly equal resentment toward one another as they feel collectively toward whites. The chilling conclusion of the pollster was "the more diversity and burgeoning minority groups we have, the more prejudice we must overcome."[10]

Chilling indeed, since large-scale migrations are creating minority groups all over the world, with ensuing prejudice and conflict. But the end result need not be a global chill, as exemplified in the career of Tiger Woods, the Masters golf champion, whose heritage is a mixture of Thai, Black American, Caucasian American, and Indian American.

C. Impact on Gender Relations

Gender relations, as well as race relations, have been affected deeply throughout history by technological developments. During the food-gathering millennia, women enjoyed equal status because as food gatherers they contributed at least as much to their families' food supplies as did their husbands. With the advent of the agricultural revolution, women gave up nomadic band life for village life; they spent most of their time at home raising children and doing housework, and no longer were they able to contribute equally to family food needs. The first industrial revolution opened new horizons for women, as factories and wage-paying jobs offered an alternative to child rearing, and housework (Chapter 26, Section VI).

Somewhat later, women benefited from the establishment of public schools, where they were able to get an education alongside male students. By the beginning of the twentieth century, women were winning the right to vote. By 1900 they had won the franchise in national elections in only 1 country; by 1950 they could vote in 69 countries; by 1975, in 129. Today, women have the vote virtually everywhere except for a few Arab countries (Oman, Qatar, Saudi Arabia, and the United Arab Emirates).

The second industrial revolution has affected women as deeply as did the first. Contraceptives made available by medical technology have given women control over their own reproductive function. No longer are they bound by traditional assumptions about what "nature intended" concerning the social roles of males and females. Motherhood can be assumed or refused. Family planning enables women to raise their children and then renew old careers or even begin new ones. However, only about 50 percent of the world's women have access to contraceptives. And some of that 50 percent cannot make effective use of the devices for various reasons, including opposition by governments or churches or husbands who want to prove their virility or to have sons to carry on the family name or to inherit the family lands.

A second important change in the status of women today is the opening of doors to education. Global illiteracy is decreasing rapidly among women as well as men. In 1960 only 59 percent of the world's women were literate, but in 1985 this number had increased to 68 percent. However, women also face the problem of differences in content as well as quality of education. From the earliest years in school, girls in all countries tend to be directed toward subjects that are of more use in the kitchen and living room than in the outside world. They are encouraged to study art, literature, domestic science, and dressmaking, whereas boys are studying engineering, mathematics, physics, and mechanics. (See map of Global Illiteracy, p. 650.)

The contrast in the content of education is an important factor in the corresponding contrast in the content of paychecks. One of the most dramatic changes in the role of women in recent years has been their influx into the global labor force. In the United States only 18.9 percent of adult women worked outside the home in 1890. By 1940 the percentage had increased

Women, newly enfranchised, voting in postwar Japan.

to 25.8 percent, by the end of World War II (1945) it had risen to 35 percent, and by 1984 to 54 percent.

Participation in the economy outside the household has been a mixed blessing for women. It has made them less dependent and has opened up new horizons and new opportunities for realizing their potential. The increased involvement of women in national economies also has correspondingly increased national productivity and wealth. In the United States, for example, two paychecks have enabled many families to enjoy larger homes, more luxurious automobiles, regular vacations, and more education for the children.

On the other hand, the new status of women has brought grievances along with the benefits. One is that having taken on outside work, women find themselves overloaded with both inside and outside work. In addition to the hours they spend on their jobs, American women work an average of 24.2 hours per week on household chores, compared to 12.6 hours by their husbands. In the former Soviet Union the disparity is greater: 25 to 28 hours per week by women, compared to 4 to 6 hours by the men. In Japan, men spend less than half an hour a day on household chores, even when their wives work.

In addition to this economic subordination, women all over the world face, in varying degrees, the constant threat of violence. In almost all cultures, violence against wives and against women in general has such deep historic roots that it is condoned as the acceptable norm. If a person is killed because of his or her politics, the act is commonly denounced as a violation of human rights. But if a person is beaten or killed because she is a female, the case commonly is dismissed as "cultural tradition." Nor is this a shortcoming only of aberrant or less-developed cultures. In the United States, a woman is beaten every fifteen seconds, and one is raped every five minutes.

In many cultures, the violence against females begins even before birth. Strong social pressure to bear sons is causing women in India and China to use amniocentesis—a genetic test designed to screen for birth defects—to determine the sex of their fetus. When the test reveals a girl, the fetus is usually aborted. Of 8,000 abortions performed at a clinic in Bombay, for example, 7,999 were female. The motivation behind this thriving business is reflected in sex-detection clinic advertisements, which proclaim that it is better to spend $38 on terminating a girl than to spend $3,800 later on her dowry. Likewise, China's single child per family policy triggered so much female infanticide that in 1982 in a village in Hupei province, the male-female ratio of one-year-olds was 503 to 100 (the norm being 106 to 100).

The end result of this female infanticide is that an estimated 100 million females are missing around the world. They are missing because they were aborted or killed at birth, or died because they were given less food than males, or because family members view a daughter with diarrhea as a nuisance, but a son with diarrhea as a medical crisis requiring a doctor. "If a boy gets sick," acknowledges an official in

Global Illiteracy

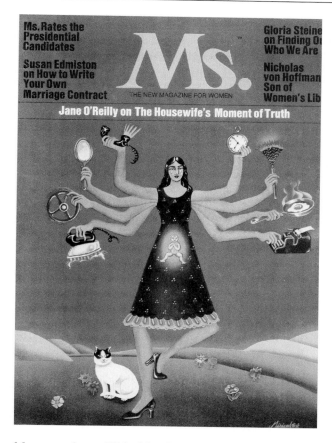

Ms. magazine published its first issue in 1972. Edited by Gloria Steinem, the magazine attempted to bring a radical feminist message to a wide audience. Ms. emphasized the need for women to have equal access with men to education, health care, and employment and tried to help Americans rethink traditional gender roles.

China's State Family Planning Commission, "the parents send him to the hospital at once. But if a girl gets sick, the parents may say to themselves, `Well, we'll see how she is tomorrow.'"

In parts of Africa and the Middle East, young girls endure another form of violence known as female circumcision. The operation removes all or part of the external genitalia, a form of mutilation that deprives the victims of all sexual feeling as well as endangering their lives during the operation and later during childbirth. The rationale of this custom is to dampen the sexual desire of young females and thus to ensure their virginity until marriage. Efforts to eradicate female circumcision are

opposed on the ground that foreign organizations and ideologies are jeopardizing "an important African tradition." The Kenyan women's magazine *VIA* responds that "There is nothing 'African' about injustice or violence, whether it takes the form of mistreated wives, mothers, or slums, or circumcision. Often the very men who. . . excuse injustice to women with the phrase, 'it is African,' are wearing three-piece pinstriped suits and shiny shoes."

In December 1997, Egyptian women won a victory when their nation's high court ruled that female circumcision was not an Islamic religious practice authorized by the Koran. This ruling encourages antimutilation campaigns in all Africa, where 2 million undergo the procedure each year.

D. Impact on War

The impact of the second industrial revolution has been most clearly evident in the field of war, and naturally so because the technology of the second industrial revolution stems directly from World War II military inventions. These wartime breakthroughs were radar (British), the nuclear bomb (American), the ballistic missile (German), and the electronic computer (American).

As important as these technological advances was the integration of the activities of military men, of scientists, and of industrialists. This proved to be a highly efficient combination, leading to what has been termed "invention on demand." Experience in battle stimulated demand for improvement of existing weapons or development of new ones, such as (during World War I) tanks, poison gas, and submarines. The demand was referred to the new scientist-military-industrialist trio, which usually responded so efficiently that military technology made unprecedented advances during the two world wars.

This arrangement was institutionalized after World War II, to the point that President Eisenhower was moved to warn of the dangers of a "military-industrial complex." The scope of the complex was demonstrated when the Strategic Defense Initiative (SDI, or "Star Wars") was adopted, and Congress began authorizing appropriations in 1983. By 1987, contracts had been signed with eighty universities (led by MIT, with $350 million) and with 460 corporations (led by Lockheed, with $1 billion).

Under these circumstances, the torrent of "demand" inventions continued unabated during the cold war years that followed World War II. Even though Einstein had warned, when the first nuclear bombs were detonated, that "we drift to unparalleled catastrophe," nevertheless an arms race proliferated, with each new invention triggering counter-inventions. The 1945 American A-bomb was followed by a Soviet one in 1949; the 1952 American H-bomb by a Soviet one in 1953; and the 1968 Soviet antiballistic missile by an American one in 1972. The end result of this arms race was the accumulation of a global arsenal of 50,000 nuclear weapons.

The implication of this stalemate was made clear by a consortium of scientists from several countries, who warned in November 1983 that if only a small fraction of existing weapons were detonated, a "nuclear winter" would ensue. Firestorms and massive amounts of smoke, oily soot, and dust would blot out the sun and plunge the earth into a freezing darkness for three months to a year or more. "Global environmental changes sufficient to cause the extinction of a major fraction of the plant and animal species on the earth are likely. In that event, the possibility of the extinction of Homo sapiens cannot be excluded."

This shocking statement prompted scientists in several countries to conduct follow-up studies. Some questioned whether the global chilling would be severe enough to be described as "winter," and proposed in its place the term "nuclear fall." On the other hand, they also agreed that nuclear war would deplete the ozone layer, which protects humans from solar ultraviolet radiation. They warned also that direct blast and radiation effects of nuclear war might cost

The Allied campaign of aerial bombardment did terrible damage to German cities. This photograph shows the devastation it delivered to the city of Cologne on the Rhine.

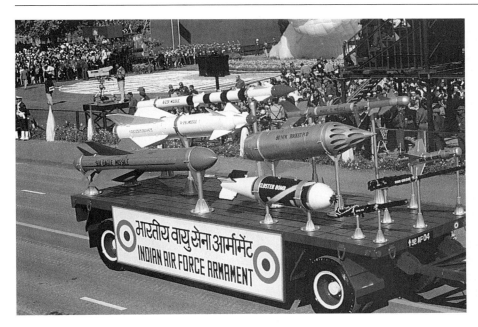

Although the two nuclear superpowers—the United States and the Russian Federation—have reduced their arsenals in recent years, global security is threatened by nuclear proliferation. Early in the twenty-first century, perhaps fifty nations—many engaged in regional conflicts—will have nuclear weapons.

several hundred million lives, but that an additional 1 billion to 4 billion of the world's 5 billion people could die of famine following worldwide crop failures. Thus a country such as India, with its huge population dependent on food imports, could suffer the heaviest loss of life, even though not a single bomb fell on its territory. Such was the dismal prospect confronting humanity at a time (1982) when $650 billion was being spent annually on arms, or $1 million each minute. Thus astronomical expenditure had brought not the desperately desired security, but the bleak alternative of nuclear fall at best, or nuclear winter at worst.

The much-discussed possibility of human self-destruction is particularly ironic, coming as it does at a time when everything imaginable by the human mind seems to be attainable by human technology. Yet this paradox fits in with our survey of human evolution, indicating that it was precisely past advances in technology that made possible the escalation of human violence from personal vendettas to full-scale warfare. (See "The Nature of Human Nature" in Chapter 2.) So long as humans were food gatherers, they had neither the incentive nor the means for large-scale fighting. They did not acquire either means or incentive until their technology

improved to the point where they had accumulated possessions worth fighting over. This occurred with the agricultural and industrial revolutions, which increased productivity dramatically and created affluent civilizations fundamentally different from all the preceding subsistence societies. Their cultivated fields, overflowing granaries, and urban centers filled with treasures were all valuable prizes for predators. Thus war became profitable and endemic, waged by nomads erupting out of their deserts and steppes, by Roman senators seeking new provinces to loot, by conquistadors overrunning whole continents with their muskets and crosses, and by their successors who won worldwide empires with their gunboats and machine guns, and most recently with their helicopters and computers.

The great paradox of our age is that as the agricultural and industrial revolutions made war profitable and rational, so our second industrial revolution has made war unprofitable and suicidal. This is why Einstein warned us that we now face the choice of new "ways of thinking" or "unparalleled catastrophe." Our species is not unique in facing such a challenge. Innumerable other species have been confronted with similar threats, and usually they have failed peared because their genetic mode of adaptation was too slow for sudden environmental change such as the onset of the Ice Age. We humans are fundamentally different because we have been able thus far to use our brains to create our own environments (by technologies such as the use of fire, the making of clothes, and the building of shelters) to suit our own needs. But now the second industrial revolution, with a powerful and dynamic technology, is creating and altering environments at an accelerating pace that requires quick and unceasing adaptation. So the supreme question now is whether we can once more use our brains adequately, this time to adapt to a new world of our own creation. In coping with this challenge, the primary advantage we enjoy over all other species that have perished in the past is that we are not buffeted by something mysterious and unknowable, such as the Ice Age. Our problem is not one of adapting to an environment beyond our control and ken, as has been the case with past species, but rather one of adapting our own human-made environment to our own human needs.

The recent adjustment of the minute hand of the "doomsday clock" of the *Bulletin of the Atomic Scientists* from three minutes to fourteen minutes before midnight offers some hope that Bertrand Russell may have been overly pessimistic in stating that "Man will sooner die than think." But any historian, reviewing the millions of needless human deaths during the last hundred years alone, would be rash to reject out of hand the validity of Russell's commentary. We cannot foresee in what direction the minute hand will move during the twenty-first century; or whether the clock still will be ticking; or whether it will be silent like the one unearthed at Hiroshima with the hands, melted and frozen, at 8:15.

SUGGESTED READINGS

Like all other ages of transition, this one also has stimulated many works on human prospects. Most recent and most thought-provoking is the interdisciplinary analysis by biologist M. E. Clark, *Adriadne's Thread: The Search for New Modes of Thinking* (St. Martin's Press, 1989). This study is especially useful in providing explanations and guidelines because the author conscientiously and ably pursues the search indicated in her subtitle. Also noteworthy are the following publications presenting various interpretations of current human prospects: A. Toffler, *Previews and Premises* (South End Press, 1984); L. S. Stavrianos, *Lifelines from Our Past* (M. E. Sharpe, 1992); M. G. Raskin, *The Common Good: Its Politics, Policies and Philosophy* (Routledge and Kegan Paul, 1986); F. M. Lappé, *Rediscovering America's Values* (Ballantine Books, 1989); and R. N. Bellah et al., *Habits of the Heart: Individualism and Commitment in American Life* (Harper & Row, 1986). Especially useful and revealing is the UN survey, *Human Development Report 1993* (Oxford University, 1993).

NOTES

1. *New York Times*, February 20, 1985.
2. Ibid., November 20 and December 11, 1984; March 3, 1986; *Los Angeles Times*, January 10, 1986.
3. *New York Times*, October 14, 1996.
4. Ibid., April, 1970.
5. Ibid., February 26, 1986.
6. *Los Angeles Times*, June 27, 1987.
7. *UN World Economic Survey 1985*, p. 31, Table 3/2.
8. *New Perspectives Quarterly* (Spring 1989), p. 4.
9. Cited by L. Heise, "Crimes of Gender," *WorldWatch*, March-April 1989, p. 19.
10. *New York Times*, March 3, 1994.

What It Means for Us Today

We have reached the end of this study of our human past. In the course of the study we have paused for stock-taking at the end of each major period. We have asked ourselves, "What does it mean for us today?" We have asked this question at the end of each of the main parts into which this text is divided. The answer for this final part is longer because more history is crowding into each year now than in past decades or centuries, and also because, living on the eve of the twenty-first century, we are looking back on thousands of years of human conduct and misconduct.

The overwhelming impression left by such a long-range survey is that we humans are classic overachievers. Making our debut long ago, probably on the African continent, as puny, relatively scarce, and seemingly defenseless creatures, our future seemed unpromising in the highly competitive arena into which we were born. We lacked the size of elephants, the strength of lions, the speed of antelopes, and the defense mechanisms of creatures such as skunks, porcupines and turtles. And yet today our species has surpassed all others, primarily because we alone have learned to manipulate the physical environment to serve our needs—to adapt the environment to our genes rather than vice versa as has been the case with all other species.

Consequently *Homo sapiens* is unique in being the creator rather than the creature of its destiny. The late space scientist Carl Sagan noted the significance of this quality.[1] Current high technology, he observed, has freed humans from the double threat of extinction by the implosion of asteroids constantly circling Earth, and of extinction by the onset of an overdue new Ice Age. The orbits of the asteroids can be tracked, and those found to be on collision course with Earth can be deflected or pulverized by blasts from nuclear missiles. Likewise a new Ice Age can be forestalled or neutralized by harnessing solar heat with huge planetary solar mirrors focusing the sun's heat to warm a freezing Earth. The combination of a planetary umbrella and a planetary heater provides some security against *Homo sapiens* as a species becoming the victim of a cosmic flyswatter that conceivably might snuff out life some time in the future on planet Earth. Further security is provided by the imminent establishment of human colonies on other planets, which would make *Homo sapiens* the first multiplanet species—a quality that could provide eminently desirable reinsurance in case of future catastrophes.

So secure appears to be the primacy of *Homo sapiens* that some scientists anticipate a utopian future. "I see," declares Willis Harman, Stanford engineering professor and systems theorist, "all sorts of wonderful, creative things happening around the world, with people creating alternative development, alternative economies, new kinds of entrepreneurship, new kinds of communities. All the pieces of a new society are being built, and they're not threatening to anybody, because it isn't a world communism movement or anything like that. It's very organic. . . . Ours is one of the great times of human existence when we're making an evolutionary leap that people will span in a single lifetime. I feel pretty confident that's what's going to happen."[2] Equally exuberant is Cal-Tech geochemist Harrison Brown: "I am just as convinced as can be that man today has much more power than he realizes. I am convinced that man has it within his power to create a world in which people the world over can lead free and abundant and even creative lives. . . . I am convinced that we can create a world which will pale the Golden Age of Pericles into nothingness."[3]

In striking contrast to these cheerful expectations are the cheerless titles of popular books now circulating internationally—titles such as *End of the World, End of the Future, End of History*. The apprehension concerning human prospects is not limited to bookstores. An international team that studied 30,000 randomly chosen men and women in the United States, Canada, Italy, Germany, France, Taiwan, Lebanon and New Zealand found that these people now are experiencing major psychological depressions three times more frequently than did their grandparents.[4]

This brings us to the great enigma of our age—the enigma of *Homo sapiens* triumphantly scaling Mount Everest, yet at the same time hobbled by self-doubt—by fear of ending not on a mountaintop but on the floor of Death Valley. The self-doubt is understandable, for the potential utopia visualized by Harman and Brown is paralleled by an existential dystopia, all too evident in newspaper headlines and on television screens. The chasm between potentiality and reality is made specific by Fordham University's annual report, *The Index of Social Health*, which monitors the well-being of American society on the basis of Census Bureau statistics regarding teenage suicide, unemployment, drug abuse, high school drop-out rate, and availability of affordable housing. The *Index* registered a drop from 75 in 1970 to 36 in 1991, which the director of the annual report labeled "awful."

Why the yawning and expanding chasm between the utopia expected by some scientists and the actually existing dystopia? The answer is to be found in our cultures. All cultures of all peoples consist of control mechanisms designed to regulate the behavior of society members. The cultures evolved gradually during the historical evolution of the societies and therefore represented their survival wisdom. The values comprising the various cultures were calculated to enhance community cohesion and survival. Consequently the values commonly incorporated in cultures favored maximum fertility for species perpetuation, maximum productivity for economic sustenance, and maximum military strength for physical survival.

Through the millennia, cultures became the essential underpinnings of their respective societies. Only through their cultures did individuals know what they could do and how to do it. Therefore any threat to cultural values became as serious as any threat to other basic necessities such as food and water. Hence the extreme reluctance to tolerate any substantive alteration or modification of traditional values. Hence also the historic persistence of cultural rigidity, even in periods such as the present, when rapid technological innovations necessitate correspondingly rapid social innovations. But technological change customarily has been accepted and welcomed because it normally raises living standards, while cultural change has been feared and resisted because it threatens traditional and comfortable values and practices.

This dichotomy has prevailed throughout history, resulting in the social stagnation amid the technological storms of our own making. The disconnection has been responsible for much of the chronic violence and bloodshed that have stained human history. It persists to the present, when the disconnection is impacting directly and ominously on many phases of our lives, as manifested incessantly on television screens and in newspaper headlines.

Example: Work

Anthropologists generally agree that our food-gathering Paleolithic ancestors had more leisure time than we enjoy currently. Present-day food gatherers, whether aborigines in Australia or the Kung of South Africa's Kalahari Desert, spend an average of only fifteen to twenty hours per week collecting food. Such a life pattern left plenty of time for social relationships, including the preparing and consumption of food with due ceremony. It was a pattern that prevailed through most of human history, but it began to change with the agricultural revolution beginning about ten thousand years ago.

That revolution triggered a chain reaction of technological breakthroughs—metallurgy, wheel, textiles, pottery, coinage—and in modern times the labor-*saving* industrial revolution of the late eighteenth century, and the labor-*replacing* high technology revolution since World War II. Each of these technological revolutions increased human productivity, but paradoxically they increased also the length of the work day. Agriculture required more labor for planting, cultivating, harvesting, and tending livestock. Likewise, with the industrial revolution, factory workers labored ten to sixteen hours a day, six days a week. Then the work day was gradually reduced, so

Members of small, simple societies, such as the Tan't Batu, who thrive in the Philippines, live in harmony with nature, such people do not have the technological means to greatly affect the natural world. Although we in complex societies like to think of ourselves as superior to such people, the truth is that there is much we can—and must—learn from them.

that in 1900 the average work week for Americans was sixty hours, and in 1935 it was cut back by law to forty hours.

After World War II, the introduction of robots and other labor-*replacing* contrivances aroused expectations for more work-time reductions. William Green, former president of the American Federation of Labor, declared flatly in 1992: "The only choice is unemployment or leisure."[5] The choice has been made, and it has been for unemployment. Corporate executives have commonly rejected proposals for shorter work days with the contention that the resulting increased labor costs would leave their corporations vulnerable to domestic and foreign competitors. Consequently, in the era of robots and computers, books were published in the United States entitled *The Overworked American*. At the same time, the Japanese coined the term "karoshi" for a fatal illness induced by overwork, which, according to Japan's National Institute of Public Health, leads to "a worsening of pre-existing high blood pressure, finally resulting in a fatal breakdown."[6] In fact, "karoshi" now is second only to cancer as a leading cause for death in Japan.

Meanwhile Green's foreboding about leisure or unemployment has been borne out by reports of a global joblessness crisis. Out of a world labor force of 2.8 billion people, at least 120 million are unemployed. Another 500 million are classified as "underemployed," meaning that they can find only marginal jobs that do not pay enough to cover even their basic needs.[7]

Example: Inequity

The historic disconnection between technological and social change is responsible not only for "karoshi" in an age of robots, but also for inequity —for global malnutrition—in an age of global glut. It was long assumed that inequity is the unavoidable consequence of human genes preprogrammed for acquisitiveness and aggression. Contrariwise, psychologist Albert Bandura concludes from recent research that human nature is neither cooperative nor predatory. Rather it is a "vast potentiality" that can be fashioned into a variety of forms by the prevailing culture.[8] Thus the nomadic food-gathering Paleolithic culture naturally discouraged acquisitiveness because accumulated private possessions would require resetting every few weeks or months when the band moved on to the next camping area.

Contrariwise material possessions became feasible and desirable with the agricultural revolution and the transition from nomadic to settled village life. The transition generated the fateful disparities between landless peasants and landed gentry, between hereditary elites and commoners. "The more advanced the technology and economy," concludes a sociologist, "the greater the social inequality tends to be."[9]

This hypothesis is borne out by the escalating inequality during our era of escalating technology and productivity. The UN *Human Development Report* for 1994 discloses that during the past half-century, world income increased sevenfold, and per capita income tripled. But this substantial gain was distributed unequally, both nationally and internationally. "Between 1960 and 1991," states the *Report*, "the share of world income for the richest 20% of the global population rose from 70% to 85%. . . the meagre share for the poorest 20% declined from 2.3% to 1.4%."[10]

The inequity is manifest not only on a global scale, but also within affluent societies, as specified in the 1985 report of the Physician Task Force on Hunger in America, headed by J. Larry Brown, chair of the Harvard School of Public Health. The group interviewed governors, teachers, ministers, and social workers, as well as hungry people themselves. They concluded that about 20 million American citizens were suffering from hunger, meaning that they were unable to purchase an adequate diet and periodically ran out of food altogether. "Hunger in America," stated the physicians, "is a national health epidemic. It is our judgment that the problem of hunger in the United States is more widespread and serious than at any time in the last ten to fifteen years. . . We believe that today hunger and malnutrition are serious problems in every region of the nation. We have, in fact, returned from no city and no state where we did not find extensive hunger."[11]

The spectacle of "karoshi" in Japan and endemic hunger in the United States forced philosopher Bertrand Russell to a chilling conclusion: "Man will sooner die than think." The validity of Russell's judgment is manifest in

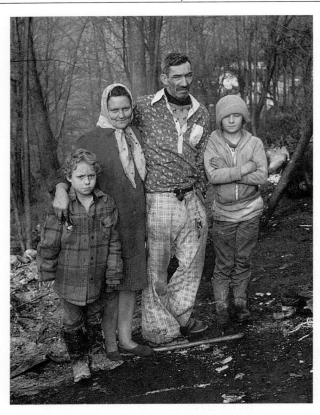

Although minorities are more likely to be disadvantaged, most of the U.S. poor are white people. Furthermore, although inner cities have the greatest concentration of poverty, rural residents are at higher risk of poverty than their urban counterparts.

the hundreds of millions who have died needlessly in our twentieth century. More lugubrious is the outlook if we view ourselves as but one link in a long species chain. Approximately 40 million different species of plants and animals now exist on planet Earth. Beyond that, somewhere between 5 and 40 billion species have existed here at one time or another. Thus only one in a thousand species is still alive, making the survival record of Earth species a 99.9 percent failure.

The multitude of species that have come and gone on our planet raises questions about our own destiny, despite our current global primacy. The obvious rejoinder is that the species that became extinct did so because they were unable to adapt to changes in their environment, such as the advent of the Ice Ages. This is where *Homo sapiens* parts company with the 99.9 percent, because our superior intelligence affords us the unique ability to manipulate our environment to suit our needs rather than the opposite as is the case with all other species. Thus we, and we alone, are the creators rather than the creatures of our destiny. But our intelligence does not assure wisdom in the manner in which we use it. Our technology enables us to build any world we wish, but thus far have we created one worth living in? Or rather, are we making uninhabitable the planet in which we were born, as environmentalists warn?

If so, are we replicating a self-destructive galactic pattern, as theorized by astrophysicist Michio Kaku? He reasons that of the 200 billion stars in our galaxy, tens of thousands must be teeming with intelligent life forms. Yet numerous and ongoing probes of stars out to 100 light years from Earth have found nothing. Some scientists speculate that intelligent life forms probably reached a point in their evolution at which they were able to purify uranium, and to self-destruct with the same "nuclear winter" that has terrified earthlings. "Perhaps other civilizations," concludes Michio Kaku, "destroyed themselves. There is no way to know, but the apparent barrenness of our sector of the galaxy may point in that direction. Now it may be our turn. . . . We on Earth could become a dead civilization for others to ponder."[12]

This speculation is scarcely reassuring, given the fact that humans hitherto have rarely refrained from any folly within their reach. But it is also a fact that today, we humans enjoy advantages that were unavailable to our ancestors and that correspondingly brighten our horizons. One advantage is our escalating technology and productivity, which have created for the first time a global glut. All of our ancestors suffered from chronic poverty, dependant as they were on finite amounts of natural wealth. Today, by contrast, we derive our wealth less from natural resources and more from technological know-how and scientific knowledge, which we have been accumulating incrementally for millennia. Consequently the available pie no longer is finite, and therefore no longer are we doomed to a pitiless struggle for survival—to a realpolitik of me first and devil take the hindmost. The traditional realpolitik, however, is far from superseded, as evident in the above statistics disclosing pervasive global inequity.

A second advantage now available is the communications revolution that makes all human advances quickly known and available to all humans. No longer must basic advances such as the mastery of agriculture and metallurgy remain for centuries and millennia purely local achievements and practices. Typically such achievements were known only in restricted and isolated regions before diffusing very slowly over wider areas. Hence the great variations in the rates at which various peoples passed from the Stone Age to the Bronze Age to the Iron Age, and so forth.

Today humans no longer are restricted to using naturally occurring local materials. We do not need to extract such materials, whether stone or copper or iron ore, out of the ground and transport them at great expense to some processing center. Rather the procedure begins in the minds of scientists in laboratories who design new materials as needed and proceed to fashion these new "designer materials." Hence the accelerating advance from the traditional Stone, Bronze, and Iron Ages to today's human-made age based on plastics, ceramics, composites, and other made-to-order materials.

The new age is based on the torrent of designer materials, tailor-made by scientists from the molecules upward. Being tailor-made, they can be, as needed, stronger and cheaper than metals and are used for constructing planes, autos, and so-called "biomaterials" (plastics, ceramics and composites), used to fashion hip joints, bone implants, artificial arteries, and even entire human-made hearts.

Human relationships are changing as basically with the animate world as with the inanimate. This is dramatically evident in the case of the smallpox virus, the most universally feared of all diseases. Appearing first in the Far East at least two thousand years ago, it reached Europe in the eighth century C.E., and then spread to the Americas after Columbus. With the Euro-

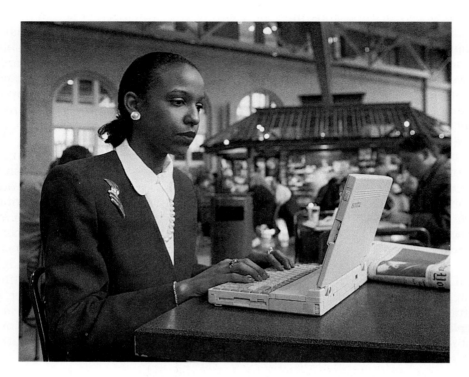

A century ago, the Industrial Revolution drew the labor force together into factories where large machinery and needed energy sources were situated. Today, a countertrend is underway as the Communications Revolution now permits people to develop ideas and to process information virtually anywhere.

pean dispersal over other continents, the virus decimated overseas populations lacking immunity. Hence the genocidal disaster suffered by Amerindians, Australian aborigines, and island populations in Polynesia and the Caribbean. The virus also persisted in Europe, reaching plague proportions, and ultimately carrying off one-third of the continent's population.

The taming of the virus began in 1796 when the English physician Edward Jenner discovered that a person inoculated and infected with cowpox was protected against smallpox. Today the smallpox-Homo sapiens relationship is completely reversed with a few stocks of the virus isolated in American and Russian laboratories. The last known case of smallpox was recorded in Somalia in 1977, and in 1980 the virus was declared eradicated in the wild.

Scientists have been recommending that the remaining stocks of the virus be destroyed lest it escape from storage, but a final decision has been deferred because of concern that the virus might be needed for future research. This concern has abated because scientists have been producing harmless clones of DNA fragments of smallpox and believe they now have the full genetic blueprint that will enable them to conduct research tests even if the virus itself were eliminated. In January 1996 the executive board of the UN World Health Organization agreed to set June 30, 1999, as the destruction date for all remaining stocks. So the killer virus, which for so long has tormented the human species, is now under lock and key, awaiting execution (and extinction) on a date set by its erstwhile victims. Thus *Homo sapiens* reigns supreme in both the animate and inanimate worlds.

"For the first time in the course of history," concludes physicist Werner Heisenberg, "man on earth faces only himself; he finds no longer any other partner or foe." The great irony of our era is that this primacy is the root cause of our global melancholia noted above. Having eliminated all possible rivals, we humans no longer confront any foes. We confront only ourselves.

This new confrontation with our inner self rather than with the outside world is a formidable undertaking. It requires not merely the acquisition of more knowledge and technology, an enterprise in which we have proven unequaled. It requires also the crowning of that knowledge with an ethical compass to provide it with direction and purpose. In the seventeenth century, when the scientific revolution was emerging, the English philosopher Francis Bacon noted its potentiality and warned against its perils. He enthusiastically endorsed the pursuit of "knowledge and skill" through science,

Sir Francis Bacon (1561–1626), is regarded as the father of empiricism and of experimentation in science. He believed that science was an instrument to be employed for "the benefit and use of life" and should be brought to the aid of the human condition.

but he added that the pursuit should be conducted with "humility and charity," and not "for pleasure of mind, or for contention, or for superiority to others, or for profit or fame, or power, or any of these inferior things; but for the benefit and use of life."[13]

The Fordham University Index and the daily exposés on television screens make clear that *thus far* we have ignored Bacon's admonition. The crucial words in this analysis are "thus far." These words raise a basic question confronting all humans. Is our current predicament a temporary hurdle which eventually we will overcome, as we have so many in the past? Or is it permanent because it is based on human genes which are preprogrammed for aggression and acquisitiveness?

If the assumption of genetic predestination is accepted, then the global melancholia becomes understandable. But not necessarily justifiable, as recent research casts doubt on this hitherto accepted predestination premise. A pioneer in this research is biologist Mary Clark who not only rejects the hypothesis of genetically based human aggressiveness and acquisitiveness but also proposes in its place a "human needs theory." This holds that "when conflict arises within a society, it is almost always because this biologically based need for bonding among its neighbors is being thwarted by one or another social arrangement."[14]

The proposition that bonding rather than conflict is a more natural human tendency was dramatically bolstered in Niota, a small Illinois town on the banks of the Mississippi. A team of convicted black and Hispanic drug dealers stationed in a nearby boot camp were sent to Niota to sandbank the levee threatened by rising waters during the 1992 Midwest floods. As they approached the town, one of the inmates remarked apprehensively, "Watch this—how long before someone calls us nigger?" Months later, reflecting on his experience, the inmate observed, "We was waiting, but it never happened." Not only did it not happen, but the opposite did happen. After working nine days from dawn to dark, the inmates won the respect and gratitude of the townspeople. "They brought us Pepsi," reminisced one of the inmates. "They let us sit down in the shade and drink from their water hose. They were just nice people. . . . They gave us roast beef and chicken dinners. Meat loaf, apple pie, as much as you wanted. And they thanked us every night." The significance of this experience was not lost on the participants, though the media did ignore it amid the hourly reports on water levels. One of the songs they sang while hurling sandbags was written by an inmate:

> They say in Niota
> The eatin's mighty fine
> They feed me twice a day
> and now they're friends of mine
> Oh, Lord, we won't let you flood
> 'cause there is lots of love
> They say in Niota
> the people's mighty fine
> Our skin's a different color
> they don't pay it mind.[15]

Minds were changed on all sides, as demonstrated when it came to clean-up time. The townspeople were offered a choice of more inmates or a group of student volunteers. The unanimous decision was for the inmates. So within a short period a diverse group of midwesterners was able to replace old fears and prejudices with mutual discovery and mutual respect.

Skeptics will argue that the conversion was possible because the entire group was forced by the rising waters to work together, and in doing so was able to transcend old fears and prejudices. This obviously is true, but it is equally true that waters are rising globally and are fostering global transcendence. The transformation is facilitated by the progressive decay of the world's dominant mega-institutions, forcing individuals to take over from increasingly dysfunctional systems. No longer can responsibilities and functions be safely entrusted to controlling centers, whether the White House, the Kremlin, or 10 Downing Street. All over the world, people necessarily are taking back authority and stewardship, creating building blocks toward the reconstruction of their societies.

Example: former Soviet Union

Grassroots environmentalists in the Soviet republics clashed with the Kremlin Establishment over the pervasive ecological degradation in their lands. The environmentalists went on to organize a movement that helped spark the democratic transformation of the Soviet Empire. Continuing their drive, they now function through the Socio-Ecological Union, seeking to hold the

A challenge for the twenty-first century lies in moving beyond the notion of discarding "waste" toward the idea of recycling materials in new and creative ways. Perhaps the containers that hold this year's drinks may become the fabric for next year's fashions.

successor Commonwealth of Independent States accountable to a broad environmental and human rights agenda.

Example: Sweden

A broad citizen movement is working to turn Sweden into a model sustainable society. With the support of leading scientists, the citizen leaders are seeking to define the nature and details of sustainability. Their conclusions are being distributed to every household and school in Sweden, with a letter from the King. Forty-nine local governments, members of the Swedish Farmers Federation, and twenty-two large Swedish companies are participating in the national reassessment and restructuring.

Example: Kenya

The women of Kenya's Greenbelt movement have established 1,500 grassroots nurseries and planted over 10 million trees. Their enterprise has inspired women in other African countries to launch similar programs.

Example: Israel

On a hilltop between Israel and the West Bank is a village of 140 residents with the name: Neve Shalom/Wahat al-Salam, Hebrew and Arabic for "oasis of peace." The village is run by a governing council of two Arabs and two Jews. It has a long waiting list of families seeking admission and is planning to establish a university that will teach conflict resolution. "Peace and coexistence" states an early settler and village member, "are so unrealistic in this country. To teach those things, you need a reality like this to show that real people can achieve them."[16]

Example: USA

A "self-help" and "mutual aid" movement is currently surging in the United States. It comprises people who face a common concern or condition and who meet voluntarily for emotional support and practical mutual assistance. The movement was inspired partly by Alcoholics Anonymous, which was formed in the mid-1930s by two alcoholics who began A.A. by helping each other. The need for the movement is indicated by the soaring membership in U.S. self-help organizations from 5 to 8 million in the 1970s, to 12 to 15 million in the 1980s. The movement includes Narcotics Anonymous, Overeaters An., Impotents An., Neurotics An., Depressives An., Batterers An., Sex Addicts An., Homosexuals An., Workaholics An., and numerous others. "People want to control something in their lives," explains a student of the movement. "They can't control international issues. But maybe they can control depression, a problem in their neighborhood, or their asthma. People do not want to be merely consumers, they want to be participants in society."[17]

   This mass animation brings to mind Thomas Jefferson, who two centuries earlier, on the occasion of the signing of the Declaration of Independence, declared exultantly: "All eyes are opened, or opening, to the rights of man. . . . the mass of mankind has not been born with saddles on their backs, nor a favored few booted and spurred, ready to ride them legitimately, by the grace of God."[18] A resurrected Jefferson doubtless would be astounded to find that on the eve of the twenty-first century, eyes were opening on all continents rather than in just a few Western countries, and the eyes were those of all classes rather than of only few educated property owners.

This burgeoning global awakening, together with the rich potentialities of modern high technology, suggests that melancholia now is incongruous. Of course this is not a time for self-deluding fantasies, but neither is it a time for gloomy foreboding. Rather it is a time for hardheaded reappraisal of existing practices and institutions, retaining what works and discarding what does not. Which is precisely what is going on now, whether in China where they are groping for a "communism with a Chinese face" or in eastern Europe where they are discarding the old planned economies but at the same time trying to preserve the old "safety nets."

The ongoing experimentation is not confined to balancing planned economies as against free markets. It also encompasses alternative forms of capitalism (such as the American variety emphasizing untrammeled free enterprise, and the German and Scandinavian varieties stressing the welfare state and worker participation in decision making), and also alternative forms of socialism (such as the distinctive Chinese combination of the free market with Communist party dictatorship, and the fluid unconformity in the former USSR where economist Nikolai Shmelev advises his fellow countrymen not to fear losing their "ideological virginity"[19]).

Such effervescence suggests a twenty-first century of great potentiality as well as great peril. Lacking a crystal ball, historians cannot predict with certainty either eventuality. But they can predict with reasonable assurance a twenty-first century that is neither utopian nor dystopian, but a century of possibilities. Which of the innumerable possibilities will actually be realized will be decided by *Homo sapiens*—the intelligent species that by virtue of its intelligence is the creator rather than the creature of its destiny. The gift of creativity, however, offers no assurance regarding the merit of what might be created, as demonstrated by the current penchant for Francis Bacon's "inferior things." This tendency may, in the course of the forthcoming century, seem to validate Bertrand Russell's dictum about humans preferring to "die rather than think." In that eventuality, another British philosopher (Edmund Burke) offers words of wisdom: "All that is required for the triumph of evil is that good men remain silent and do nothing."

If good men do not remain silent and choose to do something, what should they do? Here again we have words of wisdom to guide us, proffered by our distinguished contemporary scientist Albert Einstein. In his later years Einstein became increasingly concerned about the raison d'etre of his beloved science. In the following conclusion it is noteworthy that Einstein in the 1950s was reiterating the basic ethical premises that Francis Bacon had affirmed centuries earlier. For Bacon, science was an instrument to be employed for "the benefit and use of life." Einstein likewise insisted that "the creations of our mind shall be a blessing and not a curse to mankind."

> It is not enough that you should understand about applied science in order that your work may increase man's blessings. Concern for man himself and his fate

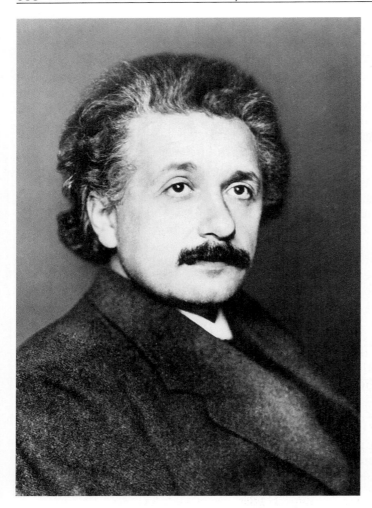

In the 1950s Albert Einstein reiterated the basic ethical premise that Francis Bacon had affirmed. Einstein insisted that "the creations of our mind shall be a blessing and not a curse to mankind."

must always form the chief interest of all technical endeavors, concern for the great unsolved problems of the organization of labor and the distribution of goods—in order that the creations of our mind shall be a blessing and not a curse to mankind. Never forget this in the midst of your diagrams and equations.[20]

Einstein believed earnestly in the feasibility of the "blessing" he prescribed, firmly rejecting the proposition of genetically preordained doom for humanity: "Human beings are not condemned, because of their biological constitution, to annihilate each other or to be at the mercy of a cruel, self-inflicted fate."[21]

If humans are not genetically self-destructive, as Einstein insists, nevertheless their rampant technology is inflicting on them successive social problems. One example is inequity, so that a number-one killer in the United States now is overeating and obesity, while in the rest of the world it is malnutrition or starvation. What the inequity means in human terms is illustrated by the photos below showing the little girl in poverty-stricken Sudan being stalked by a vulture waiting to feed on her when she no longer can defend herself and the other showing the child being pampered by her mother in the United States.

A vulture eyes a little girl who collapsed from hunger during a famine in the Sudan.

It does not follow that children born into comfortable homes will use wisely the opportunities they have in their grasp. The historical record shows that despite our past achievements, we rarely have refrained from any folly of which we were capable. Nevertheless, thanks to our genes and our technology, we are free today to be the creators of our destiny rather than its victims.

As serious as the problem of inequity, is that of war in our nuclear age. This was highlighted in May 1998 when India conducted five underground nuclear tests, and Pakistan responded immediately with comparable nuclear tests. The resulting danger of a nuclear arms race in South Asia was condemned world-wide. But an encouraging by-product has been a vigorous debate in both countries about the merits and demerits of nuclear testing, as illustrated by the conflicting messages on the placards flaunted by the demonstrators (see photos below and on page 671).

These messages illustrate the diverse reactions of Indians to their government's nuclear tests. This diversity supports Einstein's contention that humans are not "at the mercy of a cruel, self-inflicted fate." In other words, the twenty-first century is not preordained; it will be what we make it. This conclusion is supported by the success of the demonstrators in persuading their Indian and Pakistani governments to announce in September 1998 that they would sign an international treaty banning nuclear testing.[22]

Indian women cheer as Prime Minister Atal Bihari Vajpayee visits the test site at Pokaran on May 20, 1998 where India tested five nuclear devices. Vajpayee said that India was willing to "pay any price" for its security.

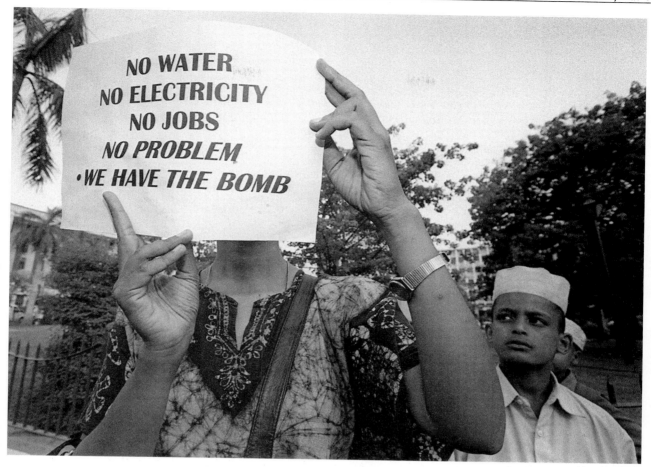

Skepticism about India's new power was expressed at an anti-nuclear march in New Delhi on May 29, 1998 after Pakistan tested five nuclear devices to counter the five tests conducted earlier in the month by India.

NOTES

1. C. Sagan, *Pale Blue Dot* (Random House, 1994); and *The Demon-Haunted World* (Random House, 1995).
2. *Business Ethics* (March-April 1992), p. 30.
3. CBS Television Network, "The Twenty-First Century," May 21, 1967.
4. *Los Angeles Times*, November 5, 1989; *New York Times*, December 8, 1992.
5. Cited in J. Rifkin, *The End of Work* (Putnam, 1995), p. 222.
6. Ibid., p. 186.
7. *Worldwatch Institute Report, State of the World,* 1997 (W. W. Norton, 1997), p. 123.
8. A. Bandura, *Aggression* (Prentice Hall, 1973), pp. 113, 322.
9. G. Lenski, *Human Societies: An Introduction to Macrosociology* (McGraw-Hill, 1974).
10. *United Nations Human Development Report 1994* (Oxford University Press, 1994), p. 35.

11. *Hunger in America. The Growing Epidemic* (Harvard University School of Public Health, 1985), pp. xiii, xiv.
12. M. Kaku, "Apocalypse When?" *Guardian* (November 20, 1991), p. 11.
13. Cited in A. Pacey, *The Culture of Technology* (MIT Press, 1983), pp. 114–15, 178–79.
14. M. E. Clark, "Meaningful Social Bonding as a Universal Human Need," in J. Burton, ed., *Human Needs Theory and Conflict Prevention*, [sic] (St. Martin's Press). More details on this subject are available in the important study by M. E. Clark, *Ariadne's Thread* (St. Martin's Press, 1989).
15. *New York Times,* July 29, 1993.
16. *Los Angeles Times,* August 31, 1997.
17. Frank Riessman, Director of National Self-Help Clearinghouse, cited in the *New York Times*, July 16, 1988.
18. Cited in H. S. Commager, "The Revolution as a World Ideal," *Saturday Review* (December 13, 1975), p. 13.
19. *New York Times,* June 25, 1987.
20. This Einstein statement was the theme of the "1985 Carnahan Conference on Harmonizing Technology with Society," held on August 22–23 1985, at the University of Kentucky, Lexington, Kentucky.
21. Albert Einstein, *Out of My Later Years* (Philosophical Library, 1950), p. 127.
22. *New York Times,* September 25, 1998.

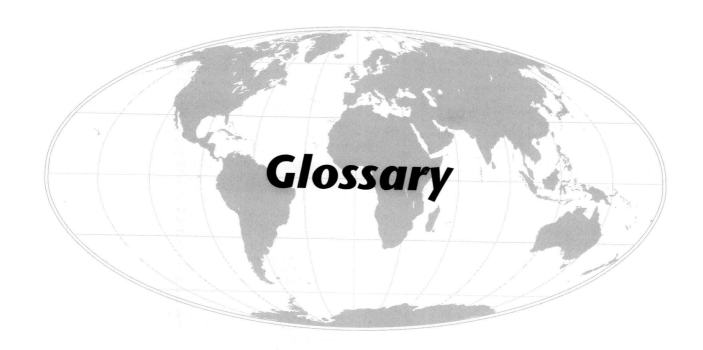

Glossary

agriculture cultivating the soil, producing crops, and sometimes raising livestock

ahisma nonviolence, a concept of India

Ainus Caucasoid people who originally inhabited the Japanese islands

alienation estrangement or withdrawal where good relationships formerly existed

ambivalent being both attracted and repelled by a person or action

Anabaptists members of a radical Protestant sect that arose in Zurich in 1524; it required adult as opposed to infant baptism, as well as nonresistance, mutual help, and separation of church and state

anachronism a person or thing that is chronologically out of place

anarchy lawlessness or disorder due to lack of governmental authority

apartheid South African policy that excludes all nonwhites from any share in political life and confines Africans to separate areas known as Bantustands (preserves for the "Bantu" Africans)

archeologist a person who determines the nature of past cultures by digging up and studying the things they have left behind

archeology the science that determines the nature of past cultures from the study of things they have left behind

arts: liberal vs. servile in the Middle Ages, liberal arts were done with the mind; servile arts involved a change in matter; e.g., a physician didn't change matter so his work was considered liberal, whereas a surgeon changed matter so his work was servile

asceticism practice of self-denial

astrologers those who study the stars and their imagined influence on human affairs

astronomy science of the heavenly bodies and of their movements

audiencas courts into which the huge vice-royalties of New Spain were divided

autarchic unit self-sufficient, independent economic unit

Bantu Negroid linguistic group originating in the Cameroon Highlands and later infiltrating the Congo Basin at the expense of the Bushmen and Pygmies; predominant ethnic group when the Europeans arrived in sub-Saharan Africa

benevolent despots rulers such as Frederick the Great of Prussia (1740–1781), Catherine the Great of Russia (1762–1796), and Joseph II of the Hapsburg

Empire (1765–1790) who used their governmental authority for the benefit of the people

Bhopal city in India where a chemical accident in a Union Carbide Corporation pesticide plant in December 1984 resulted in over 2,000 deaths

biology the science that deals with living organisms

blitzkrieg new type of "lightning war" used by the Germans in World War II; first came dive bombers, then armored tank divisions called Panzers, and finally the lighter motorized divisions and infantry

Boers inhabitants of South Africa of Dutch descent

Bolsheviks literally "majority" in Russian; Lenin's followers

bourgeoisie the middle class, e.g., merchants, industrialists, professionals, etc.

boyars large landowners in tsarist Russia

Brahmins one of the highest Hindu castes; theoretically their occupation was that of priest or teacher; see *caste*

Buddhism a movement that was begun by Guatama Buddha in India in the fifth century B.C.E.; became full-fledged religion throughout Asia

bureaucracy a body of nonelected workers in any unit of government; first appeared in China

burghers middle-class townspeople

capitalism a system in which the desire for profits is the driving motive and capital is accumulated and used to make profits in a variety of ways

caste one of many hereditary groups in India that were originally based on color and occupation; there are four broad divisions with thousands of subdivisions; still in existence in rural India despite efforts to abolish them

Chernobyl town in the Soviet Union where a damaged nuclear reactor resulted, in April 1986, in radiation contamination of air, soil, water, and food supplies in the Soviet Union and in surrounding countries

city-state independent cities that were leaders of a particular region

civilization a stage of development in which people have achieved all or most of the following: writing, arts and sciences, cities, formal political organization, social classes, taxation

class differentiation the development from a homogeneous to heterogeneous society in which there is an increasing gap between rich and poor classes of people; opposite of egalitarian society

classical liberalism program by which the growing middle class proposed to get the benefits and control in government that it wanted; see also *democratic liberalism*

class struggle Marx's proposition that it is through conflict between opposing interests of classes that humankind has passed from one type of social organization to another

cold war name given to the series of crises after World War II that resulted from bad relations between the Communist and Western worlds

colonization establishment of settlements that are ruled by foreign countries

commercial agriculture agriculture in which most of the crops produced are sold for money rather than consumed by the family

commercial bonds ties based on the interchange of material goods; trade

Common Market an economic association with six original members: Italy, West Germany, Belgium, Netherlands, Luxembourg, and France; then in 1973 Britain, Ireland, and Denmark joined

concubine a mistress, or woman who lives with a man without marriage

Confucianism name given to the teachings of Confucius and his followers; mainly a practical moral system concerned with problems of everyday life and emphasizing conformity, propriety, and social responsibility

conquistadors New World soldiers of fortune from Spain; Cortes, conqueror of the Aztec Empire, is one of the best known

contemporary happening or existing in the same period of time

corvée compulsory labor, on projects such as building roads and fortifications

Cossacks Russian frontiersmen, mostly former serfs, who fled to the wild steppe country and became hunters, fishermen, and pastoralists

Crusaders people from Christian Europe who went on expeditions during the eleventh, twelfth, and thirteenth centuries seeking to capture the Holy Land from the Moslems

Crusades expeditions from Christian Europe during the eleventh, twelfth, and thirteenth centuries seeking to capture the Holy Land from the Moslems

cultural assimilation absorption into the cultural tradition of another group and the loss of one's own cultural identity

culture the way of life of a society; the ideas, habits, arts, and institutions that are passed on from generation to generation

cuneiform pictograph writings of ancient Mesopotamia; such writing is based not on the letters of an alphabet but on symbols that represent words or ideas; see *ideographic writing*

Cynicism Greek doctrine that held that virtue is the only good; everything else—riches, honor, freedom, even life itself—is contemptible

daimyo local lords in sixteenth-century Japan who fought each other to extend their domains

democratic centralism principle adopted by Lenin for the operation of the Social Democratic party; major issues were discussed freely, and decision reached by democratic vote; once a vote was taken every party member had to support the "party line" or be expelled

democratic liberalism doctrine that holds that the state is responsible for all its citizens; reforms of democratic liberalism were the prelude to the welfare state; see also *classical liberalism*

demographic pattern pattern of human population

dharma a Hindu and Buddhist term that means morality, obligations to family and society, and religious law

diadem headband worn as a badge of royalty

dialectics a science evolved by Socrates in which provisional definitions were tested by questions until universally recognized absolute truths were reached

diffusionists people who believe that human civilization developed by diffusion from the Middle East to northwest Europe, north Africa, south Asia, and east Asia

diviner one who prophesies or foresees

Domesday Book the record of a general survey of England ordered by William the Conqueror in 1086; it listed all the economic resources of the country

dowry the property that a wife brings to her husband in marriage

Duma Russian elective national assembly created after the Russian Revolution of 1905 and swept away by the Bolshevik Revolution of 1917

dyarchy dual system of government, as in Japan, where one family did the actual work of ruling while the emperor lived in luxurious seclusion and was responsible only for ensuring that his dynasty would continue forever

dynasty a succession of rulers of the same family

ecological pertaining to ecology, the science dealing with the relations between organisms and their natural environment

Economic and Social Council UN Council whose task was fighting hunger and disease; set up such agencies as the ILO; Food and Agriculture Organization; UN Education, Scientific and Cultural Organization; World Health Organization; and International Monetary Fund

ecosystem the complex of human community and natural environment, forming a functional whole

egalitarianism belief in human equality in all fields: economic, political, and social

empire a large area, usually including several countries or peoples, all under a single political authority

enclosures land closed off in England in the fifteenth to nineteenth centuries; left yeomen without grazing land or land for wood cutting; between 1714 and 1820 over 6 million acres were enclosed

enlightened despots see *Enlightenment* and *benevolent despots*

Enlightenment movement dating from the century prior to the French Revolution of 1789; leaders believed they lived in an enlightened age of reason and progress in contrast to the previous times of superstition and ignorance

Epicureanism Greek doctrine that defined philosophy as the art of making life happy, with pleasure (defined as serenity and avoidance of pain rather than indulgence) as the highest and only good

"equal-field system" during the Sun and T'ang dynasties in China, the central government gave plots of about nineteen acres each to all able-bodied peasants; in practice, only free peasants, and not even all of these, were given land

ethnic group a group that retains its own national characteristics, language, religion, customs, and institutions

ethnocentrism regarding one's own cultural group as superior and scorning all things alien

Europeanization term used to include political domination and cultural penetration by Europe as well as actual biological replacement of one people by another, as in the relatively empty territories of the Western Hemisphere and South Pacific that were inundated by European emigrants

evolution theory that all animals and plants have their origins in preexisting types and differences gradually evolved because of modifications in successive generations

extended family two or more married couples and their children

extraterritoriality right of foreigners to be exempt from the laws of a nation in which they are living; e.g., most ambassadors and diplomats are not subject to the laws of the nation in which they live but only to the laws of their own country

fecundity to be fruitful or fertile

feudalism political system that flourished in Europe from about the ninth to fifteenth centuries; a lord gave land to vassals, who in return, gave the lord military service

fiefs feudal estates granted by kings or lords as reward for military service; see *feudalism*

fluyt flyboat; a large, cheap Dutch merchant ship that was unarmed and had great capacity for carrying goods

food gatherer a person who collects foods, e.g., picks fruits, nuts, and plants; digs up roots and shellfish; catches fish

food-gathering culture culture in which people collect food as distinct from cultures in which people grow their food

food producer a peasant or farmer who grows food instead of gathering it

footbinding the practice of wrapping tightly the feet of young girls until the arch was broken and the toes were turned under—a procedure that stunted the feet to half normal size, crippled the girls for life, and made them dependent on men

foreclosure seizing of mortgaged property after failure to repay the mortgage or loan money

Fourteen Points Wilson's specific, detailed aims including open diplomacy, freedom of the seas, removal of international trade barriers, armament reduction, and application of the principle of self-determination to subject minorities in central and eastern Europe

franchise right to vote

fresco the art of painting on a surface of plaster

geocentric based on the earth as the center of perspective in contrast to heliocentric, or sun-centered

geology the science that studies the structure of the earth and the development of this structure in the past

giaours nonbelievers; derogatory term used by the Moslems to refer to their Christian subjects

Gosplan Soviet State Planning Commission, which prepared plans on the basis of general directions from the government and statistical data received from all parts of the country

gross national product (GNP) total output of goods and services of a country

habitat one's physical environment where one normally lives and grows up

hegemony influence of authority, economic or political, of one nation or people over another

Hellenism Greek culture that spread throughout the Middle East with the conquests of Alexander the Great

helot member of the lowest social class of ancient Sparta

hidalgos Spanish aristocrats who had most of the territorial wealth, were exempt from taxes, and looked down on people engaged in commerce and industry

hierarchy organization into a series of orders or ranks with each one subordinate to the one above it

hieroglyphics picture-writing system of ancient Egypt

high culture "upper-class" culture found in schools, temples, and palaces of the cities and passed on by philosophers, theologians, and literary men

Hinduism major religion of India

hominids humanlike ancestors of modern human beings who had a brain smaller and less developed than that of humans

homogeneity of similar or uniform structure throughout

Homo sapiens "thinking" humans; includes all members of the human race

hybrid vigor the superior qualities produced by interbreeding

ideographic script writing in which symbols represent ideas or objects; found in early China, Mesopotamia, and Egypt

imperialism the rule or control, political or economic, direct or indirect, of one state, nation, or people over similar groups; see also *new imperialism*

incipient agriculture the long gradual phase during which people made the shift from partial to full dependence on agriculture

independent inventionists people who believe that civilizations developed independently in the various regions of the globe

indigenous produced, growing, or existing naturally in a particular region

infanticide killing of infants; from Latin *cide* or kill, as in regicide, or killing of a king, and genocide, or killing of an entire people

injunction an order prohibiting a specified act

Islam the religion of the Moslems, based on the monotheistic teachings of the prophet Mohammed and spread by the Arabs; not only a religion but also a political system and social code

janissaries Ottoman infantrymen

joint stock companies sold stock or shares to investors who risked only the amount invested in the shares, regardless of what losses a company might have—a characteristic that encouraged investors to risk their money, and thus mobilized the large sums necessary for European economic expansion throughout the globe

jus gentium "law of the peoples"; a new body of law accepted by the Romans and applied to all peoples

jus naturale Roman legal concept that held that natural law was above that of mere custom

Koran bible of the Islamic faith; provided guidance for all phases of life—manners, hygiene, marriage and divorce, commerce and politics, crime and punishment, peace and war

kulaks well-to-do Russian peasants who were hostile to the Soviet regime; finally eliminated when agriculture was collectivized

Kuomintang Chinese National People's party founded by Sun Yat-sen

lactation taboo birth-control practice that forbade sexual intercourse while a woman was nursing a baby

latifundai large plantations that grew up in Italy in the second century B.C.E.; worked by slaves and owned by absentee landlords

Law of Retarding Lead the best adapted and most successful societies have the most difficulty in adapting during a period of transition and change

League of Nations created by the Versailles Treaty; its two basic objectives were (1) to preserve the peace and (2) to concern itself with health, social, economic, and humanitarian problems of international scope; failed in its first objective but succeeded in its second

Legalists adherents of a Chinese doctrine very different from Confucianism or Taoism; practicing statesmen interested in strengthening the princes they served so that they could wage war and unite the country by force; all aspects of life were regulated in detail by laws that would promote the state's economic and military power

Levellers group drawn mainly from the English lower-middle-class agricultural tenants who favored a democratic government and social reform

literocracy hierarchy of learned people such as those who ruled China before the intrusion of the West

low culture "lower-class" culture found in the villages and passed on by word of mouth among illiterate peasants

mandates people of the colonies taken from the Central Powers after World War I were regarded as unable to stand on their own feet; their tutelage was entrusted to "advanced nations" that were to exercise their tutelage on behalf of the League of Nations; this tutelage was not extended to the colonies of the victorious allies

manor a self-sufficient village worked by feudal serfs who had certain rights and responsibilities but were not free to move away

materialist interpretation of history Marx's theory that in every historical epoch the mode of economic production and exchange gives rise to a particular social organization and is the basic foundation for the political and intellectual history of that epoch

Mau Mau secret East African terrorist organization made up of members of the Kikuyu tribe

Mawali non-Arab Moslems

median situated at the midpoint between the two extremes, so that when nine incomes are arranged in order, the median income is the fifth from the top and from the bottom, whereas the average income is the sum of the nine incomes divided by nine

megalopolis very large urban unit; a big city

Mensheviks literally "minority" in Russian; Lenin's opponents within the Russian Social Democratic Party

mercantile activities see *commercial bonds*

mercantilism early modern rigid regulation of economic life in contrast to no regulation or "laissez-faire" policy

Mesoamerica central and south Mexico, Guatemala, and Honduras

mestizo person in Spanish America of mixed European and Indian origin

metallurgy the technique of extracting metals from ores

millennium period of 1,000 years; plural, millennia

modernization economists define modernization as the process by which humans have gained control over their physical environment by increasing output; sociologists and anthropologists term such features as the awakening and activation of the masses; more interest in the present and future than in the past; belief that human affairs are understandable rather than the result of supernatural manipulation; and until recently, faith in the beneficence of science and technology

monasticism life centered around the monastery, or dwelling place of persons under religious vows

monoculture cultivation of a single crop

multinational corporations business corporations that conduct commercial, industrial, or banking activities in many countries, and which are today's counterpart of the earlier *joint stock companies*

muzhik a Russian peasant

nationalism allegiance to the cause of the nation rather than to the church and region as before the nineteenth century

natural geopolitical center a natural central area whose location and physical features gave it regional leadership

natural selection an important part of the process of evolution; in the struggle for existence, the organisms whose genes are best adapted to the environment are selected and will survive and reproduce; the less well adapted will die out

Neo-Confucianism a combination of Buddhism and Taoism with Confucianism; believes humankind is good and capable of becoming more perfect, and evil is the result of neglect and defective education and can be corrected

Neolithic new stone age characterized by use of smooth, ground stone implements, and dependence on agriculture or food producing rather than food gathering

New Economic Policy (NEP) plan adopted by the Soviet government in 1921 that made some concessions; e.g., peasants were allowed to sell their produce on the open market, private individuals could operate small stores and factories and keep the profits

new imperialism the great European expansion of the late nineteenth century; differed from the old imperialist control of a state over another because it did not simply demand tribute but completely transformed the conquered countries

Nirvana the goal of Buddhism, which is to end sorrow by stopping desire; done by following the "eightfold path"

North Atlantic Treaty Organization (NATO) a mutual defense organization consisting of the United States, Canada, and several western European countries who agreed that "an attack on one or more of the signers is an attack upon all"

nuclear family married couple and their children

obsolescence the condition of being obsolete or out of date or out of fashion

oligarchy government controlled by a small group

Orthodox Christianity Greek Christian religion, which rejected leadership of the pope and instead was under the patriarch of Constantinople

orthodoxy belief in accepted standards and established doctrine

ostracism a form of punishment involving isolation or exclusion from a social group

ostrogs fortified posts or blockhouses built by the Cossacks as they advanced eastward

Paleolithic old stone age, characterized by use of rough, chipped stone implements and by dependence on food gathering

paleontology the science dealing with the life of past geological periods, as known from fossil remains

Palestine Liberation Organization (PLO) an organization consisting of several Palestinian nationalist groups; all are opposed to Israel but disagree about how an independent Palestinian state should be created

Panchayat elected council of five or more, usually caste leaders and village elders, who governed the traditional Indian village

paradox something absurd, false, and self-contradicting

parochialism being narrow or restricted—literally, confined to a parish

pastoral nomads people who make a living by domesticating animals and herding them from place to place in search of pastures

patrician aristocrat, or person of high birth

Pax Mongolica literally "Mongol Peace"; during the short period of Mongol peace, overland trade flourished from the Baltic to the Pacific because the Mongols ruled the entire area and kept the peace

Pax Romana literally "Roman Peace"; period brought about by Augustus and lasting for two centuries

peripheral located away from the center

philosophes a group who believed in the existence of natural laws that regulated the universe and human society

philosophical system system of ideas, beliefs, and attitudes

photosynthesis the process by which green plants utilize the energy of sunlight to manufacture carbohydrates from carbon dioxide and water—a process on which all plant and animal life on the planet depends

pictographs early cuneiform writing consisting of conventionalized pictures representing objects

plebians common people

Pleistocene epoch a period of glacial and interglacial stages during which animals adapted to changing environmental conditions

pluralism diversity or consisting of more than one

polis see *city-state*

praetorian a soldier of the imperial bodyguard of the Roman Caesars

productivity the conversion of resources into goods and services needed by humans; increased by using better seeds and tools, moving to better land, improving economic organization, etc.

proletariat the working class in industrial societies, e.g., workers in factories, mines, the docks, etc.

Quisling a Norwegian who collaborated with Hitler and whose name became a synonym for the self-serving traitor

rationalism a way of thinking based on logical thought and reason rather than on myths or traditional religion

Reformation basic upheaval that shattered the unity of Western Christendom; Martin Luther triggered the Protestant Reformation when he reacted against abuses in the Roman church

religious sanctions rewards and punishments to enforce rules of the religious elite

Renaissance intellectual and cultural awakening in Europe during the fifteenth to seventeenth centuries; emphasis was on the human being, and the purpose of life was to develop one's potentialities

revisionism a movement among twentieth-century socialists to adopt a "revised" strategy that depends on gradual reform instead of revolution to bring about a socialist society

sans culottes literally "those who lacked the knee breeches of genteel society"; French revolutionaries who wanted a more egalitarian state with equitable division of land; government regulation of prices and wages; and a social security system

savannas tropical or subtropical grasslands; treeless plains

Scholasticism a philosophy that taught that seeking God was more important than understanding nature, theology was the queen of the sciences, and one should turn to religion for succor and consolation in the face of material disaster

secession withdrawal from an organization such as a religious community or a political party

secular states states controlled by nonreligious leaders (layperson), as opposed to states controlled by religious leaders

Security Council UN Council made up of five permanent members, the United States, USSR, Britain, France, and China, and six two-year members elected by the General Assembly whose task is to maintain peace

self-determination the principle that all peoples should have the right to self-rule

shamans medicine men or women or sorcerers; individuals in early cultures who were part-time specialists and who used magical arts for the common good

sheikhs Arabian elective tribval chiefs who were leaders in the time of war

Shiite sect a Moslem sect that repudiated the first three successors of Mohammed; Persians (Iranians) identified with this sect

shogun generalissimo; a general who commanded military forces for the Japanese emperor

Silk Road overland route from China to the Middle East along which caravans transported Chinese silk, which was in demand throughout Eurasia

sinicization becoming modified by Chinese influence

Skepticism Greek doctrine that challenged the supremacy of reason and rationalism and adopted a questioning attitude

social homogeneity social equality that was a distinctive feature of Neolithic villages; all people shared equally in the ownership of land and other natural resources

socialism ideology calling for social and economic change and political reform; the government owns and operates the means of production and the main parts of the economy, e.g., banks, mines, factories, railroads, foreign trade, etc.; emphasizes community and collective welfare rather than the individual

soviets workers' elected councils that originated in the Russian Revolution of 1905 and reappeared in the 1917 revolution; soviets supplied the government with close rapport with the masses

steppe open, treeless plains with fertile black earth

stimulus diffusion a process that occurs when two different peoples first come in contact—they don't adopt one another's specific techniques or institutions completely but instead borrow underlying ideas or principles and adapt them to their specific needs; early civilizations often developed by this means

Stoicism Greek doctrine that accepted virtue as the highest good in life; people must put aside passion, unjust thoughts, and self-indulgence and perform their duties rationally and selflessly

strategos general in charge of both civil and military affairs in the Byzantine *themes*

subsistence agricultures type of agriculture that provides only the necessities of life, leaving little surplus for selling and buying; opposite of *commercial agriculture*

subsistence security multiple-crop agriculture providing a dependable food supply; if one crop failed peasants could depend on other crops for subsistence

suffragist one who favors extending suffrage, or the right to vote, to women

Sunnite sect a Moslem sect to which Turks and other surrounding peoples belonged and which set them apart from the Persian Shiites

surplus production of more goods and services than needed

surplus value Marxist theory that workers who provided the labor receive substantially less in wages than the price charged the consumer; hence the workers cannot buy what they produce; this leads to overproduction, unemployment, and finally, depression

suzerainty authority or rule or overlordship

taiga forest belt or zone

Taoism Chinese doctrine that stressed the importance of living naturally, conforming to nature's pattern; ambition was abandoned and honors and responsibilities rejected in favor of a meditative return to nature

tax farmer financier who paid a fixed sum to the central government for the privilege of collecting taxes in a given district and then kept for personal profit as much as could be collected above that sum

technology body of knowledge and skills evolved by humans to produce goods and services

thalassocracy civilization based on sea power, such as that of the Minoan civilization of Crete

themes provinces in the Byzantine empire

theocratic states states controlled by priests or other religious leaders

totem emblem or symbol of a particular group that stood for it or imposed rules on it; rules had to be observed to assure the well-being of the group

transformation to change very much the outward appearance or the internal structure

tribes inhabitants of villages of a given region identified and distinguished from others by their distinctive language and customs

tundra barren, frozen land along the Arctic coast

United Nations (UN) organization of nations set up in 1945 to carry out two basic tasks: (1) preserve peace and security and (2) set up international economic, social, and cultural programs; originally fifty charter members, with membership doubling by 1980

UNRRA UN organization set up to provide relief of all kinds to liberated countries; originated in the spring of 1944 and was to continue until the new national administrations could assume responsibility

urbanization shift from living in the countryside to the cities; development of characteristics typical to cities

utilitarian placing practical purpose above other considerations such as beauty

Utopian Socialists school of social reformers who produced blueprints for the operation of their projected model communities but did not indicate how these principles could be put into practice in the larger society

Vedas old and sacred Hindu texts consisting of hymns, prayers, and doctrines of Hindu divinities; similar to the Bible for Christians; *Veda* means knowledge

Versailles Treaty treaty with Germany, signed on June 28, 1919, that ended World War I; this treaty, together with separate treaties with the other Central Powers, are significant for world history because they applied the principle of self-determination to Europe but failed to apply it in overseas colonies

ward a person who is in the charge of or under the guardianship of another

Warsaw Pact formal military alliance concluded in May 1955 between Russia and the east European countries

white man's burden theory that Europeans were a superior race who had the duty to direct the labor and guide the development of inferior races; allowed Europeans to cloak their imperialism with a mantle of idealistic devotion to duty

World Zionist Organization nationalist Jewish movement established in Basel in 1897; wanted a Jewish commonwealth in Palestine after the end of the Ottoman Empire

Young Turks pioneer group of Turkish nationalists who wanted a new modern government in place of the Ottoman Sultanate

Zaibatsu literally "wealth-clique"; general name given to four giant family corporations that by World War II controlled three-fourths of the combined capital of all Japanese firms, three-fourths of all trust deposits, and one-fifth of all life insurance policies

Index